THE ROUGH GUIDE TO
Central America
ON A BUDGET

written and researched by

Dawn Curtis, Amber Dobrzensky, Sara Humphreys,
Anna Kaminski, Stephen Keeling, Shafik Meghji and
Iain Stewart

roughguides.com

Contents

OPPOSITE GUNA MOLA, PANAMA PREVIOUS PAGE KEEL-BILLED TOUCAN, COSTA RICA

Introduction to
Central America

From Maya kings and Spanish conquistadors to runaway slaves and thrill-seeking surfers, Central America has tantalized adventurers for hundreds of years with its exotic blend of volcano-studded landscapes, dazzling colonial towns, jungle-smothered relics and bone-white beaches. Today the region makes a tempting target for budget travellers; prices remain low and the sheer diversity of activities is hard to match. In the space of a day you could be snorkelling off a Caribbean reef or jaguar-spotting in lush tropical forest, before spending your evening sampling local rum and dancing the night away in one of many laidback surf towns. Another day could be spent whitewater rafting, volcano hiking and soothing your aches and pains in hot springs, followed by a home-cooked dinner of stuffed tacos, rice and beans.

The nations of Central America – with the notable exception of Belize – share a common **Spanish** heritage, but their indigenous roots go far deeper. Some of the greatest **Mesoamerican ruins** – Tikal and Copán – are here, not in Mexico, and you'll find vibrant **tribal traditions** alive and well throughout the region, from the rich Maya culture of Guatemala to the Lenca of Honduras and Guna of Panama. Indeed, it's the clash of cultures – primarily indigenous, Spanish and West African – that give Central America much of its appeal. It boasts a rich **culinary tradition** that stretches from Caribbean creole to Maya-influenced Spanish-style cooking, while gorgeous **colonial cities** such as Antigua, León and Granada are memorials to the intriguing Spanish-American culture that developed here from the sixteenth century. The region's **fiestas** and **religious beliefs**, too, mix various traditions – in Guatemala, the Maya folk saint Maximón is just as venerated as more established Catholic pilgrimage sites such as Esquipulas, where the Black Christ is represented by a miraculous crucifix carved by celebrated artist Quirio Cataño in 1594.

ABOVE VOLCÁN SAN CRISTÓBAL, NICARAGUA (P.470) **OPPOSITE** CORAL REEF, THE BAY ISLANDS, HONDURAS (P.436)

However, it's the region's **natural beauty** that often surprises travellers the most. It may look insignificant on the map – at its narrowest point the isthmus is squeezed to a mere 65km across – but Central America's unique topography ensures that there's enough here to fill months of exploration. Crammed into this small area, coral-fringed Caribbean **beaches** give way to dense **jungle** that, in turn, yields to brooding **volcanic highlands**. Pounding Pacific **surf** lies within a short ride of tranquil national parks containing multi-coloured parrots, howler monkeys and tapirs.

It's a good time to visit. Central America was known for much of the twentieth century for its bitter civil wars, poverty and crime. Though crime in some areas remains high, today the whole region is free of war, and rapidly developing economies are slowly reducing levels of poverty, with infrastructure, communications and life in general improving as never before.

While towering Maya ruins find their modern-day counterpart in the skyscraper-stacked skylines of **metropolises** such as Panama City, San Salvador and Guatemala City, costs, even in the cities, remain affordable, with plenty of budget accommodation options, cheap eats and attractions charging minimal entrance fees. Though Guatemala has the largest GDP, Costa Rica and Panama are generally more expensive, with Nicaragua and Honduras the cheapest destinations.

Travelling from place to place in Central America remains easy and won't break the bank, either: a combination of the infamous "chicken buses" (repurposed US school buses), border-crossing international coaches and *lanchas* will get you wherever the fancy takes you.

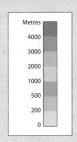

Metres
4000
3000
2000
1000
500
200
0

CARIBBEAN SEA

Puerto Lempira

Mosquitia

Río Coco

Puerto Cabezas (Bilwi)

Río Grande

Pearl
Lagoon

Little Corn

Big Corn

Bluefields

Río San Juan

COSTA
RICA

Puerto Limón

SAN JOSÉ

Bocas del Toro

Colón

Archipelago Guna Yala (San Blas)

Golfito

David

Panama Canal

PANAMA
CITY

Golfo
Dulce

PANAMA

CA-1

La Palma

Santiago

Golfo de
Panamá

COLOMBIA

Where to go

Relatively well set up for travellers, English-speaking **Belize** makes a good first stop; most travellers head to the cobalt blue waters of the Caribbean cayes and atolls to dive the longest barrier reef in the Americas, or spend a few nights on the lookout for big cats in a jaguar reserve such as **Cockscomb Basin**, or howler monkeys at the **Community Baboon Sanctuary**. Inland, **San Ignacio** is the perfect base for a range of adventure sports and a visit to the spectacular Maya site at **Caracol**, while the best place for just chilling on sandy beaches is **Placencia**. Seafood is always spectacular in Belize: and even budget travellers will find it within their means to dine like a king on freshly boiled lobsters on **Caye Caulker**. Throughout the country, West Indian culture dominates – Belize is more like its Caribbean island cousins than its Latino neighbours to the south.

You'll need to dust off your Spanish across the border in exotic Guatemala, which remains a backpacker favourite for good reason; it's here that indigenous culture, mostly Maya, is at its strongest and most expressive, with vibrant indigenous markets, arts and crafts and locals wearing traditional costume happily co-existing with travellers sipping the exceptional local coffee. There are stunning landscapes – laidback highland villages and the sky-scraping volcanoes of **Lago de Atitlán** – and jaw-dropping historical relics, from colonial **Antigua** to the mesmerizing jungle-smothered Maya ruins of **Tikal** (easily accessible from Belize). The capital, **Guatemala City**, is Central America's largest metropolis but not as intimidating as the hype suggests; its museums, restaurants and cache of colonial remnants are well worth a day or two of your time.

While its world-class Pacific surf beaches are no secret, much of **El Salvador** is off the tourist trail: Central America's smallest nation doesn't have the colour and the indigenous markets of Guatemala, but it does have the coast, from **El Tunco**, which has blossomed into a bona fide backpacker/surfer resort, to tranquil **El Cuco**, a turtle and pelican sanctuary. If you're after peace and quiet, head for the artsy flower-filled villages and coffee plantations of the **Ruta de las Flores**, or the magnificent rainforest of **Bosque El Imposible**. Foodie visitors should make an effort to get to the *feria gastronómica* in **Juayúa**, a weekly food market serving everything from iguana and snake to Mexican ice cream. The relaxed city of **Santa Ana** is an elegant stopoff, with the dazzling blue crater lake, **Lago de Coatepeque**, to explore nearby. Crammed with low-slung Spanish architecture, **Suchitoto** is the best place to soak up El Salvador's colonial past, while the **Ruta de Paz** in the east leads to poignant memorials of the country's bitter civil war, especially in bomb-ravaged **Perquín** and the massacre site at **El Mozote**. Don't ignore the capital **San Salvador** – its economy currently booming, it offers lively markets, bars and cafés more akin to the Latino culture in Miami or Puerto Rico than the rest of the region.

Honduras is also changing, but at a far slower pace – enjoy it while you can. The initially chaotic capital **Tegucigalpa** is one of the most visitor-friendly in Central America and one of the few to have retained a rich cache of colonial churches, buildings and museums in its centre. To the west, the celebrated ruin of **Copán** (often visited from Guatemala) is another enchanting Maya site, rich in carvings, and one of the region's top draws. Despite all this the

TOP TEN BEACH RESORTS

Only in Central America can you jump between Atlantic, Caribbean and Pacific beaches so quickly (in Panama the oceans are separated by just 50km), and the region has some fabulous beach resorts where you can while away long lazy days. Here are some of the best:

Bocas del Toro, Panama Explore the nine main islands, beaches and coral reefs of this sparkling archipelago, home to the Parque Nacional Marino Isla Bastimentos. See p.583

The Corn Islands, Nicaragua Sugary beaches, idyllic desert islands and a dose of languid Caribbean culture. See p.509

El Cuco, El Salvador Tranquil beaches, cheap lodgings, decent surfing and a chance to see turtles and pelicans sauntering across the sands. See p.226

Nicoya Peninsula, Costa Rica Surf Tamarindo or just swim and lounge on the golden sands at Nosara and Sámara. See p.158

Placencia, Belize Pristine white-sand Caribbean beaches, shaded by palms, where you can enjoy kayaking, snorkelling, diving, saltwater fly-fishing or whale-shark watching. See p.94

Playa El Tunco, El Salvador Laidback backpacker and surf resort, with gnarly waves and banging nightlife. See p.221

Roatan and Utila, Bay Islands, Honduras Dazzling strips of pure white sand and some of the best diving and snorkelling in the region. See p.436

San Juan de Sur, Nicaragua Another congenial backpacker surf resort, with dark-sand beaches, fresh seafood and waterfront bars. See p.491

Puerto Viejo de Talamanca, Costa Rica Tackle the challenging waves and high-octane party scene at Costa Rica's premier surf resort. See p.139

Tortuguero, Costa Rica This palm-fringed sand bar is the best place in the region to witness turtles laying eggs – a magical experience. See p.133

ABOVE PLACENCIA, BELIZE (P.94) **OPPOSITE** GRANADA, NICARAGUA (P.484)

Bay Islands are the main attraction in Honduras: the archetypal Caribbean dream of swaying palms and powdery white sand, they also provide plenty of opportunities for watersports on a budget. At the other end of the tourism scale, the largely uninhabited **Mosquitia** offers an enormous variety of wildlife, as well as the possibility of trips to remote Garífuna villages.

The up-and-coming travel destination of the Americas, **Nicaragua** makes up for its intimidating capital, **Managua**, with the beguiling Spanish colonial cities of **León** and **Granada**, both loaded with fine art, gorgeous architecture and a dynamic local and foreign student population. Nestled on the banks of vast **Lago de Nicaragua**, Granada is especially attractive and traveller-friendly, making the ideal base from which to explore the lake – serene **Isla de Ometepe** is the highlight of any excursion, its two gorgeous volcanoes separated by lush, tropical forest. Indeed, Nicaragua is richly endowed with volcano-strewn landscapes, though sun-seekers should make for its very own idyllic, low-key Caribbean island, **Little Corn**. Surfers can head for **San Juan del Sur**, now a major backpacker destination, while in the far south you can spy sloths, monkeys, caimans and parrots as you drift down the **Río San Juan**, a fantastic trip that ends up at the historic fortress of **El Castillo**.

Costa Rica is the region's most established destination. Travelling here is easy and cheap, and its million-year-old rainforests and pristine beaches are exceptionally beautiful. You can learn to surf at **Talamanca** or **Playa Tamarindo**, admire macaws in **Parque Nacional Corcovado**, or watch turtles lay their eggs on the Caribbean coast at **Tortuguero**. The capital, **San José**, offers cosmopolitan bars, restaurants and museums, while provincial **Liberia** is a cowboy town with fiestas, rodeos and even bull-running.

With its historic ties to Colombia and the US, **Panama** offers a subtle but definite contrast to the rest of the region. Costs may be a little higher here, but the range of tropical landscapes, wildlife viewing and adventure sports on offer is overwhelming. The country is perhaps best known for its history-altering **canal**, a triumph of engineering well worth seeing up close. Buzzing **Panama City** is the most exciting city in Central America, with colonial history, skyscrapers and dazzling nightlife. There are simpler pleasures here, too: few travellers will want to leave without trying Panama's tasty national dish – *sancocho* – at restaurants such as *El Rincón Tableño*. The laidback **Bocas del Toro** archipelago is celebrated for its unmissable diving and chilled-out surf scene, or you could explore the highlands around **Boquete**, home to hiking trails, hot springs and what many regard to be the world's finest coffee. Finally, the wild and unspoiled forests of **Parque Nacional Darién** and the **Guna Yala** region on the north coast, home to the Guna people, are literally the ends of the road; travellers are often disappointed to find that there is no road link between Panama (Central America) and Colombia (South America) – just the dense, tropical jungle of the **Darién Gap**. This can be dangerous to traverse by land – to continue south you'll need to travel by plane or boat.

When to go

Subtropical Central America is brimming with verdant landscapes, nourished by the semi-annual rhythms of the wet and dry seasons. Tourism is at its peak during the **dry season** – or "summer" (*verano*) – that runs from roughly December to April. The **rainy season**, often called "winter" (*invierno*), lasts from May until November. The different seasons are more distinctly felt on the Pacific side of the isthmus than they are on the Caribbean, and the major determining factor of climate here is altitude. Coming from sea level or the lowland plains to the interior highlands can grant welcome relief from high heat and humidity. Average **temperatures** here are a good 10°C (15–20°F) cooler than in low-lying areas, where humidity levels can be uncomfortable and temperatures hover in the mid-thirties (95°F) for much of the year. See the "When to visit" information at the start of each chapter for a country-specific overview.

Coming to Central America to escape the dreary winter days of chillier climes is always welcome, but it's worth considering a trip during the wet season, also known as the "green season", when tourism lulls and cut-price deals are to be found. Take extra care when planning a trip at this time of year, however, as **road conditions** can deteriorate significantly with heavy rains, making travel more difficult. However, more often than not the rain showers you'll experience will be short-lived afternoon downpours, and there's a good chance that changes in the weather will hardly interfere with your trip at all.

FROM TOP COFFEE BERRIES, HUEHUETENANGO; SQUIRREL MONKEY, CORCOVADO; ACTUN TUNICHIL MUKNAL

Author picks

Climbing ash-strewn volcanoes, surfing monstrous Pacific waves and traversing some of Central America's most bone-shaking, pot-holed roads, our hard-travelling authors have visited every corner of this magnificent region. Here are some of their personal favourite moments:

Local feasts Relish Guatemala's Huehuetenango highland coffee (see p.325) and Belize's top artisanal chocolate producers (see box, p.98), or get adventurous with lizard, snake and chocolate-covered fruit at Juayúa's *feria gastronómica* (see p.251).

Volcanic adventures El Salvador's highest volcano, Volcán Santa Ana, and nearby Volcán Izalco with its beautiful, bare lava cone, make for spectacular hikes (see p.262); you could also climb up, then board down, an active volcano by moonlight in Nicaragua (see box, p.470).

Wonderful wildlife In Costa Rica you'll encounter an amazing range of wildlife in Corcovado (see p.188), including, if you're lucky, big cats, while Panama's San San Pond Sak Wetlands offer magical opportunities to watch manatees close up (see p.585), and night tours along Nicaragua's Río San Juan (see p.502) bring you into contact with caimans that are small enough to hold.

Best hike The ascent of Cerro Chirripó – Costa Rica's highest mountain – is tough but spectacular, following a steep trail through cloudforest with amazing valley views (see p.180).

Taking to the water For rafting and kayaking head for Río Cangrejal's rapids in Honduras (see p.429), or kayak along Guatemala's incomparable Río Dulce gorge (see p.343). Winding in a motorized dugout along Panama's serpentine Río Sambú, deep in the Darién, is a real adventure (see p.557).

Indiana Jones moment After swimming through a stream to enter the Maya caves of Actun Tunichil Muknal (see p.82), you'll come upon pristine skeletal remains just as the first archeologists did.

Learning to dive The Honduran island of Utila is one of the least expensive places in the world to learn to dive – and it has a great backpacker scene (see p.437).

> Our author recommendations don't end here. We've flagged up our favourite places – a perfectly sited hostel, an atmospheric café, a special restaurant – throughout the guide, highlighted with the ★ symbol.

Festivals and Events

1 **FIESTA DE SAN JERÓNIMO, MASAYA, NICARAGUA**

See p.482

St Jerome is honoured with three months (Sept–Nov) of revelry in Masaya, beginning with the satirical Torovenado carnival.

2 **GARÍFUNA SETTLEMENT DAY, BELIZE**

See p.90

Enthusiastic celebrations to mark the arrival of the Garífuna people in Belize.

3 **DAY OF THE DEAD, SANTIAGO SACATEPÉQUEZ, GUATEMALA**

See p.298

Massive, beautiful kites are flown in the cemetery to commemorate the dead.

4 **LAS TABLAS CARNIVAL, PANAMA**

See p.567

Panama's Azuero Peninsula resounds with lively fiestas; the vibrant February carnival in Las Tablas features ornately costumed processions and communal water fights.

5 **SEMANA SANTA**

See p.288

Semana Santa, or Easter week, is the most important Catholic festival on the isthmus.

6 **FESTIVAL DE CONGOS Y DIABLOS, PORTOBELO, PANAMA**

See p.548

Afro-Panamanian fiesta celebrating the Congos of Portobelo, descendants of runaway slaves, with exuberant drumming, dancing and devil costumes.

Architectural Splendour

1 ANTIGUA, GUATEMALA
See p.288

Gorgeous, traveller-friendly colonial town, ringed by towering volcanoes.

2 CASCO VIEJO, PANAMA CITY
See p.527

The grandest Spanish colonial enclave in the region, studded with elegant palacios, churches and museums.

3 LEÓN, NICARAGUA
See p.467

The energetic old capital is home to a dazzling array of colonial buildings, churches and monuments to national poet Rubén Darío.

4 TIKAL, GUATEMALA
See p.366

The greatest Maya ruins in Mesoamerica boast six awe-inspiring pyramids towering above the rainforest.

5 CARACOL, BELIZE
See p.85

Vast Maya city in the jungle, the largest ancient site in Belize and home to the awe-inspiring Caana, the 42m-high "Sky Palace".

6 COPÁN, HONDURAS
See p.409

Magnificent Maya site, especially lauded for its ensemble of exquisite carvings and statues.

The Great Outdoors

1 SURFING, EL SALVADOR
See p.226
The Pacific coast boasts some of Central America's best surfing beaches. Las Flores, with its jungle setting and black sand, is one of the best.

2 VOLCANO-HOPPING, COSTA RICA
See p.176
Activities abound in this picture-perfect volcanic landscape.

3 RAFTING, PANAMA
See p.579
Panama's Chiriquí River offers amazing and exhilarating whitewater adventures.

4 DIVING IN THE BAY ISLANDS, HONDURAS
See p.436
Abundant marine life, clear waters and a stunning coral reef.

5 JAGUAR-SPOTTING, BELIZE
See p.93
Explore the stunning Belizean rainforest in search of these beautiful creatures.

6 VOLCANO-BOARDING
See p.470
Hike up the ashy black slopes of Cerro Negro then surf all the way down.

Indigenous Cultures

1 KEKÖLDI RESERVE, COSTA RICA
See p.139
Tours offer a glimpse of the jungle homes of the Bribrí and Cabecar peoples.

2 WESTERN HIGHLANDS, GUATEMALA
See p.309
Home to a huge and varied population of Maya groups.

3 GUNA CULTURE, GUNA YALA, PANAMA
See p.559
Experience the intriguing island life of the San Blas archipelago.

4 GARÍFUNA VILLAGES, HONDURAS
See p.90
Learn about this remarkable ethnic group, descendants of Caribs and African slaves.

5 LAGO DE ATITLÁN, GUATEMALA
See p.298
Visit the Maya villages and craft markets around this stunning lake.

6 RUTA LENCA, HONDURAS
See p.400
Soak up Lenca culture in the towns of La Esperanza and San Juan Intibucá.

Itineraries

You can't expect to fit everything Central America has to offer into one trip, and we don't suggest you try. On the following pages is a selection of itineraries that guide you through the different countries, picking out a few of the best experiences and major attractions along the way.

THE GRAND TOUR

❶ **Belizean cayes and atolls** Snorkel, scuba dive or fish off the hundreds of cayes which form part of Belize's spectacular Barrier Reef. **See p.61**

❷ **The Maya Mountain Caves, Belize** Well-preserved jungle caves, once used in Maya rituals, offer up-close encounters with ancient history. Those at Actun Tunichil Muknal (ATM) provide one of the most spectacular archeological experiences in Central America. **See p.82**

❸ **Tikal, Guatemala** Arguably the most impressive Maya ruin in Central America, this ancient city is dominated by six temples and surrounded by thousands of other structures, all surrounded by jungle. **See p.366**

❹ **Guatemala Highlands** With its volcanoes, mountain ranges, lakes and valleys, this is one of Guatemala's most beautiful areas. **See p.309**

❺ **Bay Islands, Honduras** To catch a glimpse of the elusive whale shark, head here in October or November – or simply spend days sailing or fishing on a remote island. **See p.436**

❻ **San Salvador, El Salvador** At the foot of a volcano, El Salvador's buzzing capital is a heady mix of galleries, museums and nightclubs. **See p.202**

❼ **Granada, Nicaragua** With its elegant colonial buildings, Granada is Nicaragua's architectural gem, an ideal base for exploring nearby lakes and volcanoes. **See p.484**

❽ **Isla de Ometepe, Nicaragua** This magical island, formed by two volcanoes, sits in the middle of a freshwater lake. There's jungle rainforest teeming with monkeys as well as beaches and mountains to explore. **See p.496**

❾ **Monteverde and Santa Elena, Costa Rica** These nature reserves are known as cloudforests because of their high altitude. Take a canopy tour to see lush vegetation and hundreds of wildlife species. **See p.143**

❿ **Parque Nacional Corcovado, Costa Rica** Most people come to the park in search of rare animals like ocelot and tapir, and there are also deserted beaches, waterfalls and rainforests to explore. **See p.188**

⓫ **Bocas del Toro Archipelago, Panama** Famed for surfing and snorkelling, this diverse archipelago has it all: tropical rainforests, beaches and mangroves, contrasting cultures, and the chance to dance on the sand until dawn. **See p.583**

⓬ **San Blas Archipelago, Panama** Strung out along the Caribbean coast, the vast majority of these islands are uninhabited. Come here to get away from it all. **See p.588**

MAYA RUINS

❶ **Caracol, Belize** Belize's largest Maya site, an impressive jungle city that once defeated nearby Tikal, counts among its well-restored ruins a temple that is still today the tallest man-made structure in the country. **See p.85**

ABOVE SAN JUAN DEL SUR, NICARAGUA

THE GRAND TOUR

❷ Tikal, Guatemala Tikal is the superstar Maya attraction, a couple of hours away from the Belize border. **See p.366**

❸ El Mirador, Guatemala Remote and mysterious Preclassic Maya city, much of it still enveloped in jungle. Reaching it requires time and stamina – it's best reached by foot and mule, and most opt for a five-day trip from Flores, including up to eight hours' jungle

MAYA RUINS

trekking a day – but the reward is spectacular. **See p.372**

❹ Cancuén, Guatemala This affluent Maya trading town is a little-visited but worthwhile site. The road from Flores to Cobán passes near several other Maya sights too. **See p.357**

❺ Tazumal, El Salvador Smaller than its Guatemalan counterparts, but with a certain charm, the site features both Maya and Pipil constructions. **See p.258**

❻ Copán, Honduras One of the country's main tourist destinations, Copán is smaller than Tikal but features exquisite carvings and sculpture. **See p.409**

ALONG CA-1

From Guatemala to Panama, Central America Highway 1 runs for more than 1000km past beaches, cities and jungles. The following sites are all en – or just off – route.

❶ Quetzaltenango, Guatemala This beautifully sited city, a popular spot for learning Spanish or volunteering, is ideally placed for a leisurely tour of the highlands. **See p.317**

❷ San Salvador, El Salvador El Salvador's buzzing capital is rarely peaceful. But with its

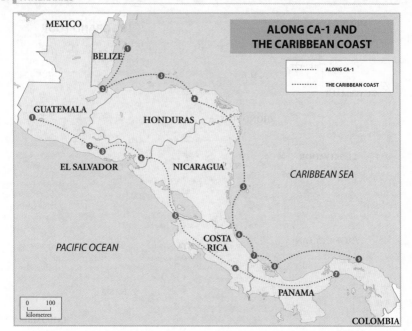

ALONG CA-1 AND THE CARIBBEAN COAST

.... ALONG CA-1
.... THE CARIBBEAN COAST

MEXICO

BELIZE

GUATEMALA

HONDURAS

EL SALVADOR

NICARAGUA

CARIBBEAN SEA

PACIFIC OCEAN

COSTA RICA

PANAMA

COLOMBIA

0   100
kilometres

Centro Histórico, green outskirts and politicized museums, it repays a visit. **See p.202**

❸ **San Vicente, El Salvador** Climb El Salvador's second-highest volcano, eye the famous clock tower and relish the stunning drive to this relaxed city. **See p.231**

❹ **Choluteca, Honduras** Steamy, substantial city containing one of Honduras's finest old colonial quarters. **See p.94**

❺ **San Juan del Sur, Nicaragua** Just off the highway in a gorgeous bay washed with rolling Pacific waves, this gringo-friendly beach town offers surfing, turtle-watching, fishing and plenty of nightlife. **See p.491**

❻ **San Isidro, Costa Rica** Hike up Mount Chirripó, Costa Rica's highest mountain, from the tiny village of San Gerardo, or simply explore the lush countryside surroundings. **See p.179**

❼ **Panama City, Panama** Both a base for visiting the nearby wildlife and famous canal and a sparkling, cosmopolitan city, this is one of the region's must-visits. **See p.527**

THE CARIBBEAN COAST

❶ **Caye Caulker, Belize** It may lack postcard-perfect beaches, but this laidback spot pulls in the younger crowds for its island-style nightlife and brilliant watersports – including snorkelling, diving, kayaking and kiteboarding. **See p.63**

❷ **Lívingston, Guatemala** Carib cuisine, punta rock and reggae make Lívingston a great place to party and an intriguing contrast to Guatemala's latino interior. **See p.341**

❸ **Bay Islands, Honduras** This 125km chain of islands off Honduras's Caribbean coast is a perfect destination for world-class (and affordable) diving, sailing and fishing. **See p.436**

❹ **Río Plátano Biosphere Reserve, Honduras** This UNESCO World Heritage Site on the remote Mosquito Coast preserves one of the finest remaining stretches of Central American rainforest. **See p.435**

❺ **Little Corn, Nicaragua** Once a haven for pirates, this tiny, unspoilt island offers swaying palm trees, white-sand beaches and warm, clear water – the perfect place to recharge. **See p.509**

❻ **Parque Nacional Tortuguero, Costa Rica** While turtle-watching is the big draw at this coastal national park, a trip along the Tortuguero Canal in a dugout canoe comes a close second. **See p.134**

❼ **Puerto Viejo de Talamanca, Costa Rica** One of the liveliest backpacker towns in Central

America, Puerto Viejo also boasts one of the best surf breaks on the Caribbean. **See p.139**

❽ Bocas del Toro Archipelago, Panama This once-isolated region offers opportunities to explore reefs and rainforests, sample diverse cultures and sip cocktails at sunset. **See p.583**

❾ Guna Yala Archipelago, Panama Part of the autonomous Guna region, these idyllic offshore islands offer a fabulous beach holiday and the chance to sample a unique culture. **See p.588**

WILDLIFE

❶ Belize's Barrier Reef Running the length of Belize's coastline, this network of coral and cayes – the second largest in the world – is home to a dazzling array of marine life. **See p.61**

❷ Cockscomb Basin Wildlife Sanctuary, Belize An excellent trail network provides exhilarating glimpses of tapirs, anteaters and, for the lucky few, jaguars. **See p.93**

❸ Biotopo del Quetzal, Guatemala Spend dawn or dusk scouring the forest for this most beautiful of birds, venerated by the Maya, and now Guatemala's national symbol. **See p.349**

❹ Bay Islands, Honduras This string of idyllic white-sand islands is one of the few places on earth where you can swim with whale sharks. **See p.436**

❺ Lago de Yojoa, Honduras Take an early-morning paddle in this picturesque lake, surrounded by mountains and home to over four hundred species of bird. **See p.398**

❻ Reserva Biológica Indio Maíz, Nicaragua Downstream from El Castillo, the Río Bartola branches off from the Río San Juan at the start of the Indio-Maíz Reserve. This vast rainforest is home to tapirs, poison-dart frogs, scarlet macaws, toucans and many hundreds of other species. **See p.503**

❼ Parque Nacional Tortuguero, Costa Rica The fantastic journey here – drifting through verdant jungle, past wooden houses on stilts – is only a sideshow to the main event: the *desove*, where hundreds of green, hawksbill and leatherback turtles haul themselves ashore each night to lay their eggs. **See p.134**

❽ Parque Nacional Corcovado, Costa Rica The most biologically diverse area in Central America harbours everything from tapirs to tayras; stumble across them on one of the park's jungle treks. **See p.188**

❾ Isla Coiba, Panama Central America's largest island boasts extraordinary biodiversity, both in its rainforests and marine surroundings, providing superlative wildlife viewing and world-class diving. **See p.572**

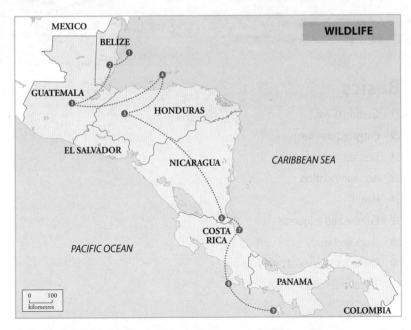

BOAT IN PUERTO VIEJO, COSTA RICA

Basics

Getting there

While you can travel to Central America overland from Mexico or by sea from Colombia, your most likely point of entry is through one of the region's international airports. Of these, the most popular gateways are **Guatemala City, San José (Costa Rica) and Panama City.**

Prices for flights to the region with established carriers can vary hugely. For the best fares on scheduled flights, book well in advance of travel, as airlines only have a fixed number of seats at their lowest prices. Fully check conditions before making a booking, however, as these cheap fares are almost always heavily restricted; the one provision nearly all carriers attach to tickets is the required duration of trip – generally the best prices allow a maximum stay of one to three months, with prices rising for a six-month duration, and again for a year's validity. It is not always cheapest to book direct with the airline; some **travel agents** (see p.29) can negotiate discounted fares, in particular for students or those under 26. It may be worth considering a **one-way ticket** if you are planning a long trip, although you may have difficulties passing through immigration without an onward ticket (see p.29).

Another option is to look into routes operated by **charter airlines** to package-holiday destinations. For the most part these are available from the US to Belize, Costa Rica and Panama, although it is also possible to reach Cancún in Mexico's Yucatán Peninsula from the UK. These charter flights allow limited flexibility, usually for a fixed period of one or two weeks, but can be picked up last-minute at very reasonable prices.

If planning a substantial amount of overland travel in Central America, consider purchasing an **open-jaw ticket** (for example, arriving in Guatemala City and returning from Panama City). Prices for open-jaw tickets are usually comparable to a straightforward return. Alternatively, **round-the-world (RTW)** itineraries can incorporate Central American destinations if you travel via the US and onward to Auckland, Sydney, etc (see box, p.28).

From the UK and Ireland

There are **no direct flights** from the UK or Ireland to Central America. Most routes are offered by US carriers – American, United and Delta – and involve connections in the States (see below). Onward flights to Central America may be operated by regional airlines such as Copa (Ⓦcopaair.com) and Avianca (Ⓦavianca.com; formerly TACA and its subsidiary LACSA). A few European airlines also offer flights through their hub cities to Guatemala City, San José or Panama City – these include Iberia (via Madrid; Ⓦiberia.com) and KLM (via Amsterdam; Ⓦklm.com). As clearing US immigration and customs can be a lengthy process, these European flights can frequently be faster. Alternatively – and less expensively – a wide network of carriers flies from Europe direct to Mexico, from where you can travel to Central America (see p.28).

Journey times from the UK and Ireland vary according to connection times, but it is possible to get door-to-door in a day. Published return **fares** from London to Central American capitals start at around £600–700 in the winter, rising substantially in the summer months.

From the US and Canada

Several US carriers operate **direct flights** to all Central American capitals. The main US hubs, offering good connections with other North American cities, are Houston (United; Ⓦunited.com), Fort Lauderdale (Spirit Airlines; Ⓦspiritair.com), Dallas (American; Ⓦaa.com) and Atlanta (Delta; Ⓦdelta.com), but there are also direct routes from New York and Los Angeles to Guatemala City,

---

TRAVEL VIA THE US: ESTA CLEARANCE

The US government requires those travellers coming to or through the US on the Visa Waiver Program to apply online for clearance via **ESTA** (Electronic System for Travel Authorization) – if you arrive at the airport without having done so, the airline won't allow you to check in.

To **apply for clearance** visit Ⓦhttp://esta.cbp.dhs.gov/esta/ at least three days before travelling; you'll need your passport to hand, and the admin fee at the time of publication is US$14. Clearance remains valid for two years. Companies advertising assistance with ESTA clearance should be ignored, as no officially recognized bodies provide this service.

Note also that Visa Waiver Program qualifiers coming to the US overland (via Mexico or Canada) do not need to have ESTA authorization – you just fill in the green I-94W form at the border instead (make sure you hand in the form when you leave).

A BETTER KIND OF TRAVEL

At Rough Guides we are passionately committed to travel. We believe it helps us understand the world we live in and the people we share it with – and of course tourism is vital to many developing economies. But the scale of modern tourism has also damaged some places irreparably, and climate change is accelerated by most forms of transport, especially flying. All Rough Guides' flights are carbon-offset, and every year we donate money to a variety of environmental charities.

San Salvador, San José and Panama City. Flights are frequent and can take as little as two hours (Miami to Belize City, for example). Low-cost carrier Jet Blue (W jetblue.com) also flies to San José (Costa Rica) from Fort Lauderdale and Orlando, and from Liberia (Costa Rica) to New York. Prices vary – advance return fares start from as little as US$300 (including taxes), though a more realistic estimate would be in the region of US$400–600.

From **Canada** you can fly direct with Air Canada (W aircanada.com) from Toronto to Costa Rica (San José; 7hr). There are also seasonal direct flights between Toronto and Montréal to Central American cities with Air Transat (W airtransat.com), and from Toronto to Liberia (Costa Rica) with WestJet (W westjet.com). Return trips between Canada and Central America start at about Can$700, although there are many travel companies offering seasonal packages with flights from Can$500. Alternatively, there are many connections to all Central American capitals via the US.

From Australia, New Zealand and South Africa

There are **no direct flights** from Australasia or South Africa to Central America, but it's easy enough to connect with flights in the US or Europe. From **Australia** and **New Zealand**, the quickest route is through Los Angeles and then Dallas or Houston (approximately 20hr; from Aus$1700/NZ$2000). From **South Africa** (Johannesburg) the options include BA (W ba.com)/ American via London and New York, Iberia via Madrid and Delta via Dakar and Atlanta (from

ZAR12,000). Connections are not great: the journey takes at least 24 hours.

From Mexico

It is fairly straightforward to travel overland **by bus** from Mexico to Guatemala or Belize. Several companies offer services with varying degrees of comfort (worth taking into consideration, given the length of most trips – Palenque to Flores is eight hours, Tulum to Belize City is nine). Popular **routes** include: Cancún/Tulum (via Chetumal/Corozal) to Belize City; Palenque (via Frontera Corozal/Bethel) to Flores, Guatemala; San Cristóbal de Las Casas (via Ciudad Cuauhtémoc/La Mesilla) to Huehuetenango; and the Mexican Pacific coast (via Ciudad Hidalgo/ Ciudad Tecún Umán) to Quetzaltenango.

Unfortunately, one annoyance experienced by many travellers (particularly crossing into Guatemala) is the demand for unofficial **"fees"** at immigration – usually it's not immigration officials that ask for this fee, but a third party. It's often easier to go with local services than one of the long-distance carriers – travelling with a busload of gringos can prove expensive. It is worth changing pesos at the border with moneychangers, as an opportunity may not arise later. Be sure to do your sums prior to agreeing to a transaction and check what you're given before handing over your cash.

It's possible, too, to **fly** from many of Mexico's airports to Central America's main cities with airlines such as Aeroméxico (W aeromexico.com), Avianca and Copa – one-way fares for Interjet's Mexico City to Guatemala City flight start at just US$85 (W interjet.com.mx).

ROUND-THE-WORLD (RTW) FLIGHTS

Round-the-world flights connect Sydney, Perth, Auckland and Johannesburg to Mexico City, Guatemala City, San José and Panama City, usually via Los Angeles or London using American Airlines or code-share partners. It is also possible to reach Australasia from both Santiago (Chile) and Buenos Aires (Argentina) as part of the same RTW tickets with BA/Qantas's Oneworld (W ba.com/W qantas.com). British Airways/Qantas and United/Air New Zealand (W airnz.co.nz) Star Alliance fares from London start at around £1500, and allow multiple stops in several continents within a certain mileage.

From South America

There is currently **no overland passage** between Central and South America due to lack of infrastructure and a guerrilla presence in the Darién jungle bordering Colombia and Panama. Known as the "Darién Gap", this break in the Carretera Panamericana (Panamerican Highway) means that intercontinental travellers will need to cross this area either **by air** or **by sea**.

Unless part of an airpass or RTW ticket, **flights** from South to Central America are typically cheaper bought in the country of departure (agents there will have access to discounted fares). However, as always, booking at the last minute can mean settling for the highest prices, so ideally you should plan at least a few weeks in advance. One-way fares from Quito/Bogotá to Panama are in the region of US$500 (considerably less with a student card).

There's a steady flow of **sea traffic** between Panama and Colombia via the Caribbean, and private sailboats often offer passage as crew for the three- to five-day journey between Colón and Cartagena (see box, p.550). Despite several attempts to establish one (most recently in 2012), there are still no regularly scheduled ferries, but many boats frequently make the run – usually depending on demand.

AGENTS AND OPERATORS

Coco Tours Honduras ☎ 504 3335 4599, ⓦ hondurascoco.com. Small, locally based tour company leading a variety of Central American tours, including cultural Garífuna visits, with a portion of profits supporting Garífuna projects.

Dragoman UK ☎ 1728 885576, US ☎ 1800 805 7680, Australia ☎ 1300 352 054, New Zealand ☎ 0800 770107, ⓦ dragoman .com. The overland adventure specialists offer a 32-day "Central America Adventure" and a 28-day trip from Guatemala to Panama City.

Exodus UK ☎ 1800 843 4272, ⓦ exodus.co.uk. Huge range of adventure travel packages, from 12-day camping trips around Belize to 15-day cycling tours of Costa Rica, Nicaragua and Panama.

Geckos Adventures Australia ☎ 613 8601 4444, ⓦ geckos adventures.com. Australian-based agency, with a number of tours led by local guides within Latin America.

Hosteltrail UK ☎ 131 208 0007, ⓦ hosteltrail.com. Backpacker hostels and tour operators throughout Central America.

Intrepid Travel UK ☎ 0800 781 1660, US ☎ 1800 970 7299, Australia ☎ 1300 018 871, New Zealand ☎ 0800 600 610, ⓦ intrepidtravel.com. Specializing in small-group, off-the-beaten-path tours through Central America, from 17 to 58 days.

Journey Latin America UK ☎ 020 8622 8469, ⓦ journeylatinamerica.co.uk. Well-established tour operator offering tailor-made itineraries as well as sound advice on travel in the region.

Keka's Travel Agency ☎ 1 800 593 5352, ⓦ kekastravel.com. Miami-based operators specializing in Latin American travel, offering low airfares and budget packages.

North South Travel UK ☎ 01245 608 291, ⓦ northsouthtravel .co.uk. Friendly, competitive travel agency, offering discounted fares worldwide. Profits are used to support projects in the developing world, especially the promotion of sustainable tourism.

Quetzaltrekkers Nicaragua ☎ 505 2311 6695, Guatemala ☎ 502 7765 5895, ⓦ quetzaltrekkers.com. Nonprofit organization providing trekking tours in Guatemala and Nicaragua, with profits directly funding children's educational and recreational projects.

REI Adventures US ☎ 1800 622 2236, ⓦ rei.com/adventures. Outdoor adventure experts offering kayaking, jungle and multisport trips to Belize, and Arenal Volcano, jungle and sea adventures to Costa Rica.

STA Travel UK ☎ 0871 230 0040, US ☎ 1 800 781 4040, Australia ☎ 134 782, New Zealand ☎ 0800 474 400, South Africa ☎ 0861 781 781, ⓦ statravel.com. Worldwide specialists in independent travel; also student IDs, travel insurance, car rental, rail passes, and more. Good discounts for students and under-26s.

Trailfinders UK ☎ 0845 058 5858, Republic of Ireland ☎ 01 677 7888, Australia ☎ 1300 780 212, ⓦ trailfinders.com. One of the best-informed and most efficient agents for independent travellers.

Tucan Travel UK ☎ 020 8896 1600, Australia ☎ 0293 266 633, ⓦ tucantravel.com. An independently owned agency offering a variety of worldwide tours, including comprehensive budget expeditions.

Wilderness Travel US ☎ 1800 368 2794, ⓦ wildernesstravel .com. Off-the-beaten-path adventure tours, safaris and treks to Costa Rica, Guatemala and Panama.

Yampu Tours UK ☎ 0800 011 2424, Australia ☎ 1800 224 201, US ☎ 1 888 926 7801, ⓦ yampu.com. Another small indie outfit, offering a large number of tours within Latin America.

Entry requirements

Nationals of the UK, Ireland, Canada, the US, Australia and New Zealand do not need visas to visit any of the seven Central American countries. Visitors are eligible for stays of either thirty days (Belize, Panama) or, in the case of Costa Rica and the CA-4 countries, ninety days (see box, p.30).

You should be able to **extend** this period by leaving the country and re-entering, or you can pay for a thirty- or ninety-day visa extension at immigration offices. You should have a valid **passport** with

CENTRAL AMERICA BORDER CONTROL AGREEMENT

Guatemala, El Salvador, Honduras and Nicaragua are party to the **Central America Border Control Agreement (CA-4)**. Under the terms of this agreement, tourists may travel within any of these four countries for a period of up to ninety days without completing entry and exit formalities at border and immigration checkpoints (though officers will still check your passport), aside from paying entry fees. The ninety-day period begins at the first point of entry to any of the CA-4 countries. Fines are applied if you exceed the ninety-day limit (at least US$115), although a request for an extension can be made for up to ninety additional days by paying a fee (around US$15–20), before the limit expires, in one of the countries themselves (to do this in El Salvador you must be sponsored by a CA-4 national). Note that you can only extend your visa once – you must leave the CA-4 area after the second ninety days expires. You can avoid the extension process by travelling to a country outside the CA-4, and then re-entering (usually after a minimum of 24 hours) – you'll then get a fresh ninety-day visa.

at least six months remaining and, officially, an onward ticket (these are seldom checked but may be a sticking point at border crossings or customs, especially entering Costa Rica).

All countries charge **entry fees** (sometimes referred to as a "tourist card") to certain nationalities, depending on relations between the countries. Investigate your destination's entry requirements before travelling, and arrive prepared with cash. For more information about specific countries and border crossings in Central America, see the relevant country's chapter, and always check with your embassy before travelling.

CENTRAL AMERICAN EMBASSIES ABROAD

Belize UK: Belize High Commission, 3/F, 45 Crawford Place, London, W1H 4LP (☎ 020 7723 3603, ⓦ belizehighcommission.com);

US: 2535 Massachusetts Ave NW, Washington DC, 20008 (☎ 202 332 9636, ⓦ embassyofbelize.org).

Costa Rica Canada: 350 Sparks St, Suite 701, ON, K1R 7S8 (☎ 613 562 2855, ⓦ costaricaembassy.com); UK: Flat 1, 14 Lancaster Gate, London, W2 3LH (☎ 020 7706 8844, ⓦ costaricanembassy.co.uk, ⓔ info@costaricanembassy.co.uk); US: 2114 S St NW, Washington DC, 20008 (☎ 202 480 2200, ⓦ costarica-embassy.org).

El Salvador Canada: 209 Kent St, Ottawa, K2P 1Z8 (☎ 613 238 2939); UK: 8 Dorset Square, London, NW1 6PU (☎ 020 7224 9800, ⓔ embajadalondres@rree.gob.sv); US: 1400 16th St NW, Suite 100, Washington DC, 20036 (☎ 202 595 7500, ⓦ elsalvador.org).

Guatemala Canada: 130 Albert St, Suite 1010, Ottawa, ON, K1P 5G4 (☎ 613 233 7237, ⓔ embcanada@minex.gob.gt); South Africa: 16/F, 2 Long St, Cape Town (☎ 021 418 2020, ⓔ mrast @solo.pipex.co.za); UK: 13 Fawcett St, London, SW10 9HN (☎ 020 7351 3042, ⓔ embgranbretana@minex.gob.gt); US: 2220 R Street NW, Washington DC, 20008 (☎ 202 745 4953, ⓔ embestadosunidos@minex.gob.gt).

BORDER CROSSINGS

Most travellers in Central America take advantage of the close proximity of the region's many distinct nations, crossing international borders regularly. While for the most part this is straightforward, "border days" can also be some of the most exhausting of your trip – follow the tips below to ease the strain.

• Always check specific entry requirements before heading for the border.
• Ensure that your passport is stamped on both entry and exit.
• Try to cross in the morning, when public transport links are more frequent and queues lighter.
• Research current exchange rates online at ⓦ oanda.com or ⓦ xe.com and be savvy when dealing with moneychangers.
• If asked for "processing fees" request a receipt (such as the stamp given by Panama). Without one, these fees are not legal. Be sure to bring a small amount of US dollars for any unexpected fees.
• Do not engage in discussion of your business with strangers. Borders are notorious hangouts for petty criminals and con men. If you are confused about how to proceed, ask a uniformed official.
• At popular crossings avoid group transport, which will slow your progress considerably. Chicken buses operate these routes as frequently as any other (although not at night).
• If given a stamped entry document do not lose it – you will require it later for departure.

Honduras Canada: 151 Slater St, Suite 805-A, Ottawa, ON, K1P 5H3 (☎ 1 613 233 8900, ⓦ hondurasemb.org); UK: 115 Gloucester Place, London, W1U 6JT (☎ 020 7486 4880); US: 3007 Tilden St NW, Suite 4M, Washington DC, 20008 (☎ 202 966 7702, ⓦ hondurasemb.org).

Nicaragua UK: Vicarage House, Suite 31, 58–60 Kensington Church St, London, W8 4DB (☎ 020 7938 2373, ⓔ emb.ofnicaragua @virgin.net); US: 1627 New Hampshire Ave NW, Washington DC, 20009 (☎ 202 939 6531).

Panama Canada: 130 Albert St, Suite 300, Ottawa, ON K1P 5G4 (☎ 613 236 7177, ⓦ embassyofpanama.ca); UK: Panama House, 40 Hertford St, London, W1Y 7TG (☎ 020 7409 2255, ⓦ panamaconsul.co.uk); US: 2862 McGill Terrace NW, Washington DC, 20008 (☎ 202 483 1407, ⓦ embassyofpanama.org).

Getting around

If you're not in a hurry and are willing to travel on public transport, you can get around most of Central America on US$1–2 per hour (probably slightly more in Belize, Costa Rica and Panama). While public transport systems are sometimes slow – and almost always crowded and sweaty – they can often also be extremely efficient: in most places you will rarely have to wait long for onward transport. On major roads, especially, buses run with high frequency and can offer a great insight into the day-to-day life of the country. Flights are relatively expensive but shuttle long-distance between major cities and can help access remote areas, such as the region's many wonderful islands.

The following is a general guide to Central American transport. More specific information can be found in the "Getting around" section of each country's "Basics" section.

By bus

Travelling **by bus** in Central America is by far the most convenient, cheap and comprehensive way to get around. The **cost** of travel depends mainly on the quality of the transport – you can look forward to paying anywhere from approximately US$1/hr for one of the region's infamous "chicken buses" to US$6/hr for a guaranteed seat on a more comfortable "Pullman"-style coach.

Chicken buses (see box p.32) generally serve as second-class, or local, services. They stop on demand, wherever passengers ask to get off or

NAVIGATING CENTRAL AMERICAN CITIES

The majority of Central American cities are laid out on a **grid system**, making navigation fairly straightforward: usually numbered calles (streets) run east–west and numbered avenidas (avenues) run north–south, with a *parque* or plaza as the point zero. For more information on navigating specific cities, see the relevant chapter.

people flag down passing services. Sometimes it can seem like you're stopping every 30m, but these buses are handy for impromptu itineraries and each country's extensive network of routes allows you to get off the beaten path with relative ease. In most places chicken buses tend to run **on demand** rather than to schedules, departing when full, though in Costa Rica, Nicaragua and Panama (where, in fact, the chicken buses, or *"diablos rojos"* are being phased out, and are rare outside the capital) schedules are more regular – in those countries it is wise to check at bus terminals before travelling for current timetable information. **Tickets** are usually bought on board, once the journey is under way, either from the conductor or from his assistant. It is always worth checking the price before boarding to avoid rip-offs, which are not unknown. **Luggage** usually goes on the roof; always keep valuables on your person and an eye on your stuff as best you can, as theft on buses is unfortunately all too common – interior overhead luggage racks are particularly risky.

Pullman buses generally cover long-distance routes and operate to a schedule, making much quicker progress and so remaining economical when you wish to cover ground more rapidly. Seats should be reserved at the appropriate ticket office in advance. Several bus companies run services from one country to another as well as within individual countries.

In addition to the sites listed below, ⓦ horariode buses.com provides a useful rundown of online bus **schedules** in Central America.

REGIONAL BUS CONTACTS

Hedman Alas ⓦ hedmanalas.com. Connecting major cities in Honduras and Guatemala.

King Quality ⓦ king-qualityca.com. Buses from Tapachula, Mexico, depart for all Central American capitals down to San José, Costa Rica.

Pullmantur ⓦ pullmantur.com. Luxury buses from San Salvador (El Salvador) to Tegucigalpa (Honduras) and Guatemala City.

CHICKEN BUSES

Central America's "**chicken buses**" are legendary. These are old school buses from North America, with a few important modifications to get them ready for the rigours of travel: most likely some Jesus stickers, elongated seats for extra bums and a speaker system for the reggaetón soundtrack. Once you find the bus you need, get on and wait for it to fill up around you; luggage (livestock, bicycles, chickens, the kitchen sink, your backpack) goes wherever it will fit. Just when you think the bus couldn't possibly get any fuller, twenty snack vendors will jump aboard, screaming at you to buy full-fat goodies. Journeys are never dull. But besides entertainment, all the madness does provide one of the best opportunities to chat to local people. Even if your Spanish is shaky, a smile and a simple "Buenas" goes a long way. Once the ice is broken, your fellow passengers will undoubtedly help you to reach your destination with ease.

Tica Bus Ⓦ ticabus.com. Tica Bus covers the most ground, spanning the region from Panama City through to Chiapas, Mexico, and stopping at most major cities.

Transnica Ⓦ transnica.com. Routes from Managua (Nicaragua) to San José (Costa Rica) and Tegucigalpa (Honduras).

Transportes Galgos Ⓦ transgalgosinter.com.gt. For travel between Tapachula in Mexico, El Salvador and Quetzaltenango and Guatemala City in Guatemala.

By plane

Although Central America has a good **international flight network**, connecting the region's key points of interest with its capital cities, unless you are severely pushed for time few flights are worth the money, since distances are usually short and accessible by bus, and prices aren't particularly cheap (around US$200/US$400 student/standard one-way for Guatemala City–San José). Regional carriers Avianca/TACA (Ⓦ avianca.com) and Copa (Ⓦ copaair .com) both offer youth fares; to be eligible you will need to have an ISIC card (see box, p.42). If you do plan to do a bit of flying, consider buying an **airpass**, which will allow short hops within Central America, as well as routes to Mexico, the US and some South American destinations. Passes can be bought in conjunction with your international ticket in your country of origin. However, these usually force you to specify your route in advance and rarely allow for trips to your preferred destinations (most travellers are not necessarily interested in visiting the region's chaotic capital cities).

Of greater interest to budget travellers are the **domestic flights** that connect the region's more populous areas to isolated tourist destinations – such as Nicaragua's Corn Islands, Panama's Bocas del Toro and Honduras's Bay Islands, all of which are more than a day's travel by bus from their respective capital cities. Internal flights can be reasonably priced, especially if bought in advance, although in general you will have to purchase them locally.

By boat

You're likely to travel **by boat** at some point if you spend any time in Central America – in some places watercraft are the only way to get around, in others they can provide a welcome break from the monotony of bumpy bus rides. Vessels range from the canoe-like *lanchas* with outboard motor to chugging ferries and speedy catamarans. Watery journeys of note include: Punta Gorda (Belize) to Lívingston (Guatemala) and onward to the Río Dulce area (see p.98); across Lago de Nicaragua to Isla de Ometepe (see p.496); down the Río San Juan to the Caribbean (see p.502). There are also some budget-friendly options through the Panama Canal (see box, p.542).

By car

Considering the prevalence of public transport and the relative expense of **car rental**, renting a vehicle is unlikely to have much appeal. If, however, you want to reach isolated spots, and can find a trusted group to share the costs and/or risks, renting a car (or 4WD) does give you some flexibility. **Prices** vary throughout the region (US$25–40/day, depending on your location, for the cheapest vehicles, with insurance extra). Always familiarize yourself with the conditions of rental before signing a contract and be aware that in the event of an accident, insurance excess levels are usually huge, sometimes up to US$1000 – meaning that you'll have to pay for fairly common damages (such as dented bumpers and burst tyres), costing several hundred dollars (the excess can sometimes be reduced by paying a higher daily insurance premium). With no insurance you'll be liable for the cost of a new car in the event of accident or theft. If you do decide to rent a vehicle you will need a full driving licence, credit card and passport. Some agencies do not rent to under-25s, although others may have an age limit of 21. Always park securely, preferably in a car park with attendant, especially in cities. There are no breakdown services available, but petrol stations are plentiful; the price of fuel is slightly higher than in the US but considerably cheaper than in Europe.

Taxis

Travelling by **taxi** in Central America is something of a gamble, but a necessary one: drivers are either some of the friendliest, most helpful folk you'll encounter or some of the biggest swindlers, but at night, especially in large cities, they provide the only safe mode of transport. Always settle a **price** before getting in (even if there is a meter, try to get an estimate), clarifying that the price is for the journey, regardless of the number of passengers or amount of luggage; throughout the region most short journeys will cost a minimum US$2–5. In terms of safety, always use registered taxis. Costa Rica and Nicaragua in particular have seen a rise in taxi-jackings; as many taxis are **colectivos**, picking up random passengers along the route, it has become all too frequent for drivers to pick up armed passengers who will forcibly ask you to hand over your cash (if you are lucky), or drive you around to drain your bank accounts with ATM withdrawals. Ask at tourist information offices and local hotels for recommended drivers, and be alert. It also pays to keep an eye on the map as your journey progresses – a possible deterrent to drivers quite literally taking you for a ride. Note that the *colectivo* taxi is unknown in Guatemala, where, as in Honduras and El Salvador, the three-wheeled tuk-tuk, or **moto-taxi**, is becoming more common.

By bike

Though many locals travel by bicycle, **bike rental** is not widely available in Central America. However, some countries, like Belize, are seeing increased bicycle tourism, and a number of travellers are also touring the region with their own

bikes. Notwithstanding the dangers of Central America's anarchic road customs, cycling in the region is facilitated by the mostly flat terrain, relatively short distances between settlements and ease of transporting bicycles aboard buses.

Accommodation

Budget accommodation in Central America is plentiful, and often of excellent quality. The best places to stay are truly memorable for their warm atmosphere, great facilities and stunning location – they are also invariably the best places to get up-to-date travel information. Others, however, can promise cockroaches, poor sanitation and noisy neighbours. It's always worth shopping around, and inspecting rooms before paying.

Do not be afraid to walk away and look at alternatives – this may even precipitate a drop in prices. **Booking ahead** is generally not necessary, except during holiday periods in busy tourist centres – plan on arriving early or calling well in advance.

Hotels and guesthouses

The mainstays of travellers' accommodation in Central America are **hotels** and **guesthouses** (and their regional equivalents: *posadas*, *pensiones*, cabinas, cabañas and *hospedajes*). *Cabinas* and *cabañas*, where accommodation is in individual structures and detached from other guests, are usually found at the beach or in the jungle.

The room rates given throughout this guide are for the **cheapest double room in high season**. A basic double room (around US$20) will have a bed, a light and probably a fan (*ventilador*). Most places offer the choice of private or shared **bathroom**; a private bath (*baño privado*) will cost a few dollars more than a shared one (*baño compartido*). **Hot water** is a rarity unless you're splurging on a swankier room; keep an eye out for gas-fired hot

---

JUNGLE LODGES

Throughout Central America you will find an array of rural **jungle lodges** in some truly magical locations. While many lodges charge fairly exorbitant prices, not all are beyond a budget traveller's means. If you have the opportunity, staying at a lodge is usually well worth the splurge and/or detour. However, as lodges are usually isolated, you will be captive to spending all your cash in one place. Lodge owners are of course wise to this and lay on all sorts of tempting treats to help relieve you of your cash.

water systems – the standard (and decidedly dodgy) electrical showerheads tend to produce tepid water at best and can also deliver electric shocks. Some hotels will provide you with towels and soap and most with toilet paper. By paying a few extra dollars you can also find rooms that come with cable TV, fridge, a/c, mosquito nets and/or balcony. Double rooms are often equivalent in price to two dorm beds (good news for couples and something for friends to consider). Private **single rooms**, on the other hand, are often only marginally discounted (if at all) from the standard price for a double. **Internet**, especially wi-fi, is becoming increasingly available throughout the region, and is often provided free to hotel guests.

Hostels

Hostels, while not particularly widespread, are increasingly common in Central America, often run by foreigners with a keen eye for backpackers' needs. These establishments offer some of the most sociable and comfortable lodgings in the region. A dorm bed should cost around US$7–12, but in capital cities (especially San José and Panama City) expect to pay around US$15. Most hostels have a few private rooms as well as dorms.

The best hostels may provide **facilities** such as a kitchen, internet and/or wi-fi access, lockers, bar and restaurant areas, TV and movies, as well as tours and activities. The lockers are a definite plus – theft does occur, so do not leave valuables lying around; you might consider travelling with your own padlock. Some hostels will even offer free board and lodging if you want to stay put and **work** for a period (see p.38).

Hostelling International cards are of little or no use in Central America.

Camping

Organized **campsites** are a rarity in Central America. However, some **national parks** do allow camping and have limited facilities such as drinking water, toilets and campfire provisions. Expect to pay around US$3–5 per person to pitch a tent (though Costa Rica can be pricier). Camping doesn't hold much appeal for locals, so don't expect to find gear on sale or for rent – you will have to carry what you need. It is also possible to pay to hang a **hammock** (your own or hired) in some areas. This may seem more appealing than an airless room, but the **mosquitoes** can be fierce – make sure you have a net.

Health

There's always a risk of illness in a country with a different climate, food and bacteria – still more so in a poor country with lower standards of sanitation than you might be accustomed to. Most visitors, however, get through Central America without experiencing anything more serious than an upset stomach as long as they observe basic precautions about hygiene, untreated water and insect bites.

Above all, it's important to get the best **advice** you can before you depart: visit your doctor or a travel clinic. You should also invest in **health insurance** (see p.42).

General precautions

There's no need to go overboard, but as you are packing consider putting together a **travel medical kit**. Components to include might be: painkillers and anti-inflammatory drugs, antiseptic cream, plasters (Band Aids) and gauze bandages, surgical tape, anti-diarrhoea medicine (Imodium or Lomotil) and rehydration salts, stomach remedies (Pepto Bismol or similar), insect repellent, sun block, anti-fungal cream, and sterile scissors and tweezers.

Once in Central America, basic hygiene will go a long way towards keeping you healthy. **Bathe** frequently, **wash your hands** before eating and avoid sharing water bottles or utensils. Make sure to eat a **balanced diet** – eating peeled fresh fruit helps keep up your vitamin and mineral intake; malnutrition can lower your resistance to germs and bacteria. Hepatitis B, HIV and AIDS – all transmitted through blood or sexual contact – are common in Central America. You should take all the usual, well-publicized precautions to avoid them. Two other causes of problems in the region are **altitude** and the **sun**. The answer in both cases is to take it easy; allow yourself time to acclimatize and build up exposure to the sun gradually. Avoid dehydration by drinking enough – water or fruit juice rather than beer or coffee, though you should take care with water (see opposite). Overheating can cause heatstroke, which is potentially fatal. Lowering body temperature (by taking a tepid shower, for example) is the first step in treatment.

Inoculations

If possible, all **inoculations** should be sorted out at least ten weeks before departure at your local health clinic. The only obligatory jab required to enter Central America is a **yellow fever** vaccination; however, this is only needed if you're arriving from a "high-risk" area – northern South America and much of central Africa – in which case you need to carry your vaccination certificate. A yellow fever shot is also highly recommended if travelling in Panama east of the canal. Long-term travellers should consider the combined hepatitis A and B and the rabies vaccines, and all travellers should check that they are up to date with the usual polio, diphtheria, tetanus, typhoid and hepatitis A jabs.

Food and water

People differ in their sensitivity to **food**. If you are worried or prone to digestive upsets then there are a few simple things to keep in mind: steer clear of raw shellfish and seafood when inland; only eat raw fruit and vegetables if they can be peeled; and avoid salads unless rinsed in purified water.

Contaminated water is a major cause of sickness in Central America, and even if it looks clean, drinking water should be regarded with caution (even when cleaning teeth and showering). That said, however, it's also essential to increase fluid intake to prevent dehydration. **Bottled and bagged water** is widely available, but always check that the seal is intact, since refilling empties with tap water for resale is not unknown. Many restaurants use purified water (*agua purificada*), but always ask.

There are various methods of **treating water** while you are travelling: boiling for a minimum of five minutes is the most effective method of sterilization, but it is not always practical, and will not remove unpleasant tastes. Water filters remove visible impurities and larger pathogenic organisms (most bacteria and parasites). To be really sure your filtered water is also purified, however, chemical sterilization – using either chlorine or iodine tablets, or a tincture of iodine liquid – is advisable; iodine is more effective in destroying amoebic cysts. Both chlorine and iodine unfortunately leave a nasty aftertaste (which can be masked with lime juice). Pregnant women or people with thyroid problems should consult their doctor before using iodine tablets or purifiers. Inexpensive iodine-removal filters are recommended if treated water is being used continuously for more than a month. Any good outdoor equipment shop will stock a range of water treatment products.

Intestinal troubles

Diarrhoea is the stomach ailment you're most likely to encounter. Its main cause is simply the change in your diet: the food in Central America contains a whole new set of bacteria, as well as perhaps rather more of them than you're used to. Don't try anything too exotic in the first few days, but do try to find some local natural yoghurt, which is a good way to introduce friendly bacteria to your system. Powdered milk, however, can be troublesome, due to being an unfamiliar form of lactose.

If you're afflicted with a bout of diarrhoea, the best cure is the simplest one: take it easy for a day or two and make sure you rehydrate. It's a good idea to carry sachets of rehydration salts, although you can make up your own solution by dissolving five teaspoons of sugar or honey and half a teaspoon of salt in a litre of water. Reintroduce only bland foods at first (rice, dry toast, etc) – papaya and coconut are also good. Diarrhoea remedies like Imodium and Lomotil should be saved for emergencies, like if you need to travel immediately. Only if the symptoms last more than four or five days do you need to worry. If you can't get to a doctor for an exact diagnosis, a last resort would be a course of Ciproxin (ciprofloxacin) – you may want to consider asking your doctor for a prescription and carrying some in your medical kit.

Cholera, an acute bacterial infection, is recognizable by watery diarrhoea and vomiting, though many victims may have only mild or even no symptoms. However, risk of infection is low: Central America was recently declared a cholera-free zone by the Pan American Health Organization.

If you're spending any time in rural areas you also run the risk of picking up various **parasitic infections**: protozoa – amoeba and giardia – and intestinal worms. These sound hideous, but they're easily treated once detected. If you suspect you have an infestation, take a stool sample to a good pathology lab and go to a doctor or pharmacist (see p.37) with the test results. More serious is amoebic dysentery, which is endemic in many parts of the region. The symptoms are more or less the same as a bad case of diarrhoea, but include bleeding. On the whole, a course of Flagyl (metronidazole or tinidozole) will cure it; if you plan to visit the isolated rural reaches of Central America then it's worth carrying these, just in case. If possible, get some, and some advice on their usage, from a doctor before you go. To avoid contracting such parasites think carefully before swimming in rivers and lakes during or just after the rainy season, when waste washes down hillsides into the water.

Malaria and dengue fever

Malaria, caused by the transmission of a parasite in the saliva of an infected anopheles mosquito (active at night), is endemic in many parts of Central America, especially in the rural Caribbean lowlands. There are several different anti-malarial **prophylactics** available, all of which must be started in advance of travel, so make sure you leave plenty of time to visit your doctor. The recommended prophylactic for all of Central America, except for the area east of the Panama Canal, is Chloroquine; east of the canal, including the San Blas Islands, it's Malarone, causing minimal side effects. Consult your doctor about which drug will be best for you. It's extremely important to finish your course of anti-malarials, as there is a time lag between bite and infection. If you do become ill after returning home, let your doctor know that you've been in a malarial risk area – **symptoms** usually occur ten days to four weeks after infection, though they can appear as early as eight days or as long as a year after infection.

In addition to malaria, mosquitoes can transmit **dengue fever**, a viral infection that is prevalent – and on the increase – throughout Central America (usually occurring in epidemic outbreaks). Thankfully, the more deadly strain of hemorrhagic dengue is less prevalent in Central America. Unlike malaria, the mosquitoes that pass dengue fever are active during the day, and there's no preventative vaccine or specific treatment, so you need to pay attention to avoiding bites (see below).

Other bites and stings

Taking steps to avoid getting bitten by insects, particularly **mosquitoes**, is essential. In general, you should sleep in screened rooms or under nets, burn mosquito coils containing permethrin (available everywhere), cover up arms and legs (though note that mosquitoes are attracted to dark-coloured clothing), especially around dawn and dusk when mosquitoes are most active, and use insect repellent containing more than 35 percent DEET.

Sandflies, often present on beaches, are tiny and very difficult to see, and hence avoid – you will become aware of their presence only when they bite, and by then it can be too late. The bites, usually found around the ankles, itch like hell and last for days. Don't give in to the temptation to scratch, as this causes the bites to get worse and last longer. Sandflies can spread cutaneous leishmaniasis, an extremely unpleasant disease characterized by skin lesions that can take months and even years to heal if left untreated.

Scorpions are common: mostly nocturnal, they hide during the heat of the day under rocks and in crevices. Their sting is painful (occasionally fatal) and can become infected, so you should seek medical treatment. You're less likely to be bitten by a spider, but the advice is the same as for scorpions and venomous insects – seek medical treatment if the pain persists or increases.

You're unlikely to see **snakes**, but wearing boots and long trousers will go a long way towards preventing a bite in the event that you do – walk heavily and they will usually slither away. Most snakes are harmless – exceptions are the fer-de-lance (which lives in both wet and dry environments, in both forest and open country, but rarely emerges during the day) and the bushmaster (found in places with heavy rainfall, or near streams and rivers), both of which can be aggressive, and whose venom can be fatal. If you do get bitten, remember what the snake looked like (kill it if it's safe to do so), wrap a lightly restrictive bandage above and below the bite area, but don't apply enough pressure to restrict blood flow and never use a tourniquet. Disinfect the bite area and apply hard pressure with a gauze pad, taped in place; then immobilize the bitten limb as far as possible. Seek medical help immediately.

Swimming and snorkelling might bring you into contact with potentially dangerous **sea creatures**. It's extremely unlikely you'll be a victim of shark attack, but jellyfish are common and all corals will sting. Some jellyfish, like the Portuguese man-o'-war, with its distinctive purple, bag-like sail, have very long tentacles with stinging cells, and an encounter will result in raw, red welts. Equally painful is a brush against fire coral: in each case clean the wound with vinegar or iodine and seek medical help if the pain persists or infection develops.

Rabies does exist in Central America. You'll see stray dogs everywhere; the best advice is to give them a wide berth. Bats can also carry the rabies virus; keep an eye out for them when entering caves. If you are bitten or scratched, wash the wound immediately with soap and running water for five minutes and apply alcohol or iodine. Seek treatment immediately – rabies is fatal once symptoms appear. If you're going to be working with animals or planning a long stay, especially in rural areas far from medical help, you may well want to consider a pre-exposure vaccination, despite the hefty cost. Although this won't give you complete immunity, it will give you a window of 24–48 hours to seek treatment and reduce the amount of post-exposure vaccine you'll need if bitten.

Getting medical help

For minor medical problems, head for the local **pharmacy** (*farmacia*) – look for a green cross. Pharmacists are knowledgeable and helpful, and many speak some English. They can also sell drugs over the counter (if necessary) that are only available by prescription at home. Most large cities have doctors and dentists, many trained in the US, who are experienced in treating visitors and speak good English. Your embassy will have a list of recommended doctors and hospitals, and we've included some in this guide, in the "Directory" sections of the main town accounts. Medical insurance (see p.42) is essential. If you suspect something is amiss with your insides, it might be worth heading straight for a **pathology lab** (*laboratorio médico*), found in all main towns, before seeing a doctor, as the doctor will probably send you there anyway. Many rural communities have a **health centre** (*centro de salud* or *puesto de salud*), where healthcare is free, although there may be only a nurse or health-worker available and you can't rely on finding an English-speaker. Should you need an injection or transfusion, make sure that the equipment is sterile and ensure any blood you receive is screened.

Medical resources for travellers

Travellers should check the latest health advice before travelling to Central America, and if suffering any symptoms after returning home.

UK AND IRELAND

Fit for Travel ⓦ fitfortravel.nhs.uk.
Hospital for Tropical Diseases ⓦ thehtd.org.
MASTA (Medical Advisory Service for Travellers Abroad) ⓦ masta-travel-health.com.
Tropical Medical Bureau ⓦ tmb.ie.

US AND CANADA

Canadian Society for International Health ⓦ csih.org.
CDC ⓦ wwwnc.cdc.gov/travel.
International Society of Travel Medicine ⓦ istm.org.
Travel Health Online ⓦ tripprep.com.

AUSTRALIA, NEW ZEALAND AND SOUTH AFRICA

Travel Doctor ⓦ traveldoctor.com.au.

Culture and etiquette

Forget those stereotypes of a scantily clad world of steamy salsa: the reality in Central America is much more conservative. Throughout the region the Church (both Catholic and Evangelical Protestant) retains a powerful influence on everyday life.

Traditional **family values** are prevalent throughout Central America: children are considered to be a blessing – a sign of virility and in many cases an economic asset – and consequently families are often large. **Homosexual** relationships are publicly frowned upon if not actively condemned; gay and lesbian travellers should be discreet.

While undeniably friendly and fun-loving (especially in the cities), local people may seem shy and unsure about the gringos squeezed into their chicken bus. You will seldom experience hostility, but it pays to greet fellow passengers with a simple "Buenas" and a smile to break the ice. **Politeness** is valued highly, so even if your Spanish is poor, take the trouble to learn key pleasantries and they'll serve you well.

Information about social customs specific to each country is given in the relevant chapter.

Dress

Most locals **dress modestly** but smartly and visitors not wishing to draw unwelcome attention should do the same. You will make a better impression if you do – especially worthwhile when you are coming into contact with officials. Flashy exhibitions of wealth are not recommended (jewellery should be left at home). Shorts (for men and women) are not generally worn away from beaches, but low-cut tops for women are becoming more usual, especially among the young. In the cities, men wearing T-shirts or untucked shirts will be considered a bit scruffy in formal settings, and even in clubs and posher bars. If visiting places of worship, especially, dress modestly – skimpy shorts and flesh-revealing tops are not appropriate. Women will probably also want something to cover their heads.

Money matters

Travellers to Central America, especially Westerners, are likely to experience the uncomfortable assumption by locals that you are in fact a multimillionaire (even if you are poorly dressed). Although you may be on a strict budget, the very fact that you have been able to travel abroad, coupled with your potential earning power back home, means you have an economic freedom unobtainable to many you will encounter. As a rule, however, you will ultimately be judged on your conduct and not your wealth: it isn't helpful, therefore, to be too liberal or too mean with your cash. Instead, show appreciation for good service by **tipping** (take tips into account when working out your budget), and paying what will satisfy both parties when haggling. **Haggling** is accepted in markets (both tourist and local) and when fixing taxi fares. Prices for tours and hotel rooms are usually fixed, though you can usually get lower accommodation rates for stays of one week or longer. Prices in shops are generally fixed, although it's usually worth asking if there are discounts if you buy more than one item.

Women travellers

Machismo is an ingrained part of Central American culture – **female travellers** will frequently experience whistling, tssking and even blatant catcalls, though probably not anything more sinister than guys showing off to their friends. Ignoring such attention is the easiest way to deal with these situations, as retorts or put-downs are often seen as encouragement. No matter how modestly you behave, though, you will probably not counteract the view that foreign women are not only desirable, but also easily attainable. Conversely, women travelling as part of a straight couple should be prepared to be invisible in many social interactions. Even if the woman is the only one to speak Spanish, for example, locals (especially men) will often automatically address their reply to the man, for fear of causing offence.

Despite this, most female travellers report positive experiences in the region. There are, however, still **precautions** to be taken. At night, try to move in groups, and remember it's always possible simply to ask for help if you feel uncomfortable.

Work and study

High unemployment and innumerable bureaucratic hurdles make the possibility of finding paid work in Central America very unlikely, although there are limited opportunities to teach English, especially in wealthier countries like Costa Rica. It's far easier to work as a volunteer – many NGOs operate in the region, relying mainly on volunteer staff. Opportunities for studying Spanish are plentiful and often fairly cheap, with a number of congenial Central American locations drawing students from all over the world.

Teaching English

There are two options for **teaching English** in Central America: find work before you go, or just wing it and see what you come up with after arriving. The latter is slightly less risky if you already have a degree and/or teaching experience. You can get a **CELTA** (Certificate in English Language Teaching to Adults), a **TEFL** (Teaching English as a Foreign Language) or a **TESOL** (Teaching English to Speakers of Other Languages) qualification before you leave home or even while you're abroad. Courses are not cheap (about £1350/US$2150/Aus$1550 for one month's full-time tuition) and you are unlikely to make this investment back very quickly on Central American wages. Once you have the necessary qualifications, check the **British Council**'s website (ⓦbritishcouncil.org) and the **TEFL** website (ⓦtefl.com) for a list of English-teaching vacancies.

Places like Guatemala City and San José in Costa Rica are your best bet for teaching in Central America, although colonial, tourist-oriented towns like Antigua in Guatemala and Granada in Nicaragua are also likely spots.

Volunteering

There are **voluntary positions** available in Central America for everything from conservation work in Costa Rica to human-rights work in Guatemala. If you have a useful skill or specialization, you might have your room and board paid for and perhaps even earn a little pocket money, although more often than not you'll have to fund yourself. If you don't have any particular skills you'll almost definitely have to pay for the privilege of volunteering, and in many cases – particularly in conservation work – this doesn't come cheap. While many positions are organized prior to arrival, it's also possible to arrange something on the ground through word of mouth. Noticeboards in the more popular backpacker hostels are always good sources of information.

Studying Spanish

Some people travel to Central America solely to **learn Spanish** and there are many cities and towns with highly respected schools. Antigua and Quetzaltenango in Guatemala, San José in Costa Rica and, to a lesser extent, Granada and San Juan del Sur in Nicaragua are all noted centres for language instruction. **Prices** vary, but you can expect to pay around US$200/week; this includes room and board with a local family, a standard feature of many Spanish courses and great for full cultural immersion. Some schools will also include activities, allowing you to take your learning out of the classroom and providing an insight into the local area. Courses usually run from Monday to Friday, but should include seven nights' homestay to include in the weekend. Cheaper courses are available – lessons without lodging or activities – but your learning curve is unlikely to be as steep.

Useful contacts

Though it is possible to arrange Spanish lessons last minute, you'll need to book several weeks or months ahead if planning to volunteer or teach English.

UK AND IRELAND

British Council ☎ 020 7930 8466. The Council's Central Management of Direct Teaching (☎ 020 7389 4931) recruits TEFL teachers for posts worldwide (check ⓦ britishcouncil.org for current vacancies).
I to I Volunteering ☎ 1800 985 4852, ⓦ i-to-i.com/volunteer. Runs a range of volunteer projects in Costa Rica, from sea turtle preservation and teaching English to working with children and building homes for underprivileged families.
Volunteer Service Overseas ☎ 020 8780 7500, ⓦ vso.org.uk. UK-based charity organization, offering volunteer opportunities across the globe.

US AND CANADA

AFS Intercultural Programs US ☎ 1 800 AFS-INFO, Canada ☎ 1 800 361 7248 or ☎ 514 288 3282; US ⓦ afs.org, Canada ⓦ afscanada.org. Cultural immersion programmes for high-school students and graduates in Costa Rica, Guatemala, Honduras and Panama.
Aide Abroad ☎ 1 888 6 ABROAD or ☎ 512 904 1137, ⓦ aideabroad.org. Voluntary placements in Central America, lasting two weeks to one year. Intermediate Spanish required.
American Institute for Foreign Study ☎ 1 866 906 2437, ⓦ aifs.com. Language study and cultural immersion in Costa Rica.
AmeriSpan ☎ 1 800 879 6640, ⓦ amerispan.com. Language programmes, volunteer/internship placements (English teaching, healthcare, environment, social work, etc) and academic study-abroad courses throughout Central America.

Amigos de las Américas ☎ 1 800 231 7796 or ☎ 713 782 5290, ⓦ amigoslink.org. Veteran nonprofit organization placing high-school and college-age students in child health promotion and other community projects in Central America.
Peace Corps ☎ 1 800 424 8580, ⓦ peacecorps.gov. US institution that recruits volunteers of all ages (minimum 18) and from all walks of professional life for two-year postings throughout Central America. All applicants must be US citizens.
World Learning ☎ 1 800 336 1616, ⓦ worldlearning.org. Accredited college semesters abroad; the large Latin American studies programme includes an ecology/conservation course in Belize and a politics-themed course in Nicaragua.

AUSTRALIA, NEW ZEALAND AND SOUTH AFRICA

AFS Australia ☎ 1300 131 736 or ☎ 02 9215 0077, ⓦ afs.org.au; NZ ☎ 0800 600 300 or ☎ 04 494 6020, ⓦ afs.org.nz; South Africa ☎ 11 447 2673, ⓦ afs.org.za. Cultural immersion programmes for high-school students and graduates.
Australian Volunteers International ☎ 03 9279 1788, ⓦ australianvolunteers.com. Postings of up to two years in Costa Rica, Guatemala, El Salvador and Nicaragua, as well as shorter-term, team-based assignments for younger volunteers.

WORLDWIDE

Cactus Language ⓦ cactuslanguage.com. Language-holiday specialist with a wide range of courses in Costa Rica, Guatemala, Honduras, Nicaragua and Panama. Prices are often lower than if applying directly to the schools.
Council on International Educational Exchange (CIEE) UK ☎ 020 8939 9057, US ☎ 1 800 40 STUDY or ☎ 1 207 533 7600; ⓦ ciee.org. Leading NGO offering study programmes and volunteer projects around the world.
Earthwatch Institute ⓦ earthwatch.org. International nonprofit organization dedicated to environmental sustainability. Voluntary positions assisting archeologists, biologists and even ethnomusicologists in Costa Rica, Nicaragua and Belize.
Gapyear.com ⓦ gapyear.com. Comprehensive resource with search engine providing links to volunteer and language teaching/learning options worldwide.
Global Volunteer Network ⓦ globalvolunteernetwork.org. Voluntary placements on community projects worldwide.
Global Vision International Australia ☎ 1300 795 013, ⓦ gviaustralia.com.au; US ☎ 1888 653 6028, ⓦ gviusa.com; UK ☎ 017 2725 0250, ⓦ gvi.co.uk. Worldwide placements, many in Central America, including marine conservation and teaching work.
Idealist ⓦ idealist.org. A comprehensive portal of global volunteering positions, connecting applicants with jobs and volunteer placements within the nonprofit sector.
Peace Brigades International ⓦ peacebrigades.org. NGO dedicated to protecting human rights, with placements accompanying human-rights workers in Guatemala. Costs (including a small monthly stipend) are covered, although fundraising is encouraged. Applicants need to be 25 or older and fluent in Spanish.

Projects Abroad US ☎ 1 888 839 3535, ⓦ projects-abroad.org; Australia ☎ 1300 132 831, ⓦ projects-abroad.com.au; Canada ☎ 1 877 921 9666, ⓦ projects-abroad.ca; South Africa ☎ 21686 0916, ⓦ projects-abroad.org.za; UK ☎ 1903 708300, ⓦ projects-abroad.co.uk. The leading global organizer of overseas volunteer work, ranging from teaching and conservation, to healthcare and sports.

Raleigh International ☎ 020 7371 8585, ⓦ raleighinternational .org. Long-established youth-development charity working on community and environmental projects worldwide. Opportunities for both young volunteers (17–25) and older skilled staff (over 25). Central American projects in Costa Rica and Nicaragua.

Crime and personal safety

While political violence has decreased over recent years, crime rates in Central America continue to rise, and tourists make handy targets. Though the majority of crime is opportunistic theft – bag-snatching or pickpocketing – some criminals do operate in gangs and are prepared to use extreme violence. It is commonly accepted that Guatemala tops the list for crimes committed against tourists, but it is possible to be the victim of crime anywhere in the region, especially if you let your guard down.

General precautions

As you're packing, keep the sentimental value of what you take with you to a minimum. Do not wear **jewellery**, and carry only a small amount of **cash** in your wallet. Larger volumes of cash and credit cards should be kept close to your body – in a money belt, hidden pocket or even in your shoes. Scan any important **documents** (passport, insurance, etc) and email them to yourself, so you can access them even if you lose everything. It's worth carrying a paper copy too, so that you can leave the originals in a hotel safe. There is always a dilemma about whether to carry **electronic devices** (such as a camera, tablet or MP3 player) on your person or leave them in your hotel. If you choose to leave them, make sure they're not accessible – you could always pack a small padlock and short length of chain (or cable lock), so that you can create a DIY safe in a wardrobe or under a bed.

It's very important in Central America to **keep an eye on your belongings** at all times. Never put anything down or let your possessions out of your sight unless you're confident they are in a safe place. The highest-risk areas for opportunistic theft are large urban centres, bus stations, at ATMs and at border crossings. **Buses** are also a focus for petty thievery. When travelling by bus you'll often be separated from your main bag – it will usually end up on the roof. This is generally safe enough (and you'll probably have little option in any case). Theft of the bag itself is unlikely, but opportunist thieves may dip into zips and outer pockets, so don't leave anything you'd miss accessible. Some travellers choose to put their pack into a sack to disguise it, prevent pilfering and also keep it clean and dry – not a bad idea. If you carry a day-pack, fill it wisely and keep it on your person (preferably strapped to you). Do not use overhead racks on buses. Needless to say, there is a greater risk of crime after dark, so try to arrive in new towns in daylight so that you're not wandering unlit streets with all your gear. Bear in mind, too, that the threat of petty crime does not exclusively come from the local population – unscrupulous fellow travellers have been known to help themselves to anything of value.

Violent crime does occur in Central America. Muggings at knifepoint, armed robbery and rape are all dangers to be aware of. If threatened with a weapon, do not resist. You can reduce your chances of falling victim to these crimes by staying in populated areas or around other travellers. However, it should be noted that tourist shuttles are actually more likely to be a target for hijackers, especially at night.

Armed **hold-ups of cars** are rare but do happen (typically small groups of masked men with guns will try to block the road). You're especially vulnerable if you drive alone – avoid isolated roads and try to travel with a group. These *banditos* are unlikely to take your car – they want your cash. Most locals advise that you should simply drive on without stopping (especially if you are already going fast), as they're unlikely to shoot. It's a tough call, but if you do stop, do not resist and just pay up.

Drugs

Drugs of all kinds are available everywhere. Buying or using really isn't worth the risk: penalties are very strict. If you are arrested with drugs your embassy will probably send someone to visit you, and maybe find an English-speaking lawyer, but otherwise you're on your own. Practically every capital city has foreigners incarcerated for drug offences who'd never do it again if they knew what the punishment was like. **Drug gangs** are a major problem, especially in Honduras, Guatemala and El Salvador, and are responsible for much of the high crime rates.

Reporting a crime

If you are unfortunate enough to suffer a crime, report the incident immediately to the **police** – if there is a tourist police force, try them first – if only to get a copy of the report (*denuncia*), which you'll need for insurance purposes. The police in Central America are poorly paid and, in the case of petty crime, you can't expect them to do much more than make out the report. If you can, also report the crime to your embassy – it helps the consular staff to build up a higher-level case for the better protection of tourists.

Travel essentials

Costs

Your **daily expenses** are likely to include accommodation, food and drink and transport. You may wish to budget separately for activities, as one-off costs (for example, a day's snorkelling or diving) can be high and would blow a daily budget. In general,

PRICES IN THIS GUIDE

At the beginning of each chapter you'll find a guide to "rough costs", including food, accommodation and travel. Prices are quoted in US dollars for ease of comparison. Within the chapter itself prices are quoted mainly in local currency, though as US dollars are widely accepted prices are often quoted in that currency instead. Note that prices and exchange rates change all the time; we have done our best to make sure that all figures are accurate, but as tourism increases throughout the region it's likely that prices will rise incrementally.

the cheapest countries in the region are Honduras, Nicaragua, Guatemala and El Salvador, while Belize, Costa Rica and Panama are more expensive. However, even in these countries it is still possible to travel on a budget of around US$35 per day, with the most significant difference being the cost of public transport and accommodation.

Generally speaking, the price quoted in restaurants and hotels is the price you pay. However, in some more upmarket establishments an additional **tax** will appear on your bill; it's worth checking if tax is included from the outset. Service is almost never included, and, while not expected, **tipping** for good service can make a huge impact on the basic

BUDGET TIPS

• Slow down. Racing from place to place eats into your budget, as you'll be forking out for transport and tours every day.

• Eat and drink as the locals do. Local staples can be half the price of even the most reasonable tourist menu. Set lunches in traditional *comedores* are great value.

• Cut down your beer bill. When buying booze it's cheapest to get it from small *tiendas* (shops) and take back the bottles to claim the deposit. Litre bottles are more economical than the 330ml ones.

• Refill your water bottle. Many hostels/hotels offer water refills for free or a small fee. Alternatively, in some countries you can buy 500ml bags (*bolsitas*) of water. If you're not moving around, invest in larger gallon bottles.

• Use local transport. Tourist shuttles should be the exception, not the norm.

• Let your money work for you. Try to get a bank account that allows free withdrawals at foreign ATMs. This also allows you to carry small amounts of cash, as ATMs are plentiful.

• Share costs with other travellers. The price of a private room for two is often cheaper than two dorm beds; a triple is even better value.

• Walk as much as possible, during the day at least. Taxis are often very expensive (though often the only safe option at night, when you should take them).

• Shop in markets, bakeries and supermarkets. Self-catering is worthwhile if you're staying in one place and can eat your leftovers for breakfast.

• Learn to haggle – bargaining can be fun. Don't be afraid to confront taxi drivers or chancers who you suspect are trying to rip you off. However, don't be too aggressive – a traveller from a comparatively rich country arguing over a few cents is not cool.

YOUTH AND STUDENT DISCOUNTS

There are few youth or student discounts in the region. Indeed, often you will find yourself charged more than locals simply because you are a foreigner. It is always worth enquiring if discounts are available, however, as on occasion entrance fees may be tiered (and applicable to foreigners as well as nationals). If a discount is applicable you will need to show **ID**. Most useful is the International Student Identity Card (**ISIC**), which can also be used to obtain discounts on flight bookings. You can get these from STA Travel (see p.29) and affiliated agencies with current official ID issued by your school/university (enrolling at a Spanish language school is generally not sufficient to obtain official student ID).

wage. Prices for accommodation (as well as some airfares and organized tours) can be considerably cheaper in **low season** (generally Sept–Dec), when it's always worth negotiating to obtain the best price (prices quoted in this guide are based on high-season rates).

Tiered pricing (charging foreigners more than nationals) is becoming more common, in particular for entrance fees. This is based on the premise that tourists can afford to pay considerably more to visit attractions than those on local salaries.

Electricity

All countries in the region use sockets accepting the flat two-pronged plug common to the majority of the Americas; Ⓦ kropla.com is a useful website with information about adapters and converters. Standard **voltage** is 110–120v. Be wary of **electric showerheads**, often with protruding wires, in budget accommodation. If it isn't working (more than likely), do not touch the fitting. You may want to consider using a towel to turn off the conductive taps, too.

Gay and lesbian travellers

Apart from in Belize – where homosexual acts are illegal, and which officially bans gay foreigners from entering the country (though these laws have yet to be enforced, and are soon to be challenged before the Supreme Court) – consensual homosexual acts are **legal** throughout Central America (and in Mexico, which is far more liberal). In reality, however, homosexuality is barely tolerated by conservative Central American society, and harassment does exist in certain areas. Gay and lesbian travellers are unlikely to experience problems, however, if they remain discreet. Unsurprisingly, there is little in the way of an open gay community or scene. In the more cosmopolitan capital cities a few gay clubs exist, although these are almost entirely geared towards men.

Insurance

It's important to take out an **insurance policy** before travelling to cover against theft, loss, illness or injury. Before paying for a new policy, however, check whether you are already covered on any existing home or medical insurance policies that you may hold. A typical travel insurance policy usually provides cover for the loss of baggage, tickets and – up to a certain limit – cash or cheques, as well as cancellation or curtailment of your journey. Most of them exclude so-called dangerous sports unless an extra premium is paid: in Central America this can mean scuba diving, whitewater rafting, surfing and trekking. It is also useful to have a policy providing a 24-hour medical emergency number.

When securing baggage cover, make sure that the per-article limit – typically under £500/US$1000 – will cover your most valuable possession. If you need to **make a claim**, you should keep receipts for medicines and medical treatment as well as any high-value items that are being insured. In the event that you have anything stolen, you must obtain a *denuncia* from the police.

Several companies now offer tailored "backpacker" insurance, which provides low-cost coverage for extended durations (beyond the standard thirty-day holiday policies). These include Rough Guides' own recommended insurance (see box opposite).

Internet

Central America is increasingly **well connected** to the internet and you should have little difficulty getting online. Even smaller towns usually have at least one internet café, often populated by noisy gaming schoolkids, and hostels, restaurants and hotels are increasingly offering free wi-fi. Many internet cafés are well equipped with webcams and headphones as well as the facility to download digital photos onto CD. Check Ⓦ kropla.com for details of how to use your laptop when abroad.

ROUGH GUIDES TRAVEL INSURANCE

Rough Guides has teamed up with ⓦWorldNomads.com to offer great **travel insurance** deals. Policies are available to residents of more than 150 countries, with cover for a wide range of **adventure sports**, 24hr emergency assistance, high levels of medical and evacuation cover and a stream of **travel safety information**. ⓦroughguides.com users can take advantage of their policies online 24/7, from anywhere in the world – even if you're already travelling. And since plans often change when you're on the road, you can extend your policy and even claim online. In addition, buying travel insurance with WorldNomads.com can also leave a positive footprint and donate to a community development project. For more information go to ⓦ**roughguides.com/travel-insurance**.

Mail

Stamps are rarely available outside the post office (*correo*), although it can be worth asking if you are buying a postcard, for example, as occasionally souvenir shops and stationers do stock them. Sending mail from the main post office in any capital city is probably the best way to ensure speedy and efficient delivery. The cost and speed of mailing items varies from country to country, but is by far cheapest and quickest from Panama. To receive mail by **poste restante** you should address it to yourself at "Lista de Correos" at the "Correo Central" in the capital city of the appropriate country.

Maps

The best **overall map** of Central America, covering the region at a scale of 1:1,100,000, is produced by Canada's International Travel Maps and Books (ⓦitmb.com). They also publish individual country maps at various scales. Maps are generally hard to find once you get to Central America, so it's wise to bring them with you when possible.

Money

Cash payments are the norm in Central America, with the most convenient way to access money being via an **ATM** (*cajero automático*). Most machines accept Visa and MasterCard credit cards, as well as Visa debit cards, and are increasingly widespread throughout the region. However, it is always advisable to check the Directory sections of specific destinations in this guide in advance of travel to confirm that smaller settlements have an ATM, as not all do. If you are relying on ATMs, it's worth having a back-up card in case the first is lost or stolen. If you plan to be travelling for a significant period, it is worth thoroughly researching your bank's terms for cash withdrawals abroad – some make no charge at all, allowing you to make frequent withdrawals and

carry only small amounts of cash around urban areas. As a possible alternative some banks will give **cash advances** over the counter (sometimes for a small fee). Try to hoard notes of small denominations; you will constantly encounter problems obtaining change from local businesses, often stalling transactions as no one has anything smaller than a US$1 bill (or its equivalent). In general, budget-friendly hotels and restaurants do not take **credit cards**, though a few mid-range establishments and tourist handicraft shops may accept them. **Travellers' cheques** are increasingly difficult to change for the same reason, but are good to carry as a back-up. Note that most Central American ATMs do not accept five-digit PINs; contact your bank at home in advance if you have one.

Belize, Guatemala, Honduras, Nicaragua and Costa Rica each have their own **national currency**, while El Salvador and Panama both use the US dollar (in Panama the dollar is divided into 100 balboas – although US cents are also legal tender). However, **US dollars** are accepted throughout Central America and in many places prices for tourist services (language school fees, plane tickets, tour fees) are quoted exclusively in them. Indeed, some ATMs (particularly those in Nicaragua) will actually dispense dollars on request. Local currency is always accepted at the current exchange rate, though, so there is no need to carry huge amounts of dollars in cash, though it is certainly useful to carry some to exchange at border crossings. Generally speaking, you should also get rid of any remaining unwanted local currency at border crossings, as it will be more difficult to exchange the further away from the border you are. Try to research the current exchange rates before dealing with moneychangers (ⓦoanda.com or ⓦxe.com).

Phones

It's easy enough to phone home from most cities and towns in Central America. Each country has a national telecommunications company with offices throughout the country. It's also worth keeping an eye out for internet cafés that offer **Skype**, for excellent-value international calls. **Mobile phones** are as prolific as they are in the developed world; despite living in relative poverty, the rural population can often be spotted checking their text messages. You may find that taking your own phone comes in useful in emergencies, but on the other hand, it does become one more item to keep secure. Also remember that rates to receive calls and messages while abroad are often extortionate. Alternatively, you may consider buying a phone locally, as packages that include call-time are reasonable. However, practically speaking, if you only anticipate making the odd call, forget the mobile and simply use local **payphones**, which are usually easy to come by (the exception is El Salvador, where they have largely been replaced by mobiles).

Shopping

When it comes to shopping you'll find that what's on offer is either significantly cheaper or significantly different to what's available back home – from places like the Guatemalan highlands, where indigenous **craft markets** abound, to Panama City, where glitzy **shopping malls** offer cut-price designer clothing and shoes. Throughout the region you can also buy locally sourced **coffee**, thereby supporting local farmers.

In markets **haggling** is standard. Try not to get cornered by stallholders, who will try to pressure you into buying on the spot. It is always wise to compare various sellers' best prices before agreeing to a sale. If you're looking for crafts, it's also worth scouting out official **tourist shops** (where prices are fixed) to get a ballpark figure to try and beat in markets. If you plan to buy several items you will get the best prices if you buy in bulk from the same seller. Haggling is not commonplace in shops. However, if you are unsure about whether or not prices are fixed, simply ask if discounts apply: "*Hay descuentos?*"

Time

Panama is GMT –5, and all the other countries are GMT –6, in the **Central Time Zone** (same as Central Standard Time in the US). In recent years, Central American governments have gone back and forth on the issue of whether or not to apply daylight savings as an energy-saving measure, and will no doubt continue to do so in the future.

Tourist information

Official sources of tourist information in Central America are spotty at best. For budget travellers, often the best way to obtain the latest advice is to talk to other backpackers about their experiences. Similarly, popular **hostels** usually have notice boards and the best have clued-up staff with local knowledge. All Central American countries do have their own official **tourist offices**, which we have detailed in each individual Basics chapter, but the prevalence of these on the ground is not great. However, the following tourist-office websites provide a useful reference, especially for pre-trip planning. See also the "… Online" boxes in the individual Basics chapters for further suggestions.

USEFUL WEBSITES

Ⓦ **2backpackers.com** Blog from a well-travelled couple who have journeyed extensively across Central America (and pretty much everywhere else).

Ⓦ **centralamericanpolitics.blogspot.com** Blog that follows Central American politics by associate professor of political science at the University of Scranton (US), currently living in Guatemala.

Ⓦ **cotal.org.ar** Confederation of Latin American Tourist Organizations.

Ⓦ **horariodebuses.com** Useful online bus schedules for Central (and South) America.

Ⓦ **lanic.utexas.edu/country/central/** Latin American Network Information Center.

Ⓦ **latinnews.com** Real-time news feed with major stories from all over Latin America in English.

Ⓦ **onlinenewspapers.com** One page of news per country, with hyperlinks to Spanish and English papers.

Travellers with disabilities

Central America is not the most accessible part of the world for travellers with disabilities. On the whole, it's the top-end hotels and services that may offer equipped facilities – out of the price range for most budget travellers. However, for the most part, Central American society is community-orientated and strangers take pleasure in helping and facilitating the passage of others. **Costa Rica** (where tourist facilities are well developed) and **Panama** (where there is a large expat community) have the best infrastructure, relative to the rest of the region. Specialist websites advising travellers with disabilities include Ⓦ able-travel.com, Ⓦ globalaccessnews .com and Ⓦ disabledtraveladvice.co.uk.

BLUE HOLE

Belize

HIGHLIGHTS

❶ Caye Caulker A watersports haven with a relaxed island nightlife. **See p.63**

❷ Blue Hole Dive the inky waters of this coral-encrusted cavern. **See p.70**

❸ San Ignacio Excellent base for Maya ruins and adventure trips. **See p.79**

❹ Caracol Explore Belize's greatest and most extensive Maya site. **See p.85**

❺ Cockscomb Basin Wildlife Sanctuary Hike deserted jungle trails in this jaguar reserve. **See p.93**

❻ Placencia Relax on Belize's most beautiful white-sand beaches. **See p.94**

HIGHLIGHTS ARE MARKED ON THE MAP ON P.47

ROUGH COSTS

Daily budget Basic US$35/occasional treat US$70

Drink Beer US$2

Food Jerk chicken US$5

Hostel/budget hotel US$15/US$25

Travel Belize City–San Ignacio (120km) by bus: 2hr 30min, US$4

FACT FILE

Population 308,000

Language English (official), Kriol (unofficial)

Currency Belize dollar (Bz$)

Capital Belmopan (population: 20,000)

International phone code ☏ 501

Time zone GMT –6hr

1

Introduction

With far less of a language barrier to overcome than elsewhere in Central America, Belize, perched on the isthmus's northeast corner, is the ideal first stop on a tour of the region. And, although it is among the most expensive countries in Central America, its reliable public transport, numerous hotels and restaurants and small size make it an ideal place to travel independently.

Belize offers some of the most **breathtaking scenery** anywhere in the region: thick tropical forests envelop much of the country's southern and western regions, stretching up towards the misty heights of the sparsely populated Maya Mountains, while just offshore radiant turquoise shallows and cobalt depths surround the **Mesoamerican Barrier Reef**, the longest such reef in the Americas. Here too are the jewels in Belize's natural crown: three of the four **coral atolls** in the Caribbean.

Scattered along the barrier reef, a chain of islands – known as **cayes** – protect the mainland from the ocean swell, and make wonderful bases for **snorkelling and diving**; the cayes are most travellers' top destination in the country. **Ambergris Caye** and **Caye Caulker** are the best known, though many of the less developed islands, including the picture-perfect **Glover's Atoll**, are gaining in popularity. The **interior** has remained relatively untouched, thanks to a national emphasis on conservation: in the west, the dramatic landscape – especially the tropical forests and cave systems – of the **Cayo District** provides numerous

opportunities for adventure-seekers and culture vultures. Inexpensive **San Ignacio**, the region's transport hub, gives access to the heights of the **Mountain Pine Ridge Forest Reserve** and the rapids of the **Macal** and **Mopan rivers**, as well as the impressive Maya sites including **Caracol**, **Xunantunich** and **Actun Tunichil Muknal**. **Dangriga**, the main town of the south-central region, serves as a jumping-off point for heavenly **Tobacco Caye** and the **Cockscomb Basin Wildlife Sanctuary**; to the south, the small fishing village of **Hopkins** and more developed **Placencia peninsula** have some of the country's best **beaches**. Belize's most isolated region – the far south – is dominated by the Maya Mountains, which rise to more than 1100m and shelter some of the world's finest **cacao** farms.

CHRONOLOGY

200–800 AD Classic period: Maya culture flourishes throughout Belize.

800–900 AD Maya cities across central and southern Belize decline, though Lamanai and other northern cities continue to thrive throughout the Postclassic period (900–1540 AD).

1530s The Spanish, led by Francisco de Montejo, engage in the first of numerous unsuccessful attempts to conquer the Maya of Belize.

1544 Gaspar Pacheco subdues Maya resistance and founds a town on Lake Balcar.

1570 Spanish mission is established at Lamanai.

1638 The Maya rebel, forcing the Spanish to abandon the areas they have settled.

1630–70 British buccaneers, later known as Baymen, plunder Spanish treasure ships along the Belizean coast, then begin to settle the coastline and harvest logwood, used for textile dyes in Europe. They rely heavily on slave labour from Africa.

1700s Spain and Britain clash over control of Belize. In 1763, Spain officially grants British settlers logging rights, but does not abandon territorial claims on the region.

1798 The British defeat the Spanish in the Battle of St George's Caye, gaining control of the region.

1838 Slavery is abolished.

1839 Citing Spanish territorial claims, newly independent Guatemala asserts sovereign authority over Belize.

1847 Mexican refugees fleeing the Caste Wars in the Yucatán arrive in Belize.

1859 Britain and Guatemala sign a treaty that acknowledges British sovereignty over Belize.

1862 Belize officially becomes a British colony, and part of the Commonwealth, called British Honduras.

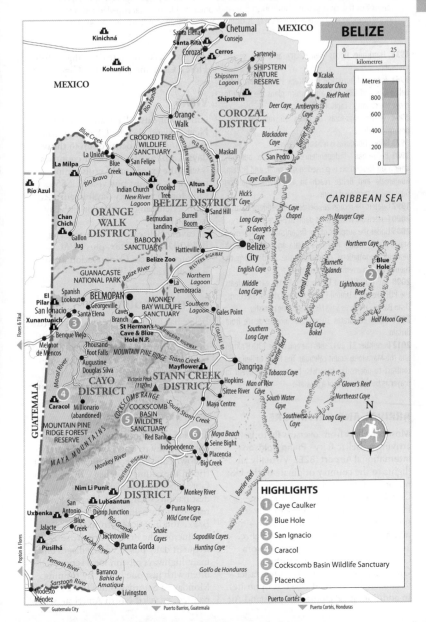

BELIZE

0 _____ 25
kilometres

HIGHLIGHTS

1 Caye Caulker

2 Blue Hole

3 San Ignacio

4 Caracol

5 Cockscomb Basin Wildlife Sanctuary

6 Placencia

1

BELIZE'S ETHNIC GROUPS

For a tiny nation, Belize is home to several strongly identified **ethnic groups** – including the Maya and Garinagu (or Garífuna) cultures. **Creoles** – descendants of the slaves and slave owners that arrived during the area's logging boom in the 1800s – make up about a fifth of the country's population, with both the language and food widespread throughout the country. Belizean Kriol, with roots in English and various African languages, is spoken by around 70 percent of the population – although the language is not formally acknowledged, it is unanimously recognized as a glue that unites most of Belize's multicultural population.

1931 Hurricane floods Belize City and kills several thousand.

1961 A second hurricane (Hurricane Hattie) devastates Belize City and kills 262, after which plans are made to move the country's capital to Belmopan.

1964 British Honduras becomes an internally self-governing colony.

1973 British Honduras is renamed Belize.

1981 Belize gains independence from Britain, but only after a UN Resolution is passed in its favour, and Britain, Guatemala and Belize reach an agreement regarding Guatemala's territorial claims.

1992 Guatemala recognizes Belize's independent status.

2000 Guatemala reasserts its claim to Belizean territory.

2005 Under the auspices of the Organization of American States (OAS), Belize and Guatemala agree to establish peaceful negotiations concerning the border dispute, though the issue remains unresolved.

2008 The UDP (United Democratic Party) easily defeats the PUP (People's United Party) in the national elections; Dean Barrow replaces Said Musa as prime minister.

2011 Belize celebrates 30 years of independence from Britain.

2012 December 21, 2012 sees the end of the 13th B'Aktun and the Maya long-count calendar. The Maya of Belize, in contrast to doomsday theorists, honoured the event in prayer as the beginning of a new era.

ARRIVAL AND DEPARTURE

Most travellers from overseas **fly** to Belize, arriving at Belize City's **Philip Goldson International Airport (BZE)**. Virtually all flights to the country originate in the US; major operators include American, Continental, Delta and US Airways. However, it is usually cheaper to fly to southern Mexico – usually Cancún – and take a **boat** or cross by land into Belize. You can also enter Belize by land from Guatemala, though from southern Guatemala or Honduras it's often easier to enter Belize by **boat** (see box opposite). In addition, **local airlines** Maya Island Air

and Tropic Air operate daily flights from Flores, Guatemala, to Belize City.

VISAS

Citizens of Australia, Canada, the EU, New Zealand and the US do not need **visas** for stays in Belize of up to **thirty days**. Citizens of most other countries – with the exception of cruise-ship passengers – must buy visas (US$50; valid for up to ninety days) in advance from a Belizean consulate or embassy (see p.61).

Leaving Belize, you'll have to pay a Bz$30/US$15 **exit tax**, plus a PACT – Protected Areas Conservation Trust – fee of Bz$7.50/US$3.75.

GETTING AROUND

Belize has just three major highways (the Northern, Western and Southern), but the majority of the country is well served by **public transport**. The unpaved side roads are sometimes in poor repair, though they are usually passable except in the worst rainstorms.

BY BUS

Buses are the cheapest, and most efficient, way to travel in Belize – nearly all towns are connected, and the longest trip in the country (Belize City to Punta Gorda; 5–7hr) costs just Bz$28, while destinations such as San Ignacio can be reached from Belize City (2–3hr) for Bz$7. You buy **tickets** from the conductor. The main towns are served by frequent daily buses, while villages off the main highways rely on **local services**, often with just one bus a day running Monday to Saturday only. These brightly painted, recycled North American school buses, known to travellers as "chicken buses" (see box, p.32), will pick up and drop off anywhere along the roadside. The most frequent services operate along the Western and Northern highways (though these roads have been officially renamed the George Price Highway and the Phillip Goldson Highway respectively, most people still use the old names), usually from very early in the morning to mid-evening. The Hummingbird and Southern highways, to Dangriga, Placencia and Punta Gorda, are not quite so well provided for, though services are improving.

BY CAR

In the most remote parts of Belize bus services will probably only operate once a day, if at all, and unless you have your own transport – which is expensive – you will need time and patience to cope with the inconvenient schedules. If **car rental**, which starts at about US$68/day (without insurance), is beyond your budget, you may be able to ask around and find a local **"cab"** – a resident with a car – to drive you. This kind of "ride" should cost the price of the fuel plus a small tip; agree on a rate beforehand. Otherwise, hitching may be your only option, but if you go for this you should be extremely cautious – there are always risks involved, especially for female travellers.

All official **taxis** in Belize are licensed, and can be identified by their green plates. They operate from special ranks in the centre of all mainland towns. There are no meters, so establish your fare in advance; within towns a Bz$6–10 **fixed**

rate should apply. It is also possible to negotiate official taxi rides between cities, though this option can be quite expensive: usually at least US$75–100/ person for a three-hour ride.

BY BIKE

Cycling can be a great way to reach Belize's more isolated ruins and towns. **Bikes** are increasingly available for rent – usually around Bz$15–25/day – especially in San Ignacio and Hopkins. Though biking along major highways is certainly possible, it is uncommon, and drivers will not be watching for cyclists; it is therefore important to remain exceptionally alert during the day and to avoid cycling at night. You'll find repair shops in all towns. One thing to note, however, is that Belizean buses don't have roof racks; if there's room, the driver might let you take your bike onto the bus.

BY BOAT

If you plan on visiting the cayes, you'll have to travel by **boat**, which will likely be a fast **skiff**, or partially covered speedboat. **Tickets**, usually Bz$25–45, can be bought in advance for domestic routes, but it's generally worth showing up half an hour before departure time to ensure your seat. Numerous boats make multiple daily runs between Belize City, Caye Caulker and Ambergris Caye, and one connects Ambergris Caye with Corozal (see p.75).

BY PLANE

Though it is quite expensive, some budget travellers do choose to travel by

---

LAND AND SEA ROUTES TO BELIZE

There are **two land border crossings** into Belize: one from Chetumal, **Mexico**, to Santa Elena (see box, p.77), and one from Melchor de Menchos, **Guatemala**, to Benque Viejo del Carmen (see box, p.363).

There are numerous **sea routes** to Belize from **Mexico**, **Guatemala** and **Honduras**. One ferry shuttles travellers between Chetumal and San Pedro (see p.68), while another runs from Puerto Cortés, Honduras, via Dangriga (see box, p.420) to Belize City. Connections to Guatemala include daily skiffs between Punta Gorda and Puerto Barrios, and services between Punta Gorda and Lívingston (see p.98), while a weekly boat moves tourists between Placencia and Puerto Cortés, Honduras (see p.96).

The exit fee at any border is Bz$37.50 (around US$19).

1

air, as flights are not only much faster than buses, but also connect destinations unreachable by road. Maya Island Air (☎223 1140, ⓦmayaregional.com) and Tropic Air (☎226 2012, ⓦtropicair.com) each operate numerous daily flights from both the municipal and international airports in Belize City to San Pedro, Caye Caulker, Dangriga, San Ignacio, Placencia and Punta Gorda. Flights also run from San Pedro to Corozal. Prices start at around Bz$70–90.

ACCOMMODATION

While Belizean **accommodation** is generally expensive by Central American standards, there are budget hotels in all the towns, and the most popular backpacker destinations – Caye Caulker, San Ignacio, Hopkins and Punta Gorda – have a great deal of choice and are often less expensive than the rest of the country. **Finding a room** is usually no problem, though at Christmas, New Year and Easter, booking ahead is advisable.

Hostels are still quite thin on the ground in much of Belize, though some dormitory accommodation (usually US$10–15) is available in Caye Caulker, Dangriga, Hopkins and San Ignacio. In other cities and towns most budget travellers rely on **budget hotels**, which usually charge from US$25 for a double, depending on the city. For this price you should get a private bathroom, TV and a fan; a/c will add at least US$10 more to the cost per night. Check out Belize Explorer (ⓦbelizeexplorer.com), which lists most of the country's accommodation for under US$70, for ideas.

There are also a few proper **campsites** in Belize, most of which charge US$5–10 for pitching a tent, and some mid-priced hotels in smaller villages and on the coast will allow you to camp on their grounds for about the same rate. In order to camp in any protected area (fees around US$10), you'll have to get permission from park authorities – in person, at the ranger's office, or through an organized tour.

In smaller communities, such as Sarteneja, Baboon Community Sanctuary, and in the Toledo district,

homestays – usually under US$30 and including meals – are an alternative solution to hotels. Ask at regional offices of the Belize Tourist Board, or see individual listings of the areas mentioned above for contact information.

The accommodation prices quoted throughout this chapter are **inclusive of tax**.

FOOD AND DRINK

Belizean food is a mix of Latin American and Caribbean, with Creole flavours dominating the scene in local restaurants, but with a number of international options as well – numerous Chinese restaurants and the odd Indian curry house can be found across the nation. The basis of any Creole main meal is **rice and beans**, and this features heavily in smaller restaurants, where most meals cost around Bz$8–12. The white rice and red beans are cooked together in coconut oil and usually served with stewed chicken or beef, or fried fish; there's always a bottle of hot sauce on the table for extra spice.
Seafood is almost always excellent. Red snapper and grouper are the most commonly seen on restaurant menus, but you might also try a barracuda steak, conch fritters or a plate of fresh shrimp. In San Pedro, Caye Caulker, San Ignacio and Placencia the food can be exceptional, and the only concern is that you might get bored with **lobster**, which is served in a vast array of dishes. Note that the **closed season** for lobster fishing is from mid-February to mid-June; if you do order some during this period, it will either be illegal or frozen.

Breakfast (Bz$6–10) is usually served from 7am to 10am and generally includes eggs and flour tortillas, or fry jacks, a deep-fried dough often stuffed with meat/veg fillings. The **lunch hour** (noon–1pm) is observed with almost religious devotion – you will not be able to get anything else done at that time. **Dinner** is usually eaten quite early, between 6 and 8pm; few restaurants stay open much later.

Vegetables are scarce in Creole food, but there's often a side dish of potato or coleslaw. There are few specifically **vegetarian** restaurants, but in touristy areas many places offer a couple of vegetarian dishes and the ubiquitous Chinese restaurants always have a few veggie dishes on offer.

DRINK

Tap water, in the towns at least, is safe but highly chlorinated, and many villages (though not Caye Caulker) have a potable water system. Many travellers nonetheless choose to buy filtered bottled water, which is sold everywhere for around Bz$2 per bottle. **Fruit juices** are widely available, with fresh orange, lime, watermelon and pineapple being the most popular options. **Coffee**, except in the best establishments, will almost certainly be instant, though decent **tea** is quite prevalent. Belikin, Belize's (only) national **beer**, comes in several varieties: regular, a lager-type bottled and draught beer; bottled stout; Lighthouse and Premium lagers; and seasonal brews. The Belikin factory offers tours and sampling sessions (see p.58). Home-made **wines** of varying strengths, including cashew nut and blackberry, are bottled and sold throughout the country, and you can also get hold of imported wine, though it's not cheap. Local **rum**, in numerous dark and clear varieties, is inexpensive. The legal drinking age in Belize is 18.

One last drink that deserves a mention is **seaweed**, a milkshake-style blend of seaweed, milk, cinnamon, sugar and cream. You'll find it at local restaurants and cafés in seaside towns and cities along the coast.

CULTURE AND ETIQUETTE

Belizeans are generally welcoming and accustomed to tourists, though it's important to remember that the country is, on the whole, quite **conservative**. Dress, except among professionals, is usually casual, though tourists – especially women – who wear revealing clothing will probably be looked down upon, particularly in Belize's many churches.

The country's laidback attitude usually carries over into conversation; when approaching Belizeans, it's best to be friendly, relaxed and patient. **Women travellers** may receive advances from local men. Ignoring such attentions completely will sometimes only be met by greater persistence; walking away while flashing a quick smile and wave usually gets the message across, while remaining polite.

Belizeans are not particularly accepting of **homosexuality** – indeed, homosexual acts between men are officially illegal – and rarely open about sexual orientation; some may find the community in San Pedro more tolerant than elsewhere. Though it is unlikely that locals will express disapproval, it is a good idea for gay travellers to avoid public displays of affection. Those wishing to visit gay-friendly venues should visit ⓦgayfriendlybelize.com for current information.

Belizeans rarely **tip**, though foreigners are usually expected to give around ten percent in taxis and in restaurants. **Haggling** is also uncommon and will usually be considered rude, except at street markets.

KRIOL WORDS AND PHRASES

Belizean **Kriol**, derived mainly from English, is the native language of the majority of the country's inhabitants. Some 70 percent of the population speak it, and it's not unusual to hear English and Kriol being used interchangeably in conversation.

Aarait Fine
Dah how yuh di du? How are you?
Fu chroo? For real?
Gud maanin Good morning
Hall yuh rass! Get the hell out!
Humoch dis kaas? How much does this cost?
I gwen I'm going

Ih noh mata It doesn't matter
Mee noh andastan I don't understand
Mee noh know I don't know
Mi naym dah ... My name is ...
Weh di go'ahn? What's up?
Weh I deh? Where am I?
Weh taim yuh gat? What time is it?
Weh yuh naym? What's your name?

1

SPORTS AND OUTDOOR ACTIVITIES

Football (soccer) and **basketball** are very popular in Belize, though the country's size and resources limit teams to the semi-professional level, and visitors will find few spectator events.

However, Belize is a haven for a wide range of **outdoor activities**. Many travellers will participate in some form of **watersports**, including snorkelling, diving, windsurfing, kayaking and sailing. Companies in San Pedro, Caye Caulker and Placencia offer **diving courses** and lead multi-day kayaking and sailing trips to the cayes. In the Cayo region, operators organize **hiking** trips through the local jungle and Mountain Pine Ridge Forest, as well as **horseriding** excursions to Maya ruins and other sights. Stunning cave systems dot the south and west and **caving tours** are becoming more widespread and popular. There are a number of operators in San Ignacio (see box, p.81).

COMMUNICATIONS

Though most towns have post offices, and the service is more efficient (and expensive) than in the rest of Central America, Belizean **postal services** can still be unreliable. Sending letters, cards and parcels home is straightforward; prices start at Bz$0.75 for a letter and Bz$0.40 for a postcard.

Belize has a modern phone system, with **payphones** plentiful throughout the country. These can only be used with **phonecards**, which are widely available from BTL (Belize Telecommunications Limited) offices, as well as hotels, shops and stations. Phonecards can be used for both local and international calls. There are **no area codes** in Belize, so you need to dial all seven digits. Making a reverse charge (collect) call home is easy using the Home Country Direct service, available at BTL offices, most payphones and larger hotels – dial the access code (printed on some payphones and in the phone book) to connect with an operator in your home country. **Mobile phones** are common in Belize, and almost all of the country receives excellent service. North Americans can usually connect to local systems with their regular service, albeit at very high roaming charges. Alternatively, BTL sells SIM cards to visitors with compatible international phones. **Web access** is readily available in all the main towns and for guests at many hotels, though it can be expensive in tourist areas – up to Bz$12/hr.

CRIME AND SAFETY

Though Belize does have a relatively high **crime** rate, general crime against tourists is rare, especially in comparison to other Central American countries, and **violent crime** against tourists is seldom experienced, even in Belize City (see box, p.55). The last decade saw several attacks on tourist groups near the Benque/ Melchor border with Guatemala, but tour operators now take precautions to prevent this; solo trekkers should be on alert, however, and it is not recommended to hike alone in this region. Elsewhere in the country, theft does occur, the majority of cases involving **break-ins** at hotels. Bear this in mind when you're searching for a room; doors should have good locks and it's even better if the room has a safe – valuables should never be left lying around, in any case. Out and about there's always a slight danger of **pickpockets**, but with a bit of common sense you've nothing to fear. **Verbal abuse** is not uncommon, especially in Belize City. The vast majority of this harassment is harmless, though the situation can be more threatening for **women travelling alone**; most hecklers, however, will be satisfied with a smile and wave as you move quickly onwards. If you need to **report a crime**, your first stop should be the tourism police, ubiquitous in Belize City and becoming more common in many tourist hotspots, including San

EMERGENCY NUMBERS

Ambulance ☎ 223 3292 (B.E.R.T.; Belize Emergency Response Team)
Ambulance and fire (Belize City) ☎ 90
Police ☎ 90 or ☎ 911
Tourism police (Belize City) ☎ 227 6082

Ignacio, Caye Caulker, Ambergris Caye and Placencia.

Many of the country's violent crimes are related to the **drug trade**, of which Belize is an important link in the chain between South and North America. Marijuana, cocaine and crack are all readily available, and whether you like it or not you'll receive regular offers. All such substances are **illegal**, and despite the fact that dope is often smoked openly in the streets, the police do arrest people for possession – they particularly enjoy catching tourists. If you are arrested you'll probably spend a couple of days in jail and pay a fine of several hundred US dollars; expect no sympathy from your embassy.

HEALTH

Health standards in Belize are quite high for the region, and Belize City has **hospitals** as well as a number of **private physicians** (see p.61). All other large towns have well-stocked **pharmacies and clinics**, which are usually free, though many will expect a donation for their services.

INFORMATION AND MAPS

Information on travelling in Belize is abundant, though often only available online, as even some major towns (except Belize City, Punta Gorda, Placencia and San Pedro) don't have a local tourist office. The office of the country's official source of tourist information, the **Belize Tourism Board** (BTB; ⓦtravelbelize.org), in Belize City, is not particularly useful, though their website is excellent (see p.59). The **Belize Tourism Industry**

Association (BTIA; ⓦbtia.org), which regulates many of the country's tourism businesses, has helpful representatives in touristed areas; they can put you in touch with local businesses and tour operators.

Local **maps** can be difficult to find and are often nonexistent in smaller towns and villages (where most streets don't have names), though the better hotels will usually be able to provide them to guests.

MONEY AND BANKS

The national currency is the **Belize dollar**, which is divided into 100 cents and fixed at two to one with the US dollar (US$1 = Bz$2); US dollars are also widely accepted, either in cash or travellers' cheques, and it can be cheaper to pay this way (see p.54). On account of this dual-currency system, always check whether the price you are quoted is in Belizean or US dollars; we have noted prices in local currency unless an operation has specifically quoted their fees in US dollars.

Credit and debit cards are widely used in Belize. Visa is the best option, though many establishments also accept MasterCard. Before you pay, check with the establishment if there's a charge for using plastic, as you might have to pay an extra five or seven percent for the privilege. Any bank can give you a Visa/ MasterCard **cash advance**, and most of them have **ATMs** that accept foreign-issued cards, although your own bank is likely to charge a fee for use abroad.

Taxes in Belize are quite high: sales tax is 12.5 percent and hotel tax is 9 percent. The hotel prices we quote throughout this chapter include tax.

BELIZE ONLINE

ⓦ **belizeaudubon.org** The latest information on Belize's growing number of reserves, national parks and associated visitor centres.

ⓦ **belizebus.wordpress.com** Excellent guide to transport routes and timetables.

ⓦ **belizefirst.com** Online magazine dedicated to Belize, featuring accurate reviews and articles about hotels, restaurants and destinations.

ⓦ **spear.org.bz** In-depth information on social, cultural, political and economic matters concerning Belize.

ⓦ **travelbelize.org** Belize's official tourism website offers excellent advice on travelling in Belize and can even help book accommodation and tours.

1

You'll find at least one **bank** in every town. Although the exchange rate is fixed, banks in Belize will give slightly less than Bz$2 for US$1 for both cash and travellers' cheques, so it can be a good idea simply to **pay in US dollars** if they are accepted and if you have them. Other than banks, only licensed *casas de cambio*, which can be difficult to find, are allowed to **exchange currency**, though there's usually a shop where locals go. To buy US dollars, you'll have to show an onward ticket.

OPENING HOURS AND HOLIDAYS

It's difficult to be specific about **opening hours** in Belize, but in general **shops** are open from 8am to noon and 1pm to 5pm. The **lunch hour** (noon–1pm) is almost universally observed. Some shops and businesses work a half-day on Saturday, and everything is liable to close early on Friday. **Banks** (generally Mon–Thurs 8am–2pm, Fri 8am–4pm) and government offices are only open Monday to Friday. **Post offices** are usually open Monday to Friday 8am to noon, and 1pm to 4pm. Watch out for **Sundays**, when shops and restaurants outside tourist areas are likely to be closed, and fewer bus services and internal flights operate. **Archeological sites**, however, are open every day. Virtually everything will be closed on the main **public holidays**, but note that if the holiday falls mid-week, it is observed on the following Monday.

PUBLIC HOLIDAYS

Jan 1 New Year's Day
March 9 Baron Bliss Day
March/April (variable) Good Friday, Holy Saturday, Easter Monday
May 1 Labour Day
May 24 Commonwealth Day
Sept 10 St George's Caye Day/National Day
Sept 21 Independence Day
Oct 12 Columbus Day (Pan America Day)
Nov 19 Garífuna Settlement Day
Dec 25 Christmas Day
Dec 26 Boxing Day

FESTIVALS

Belize's calendar is full of **festivals**, ranging from the local to the national. The calendar here includes a few highlights – but you'll find plenty of entertainment whenever you come.

February Carnaval is celebrated in the week before Lent with a week of dancing, parades, costumes and drinking.
March Celebrations throughout the country in honour of Baron Bliss Day – March 9 (see box opposite); La Ruta Maya River Challenge in San Ignacio.
May Cashew Festival in Crooked Tree; Toledo Cacao-Fest in Punta Gorda; Coconut Festival in Caye Caulker.
June Caye Caulker Lobster Festival; three-day Día de San Pedro festival in San Pedro; Placencia Lobster Festival.
July Belize international film festival in Belize City.
August Week-long Deer Dance Festival in San Antonio; Costa Maya festival in San Pedro.
September Celebrations commemorating St George's Caye Day (Sept 10) and Independence Day (Sept 21).
November 19 Garífuna Settlement Day.

Belize City

Even to the most hardened cosmopolite **BELIZE CITY** – the country's largest city, though not the capital – can be a daunting place. Dilapidated wooden buildings stand right on the edge of the road, offering pedestrians little refuge from the incessant traffic, and local attention ranges from simple curiosity and good-natured joking to outright heckling. Still, travellers who approach the city with an open mind may actually enjoy themselves. The streets, which certainly are chaotic, buzz with an energy that arises from the diversity of the city's seventy thousand or so citizens. And Belize City is, without a doubt, an experience; those who manage to feel comfortable here should have no problems anywhere else in the country.

WHAT TO SEE AND DO

Belize City is divided into northern and southern halves by **Haulover Creek**, a branch of the Belize River. The few sights are within **walking** distance of one another, and can all be visited within an afternoon. The pivotal (literally) point of the city centre is the Liverpool-made

SAFETY IN BELIZE CITY

Due to increasing gang activity, walking in the city's south side is not recommended at any time, but walking in the touristy areas of Belize City in **daylight** is perfectly safe if you use common sense: be civil, don't provoke trouble by arguing too forcefully and never show large sums of money on the street. Women should dress conservatively: female travellers, especially those wearing short shorts or skirts, are likely to attract mild verbal harassment from local men. However, the presence of a specially trained **tourism police** (❶ 227 6082), together with the legal requirement that all tour guides be licensed, generally prevents serious crime.

The chances of being mugged do increase **after dark**, but you'll find that you can walk – with others – around the main tourist drag in relative safety; you'll certainly encounter tourism police in this area. If you're venturing further afield, or if you've just arrived by bus at night, travel by taxi.

Swing Bridge, the only manually operated swing bridge left in the Americas. Formerly opened twice a day, it is now only operated on request due to the decrease in river traffic. **East** of the bridge is the most touristy part of town, with a scenic stretch of seafront and the majority of the city's decent hotels and restaurants. Immediately **south** of the Swing Bridge is Albert Street and the commercial zone, home to the city's banks, shops and a couple of supermarkets. This commercial centre sits on the fringes of a rougher area of the city (see box above), so be wary of straying from the recommended sights.

Image Factory

The **Image Factory**, north of the Swing Bridge at 91 N Front St (Mon–Fri 9am–5pm, Sat 10am–1pm; free, donations welcome; ❶ 223 4093, ⊛ imagefactory belize.com), hosts displays by Belize's hottest contemporary artists. The gallery holds outstanding, frequently provocative exhibitions, and you often get a chance to chat with the artists themselves. The factory is also home to one of the best **bookstores** in the country (see p.61).

Tourism Village

If you continue east along North Front Street from the Image Factory, you'll encounter an advance guard of trinket sellers, street musicians, hustlers and hair-braiders, announcing you're near **Tourism Village**, Belize's **cruise-ship terminal**. The Village itself can only be accessed by ship passengers; across the street, the **Fort Street Plaza** serves as an

extension of the Village and includes a restaurant, bar and additional shops. On ship days, a number of vendors line the streets in this area, though the items tend to be overpriced; be prepared to haggle here.

The seafront

Beyond the Tourism Village, the road follows the north shore of the river mouth, reaching the **Fort George Lighthouse**, which marks the tomb of **Baron Bliss**, Belize's greatest benefactor (see box below). On the seafront itself, **Memorial Park** honours the Belizean dead of the world wars, and in the streets around the park you'll find several colonial mansions, many of which now house upmarket hotels. At the corner of Hutson Street and Gabourel Lane a block from the sea is the former **US Embassy**: a superb "colonial" building actually constructed in New England in the nineteenth century, then dismantled and shipped to Belize.

BARON BLISS

Throughout Belize you'll come across time and again the name of **Baron Bliss**, an eccentric Englishman with a Portuguese title. A keen fisherman, he arrived off the coast of Belize in 1926 after hearing that the local waters were rich with game. Unfortunately, he became ill and died without ever making it ashore. Despite this, he left most of his considerable estate to the colony and, in gratitude, the authorities declared March 9, the date of his death, **Baron Bliss Day**.

1

BELIZE CITY

● EATING	
Bluebird	13
Chap's	3
KC's Deli	12
Ma Ma Chen	8
Martin's	10
Moon Clusters	7
Nerie's Restaurant II	9
Sumathi	4

● DRINKING & NIGHTLIFE	
Cesar's Palace	1
Club Next	5
Riverside Tavern	6
Thirsty Thursdays	2
Tropicana Lounge	11

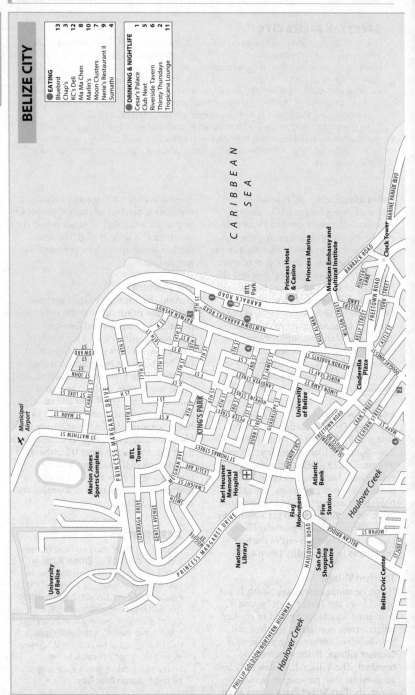

CARIBBEAN SEA

Princess Hotel & Casino

Princess Marina

Mexican Embassy and Cultural Institute

Clock Tower

MARINE PARADE BLVD

BTL Park

BARRACK ROAD

NEWTOWN BARRACKS ROAD

BARRACK ROAD

HUNTERS LANE

FULLERS LAND

WILSON STREET

KELLY STREET

FREETOWN ROAD

YORK STREET

CASTLE ST

DOUGLAS JONES ST

9TH ST

8TH ST

7TH ST

6TH ST

5TH ST

4TH ST

3RD ST

2ND ST

BAYMEN AVENUE

14TH ST

10TH ST

13TH ST

11TH ST

18TH ST

15TH ST

17TH ST

16TH ST

EDW RD

ST JOHN

ST LUKE ST

ST CHARLES ST

ST MARK ST

ST MATTHEW ST

CALE ALMAR

MAYOR ROBERTS ST

NURSE SEAY ST

SIMON LAMB ST

Cinderella Plaza

HOPKINS STREET

VERNON STREET

LANDIVAR STREET

JAMES ST

SEAY ST

KING'S PARK

GUADALUPE ST

PETER STREET

DUNN STREET

HYDE'S LANE

7TH ST

6TH ST

5TH ST

University of Belize

FREETOWN ROAD

CRAN STREET

CLEGHORN STREET

MAPP ST

Municipal Airport

PRINCESS MARGARET DRIVE

19TH ST

8TH ST

H ST

K ST

F ST

D ST

ST THOMAS STREET

ST

Marion Jones Sports Complex

BTL Tower

LIZARRAGA DRIVE

GENTLE AVENUE

WIGHAM AVE

LESLIE AVE

WIGHAM ST

SMITH ST

VOGUE ST

Karl Heusner Memorial Hospital

HUESNER CRES

National Library

HAULOVER ROAD

BELCAN BRIDGE

PRINCESS MARGARET DRIVE

Flag Monument

Fire Station

San Cas Shopping Centre

Atlantic Bank

Belize Civic Center

SLAUGHTERHOUSE RD

MOPAN ST

STUDIS ST

University of Belize

Haulover Creek

PHILLIP GOLDSON/NORTHERN HIGHWAY

Haulover Creek

Belikin Brewery, Discovery Expeditions, International Airport (18km), Orange Walk (87km) & Corozal (135km)

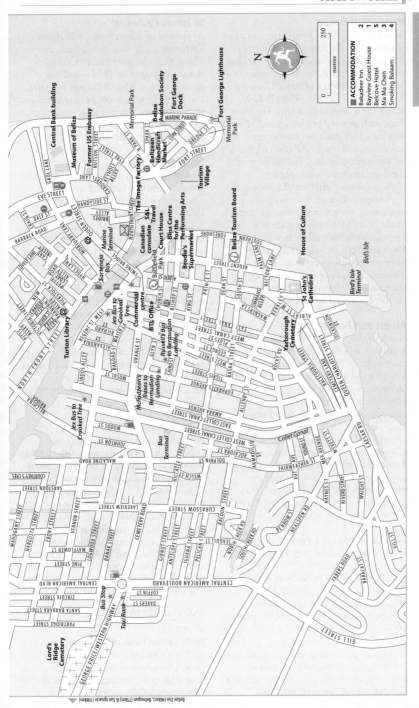

ACCOMMODATION

Bakadeer Inn	2
Bayview Guest House	1
Belcove Hotel	5
Ma Ma Chen	3
Smoking Balaam	4

0 metres 250

N

Central Bank building

Museum of Belize

Former US Embassy

Memorial Park

Belize Audubon Society

Fort George Lighthouse

Fort George Dock

MARINE PARADE

Belizean Handicraft Market

Memorial Park

The Image Factory

Tourism Village

Canadian consulate

S&L Travel

Court House

Bliss Centre for the Performing Arts

Belize Tourism Board

Marine Terminal

Battlefield Park

Blodie's Supermarket

House of Culture

Turton Library

Sarteneja Bus

Commercial centre

BTL Office

Russell's Bus

Christ to Bermudian Landing

St John's Cathedral

Bird's Isle

Bird's Isle Terminal

Jex Bus to Crooked Tree

McFadzean's Buses to Bermudian Landing

Yarborough Cemetery

Bus Terminal

Collet Canal

Lord's Ridge Cemetery

Bus Stop

Taxi Rank

GEORGE PRICE/WESTERN HIGHWAY

CENTRAL AMERICAN BOULEVARD

1

Museum of Belize

At the north end of Queen Street, in front of the Central Bank building, the city's former colonial prison, built in 1857, has undergone a remarkable transformation to become the **Museum of Belize** (Tues–Fri 9am–4.30pm, Sat 9am–4pm; Bz$10; ☎ 223 4524, ⊛ nichbelize.org). The lower floor, with exposed brickwork and barred windows, includes a reconstruction of a cell as well as a small exhibition on the jail's former occupants. The majority of the floor, however, is devoted to photographs and artefacts chronicling the city's history. Though these are quite interesting, the star attractions are upstairs, in the Maya Masterpieces gallery: a first-class collection of the best of Belize's **Maya artefacts**, including some of the finest painted Maya ceramics anywhere. Visitors can also peruse a comprehensive collection of Belizean stamps and an excellent selection of the country's insects.

Albert and Regent streets

South of the Swing Bridge, **Albert Street** is Belize City's main commercial thoroughfare, lined with banks and souvenir shops. On the parallel **Regent Street** are several former colonial administration and court buildings, collectively known as the **Court House**. Completed in 1926, these well-preserved examples of colonial architecture, with columns and fine wrought iron, overlook **Battlefield Park** (named to commemorate the noisy political meetings that took place here before independence), really just a patch of grass and trees with a dry ornamental fountain in the centre.

Bliss Centre for the Performing Arts

A block behind the Court House, on the waterfront at 2 Southern Foreshore, the **Bliss Centre for the Performing Arts** (Mon–Fri 8am–5pm; free; ☎ 227 2110, ⊛ nichbelize.org) not only hosts an eclectic mix of plays and concerts in its 600-seat auditorium, but also holds the country's national art collection, puts on temporary exhibitions and has a café/bar. Performances showcase local talent, including children's groups, solo acts and Garífuna dancers and drummers.

St John's Cathedral

At the end of Albert Street is **St John's Cathedral** (daily 6am–6pm; free), the oldest Anglican cathedral in Central America – begun in 1812 – and one of the oldest remaining buildings in Belize. Its red bricks were brought over as ballast in British ships – and it does look more like a large English parish church than most of the other buildings here.

House of Culture

East of the cathedral, on the seafront, the renovated former Government House, now renamed the **House of Culture** (Mon–Thurs 8.30am–5pm, Fri 8.30am–4.30pm; Bz$10; ☎ 227 3050, ⊛ nichbelize.org), is one of the most beautiful spots in Belize City, with its manicured lawns and sea views. Built in 1814, the structure served as the British governor's residence until Belizean independence in 1981. The main room downstairs exhibits the possessions of former governors as well as colonial silverware, glasses and furniture; temporary historical and cultural exhibitions are also on this floor. Upstairs are rooms for painting, dance and drumming workshops, art exhibitions and musical performances.

Belikin Brewery

Beyond the city limits, immediately opposite the airport runway, is the **Belikin Brewery** – the source of Belize's national beer. A visit to the factory (Mon–Fri 9am–4.30pm; US$15pp; ☎ 225 2058, ⊜ belikin.factory@bowenbz.com) includes a tour of the high-tech facilities, topped off with a hearty sampling session in the pub-style "Tap Room". Belikin classic, Premium, Stout and Lighthouse Lager are available for tasting, as well as seasonal brews including cacao and sorrel. The gift shop sells souvenirs.

ARRIVAL AND DEPARTURE

BY PLANE

Phillip Goldson International Airport International flights (see p.48) land at Phillip Goldson International Airport, 17km northwest of the city. Taxis are the only way to get into town; they cost Bz$50. There's a branch of the Belize Bank (with ATM) in the terminal.

Municipal airport Domestic flights to and from San Pedro, San Ignacio, Placencia, Dangriga, Caye Caulker and Punta Gorda (see p.49) come and go from the municipal airport, a few kilometres north of town on the edge of the sea; taxis from here to the city centre charge Bz$10.

BY BUS

Terminals Most buses depart from the central bus terminal at 19 West Collet Canal St (☎ 227 2255), which is in a fairly run-down area on the western side of the city. It's only 1km or so from the centre, so you can walk to any of the recommended hotels, but take a taxi at night. Other smaller companies leave from different points in the city (see box below).

Schedules Most services operate daily, though departure times may be erratic on Sundays. The shop inside the Marine Terminal at the swing bridge has reliable information on bus (and boat) schedules, and sells tickets for the express buses to Chetumal, Flores and Guatemala City.

Destinations Belmopan (NTSL, JA, BBOC; hourly 5am–9pm [express]; 1hr 15min); Benque Viejo del Carmen, for the Guatemalan border (NTSL, BBOC; hourly 5am–9pm [express]; 3hr 30min); Bermudian Landing, for the Community Baboon Sanctuary (MF, RU; Mon–Sat noon, 4pm & 5pm; 1hr 15min); Chetumal, Mexico (NTSL; hourly 5am–7pm [express]; 3hr 30min); Corozal (NTSL, BBOC; hourly 5am–7pm [express]; 2hr 30min); Crooked Tree (JX; Mon–Sat 10.55am & 4.30pm; 1hr 30min); Dangriga (JA; 12 daily 6am–5pm [express]; 3hr 30min via Belmopan); Orange Walk (NTSL, BBOC; hourly 5am–7pm [express]; 1hr 30min); Placencia (JA; 4 daily, via Belmopan and Dangriga; 5–7hr); Punta Gorda (JA; 12 daily, all via Belmopan and Dangriga [express]; 5–8hr); San Ignacio (NTSL, BBOC; hourly 5am–9pm, via Belmopan; 2hr 30min); Sarteneja (SC; Mon–Fri 4 daily [10.30am, noon, 4pm, 5pm]; 3 on Sat [10.30am, noon, 4pm]).

BY BOAT

Caye Caulker Water Taxi Association Skiffs to Caye Caulker (45min) and Ambergris Caye (1hr 15min) depart from the Marine Terminal on the north side of the Swing Bridge (daily 8am–4.30pm, at least every 1hr 30min; ☎ 223 5752, ✆ cayecaulkerwatertaxi.com).

San Pedro Water Jets Express Several daily runs to the cayes from a terminal at Bird's Isle (☎ 226 2194, ✆ sanpedrowatertaxi.com).

Pride of Belize A new ferry that makes a weekly run between the city and Puerto Cortés, Honduras, via Dangriga (Sat 9am; Bz$145; ☎ 600 3259, ✆ prideofbelize.com).

Information and schedules The shop inside the Marine Terminal has boat schedules.

GETTING AROUND

Walking The best way to get around Belize City's compact centre is on foot; even going from one side to the other should only take around 20min. Increasing gang violence on the city's south side makes much of the rest of the city highly undesirable for walking, so ask your hotel for advice on areas to avoid and use taxis after dark.

By taxi Identified by green numberplates, taxis charge Bz$7–9 for one or two passengers within the city limits.

INFORMATION AND TOURS

Belize Tourism Board 64 Regent St (Mon–Thurs 8am–5pm, Fri 8am–4pm; ☎ 227 2420, ✆ travelbelize.org). The staff here are not particularly helpful, but the office does hand out city maps, hotel guides and brochures; they can also recommend tour guides for nearby sights.

Tour operators A number of operators organize day-trips from Belize City, the most popular going to the Maya ruins at Altun Ha (US$45–60). Reliable options include S & L Travel, 91 N Front St (☎ 227 7593, ✆ sltravelbelize.com),

---

BUS COMPANIES AND STOPS

Belize's main bus company is National Transport Services Limited (NTSL). Note that the company's original name – Novelo's – still appears on some signs. Other, smaller companies also serve specific destinations, leaving from a variety of stops. The following are the main operators.

BBOC A co-operative of bus companies running services along the Northern and Western highways from the terminal.

James Bus (JA; ☎ 722 2049) Buses for Dangriga and Punta Gorda (via Belmopan), leaving from the terminal.

Jex Bus (JX; ☎ 225 7017) Departs for Crooked Tree from Regent St West (Mon–Sat 10.55am) and Pound Yard, Collet Canal (Mon–Fri 4.30pm & 5.15pm).

McFadzean's Bus (MF) Departs for Bermudian

Landing (via Burrell Boom) from Euphrates Ave, off Orange St, near the main bus depot.

NTSL (☎ 227 6372) Serving all major destinations from the terminal.

Russell's Bus (RU) Departs for Bermudian Landing from Cairo St, near the corner of Cemetery Rd and Euphrates Ave.

Sarteneja Bus Company (SC) Buses to Sarteneja via Orange Walk, from the south side of the Swing Bridge.

1

and Discovery Expeditions, 5916 Manatee Drive (☎ 223 0748, ⓦ discoverybelize.com).

ACCOMMODATION

Accommodation in Belize City is more expensive than elsewhere in the country, so prices for even budget rooms can come as quite a shock. There's usually no need to book in advance unless you're eager to stay in a particular hotel – you'll always be able to get something in the price range you're looking for. Keep in mind, however, that the further south and west you go, the more dangerous the area becomes; if you are travelling alone you may want to stay north of the river near Queen Street, the city's most populated area.

NORTH OF THE RIVER

Bakadeer Inn 63 Cleghorn St ☎ 223 0659. Safe and clean, with accommodating staff and comfortable, brightly painted rooms with private bath. US$35

Bayview Guest House 58 Baymen Ave ☎ 223 4179. Well located for sampling the city's nightlife, the *Bayview* offers eight weary but clean rooms with private bath, and shared kitchen facilities. US$25

Ma Ma Chen 7 Eve St, near the end of Queen St ☎ 223 4568. A Taiwanese couple runs this quiet, simple guesthouse/restaurant. Very basic rooms (some with a/c and private bath) line a hallway in the family home. US$30

Smoking Balaam 59 North Front St ☎ 601 4510. The four basic upstairs rooms, with fan and shared bath, in this creaky canal-front building are among the cheapest in the city. Downstairs, the internet café is a convenient spot to check emails while eating breakfast. US$20

SOUTH OF THE RIVER

★ **Belcove Hotel** 9 Regent St West ☎ 227 3054, ⓦ belcove.com. Basic, very clean rooms, some with a/c and private bath. Although it's on the edge of the dangerous part of town, the hotel itself is quite safe and enjoys great views of Swing Bridge from the balcony. US$33

EATING

Belize City's selection of restaurants is quite varied, though simple Creole food (rice and beans) still predominates at the lower end of the price scale. Note that many restaurants close early in the evening and on Sundays.

NORTH OF THE RIVER

Chap's 160 New Town Barracks. Good Mexican food with great lunch specials (from Bz$10), served on a breezy patio. Tues–Thurs 11am–10pm, Fri & Sat 11am–midnight, Sun noon–6pm.

Ma Ma Chen 7 Eve St ☎ 223 4568. Simple vegetarian restaurant, with adjoining guesthouse (see above),

★ TREAT YOURSELF

Sumathi 190 Newtown Barracks Rd. An excellent, authentic Indian curry house in the heart of the city; prices are steep, from US$10 a plate, but the large portions are delicious and good for sharing. Closed Mon.

serving tasty Taiwanese food, including spring rolls for Bz$8 and rice dishes for Bz$10. Daily 8am–7pm.

Moon Clusters 36 Daly St. One of the only true coffee shops in Belize City; another branch on Albert St serves an identical menu of coffees and cakes in a less inviting space. Relax in the bright and quirky interior with an excellent cup for Bz$7. Mon–Sat 7.30am–5pm.

Nerie's Restaurant II Corner of Queen and Daly sts ☎ 223 4028. Great Belizean food at reasonable prices: main dishes run from Bz$8 for rice and beans to Bz$12 for fish. Daily 8am–7pm.

SOUTH OF THE RIVER

Bluebird 35 Albert St. The best ice-cream bar in the city with a variety of exotic flavours, including ginger and soursop, at Bz$2 a scoop. Mon–Sat 7am–6pm.

KC's Deli Downtown Plaza mall, Albert St. A basic local snack stop, with standard fast-food options and decent daily lunch specials for under US$6. Mon–Sat 7am–6.30pm.

★ **Marlin's** 11 Regent St West, next to the *Belcove Hotel*. Great, inexpensive local cuisine, with an emphasis on seafood, served in large portions on a veranda overlooking the river. Traditional rice and beans, soups or breakfasts for Bz$6–12. Mon–Sat 9am–7pm.

DRINKING AND NIGHTLIFE

Belize City's nightlife really comes into its own on Fridays and Saturdays; any other night of the week, you're likely to find the city deserted after 9pm, with only a few hard-drinking (and often rowdy) locals frequenting the bars that are open. On weekends, however, there are plenty of venues to choose from, playing everything from techno to Latin grooves to punta, soca and reggae. Even then, though, don't arrive much before midnight, or you'll find many places empty. A relatively safe area of town with a variety of bars and clubs is the strip of Barracks Newtown Road from the *Princess Hotel* to *Caesar's Palace* bar.

Caesar's Palace Newtown Barracks Rd, across from BTL Park. An energetic crowd comes here to dance to Latin, techno and reggae after 10pm on Fri and Sat.

Club Next In the *Princess Hotel* ☎ 223 2670, ⓦ princessbelize.com. A lively local favourite. DJs play a variety of music and the dance floor is packed late on Fri and Sat nights. Bz$20 cover.

Riverside Tavern 2 Mapp St. Owned by the Belikin brewery, this is one of the classier spots in town. Popular with locals and tourists alike, it has a spacious outdoor patio and decent cocktail menu, as well as draught beer on tap. Mon–Wed 11am–10pm, Thurs 11am–midnight, Fri 11am–2am, Sat noon–2am.

Thirsty Thursdays 164 Newtown Barracks Rd ☎223 1677. A buzzing bar set on a large balcony, where you'll find polished young Belizeans bouncing to electro-pop and hip-hop, and sipping drinks from the long cocktail list (from Bz$6) – be prepared to pay a cover charge (from Bz$15, with "ladies" half price). Thurs–Sat 5pm–2am.

Tropicana Lounge 5 Fort St ☎601 9001. A local crowd gathers here to shake up the dance floor, with dancehall, reggae and punta encouraging extreme booty shaking – if you haven't already experienced punta dancing, this might be a good place to start. Tues–Sat 1pm–1am.

ENTERTAINMENT

Cinema At the *Princess Hotel*, on Newtown Barracks Rd. The only cinema in the city, with one showing nightly of a recent Hollywood blockbuster. It is also the venue for Belize's annual Film Festival.

Performing arts The cultural centre of Belize is the Bliss Centre for the Performing Arts (see p.58), which stages a variety of events – from plays to concerts – in its large auditorium. The House of Culture (see p.58) also hosts exhibitions and events, including classical concerts, in its intimate upstairs rooms. Both venues are affordable (from free to Bz$30), but shows can be sporadic. Check ⓦnichbelize.com for schedules.

SHOPPING

The Angelus Press 10 Queen St ☎223 5777. Good bookshop with a wide range of Belize-related books and maps. Mon–Fri 7.30am–5.30pm, Sat 8am–noon.

Crafts and souvenirs For items like T-shirts, shells, wooden carvings and beaded jewellery, head to the market space opposite the Tourism Village (see p.55); or the National Handicraft Center, 2 South Park St (Mon–Fri 8am–5pm, Sat 8am–4pm), which sells high-quality Belizean arts and crafts at fair prices.

The Image Factory 91 N Front St ☎223 4093, ⓦimagefactorybelize.com. This superb gallery (see p.55) also has a well-stocked bookstore, with a good selection of Belizean literature, travel guides and current pop fiction novels. Mon–Fri 9am–5pm.

Supermarket Albert St, south of the Swing Bridge, is the city's central commercial district. A number of supermarkets line the street, including the city's largest, Brodie's, which is quite expensive, as most of the selection is imported.

DIRECTORY

Banks and exchange The main banks have branches on Albert St (usually Mon–Thurs 8am–2pm, Fri 8am–4.30pm). Most have ATMs that accept foreign-issued cards. For Guatemalan quetzales and Mexican pesos try Kaisa International in the Marine Terminal.

Consulates Current addresses and phone numbers can be found under "Diplomatic Listings" in the green pages of the telephone directory. Canada ☎223 1060; Guatemala ☎223 3150; Honduras ☎224 5889; Mexico ☎223 0193. Most are normally open in the mornings from Monday to Friday. The US embassy (☎822 4011) and British High Commission (☎822 2146) are in Belmopan (see p.78).

Health Karl Heusner Memorial Hospital, Princess Margaret Drive, near the junction with the Northern Highway (☎223 1548). There are a number of pharmacies on Albert St.

Immigration In the Government Complex on Mahogany St, near the junction of Central American Blvd and the Western Highway (Mon–Thurs 8.30am–4pm, Fri 8.30am–3.30pm; ☎222 4620). Thirty-day extensions of stay (the maximum allowed) cost US$30.

Internet The Angelus Press, 10 Queen St (Bz$4/hr), and Turton Library, N Front St (☎227 3401; Bz$2.50/hr), are central options. Many hotels offer internet access to guests.

Laundry Belize Dry Cleaners, 3 Dolphin St (Mon–Fri 7am–6pm; reduced hours Sun; ☎227 3796), has a full or self-service laundromat.

Police The main police station is on Queen St, a block north of the Swing Bridge (☎227 2210). Alternatively, contact the Tourism Police (see box, p.55).

Post office North Front St, opposite the Marine Terminal (Mon–Fri 8am–noon & 1–4pm).

Telephones There are payphones (operated using pre-paid cards) dotted all around the city. The main BTL office, 1 Church St (Mon–Fri 8am–6pm), also has fax and email services.

The cayes and atolls

Belize's spectacular **Barrier Reef**, with its dazzling variety of underwater life, string of exquisite **cayes** (pronounced "keys") and extensive opportunities for all kinds of watersports, is the country's main attraction for most first-time visitors. The longest barrier reef in the western hemisphere, it runs the entire length of

1

the coastline, usually 15 to 40km from the mainland, with most of the cayes lying in shallow water behind the shelter of the reef. **Caye Caulker** is the most popular destination for budget travellers. The town of **San Pedro** on **Ambergris Caye**, meanwhile, has transformed from a predominantly fishing community to one dominated by tourism. There are still some beautiful spots though, notably the protected sections of reef at either end of

the caye: **Bacalar Chico National Park** and **Hol Chan Marine Reserve**.

Beyond the barrier reef are two of Belize's three **atolls**, the **Turneffe Islands** and **Lighthouse Reef**, regularly visited on day-trips from San Pedro and Caye Caulker. Lighthouse Reef encompasses two of the most beautiful diving and snorkelling sites in the country – **Half Moon Caye Natural Monument** and the **Great Blue Hole**, an enormous collapsed cave.

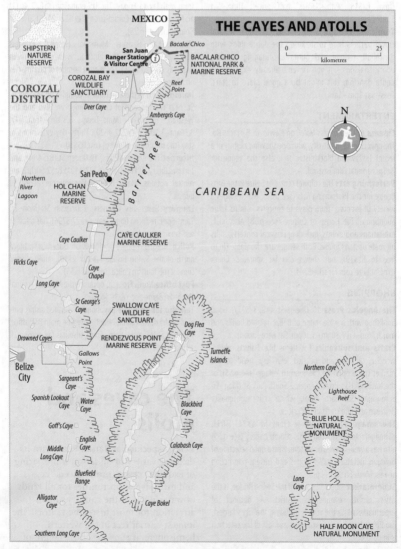

THE CAYES AND ATOLLS

MEXICO

SHIPSTERN NATURE RESERVE

San Juan Ranger Station & Visitor Centre

Bacalar Chico

BACALAR CHICO NATIONAL PARK & MARINE RESERVE

0   25
kilometres

COROZAL DISTRICT

COROZAL BAY WILDLIFE SANCTUARY

Deer Caye

Reef Point

Ambergris Caye

N

Northern River Lagoon

San Pedro

HOL CHAN MARINE RESERVE

Barrier Reef

CARIBBEAN SEA

Caye Caulker

CAYE CAULKER MARINE RESERVE

Hicks Caye

Caye Chapel

Long Caye

St George's Caye

SWALLOW CAYE WILDLIFE SANCTUARY

Dog Flea Caye

Drowned Cayes

RENDEZVOUS POINT MARINE RESERVE

Gallows Point

Turneffe Islands

Belize City

Sargeant's Caye

Northern Caye

Spanish Lookout Caye

Water Caye

Lighthouse Reef

Goff's Caye

Blackbird Caye

BLUE HOLE NATURAL MONUMENT

English Caye

Middle Long Caye

Calabash Caye

Bluefield Range

Long Caye

Alligator Caye

Caye Bokel

Southern Long Caye

HALF MOON CAYE NATURAL MONUMENT

SAFEGUARDING THE CORAL REEF

Coral reefs are among the most **fragile ecosystems** on earth. Colonies grow less than 5cm a year; once damaged, the coral is far more susceptible to bacterial infection, which can quickly lead to large-scale irreversible deterioration. All licensed **tour guides** in Belize are trained in reef ecology, and should brief you on reef precautions. If exploring independently, keep the following points in mind:

• Never anchor boats on the reef – use the permanently secured buoys.

• Never touch or stand on the reef.

• Don't remove shells, sponges or other creatures, or buy reef products from souvenir shops.

• Avoid disturbing the seabed around corals – clouds of sand smother coral colonies.

• If you're a beginner or out-of-practice diver, practise away from the reef first.

• Don't use suntan lotion in reef areas – the oils remain on the water's surface; instead, wear a T-shirt to guard against sunburn.

• Don't feed or interfere with fish or marine life; this can harm not only sea creatures, but snorkellers and divers too – large fish may attack, trying to get their share.

CAYE CAULKER

A firm favourite on the backpacker trail, **CAYE CAULKER**, 35km northeast of Belize City, is relaxed, easy-going and more than merits its "Go Slow" motto. The **reef**, 1.5km offshore, is a **marine reserve**, offering unbelievable opportunities for any imaginable watersport. Though the number of expensive places is increasing, in general the island is affordable, with an abundance of inexpensive accommodation and tour operators. Though it's hard to imagine today, up until about fifteen years ago, tourism existed almost as a sideline to the island's main source of income, **lobster fishing**. The money might be coming from tourists these days but there are still plenty of the spiny creatures around, most notably at the annual **Lobster Fest**, normally held in the third weekend of June to celebrate the start of the season.

WHAT TO SEE AND DO

Caye Caulker is a little over 8km long. The settlement is at the southern end, which curves west like a hook; the northern tip, meanwhile, forms the **Caye Caulker Forest Reserve**, designated to protect the caye's littoral forest, one of the rarest habitats in Belize. Although there's a reasonable beach along the front of the caye (created by pumping sand from the back of the island), the waterfront is heavily developed, and the sea nearby is full of seagrass. If you want to go for a dip you'd do best to head for "**the Split**",

at the northern end of the village – a narrow (but widening) channel cut by Hurricane Hattie in 1961; it's a popular place to relax and swim.

Snorkelling

Snorkelling the reef is an experience not to be missed; its coral canyons are home to an astonishing range of fish, including eagle rays and perhaps even the odd shark (almost certainly harmless nurse sharks). Because of the reef's fragility, visits to the marine reserves and the reef itself must be accompanied by a licensed guide (see p.65). **Trips** are easily arranged at the island's snorkel and dive shops – expect to pay from US$40 per person for a half day and from US$65 for a full day. Most day-trips stop at the reef as well as **Hol Chan Marine Reserve** (see p.68) and **Shark-Ray Alley**.

Sea-kayaks (see p.65) are useful for independent snorkelling closer to the island, where some coral is visible.

Diving

Diving here is also excellent, and instruction and trips are usually cheaper than in San Pedro: open-water certification starts at US$300, two-tank dives at US$70, trips to the **Blue Hole** (see p.70) at US$280 and trips to the **Turneffe Islands** (see p.70) at US$200. Most places in town offer enthusiastic, knowledgeable local guides, regular fast boat trips and a wide range of diving courses.

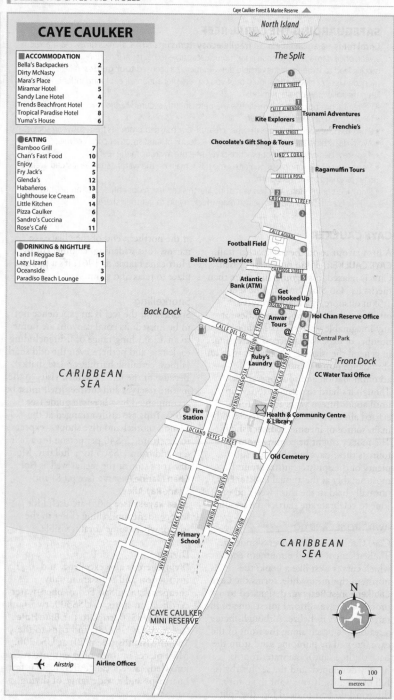

CAYE CAULKER

Caye Caulker Forest & Marine Reserve ▲

North Island

The Split

ACCOMMODATION
Bella's Backpackers	2
Dirty McNasty	3
Mara's Place	1
Miramar Hotel	5
Sandy Lane Hotel	4
Trends Beachfront Hotel	7
Tropical Paradise Hotel	8
Yuma's House	6

EATING
Bamboo Grill	7
Chan's Fast Food	10
Enjoy	2
Fry Jack's	5
Glenda's	12
Habañeros	13
Lighthouse Ice Cream	8
Little Kitchen	14
Pizza Caulker	6
Sandro's Cuccina	4
Rose's Café	11

DRINKING & NIGHTLIFE
I and I Reggae Bar	15
Lazy Lizard	1
Oceanside	3
Paradiso Beach Lounge	9

HATTIE STREET

CALLE ALMENDRO

Kite Explorers

Tsunami Adventures

Frenchie's

PARK STREET

Chocolate's Gift Shop & Tours

LIND'S CORAL

CALLE LA POSA

Ragamuffin Tours

CROCODILE STREET

CALLE AGUADA

Football Field

Belize Diving Services

CHAPOSE STREET

Atlantic Bank (ATM)

Get Hooked Up

PASERO STREET

Anwar Tours

Hol Chan Reserve Office

Back Dock

CALLE DEL SOL

Central Park

Ruby's Laundry

Front Dock

CC Water Taxi Office

CARIBBEAN SEA

Fire Station

Health & Community Centre & Library

LUCIANO REYES STREET

Old Cemetery

AVENIDA LANGOSTA

AVENIDA HICACO (FRONT) STREET

AVENIDA PUEBLO NUEVO

Primary School

AVENIDA MANGLE (BACK STREET)

PLAYA ASUNCIÓN

CARIBBEAN SEA

CAYE CAULKER MINI RESERVE

N

✈ *Airstrip*   Airline Offices

0	100
	metres

Sailing and other activities

One romantic way to enjoy the sea and
the reef is to spend the day on a **sailboat**,
which costs around US$60 per person,
and usually includes several snorkelling
stops and lunch, arriving back as the sun
goes down.

Kayaking is another good option for
those wishing to snorkel without a guide.
Some hotels lend kayaks to guests for
free, and a number of establishments
along Front Street rent them: Tsunami
Adventures (see below) charge only
Bz$25/hr, and most shops rent snorkel
gear for about Bz$20.

ARRIVAL AND INFORMATION

By plane The airstrip is about 1km (a 15min walk) south
of the town centre. Alternatively, you can take one of the
island's numerous golf carts (Bz$8–10), which usually
wait to meet flights.

By boat Boats pull into the front dock, which is in the
middle of the island's eastern edge and within easy
walking distance of all of the hotels listed below. Boats
operated by the Caye Caulker Water Taxi Association
(ⓣ 223 5752, ⓦ cayecaulkerwatertaxi.com) arrive and
depart for Belize City (45min; Bz$20) at least every 1hr
30min from 8am to 4pm (5pm on weekends and
holidays), and for San Pedro (30min; Bz$20) at least
every 2hr from 8am to 5pm. San Pedro Water Jets
Express (ⓣ 226 2194, ⓦ sanpedrowatertaxi.com) also
provides several daily runs between Belize City and San
Pedro.

Tourist information There's no official tourist office,
but the town's websites (ⓦ gocayecaulker.com and
ⓦ cayecaulkerbelize.net) are helpful.

TOURS AND ACTIVITIES

SNORKELLING
Anwar Tours North of the front dock (ⓣ 226 0327,
ⓦ anwartours.page.tl).

Chocolate's Manatee Tours Chocolate's Gift Shop,
northern end of Front St. Snorkelling tours combined with
a visit to Swallow Caye Wildlife Sanctuary, on a mangrove
caye near Belize City, to view the manatees (US$60; ⓣ 226
0151, ⓔ chocolateseashore@gmail.com).

Raggamuffin Tours Near the north end of Front St.
Options include sunset cruises for US$25pp (8 minimum)
with rum cocktails and chips with salsa included (ⓣ 226
0348, ⓦ raggamuffintours.com).

Tsunami Adventures Near the Split (ⓣ 226 0462,
ⓦ tsunamiadventures.com).

DIVING
Belize Diving Services Back St (ⓣ 226 0143,
ⓦ belizedivingservices.net).

Frenchie's Towards the northern end of the village
(ⓣ 226 0234, ⓦ frenchiesdivingbelize.com).

GENERAL WATERSPORTS
Get Hooked Up Cnr Avda Langosta & Pasero St. Fishing
trips and rents gear, and rents bicycles for US$12/day
(ⓣ 226 0270).

Kite Explorers Front St, by the Split. Watersports centre
with SUP boards to rent ($10/hr), as well as kitesurfing
and windsurfing lessons and rentals (ⓣ 635 4697,
ⓦ kiteexplorer.com).

ACCOMMODATION

Some of Caye Caulker's hotels have been renovated to provide
more upscale accommodation, but the island still has an
abundance of simple, inexpensive rooms with shared bath.
Book in advance, especially at Christmas and New Year.

Bella's Backpackers Crocodile St ⓣ 226 0360, ⓔ monkey
bite38@yahoo.com. These dorm beds and semi-private
rooms, set in a rambling wooden building, attract a curious
crowd of hippies and hipsters. There's a communal kitchen
and common room, free use of the canoes and rusty bicycles
for guests, and wi-fi access. You can also camp in the yard.
Camping per tent Bz$15, dorm US$10, double US$25

Dirty McNasty Crocodile St across from *Bella's*,
ⓦ dirtymcnastys.com. A party hostel with basic dorms
and private rooms; the on-site bar/lounge was under
construction at the time of research but promises to be
buzzing. Dorm US$11, double US$30

Mara's Place Near the Split ⓣ 600 0080, ⓔ maras
_place@hotmail.com. Comfortable, clean, quiet cabins
with private bath, TV and porch. There's also a communal
kitchen and private sundeck. US$45

Miramar Hotel Front St ⓣ 206 0357. Basic rooms, some
with private bath, in a wooden building with a large
balcony overlooking the sea; there's one hot shower on the
second floor. US$15

★ **Sandy Lane Hotel** Middle St ⓣ 226 0117. Basic,
well-worn wooden rooms and cabañas, some with shared

1

bath and some en suite. The best deal on the island. US$15
Trends Beachfront Hotel Immediately right of Front
Dock ☎ 226 0094, ⊛ trendsbze.com. Large rooms, some
with balconies, with comfortable beds and private baths in
a pastel-painted wooden building. US$25
Tropical Paradise Hotel At the southern end of Front St
☎ 226 0124. A wide range of rooms, all with hot showers,
private baths and fans, and some with a/c, in a series of
brightly painted wooden buildings. The restaurant serves
inexpensive meals. US$50
Yuma's House 75m north of Front Dock, along the beach
☎ 206 0019, ⊛ yumashousebelize.com. Dorm beds and
small, shared-bath rooms in an atmospheric wooden beach
house with communal kitchen. Downstairs offers plenty of
chill-out hammocks and chairs in a pretty sand garden.
Reservations necessary. Dorm US$14, double US$29

EATING

Restaurant prices in Caye Caulker tend to be higher than in
the rest of the country, and it can be difficult to find a meal
for less than Bz$15. Still, lobster (in season) and seafood
are generally good value. Beachfront grill-stands line the
sand on the island's east side, where BBQ plates go for
Bz$8–20, while "walking bakeries" sell home-made
banana bread, coconut cakes and other goodies from carts
on the street. You can also self-cater, stocking up at several
shops and supermarkets. Note that the tap water is unfit to
drink; rainwater and bottled water are widely available.
Bamboo Grill On the beach. Good Belizean cuisine and
seafood (Bz$17–35) served at high tables with wooden
swings. The bar stays open late.
Chan's Fast Food C Del Sol at Avda Langosta. Fast-food
hole-in-the-wall, with two small tables and the cheapest
eats in town; a hearty takeaway box of Belizean or Chinese
food goes for Bz$7–15. Daily 7am–9pm.
Enjoy Front St next to *Oceanside*. This street-side venue

★ TREAT YOURSELF

Habañeros Front St ☎ 226 0487. The
island's poshest restaurant: attentive staff
serve up superb seafood and creative,
Latin-inspired dishes (Bz$30–50),
accompanied by fine wines on a romantic,
open-air veranda. Reservations
recommended. Closed Thurs.

Sandro's Cuccina Pasero St. This
authentic Italian restaurant makes the
most of local ingredients, with gourmet
touches. The open-air seating allows
diners to watch the passionate chef
prepare delicious pastas, seafood and
meats for Bz$14–35. Reservations
necessary. Thurs–Tues 5–9.30pm.

isn't known for its decor, despite the sandy floors and
swing-chairs at the bar. Instead, it's the large portions –
with seafood plates from Bz$20 – and 2-for-1 happy hour
rum deals that pack it out at night. Daily noon–11pm.
★ **Fry Jack's** Across from the bank on Avda Langosta.
The tiny shack adjoining the *Get Hooked Up* office serves
the eponymous popular Belizean breakfast food, stuffed
with a variety of fillings, for Bz$2–4. There's no seating,
but it's great for breakfast on the run.
Glenda's Back St. Busy brunch spot, known for cinnamon
rolls and breakfast sandwiches (Bz$4–10).
Lighthouse Ice Cream Front St. Cool off with the
second-best home-made ice cream in Belize – beaten only
by *Tutti Frutti* in Placencia (see p.97). Try local flavours like
soursop or coconut.
Little Kitchen Behind the fire station, off Luciano Reyes
St. This out-of-the-way upstairs café offers some of the
cheapest food on Caye Caulker, with excellent seafood for
Bz$10–30 – try the conch fritters. Expect slow service.
Daily noon–9pm.
Pizza Caulker Pasero St ☎ 206 0666. Decent, medium-
crust pies; daily specials include a slice of pizza and beer for
Bz$9. Daily 3–10pm.
Rose's Café C del Sol at Front St. One of the best places in
town to eat lobster; the good (seasonal) selection starts at
Bz$30 a plate. Daily 6.30am–11pm.

DRINKING AND NIGHTLIFE

Many bars offer a happy hour from 3–7pm, with local
spirits being the least expensive option.
I and I Reggae Bar Luciano Reyes St. A favourite among
tourists and locals, with strong cocktails and a sweaty
dance floor. The breezy rooftop space closes at 10pm, at
which point the crowd starts to drift to *Oceanside*.
Lazy Lizard On the Split. A typical night out on the island
begins with a sunset drink at the Split's *Lazy Lizard* beach
bar, the main social gathering spot on the island.
Oceanside Front St. A dark indoor club, with a sand dance
floor, attracts a rowdy mix of locals and tourists –
especially as the night draws on. Daily 9pm–4am.
Paradiso Beach Lounge North of Front Dock, on the
beach. They host a popular "movies under the stars" event
here in the high season (Bz$10).

DIRECTORY

Bank Atlantic Bank, just north of the centre, has a 24hr
ATM.
Internet Cayeboard Connection (daily 8am–9pm) on
Front St also has a book exchange, while La Perla del Mar
(7am–9pm) on Avda Langosta has icy-cold a/c and good
coffee; both charge $12/hr to connect.
Laundry Drop-off services at Ruby's, C del Sol, roughly
from 9am–5pm (closes for lunch).
Post office Front St.

AMBERGRIS CAYE AND SAN PEDRO

AMBERGRIS CAYE is the most northerly and, at almost 40km long, by far the largest of the cayes. The island's main attraction is the former fishing village of **SAN PEDRO**, facing the reef just a few kilometres from the caye's southern tip. San Pedro is a small town, but its population – more than nine thousand – makes it the biggest on any of the cayes. As the result of massive recent development, it has lost much, though not all, of its Caribbean charm: it still retains a relaxed atmosphere, despite the fact that some of the most exclusive hotels, restaurants and bars in Belize have been built here. The island has a few budget places, but much of the accommodation caters to high-end tourists. To save money, consider staying on Caye Caulker and doing a day-trip here.

WHAT TO SEE AND DO

San Pedro's main streets are only half a dozen blocks long and the town does not boast any particular sights. Activity

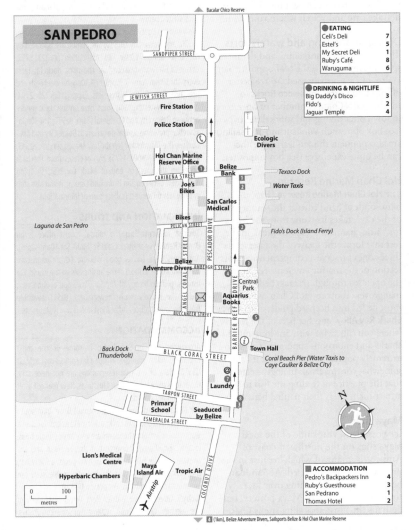

Bacalar Chico Reserve

SAN PEDRO

SANDPIPER STREET

JEWFISH STREET

Fire Station

Police Station

Hol Chan Marine Reserve Office

CARIBEÑA STREET

Joe's Bikes

Bikes

PELICAN STREET

Laguna de San Pedro

Belize Adventure Divers

AMBERGRIS STREET

ANGEL CORAL STREET

PESCADOR DRIVE

BUCCANEER STREET

BARRIER REEF DRIVE

BLACK CORAL STREET

TARPON STREET

Laundry

Primary School

Seaduced by Belize

ESMERALDA STREET

Back Dock (Thunderbolt)

Lion's Medical Centre

Hyperbaric Chambers

Maya Island Air

Tropic Air

COCONUT DRIVE

Airstrip

Ecologic Divers

Belize Bank

Texaco Dock

Water Taxis

San Carlos Medical

Fido's Dock (Island Ferry)

Central Park

Aquarius Books

Town Hall

Coral Beach Pier (Water Taxis to Caye Caulker & Belize City)

N

0   100
metres

EATING	
Celi's Deli	7
Estel's	5
My Secret Deli	1
Ruby's Café	8
Waruguma	6

DRINKING & NIGHTLIFE	
Big Daddy's Disco	3
Fido's	2
Jaguar Temple	4

ACCOMMODATION	
Pedro's Backpackers Inn	4
Ruby's Guesthouse	3
San Pedrano	1
Thomas Hotel	2

4 (1km), Belize Adventure Divers, Sailsports Belize & Hol Chan Marine Reserve

1

focuses on the **sea** and the **reef**, with everything from simple sunbathing to windsurfing, sailing, fishing, diving, snorkelling and glass-bottomed-boat rides on offer. **Beaches** on the caye are narrow and the sea immediately offshore is shallow, with a lot of seagrass, so in town you'll usually need to walk to the end of a dock if you want to **swim**. Be careful, though: there have been accidents in San Pedro in which speeding boats have hit people swimming from the docks. A line of buoys indicates the "safe area", but speedboat drivers can be a bit macho, so do take care and watch where you swim.

Diving, snorkelling and watersports

The most central snorkelling and diving spot on Ambergris is the **reef** opposite San Pedro, but it's heavily used. You're better off heading north, to **Mexico Rocks**, or south, to **Hol Chan**. A number of operators in town offer diving and snorkelling trips (see box opposite). **Windsurfing** and **sailing** are also popular, though learning either can be quite expensive (see box opposite).

Hol Chan Marine Reserve

The **Hol Chan Marine Reserve** (Bz$50), 8km south of San Pedro at the southern tip of the caye, takes its name from the Maya for "little channel" – it is this break in the reef that forms the focus of the reserve. Its three zones preserve a comprehensive cross section of the marine environment, from the open sea through seagrass beds and mangroves. Tours to Hol Chan, which must be led by a licensed guide, also stop at **Shark-Ray Alley**, another part of the reserve, where you can swim with 3m-long **nurse sharks** and enormous **stingrays**. This is an extremely popular attraction, but it's also somewhat controversial: biologists claim that the practice of feeding the fish to attract them alters their natural behaviour.

Maya sites

It's possible to visit some of the local **Maya sites** on the northwest coast of Ambergris, many of which are just in the process of being excavated. At **San Juan** beach you'll be scrunching over literally thousands of pieces of Maya pottery, but perhaps the most appealing site is **Chac**

Balam, slightly further north on the western tip of the island, a ceremonial and administrative centre with deep burial chambers.

ARRIVAL AND DEPARTURE

By plane The airport is just south of the city centre, within easy walking distance of any of the recommended hotels, though golf buggies and taxis also line up to give you a ride for around Bz$8–10.

By boat Boats from Belize City and/or Caye Caulker dock at the Coral Beach pier on the front (reef) side of the island at the eastern end of Black Coral St. From this central dock, you're pretty much within walking distance of most of the hotels listed below.

Destinations Boats from San Pedro to Caye Caulker (30min; Bz$20) and Belize City (Bz$30; 1hr 20min) are operated by the Caye Caulker Water Taxi Association (☎ 223 5752, ⊚ cayecaulkerwatertaxi.com) at the front dock (at least every 1hr 30min 7am–3.30pm, or 4.30pm on weekends and holidays). San Pedro Water Jets Express (☎ 226 2194, ⊚ sanpedrowatertaxi.com) stops here on the daily service between Belize City and Chetumal (8am; Bz$70; 1hr 30min) as well as providing several daily runs to Belize City and Caye Caulker. The *Thunderbolt* (erratic low-season service; Bz$45; ☎ 422 0226 or ☎ 601 4475; 2hr) operates from the back dock, on the western end of Black Coral St, shuttling passengers between San Pedro and Corozal; it will also stop in Sarteneja on request (call for current information).

INFORMATION AND TOURS

Tourist information The official tourist office is on Barrier Reef Drive at Black Coral St (Mon–Sat 10am–1pm). Ambergris Caye has a good website (⊚ ambergriscaye .com) with links to most of the businesses on the island. For listings, pick up a copy of *The San Pedro Sun* or *Ambergris Today*, the island's tourist newspapers (Bz$1), available from the tourist office and at most hotels and restaurants.

ACCOMMODATION

Accommodation in San Pedro is some of the most expensive in the country – all but a few places cost at least US$70. Most of the year reservations are not necessary, though it's risky to turn up at Christmas, New Year or Easter unless you've booked.

★ **Pedro's Backpacker Inn** Coconut Drive, 1km south of town ☎ 226 3825, ⊚ backpackersbelize.com. A bit of a walk from town, and the rooms are very basic (single beds, lockers and shared showers), but they're clean and the cheapest on the island. There are two pools, a lively bar, bike rental and wi-fi, and the knowledgeable staff can organize a range of tours. Per person US$10

Ruby's Guesthouse Barrier Reef Drive, just north of the airstrip ☎ 226 2063, ⊚ ambergriscaye.com/rubys.

TOURS AND ACTIVITIES

In addition to the specialist activities detailed below, several operators also offer inland tours to Maya ruins, manatee tours and fishing trips.

Diving For qualified divers, a two-tank local dive from Ambergris Caye costs around US$80. Open-water certification courses are around US$435, while a more basic, single-dive resort course costs from US$140; both include equipment. For diving trips and courses try Belize Diving Adventures (☎226 3082, ⓦbelizedivingadventures.net), Ecologic Divers (☎226 4118, ⓦecologicdivers.com), or Seaduced by Belize (☎226 2254, ⓦseaducedbybelize.com).

Snorkelling All the dive shops in San Pedro also offer snorkelling trips, costing around US$25–35 for 2–3hr and US$40–55 for 4–5hr, and many will rent snorkelling supplies; trips to the Blue Hole (see p.70) cost around US$250 and trips to the Turneffe Islands (see p.70) US$185.

Windsurfing and sailing The best rental and instruction for both is offered by SailSports Belize (☎226 4488, ⓦsailsportsbelize.com), on the beach at *Caribbean Villas Hotel*. Sailboard rentals cost US$22/hr and catamaran rentals from US$38/hr, with discounts for multiple hours. They also offer kitesurfing and sailing lessons.

Family-run hotel on the seafront; rooms with a/c, with private baths and on the higher floors cost more, but all are good value, especially those in the annexe on the lagoon. US$20

San Pedrano Cnr Barrier Reef Drive & Caribeña St ☎226 2054, ⓔsanpedrano@btl.net. Family-run hotel in a wooden building set back slightly from the sea, with comfortable rooms with bath (some with a/c and all with TV) and breezy verandas. US$35

Thomas Hotel Barrier Reef Drive, north of the centre ☎226 2061. Rooms here (some with a/c) are a good deal, with private baths, fridges and TVs. US$33

EATING

Restaurant prices in San Pedro are generally higher than elsewhere in Belize. Most restaurants offer a lot of seafood, and you can also rely on plenty of steak, shrimp, chicken, pizza and salads. In the evening, several inexpensive fast-food stands open for business along the front of Central Park. Self-catering isn't much of a bargain: there's no market and the supermarkets are stocked with expensive imported canned goods.

Celi's Deli Opposite the *Hotel Holiday* on Barrier Reef Drive. Home-made tortillas, Johnny cakes – a cornmeal flatbread – and meat pies make *Celi's* a local favourite, as well as cheap tacos, burritos and sarnies for Bz$2–10. Daily 5am–5pm.

Estel's On the beach just south of the park ☎226 2019. This locally owned, laidback restaurant serves breakfast all day and Belizean food at lunch for Bz$6–30. Fri–Wed 6am–5pm.

★ **My Secret Deli** Caribeña St opposite Joe's Bikes ☎226 3223. The best budget restaurant and busiest lunchtime spot on Ambergris, serving large plates of Belizean food for Bz$5–12; the conch soup is a local speciality. Mon–Sat 7am–3pm & 6–9pm, Sun 11.30am–3pm.

Ruby's Café Barrier Reef Drive, next to *Ruby's Guesthouse*. Delicious home-made cakes, pies and sandwiches, and freshly brewed coffee. Popular with locals. Daily 5am–5pm.

Waraguma Towards the south end of Pescador Drive. Seafood burritos and kebabs (Bz$15–25) are the main draw here, while tasty *pupusas* or stuffed tortillas (Bz$3–7) make a good snack between meals. Daily 11am–10pm.

DRINKING AND NIGHTLIFE

San Pedro, with a lively tourist/expat crowd, is the tourist entertainment capital of Belize, and if you check locally, you'll find live music on somewhere every night of the week. Most of the hotels have bars, several of which offer happy hours.

Big Daddy's Disco On the beach just south of the park. Locals flock to this beach bar and club for reggae and Latin music on weekend nights. Drinks can be expensive, so ask for a price list before choosing. Daily 11am–2am.

Fido's Barrier Reef Drive. An American comfort food restaurant by day, by night *Fido's* becomes one of the most popular evening spots in San Pedro, frequently hosting live bands and karaoke nights till midnight.

Jaguar's Temple Barrier Reef Drive, opposite the park. This large, colourfully painted club has a heaving dance floor and is open late. Thurs–Sat 9pm–4am.

DIRECTORY

Banks Belize Bank near Central Park on Barrier Reef Drive has an ATM, and the other banks will give cash advances, but travellers' cheques and US dollars are accepted – even preferred – everywhere.

Bicycles Joe's Bikes, on Caribeña St, rents bikes for Bz$5/hr or Bz$20/day.

Books Aquarius Books on Pescador Drive has a selection of used paperbacks, mainly thriller and romantic novels, for less than Bz$5 (Mon–Sat 9am–4pm).

1

Internet Caribbean Connection, on Barrier Reef Drive, offers access for Bz$10/hr (daily 7am–10pm).
Laundry Nellie's Laundromat, Pescador Drive, charges about $6 a load (Mon–Sat 7am–9pm, Sun 8am–2pm).
Post office Pescador Drive.

TURNEFFE ISLANDS

Although Caye Caulker and San Pedro are the only villages on the reef, there are a couple of dozen other inhabited islands, as well as some excellent diving spots. The virtually uninhabited **TURNEFFE ISLANDS**, 40km from Belize City and south of cayes Caulker and Ambergris, comprise an oval archipelago of low-lying mangrove islands around a shallow lagoon 60km long. These are enclosed by a beautiful coral reef, which offers some of the best **diving** and snorkelling in Belize. The island boasts several resorts, all of which are out of the reach of the typical budget traveller, but you can still visit this incredible spot on a day-trip from San Pedro (see p.67) and Caye Caulker (see p.63).

LIGHTHOUSE REEF

About 80km east of Belize City is Belize's outermost atoll, **LIGHTHOUSE REEF**, home to the popular underwater attractions of the **Blue Hole** and **Half Moon Caye Natural Monument**.

The Blue Hole

The **Blue Hole**, technically a karst-eroded sinkhole, is more than 300m in diameter and 135m deep, dropping through the bottom of the lagoon and opening out into a complex network of caves and crevices; its depth gives it an astonishing deep-blue colour that is, unfortunately, best appreciated from the air. Though visibility is generally limited, many divers still find the trip worthwhile for the drop-offs and underwater caves, which include stalactites and stalagmites. Unfortunately for budget travellers, trips to the Blue Hole – which must be led by a licensed guide or company – usually cost at least US$200.

Half Moon Caye Natural Monument

The **Half Moon Caye Natural Monument**, the first marine conservation area in Belize, was declared a national park in 1982 and became one of Belize's first World Heritage Sites in 1996. The 180,000-square-metre caye is divided into two distinct ecosystems. In the west, guano from sea birds fertilizes the soil, enabling the growth of dense vegetation, while the eastern half has mostly coconut palms. A total of 98 bird species has been recorded here, including frigate birds, ospreys and a resident population of four thousand red-footed boobies, one of only two such nesting colonies in the Caribbean. Upon arrival (most people come as part of a tour), visitors must pay the Bz$20 entrance fee at the visitors' centre; you can **camp** here (☎223 5004; US$10/person), but you need to call ahead for permission.

The north

The level expanses of northern Belize are a mixture of farmland and rainforest, dotted with swamps, savannas and lagoons. Most visitors come to the region for its **Maya ruins** and **wildlife reserves**. The largest Maya site, **Lamanai**, served by regular boat tours along the New River Lagoon, features some of the most impressive pyramids and beautiful scenery in the country. The site of **Altun Ha**, meanwhile, is usually visited on a day-trip from Belize City. The northern reserves also host an astonishingly diverse array of wildlife. At the **Community Baboon Sanctuary**, a group of farmers have combined agriculture with conservation to the benefit of the black howler monkey, and at the stunning **Crooked Tree Wildlife Sanctuary**, rivers and lagoons offer protection to a range of migratory birds.

Many of the original residents in this region were refugees from the nineteenth-century Caste Wars in Yucatán, and some of the northernmost towns are mainly **Spanish-speaking**. The largest settlement today is **Orange Walk**, the country's main centre for sugar production. Further north, near the border with Mexico, **Corozal** is a small Caribbean town, strongly influenced by Maya and mestizo culture.

COMMUNITY BABOON SANCTUARY

A 45-minute drive north of Belize City, the **COMMUNITY BABOON SANCTUARY** (ⓦhowlermonkeys.org), to the west off the Northern Highway, is one of the most interesting conservation projects in Belize. It was established in 1985 by Dr Rob Horwich and a group of local farmers (with help from the World Wide Fund for Nature), who developed a code of conduct of sustainable living and farming practices. A mixture of farmland and broad-leaved forest along the banks of the Belize River, the sanctuary coordinates seven villages, of which **Bermudian Landing** is the most conveniently accessed, and more than a hundred landowners, in a project of conservation, education and tourism.

The main focus of attention is the **black howler monkey** (known locally as a "baboon"). These primates generally live in groups of between four and eight, and spend the day wandering through the canopy, feasting on leaves, flowers and fruits. At dawn and dusk they let rip with their famous howl: a deep and rasping roar that carries for many kilometres. The sanctuary is also home to more than two hundred bird species, as well as iguanas, peccaries and coatis. You can find exhibits and information on the riverside habitats and animals you are likely to see in the **natural history museum** – Belize's first – at the visitors' centre in Bermudian Landing.

ARRIVAL AND INFORMATION

By bus Three daily buses connect Belize City (leaving the city at noon, 4pm & 5pm; 1hr 15min; Bz$4) and the village of Bermudian Landing. The central stop is at the sanctuary's visitors' centre, only a few minutes' walk from all our recommended accommodation.

Tourist information The reserve's visitors' centre (daily 8am–5pm; ☎ 245 2007) is at the west end of Bermudian Landing. The Bz$14 entrance fee includes a guided nature walk and a tour of the small natural history museum. The reserve also organizes a range of inexpensive activities including horseriding, canoeing and night hikes.

ACCOMMODATION AND EATING

Apart from the *Howler Monkey Lodge*, there are extremely limited catering options – bring your own food if staying elsewhere.

Camping If you have your own tent, you can camp at the visitors' centre. Per person U̲S̲$̲5̲

Homestays Ask at the visitors' centre, or email centre staff (ⓔ cbsbelize@gmail.com) about homestays with local families. Rates include three meals a day. Per person from U̲S̲$̲4̲0̲

Howler Monkey Lodge On the river near the visitors' centre ☎ 220 2158, ⓦ howlermonkeylodge.com. Wooden cabins sleeping up to six have private baths, a/c, and access to a swimming pool; guided kayak trips can also be arranged. Rates include three meals. Per person U̲S̲$̲6̲0̲

ALTUN HA

Some 55km north of Belize City and just 9km from the sea, the remarkable Maya site of **ALTUN HA** (daily 8am–5pm; Bz$10) was occupied for twelve hundred years until it was abandoned around 900 AD. Its position near the Caribbean suggests that it was sustained as much by trade as by agriculture – a theory upheld by the discovery here of obsidian and jade, neither of which occurs naturally in Belize.

Altun Ha clusters around two Classic-period plazas. Entering from the road, you come first to **Plaza A**, enclosed by large temples on all sides. A magnificent tomb was discovered beneath Temple A-1, the **Temple of the Green Tomb**. Dating from 550 AD, this yielded jades, jewellery, stingray spines, skin, flints and the remains of a Maya book. The adjacent **Plaza B** is dominated by the site's largest temple, the **Temple of the Masonry Altars**. Several tombs have been uncovered within the main structure; in one, archeologists discovered a carved jade head of Kinich Ahau, the Maya sun god. Just under 15cm high, it is the largest carved jade found in the Maya world; a replica is on display in the Museum of Belize (see p.58).

ARRIVAL AND INFORMATION

By bus Altun Ha is difficult to reach independently. In theory there are buses from the Belize City terminal to the village of Maskall, passing the turn-off to the site at the village of Lucky Strike, but service is erratic.

Tours Travel agents such as Experience Belize (ⓦ experiencebelizetours.com) can arrange the trip (US$45 per person), and tourists also visit on day-trips from San Pedro and Caye Caulker (from US$95 per person).

1

CROOKED TREE WILDLIFE SANCTUARY

Midway between Belize City and Orange Walk, a branch road heads west to **CROOKED TREE WILDLIFE SANCTUARY** (daily 8am–4.30pm; Bz$8), a reserve that encompasses swamps, wetlands and four separate lagoons. Designated Belize's first Ramsar site (to protect wetlands of international importance), the sanctuary provides a resting place for thousands of migrating and resident birds, such as snail kites, tiger herons, snowy egrets, ospreys and black-collared hawks. The reserve's most famous visitor is the **jabiru stork**, the largest flying bird in Latin America, with a wingspan of 2.5m. The **best months** for birdwatching are late February to June, when the lagoons shrink to a string of pools, forcing wildlife to congregate for food and water.

In the middle of the reserve, straggling around the shores of a lagoon, is the village of **Crooked Tree**, which is linked to the mainland by a **causeway**. One of the oldest inland villages in the country, Crooked Tree is also one of Belize's loveliest, with well-kept houses and lawns dotted along tree-lined lanes. Though guided tours to the lagoon are quite expensive (at least US$50–80), numerous trails, signposted from the roads, wind around the island and along the shoreline, where you'll see plenty of birds and wildlife even without a guide.

ARRIVAL AND INFORMATION

By bus Buses from Belize City (Mon–Fri 3 daily, 1 on Sat; 1hr 30min; Bz$4) make a loop around the village of Crooked Tree before heading to the causeway. Alternatively, frequent buses run between Belize City and Orange Walk from the junction with the Northern Highway.

Tourist information The wildlife sanctuary visitors' centre (8am–4.30pm) is at the end of the causeway in Crooked Tree. Pay the reserve's Bz$8 entrance fee here.

ACCOMMODATION AND EATING

Most of the accommodation in Crooked Tree is in mid-priced hotels, though some of these also have camping space.

3-J's In the centre, in a green building on the bus route. Friendly place serving Creole meals and fast food for less than US$8. Closed in low season, and keeps erratic hours.

★ TREAT YOURSELF

Bird's Eye View Lodge On the lakeshore, clearly signposted through the village ☎ 225 7027, ⓦ birdseyeviewbelize.com. Worth the splurge for its idyllic, isolated location right on the lagoon. Comfortable rooms, some with balconies, have private baths and a/c, or you can pitch a tent in the grounds. The restaurant serves good meals around the clock, and safari tours of the sanctuary, as well as trips to nearby Maya sites, can be arranged. Camping per person US$10, double US$80

Carrie's Kitchen Village centre, behind the hurricane shelter. A local gem, serving good Belizean food for less than Bz$8. Mon–Sat 10am–9pm.

Tillet's Village Lodge In the centre of the village along the bus route ☎ 245 7016, ⓦ tilletvillage.com. Good-value hotel set amid lovely gardens. Rustic cabins have private baths, hot water and fans; comfortable rooms – with fan or a/c – share a balcony. There's a small shop, a restaurant serving three daily meals, and tours can be arranged. Double US$35, cabin from US$50

ORANGE WALK

Like many of Belize's northern cities, **ORANGE WALK**, the largest town in the region, was founded by mestizo refugees fleeing the Caste Wars in the Yucatán. Long before their arrival, however, the area around Orange Walk had been worked as some of the most productive arable farmland in Belize – aerial surveys have revealed evidence of raised fields and a network of irrigation canals dating from ancient Maya times. Today, Orange Walk is a thriving community by Belizean standards, and though there aren't any sights in town as such, it's a pleasant, low-key base for those looking to explore one of the region's highlights: the nearby ruins at Lamanai.

WHAT TO SEE AND DO

At the centre of town, on the distinctly Mexican-style formal plaza, the town hall is referred to as the Palacio Municipal, reinforcing the town's strong historical links to Mexico. The only formal attraction is the **Banquitas House of Culture** (Mon–Thurs 8.30am–5pm, Fri

8.30am–4.30pm; free; ☎ 322 0517, ⓦ nichbelize.org), on the riverbank near the bridge, which houses a permanent exhibition charting the history of Orange Walk District from Maya times to the present, as well as travelling exhibitions from NICH (the National Institute of Culture and History).

ARRIVAL AND INFORMATION

By bus Hourly buses from Belize City and Corozal pull up on the main road in the centre of town, officially Queen Victoria Ave but always referred to as the Belize–Corozal Rd. Services to and from Sarteneja stop opposite *St Christopher's Hotel* on Main St. Local buses to the surrounding villages leave from the market area, behind the town hall and fire station.

Destinations Belize City (hourly; 1hr 30min); Chetumal (hourly; 2hr); Corozal (hourly; 1hr); Sarteneja (3 daily Mon–Sat; 2hr).

Internet Access is cheap and plentiful; K & N Printshop, on the Belize–Corozal Rd two blocks south of the post office, is open daily (7am–noon & 2–5.30pm) and charges Bz$4/hr.

Post office Right in the centre of town, on Queen Victoria Ave.

Tour operators A number of operators organize day-trips to Lamanai (see p.74). The most informative is Jungle River Tours, 20 Lovers Lane (☎ 302 2293, ⓔ lamanaimayatour@btl.net).

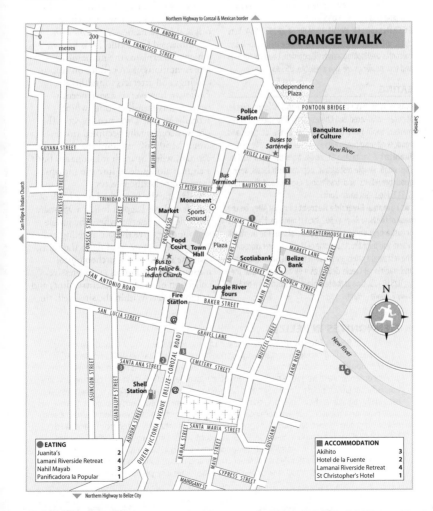

ORANGE WALK

Northern Highway to Corozal & Mexican border

0   200
metres

SAN ANDRES STREET
SAN FRANCISCO STREET
SAN FELIPE & Indian Church

Independence Plaza

PONTOON BRIDGE

Police Station

CINDERELLA STREET

Banquitas House of Culture

New River

GUYANA STREET

MEJIBA STREET

Buses to Sarteneja

AVILEZ LANE

Sarteneja

SYLVESTER STREET

TRINIDAD STREET

DUNN STREET

ST PETER STREET

Bus Terminal

BAUTISTAS

1
2

Monument

PROGRESSO

Market   Sports Ground

BETHIAS LANE

FONSECA STREET

SLAUGHTERHOUSE LANE

Food Court   Town Hall

Plaza

LOVERS LANE

MARKET LANE

Scotiabank

Belize Bank

RIVERSIDE STREET

Bus to San Felipe & Indian Church

SAN ANTONIO ROAD

PARK STREET

CHURCH STREET

Fire Station

Jungle River Tours

MAIN STREET

BAKER STREET

SAN LUCIA STREET

N

@

GRAVEL LANE

QUEEN VICTORIA AVENUE (BELIZE–COROZAL ROAD)

MUFFET STREET

3

SANTA ANA STREET

CEMETERY STREET

FARM ROAD

New River

3

ASUNCION STREET

Shell Station

GUADALUPE STREET

@

4 4

AURORA STREET

SANTA MARIA STREET

BANAK STREET

MAIN STREET

LOUISIANA

MAHOGANY ST

CYPRESS STREET

● EATING	
Juanita's	2
Lamani Riverside Retreat	4
Nahil Mayab	3
Panificadora la Popular	1

■ ACCOMMODATION	
Akihito	3
Hotel de la Fuente	2
Lamanai Riverside Retreat	4
St Christopher's Hotel	1

Northern Highway to Belize City

1

ACCOMMODATION

Akihito 22 Queen Victoria Ave ☎ 302 0185. Basic, cheap accommodation – dorm beds, and some rooms with private baths and a/c – in a concrete building a few blocks south of the centre. Dorm US$8, double US$15

★ **Hotel de la Fuente** 14 Main St ☎ 322 2290, ⓦ hoteldelafuente.com, ✉ info@hoteldelafuente.com. Bright rooms in this great-value hotel include private baths, mini-fridges, coffee makers, wi-fi and a/c. All local tours can be arranged with the front desk. A new riverside site, closer to Lamanai, was under construction at the time of research. US$35

Lamanai Riverside Retreat Lamanai Alley, on the bank of the New River ☎ 302 3955. Some camping space, and basic riverside cabins, with private bath, sleeping up to four. There's an excellent restaurant, too (see below). Camping US$10, cabin US$40

St Christopher's Hotel 10 Main St ☎ 302 1064. Very clean, attractive rooms with TVs, private baths, wi-fi and balconies overlooking a riverside garden. Laundry services and tour bookings are also available. US$35

EATING

Orange Walk has numerous restaurants offering Creole, Mexican-influenced and Chinese food. The street near the market, behind the town hall, has a line of cafés and vendors offering cheap eats for Bz$2–8.

Juanita's 8 Santa Ana St, across from the Shell station. This small, simple restaurant, popular with locals, serves good breakfasts and traditional Creole food for under Bz$12. Mon–Sat 6am–2pm.

★ **Lamanai Riverside Retreat** Lamanai Alley, on the bank of the New River ☎ 302 3955. Enjoy breakfast, dinner or just a beer on an outdoor patio right on the riverbank where you might just spot one of the local river crocodiles. The restaurant offers a wide variety of Mexican-influenced and traditional Creole dishes as well as burgers and fries for Bz$10–25. One of the few places in town open on Sun. Daily 7.30am–10pm.

Nahil Mayab Guadelupe St & Santa Ana St, ☎ 322 0831. "Maya-inspired" plates and American food for Bz$10-30; brave the insects in the pretty garden patio if the a/c is too cool to handle. Mon 10am–3pm, Tues–Thurs 10am–11pm, Fri & Sat 10am–11.30pm.

Panificadora la Popular Bethias Lane. An excellent bakery that's been around for decades, serving fresh bread and cakes (Bz$2–10). Daily 6.30am–7pm.

LAMANAI

Extensive restoration, a spacious museum and a stunning jungle setting make **LAMANAI** (Mon–Fri 8am–5pm, Sat, Sun & holidays 8am–4pm; Bz$10) the most impressive Maya site in northern Belize. It is also one of the few sites whose original Maya name – *Lama'an ayin* ("Submerged Crocodile") – is known, which also explains the numerous representations of crocodiles on stucco carvings and artefacts found here. *Lamanai*, however, is a seventeenth-century mis-transliteration, which actually means "Drowned Insect". The site was continually occupied from around 1500 BC up until the sixteenth century, when Spanish missionaries built a church alongside to lure the Indians from their "heathen" ways.

Today the site is perched on a bank of the New River Lagoon inside a 950-acre archeological reserve, where the jungle surroundings give the site a feeling of tranquillity. Before heading to the ruins, visit the spacious new **archeological museum**, which houses an impressive collection of artefacts, eccentric flints and original stelae. Within the site itself, the

---

MENNONITES IN BELIZE

Members of Belize's **Mennonite** community, easily recognizable in their denim dungarees, can be seen trading produce and buying supplies every day in Orange Walk and Belize City. The Mennonites, a Protestant group noted for their pacifist beliefs and rejection of modern advancements, arose from the radical Anabaptist movement of the sixteenth century and are named after Dutch priest Menno Simons. Recurring government restrictions on their lifestyle, especially regarding their objection to military service, have forced them to uproot themselves and move on repeatedly. Having emigrated to Switzerland, they then travelled to Prussia, and in 1663 a group moved to North America. After World War I they migrated from Canada to Mexico, eventually arriving in Belize in 1958. In recent years, farm-produced prosperity has caused drastic changes in their lives: the Mennonite Church in Belize is increasingly split between a modernist section – who use electricity and power tools, and drive trucks, tractors and even cars – and the traditionalists, who prefer a stricter interpretation of beliefs.

most remarkable structure is the N10-43 (informally the "High Temple"), a massive **Late Preclassic temple** that is more than 37m tall and the largest from the period in the Maya region. The view across the surrounding forest and along the lagoon from the top of the temple is magnificent, and well worth the daunting climb.

ARRIVAL AND DEPARTURE

By river tour The easiest, most pleasant way to get to Lamanai is by river, and the cheapest and most informative way to do this is as part of an organized tour. Various operators in Orange Walk (see p.73) offer day-trips, departing around 9am; the price (US$40–50) will usually include lunch.

SARTENEJA AND SHIPSTERN NATURE RESERVE

Across Chetumal Bay from Corozal, the largely uninhabited **Sarteneja peninsula** is covered with dense forests and swamps that support an amazing array of wildlife. **SARTENEJA**, the peninsula's only settlement, is a peaceful, Spanish-speaking, lobster-fishing community.

All buses to Sarteneja pass the entrance to **SHIPSTERN NATURE RESERVE** (daily 8am–4pm; Bz$15; ⓦshipstern.org), 5km before the village, though you can also get here by renting a bike from *Fernando's* or *Backpackers Paradise* in Sarteneja (see below). The reserve encompasses an area of eighty square kilometres, including large areas of tropical moist forest, some wide belts of savanna, and most of the shallow Shipstern Lagoon, dotted with mangrove islands. The **visitors' centre** offers a variety of guided walks, though even if you choose the shortest, you'll encounter more named plant species here than on any other trail in Belize. Shipstern is also a birdwatcher's paradise: the lagoon system supports blue-winged teal, American coot and huge flocks of lesser scaup, while the forest is home to keel-billed toucans and at least five species of parrot. Other wildlife in the reserve includes crocodiles, jaguars, peccaries and an abundance of wonderful butterflies.

ARRIVAL AND INFORMATION

By boat The *Thunderbolt* skiff run (ⓣ422 0226 or ⓣ601 4475) between Corozal and Ambergris Caye will call at Sarteneja if there's sufficient demand, pulling into the main dock on North Front St.

By bus Buses pull into Sarteneja at its southern end and make a loop around town.

Destinations Belize City (several daily Mon–Sat 4–6.30am, 1 on Sun 6am; 3hr 30min); Chetumal (daily, usually 6am; 3hr 30min). All buses to and from Sarteneja pass through Orange Walk.

Tour operators All the accommodation options can arrange local trips and tours, or try *Sarteneja Adventure Tours* (ⓣ633 0067, ⓦsartenejatours.com) for excursions and homestays.

ACCOMMODATION AND EATING

★ **Backpackers Paradise** La Bandera Rd ⓣ423 2016, ⓦbackpackers.bluegreenbelize.com. Super-cheap cabañas and camping just a 5min drive out of town; ask the bus driver to drop you off at the Sarteneja Monument, or arrange a pier pick-up in advance. There's also bike rental (Bz$10/day), horseriding tours (Bz$18/hr) and free wi-fi. Owner/Chef Nathalie's excellent on-site restaurant serves local, vegetarian and French dishes throughout the day for Bz$8–20. Camping <u>US$4</u>, cabaña <u>US$14–33</u>

Fernando's Guesthouse North Front St, 100m along the shoreline from the main dock ⓣ423 2085, ⓦfernandosseaside.com. Large, tiled rooms, with fan or a/c and private baths, share a veranda overlooking the sea. Snorkelling and nature tours can be arranged, and bike rentals are available. <u>US$35</u>

Liz's Fast Food At the eastern end of the village. Come here for traditional Belizean food (Bz$6–12). Closed Sun.

COROZAL

South from the Mexican border, the road meets the sea at **COROZAL**, near the mouth of the New River. The **ancient Maya** prospered here by controlling river- and seaborne trade, and the impressive site of **Cerros** is nearby, if complicated to reach. Present-day Corozal was founded in 1849 by refugees from Mexico's Caste Wars, although today's grid-pattern town, a neat mix of Mexican and Caribbean, is largely a result of reconstruction in the wake of Hurricane Janet in 1955.

WHAT TO SEE AND DO

There's little reason to spend time in Corozal unless you are trying to get to Cerros. However, it is an ideal place for a few days of quiet relaxation. The breezy shoreline **park** is good for a stroll, while on the tree-shaded main plaza, the **town**

1

hall is worth a look inside for a mural by Manuel Villamar Reyes, which vividly describes local history. The **Corozal House of Culture** (Mon–Fri 8am–5pm; free), a historical waterfront building, has a small museum and gallery space. In the block west of the plaza you can see the remains of **Fort Barlee**, built to ward off Maya attacks in the 1870s.

Santa Rita

The small Maya site of **Santa Rita** (daily 24hr; free) is within walking distance of the centre, about fifteen minutes northwest of town; follow the main road towards the border, bear right at the fork and turn left at the Super Santa Rita store. Though it is an interesting enough spot if you have time to kill, the site is no longer maintained and does not justify extending your stay in Corozal. Founded around 1500 BC, Santa

Rita was in all probability the powerful Maya city later known as Chactemal. The main remaining building is a small pyramid, and excavations here have uncovered the burial sites of an elaborately bejewelled elderly woman and a Classic-period warlord.

ARRIVAL AND INFORMATION

By plane Flights from San Pedro arrive at the airstrip 2km south of town. Taxis meet flights and charge Bz$8–10 for a trip to the centre.

By boat The *Thunderbolt* skiff (☎ 422 0226 or ☎ 601 4475, Bz$45; erratic low-season service; 2hr) arriving from San Pedro pulls into the main dock on 1st Ave, just two blocks southeast of the town centre.

By bus The Northern Transport depot is near the northern edge of town, opposite the Shell station. In addition to local services between Belize City and Corozal, express buses pass through Corozal en route to Chetumal, Mexico, roughly hourly in each direction. Buses for surrounding

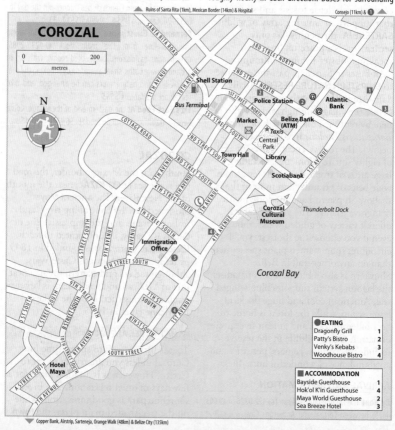

▲ Ruins of Santa Rita (1km), Mexican Border (14km) & Hospital   Consejo (11km) & ❶ ▲

COROZAL

0   200
metres

N

Shell Station

Bus Terminal

Police Station

Atlantic Bank

Market

Belize Bank (ATM)

Taxis

Town Hall

Central Park

Library

Scotiabank

Corozal Cultural Museum

Thunderbolt Dock

Immigration Office

Corozal Bay

Hotel Maya

●EATING	
Dragonfly Grill	1
Patty's Bistro	2
Venky's Kebabs	3
Woodhouse Bistro	4

■ACCOMMODATION	
Bayside Guesthouse	1
Hok'ol K'in Guesthouse	4
Maya World Guesthouse	2
Sea Breeze Hotel	3

▼ Copper Bank, Airstrip, Sarteneja, Orange Walk (48km) & Belize City (135km)

INTO MEXICO: SANTA ELENA

It's less than 4hr by bus along the Northern Highway from Belize City to **Chetumal**, Mexico, via the border crossing at **Santa Elena**.

Entering Belize, you'll find Mexican immigration and customs posts on the northern bank of the Río Hondo, 12km from Chetumal; when you're finished there, the bus will pick you up again to take you to Belizean immigration.

Leaving Belize, you'll have to pay an exit tax of Bz$30 and the PACT conservation fee of Bz$7.50. Upon entering Mexico, any traveller staying for more than a week, or those transiting Mexico to travel onwards to another country, must pay the FMT (Migratory Form for Foreign Tourists) fee of about 300 pesos (roughly Bz$45); this form is your proof of immigration and should not be lost. **Moneychangers** wait on the Belize side of the border; make sure to get rid of your Belize dollars before crossing into Mexico.

villages (including Copper Bank) leave from the market area.

Destinations Belize City (hourly 4am–6pm; 2hr 30min); Chetumal (hourly 6am–9pm; 1hr); Orange Walk (hourly; 1hr).

Tour operators For organized tours to local nature reserves and archeological sites, contact Henry Menzies (☎422 2725, ⊛belizetransfers.com); he's also an expert on travel to Mexico.

Tourist information Corozal has no tourist office, but the city's website (⊛corozal.com) is useful.

ACCOMMODATION

Bayside Guesthouse 31 3rd Ave ☎625 7824, ⊛baysideguesthouse.webplus.net. Four tastefully decorated rooms with private baths, fans and coffee makers; one has a/c. Off-road parking and evening meals also available. Rates include breakfast. <u>US$46</u>

Hok'ol K'in Guesthouse 89 4th Ave ☎422 3329. Decent option right on the seafront. Eleven large rooms include private baths, fans and balconies; some have a/c. The downstairs restaurant and bar serves inexpensive meals (Bz$5–15) and cold beer. <u>US$52</u>

Maya World Guesthouse 16 2nd St North ☎666 3577, ⊜byronchuster@gmail.com. Very basic budget hotel with private baths and fans. There's a communal kitchen and pleasant veranda too. <u>US$28</u>

★ **Sea Breeze Hotel** 23 1st Ave ☎422 3051, ⊛theseabreezehotel.com. One of the best budget choices in Belize, with friendly staff, a low-key bar, clean, secure accommodation and free use of bicycles. Rooms include private baths, fans and cable TV; some have a/c. Guests can charter owner Gwyn's speedboat for trips to Cerros (see below) for US$30 per person. <u>US$20</u>

EATING

Dragonfly Grill 2 2nd Ave. North American comfort food, including good breakfasts and BBQ specials for under US$7, served in a cheery open-air setting with free wi-fi access. Fri–Tues 10am–10pm.

Patty's Bistro 7 2nd St North ☎402 0174. Good Belizean, Mexican and American food – from cheeseburgers to fish soups – for Bz$7–25. Daily noon–9.30pm.

Venky's Kebabs 5th Ave by 5th St South ☎402 0536. Ignore the uninspiring interior and concentrate on *Venky's* very good Indian food. Expect to pay Bz$15 for generous portions, with both meat and vegetarian options available. Daily 10.30am–9.30pm.

★ **Woodhouse Bistro** 1st St. One of the best Asian restaurants in Belize, with an extensive Chinese-oriented menu (Bz$8–20), funky decor, and open-air seating with pleasant ocean views. Mon & Wed–Sun 11am–10pm.

DIRECTORY

Bank Belize Bank (with 24hr ATM), on the north side of the plaza.

Immigration The office is on 5th Ave opposite *Venky's Kebabs*.

Internet Easy to find; look for signs along 4th and 5th aves (Bz$4/hr).

Post office On the west side of the plaza.

CERROS

Built in a strategic position at the mouth of the New River, the late Preclassic centre of **CERROS** (daily 8am–5pm; Bz$10) was one of the first places in the Maya world to adopt the rule of kings. Despite this initial success, however, Cerros was abandoned by the Classic period. The ruins of the site now include three large acropolis structures, ball courts and plazas flanked by pyramids. The largest building is a 22m-high temple, whose intricate stucco masks represent the rising and setting sun.

Mosquitoes around the Cerros site are particularly pesky – prepare accordingly.

1

ARRIVAL AND DEPARTURE

By boat The most comfortable and reliable way to reach the ruins is by boat. Hotels in Corozal (ask at the *Sea Breeze Hotel* or *Hok'ol K'in Guesthouse*) can advise on charters, which operate either with a guided tour (from US$75 per person) or without (from US$30 per person).

ACCOMMODATION AND EATING

Cerros Beach Resort ☏ 623 9763, ⓦ cerrosbeachresort .com. If you want to stay in the atmospheric surroundings of the ruins for a night or two, try these charming cabañas with private bath, TV and wi-fi. There's also a bar/ restaurant serving local and international cuisine at Bz$8– 25 to guests and day-trippers. US$60

The west

Heading west from Belize City towards the Guatemalan border, you'll traverse varied landscapes, from open grassland to dense tropical forest. A fast, paved road, the **Western Highway**, runs the entire way, taking you from the heat and humidity of the coast to the cooler, lush foothills of the Maya Mountains.

Before reaching Belize's tiny capital, **Belmopan**, the road passes two excellent attractions: the **Belize Zoo** and the **Monkey Bay Wildlife Sanctuary**. West of Belmopan, following the Belize River valley, the road skirts the **Maya Mountains**. You're now in **Cayo District**, the largest of Belize's six districts and arguably the most beautiful. South of the road, the **Mountain Pine Ridge** is a pleasantly cool region of hills and pine woods. **San Ignacio**, on the Macal River, makes an ideal base for exploring the forests, rivers and ruins of western Belize, including **Caracol**, the largest Maya site in Belize, and the region's many dramatic **caves**, often filled with Maya artefacts.

BELIZE ZOO

The **BELIZE ZOO**, at Mile 29 on the Western Highway (daily 8am–5pm; Bz$30; ⓦ belizezoo.org), is easily visited on a half-day trip from Belize City or as a stop on the way west. Probably the finest zoo south of the USA, and long recognized as a phenomenal conservation achievement, the zoo opened in 1983. Now organized

around the theme of "a walk through Belize", the zoo offers the chance to see the country's native animals at close quarters. Residents include tapirs, a wide variety of birds and all the Belizean cats. These animals, many of which have been rescued and cannot be released into the wild, enjoy spacious and natural enclosures – the most authentic slice of natural habitat that such animals are ever likely to occupy.

ARRIVAL AND DEPARTURE

By bus Take any bus between Belize City and Belmopan and ask the driver to drop you at the signed turn-off, a 200m walk from the entrance; you can leave your luggage at the visitors' centre.

ACCOMMODATION

Jungle Lodge On the opposite side of the highway from the zoo, about 300m back towards Belize City ☏ 822 8003, ⓔ info@belizezoo.org. If you'd like to stay overnight in the area, try the zoo's lodge, which offers wooden dorms with shared baths and hot showers, as well as pricier private cabins. Guests can take a night-time tour of the zoo for Bz$30pp. Dorm US$30, cabin US$67

GUANACASTE NATIONAL PARK

Just off the highway at the turn-off towards Belmopan is tiny **GUANACASTE NATIONAL PARK** (daily 8am–4.30pm; Bz$5), a 52-acre area of beautiful tropical forest. Several short, circular trails leave from the **visitors' centre**, winding through the forest and passing the Belize and Roaring rivers; there's even a spot for swimming. Although a visit here isn't necessary if you're planning on spending time in Belize's other forested areas, Guanacaste provides an excellent introduction to the country's flora and fauna and is exceptionally accessible; any bus heading west can drop you off at the visitors' centre, where you can leave your belongings while you explore.

BELMOPAN

At Guanacaste, the Hummingbird Highway (see p.87) splits from the Western Highway and heads south to **BELMOPAN** (and, eventually, Dangriga). The city was founded in 1970, after Hurricane Hattie swept much of Belize City into the sea. The government decided to use the disaster as a chance to move to higher ground and, in a bid to focus development on the interior, chose a site at the geographical heart of the country. The name of the city combines the words "Belize" and "Mopan", the language spoken by the Maya of Cayo, and the layout of the main government buildings is modelled loosely on a Maya city, with buildings grouped around a central plaza. When built, Belmopan was meant to symbolize a new era, with tree-lined avenues, banks, embassies and communications worthy of a world centre. Few people, however, chose to move here, and Belmopan remains the smallest capital city in the world. Although the population is growing slowly, there's little reason to stay any longer than it takes your bus to leave.

ARRIVAL AND DEPARTURE

By bus Buses from Belize City to San Ignacio, Benque Viejo, Dangriga and Punta Gorda all pass through Belmopan, so there's at least one service in either direction every 30min. All buses stop at the terminal, which is in the city centre and within walking distance of most of the city's hotels.

Destinations Belize City (every 20min, until 7pm; 1hr 15min); Benque Viejo del Carmen, for the Guatemalan border (every 30min; 1hr 30min); Dangriga (every 2hr, until 6pm; 1hr 40min); Punta Gorda (every 2hr; 6hr); San Ignacio (every 30min, until 10pm; 1hr 15min).

ACCOMMODATION AND EATING

Belmopan's accommodation is for the most part expensive and aimed at visiting dignitaries and professionals. Many restaurants are closed on Sunday, so snacks from the bus terminal may be your only option if you're passing through, unless you are willing to wander quite a bit further afield.

Caladium Beside the bus terminal. Good Belizean food, with a Bz$12 daily special, in a/c surroundings. Mon–Sat 7.30am–8pm.

Corkers Hibiscus Plaza. Good pastas, salads and pub grub served indoors or on the outside patio. Mon–Wed 11am–8pm, Thurs–Sat 11am–late.

El Rey Inn 23 Moho St ☏ 822 3438, ⓦ elreyhotel.com. A variety of options; the budget rooms have a fan and private bath. It is quite a long walk from the bus station (20–30min), so consider taking a taxi (Bz$7). US$45

DIRECTORY

Banks Banks (with ATMs) are close to the bus terminal.
Immigration The office is in the main government building by the fire station.
Internet PC.Com, next to *Caladium*, across from the bus station (Mon–Fri 8am–5pm, Sat 9am–12.30pm; Bz$4/hr).

SAN IGNACIO

On the west bank of the Macal River, about 35km from Belmopan, **SAN IGNACIO** is a friendly, relaxed town that draws together the best of inland Belize. Surrounded by fast-flowing rivers and forested hills, it's an ideal base from which to explore the region, offering a pleasant climate, good food, inexpensive hotels and frequent bus connections. The town and surrounding area are usually referred to as **Cayo** by locals, the same word that the Spanish used to describe the offshore islands – an apt description of the area, which is set on a peninsula between two converging rivers. The early Spanish Conquest in 1544 made little impact here, and the area was a centre of rebellion in the following decades. **Spanish friars** arrived in 1618, but the population continued to practise "idolatry", and in 1641 Maya priests threw out some Spanish clerics. Tipu, the region's capital, retained a measure of independence until 1707, when the population was forcibly removed to Guatemala.

WHAT TO SEE AND DO

Aside from a visit to the ruins at **Cahal Pech**, or the **Iguana Conservation Project**, there's little to do in San Ignacio proper, though relative to other Belizean towns, you can spend many pleasant days here; it's a relaxed and inexpensive base for exploring nearby sights. Numerous independent local operators (see box, p.81) offer superb guided trips to nearby attractions, including Actun Tunichil Muknal (see p.82) and Caracol (see p.85). There's some turnover among tour operators, so it's always worth asking at your hotel about what's currently being offered.

Cahal Pech

The hilltop Maya site of **Cahal Pech** (daily 6am–5.30pm; Bz$10), about twenty minutes' walk west of San Ignacio centre, on the uphill road to Benque Viejo, is well worth a visit. There's a good chance you'll have the forested ruins all to yourself, and although the structures are not particularly tall, the maze of restored corridors, stairways, plazas and temples is enchanting. Cahal Pech was the royal acropolis-palace of an elite Maya family during the Classic period, and there's evidence of monumental construction

from at least as early as 400 BC, though most of the remaining structures date from the eighth century AD. The **visitors' centre and museum** has a scale model of the site, excellent displays and a variety of artefacts. Entering the site itself, you arrive at **Plaza B**, where your gaze is drawn to Structure 1, the **Audiencia**, the highest building at Cahal Pech. From the top, the ruins of

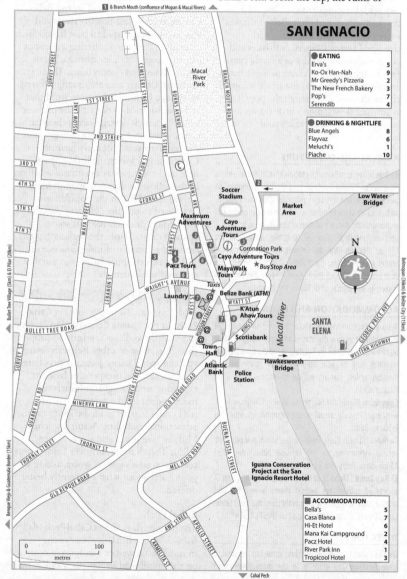

SAN IGNACIO

EATING
Erva's	5
Ko-Ox Han-Nah	9
Mr Greedy's Pizzeria	2
The New French Bakery	3
Pop's	7
Serendib	4

DRINKING & NIGHTLIFE
Blue Angels	8
Flayvaz	6
Meluchi's	1
Piache	10

ACCOMMODATION
Bella's	5
Casa Blanca	7
Hi-Et Hotel	6
Mana Kai Campground	2
Pacz Hotel	4
River Park Inn	1
Tropicool Hotel	3

Xunantunich (see p.86) are clearly visible to the southwest. Behind Structure 1, in **Plaza A**, is a restored three-storey temple, as well as other sacred buildings.

Iguana Conservation Project

The **Iguana Conservation Project** (daily 8am–4pm; Bz$12), housed within the *San Ignacio Resort Hotel* grounds, works to breed and raise endangered green iguanas before releasing them into the wild. The interactive exhibit of live critters is frequented by large groups of tourists and students; the Adopt an Iguana programme allows visitors to sponsor and name one of these dragon-like reptiles.

ARRIVAL AND INFORMATION

By plane If you're arriving at the new airstrip, on the road to Benque – about a 15min drive from town – it's best to arrange transport through your accommodation in advance; taxis may also be waiting to shuttle visitors to town (from Bz$10). For domestic and international air tickets head to Exodus Travel, 2 Burns Ave (☎824 4400 ⓦaquallos.com/exodustavel).

By bus Services to and from Belize City stop in the centre of town just south of Coronation Park, within easy walking distance of all of the recommended hotels. There's also a useful shuttle service between Belize International Airport and San Ignacio (from US$35pp; ⓦbelizeshuttlesandtransfers.com).

Destinations Belize City via Belmopan (every 30min 4am–6pm; 3hr); Benque Viejo del Carmen, for the Guatemalan border (every 30min; 15min).

By taxi To get to or from the Guatemalan border, it's most comfortable to get a shared taxi. The Savannah Taxi Coop (☎824 2155) has drivers that will carry up to four passengers for Bz$25.

Tourist information A new branch of the BTB was under construction at the time of research. When finished, it will be within the tourist complex in Coronation Park, opposite the bus station. The town's website (ⓦsanignaciotown.com) is also helpful, and most hotels will offer good information on local tours.

ACCOMMODATION

San Ignacio has some of the best-value budget accommodation in the country, and you'll almost always find space.

Bella's 4 Galves St ☎843 4644 or ☎671 2248, ⓔbellashostel.belize@yahoo.com. The only real hostel in town offers dorm beds, a few private rooms, communal kitchen and several common areas to relax in. Tours and trips can also be arranged. Dorm US$11, double US$23

Casa Blanca 10 Burns Ave ☎824 2080, ⓦcasablancaguesthouse.com. Very popular hotel with immaculate rooms, all with private bath and cable TV (some with a/c) and a comfortable sitting area with fridge, coffee and tea. Tours can also be arranged here (see box below); booking advisable. US$30

★ **Hi-Et Hotel** 12 West St ☎824 2828, ⓔthehiet@btl .net. Popular, comfortable hotel with shared-bath rooms

---

TOURS AND ACTIVITIES AROUND SAN IGNACIO

There is an abundance of tour operators in this region, based between San Ignacio and the border. The range below includes speciality companies, budget companies, and the most experienced operators.

Cayo Adventure Tours 29 Burns Ave ☎824 3246, ⓦcayoadventures.com. Experiences operators with customized trips to the caves and ruins, as well as birding and nature tours.

K'Atun Ahaw Tours *Casa Blanca* ☎824 2661, ⓦbelizeculturetours.com. Specializing in day-trips to Tikal, Elias Cambranes also leads trips to the caves and ruins at Xunantunich and Caracol (US$75–115).

Maximum Adventures Next to *Serendib* on Burns Ave ☎623 4880, ⓦsanigenciobelizetours.com. With his small family-run operation, Max offers tours to all the local sights at some of the best prices in the region; trips to Actun Tunichil Muknal and Barton Creek cave and zipline go for US$85/person.

MayaWalk Tours 19 Burns Ave ☎824 3070 or ☎663 9695, ⓦmayawalk.com. This extremely popular tour

operation, with a/c minibus shuttles and experienced guides, can whisk you to all the major sights in the region. Trips cost about US$20 more (per person) than other local operations, but you're paying for speed and comfort. Entry fees, equipment, lunch and snacks are all included in the price. There's also a bar, restaurant and dorms with shared-bath dorms (US$12pp).

★ **Pacz Tours** 30 Burns Ave ☎824 0536, ⓦpacztours .net. A wide variety of informative tours, including trips to Actun Tunichil Muknal and Caracol (US$110), with the most experienced operator in the area.

River Rat Expeditions Benque del Viejo town, on the road to the border beyond Xunantunich ☎628 6033, ⓦriverratexpeditions.com. Informative guides with off-road transport, specializing in trips to archeological sites and ruins.

1

in a charming old wooden building. Upstairs rooms come with a tiny balcony, and there are larger rooms with private bath in an adjoining concrete building. Book ahead. US$13

Mana Kai Campground Branch Mouth Rd ☎ 624 6538. Centrally located campsite with hammocks, showers and outdoor cooking, and sweet private cabins (sleeping up to four) with shared or private bath. Camping per person US$5, cabin from US$20

Pacz Hotel 4 Far West St ☎ 604 4526, ✉ paczghouse @btl.net. Five clean, comfortable rooms (some with private bath) at bargain rates. The sitting room has a fridge and cable TV. Good for local information. US$18

River Park Inn 1km along the Branch Mouth Rd ☎ 824 2116, ⊕ riverparkinnbelize.com. Campsite with showers, flush toilets and a kitchen, plus simple cabins with shared hot-water showers. Camping US$5, cabin US$35

Tropicool Hotel 30 Burns Ave ☎ 804 3052, ✉ tropicoolgift@gmail.com. Bright, clean rooms with shared hot-water baths, and wooden cabins (sleeping up to four) with private showers and cable TV. The sitting room has a TV and a laundry area. Double US$18, cabin US$40

EATING

San Ignacio has an abundance of good, inexpensive restaurants. The Saturday market is also the best in Belize, with local farmers bringing in fresh produce.

Erva's 4 Far West St, under *Pacz Hotel*. Traditional Belizean dishes for less than Bz$20, popular with both budget travellers and locals. Mon–Sat 8am–3pm & 6–10pm.

Ko-Ox Han-Nah 5 Burns Ave. Small restaurant with an international menu – everything from Belizean to Burmese, accompanied by fresh salads – at great prices; get here early. Mains Bz$10–30. Mon–Sat 6am–9pm.

Mr Greedy's Pizzeria 34 Burns Ave. A central location, free wi-fi, game nights, and decent thick-crust pies from US$9 make *Greedy's* an appealing choice. The happy-hour drinks specials also make this a popular watering hole; the bar is open long after the kitchen closes. Daily 6am–midnight.

The New French Bakery Coronation Park. Popular local bakery, with fresh breads, cakes and cookies, and pizza by the slice for Bz$2. Mon–Sat 6.30am–6pm.

Pop's Far West St. Huge, inexpensive breakfasts and bottomless cups of coffee for Bz$10, as well as traditional Belizean dishes. Daily 6.30am–3pm.

★ **Serendib** 27 Burns Ave. Excellent curries and Sri Lankan-style cuisine for Bz$10–22. Mon–Sat 6am–10pm.

DRINKING AND NIGHTLIFE

As tourism to San Ignacio increases, so does the number of bars, some of which can get quite rowdy later at night. The town is also a popular weekend spot for many Belizeans, and there's live music and dancing every Friday and Saturday night.

Blue Angels Hudson St. This dark upstairs club has the only real dance floor in town, usually filled with sweaty bodies. Locals head here to grind and wind to dancehall; it's quite rough around the edges, offering an authentic taste of Belizean nightlife.

Flayvaz Burns Ave, across from *Maya Walk Tours*. A laidback restaurant by day – offering decent grub, free wi-fi, and an on-site tour operation – becomes a mellow reggae bar at night, with live music in the garden courtyard.

★ **Meluchi's** Joseph Andrew Drive, overlooking the cemetery. Good happy-hour specials, decent bar snacks and frequent events – from live music to late-night karaoke – ensure a steady stream of locals and visitors.

Piache Buena Vista St, across from the casino. This large, thatch-roof bar is the busiest watering hole in town, where locals mix with gaggles of tourists on the open-air dance floor.

DIRECTORY

Banks and exchange Belize, Scotia and Atlantic banks are on Burns Ave; all have 24hr ATMs. Moneychangers will approach anyone they think is heading west to exchange for Guatemalan quetzals; they also board buses bound for Benque before departure.

Internet Tradewinds, above the post office (Mon–Sat 7am–10pm, Sun 10am–10pm; Bz$4/hr).

Laundry Drop-off laundry at *Martha's Guest House*, on West St.

Post office Next to Courts furniture store on Hudson St in the centre of town.

AROUND SAN IGNACIO

San Ignacio makes a great base from which to explore the **Cayo District**'s impressive **Maya ruins** and stunning natural scenery. You'll be required to hire a local guide in order to visit several of the region's highlights, though this is often a good idea anyway, to get the best experience (see box, p.81).

Actun Tunichil Muknal

In Roaring Creek valley, **Actun Tunichil Muknal** or "ATM" (tours from US$85, including snack or lunch, US$25 entry fee and transport to and from San Ignacio; you must be accompanied by a licensed guide to enter) was named "Cave of the Stone Sepulchre" for the astonishingly well-preserved skeletons, sixteen in total, of Maya human sacrifices found here. As the cave has historically been inaccessible to looters, little has been touched since the Maya stopped using it more than a millennium ago, and the plethora of Maya pottery lying about is spellbinding. Once ritually used as a gateway to the underworld, the cave, with its stunning calcified rock formations – due to the limestone layers overhead; a geologist's dream – seems as dramatic today as it would have to the ancient Maya. Perhaps the most remarkable sight is the full skeleton of a young woman

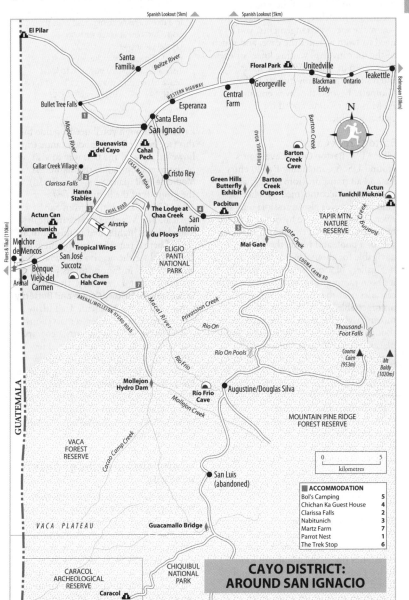

Spanish Lookout (5km)   Spanish Lookout (5km)

El Pilar
Santa Familia
Belize River
Bullet Tree Falls
Mopan River
Buenavista del Cayo
Santa Elena
San Ignacio
Cahal Pech
Callar Creek Village
Clarissa Falls
Hanna Stables
CHIAL ROAD
Actun Can
Xunantunich
Melchor de Mencos
Tropical Wings
San José Succotz
Benque Viejo del Carmen
Arenal
Che Chem Hah Cave
ARENAL/MOLLEJON HYDRO ROAD

Floral Park   Unitedville   Teakettle
Georgeville   Blackman Eddy   Ontario
WESTERN HIGHWAY
Central Farm
Esperanza
Cristo Rey
Green Hills Butterfly Exhibit
Barton Creek Outpost
Pacbitun
The Lodge at Chaa Creek
San Antonio
du Plooys
Airstrip
ELIGIO PANTI NATIONAL PARK
Mai Gate
Macal River
Privassion Creek
Río On
Río On Pools
Río Frio
Mollejon Hydro Dam
Río Frio Cave
Augustine/Douglas Silva
Mollejon Creek

N

Barton Creek
Barton Creek Cave
Actun Tunichil Muknal
TAPIR MTN. NATURE RESERVE
Slate Creek
COOMA CAIRN RD
Thousand-Foot Falls
Cooma Cairn (953m)
Mt Baldy (1020m)
MOUNTAIN PINE RIDGE FOREST RESERVE

Belmopan (10km)

CHIQUIBUL ROAD
CASA MAYA ROAD

GUATEMALA
Flores & Tikal (110m)

VACA FOREST RESERVE
Cacao Camp Creek
San Luis (abandoned)
VACA PLATEAU
Guacamallo Bridge

CARACOL ARCHEOLOGICAL RESERVE
CHIQUIBUL NATIONAL PARK
Caracol

0   5
kilometres

ACCOMMODATION	
Bol's Camping	5
Chichan Ka Guest House	4
Clarissa Falls	2
Nabitunich	3
Martz Farm	7
Parrot Nest	1
The Trek Stop	6

CAYO DISTRICT: AROUND SAN IGNACIO

1

lying below a rock wall – and nearby the stone axe that may have killed her.

The cave is protected by a stiff entry fee (always included in tour prices), with only a handful of guides licensed to lead tours and a restriction on the number of daily visitors. It's one of the priciest excursions in Belize, and note that unless you make special arrangements, you'll need to **swim** to enter the cave, and much of the tour involves wading knee- or even chest-deep in water. With the most interesting sights lying almost half a kilometre beyond the cave's entrance, ATM is not recommended for claustrophobics.

Barton Creek Cave

Like ATM, **Barton Creek Cave** (tours around US$65, including Bz$20 entry fee and all transport from San Ignacio; you must be accompanied by a licensed guide to enter) is also accessible only by river, though this time by canoe. Framed by jungle, the cave's entrance is at the far side of a pool, and inside the river is navigable for about 1600m before ending in a gallery blocked by a huge rockfall. If it's been raining, a subterranean waterfall cascades over the rocks – a truly unforgettable sight. The clear, slow-moving river fills most of the cave width, though the roof soars 100m above you in places. Several **Maya burial sites** and pottery vessels line the banks, the most awe-inspiring indicated by a skull set in a natural rock bridge used by the Maya to reach the sacred site.

The **Barton Creek Outpost** (ⓦbartoncreekoutpost.com) is a picnic and recreation spot for day-trippers arriving with tours; visitors can explore numerous jungle trails and play Tarzan on the rope swing, or take in the impressive views of the area on the two-station zipline.

Along the Macal River

Steep limestone cliffs and forested hills edge the lower **Macal River**, whose main tributaries rise in the Mountain Pine Ridge Forest Reserve and the Chiquibul Forest. In the upper reaches the water is sometimes suitable for whitewater

★ **TREAT YOURSELF**

Martz Farm Mile 8.5 Hydro Rd ⓣ614 6462 or ⓣ663 3849, ⓦmartzfarm.com. Much further upriver from the other, pricier places on the Macal, but well worth the effort, with accommodation in comfortable thatched en-suite cabins, or in a treehouse or bunkhouse with shared bath, perched above a rushing, crystal-clear creek. For US$25 more per night all meals are included. The staff can also arrange guided day-trips to local Maya ruins and natural sights. Bunkhouse US$40, treehouse US$55, cabin US$65

kayaking, though you'll need a guide for this (see box, p.81). A guided canoe trip, however, is by far the best way to visit one of the river's top sights, the **Rainforest Medicine Trail** (daily 8am–5pm; Bz$6), in the grounds of the luxurious *Lodge at Chaa Creek*, 5km upriver from San Ignacio. The Maya's extensive medical knowledge is highlighted in this natural trail of herbal remedies: among the plants here you'll see the negrito tree, whose bark was once sold in Europe for its weight in gold as a cure for dysentery. The **Chaa Creek Natural History Centre and Butterfly Farm**, next to the Medicine Trail (daily 8am–5pm; Bz$20), offers a marvellous introduction to Cayo's history, geography and wildlife. At *du Plooy's* resort, a few kilometres upstream from the swanky *Lodge at Chaa Creek* resort, the ambitious **Belize Botanic Gardens** (daily 7am–5pm; Bz$15; ⓣ824 3101, ⓦbelizebotanic.org) aim to conserve many of Belize's native plant species in small areas representative of their habitats.

MOUNTAIN PINE RIDGE FOREST RESERVE

South of San Ignacio, the **MOUNTAIN PINE RIDGE FOREST RESERVE** comprises a spectacular range of rolling hills, jagged peaks and gorges interspersed with areas of grassland and pine forest. In the warm river valleys the vegetation is gallery forest, giving way to rainforest south of the Guacamallo Bridge, which crosses the upper Macal River. One of the most scenic of the many small rivers in the Pine Ridge is the **Río On**, rushing over cataracts and into a gorge. On the northern side of the ridge are the **Thousand-Foot Falls**, actually more than 1600ft (488m) and the highest in Central America. The reserve also includes limestone areas riddled with caves, the most accessible being the **Río Frio**. The area is virtually uninhabited but for a few tourist lodges and one small settlement, **Augustine/Douglas Silva**, site of the reserve headquarters.

With few roads, it can be very difficult to get around the reserve. The whole area is perfect for **hiking** and **mountain biking**; hitching is another option.

San Antonio

Nestled in the Macal River valley, **SAN ANTONIO** is the southernmost settlement outside the reserve. It's a good place to learn about traditional Maya practices: the village was the home of famous Maya healer Don Eligio Panti, and there's a small, informal museum in the village dedicated to his life and work. In addition, the **Tanah Museum**, on the road to the village near the *Chichan Ka Guest House* (see below), with its popular gift shop, has exhibits on village life.

The reserve

Not far beyond San Antonio, the two entrance roads meet and begin a steady climb to the **reserve**. About 5km uphill from Fidencio and Petronila Bol's campsite (see below) is the **Mai Gate**, a checkpoint with information about the reserve, toilets and drinking water. There are plans to levy an **entrance fee**, but for the moment all the guards do is write your name in the visitors' book (to ensure against illegal camping).

Once in the reserve, pine trees replace the dense, leafy forest. After 3km a road heads off to the left, running for 16km to a point overlooking the **Thousand-Foot Falls** (US$2). The setting is spectacular, with thickly forested slopes across the steep valley. The waterfall is about 1km from the viewpoint, but try to resist the temptation to climb around for a closer look, as the slope is a lot steeper than it first appears.

Around 11km further on from the junction to the falls lies one of the reserve's main attractions, the **Río On Pools** – a gorgeous spot for a swim. Another 8km from here and you reach the reserve headquarters at **Augustine/Douglas Silva**. You can **camp** here and the village store has a few basic supplies. The huge **Río Frio Cave** is a twenty-minute walk from Augustine/Douglas Silva, following the signposted track from the parking area through the forest to the main cave. Sandy beaches and rocky cliffs line the Río Frio on both sides as it flows through the cave.

ARRIVAL AND DEPARTURE

Arrival There are two entrance roads to the Mountain Pine Ridge Reserve, one from the village of Georgeville, on the Western Highway, and the other from Santa Elena, along the Cristo Rey road and through the village of San Antonio. If you're fit, a good way to get around is to rent a mountain bike in San Ignacio; you can take it on the bus to San Antonio. There are also buses from San Ignacio to San Antonio via Cristo Rey (Mon–Sat 4 daily).

Tours Tours can be arranged from San Ignacio (see box, p.81) and with *Bol's* (see below).

ACCOMMODATION AND EATING

Bol's Camping 1km beyond the junction of the two entrance roads to the reserve ☏ 664 3462. Basic campsite run by Fidencio and Petronila Bol. Fidencio, who also operates Bol's Jungle Tours, can guide you to several nearby caves. <u>US$10</u>

Chichan Ka Guest House On the road approaching San Antonio from San Ignacio ☏ 669 4023, ✉ tanah_info @awrem.com. The García sisters, nieces of the famous local healer Don Eligio, run this inexpensive guesthouse; buses from San Ignacio stop outside. The sisters also serve traditional meals, offer courses in the gathering and use of medicinal plants and are renowned for their slate carvings – their gift shop is a favourite tour-group stop. <u>US$15</u>

Reserve HQ camping You can camp at the reserve headquarters at Augustine/Douglas Silva; talk to a ranger at the station here for permission to pitch your tent. <u>US$20</u>

CARACOL

Beyond Augustine/Douglas Silva, the Maya Mountains rise up to the south, while to the west is the wild Vaca plateau. Here the ruins of **CARACOL** (daily

1

8am–4pm; Bz$20), the most magnificent Maya site in Belize, and one of the largest in the Maya world, were lost for more than a thousand years until their rediscovery in 1936. Two years later they were explored by A.H. Anderson, who named the site Caracol – Spanish for "snail" – because of the large numbers of snail shells found on the site. The first detailed, full-scale excavation began in 1985, and research and restoration continue today.

Most people arrive with a guided tour from San Ignacio (see box, p.81), as there is no public transport to, or even near, the site. If you manage to make it here on your own, you'll be guided around by one of the guards. The **visitors' centre** is one of the best at any Maya site in Belize and an essential first stop. Of the site itself, only the core of the city, comprising thirty-two large structures and twelve smaller ones grouped round five main plazas, is open to visitors – though even this is far more than you can effectively see in a day. The most massive structure, **Caana** ("Sky Place"), is 42m high and still one of the tallest buildings in Belize. Hieroglyphic inscriptions here have enabled epigraphers to piece together a virtually complete dynastic record of Caracol's rulers from 599 AD. One altar records a victory over Tikal in 562 AD – a triumph that sealed the city's rise to power.

Caracol hosted a special solstice celebration on December 21, 2012. The event – which included a detailed tour of the ruins, a slideshow on Maya archeology in Belize, participation in Maya B'Aktun ceremonies, and camping on the grounds – was so successful that plans are being made to reopen the site for future **solstice ceremonies**; contact NICH, the National Institute for Culture and History (ⓦnichbelize.org), for more.

ALONG THE MOPAN RIVER

Rushing down from the Guatemalan border, the **Mopan River** offers some attractive and gentle **whitewater rapids**. Accommodation here is cheaper than the more upscale Macal River lodges, and all of the places reviewed below can arrange river trips, as well as tours throughout Cayo.

ACCOMMODATION

Clarissa Falls 2km along a signed track off the Western Highway, about 7km west of San Ignacio ☎824 3916, ⓦclarissafalls.com. Restful place on the river with simple, clean cottages with private bathrooms, plus camping with shared hot-water showers. There's also a restaurant, and the staff can arrange a variety of tours. Camping U̲S̲$̲8̲, cottage per person U̲S̲$̲3̲7̲.̲5̲0̲

★ **Nabitunich** Signed on the right, opposite the airport entrance ☎661 1536, ⓦhannastables.com. With unbeatable views of the Xunantunich ruins and surrounding countryside, the peaceful San Lorenzo farm – attached to Hanna Stables – provides a wonderful base for horseback trips and bird viewing. Accommodation in simple private cottages includes three family-style meals a day in the central lodge, which also houses a library and games room; dorm beds are available in the bunkhouse, with meals for US$6 each. The sizeable property also encompasses a long stretch of the Mopan River, which can be explored by kayak, tube, horse or foot. Laundry (US$5/load) and wi-fi also available. Dorm U̲S̲$̲1̲5̲, cottage per person including meals U̲S̲$̲4̲5̲

Parrot Nest Bullet Tree Falls, at the end of the track just before the bridge ☎669 6068, ⓦparrot-nest.com. Six cabins (two up a tree and one with private bath) set in beautiful gardens on the riverbank, with shared, hot-water baths. Filling meals are available, and there's free tubing and a free shuttle to San Ignacio. U̲S̲$̲4̲9̲

XUNANTUNICH

On the Western Highway, around 12km west of San Ignacio, the quiet village of **San José Succotz** is home to the ruins of **XUNANTUNICH** (pronounced Shun-an-tun-ich), "the Stone Maiden" (daily 8am–5pm; Bz$10). This impressive Maya site is also one of the most accessible in Belize; any bus heading west from San Ignacio can drop you at the cable-winched ferry that crosses the river (daily 8am–5pm; free). From the other side, a steep road leads through the forest for about 2km to the site. Note that the river occasionally floods in the rainy season, so check in advance that the site is open before making a trip.

Your first stop should be the **visitors' centre**, with a scale model of the ruins. The site itself, on an artificially flattened hilltop, includes five plazas, although the surviving structures are grouped around just three. Recent investigations have found evidence of Xunantunich's role in the power politics of the Classic period,

INTO GUATEMALA: BENQUE VIEJO DEL CARMEN

The westernmost town in Belize, just 2km before the Guatemalan border, is **Benque Viejo del Carmen**. This quiet town is served by constant **buses** (which terminate here); to get to the border itself you'll need to take a **shared taxi** (Bz$10).

Leaving Belize you pay an exit tax of Bz$30, plus the PACT Conservation fee of Bz$7.50. There's no charge to enter Guatemala for North Americans or citizens of the EU, Australia and New Zealand; if you do require a visa (up to US$10), they can sometimes be issued here, though it's a good idea to check if you need one in advance. The Guatemalan border town of **Melchor de Mencos** has little to recommend it, so it is best to continue as soon as you're ready. **Moneychangers** will be waiting on either side of the border; you might want to bargain with them to get the best rate.

Minibuses (US$10–15) to **Flores** or **Tikal** usually wait just over the border, and *colectivo* minibuses to Flores wait just over the bridge at the border; regular second-class buses pass the junction just beyond the bridge.

during which it probably joined Caracol and Calakmul in an alliance against Tikal. By the Terminal Classic period, Xunantunich was already in decline, though still apparently inhabited until around 1000 AD.

The track from the entrance brings you out into Plaza A-2, with large structures on three sides. Plaza A-1, to the left, is dominated by **El Castillo**, at 40m the city's tallest structure. The climb up can be daunting, but the views from the top are superb, with the forest stretching out all around and the rest of the ancient city beneath you.

ACCOMMODATION AND EATING

The Trek Stop Signed on the road, 12km west of San Ignacio ⓣ823 2265, ⓦthetrekstop.com. A wonderful budget place to stay, with clean cabins and a campsite. The restaurant serves large portions and has good vegetarian choices, and there's a shared kitchen, free wi-fi, and bikes, kayaks and tubes available for rent. Camping US$5, double US$24

The south

South of Belmopan lies Belize's most rugged terrain. Population density in this part of Belize is low, with most of the towns and villages located on the water. **Dangriga**, the largest settlement, is home to the **Garífuna** people and is the transport hub for much of the region. Further south, the **Placencia peninsula** is the area's focus for coastal tourism, boasting some of Belize's only true beaches, and is also the departure point for the south's idyllic cayes. The Southern Highway comes to an end in **Punta Gorda**, from where you can head to Guatemala or visit **ancient Maya sites** and present-day **Maya villages.**

Inland, the **Maya Mountains** form a solid barrier to land travel except on foot or horseback. The Belizean government, showing supreme foresight, has placed practically the whole massif under some form of protection. The most accessible area of rainforest is the **Cockscomb Basin Wildlife Sanctuary**, a reserve designed to protect the area's sizeable jaguar population.

THE HUMMINGBIRD HIGHWAY

Southeast from Belmopan, the **HUMMINGBIRD HIGHWAY** heads towards Dangriga, passing through magnificent scenery. On the right the eastern slopes of the **Maya Mountains** become visible, forming part of a ridge of limestone mountains riddled with underground rivers and **caves**, several of which are accessible. Many contain Maya artefacts – burials, ceramics and carvings.

St Herman's Cave

About 19km out of Belmopan the road crosses the **Caves Branch River**, a tributary of the Sibun River. Just beyond, by the roadside on the right, is **St Herman's Cave** (daily 8am–4.30pm; Bz$8, includes entrance to the Blue Hole National Park). You pay the entrance fee at the visitors'

1

centre, after which a ten-minute walk on a marked trail leads to the cave entrance, beneath a dripping rock face; you'll need a flashlight to enter, heading down steps that were originally cut by the Maya. Inside, clamber over the rocks and splash through the river for about 300m, admiring the stunning natural formations, before the section of the cave accessible without a guide ends. To go further, consider hiring a guide (see below).

Blue Hole National Park

Two kilometres beyond St Herman's Cave, accessible from the highway or via a marked trail from the visitors' centre, is **Blue Hole National Park**, centred on a beautiful pool whose cool turquoise waters are perfect for a refreshing dip. The "Hole" is actually a short stretch of underground river, whose course is revealed by a collapsed cavern. Other trails depart from here, including the Hummingbird Loop.

ARRIVAL AND INFORMATION

By bus All buses between Belmopan and Dangriga can drop you at St Herman's Cave or the Blue Hole.
Guides The best independent guide to the Hummingbird Highway is Marcos Cucul, based in Belmopan (☎ 600 3116, ⓦ mayaguide.bz).
Cave and rappelling trips The luxurious *Caves Branch Jungle Lodge* (☎ 822 2800, ⓦ cavesbranch.com), 20km south of Belmopan, runs excellent trips – they're not cheap (from US$85/person), but well worth it for the experienced and knowledgeable staff.

ACCOMMODATION

Camping ⓦ belizeaudubon.org. Behind the visitors' centre at St Herman's Cave, trails lead through the surrounding forest and, after 4km, to a campsite. **US$10**

DANGRIGA

From the junction of the Hummingbird and Southern highways, it's 10km to **DANGRIGA** (formerly known as Stann Creek), the district capital and the largest town in southern Belize. Dangriga is the cultural centre of the **Garífuna**, a people of mixed indigenous Caribbean and African descent, who overall make up about eleven percent of the country's

population. The town is also home to some of the country's most popular artists, including painters and drum-makers, and you may catch an exhibition or performance. Still, for most travellers the town is of little interest unless you're here during a festival, though it makes a very useful base for visiting **Tobacco Caye** offshore and the **Mayflower Bocawina National Park** (see p.91) and the **Jaguar Reserve** near Hopkins (see p.93).

Pen Cayetano's studio gallery

One worthwhile sight in town, especially if you're interested in Garífuna culture, is the internationally renowned musician and artist **Pen Cayetano's studio gallery** on Aranda Crescent (Tues–Sat 9am–noon & 2–5pm, Sun 9am–noon; US$5; ☎ 628 6807). Examples of Cayetano's best known work – colourful and energetic landscapes and portraits – hang in a lovingly restored colonial house, along with more recent pieces and needlework examples. The space is also home to a mini museum of musical instruments, traditional utensils and folkloric objects.

ARRIVAL AND DEPARTURE

By plane Dangriga's airstrip, served by at least eight daily flights on the route from Belize City to Punta Gorda, is on the shore just north of the *Pelican Beach Hotel*, 2km north of town; taxis into town cost Bz$8–10.
By bus NTSL and James buses pull up at the terminal 1km south of the centre. Though taxis are usually available for Bz$5–7, all of the hotels we recommend are an easy 10–15min walk from the terminal.
Destinations Belize City, mostly via Belmopan (at least every 2hr; 2–3hr); Placencia (6 daily; 1hr 45min); Punta Gorda (8–10 daily; 2hr 30min). The 10.30am and 5.15pm buses to Placencia also pass through Hopkins (Mon–Sat only; 30min) and continue south via the Sittee River.
By boat Boats to Tobacco Caye (40min; from Bz$35) leave from the bridge near the *Riverside Restaurant*, though there are no scheduled departures; ask in the restaurant for captains Buck or Doggy. Water-taxis may make the same run into Honduras as the *Pride of Belize* ferry (see box, p.59) for about Bz$120/person; ask at *Riverside Restaurant*.

INFORMATION AND TOURS

Tourist information There's no tourist office in Dangriga, but the *Riverside Restaurant* (see p.90) can answer questions on transport and local information. The town's website (ⓦdangrigalive.com) is also very helpful and has a downloadable map.

Tour operators Island Expeditions (ⓦislandexpeditions .com), on the Southern Foreshore, rents sea-kayaks (singles Bz$70/day, doubles Bz$110/day), and will also shuttle you and your boat out to the nearby cayes.

Garífuna culture Naomi Morales (☏600 6141) invites groups into her home for a full-day course in baking traditional Garífuna cassava bread – a great way to learn a bit more about the culture (Bz$200 per tour, for up to 25 people).

ACCOMMODATION

★ **D's Hostel** 1 Sharp St, near the beach ☏502 3324, ⓦvalsbackpackerhostel.com. Though the dorms in this concrete building are not the most attractive, they are clean, and the hostel offers same-day laundry service, internet and wi-fi, free waffle breakfast, a book exchange, bike rental and lovely views of the sea from the rooftop. The friendly owner, Dana, can arrange local tours and Garífuna language and culture classes. <u>US$12.50</u>

Pal's Guesthouse 868 Magoon St ☏522 2365,

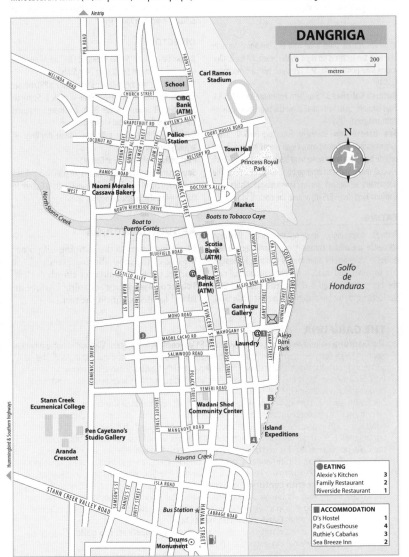

DANGRIGA

0   200
metres

Airstrip

PIN ROAD
MELINDA ROAD
CHURCH STREET
School
Carl Ramos Stadium
CIBC Bank (ATM)
FRONT STREET
GRAPEFRUIT RD
KUYLEN'S ALLEY
COURT HOUSE ROAD
Police Station
COCONUT RD
CITRON STREET
GIBNUT ALLEY
LEMON STREET
PLUM STREET
ORANGE ST
RECTORY RD
Town Hall
Princess Royal Park
RAMOS ROAD
WEST ST
Naomi Morales Cassava Bakery
DOCTOR'S ALLEY
COMMERCE STREET
North Stann Creek
NORTH RIVERSIDE DRIVE
Market
Boats to Tobacco Caye
Boat to Puerto Cortés
Scotia Bank (ATM)
BLUEFIELD ROAD
CASTILLO ALLEY
REAR PINE ST
PINE STREET
CANAL STREET
CEDAR STREET
OAK STREET
Belize Bank (ATM)
ALEJO BENI AVENUE
KNOPP'S STREET
MAGOON ST
OAK TREE ST
SOUTHERN FORESHORE
Golfo de Honduras
MOHO ROAD
ST VINCENT STREET
Garinagu Gallery
GANEY STREET
HOWARD'S STREET
MADRE CACAO RD
MAHOGANY ST
TUBROOSE STREET
Laundry
Alejo Beni Park
SHARP STREET
SALMWOOD ROAD
ECUMENICAL DRIVE
POLACK STREET
YEMERI ROAD
Stann Creek Ecumenical College
Wadani Shed Community Center
ZERICOTE STREET
Pen Cayetano's Studio Gallery
MANGROVE ROAD
Island Expeditions
Aranda Crescent
Havana Creek
Hummingbird & Southern highways
STANN CREEK VALLEY ROAD
ISLA ROAD
SAMSON'S ST
DANIEL'S ST
UNITY STREET
Bus Station
CABBAGE ROAD
HAVANA STREET
Drums Monument

N

Golfo de Honduras

● EATING

Alexie's Kitchen	3
Family Restaurant	2
Riverside Restaurant	1

■ ACCOMMODATION

D's Hostel	1
Pal's Guesthouse	4
Ruthie's Cabañas	3
Sea Breeze Inn	2

1

INTO HONDURAS

A **ferry** from Belize City (☎600 3259, ⓦprideofbelize.com) passes through Dangriga on its way to **Puerto Cortés**, Honduras, every Sat morning at 10.30am, stopping at the north bank of the river. Tickets from Dangriga to Puerto Cortés are Bz$110, while the total run between Puerto Cortés and Belize City costs Bz$145. These are a number of other boats between Belize and Honduras (see p.420).

ⓦpalsbelize.com. Quiet hotel with two buildings; the nicer one with ten rooms is set right on the beach. All basic, tiled rooms have private baths and TVs; those with a/c cost more. __US$40__

Ruthie's Cabañas 31 Southern Foreshore ☎502 3184. Four bargain, thatched cabañas on the beach with private bath and porch. __US$28__

Sea Breeze Inn Southern Foreshore ☎522 3766, ⓔpinkycullerton@gmail.com. Clean rooms with wi-fi and private baths in a large waterfront beach house; those with a/c cost more. Staff can arrange boats to Tobacco Caye. The downstairs restaurant serves international dishes and Garífuna food (from Bz$10) around the clock. __US$35__

EATING

Perhaps surprisingly, few restaurants in Dangriga specialize in Garífuna cuisine, though some serve a few dishes – it's generally more readily available in Hopkins (see opposite). BBQ stands in the park, market, and near the bus station sell good chicken plates for less than Bz$10; *Elena's* by the bus station is the busiest grill in town.

Alexie's Kitchen Madre Cacao Rd. Large open-air local restaurant serving good Creole breakfasts, lunches and dinners for Bz$8–10. Mon–Sat 7am–10pm.

Family Restaurant St Vincent St. opposite Scotia Bank. An a/c oasis in baking-hot Dangriga, with greasy Chinese dishes and fast food for less than Bz$15; the long menu has several vegetarian options. Daily 11am–11pm.

Riverside Restaurant On the south bank of the river by the bridge ☎523 3499. Tasty Creole cuisine, including great breakfasts and a daily special, for Bz$10–25. Also a great place to find tourist information. Mon–Sat 6.30am–9pm, Sun 7am–3pm.

DIRECTORY

Banks Belize Bank, Scotia Bank and CIBC are all near the bridge on St Vincent St; all have 24hr ATMs.

Internet The internet café in *D's Hostel* (see p.89) charges Bz$4/hr. DK Internet (Mon–Sat 9am–noon & 3–5pm), on St Vincent St opposite Belize Bank, has more computers and charges the same, but is closed on Sun.

Laundry *D's Hostel* (see p.89) has a same-day drop-off laundry service.

Post office Mahogany St at Ganey St.

Souvenirs Pen Cayetano's Gallery (see p.88) has painted and woven crafts for sale. The Garinagu Crafts & Gallery on Oak St (Mon–Fri) is also an option.

AROUND DANGRIGA

Dangriga serves as the jumping-off point for one of the most alluring islands a budget traveller could ever afford; **Tobacco Caye**, a tiny, stunning Caribbean island located right on the reef.

THE GARÍFUNA

The **Garífuna** trace their history to the island of **St Vincent**, in the eastern Caribbean, where two Spanish ships carrying slaves from Nigeria to America were wrecked off the coast in 1635. The survivors took refuge on the island, which was inhabited by **Caribs**, themselves recent arrivals from South America. At first the Caribs and Africans fought, but the Caribs had been weakened by disease and wars against the native Kalipuna, and eventually the predominant race became black with some indigenous blood, known by the English as the **Black Caribs**, or Garífuna.

For most of the seventeenth and eighteenth centuries St Vincent fell nominally under British control, though in practice it belonged to the Garífuna, who fended off British attempts to gain full control until 1796. The British colonial authorities, however, would not allow a free black society, so the Carib population was hunted down and transported to **Roatán**, off the coast of Honduras (see p.441). The Spanish Commandante of Trujillo, on the Honduran mainland, took the surviving Black Caribs to Trujillo, where they became in demand as free labourers, fishermen and soldiers.

In the early **nineteenth century** small numbers of Garífuna moved up the coast to Belize. The largest single migration took place in 1832, when thousands fled from Honduras after they supported the wrong side in a failed revolution to overthrow the government. It is this arrival that is today celebrated as **Garífuna Settlement Day** on November 19 each year.

To learn more about this distinctive culture, visit **Pen Cayetano's studio gallery** (see p.88) or try a cassava bread-making lesson (see p.89).

Tobacco Caye

Columbus Reef, a superb section of the Barrier Reef, lies about 20km offshore from Dangriga. Idyllically perched on its southern tip, **TOBACCO CAYE** is the easiest of the cayes in the area to visit and has a number of places to stay. The island is tiny: stand in the centre and you're only a couple of minutes from the shore in any direction, with the unbroken reef stretching north. The reef is so close to shore that you won't need a boat to go **snorkelling** or **diving**.

ARRIVAL AND INFORMATION

By boat Boats to Tobacco Caye (40min; Bz$30) leave daily from near the bridge in Dangriga, though there are no scheduled departures (see p.88).

Diving and snorkelling gear Several of the resorts, including *Reef's End Lodge*, have dive shops that rent gear even to those who are not guests; snorkelling gear costs US$7.50 and diving gear US$25.

ACCOMMODATION AND EATING

Accommodation on the remote caye is increasingly expensive and there are no independent restaurants, but most packages include three meals.

Lana's on the Reef ☎ 532 2424, ⓦ lanasonthereef.com, ⓔ bookings@lanasonthereef.com. *Lana's* four simple rooms, with fans and private baths, are the best deal on Tobacco Caye. Per person, including meals US$40

Reef's End Lodge ☎ 670 3913, ⓦ reefsendlodge.com. A dive and adventure resort offering good-value packages for stays of three nights or more. Three nights, per person, including room, all meals, transfers and six dives with basic equipment US$477

Mayflower Bocawina National Park

On the road between Dangriga and Hopkins, beyond Silk Grass Village, is the **MAYFLOWER BOCAWINA NATIONAL PARK**, a 7000-acre reserve of broadleaf forest at the base of the Maya Mountains. The entry fee is payable at the **visitors' centre** (8am–4pm; Bz$10), where you can find trail maps and information on the local flora and fauna. The park is home to the longest **zipline** in Belize, with twelve platforms set over a dense patch of jungle; full-moon night-time tours are a breathtaking experience. **Rappelling** is also offered – for several skill levels – at the park's pristine waterfalls such as Antelope (152m) and

Big Drop (120m), and the area offers many unexcavated Maya sites to explore.

ARRIVAL AND INFORMATION

Tours Bocawina Adventures and Eco-tours (☎ 670 2622, ⓦ bocawinaadventures.com) run tours of the park, as well as a zipline and rappelling (US$65). Contact the main office at the (pricey) *Mama Noots* ecolodge (☎ 670 8019, ⓦ mamanootsbelize.com) in the park to arrange visits.

Independent visits *D's Hostel* in Dangriga (see p.89) can help arrange independent visits.

HOPKINS

Home to well over a thousand **Garífuna**, the small village of **HOPKINS**, south of Dangriga and stretching along a bay, is a great place to learn more about this unique culture. Garífuna continues to be widely spoken here, and Garífuna Settlement Day on November 19, is celebrated enthusiastically. You can see **drumming** at the Lebeha Drumming Centre (see p.92), and there are numerous artists' workshops dotted throughout the village. The **beach** is an obvious draw, but there are also plenty of opportunities to get active and explore the area at leisure – the lagoon just north of the village is a great place for kayaking.

There are no **street names** in Hopkins; the main point of reference is the junction where the road from the Southern Highway enters the village – dividing Hopkins into north and south – and signs point the way to many hotels and restaurants.

ARRIVAL AND INFORMATION

By bus The 10.30am & 5.15pm buses from Dangriga (Mon–Sat; departing to Dangriga at 7am & 2pm) make a loop around town before heading south to the Sittee River; let the bus driver know beforehand where you want to get off. Alternatively, any bus on the Southern Highway can drop you at the turn-off to the village. From here it's quite easy and common to hitch a ride into town; a taxi may also be waiting by the bus stop to run tourists into town for Bz$10.

Tourist information There's no tourist office, but the town's websites (ⓦ visithopkins.com and ⓦ visithopkins villagebelize.com) have helpful listings.

TOURS AND ACTIVITIES

Bike/motorbike rental You can rent bicycles (Bz$20/day) from Fred's Bikes or Tina's Bicycles, both of which are in south

1

Hopkins. Motorbike Rentals (☎665 6292, ⓦalternate adventures.com), opposite *Thongs Cafe*, rents motorbikes.

Kayaking and windsurfing Rent kayaks (Bz$15/hr) at *Driftwood Beach Bar* (see opposite) or *Tipple Tree Beya* (see below). *Windschief* (see below) offers windsurfing lessons (Bz$60/hr), and rental (Bz$60/day).

Snorkelling and diving Many hotels can arrange snorkelling trips to the reef, while Hopkins Underwater Adventures (☎633 3401, ⓦhopkinsunderwater adventures.com) at Parrot Cove Lodge, south of the village, runs diving trips to South Water and other cayes (from US$120/2 dives). Motorbike Rentals (see above) supplies snorkel gear (US$7/day).

Tours Motorbike Rentals (see above) runs tours and provides a book exchange.

ACCOMMODATION

There are plenty of accommodation options here, with hotels, cabañas and resorts at all price ranges lining the beach.

Funky Dodo South of the centre ☎667 0558, ⓦthefunkydodo.com. A party hostel where guests linger for days, with simple shared-bath dorms and private rooms in a central location near the shore. Amenities include a bar, communal kitchen, laundry services, free wi-fi and cosy chill-out spots. Dorm Bz$15, double Bz$38

Kismet Inn Beachfront at the northern tip of the village ☎651 9368, ⓦkismetinn.com. Quirky, aquatic-themed rooms – most with shared bath – plus a self-contained cabin with organic architecture occupy this quiet stretch of beach; campers are also welcome. *Kismet* also offers a veggie and seafood restaurant, communal kitchen access (Bz$5), wi-fi, and free bikes for guests, and snorkel or fishing tours can also be arranged. Camping US$10, room/cabin per person US$15

Lebeha Drumming Center North end of the village ☎665 9305, ⓦlebeha.com. A variety of accommodation here: shared-bath dorms are the cheapest, but there are also rooms by the road and some lovely wooden beach cabins with private bath. Drumming lessons upon request, and wi-fi available. Dorm Bz$16, double Bz$30, cabin US$50

Tania's Guest House South of the centre, just beyond the basketball court ☎523 7058, ✉taniaprim@yahoo .com. Exceptionally friendly staff and clean, basic rooms with private bath in a wooden building. US$23

Tipple Tree Beya On the beach, south end of the village ☎520 7006, ⓦtippletree.com. Comfortable rooms in a wooden building have private bath, fridge and coffee maker; one private cabin has a kitchen. The beautifully kept beachside location makes it worth the slight splurge. Double US$35, cabin US$55

★ **Windschief** On the beach, south of the centre ☎523 7249, ⓦwindschief.com. Two cabins, one with a double bed and the other with two double beds, have private bath, fridges, coffee makers, wi-fi, and access to the well-stocked beach bar. Windsurfing available (see above). US$30

Yugadah Inn Southern end of the village ☎503 7089. This local restaurant (see opposite) offers four tiny rooms with no real lighting and shared bath – the cheapest digs in town. US$11

EATING, DRINKING AND NIGHTLIFE

Hopkins has a good variety of restaurants serving everything from simple Creole plates to traditional Garifuna meals as well as international cuisine. On most

HOPKINS

● EATING, DRINKING & NIGHTLIFE

Chef Rob's Gourmet Cafe	6
Driftwood Beach Bar & Pizza Shack	1
Iris' Place	5
King Cassava	2
Thongs Café	3
Yugadah Inn	4

■ ACCOMMODATION

Funky Dodo	3
Kismet Inn	1
Lebeha Drumming Center	2
Tania's Guest House	5
Tipple Tree Beya	7
Windschief	4
Yugadah Inn	6

Supermarket

CARIBBEAN SEA

Belize Bank (ATM)

Dock

HOPKINS ROAD

Motorbike Rentals

Catholic Church

School

Miller's Arts & Crafts

Fred's Bikes

N

Dave's Carvings

Alex's Seashell Art

Tina's Bicycles

0   250
metres

⑥, Sittee River Marina, Parrot Cove Lodge & Hopkins Underwater Adventures ▼

★ TREAT YOURSELF

Chef Rob's Gourmet Café *Parrot Cove Lodge*, a little more than 3km south of the village centre ☎ 523 7225. Rob's four-course extravaganza (Bz$55) is based upon a creative, daily-changing menu with a strong Caribbean influence and freshly sourced, local produce. Dine beachside, tuck into a rib-eye steak with spiced rum sauce or red snapper fillet with lobster sauce, and enjoy a peaceful Hopkins evening. Tues–Sun lunch & dinner.

nights the *Lebeha Drumming Center* (see opposite) hosts a performance of Garífuna drumming; stop by in advance to check the schedule.

★ **Driftwood Beach Bar & Pizza Shack** At the northern end of the village on the beach Ⓦ driftwoodpizza.com. Set on a gorgeous strip of sand, this laidback beach bar serves delicious pizzas (Bz$16–30) and daily lunch specials for Bz$10. They host regular barbecues, full-moon parties, drumming nights, volleyball games and jam sessions; the place is so popular that a second southside branch is in the works. Thurs–Tues 11am–10pm.

Iris' Place At the southern end of the village. Inexpensive local cuisine, veggie plates and delicious large breakfasts for Bz$4–20.

King Cassava Central Junction. For a drink with the locals, head to *King Cassava*, which often has live music at weekends. The kitchen serves Mexican food (BZ$10–16) and fry jacks for breakfast. Wed–Mon 9am–9pm, open later on weekends.

Thongs Cafe Two blocks south of *King Cassava* Ⓦ thongscafe.com. International breakfasts, baked goodies, and salads and sarnies for less than Bz$15, in a cosy coffee shop setting. Dinners are served on weekends, and there's a small gift shop and free wi-fi as well. Wed, Thurs & Sun 8am–2pm, Fri & Sat 8am–2pm & 6–9pm.

★ **Yugadah Inn** Southern end of the village ☎ 503 7089. The Nuñez sisters serve some of the tastiest Garífuna food in Belize, great seafood dishes from US$8, and a knockout rum punch. If it's traditional grub you're after, it's best to drop by or call in advance – *hudut* (coconut-based fish stew served with mashed plantain) and the like are cooked on request, and you'll need to give at least an hour's notice. Daily 6am–10pm.

DIRECTORY

Bank Belize Bank has a 24hr ATM by the main street junction.

Internet Many hotels and guesthouses have free wi-fi for guests, or you can connect at *Windschief*'s café for Bz$8/hr (closed Sun).

GLOVER'S REEF

GLOVER'S REEF, the southernmost of Belize's three coral atolls, lies around 40km off the coast from Hopkins. Roughly oval in shape, it stretches 35km north to south, with a number of cayes in its southeastern section. Famous for its wall diving, which is thought to be among the best in the world, the atoll also hosts a stunning lagoon, which offers spectacular snorkelling and diving, as well as a staggering diversity of wildlife. The entire atoll is a **marine reserve** (US$15 entry fee, usually payable to your accommodation or tour guide), with a research station on Middle Caye.

Activities include sailing, sea kayaking, fishing, snorkelling, and diving (including dive training), which is spectacular, thanks to a huge underwater cliff and some tremendous wall diving.

ACCOMMODATION AND EATING

Glover's, offering budget accommodation, is something of an anomaly among the remote atolls.

Glover's Atoll Resort Northeast Caye ☎ 520 5016, Ⓦ glovers.com.bz. Thatched cabins, over the water or on the beach, overlooking the reef, dorm beds in a wooden house, and camping space. All rates include transport from the Sittee River in the resort's boat (leaves Sun 9am, returns following Sat; 3hr) and use of the communal kitchen; nightly rates are also available. Meals are not included, so you can either bring your own food or eat at the restaurant. The staff pretty much leave you to your own devices – you can choose to enjoy the simple desert-island experience or take part in activities, which are charged separately. Per person per week: camping **US$110**, dorm **US$167**, cabin **US$280**

COCKSCOMB BASIN WILDLIFE SANCTUARY

On the mainland, the jagged peaks of the **Maya Mountains** rise to the west of the Southern Highway. The tallest summits are those of the Cockscomb range, which includes **Victoria Peak** (1120m), the second-highest mountain in Belize. Beneath the ridges is a vast bowl of stunning rainforest, more than four hundred square kilometres of which is protected by the **COCKSCOMB BASIN WILDLIFE SANCTUARY** – better known as the **Jaguar Reserve** (daily 7.30am–4.30pm; Bz$10; Ⓦ belizeaudubon.org). The basin

1

could be home to as many as sixty of Belize's 800-strong **jaguar population**, but although you'll almost certainly come across their tracks, your chances of actually seeing one are very slim, as they are mainly active at night and avoid humans. More than 290 species of **bird** have also been recorded here, including the endangered scarlet macaw, the great curassow and the king vulture.

The sanctuary is at the end of a rough 10km road that branches off the main highway at the village of **Maya Centre**, runs through towering forest and fords a couple of streams before crossing the Cabbage Hall Gap and entering the Cockscomb Basin. Here, you'll find the reserve **headquarters** (see below), where you can pick up maps (they also offer accommodation). Beyond the headquarters, a system of very well-maintained trails of varying lengths winds through tropical moist forest, crossing streams and leading to a number of picturesque waterfalls and ridges. For those who have the time – and have made the necessary preparations – it's also possible to take the four- or five-day hike and climb to the summit of Victoria Peak. If you're looking for a more relaxing experience, however, you can float down South Stann Creek in an inner tube, available for rent (Bz$10) at the headquarters.

ARRIVAL AND INFORMATION

By bus All buses between Dangriga and Punta Gorda pass Maya Centre. If visiting the reserve, you need to sign in and pay the entrance fee at the craft centre at the junction of the road leading up to the Cockscomb. From the craft centre, you can catch a ride with a taxi or truck to the reserve headquarters; this usually costs about Bz$30–40 each way for up to 5 people. The 10km walk to the reserve from this point is relatively easy but will take several hours.

Information Julio's Store, just beyond the Maya souvenir shop at the highway intersection, sells basic supplies and cold drinks (there's no shop in the reserve). It's also a bar with internet access.

Tours The owner of Julio's Store (see above) runs Cockscomb Maya Tours (☎ 660 3903, ⓦ cockscombmayatours.com) and can arrange guides and transport into the reserve.

ACCOMMODATION AND EATING

There's camping at the reserve headquarters, and, for the same price, at two other designated sites along the trails – for

which you'll need to get a permit at the reserve headquarters. Maya Centre has several inexpensive places to stay, all of which can arrange meals, tours, guides and transport.

Nu'uk Che'il Cottages Maya Centre, 500m up the track to the reserve ☎ 520 3033. Spartan rooms with private bath, and a large wooden cabin with shared showers and dorm beds. The restaurant serves Maya cuisine (Bz$5–15), and the owner has developed a medicinal plant trail out back. Dorm US$10, double US$30

Reserve headquarters Cockscomb Basin ⓦ belize audubon.org. A variety of accommodation, including private furnished cabins for four or six people, wooden dorms and camping space. There is no restaurant at the headquarters, so bring supplies. Camping US$10, dorm US$20, cabin US$55

★ **Tutzil Nah Cottages** On the highway just before the junction ☎ 520 3044, ⓦ mayacenter.com. Two clean, flower-framed cabins, one wood and one concrete, housing four rooms with choice of shared or private bath. It's run by the Chun brothers, who are also excellent guides to the reserve. The family also runs a small grocery store at the front. US$16

PLACENCIA

Some 16km south of Maya Centre, a newly paved road cuts east from the Southern Highway, heading through pine forest and banana plantations before reaching the sea and snaking south down the narrow **Placencia peninsula**. Immensely popular for its sandy beaches, which are among the best in Belize, this once lush area has become increasingly developed, with a plethora of concrete condominiums replacing what was once thick green vegetation. What with the property boom, and the imminent addition of a cruise-ship dock, locals fear that the peaceful peninsula will soon be but a distant memory. Though accommodation throughout most of the peninsula is limited to upscale resorts and hotels, **PLACENCIA** village itself has several decent budget options. Shaded by palm trees and cooled by the sea breeze, the village is still an ideal spot to relax.

WHAT TO SEE AND DO

Apart from simply hanging out on the beach, Placencia is a good, if expensive, base for **snorkelling** and **diving** trips to the southern cayes and reef or a day-trip to the **Monkey River**.

Other trips from Placencia can include anything from an afternoon on the water to a week of camping, fishing and sailing. Placencia's lagoon is also ideal for exploring in a **canoe** or **kayak**; you may spot manatees.

Diving and snorkelling

Diving options from Placencia are excellent, but the distance to most dive sites (at least 30km) means that trips here can be more expensive than elsewhere (see p.96). You could visit uninhabited

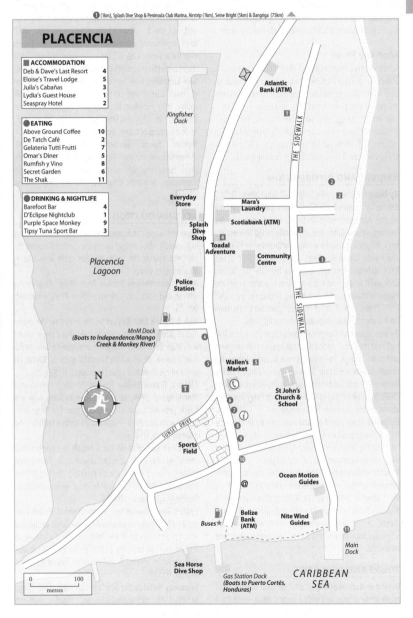

❶ (1km), Splash Dive Shop & Peninsula Club Marina, Airstrip (1km), Seine Bright (5km) & Dangriga (75km) ▲

PLACENCIA

ACCOMMODATION	
Deb & Dave's Last Resort	4
Eloise's Travel Lodge	5
Juila's Cabañas	3
Lydia's Guest House	1
Seaspray Hotel	2

EATING	
Above Ground Coffee	10
De Tatch Café	2
Gelateria Tutti Frutti	7
Omar's Diner	5
Rumfish y Vino	8
Secret Garden	6
The Shak	11

DRINKING & NIGHTLIFE	
Barefoot Bar	4
D'Eclipse Nightclub	1
Purple Space Monkey	9
Tipsy Tuna Sport Bar	3

Atlantic Bank (ATM)

Kingfisher Dock

THE SIDEWALK

Placencia Lagoon

Everyday Store

Mara's Laundry

Scotiabank (ATM)

Splash Dive Shop

Toadal Adventure

Community Centre

THE SIDEWALK

Police Station

MnM Dock (Boats to Independence/Mango Creek & Monkey River)

N

Wallen's Market

St John's Church & School

Sports Field

SUNSET DRIVE

Ocean Motion Guides

@

Belize Bank (ATM)

Buses ★

Nite Wind Guides

Main Dock

Sea Horse Dive Shop

Gas Station Dock (Boats to Puerto Cortés, Honduras)

CARIBBEAN SEA

0   100
metres

1

Laughing Bird Caye National Park, beyond which lie the exquisite **Silk Cayes**, where the Barrier Reef begins to break into several smaller reefs and cayes, or nearby **Gladden Spit**, now a marine reserve created to protect the enormous **whale shark**. You can **snorkel** near Placencia Island, just off the tip of the peninsula; here you'll see a variety of fish and corals.

Monkey River

One of the best inland day-trips from Placencia (see below) takes you by boat to the virtually pristine **Monkey River**, which teems with fish, birdlife, iguanas and, as the name suggests, howler monkeys. The 20km, thirty-minute dash through the waves is followed by a leisurely glide up the river and a walk along forest trails.

ARRIVAL AND INFORMATION

By boat The *Hokey Pokey* ferry (6–7 daily; 20min; Bz$10) departs for Independence/Mango Creek from the MnM Dock on the northwest edge of town, where buses on the Dangriga–Punta Gorda line are usually timed to meet the ferry. *D Express* provides a weekly shuttle between Placencia and Puerto Cortés, Honduras (4hr 30min; US$60; ☎663 5971, ⓦbelizeferry.com), departing from the Gas Station dock on Fri at 9am; you can buy tickets in advance from the Placencia Tourism Centre (see below). Both docks are within a 10–15min walk of any of the recommended hotels. Main Dock is used by cruise ships and commercial boats.

By bus Buses from Dangriga (3 daily Mon–Sat, 1 Sun; 2hr) pull in at the petrol station near the beach at the southern end of the village. Three daily buses bound for Dangriga usually depart at 6.15am, 7am and 1pm. All buses on the Dangriga–Punta Gorda line stop at Independence/Mango Creek, from where you can take the *Hokey Pokey* ferry (see above) for the short ride to Placencia.

By plane Maya Island Air and Tropic Air fly to Placencia from Belize City (about 45min). Taxis are usually waiting to take you the 3km from the airstrip south to the village, or someone in the airport can call one for you.

Tourist information The Placencia Tourism Centre, Placencia Village Centre near *Gelateria Tutti Frutti* (Mon–Fri 9–11.30am & 1–5pm; ☎523 4045, ⓦplacencia.com), is probably Belize's best tourist office. It distributes *Placencia Breeze*, a free local newspaper filled with transport schedules, local listings and a good map of the village and peninsula.

TOURS AND ACTIVITIES

Diving and snorkelling Splash Dive Shop, in the marina north of the village, and with a central office across from

Scotia Bank (☎523 3058, ⓦsplashbelize.com), is the best-equipped diving operation in Placencia, staffed by certified tour guides. Sea Horse Dive Shop, in town near the gas station (☎523 3166, ⓦbelizescuba.com), also offers instructions and excursions at competitive rates. Diving trips start around US$120 for a two-tank dive, and US$430 for open-water certification; snorkelling trips start at about US$70/person including equipment, transport and a snack. Nite Wind Guides (☎523 3847, ⓔdoylegardiner@yahoo.com) and Ocean Motion Guides near the main dock (☎523 3363, ⓦoceanmotionplacencia .com) both offer snorkelling and manatee-watching trips.

Sea-kayaking Dave Vernon, of Toadal Adventure at *Deb & Dave's Last Resort* (☎523 3207, ⓦtoadaladventure .com), offer excellent four- to six-day river- and sea-kayaking trips; they also rent equipment (Bz$70–80/day), as do a number of hotels, including *Seaspray*.

Nature tours Barebones Tours (☎677 9303, ⓦbarebonestours.com), operating from their Monkey River base, organize nature tours, overnight jungle adventures, and trips down the Monkey River (around US$65).

ACCOMMODATION

There are numerous inexpensive accommodation options in Placencia. Most budget rooms are clustered around the northern end of the Sidewalk. You could also stay in Monkey River village.

Anna's guesthouse Monkey River village. Basic rooms with shared bath, and simple meals at *Alice's* restaurant. US$25

Deb & Dave's Last Resort On the road, near the centre ☎523 3207, ⓔdebanddave@btl.net. Four clean rooms with shared hot-water bath are in a secluded annexe to the family home, all set within beautiful gardens. Kayaks for rent and excellent tours, too (see above). US$25

Eloise's Travel Lodge Next to St John's Church and School ☎503 3299. An old wooden building near the beach favoured by budget travellers, barebones rooms – those with private bath cost extra – with shared kitchen facilities and a breezy porch. US$15

★ **Julia's Cabañas** On the Sidewalk just north of the centre ☎503 3478, ⓦjuliascabanas.com. Rooms and brightly painted cabañas with private bath, TVs, fridges and coffee makers. Drop-off laundry service available. Double US$35, cabaña US$65

Lydia's Guest House Near the north end of the Sidewalk ☎523 3117, ⓦlydiasguesthouse.com. Clean, secure and affordable rooms with shared bath and use of a kitchen, in a quiet location near the beach; pricier private cabañas also available. Free wi-fi and breakfast (about US$6) on request. US$25

Seaspray Hotel On the beach, in the centre of the village ☎523 3148, ⓦseasprayhotel.com. Popular, well-run hotel in a great location, with a variety of excellent accommodation, all with private bath and fridge, and some with TV, kitchenette and balcony. There are hammocks on the beach and kayaks for rent. US$25

EATING

There are plenty of good restaurants in Placencia, but things change fast, so ask locally for the latest recommendations. Most places close early and you'll certainly have more of a choice if you're at the table by 8pm.

Above Ground Coffee On the road, south of the sports field; find them on facebook. A cosy tree-house café with freshly baked cakes and cookies, free wi-fi and great Guatemalan coffees (Bz$5–9). Mon–Sat 7am–4pm, Sun 8am–noon.

★ **De Tatch Café** On the beach, near *Seaspray Hotel*. Excellent international and Belizean cuisine and seafood (Bz$10–35), served in a quiet, open-air restaurant right by the sea; the Bz$12 lunch special is a bargain. Wi-fi available. Thurs–Tues 8am–9.30pm.

★ **Gelateria Tutti Frutti** Near the southern end of the road. Without doubt the best ice cream in Belize, available in dozens of flavours and starting at Bz$4. Thurs–Tues 9am–9pm.

Omar's Diner On the road next to *Barefoot Bar*. Inexpensive menu of filling breakfasts, Mexican cuisine and seafood, served on an open-air deck. Breakfast and lunch Bz$7–12, dinner Bz$16–30. Sun–Fri 8am–9pm.

Secret Garden Opposite the sports field ⓦ secret gardenplacencia.com. Set back from the road in a quiet, secluded spot, this restaurant and spa serves great breakfasts and fresh European and Belizean dishes (Bz$10–30) in a bohemian setting. Closed Mon.

The Shak Opposite the dock, at the end of the road ⓦ shakbeachcafe.com. Small beachfront restaurant serving smoothies, salads, sandwiches and good all-day breakfasts for Bz$10–25. Mon–Thurs 8am–7pm, Fri–Sun 8am–9pm.

DRINKING AND NIGHTLIFE

Although most of the restaurants also serve drinks, there are a few places with live music and more of a bar atmosphere.

> ### ★ TREAT YOURSELF
>
> **Rumfish y Vino** Opposite the sports field ☏ 523 3293, ⓦ rumfishyvino.com. Friendly staff, an inventive tapas menu (Bz$12–30) and an extensive drinks list make this self-professed "gastro-bar" the crown jewel in Placencia's dining scene. The candlelit surroundings and atmospheric veranda are as enjoyable as the food. Daily 2–10pm.

Barefoot Bar On the road near the MnM dock. Old favourite in a brightly decorated and prominent location. Very popular bar serving great cocktails (happy hour 5–6pm) and bar food. Open late most nights.

D'Eclipse Nightclub Near the airstrip. The peninsula's only true clubbing experience attracts a good mix of locals and visitors. Busy at weekends from midnight.

Purple Space Monkey Opposite the sports field. The massive street-side bar and happy-hour rum specials (Bz$3.50) make this a great spot for drinking and people-watching. The restaurant also has a posh menu of sushi and fusion plates (Bz$10–40).

Tipsy Tuna Sports Bar On the beach. This lively bar and restaurant is often packed and sometimes hosts live music on weekends. Happy hour (daily 5–7pm) includes free banana chips. Fre wi-fi available.

DIRECTORY

Banks Atlantic Bank and Scotia Bank can exchange currency and have 24hr ATMs.

Internet Placencia Office Supply, on the road south of the centre, has numerous computers and a reliable connection (Mon–Fri 8am–7pm, Sat 8am–5pm); there's also access at *De Tatch Café* and *Tipsy Tuna*.

Laundry *Julia's Cabañas* has a drop-off laundry service; Mara's Laundry behind Scotia Bank also offers full laundry services for Bz$15/load.

Post office On the road, at the northern end of the village.

THE FAR SOUTH

Beyond Independence, the Southern Highway leaves the banana plantations, first twisting through pine forests, crossing numerous creeks and rivers, and arriving in the sparsely populated **Toledo District**, Belize's least developed region. Here, the Mopan and Kekchi, the country's two main Maya groups, comprise almost half the population.

Nim Li Punit

Just 1km off the Southern Highway, about 73km south of the Placencia junction, lies **Nim Li Punit** (daily 9am–5pm; Bz$10), a Late Classic Maya site, possibly allied to nearby Lubaantun and to Quiriguá in Guatemala (see p.338). The ruins stand on top of a ridge, surrounded by the fields of the nearby Maya village of **Indian Creek**. The **visitors' centre** has a good map of the site and explanations of some of the carved texts found here, which include eight

1

RANGER FOR A DAY

The **Ya'axche Conservation Trust** (☎ 722 0108, ⓦ yaaxche.org) runs an interesting "ranger for a day" programme from their Toledo HQ. Guests spend the day patrolling the Golden Stream Corridor Preserve, learning about medicinal plants, checking for signs of illegal activity and monitoring the region's biodiversity. The US$45 fee directly funds the locally staffed park ranger programme.

stelae, among them **Stele 15**, which, at more than 9m, is the tallest yet found in Belize. The site is an easy day-trip from Punta Gorda.

ACCOMMODATION

If you fancy a remote stay in Toledo's wilderness, you can choose from several high-end places along the final 22km of the Southern Highway to Punta Gorda.

Sun Creek Lodge Sun Creek, 3km south of the Dump junction ☎ 604 2124, ⓦ suncreeklodge.com. A good budget bet, with four beautiful thatched cabañas and a villa, all with electricity and some with private bath, set in a lively patch of jungle. One of the owners knows the area exceptionally well and can organize tours. Wi-fi access available in the lodge, and breakfast is included. From US$40

PUNTA GORDA

The Southern Highway comes to an end in **PUNTA GORDA**, known locally as PG, the heart of the isolated Toledo District. The town, the focal point for many local villages and farming settlements, is

populated by a mixture of eight thousand Creoles, Garífuna and Maya – who make up more than half the population of the district. Apart from its **chocolate**-related sights (see box below) there are few other attractions in PG itself, but it makes an excellent base from which to explore the nearby Maya villages and ruins.

ARRIVAL AND DEPARTURE

By plane Maya Island Air and Tropic Air operate several daily flights from Belize City (via Dangriga and Placencia), landing at the airstrip five blocks west of the main dock and a 5–10min walk from any of the recommended hotels.

By bus Buses from Belize City via Belmopan and Dangriga (5–10 daily Mon–Sat, 3 daily Sun; 5hr–6hr 30min) circle the town, usually stopping at the petrol station at the northeast edge of the centre, which is within easy walking distance of all the recommended hotels. Belize City buses via Dangriga and Belmopan (12 daily; 5–7hr) depart from the station off Front St; the express bus departs at 6am from the petrol station. Buses to the Maya villages leave from the market area, usually around noon: San Antonio (2 daily, usually Mon–Sat only); San Pedro Columbia (for Lubaantun; Mon–Sat); Jalacte and Pueblo Viejo (for Uxbenka; 4–8 weekly); San Benito Poite (for Blue Creek; 4 weekly).

By boat Skiffs from Puerto Barrios and Lívingston, Guatemala, use the main dock near the centre of the seafront.

Departures Puerto Barrios, Guatemala (5 daily; 1hr; Bz$50); Lívingston, Guatemala (2 weekly; 10am Tues & Fri; 1hr; Bz$60).

INFORMATION AND TOURS

Tourist information The Belize Tourism Industry Association (☎ 722 2531) has a large office in a pretty

THE HOME OF FAIRTRADE CHOCOLATE

The Toledo Cacao Growers' Association, set up in conjunction with the British chocolate company *Green & Black's*, became the world's first fairtrade cacao producers in 1993, and the product of this partnership, **Maya Gold chocolate**, is now sold internationally. 2007 marked the first ever **Cacao Festival** (ⓦ tcgabelize.com), which has quickly established itself as an annual fixture in the town's calendar, and several home-grown brands of chocolate have sprung up in the district. A great example is the **Cotton Tree Chocolate Factory** on Punta Gorda's Front St (☎ 621 8776, ⓦ cottontreechocolate.com, erratic hours), which offers complimentary tasting sessions and short free tours of their tiny workshop.

About half an hour north of PG on the road to San Felipe, you'll find **Ixcacao** (☎ 742 4050, ⓦ cyrilaschocolate.org), a Maya family-run farm producing world-class chocolate. Every ingredient, from the hand-churned sugar cane to the coconut and spices, is produced locally. Drop by for a tour (Bz$20) and have a go at making your own chocolate. If you want both the farm tour and cacao-making tutorial, it may be easier to spend a night in the rustic bunkhouse (see opposite). Cacao products, from chocolate to wine, and Maya crafts are on sale in the tiny shop downstairs.

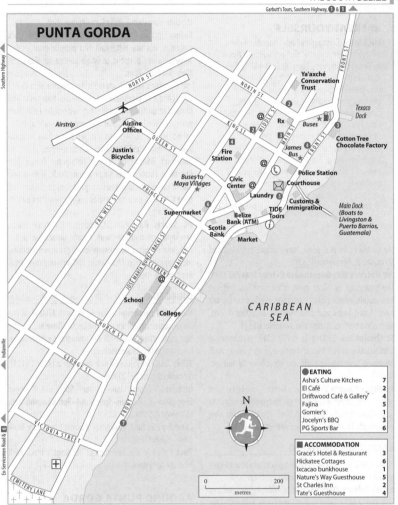

Garbutt's Tours, Southern Highway, ❶ & ❶

PUNTA GORDA

Southern Highway

NORTH ST

Ya'axché
Conservation
Trust ❷

FRONT ST

*Texaco
Dock*

NORTH ST

Airstrip

Airline
Offices

QUEEN ST

KING ST

MIDDLE ST

@

Rx

Buses ★

Cotton Tree
Chocolate Factory

Justin's
Bicycles

MAIN ST

James ❹
Bus ★

PRINCE ST

Fire
Station

@

FAR WEST ST

Buses to
Maya Villages

Civic
Center @

Police Station

Courthouse

WEST ST

Supermarket ❻

Laundry ❺

Customs &
Immigration

*Main Dock
(Boats to
Livingston &
Puerto Barrios,
Guatemala)*

Belize
Bank (ATM)

TIDE
Tours

ⓘ

JOSE MARIA NUÑEZ (BACK) ST

Scotia
Bank

Market

CLEMENT STREET

@

Indianville

School

College

CARIBBEAN
SEA

CHURCH ST

GEORGE ST

❸

VICTORIA STREET

Ex-Servicemen Road & ❻

N

❼

CEMETERY LANE

✚

● EATING
Asha's Culture Kitchen	7
El Café	2
Driftwood Café & Gallery	4
Fajina	5
Gomier's	1
Jocelyn's BBQ	3
PG Sports Bar	6

■ ACCOMMODATION
Grace's Hotel & Restaurant	3
Hickatee Cottages	6
Ixcacao bunkhouse	1
Nature's Way Guesthouse	5
St Charles Inn	2
Tate's Guesthouse	4

0   200
metres

colonial building; staff can help with transport schedules and in setting up tours of the outlying cayes and sites in Toledo District.

Tour operators The local TIDE (Toledo Institute for Development and the Environment; 14 Front St ☎722 2129, ⓦtidetours.org) is involved with many conservation projects and also offers cacao, mountain-bike and kayak tours and camping trips to Payne's Creek National Park. Garbutt's tours (☎604 3548, ⓦgarbuttsfishinglodge. com) is a family-run business operated from the small marina at the entrance to town. As well as running local scuba, snorkel and marine tours, the Garbutt brothers rent kayaks and seaside cabins, and run affordable trips to the pristine Lime Caye.

ACCOMMODATION

Accommodation in Punta Gorda is generally inexpensive. Out of town, *Nature's Way Guest House* (see p.100) organizes guesthouse and homestay accommodation in surrounding villages, in conjunction with the Toledo Ecotourism Association (TEA).

Grace's Hotel & Restaurant 19 Main St ☎702 2414, ✉gracemcp@hotmail.com. Functional, clean rooms with private bath in the centre of town; those with a/c cost twice as much. The restaurant, open daily, serves a large menu including hearty Belizean dishes for less than Bz$15. <u>US$25</u>
Ixcacao bunkhouse About 30min north of PG on the road to San Felipe ☎742 4050, ⓦcyrilaschocolate.org. Bunkhouse accommodation available to anyone touring

1

★ **TREAT YOURSELF**

Hickatee Cottages Less than 2km west of the centre, on the Ex-Servicemen Road beyond Cemetery Lane ☎ 662 4475, ⊕ hickatee.com. The lush jungle setting of this small B&B makes it a great base for birding and wildlife exploration – just don't forget your insect repellent. There's a small pool, wi-fi, restaurant, an abundance of nature trails, and free bicycles for exploring the area; all local tours are easily arranged here. A stay in the rustic-chic private cabañas, with solar-powered ceiling fans and hot-water showers, includes breakfast plus transfers to and from town (arranged in advance). US$75

the facilities (see box, p.98). Rates include breakfast and Maya dinner. Per person US$20

★ **Nature's Way Guesthouse** 65 Front St ☎ 702 2119. The best place in PG to meet other travellers and get information, where eight clean rooms overlooking the sea have shared baths and cold showers. Breakfast (US$6), wi-fi and a book exchange also available. US$25

St Charles Inn 23 King St ☎ 722 2149, ✉ stcharlespg @btl.net. One of PG's smartest options, with friendly staff. All rooms have private bath, and most have TV and a/c. US$40

Tate's Guesthouse 34 José María Nuñez St, two blocks west of the town centre ☎ 722 0147, ✉ tatesguesthouse@yahoo .com. Quiet, friendly, family-run hotel. Spotless rooms have private bath, TV and wi-fi access; some with a/c. US$25

EATING AND DRINKING

Punta Gorda has several excellent places to eat with very reasonable prices; it's hard not to eat well here.

Asha's Culture Kitchen Front St, 400m beyond *Nature's Way* ☎ 632 8025. Fresh seafood and Creole BBQ dishes for Bz$10–25, served on a large deck over the water. Mon & Wed–Sat 8am–midnight, Sun 2pm–midnight.

El Café North St, behind *Charlton's Inn*. Small diner serving good breakfasts, burgers and Belizean cuisine for Bz$3–12. Daily 6.30am–2pm.

★ **Driftwood Café & Gallery** 9 Front St, near the Cotton Tree Chocolate Factory – find them on facebook. The best coffee in town and great (if pricey) food; vegan chocolate chilli (US$7), callaloo omelettes and a Bz$5 frozen mocha shake (made with real java and local organic cacao) drive this simple café towards gastro ranks. There's free wi-fi and a small art gallery inside. The café also serves as the HQ for Emmeth Young's Maroon School of Creole drumming; ask here about lessons, drum-making workshops, and a stay at the centre (under construction at

the time of research). Daily 7am–4pm.

Fajina Upstairs from the craft shop, opposite the dock entrance. This tiny restaurant is a popular local choice, serving hearty portions of Maya cuisine for Bz$5–10. Mon–Sat 6am–7pm.

★ **Gomier's** Across from the town entrance sign ☎ 722 2929 (find it on facebook). An unexpected vegetarian and seafood restaurant in a simple thatched *palapa*. Exotic fruit juices, seaweed shakes, and fresh veggie or seafood dishes for Bz$10–20. Gomier can also teach you how to make your own tofu (Bz$75pp). Mon–Sat 8am–9pm.

Jocelyn's BBQ Front St, just before the Cotton Tree Chocolate Factory. This small green shack, with a few plastic tables and chairs, serves great stewed chicken and fried fish (with coco-rice and beans) for less than Bz$10. Daily 7.30am–6pm.

PG Sports Bar Main St, opposite the clock tower. Weekend watering hole with a huge indoor bar, and a dark, sweaty dance floor where locals get down to punta, soca, reggae and rap. Mon–Thurs 7.30pm–midnight, Fri & Sat 7.30pm–4am.

DIRECTORY

Bank and exchange Belize Bank (with ATM) is on the main square across from the Civic Center. There will usually be a moneychanger outside the immigration office when international boats are docking.

Bikes Justin, at Prince St near the airstrip (☎ 663 9173), rents bicycles for Bz$20/day.

Internet V-Comp (Mon–Sat 8am–8pm) and KC Photo Shop (Mon–Sat 7.30am–9pm, Sun 4–9pm), both on Main St, charge Bz$6/hr.

Laundry PG Laundry, on Main St across from Belize Bank (Mon–Sat 8am–5pm).

Post office In the government buildings a block back from the ferry dock.

AROUND PUNTA GORDA

As the only transport hub in the far south, Punta Gorda serves as an important base for all of the region's sights, including the beautiful and tranquil islands of the **Port Honduras Marine Reserve**, the Maya ruins of **Lubaantun** and **Uxbenka**, and traditional Maya villages such as **San Antonio**.

Port Honduras Marine Reserve

Six hundred square kilometres of the bay and coast north of Punta Gorda are now protected as the **Port Honduras Marine Reserve**, partly to safeguard the many **manatees** living and breeding there. The main reef has started to break up here, leaving several clusters of islands, each surrounded by a small independent reef. Hundreds of these tiny islands lie in the mouth of a large bay, whose shoreline is a maze of mangrove swamps.

North of Punta Gorda are the **Snake Cayes**, idyllic and uninhabited Caribbean islands that draw a small number of visitors for their stunning beaches. Further out in the Gulf of Honduras are the **Sapodilla Cayes**, now a **marine reserve** (Bz$20 entrance fee), of which the largest caye, **Hunting Caye**, is frequented by Guatemalan as well as Belizean day-trippers; though most visitors simply choose to relax on the beach, the reef, located only a few hundred metres offshore, provides excellent opportunities for snorkellers.

Some of these islands already have accommodation, and more resorts are planned, though at present the cayes and reserve receive relatively few foreign visitors and are fascinating to explore on a day-trip from Punta Gorda; contact TIDE (see p.99) for more information on how to visit the reserve and cayes.

San Antonio

Perched on a small hilltop, the Mopan Maya village of **San Antonio** is one of the few towns served by daily buses from Punta Gorda (usually Mon–Sat only). The founders of San Antonio came from the village of San Luis, just across the border in Guatemala, and they maintain many age-old traditions, including their patron saint, San Luis Rey, whose beautiful church stands in the centre of the village.

The area around San Antonio is rich in wildlife, dominated by jungle-clad hills and swift-flowing rivers. Though most visitors come to town to relax and to learn about Maya village life, this stunning region also provides excellent **hiking** opportunities.

ACCOMMODATION

Bol's Hilltop Hotel San Antonio ☎ 702 2144 (community phone). Basic rooms with shared bath and superb views;

also a good place to get information on local natural history and archeology. US$10

Blue Creek

Some 40km northwest of Punta Gorda lies the Mayan village of **BLUE CREEK**, whose main attraction is a beautiful stretch of water running through magnificent rainforest. To get to the best swimming spot, a lovely turquoise pool, walk for ten minutes upriver along the right-hand bank. The creek's source, **Hokeb Ha** cave, is another fifteen minutes' walk upriver through the privately owned **Blue Creek Rainforest Reserve**. A guide can take you to Maya altars deep in the cave. To get to Blue Creek, take the village bus from Punta Gorda to San Benito Poite.

Uxbenka

Some 7km west of San Antonio, towards the village of **Santa Cruz**, which is served by four weekly buses, the ruins of **UXBENKA**, a small Maya site, are superbly positioned on an exposed hilltop with great views towards the coast. As you climb the hill before the village you'll be able to make out the shape of two tree-covered mounds and a plaza, and there are several stelae protected by thatched shelters.

If you do make it out here you can enjoy some wonderful **waterfalls** within easy reach of the road. Between Santa Cruz and Santa Elena, the **Rio Blanco Falls** tumble over a rocky ledge into a deep pool, and at **Pueblo Viejo**, 7km further on, an impressive series of cascades provides a spectacular sight. Trucks and buses continue 13km further west to **Jalacte**, at the Guatemalan border, used regularly as a crossing point by nationals of both countries, though it's not currently a legal entry or exit point for tourists.

Lubaantun

The Maya site of **LUBAANTUN** (daily 8am–5pm; Bz$10) is an easy visit from Punta Gorda via the bus to **San Pedro Columbia**. To get to the ruins, head through the village and cross the Columbia River; just beyond you'll see

1

the track to the ruins, a few hundred metres away on the left. Some of the finds made at the site are displayed in glass cases at the **visitors' centre**, including astonishing, eccentric flints and ceramics.

Lubaantun ("Place of the Fallen Stones") was a major Late Classic Maya centre, though it was occupied only briefly, likely from around 750 to 890 AD. The ruins stand on a series of ridges which Maya architects shaped and filled, building retaining walls up to 10m high. The whole site is essentially a single acropolis, with five main plazas, eleven major structures, three ball courts and some impressive pyramids surrounded by forest.

Lubaantun's most enigmatic discovery came in 1926, when the famous **Crystal Skull** was "found" beneath an altar by Anna Mitchell-Hedges, the daughter of the British Museum expedition's leader. Carved from pure rock crystal, the skull's origin and age remain unclear, though much contested.

ACCOMMODATION

Maya Mountain Research Farm About 3km upriver from San Pedro Columbia ✆ mmrf.bz.org. Arriving here is an adventure in itself – you can paddle in on a canoe, or swim down the (crocodile-free) river. Concealed within the folds of the namesake mountains, this unique setup provides permaculture students, volunteers and eco-warriors with a rare opportunity to fall off the grid and absorb the wilderness of the area – without leaving a damaging footprint. The rustic wooden cabins barely interfere with the engulfing jungle cacao farm, which borders a pristine stretch of the Rio Grande, and meals are cooked on a wood-fired stove and shared in a large *palapa*; as a touch of luxury, you can also pick up a wi-fi signal. Other activities include hiking, tubing, and exploration of the unexcavated ruins surrounding the base camp. Per person, three meals included US$50

TURTLES AT TORTUGUERO

Costa Rica

HIGHLIGHTS

❶ **Tortuguero** Glimpse turtles galore at this isolated village and surrounding national park. See p.133

❷ **Puerto Viejo de Talamanca** Great surfing, good reggae and a lively scene. **See p.139**

❸ **Monteverde** Hike or zipline in ancient, brooding cloudforest. **See p.143**

❹ **Nicoya Peninsula** Surf Costa Rica's best waves and find your perfect beach. **See p.158**

❺ **Parque Nacional Chirripó** Spectacular hiking on Costa Rica's highest mountain. **See p.180**

❻ **Parque Nacional Corcovado** Rainforest hikes, amazing wildlife and remote beaches. **See p.188**

HIGHLIGHTS ARE MARKED ON THE MAP ON PP.106–107

ROUGH COSTS

Daily budget Basic US$40/occasional treat US$85

Drink Beer US$2.50, coffee US$1.50

Food *Casado* US$6

Hostel/budget hotel US$16/US$40

Travel San José–Puerto Viejo (210km) by bus: 4hr 30min, US$12

FACT FILE

Population 4.3 million

Languages Spanish, Creole, Bribrí

Currency Costa Rica colón (CRC; c)

Capital San José (population: 288,000)

International phone code ☎ 506

Time zone GMT –6hr

2

Introduction

Costa Rica can appear almost unfairly blessed with natural attractions. Within its boundaries lie lush rain- and cloudforests, smouldering volcanoes, long sandy beaches, and a simply stunning biological diversity, as well as tranquil colonial towns and chilled-out coastal resorts. In sharp contrast to the turbulence experienced by many of its neighbours, the country has become synonymous with stability and prosperity – Costa Ricans, or Ticos, enjoy the highest rate of literacy, health care, education and life expectancy in the isthmus. The country has a long democratic tradition of free and open elections, no standing army (it was abolished in 1948) and even a Nobel Peace Prize to its name, won by former president Oscar Arias.

Indeed, Costa Rica's past and present are so quiet, comparatively, that it's often said that the nation lacks a history or identity. This is far from the truth: Costa Rica's character is rooted in its distinct **local cultures**, from the Afro-Caribbean province of Limón, with its Creole cuisine and Caribbean English, to the traditional values embodied by the *sabanero* (cowboy) of Guanacaste.

For travellers, though, Costa Rica is the prime **ecotourism** destination in Central America. Every year many thousands of visitors come to experience the extreme biodiversity offered by its 161 parks and reserves, from **Monteverde** to **Corcovado** to **Chirripó** to **Tortuguero**; hiking, rafting and zipline canopy tours are the most popular activities for exploring the enormous array of exotic flora and fauna.

There's also the country's incredibly varied landscape: active volcanoes, such as **Arenal**, **Irazú**, **Poás** and **Rincón de la Vieja**, punctuate its mountainous spine, while the beaches on both coasts – **Santa Teresa**, **Jacó**, **Tamarindo** and **Puerto Viejo de Talamanca**, among others – provide excellent surfing. Finally, there's a cultural diversity; this one small country incorporates the cowboys of **Liberia**, the Afro-Caribbean rhythms of **Cahuita** and **Limón** and the indigenous reserves of the Bribrí. The potent combination of sights and activities, accessibility and relative safety means, Costa Rica can sometimes be expensive and crowded, but no trip to Central America would be complete without stopping here.

WHEN TO VISIT

The main rainy season runs from May to November, peaking in September and October (on the Caribbean coast, rain falls April to August and November to December). These months are less crowded and generally cheaper, as hotels, tours and activities lower their prices to attract the smaller numbers of tourists. **Peak season** (December, January and Easter) is by and large the driest and the most expensive time to visit – accommodation and transport require advanced bookings during these times.

CHRONOLOGY

11,000 BC First human settlement in Costa Rica

1000 BC Several autonomous tribes inhabit Costa Rica, the Chorotegas being the most numerous. Foundations are laid at the Guayabo settlement, which is mysteriously abandoned around 1400 AD.

100 BC Costa Rica becomes part of the trade network that stretches from Mexico to the Inca empire.

1502 AD Christopher Columbus lands on the Caribbean coast and is allegedly the one who dubs the land 'Costa Rica' ('Rich Coast').

1506 Columbus's rival, Diego de Nicuesa, is dispatched by Spain's King Fernando to govern the region; expedition fails.

1522 A third Spanish expedition sails from Panama to settle the region. The indigenous people begin a campaign of resistance.

1540 The Spanish establish the Kingdom of Guatemala, which includes most of Central America as well as the Mexican state of Chiapas. After it's discovered that there is no gold in the region, Spain largely ignores Costa Rica for the next several hundred years.

1563 Cartago founded as the first permanent settlement.

1723 Volcán Irazú erupts, nearly destroying the capital at Cartago.

1737 San José founded; rivalry with Cartago eventually leads to civil war.

1821 Costa Rica wins independence from Spain.

1823 San José named the federal capital after the liberal josefinos (citizens of San José) violently clash with the conservative citizens of Cartago. Costa Rica becomes a state in the Federal Republic of Central America.

1824 Juan Mora Fernandez becomes the nation's first elected head of state. He encourages coffee cultivation with land grants, thereby creating an elite class of coffee barons. The Nicoya-Guanacaste region becomes part of Costa Rica.

1838 Costa Rica withdraws from the Federal Republic, and declares sovereignty.

1843 Coffee becomes the nation's major export crop after British merchant William Le Lacheur establishes a direct trade route between Costa Rica and England.

1856 American adventurer William Walker invades Costa Rica with dreams of annexing Central America to the US, but is defeated in the Battle of Santa Rosa by national hero Juan Santamaría.

1870 General Tom Guardia seizes power, ruling as dictator for 12 years. In contrast to his ascent, his policies include curbing military power and taxation on coffee earnings to fund public works.

1889 First democratic elections held, though neither women nor blacks are allowed to vote.

1914 The opening of the Panama Canal boosts Costa Rica's economy, now dominated by the banana trade.

1919 Dictator Federico Tinoco Granados violently deposed.

1940 President Calderón Guardia enacts minimum-wage laws and restricts the working day to 8 hours.

1948 President Rafael Calderón Guardia refuses to relinquish power after losing election to Otilio Ulate. Civil war erupts; "Don Pepe" Figueres defeats Calderón, becomes interim president, then returns power to Ulate. Later elected to two terms as president, Figueres abolishes the armed forces, establishes citizenship rights for black people and institutes the female vote.

1981 Economic crisis – Costa Rica defaults on loan interest payments, accruing one of world's highest per capita debts – and instability, caused by civil war in Nicaragua.

1983 Reserva Natural Absoluta Cabo Blanco becomes Costa Rica's first protected area.

1987 Costa Rican President Oscar Arias Sánchez is awarded the Nobel Peace Prize for his efforts in ending the Nicaraguan civil war.

2007 Costa Rica signs controversial CAFTA (a free-trade agreement with the US and Central American neighbours) after several years of fiery debate.

2010 Laura Chinchilla succeeds her political mentor Oscar Arias Sánchez to become the country's first female president.

2012 Major earthquake occurs off the coast near the Nicoya Peninsula, measuring 7.6 on the Richter scale. Also, Laura Chinchilla's ratings are the lowest of all the presidents in the Americas.

ARRIVAL AND DEPARTURE

Visitors flying to Costa Rica usually arrive at **Juan Santamaría International Airport** (SJO) in Alajuela (17km from San José). Iberia (wiberia.com) is currently the only airline offering direct flights from Europe (Madrid), while American Airlines (waa.com), Delta (wdelta.com), United (wunited.com) and US Airways (wusairways.com) connect Costa Rica to numerous North American cities, including Chicago, Houston, Miami, New York and Toronto, as well as various Central American destinations. Flights from North America and Nicaragua also arrive at **Liberia International Airport** in Guanacaste – a convenient jumping-off point for the Nicoya Peninsula – as do some charter flights from Europe during the high season. A return ticket is technically required for everyone entering the country but is rarely checked at the airport; if entering by land, you are more likely to be asked to produce an onward ticket. Tourists leaving the country by air must pay a US$26 **departure tax** at the airport.

Most travellers entering by **land** arrive with Tica Bus (wticabus.com) and TransNica (wtransnica.com), which provide services from Guatemala City, Tegucigalpa (Honduras), Managua via Granada (Nicaragua) and San Salvador (El Salvador) to San José via Liberia. Services from Changuinola, David and Panama City (Panama) go straight to San José. Cheap local buses run to the border, but it's worth paying more for an international bus, as it saves you the hassle of finding onward transport across the border; plus, they tend to cross

2

2

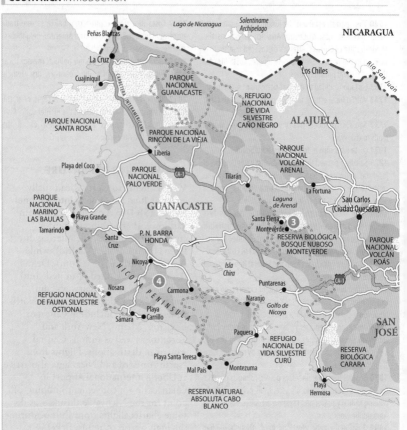

NICARAGUA

Lago de Nicaragua
Solentiname
Archipelago

Peñas Blancas

La Cruz

Cuajiniquil

Los Chiles

Río San Juan

PARQUE
NACIONAL
GUANACASTE

REFUGIO
NACIONAL
DE VIDA
SILVESTRE
CAÑO NEGRO

ALAJUELA

PARQUE NACIONAL
SANTA ROSA

PARQUE NACIONAL
RINCÓN DE LA VIEJA

Liberia

PARQUE
NACIONAL
VOLCÁN
ARENAL

Playa del Coco

Tilarán

La Fortuna

San Carlos
(Ciudad Quesada)

PARQUE
NACIONAL
PALO VERDE

GUANACASTE

Laguna
de Arenal

PARQUE
NACIONAL
MARINO
LAS BAULAS

Playa Grande

Santa Elena
Monteverde

RESERVA BIOLÓGICA
BOSQUE NUBOSO
MONTEVERDE

PARQUE
NACIONAL
VOLCÁN
POÁS

Tamarindo

Santa
Cruz

P. N. BARRA
HONDA

Nicoya

Isla
Chira

Puntarenas

Nosara

Carmona

Naranjo

Golfo de
Nicoya

SAN
JOSÉ

Refugio Nacional
de Fauna Silvestre
Ostional

Playa
Carrillo

Sámara

Paquera

REFUGIO
NACIONAL DE
VIDA SILVESTRE
CURÚ

RESERVA
BIOLÓGICA
CARARA

Playa Santa Teresa

Mal País

Montezuma

Jacó

Playa
Hermosa

RESERVA NATURAL
ABSOLUTA CABO
BLANCO

N

ISLA DEL COCO IS 500 KM S.W. OF COSTA RICA
ISLA DEL COCO

PACIFIC OCEAN

Bahía Chatham

Bahía Wafer

PARQUE NACIONAL
ISLA DEL COCO

Bahía Yglesias

0   3
kilometres

HIGHLIGHTS

1 Tortuguero

2 Puerto Viejo de Talamanca

3 Monteverde

4 Nicoya Peninsula

5 Parque Nacional Chirripó

6 Parque Nacional Corcovado

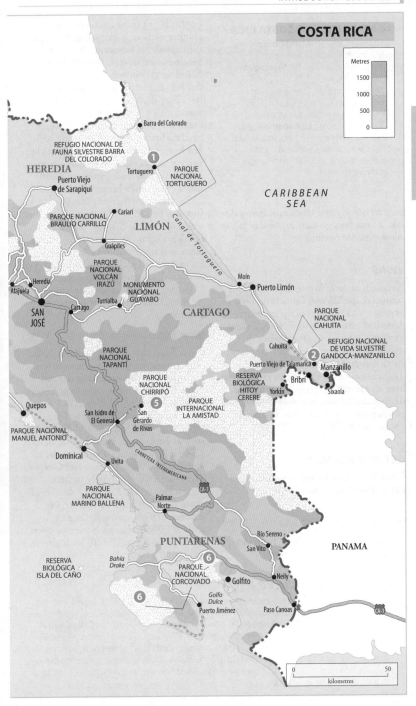

COSTA RICA

Metres
1500
1000
500
0

2

Barra del Colorado

REFUGIO NACIONAL DE FAUNA SILVESTRE BARRA DEL COLORADO

HEREDIA

Puerto Viejo de Sarapiquí

Tortuguero ❶

PARQUE NACIONAL TORTUGUERO

CARIBBEAN SEA

Cariari

PARQUE NACIONAL BRAULIO CARRILLO

LIMÓN

Guápiles

Canal de Tortuguero

PARQUE NACIONAL VOLCÁN IRAZÚ

Heredia

Alajuela

SAN JOSÉ

Cartago

Turrialba

MONUMENTO NACIONAL GUAYABO

Moín

Puerto Limón

CARTAGO

PARQUE NACIONAL CAHUITA

PARQUE NACIONAL TAPANTÍ

Cahuita

REFUGIO NACIONAL DE VIDA SILVESTRE GANDOCA-MANZANILLO

Puerto Viejo de Talamanca ❷ Manzanillo

Bribri

PARQUE NACIONAL CHIRRIPÓ ❺

RESERVA BIOLÓGICA HITOY CERERE

Yorkín

Sixaola

Quepos

San Isidro de El General

San Gerardo de Rivas

PARQUE INTERNACIONAL LA AMISTAD

PARQUE NACIONAL MANUEL ANTONIO

Dominical

Uvita

CARRETERA INTERAMERICANA

PARQUE NACIONAL MARINO BALLENA

Palmar Norte

CA-1

Río Sereno

PUNTARENAS

San Vito

PANAMA

RESERVA BIOLÓGICA ISLA DEL CAÑO

Bahía Drake

❻

PARQUE NACIONAL CORCOVADO

Golfito

Neily

❻

Golfo Dulce

Puerto Jiménez

Paso Canoas

CA-1

0   50
kilometres

2

LAND ROUTES TO COSTA RICA

Costa Rica has several **land borders** with neighbours Nicaragua and Panama. The main border crossing with **Nicaragua** is at Peñas Blancas (see box, p.172) via Liberia. Further east, there is another crossing at Los Chiles (see box, p.177), though it also involves a boat trip.

The main crossing for **Panama** is at Paso Canoas (see box, p.190). Sixaola (see box, p.143), on the Caribbean coast, is a smaller crossing, as is Río Sereno in the southern highlands.

borders quickly and efficiently. If you do take a local bus, go early in the day to allow time for queuing.

VISAS

Nationals of most Western European countries, the US and Canada do not require a **visa** for stays of up to ninety days. Irish, Australian and New Zealand nationals require visas for stays of thirty to ninety days. For the latest visa info, check out ⓦwww.visitcostarica.com.

All visitors to Costa Rica are required to have a **passport** that is valid for at least six months. By law, you should have your passport on you at all times, though a photocopy suffices.

GETTING AROUND

Costa Rica's inexpensive, comprehensive public **bus** system covers even remote areas.

BY BUS

San José is the hub for virtually all **bus** services in the country; it's often

impossible to travel from one place to another without backtracking through the capital. No buses run the three days before Easter Sunday. **Timetables** can be found on ⓦvisitcostarica.com. You are unlikely to pay more than 6000c, even for a long-distance journey. **Tickets** are issued with a seat number and a date; make sure the date is correct. If you're heading for a popular destination with few bus connections, buy a return ticket as soon as you arrive to guarantee a seat.

A network of more expensive **shuttle buses** – Grayline's Fantasy Bus (ⓣ2220 2126, ⓦgraylinecostarica.com) and Interbus (ⓣ2283 5573, ⓦinterbusonline .com) – connects San José with Costa Rica's main tourist destinations. These are faster and more comfortable than public buses, and will pick up and drop off door to door. They tend to charge around US$45–75 for a mid- to long-range journey (from San José to Tamarindo, for example).

BY PLANE

Costa Rica's two domestic **airlines**, Sansa (ⓦflysansa.com; from Juan Santamaría International Airport in Alajuela) and NatureAir (ⓦnatureair.com; from Tobías Bolaños International Airport in Pavas, 6km from San José), offer scheduled services between San José and destinations such as Tortuguero, Bahía Drake, Golfito, Liberia, Playa Nosara, Playa Sámara, Tamarindo, Puerto Jiménez and Quepos. Planes are small and highly weather-dependent, so schedules are vulnerable to change. Tickets must be reserved in advance in high season. Rates start from around US$60, though NatureAir offers "*loco*" prices (from US$30) for flights that are not fully booked.

ADDRESSES IN COSTA RICA

As in most Central American countries, Costa Rica's major cities are laid out in a **grid**, with the main plaza in the middle. Calles run north–south, and avenidas east–west. Generally the calles **east** of the plaza are odd-numbered and the ones **west** even-numbered; the **Calle Central** (sometimes called C 0) is usually immediately east of the Parque Central. Avenidas are usually even-numbered **south** of the park, and odd-numbered **north**. Exact **street numbers** tend not to exist; a city address written in the Guide as "C 16, Av 1/3", for example, means the place you're looking for is on Calle 16, between avenidas 1 and 3. In smaller towns addresses tend to be given in terms of landmarks.

BY CAR

Car rental and petrol in Costa Rica can be expensive, though having your own transport is really useful for visiting some of the country's more exciting sights, such as the Central Valley's volcanoes, the Nicoya Peninsula and the Osa Peninsula. Few buses serve these routes, and the timetables of those that do often leave you with little time for exploration.

Road **conditions** are often poor, especially in more remote areas – in dry season, most roads are passable by regular vehicles (though 4WDs are recommended); in the rainy season, most rental companies will insist that you rent a 4WD. Off the Interamericana and other major, paved roads, be prepared for potholes, dirt-and-gravel roads, narrow single-lane carriageways lacking hard shoulders, streams to be crossed and obstructions such as cattle.

In peak season, rental **costs** vary from around US$260 per week for an economy car, and from US$400 for a 4WD (both including full insurance), and you can expect to pay roughly US$70 a tank on a mid-sized vehicle. Reserving and paying for the car rental online makes for substantial savings. Major international rental companies – Avis, Hertz, Budget, Europcar – are based at and near the San José and Liberia international airports; some have other branches in Tamarindo, Jacó and other popular destinations. **Local rental companies** such as Alamo (☎2242 7733, ⓦalamocostarica.com) or Avanti (☎1 800 497 3659, ⓦavantirentacar.com) offer competitive rates.

Buying basic insurance is mandatory, even if you have your own; note that basic insurance in Costa Rica tends only to cover damage by you to other people's vehicles, not to your own car. Full insurance can cost upwards of US$25 per day. **Theft** from vehicles is common, so never leave any valuables in your rental car.

Taxis are plentiful in urban areas – look for red vehicles with yellow triangles containing the licence number marked on the front passenger door, and a taxi sign on the roof. In San José, taxis are metered, while elsewhere, fares are agreed on in advance. In rural areas, 4WDs are often used as taxis and in some towns you'll find *colectivos* (shared taxis).

Hitchhiking is reasonably common among locals in rural areas. It's not necessarily safe, however, so if you hitch, try to do so in pairs. Offer to pay the driver.

BY BICYCLE

Costa Rica is the easiest of all Central American countries to explore by bike, and **cycling** is an inexpensive and popular way to get around. Most beach towns have at least one bicycle rental outlet, with prices from US$10–15 a day. The quality of the bikes varies greatly, so check the equipment before you pay.

ACCOMMODATION

Although Costa Rica is one of the most expensive countries in Central America, there are plenty of **budget** B&Bs, hostels and campsites. Most towns have a range of places to stay, and even the smallest settlements have a basic *pensión* or *hospedaje*. US$12–20 a night covers a dorm or basic room in a hostel, while for around US$30–50 a night you'll get a more comfortable en-suite room, with a fan and possibly even a TV and phone, in a B&B environment. There are plenty of youth hostels all over Costa Rica; most come with a range of amenities that backpackers have come to expect – wi-fi, laundry service, book exchange, TV lounge, fans or a/c, tour booking services and even swimming pools.

When looking at prices, ask if the national **hotel tax** (16.39 percent) has been added to the published price. Most hostels and hotels price their rooms in US dollars, though you can pay in dollars or colones. Reservations are a necessity in high season (Dec–April).

Camping is fairly widespread. In the beach towns especially, you will usually find at least one well-equipped private campsite, and many budget hotels let you pitch your tent in the grounds. Although not all national parks have campsites, those that do are of generally high quality, with at least some basic facilities,

2

and cost around US$5 per person per day; all supplies must be carried in and all rubbish carried out. Never leave valuables in your tent. Camping rough is illegal.

FOOD AND DRINK

The cheapest places to eat are **sodas** – the local greasy spoons – which serve three meals a day, with *platos del día* (daily specials) costing around US$5. There's a wide range of **restaurants**, particularly in tourist hotspots; expect to pay from US$10 for a main course in the capital, and almost double that in some coastal towns. A town's central **market** is a good place to stock up on fresh produce, with stalls offering quick and cheap meals. Larger cities boast a full array of American fast-food chains, as well as inexpensive Chinese joints. Generally, restaurants **open** early, around 7am, and most are empty or closed by 10 or 10.30pm. When ordering, check whether or not tax is included in the price.

Tican cuisine is economical and filling, with staples such as **gallo pinto** ("painted rooster"), a breakfast dish of rice and beans, and **casados** ("married"), combinations of rice, beans, salad, plantain and meat or fish that are frequently large enough for two to share. Fried/roast chicken is another national favourite. You will also find excellent fresh **fish**, including *pargo* (red snapper), *atún* (tuna) and *corvina* (sea bass), with Tican-style *ceviche* a speciality. Fresh **fruit** is cheap and plentiful – try *mamones chinos* (a kind of lychee), *maracuya* (passion fruit) and *marañón*, whose seed is the cashew nut.

Most menus will have a **vegetarian** option, particularly in international restaurants where the menus are geared towards foreign customers.

DRINK

Costa Rica is famous for its **coffee**, which is a good souvenir to take home – and it is not hard to locate a decent *café negro*. Also good are the **juices** or *refrescos naturales*, combining fresh tropical fruit, ice and either milk (*leche*) or water (*agua*); *batidos* (smoothies) are a delicious variation, and in Guanacaste you can also get the distinctive rice milk-based **horchata**. **Tap water** is safe to drink in most places.

Costa Rica has several local brands of lager **beer**. Most popular, and cheapest, is Imperial, but Bavaria Gold is the best of the bunch. Pilsen and Rock Ice (beer with lemon flavour) are also worth a try; pricier imported beers are available in bars, restaurants and hotels.

For an after-dinner drink, try creamy, Baileys-style coffee **liqueurs** such as the famous Café Rica. For those with a stronger stomach, there is an indigenous sugarcane-based spirit, **guaro**, of which Cacique is the most popular brand.

CULTURE AND ETIQUETTE

Costa Rica is a friendly country, and many Ticos speak at least some English. Though officially a **Catholic** nation, the degrees of orthodoxy are hugely varied and many denominations of Christianity are observed. Attitudes are still fairly conservative, so do not be tempted to sunbathe nude or topless.

Macho attitudes still exist. **Gay and lesbian** travellers should be discreet, but an increasing number of gay-friendly hotels and nightclubs, particularly in the capital, tells of a gradual shift in mentality; ⓦcostaricagaymap.com is a useful website. Solo **women** can travel alone with relative confidence. While gringa-enticement is a rather competitive and popular way to pass the time, it is usually harmless and can be ignored.

Prostitution is legal in Costa Rica; underage prostitution is not. Larger beach towns such as Jacó have a reputation as magnets for foreign men drawn by local underage girls. Do not be tempted to partake of this socially destructive trade.

SHOP TILL YOU DROP

Costa Rica's indigenous tribes excel when it comes to **crafts**. Look out for replicas of the Sarchí ox-cart, colourful Boruca masks – either devil masks or those with jungle motifs – Chorotega pottery, baskets woven by the Huetar, tiny Bribrí canoes and cocoa products.

TICO WORDS AND PHRASES

Pura vida Literally "pure life" – a general greeting used to mean "cool", "all right", "all good" and so on.

Friendly **bargaining** is worth a try at craft markets, but is not the done thing elsewhere. As for **tipping**, most restaurants include a ten percent service charge in the bill. After a guided tour, a small tip to the guide is the norm.

SPORTS AND OUTDOOR ACTIVITIES

With a national team that has qualified for several World Cups, **fútbol** (or soccer) is Costa Rica's most popular spectator sport.

The nation's **surf** – some of the best in Central America – is one of its biggest draws. More than fifty well-known breaks dot the Pacific and southern Caribbean coasts, and all beach communities offer a selection of teachers and board rental companies; Jacó, Mal País and Puerto Viejo de Talamanca are the most popular beach locations. The teeming oceans also bring in masses of scuba-divers. **Snorkelling** is the most economical way to get up close to the marine life; the best areas for exploring brilliant corals are Cahuita and Manzanilla. **Kayaking** is a good way to explore the country's many lagoons, rivers and mangroves; paddling around Golfo Dulce from Puerto Jiménez, you may even see whales, while Bahía Drake's mangroves are also rich with animal life. Costa Rica also boasts

world-class **whitewater rafting** (Class II–V) particularly along Ríos Reventazón and Pacuare in Central Valley, with gentler options near Manuel Antonio.

There are also many land-based activities on offer. Costa Rica is one of the best places in the world for zipline **canopy tours**, the best of which are in Monteverde. There's superb **hiking** to be had, too – from short jaunts in the smaller national parks to multiday jungle treks in Parque Nacional Corcovado, while Volcán Chirripó remains the country's most challenging two-day ascent. **Horseriding** is also frequently offered for volcano tours and elsewhere, but check the condition of the horses before you pay.

COMMUNICATIONS

The Costa Rica postal system is reasonably efficient and reliable. Letters and postcards take around a week to reach the US, and around ten days to reach Europe.

Public **phones** require Chip or Colibrí phonecards (*tarjetas telefónica*), which come in 1000c, 2000c and 3000c denominations and are available from most grocery stores, street kiosks and pharmacies. There are no area codes and all phone numbers have eight digits. ☎2 precedes all landline numbers, while mobile phone numbers are prefixed with ☎8. With the proliferation of free wi-fi, free internet phone calls via Skype are by far the best way to go.

Top-up **SIM cards** for unlocked mobile phones are readily available for around

NATURAL HAZARDS

The downside to the fantastic watersports on offer in Costa Rica is the threat of the sea: powerful **rip currents** combined with a lack of lifeguards on many beaches result in around two hundred incidents of **drowning** per year. Popular beaches will have signs or flags warning of danger zones, and you should always ask about swimming conditions before jumping in. If you are caught in a rip tide, don't struggle against the current – that's how the majority of drownings occur. Let the current carry you out beyond the breakers where the rip current ends, then swim parallel to the shore until the waves can carry you back to the beach.

Costa Rica has a number of active **volcanoes**, and is an earthquake-prone country. The last major earthquake occurred off the coast near the Nicoya Peninsula in 2012 (see p.105).

Wildlife in Costa Rica's national parks – venomous snakes, big cats and others – can pose a threat, which is why trekking solo in Parque Nacional Corcovado is not recommended.

2

2500c and enable you to make inexpensive local calls. A basic mobile phone in Costa Rica costs from 30,000c. To buy either a SIM card or a mobile phone, bring your passport.

The inexpensive **internet cafés** once commonly found in towns (around US$1–1.50/hr) are becoming rarer with the proliferation of free wi-fi hotspots. Most hostels and hotels provide free internet and/or wi-fi.

CRIME AND SAFETY

Costa Rica is a relatively safe country and crime tends to be **opportunistic** rather than violent. Pickpocketing and luggage theft are the greatest threats. Purse-snatching and pickpocketing is an issue in San José and other larger cities, particularly in bus terminals and markets. If you do have anything stolen you should report it immediately at the nearest police station (*estación de policía*, or *guardia rural* in rural areas), where you file a report. Tourist-related crime, such as overcharging, can be addressed to the ICT in San José (see p.119).

Car-related crime, particularly involving rental vehicles, is on the rise, so park vehicles securely, especially at night. A common scam is to pre-puncture rental-car tyres, follow the car and pull over to "offer assistance"; beware of good Samaritans on the roadside.

Pedestrians (and drivers) should also beware of aggressive driving on the part of some locals, and a disregard for pedestrian crossings.

The **drug trade** that affects Costa Rica's neighbouring countries has not passed Costa Rica by, and dealers in the likes of Jacó and Tamarindo do occasionally approach travellers. Drug possession carries stiff penalties in Costa Rica.

EMERGENCY NUMBERS

All emergencies ☎911
Cruz Roja (ambulance) ☎128
Fire ☎118
Police ☎117

HEALTH

The quality of **medical care** in Costa Rica is generally good, with facilities in San José the best in the country, but rather limited in remote corners. Well-stocked **pharmacies** are found in most towns; they generally open from 8am to 4.30pm. There are also 24hr pharmacies in private hospitals in San José and several other big towns. Strong insect repellent (50 percent DEET) is a must, since mosquitoes carry dengue fever; there is also a very small risk of malaria in Limón Province. Vaccinations against hepatitis A and typhoid are recommended.

INFORMATION AND MAPS

One of the best sources of **information** about Costa Rica is the Instituto Costarricense de Turismo, or ICT (Ⓦvisitcostarica.com), with two offices in San José. The handful of smaller regional ICT offices dotted around the country are of limited use; you'll have to rely on locally run initiatives, guesthouses and tourist agencies for information.

For **maps**, Ⓦmaptak.com has handy, downloadable plans of the provinces and their capitals, as does the *Costa Rica Guide* (see box below). The Fundación Neotrópica (Ⓦneotropica.org) 1:500,000 map, available from San José bookshops, shows national parks and protected areas. The best road map of Costa Rica is the waterproof MapCR.com map, revised annually and available from good bookshops, such as San José's 7th Secret Books (see p.121).

COSTA RICA ONLINE

Ⓦ**costarica-nationalparks.com** A thorough guide to the country's parks and reserves.
Ⓦ**costaricaguide.info** Excellent free maps, with useful directories, bus schedules and transport information, and plenty of budget listings.
Ⓦ**ticotimes.net** Central America's leading English-language newspaper.
Ⓦ**visitcostarica.com** The official tourist site for Costa Rica, with bus schedules, hotels, maps and useful contact numbers.

STUDENT AND YOUTH DISCOUNTS

Students with ISIC (@isic.org) cards may be entitled to small museum and tour discounts. International Student Exchange (@isecard.com) cards also entitle students to certain discounts.

MONEY AND BANKS

The official currency of Costa Rica is the **colón** ("c"; plural colones), but given the ubiquity of US dollars (US$) – which are accepted by guesthouses, shops, many restaurants, and tourist sights across the nation (many services are priced in dollars) – colones are generally only necessary for local transport and food in cheap restaurants. **Coins** come in denominations of 5, 10, 25, 50, 100 and 500, while **banknotes** come in denominations of 1000, 2000, 5000, 10,000, 20,000 and 50,000 colones. Many establishments will not accept torn notes; these can be exchanged at banks.

ATMs (*cajeros automático*) are found in larger towns; some dispense US dollars as well as colones. International Visa and MasterCard debit cards are accepted at any ATM. **Credit cards** are necessary to rent a car, accepted by many hotels, restaurants and businesses, and can be used for obtaining cash advances, though you'll be paying a high transaction fee. Visa is more widely accepted than MasterCard. **Travellers' cheques** are increasingly redundant and should only be bought in US dollars. Bring plenty of cash when visiting smaller towns, as banking facilities can be scarce.

OPENING HOURS AND PUBLIC HOLIDAYS

Shops and businesses are open weekdays from 9am to 6pm (**malls** usually open between 10am and 9pm), with shorter hours on Saturdays. **Pharmacies** are open from 8am to 4.30pm. **Banking hours** are Monday to Friday, 9am to 4pm, while **post offices** open from Monday to Friday from 7.30am to 6pm, with limited Saturday hours (8am–noon) in San José and Liberia.

PUBLIC HOLIDAYS

Jan 1 New Year's Day
March/April Holy Thursday, Good Friday, Holy Saturday, Easter Monday
May 1 Labour Day
July 25 Guanacaste Day (Guanacaste Province only)
Aug 15 Mother's Day/Assumption Day
Sept 15 Independence Day
Dec 25 Christmas Day

Many **museums** shut on Mondays, and all banks, post offices, museums and government offices close on the main **public holidays**.

FESTIVALS

Costa Rica celebrates many **festivals**, or *feriados*, throughout the calendar year. Below are some of the highlights:

January Las Fiestas de Palmares is celebrated over two weeks with concerts, carnival rides and running of the bulls.
March Festival Imperial in Alajuela hosts the biggest rock festival in the country, attracting some 30,000 revellers.
April Día de Juan Santamaría honours Costa Rica's national hero with week-long festivities including parades and concerts.
August 2 La Virgen de los Ángeles – the nation's Patron Saint, La Negrita, is honoured with a religious procession from San José to Cartago.
September Parties and events all over the country to celebrate Costa Rican Independence Day.
October 12 Día de la Raza – celebrations, particularly in Límon Province, to mark Columbus's landing on Isla Uvita.
December Las Fiestas de Zapote – the last week of the month is a non-stop street party in San José's southeastern suburb, with music, bullfights, rides and games.

San José

Sitting in the middle of the fertile Valle Central, sprawling **SAN JOSÉ** has a spectacular setting, ringed by soaring mountains and volcanoes on all sides. The city's car-dealership architecture and bumper-to-bumper traffic aside, San José – while not a destination in its own right – is a pleasant enough city to spend a

▲ Juan Santamaría Airport & Alajuela

● DRINKING & NIGHTLIFE		● EATING		■ ACCOMMODATION	
Déjà Vu	7	Donde Carlos	6	In & Basic Hostel Lounge	2
Ebony	1	Soda Tapia	3	Mi Casa Hostel	1
Jazz Café	4				
Stan's Irish Pub	5				
Vertigo	2				

★ BUS STOPS

Alajuela, Volcán Poás & International Airport	L	Los Chiles & Zarcero	C
Cahuita, Puerto Viejo de Talamanca & Sixaola	A	Nicoya, Sámara & Tamarindo	I
		Peñas Blancas & La Cruz	J
Cartago	N	Puerto Jiménez	B
Golfito	F	Puerto Viejo de Sarapiquí	M
Guápiles	A	Santa Cruz, Playa Hermosa & North Guanacaste Beaches	A
Jacó, Quepos	K		G
Liberia & Playa del Coco	E	Sarchí	H
Limón	A	Tilarán & Monteverde	D

couple of days. You may well have to, given that it's the country's major transport hub and the easiest place to organize tours to other parts of the country, as well as day-trips to Valle Central destinations. A historical centre with attractive colonial buildings, several excellent museums and a lively dining and nightlife scene gives you plenty to occupy your time here, and the temperature – a constant 24ºC or so year-round – is pleasant.

WHAT TO SEE AND DO

The majority of San José's attractions are within walking distance of each other, scattered around the city centre. The **Parque Central** lies at the centre of the city, but the **Plaza de la Cultura** is San José's social core. The area around it is subdivided into little neighbourhoods (**barrios**). A bus ride from San José is Escazú, a hillside suburb with picturesque narrow streets, home to expats, wealthy Ticos and some excellent shops.

Museo de Oro Precolombino y Numismática

The Plaza de la Cultura cleverly conceals one of San José's treasures, the bunker-like underground museum complex – **Museo de Oro de Precolombino y Numismática**, or Pre-Columbian Gold and Money Museum (daily 9.15am–5pm; US$11; ⊕ museosdelbancocentral.org). In addition to early global currency, Costa Rican coins through the ages and coffee tokens used for paying coffee plantation workers, the real highlights are the priceless pre-Columbian gold creations. The vast

2

Centro Comercial
El Pueblo
❶

Río Torres

SAN JOSÉ

Terminal Caribe

Bishop's
Castle

AVENIDA 13

AVENIDA 11

AVENIDA 9

AMÓN

Parque
Zoológico
Simón Bolívar

AV 11 BIS

AVENIDA 13

AVENIDA 9

Fundación
de Parques
Nacionales
Office

Museo de
Jade

OTOYA

Parque
España

Parque
Morazán

Biblioteca
Nacional

Centro Nacional
de la Cultura

Parque
Nacional

Museo de Oro
Precolombino
y Numismática

AVENIDA 3

Palacio Nacional

ESCALANTE

BARIO
DENT

PLAZA
DE LA
CULTURA

Teatro Nacional

AVENIDA CENTRAL

AVENIDA 1

Cathedral

PLAZA
DE LA
DEMOCRACÍA

Museo
Nacional

AVENIDA 1

Parque
Central

ⓘ

Tica Bus Terminal

LA
CALIFORNIA

AVENIDA CENTRAL

AVENIDA 6

Church La Soledad

AVENIDA 2

LOS
YOSES

SEE 'CENTRAL SAN JOSÉ' MAP

AVENIDA 8

AVENIDA 10

AV 10

AVENIDA 12

AVENIDA 16

AVENIDA 18

AVENIDA 20

Pacific Rail
Station

0   200
metres

display includes the largest array of animal-shaped gold ornaments and figurines in Central America – funerary offerings, ceremonial decorations and much more. Displays on metallurgy techniques in Central America reveal which indigenous groups were responsible for which stylistic designs.

Teatro Nacional

San José's heavily columned, Neoclassical **Teatro Nacional** (Tues–Sun 9am–4pm, free tours every hour; US$11; ⓦteatronacional.go.cr), built in 1897, sits on the corner of C 5 and Av 2, behind the Plaza de la Cultura. The theatre's marbled stairways, gilt cherubs and red-velvet carpets would look more at home in Old Europe than in Central America, and remain in remarkably good

condition, despite the humidity and a succession of earthquakes. Above the staircase is a vast painting depicting coffee and banana harvests (reproduced on the 5 colón note in the 1950s); you can tell that the artist had never actually seen a banana harvest by the awkward way his subjects hold them. During the day you can wander around the post-Baroque splendour, or treat yourself to excellent coffee and cakes at the elegant **café**.

Museo de Jade

Three blocks northeast of the Plaza de la Cultura, at Av 7, C 9/11, on the north side of Parque España, is one of the city's finest museums, the **Museo de Jade** (Mon–Fri 8.30am–3.30pm, Sat 9am–1pm; US$9). Jade is the star here, and the displays are subtly backlit to

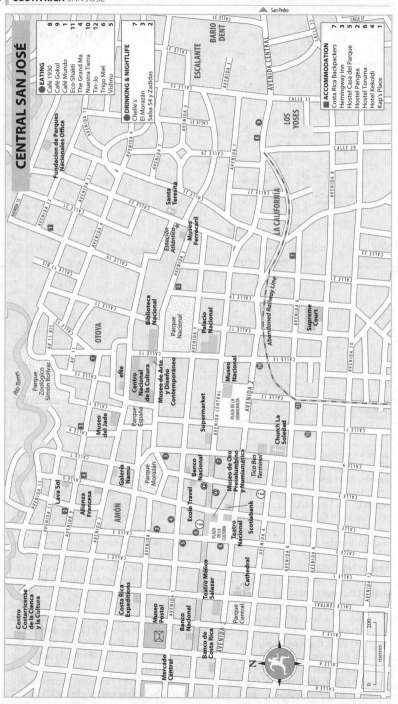

CENTRAL SAN JOSÉ

San Pedro

● EATING
Café 1930	8
Café Gokul	9
Café Mundo	1
Eco-Shakti	11
The Grand Ma	4
Nuestra Tierra	10
Tin-Jo	6
Trigo Miel	12
Vishnu	5

● DRINKING & NIGHTLIFE
Chelle's	7
El Morazán	3
Salsa 54 y Zadidas	2

■ ACCOMMODATION
Costa Rica Backpackers	7
Hemingway Inn	3
Hostel Casa del Parque	5
Hostel Pangea	2
Hostel Toruma	6
Hotel Kekoldi	4
Kap's Place	1

BARIO DENT

ESCALANTE

LOS YOSES

LA CALIFORNIA

Fundación de Parques Nacionales Office

Santa Teresita

Estación Atlántico

Museo Ferrocarril

Biblioteca Nacional

Parque Nacional

Palacio Nacional

Supreme Court

OTOYA

eÑe

Centro Nacional de la Cultura

Museo de Arte y Diseño Contemporáneo

Museo Nacional

Abandoned Railway Line

Río Torres

Parque Zoológico Simón Bolívar

Museo del Jade

Parque España

Supermarket

PLAZA DE LA DEMOCRACIA

Church La Soledad

Galería Namu

Parque Morazán

Banco Nacional

Museo de Oro Precolumbino y Numismática

Tica Bus Terminal

AMÓN

Lava Sol

Alianza Francesa

Ecole Travel

Teatro Nacional

Scotiabank

PLAZA DE LA CULTURA

Centro Costarricense de la Ciencia y la Cultura

Costa Rica Expeditions

Museo Postal

Banco Nacional

Teatro Mélico Salazar

Cathedral

Parque Central

Banco de Costa Rica

Mercado Central

N

0   200   metres

show off the multicoloured and multitextured pieces to full effect. You'll see some **axe-gods** – anthropomorphic bird/human forms shaped like an axe and worn as a pendant – elaborate necklaces, bird and animal representations, and fertility symbols. Besides jade, extensive displays feature fine pre-Columbian gold work, elaborately carved stone *metates* (grinding tables) and stone seats with animal motifs, pottery with jaguar and graphic fertility motifs, shamanic paraphernalia (including a two-pronged clay tube used to inhale hallucinogens), and skulls with unusually serrated teeth.

Museo de Arte y Diseño Contemporáneo

Sprawling across the entire eastern border of the Parque España, the former National Liquor Factory, dating from 1887, houses the Centro Nacional de la Cultura, home to the cutting-edge **Museo de Arte y Diseño Contemporáneo** (Mon–Sat 9.30am–5pm; 2000c, free on Mon; ⓦmadc.ac.cr). Constantly changing exhibits include photography, paintings, abstract sculpture and installations by domestic artists as well as works from across Latin America.

Museo Nacional

Just off the Plaza de la Democracia, the **Museo Nacional** (Tues–Sat 8.30am–4.30pm, Sun 9am–4.30pm; US$8; ⓦmuseocostarica.go.cr) is housed in the old Bellavista Fortress where, after the 1948 civil war, President José Figueres Ferrer proclaimed the abolition of the Costa Rican army. The rooms, arranged in a labyrinthine fashion around a beautiful flowering courtyard, showcase exhibits ranging from the country's most important archeological pieces – ornate mortuary slabs, *metates* covered in elaborate designs and fertility-themed pre-Columbian pottery – to wonderfully intricate anthropomorphic gold figures and the pen that President Figueres used to sign the 1949 constitution.

Mercado Central

The majority of Josefinos do their shopping in the **Mercado Central** (Mon–Sat 6am–6pm), which covers the two blocks between Av Central/3 and C 6/8. Entering its labyrinthine interior you're confronted by all manner of household goods, bags of coffee, Costa Rica-themed T-shirts and much, much more. In the annexe, colourful arrangements of fruits and vegetables sit alongside dangling sides of beef and silvery ranks of fish. The glut of *sodas* inside the market means it's the best place in town to get a cheap bite and for a spot of people-watching. Don't bring any valuables.

Parque la Sabana

At the west end of Paseo Colón, a wide boulevard of shops, restaurants and car dealerships, the vast expanse of green known as **Parque la Sabana** was San José's airport until the 1950s, and is now home to the country's key art museum. Housed in a converted air terminal, the attractive **Museo de Arte Costarricense**, Av 0, C 42 (Tues–Sun 10am–4pm; free; ⓦmusarco .go.cr), has a good collection of contemporary Costa Rican art, as well as the Jardín de Esculturas (sculpture garden) and Salón Dorado (golden room), which contains a huge mural painted by French artist Louis Ferón in 1940.

ARRIVAL AND DEPARTURE

BY PLANE

Together, Juan Santamaría and Tobías Bolaños airports have comprehensive links to all parts of the country, domestic destinations including Liberia, Tortuguero, Jacó, Puerto Jiménez, Golfito, Tamarindo, Quepos, Puerto Limón, Montezuma and Sámara. The international airport also receives flights mainly from North America (see p.105).

Juan Santamaría International Airport Costa Rica's main airport (☎2437 2400, ⓦaeris.cr) is 17km northwest of San José. Interbus (ⓦinterbusonline.com) runs door-to-door shuttles for US$15; reserve in advance. The red Taxi Aeropuerto (☎2221 6865, ⓦtaxiaeropuerto.com) taxis can also be reserved in advance; expect to pay US$35 and US$45. Buses to downtown San José depart from the airport bus stop just outside the terminal. Many hostels and guesthouses offer pick-up services (around US$30).

Tobías Bolaños Airport Nature Air uses Tobías Bolaños (☎2232 2820), around 7km northwest of the city centre. Buses run to San José every 30min. A taxi into the centre costs around US$20, or else you can get a ride with Interbus (see above) for US$15.

2

BY BUS
Terminals There is no central bus terminal, though the four main bus terminals that you're likely to use are Terminal Coca-Cola (Av 1, C 16/18; destinations all over Costa Rica); Gran Terminal del Caribe (C Central north of Av 13; destinations along the Caribbean coast); Terminal Musoc (Av 22, C Central/1; buses to San Isidro and northern destinations); Terminal San Carlos (Av 9 at C12; destinations in the north and northwest, such as Monteverde and La Fortuna).

Domestic destinations Alajuela (Station Wagon or Tuasa: every 10min, 4.30am–10.45pm; 40min); Cahuita (Mepe: 5 daily, 6am, 10am, noon, 2pm & 4pm; 4hr); Cariari (Gran Terminal del Caribe, for Tortuguero: 8 daily, 6.10am–7pm; 2hr 15min); Cartago (Lumaca: hourly 5.15am–10pm; 45min); Dominical and Uvita (Transportes Morales: 2 daily, 6am & 3pm; 7hr); Golfito (Tracopa: 2 daily at 7am & 3pm; 8hr); Heredia (MRA: every 10min 5am–11pm; 20min); Jacó (Transportes Jacó: 5 daily, 7.30am, 10.30am, 1pm, 3.30pm & 6.30pm; 3hr); La Fortuna/Arénal (Terminal San Carlos: 3 daily, 6.15am, 8.30am & 11.30am; 4hr); Liberia (Pulmitan: hourly 5am–8pm; 4hr 30min); Los Chiles (Terminal San Carlos: 2 daily, 5.30am & 3.30pm; 5hr); Mal País (Hermanos Rodriguez: 2 daily, 7am & 3.30pm; 5hr 15min); Manzanillo (Mepe: 1 daily, noon; 4hr 45min); Monteverde/Santa Elena (Tilarán: 2 daily, 6.30am & 2.30pm; 4hr 30min); Montezuma (Terminal Coca-Cola: 7 daily, 6am–6pm; 6hr); Nicoya (Empresas Alfaro: 5 daily, 6.30am–5pm; 5hr); Nosara (Empresas Alfaro: 1 daily, 6am; 6hr); Palmar Norte for connections to Sierpe and Bahía Drake (Tracopa: 7 daily, 5am–6.30pm; 5hr); Paso Canoas (Tracopa: 4 daily, 5am, 1pm, 4.30pm & 6.30pm, Sun also 10pm; 6hr); Peñas Blancas (Transportes Deldú: 7 daily 4am–4pm; 6hr); Playa del Coco (Pulmitán: 3 daily, 8am, 10am & 4pm; 5hr); Playa Sámara (Empresas Alfaro: daily

12.30pm; 5hr); Puerto Jiménez (Blanco Lobo: 2 daily, 6am & noon; 8hr; book in advance during high season); Puerto Limón (Autotransportes Caribeños: every 30min, 5am–7pm; 3hr); Puerto Viejo de Sarapiqui (Mepe: 9 daily, 6.30am–6pm; 2hr); Puerto Viejo de Talamanca (Mepe: 5 daily, 6am, 10am, noon, 2pm & 4pm; 4hr 30min); Puntarenas (Empresarios Unidos: hourly 6am–7pm; 2hr 30min); Quepos/Manuel Antonio (Transportes Morales: 4 daily, 6am, noon, 6pm & 7.30pm); San Isidro de General (Tracopa: hourly 5am–6pm; 3hr); Sarchí (from C 18, Av 5/7: 3 daily, Mon–Fri 12.15pm, 5.30pm & 5.55pm, Sat noon; 1hr 30min); Sixaola (Mepe: 4 daily, 6am, 10am, 2pm & 4pm; 6hr); Tamarindo (Empresas Alfaro: 2 daily, 11.30am & 3.30pm; 5hr); Turrialba (hourly 5am–10pm; 2hr); Volcán Irazú (Metropoli: 1 daily, 8am, returning 12.30pm; 2hr); Volcán Poás (Tuasa: 1 daily, 8.30am, returning 2pm; 2hr).

International destinations Changuinola/Bocas del Toro, Panama (Panaline: daily, 10am, 8hr; Transportes Bocatoreños: daily, 9am; 6hr); Guatemala City (Tica Bus: 3 daily, 6am, 7am & 12.30pm; 60hr); Managua, via Antigua, Nicaragua (King Quality: 1 daily, 3am; 8hr; Tica Bus: 3 daily, 6am, 7.30am, 12.30pm; 9hr; TransNica: 4 daily, 4am, 5am, 9am & noon; 9hr); Panama City (Panaline: 1 daily, 1pm; 15hr; Tica Bus: 2 daily, noon & 11pm; 15hr); San Salvador (King Quality: 1 daily, 3am; 54hr; Tica Bus: 3 daily, 6am, 7.30am & 12.30pm; 54hr); Tegucigalpa, Honduras (Tica Bus: 3 daily, 6am, 7.30am & 12.30pm; 48hr; King Quality: daily, 3am; 48hr).

GETTING AROUND

By bus The bus network, connecting central San José with virtually all of the city's suburbs, generally runs daily 5am–10pm. Most buses to San Pedro (labelled "Mall San Pedro") leave from Av Central, C 9/15, and those for Paseo

BUS COMPANIES

ATC C 12, Av 7/9 (☎2255 0567, ☎2255 4318 or ☎2255 4300).

Blanco Lobo C 12, Av 9/11 (☎2221 4214).

Empresas Alfaro Av 5, C 14/16 (☎2222 2666).

Empresarios Unidos C 16, Av 12 (☎2222 8231).

Hermanos Rodriguez Terminal Coca-Cola (☎2642 0219).

King Quality C 12, Av 3/5 (☎2258 8834, ⓦking-qualityca.com).

Lumaca C 13, Av 6/8 (☎2537 2320).

Mepe Gran Terminal del Caribe (☎2257 8129).

Metropoli Av 2, C 1/3 (☎2536 6052).

Microbuses Rapiditos Heredianos (MRA) C 1, Av 7/9 (☎2233 8392).

Panaline C 16, Av 3/5 (☎2256 8721).

Pulmitán C 24, Av 5/7 (☎2222 1650 or ☎2666 3818).

Station Wagon Av 2, north of Iglesia de la Merced (☎2441 1181).

Tica Bus C 9, Av 4 (☎2221 0006, ⓦticabus.com).

Tilarán C 12, Av 7/9 (☎2222 3854).

Tracopa Av 5, C 18/20 (☎2771 4214).

TransNica C 22, Av 3/5 (☎2223 4242, ⓦtransnica.com).

Transportes Caribeños Gran Terminal del Caribe (☎2221 2596).

Transportes Deldú Av 9, C 10/12 (☎2256 9072).

Transportes Jacó Terminal Coca-Cola (☎2223 1109).

Transportes Morales Terminal Coca-Cola (☎2223 5567).

Tuasa Av 2, C 12/14 (☎2222 5325).

TOUR OPERATORS IN SAN JOSÉ

San José is home to scores of **tour and activity operators**. Those listed here are experienced and reliable, and are all licensed (and regulated) by the ICT. Be wary of fly-by-night operations, of which there are many.

Costa Rica Expeditions C 0, Av 3 ☎ 2257 0766, ⓦ costaricaexpeditions.com. This US-based firm is the most established and experienced of the major tour operators, with an extensive range of tours catering to most budgets.

Ecole Travel C 7, Av 0/1 ☎ 2234 1669, ⓦ ecoletravel .com. Small agency, popular with budget travellers, offering two-night tours to Tortuguero (US$219), full-day rafting on Río Pacuare (US$85) and three-day Corcovado (US$289) tours, as well as day-trips for US$70–90.

Expediciones Tropicales ☎ 2257 4171, ⓦ costarica info.com. Another budget traveller favourite with knowledgeable guides, running the popular "combo" full day-tour of Volcán Poás, as well as day tours to Volcán Irazú, the Orosí Valley and Lankaster Gardens, Grecia and Sarchí and more.

Specops ☎ +1 941 346 2603, ⓦ specops.com. Adventure education group, comprising US Special Forces veterans and expert Costa Rican guides, specializing in white-knuckle thrills, jungle-survival courses and adventure film and photography.

2

Colón and Parque la Sabana (labelled "Sabana-Cementerio") from the bus shelters on Av 2, C 5/7. All buses have their routes clearly marked on their windshields, and usually the fare, too.

By taxi Licensed vehicles are red with a yellow triangle on the side, and have "SJP" licence plates. San José taxis are metered (ask the driver to *toca la maría, por favor*); it's illegal not to use a meter, though some drivers will claim that theirs is broken in an attempt to extract more money from you, in which case you negotiate the fare upfront. Short rides cost 1500–2500c, and about double that out to the suburbs. There's a 20 percent surcharge after 10pm.

INFORMATION

Tourist information There's a small tourist information stand by the luggage claims in the international airport. San José's tourist office (Mon–Fri 9am–5pm; ☎ 2299 5800, ⓦ visitcostarica.com), C 5, Av Central/2, has free maps and booklets detailing the (ever-changing) national bus schedule. They also hand out *San Jose Volando* (ⓦ sanjosevolando.com), a free monthly culture guide in English.

ACCOMMODATION

Reserve in advance in high season (Dec–May) and on holidays. Free wi-fi and/or internet, and laundry services, are offered at most hostels and guesthouses.

HOSTELS

Costa Rica Backpackers Av 6, C 21/23 ☎ 2221 6191 or ☎ 2223 2406, ⓦ costaricabackpackers.com; map p.116. Lively hostel with simple dorms and facilities including a restaurant and bar (happy hour 5–7pm), and rooms clustered around a garden with outdoor kitchen, hammocks and a pool. Pick-up from bus stations available. Dorm US$13, double US$32

Hostel Casa del Parque Av 3 at C 19 ☎ 2233 3437, ⓦ hostelcasadelparque.com; map p.116. Centrally located, next to the Parque Nacional, this Art Deco house has five spartan rooms and a dorm, an attractive courtyard for socializing and staff who treat you like old friends. Great café serving organic food, too. Dorm US$10, double US$34

Hostel Pangea Av 7, C 3/3b ☎ 2221 1992, ⓦ hostel pangea.com; map p.116. San José's party hostel boasts a pool, rooftop restaurant, bar and dance floor. As well as simple dorms, there are rooms with private or shared facilities and brand-new posh "suites" with plasma-screen TVs and king-sized beds. Walls are thin, though. Dorm US$14, double US$40

Hostel Toruma Av Central, C 29/31 ☎ 2234 8186, ⓦ hosteltoruma.com; map p.116. In a colonial building once home to a former Costa Rican president, this hostel is smarter than most, with high ceilings, tiled floors and a pool. The dorms are clean and the doubles have safes. No kitchen, but there's a small restaurant on site and the staff are very accommodating. Dorm US$13, double US$50

In & Basic Hostel Lounge Los Yoses; take a taxi and ask for 200m Sur y 75m Oeste del Spoon ☎ 2233 2693 or ☎ 2234 2998, ⓦ inandbasic.com; map pp.114–115. Secure and friendly hostel in the suburb of Los Yoses. Owners give plenty of travel advice, rates include all-you-can-eat pancake breakfast and common areas encourage socializing. Dorm US$14, double US$36

Mi Casa Hostel Sabana Norte, 150m north of ICE Building ☎ 2231 4700, ⓦ micasahostel.com; map pp.114–115. Close to Parque La Sabana, this chilled-out hostel with a homey vibe lives up to its name. The staff are wonderfully helpful, the vintage furnishings are a nice touch and you can linger in the garden with a cold beer from the on-site bar. Dorm US$13, double US$34

2

HOTELS AND B&BS

Hemingway Inn C 19, Av 9 ☎ 2221 1804, ⓦ hemingway inn.com; map p.116. Just north of the centre in the quiet Barrio Amón, this rambling 1920s guesthouse features seventeen individually decorated singles (US$35) and doubles (with safes), each named after a famous American author. Nice garden, too. **US$50**

Hotel Kekoldi Av 9, C 5/7 ☎ 2248 0804, ⓦ kekoldi.com; map p.116. Along the city's abandoned railroad tracks, this small, quiet lodge has simple rooms with shared or private baths, plus a kitchen, library, help with tours and car rental, and a lush patio garden with two pet ducks. Continental breakfast included. It can be hard to find: tell your taxi driver it's a *calle sin salida* (dead-end road). **US$80**

★ **Kap's Place** C 19, Av 11/13 ☎ 2221 1169, ⓦ kapsplace .com; map p.116. Run by Karla Arias (a bottomless source of information), this welcoming hotel has a range of colourful rooms of varying size and price, plus a kitchen, terrace and living room to relax in. Tours, table football, yoga and dance classes are available. Quiet time is 8pm–8am. **US$40**

EATING

Cosmopolitan San José has an excellent eating scene, running the gamut from swanky international restaurants to cheap Tico *sodas* and snack bars, with plenty of American fast-food branches as well. Be aware that in restaurants, the 23 percent tax tends to be added on top of the menu prices. At the Mercado Central you'll find lots of small *sodas* serving cheap and filling *ceviche*, *tamales*, *casados* and more. There are many American fast-food joints along Paseo Colón and at the food court at the San Pedro mall (see opposite). Good supermarkets include Más X Menos (Av 0, C 9/11; daily 8am–9pm; another branch in San Pedro on Av 0, 300m north of the church) and Pali (Paseo Colón, C 24/26; Mon–Thurs 8.30am–7pm, Fri & Sat 8.30am–8pm, Sun 8.30am–6pm).

Café 1930 *Gran Hotel Costa Rica, Av 2, C 3/5; map p.116.* The closest thing in San José to a European street café, with great coffee (from 1000c). While the food isn't cheap (upwards of 4000c), this is a good place to sit and watch the buskers and street performers in the Plaza de la Cultura. Daily 24hr.

Café Gokul Av Central, C 9/11; map p.116. Inside Teatro Giratables, this restaurant offers good vegetarian Indian cuisine, including tasty samosas, spicy paneer curries and creamy lassis. Mains around 3800c. Daily noon–9pm.

★ **Café Mundo** C 15, Av 9; map p.116. Italian-themed restaurant popular with expats, as much for the great location as their extensive wine list and decent pizza and pasta. The half-size portions of pasta (from 3000c) are a bargain, as is the daily lunch special (3700c). There's also a busy bar (attracting a largely gay clientele). Mains 4000–12,000c. Mon–Fri 11am–10.30pm, Sat 5pm–midnight.

Eco-Shakti Av 8, C 13; map p.116. Peaceful diner with a health-conscious slant: granola for breakfast, veg and fruit

★ TREAT YOURSELF

Donde Carlos San Pedro; ask the taxi driver to take you to 100 Norte de la Iglesia de Fátima ☎ 2225 0819, ⓦ dondecarlos.com; map pp.114–115. You'll smell the grilled meats long before you reach this unassuming-looking Argentine steakhouse. Expect white linen, professional service, and some of the best steaks in the city. Filet mignon, baby beef, tenderloin, ribeye and New York strip are all seared expertly to your specifications. Mains around 12,000c. Mon–Fri 12.30–3pm & 6.30–11pm, Sat noon–11pm, Sun noon–7pm.

juices, herbal teas and numerous veggie options (and fish dishes), as well as a good-value lunch menu (3800–4700c), featuring a soup, salad, vegetarian *casado* and drink. Mon–Fri 7am–7pm, Sat 8am–6pm.

The Grand Ma Av 1, C 3/5; map p.116. Images of palm leaves and the eponymous Grand Ma cover the windows outside, while inside you find tastes of the Caribbean coast (often elusive in the capital): the spicy chicken, rice and peas (from 2800c) is a good bet. Daily noon–9pm.

Nuestra Tierra Av 2, C 15; map p.116. Close to the National Museum, this well-loved Tico restaurant specializes in two things: a faux-rustic atmosphere and waiters straining under huge platters of *casados* and grilled meats. Mains 5000–11,000c. Daily noon–11pm.

Soda Tapia C 24, Av 2; map pp.114–115. A bright retro-style diner with a huge menu featuring everything from burgers and grilled sandwiches (from 1800c) to large helpings of *casados* and old-style ice-cream sundaes. Mon–Thurs 6am–2am, Fri & Sat 24hr, Sun 6am–midnight.

Tin-Jo C 11, Av 6/8; map p.116. Popular Chinese restaurant with an ambitious menu that includes Japanese, Vietnamese, Indian and Thai dishes as well as those from the mother country. Unsurprisingly, the Chinese dishes stand out: the hot and sour soup and the sizzling dishes are great and portions are very generous. Mains 5500–10,000c. Mon–Sat 11.30am–3pm & 5.30–10pm, Sun 11.30am–10pm.

Trigo Miel C 3, Av 0/1; map p.116. The best-stocked branch of the national bakery chain, with a front window filled with cream cakes. Slices of these, plus sandwiches, pastries and savoury snacks (400–1000c), can be eaten in or taken away. Daily 7am–6pm.

Vishnu Av 1, C 1/3; map p.116. There are no Indian dishes in sight, but this cheery vegetarian *soda* does serve healthy *platos del día*, soya burgers, salads, sandwiches and breakfast options. You can have a good feed for 2000–3500c.

DRINKING AND NIGHTLIFE

San José's nightlife is varied, with scores of bars. Some of the best are to be found in the neighbourhoods of Las Yoses and San Pedro – the latter geared towards the university population. Cover charges in clubs average around 3500c and often include a free drink; the action doesn't really kick off until after midnight. Incidentally, in San José, the term "nightclub" generally implies some form of erotic entertainment (prostitution being legal in Costa Rica), while a *discoteca* will be somewhere to dance (with your clothes on). Just so you know.

Chelle's Corner Av Central, C 9; map p.116. Dating back more than 100 years, *Chelle's* features wood-panelled walls, red leather seats and plenty of local colour. Beers from 1100c, *casados* to absorb the alcohol from 3000c. Daily 24hr.

Déjà Vu C 2, Av 14/16; map pp.114–115. One of the hottest gay clubs (drag night on Sat) in town, with two large dance floors of banging electronic music, as well as the more intimate *Sinners* bar. Take a taxi.

Ebony Centro Comercial El Pueblo; map pp.114–115. A young crowd fills *Ebony* to bump'n'grind to salsa, dancehall, hip-hop and reggaetón; Ladies' Night on Thurs is buzzing.

Jazz Café Av Central, San Pedro ⓦ jazzcafecostarica.com; map pp.114–115. The best place in San José to hear live jazz, blues and Latin, with an intimate atmosphere and consistently good acts. Music 10pm–2am; cover charge 2500–5500c.

El Morazán C 9, Av 3; map p.116. Classy bar next to Parque Morazán, attracting a trendy, arty clientele with its extensive cocktail list and occasional live music on weekends.

Salsa 54 y Zadidas C 3, Av 1/3; map p.116. Great *salsateca* playing a mix of salsa, merengue, cumbia and more. The dancers are seriously good, so if you've got two left feet, you'd better watch from the sidelines.

Stan's Irish Pub 150m west of the Casa Presidential, Zapote, just south of San Pedro; map pp.114–115. The owners have made a reasonable stab at creating a pub-style atmosphere (there's even a darts board), but the real draw is the range of more than sixty beers (around 1400c) including – of course – Guinness.

Vertigo Paseo Colón, Av 38/40 ⓦ vertigocr.com; map pp.114–115. Swanky European-style club with house, trance and techno keeping the vast dance floor – both local and international DJs – moving. Upstairs you can sink into a red sofa in the chill-out lounge.

ENTERTAINMENT

Josefinos love the theatre, and you often need a strong grasp of Spanish to follow the rapid, colloquial dialogue (though you can find some performances in English). Check the *Tico Times* for listings. Going to the cinema in San José is a bargain, with tickets costing around 2000–3200c.

Cinemas generally show subtitled versions of the latest American movies; the few that are dubbed will have the phrase "*hablado en Español*" in the newspaper listings or on the posters.

Cinema CCM (ⓦ ccmcinemas.com) in Mall San Pedro (Av 0, C 47) is a huge complex screening international films. Sala Garbo (Av 2, C 28, ⓦ salagarbocr.com) is a small venue with two screens showing foreign-language art-house movies.

Theatre Teatro Mélico Salazar, Av 2, C Central/2 (ⓣ 2233 5424, ⓦ teatromelic.gov.cr) draws great musical talents from Costa Rica and further abroad, along with ballet, theatre and dance performances. Teatro Nacional, Av 2, C 3/5 (ⓣ 2221 1329, ⓦ teatronacional.go.cr), is the most important theatre in the country, with productions ranging from Shakespeare, symphony orchestra and ballet to Chinese acrobatics and Latin American music.

SHOPPING

7th Street Books C 7, Av 0/1. New and used books, with English literature and a wide range of books on Costa Rica, as well as the best maps of the country. There's an excellent juice and smoothie café attached. Mon–Sat 9am–6pm, Sun 10am–5pm.

eÑe Av 7, C 13. Various Costa Rican designers, with quality clothing, jewellery, bags, and contemporary artwork for sale.

Galería Namu Av 7, C 5/7, ⓦ galerianamu.com. Fair-trade gallery stocking quality indigenous crafts and art from all over Costa Rica; come here for Corotega ceramics, Boruca devil masks, Huetar woodcarvings, woven Wounaan goods and more.

Mercado Nacional de Artesanía y Pintura C 22, Av 2 bis in the Plaza de la Democracia. Touristy street market featuring hats, T-shirts, Sarchí ox-carts, jewellery, woodwork, hammocks and fabrics. Daily 8am–6pm.

Plaza Esmerelda Pavas, in the city suburbs. Huge crafts co-operative where you can watch cigars being rolled, necklaces set and Sarchí ox-carts painted. Closed Sun.

DIRECTORY

Banks All currency exchange in San José is done at banks. There are numerous banks in the centre. Try Banco de Costa Rica, Av 2, C4/6; Banco Nacional, Av Central, C2/4; or ScotiaBank, C 5, Av 0/2 (Mon–Fri 8.30am–6.30pm, Sat 9am–1pm).

Embassies and consulates Canada, Oficentro Ejecutivo La Sabana, 3rd floor, Edificio 3, Sabana Sur (ⓣ 2242 4400); UK, 11th floor, Edificio Centro Colón, Paseo Colón, C 38/40 (ⓣ 2258 2025); US, opposite the Centro Comercial in Pavas, or Av 0, C 120 (ⓣ 2519 2000).

Health The main free public hospital is San Juan de Dios, Paseo Colón, C 14–16 (ⓣ 2257 6282). The private hospital, Clínica Biblica, Av 14/16, C 0/1 (ⓣ 2522 1000, emergencies

2522 1030), is open 24hr, with a pharmacy and English-speaking doctors. Farmacia Fischel has branches at Av 3, C 2 (Mon–Sat 7am–7pm, Sun 9am–5pm), and Av 2, C 5/7 (Mon–Fri 7am–8pm, Sat 8am–7pm, Sun 8am–6pm).

Internet If your accommodation doesn't offer free wi-fi or internet, try Café Digital, on the south side of Av Central (Av 0), halfway between C 5 and C 7.

Laundry Offered by most lodgings. Otherwise, try Lava Sol C 5, Av 9/11.

Post office The Correo Central is at C 2, Av 1/3.

The Valle Central and the Highlands

Despite its name – literally "Central Valley" – Costa Rica's **Valle Central** is actually an intermontane plateau poised at an elevation of between 3000 and 4000m. The area supports roughly two-thirds of Costa Rica's population, as well as its four most important cities – San José and the provincial capitals of **Alajuela**, **Heredia** and **Cartago**, though none warrants more than a flying visit. Beyond the cities it's a largely agricultural region, with green coffee terraces shadowed by the surrounding mountains, many of which are volcanoes. These volcanoes, especially **Irazú** and **Poás** and the national parks around them, are the chief attractions, but there's also excellent **whitewater rafting** near **Turrialba**, and the **Monumento Nacional Guayabo**, the country's most important archeological site.

Most people use San José as a base for forays into the Valle Central. If you do want to get out of the city and stay in the Valle Central, the nicest places are the **lodges** scattered throughout the countryside.

ALAJUELA

With a population of just over 46,000, **ALAJUELA** is Costa Rica's second-largest city; it's also close to the airport and just thirty minutes from downtown San José.

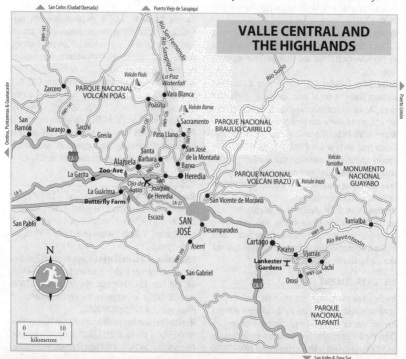

VALLE CENTRAL AND THE HIGHLANDS

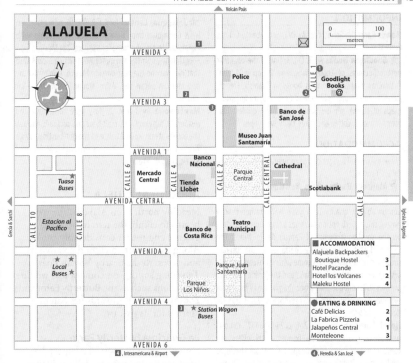

ALAJUELA

2

For the most part, it's a hot urban sprawl, but it's a handy place to stay overnight if you're flying in late or flying out early. You can also use it as a base for visiting some of the surrounding sights, though those can just as easily be visited from San José.

WHAT TO SEE AND DO

The city's few attractions are close to the **Parque Central**. The most impressive sight is the sturdy-looking former jail, Av 3, C 0/2, which houses the **Museo Juan Santamaría** (Tues–Sat 10am–5pm; ⓦmuseojuansantamaria.go.cr). Dedicated to Alajuela's most cherished historical figure – drummer-boy-cum-martyr Juan Santamaría, who sacrificed his life to save the country from American adventurer William Walker in 1856 – the museum's curiously monastic atmosphere is almost more interesting than the small collection itself, which runs the gamut from mid-nineteenth-century maps to crumbly portraits of figures involved in the battle of 1856. Three blocks south of the

museum is a small **plaza** also named after Santamaría, decked out with murals. On the east side of the Parque Central is the **cathedral**, the final resting place of two of Costa Rica's presidents, which was badly damaged in the 1991 earthquake.

ARRIVAL AND DEPARTURE

By plane Juan Santamaría International Airport is less than 3km from the city. Many hotels and hostels will arrange a free pick-up with notice; otherwise take a bus from outside the airport or a taxi (US$7–9).

By bus Most small terminals are in the streets southwest of the Mercado Central and there are two Tuasa bus terminals across the street from each other.

Destinations Butterfly Farm (Av 2 at C 8: hourly 8.30am–7.30pm; 30min); Heredia (C 8, Av Central/1: every 15min 5am–10pm; 20min); Sabanilla, for Doka Coffee Farm (C 10, Av 2/Central: Mon–Fri every 30min 6am–5.30pm; 20min); San José (Tuasa West: C 8, Av Central/1; every 10min 5am–11pm; 45min, via the airport; Station Wagon: Av 4, C 2/4; every 10min 4am–midnight; 45min); Sarchí (C 8, Av Central/1: every 30min from 5am–10pm; 30min); Volcán Poás (Tuasa West: C 8, Av Central/1; 9.15am; 1hr 15min); Zoo-Ave (frequent; 15min).

2

INFORMATION

Banks Banco Nacional, C 2, Av 0/1; Scotiabank, C 1, Av Central.

★ **Goodlight Books** Av 3, C 1/3. One of the country's best collections of English-language fiction and non-fiction, as well as numerous books in Spanish, French, German and Italian, plus maps (including rudimentary maps of town), phrase books and travel guides. Plus internet access, coffee and cakes. Daily 9am–6pm.

ACCOMMODATION

There are several budget digs of comparable quality along Av 3, C Central/2.

★ **Alajuela Backpackers Boutique Hostel** Av 4 at C 4 ☎ 2441 7149, ⍟ alajuelabackpackers.com. Comparable in quality to a good hotel rather than a hostel, this superb option occupies a four-storey building on the southwest corner of Parque de los Niños. The secure dorms have private bathrooms, the private singles, doubles and triples come with ultra-comfortable orthopaedic mattresses and a/c, and the junior suites are plusher still. Collapse onto a beanbag in the TV lounge or socialize in the upstairs bar. Exemplary. Dorm US$15, double US$54

Hotel Pacande Av 5, C 2/4 ☎ 2443 8481, ⍟ hotel pacande.com. This Tico-run budget hotel offers ten compact private rooms (the cheapest with shared bath), as well as more stylish ones with private facilities, TV and dark wood furnishings (though most lack natural light). Staff are welcoming and rates include breakfast. US$30

Hotel los Volcanes Av 3, C Central/2 ☎ 2441 0525, ⍟ hotellosvolcanes.com. Refurbished, rambling 1920s house with spacious, wood-panelled, somewhat musty rooms and an attractive garden and open-air kitchen out back. Free drop-off at the airport. US$35

Maleku Hostel 50m west of the main entrance of the new hospital ☎ 2430 4304, ⍟ malekuhostel.com. This small and cheerful family home is one of the best budget options in town: compact dorms and private rooms (shared baths) are immaculate, and there's lots of useful travel advice, as well as free breakfast, internet and airport drop-off. Dorm US$15, double US$38

EATING AND DRINKING

Café Delicias Av 3 at C 1. A sweet little café, with Café Britt coffee (from 800c), tempting cheesecakes and pineapple pastries (750–1350c), sandwiches and light meals. There's another branch on the corner of C 9 and Av 6. Mon–Sat 8am–8pm.

La Fabrica Pizzeria Plaza Real. The thin-crust pizzas, baked in a wood-fired oven at this informal restaurant, are excellent value and delicious. Veggie-lovers shouldn't miss the spinach pizza. Mains from 4000c. Daily noon–9pm.

★ **Jalapeños Central** Av 5, C 2. This friendly place, run by a Colombian from New York, gets packed out with expats and locals who come for the excellent Mexican food – enchiladas, burritos and guacamole, with a *sopa Azteca* that just may be the best outside Mexico. Don't miss the non-Mexican pecan pie. Mains around 3500c. Mon–Sat 11.30am–9pm.

Monteleone Av 3 at C 2. Busy little corner bar and restaurant, famous for its craft beer and cocktails, though the food – steaks, grilled fish, and the gut-busting *chifrijo Tico* – is well worth a visit in its own right. Mains from 3500c. Daily 4–11pm.

AROUND ALAJUELA

Heading **north** from Alajuela, the road begins to climb, the terrain becomes greener and the air considerably cooler. Along this ascent you'll find great vistas and access to the nearby Volcán Poás. Travelling **south**, you come across wildlife attractions such as the **Butterfly Farm** and **Zoo-Ave**, while westwards lies Sarchí, famous for its ox-cart.

La Guácima Butterfly Farm

Some 12km southwest of Alajuela, **La Guácima Butterfly Farm** (daily 8.30am–5pm; 2hr tours 8.30am, 11am, 1pm & 3pm; US$20; ⍟ butterflyfarm.co.cr) breeds valuable pupae for zoos and botanical gardens all over the world. The farm also has beautiful views over the Valle Central. Butterflies are most active early in the day, and thousands of them fluttering about like colourful tornadoes is a glorious sight. Afternoons are better for photographing them, as they are more sedate. In the wet season, arrive early, as the rain forces the butterflies to hide.

Many lodgings in San José organize **tours** here, and buses from San José (40min) leave every hour from C 8, Av 2/4, returning at 8.25am, 12.25pm, 3.25pm and 5.25pm; you can also get here from Alajuela (see p.122).

Zoo-Ave

The well-run animal park, **Zoo-Ave** (daily 9am–5pm; US$20; ⍟ zooavecostarica .org), 10km west of Alajuela in La Garita, is an excellent introduction to more than 115 species of Costa Rican birds, including macaws. Besides the aviary, there's a zoo featuring mostly rescued animals, including monkeys, reptiles and cats, and an animal-breeding centre that aims to reintroduce rehabilitated animals into the wild.

Buses run to Zoo-Ave from Alajuela (see p.122); to go back, flag down an Alajuela bus on the main road where you arrived.

Sarchí

Touted as the centre of Costa Rican arts and crafts, the commercialized village of **SARCHÍ**, 30km northwest of Alajuela, has a pretty setting. The most famous item produced here is the **Sarchí ox-cart**, a kaleidoscopically painted square cart of Moorish origin; you can check out what is allegedly the world's largest ox-cart in Sarchí Norte, the heart of this spread-out village, and buy small models of it.

Large *fábricas* (workshops*)* line the main road from **Sarchí Sur**, separated from **Sarchí Norte** by the river.

ARRIVAL AND DEPARTURE

By bus Buses run to Sarchí from Alajuela (see p.122), with buses back (via Grecia) leaving from Sarchí Norte. Buses to San José run every 30min 5am–10pm.

EATING

Las Carretas Sarchí Sur, next to the Fábrica de Carretas Joaquín Chavarrí. Locally famous restaurant, popular for its *comida típica* and its Sunday buffet (6500c).

PARQUE NACIONAL VOLCÁN POÁS

PARQUE NACIONAL VOLCÁN POÁS (daily 8am–4pm; US$10), 55km from San José and 37km north of Alajuela, is one of the most easily accessible active volcanoes in the world. Its history of eruptions dates back eleven million years – the last gigantic blowout was on January 25, 1910, when it dumped 640,000 tonnes of ash on the surrounding area – and the last bit of minor activity in 1995 resulted in brief closure of the park. The best time to visit is early in the morning, before the mists sweep in and obscure the view (from as early as 10am). Since tour buses don't arrive until after 10am, it's worth renting a car to get out here. Due to the

altitude, it tends to be cold and rain is not uncommon, so dress appropriately.

WHAT TO SEE AND DO

Poás (2704m) has blasted out three craters in its lifetime, and due to more or less constant activity, the appearance of the **main crater** is subject to change – it's 1300m wide and filled with milky turquoise water from which sulphurous gases waft.

Park trails

The park has several well-maintained, short and unchallenging **trails**, which take you through an otherworldly landscape, dotted with smoking fumaroles and tough ferns and trees trying valiantly to hold up against regular sulphurous scaldings.

The paved **Crater Overlook** trail (750m; 15min) winds its way from the visitors' centre to the main crater, along a paved road. Side-trail **Sendero Botos** (1.4km; 30min) heads up through the forest to the pretty, emerald Botos Lake, which fills an extinct crater and makes a good spot for a picnic. Named for the pagoda-like tree commonly seen along its way, the **Escalonia** trail (about 1km; 30min) starts at the picnic area (follow the signs), then takes you through the forest, where the ground cover is less stunted compared to that at the crater, back to the visitor car park.

Wildlife-watching

A wide variety of **birds** plies this temperate forest, among them the ostentatiously colourful quetzal, robins and several species of hummingbird. Although a number of large mammals live in the park, including coyotes and wildcats, you'll be very lucky to spot them. The small, green-yellow **Poás squirrel**, endemic to the area, is far more common.

Poás is also home to a rare version of cloudforest called dwarf or **stunted cloudforest**, a combination of pine-needle-like ferns, miniature bonsai-type trees and bromeliad-encrusted cover, all of which has been stunted by an

2

onslaught of cold, continual cloud cover and acid rain from the mouth of the volcano.

ARRIVAL AND DEPARTURE

By bus A daily Tuasa bus leaves San José at 8.30am from Av 2, C 12/14, calling at Alajuela at 9.15am (1hr 30min–2hr). It returns at 2.30pm. Most buses stop at one of the many roadside restaurants.

By taxi To reach Poás before both buses and clouds, drive or take a taxi from Alajuela (roughly US$40) or San José (around US$60).

INFORMATION AND TOURS

Tourist information The visitors' centre, next to the car park at the entrance, has a thorough display on the park's fauna and flora, a trail map, bathrooms and cafeteria.

Tours Many visitors come on tours (see box, p.119) from San José (approximately US$55/person for a 4–5hr trip).

HEREDIA

Just 11km northeast of San José is the lively town of **HEREDIA**, boosted by the student population of the Universidad Nacional (UNA) at the eastern end of town. The centre has a few historical buildings worth visiting, and can also be used as a base for trips to Volcán Barva and Braulio Carillo National Park, though the latter can just as easily be visited from San José.

WHAT TO SEE AND DO

Heredia is centred on the quiet **Parque Central**, draped with huge mango trees and overlooked by the plain **Basílica de la Inmaculada Concepción**, whose unexcitingly squat design – "seismic Baroque" – has kept it standing since 1797, despite several earthquakes. North of the plaza, the old Spanish tower of **El Fortín**, "the Fortress", features odd gun slats which fan out and widen from the inside to the exterior, giving it a medieval look; you cannot enter or climb it.

East of the tower on Avenida Central is the **Casa de la Cultura**, a well-maintained colonial house featuring permanent historical displays

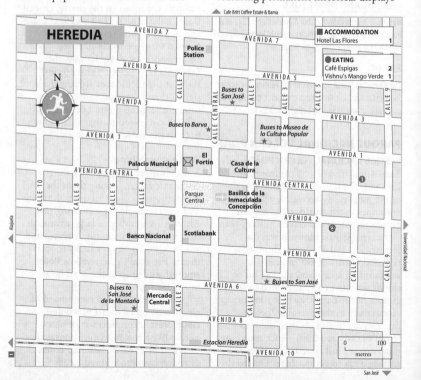

Cafe Britt Coffee Estate & Barva

HEREDIA

N

AVENIDA 7
AVENIDA 7
Police Station
AVENIDA 5
AVENIDA 5
Buses to San José
AVENIDA 3
AVENIDA 3
Buses to Barva
Buses to Museo de la Cultura Popular
El Fortín
AVENIDA 1
Palacio Municipal
Casa de la Cultura
AVENIDA CENTRAL
AVENIDA CENTRAL
Parque Central
Basílica de la Inmaculada Concepción
AVENIDA 2
Banco Nacional
Scotiabank
AVENIDA 4
Buses to San José
AVENIDA 6
Buses to San José de la Montaña
Mercado Central
AVENIDA 8
Estación Heredia
AVENIDA 10

CALLE CENTRAL, CALLE 2, CALLE 1, CALLE 3, CALLE 5, CALLE 9
CALLE 10, CALLE 8, CALLE 6, CALLE 4, CALLE 7

Alajuela
Universidad Nacional

■ ACCOMMODATION
Hotel Las Flores 1

● EATING
Café Espigas 2
Vishnu's Mango Verde 1

0   100
metres

San José

as well as local paintings and sculpture (opening hours vary).

ARRIVAL AND DEPARTURE

By bus Buses arrive and depart from bus stops in the southern part of town, mostly near the Mercado Central. Destinations Alajuela (every 15min 6am–10pm); Paso Llano for Volcán Barva and PN Braulio Carrillo (Transportes del Norte, southern side of the Mercado Central: Mon–Fri 4.50am, 6.15am, 7.40am, 1pm & 5pm; 1hr 15min); San José (Av 8, a block southeast of the market: every 30min 4.40am–11pm; 45min).

ACCOMMODATION AND EATING

There is little point in staying in Heredia, given San José's proximity and superior facilities. There are, however, a couple of good accommodation and dining options in the centre.

Café Espigas C 2, Av 2, southwest corner of the Parque Central. Serving meal combos that include *pintos* (3000c), *casados* (3350c), sandwiches and burgers, this café specializes in Britt Finca coffee (from 700c). Daily 7am–9pm.

Hotel Las Flores Av 12, C 12/14 ☎2261 8147, ⓦhotel-lasflores.com. A 10min walk from the centre, *Las Flores* is Heredia's best option, offering green-hued doubles with private baths, TV and small balconies (though no views). Staff are cheerful and there's a small *soda* downstairs. US$35

Vishnu's Mango Verde C 7, Av Central/1. Bright and bustling vegetarian *soda* with inexpensive salads, sandwiches and pastas (1500–3000c), as well as juices and smoothies. Mon–Sat 8am–7pm.

PARQUE NACIONAL BRAULIO CARRILLO AND VOLCÁN BARVA

The little-visited **PARQUE NACIONAL BRAULIO CARRILLO** (daily 7am–4pm; US$10), 35km northeast of San José, covers 325 square kilometres of virgin rain- and cloudforest. The growth here gives you a good idea of what much of Costa Rica used to look like fifty years ago, when approximately three-quarters of the country was virgin rainforest.

This part of the country receives a lot of **rainfall**, so come prepared for precipitation and some serious mud even during the "dry" season (Jan–April).

The trails

A rather challenging trail ascends the dormant **Volcán Barva** from the Barva ranger station through dense deciduous cover before reaching the cloudforest at the top. It takes around three hours to reach the top, but you're rewarded by great views, with two attractive lagoons at the volcano's summit. The straightforward **Sendero La Botella** (2.8km) rambles past several small waterfalls from Quebrada González ranger station, while from Zurquí you can either enjoy a gentle hike along the **Sendero Histórico**, which follows Río Hondura to its meeting point with Río Sucio, or else do a short, steep 1km hike to a *mirador*.

ARRIVAL AND DEPARTURE

The Barva ranger station can be accessed from Heredia via Paso Llano, and the village of Sacramento, 4km from the entrance, is accessible by bus from Heredia, but there's no public transport beyond here. A 4WD is necessary to drive the rest of the way, or else you have to walk in. While you can easily get dropped off at either the Zurquí or the Quebrada Gonzáles ranger stations along Hwy 32 by any bus passing between San José and Guápiles, it might be difficult to catch a ride on the way back.

INFORMATION

Ranger stations The park has five staffed ranger stations, the three main ones being Barva (southwestern entrance), Zurquí (southern entrance) and Quebrada González (northeast entrance). The Volcán Barva climb is accessed via the Barva ranger station (☎2266 1883; US$10; 7am–4pm). These three have parking (don't leave valuables in the car), picnic areas and well-marked trails around them.

Hikes Register at the ranger stations before setting off, and try to arrange a guide for longer hikes, as there have been some incidents of robbery.

Accommodation and eating there are basic huts and camping facilities (US$3) available, but you need to bring your own drinking water.

CARTAGO

CARTAGO, meaning "Carthage", was Costa Rica's capital for three hundred years before the centre of power was moved to San José in 1823. Founded in 1563 by Juan Vázquez de Coronado, the city, like its ancient namesake, has been razed a number of times, although in this case by **earthquakes** rather than Romans – two, in 1823 and 1910, practically demolished the place.

2

WHAT TO SEE AND DO

For the most part, the city is an unattractive, congested concrete sprawl, rebuilt after the last major earthquake with little concern for aesthetics, but is worth a quick stop to visit the **Basílica de Nuestra Señora de Los Angeles**, particularly in August.

Basílica de Nuestra Señora de Los Angeles

Cartago's highlight is the **Basílica de Nuestra Señora de Los Angeles**, C 16 and Av 2, dating back to 1635 and rebuilt in a decorative Byzantine style after the original was destroyed in an earthquake in 1926. Millions of Costa Ricans make an annual pilgrimage here on August 2 to honour the statue of **La Negrita** (or the Black Virgin), the nation's patron saint since 1824. La Negrita is a representation of the Virgin Mary, allegedly found on this spot by a native woman in 1635; legend has it that when the woman tried to take the statuette with her, it reappeared in the spot where it was found. A shrine was built on the spot, where she now resides on a gilded perch at the main altar.

Iglesia de la Parroquía

From the basilica it's a five-minute walk west to Cartago's other attraction – the

Iglesia de la Parroquía (known as "Las Ruinas"), which sits on the eastern end of the concrete Parque Central. Built in 1575, the church was repeatedly destroyed by earthquakes, but stubbornly rebuilt by the Cartagoans each time, until the giant earthquake of 1910 finally vanquished it. Only the elegantly tumbling walls remain, enclosing pretty subtropical gardens. The ruins are not open to the public, but can be viewed from the Parque Central.

ARRIVAL AND DEPARTURE

By bus Buses arrive and depart from various stops around town.

Destinations San José (every 10min 5am–midnight; 45min), from the bus station just north of the central market and from Av 4/6, C 2/4; Turrialba (hourly Mon–Fri 6am–10pm; 5 daily Sat & Sun; 1hr 30min), from the corner of C 8 and Av 3; Volcán Irazú (daily 8.30am, returning 12.30pm; 1hr).

ACCOMMODATION AND EATING

Lodgings in Cartago are limited, and unless you wish to be here for the annual pilgrimage, it's best to visit the city as a day-trip from San José.

Hotel Dinastia C 3, Av 6/8, 100m north of the central market ☎2551 7057. Friendly hotel offering clean, spartan rooms with private baths; look at a few, as not all have natural light. **US$30**

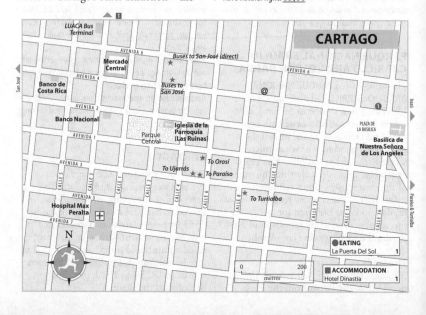

CARTAGO

LUACA Bus Terminal

AVENIDA 6

Mercado Central

Buses to San José (direct)

Buses to San José

San José

Banco de Costa Rica

AVENIDA 4

AVENIDA 6

AVENIDA 2

Banco Nacional

@

AVENIDA 1

Parque Central

Iglesia de la Parroquía (Las Ruinas)

PLAZA DE LA BASÍLICA

Basílica de Nuestra Señora de Los Angeles

Irazú

AVENIDA 3

To Orosí

To Ujarrás

To Paraíso

CALLE 10

Paraíso & Turrialba

AVENIDA 5

To Turrialba

CALLE 12

CALLE 14

CALLE 16

Hospital Max Peralta

CALLE 3

CALLE 1

CALLE 2

CALLE 4

CALLE 6

CALLE 8

AVENIDA 7

N

0   200
metres

● EATING
La Puerta Del Sol   1

■ ACCOMMODATION
Hotel Dinastia   1

A TOUR OF THE VALLE DE OROSÍ

If anything is worth renting a car for, then it's got to be a day-trip around the lovely river valley of **Orosí**, a 60km scenic loop complete with coffee plantations, fabulous mountain vistas, a remote national park, Costa Rica's largest dam and man-made lake and quite possibly the best botanical gardens you'll see anywhere. The road begins in the village of **Paraíso**, 8km south of Cartago. On the way, 3km before you reach Paraíso, it's well worth stopping off at the **Lankester Gardens** (daily 8.30am–4.30pm; US$7; ☎2511 7939, ⊛jbl.ucr.ac.cr) – home to more than 1100 species of orchids, best seen during the dry months of March and April. Orchids aside, there are plenty of other tropical species and a sculpted Japanese garden.

Heading south from Paraíso, you pass through **Orosí**, with a particularly photogenic 1743 church that survived Costa Rica's umpteen earthquakes. Five kilometres before Orosí, stop at the **Miradór Orosí** (daily 8am–5pm) for the splendid views.

From Orosí, the road runs south for another 10km or so, arriving at **Parque Nacional Tapantí** (daily 8am–4pm, US$10), Costa Rica's wettest national park, with the Cerro de la Muerte (Mountain of Death) looming above it. The park is home to more than 300 bird species, some of which you'll see if you hike the three trails, the longest of which is a rugged 2km.

Doubling back to Orosí, take the road that runs parallel to the Río Orosí and curves around the **Lago de Cachí**, the man-made lake created by the massive Cachí Dam.

Once you pass through the village of Ujarrás, you can double back to Paraíso. Though not technically part of the Orosí loop, it is well worth taking the road towards Turrialba for 2km until you reach **Finca Cristina** (☎2574 6426, ⊛cafecristina.com), an organic coffee farm where you can pick up freshly roasted beans.

EATING

La Casona del Cafetal 2km north of the Cachí dam, ⊛lacasonadelcafetal.com This restaurant on a coffee plantation is a worthy lunch stop, with a lavish Sunday buffet and coffee flan for dessert. Daily 11am–6pm.

La Puerta Del Sol Av 4, between C14/16, across from the basilica. Popular restaurant with cosy booths serving a wide range of Tico breakfast options (around 2000c), burgers and sandwiches (1500–2700c), and *casados* (from 3100c). Sun–Thurs 8am–10pm, Fri & Sat 8am–midnight.

PARQUE NACIONAL VOLCÁN IRAZÚ

Some 19km northeast of Cartago, **PARQUE NACIONAL VOLCÁN IRAZÚ** (daily 8am–4pm; US$10) makes for a long, but scenic, trip from the city. The park's blasted-out lunar landscape is dramatic, and Volcán Irazú, its centrepoint, is the tallest and largest active volcano in the country (3432m). The main crater, 1050m in diameter and 300m deep, is flanked by two smaller craters: the inactive Diego de la Haya is creepily impressive, its deep depression filled with a strange green lake, while the smallest crater, Playa Hermosa, is slowly being taken over by vegetation. From the viewpoint there are fantastic views to the Caribbean on clear days. Two marked **trails** lead to the crater from the entrance, where you'll find the ranger's booth.

ARRIVAL AND INFORMATION

By bus A daily bus runs to the park from the *Gran Hotel Costa Rica* in San José (daily at 8am) – be there early in high season to get a seat – picking up passengers at Las Ruinas in Cartago around 8.30am; it arrives as Irazú at around 10am and leaves for San José at 12.30pm.

Tours Tours to the volcano (around US$45–60) can be arranged by a number of San José operators (see box, p.119).

Visitors' centre The park has a visitors' centre with information, toilets and a snack bar.

TURRIALBA

The pleasant agricultural town of **TURRIALBA**, 45km east of Cartago on the eastern slopes of the Cordillera Central, has sweeping views over the rugged eastern Talamancas and is Costa Rica's **whitewater rafting** central, with world-class rapids on the nearby Río Reventazón and Río Pacuare (see box, p.130). Enjoy the Valle Central rivers while you can, as both are under threat of damming.

ARRIVAL AND DEPARTURE

By bus The bus terminal is at the western entrance of town, off Hwy 10.

2

WHITEWATER RAFTING IN THE VALLE CENTRAL

The two main rivers for whitewater rafting in the Turrialba area are Río Reventazón and Río Pacuare. While Costa Rica Expeditions and Expediciones Tropicales (see box, p.119) both offer rafting day-trips from San José, you spend a lot of time in transit and it's cheaper to arrange rafting excursions in Turrialba itself.

Río Reventazón The main river for rafting, with water levels pretty much constant year-round due to water releases from the dam (barring Sundays) and the biggest rafting challenges in Costa Rica. There are roughly four rafting sections to this river: El Carmen (Class II float for complete novices), Florida (Class III, scenic float with some whitewater action), Pascua (Class IV – 15 thrilling rapids that can be tackled by both novices and professionals) and Peralta (Class V – challenging and for pros only; not always available due to safety issues).

Río Pacuare The Lower Pacuare (Class II–IV) offers a particularly scenic stretch with a good mix of easy floats and challenging rapids. The scenery along the Upper Pacuare is just as gorgeous, though with its Class III–IV runs, you'll be keeping most of your attention on the water. The Pacuare is best rafted between June and October; between October and December, when the water is highest, some Class IV runs become Class V runs – for advanced rafters only.

Destinations Cartago (9–10 daily; 1hr 20min); San José via Cartago (every 45min, 5am–6.30pm; 2hr); Siquirres, for transfers to Puerto Limón (9 daily 6am–6pm; 1hr 45min).

ACCOMMODATION

Casa de Lis Hostel Av Central near C 2 ☎ 2556 4933, ⓦ hostelcasadelis.com. Small, super-central hostel with volcano views from the roof terrace, bright, spotless rooms and a tranquil vibe. Book ahead, as it fills up quickly. Dorm US$10, double US$25

Hotel Interamericano Av 1 near C 1 ☎ 2556 0142, ⓦ hotelinteramericano.com. Experienced and novice rafters alike gravitate towards this basic hotel south of the old train tracks, with inexpensive basic singles (from US$12), doubles, triples and quads on offer. Bilingual Luis can help you organize your wet'n'wild adventure. US$22

Turrialba B&B C 1, half a block north of the main square ☎ 2556 6651. Wonderfully friendly B&B with large, tiled en-suite a/c rooms, a cavernous dining area, an excellent book exchange and a jacuzzi on the patio bedecked with lush greenery. US$60

EATING AND DRINKING

La Kasbah In front of the bus terminal. Excellent Turkish dishes – the grilled meats and anything with aubergine stand out – accompanied by some of the best music in town. The bar gets very lively and DJs take over after 10pm. Thurs–Sat 6.30pm–late.

Panaderia La Castellana Av 4 at C 2. Inexpensive Tico specials and pizza by the slice around the clock, as well as pastries and desserts, and some dishes available in half portions. Mains around 4000c. Daily 24hr.

Wok'n'Roll C 1, opposite *Turrialba B&B*. Bright, Chinese-run diner serving palatable sushi, though what they do best are the Chinese noodle and rice dishes. You can't go wrong with the Singapore-style fried noodles (3500c). Daily noon–10pm.

MONUMENTO NACIONAL ARQUEOLÓGICO GUAYABO

Costa Rica's most important archeological site, the **MONUMENTO NACIONAL ARQUEOLÓGICO GUAYABO** (daily 8am–4pm; US$8) lies 19km northeast of Turrialba. Guayabo belongs to the archeological-cultural area known as **Intermedio**, which begins roughly in the province of Alajuela and extends to Venezuela, Colombia and parts of Ecuador. Archeologists believe that Guayabo was inhabited from about 1000 BC to 1400 AD by around twenty thousand people; in 1400 AD the city was mysteriously abandoned and never found by the conquering Spanish; its remains were only found in 1968. Visually, the site is not terribly impressive; what you see are stone residential mounds, some petroglyphs, an aqueduct and cisterns that technically still function after centuries of disuse. At the **visitor centre** you can see a model of what the city may have looked like.

ARRIVAL AND DEPARTURE

By bus Buses run to Guayabo from Turrialba from 100m south of the main bus terminal (Mon–Sat 3 daily, 11.15am, 3.10pm & 5.20pm, returning at 5.15am, 7am, 12.30pm & 4pm; Sun 3 daily, 9am, 3pm & 6.30pm, returning 7am, 12.30pm & 4pm; 1hr), though the inconvenient timetable means you either have not enough or too much time at the site.

By car Driving from Turrialba takes about 30min. The last 3km is on a bad gravel road – 4WD recommended. Taxis charge around US$20 from Turrialba.

Limón Province and the Caribbean coast

Sparsely populated **Limón Province** sweeps south in an arc from Nicaragua down to Panama. Hemmed in to the north by dense jungles and swampy waterways, to the west by the mighty Cordillera Central and to the south by the even wider girth of the Cordillera Talamanca, the region has a Caribbean feel. This is largely due to the presence of the descendants of former Jamaican slaves and Panamanian and Colombian turtle hunters, and their unique creole – **Mekatelyu** – is still spoken today.

Limón holds much appeal for ecotourists, having the highest proportion of protected land in the country. At **Tortuguero** you can watch giant sea turtles lay their eggs, while at **Cahuita** and **Manzanillo** you can snorkel coral reefs and surf at **Puerto Viejo**. In addition, more than anywhere else in Costa Rica, the Caribbean coast exudes a sense of **cultural diversity**: besides the Afro-Caribbean population, the coast is home to communities of several indigenous peoples from the **Bribrí**, **Kèköldi** and **Cabécar** groups. Visits to their communities are some of the most interesting experiences you may have in Costa Rica.

Limón province sees a lot of **rain** throughout the year – less so in February/ March and September/ October, but be prepared nonetheless.

GETTING AROUND

Getting around northern Limón Province requires patience. While from Puerto Limón to the Panama border at Sixaola there is one main road, regularly plied by buses, north of Puerto Limón there is no public land transport at all: instead, private *lanchas* ply the coastal canals connecting Moín, 8km north of Puerto Limón, to Tortuguero and Río Colorado near the Nicaraguan border. Regular boat transfers also run to Tortuguero from Cariari, a banana town reachable from Guápiles, en route to Puerto Limón. There are also daily flights in tiny planes from San José to Tortuguero.

PUERTO LIMÓN

PUERTO LIMÓN, 165km east of San José, is Costa Rica's main port, with brightly painted houses, a somewhat neglected air and a reputation as Central America's prime drug-trafficking gateway. Police presence has been beefed up here over the last few years, which has led to a slight decrease in the crime rate, but you should still watch your back – mugging and pickpocketing are not uncommon, though most crime does not affect visitors. It's possible to bypass Limón altogether – there are direct buses from San José to Cahuita and Puerto Viejo, with **boats** to Tortuguero from Moín easily organized from Cahuita – but if you're travelling to Tortuguero independently, you may wish to stay in Limón overnight, especially if you coincide with **El Día de la Raza** (see box below).

WHAT TO SEE AND DO

Limón's palm-shaded **Parque Vargas**, by the *malecón* (sea wall), has a certain appeal. The partly pedestrianized **Avenida 2**, known locally as the "market street", is the main drag, touching the north edge of Parque Vargas, at the easternmost end

CARNAVAL IN LIMÓN

Though in the rest of the Americas **Carnaval** is usually associated with the days before Lent, Limón takes Columbus's arrival in the New World – October 12 – as its point of celebration. **El Día de la Raza** (Columbus Day), celebrating Columbus' landing on Isla Uvita, is basically an excuse to party.

The carnival features a variety of events, from Afro-Caribbean dance to Calypso music, bull-running, children's theatre, colourful *desfiles* (parades) and firework displays. Most spectacular is the **Gran Desfile**, usually held on the Saturday before October 12, when revellers in Afro-Caribbean costumes parade through the streets. This is the most popular time of year to visit Limón, so book rooms well in advance.

2

PUERTO LIMÓN

PORTETE & PLAYA BONITA

Isla Uvita

Puerto Limón

PORTETE

Playa Bonita

Main Docks

Tortuguero Canal

Lanchas to Tortuguero

Moín

0 — 2 kilometres

ACCOMMODATION
Hotel Acón   2
Hotel Playa Bonita   1

EATING
Kalisi   2
Soda Bío Bío Natura   1

N

CARIBBEAN SEA

0 — 100 metres

Malecón (Sea Wall)

Scotiabank

Supermarket

BAC Bank

Mercado Central

Police

Museo Ethnohistoric

Cathedral

Baseball Field

Buses to Moín

Bus Terminal

Town Hall

Mural

Parque Vargas

Banco de Costa Rica

Coopelimón Buses to San José

Docks

Buses to Cahuita, Puerto Viejo & Sixaola

AVENIDA 6
AVENIDA 5
AVENIDA 4
AVENIDA 3
AVENIDA 2
AVENIDA 1

CALLE 1
CALLE 2
CALLE 3
CALLE 4
CALLE 5
CALLE 6
CALLE 7
CALLE 8
CALLE 9

Hospital & Moín (See inset)

Buses to San José & Moín

cahuita, Puerto Viejo & San José

of C 1 and Av 1/2, and the south side of the **Mercado Central**; you can pick up CDs of local reggaetón bands from vendors along the street. The aptly named **Playa Bonita**, 4km northwest of town, is an attractive stretch of sand.

ARRIVAL AND DEPARTURE

By boat Regular (dry season) boats run between Tortuguero and the dock at Moín, 7km northwest of town. Moín is served by Tracasa buses (see below); taxis cost around US$7.

By bus Transportes Caribeños services from San José, Moín and Guápiles arrive at the Gran Terminal del Caribe at Av 1, C 7/8. Arrivals from the south – Cahuita, Puerto Viejo and Panama (via Sixaola) – terminate at the Transportes Mepe Terminal at C 6, between Av 1 & 2, on the east side of the stadium.

Destinations from Gran Terminal del Caribe Guápiles (almost hourly 5am–6pm; 2hr); Moín (Mon–Sat hourly 5.30am–6.30pm, Sun every 2hr 5.30am–6.30pm; 30min); San José (hourly 5am–7pm; 3hr).

Destinations from Transportes Mepe Terminal Bribrí & Sixaola (hourly 5am–7pm 3hr); Cahuita (almost hourly 5am–7pm; 1hr); Manzanillo (5 daily Mon–Fri; 2hr); Puerto Viejo (almost hourly 5am–7pm; 1hr 30min).

By shuttle Interbus (🖰interbusonline.com) shuttles travelling from San José to Cahuita and Puerto Viejo can drop you off in Limón en route.

ACCOMMODATION AND EATING

The more attractive (and safer) options are found along the road between Limón and Moín. A taxi here costs about 1500c, and the bus to and from Moín also runs along the road. Hotel prices rise by as much as fifty percent for Carnaval week. The cheapest places to eat are the *sodas* inside the Mercado Central (Mon–Sat only).

Hotel Acón Av 3, C 2/3 ☎ 2758 1010. A large, rambling hotel in the centre housing sizeable but rather dark rooms with private bathrooms, TVs and a/c. The *Aquarius* disco here is one of the busiest in town. Private parking available. US$45

Hotel Playa Bonita Playa Bonita, 2.5km from Moín ☎ 2795 1670, 🖰hotelplayabonita.com. Large seaside hotel with secure parking, comfortable rooms with TV and a/c, and a restaurant menu running the gamut from seafood to burgers. US$60

Kalisi C 6, Av 3/4. Family-run cafeteria serving up daily specials of either spicy chicken or beef with generous sides of rice and beans, as well as the ubiquitous *gallo pinto* breakfasts. Mon–Fri 7.30am–7.30pm, Sat 8am–7.30pm, Sun 8am–5pm.

Soda Bio Natura C 6, Av 4. A healthy option with good breakfasts, all manner of soy products, and snacks including thirst-quenching *batidos* (800c) and avocado toast (1000c). Mon–Sat 8am–5.30pm.

TORTUGUERO

The peaceful village of **TORTUGUERO** lies on a thin spit of land between the sea and the Canales de Tortuguero, at the corner of one of Costa Rica's great natural attractions – **Parque Nacional Tortuguero**. Despite its isolation – 254km from San José and 83km northwest of Limón – the area is extremely popular, mainly because of its spectacular biodiversity. An abundance of species is found here, including fifty kinds of **fish**, more than one hundred **reptiles**, more than three hundred species of **birds** and sixty species of **mammals**, several of which, including the manatee, are under threat of extinction. Most notably, the beach here is one of the world's main nesting sites for **green sea turtles**, as well as the rarer **hawksbill**, **leatherback** and **loggerhead turtles**.

WHAT TO SEE AND DO

While turtle season is the most popular time to visit Tortuguero, the village receives visitors most of the year, since getting here

TURTLE TIME

Every year Tortuguero is overrun with visitors who come for one reason – to see marine turtles lay their eggs (an event called the **desove**). Although Tortuguero is by no means the only place in Costa Rica to see marine turtles nesting, four of the largest kinds of endangered sea turtles regularly nest here in large numbers. Along with the **green** (verde) turtle you might see the **hawksbill** (carey), with its distinctive hooked beak, and the ridged **leatherback** (baula), the largest turtle in the world, which can easily weigh 300kg – some are as heavy as 400kg and reach 3m in length. The rarest of them all is the **loggerhead** (boba); there are only one or two sightings per season. The green turtles and hawksbills nest in the greatest numbers from July to mid-September (August is the peak month); the leatherbacks come ashore (in far smaller numbers) from March to May.

2

via the **Canales de Tortuguero** – a waterway created by connecting existing rivers and lagoons, allowing sheltered passage to Tortuguero via coastal villages – is an adventure in itself. During the journey you get to see a lot of wildlife, though not as much as you see during guided boat trips at dawn from Tortuguero village itself. Animal- and birdwatching aside, the park also offers hiking and nature walks.

Tortuguero village

Covered in wisteria, oleander and bougainvillea, **Tortuguero village** has the air of a dilapidated tropical garden, with houses protruding from the greenery along the dirt footpaths, and the beach on its eastern side buffeted by rough Atlantic surf. It is centred on the main **dock**, or *muelle*, where all the boats arrive. Two dirt paths run north–south through the village – the "main street" and "Avenida 2", or secondary street – from which narrow paths go off to the sea on the eastern side and the canal on the western. The beach is not suitable for swimming due to riptides. At the north end of the village, past the tiny waterfront park with giant bird sculptures, beyond *Miss Junie's* hotel, the **Natural History Visitors' Centre** (Mon–Sat 10am–noon & 2–5pm, Sun 2–5pm; 1200c; ⓦconserveturtles.org), run by the Sea Turtle Conservancy, has a small, informative exhibition on the life cycle of sea turtles and a video explaining the history of turtle conservation in the area.

Parque Nacional Tortuguero

Entrance to the **Parque Nacional Tortuguero** is at the **Cuatro Esquinas Station** (5.30am–4pm; US$10; ☏2710 2929), just south of the village and reached by the main path (right from the main dock). You have to pay the entry fee whether you wish to hike in the park or take part in one of the guided boat trips. Due to damage to the path and lack of government funding, the self-guided **El Gavilán trail** (1km), which starts at the entrance and skirts a small swamp, covering the width of the land from lagoon to sea, is currently only partially open. However, it is possible to cover the

better-maintained routes used on the evening turtle tours (see below). Exploring the park can be a muddy experience and rubber boots are mandatory; numerous places in town rent or lend them out (US$2/day).

Turtle tours

During turtle season, you can watch the turtles lay their eggs by taking part in a rigorously controlled and extremely well-organized guided **turtle tour** (US$20 for two hours), which leave nightly at 8pm and 10pm from the village. Make sure you get a Turtle Spotter Program sticker when you book: this ensures a proportion of your money goes towards supporting turtle conservation projects. Visitor permits are allocated to guides via a daily lottery at 4.45pm; to guarantee yourself a place, make sure you reserve before 4.30pm on the day in question. The turtle viewing area is divided into five sectors; the two sectors furthest from the village are part of the national park, so you have to pay the US$10 park entry fee on top of the turtle tour fee (unless you already have one from earlier in the day). Since the furthest sectors are the quietest, there's a greater likelihood of seeing turtles there. Visitors must wear dark clothing, refrain from smoking and are not allowed to bring cameras or torches. Tours are conducted in silence, with visitors waiting in special shelter sites close to the beach. When a turtle is spotted by scouts, they radio the guides, who then bring you round the back of the turtle, one by one, to witness the turtle laying its eggs in the nest it has dug. Tours after midnight are illegal.

Boat trips

Worth the trip to Tortuguero in their own right are the **boat trips** (US$20, plus park entry fee) through the area's canals and *caños*, or lagoons, to spot animals including spider, howler and white-faced capucin monkeys, caimans, iguanas and Jesus Christ lizards, and birds including herons, cranes and kingfishers. You're likely to be offered a boat trip as soon as you set foot in Tortuguero. These fall into two categories: canoe trips, where you have to do some of the paddling, and electric boat trips. Canoe guides may tell you that motor boats are not allowed in the narrow Caño Chiquero and Caño Moro – the best for wildlife watching – which is true of regular boats, but does not apply to the silent electric boats. Bring a poncho for the sudden downpours.

Cerro Tortuguero

As a result of damage to its footpaths (and lack of government funding for their upkeep), **Cerro Tortuguero**, an ancient volcanic deposit looming above the flat coastal plain 6km north of the village, is officially closed. However, it's worthwhile to join local guide Ross (see box below) on one of his incredible nature walks around the base of Cerro Tortuguero.

ARRIVAL AND DEPARTURE

Getting to Tortuguero independently requires a bit of forward planning. You can either do a combination bus/boat route, or you can fly (though then you miss out on half the adventure). If you don't want the hassle of getting there independently, go with one of the numerous companies that offer transfers (around US$60) from San José and La Fortuna (via Cariari) and from Cahuita and Puerto Viejo de Talamanca (via Moín). There are two ways of travelling by bus and boat: from San José to Cariari and Cariari to Tortuguero, or from the Caribbean coast and then from Moín to Tortuguero (see p.133).

From San José to Cariari by bus Take a bus from the Gran Terminal del Caribe at 6.30am, 9am, 10.30am or 1pm to Cariari's *estacion nueva*, then walk five blocks north to the Terminal Caribeño (also known as *estacion vieja*). On the return journey, buses depart Cariari at 7.30am,

8.30am, 11.30am, 1pm, 3pm and 5.30pm). In peak season, buy bus tickets a day or two in advance.

From Cariari by bus and boat In Cariari you have two options: go with Coopetraca (☎ 2767 7590 or ☎ 2767 7137) or Clic Clic (☎ 2709 8155 or ☎ 8844 0463); both charge 3000c for the bus-boat combo, the only difference being that with Clic Clic you pay for the bus to La Pavona in Cariari, and then pay for the boat separately once you get to the dock, with myriad boat companies soliciting your custom. With Coopetraca, you pay the whole amount upfront. Buses (1hr–1hr 30min; 1000c) depart at 6am, 9am, 11.30am and 3pm, returning when the boats from Tortuguero arrive in La Pavona. Boats leave from the La Pavona dock at 7am, 12.30pm and 4pm, returning at 6am, 11.30am and 3pm. A one-way ticket costs 2000c.

From Moín by boat Unlike from La Pavona, boat services from Moín serve tourists rather than locals and, as such, there are no scheduled departures, though during peak season, a number of boats depart daily to and from Tortuguero at around 10am. A return boat ticket costs US$60–70 (4hr). Operators include Tropical Wind (☎ 2798 6059), but there's no real advantage to one operator over another. Even in peak season, it's better to call and ask about departures in advance, though it's possible to just turn up and get a seat on a boat. In low season, it's easier to go via Cariari.

By plane Sansa (☎ 2229 4100, ⊕ flysansa.com) and NatureAir (☎ 2299 6000, ⊕ natureair.com) have daily flights from San José to Tortuguero (departing 6–7am; 30min). The tiny planes are particularly weather-susceptible, so bad weather can delay or ground the flights. Flights land at the airstrip 4km north of Tortuguero village; water-taxis cost US$5 per person.

INFORMATION AND TOURS

Tourist information See the excellent ⊕ tortuguerovillage.com for maps, tour information and listings.

TOUR OPERATORS IN TORTUGUERO

There are many **tour operators** in Tortuguero offering competitively priced boat trips. Avoid the beach boys who accost you at the dock or around town. Canoe guides are mostly interchangeable.

Ballard Excursions ☎ 2709 8193 or ☎ 8320 5232, ⊕ ballardross1@gmail.com. What you learn from Canadian botanist Ross Ballard during wonderfully informative nature walks around Cerro Tortuguero ($20) will stay with you forever. Also night tours and overnight stays in the nearby biological station.

Casa Marbella See p.136. Excellent trips in an electric boat with knowledgeable bilingual guide

Rodrigo "Chacalín" and nice extra touches, such as ponchos, provided.

Castor Hunter Thomas ☎ 8870 8634, ⊕ castor hunter.blogspot.com. Guide with more than two decades of experience in leading canoe, turtle and hiking tours.

Tinamon Tours ☎ 2709 8004, ⊕ tinamontours.com. Biologist Barbara Hartung provides quality canoe, hiking, cultural and several other tours in English, German, French or Spanish.

ACCOMMODATION

All accommodation options reviewed here offer free wi-fi. Camping wild is not allowed in Tortuguero.

Cabinas Balcon del Mar On the beachfront, just south of *Cabinas Icaco* ☎ 2709 8124 or ☎ 8870 6247. Some of the rooms are tiny, dark and inadequately ventilated, while others have private bath and even balconies to catch the sea breeze. There's free wi-fi, and the larger apartments come with kitchenettes. Double US$10, apartment US$25

Cabinas Miss Miriam II Across the field from El Icaco, 50m by the beach ☎ 2709 8107 or ☎ 8873 2671. Spick-and-span rooms with tiled floors, attractive courtyard with hammocks and a quiet location near the sea. Confirm your reservations, though, as there have been complaints of overbooking. US$30

Cabinas Princesa Resort Just east of the El Gavilán store ☎ 2709 8131. The most attractive of the three *Princesa* locations in town, with spartan wood-and-concrete rooms on the oceanfront, an attractive garden, two pools and a Tico restaurant. Double US$40

Cabinas Tortuguero Across from the *Taberna* ☎ 2709 8114, ✉ cabinas_tortuguero@yahoo.com. Eleven brightly painted bungalows, some with shared, some with private baths, plus fans and hammocks on the veranda, set in a lovely garden. US$18

★ **Casa Marbella** 100m north of the dock ☎ 8833 0827, ⒲ casamarbella.tripod.com. This waterfront B&B, professionally run by Canadian biologist Daryl who is a treasure trove of local knowledge, boasts airy, spacious rooms with private baths and fans; the corner room upstairs has the best river views. Rates include breakfast. One of the best places for tours (see box, p.135). US$45

Hotel Miss Junie's At the northern end of the main street ☎ 2709 8102, ⒲ iguanaverdetours.com. Offering a touch more comfort than other options in the village, this attractive lodge, set in lush grounds, has airy wood-panelled rooms with private bathroom, security boxes and fans; those on the first floor at the front are the best of the bunch. Rates include breakfast; the on-site restaurant is a local institution. US$50

El Icaco On the beachfront, east of the village centre ☎ 2709 8044, ⒲ hotelelicaco.com. This popular beachfront place has lime-green rooms, all en-suite with hot water and fan, a communal kitchen, TV lounge and wonderfully relaxing hammock area. Rates include breakfast. US$35

EATING AND DRINKING

Buddha Café Near the dock. Wonderfully tranquil riverfront setting and an imaginative international menu. Choose from daily specials, such as *ceviche*, pizza, crêpes and more. The home-made brownie with ice cream is to die for. Mains 3500c. Daily 11am–9pm.

La Culebra Next to the main dock. This innocuous-looking purple riverfront building becomes the town's most popular watering hole by night: expect a boisterous local crowd and deafening tunes. Beer 1200c.

Dorling Bakery Across from The Jungle souvenir shop. Grab a seat out back in the riverside garden and tuck into a slice of home-made cake – chocolate, carrot, banana and lemon – or a meat-filled pastry or sandwich. The only spot open before the morning boat tours set off. Daily 5am–7pm.

Miss Junie's *Hotel Miss Junie's*, at the northern end of the main street ☎ 2709 8102, ⒲ iguanaverdetours.com. Run by the village matriarch, this local institution is the place to treat yourself to local delights such as Caribbean lobster with coconut rice, grilled chicken and fresh whole fish. Mains from 4500c. Daily 7–9am, noon–2.30pm & 6–9pm.

Miss Miriam's Next to the football pitch. Run by the daughter of Miss Miriam, this place serves up heaped portions of Nicaraguan-Caribbean food (mains from 3500c), such as giant river shrimp, fried fish and spicy chicken.

Soda La Fe Near the entrance to the park. Ideal for pre- or post-park refreshments, this tiny *soda* has filling *pintos* (from 1600c) and *casados* (from 2800c), as well as *empanadas* (650c). Daily noon–9pm.

Wild Ginger Walk towards the beach from the canalfront plaza with the giant birds, then take a left just before you reach it and carry on for 50m. Wonderfully friendly Tico-Californian outpost, with imaginative fusion dishes making the most of local ingredients and great desserts. Mains 5000c. Daily noon–9pm.

DIRECTORY

Banks and exchange There is no bank, and few businesses accept credit cards, so bring plenty of cash.

Health Ebais, across from the dock, serves as a basic clinic, but the doctor only visits once a week.

Internet Most accommodation offers wi-fi and there are a couple of spots with computers around the village. Internet connections can be affected by heavy rains.

CAHUITA

The tiny coastal village of **CAHUITA**, 43km southeast of Limón, comprises just two puddle-dotted, gravel-and-sand roads running parallel to the sea, intersected by a few cross-streets. With its resident Rastas and laidback vibe it feels more like a Caribbean outpost than part of Central America. Though the principal attraction here is the village's proximity to the **Parque Nacional Cahuita** (see p.139), the fairly empty stretches of sand along the water make the local beaches perfect for relaxing and sunbathing as well.

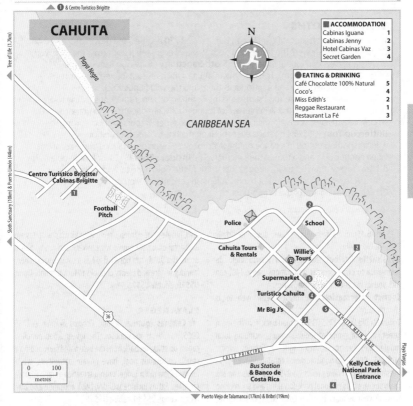

CAHUITA

▲ ❶ & Centro Turístico Brigitte

Tree of Life (1.7km)

Playa Negra

CARIBBEAN SEA

Sloth Sanctuary (108km) & Puerto Limón (44km)

ACCOMMODATION
Cabinas Iguana	1
Cabinas Jenny	2
Hotel Cabinas Vaz	3
Secret Garden	4

EATING & DRINKING
Café Chocolatte 100% Natural	5
Coco's	4
Miss Edith's	2
Reggae Restaurant	1
Restaurant La Fé	3

2

**Centro Turístico Brigitte/
Cabinas Brigitte**

**Football
Pitch**

Police

School

**Cahuita Tours
& Rentals**

**Willie's
@ Tours**

Supermarket

Turística Cahuita

Mr Big J's

CAHUITA MAIN ROAD

Playa Vargas

CALLE PRINCIPAL

**Bus Station
& Banco de
Costa Rica**

**Kelly Creek
National Park
Entrance**

0 ___ 100
metres

▼ *Puerto Viejo de Talamanca (17km) & Bribrí (19km)*

WHAT TO SEE AND DO

Cahuita's main street runs from the National Park entrance at **Kelly Creek** to the northern end of the village, marked roughly by the football pitch. Beyond here it continues 2 or 3km north along Playa Negra (Black Sand Beach).

Tree of Life

The excellent combined wildlife rescue centre and botanical garden **Tree of Life** (Tues–Sun: Dec to mid-April 9.30am–3pm; July & Aug 11am guided tour only; US$12; Ⓦtreeoflifecostarica.com), 2km out of town on the Playa Negra road, takes in wild animals that have been victims of loss of habitat, hunting and the pet trade. Animals that can be are rehabilitated, before being released into the wild, while those that cannot are given a home here. Resident creatures include coati, capuchin monkeys, an orphaned jaguarundi, howler monkeys, peccaries and more. Todd and Patricia also run breeding programmes for turtles and iguanas, and their twelve acres of botanical gardens include labelled edible plants, such as cinnamon, as well as hundreds of tropical species.

Playa Negra

The blue-flag, black-sand **Playa Negra**, northwest of town, is suitable for swimming and good for anyone learning to surf; boards are available to rent (US$5/hr) from *Cabinas Brigitte*, as well as a couple of other spots.

ARRIVAL AND INFORMATION

By bus Buses pull in at the station next to the Banco de Costa Rica.

Destinations Bribrí/Sixaola (hourly 6am–7pm; 2hr); Limón (5 daily 6am–6.15pm; 1hr–1hr 30min); Manzanillo (5 daily; 1hr–1hr 15min); Puerto Viejo (5 daily

2

VISIT THE SLOTHS

What creature wears a beatific smile, can turn its head 270 degrees, and moves at a speed of 2m per minute? Answer? The three-toed sloth. If you've ever seen a sloth cross the road, you'll understand the need for the expertly run **Sloth Sanctuary** (Tues–Sun 8am–2pm; ☎2750 0775, ⓦslothsanctuary.com), 11km north of Cahuita, which takes in injured and orphaned sloths, rehabilitates them and reintroduces them into the wild (if possible).

Diurnal, vegetarian three-toed sloths and their omnivorous nocturnal cousins, the two-toed sloths, reside here under the watchful eye of founder Judy, her daughter and grandson, all of whom are actively involved in their care. There are two types of tours to choose from. The **Buttercup Tour** (US$25; 2hr; starts every hour on the hour) consists of an hour-long wildlife-spotting outing in a canoe on the river, followed by an entertaining and educational video about sloths and a tour of the sanctuary. The **Insider's Tour** ($150 for four people; 7am & 11am; reservations required) adds to that a visit to the sloth hospital and private nursery, where you get to meet the tiniest babies. A fantastic experience. You can get here from Cahuita by taking any of the Limón-bound buses or a taxi.

6.15am–6.45pm; 30min–1hr); San José (5 daily 7am–4.30pm; 4hr).

By shuttle Interbus shuttles from Puerto Viejo de Talamanca to other popular destinations (see p.140) can pick you up in Cahuita; book in advance.

Tourist information The most useful website is ⓦcahuita.cr.

Tours Mr Big J's (☎2755 0353), a road back from the main street, offers a range of regional tours, including local jungle hikes; Centro Turistico Brigitte at *Cabinas Brigitte* (☎2755 0053, ⓦbrigittecahuita.com) specializes in horseriding trips; Willie's Tours (☎2755 1024), also on the main street, offers national park, kayaking and snorkelling tours as well as tours to other Costa Rican destinations, one-/two-day trips to Panama's Bocas del Toro, and transfers to/from Tortugero via Moín (see p.133).

ACCOMMODATION

There's accommodation along Playa Negra as well as in the village, though that road is poorly lit at night.

IN THE VILLAGE

★ **Cabinas Jenny** At the beach end of the side street leading past the tiny plaza ☎2755 0256, ⓦcabinasjenny .com. The beautiful top-floor rooms have high wooden ceilings, mosquito nets, fans and kitchenettes, plus thoughtful touches such as filtered drinking water. Each comes with a private balcony overlooking the sea. The ground-floor rooms are simpler and cheaper, with fans and hammocks on porches. US$27

Hotel Cabinas Vaz Between the bus station and the main street. ☎2755 0218, ⓔhotelvaz@gmail.com. The en-suite rooms may be impersonal and motel-style, but they're spotless and most have a/c. Guests have access to a pool. US$35

Secret Garden Down the side street just before Kelly Creek ☎2755 0581, ⓔkoosiecosta@live.nl. Behind the

lush, jungle-style garden strewn with kitsch statuettes are a handful of simple rooms with private bathroom, plus a dorm. The Dutch-run hostel also has a communal kitchen, laundry service and plenty of books to flick through. Dorm US$10, double US$25

PLAYA NEGRA

★ **Cabinas Iguana** Beyond *Cabinas Brigitte* ☎2755 0005, ⓦcabinas-iguana.com. The lovely wood-panelled cabins on stilts, set back from the beach and surrounding a small, curvaceous pool, have private bathrooms, while rooms in the main lodge, with a screened veranda, share facilities. Extras include laundry, book exchange and bike rental. Lodge US$30, cabins US$55

EATING AND DRINKING

Café Chocolatte 100% Natural Main street. Your first stop for great coffee, fresh juices, and mega sandwiches with a variety of fillings (including veggie options) to wrap up for your hike in the park. Sandwiches from 4000c. Mon–Fri 6.30am–2pm.

Coco's At the main junction in the town centre. You'll hear this eye-catching bar, decked out in a Rasta colour scheme, before you see it; a popular spot for a cold beer (1200c) or a potent rum punch (3000c), it attracts a lively clientele after dark. There's also occasional live music, and wonderfully fresh food, from *ceviche* to the squid with *tostones* (mashed, fried plantain). Daily noon–late.

Miss Edith's A block away from main street, beyond the post office. Tucked away off the main drag, this simple restaurant is the domain of one of the village's matriarchs, who works her magic daily. Expect mouth-searing jerk chicken, stewed fish and other Caribbean delights. Mains from 3000c. Daily 7am–8pm.

Reggae Restaurant Attached to the *Reggae Cabinas*, Playa Negra. The location, just opposite the beach, makes this a great place to grab a cold beer (1200c) or enjoy home-cooked food – from the signature prawns in coconut milk to *casados*. Mains from 2500c. Daily 7–11am & noon–9pm.

Restaurant La Fé On the main street, near the main intersection. Popular Tico-run restaurant famous for its spicy coconut sauce (perfect with seafood), offering Tico standards and generous breakfasts. Mains from 3500c. Daily 7am–11pm.

DIRECTORY

Bank Banco de Costa Rica, next to the bus station, a couple of blocks from the main street, has an ATM.
Bicycle rental Bicycles can be rented from *Cabinas Brigitte* or Mr Big J's (5000c/day).
Laundry Mr Big J's, a block from the main street (3500c/bag).

PARQUE NACIONAL CAHUITA

PARQUE NACIONAL CAHUITA (daily 6am–5pm; entry by donation at Kelly Creek, or US$10 if entering at Puerto Vargas) is one of the country's smallest protected areas, covering the wedge-shaped piece of land from Punta Cahuita back to the main highway and, crucially, the **coral reef** about 500m offshore. Given that this is one of the last living reefs in Costa Rica, snorkelling is only allowed with a guide; local tour operators offer **snorkelling trips** (around US$30). On land, Cahuita shelters the litoral, or coastal, rainforest, a lowland habitat of semi-mangroves and tall canopy cover that backs the white-sand beaches of Playa Blanca and Playa Vargas. **Birds**, including ibis and kingfishers, are in residence, along with white-faced capucin and howler monkeys, coati, raccoons, sloths and snakes.

The park's one **trail** (8km), skirting the beach, is an easy, flat walk, alternating between sandy path and raised boardwalk, with a 1.5km gravel road leading from the Puerto Vargas ranger station to the main road. The Río Perezoso, about 2km from the Kelly Creek entrance, or 5km from the Puerto Vargas trailhead, is not always fordable in the the rainy season. Be aware of rip currents at both beaches and look for green flags indicating safe swimming spots; if starting from Kelly Creek, the first 500m or so of Playa Blanca are not safe.

ARRIVAL AND DEPARTURE

Entrances The park has two entrances: at Kelly Creek, at the southern end of Cahuita village, and at Puerto Vargas, 5km south of Cahuita.

EATING

Boca Chica Restaurant If you do the hike in the morning from Kelly Creek, you will reach this peaceful French-run restaurant at the end of your walk, near the main highway. They offer three set dishes daily (5000c).

PUERTO VIEJO DE TALAMANCA

It's **surfing** that really pulls the crowds to the languorous hamlet of **PUERTO VIEJO DE TALAMANCA**, which offers some of the most challenging waves in the country, including the famous "**Salsa Brava**". The **village** itself lies between the thickly forested hills of the Talamanca mountains

---

ATEC, THE KÉKÖLDI AND THE YORKÍN RESERVES

Skirted by the **Kéköldi Reserve** (ⓦkekoldi.org), inhabited by about two hundred Bribrí and Cabécar peoples, Puerto Viejo retains strong links with **indigenous culture**. The Asociación Talamanqueña de Ecoturismo y Conservación, or **ATEC**, is a grassroots organization set up by members of the local community. As well as being able to tell you where to buy locally made products, the group arranges some of the most interesting **tours** in Costa Rica. Day-trips to the reserve cost US$35, and include a guided hike, visit to the iguana farm and lunch; these can also be extended for overnight stays. Even more rewarding is the day-trip to the remote Bribrí community of Yorkín, reachable by canoe from a village west of the town of Bribrí. The tour of the community is normally led by Bernarda, a remarkable woman who set out to stamp out machismo in her village when she was just nineteen, and who has succeeded, making her village unique in Costa Rica. You learn about traditional pursuits, such as cocoa growing, and get to practise grinding the beans before drinking the freshest hot chocolate of your life. If you're spending a few days in the region, an ATEC-arranged trip is a must – contact the Puerto Viejo office (☎2750 0191; on the main street) at least one day in advance.

2

and the sea, where locals bathe and kids frolic with surfboards. The main drag is crisscrossed by a few dirt streets and an offshoot road that follows the shore. As in Cahuita, many expats have been drawn to Puerto Viejo and have set up their own businesses; and, like Cahuita, most locals are of Afro-Caribbean descent. The village's backpacker and surf-party culture ensures a lively, youthful nightlife, but there is also a **drugs scene**, and **crime**, particularly theft, can be a problem: never take valuables to the beach (and stay off it at night), make sure your accommodation is secure and take care after dark.

WHAT TO SEE AND DO

It is hard to spend time here without hitting the waves; the best **surf** is from December to March and July to August. There are plenty of places to **rent boards** and book lessons (see below) and the surf ranges from beginner waves on Playa Negra to the advanced, reef-side break of Salsa Brava, offering both lefts and rights. For surf **lessons**, Hershel of Caribe Surf (☎8878 1739 or ☎8357 7703) is a great instructor, and the long-running Van Dyke Surf School (*Hotel Pueblo Viejo*; ☎2750 020) also has an excellent reputation.

ARRIVAL AND DEPARTURE

By bus Buses arrive and depart from the stop across from *Maritza's Bar* on the main street in the village centre.

Destinations Buses link the village with Bribrí/Sixaola (hourly 6.30am–7.30pm; 30min/1hr 30min); Cahuita (hourly 5.30am–7.30pm; 30min); Manzanillo (5 daily, 6.45am, 7.15am, 11.45am, 4.15pm & 7.15pm; 30min); Puerto Limón (hourly 5.30am–7.30pm; 1hr 30min) San José (3 daily, 9am, 11am, 4pm; 4hr 30min–5hr).

INFORMATION AND TOURS

★ **ATEC** On the main road, opposite *Café Viejo* ☎2750 0398, ⓦateccr.org. An excellent local organization (see box, p.139) offering fascinating trips to nearby indigenous settlements (US$70), as well as private surf lessons (US$60/2hr) and dolphin-watching (US$55).

Aventuras Bravas *Rocking J's* ☎2750 0626, ⓦaventurasbravas.com. Booking agent offering an exhaustive range of activities, including surf lessons (group US$45), rafting (US$99), and kayak rentals (US$20/day) and trips (US$30). Also runs a shuttle to/from Bocas del Toro in Panama (US$40).

Terraventuras Main street, next to the Old Harbour Supermarket ☎2750 0750, ⓦterraventuras.com. Countrywide adventure tours, plus their own canopy tour and overnight trips to Tortuguero.

Tourist information The most useful websites are ⓦpuertoviejosatellite.com and ⓦgreencoast.com, with info on accommodation, activities and eating out. The tour operators listed here can also be helpful.

ACCOMMODATION

If you're staying at or close to *Kaya's Place* and *Rocking J's*, walk with other people or consider taking a taxi back from town after dark, as muggings occasionally occur.

Cabinas Jacaranda 25m north of the football pitch ☎2750 0069, ⓦcabinasjacaranda.net. Follow the

PUERTO VIEJO DE TALAMANCA

■ ACCOMMODATION	
Cabinas Jacaranda	4
Hotel Puerto Viejo	2
Hotel Pura Vida	5
Kaya's Place	6
Rocking J's	1
La Ruka Hostel	3

CARIBBEAN SEA

Buses to Cahuita, Limón, Sixaola, Manzanillo & San José

Playa Negra

AVENIDA 71

Cahuita & Bribrí

mosaic-tiled floor from the front gate and you discover a mini Eden: simple rooms for between one and four people feature colourful murals, wooden furniture, fans and safes, and most have private baths; there are also verdant gardens, where you can have a massage or take a yoga class, plus a kitchen and free internet. US$34

Hotel Puerto Viejo Next to *Baba Yaga* ☎ 2750 0620. Long-running hostel with rows of tiny wooden *cabinas* with powerful fans, most with shared bath, and a large communal kitchen. The bar is a surfers' favourite and owner Kurt rents out surfboards. Per person US$10

★ **Hotel Pura Vida** Across the street from the football field ☎ 2750 0002, ⊚ hotel-puravida.com. On a quiet street, this fantastic Chilean-German guesthouse oozes tranquillity – from its appealing patio overflowing with greenery, with hammocks, easy chairs and pets sprawled on the tiled floors, to the large, airy, fan-cooled rooms, some with own bathrooms. Hearty breakfast US$7. US$32

Kaya's Place Playa Negra, west of town ☎ 2750 0690, ⊚ kayasplace.com. Arty murals, thatched roofs and carved driftwood give *Kaya's Place* a distinct rustic-chic character; each room is unique, but the ocean-view rooms on the first floor are worth splurging on as the cheapest ones don't get much natural light. US$27

Rocking J's On the main road, 100m beyond Tuanis Bikes ☎ 2750 0657, ⊚ rockingjs.com. The epicentre of backpacker life in Puerto Viejo, *Rocking J's* has a bewildering array of options for shoestringers, as well as more upmarket options – the suites and the Stables. The beachside compound also has a big garden, chill-out areas, a restaurant and bar with live music every Friday and frequent parties. You won't get much sleep, but then, that's not the point. Hammocks US$7, camping US$8, dorm US$11, cabinas US$26, treehouse US$26

La Ruka Hostel 600m along road to Playa Cockles ☎ 2750 0617, ⊚ larukahostel.com. Staying at *La Ruka* (named after resident three-legged dog) is like staying at a friend's house; many guests end up lingering longer than they thought. There's a great common area, hung with hammocks, and friendly owners Dani and Dave hold occasional parties. All rooms share facilities. Dorm US$10, double US$25

EATING

Beach Hut On the main road just before *Stanford's*. A beachside bar and restaurant serving English-style fry-ups all day long, gourmet burgers, stuffed baguettes and light dishes such as the mango and avocado shrimp salad with spicy cayenne vinaigrette or seared tuna steak. Mains around 4000c. Daily noon–midnight.

Bread & Chocolate Half a block off the main street, next to *Cabinas Larry*. Delectable home-made cakes, home-made peanut butter sandwiches…in fact, home-made everything, because most things, soups and mains included, come made completely from scratch at this lovely café. Don't miss out on the do-it-yourself coffees either. Sandwiches 3000c. Tues–Sat 6.30am–6.30pm, Sun 6.30am–2.30pm.

★ **Caribeans** Near to *Mango Sunset* bar. Boost your karma – and your waistline – with a visit to this delightfully run organic and fair-trade coffee and chocolate café. They brew a killer coffee (900–1900c), and the 80 percent cocoa chocolate is outstanding: try it in a muffin, cupcake, brownie or ice-cream sundae.

Chile Rojo First floor of the shopping arcade opposite ATEC. The best way to approach this otherwise budget-busting pan-Asian restaurant/bar is to come with an empty stomach on Monday for the all-you-can-eat sushi

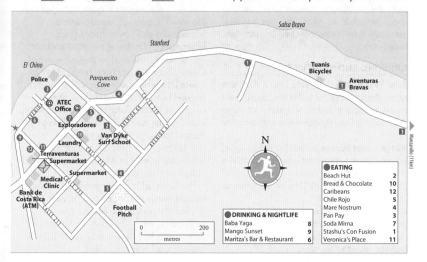

● DRINKING & NIGHTLIFE	
Baba Yaga	8
Mango Sunset	9
Maritza's Bar & Restaurant	6

● EATING	
Beach Hut	2
Bread & Chocolate	10
Caribeans	12
Chile Rojo	5
Mare Nostrum	4
Pan Pay	3
Soda Mirna	7
Stashu's Con Fusion	1
Veronica's Place	11

2

and (mostly) Chinese buffet (6500c). The rest of the week, Thai curries and other delights grace the à la carte menu. Thurs–Tues noon–11pm.

Mare Nostrum Main road, not far from *Chile Rojo*. The best budget seafood in town, with an overwhelmingly large menu; the fresh fish (4500–5500c), paella (3800–4800c) and sangria are all specialities. Daily noon–10pm.

Pan Pay On the seafront across from the police station. A popular breakfast spot offering the best croissants in town, plus delicious Spanish omelettes (1500c for a hefty slice with bread), good, low-cost coffee and takeaway sandwiches (1800–2700c). Daily 7am–7pm.

Soda Mirna Next to ATEC on main road. As well as a token *casado* or two, this great little spot serves up such Caribbean delights as spicy chicken with rice and beans, pork ribs and seafood dishes made fiery by the home-made hot sauce. Mains from 3000c. Daily noon–10pm.

Veronica's Place 50m southeast of the bus stop. The only strictly vegetarian place in town, offering reasonably priced Caribbean food (2900–4000c), using plenty of fresh produce from Veronica's own organic farm. There are plenty of vegan options too, as well as "magic" revitalizing juices, home-made ice cream, and even traditional remedies for if you're feeling poorly. Sun–Thurs 8am–9pm, Fri 8am–4pm.

DRINKING AND NIGHTLIFE

Baba Yaga Next to *Hotel Puerto Viejo*. A Rasta joint named after the witch in Russian folk tales, offering drinks promotions and a massive sound system – on reggae (Sun) and ladies' (Tues) nights the crowds spill out onto the street.

Mango Sunset Opposite the bus stop. Welcoming bar, with great live rock, reggae and Latin music (notably on Wed) and lots of drinks promotions to get you in the mood (think US$1.50 tequila shots). There are also dartboards and Sky TV for sports events.

Maritza's Bar & Restaurant 50m northeast of the bus stop. Across from the beach, with indoor and outdoor seating, this place has a DJ or live music most nights (including salsa on Sat and calypso on Sun).

DIRECTORY

Bank Banco de Costa Rica, diagonally across from the *Super Puerto Viejo* supermarket, has an ATM.

Bicycle rental Tuanis Bicycles on the road to Manzanillo, just before *Rocking J's* (2700c/day); *Café Rico* (3500c/day).

Health There are two clinics in the area: Sunimedica (☎ 2750 0758), next to the post office, and the larger Hone Creek Clinic (☎ 2750 8022), 5km north of town. Farmacia Amiga, in the small commercial centre next to the post office, is the town pharmacy.

SOUTH TO MANZANILLO

The 12km of coast between Puerto Viejo and **MANZANILLO** village – dotted by the tiny hamlets of **Playa Cocles**, **Playa Chiquita**, **Punta Uva** and **Punta Mona** – is one of the most beautiful stretches in the country.

WHAT TO SEE AND DO

Though not spectacular for swimming, the **beaches** in this area are exceedingly picturesque. The whole stretch can be reached by bicycle from Puerto Viejo; a cycle tour of the beaches can easily be done as a day-trip.

Refugio Nacional de Vida Silvestre Gandoca-Manzanillo

The little-visited but fascinating **Refugio Nacional de Vida Silvestre Gandoca-Manzanillo**, bordering the Río Sixaola and the Panamanian border, incorporates the small hamlets of Gandoca and Manzanillo and covers fifty square kilometres of land and a similar area of sea. It was established to protect some of Costa Rica's last few **coral reefs**, of which **Punta Uva** is the most accessible. You can **snorkel** here, or **dive**, and there are a couple of good hiking trails – a coastal walk leading east from Manzanillo to **Punta Mona**, an excellent place for snorkelling, and a more challenging 9km hike leading west of Manzanillo to the village of Gandoca.

The first trail is straightforward enough, but for the second one you'll need a guide. The park office (in the green wooden house at the entry to Manzanillo; 8am–noon & 1–4pm; ☎ 2759 9100) can provide trail maps.

INTO PANAMA: SIXAOLA

The **Sixaola–Guabito border** is open daily from 8am to 6pm Panama time or 7am–5pm Costa Rican time (Panama is 1hr ahead); border posts close for lunch for an hour around 1pm, so you'll be hanging around at that time. Get to the border as early as possible, especially since there's nowhere decent to stay in Guabito. Citizens of some nationalities may require a **tourist card** (US$5; valid for thirty days) to enter Panama (see p.518).

In **Panama**, if you're arriving from Bocas del Toro, your best bet is to take the ferry to Changuinola (20km; 45min) and then grab a taxi to the bus station or the border (US$7). There's one direct bus from Changuinola to San José (10am daily; 8hr), but if you miss that, you can catch one of the hourly buses heading up the Caribbean coast.

Manzanillo

Playa Manzanillo has a large shelf of coral reef just offshore, which teems with marine life and offers some of the best snorkelling in Costa Rica. The village of **MANZANILLO** itself is small and charming, with stunning beaches, laidback locals and a couple of great places to eat and hang out.

ARRIVAL AND DEPARTURE

By bus Buses depart from along Manzanillo's main street. Destinations Puerto Limón via Puerto Viejo and Cahuita (5 daily, 5am, 7am, 8.30am, 12.45pm & 5.15pm; 2hr 30min); San José (1 daily, 7am; 5hr).
By bike Renting a bike (see p.142) is a good option; it takes about 90min to cycle from Puerto Viejo; the road runs alongside the beaches.

ACCOMMODATION AND EATING

Cabinas Bucus Behind *Cabinas Manzanillo* ☎ 2759 9143, ⓦ costa-rica-manzanillo.com. Four pristine doubles with wooden shutters, balconies and private stone bathrooms, in a lovely spot backing on to jungle, run by local guide Omar and his German wife Melte, who lead informative tours. US$30
Cabinas Manzanillo On the northern edge of Manzanillo ☎ 2759 9033. Reliable, low-key hotel run by incredibly helpful owners, with eight spotless, bright rooms, all with powerful fans, private bath and TV; those upstairs have better jungle views. US$40
★ **Maxi's** Near the beach in central Manzanillo. Manzanillo's – generally thumping – heartbeat, locally renowned *Maxi's* has an upstairs restaurant that attracts visitors from far and wide with its superlative seafood – huge portions of grilled fish, lobster and other delights fresh from the sea. Mains 3000–12,500c. Daily 6am–late.
Miraflores Eco-Lodge Playa Chiquita, halfway between Puerto Viejo and Manzanillo ☎ 2750 0038, ⓦ mirafloreslodge.com. Comfortable, rustic lodge opposite the beach, run by botanist Pamela. The upstairs rooms are brighter, with high bamboo ceilings, and there's

a café, library and beautiful, labyrinthine gardens. The owner also has excellent contacts with local Kéköldi Bribrí communities and runs imaginative tours. US$50

The Central Pacific

From cool, undulating forests to rolling waves and scorching sands, the physical attributes of the **Central Pacific** region are some of the most varied and impressive in the country. Every year thousands of travellers make the rugged, 170km journey northwest from San José to the **Monteverde** and **Santa Elena** reserves, to meander on foot through some of the Americas' last remaining pristine cloudforest or to take part in one of the high-adrenaline canopy tours for which the area is famous. Meanwhile, only a hundred or so kilometres away, facing out onto the Pacific, **Jacó** is Costa Rica's party town and a hugely popular **surfing destination**. Further south along the coast, tiny **Parque Nacional Manuel Antonio** draws visitors eager to walk its trails in search of monkeys and rare birds, and discover the park's secluded beaches.

SANTA ELENA AND MONTEVERDE

The hub of the mountainous Monteverde region, and one of the most appealing (and most visited) destinations in Costa Rica, is the small Tico village of **SANTA ELENA** and the tiny settlement of **MONTEVERDE**, settled in the 1950s by Quakers who left Alabama to avoid military service. The two nestle in a

2

MONTEVERDE AND SANTA ELENA

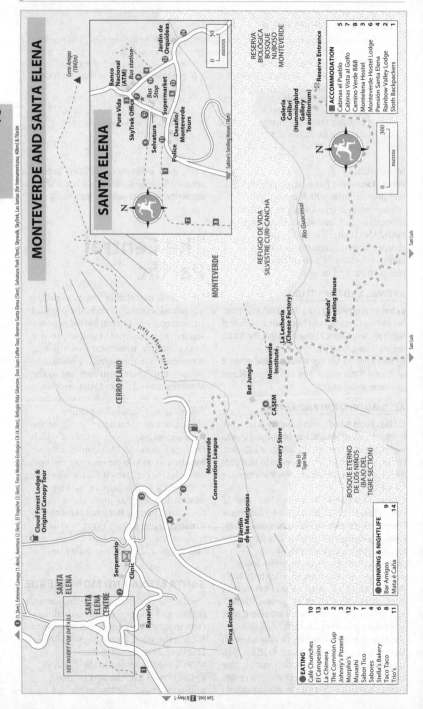

SANTA ELENA

Cerro Amigos (1842m)

Banco Nacional (ATM)
Bus station
Jardin de Orquideas
Pura Vida
SkyTrek Office
Bus Stop
Supermarket
@
Selvatura
Desafío/ Monteverde Tours
Police

Sabine's Smiling Horses (1km)

RESERVA BIOLÓGICA BOSQUE NUBOSO MONTEVERDE

Galería Colibrí (Hummingbird Gallery & auditorium)

Reserve Entrance

ACCOMMODATION
Cabinas el Pueblo	5
Cabinas Vista al Golfo	7
Camino Verde B&B	8
Montelena Hostel	3
Monteverde Hostel Lodge	6
Pensión Santa Elena	4
Rainbow Valley Lodge	2
Sloth Backpackers	1

N

MONTEVERDE

REFUGIO DE VIDA SILVESTRE CURI-CANCHA

Río Guacimal

San Luis

San Luis

Friends' Meeting House

La Lechería (Cheese Factory)

Monteverde Institute

Bat Jungle

CERRO PLANO

Cloud Forest Lodge & Original Canopy Tour

Monteverde Conservation League

CASEM

Grocery Store

Bajo B Tigre Trail

BOSQUE ETERNO DE LOS NIÑOS (BAJO DEL TIGRE SECTION)

El Jardín de las Mariposas

Serpentario

Clinic

Ranario

Finca Ecológica

SANTA ELENA

SANTA ELENA CENTRE

SEE INSERT FOR DETAILS

1.2km), Extreme Canopy (1.4km), Aventura (2.5km), El Campesino, El Trapiche (2.5km), Finca Modelo Ecológica CA (4.3km), Refugio Vida Silvestre, Don Juan Coffee Tour, Reserva Santa Elena (5km), Selvatura Park (7km), Skywalk, SkyTrek, Las Juntas (for Interamericana; 40km) & Tilarán

San José & Hwy-1

EATING
Café Chunches	10
El Campesino	13
La Chimera	5
The Common Cup	2
Johnny's Pizzeria	3
Morpho's	12
Musashi	7
Sabor Tico	1
Sabores	4
Stella's Bakery	6
Taco Taco	8
Trio's	11

DRINKING & NIGHTLIFE
Bar Amigos	9
Mata é Caña	14

beautiful, mountainous landscape near three small nature reserves, connected by a narrow, winding, dusty, yet wonderfully picturesque 5km stretch of road lined with lodgings, restaurants and craft shops. If walking it, be very careful of the traffic.

Reserva Santa Elena is easily reachable from its namesake village, while Monteverde is the gateway to the **Reserva Biológica Bosque Nuboso Monteverde** and the new **Reserva Cariari**. In addition to hiking in the reserves, visitors can join guided animal-spotting night walks, or stop by the snake, frog and butterfly sanctuaries. The forests here are criss-crossed with canopy wires, with enough action-packed activities to satisfy the most jaded of adrenaline junkies; you could also visit **Monteverde cheese factory**, responsible for Costa Rica's best cheese, or a nearby **finca** (coffee farm) to learn about coffee and cocoa production.

WHAT TO SEE AND DO

The heart of Santa Elena consists of three streets in a triangle, among which sits a plethora of hostels, cafés and tour agencies; east of here, Monteverde spreads out along the mountain road. Attractions are found on the outskirts of Santa Elena, along the mountain road and in the forests surrounding the two settlements.

Reserva Santa Elena

Less visited than the Monteverde reserve, **Reserva Santa Elena** (daily 7am–4pm; US$14; ☎ 2645 5390, ⓦ reservasantaelena .org), 6km northeast of the village of Santa Elena, is an area of exceptional natural beauty, and offers a glimpse of the rich biodiversity of the cloudforest. Established in 1992, the park strives to be self-funding, assisted by donations and revenue from entrance fees, and gives a percentage of its profits to local schools. Much of the maintenance and many of the building projects depend on volunteers, usually foreign students. The trails are well signposted and maintained, but are often muddy, as they're deliberately unpaved and the area is very moist. There's a greater chance of spotting birds and animals early in the mornings; guided tours (daily at 7.30am & 11.30am; US$15) are available.

Of the five **trails**, the highlights are the 3.4km Sendero Encantado, along which quetzals are frequently spotted, and the longest trail – the Sendero Caño Negro (4.8km; 3hr) loop – a reasonably demanding walk with steep ups and downs, and more chances to spot wildlife. There are boots and rain gear for rent, information about the trails and a small café and gift shop at the **visitors' centre** at the park entrance.

CHOOSE YOUR ZIPLINE

Many people visit the Monteverde region purely to experience a high-adrenaline **canopy tour**. Several agencies can take you into the parks to whizz along ziplines far above the ground, or leap into the abyss using an enormous Tarzan swing.

Aventura 3km north of Santa Elena towards the reserve ☎ 2645 6388, ⓦ monteverdeadventure.com. For serious zipliners, Aventura (7am–4pm; US$45) offers an excellent array of ziplines (19 platforms in total), a Superman zipline (you're suspended from your back, so that you can "fly"), included in the entry price, a Tarzan swing that's a little smaller than Extremo Canopy's and a 15m rappel.

Extremo Canopy ☎ 2645 6058, ⓦ monteverde extremo.com. True to its name, this extreme ziplining adventure (8am–4pm; US$40) is all about the adrenaline. Highlights include a Superman canopy ride (US$5) and a 45m Tarzan swing – you're practically bungee-jumping before the cable stops your freefall.

Original Canopy Tour In the grounds of *Cloud Forest Lodge*, ☎ 2645 5243, ⓦ canopytour.com. The company that started it all (7.30am–4pm; adults US$45), offering thirteen ziplines and a rappel, as well as 5km of hiking trails.

Selvatura Opposite the bus stop ☎ 2645 5929, ⓦ selvatura.com. Besides a host of non-zipline attractions (see p.146), Selvatura (7.30am–4pm; US$45) offers 3km of cables, seventeen ziplines and a more modest Tarzan swing than the competition.

SkyTrek Next to the bus stop ☎ 2645 5238, ⓦ skytrek .com. One of the most popular canopy tours (7.30am–5.30pm; US$66), with eleven cables, including one that's an incredible 770m long with speeds reaching 64km/h. SkyTram cable car included in the price; more expensive packages include SkyWalk (aerial walkways).

Shuttles (US$2) run here from Santa Elena daily at 6.30am, 8.30am, 10.30am and 12.30pm, returning at 9am, 11am, 1pm, 3pm and 4pm.

Selvatura Park

A couple of hundred metres down the road towards Santa Elena from Reserva Santa Elena, the **Selvatura Park** (daily 9am–5pm; ☏ 2645 5757, ⓦ selvatura.com) is a catch-all attraction featuring a canopy tour (see box, p.145), treetop walkways (US$30), butterfly garden (US$15), hummingbird garden (US$5) and reptile and amphibian exhibition (US$15). You can choose exactly which activities you want, and while the Serpentario (see below), Ranario (see below) and the Jardín de Mariposas (see below) are better places to see reptiles, amphibians and butterflies, the hummingbird garden is particularly worth it, with more than a dozen multicoloured species hovering over the sugar water feeders. Several shuttles daily run to and from Santa Elena.

Jardín de Orquídeas

The **Jardín de Orquídeas** (daily 8am–5pm; US$10; ⓦ monteverdeorchidgarden.com), in the centre of Santa Elena, boasts more than 450 different species of orchid; February is the best month to visit to see them all in bloom. You're given a magnifying glass to appreciate the world's smallest orchid.

Serpentario

On the outskirts of Santa Elena, on the road towards Monteverde, the **Serpentario** (daily 9am–8pm; US$9) showcases a number of scaled, slithering delights, some of which, including the pit viper, are found wild in the area. Highlights include the deadly fer-de-lance, a tangle of boa constrictors and the beautiful eyelash pit viper, with a protrusion above the eyes that any supermodel would be proud of.

Ranario

The **Ranario – Frog Pond** – on the outskirts of Santa Elena, showcases a fascinating array of frogs and toads, including the incredible transparent frog (9am–8.30pm; US$12 including guided

tour). Most species are more active in the evenings.

El Jardín de las Mariposas

El Jardín de las Mariposas, the Butterfly Garden (daily 9.30am–4pm; US$9 includes 1hr guided tour; ⓦ monteverdebutterflygarden.com), lets you walk among the butterfly species from Costa Rica's varying climatic regions, including the brilliant turquoise morpho and other eye-catching species. Try to arrive between 10am and 2pm, when the butterflies are most active. It's a ten-minute taxi ride from the main road.

Bosque Eterno de Los Niños

A huge, 220-square-kilometre private reserve, the **Bosque Eterno de Los Niños**, or Children's Eternal Rainforest (☏ 2645 5003, ⓦ acmcr.org), close to the Monteverde settlement, exists thanks to the Children's Rainforest Movement fundraising initiative that started in 1987, and is a spectacular example of children's pocket money put to good use. Most of the land, covered in primary and secondary rainforest, is set aside for conservation and research, but visitors are allowed to hike along one beautiful trail – the **Bajo El Tigre trail** (daily 8am–4pm; US$8; guided tours US$28 without transfers, US$31 with; book a day in advance), which is physically separated from the rest of the reserve, and is a short, easy trek at lower elevations than in the cloudforest reserves, and with premontane forest (rare in Costa Rica) and great views out to the Golfo de Nicoya. Sunsets can be spectacular.

For a different experience, take one of the reserve's **night walks** (daily 5.30pm; 2hr; US$23 including transfers). The informative tour gives you a good chance of seeing nocturnal animals, including porcupines, tarantulas, armadillos, agoutis, sloths and a marvellous variety of insects and roosting birds. The trail begins just before the cheese factory (see opposite).

The Bat Jungle

The **Bat Jungle** (daily 9am–7.30pm; US$12; ☏ 2645 6566), next to *Stella's Bakery*, fifteen minutes from Santa Elena along the road to Monteverde, is an exceptionally well-run enterprise by biologist Richard Laval. His daily guided tours dispel myths and dole out fascinating facts; for example, the only way to get bitten by a vampire bat is if you sleep naked next to livestock (their preferred meal), and that mascara is made from bat poop. You get to see several species of local bats behind glass in a darkened enclosure and hear their excited noises during feeding time (9am, noon & 3pm). Don't miss the excellent *Café Caburé* upstairs, either.

La Lechería

At **La Lechería**, or Monteverde Cheese Factory (1hr 15min tours Mon–Sat 9am & 2pm; US$10; reservations required; ☎2645 5522), informative tours teach you about the Quaker origins of the factory and the traditional processes by which they make their own cheeses – including their own versions of Edam, Gouda, Cheddar and Provolone, among others. It all ends up with a cheese-tasting, and there's a shop and café on the premises.

Refugio de Vida Silvestre Curi-Cancha

The privately owned **Refugio de Vida Silvestre Curi-Cancha** (daily 7am–3pm & 6–8pm; US$10; ☎2645 6915), a reserve accessed via a trail behind La Lechería, is the area's newest, with some trails still in construction. A compact area, with narrow forest trails nowhere near as busy as those in the Monteverde and Santa Elena reserves, it offers a better chance of wildlife viewing, with quetzals, coyotes and coatis in residence. You can either join a guided tour (7.30am; US$17), or ramble the mostly flat, well-signposted trails – seven of them, ranging from 600m to 2.2km in length – on your own. To get here, take one of the five daily buses to Monteverde (see p.148); there are also five daily shuttles to Monteverde that can drop you off (see p.148).

Reserva Biológica Bosque Nuboso Monteverde

The world-renowned Monteverde Cloudforest Reserve, or **Reserve Biológica Bosque Nuboso Monteverde** (daily 7am–4pm; US$18; ☎2645 5122, ⓦcct .or.cr), a joint conservation effort of the Quakers, the International Children's Rainforest project and others, protects the last sizeable pocket of primary cloudforest in Central America. Stretching over 105 square kilometres, it supports six different **ecocommunities**, hosting an estimated 2500 plant species, more than 100 species of mammals, some 490 butterfly species and more than 400 species of birds, among them the resplendent **quetzal**. Though the cloudforest cover – dense, low-lit, heavy and damp – can make it difficult to see the animals, the park is nonetheless the most popular of the area's three nature reserves and an essential stop during any trip to Costa Rica.

The free **map** you're given on arrival will help you navigate the 13km of well-signposted trails (nine in total). Some are paved, while the more remote trails are unpaved and muddy year-round. **Temperatures** are cool (15° or 16°C). Be sure to carry rain gear, binoculars and insect repellent. It's just about possible to get away without **rubber boots** in the dry season, but you will definitely need them in the wet. The reserve office rents both boots and binoculars (US$2).

Of the **trails**, the most popular option for day hikes is **El Triángulo**, east of the entrance – this consists of Sendero Pantanoso (1.6km), passing through pine forest and bog and straddling the continental divide; the interpretive Sendero Bosque Nuboso (1.9km), which starts at the ranger station and passes through cloudforest; and Sendero Río (2km), which rambles past several small waterfalls. Keen birdwatchers shouldn't miss **El Camino** (2km), which runs parallel to the Sendero Bosque Nuboso, and if you're after a good view, you can either take **Sendero Mirador La Ventana** to a mesmerizing viewpoint (1550m) overlooking the continental divide, or **Sendero Chomogo** (1.8km), which crosses El Triángulo to a height of 1680m. If you're fit and serious about wildlife spotting, you may consider the longer, rugged, less developed trails beyond El Triángulo; for some of these you'll need a guide.

The reserve runs highly recommended **guided walks** (7.30am & 8.30am; 2hr

2

2

30min; US$17; evening walks 7.15pm; 2hr; US$20 including transport; reservations ☎2645 5112), as well as five-hour birdwatching tours (6am, leaving from *Stella's Bakery* in Monteverde; US$64). Additional daytime walks are sometimes put on in high season, but it's worth booking a day in advance, as groups are limited to ten people.

In an attempt to limit human impact and conga-line hiking, a number of **rules** govern entrance to Monteverde, including a quota of 160 visitors at any one time. In high season, consider booking tickets a day in advance (bookings aren't available more than 24 hours in advance). Things get noisy and crowded between 8 and 11am, when the tour groups arrive.

You can reach the reserve either by public bus (see p.148) or by shuttle (departing Santa Elena 7am, 7.30am, 10.30am, 1.30pm & 3.30pm, returning 7.30am, 8am, 11am, 2pm & 4pm; US$5 return).

ARRIVAL AND DEPARTURE

By bus All buses depart from in front of Banco Nacional at the northern apex of the triangle, with the exception of the San José and Tilarán buses, which leave from the bus station, just around the corner from the bank. Watch your luggage on buses; thefts are common.

Destinations Monteverde (5 daily, 6.15am, 7.30am, 9.30am, 1.30pm & 3pm, returning from La Lechería at 6.40am, 8.30am, 11.30am, 2pm & 4pm; 30min); Puntarenas (3 daily, 4.20am, 6am & 3pm; 3hr); San Jose (2 daily, 6.30am & 2.30pm; 5hr); Tilarán (2 daily; 2hr 30min). From Tilarán there are buses to La Fortuna and Arénal (7hr) – though it's much quicker and better to take the boat-jeep-boat transfer (see box, p.175). For all other destinations, catch any bus to the Interamericana and flag down the bus you want.

By shuttle Two local shuttles can pick you up from your lodgings: one to Santa Elena reserve and another to the Monteverde reserve. Interbus shuttles (☏interbusonline .com) do countrywide transfers (mostly morning departures) to San José (US$40), Jacó (US$55), La Fortuna (US$35), Manuel Antonio (US$55), Montezuma (US$55), Santa Teresa and Mal País (US$55) and Tamarindo (US$55). Destinations Monteverde reserve (7am, 7.30am, 10.30am, 1.30pm, 3.30pm; returning 7.30am, 8am, 11am, 2pm & 4pm; US$5 return); Santa Elena reserve (6.30am, 8.30am, 10.30am, 12.30pm, returning 9am, 11am, 1pm, 3pm & 4pm; US$4 return). Confirm latest schedules at your lodgings.

By taxi 4WD taxis congregate next to the tourist office. Trips from Santa Elena to Monteverde cost around 3500c; shorter trips are typically around 1500–2000c.

By car The roads around Monteverde and Santa Elena are accessed via the Rancho Grande turn-off (18km north of Puntarenas), at the Río Lagarto turn-off around 15km northwest of Rancho Grande in the direction of Liberia, via Las Juntas (another 10km or so towards Liberia), or via Tilarán if coming from the north.

INFORMATION

Tourist information *Pensión Santa Elena*, next to Banco Nacional, offers excellent impartial advice to everyone, not just guests, and may be able to help you save a few dollars by booking things for you.

ACCOMMODATION

The region's budget accommodation is concentrated in and around Santa Elena. Most lodgings offer tourist information and can book tours. All accommodation reviewed below offers free wi-fi. In the drier months, advance reservations are essential.

Cabinas el Pueblo Down a dirt track beyond the Super Compro supermarket ☎2645 5273 or ☎2645 6192, ☏cabinaselpueblo.com. Attractive little family-run establishment just far away enough from the centre to miss the traffic noise. The cabins with shared bathroom are small and pared down; those with private baths have more character, as well as small TVs and fridges. Breakfast is included. US$25

Cabinas Vista al Golfo A 15min walk up the hill behind the Super Compro supermarket ☎2645 6321, ☏cabinasvistaalgolfo.com. One of the best-value hotels in town, offering spick-and-span rooms with shared or private baths; pay extra to get a TV, fridge and balcony. As well as a kitchen and hammocks, there's an upstairs terrace with stunning views of the Gulf of Nicoya. Rates include breakfast. Dorm US$10, double US$20

Camino Verde B&B Along the dirt road behind the Super Compro supermarket ☎2645 5641, ☏hotelcamino verde.com. These simple, bright rooms, surrounding a shared kitchen and with views of the Gulf of Nicoya, make fine use of attractive natural woods, and some have private baths. The rooms nearest the office are the best. Rates include breakfast. Dorm US$14, double US$30

Montelena Hostel Above Tico y Rico ☎2645 6549, ☏hostelbookers.com. Large sociable hostel right in the middle of Santa Elena. The good-sized dorms with tiled floors, spacious private rooms and guest kitchen make up for the fact that the place gets noisy. Dorm US$8, double US$22

Monteverde Hostel Lodge 75m east of Banco Popular ☎2645 5170, ☏monteverdehostellodghe.com. The town's deluxe backpacker option, this wood-panelled lodge offers comfortable dorms, singles (US$25), doubles, triples and quads. All rooms are en suite with cable TV, and there's a well-stocked kitchen and a communal vibe. Dorm US$12, double US$44

TOURS IN SANTA ELENA

Operators in town offer a variety of excursions. Note that most of the hotels and lodges are able to get you slightly cheaper rates than those listed below.

COFFEE TOURS

Don Juan Coffee Tour On the road out to Tilarán ☏ 2645 7100, ⍟ donjuancoffeetour.com. The Monteverde area is one of Costa Rica's most important coffee-producing regions; learn all about the process on this well-managed organic farm (8am, 10am, 1pm & 3pm; 2hr; adults US$25 including transfers).

★ **El Trapiche** North of Santa Elena ☏ 2645 7780, ⍟ eltrapichetour.com. Tours of this friendly, family-run coffee farm (Mon–Sat 10am & 3pm, Sun 3pm; US$30) come highly recommended. During the 2hr tour you learn all about the coffee and cocoa processing, ride a traditional ox-cart and watch the oxen work the sugar-cane press. You'll also get a cup of some of the best coffee ever, as well as fresh cocoa, sugar-cane juice and sugar-cane spirit, so you'll leave on a caffeine- and sugar-induced high.

HORSERIDING

Desafío/Monteverde Tours Opposite the Super Compro supermarket, Santa Elena ☏ 2645 5874, ⍟ monteverdetours.com. Specializes in horseback tours, including a 2hr 30min ride through forest and farmland (US$40), a day-trip to the San Luís waterfalls (US$80) and an all-day "cowboy" ride (US$79).

★ **Sabine's Smiling Horses** 1km south of Santa Elena cemetery ☏ 2645 6894, ⍟ horseback-ridingtour .com. Multiligual Sabine (English, French, German) whose horses are in excellent condition, arranges a number of horse treks, including the popular 3hr waterfall tour (US$50), monthly full-moon tours, and multi-activity combos.

CANYONING

Finca Modela Ecologica North of Santa Elena, en route to La Cruz ☏ 2645 5581, ⍟ familiabrenestours .com. A 2hr tour (8am, 11am & 2pm; US$50) including swimming, bouldering, hiking, ziplining and a rappel down the largest of the six waterfalls on the property.

NIGHT TOURS

★ **Refugio Vida Silvestre** En route to Tilarán ☏ 2645 6996, ⍟ monteverdewildliferefuge.com. Given that 70 percent of the local wildlife is nocturnal, wildlife spotting after dark is particularly rewarding. While both the Monteverde reserve (see p.147) and the Children's Eternal Forest (see p.146) offer night walks, Refugio Vida Silvestre (5.30–7.30pm & 7.30–9.30pm; US$27 including transport) specializes in them. During the 2hr guided tour you can expect to see two-toed sloths, kinkajou, tarantulas, pit vipers, frogs and more.

★ **Pensión Santa Elena** Next to Banco Nacional ☏ 2645 5051, ⍟ pensionsantaelena.com. The best and most popular cheapie in town. The staff are extremely knowledgeable, and accommodation runs the gamut from camping to stylish private rooms with bath (try to get one of the nifty split-level ones), with access to a guest kitchen. Camping US$7, dorm US$8, double US$20

★ **Rainbow Valley Lodge** 15min walk west of Santa Elena ☏ 2645 7015, ⍟ rainbowvalleylodge.cr.com. Run by Rolf the ultra-helpful Minnesota native, this wonderfully tranquil retreat consists of two self-sufficient doubles with coffee makers and fridges and killer views down the mountainside. There's also a fully equipped cabin and a visiting coati. Rolf has maps and discount coupons for practically everything. Double US$35, cabin US$60

Sloth Backpackers Just on the outskirts, on road heading west ☏ 2645 5793, ⍟ monteverdesloth backpackers.com. You can't miss this friendly hostel, with its eye-catching murals. It's compact, well run by a local Tico girl, and besides the town's best free breakfast (pancakes, eggs, toast, fruit), it's a great place to socialize and book tours. Dorm US$10, double US$20

EATING

If you're self-catering, stock up at the enormous Super Compro supermarket in Santa Elena.

Café Chunches Opposite *Pensión Santa Elena*. Popular with expats, the short menu at this mellow café features sandwiches and salads (1500–2500c), excellent breakfasts (from 2500c), daily specials, and sumptuous banana bread and chocolate brownies (480–850c). The teas and coffees are also top-notch. Local artwork covers the walls and there's plenty of reading material available. Mon–Fri 8am–7pm, Sat 8am–6pm.

El Campesino Near *Hotel el Sueno* in the centre of Santa Elena. Homey little restaurant decorated by someone who loves stuffed animals, with a vast menu featuring excellent *comida típica* (*pintos* 2300c), rice dishes (3500c) and *ceviche* (3000c). Portions are big, so come hungry. Daily 11am–11pm.

The Common Cup 50m north of the Serpentario. The coffee in this friendly little café is anything but common; the barista is an expert in latte art. Besides gourmet coffee there are breakfasts (3000c), panini (3000c), soups and fresh juices (1500c) in glasses the size of tureens. Daily 7am–6pm.

2

★ TREAT YOURSELF

La Chimera Halfway between Santa Elena and Monteverde ☎ 2645 6081. Subdued mood lighting, an excellent wine selection and superb fusion tapas (from 2000c) – try slow-cooked pork and white bean stew, coconut shrimp with a mango-ginger dip and anything featuring aubergine. Daily noon–3pm & 6–9.30pm.

Johnny's Pizzeria 15min walk towards Monteverde. Not the cheapest of the local pizzerias, but by far the best, with wood-fired thin-crust offerings including the signature "Monteverde" (prosciutto, organic leeks and green olives) and plenty of veggie options. Mains from 5500c. Daily 11.30am–10pm.

Morpho's Near *Pensión Santa Elena*. Tico and international dishes served in a semi-tacky rainforesty interior. Dishes such as sea bass in avocado sauce stand out; finish off with the unbelievably rich frozen peanut butter pie. Mains 3500–8900c. Save your bill – it gets you a US$2 discount at the Orchid Gardens. Daily 11am–9pm.

Musashi In the heart of Santa Elena. Lunchtime bento box specials, soba, teriyaki and teppanyaki dishes, as well as sushi, expertly prepared by Venezuelan sushi chef. Mains from 3500c. Tues–Sun 11am–11pm.

★ Sabor Tico 10min walk along the road to the Santa Elena reserve. The best Tico food in town is served at this family-run restaurant, with hungry diners piling in for the massive *casados* (2500c) and giant fruit juices. Prepare yourself for a leisurely meal when this place is packed. Daily noon–9pm.

★ Sabores 20min walk from Santa Elena, towards

the Jardín de Mariposas ⓦ monteverdeicecream.com. Benchmark-setting Monteverde ice-cream parlour that produces seventeen delicious flavours (from 1700c). Also milkshakes, iced coffees and "monkey bananas" (450c). Wed–Mon noon–8pm.

Stella's Bakery 500m in the direction of Monteverde from the Bat Jungle. Freshly baked pastries, pies, brownies, muffins and more. Daily 6am–10pm.

Taco Taco Next to *Pensión Santa Elena*. Great little hole-in-the-wall featuring tacos, quesadillas and burritos, filled with roasted vegetables, chicken or spiced pork (*al pastor*). Mains from 2500c. Daily noon–8pm.

Trio's Near the Super Compro supermarket. Minimalist decor with subdued lighting, black leather seats, huge windows and an inventive menu. Expect unusual soups (such as carrot, sweet potato, coconut and tamarind), gourmet sandwiches and wraps, and standout mains like ribs with guava glaze and chicken stuffed with figs and goat's cheese. Sandwiches from 2500c, mains from 5500c. Daily noon–11pm.

DRINKING AND NIGHTLIFE

Bar Amigos Behind *Camino Verde B&B*. If you embrace the disco balls, thumping reggaetón and vast dance floor, this ski-lodgesque Tico nightclub can be good fun. Drunken hedonism aside, you can just grab a beer and watch US sports on the big screen.

★ Mata é Caña 40m beyond *Morpho's*, towards Cerro Plano. Run by the folks behind *Pensión Santa Elena*, this bar has a friendly, relaxed vibe, with live music, DJs and screenings of sports events.

DIRECTORY

Banks Banco Nacional, at the northern apex of the triangle, has an ATM, as do Banco de Costa Rica and Banco Popular.

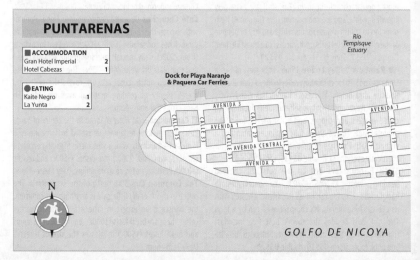

PUNTARENAS

■ ACCOMMODATION	
Gran Hotel Imperial	2
Hotel Cabezas	1

● EATING	
Kaite Negro	1
La Yunta	2

Río Tempisque Estuary

Dock for Playa Naranjo & Paquera Car Ferries

AVENIDA 3

AVENIDA 1

CALLE 35

CALLE 33

CALLE 31

CALLE 29

AVENIDA 1

AVENIDA CENTRAL

CALLE 27

CALLE 25

CALLE 23

CALLE 21

CALLE 19

AVENIDA 2

AVENIDA 1

N

GOLFO DE NICOYA

Health Red Cross (☎2645 6128; 24hr); hospital just north of town. Vitosi pharmacy (Mon–Sat 8am–8pm, Sun 9am–8pm) is across the street from the Chamber of Tourism.

Internet In addition to the accommodation options, a café next door to *Maravilla* restaurant offers access (1000c/hr).

Post office Opposite the shopping mall.

PUNTARENAS

Built on a sand spit just a few blocks wide, heat-stunned **PUNTARENAS**, 110km west of San José, has the look of raffish abandonment that haunts so many tropical port cities. The vast majority of visitors pass through without stopping, as the town is of most use for its transport connections between the southern Nicoya Peninsula and the mainland. While Montezuma-bound travellers can bypass Puntarenas altogether by taking a speedboat from Jacó (see p.152), Puntarenas does have something of a decaying charm, and you can spend a couple of relaxing hours here, waiting for your boat or bus, soaking up the sun and local atmosphere, admiring the quaint little **church** (Av Central, C 5/7) and checking out the vibrant **food market** (in the northeast corner of town, off Av 3).

ARRIVAL AND DEPARTURE

By boat The dock for the car and passenger ferries from Paquera and Playa Naranjo, on the Nicoya Peninsula, is on the northwestern point of town (Av 3, C 31/33). Playa Naranjo is serviced by Coonatramar (☎2661 1069, ⓦcoomntramar.com), while Paquera is reached via Ferry Peninsular (☎2641 0118).

Destinations Paquera (for links to Montezuma, Santa Teresa and Mal País; every 2hr 9am–8.30pm); Playa Naranjo (for links to Nicoya and the western peninsula; 4 daily, 6.30am, 10am, 2.30pm & 7.30pm). Schedules are subject to change; check times at the ferry office by the dock.

By bus Buses from San José arrive at the bus station on the corner of C 2 and Paseo de los Turistas. Services to other destinations depart from across the street.

Destinations Jacó (4 daily, 5am, 11am, 2.30pm & 4.30pm; 1hr 30min); Liberia (8 daily; 3hr); San José (hourly 4.15am–9pm; 2hr 30min); Quepos (6 daily, 5am, 8am, 11am, 12.30pm, 2.30pm & 4.30pm; 3hr 30min); Santa Elena/Monteverde (2 daily, 1.15pm & 2.30pm; 2hr 30min).

To the Nicoya Peninsula Ferries from Puntarenas go to two destinations on the Nicoya Peninsula: Paquera and Playa Naranjo. There is nothing in Naranjo, and you won't have to hang around, as buses to Nicoya (4 daily, 7am, 10.50am, 2.50pm & 7pm; 3hr) meet the ferries. Buses to the beaches along the southern tip only run from Paquera, though it's possible to get from Playa Naranjo to Paquera via 4WD taxi (US$50 or so). Buses to Montezuma (2hr) meet the ferries to Paquera, so there's no need to hang around in Paquera itself. Pay no attention if taxi drivers try to persuade you that the bus isn't coming.

ACCOMMODATION AND EATING

There's little reason to linger in Puntarenas overnight, but there are a couple of reasonable, inexpensive hotels. The

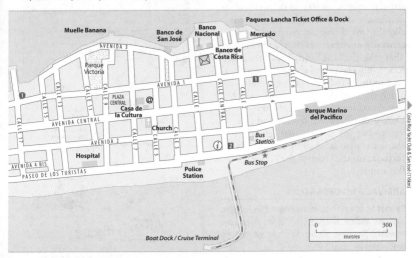

Muelle Banana · Paquera Lancha Ticket Office & Dock · Banco de San José · Banco Nacional · Mercado · AVENIDA 3 · Parque Victoria · Banco de Costa Rica · AVENIDA 1 · PLAZA CENTRAL · @ · Casa de la Cultura · AVENIDA CENTRAL · Church · Parque Marino del Pacífico · AVENIDA 2 · Hospital · Bus Station · AVENIDA 4 BIS · PASEO DE LOS TURISTAS · Police Station · Bus Stop · Boat Dock / Cruise Terminal · 0 — 300 metres · Costa Rica Yacht Club & San José (116km)

2

cheapest, freshest eats are found at the food stands at the Mercado Central.

Gran Hotel Imperial Paseo de los Turistas, C 0/2 ☏ 2661 0579. This faded, wooden-boarded hotel is something of an oddity: the peeling paint in the basic rooms (all with private bath, fans and TVs, some with balcony) is electric pink, while the lobby and hallways are strewn with fashion magazines and pot plants. Handy for the bus stations. <u>US$40</u>

Hotel Cabezas Av 1, C 2/4 ☏ 2661 1045. The best budget option in town, this bright and sunny hotel offers clean and compact rooms (with private or shared bathrooms and TVs) and excellent security. The *dueña* is quite the matriarch, but it adds to the familial ambience. <u>US$25</u>

Kaite Negro Av 1 at C 17. Delicious, typical Tico food, fresh fish (from 2800c), *bocas* (snacks) and a dynamic atmosphere (especially at weekends, when there's live music). Also an excellent cocktail bar.

La Yunta Paseo de los Turistas, C 19/21 ☏ 2661 3216. As the mounted bull heads and cattle prints on the walls suggest, steaks (from 4500c) are the focus here – and are expertly seared. The seafood is equally appealing, but more expensive (from 5500c). Daily noon–10pm.

JACÓ

The thriving resort of **JACÓ** can make no claim to either class or exclusivity: stretching 3km along a main road parallel to the **beach**, it's little more than a brash strip of souvenir shops, bars, restaurants and hotels. As the closest beach to the capital, it's long been a very popular summer weekend destination for *Josefinos*, and now foreign investment is allowing for almost unrestrained (and generally unattractive) development. That said, the long sandy beach remains reasonably clean, and the **surf** is good year-round – indeed, surfing is pretty much the only thing to do here, and the town is built around the industry. Dozens of places rent **boards** and give lessons (see p.153). Alternatively, there's also some nice snorkelling around **Isla Tortuga**, off the coast of the Nicoya Peninsula.

ARRIVAL AND DEPARTURE

By boat Jet-boats to Montezuma (several daily, including 10.45am; confirm schedule; 1hr) depart from Playa Herradura, 2km north of town. Most tour operators will book a ticket for you (US$40).

By bus Buses for San José leave from the Plaza Jacó mall, at the northern end of town. Buses for destinations north leave from in front of the Más x Menos supermarket; for destinations south, wait across the street.

Destinations Puntarenas (from outside Banco Nacional; 4 daily, 6am, 9am, noon & 4.30pm; 1hr 30min); Quepos (4 daily, 6am, noon, 4.30pm & 6pm; 1hr 30min); San José (5 daily, 5am, 7.30am, 11am, 3pm & 5pm; 3hr).

By shuttle Interbus (ⓦ interbusonline.com) offers daily shuttles to San José (US$35), Manuel Antonio (US$35), Monteverde (US$45), Montezuma (US$55) and Santa Teresa and Mal País (US$55).

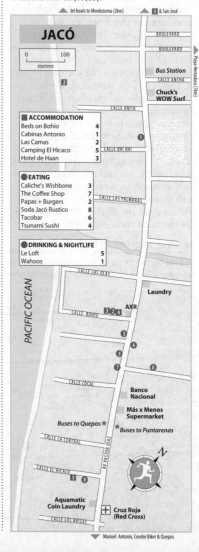

JACÓ

0 — 100 metres

Jet boats to Montezuma (2km) | & San José

BOULEVARD
BOULEVARD
Bus Station
CALLE ANCHA
Chuck's WOW Surf
CALLE ANITA
CALLE BRI BRI
CALLE LAS PALMARAS
CALLE LAS OLAS
Laundry
AXR
CALLE BOHÍO
CALLE COCAL
Banco Nacional
Más x Menos Supermarket
Buses to Quepos ★
★ Buses to Puntarenas
CALLE LA CENTRAL
CALLE EL HICACO
Aquamatic Coin Laundry
Cruz Roja (Red Cross)
CALLE LAS BRISAS
PACIFIC OCEAN
AV PASTOR DÍAZ
Playa Herradura (7km)

Manuel Antonio, Condor Biker & Quepos

■ ACCOMMODATION
Beds on Bohío	4
Cabinas Antonio	1
Las Camas	2
Camping El Hicaco	5
Hotel de Haan	3

● EATING
Caliche's Wishbone	3
The Coffee Shop	7
Papas + Burgers	2
Soda Jacó Rustico	8
Tacobar	6
Tsunami Sushi	4

● DRINKING & NIGHTLIFE
Le Loft	5
Wahoos	1

SAFETY IN JACÓ

Though in recent years the local council has done much to clean Jacó up, there is still a thriving prostitution and drug scene. While prostitution (for over 18s) is legal in Costa Rica, child prostitution is not, and Jacó does have a reputation for attracting middle-aged cruisers who come in search of underage girls. That aside, Jacó is not an unsafe place, and the worst most travellers will come across is petty thievery, pickpocketing and having items stolen from locked cars. Parts of the **beach** can be a bit dodgy at night.

INFORMATION AND TOURS

Tourist information Check out ⓦ jacoguide.com and look for the colourful *Jacó's Map*, printed monthly and complete with tide charts – invaluable for surfers.

Tour operators For surfboard rental, try Chuck's WOW Surf, Av Pastor Díaz at C Ancha (☎ 2643 3844, ⓦ wowsurf .com; board rental US$15–40/day, lessons US$65). Experienced local surfer Gustavo Castillo (☎ 2643 3574 or ☎ 8829 4697), based on the beach in front of *Bohío Grill*, offers lessons for a similar price.

ACCOMMODATION

Make advance reservations during the high season (Dec–April), especially at weekends.

Beds on Bohío C Bohío, behind *Papas + Burgers* ☎ 2643 5251, ⓦ hostelworld.com. Run by young, energetic owners, this is a friendly surfer hangout with lovely staff, a guest kitchen and mod cons. Unfortunately the place could be cleaner and better mattresses wouldn't go amiss. Dorm US$12, double US$40

Cabinas Antonio North of the *Pizza Hut* and bus station ☎ 2643 3043. Friendly, peaceful cabins, popular with budget travellers and Tico families, boasting a lovely pool, a/c, cold-water showers and private parking. There's a laundry next door and you're only a few metres from the beach. US$40

Las Camas Jaco Sol, next to *Sol Dorado* ☎ 8533 7619, ⓦ lascamashostel.com. Hungarian-run cheapie that feels more like a friend's house than a hostel; a good place to socialize. It's not exactly sparkling clean and the *camas* (beds) themselves could be more comfortable. Dorm US$11, double US$24

Camping El Hicaco C Hicaco. Big, tree-shaded campsite (bring your own tent) next to a high-rise hotel. Good central location, though showers, lockers and parking all cost extra. Don't leave any valuables inside your tent. US$5

Hotel de Haan C Bohío ☎ 2643 1795, ⓦ hoteldehaan .com. Just off the main strip, *Hotel de Haan* has a great pool area and is particularly popular with a surfing crowd.

Rooms are cavernous and pretty rustic; there's a kitchen, free internet and laundry service, and surf lessons are available. Dorm US$19, double US$44

EATING

Más x Menos supermarket, on the main Av Pastór Díaz, is particularly well stocked; imported foods are available.

Caliche's Wishbone Av Díaz. Californian-style Tex-Mex with no additives or preservatives but plenty of creative dishes (try the tuna steak with mango salsa), as well as vegetarian options: tofu salad, monster baked potatoes with a variety of toppings, and pizza. The guacamole's awesome, too. Mains from US$7. Daily except Wed noon–10pm.

The Coffee Shop Av Pastor Díaz, across from *Los Amigos*. Freshly baked bread and cinnamon rolls, sandwiches, bagels with cream cheese (2000c) and other Western dishes, along with seriously good coffee (1000c; they roast and grind their own). Daily 7am–2pm.

Papas + Burgers C Bohío. As the name suggests, this place is all about the bap and the beef, and the burgers here aren't at all bad, judging by the surfer crowd that packs the lively terrace. Daily noon–10pm.

Soda Jacó Rustico C Hicaco. The pick of Jacó's *sodas*, packed daily with locals and visitors. An enormous *casado* and a fruit juice or soft drink will leave you with change from 3000c. Daily 11.30am–9pm.

★ **Tacobar** C Pops. There are few dishes in the world more perfect than an expertly prepared fish taco, and that's exactly what you get at this breezy open-air restaurant. Place your order for the type of fish (wahoo, tuna, mahi mahi) and the number of tacos you want and then help yourself to the salad bar and a variety of sauces. Wash it down with an epic mint lemonade. Perfection. Daily 8am–6pm.

Tsunami Sushi Av Pastor Díaz, near the Banco de Costa Rica. Excellent super-fresh sushi, as well as *gyoza*, spring rolls, noodles and teriyaki, served to a pounding beat; for a quieter meal, opt for seats outside. Nightly specials with many sushi sets going for half price (3000c). Sun–Thurs 5–10pm.

DRINKING AND NIGHTLIFE

Le Loft Av Pastor Díaz. A slice of urban sophistication in the middle of Jacó, this swanky nightclub featuring local DJs is a place to dress up for.

Wahoos Av Pastor Díaz, just before *Chuck's* and *Sunrise*. Bilingual karaoke on Fri and Sat, plus rock and reggae nights, and screenings of all the big US sports events. The hefty cocktail list helps to generate a friendly, relaxed atmosphere.

DIRECTORY

Banks There are several banks along the main strip, including Banco Nacional.

Bike/scooter rental Condor Biker rents out mountain bikes (US$15–12/day; US$100 deposit). There are several scooter and ATV rental outlets, including AXR on C Bohío.

2

Health The Red Cross (☎ 2643 3090) maintains a clinic on the southern end of the strip between C El Hicaco and C Las Brisas.

PLAYA HERMOSA

A quieter alternative to Jacó, peaceful **PLAYA HERMOSA** is just 7km away. Offering a long stretch of darkish sand that has a challenging, often fierce, break, the village is pricier than Jacó and geared towards serious surfers.

ARRIVAL AND DEPARTURE

By bus The bus from Jacó to Quepos runs through Playa Hermosa – ask the driver for the right stop – or you can take a taxi (around 4500c).

ACCOMMODATION AND EATING

Cabinas Las Arenas ☎ 2643 7013, ⓦ cabinaslasarenas .com. Rustic wooden cabins with private bathrooms and fans; an ideal place to meet other surfers, with a familial atmosphere. US$49

Dos Gringos Hearty food (mains 5800–8200c) and surf videos.

QUEPOS

Compact **QUEPOS**, backed against a hill and fronted by a muddy beach, can look pretty ramshackle, but it's got a friendly Tico vibe to it, and makes an excellent base for visiting the region's celebrated national park, given its concentration of good inexpensive accommodation, bars and restaurants.

THINGS TO SEE AND DO

You can go whitewater rafting, sea-kayaking, horseriding and dolphin-watching, but for most visitors, the town's biggest draw is its proximity to Parque Nacional Manuel Antonio and its beaches, 7km south.

Rainmaker Aerial Walkway

The **Rainmaker Aerial Walkway** (US$15, US$35 with guide; ☎ 2777 3565, ⓦ rainmakercostarica.org), 1km northwest of Quepos, is an excellent canopy walk that passes through a privately owned chunk of rainforest. From the platforms high up in the treetops you get great views of the surrounding primary and secondary rainforest, and there's excellent bird-spotting to be had. The canopy walk aside, there are also several excellent hiking trails in the reserve.

ARRIVAL AND DEPARTURE

By plane Sansa and NatureAir connect Quepos to San José and Liberia. The airport is 5km out of town.
By bus All buses arrive at and depart from the bus terminal in the town centre, next to the Banco de Costa Rica. In high season, buy your tickets to San José in advance.
Destinations Jacó (4 daily, 4.30am, 7.30am, 10.30am & 3pm; 1hr 30min); Manuel Antonio (every 30min 6am–7.30pm; 30min); Puntarenas (3 daily, 8am, 10.30am & 3.30pm; 3hr 30min); San Isidro, via Dominical (3 daily, 5.30am, 11.30am & 1.30pm; 3hr); San José (7 daily, 5am, 8am, 10am, noon, 2pm, 4pm & 7.30pm; 3hr); Uvita via Dominical (2 daily, 10am & 7pm; 4hr 30min).
By shuttle Interbus (☎ 2777 7866, ⓦ interbusonline .com) runs shuttles to Jacó (US$35), La Fortuna (US$35), Monteverde (US$45), Montezuma (US$55), San José (US$45) and Santa Teresa and Mal País (US$55); reserve in advance.

INFORMATION AND TOURS

Tourist information Check out the Jaime Peligro bookshop (Mon–Sat 9.30am–5.30pm, ⓦ queposbooks .com) with its excellent selection of local guides, maps and other useful tourist info on the area.
Tours There are a couple of good Class III and IV whitewater runs in the area; h2o Adventures (☎ 2777 4092, ⓦ riostropicales.com) organize rafting trips. All-rounder Iguana Tours (☎ 2777 1262, ⓦ iguanatours.com) can make the necessary arrangements for sea-kayaking, horseriding or dolphin-watching.

ACCOMMODATION

There are good budget lodgings both in Quepos proper and en route to Manuel Antonio.
Backpackers Manuel Antonio On the main road, halfway between Quepos and Manuel Antonio ☎ 2777 2507, ⓦ backpackersmanuelantonio.com. This sociable hostel boasts hot-water showers, spotless dorms, private rooms (shared baths), a splash pool and a good location (handy for the bus, *Angel* restaurant, the supermarket and laundry). Dorm US$12, double US$35
Central Backpackers 500m along the road to Manuel Antonio, ⓦ centralbackpackers.hostel.com Small, secure new hostel with a super-helpful and knowledgeable manager who happens to be a good cook to boot. The rooms are spotless and family-style dinners encourage bonding between guests. Dorm US$13, double US$38
★ **Vista Serena Hostel** Halfway along the road to Manuel Antonio ☎ 2777 5162, ⓦ vistaserena.com. Run by

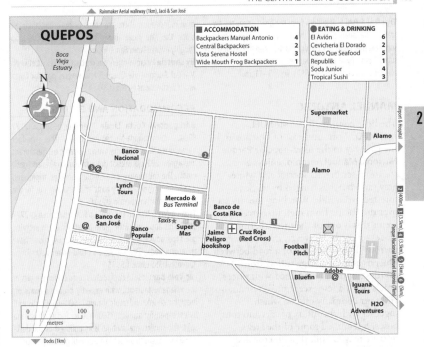

QUEPOS

Boca Vieja Estuary

■ ACCOMMODATION	
Backpackers Manuel Antonio	4
Central Backpackers	2
Vista Serena Hostel	3
Wide Mouth Frog Backpackers	1

● EATING & DRINKING	
El Avión	6
Cevicheria El Dorado	2
Claro Que Seafood	5
Republik	1
Soda Junior	4
Tropical Sushi	3

Supermarket

Alamo

Banco Nacional

Alamo

Lynch Tours

Mercado & Bus Terminal

Banco de Costa Rica

Banco de San José

Taxis

Banco Popular

Super Mas

Jaime Peligro bookshop

Cruz Roja (Red Cross)

Football Pitch

Bluefin

Adobe

Iguana Tours

H2O Adventures

0   100
metres

Docks (1km)

Airport & Hospital

Parque Nacional Manuel Antonio (7km)

---

a helpful bilingual Tico mother and son, this hillside haven of calm is a wonderful place to relax and watch the sunset from the hammocks on the terrace. Shoestringers can choose from economy fourteen-person dorms and premium four-person ones (all with bathroom); if you want more privacy, opt for a fully equipped bungalow. Dorm US$10, bungalow US$45

Wide Mouth Frog Backpackers Two blocks west of the bus station ☏ 2777 2798, ⦿ widemouthfrog.org. Behind the high security gate is a veritable oasis. Basic, clean rooms form a quad around the pool. Staff are informative, and there's a big kitchen, internet room, TV lounge, and friendly dogs underfoot. The one gripe is that some rooms are stuffy as only part of the window will open, and you have to pay US$1 to exchange a book. Rates include breakfast. Dorm US$11, double US$30

EATING AND DRINKING

Super Mas (opposite the bus terminal) is a well-stocked supermarket with some exotic imported ingredients. Some of the best dining options are along the road to Manuel Antonio.
El Avión 2km from Manuel Antonio village. If you're wondering how this 1954 Fairchild C-123 plane got here, story has it that it was due to be passed on to the Nicaraguan Contras in the 1980s, but never made it due to the Oliver North scandal. The Contras' loss is your gain; this airplane-cum-bar is a great spot for a sunset beer.

Cevicheria El Dorado One block north of the bus terminal. Forget the nondescript decor at this tiny spot; it's the tasty *ceviche* you've come for. Fresh catch of the day is paired with lime juice and coriander, with a few cooked plantain slices on the side. Mains around 2500c. Mon–Sat 11am–9pm.

Republik On the road parallel to the sea. Swish bar/club with a long list of potent cocktails (2300–3800c; the mojitos are particularly good), a chic retro decor and ladies' night on Thurs. The party often lasts till 4am.

Soda Junior Just north of the bus station. This tiny, Tico-run *soda* is the best place in town for inexpensive fried chicken and lip-smacking *casados*. Breakfast from 1700c, mains from 2500c. Daily 8am–9pm.

★ TREAT YOURSELF

Claro Que Seafood By the *Hotel Sí Como No*, 2km north of Manuel Antonio. Killer views and imaginative fusion dishes, crafted largely from organic ingredients, are the order of the day at this breezy, casual restaurant. Expect the likes of coconut squid with home-made tartar sauce and macadamia-encrusted mahi mahi with blackberry sauce. Mains from 5500c. Daily noon–9pm.

2

Tropical Sushi Half a block from the beach, near the fire station. The Japanese chef at this authentic sushi joint crafts some excellent rolls (try the dragon roll), and the sashimi is super-fresh. If you favour quantity over quality, go for the all-you-can-eat option for US$23. Daily 5–11pm.

MANUEL ANTONIO

The little community of **MANUEL ANTONIO**, 7km southeast of Quepos and the gateway to the ultra-popular **Parque Nacional Manuel Antonio**, enjoys a stunning setting, its spectacular white-grey sand beaches fringed by thickly forested green hills. Watching the sun set over the Pacific from high up here, it seems this is one of the most charming places on earth. However, the winding, narrow 7km bottleneck of a road between Quepos and the village suffers from overdevelopment – it's lined with pricey hotels (with a few exceptions), restaurants and tour company offices, which, together with the influx of cars and tour buses, has tainted some of the area's pristine magic. Still, though crowded most of the time, the park remains one of Costa Rica's loveliest destinations, with wildlife-spotting aplenty.

WHAT TO SEE AND DO

Tiny Manuel Antonio village is booming, with an ever-increasing stream of visitors heading to the park (see below). Other **activities** include body-boarding and sea-kayaking, with equipment rental along the main sandy swathe of Playa Espadilla; be aware of rip currents. Beginner **surfers** can also take to the waves here, with plenty of surfing instruction (of varying quality) and board rental available. Cross the rocky headland at the western end of Playa Espadilla and you'll find yourself on **La Playita** – Costa Rica's prime gay beach (not accessible during high tide). Access to the beaches is free, so beware of scammers trying to tell you otherwise, and be particularly cautious with your belongings, as **theft** along the beaches is a depressingly common occurrence.

ARRIVAL AND DEPARTURE

By bus Buses between Quepos and Manuel Antonio drop passengers off 200m before the park entrance at the mini-roundabout. There are stops in both directions all along the 7km route (buses run in a continuous loop roughly every 30min 6am–10pm).

By shuttle Interbus offers direct shuttle service between Manuel Antonio (via Quepos) and several popular Costa Rican destinations (see p.108).

ACCOMMODATION AND EATING

Backpackers Costa Linda Near the beach, ☎ 2777 0304, ⓦ costalinda-backpackers.com. This budget paradise is a hive of activity, with a sociable bar/restaurant and a great 2000c breakfast (fresh fruit, pancakes and *gallo pinto*). The cell-like rooms – singles, doubles, triples and quads – however, are very basic and some are not for the claustrophobic. Per person **US$10**

Tico Lodge 200m up the road up from the beach ☎ 2777 5085. This appealing little place boasts excellent security, good tour advice and laundry service. The cosy rooms have terracotta decor, TVs, fridges and cold-water bathrooms. A/c costs US$5 extra. **US$35**

★ **Vela Bar** Close to *Backpackers Costa Linda*. The pick of the village restaurants, with expertly prepared *mariscos*, including *ceviche* and creole shrimp (5500–6500c), as well as less expensive *casados* (3500–4500c) and a fine banana split. The service, meanwhile, is as polished as the dark-wood tables, which are set in a peaceful garden terrace.

PARQUE NACIONAL MANUEL ANTONIO

Despite being the smallest, at just 16km square, **PARQUE NACIONAL MANUEL ANTONIO** (Tues–Sun 7am–4pm; US$10; ☎ 2777 0644) is Costa Rica's most popular National Park. It preserves lovely **beaches**, **mangroves** and humid tropical **forest**. You can also see the unique *tómbolo* of **Punta Catedral**: a rare geophysical formation, a *tómbolo* is created when an island becomes slowly joined to the mainland through accumulated sand deposits. **Wildlife** – including sloths, snakes, green kingfishers, laughing falcons, iguanas, capuchin, howler and spider monkeys – is in abundance, though you'll be hard pressed to spot the park's shyest primate, the squirrel monkey.

Within the park you'll come across many signs imploring you not to feed the monkeys (or any other wildlife), and you should take that warning very seriously, as feeding wild creatures leads to their dependence on handouts, sickness and even death.

PARQUE NACIONAL MANUEL ANTONIO

WHAT TO SEE AND DO

A network of several well-marked trails allows you to explore deep into the park; you can walk all the trails within half a day. From the entrance, the wide **Sendero Perezoso** (1.8km) leads to the rocky headland of the **Punta Catedral**, preceded by the wide, beautiful crescent of **Playa Manuel Antonio**, popular with swimmers and capucin monkeys. At the western end of the beach is a semicircle of rocks, visible at low tide and believed to be a **turtle trap** of pre-Columbian origins; at low tide, turtles would be unable to swim out. The **Sendero La Trampa** starts here, linking with the 1.4km loop of **Sendero Punta Catedral** that winds its way around the headland, with several viewpoints overlooking the beaches and rocky islets beyond. The trail exits at **Playa Espadilla Sur**, a long beach with usually very calm waters, just a minute's walk from Playa Manuel Antonio. From the main Sendero Perezoso, instead of heading down to the beaches, you can take the other trail that

splits in two: the upper branch heads up to **El Mirador** (1.3km) – a bluff that overlooks Puerto Escondido and a mirage-like beach beyond – while the other fork leads down to the small **Playa Gemellas**, good for sunbathing and swimming. **Playa Puerto Escondido** is only accessible from Playa Gemellas at low tide; sometimes the trail is closed altogether.

ARRIVAL AND INFORMATION

By bus Frequent buses run from Quepos to Manuel Antonio village (see opposite).

By car If you're thinking of driving to the park from Quepos, don't. Parking costs an exorbitant 3000c and there have been reports of break-ins and thefts. Take one of the frequent buses instead.

Park information To beat the inevitable crowds, get to the park for opening time. The entrance is accessed on foot from Manuel Antonio village. Pay your entrance fee at the Coopalianza office, around 75m short of the entrance. Guides (US$25 for 2hr), available at the entrance, can be very helpful when it comes to spotting wildlife in the dense foliage; only certified guides are allowed inside the park.

2

The Nicoya Peninsula

The Nicoya Peninsula is one of the most popular tourist destinations in Costa Rica. Many come for the beaches, which are some of the best in the country. The likes of **Tamarindo**, **Santa Teresa** and **Playa del Coco** have long been popular with surfers for the country's best wave action, while quieter stretches like **playas Nosara and Sámara** offer more space for contemplation of the beautiful coastline. Some of the beaches in Guanacaste Province, in the northern section of the peninsula, can be difficult to reach on public transport, but the rewards are great for those with 4WDs who brave the challenge. Similarly, unless you have your own vehicle, pretty much the only way to reach **Montezuma** or Santa Teresa, two of the most popular beach hang-outs in the country, in the isolated southern part of the peninsula, is by boat from Jacó or Punta Arenas, followed by a bone-shaking ride along rough and rugged dirt roads.

GETTING AROUND

It can be tricky getting from south to north Nicoya. When it comes to public transport, Montezuma, Playa Santa Teresa and Mal País are rather cut off from the rest of the peninsula. Minor beachside roads leading northwest to Sámara are impassible by anything but a 4WD, with rivers to be crossed at low tide only. North of Montezuma, the paved road ends at Paquera. If you're driving, the unpaved road connecting Paquera and Playa Naranjo is dirt-and-gravel, steep and winding in places and potholed. In dry season, a regular vehicle can make it, but in the rainy season, only a 4WD will do. If travelling by public transport, you have no choice but to take a ferry from Paquera to Puntarenas (see p.151), and then another to Playa Naranjo.

MONTEZUMA

The colourful beach town of **MONTEZUMA** lies near the southwestern tip of the Nicoya Peninsula, about 40km south of Paquera. Sandwiched between hills covered in lush vegetation and white-sand coves framed by aquamarine sea, the once remote fishing village is still relatively cut off from the rest of the country by bad roads, and attracts a laidback crowd who come here for sun, sea, yoga classes and a more tolerant outlook than in other parts of the country.

WHAT TO SEE AND DO

Some of the loveliest **beaches** in the country stretch out in either direction: white sands, dotted with jutting rocks and leaning palms and backed by lush greenery, including rare Pacific lowland tropical forest. Montezuma makes a good base for a day excursion south to the **Cabo Blanco** reserve (see p.160), and, for a shorter walk, the environs are laced with a number of **waterfalls**.

Beaches

The beach in front of the football field is excellent for sunbathing, while if you're looking to snorkel, your best bet is **Playa Las Manchas**, 1km west of the village (low tide only). Despite the inviting coastline, **swimming** isn't very good on the beaches immediately north of Montezuma – the waves are rough and the currents strong. It's better to continue north towards Playa Grande along an attractive, winding **nature trail** (1.5km; 30min), which dips in and out of several coves. There's reasonable swimming here, and decent surfing, as well as a small waterfall at its eastern edge.

Waterfalls

The trail to a trio of **waterfalls** starts just west of the village, towards Cabo Blanco, from a car park opposite the *Hotel Amor del Mar*. The first waterfall is a five-minute walk along a dirt path; in dry season you might only see a few trickles of water here. To get to the second, main, waterfall, you can follow the footpath along the river, which involves some scrambling up and down boulders (10min); there's also a precarious, narrow footpath that climbs to a smaller waterfall on top of the second one. (This walk requires the agility and balance of a monkey, given the sheer drop.) The deep pool surrounding the second waterfall is perfect for swimming and diving, and, as at the third waterfall, there's a fun rope swing above it. Always take care with

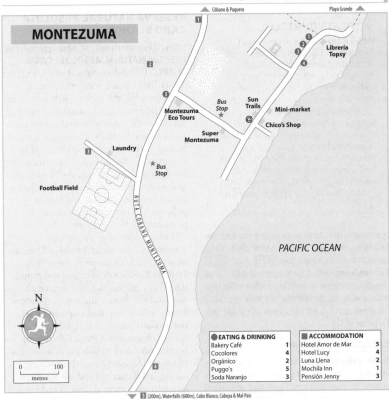

MONTEZUMA

Cóbano & Paquera

Playa Grande

Librería Topsy

Bus Stop

Sun Trails

Mini-market

Montezuma Eco Tours

Chico's Shop

Super Montezuma

Laundry

Bus Stop

Football Field

RUTA CÓBANO MONTEZUMA

PACIFIC OCEAN

N

0   100
metres

● EATING & DRINKING		■ ACCOMMODATION	
Bakery Café	1	Hotel Amor de Mar	5
Cocolores	4	Hotel Lucy	4
Orgánico	2	Luna Llena	2
Puggo's	5	Mochila Inn	1
Soda Naranjo	3	Pensión Jenny	3

▼ 5 (200m), Waterfalls (600m), Cabo Blanco, Cabuya & Mal País

waterfalls, especially in the wet season, on account of **flash floods**, and under no circumstances try to climb them; several people have died that way.

ARRIVAL AND INFORMATION

By boat There are daily fast ferries to Jacó (9.30am; 1hr; US$45); book with any tour agency.

By bus Services arrive and depart from across the football field. To get to Santa Teresa and Mal País, you need to change at Cóbano.

Destinations There are services to Cabo Blanco (2 daily, 8.15am, 4.30pm; 45min), Cóbano (6 daily 8am–8pm; 30min), Paquera (6 daily, 5.30am, 8am, 10am, noon, 2pm & 4pm; 2hr) and San José (2 daily, 6.15am & 2pm; 6hr).

By car In the rainy season, the steep, unpaved road between Cóbano and Montezuma requires a 4WD.

Tour operators Montezuma Bike Tours (☎ 8871 1540, ⓦ montezumabiketours.com) offers mountain-biking adventures (up to 4hr long), tackling rugged mountain and beach terrain. For snorkelling (US$55) and diving off Isla Tortuga, try Montezuma EcoTours (☎ 2642 1000, ⓦ montezumaecotours.com).

ACCOMMODATION

Montezuma is a popular destination, so book in advance. Unfortunately, none of the lodging options is particularly good value. Camping on the beach is illegal.

Hotel Lucy 500m south of the centre ☎ 2642 0273. A Montezuma stalwart and one of the village's best cheapies: it has a nice veranda draped with hammocks upstairs, and clean and simple rooms, some with private cold-water bathrooms (those upstairs have sea views); make sure your door locks properly, though. Dorm U̲S̲$̲1̲1̲, double U̲S̲$̲3̲8̲

Luna Llena ☎ 2642 0390, ⓦ lunallenahotel.com. Catching the breeze on the hilltop above the village, this friendly German-American run hostel consists of a mix of rooms (some rather small), most with shared facilities, and a single dorm with mattresses that could do with replacing. There's no a/c, but there are two guest kitchens and a communal space to relax in. Dorm U̲S̲$̲1̲5̲, double U̲S̲$̲3̲8̲

Mochila Inn 150m down the road to Cóbano ☎ 2642 0030. This secluded hostel is a sanctuary for wildlife, especially monkeys, which come by for lunch. Reggae plays gently in the communal area, and the mood is

2

supremely relaxed. Accommodation is pretty basic and back-to-nature – there are even outdoor privies, which can be an adventure at night. Dorm US$10, double US$25

Pensión Jenny North of the football field ☎ 8835 3114. Though it must be pretty much the only place in Costa Rica without wi-fi, this pleasant blue-and-white guesthouse has several spartan but spotless rooms with shared bath. Per person US$20

EATING AND DRINKING

Bakery Café Opposite Librería Topsy. Pretty murals lend a relaxed vibe to this open-walled café, which is particularly good for breakfast: great eggs, French toast, yoghurt and granola, and pancakes (all around 2500c) are on offer. Daily 8am–3pm.

Cocolores In a garden by the beach. A justifiably popular restaurant offering a varied international menu with European, Middle Eastern and Latino dishes including a great coconut fish curry. Good value considering the excellent quality (mains from 4500c), though service is not a strong point. Tues–Sun 4.30–9.30pm.

Orgánico Next to *Soda Naranjo*, before the *Bakery Café*. This health-conscious café entices you in with its excellent range of healthy (and extremely tasty) falafels, salads, sandwiches and other dishes (try the Thai-spiced burger). The smoothies and milkshakes are not to be missed either. Mains around 4000c. Daily 8am–9pm.

Puggo's North of the football field. Colourful restaurant specializing in Middle Eastern cuisine, so get your fill of falafel, grilled meat kebabs, and *baba ghanoush* here, as well as a few token gringo-pleasers. Service is very slow. Mains from 4000c. Daily noon–11pm.

Soda Naranjo Opposite *Cocolores*. Hidden behind a wall of leafy foliage, this low-key *soda* serves delicious *casados* and fresh fish dishes at some of the best prices in town (mains around 3500c). The range of fruit juices is excellent, too. Mon–Sat 7am–9.30pm.

RESERVA NATURAL ABSOLUTA CABO BLANCO

Some 7km southwest of Montezuma, the **RESERVA NATURAL ABSOLUTA CABO BLANCO** (Wed–Sun 8am–4pm; US$10) is Costa Rica's oldest protected piece of land, covering the entire southwestern tip of the peninsula, and established in 1963 thanks to the environmental campaigns of a Danish/Swedish couple. The natural beauty of the area is complemented by the array of wildlife found here, including howler monkeys, agouti, sloths, peccaries and snakes, while local seabirds include brown boobies, frigates and brown pelicans, the islands off the coast providing ideal nesting grounds.

Hiking, swimming and wildlife-watching are the main activities. There are only two trails in the park: the 4.5km **Sendero Sueco**, a demanding and muddy hike that takes around two hours each way, and the shorter and gentler **Sendero Danes**, a 2km loop that starts and ends on the Sendero Sueco. The highlight of Sendero Sueco is the **Playa Cabo Blanco** – a pristine sand-and-pebble beach at the end of the trail, against a backdrop of jungle, jutting headlands and teal waters. Don't forget to leave around 2pm to make it back to the ranger station for closing time.

ARRIVAL AND INFORMATION

By bus A bus rattles between Montezuma and Cabo Blanco twice daily (8.15am & 3.30pm from Montezuma, heading back at 9am & 4pm; double-check the schedule); fewer departures during rainy season.

By taxi A taxi from Montezuma costs around US$18.

By bike You can cycle down to Cabo Blanco on a mountain bike; there are rental operators in Montezuma (see p.158).

By 4WD or quad bike From Mal País, the park is reached via a beautiful, narrow and steep unpaved road running through the jungle; 4WDs or quad bikes only.

Facilities You can't stay in the park, so have return transport planned, and take plenty of sunblock and water.

MAL PAÍS AND PLAYA SANTA TERESA

The long beach of **PLAYA SANTA TERESA**, at the tip of the peninsula on the Pacific side, is luring increasing numbers of travellers with its picturesque setting and some of the best surfing in Costa Rica. By contrast, the almost deserted stretch of road, dotted with the odd hotel, house and restaurant, coupled with a breathtaking coastline that makes up neighbouring **MAL PAÍS**, remains virtually untouched. Though there's been a fair amount of development in the area as a whole, the atmosphere is still chilled and friendly, with a barefoot surfers' vibe. Despite the villagey feel, the area is pretty cosmopolitan, and you'll find lots of good places to **eat**, even on a budget.

ARRIVAL AND INFORMATION

By bus Buses arrive at and depart from Playa Carmen (the intersection where the right fork takes you to Santa Teresa, and the left to Mal País); services sometimes continue into Mal País and/or Santa Teresa themselves.

Destinations Cóbano (for connections to Montezuma; 4 daily, 7am, 11.30am, 2pm & 6.30pm; 45min); San José (2 daily, 6am & 2pm; 6hr).

By car The road between Cóbano and Santa Teresa/Mal País is unpaved, and rutted and steep in places, so a 4WD is recommended year-round.

By shuttle Interbus (ⓦ interbusonline.com) runs shuttles to San José (US$45); it might be possible to catch one to Santa Teresa, too. Book ahead.

By taxi Taxis to Cóbano cost around US$35.

Banks Playa Carmen (at the intersection of the roads from Cóbano, Mal País and Santa Teresa) is home to a Banco Nacional and a Banco de Costa Rica.

ACCOMMODATION

Cuesta Arriba 300m north of the football pitch, Santa Teresa ⓣ 2640 0607, ⓦ cuestaarribahoste.com. In a peaceful spot, this seems like more of a luxury villa than a hostel, with whitewashed walls, a pool, spacious communal areas festooned with hammocks and large, bright dorms with sturdy bunks and good mattresses. A basic breakfast is thrown in – our only quibble is that the a/c private rooms (separate from main building) are rather compact. Dorm US$12, double US$65

★ **Hotel Meli Melo** Around 2km along Santa Teresa's main road from the intersection ⓣ 2640 0575, ⓦ hotel melimelo.com. Delightful guesthouse run by a friendly French couple who are attentive to guests' needs. The spacious rooms, surrounded by lush vegetation, have all mod cons, as well as unusual bathrooms and access to an outdoor kitchen. Bikes available to borrow. US$55

Pura Vida Mini Hostel Just off the main street, Santa Teresa ⓣ 2640 0912, ⓦ minihostelsantateresa.com. If you're in Santa Teresa with a view to partying all night and surfing all day, sleep not being terribly important, this lovely spot is your best bet for meeting like-minded people. For marginally greater security than in the main house, opt for one of the thatched cabins by the pool or one of the a/c bungalows. The communal kitchen is a bonus. Dorm US$15, double US$32, cabin per person US$16

Tranquilo Backpackers Just off the main street, Santa Teresa ⓣ 2640 0589, ⓦ tranquilobackpackers.com. Matching the high standards of its sister hotel in San Jose, the friendly *Tranquilo* provides simple four- to six-bed dorms and a few spacious private doubles, plus a sociable atmosphere, board and bike rentals, and famous pancake breakfasts. Camping US$7, dorm US$11, double US$35

Wave Trotter Surf Hostel Up the hill behind *El Pulpo* in Santa Teresa ⓣ 2640 0805, ⓦ wavetrotterhostel.com. Run by two Italian guys (and Coco the dog), this is a surfer's paradise, complete with boards lining the walls and chilled beats echoing through the communal area. The only thing that tops the hot-water showers and clean, comfortable (if spartan) dorms and private rooms is the welcoming, familial atmosphere. Dorm US$12, double US$30

EATING AND DRINKING

Baraka Café Santa Teresa. This chilled-out café serves tremendous breakfasts: creamy lattes come in huge, comforting mugs, there are fabulous tostadas with real raspberry jam and even the *pinto* tastes like a delicacy. Expect to pay 2000–3300c. Daily 7am–4pm.

SURFING IN SANTA TERESA

Santa Teresa and its surrounds have some of the best suring on the peninsula. **Playa Hermosa** (not to be confused with Playa Hermosa near Playa del Cocos), north of Santa Teresa, is an excellent beach for beginners with consistent right and left breaks. **Playa El Carmen**, straight down from the main intersection, is suitable for beginners also, while **Playa Santa Teresa** boasts a fast break that's for advanced surfers.

Given the abundance of surf shops and surf schools, **prices** are competitive, and you can expect to pay around US$45 for a 2hr surfing lesson and around US$15/20 for half-/full-day board rental.

Jobbie's Surf Shop ⓣ 8703 4048. A recommended, Canadian-run rental/surf school.

Natu Surf School ⓣ 0240 0714. Long-running and reliable school.

2

Burger Rancho Santa Teresa. The burgers here (2500–4500c) are the real deal – unlike in so many places in Costa Rica – and can be washed down with a delicious milkshake or smoothie. Daily 5–10pm.

Caracoles Mal País. The best *soda* in the area, with tables set in the large grounds by a beach overrun with hermit crabs. Choose from classic *casados* or more inventive mains – Caribbean-style prawns, perhaps, or soya-glazed tuna steak. Mains from 3000c. Daily noon–9pm.

★ **Chop It** Playa Carmen Mall, near the intersection. Come to this tiny spot for lunch or brunch; choose from over a dozen ingredients to create a mega salad or grilled taco with filling, or opt for a gourmet burger (including the veggie Portobello mushroom burger with goat's cheese and red onion jam). Then head next door for some authentic *gelato*. Mains 3500c. Tues–Sun 11am–4pm.

★ **Koji's** Playa Hermosa, 50m south of the Hermosa Valley School ☎ 2640 0815. Who'd have thought that this remote location would play host to some of the best sushi in the country? Chef Koji, a master of his craft, delivers wonderful signature rolls, super-fresh sashimi and beautifully grilled and mouth wateringly tender octopus. Wash it all down with a local microbrew. Reserve ahead or else pitch up at the bar. Dishes from 3000c. Wed–Sun 5.30–9.30pm.

PLAYA SÁMARA

SÁMARA, one of the more peaceful, though increasingly upmarket, beach resorts on the Nicoya Peninsula, lies 30km southwest of Nicoya. Compared to other Pacific beach towns, it's quite remote and relatively inaccessible, which makes for a pleasantly relaxing atmosphere. The long, dark-sand beach here is one of the country's calmest for swimming – there's a reef about 1km out that takes the brunt of the Pacific's power. The moderate waves also make Sámara a great place to learn to

---

★ **TREAT YOURSELF**

Brisas del Mar Up on the hill at the *Hotel Buenos Aires*, Santa Teresa ☎ 2640 0941. This breezy open-air terrace overlooking Santa Teresa is the perfect place to canoodle with your sweetie over cocktails or to enjoy a fabulous dinner, the daily specials chalked up on the board. Expect the likes of Creole shrimp stack with chilli cornbread, grilled fish with a ginger-mango glaze and beef stroganoff with a twist. Leave room for the exquisite desserts. Mains from 7000c. Tues–Sun 4–10pm.

---

surf, and there's a great cluster of **dive sites**, easily reachable by boat.

ARRIVAL AND DEPARTURE

By bus Buses to San José depart from the main intersection south of the *Entre Dos Aguas* B&B. Nicoya-bound buses leave from the corner shop by the football field.

Destinations Nicoya (hourly 5.30am–6.30pm; 1hr); San José (2 daily, 4.30am & 8.30am; 5hr).

By shuttle Interbus (ⓦinterbusonline.com) runs shuttles to San José via Montezuma (US$45); book ahead.

ACTIVITIES

Surf schools and dive centres Matteo Caretti at the Marea Surf Shop, C Principal (☎ 8887 3059 or ☎ 2656 1181), is a kind, reassuring and professional instructor (private class US$35/hr). Renting boards or taking lessons from C&C Surf School (☎ 2656 0590) ensures that 10 percent of the proceeds go to a local turtle conservation project, and if you don't want to embarrass yourself in front of other novices, you can opt for private lessons (US$45). Pura Vida Dive Center (☎ 8523 0043, ⓦpuravidadive.com), across the street from *Posada Matilori*, runs trips to local dive sites (around US$105 for a two-tank dive).

ACCOMMODATION

Camping Cocos Beyond *El Ancla* hotel ☎ 2656 0496. In a fabulous palm-dotted beach location, this ultra-popular campsite has basic *servicios* and provides electricity until 10pm. Keep an eye on your stuff, as the beach is notorious for thieves at night. US$7

Hotel Playa Sámara Behind the football pitch ☎ 2656 0190. Rudimentary rooms with clean beds, tiled floors and thimble-sized private bathrooms but little else. Not for light sleepers; there's a club next door. US$30

Posada Matilori First left along the beach road, then first right ☎ 2656 0984. Brightly painted guesthouse with spotless (small) rooms with orthopaedic mattress, TV, safe, fan or a/c and shared bath. There's a well-equipped kitchen and free boogie boards; the friendly multilingual owner is extremely helpful. Dorm US$17, double US$30

Tico Adventure Lodge ☎ 2656 0628, ⓦticoadventure lodge.com. Stunning American-run lodge built around the trees on the property. There's plenty of greenery, and while the a/c rooms don't benefit from much natural light, they are spotless and comfortable, there's free coffee all day long and the owner is a great source of local info. US$50

EATING AND DRINKING

Ahora Sí At the Natural Center for Yoga. This organic shop and café is a super spot for breakfast – from granola to eggs the way you like them – and for healthy vegetarian lunches: the home-made gnocchi are particularly good. Lunch mains from 3000c. Daily 7.30am–4pm.

★ **El Dorado** 150m beyond the Banco Nacional. Outstanding Italian food (3500–9000c), wine and hospitality. In true Mediterranean style, the Italian owners run things exactly as they would back home and the dishes are executed with precision and flair. Daily noon–10.30pm; closed during the low season.

Al Manglar Near the north end of the beach. Unpretentious open-air place serving great pizza and other Italian dishes (try the gnocchi). Mains from 4500c. Daily 5–10pm.

Lo Que Hay Just off the beach. At this mellow spot, you can watch the game on the big screen while munching your way through awesome tacos (try the delicious fish variety) as well as fajitas and other backpacker-friendly food. Mains from 3000c. Daily 7am–late.

La Vela Latina Near *El Ancla* hotel, on the beach. Sit in rocking chairs as the friendly staff mix you one of their cracking daiquiris (2500c) or another expertly blended cocktail. Daily 11am–midnight.

PLAYAS NOSARA

The stimulating 25km drive from Sámara north to the **PLAYAS NOSARA** runs along shady, secluded dirt-and-gravel roads punctuated by a few creeks – a 4WD is essential year round. Generally referred to collectively, there are three beautiful, rugged beaches in the area – Nosara, Guiones and Pelada – of which **Playa Guiones** is the most impressive, and most popular with surfers. The beach settlement itself is spread over a large area; the main **village** of Nosara is 3km inland, home to a small airstrip. Some attempts have been made to limit development in the area – a good deal of the land around the Río Nosara has been designated a wildlife refuge – and the vast majority of people who come to Nosara are North Americans and Europeans in search of quiet and natural surroundings.

ARRIVAL AND INFORMATION

By plane There are two daily flights from San José with Sansa and NatureAir.

By bus Buses depart from the corner shop by the football field.

Destinations Nicoya (5 daily, 5am–3pm; 2hr); San José (1 daily, 2.45pm; 6hr). For Sámara take the bus to Nicoya and stop at Bomba de Sámara (ask the driver). From here you can jump on buses passing through to Sámara from Nicoya.

By car A dusty, bumpy, potholed dirt road branches off towards Nosara from the paved Nicoya–Samara road 5km before Samara; in dry season, a regular car will get you as far as Playa Nosara, but 4WD is required to reach the beaches further along.

Tourist information Two useful websites are ⓦ nosara .com and ⓦ surfingnosara.com.

ACCOMMODATION

Casa Tucan On the beach road in Playa Guiones, 100m from Banco de Costa Rica ☎ 8611 7954. This friendly Tico-run place has everything: spacious rooms, relaxing pool area and in-house bar and restaurant, all in a lush garden a stone's throw from the beach. Good for groups. US$80

Gilded Iguana Behind Playa Guiones ☎ 2682 0450, ⓦ thegildediguana.com. Scores highly thanks to its large rooms with polished floors and high ceilings, private baths, fridges and colourful paintings, as well as its curvy pool, hammocks and bar/restaurant. Family rooms are particularly good value for groups. US$50

★ **Kaya Sol** Behind Playa Guiones ☎ 2682 0080, ⓦ kayasolsurfhotel.com. With a mix of clean and airy dorms, spacious, tastefully decorated private rooms in bungalows with their own baths, and longer-stay accommodation with kitchens, *Kaya Sol* is justifiably popular. A lovely pool with mini-waterfall, hummingbirds in the garden and an excellent restaurant complete the package. Dorm US$13, double US$50

Solo Bueno On the road to Playa Guiones ☎ 2682 1284, ⓦ malekuhostel.com. The owners of this place are surf addicts, and it shows in the ambience and decor – dorms are basic and the reception area packed with hammocks. You can camp in the grounds (tents for rent) and there are boards and bikes for hire, as well as yoga and surf classes and regular Twister sessions. Camping US$7, dorm US$16

EATING AND DRINKING

If self-catering, try the Super Nosara supermarket, in Nosara proper to the south of the football field.

Beach Dog Cafe By the beach. Crowd-pleasers at this chilled-out surfers' café include awesome smoothies, killer fish tacos and ample breakfasts – from eggs to French toast. Phonecalls to the US and Canada are free. Mains from 3300c. Thurs, Fri & Sun–Tues 8am–3pm, Wed & Sat 8am–10pm.

La Casona At the entrance to Nosara proper. This family-run place is a great spot for a tasty and relaxed evening meal; *comida típica* is in the 2500–4400c range. Daily noon–9pm.

Gilded Iguana *Gilded Iguana* hotel. Upmarket gringo bar with Mexican food and well-priced lunch specials, including fish tacos, fajitas and fish and chips. Mains from 3500c. Daily; live music Tues & Sat.

Robin's Café 50m beyond Banco de Costa Rica. Enjoy delicious organic sandwiches and wraps (2500–3500c), crêpes, pastries, and home-made ice cream in the little garden in front of this café. Raw-food fans will appreciate the non-cooked specials. Free wi-fi. Mon–Sat 8am–5pm, Sun 10am–4pm.

2

2

REFUGIO NACIONAL DE FAUNA SILVESTRE OSTIONAL

Some 8km northwest of Nosara, Ostional and its chocolate-sand beach make up the **REFUGIO NACIONAL DE FAUNA SILVESTRE OSTIONAL**, one of the most important nesting grounds in the country for **Olive Ridley turtles**, which come ashore here to lay their eggs between May and November. If you're in town during the first few days of the *arribadas* – the mass arrival of turtles to lay eggs – you'll see local villagers carefully stuffing bags full of eggs and slinging them over their shoulders. This is quite legal: villagers of Ostional and Nosara are allowed to harvest eggs, for sale or consumption, during the first three days of the season only. You can't swim here – the water's too rough and there are sharks.

It takes about fifteen minutes to drive the gravel-and-stone road from Nosara to the refuge; alternatively, you can bike it or take a taxi (around 2000c); hitchhiking seems to be popular also.

NICOYA

Busy **NICOYA** is one of the largest settlements on the peninsula. Located inland, it has little to offer travellers besides being a handy place to change buses. You won't need to spend the night, as onward bus connections are frequent.

ARRIVAL AND DEPARTURE

By bus The bus station is at Nicoya's southernmost point, just before the road bridge leading out of town. Services from Liberia pull into a stand 300m north of the main bus station. Destinations Liberia (every 30–60min 3.30am–10pm; 2hr 30min); Playa Naranjo (for connecting ferry to Puntarenas; 4 daily, 5am, 9am, 1pm & 5pm; 3hr); Playa Nosara (Mon–Sat 5 daily, 4.45am, 10am, 1pm, 3pm & 5.30pm; Sun 4 daily, 10.30am, 1pm, 3pm & 4.30pm; 2hr);

Sámara (12 daily 5am–9pm; 2hr); San José (Mon–Sat 10 daily 3am–5pm; Sun 5 daily; 4hr 30min).

EATING

Cafetería Daniela C3 at Av 2. If you're stuck in town for a couple of hours, sate your hunger pangs here with great fajitas (3500c), *casados* (from 2500c) and *pintos* (from 1800c). Mon–Sat 7–9pm.

PLAYA TAMARINDO

Stretching for a couple of kilometres over a series of rocky headlands, **PLAYA TAMARINDO** ("Tamagringo") is one of the most popular Pacific coast beaches, though it couldn't be any less Costa Rican in character – rampant development and swarms of tourists looking for a good time are its dominant features. There's a decent selection of restaurants, a lively surfing scene and, in high season, a strong party vibe.

WHAT TO SEE AND DO

Tamarindo is the perfect beach for beginner **surfers**: gentle waves push against the grey-white sands on a daily basis, all year round. Intermediates can tackle the wave that breaks in front of the *Tamarindo Diria Hotel*, while serious surfers will want to head a few kilometres south to Playa Langosta or north to Playa Grande (see p.166). Numerous places **rent surfboards** – typically US$15–20 for a day's rental of a longboard. You can also take river estuary **tours** through the mangroves of nearby Parque Nacional Marino Las Baulas (see p.167) and moonlight turtle tours to the same park (Nov to mid-Feb), as well as windsurfing and snorkelling elsewhere.

ARRIVAL AND INFORMATION

By plane There are up to four flights per day from San José with Sansa and NatureAir.

LEARNING TO SURF IN PLAYA TAMARINDO

Several good operators in town offer **surfing lessons**, which should cost US$40–50. Check the student-to-instructor ratio when booking surfing lessons; 2:1 is best.

Mato's Surf Shop ☎ 2653 0845, ⓦ matossurfshop .com. Going strong for more than twelve years, with bargain 2hr lessons for US$35.

Witch's Rock Surf Camp Towards the northern end of the beach ☎ 2653 0239, ⓦ witchrocksurfcamp.com. Regular trips to Ollie's Point and Witch's Rock, and surfing lessons for all capabilities.

By boat An estuary separates Tamarindo from Playa Grande, and though the distance is easily swimmable and the water quite shallow, the estuary is also home to crocodiles. Take one of the many loitering boats across (US$1).

By bus San José-bound buses arrive at the Empresas Alfaro office behind the *Babylon* bar; all other buses leave from *Zullymar Hostel*, across the street.

Destinations Liberia (12 daily, 4.30am–6.30pm; 1hr 30min–2hr); San José (2 daily, 5.30am & 2pm; 6hr); Santa Cruz, for points south (6 daily, 6am–4pm; 1hr 30min).

By shuttle Tamarindo Shuttle (☎2653 2626, ⓦtamarindoshuttle.com) offers a door-to-door service from Liberia's airport (US$20; 1hr 30min). There are also

direct shuttles to Tamarindo from Santa Elena/Monteverde (see p.148) and San José (see p.118).

Tours Papagayo Excursions, 1km north of the town centre on the road to Liberia ☎2653 0254, ⓦtamarindo.com/papagayo. For river estuary and turtle tours, plus canopy, snorkelling, horseriding and kayaking trips, this friendly and professional outfit offers competitive rates.

ACCOMMODATION

Wherever you stay, you should make sure to make reservations well in advance for high season.

Beach House Hostel At the north end of main road ☎2653 2848, ⓦbeachhousetamarindo.com. Staying at

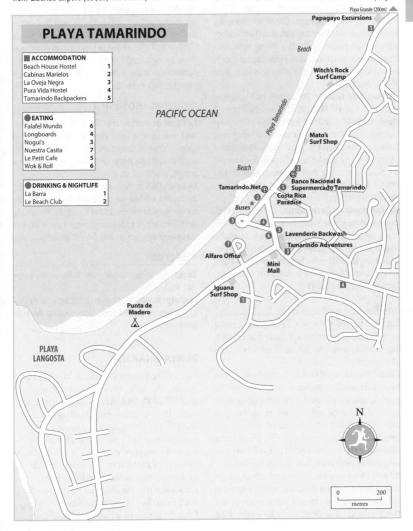

PLAYA TAMARINDO

■ ACCOMMODATION
Beach House Hostel	1
Cabinas Marielos	2
La Oveja Negra	3
Pura Vida Hostel	4
Tamarindo Backpackers	5

● EATING
Falafel Mundo	6
Longboards	4
Nogui's	3
Nuestra Casita	7
Le Petit Cafe	5
Wok & Roll	6

● DRINKING & NIGHTLIFE
La Barra	1
Le Beach Club	2

PACIFIC OCEAN

Playa Grande (200m)
Papagayo Excursions
Beach
Witch's Rock Surf Camp
Playa Tamarindo
Mato's Surf Shop
Beach
Banco Nacional & Supermercado Tamarindo
Tamarindo.Net
Costa Rica Paradise
Buses
Lavendería Backwash
Tamarindo Adventures
Alfaro Office
Mini Mall
Iguana Surf Shop
Punta de Madero
PLAYA LANGOSTA

N

0 200
metres

2

this laidback hostel is a bit like having your very own beach villa – there's a great communal terrace, a/c, proper mattresses and wonderful beach views. Totally chilled surf vibe – so peaceful, in fact, that monkeys swing by in the mornings. Dorm US$14, double US$35

Cabinas Marielos On the main road ☎2653 0141, ⓦcabinasmarieloscr.com. Set back from the main road, among tropical gardens, these charming cabins have floral curtains, security boxes, a/c and bathrooms accessed via saloon-style doors (the bathroom walls don't reach to the ceiling, so they're not the most private). There are also some cheaper rooms with fan. The well-informed owner runs turtle tours. US$45

La Oveja Negra Next to Tamarindo Adventures ☎2653 0025, ⓦlaovejanegrahostel.com. Chilled-out place with a huge common area decorated with a surfboard collage and sporting a massive TV. Run by a friendly surfer dude, it's not the place to catch up on your snoozing, but if you're looking to surf and party, you're in the right place. Dorm US$12, double US$30

★ **Pura Vida Hostel** 500m up main road leading up from beach road ☎8747 8780, ⓦpuravidahostel.com. A stand-out hostel – and not just because of the huge thatched *palapa* that shades the communal lounge area. Sociable without being a party hostel, *Pura Vida* is presided over by a knowledgeable hostess; the dorms and doubles are immaculate, there are hammocks and rocking chairs to relax in, and they offer plenty of extras to liven up your stay. Dorm US$15, double US$45

★ **Tamarindo Backpackers** ☎2653 4545, ⓦtamarindobackpackers.com. On a secluded dead-end street, this wonderfully friendly hostel boasts a kidney-shaped pool in a lush garden filled with creeping plants, a/c in dorms as well as rooms, hammocks perpetually filled with relaxing travellers and a chilled-out atmosphere. Dorm US$15, double US$45

EATING

Tamarindo has one of the most diverse eating scenes in Costa Rica, but prices can be high; there's a supermarket, Supermercado Tamarindo, just before the turn towards Playa Langosta.

Falafel Mundo Just off the loop. Tiny joint with just two tables and a handful of wooden stools at the counter. The menu is similarly small: falafel or *shawarma* kebabs in pita bread (3000–3500c), with hummus an optional (and highly recommended) extra. Daily 9am–11pm.

Longboards Near the main T-junction. This popular joint is all about the BBQ ribs, superb pulled pork and other meaty delights. Mains from 2500c. Thurs–Tues 11am–10pm.

Nogui's On the loop. Casual restaurant, virtually on the beach, serving excellent breakfasts, decent sandwiches and snacks, though it's the fine fish and seafood that brings in the repeat customers – from the wonderful fish

tacos to whole grilled fish. It's a great place to enjoy the sunset with a cold beer (1400c). Mains from 4500c. Daily 11am–11pm.

Nuestra Casita Tucked off the main road. This adorable Tico spot dishes up a brilliant *típico* breakfast for 1500c, and *casados* from 2000c in a secluded area away from the mad buzz of town. Well worth the time it takes to find it. Daily 8am–9pm.

Le Petit Cafe Plaza Tamarindo. A great little spot for breakfast or lunch, this café, on a square, serves an excellent pastrami Reuben (3260c) as well as tasty smoothies and spiced pumpkin lattes – service can be grumpy, though. Mon–Sat 8am–5pm.

★ **Wok & Roll** Opposite Plaza Tamarindo. Amazingly, you can find authentic Korean food in Costa Rica – order the house special of sticky ribs with rice and kimchi (7000c), or, if chilli-tinged pickled cabbage is not your thing, try the bulgogi (5000c), tom yum goong (4500c), noodle dishes and – a concession to Western palates – pecan pie. Daily noon–10pm.

DRINKING AND NIGHTLIFE

La Barra On the main road. This funky little bar/club is most popular with Ticos, although they're more than happy to share the dance floor. Merengue and salsa carry on till around 1am, when the DJ begins to mix the latest pop hits. Good fun. Daily.

Le Beach Club On the beach. Perfect for drinking during the day and watching the sun set over the sea, this beach bar has installed hammocks and even beds right on the sand. DJs take over on Saturdays, when it seems like half the town gathers here to party. Daily 11am–late.

DIRECTORY

Banks There are several banks with ATMs, notably on the main road.

Laundry Lavandería Backwash (2000c/kg) is on the left as you turn up towards Playa Langosta from the main beach road.

PLAYA GRANDE

Part of the Parque Nacional Marino Las Baulas, the long, wide crescent of sand that is **PLAYA GRANDE** stretches for nearly 5km. Besides the superb **surfing** beach, the village – a straggle of houses, guesthouses and restaurants spread out along a couple of roads – is a wonderfully low-key place to stay, being the antithesis of Tamarindo's unbridled hedonism across the narrow channel to the south. And then there are the **turtles** – Playa Grande is part of a nature reserve that protects the highly endangered leatherback turtles (see below).

ARRIVAL AND INFORMATION

By bus There are no buses from Playa Grande, but you can take a bus from Tamarindo (see p.164).

By boat You can cross the estuary from Tamarindo (US$1) and then walk up the beach.

Surf schools Playa Grande Surf School at *Mi Casa Hostel* offers lessons for all abilities and rents boards, as does Playa Grande Surf Camp.

ACCOMMODATION AND EATING

El Huerto Next door to *Indra Inn*. This excellent Mediterranean restaurant hits the spot with its Spanish tortillas and perfectly *al dente* home-made pasta, but the biggest accolade is reserved for their beautiful melt-in-your-mouth wood-fired pizzas (from 5000c). Daily except Wed 6.30–10.30pm.

⭐ **Indra Inn** On main road at the entrance to Playa Grande ☎2653 0938 or ☎2653 4834, ⊛indrainn.com. Run by the friendly team of Matt, Natalya and Marshmallow the dog, this brightly painted guesthouse has spacious a/c rooms and a sociable bar area where guests and staff congregate in the evenings. An ample breakfast is included and the hosts are a great source of local info. US$60

⭐ **Mamasa** On main road 200m before *Indra Inn*. Perch on a carved wooden seat under the thatched *palapa* and order a BLT with Cajun mahi mahi, home-made bagels with cream cheese or granola with yogurt and lemongrass honey. There's no better place for lunch/brunch/Saturday-night specials, and service is super-friendly. Sandwiches 4000c. Tues–Fri & Sun 10am–2pm, Sat 10am–2pm & 5.30–9pm.

El Manglar & Mi Casa Hostel Near the southern end of the beach ☎2253 0952, ⊛micasahostel.com. This sociable surfer magnet is two places in one: a hostel with a clean but basic dorm and a hotel with a/c en-suites and pricier villas, all surrounding a pool in the middle of a lush garden. Dorm US$15, double US$40

Playa Grande Surf Camp South end of the beach ☎8870 4164, ⊛playagrandesurfcamp.com. Very near the beach, this surfers' haven has three cosy A-frame cabañas with a/c sitting by the pool, and fan-cooled cabins with hammocks on the patio. You can grill your own dinner on the barbecue or use the guest kitchen. Cabaña US$45, cabin per person US$15

⭐ **Rip Jack Inn** ☎2653 0480, ⊛ripjackinn.com. Homey, relaxed upstairs restaurant, with cats on the bar and imaginative dishes chalked up on the board. For lunch (mains around 4500c), there are sandwiches, fish tacos and big juicy burgers; evening dishes (mains from 7000c) include the likes of clam and mussel linguini and papaya ginger shrimp with softshell crab. Daily noon–10.30pm.

PARQUE NACIONAL MARINO LAS BAULAS

On the Río Matapalo estuary between Conchal and Tamarindo, **PARQUE NACIONAL MARINO LAS BAULAS** (daily 8am–noon & 1–5pm; open for guided night tours in season; US$10 out of season, US$25 in season including tour; ☎2653 0470) is less a national park than a reserve, created to protect the nesting grounds of endangered **leatherback turtles**. These wondrous giants, which come ashore to nest from October to mid-February, have laid their eggs at **Playa Grande** for possibly millions of years, and it's now one of the few remaining such nesting sites in the world. Turtle sightings are likely on one of the **guided tours**, but not guaranteed on a nightly basis; you wait at the visitor centre, and if a turtle is spotted by a scout, the information is relayed by radio to your guide who will then escort you to the area. Tours are conducted in silence; cameras and smoking are not allowed on the beach.

Around 200m from the park entrance, the **El Mundo de la Tortuga** exhibition (daily 2–6pm, later when turtles are nesting; US$5) includes an audio-tour in English and some stunning turtle photographs. You'll learn about the leatherbacks' habitats and reproductive cycles, along with the threats they face and current conservation efforts. If you come on one of the turtle-watching tours, the exhibition is included in the tour price.

ARRIVAL AND INFORMATION

On foot/by boat There is no public transport to the park, so you can either walk from your lodgings in Playa Grande or visit by boat from Tamarindo, a service that usually comes as part of tour packages, or can be booked when you call to reserve your entrance ticket.

Turtle tours Tours, which run between October and mid-February, typically take place from 9pm up until 2am at the latest. Tickets can be bought at the southern entrance, where the road enters the park near the *Villa Baulas*. Booking in advance is highly recommended, as numbers are strictly limited.

PLAYA DEL COCO

Some 35km west of Liberia, **PLAYA DEL COCO** was the first Pacific beach to hit

2

the big time with weekending Costa Ricans from the Valle Central. It's turned out to be something of a nightmare: a cross between an upmarket resort filled with brash hotels, casinos and restaurants, and a hot spot for budget travellers in search of Jägermeister and a dance floor. However, **surfers** use the place as a jumping-off point for nearby Witch's Rock and playas Hermosa and Panamá, the **nightlife** is lively, and there are some good **diving** operators, so it could be worth spending a day or two here.

WHAT TO SEE AND DO

The main road down to the beach is a noisy melange of roaring 4WDs and souvenir markets, while the area nearer the beach is a little quieter, with the football pitch and some funky bars that are packed out most nights. The dark-sand beach is not the cleanest, so it's best to take the bus or taxi to the lovely, neighbouring, **Playa Hermosa**, with its clear blue waters and volcanic sand. Diving is popular; dive centres take you to the islands off the coast, such as **Isla Santa Catalina**, 20km offshore.

ARRIVAL AND INFORMATION

By bus Buses stop at the terminal opposite Deep Blue Diving Adventures on the main street.
Destinations Liberia (7 daily 5.15am–8pm; 1hr); San José (3 daily, 4am, 8am & 2pm; 5hr).
Tour operators Dutch-owned Rich Coast Diving, on the main road about 300m from the beach (☎ 2670 0176, ⊛ www.richcoastdiving.com), organizes snorkelling (US$50) and scuba trips to Bat Islands, and offers the chance to dive with bull sharks (from US$75) and to frolic with manta rays at Las Catalinas. Summer Salt Dive Centre, next to *Jardín Tropical* (☎ 2670 0308, ⊛ www.summer-salt.com), is a reputable Swiss-run outfit that also offers dolphin- and whale-watching excursions.

ACCOMMODATION

Cabinas Coco Azul Behind the church ☎ 2670 0431. Friendly cheapie, offering clean rooms with hot-water private bathrooms and fans or a/c set around a garden with mango trees. The rooms on the ground floor get little natural light. U̅S̅$̅3̅5̅
Hotel Mar & Mar On the waterfront ☎ 2670 1212. Just a few metres from the beach, this breezy motel-style option comes with large, bright, fan-cooled rooms, and

hammocks swaying in the breeze on the upstairs terrace. Breakfast is 2500c. U̅S̅$̅2̅0̅
Pure Vibes 200m north of *Lizard Lounge*, 5min from main street. Though the dorms are basic and rather cramped, this large hostel is well geared towards sociable travellers: there's a large L-shaped pool with swim-up bar, the bar staff treat you like friends and the manager holds his famous Jamaican BBQs at the on-site Jamaican-themed restaurant. Other thoughtful touches include bikes for rent. Dorm U̅S̅$̅1̅5̅, double U̅S̅$̅4̅5̅
★ **Ruby's** On the road leading to Mapache ☎ 2389 6746. Quiet, comfortable and friendly, this family-run hotel boasts bright rooms with firm mattresses, a/c and an attractive courtyard with barbecue and shaded tables. Security is tight, and the American owner is relaxed and unobtrusive. Although on the main road, it is quiet and just a 10min walk to the town's best bars. U̅S̅$̅4̅0̅

EATING AND DRINKING

Beach Bums At the northern end of the beach. This large barn, decorated with surfboards, assorted flotsam and jetsam and graffiti, is the town's best bar, perpetually haunted by surfers and leather-skinned expats. Great spot for a beer, bar snacks and live music (Wed–Sun). Daily 11am–midnight.
La Dolce Vita Pueblito Sur. As close as you get to authentic Italian in this town, serving crisp wood-fired pizzas, home-made pasta and fresh fish dishes. Mains from 4500c. Daily 8am–10pm.
Jardín Tropical Overlooking the park at the far end of town. The best breakfast in town – a hearty *gallo pinto* will set you back 2500–3000c – and generous lunchtime *casados*. Daily 8am–4pm.
La Vida Loca At the south end of the beach. Supersized nacho platters, huge burgers, chilli dogs and pizza at this lively gringo heaven. The bar is really hopping in the evenings. Mains from 2500c. Daily 11am–11pm.

Guanacaste

Guanacaste Province, bordered to the north by Nicaragua, and by the Pacific Ocean to the west, is distinctly different from the rest of Costa Rica – indeed, if not for a very close vote in 1824, Guanacaste might have been part of Nicaragua. While the traditional **sabanero** (cowboy) culture, music and folklore for which the region is famous have been overtaken by tourism, there is still undeniably something special about the place. The **landscape** has an arid beauty to it, despite much of it having come about essentially through the slaughter of tropical dry forest: the wide, rolling plains and the brooding humps of volcanoes are washed in muted earthy tones. While the province's beaches (roughly two-thirds of the Nicoya Peninsula is in Guanacaste) attract the most visitors, the mud pots and stewing sulphur waters of **Parque Nacional Rincón de la Vieja** and the tropical dry forest cover of **Parque Nacional Santa Rosa** draw scores of nature aficionados to the interior every year, while the town of **Liberia** is seeing more international traffic these days thanks to its expanded international airport and proximity to the Nicoya Peninsula.

LIBERIA

Most travellers use **LIBERIA** as a jumping-off point for the national parks of **Rincón de la Vieja**, **Santa Rosa** and **Palo Verde**, an overnight stop to or from the **beaches** of the Nicoya Peninsula or a convenient stopover on the way to Nicaragua.

Liberia also boasts several lively **festivals**. In February, **Expo Pérez Zeledón** sees ten days of parades, bands, fireworks and bull-running. On July 25, **El Día de la Independencia** celebrates Guanacaste's independence from Nicaragua with parades, rodeos, fiestas and roving marimba bands.

WHAT TO SEE AND DO

The town is arranged around its large **Parque Central**, properly called Parque Mario Cañas Ruiz. This is one of the loveliest central plazas in the country, ringed by benches and tall palms that shade gossiping locals. Its startlingly modern **church** seems somewhat out of place.

About 600m away at the eastern end of town, the colonial **Iglesia de la Agonía** is more arresting, with a mottled yellow facade. On the verge of perpetual collapse – it has had a hard time with earthquakes – it's almost never open. The town's most interesting street is **Calle Real** (also known as Calle Central or Calle 0). In the nineteenth century this was the entrance to Liberia, and practically the entire thoroughfare has been restored to its original – and strikingly beautiful – colonial simplicity.

ARRIVAL AND INFORMATION

By plane Liberia's international airport is 12km west of the town. Flights arrive largely from North America. A taxi

LIBERIA

Terminal Liberia

& Rincón de la Vieja (8km)

Nicaraguan Border, Santa Rosa

Airport, Nicoya & Beaches

Mercado Central

Pulmitan Terminal

Banco Nacional

Tica Bus stop

Bancredito

Banco Popular & Banco de San José

Toyota Rent a Car

Super-market

Centro Commercial Santa Rosa

INTERAMERICANA

Police

Parque Central

Banco de Costa Rica

Gobernación

Iglesia de la Agonía

Río Liberia

AVENIDA CENTRAL

N

San José

0   200
metres

EATING
Café Liberia	4
Copa de Oro	5
Liberia Supremacy	2
Morales House	6
Rancho Dulce	3
Smoothies & Wraps	1

ACCOMMODATION
Hostal Ciudad Blanca	4
Hotel Los Angeles	1
Hotel Liberia	2
Hotel Posada del Tope	3
Hotel La Siesta	5

2

into Liberia costs around US$25. There are no buses. Destinations include Miami, New York, Atlanta, Denver, Toronto and Brussels, with domestic flights (Sansa and Nature Air) to San José, La Fortuna, Tamarindo and Nosara. **By bus** All buses (except those from and to San José and Playa del Coco) arrive at the Terminal Liberia (Av 7, C 12/14) at the northwestern edge of town. The Pulmitan Terminal (Av 5, C 10/12) is one block southeast of Terminal Liberia. International Tica Bus (w ticabus.com) departures for Managua via Antigua, Nicaragua, arrive and depart from in front of *Hotel Bromadero* (next to the *McDonald's* by the main crossroads); tickets must be booked in advance through *Hotel Liberia*.

Destinations La Cruz/Peñas Blancas (Nicaraguan border; 14 daily 5am–6pm; 1hr 45min); Managua via Antigua, Nicargua (4 daily 6am, 9am, 10.30am, 3.30pm; 5hr); Nicoya (Mon–Sat every 30min 3.30am–9pm, Sun hourly 8am–6pm; 2hr); Playa del Coco (hourly 5am–11am, then 12.30pm, 2.30pm & 6.30pm; 1hr); Playa Panamá via Playa Hermosa (8 daily 4.30am–5.30pm; 1hr 15min); Playa Tamarindo (hourly 3.50am–6pm; 1hr 30min–2hr); Puntarenas (8 daily 5am–3.30pm; 3hr); San José (hourly 4am–8pm; 4hr 30min); Santa Rosa (take the bus for the Nicaraguan border and ask to be dropped at the park; 40min).

Tourist information Staff at *Hotel Liberia* and *Hotel Posada del Tope* can answer questions on the local area and provide information on a shuttle service to Rincón de la Vieja (US$25).

ACCOMMODATION

All the accommodation options reviewed below offer free wi-fi.

Hostal Ciudad Blanca Av 4, C 1/3 **☎** 2666 3962. The facade of this restored colonial mansion is grander than the a/c rooms, which are comfortable enough but not all adequately ventilated. For sound sleepers only, as the animals in the yard (including roosters!) can get noisy. US$40

Hotel Los Angeles Av 7, C 2/4 **☎** 2665 5900. Friendly, central motel with secure parking and anonymous, spotless rooms with a/c and TV. Substantial discounts for solo travellers. US$40

Hotel Liberia C 0, 75m south of the Parque Central **☎** 2666 0161. In a historic home, this cheapo hotel has a good setup for backpackers: hammocks in the sunny courtyard, wi-fi, laundry, book exchange and informative staff. The simple rooms, on the other hand, could seriously use some sprucing up. Dorm US$12, double US$26

Hotel Posada del Tope C 0, 150m south of the municipal government building **☎** 2666 3876. Popular place in a beautiful old house. The bare-bones rooms in the main building are stuffy and could be cleaner; opt for the brighter and only slightly more expensive ones across the street in the annexe, which are set around a charming courtyard. All have fans and share bathrooms. Per person from US$10

★ **Hotel La Siesta** C 6, Av 4/6 **☎** 2666 0606, **e** lasiesta liberia@hotmail.com. Attractive hotel with comfortable a/c doubles with private bathrooms and cable TV, set around a courtyard with a fountain and small pool. There are also simpler fan rooms, with TV and private showers and toilets (though, bizarrely, no sinks), in a nearby annexe. Plus laundry, free internet and one of the best restaurants in town. US$50

EATING AND DRINKING

Local treats include *natilla* (sour cream) eaten with eggs or *gallo pinto* and tortillas. For a real feast, try the various *desayunos guanacastecos* (Guanacastecan breakfasts). For rock-bottom-cheap lunches, head for the stalls at the market by the Liberia bus terminal. There's a large supermarket on C 0, Av 3/5.

Café Liberia C 0, next to *Hotel Liberia*. In a stunning nineteenth-century property, with grand wooden doors and a frescoed ceiling, *Café Liberia* has perfectly brewed cappuccinos and lattes, plus crêpes, bagels, salads and sandwiches (including a few vegetarian options). Mains from 1500c. Mon–Fri 8am–7pm, Sat 10am–6pm.

Copa de Oro C 0, Av 2. Unassuming joint with sport on the TV, quick service and an intriguing mural on the far wall. The menu features hearty *casados* (3500c), *ceviche*, and the house special – *arroz copa de oro* (seafood rice). Wed–Mon 11am–10pm.

Liberia Supremacy Av 1, C 5/7. Reggae on the stereo, cheap beer on tap, a young crowd, and posters of the usual suspects: Che, Marley et al.

Morales House Av 1 at C 14. Rub shoulders with cowboys at this rustic bar decked out with bulls' heads and with *ranchera* music on the stereo. Single women might not feel too comfortable.

Rancho Dulce C 0, Av Central. With its bamboo walls, tiny stools and laidback air, *Rancho Dulce* feels more like a beach bar than a *soda*. Throughout the day it does a roaring trade in excellent *casados* (from 1800c), sandwiches and *refrescos*. Daily 8am–10pm.

Smoothies & Wraps C 0 at Av 3. A corner hole-in-the-wall, serving exactly what the name suggests. Some of the imaginative smoothies (from 1500c) are practically a meal in themselves. Daily noon–8pm.

DIRECTORY

Banks Av Central is lined with several banks, including Banco Nacional and Banco de Costa Rica, both across from the Parque Central.

Health Hospital Dr Enrique Baltodano Briceño (**☎** 2666 0011, emergencies **☎** 2666 0318) is in the northeastern part of town, behind the stadium.

Post office Between Av 3 and Av 5, in the white house across from the empty square field bordered by mango trees.

PARQUE NACIONAL RINCÓN DE LA VIEJA

The earth around **PARQUE NACIONAL RINCÓN DE LA VIEJA** (US$10; ☎2661 8139), northeast of Liberia, is actually alive and breathing: **Volcán Rincón de la Vieja**, the park's namesake, is very much active. Though it last erupted in 1991, rivers of lava continue to boil beneath the thin epidermis of ground, while **mud pots** (*pilas de barro*) bubble, and puffs of steam rise out of lush foliage, signalling sulphurous subterranean springs. The dramatically dry surrounding landscape, meanwhile, varies from rock-strewn savannah to patches of tropical dry forest and deciduous trees, culminating in the blasted-out vistas of the volcano crater itself. This is great terrain for **camping**, **riding**, **hiking** and **wallowing in mud**, with a comfortable, fairly dry heat – although it can get damp and cloudy at the higher elevations around the crater. **Birders**, too, will enjoy Rincón de la Vieja, as there are more than two hundred species in residence.

WHAT TO SEE AND DO

The park has **hiking trails** for all levels, which begin from one of the two *puestos* (ranger stations) – **Santa María** to the east, and **Las Pailas** to the west. *Puesto* Santa María is an old colonial house, rumoured to once be the country retreat of US President Lyndon Johnson, and has some rustic sleeping arrangements (see below).

The hiking trails

Most treks start from Las Pailas, although the main one – the demanding uphill track to the volcano's **crater**, which can be tackled on foot, horseback or a combination of the two – can be embarked on from both. This is one of the best hikes, if not *the* best hike, in the country. A variety of elevations and habitats reveals hot springs, sulphur pools, bubbling mud pots and fields of purple orchids, plus of course the great smoking volcano at the top. It is possible to hike without a **guide**, but should you wish to organize a guided trek ask at Las Pailas (☎2661 8139). Alternatively, several hotels in Liberia offer treks. Ring ahead before

you start out, as the trail is often closed due to low visibility or high winds.

From the Las Pailas entrance, a very satisfying 6km circular trail takes you around some unusual natural features, with bubbling mud pots and a mini-volcano as well as steaming sulphurous vents that make for a highly atmospheric experience. There are more **gentle walks** in the Las Pailas sector, and one in the Santa Maria sector, that take you to fumaroles and mud pots, and you can also hike to two waterfalls, the *cataratas escondidas*.

ARRIVAL AND INFORMATION

There is no public transport to the park. If you drive, a 4WD is recommended year-round, and compulsory in the wet season.

Las Pailas ranger station Las Pailas (Tues–Sun 7am–5pm) – the western entrance – is the most common gateway. Transfers from *Hotel Posada del Tope* and *Hotel Liberia* (see opposite) cost US$25; a 4WD taxi from Liberia will be around US$40. If you drive yourself, travel through the hamlet of Curubandé, 5km north of Liberia off the Interamericana. The 20km road (1500c/person to pass through a private section) is a decent gravel road, passable by regular car in dry season.

Santa María ranger station Santa María (daily 7am–5pm) is in the east. Transfers are available from Liberia hotels (see opposite); a 4WD taxi from Liberia will cost US$60 or so. Driving, go through Liberia's Barrio La Victoria in the northeast of the town (ask for the *estadio* – the football stadium), from where it's a signed, bumpy, 24km drive along a rugged dirt-and-gravel road to the park.

ACCOMMODATION

Most budget travellers stay in Liberia: reasonably priced accommodation around the park is scarce, and there are no restaurants.

Camping There are campsites at both ranger stations – Santa María is better equipped, with pit toilets, showers and grills, but you must bring your own food and drinking water. Be prepared for cold nights, strong winds and fog. **US$4**

Rinconcito Lodge On the road to Santa María ☎2666 2764, ⊛rinconcitolodge.com. The cheapest option close to the park, this eco-farm has simple, good-value *cabinas* with hot-water private baths. Horseriding and trekking tours are also on offer (US$40–55), and the owners are friendly and helpful. Meals and packed lunches are available. **US$39**

PARQUE NACIONAL SANTA ROSA

PARQUE NACIONAL SANTA ROSA (daily 8am–4pm; US$10; ☎2666 5051), 35km

2

north of Liberia, is popular thanks to its good trails, great surfing (though poor swimming) and turtle-spotting opportunities.

Santa Rosa has an amazingly diverse **topography** for its size, ranging from mangrove swamp to rare tropical dry forest and savannah, and a staggering array of mammals, birds, amphibians and reptiles. Jaguars and pumas prowl the park, though you're unlikely to see them; coati, coyotes and peccaries, on the other hand, are often found snuffling around watering holes. Between July and November (peaking in September and October), the sight of hundreds of **Olive Ridley turtles** (*lloras*) nesting on Playa Nancite puts all other animal sightings into the shade; a maximum of twenty visitors is allowed access to the nesting area each day (call ahead to reserve).

Though too rough for swimming, the picturesque **beaches** of Naranjo and Nancite, about 12km down a bad road from the administration centre, are popular with serious **surfers**.

ARRIVAL AND INFORMATION

Park entrance The park's entrance hut is signed from the Interamericana; it is a 7km walk from here to the campsite and administration centre, so it's much more convenient to enter the park if you have your own vehicle.

By bus Buses from Liberia (use the Peñas Blancas/La Cruz service) run past the entrance. Tell the driver well in advance that you want to stop at the park.

Tourist information The visitors' centre at the entrance is effectively the main reception (☏ 2666 5051).

ACCOMMODATION AND EATING

The camping facilities (pay at the administration centre) are some of the best in the country. Watch your fires (the area is a tinderbox in the dry season), take plastic bags for your food, don't leave anything edible in your tent (it will be stolen by scavenging coati) and carry plenty of water. Make sure to stock up on food before entering the park. You can buy drinks at the administration centre, but little else.

La Casona camping Near the administration centre. This campsite has bathrooms and grill pits. US$4

Playa Naranjo camping On the beach. Camping with picnic tables and grill pits, a ranger's hut with outhouses and showers – and, from time to time, a boa constrictor in the roof. Only open outside the turtle-nesting season. US$4

The Zona Norte

Costa Rica's **Zona Norte** ("northern zone") spans the hundred-odd kilometres from the base of the Cordillera Central to just short of the mauve-blue mountains of southern Nicaragua. Formerly cut off from the rest of the country by a lack of good roads, the Zona Norte has developed a unique character, with independent-minded farmers and Nicaraguan refugees making up large segments of the population. Many people from the north hold a special allegiance to, and pride in, their area. Less obviously picturesque than many parts of the country, the entire region nonetheless has a distinctive

INTO NICARAGUA: PEÑAS BLANCAS

Peñas Blancas (daily 6am–8pm) is the main crossing point into Nicaragua and the only one you can cross by land. This is a border post rather than a town, so there's nowhere to stay. Arrive as early as possible and expect to spend at least an hour to get through the procedures, though if you're travelling via Tica Bus (see p.105), proceedings are speeded up considerably and all passengers are processed together. Travellers must fill in exit and entry forms; Tica Bus gives those out beforehand. Some nationalities require Nicaraguan visas; check visa requirements (see p.450) beforehand. Exit stamps are given on the Costa Rican side.

For travellers entering Nicaragua from Costa Rica, there is a fee of US$10; if you're leaving Nicaragua, you pay US$2. Moneychangers are always on hand and have colones, córdobas and dollars; make sure you know roughly what the exchange rate should be in advance. It's 1km between the Costa Rican and Nicaraguan immigration offices; if you've only caught the bus as far as the border, you can either walk across or get a lift in one of the golf carts (tip required). If you're coming from Nicaragua, the last San José bus (45min) leaves at 7pm and the last Liberia bus at 6.30pm (45min).

appeal, with lazy rivers snaking across steaming plains and flop-eared cattle languishing beneath the trees.

Most travellers only venture here to see **Volcán Arenal**. Further north, the remote flatlands are home to the increasingly accessible **Refugio Nacional de Vida Silvestre Caño Negro**, which harbours an extraordinary amount of birdlife. There's a serviceable **bus** network, though if you're travelling outside the La Fortuna or Sarapiquí areas, consider renting a car. The area around Arenal is best equipped for visitors; between Boca de Arenal and Los Chiles in the far north, there is a real shortage of **accommodation**.

LA FORTUNA AND AROUND

That the north attracts the numbers of visitors it does is mainly due to majestic **Volcán Arenal**, one of the most active volcanoes in the western hemisphere. Just 6km away, **LA FORTUNA** is a compact, simple agricultural town that's become a major tourist hub due to its perfect location as a jumping-off point for volcano-based activities.

Beware of opportunistic **theft** in La Fortuna and avoid "guides" offering their services on the street.

WHAT TO SEE AND DO

Besides the **volcano** looming beyond the town – when you can see it, that is; the summit is often shrouded in clouds for days at a time – the area around La Fortuna offers ample **outdoor activities** – from rugged cycling tours and canopy tours to nature walks, hot spring spas and paddleboarding on Lake Arenal. Due to the proliferation of **tour companies**, it pays to shop around to get a good price; make sure you know exactly what's included in any tour you consider.

Hot springs

Several lodges along the road from La Fortuna to Arenal offer visitors the opportunity to soak in the volcano-tinged sulphurous **hot springs**. **El Tabacón** (daily 10am–10pm; US$60 for a day pass, US$45 for a 6–10pm pass; US$95 for day pass with lunch and dinner; ⓦwww .tabacon.com) is the most expensive, complete with lush tropical setting, waterfalls gushing down fake cliffs and a series of beautiful natural pools – both hot and cold – to relax in and numerous spa treatments available. **Baldi Hot Springs** is the least expensive (daily 10am–10pm; US$31; with dinner buffet US$51; ⓦbaldihotsprings.cr) and features a

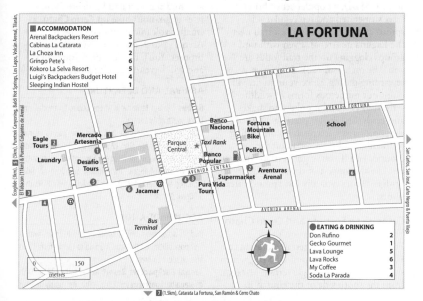

2

TOURS AND ACTIVITIES IN LA FORTUNA

Competition between **tour agencies** in La Fortuna is fierce: for the best experience, make sure you go with an established tour operator, rather than the freelance "guides" who may approach you, some of whom have been involved in serious incidents over the years. The vast majority of operators offer the same standard trips on top of their specialities: guided hikes in Parque Nacional Arenal combined with hot springs visits, canopy tours, rafting, day-trips to Caño Negro, and transfers to Monteverde. The following outfits are particularly recommended.

Aventuras Arenal Av Central ☎ 2479 9133, ⓦ arenaladventures.com. Long-standing operator offering professionally run biking, horseback and watersports excursions, plus transport to just about anywhere in the country.

★ **Desafío Tours** C 2 ☎ 2479 9464, ⓦ desafio costarica.com. Friendly, efficient and community-aware rafting specialists who run trips on the Río Toro (US$90) and guided hikes up Cerro Chato (US$80), among other excursions. Their Monteverde transfer can include a horseriding or mountain-biking excursion along the way (US$90).

Ecoglide ☎ 2479 7120, ⓦ arenalecoglide.com. The most extensive of the canopy tours in the area, offering twelve ziplines and a Tarzan swing (US$55)

Jacamar Av Central, next to *Lava Rocks* ☎ 2479 9767, ⓦ arenaltours.com. Volcano tours, trips to Caño Negro and a number of nature hikes.

PureTrek Canyoning West of town, en route to *Arenal Nayara Hotel & Gardens* ☎ 2479 1315, ⓦ puretrek.com. Rappelling specialist, offering guided rappels down your choice of four waterfalls (US$100).

---

number of hot and warm pools that you meander between, as well as two exhilarating water slides. Agencies in town (see box above) can often get you a cheaper price in conjunction with other excursions.

Puentes Colgantes de Arenal

Puentes Colgantes de Arenal (daily 7.30am–4.30pm; ⓦ hangingbridges.com; adult US$24), a popular set of bridges – six suspended and ten regular – is spread along a 3km rainforest trail near the Laguna de Arenal. Even with tour groups clogging up the trail (odds are you'll be on a tour too), this is a very rewarding outing, since your guide will point out numerous forms of wildlife – from insects and monkeys to snakes and birds. The trail is pretty gentle, though there's a steep-ish uphill leading to the highest bridge, 25m off the ground, and if you've got vertigo you may not like the longest of the suspended bridges. Tours typically last around three hours.

Catarata La Fortuna and Cerro Chato

You can make an excursion to La Fortuna's stunning waterfall, **Catarata La Fortuna** (daily 8am–5pm; US$10), which sits amid beautiful jungle terrain just 6km from the south side of the church in

town. A taxi (3500–4000c) can take you right to the entrance office, or it's a good uphill walk on foot (1hr from La Fortuna). Once in, it is a steep climb down a winding path and staircase and a gruelling return journey, but the waterfall is spectacular and makes for a wonderfully refreshing swim.

At the entrance to the *cataratas* you'll also find the start of a hardcore 5km, five- to six-hour hike up **Cerro Chato**, a smaller volcanic peak that clings to Arenal's skirts, and offers views of its big brother. You'll be crossing private land and will have to pay US$10.

ARRIVAL AND DEPARTURE

By bus The bus terminal is at the Centro Comercial, one block south of Av Central.

Destinations Monteverde (take the 8am bus to Tilarán, changing there for the 12.30pm bus to Monteverde; 6–8hr); San Carlos (for frequent San José connections; 6 daily 6.15am–4.45pm; 1hr 30min); San José (2 daily, 12.45pm & 2.45pm; 4hr 30min); Tilarán (2 daily, 8.30am & 5.30pm; 3hr 30min).

ACCOMMODATION

Budget accommodation is concentrated in town, with a few possibilities on the road leading to the waterfall and also en route to Arenal.

Arenal Backpackers Resort Av Central ☎ 2479 7000, ⓦ arenalbackpackersresort.com. With its neatly tended lawns, pool lined with palm trees, and wet bar, *Arenal Backpackers* certainly has plenty of amenities. The thin walls, coupled with a lively atmosphere, mean that you won't be getting much sleep, however. Rooms (with private bath, a/c and TV) and dorms are spacious, clean and bright, while the deluxe tents (sleeping two) come with mattresses and bedding (and that old tent smell). The security is excellent, but the staff could be more helpful. Camping US$35, dorm US$15, double US$35

Cabinas La Catarata 700m up the road towards the waterfall, a 15min walk from La Fortuna ☎ 2479 7790. This friendly property has four fully equipped cabins (sleeping 2–6), each with a terrace and hammocks overlooking a lush piece of land with a river running through it – ideal for birdwatching. The considerate hosts are super-friendly; a hearty breakfast (US$5) is served across the road, in front of their house. A taxi costs around US$2. US$30

La Choza Inn Av Fort, C 2/4 ☎ 2479 9361, ⓦ lachozainnhostel.com. In a quiet part of the town, this efficiently run hotel has airy dorms and comfortable doubles (a/c, TV and fridge cost extra); the communal kitchen is particularly well equipped and the staff go out of their way to make you feel welcome. Dorm US$10, double US$50

Gringo Pete's C 7, just north of Av Arenal ☎ 2479 8521, ⓦ gringopeteshostel.com. Long-running hostel catering to shoestring travellers. The boxy private rooms have little natural light but the dorm is large and the prices are fantastically low. There are sociable communal areas, kitchen and free coffee, and the staff throw an occasional BBQ. Dorm US$8, double US$22

Luigi's Backpackers Budget Hotel Av Central, a block west of *Lava Lounge* ☎ 2479 9898, ⓦ luigishotel.com. This motel-style budget hotel is certainly focused on creature comforts: the beds have orthopaedic mattresses, and there's a/c, coffee makers and access to a large pool and jacuzzi. The attached restaurant serves pizza (as you might expect from a guy called Luigi). US$60

★ **Sleeping Indian Hostel** Av Fort ☎ 2479 8431. Housed above a great little café, this quiet hostel consists of several airy private rooms around a large and appealing common area, complete with hammocks and a guest kitchen. Staff are very friendly and helpful. US$35

★ **TREAT YOURSELF**

Kokoro La Selva Resort Between La Fortuna and Laguna de Arenal ☎ 2479 1222, ⓦ kokoroarenal.net. Set amid lush grounds with several short walking trails, this lovely family-run property consists of large, attractively designed cabins (2–5 people) and cheaper multi-person rooms, all with access to the pool. The hot tub is fed by the hot springs that run through the property and the large lounge area is in the style of a giant *palapa*. Lunch and dinner served on request and there's a shuttle into La Fortuna. Treehouses, currently being built, will come with a shared guest kitchen. Double US$85, cabin US$115

EATING AND DRINKING

Gecko Gourmet Just west of the church. Catering to homesick gringos, this café has breakfast burritos (3500c), smoked salmon and cream cheese bagels (3000c), meatloaf, BBQ pulled pork and BLT sandwiches (4000c), as well as fine coffee and smoothies (try the mocha with peanut butter). Daily 7am–3.30pm.

Lava Lounge Av Central, C 2/4. By day this breezy Tiki bar-style restaurant with a *palapa* roof serves excellent fajitas, salads, chunky sandwiches and veggie wraps (3000–5000c), and at night it turns into a relaxed bar with a soundtrack of reggae and chilled beats. Daily 11am–10.30pm.

Lava Rocks Opposite the church. Not to be confused with *Lava Bar and Grill*, this place has wonderfully nice staff and well-executed *comida típica* (*casados* and rice dishes from 3750c. Daily 11.30am–9.30pm.

My Coffee Av Central, C 1/2. Besides the ubiquitous *gallo pinto*, breakfast offerings include French toast, pancakes, eggs done the way you like them and hefty omelettes. Great coffee, too. Mains from 3000c. 8am–8pm.

Soda La Parada Av Central, opposite Parque Central. One of the best *sodas* in town, always crowded. It's perfect for an early breakfast of *gallo pinto* or a range of heaped *casados* (3500c), which is what this place does best; they also offer so-so burgers and pizza. Daily 7am–11pm.

LA FORTUNA TO MONTEVERDE: JEEP-BOAT-JEEP TRANSFERS

The most interesting way to travel between La Fortuna and **Monteverde** (see p.143) is by a **"jeep–boat–jeep" transfer**, a time-saving and spectacularly pretty connection taking 2–3hr. This involves taking a minivan (*not* jeep!) to the Laguna del Arenal, crossing it by boat, and then boarding another minivan for the rest of the journey to Santa Elena/Monteverde. The journey shows off both the breathtaking mountain pastures of Monteverde and your first (or last, depending on the direction) glimpse of majestic Volcán Arenal. The transfer is easily arranged through lodgings and tour agencies, but since prices range from US$20–35, it's best to shop around.

2

DIRECTORY

Bicycle rental Fortuna Mountainbike, C 3, rents decent mountain bikes (US$15/20 half/full day) and arranges day tours.

Health Centro Médico Arenal Vital, C 1, in the *Hotel Las Colinas* (☏ 2479 7027), is a private clinic with English-speaking staff, open around the clock.

Laundry There's a laundry service a block before *La Choza Inn* (US$4/kg).

Taxis There's a rank on the east side of the Parque Central. Agree on a price before getting in.

PARQUE NACIONAL VOLCÁN ARENAL

Volcán Arenal is spectacular, whether admired from La Fortuna, where its slopes are still a lush green, or from the barren and desolate western face, where the foliage has been gradually scorched by the ash and lava that once tumbled down the side every day. This volcano was presumed dormant, as it sat there, minding its own business, until 1968, when it spectacularly blew its top, its lava flows wrecking three villages and killing thousands of livestock, as well as eighty people. Since then, it had been spewing molten rock on pretty much a daily basis, before falling suspiciously silent in 2010 – watch this space. You can get closer by heading to the **PARQUE NACIONAL VOLCÁN ARENAL** (daily 8am–4pm); though fences are in place to keep you from tackling the volcano's slopes, the park does have some good **trails**.

The trails

Easy walks in the park include the **Sendero Los Heliconias** (1km), which starts from the ranger station and leads past the 1968 old lava flow, with the option of a 1.5km trail branch leading to a viewpoint, and **Sendero Las Cascadas** (1km; US$4), in the grounds of the Arenal Observatory Lodge, which leads down to a roaring waterfall. **Sendero Los Coladas** splits off from the Sendero Las Heliconias and skirts the bottom of volcano for 2km, taking you past the more recent (1993) lava flow and joining the **Sendero Los Tucanes**, an easy 3km through lush rainforest. A little tougher, the **Old Lava Flow Trail** (2km) starts at the park headquarters and rambles up and down along the huge 1993 lava flow. That hike is easily combined with the **Sendero El Ceibo** (1.8km), a jolly ramble through secondary forest. The park's toughest hike is the 4km **Sendero Cerro Chato** (US$4), which runs from the Arenal Observatory Lodge and climbs steeply to the top of dormant Cerro Chato, where you're rewarded with great views of neighbouring Arenal and a stunning 1100m-high volcanic lake. Finally, there's **Arenal 1968** (daily 7am–10pm; US$10), a private network of short trails centred around the 1968 lava flow, located 1.2km before the ranger station. In addition, **night tours** of the park leave La Fortuna every evening at about 3 or 4pm; wait for a clear evening before signing up with an operator in town (see box, p.174).

ARRIVAL AND INFORMATION

Tours Many visitors come to the park on a tour; note that, unlike the full-day tours, half-day tours involve very little hiking.

By bus No buses head in to the park, but you can catch the 8am bus from La Fortuna to Tilarán, get dropped off at the park entrance (where you'll find the ranger station/information centre; several trails start from here) and then catch the return bus at 2pm.

By car Head west from La Fortuna for 15km, then, at a fork in the road, take a signposted left turn and follow the dirt-and-gravel road for 2km to the entrance. The *Arenal Observatory Lodge* hotel, where several trails set off, is another 3km along that road.

By taxi The 17km taxi ride from La Fortuna to the park entrance will cost around US$35.

LOS CHILES

LOS CHILES, a humid border settlement 3km from Nicaragua, is becoming more popular with travellers, thanks to its proximity to **Caño Negro**, 25km downstream on the Río Frío (see below), and also to the Nicaraguan border, which can only be crossed by boat.

ARRIVAL AND INFORMATION

By boat The boat docks are 1km west of the bus station. Turn left at *Cruz Roja* on the main street, then head right downhill along Av 0 to the waterfront.

By bus The bus terminal is behind *Soda Pamela* on Av 1, near the intersection with Hwy 35. Bus timetables change frequently, so confirm before setting off.

Destinations San Carlos (Ciudad Quesada; 12 daily 4.30am–6pm; 2hr); San José (2 daily, 5.15am & 3pm; 6hr); Upala via Caño Negro (3 daily, 5am, 2pm & 4.30pm; 2hr 30min).

Bank Banco Nacional (with ATM) is on the north side of the soccer pitch, Av 1, C 0/1.

Tourist information You can check bus schedules and boat timetables at your lodgings.

ACCOMMODATION AND EATING

Cabinas Jabiru One block west and north of the bus station ☎ 2471 1211. The economical rooms here, each with private bath, TV, fridge and a/c, may not be the most memorable you'll ever stay in, but they're fine for a day or two. US$30

Rancho Tulipan 100m from the dock ☎ 2471 1414. The plushest lodgings in town (which isn't saying much), with comfortable singles, doubles, triples and quads with private bathrooms, TVs and a/c, set amid a garden filled with medicinal plants. The decent restaurant serves Tico and Continental food (mains from 3000c). US$50

Soda Pamela Opposite the bus station. *Pintos, casados, empanadas* and fried chicken served by ultra-friendly English-speaking staff. Mains from 2200c. Daily 6am–7pm.

REFUGIO NACIONAL DE VIDA SILVESTRE CAÑO NEGRO

The largely pristine 102-square-kilometre **REFUGIO NACIONAL DE VIDA SILVESTRE CAÑO NEGRO** (daily 8am–4pm; US$10; ☎ 2471 1309), 25km west of Los Chiles, is one of the best places in the Americas to view huge concentrations of both migratory and indigenous birds – over 365 species – along with mammalian and reptilian river wildlife. The protected area consists of wetlands, fed by Río Frío, the river swelling up to form a lake during the wet season. Until recently its isolation – it's 192km from San José – kept the park well off the beaten track, but nowadays more visitors are coming to the area. You can visit on a long day excursion from La Fortuna (see box, p.174) or from Los Chiles (see above), and it's far easier to get to the park solo than it used to be. Staying overnight gives you an advantage over the day-trippers, as early morning is the best time to see wildlife (get going around 6am).

ARRIVAL AND DEPARTURE

By boat During rainy season (and some of the dry season) it's possible to catch a boat for travel down the Río Frío from Los Chiles (US$20/person).

By bus Buses arrive and leave from the office of the local guide co-operative Real Tour, in the centre of Caño Negro. There are three buses a day to Los Chiles (at 6am, 3pm & 5.30pm); confirm timetables before setting off.

By car Caño Negro is reachable by rough dirt-and-gravel road between Los Chiles and Upala. It's accessible by regular vehicle during dry season, but a 4WD is mandatory in the rainy season. Coming from Los Chiles, turn before the phone signal tower.

INTO NICARAGUA: LOS CHILES

Currently, the only way to reach Nicaragua from the **Los Chiles** crossing is by **boat** (1hr) on the Río Frío. At least two boats daily (12.30pm & 3.30pm; 1hr 30min) leave the docks in Los Chiles for San Carlos de Nicaragua (see p.500), depending on demand and tides, with return boats at around 10.30am and 4pm. Boats connect with buses for the 14km ride to San Carlos. You need to get an exit stamp from the Costa Rican immigration office, opposite Rancho Tulipan, first. Most nationalities don't need visas for Nicaragua, but check first (see p.450). Make sure the **Nicaraguan border patrol**, 3km upriver from Los Chiles, stamps your passport, as you will need proof of entry when leaving Nicaragua. You'll also need some cash upon arrival in San Carlos; change a few colones for córdobas at the Los Chiles bank. From San Carlos it's also possible to cross the lake to **Granada** and on to **Managua**. There is a US$10 charge to enter Nicaragua. The border crossing is open 8am–5pm.

2

INFORMATION AND TOURS

Tourist information The entrance fee (US$10) is payable at the Real Tour office (daily 8am–4pm). The ranger station is at Estación Biológica Caño Negro, 6km north of the church.

Tour operators Several agencies in La Fortuna (see box, p.174) offer day-trips here, though these miss out on the best time of day for wildlife-viewing. If you get here under your own steam, hiring an experienced local guide (from US$20) is well worth the money; the local guide co-operative, Real Tour, in the centre of town (☎ 2471 1621; daily 8am–4pm), can put you in touch with a guide, and you'll find guides waiting around the dock area. Tours cost around US$70 for a two-hour excursion along the Río Frío of up to three people, though you can take longer boat tours as well, with guides pointing out birds, caimans, monkeys, iguanas, sloths and other wildlife.

PUERTO VIEJO DE SARAPIQUÍ

Steamy, tropical and carpeted with fruit plantations, the eastern Zona Norte bears more resemblance to the hot and dense Caribbean lowlands than the plains of the north and, despite the toll of deforestation, still shelters some of the country's best-preserved premontane rainforest. The largest settlement, **PUERTO VIEJO DE SARAPIQUÍ**, is principally a river transport hub and a place for the region's banana, coconut and pineapple plantation workers to stock up on supplies. If you're driving from the Valle Central to the Caribbean coast, Puerto Viejo makes a convenient (if not terribly exciting) stopover.

There are two options when it comes to getting here from the Valle Central. The western route, taking just over three hours, goes via Varablanca and the La Paz waterfall, passing the hump of Volcán Barva. This route offers great views of velvety green hills clad with coffee plantations, which turn, eventually, into rainforest. It's faster (1hr–1hr 30min), but marginally less scenic, to travel via the **Guápiles Highway**. The region receives a lot of **rain** – as much as 4500mm annually – so wet-weather gear is essential.

ARRIVAL AND DEPARTURE

By bus The bus station is in the centre of town on the main road by the football pitch.

Destinations Guápiles (for connections to Puerto Limón; 10 daily 5.30am–7pm; 1hr); San José (11 daily 5am–5.30pm; 2hr).

ACCOMMODATION AND EATING

Mi Lindo Sarapiquí On the corner of the football pitch ☎ 2766-6281. A good budget option, with clean, spacious rooms, private hot showers and a friendly atmosphere. The restaurant is very popular too, particularly for its seafood. US$40

★ **Posada Andrea Cristina** 1km west of town on the road to Chilamate ☎ 2766 6265, ⊛ andreacristina.com. A tropical haven, with lovely, quirky cabins, bungalows and a wonderful room in a treehouse set among jungle plants. The hospitable owner has a wealth of information on conservation projects, runs river and trekking tours, offers Spanish classes and serves excellent (mainly vegetarian) food. US$55

Restaurante Real 150m east of *Hotel El Bambú*. Plastic tablecloths, sports on TV and surprisingly good Chinese food, from won ton soup to *camarones al ajillo* (prawns in garlic sauce). They also do roast chicken by the quarter. Mains around 3000c. Daily 7.30am–10pm.

The Zona Sur

Costa Rica's **Zona Sur** ("southern zone") is the country's least-known and most challenging region. Geographically, it's a diverse area, ranging from the agricultural heartland of the Valle de El General to the high peaks of the Cordillera de Talamanca. South of Cerro Chirripó, one of the highest peaks in Central America – Costa Rica's highest mountain and arguably most challenging hike – the cordillera falls away into the lowlands of the Valle de Diquis and the coffee-growing Valle de Coto Brus, near the Panama border.

The region's chief draw is the **Parque Nacional Chirripó**, which draws thousands of hikers who come with the goal of conquering **Cerro Chirripó**, a demanding high-altitude trek. The National Park is accessed through the little mountain town of San Gerardo de Rivas, and getting there is half the adventure. More accessible, the **Playa Dominical** area of the Pacific coast is a surfing destination of tremendous tropical beauty, while tiny **Uvita**, nearby, is the gateway to the whale-watching mecca of **Parque Nacional Marino Ballena**.

SAN ISIDRO DE GENERAL

An important crossroads for anyone passing through on their way to the Osa Peninsula, Panama or the west coast, **SAN ISIDRO DE GENERAL** is a large, hot urban sprawl, reached via a particularly winding and scenic mountain road from Cartago. Odds are you'll only stop here long enough to change buses.

ARRIVAL AND DEPARTURE

By bus From the Tracopa terminal (☎ 2771 0468), two blocks east of Parque Central on the Interamericana, buses run to San José, Palmar Norte and Paso Canoas (for Panama). From Terminal Quepos (☎ 2771 2550), on the street south of the Tracopa terminal, buses depart for Quepos, Dominical, Uvita, and Puerto Jiménez via Palmar Norte. To get to San Gerardo de Rivas, go to the local bus terminal on Av 6. Book tickets in advance for popular long-distance buses.

Destinations Dominical (3 daily, 7.30am, 9am & 5.30pm; 2hr 30min); Palmar Norte (10 daily 4.45am–9.30pm; 2hr); Paso Canoas (6 daily 8.30am–9pm; 5hr); Puerto Jiménez (2 daily, 6.30am & 3pm); Quepos (2 daily, 7am & 1.30pm; 3hr); San Gerardo de Rivas (3 daily, 9.30am, 2pm & 6.45pm; 1hr 30min); San José (9 daily 7.30am–7.30pm; 3hr); Uvita (2 daily, 8.30am & 4pm; 1hr 30min).

ACCOMMODATION AND EATING

There are a few basic Tico restaurants scattered along C Central.

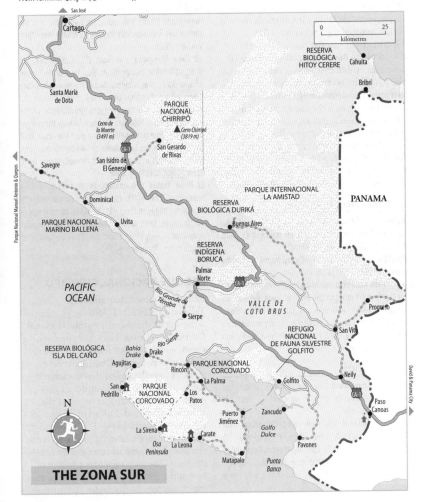

THE ZONA SUR

Hotel Chirripó On the south side of Parque Central ☎ 2771 0529, ⓦ hotelchirripo.com. Your best bet should you need to stay, with the cheapest rooms sharing a bathroom, and the swishest en suites coming with a/c (singles from US$16). US$22

SAN GERARDO DE RIVAS

The mountain village of **SAN GERARDO DE RIVAS**, 22km east of San Isidro, is the gateway to the popular **Parque Nacional Chirripó**, home of Costa Rica's tallest mountain and most demanding climb.

WHAT TO SEE AND DO

While most visitors tend to come for the challenge of tackling Mt Chirripó, there is much more to the area around San Gerardo than just the one mountain. **Cloudbridge Reserve**, a private swathe of forest accessible by the road that runs past the Mt Chirripó trailhead, has several attractive, undemanding trails, one of them leading to a spectacular waterfall (30min). There's also a spectacular **day hike**, taking in a local art gallery and a trout farm where you can grab some lunch; walk up the Mt Chirripó trail and take the right fork at the T-junction. *Casa Mariposa* (see below) has the hike details.

ARRIVAL AND DEPARTURE

By bus Buses for San Isidro depart from the football field, around 1.2km short of the Chirripó trailhead (3 daily, 5.15am, 11.30am & 4pm; 1hr 30min).

By 4WD taxi It's possible to get a taxi from San Isidro for around US$40.

By car The road from San Isidro to San Gerardo is paved for the first 10km up to the town of Rivas. Beyond, it's steep, gravelled, potholed and bumpy, and while a regular car can just about make it in the dry season, it's a tough drive, so a 4WD is preferable year-round and mandatory outside dry season.

INFORMATION

Tourist information *Casa Mariposa* (see below) has extensive information on the surrounding area, bus timetables and more.

Parque Nacional Chirripó ranger station 1km before the football field (daily 6.30am–noon & 1–4.30pm; ☎ 2200 5348). Come here to check availability at the *Crestones Base Lodge*, pay park fees, confirm reservations and book porters. The rangers very rarely answer the phone.

Internet All lodgings reviewed below offer free internet or wi-fi.

ACCOMMODATION AND EATING

San Gerardo consists of a loose string of lodgings and restaurants, spread over 2km or so. The "centre" of the village is the football field.

Cabinas El Descanso ☎ 2742 5061, ⓦ hoteleldescansocr .com. Friendly, family-run place with rather basic, spartan rooms on the ground floor and brighter, larger, more expensive rooms with balcony upstairs. The on-site restaurant serves generous portions of home-cooked food. US$30

Café Bambú Opposite the church. Friendly café luring hungry hikers with pizzas (from 1500c), pastries, lattes and fruit smoothies. There are also cakes (500c), pies, home-made breads and cookies to take away, and the atmosphere is wonderfully friendly. Fri & Sat 11am–7pm, Sun 9am–6pm.

★ **Casa Mariposa** 40m from the trailhead ☎ 2742 5037, ⓦ hotelcasamariposa.net. Run by knowledgeable Jill and John, this wonderfully homey hostel has cosy rooms with orthopaedic mattresses centred around the lounge/kitchen area that everyone gravitates to in the evenings, a dorm built into the rock face up the garden path and a large stone bath for that post-hike soak. Your hosts are by far the best source of info on the area, and hikers shouldn't miss out on Jill's famous energy balls. Dorm 7000c, double 18,000c

El Urán Hotel y Restaurants Next door to *Casa Mariposa* ☎ 2742 5003, ⓦ hoteluran.com. Conveniently located for hiking in the park, this hostel offers a mix of simple rooms, some with shared facilities, and a popular restaurant serving heaped portions of *casados* and other simple dishes. Per person 9280c

PARQUE NACIONAL CHIRRIPÓ

Part of the remote Cordillera de Talamanca, **CERRO CHIRRIPÓ** (3820m) – the star of the popular **Parque Nacional Chirripó** – is Costa Rica's most demanding **climb**, which the vast majority of hikers tackle over two days. During the hike, trekkers pass through different climatic zones – from the lush cloudforest that covers the mountainsides between the altitudes of around 2400m to 3400m to the sparce *páramo* beyond that point, with rocky landscapes, covered in sparse, hardy scrubland, and glacial lakes dominating the view. The park supports a wealth of **bird and animal life**; you may spot pumas, tapirs, coyotes, harpy eagles and quetzals.

You have to take all your supplies with you, including warm and waterproof clothing (it gets extremely cold at the top), food, three-season sleeping bag (which can be rented in San Gerardo along with cooking equipment), cooking stove, fuel and plenty of food and water.

The most popular time to climb Cerro Chirripó is the **dry season** (late Dec–April), though it can still rain at any time. In May the park is closed completely. The park is busiest during the holidays and weekends, so weekdays are your best bet; allow at least three days for your stay in San Gerardo and the two-day hike.

Climbing Cerro Chirripó

We won't lie: **climbing Cerro Chirripó** is a tough hike, not least because it's a high-altitude climb – you'll be going from 1350m in San Gerardo to a height of 3820m. The 16km hike to the summit is also mostly steep, with relentless uphills most of the way. However, this is a beautiful trail, with sweeping views of the valley below peeking through the trees, and, at the top, a stupendous view of the Caribbean on one side and the Pacific on the other. The hike is usually done over the course of two days; on **Day 1** you hike to the *Crestones Base Lodge*, 10km up the mountain, which can take from five to fourteen hours, depending on your general fitness, while on **Day 2**, hikers make a push for the summit in the wee hours of the morning in order to watch the sunrise from the top and then make their way down to San Gerardo – the descent often takes as long as the ascent. Super-fit hikers have been known to do the hike in one day, descending to San Gerardo late at night, but it's not recommended, as exhaustion combined with trail hazards can easily lead to injury.

The **trailhead** is around 40m beyond *Casa Mariposa* (see opposite) on your right; the trail entrance is quite narrow, and there are several trails around the lodge, so make sure you don't miss it in the dark (most people begin the hike around 5am).

While the hike to the summit is a wonderful challenge, it's particularly rewarding to linger at the top for an extra day and hike some of the other trails, such as the ones to **Cerro Ventisqueros** (3812m) and **Cerro Terbi** (3760m); enquire about trail conditions at the lodge.

ARRIVAL AND DEPARTURE

By bus Parque Nacional Chirripó is only accessible by bus via San Gerardo de Rivas (see opposite). Buses pull in at the football field, around 1.2km short of the trailhead.

INFORMATION

Permits In San Gerardo, the Parque Nacional Chirripó ranger station (see opposite) is your essential stop for securing a park permit and booking a space at the *Crestones Base Lodge* up Cerro Chirripó. Since spaces at the lodge are limited, you have to come here at least a day before you intend to ascend the mountain. Each day there should technically be ten slots available on a first-come, first-served basis, but that's not always the case, so get here before opening time just to make sure. In theory, you can make a reservation over the phone, but the rangers are known not to pick up.

Entry fees US$20 for two days, plus US$20 for each additional day. Bunks at the lodge cost US$10 per night. If you want to hire porters to take your luggage up the mountain, you need to bring it to the rangers' office before closing time the day before you intend to hike.

ACCOMMODATION

Crestones Base Lodge Book through the park office in San Gerardo (see opposite). This basic lodge with solar-powered electricity offers simple bunks to sleep sixty people. Drinking water is provided, but everything else has to be brought with you – from sleeping bags to food. Per person US$10

DOMINICAL

In spite of large-scale development in the surrounding area, **DOMINICAL**, 44km south of Quepos (see p.154), remains a one-horse town or, rather, a one-street surfing village, where every other person you meet along the main road – a bumpy dirt track running to the beach – seems to be barefoot and carrying a surfboard.

Thousands of (mainly American) **surfers** flock in every year to ride the beach and point breaks and to hit the many beachfront bars. Novice surfers can take lessons from the many surf shops on offer; Costa Rica Surf Camp (☎2787 0393, ⓦcrsurfschool.com) comes highly recommended for the quality of its instructors and the 2:1 student-teacher ratio, while at Sunset

2

Surf (⒲sunsetsurfdominical) some lesson slots are set aside for women only. **Swimming** is ill-advised due to strong riptides; watch for the red flags marking the area and only swim where lifeguards are present.

ARRIVAL AND INFORMATION

By bus Buses collect passengers along the main strip. Destinations Palmar, where you can make connections to the Osa Peninsula (2 daily, 4.30am & 10.30am; 2hr); Quepos (6 daily, 7.30am, 8am, 10.30am, 1.45pm, 4pm & 5pm; 2hr); San Isidro (2 daily, 6.15am & 2pm; 1hr 30min); San José (2 daily, 5.30am & 1.30pm; 4hr 30min).

Banks There are no banks in town, so bring enough cash to cover your stay.

Tourist information There's a small Infotour office on your right-hand side as you enter the village. They give out rudimentary maps of Dominical.

ACCOMMODATION

Cabinas San Climente On the main road just before the right turn down to the beach ☎ 2787 0158. Simple, clean and secure wooden cabins, ranging from very basic to more spruced up. You pay more for private bathrooms, hot water, a/c and sea views. US$25

Camping Antorchas Just off the beach road ☎ 2787 0307. As well as camping spots, there are a few basic dorms with private or shared bathrooms. The campsite has a kitchen, cold showers and lockers. Camping US$5, dorm US$10

Posada del Sol Halfway along the main strip ☎ 2787 0082. Adorable, secure guesthouse with just five rooms (including a microscopic single), and surfer-friendly touches, such as sinks for washing wetsuits and clothes lines to dry them. A laidback retreat rather than a party spot. US$25

Tortilla Flats On the beach ☎ 2787 0033. Popular surfers' hotel spread over several buildings. Brightly decorated rooms come with attached baths, and there's a hammock-festooned terrace upstairs. Crowds gather every evening at the beachfront restaurant/bar to watch the sunset and party. US$30

EATING AND DRINKING

Chapy's Healthy Subs & Wraps Halfway along the main strip. The most gratifying lunch spot in the village, Chapy's does enormous focaccia sandwiches and wraps with fillings ranging from smoked salmon and cream cheese to spicy hummus and grilled vegetables. Mains 3500c. Mon–Sat 9am–3pm.

Maracutú Middle of the mains trip. Funky Italian restaurant offering mouthwatering vegan, vegetarian and fish dishes (3400–6000c), and surf videos on loop. Wed is

reggae night, and on Tues there's an open jam session. Daily noon–11pm.

Soda Nanyoya Tucked away behind the town's fruit stand. You may have to queue for a table at this breezy, open-walled bar/restaurant, but it's probably the freshest orange juice you'll ever taste, and the best *pinto* breakfast (1500c) in town at blissfully low prices. BYOB at night. Daily 8am–9pm.

Tortilla Flats *Tortilla Flats* hotel, on the beach. The prime spot in town to watch the sun set while nursing a cool beer (happy hour 4–6pm), complemented by tacos and foot-long subs (from 2500c).

UVITA

Tiny **UVITA**, 17km south of Dominical, and the gateway to the **Parque Nacional Marino Ballena**, consists of a few houses, lodgings, shops and restaurants, scattered along a couple of roads. The area just off the Interamericana is referred to as "Uvita", while the street nearest to the beach is "Playa Uvita". You can reach the park by sticking to the main paved road that runs from the Interamericana right up to the entrance, or else by taking the dirt-and-gravel road that heads south (with *Flutterby House* signposted off it) from that main paved road. The national park aside, the waves here attract novice **surfers**, and the vast deserted beaches make a change from those up north, where you find yourself fighting your fellow sunbathers for a small patch of sand.

ARRIVAL AND DEPARTURE

By bus Buses arrive and depart from the corner where the main road through Uvita meets the dirt road towards *Flutterby House*.

Destinations Dominical (9 daily 4.45am–6pm; 20min); Palmar, where you can connect to Sierpe and Bahía Drake (2 daily, 5am & 11am; 1hr 30min); Quepos (5 daily, 4.45am, 5.15am, 11am, 1.15pm & 4pm; 2hr); San Isidro (2 daily, 6am & 1.45pm; 2hr); San José (2 daily, 5.15am & 1.15pm; 5hr).

ACCOMMODATION AND EATING

There are a couple of small grocery shops stocking basic foodstuffs.

★ **Flutterby House** Follow the signposts from the main road through Uvita ⒲flutterbyhouse.com. Behind the gates is a ramshackle paradise of treehouses and basic cabins with mozzie nets, the lush grounds alive with surfers, slack rope walkers and dogs. Run by two Californian sisters, this place is as sustainable as it gets, with the innovative toilets due to be used to power the methane stoves in the large guest kitchen. There are surfboards for rent, a lively bar and a wonderfully laidback vibe. Cabin US$40

★ **Sabor Español** Just off the road to the beach, behind *Flutterby House*. Super-friendly Spanish-run restaurant serving flavourful standards such as gazpacho, *tortilla de patatas*, paella (2 person minimum), and outstanding dishes such as whisky-flambéed shrimp. For dessert, there's the non-Spanish but very welcome crêpes with Nutella and ice cream. Mains from 4500c. Daily noon–4pm & 6.30–9.30pm.

Tucan Hotel On the main road just before the right turn down to the beach ☎ 2743 8140, ⓦ tucanhotel.com. A wonderful catch-all, where shoestringers can bed down in a tent, hammock, dorm or private rooms with a/c. The on-site café caters to vegetarians and vegans and there's free coffee and a beach shuttle thrown in. Tent US$6, hammock US$6, dorm US$10, double US$25

PARQUE NACIONAL MARINO BALLENA

The beautiful **Parque Nacional Marino Ballena**, covering the vast beaches that end in Punta Uvita – appropriately enough, given the name of the park, shaped like the tail of a whale – and the waters surrounding Isla Ballena, protects a variety of marine fauna, including bottlenose dolphins, turtles and **migrating humpback whales**. The vast main beach is a spectacular vantage point from which to watch the sunset, and there's good snorkelling to be had off Punta Uvita (best at low tide). During the humpback whale season (Aug–Oct & Dec–April), you may well see pods of the giants breaching off the coast, while turtle season (May–Oct) attracts hawksbill and olive ridley turtles that come to lay eggs on the beach.

ARRIVAL AND INFORMATION

Park entrances The main beach is accessible either from the official entrance next to the ranger stations at the end of the paved road through Uvita (daily dawn–dusk; US$10; parking US$2), or at the unofficial entrance at the end of the dirt road behind *Flutterby House* (see opposite).

Camping You can bed down at the basic free campsite (cold showers and toilets), 300m from the official park entrance, but you have to bring all supplies with you.

Península de Osa and Golfo Dulce

Costa Rica's **Osa Peninsula** is the country's remotest and wildest region, and one of the most biologically diverse on earth, making it a hugely exciting destination for birdwatchers and animal lovers alike. While the peninsula's two main settlements – Puerto Jiménez and Drake – are linked to the rest of the country by ever-improving roads, there is an off-the-grid feel to them, and getting around much of the peninsula is still an adventure. The region experiences **rain** even during the dry season, and during the wettest part of the year (Oct–Dec), spectacular thunderstorms canter in from the Pacific and travel by road becomes tricky.

Curled around the **Golfo Dulce** – a prime spot for spotting whales, whale sharks and other marine fauna – the Osa Peninsula is covered in dense, pristine rainforest that is part of the **Parque Nacional Corcovado**, the country's top wildlife-spotting and hiking destination. On its western side is the remote and picturesque **Bahía Drake**, home to the village of **Drake** and only accessible by boat and rough road. More accessible, **Puerto Jiménez** is the peninsula's main town, sitting directly across the Golfo Dulce from the former banana port of **Golfito**.

GOLFITO

A former banana port, just 33km north of the Panamanian border, gently decaying **GOLFITO** stretches along the water at the cusp of the glorious Golfo Dulce. Golfito's history is intertwined with the **United Fruit Company**, which first set up here in 1938. When it pulled out in 1985 the town became one of the most unsavoury places in Costa Rica. These days, Golfito is a tax-free zone for imports from Panama, with a purpose-built **Zona Americana** – a huge shopping centre – where Ticos come for 24-hour shopping sprees. The tax-free benefit does not extend to foreigners, who only come

2

to Golfito if they are into sports fishing or prostitution, or if they are heading straight to Panama from the Osa Peninsula or vice versa. South of the Zona Americana, and the more affluent part of town, is the **pueblo civil**, where there are a couple of places to stay if you must, a smattering of restaurants and the *lancha* across the Golfo Dulce to Puerto Jiménez and the Osa Peninsula.

ARRIVAL AND DEPARTURE

By boat Boats link Puerto Jiménez and Golfito's tiny *muellecito* (little dock) behind *Hotel Golfito*. From Golfito there are five fast boats daily (7.30am, 10am, 1pm, 2.30pm & 3.15pm; 35min; 3000c) and one slow boat at 11.30am (2hr). Boats leave early if full, so get to the dock 20min before departure time (which you should confirm beforehand).

By bus Most services stop at the depot opposite the little park in the northern part of Golfito. Buy your onward ticket in advance, particularly for San José.

Destinations Neilly (hourly 6am–7pm; 1hr 30min); San José (2 daily, 5am & 1.30pm; 7hr; leaves from terminal near Muelle Bananero).

ACCOMMODATION

Hotel Golfito Next to the gas station on the way into town ☎ 2775 0047. Simple budget hotel in front of the *muellecito*: rooms are clean, with private cold-water bathrooms and sturdy fans (a/c costs extra). The communal balcony sits virtually on the water, and has beautiful views. U͟S͟$͟2͟5͟

Mar Y Luna 500m before the *pueblo civil* on the main road ☎ 2775 0901, ⊛ hotelmarylunaandsuites.com. Bright, very comfortable doubles with private bath, a/c, TV and sea views, and larger rooms with kitchenettes. It also boasts a renowned seafood restaurant with decking virtually on the sea. U͟S͟$͟4͟0͟

EATING AND DRINKING

8º Latitude On the little street that starts by *Buenos Días*. Run by an eccentric American couple, this compact, friendly expat favourite is the perfect place for a cold beer (around 1200c).

Blue Marlin By the *muellecito*. You only need to walk a few steps from the boat for some of the best food in town. The *ceviche* is OK, but the ample portions of seafood rice are superb, as is the fish soup, and the *patacones* (plantain fritters) are among the best in Costa Rica. Mains around 2500c. Daily 11am–4pm.

Buenos Días Across the road from the *muellecito*. Cheerful American diner-style café serving *gallo pinto*, hash browns and more for breakfast (from 2000c), and *casados* and burgers (from 3000c) the rest of the day. Daily 6am–10pm.

PUERTO JIMÉNEZ

Most visitors to the Parque Nacional Corcovado base themselves in the tiny

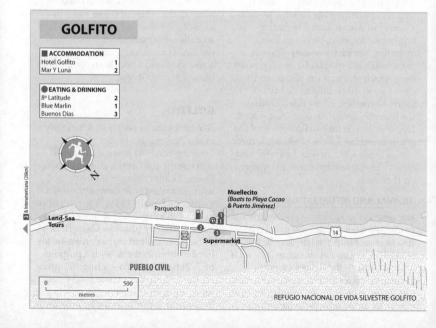

GOLFITO

◼ ACCOMMODATION	
Hotel Golfito	1
Mar Y Luna	2

● EATING & DRINKING	
8º Latitude	2
Blue Marlin	1
Buenos Días	3

Muellecito
(Boats to Playa Cacao & Puerto Jiménez)

Parquecito

Land-Sea Tours

2 & Interamericana (26km)

Supermarket

14

PUEBLO CIVIL

0   500
metres

REFUGIO NACIONAL DE VIDA SILVESTRE GOLFITO

town of **PUERTO JIMÉNEZ**, the main gateway for hiking in the park. You're likely to see wildlife in the town itself – from nesting macaws and visiting monkeys to crocodiles in the mangroves. Jiménez has plenty of **activities** of its own to keep you busy for a few days, among them kayaking on the Golfo Dulce, boat trips with dolphin- and whale-spotting possibilities and day excursions to various community projects (see below).

From Jiménez, *colectivos* run to Carate, 43km southwest, where the most popular of **Corcovado's hiking trails** begins (see p.189).

ARRIVAL AND DEPARTURE

By bus The bus station, with departures to San Isidro (daily, 1pm; 5hr) and San José (2 daily, 5am & 11am; 8hr), is at the western side of the village, a block from the football field.

By colectivo *Colectivo Transportación* (☎8837 3120) officially runs from *Soda Deya* to Carate (2 daily, 6am & 1.30pm; 1hr 30min) via Cabo Matapalo, but confirm departures, as some services don't run.

By car The road to Puerto Jiménez from the Interamericana is almost completely paved, though there is a severely potholed section between the Interamericana and Rincón.

By 4WD taxi Central Taxi Center (☎2735 5481) can drive up to four people to Carate for US$80.

INFORMATION AND TOURS

Bank Banco Nacional is on the main road in town.

Escondido Trex ☎2735 5210. Excellent-value kayaking (from US$50), snorkelling (US$50), dolphin-spotting (US$65) and mangrove tours (US$77), all with very knowledgeable guides. Those with a head for heights should try the waterfall rappelling (US$100) or climbing a giant *areno* tree (US$100).

Osa Wild Run by experienced tropical biologist Ifi, Osa Wild (☎2735 5848, ⊛osawildtravel.com) is your best source of information on Parque Nacional Corcovado. Guided hikes in the park are arranged (from U$55/person/day), as are day-trips to various community-oriented initiatives around Osa, such as a local coffee farm.

Tourist information Oficina de Área de Conservación Osa, opposite the airstrip (☎2735 5580, Mon–Fri 8am–noon & 1–4pm), is the government body in charge of Corcovado National Park. The number of people allowed in the park at any one time is limited; you need to reserve your slot here in advance (max 5 days/4 nights), pay your park entry fee and collect the receipt that you'll have to show to park rangers. Sometimes it's possible to get permission to enter the park the day before you want to go; if reservations are not paid for by 1.30pm, then spaces are up for grabs.

ACCOMMODATION

Wherever you want to stay, make sure to book in advance in the dry season.

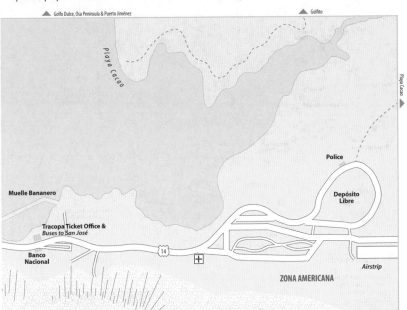

Cabinas Back Packers Half a block west of main supermarket ☏ 2735 5181. Run by a friendly Colombian, this sparkling clean budget spot features tiled doubles (some with TVs) with shared facilities, plus a large kitchen for guest use and free wi-fi. US$20

★ **Cabinas Celvante Jungle Hostel** 3km southwest of Puerto Jiménez ☏ 8607 0733 or ☏ 8607 0316. In a lush jungle setting, this superb hostel boasts not only its own organic farm, but also all sorts of sustainable practices, a great common area and bar and walking trails nearby. The owners run a twice-daily shuttle to Jiménez. Camping US$14, dorm US$14, double US$35

Cabinas The Corner A block west of the main street and a block south of the bus station ☏ 2735 5328, ⓦ jimenezhotels.com/cabinasthecorner. In addition to the plain fan-cooled four- and five-bed dorms are a couple of rudimentary doubles with private baths – all with free wi-fi. It's a good place to meet other travellers and the *dueña* is a keen – and vocal – conservationist. Dorm US$6, double US$12

★ **Cabinas Marcelina** On the main street, near the Catholic church ☏ 2735 5286. This comfortable pink guesthouse is an idyllic hideaway from the dusty streets: all rooms are en suite, and most look onto the sweet breakfast garden filled with tropical flowers. US$50

Hotel Oro Verde Just off the main road ☏ 2735 5241. Rooms are somewhat musty, with optional hot water and a/c. Bring earplugs, as it can be noisy. Try to nab one of the best rooms with terrace access. In-house tour guide Josh is bubbling with enthusiasm for the national park. Per person US$20

EATING

Cafe Monka On the main street. The best place for breakfast in town, with excellent coffee and granola with yogurt and *huevos rancheros* (Mexican-style eggs with salsa) served alongside traditional *gallo pinto*, and sandwiches for lunch. Mains 2000c. Daily 7.30am–5pm.

★ **Jade Luna** On the main street. Legendary local ice cream; flavours range from mint oreo to *dulce de leche* with macadamia (2000c per pot). Daily 8am–5pm.

★ **Pizzamail.it** By the football field. Superb, authentic Italian thin-crust pizzas and calzones, with imported ingredients that you may have been hankering for, such as

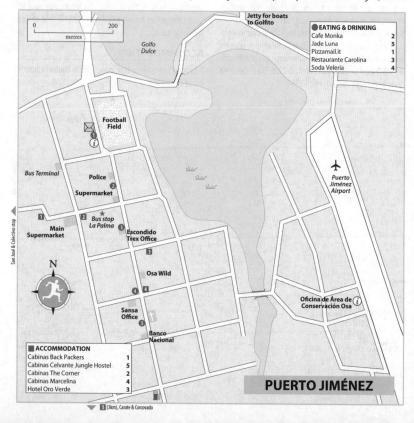

EATING & DRINKING

Cafe Monka	2
Jade Luna	5
Pizzamail.it	1
Restaurante Carolina	3
Soda Veleria	4

ACCOMMODATION

Cabinas Back Packers	1
Cabinas Celvante Jungle Hostel	5
Cabinas The Corner	2
Cabinas Marcelina	4
Hotel Oro Verde	3

PUERTO JIMÉNEZ

olives and capers. Even the smallest pizza is plenty for one person. Mains from 4000c. Daily 4.30–10pm.

Restaurante Carolina Main street, a block and a half south of the football field. A catch-all restaurant popular with visitors, guides and locals, offering grilled meats, soups and *casados*. Mains from 4000c. Daily noon–10pm.

Soda Veleria On the main street. Friendly *soda*, popular with locals, serving large portions of home-cooked *casados* and fresh juices. Mains from 2000c. Daily noon–9pm.

BAHÍA DRAKE

BAHÍA DRAKE (named after Sir Francis Drake who visited in 1579) is one of the most stunning – and remote – areas in Costa Rica, with fiery-orange Pacific sunsets and the blue wedge of **Isla del Caño** floating just off the coast. **Agujitas**, the village, consists of just two streets – the main one running uphill, and the other running roughly parallel to the beach. It's a wonderful base for the majority of travellers who come to the area to explore **Parque Nacional Corcovado**.

WHAT TO SEE AND DO

Corcovado's **San Pedrillo** entrance is within hiking distance from the Agujitas – 10km (4–5hr each way) along the coastal trail. Upon your return, you can relax in some excellent budget digs (or stay in one of the area's upscale ecolodges) and sample surprisingly varied cuisine.

Isla del Caño, 20km west of Agujitas, is one of Costa Rica's top snorkelling and diving destinations, and diving/snorkelling trips are easily arranged through your lodgings. You can also take to the water of **Río Agujitas**, easily reachable from the village; kayaking is a good way to spot the abundant birdlife, as well as caimans. Finally, Bahía Drake is the launchpad for ultra-popular boat trips to **La Sirena**, at the heart of Parque Nacional Corcovado, from where you can go on guided wildlife-spotting rambles in the park without the need for any strenuous hiking (see p.189).

ARRIVAL AND DEPARTURE

By plane The Drake airstrip, 2km north of Agujitas, is served by daily flights from San José with NatureAir and

Sansa. There are also charter flights from Puerto Jiménez, Golfito, Carate and La Sirena with Alfa Romeo Aero Taxi (see p.190).

By bus From the north, take a Puerto Jiménez-bound bus to Rincón, from where a morning bus (Mon–Sat) heads to Bahía Drake; check the latest times with Fundación Corcovado (see below) beforehand. There's a 5am Transcopa bus from San José that stops in Palmar Norte, from where there are frequent *colectivos* to Sierpe. From the south, *colectivos* run from Puerto Jiménez to La Palma, from where there are morning and afternoon buses to Drake; check the latest times first in Puerto Jiménez. From Drake, a 4.15am bus leaves from in front of the supermarket during dry season, stopping at Rincón to coincide with the San José-bound bus from Jiménez and reaching La Palma at 7am, with a connecting bus to Jiménez around 8am.

By boat Speedboats ply their way through mangrove channels and along the ocean between Agujitas and Sierpe, a village reachable by minor road off the Interamericana. Boats run from Sierpe at 11am, noon and 3.30pm, heading back from Bahía Drake at 6.45am, 7.15am and 2.30pm (US$20 one-way). You can also negotiate a private boat transport to/from Sierpe.

By car The road from Rincón to Bahía Drake is a bumpy gravel road with several river crossings, so a 4WD is mandatory.

INFORMATION AND TOURS

Tourist information ⓦ gringocurtandticoesteban.com.

Fundación Corcovado ☎ 2297 3013, ⓦ corcovado foundation.org. A volunteer organization set up to maintain the park, improve local amenities and rally against encroaching developers. The beachfront office doubles as an unofficial tourist information office.

Tours Most lodgings offer tours, from snorkelling to horseriding, for US$75–100. Corcovado Expeditions, set back from the beach just next to the Fundación Corcovado (☎ 8818 9962, ⓦ corcovadoexpeditions.net), has trips to Isla del Caño and Corcovado (both US$75), and mangrove and canopy tours. Tracie the "Bug Lady" runs popular night-time jaunts (ⓦ thenighttour.com; US$35); advance reservations highly recommended.

Banks There are no banks or ATMs in Drake. Some lodgings accept cards.

ACCOMMODATION

There are many upscale ecolodges in the Bahía Drake area, with budget accommodation concentrated in Agujitas village. Most places offer wi-fi.

Cabinas Murillo On the road running parallel to the beach ☎ 8892 7702, ⓦ drakecorcovadocabins.com. Centrally located, this quiet, Tico-run place offers one of the best bargains in the village. It's worth paying a little

2

extra for the rooms higher up the hillside offering great views of the bay. Guest kitchen and free wi-fi available. Double US$40, two-person cabin US$50

Casita Corcovado Up from the road running parallel to the beach ☎2775 0627 or ☎8996 9987, ⓦcasitacorcovado.com. Up on a bluff, this attractive, ecologically sound three-bedroom cottage offers splendid bay views and hammocks swaying in the sea breeze. Rooms can be rented individually, or the cottage as a whole, and Jamie and Craig make you feel very welcome. Substantial discounts for solo travellers. Double US$70, cottage US$190

★ **Jumanji Bungalows** Follow the road up from the village for around 15min ☎2775 1556, ⓦjumanji bungalows.com. This small, secluded jungle hotel has just two doubles, with plenty of personalized attention from the gregarious hosts. There's a small swimming pool and the on-site gourmet restaurant serves a fantastic breakfast (US$10) and excellent French/Italian cuisine. US$35

★ **Hotel Finca Maresia** 2km outside Agujitas ☎2775 0279, ⓦfincamaresia.com. On undulating land surrounded by tropical forest, this is a delightful collection of bungalows with orthopaedic mattresses, private baths and balconies, plus simpler rooms with shared baths. There's a wonderfully serene vibe and staff can arrange pick-ups and excellent tours. Rates include breakfast. Double US$50, bungalow US$90

Pura Vida Bahía Drake In the centre of the village ☎8720 0801, ⓦpuravidadrakebay.com. Locally known as "Martina's Place", this cheerful yellow house offers a fan-cooled double and an apartment for up to four people, as well as a glamping option – double beds set up in large tents outside. German and English spoken. Double US$20, apartment US$30

EATING

Empanadas Argentinas Main street. True to its name, this friendly place serves up Argentine-style *empanadas* (2000c), as well as more substantial mains. This is also as close as Drake gets to having a nightlife, with the Argentine musician owners occasionally taking to the tiny stage. Daily 4–10pm.

★ **Gringo Curt's Seafood and Visitor Center** Main street. This friendly spot does only a handful of dishes, but what a handful! Expect gargantuan portions of fish tacos, an obligatory pasta dish for vegetarians, and the tour de force – a slab of beautifully seasoned fish, baked in a banana leaf and complete with sautéed veggies – a rarity in Costa Rica. A main is enough for two people. Mains 4500–7000c. Daily 11am–9pm.

Mar y Bosque Main street. This lovely, open-air *soda*, run by the descendants of the original Bahía Drake settlers, overlooks a butterfly-filled garden. It's great all day: for breakfast go for a delicious juice or smoothie to wash down your pancakes or *pinto* (2000c); the more substantial *casados* (2000c plus) are equally good. Esteban, the son of the owner, offers informative trips into Corcovado. Mon–Sat 7am–9pm.

Restaurante Jade Mar Main street. This open-sided strip-lit place is always busy with locals and visitors. The extensive menu is a catch-all offering steaks, fresh seafood (including lobster), pizza and pasta. Mains from 4500c.

PARQUE NACIONAL CORCOVADO

Created in 1975, **PARQUE NACIONAL CORCOVADO** (daily 8am–4pm; US$10; ☎2735 5036) protects a fascinating and complex area of land, which houses 2.5 percent of the world's total biodiversity. It's a beautiful park, with deserted beaches, waterfalls, high canopy trees and the best **wildlife-spotting** opportunities in the country. Exploring Corcovado, however, is not for the faint-hearted, due to the heat, distances involved and natural hazards. The **terrain** includes exposed beaches, rivers to be forded, mangroves, *holillo* (palm) swamps and dense forest, although most of it is at lowland elevations. **Trails** are relatively

---

WHO'S WHO OF CORCOVADO'S WILDLIFE

Felines All of Costa Rica's cats are respesented in Corcovado: the big ones – jaguar, puma, ocelot – and the little ones: jaguarundi, margay and oncilla.

Monkeys You are more likely to spot the white-faced capuchins and spider monkeys, but howlers and squirrel monkeys also reside here.

Other mammals Baird's tapir is the most impressive of the herbivores, but you may also see peccaries, deer, sloths, and several species of anteater, including the ultra-rare and elusive silky (or pygmy) anteater.

Creepy crawlies Insects to beware of are the bullet ant, army ant, tarantula hawk (a wasp with an extremely painful sting) and ticks (though they don't carry lyme disease here).

Reptiles Besides crocodiles and spectacled caiman that dwell in some of the rivers, you may come across the extremely venomous fer-de-lance snake.

2

TREKKING IN CORCOVADO

You have to **reserve a space** in Corcovado in advance – this will include meals and either camping space or lodging at the *puesto* of your choice. To reserve, contact the park's Puerto Jiménez office (see p.185) at least two weeks in advance, or go through a tour agency. Within the park, all ranger stations have camping areas, drinking water, information, toilets and telephone or radio; La Sirena even has (slow) wi-fi. Wherever you enter, jot down the details of the **marea** (tide tables), which are posted at ranger stations. You'll need to cross most of the rivers at low tide; to do otherwise is dangerous. Rangers can advise on conditions.

Don't underestimate the difficulty of hiking in 100 percent humidity and temperatures of at least 26°C (without the benefit of the sea breeze on the Los Patos trail). Plan to hike early – though not before dawn, due to snakes – and shelter during the hottest part of the day. Rangers at each *puesto* always know how many people are on a given trail, and how long those hikers are expected to be. If you are late getting back, they'll go looking for you. Few rangers speak English, so if hiking independently, a knowledge of some **Spanish** is essential.

Essentials include sunscreen, insect repellent, a hat and a waterproof bag for your clothes, as you'll have to cross several rivers. Take plenty of **water** – and we mean plenty; several hikers have died in the park due to dehydration – and food; stock up either in Jiménez or Drake. Don't leave any trash in the park or at the ranger stations, as waste is a problem.

Finally, although unlikely, there is some chance of getting attacked by wild **animals**. If peccaries display threatening behaviour, climb a tree; if a puma attacks, make yourself as big as possible, shout and fight.

easy to follow, particularly in the dry season, though some hikers have been known to get lost. The coastal areas of the park receive around 3800mm of **rain** a year, with precipitation rising to about 5000mm in the higher elevations of the interior. There is a dry season (Dec–March), but the inland lowland areas, especially those around the lagoon, can be amazingly **hot** during this period.

WHAT TO SEE AND DO

The park has three main trails: the most popular starts in the village of **Carate**, 43km southwest of Jiménez, and runs to the **La Sirena** ranger station at the heart of Corcovado via the **La Leona** ranger station, 2.5km from Carate and one of three official entrances to the park. From Bahía Drake, it's a 10km hike to the **San Pedrillo** ranger station – the park's western entrance. From here there's a popular 25km trail to La Sirena, which at the time of writing was closed indefinitely. Finally, there's an 18km trail from the **Los Patos** ranger station to La Sirena.

La Leona to La Sirena

The mostly flat 16km trail from **La Leona to Sirena** runs mostly inland from the beach, though there are several exposed stretches of beach that you have to walk

on, including the 2.5km walk from Carate to La Leona, so get an early start. The hike takes 7–8 hours and you are likely to spot such wildlife as **scarlet macaws** that roost in the coastal trees, **monkeys** – particularly white-faced capuchins and spider monkeys – and even tapirs and peccaries. There have also been several recent spottings of pumas near La Sirena.

La Sirena to San Pedrillo

The trail from **La Sirena to San Pedrillo** is the toughest of them all. The trail was closed indefinitely at the time of writing, following the death of several hikers, but if it reopens, get the latest information from the La Sirena rangers before you set out.

A large part of the 25km stretch runs along the exposed beach, and the two-day hike is exhausting. You have to take more than enough water to last you, as well as a tent, sleeping bag and mosquito net. It is recommended to walk much of the beach trail at night, as the heat during the day must not be underestimated. There are three rivers to ford, the most dangerous just 1km beyond La Sirena. **Río Sirena** is the deepest of all the rivers on the peninsula and can only be crossed with caution at low tide; the brackish water at the mouth of the estuary is home to bull sharks – an aggressive species that

2

INTO PANAMA: PASO CANOAS

The only reason to come to **PASO CANOAS** is to cross the border into Panama. The border crossing is open 24hr and the process is straightforward. If you're driving, you may find yourself waiting in queues. If taking the international Tracopa or Tica Bus service, your processing will be quick. For travel into Panama, pick up a **tourist card** (US$5) – check also visa requirements (see p.518). You may be required to produce proof of onward travel from Panama.

There are direct Tica Bus services from San José to Panama City (15hr) and daily Tracopa services between San José and **David**, the first city of any size in Panama, about 90min beyond the border. Buses run from the Panamanian border bus terminal hourly until 5pm. From David it's easy to pick up local services to Panama City.

---

occasionally attack humans – and crocodiles. Beyond the third river – La Llorona – the trail splits in two; most hikers follow the shorter beachside trail to San Pedrillo, while the other route runs inland and adds 2km to your hike.

La Palma to Los Patos

The small hamlet of **La Palma**, 24km north of Puerto Jiménez and linked to it by bus, is the starting point for the walk to the **Los Patos** *puesto*. It's a 14km hike, much of it through hot lowland terrain (though it might be possible to arrange a 4WD taxi to take you some of the way).

There are numerous river crossings along the trail, and you need to be careful not to miss the correct turn to the *puesto*. To get to Los Patos from Jiménez, drive 10km north and take the second left, a dirt track, signed to El Tigre and Dos Brazos. Taxis cost around US$20.

Los Patos to La Sirena

The trail across the peninsula from **Los Patos to La Sirena** is 18km long. It is recommended that you hike from Los Patos to La Sirena to get the toughest part out of the way first. It's a demanding walk, with two river tributaries to ford and steep uphills and downhills for the first 6km, taking you into high, wet and dense secondary forest. The remaining 12km or so is flat and easy to follow, and since you're passing through the heart of Corcovado, there's a good chance of seeing some of the park's elusive mammals (or at least their tracks).

ARRIVAL AND DEPARTURE

By air Alfa Romeo Aero Taxi (☎2735 5353, ⓦwww .alfaromeoair.com) is a charter service connecting Puerto Jiménez, Bahía Drake, Golfito, Carate and La Sirena; flights cost around US$100.

By boat There are regular boat day-trips from Bahía Drake to La Sirena; you can take the boat one-way and then hike from La Sirena to La Palma or Carate, though you will need to get a permit from the park office in Puerto Jiménez.

By colectivo and 4WD taxi Daily *colectivos* run from Puerto Jiménez to Carate (see p.185) along a bumpy, rutted road. If you want to get to Carate earlier in the morning, share a 4WD taxi from Jiménez with other hikers (see p.185).

INFORMATION

Health Night walks in the jungle are forbidden – there is no way to get you out of the park after dark, and were you to get bitten by a venomous snake you would die.

Tour operators To increase your chances of seeing the park's wildlife, it's well worth investing in the services of a guide: rates are around US$55/person/day. Osa Wild are particularly good (see p.185).

ACCOMMODATION AND EATING

If you want to make a very early start from Carate, you can camp en route to La Leona for a nominal fee. Book meals in advance at the La Sirena canteen, or bring your own utensils, portable stove and fuel.

Camping You can camp at all the ranger stations. Bring tent, mosquito net, sleeping bag, food and water. US$5

La Sirena accommodation block La Sirena ranger station. Musty dorms and old foam mattresses are provided, but no bedding. US$15

La Sirena canteen La Sirena ranger station. You can eat expensive but good meals here (lunch US$20, dinner US$25); book in advance at the Jiménez office.

PACIFIC SURFING

El Salvador

HIGHLIGHTS

❶ Pacific beaches Sample the surf or lounge on the sands. **See p.217**

❷ Perquín Visit the haunting Museo de la Revolución Salvadoreña. **See p.238**

❸ Suchitoto Stunning lake views in the country's finest colonial town. **See p.241**

❹ Parque Nacional El Imposible Pristine mountain forest; a haven for wildlife. **See p.250**

❺ Ruta de las Flores Winding mountain road and artistic towns. **See p.251**

❻ Lago de Coatepeque Awe-inspiring crater lake hemmed in by volcanoes. **See p.261**

HIGHLIGHTS ARE MARKED ON THE MAP ON P.193

ROUGH COSTS

Daily budget Basic US$26/occasional treat US$40

Drink Coffee US$0.75, Pilsner beer US$1.50

Food *Pupusa* US$0.50

Hostel/budget hotel US$12/US$20

Travel San Salvador–San Miguel by bus (138km): 2hr 30min, US$2.50

FACT FILE

Population 6.2 million

Language Spanish

Currency US dollar (US$)

Capital San Salvador (population: 2.4 million)

International phone code ☎503

Time zone GMT -6hr

Introduction

The smallest and most densely populated country in Central America, El Salvador is also the region's least visited nation. Known less for its world-class surf and stunning forest reserves than the vicious civil war it suffered in the 1980s and gang violence since the 1990s, the country has long struggled to gain tourists' trust. Those who do make it here, however, are well rewarded by the hospitality of its proud inhabitants and the sheer physical beauty of the place. Almost every journey in El Salvador yields photogenic vistas: majestic cones of towering volcanoes, gorgeous colonial towns, rolling coffee plantations and rugged mountain chains.

Booming **San Salvador** is one of Central America's most developed cities, boasting an enticing spread of galleries, museums, restaurants and a sophisticated nightlife. Within easy reach are the fascinating ruins at **Joya de Cerén** and a glorious sweep of the **Pacific coast**, including surfers' favourite **Costa del Bálsamo**. Some beaches offer true seclusion, while others receive the best waves in all of Central America.

Further east is the turtle-rich haven of **El Cuco** and the idyllic islands of the **Golfo de Fonseca**, while inland the small but affable city of **San Vicente** gives access to delightful artistic villages like floral **Alegría**, high above the central plains. Larger **San Miguel** hosts one of the biggest carnivals in Central America

while the **Ruta de Paz** traverses the poor and rugged Morazán region towards the poignant war museum at **Perquín** and the town of **El Mozote**, the site of one of the civil war's worst atrocities – unmissable for anyone interested in El Salvador's recent history.

In the west, the laidback grandeur of **Santa Ana** lies between the exquisite **cloudforests** of Montecristo and El Imposible. For climbers, the nearby **volcanic peaks** of Izalco and Cerro Verde provide good hiking, while at their base is the mesmerizing deep-blue crater lake of **Coatepeque**; for gastronomes, the **Ruta de las Flores** features **Juayúa**'s famous food festival, as well as other blossom-smothered mountain towns.

The north, though rough and wild, hosts the still unspoiled colonial gem of **Suchitoto**, above the glorious crater lake of Suchitlán, while **La Palma**, near the Honduran border, is famous for its naïf crafts, producing wooden handicrafts, pottery and hammocks.

WHEN TO VISIT

The **dry season** (Nov–March) is the best time to visit El Salvador: northeasterly winds make for less humid air, more accessible dirt roads, sandier beaches and less daunting waves. Humidity builds throughout late March and April into the **wet season** (May–Oct), which is fed by Pacific low-pressure systems and sees clear mornings cloud over to late afternoon and overnight downpours. This is the season for big waves, flowering orchids and spectacular lightning storms, but travel can be difficult and flooding and hurricanes are not unknown. **Temperatures** are always regulated by altitude.

CHRONOLOGY

Pre-8000 BC Paleo-Indian cave dwellers around Corinto are the first known inhabitants.

Pre-1200 BC Maya arrive from Guatemala.

900 AD Maya culture mysteriously collapses.

900–1400 AD Waves of Nahuat-speaking settlers, later dubbed "Pipils", migrate from Mexico, establishing seats of power at Cihuatán, Tehuacán and Cuscatlán.

1524 Pedro de Alvarado crosses the Río Paz to conquer the area for Spain; he names the region "El Salvador" (literally "The Saviour"), in honour of Jesus.

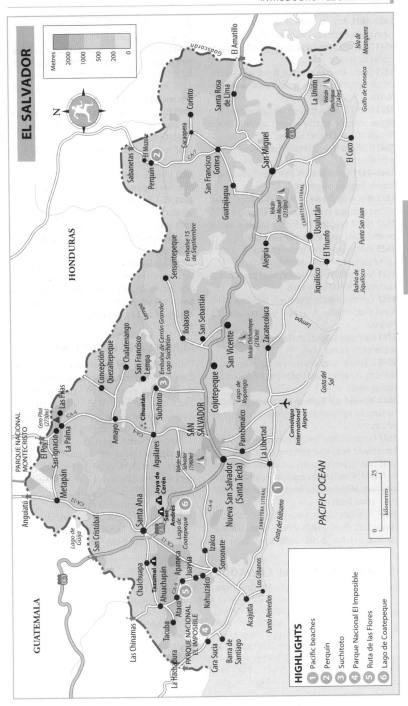

EL SALVADOR

N

Metres
2000
1000
500
200
0

3

GUATEMALA

HONDURAS

Cerro Pital
(2730m)

PARQUE NACIONAL
MONTECRISTO

Anguiatú

Lago de
Güija

El Amatillo

Godscordn

El Poy

Las Pilas

CA-4

Metapán

San Cristoba

Chalchuapa

Tacuba

Ahuachapán

Ataco

Apaneca

Juayúa

CA-8

Nahuizalco

Las Chinamas

La Hachadura

PARQUE NACIONAL
EL IMPOSIBLE

Cara Sucia

Barra de
Santiago

Acajutla

Sonsonate

Izalco

San Ignacio

La Palma

Concepción
Quezaltepeque

Chalatenango

San Francisco
Lempa

Amayo

Lempa

Embalse de Cerrón Grande/
Lago Suchitlán

Suchitoto

Cihuatán

Aguilares

Volcán San
Salvador
(1960m)

SAN
SALVADOR

Santa Ana

Tazumal

Lago de
Coatepeque

CA-1

San
Andrés

Joya de
Cerén

Nueva San Salvador
(Santa Tecla)

La Libertad

CARRETERA LITORAL

Costa del Bálsamo

PACIFIC OCEAN

Punta Remedios

Sabanetas

El Mozote

Perquín

CA-7

Cacaopera

Corinto

Santa Rosa
de Lima

San Francisco
Gotera

Guatajiagua

San Miguel

Usulután

Alegría

Jiquilisco

El Triunfo

Volcán
San Miguel
(2130m)

CARRETERA LITORAL

Bahía de
Jiquilisco

Punta San Juan

La Unión

Volcán
Conchagua
(1243m)

Golfo de Fonseca

Isla de
Meanguera

El Cuco

Sensuntepeque

Embalse 15
de Septiembre

Ilobasco

San Sebastián

San Vicente

Volcán Chichontepec
(2182m)

Zacatecoluca

Cojutepeque

Lago de
Ilopango

Panchimalco

Comalapa
International
Airport

Costa del
Sol

Lempa

kilometres
0   25

HIGHLIGHTS
① Pacific beaches
② Perquín
③ Suchitoto
④ Parque Nacional El Imposible
⑤ Ruta de las Flores
⑥ Lago de Coatepeque

3

1600–1800 Hacienda feudalism creates a rich Spanish ruling elite and indentured indigenous labour force.

1811 Father José Delgado leads an unsuccessful revolution against the Spanish.

1821 Central American provinces, including El Salvador, declare independence from Spain, but are annexed by Mexico.

1823 Central American countries win independence from Mexico under Salvadoreño Manuel José Arce; Federal Republic of Central America is created.

1841 El Salvador declares independence; Federal Republic is dissolved.

1840–1931 Coffee becomes main export crop; private interests dominate government.

1873 Massive earthquake on March 19 destroys the last vestiges of colonial San Salvador; it gets hit again in 1917.

1927 Liberal candidate Pío Romero Bosque is elected president, takes steps to dismantle oligarchies.

1929 Economy collapses in response to Wall Street crash; Liberal plans for democracy derailed.

1931 General Maximiliano Martínez seizes power in coup, starting fifty years of military rule.

1932 Communist-led rebellion sees thousands killed. Government response is a week-long massacre, "La Matanza".

1961 Right-wing National Conciliation Party (PCN) comes to power after a military coup.

1969 El Salvador attacks Honduras in the six-day "Soccer War" (over immigration and land reform, but sparked by a football match).

1972 Reformist José Napoleón Duarte wins presidential elections; but he is immediately deposed and exiled by the military.

1977 As many as three hundred unarmed civilians shot in front of world media while protesting in San Salvador.

1980 Leftist opposition parties and guerrilla groups form the FMLN-FDR, while right-wing death squads wage terror campaigns. Archbishop Óscar Romero is assassinated; full-scale civil war breaks out.

1981 US pumps aid to military to stem "spread of Communism", despite its links to death squads. El Mozote massacre (see box, p.240). Death squad leader and all-round pathological killer Roberto D'Aubuisson founds ARENA (National Republican Alliance).

1984 Duarte defeats D'Aubuisson to become first civilian president since 1932 (his campaign is financed by the CIA), but he fails to stop human rights abuses by the army.

1986 Another massive quake devastates the nation; between 1000 and 1500 people are killed.

1989 Fighting intensifies; San Salvador is occupied, and six Jesuit priests are assassinated. ARENA candidate Alfredo Cristiani elected president.

1992 Peace accords finally signed, presided over by the UN and the Catholic Church.

2001 US dollar replaces the colón. Two earthquakes kill more than 1000 people and destroy infrastructure.

2005 CA-4 free-trade agreement signed between El Salvador, Honduras, Guatemala and Nicaragua.

2009 Mauricio Funes, ex-journalist and leader of FMLN party, wins presidential elections, ending twenty years of ARENA rule.

2012 Truce between rival criminal gangs (*maras*), the Mara Salvatrucha and Calle 18, results in a 40 percent reduction in crime and a dramatic drop in murders; Funes government suffers setback in parliamentary elections, which give ARENA a narrow victory.

ARRIVAL AND DEPARTURE

Visitors **flying** to El Salvador will arrive at **Comalapa International Airport (SAL)**, about 50km southeast of San Salvador. The main hub for TACA Airlines (⊛taca .com), it's one of the busiest in Central America, with daily flights from numerous North American cities (principally Dallas, Houston, LA, Miami, New York and Mexico City) as well as the rest of Central America, South America and the Caribbean. The only direct service from Europe is the Iberia (⊛iberia.com) flight from Madrid.

You can enter El Salvador by land from Guatemala and Honduras (see box

LAND ROUTES TO EL SALVADOR

The main border crossings with **Honduras** are in the east at El Amatillo (see box, p.395), convenient for connections to Tegucigalpa, and at El Poy (see box, p.404) in the northwest.

The main border with **Guatemala** is at La Hachadura (see box, p.250) in the southwest, best for the Pacific beaches and used by international buses from Mexico. Another Guatemala crossing is at Las Chinamas (see box, p.257), near Ahuachapán, used by international buses from Guatemala City. The crossing at Anguiatú (see box, p.338), in the north near Metapán, is used by buses from Esquipulas. A smaller crossing at San Cristóbal (see box, p.338) is close to the city of Santa Ana. Note that you should not be charged a border entry fee, since your Honduran or Guatemalan tourist card is valid in El Salvador (this also applies for leaving El Salvador).

opposite). Almost all **international buses** arrive in San Salvador (see p.210). Chicken buses run from border crossings to nearby towns in the daylight hours.

The only international **boats** run from Nicaragua across the Golfo de Fonseca to La Unión (see box, p.228).

VISAS

Visas for El Salvador are not currently required for citizens of the UK, US, Canada, Australia, Ireland, Israel, New Zealand, South Africa and most other European countries. A US$10 border **entry fee** is levied at the airport, but only for nationals of Australia, Canada and the US. Under the **CA-4 agreement**, there is one tourist card for El Salvador, Guatemala, Honduras and Nicaragua (see box, p.30) – make sure you get a ninety-day allowance rather than a thirty-day one. If you are applying for a formal extension, visit the Dirección General de Migración y Extranjería (Sección de Visas y Prórrogas), 9A C Pte & 15 Av Nte, in the Centro de Gobierno, San Salvador (Mon–Fri 8am–4pm). See ⓦ migracion .gob.sv for details.

GETTING AROUND

El Salvador's only form of public transport is the **bus**, which is without doubt the cheapest way to travel. The size of the country, and the efficient road layout around the Carretera Panamericana, mean that you can get from one point to another within the country in less than a day. Most long-distance journeys route through San Salvador, often requiring at least one change of bus if travelling to smaller towns.

BY BUS

Buses are subsidized and extremely cheap: an *especial* bus from San Salvador to Sonsonate (1hr 30min) costs just US$1.30. Centrally placed San Salvador, with its three busy bus terminals (see p.210), is the hub of all bus travel in the country. All other towns of any

significant size have at least one bus terminal. Services run in daylight hours, with rare exceptions going just after dusk, so plan your overnight stops carefully.

All routes are covered by the same "**chicken buses**" you'll see in other Central American countries (see box, p.32). More comfortable, **modern buses** are gradually being introduced to major routes, dubbed *especial* and often air-conditioned, though these are less frequent. Best of all are the **coach-style** *super especial* buses that run between San Salvador and San Miguel, which are air-conditioned and rarely stop en route (though quality often varies in both *especial* and *super especial* classes). No buses have toilets on board (that work, at least).

By shuttle bus and international bus

Special **shuttle bus** services (typically minibuses) for travellers are nowhere near as common in El Salvador as, say, Guatemala, but you'll find several companies running between El Tunco and nearby beaches to San Salvador, the airport and direct to Antigua in Guatemala. If you're looking for a more luxurious ride between San Salvador and Santa Ana, contact Tica Bus or King Quality (see box, p.210), which usually make a stop in Santa Ana on their way to and from Guatemala City – this will cost around US$35, however. Other international services from San Salvador to Managua (Nicaragua) and Tegucigalpa (Honduras) rarely make stops elsewhere in El Salvador (see p.210).

BY CAR

Licensed **taxis** in El Salvador are yellow and black. They can be hailed or found in large towns and cities around the main plazas, shopping centres or bus stations. There are no meters, so **fares** should be agreed before you set off. Expect to pay US$5–6 for most trips within San Salvador and US$3–5 in other cities, but you can bargain a bit if you are polite. Licensed taxis will also drive **long distance**; ultra convenient, fast, but not cheap unless you have a group – figure on US$40–45 for an hour to ninety-minute

3

journey (San Salvador to San Vicente or Suchitoto, for example). Avoid people offering lifts in other types of car.

It can be helpful to **rent a car** if you want to explore some of the country's more remote areas, especially stretches of the Pacific coast. Western companies such as Hertz (☎2339 8004) and Avis (☎2339 9268) **rent** at Western prices (from US$45/day with insurance); local garages often charge half those rates (rarely more than US$20/day). Recommended local rental companies include: Sandoval (☎2225 0392, ⓦrentacarsandoval.com) and Quick Rent A Car (☎2229 0020, ⓦquickrentacar.com.sv). Note that even if you opt to pay for **insurance** when you rent a car (US$12–15 extra per day), the deductible will still be hefty (typically US$1000), meaning that you'll end up paying for a damaged bumper or a flat tyre.

When driving, look out for abrupt coned-off lanes on the motorway – these are **police stops**, where you may be asked to present your passport, driving licence and car documents. If you need assistance, stop at one of the petrol stations or mechanics that are widespread along the road. Avoid driving at night; **cows** often wander onto main roads, including the Panamericana, and it's hard to see **potholes**. Also, dirt roads can become impassable during the rainy season, even with a 4WD; ask locally about conditions before you set off. Armed **hold-ups** of private cars are extremely rare nowadays (though be

careful on lonely stretches of road, such as the Carretera del Litoral between El Zonte and Sonsonate), but keep US$20 or so aside just in case, and offer no resistance. It's good to rent an old-looking car, so as not to draw attention to yourself – driving solo will also make you a more tempting target. In cities, thefts of cars, or items left in them, do occur, so it's wise to leave your car in a guarded or locked car park overnight.

Hitching is common off the highways. That said, it carries obvious risks, and we don't recommend it. If you do hitch, it's polite to offer payment – about the same as the bus fare – for the journey.

BY BIKE

Bikes offer great freedom in rural areas, and you can take them on buses. There are no formal rental places, but it is possible to do deals with locals, tour operators and at hotels; rates are around US$5/hr or US$15/day. Otherwise, a cheap mountain bike shouldn't cost more than US$50 to buy from a general store in any of the bigger towns.

BY BOAT

Although only the islands of the Golfo de Fonseca and the islands of the Bahía de Jiquilisco require **boat** access, there are plenty of other opportunities to get out on the water. Scheduled services are always much cheaper (US$1–5), but *lancha* owners and fishermen need little persuasion to provide private lifts and tours of the country's lakes and mangrove swamps. This is usually done as a set fee

---

ADDRESSES IN EL SALVADOR

Navigating Salvadoran cities is initially confusing but ultimately logical. As elsewhere, most cities are organized on the **grid** plan: streets running north–south are **avenidas**, those running east–west are **calles**. The main avenida and calle will have individual names (along with a few of the others) and the heart of any city is at their intersection – usually, though not always, at the Parque Central, the main square. North or south of this intersection avenidas are Norte (Nte) or Sur, while east or west calles are Oriente (Ote) or Poniente (Pte). Avenidas lying to the east of the main avenida are numbered evenly, increasing the further you go out; west of the avenida the numbers are odd. Similarly, calles have even numbers south of the main calle and odd numbers north. **Addresses** can be given either as the street name/number, followed by the building number, or as the intersection of two streets. So: "12A C Pte 2330, Col Flor Blanca" is no. 2330, Calle 12 Poniente in the district (*colonia*) of Flor Blanca, while "10A Av Sur y 3 C Pte" is the intersection of 10A Avenida Sur and Calle 3 Poniente.

for the boat (usually about US$35–45, depending on duration), so getting into a sizeable group reduces the cost.

ACCOMMODATION

El Salvador's **accommodation** industry is slowly waking up to the traveller market: new places are appearing all the time, and very few destinations have nowhere at all to stay. However, the number of **hostels** with dorm rooms is still relatively small, so it's best to budget for cheap **hotels**. Prices are relatively high compared to the rest of Central America: in San Salvador a clean, secure, double room comes to at least US$30, often more, while outside the capital you can expect to pay at least US$15–20, or US$25–30 for air conditioning. Lots of hotels rent multi-bed rooms (intended for Salvadoran families), where you can pack in like sardines – these can be a good way to cut costs if you're with a group. Discounts on longer stays are also often available. Rooms vary within an establishment, so look around. Hot water is rare in the cheaper places.

The Ministerio de Trabajo, C Nuevo Dos 19 in San Salvador (☎2298 8739), runs four centres providing **free accommodation** around the country.

Campsites are available at most lakes, national parks and several towns and beaches. Salvadoreños with spare land may be willing to let you pitch a tent – offer around US$5. Hammock-slinging is possible on some beaches (though steer clear of the sketchier beaches around La Libertad, for safety reasons) and at some beach hotels (also for about US$5). The hotels will usually put your bag somewhere safe, if you ask.

Accommodation fills up around Santa Semana (the week before Easter), Christmas, the Fiestas Agostinas (the last week of July and first week of August) and/or at the time of local festivals; at these times **reserve** in advance.

FOOD AND DRINK

Eating well in El Salvador is far more about fresh ingredients than refined cooking. The main meal of the day is **lunch** (*almuerzo*), which most locals eat in a *comedor*, where *típicos* (local dishes of meat or fish, rice, vegetable or salad) and coffee go for around US$3–4, or a *pupusería*, where you can get **pupusas** – small tortillas served piping hot and filled with cheese (*queso*), beans (*frijoles*), pork crackling (*chicharrón*), or all three – for around US$0.50 (US$0.75–1 in San Salvador). *Pupusas* are normally made fresh from cornmeal, and are served with hot sauce, tomato juice and/or *curtido*, a serving of pickled cabbage, beetroot and carrots. The cleanliness and quality of establishments vary, but are usually OK, though with no frills; if doubtful, choose one that's busy and cooks unfrozen meat.

A standard **breakfast** (*desayuno*) – it's rare to be offered anything else – is composed of *frijoles* (refried black beans), *queso* (white cheese) and *huevos* (eggs, either fried or scrambled), along with coffee. Although San Salvador's western suburbs are the only place to find the full gamut of international cuisine, most towns have a handful of **restaurants**. Chinese, Italian and Tex-Mex, and Argentine meat-grilling restaurants are the most widespread, though their authenticity varies. **Vegetarians** will find dedicated restaurants only in the biggest cities, and should be prepared to eat a lot of beans and cheese. There are also US **fast-food chains** – set meals for about US$5 – throughout the country, usually clustered along the Panamerican Highway or in the increasingly ubiquitous malls. Fried chicken is the *plat du jour*; the Guatemalan (but US-based) *Pollo Campero* chain is the best of the Central American franchises (⊕campero.com). El Salvador had the dubious honour in late 2010 of opening Central America's first branch of *Starbucks*, in Plaza Santa Elena on the outskirts of the capital (there are now four branches in the city).

In addition to *pupusas*, other Salvadoreño **specialities** include *mariscada* (huge bowls filled with fish and crustaceans in a creamy soup), *tamales* (meat or chicken wrapped in maize dough and boiled in a leaf), *ceviche* (raw, marinated fish) and *sopa de frijoles* (black

3

3

or red bean soup). On the coast, *conchas* (cockles or any other shellfish) are served raw with lemon juice, tomato, coriander and Worcestershire sauce (*salsa inglesa*). Try the *ostras* (oysters), especially in popular places to eat by the sea; they are fresher here than in most Western restaurants.

DRINK

Local **coffee** is very good, usually drunk black and strong at breakfast and mid-afternoon with *tamales*. In small villages it will be boiled up with sugar cane and called *lista*. El Salvador's tropical fruits make delicious **juices**. *Jugos* are pure juices – most commonly orange, papaya, pineapple and melon – mixed with ice. *Licuados* (sometimes called *batidos*) blend juice with sugar, ice and sometimes milk, while *frescos* are fruit-based sweet drinks made up in bulk and served with lunch or dinner. Unless you ask otherwise, sugar will be added to *jugos* and *licuados*. *Horchata* is a dense milk drink with a base of rice, sweetened with sugar and cinnamon.

The usual brands of **soft drinks** are available. **Water** is safe to drink in San Salvador only; elsewhere check that the water and ice used in drinks is purified. Bottled mineral water and small bags of pure spring water are available almost everywhere, while most hotels provide drinking water. El Salvador produces five good **beers** – the most important decision you will have to make is between Pilsner and Golden Light. True lager followers will go for the excellent and textured former. **Aguardiente** is a sugar cane-based liquor, fiery but quite smooth, produced under government control and sold through outlets called *expendios*; Tic-Tac is a favourite label.

CULTURE AND ETIQUETTE

Salvadoreños are generally confident, principled, hardworking and keen to laugh; they will often vie to help travellers. This said, not many tourists pass through the country, especially rural areas, so you may be regarded as something of a novelty and children especially may stare and touch your hair. More than eighty percent of the population is **Catholic**, though Evangelical Protestantism is on the rise.

You should be confident and **polite**: say "Buenos dias" (morning) or "Buenas tardes" (afternoon) when you catch someone's eye or enter a room, shake hands when meeting and do not offend by being paranoid about your safety or belongings. Women should not react to macho male posturing, as this is seen as flirtatious; understand that if you dress to be noticed, you will be. Remember to

---

SALVADORAN WORDS AND PHRASES

The Salvadoran slang, called **Caliche**, is formed from Nahuat and English roots. You'll probably hear it spoken on your travels, particularly by kids and *campesinos*, and you'll always raise a smile if you try a few words yourself.

Ahuevo/cabal (That's) right
Ba! Yes/sure/fine!
Bayunco Rowdy, immature, crazy
Birria/polarizado Beer
Brosa/chero/chera Friend/friend (m)/ friend (f)
Cachimbo/vergo Loads of ...
Ceviche It's alright
Chavo/chava Boy/girl (informal)
Chele A "white" person with blond hair
chivo/chivisimo Cool/very cool
chucho/chucha Male dog/female dog
Chuco/chuca Dirty
Cora A quarter of a dollar

Guanaco A nickname for anyone from El Salvador
Huevón/huevonazo/huevonada Lazy/ very lazy/lazy thing
Mara Gang or group of friends
Marero Gang member
Paloma Penis, or something cool
Palomísima/vergonísimo Very cool
Púchica Wow!
Salú Goodbye
Talega Drunk
Vacilar Chill out, have fun
Vergón Cool or amazing (from "verga", penis)
Yuca Something difficult (literally, a root plant)

wear sleeves and trousers and to remove hats when entering a church (women should cover their heads). It is also considered rude to point at anything or anyone inside a church. Always ask permission before taking **photos** of people in indigenous areas, though you will generally find lots of eager posers.

Tipping at restaurants is not expected at the cheaper places, and may not be received well. More Western-style restaurants (especially in San Salvador) may add around a ten-percent service charge, and you can increase this should you want to; tipping in bars in the capital goes down well too. Free guides should also be tipped. There is no need to tip anyone else, but if you are not awkward about it then they won't be offended. Gentle **haggling** is acceptable – sometimes it works, sometimes it doesn't.

SPORTS AND OUTDOOR ACTIVITIES

Fútbol (soccer) is by far the biggest spectator sport in El Salvador. There are two domestic seasons every year: the first (the *clausura*) runs every weekend from February to mid-May, the second (called *apertura*) goes from September to mid-December; both are followed by play-offs and finals. The big **teams** of the last few years are Águila from San Miguel, FAS from Santa Ana, Firpo from Usulután and Isidro Metapán. The quality of football is mixed but the crowds are awesome; don't bring anything valuable, and always sit with and cheer for the home side. See ⊕fesfut.org.sv for fixtures and information. Great attention is paid to the international scene, too: the whole country has arranged itself behind two Spanish clubs, FC Barcelona and Real Madrid, though Barcelona is currently far more popular and regarded as the 'people's' (ie poor man's) team. **Baseball** is popular as well; San Salvador has a stadium, opposite the Artesan Market on Alameda M.E. Araujo, with games on Sundays. Football, baseball and basketball games take place on widespread municipal facilities, in parks and on beaches across the country. If it is not a training session you will be more than welcome to join in.

El Salvador's 320km of coastline is widely accepted to have the best **surfing** in Central America and is known for several world-famous breaks. The best areas are on the Costa del Bálsamo (see p.221) and the eastern beaches around El Cuco (see p.226). See ⊕surfingelsalvador .com for surf reports, beach reviews and general information. The best **hiking** is in the national parks. For good challenges try the Parque Nacional Montecristo cloudforest (see p.264), up the volcanoes of the Cerro Verde (see p.262) and through the dramatic, dry rainforest of the Parque Nacional El Imposible (see p.250). **Diving** here is not as good as in the Bay Islands or Belize, but there is the opportunity to see underwater thermal vents in a crater dive on Lago de Ilopango (see p.217), and the only Pacific coral diving in Central America is off Los Cóbanos (see p.249), along with a couple of good wreck dives. See ⊕elsalvador divers.com for more information.

COMMUNICATIONS

Mail (letters) from San Salvador generally takes about one week to the US and nine or so days to Europe; there are parcel services available, but you should use a courier service if sending anything of value. The use of **mobile phones** is huge in El Salvador, and unless you have one, you are unlikely to be able to make phone calls other than via expensive hotel phones. By far the cheapest option, however, is web-based calls; almost all internet places are now equipped with headsets.

If you don't want to pay for roaming on your own phone (or don't have one), the cheapest local pay-as-you-go **mobile phone** costs around US$15 and can make and receive international calls. If you have an **unlocked** GSM phone you can just buy a local **SIM card** for US$5 (CDMA phones cannot use SIMs). There are several GSM networks; Movistar (⊕movistar.com.sv), Tigo (⊕tigo.com.sv) and Claro (⊕claro.com

.sv) are the **primary operators** – Claro also covers the rest of Central America (with the exception of Belize). **Claro** (formerly "Telecom") also has offices in every town, where you can get set up – bring your passport. **Public phones** are effectively defunct in El Salvador. The **telephone code** for the whole of El Salvador is ☎503.

Internet of varying speeds is now available everywhere. Rates range from US$0.50–1 for 15–30min (the range varies wildly, and is often higher in hotels).

CRIME AND SAFETY

El Salvador has a reputation for guns, gangs and danger, which, while not unfounded, is no longer a problem in areas frequented by most tourists. *Maras* (**gangs**) exist across the country (mainly in the grim eastern suburbs of San Salvador), but really dangerous characters generally concern themselves with the more profitable fields of drugs, extortion and human trafficking; they don't look for tourists, nor will they be found in any of the neighbourhoods you are likely to visit. In 2012 the main gangs – Mara Salvatrucha and Calle 18 – negotiated a truce that has resulted in a dramatic drop in crime and killings.

Generally, you should be fine if you stay confident (say "Buenos" to people), and stay in groups and in busy areas. This in particular for **women travellers**, who should ignore the usual catcalls and loud blown kisses, as attempts to scold will be seen as flirtatious; the less attention you pay, the less attention you will receive. Male or female, if you are being pestered, don't show animosity, and head for a busy café or restaurant. Although muggings are extremely rare, you should avoid wearing expensive clothing and flashing valuables, and, if you are mugged, never

fight back. It's worth keeping US$10–20 in a pocket while travelling, as this will be enough for most *banditos* – highway robbery is rare but does happen on isolated roads. Be especially careful after nightfall in Sonsonate and San Salvador's *centro*; La Unión and San Miguel can also be dodgy.

The **National Civilian Police** (PCN) is one of the best forces in Central America, with little corruption and a good presence in cities, at least until nightfall. Additionally, an often English-speaking **tourist police** operates nationwide to guide treks, assist and advise (☎2245 5448).

Statistically, the biggest threats to tourists in El Salvador are the **riptides** on its beaches. It is best not to go out too far on your own, and ask locally about the conditions. If you are unable to swim back, try not to panic, swim parallel to the shoreline and wait for the rip to die down. There is no coastguard, so call the police in an emergency, or better still find the nearest surfer.

HEALTH

Pharmacies are widespread, especially in San Salvador, and most of them will have a wide range of antibiotics for stomach troubles. Two private **hospitals** in San Salvador provide the best medical services in the country (see p.214); in the east, San Miguel's Hospital Clínica San Francisco (see p.237) is another good private hospital. All three have 24hr emergency rooms. Make sure you have comprehensive medical cover in your **insurance policy**; any kind of medical treatment is likely to be expensive, and you will probably be asked to pay up front whether or not you are insured. Have insurance documents or cash at the ready if you need treatment.

INFORMATION AND MAPS

The national tourist board, **Corsatur** (ⓦelsalvador.travel), has its main office in San Salvador at Alameda Manuel Araujo, Pasaje y Edificio Carbonel 2, Colonia Roma (Mon–Fri

---

EMERGENCY NUMBERS

Cruz Roja (ambulance) ☎2222 5155
Fire ☎2271 2227 or ☎2271 1244
Police ☎911

NATIONAL PARK INFORMATION

Officially, there is a permission-granting ritual that must be performed before you enter any of El Salvador's national parks, though if you go with a guide on an organized visit, wardens will usually waive this. Confusingly, parks are administered by three different agencies. All three also allow entry to, and have information about, other preserved areas as well.

Instituto Salvadoreño de Turismo (ISTU) 41 Av Nte & Alameda Roosevelt 115, San Salvador ☏ 2222 8000, ⓦ istu.gob.sv. Manages Parque Nacional Walter T. Deininger, and has information about all the country's national parks. Mon–Fri 8am–4pm, Sat 8am–noon.

Ministerio de Medio Ambiente y Recursos Naturales Edificio MARN (Instalaciones ISTA), 2 C & Colonia Las Mercedes, San Salvador ☏ 2267 6276,

☏ 2267 6259, ⓦ marn.gob.sv. Issues permits to the Parque Nacional Montecristo in person or by fax. Mon–Fri 7.30am–12.30pm & 1.30–3.30pm.

SalvaNatura 33 Av Sur 640, Colonia Flor Blanca, San Salvador ☏ 2279 1515, ⓦ salvanatura.org. Manages the Parque Nacional El Imposible and Parque Nacional Los Volcanes, with books and useful maps for sale, and some free leaflets. Mon–Fri 8am–12.30pm & 2–5.30pm.

8.30am–12.30pm & 1.10–4.30pm; ☏ 2243 7835). The staff (who only speak basic English) will help with enquiries if you persist. Other outposts ("Centro de Amigos del Turista" or CAT) exist in La Palma, Suchitoto, La Unión and Puerto La Libertad, and there's a seldom-manned desk at the airport. Small towns like Apaneca and Perquín have their own kiosks that issue little more than pamphlets in Spanish, but often the best tips come directly from hostel and hotel owners.

Maps of El Salvador are rare and generally terrible, except for those in this guide, and those produced on the second floor of the Centro Nacional de Registros, 1A C Pte and 43 Av Nte 2310, San Salvador (Mon–Fri 8am–noon & 1–4pm; ☏ 2261 8400, ⓦ cnr.gob.sv). ITMB's 1: 250,000 *El Salvador* map is also a useful resource, but still carries some inaccuracies.

MONEY AND BANKS

El Salvador has officially used the **US dollar** (US$) since 2001. All US dollar notes and coins are currently in free circulation, but try to stockpile US$1 and US$5 bills, as anything over US$10 is likely to send the shopkeeper running down the street in search of change.

ATMs (*cajeros*) are becoming increasingly widespread, particularly in tourist destinations. Keep a stash of cash, however, for Perquín, Tacuba, some parts of the Ruta de las Flores and the eastern craft towns.

Elsewhere, the main **banks** – Banco Agrícola, Banco Hipotecario, Scotiabank and Citibank – have ATMs, which charge a handling fee of around US$2–3. Payment by **credit card** is unheard of at the budget level, but if you do encounter an establishment that will take your card there will be a charge of five percent

EL SALVADOR ONLINE

ⓦ **buscaniguas.com.sv** Long-standing portal – in Spanish only – with useful listings, including hotels, restaurants and entertainment, plus interesting blog pages.

ⓦ **elsalvador.travel** The official tourist site, with good information and a directory of businesses, hotels, restaurants and a calendar of events in English.

ⓦ **fotosdeelsalvador.com** An appetite-whetting archive holding thousands of

photos from across the country (info in Spanish only).

ⓦ **laprensagrafica.com** and ⓦ **elsalvador.com** The websites for the two big conservative daily papers (Spanish only).

ⓦ **luterano.blogspot.com** An excellent English-language blog, updated almost daily, summarizing current affairs and adding well-informed commentary.

3

(more expensive places will not levy this charge). **Travellers' cheques** are less widely recognized, and at present can only be changed in banks. There are **casas de cambio** (generally daily 9am–5pm) along Alameda Juan Pablo II in San Salvador, in Santa Ana and San Miguel and at the borders. There are Western Union and Moneygram outlets in almost every mid-size town.

OPENING HOURS AND PUBLIC HOLIDAYS

Opening hours throughout the country vary. The big cities and major towns generally get going quite early in the morning, with government offices working from 8am to 4pm and most businesses from 8.30/9am to 5/5.30pm, with some closing for an hour at lunch. **Post offices** across the country are generally open Monday to Friday 8am to 5pm and Saturday 8am to noon. **Banks** are open Monday to Friday, from 8.30am or 9am until 4pm or 5pm (some of them close from 1 to 2pm). Some banks in the larger cities also open between 8am and noon on Saturday. Hotels in smaller places lock up for the night at around 9 or 10pm, and you may be banging on the door for a while and paying extra if you don't warn them of your late arrival. On **public holidays** everything shuts down, with some businesses also closing on the day of local fiestas. Museums and archeological sites all close on Mondays.

FESTIVALS

Ferías (festivals) in El Salvador, as in the rest of the continent, are very important. Almost every town will have its own annual celebration, honouring the saint most connected to the place in question. The following calendar lists a few highlights.

January 8–15 Cristo Negro and Feria Gastronómica Internacional in Juayúa. Street fiesta with the best range and quality of food.

February Festival Internacional de Arte y Cultura in Suchitoto. A month-long celebration of classical music, opera, art and theatre.

> ### PUBLIC HOLIDAYS
> **Jan 1** New Year's Day
> **March/April** Easter (Thurs–Easter Sun)
> **May 1** Labour Day
> **Aug 1–6** El Salvador del Mundo
> **Sept 15** Independence Day
> **Oct 12** Columbus Day
> **Nov 1** Day of the Dead
> **Nov 2** All Saints' Day
> **Dec 24 & 25** Christmas
> **Dec 31** New Year's Eve

March/April Santa Semana in Izalco. Popularly known as the best place for the Easter processions and street paintings.

May Las Flores y Las Palmas in Panchimalco (second Sun). Celebrates flower and palm-tree cultivation with music, dancing and fireworks.

August 1–5 Fiestas Patronales de San Salvador. Street parties and parades shut down the capital on Aug 1, 3 and 5.

August 1–6 Festival del Invierno in Perquín. Exciting, young and bohemian music and arts festival in this mountain town.

November 14–30 Carnaval celebrated in San Miguel. One of the biggest fiestas in Central America, with processions and music floats, dancing and drinking.

San Salvador

Sprawling across the Valle de las Hamacas at the foot of the mighty Volcán San Salvador is the urban melee of **SAN SALVADOR**, El Salvador's mercurial capital. Established here by the Spanish in 1545, it remained a relatively minor place until 1785, when it was named the first *intendencia* (semi-autonomous governing unit) within the Captaincy General of Guatemala (which nominally controlled all of Central America). Father José Delgado first made the call for independence here in 1811, and the city was the only capital of the Central American Federation, before being named capital of El Salvador when the federation dissolved in 1840. Not much remains of this illustrious history: a series of earthquakes throughout the nineteenth and twentieth centuries levelled most of the centre. Little you can see predates the nineteenth century.

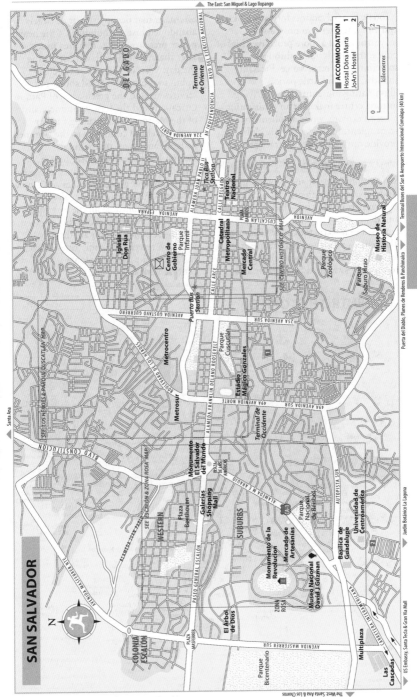

The East: San Miguel & Lago Ilopango

SAN SALVADOR

ACCOMMODATION
Hostal Doña Marta 1
JoAn's Hostel 2

Terminal de Oriente

Terminal Buses del Sur & Aeropuerto Internacional Comalapa (40 km)

Puerta del Diablo, Planes de Renderos & Panchimalco

Jardín Botánico La Laguna

US Embassy, Santa Tecla & Gran Vía Mall

Santa Ana

SEE LOS PRÓCERES & PARQUE CUSCATLÁN MAP

SEE ESCALÓN & ZONA ROSA MAP

BLVD CONSTITUCIÓN

AVENIDA MASFERRER SUR

COLONIA ESCALÓN

Parque Bicentenario

PLAZA MASFERRER

El Árbol de Dios

ZONA ROSA

Museo Nacional David J. Guzmán

Monumento de la Revolución

Mercado de Artesanías

PASEO GENERAL ESCALÓN

WESTERN

Plaza Beethoven

Galerías Shopping Mall

SUBURBS

ALAMEDA M ARAUJO

AVENIDA MASFERRER SUR

Basílica de Guadalupe

Parque Nacional de Béisbol

Universidad de Centroamérica

AUTOPISTA SUR

Multiplaza

Las Cascadas

CARRETERA INTERAMERICANA

Monumento El Salvador del Mundo

BOULEVARD DE LOS HÉROES

Metrosur

Metrocentro

AVENIDA GUSTAVO GUERRERO

Parque Cuscatlán

Estadio Mágico González

ALAMEDA FRANKLIN DELANO ROOSEVELT

49A AVENIDA NORTE

49A AVENIDA SUR

Terminal de Occidente

Puerto Bus Station

CALLE ARCE

AVENIDA ESPAÑA

Iglesia Don Rúa

Centro de Gobierno

Parque Infantil

Catedral Metropolitana

Mercado Central

SEE CENTRO HISTÓRICO MAP

25A AVENIDA SUR

AVENIDA CUSCATLÁN

Teatro Nacional

Tica Bus Station

CALLE DELGADO

ALAMEDA JUAN PABLO II

22A AVENIDA NORTE

AV INDEPENDENCIA

BLVD DEL EJÉRCITO NACIONAL

EL COYOTE

Parque Zoológico

Parque Saburo Hirao

Museo de Historia Natural

N

3

kilometres

Today, San Salvador is forward-looking and vibrant; after two progressive mayorships and a more proactive chief of police, the city is going through something of a renaissance. Pleasant suburbs, peaceful little parks, illuminating museums and a thriving historic centre make for an exhilarating place to explore, while a bohemian arts scene, plentiful bars and lively clubs provide fun night-time distractions.

WHAT TO SEE AND DO

San Salvador's social and geographical landscape is conveniently linear. The eastern part of the city – industrial, poor and dangerous – morphs into the crowded **Centro Histórico**, or **El Centro**. The centre's churches and theatre are some of the country's best, though completely swamped by markets and *comedores* that occupy streets of largely abandoned historic buildings – the heavy police presence makes this area much safer than it might feel, at least during the day. West of here the roads creep uphill to the more relaxed shops and services around the green acres of **Parque Cuscatlán**, and the heady commercialism of the **Metrocentro**. Heading further west, the climb continues to the trimmed hedges, fancy bars and cultural monoliths of the **Zona Rosa**, before finishing at the fine restaurants, exclusive nightclubs and guarded castles of **Colonia Escalón** – the upscale strip malls and condos now continue all the way into **Santa Tecla**. Floating above this east-to-west progression are the arty, studenty, traveller-friendly cafés, hostels and late-night bars of **Colonia Centroamérica**.

▲ Iglesia Don Rua (2 blocks)

CENTRO HISTÓRICO

0   300   metres

EATING & DRINKING	
Koradi	3
Panadería Latino	4
Pan Salvador	2
Pupusería Doña Isabel	1

ACCOMMODATION	
International Custodio	2
Villa Florência Centro Histórico	1

▼ Parque Zoológico Nacional & Museo de Historia Natural

Plaza Barrios

Though at the heart of the raging *Centro Histórico,* the rejuvenated **Plaza Barrios** remains relatively tranquil. A plaque on a white base on the north side commemorates the six Jesuit priests murdered at La UCA in 1989 (see p.209), while an imperious equestrian statue of **Gerardo Barrios** (president 1859–63) commands the centre. The bronze image was one of several commissions here for Swiss-born sculptor Francisco Durini, better known for his beautification of Quito, Ecuador, in the early 1900s.

Palacio Nacional

On the western edge of the Plaza Barrios stands the **Palacio Nacional** (Mon–Fri 8am–4pm; US$3), built between 1905 and 1911, having replaced an earlier edifice that was destroyed by fire. Briefly home to the president's office and Supreme Court, El Salvador's Legislative Assembly was based here until 1974, and all other government offices – save the National Archives – moved out after the quake of 1986. Since then, restoration of the Neoclassical palace has been ongoing, with the wonderfully ornate upper galleries serving as a **museum** for the building and the history of San Salvador (the ground level remains the National Archives offices). Everything is labelled in Spanish and English.

Catedral Metropolitana

The most imposing structure on Plaza Barrios is the **Catedral Metropolitana** (Mon–Fri & Sun 6am–6pm, Sat 6am–1pm & 4–6pm; donations optional). The cathedral dates back to 1888, but has been severely damaged on a number of occasions, most notably by fire in 1951. Repairs were suspended in 1977 by **Archbishop Óscar Romero**, who argued that funds allocated for the work should be diverted to feeding the country's poor. Romero's murder in March 1980 (which took place at La Hospital Divina Providencia, in the western suburbs) is widely perceived as the event that sent the country spiralling into civil war: mourners carrying his body to the cathedral were fired upon by government troops stationed on top of the surrounding buildings, and many were slaughtered. Work on the building resumed after the civil war, and was finally completed in 1999. You can visit Romero's resting place in the cavernous *cripta* (Mon–Sat 8am–11.45am & 2–4.45pm, Sun 8am–4.45pm; free) below the cathedral, via a separate entrance on the east side of the building. Located behind a small shrine and framed by portraits of the archbishop, the Modernist bronze **tomb** was designed by Italian artist Paolo Borghi.

Teatro Nacional

Across from the cathedral is the elegant French Renaissance-style **Teatro Nacional**, though the entrance faces the compact **Plaza Morazán**, one block north. Built between 1911 and 1917 and reflecting the global vogue for French culture in the early twentieth century, the restored interior – all red plush, marble and decorative plasterwork – harks back to grander times. The magnificent modern ceiling frieze by Salvadoran artist Carlos Cañas depicts Rubenesque maidens cavorting in the clouds. Regular musical and theatrical events are held here, including performances by the national orchestra most fortnights; tickets are heavily subsidized and sometimes free (seeing a performance is the only way to get inside). Upcoming events can be found in the Friday edition or website of the national newspaper *Diario del Hoy* (ⓦelsalvador.com).

Iglesia el Rosario

Two blocks east of Plaza Barrios is spacious **Plaza Libertad**, where the central statue of feather-winged Liberty (1911), by Francsico Durini, stands watch over the scrappy markets that surround the square. Dominating the east side, the smog-stained, ugly concrete facade of the **Iglesia el Rosario** (Mon–Sat 6.30am–noon & 2–6.30pm, Sun 8.30am–noon & 2–6.30pm) looks like an industrial turbine. Do not let this put you off, as the

3

interior is the most spectacular and original in the country, created in 1971 by artist and architect Rubén Martinez. Sunlight passing through banks of modern stained glass set in the arc of the roof casts acid-bright colour dispersions across the brick walls, contorted metal sculptures, doll-like shrines and the chequered floor.

Iglesia Calvario

One block south and two blocks west of Plaza Barrios, in the jaws of the chaotic street market, is the dark, neo-Gothic **Iglesia Calvario** (daily 7am–5pm), constructed between 1911 and 1950 but managing to look far older. It's a handsome building, with a smattering of blue-and-yellow stained glass from Italy inside, but not much else to see.

Museo Universitario de Antropología (MUA)

The enlightening **Museo Universitario de Antropología** (Mon–Fri 9am–1pm & 3–5pm; Sat 9am–noon; free; bus #42), west of Plaza Barrios along Calle Arce (at 17 Av Nte), in the campus of Universidad Tecnológica de El Salvador (UTEC), is smaller than the Museo Nacional, but contains a more focused collection – it also houses some of the most beautifully decorated **Mesoamerican ceramics** in the region. Most of these date from the Classic period (600–900 AD) and are displayed in the ground-floor galleries along with traditional dresses. Upstairs the Sala de Migración contrasts the prehistoric migration of pre-Columbian Americans north to south with the modern, perilous overland migration made by thousands of El Salvadoran workers to the US each year. There's also a fascinating diagram showing what the Spanish regime meant by "mestizo" and "mulatto", and a rare collection of the defunct colón banknotes and coins. Also upstairs, a gallery houses a display of personal effects and music dedicated to the composer **Francisco "Pancho" Lara Hernández** (1900–89), best known for the folk song *El Carbonero*, often regarded as the nation's second national anthem. Labelling is comprehensive throughout the museum, but in Spanish only.

Parque Cuscatlán

Parque Cuscatlán, a short walk west of the Museo Universitario de Antropología, is a large expanse of shady walkways and grass lawns that not only offers respite from the heat and noise, but is also home to several intriguing sights. Engraved into the park's northern embankment, the **Monumento a la Memoria y la Verdad** (Tues–Sun 6am–6pm; free) lists the names of the thousands who died or "disappeared" leading up to and during the civil war of 1980–92. Nearby, the **Sala Nacional de Exposiciones** (daily 9am–noon & 2–5pm; free) hosts high-quality rotating art exhibitions, while at the eastern end of the park the **Tin Marín Museo de los Niños** (Tues–Sun 9am–5pm; US$2.50; ⊛tinmarin.org) may well be the best kids' museum ever, with fun activities including painting a VW Beetle, sitting in a cockpit of a Boeing 727, or visiting a planetarium (an extra US$1).

Museo de la Palabra y la Imagen

Several blocks north of Parque Cuscatlán via 45 Avenida Norte, the curious **Museo de la Palabra y la Imagen** (Mon–Fri 8am–noon & 2–5pm, Sat 8am–noon; US$2; ⊛museo.com.sv) is tucked away on a side road (at 27 Av Nte 1140). It's nominally a museum of literature dedicated to Salvador Efraín Salazar Arrué (1899–1975), aka **Salarrué**, the seminal Salvadoran writer, poet and painter – displays contain his personal effects and examples of his drawings and writings, including the much loved *Cuentos de Cipotes* ("Children's Stories") and *Cuentos de Barro* ("Tales of Clay"). Of more interest to foreign visitors are the small galleries at the back containing graphic displays on the civil war. The war photography is moving, shocking and high-quality. There's also a re-creation of the "Cueva de las Pasiones", the cave where **Radio Venceremos**, the clandestine guerrilla radio station that counterbalanced government media propaganda during the civil war, was hidden in 1982. The newest exhibit focuses on Salvadoran emigration to the US.

Colonia Centroamérica

Heading northwest from the Museo de la Palabra, across Boulevard los Héroes and

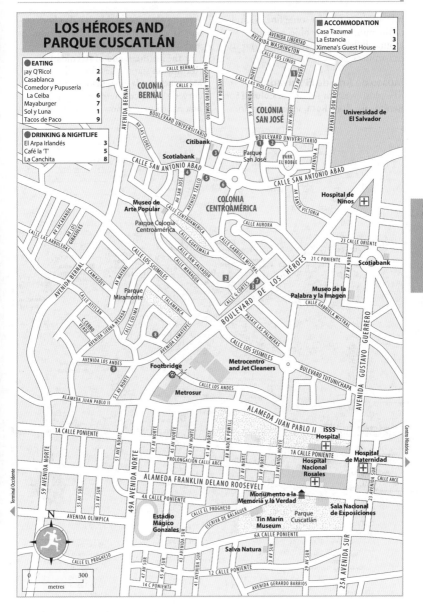

LOS HÉROES AND
PARQUE CUSCATLÁN

ACCOMMODATION
Casa Tazumal ... 1
La Estancia ... 3
Ximena's Guest House ... 2

EATING
¡ay Q'Rico! ... 2
Casablanca ... 4
Comedor y Pupusería
  La Ceiba ... 6
Mayaburger ... 7
Sol y Luna ... 1
Tacos de Paco ... 9

DRINKING & NIGHTLIFE
El Arpa Irlandés ... 3
Café la 'T' ... 5
La Canchita ... 8

3

up Calle Centroamérica, takes you into the arty and laidback **Colonia Centroamérica**, the most traveller-friendly area of town. Straight up the hill on the street, the **Parque Colonia Centroamérica** has two free floodlit basketball courts, as well as benches and gnarled trees or: to enjoy; it's the only park that's safe after dark. At the northern end of the park, the **Museo de Arte Popular** (Tues–Sat 10am–5pm; US$1; ⓦartepopular.org) has an engaging collection of Salvadoran folk art, in particular some fine examples of the miniature clay objects made around Ilobasco and known as *sorpresas,* or surprises (see p.230).

Museo de Arte de El Salvador

The plush western suburb of **Colonia San Benito**, aka **Zona Rosa**, is San Salvador's evening playground, but it's also home to San Salvador's most expressive monument and one of its best museums.

At the northern end of Avenida La Revolución stands the 25m-tall **Monumento a la Revolución**, a vast, curved slab of concrete bearing a mosaic of a naked man (known as "El Chulón")

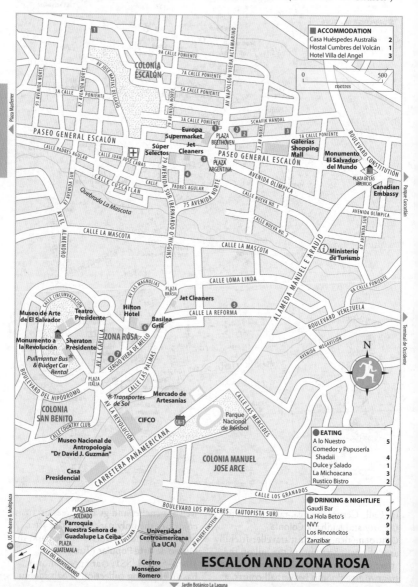

ACCOMMODATION

Casa Huéspedes Australia	2
Hostal Cumbres del Volcán	1
Hotel Villa del Angel	3

EATING

A lo Nuestro	5
Comedor y Pupusería Shadaii	4
Dulce y Salado	1
La Michoacana	3
Rustico Bistro	2

DRINKING & NIGHTLIFE

Gaudí Bar	6
La Hola Beto's	7
NVY	9
Los Rinconcitos	8
Zanzibar	6

ESCALÓN AND ZONA ROSA

with head thrown back and arms uplifted. Completed in 1954 to commemorate the uprising that ousted General Salvador Castaneda Castro from power six years earlier, the monument now lies inside the grounds of the **Museo de Arte de El Salvador** (Tues–Sun 10am–6pm; US$1.50, free Sun; Ⓦmarte .org.sv; bus #34), a superb digest of Salvadoran art from 1870 to the current day. The primary exhibit is "Al Compás del Tiempo", due to run unchanged until December 2016; highlights include one of **Fernando Llort**'s folksy naïf works, *Domingo en la Plaza* (1979), a good selection of **José Mejía Vides**' paintings, including a romantic view of Panchimalco, and the vivid realism of *Trabajadores* (1946) by **Julia Díaz** (who opened the nation's first art gallery in 1958). Don't miss the haunting Modernist collection in Sala 3, influenced by the civil war in the 1980s – *El Sumpul* (1984) by **Carlos Cañas** captures the horror with a pile of dead bodies, while **Titi Escalante** re-imagines Matisse's dancers with a ghoulish bronze sculpture. If you book two to four days in advance you can get a free English-speaking guide.

Museo Nacional de Antropología "Dr David J. Guzmán"

The southern end of Avenida La Revolución sports the **Museo Nacional de Antropología "Dr David J. Guzmán"** (Tues–Sun 10am–6pm; US$3; Ⓦcultura .gob.sv/muna; bus #30-B), named after an eminent Salvadoreño biologist and home to the nation's largest collection of cultural artefacts and anthropological displays. The two lower-floor galleries contain temporary exhibits and a hall dedicated to the history of agriculture through ancient pottery, tools, ploughs and the like, with special sections on Salvador's balsam, indigo and coffee industries. Labels here are in Spanish only (this may change), but the two galleries upstairs now feature full bilingual descriptions. The Sala de Religión boasts some truly magnificent exhibits, including the **Monolito del Jaguar**, a five-tonne representation of a jaguar's head on a stone disc, some delicate

obsidian items and bizarre objects such as the conch "shell trumpet" and ancient Pipil stone sculptures of mushrooms (the hallucinogenic variety were closely associated with death and the underworld). Grab a coffee in the museum courtyard afterwards, where *Bistro San Lorenzo* does a variety of meals and desserts.

Parroquia Nuestra Señora de Guadalupe La Ceiba

At the southern end of Avenida la Revolución is the **Carretera Panamericana** – turn right and a short walk from here is possibly the most captivating church in San Salvador, the **Parroquia Nuestra Señora de Guadalupe La Ceiba** (office hours Mon–Fri 8am–noon & 2–5.15pm, Sat 8am–noon; free; ☏2243 3686; bus #42, #44, #101). Started in 1913 and consecrated in 1953, the basilica is dedicated to Our Lady of Guadalupe, the much-revered indigenous Mexican apparition of the Virgin Mary and patroness of the Americas. Inside are lovely stained-glass windows, as well as a 1950s mural of the Virgin and angels over the altar. The church tends to be locked when the office is closed, unless there is a **Mass** (Mon–Sat 7am and 5.30pm; Sun 7am, 9am, 11am & 4pm).

La UCA

Stretching behind Nuestra Señora de Guadalupe is the campus of the private, Jesuit-run **Universidad Centroamericana** ("La UCA"), pleasantly laid out amid shady grounds and sports fields. The small but moving **Centro Monseñor Romero** (Mon–Fri 8am–noon & 2–6pm, Sat 8am–11.30am; free; Ⓦuca.edu.sv/cmr) at the southern end of the campus commemorates the assassinated Archbishop Romero, along with the six Jesuit priests, their housekeeper and her daughter who were murdered here by the infamous Atlacatl Battalion in November 1989. The Sala de los Martires (labelled in Spanish only) houses clothing, photographs and personal effects of Romero and the priests, along with those of other human-rights workers killed during the years of conflict. Among the

3

more chilling exhibits is a display of glass jars containing the ashes of six victims, arranged in the shape of a cross, and the bloodied handkerchief of Father Rutilio Grande, murdered in 1977. Enter La UCA along Blvd Los Proceres, or Blvd La Sultana.

ARRIVAL AND DEPARTURE

BY PLANE

Comalapa International Airport The airport (☎ 2366 9455, ⓦ aeropuertoelsalvador.gob.sv) is a 45min drive southeast of San Salvador city centre (note that if you are heading to El Tunco, it's much faster to arrange a pick-up direct from the airport).

Buses Buses #14, #15 and #29, among others, stop by the highway turn-off to the airport; #29 then stops in the city centre. These buses only cost US$1.50, but can take 1hr to get into the city and are very crowded. After 7pm, taxis are the only way to get to San Salvador.

Taxis Acacya (☎ 2271 4937 or ☎ 2222 1202) have a booth at the airport and charge US$25 day or night to the capital, regardless of numbers. They also run a *colectivo* service (8am, 9am, noon, 1pm, 5pm & 6pm from the airport; 6am, 7am, 10am & 2pm to the airport; US$3), leaving and arriving at their offices at 19A Av Nte & 3A C Pte 1107.

BY BUS

San Salvador has three chaotic domestic terminals. International buses depart from individual offices, mostly in the western half of the city (see box below).

INTERNATIONAL BUSES

Tickets to Guatemala City range from US$30–55, while Managua (Nicaragua) and Tegucigalpa (Honduras) will be US$50–60. Pullmantur runs double-deckers, and, along with King Quality, generally offers the most luxurious service. Buy tickets at the relevant offices (see box below). Shuttle buses also run to Antigua, Guatemala, though it's easier to pick these up in El Tunco (see p.221).

Destinations Guatemala City (King Quality: daily; 5hr; Puerto Bus: 18 daily Mon–Sat, 4 daily Sun; 5hr; Pullmantur: 4 daily; 4hr 30min; Transporte de Sol: daily 7am & 4pm; 4hr 30min); Managua, Nicaragua (Puerto Bus: daily; 11hr;

Transporte de Sol: daily 6.15am; 12hr); Panama City via San José, Costa Rica, and Managua, Nicaragua (Tica Bus: daily; 36hr/18hr/11hr); San José, Costa Rica (Puerto Bus: daily; 18hr); San Pedro Sula, Honduras (Puerto Bus: 2 daily; 6hr); Tapachula, Mexico (Puerto Bus: daily; 10hr; Tica Bus: daily, via Guatemala City; 10hr/5hr); Tegucigalpa, Honduras (King Quality: 2 daily; 6hr 30min; Puerto Bus: 3 daily; 6hr 30min; Pullmantur: 1 daily; 6hr 30min).

DOMESTIC BUSES

Note that you can also pick up buses to La Libertad and El Tunco at Parque Bolívar, which is much more convenient to the centre than the Terminal de Occidente.

Terminal de Occidente Blvd Venezuela (connected to the centre by buses #4, #27, #34 and #7C; bus #44 goes to Blvd los Héroes and #34 to the Terminal de Oriente). Serves the south and west of the country.

Destinations Ahuachapán (#202; frequent; 3hr 30min); San Juan Opico, for Joya de Cerén (#108; frequent; 1hr); La Libertad (#102; every 10min 4.30am–8pm; 1hr; the *especial* #102-A goes all the way to Sunzal via El Tunco every 30min, 6am–8.15pm; 1hr); Metapán (#201A; every 30min; 3hr 30min); Santa Ana, via San Andrés ruins (#201; every 10min, 4am–8.10pm; 1hr 15min–2hr; *especial* 1hr 15min); Sonsonate (#205; every 15min, 4.30am–4.15pm; 1hr 45min; *especial* 1hr 15min).

Terminal de Oriente Blvd del Ejército (connected to the centre by buses #3, #5, #7, #8, #9, #28, #29, #34 and #42; and #29 and #54 to Blvd los Héroes). Serves the east and north of the country. Destinations Chalatenango (#125; every 10min, 4am–6.30pm; 2hr); Ilobasco (#111; every 15min; 1hr 20min); La Palma/El Poy (#119; every 30min; 4hr 30min); La Unión (#304; every 30min; 3–4hr; *especial* 1pm; 3hr); San Francisco Gotera (#305; direct; 3 daily; 3–4hr); San Miguel (#301; hourly 3–11am, less frequent 11am–5.10pm; 3–4hr; *especial & super especial* services every 15min 3.30am–5pm; 2hr 40min); San Vicente (#116; frequent; 1hr 30min; *especial* 8 daily; 1hr); Suchitoto (#129; every 20min, 4.30am–8.15pm; 1hr 30min); Usulután (#302; 2 daily; 2hr 30min).

Terminal del Sur On the Autopista a Comalapa (connected to the centre by buses #11B, #21 and #26). The stop for buses along the eastern Carretera del Litoral to Zacatecoluca and Usulután.

INTERNATIONAL BUS COMPANIES AND STOPS

King Quality Alameda Juan Pablo II & 19 Av Nte; linked to the city centre by bus #52 (☎ 2271 1361).

Puerto Bus Alameda Juan Pablo II, by the Centro de Gobierno; linked to the city centre by bus #52 (☎ 2271 1361).

Pullmantur *Hotel Sheraton Presidente*, Av La Revolución, Colonia San Benito (☎ 2243 1300, ⓦ pullmantur.com).

Tica Bus By the *Hotel San Carlos* at Concepción 121 in the Centro Histórico; linked to the city centre by bus #29 and #34 (☎ 2222 0848).

Transporte de Sol Av La Revolución (☎ 2243 1345).

USEFUL BUS ROUTES IN SAN SALVADOR

#29 From Terminal de Oriente to Metrocentro via Centro Histórico.

#30B Along Blvd de los Héroes, up Alameda Roosevelt and part of Paseo Escalón, then turning west to run past the Zona Rosa.

#34 From Terminal de Oriente through Centro Histórico to Terminal de Occidente and out along the Carretera Panamericana, past the Mercado de Artesanías.

#44 Along Blvd de los Héroes, onto 49A Av Sur close to the Terminal de Occidente, past the Universidad de Centroamérica and out past the US Embassy to Santa Elena.

#52 Along Alameda Juan Pablo I, past Metrosur and on to El Salvador del Mundo (opposite the Telecom office), then up Paseo Escalón past the Galerías shopping mall.

#101A/B/C/D From Centro Histórico up Alameda Roosevelt to Plaza de las Américas, then on to Santa Tecla.

Destinations Costa del Sol (#495; every 30min; 2hr 30min); Puerto El Triunfo (#185; 6 daily; 2hr); Usulután, for Puerto El Triunfo (#302; frequent; 2hr 30min); Zacatecoluca, for Costa de Sol (#133; frequent; 1hr 30min).

GETTING AROUND

By bus The city bus network runs from 6am until around 8pm and is comprehensive, frequent and cheap – it's US$0.25 to anywhere in the city. Pay the driver if there is a gate, or the roaming, shouting driver's assistant if not. Most stops are not marked, so look for large public buildings, shopping centres or groups of people waiting by the road; usually you can also hop on or off if they stop in traffic.

By taxi Yellow city taxis ply the streets and wait around bus terminals, markets and major hotels and shopping areas. They cost US$5–10 depending on how far you go (in the centre trips will be US$5–6), which you should agree on before getting in. Always take taxis after dark.

INFORMATION AND TOURS

Tourist information The Ministero de Turismo (MITUR) and Corsatur offices are at Edificio Carbonell #1, Alameda M.E. Araujo, Colonia Roma (Mon–Fri 8.30am–12.30pm & 1.10–4.30pm; ☎ 2243 7835, ⓦ elsalvador.travel); they give out basic maps and advertisement-laden "guides".

Tour operators Akwaterra (☎ 7888 8642, ⓦ akwaterra .com) speak English and run active ecotours on land and sea – everything from kayaking and surfing to horseriding, paragliding and mountain biking. El Salvador Divers, 3A C Pte 5020-A at 99A Av Nte (☎ 2264 0961, ⓦ elsalvador divers.com), offers diving trips along the Los Cóbanos/Los Remedios stretch of the Pacific coast and crater diving at Lake Coatepeque, plus PADI courses and equipment rental.

ACCOMMODATION

The Centro Histórico is not generally conducive to peace of mind or a pleasant stay, and there is very little to do there at night but wait for a morning bus. The western suburbs are safe, with plenty to see and do, but there are few

genuinely budget options apart from in the southern sections. North of Blvd de los Héroes is the middle ground, and much better for travellers: it's safe and with a good amount of nightlife and eating options.

CENTRO HISTÓRICO

International Custodio 10A Av Sur 109 ☎ 2502 0678, ⓔ peraltavictor62@hotmail.com; map p.204. One of the centre's cheapest options, with friendly service, great views from the roof, clean sheets and decent fans. Credit cards are accepted and the manager, who speaks good English, can give advice on the area. Reductions available on extended stays. Double: shared bath US$12, with bath US$16

Villa Floréncia Centro Histórico 3A C Pte 1023, between 17 & 19 Av Nte ☎ 2221 1706; map p.204. One of several similar hotels in the area behind the Puerto Bus terminal. With large, bright, airy en-suite rooms, cable TV, free wi-fi and communal seating areas, this is the best of the bunch. Double: with fan US$20, with a/c US$35

BLVD DE LOS HÉROES AND PARQUE CUSCATLÁN

★ **Casa Tazumal** 35A Av Nte 3 ☎ 2235 0156, ⓦ hotel tazumalhouse.com; map p.207. Pricier but homely option with plenty of perks – free wi-fi, airport or bus terminal pick-up, good food and laundry service (US$5) – in addition to clean rooms with cable TV and firm beds. US$43

La Estancia Av Cortés 216 ☎ 2275 3381; map p.207. Relaxed hostel on a quiet residential street just off Blvd de los Héroes, with a large cable-TV area (you'll pay extra for basic breakfast, use of the kitchen, water and coffee machine). The dorm bunks spill out into the corridor and the clean en-suite rooms are small and in need of renovation, but great value, especially the room with a private terrace. Dorm US$12, double US$20

Hostal Doña Marta Pje Maracaibo, Casa 1-b, off Blvd Venezuela, Colonia Venezuela ☎ 2301 3006, ⓦ hostal donamarta.blogspot.com; map p.203. This friendly,

3

family-run place (0.5km south from Parque Cuscatlán) runs like a B&B, presided over by the lovable Doña Marta herself. Rooms are basic but cosy, and Marta's cooking is fantastic. Free wi-fi. Dorm US$13, double US$30

Ximena's Guest House C San Salvador 202, Colonia Centroamérica ☎2260 2481, ⓦximenasguesthouse.com; map p.207. The original San Salvador hostel is not necessarily still the best. Beds are lumpy or saggy and the electric hot water (which you pay extra for) is shockingly inconsistent. It remains a travellers' favourite though, not least for the wide range of breakfasts, helpful English-speaking owner and sociable evening atmosphere. Dorm US$8, double US$30

COLONIA ESCALÓN AND THE ZONA ROSA

Casa Huéspedes Australia 1A C Pte 3852 ☎2298 6035; map p.208. Lacks the atmosphere of the Blvd de los Héroes hostels, but is certainly cleaner and more comfortable; offers free breakfast and wi-fi, and the showers are big and hot. It's incredible value for Escalón, but choose the cheapest rooms, as there is no massive difference in the more expensive ones. US$40

Hostal Cumbres del Volcán 85A Av Nte 637 ☎2207 3705, ⓦcumbresdelvolcan.com; map p.208. Great location in Escalón, with comfy dorm bunks or singles (US$10), and private triples/doubles with bathroom and a/c. Breakfast, free wi-fi (and computers), kitchen and help with transport and tours offered. Dorm US$8, double US$35

JoAn's Hostel C del Mediterraneo 12, Colonia Jardines de Guadalupe ☎2207 4292, ⓦjoanshostel.hostel.com; map p.203. This newish hostel (just south of La UCA) offers simple modern rooms and dorms, free wi-fi, communal kitchen, lounge with cable TV and a terrace with barbecue. Dorm US$13, double US$36

EATING

Cheap eats abound in the Centro Histórico; south of Plaza 17 de Julio (aka Plaza Hula-Hula) is a collection of popular outdoor food stalls (with tables). Prices and quality increase in the western suburbs. The Blvd de los Héroes itself is dominated by fast-food chains (you are never far

from a *Wendy's* or a pizza chain in San Salvador), but there are good options off the main drag. Other budget options include the *Eat and Run* chain at petrol stations and the food courts in the malls (see p.214).

CENTRO HISTÓRICO

Koradi 9A Av Sur 225, at 4A C Pte ☎2221 2545; map p.204. One of the few places catering to vegetarians, with soya burgers (US$3), wholewheat pizzas and fresh juices. Mon–Fri 7am–5.30pm, Sat 7am–5pm.

★ **Panadería Latino** C Delgado, between 2A Av Nte & Av Providencia Ayala; map p.204. Almost blocked in by market stalls, this local institution and no-frills canteen is justly popular for its vast ranges of dishes – tacos, chicken, eggs, etc – for under US$1. Daily 6am–8pm.

Pan Salvador C Arce, between 7A & 9A Av Nte (no sign); map p.204. Popular with local workers, this busy *comedor* and bakery, filled with the aroma of baking cakes, serves meat dishes for around US$1–2, with a quarter chicken for US$2.25 and coffee for US$0.75. Expect long lines at meal times. Daily 6am–6pm.

Pupusería Doña Isabel 9A Ave Nte, between C Rubén Darío & C Arce; map p.204. Popular no-frills *pupusa* canteen, serving freshly made *pupusas* (US$0.75) stuffed with all the usual: cheese, pork and beans. Mon–Sat 7am–6.30pm, Sun 7am–noon.

BLVD DE LOS HÉROES AND PARQUE CUSCATLÁN

¡ay Q'Rico! Blvd Universitario 217 ☎2225 6905; map p.207. Popular among the local students for its cheap daily menus (US$2–3), served with free beer. Also a wide selection of seafood and poultry dishes with a touch of Mexican flavour. Cash only. Mon–Sat 11.30am–3pm & 5pm–2am.

Casablanca C San Antonio Abad & Av San José ☎2235 1489 (no sign); map p.207. A well-prepared canteen menu (US$3–5), with large soup portions, served in a cool and open room shielded from the traffic by climbing plants. Mon–Sat 7am–5pm.

Comedor y Pupusería La Ceiba C San Antonio Abad 721 ☎2208 0344; map p.207. Best place for a plate of filling *pupusas* in the area (US$0.75), served from 5.30pm – before that expect tasty but standard *comedor* food, from fried chicken to *tamales* and tortas. Mon–Sat 7am–9pm.

Mayaburger C G. Cortés, at Mistral; map p.207. This trustworthy hole-in-the-wall burger joint outstrips the big franchises both on price (a two-burger sandwich, onions and salad are US$4; regular burgers US$1.75) and taste – plus, it's open 24/7. Daily 24hr.

Sol y Luna Blvd Universitario, at Av C ☎2225 6637; map p.207. Rare but decent veggie and vegan-friendly restaurant, open for lunch only and serving a tasty buffet

map p.208

★ TREAT YOURSELF

A lo Nuestro C La Reforma 225A ☎ 2223 5116; map p.208. If you want to taste the true potential of what many view as El Salvador's "simple" cuisine, head to this gourmet restaurant. The refined Salvadoran menu is a delight, and the ambience romantic, with table linen and low lighting. Mains US$12–25. Mon–Thurs noon–2.30pm & 7–10.30pm, Fri noon–2.30pm & 7–11pm, Sat 7–11pm.

that changes daily, including a choice of two fresh juices (US$5–6). Mon–Sat noon–3.30pm.

Tacos de Paco C Andes 2931 ☎ 2260 1347; map p.207. Tasty Mexican tacos (US$4–5) served in a room that has original art on the walls and hosts poetry readings on Wed evenings at 6pm. Daily noon–3pm & 5–10pm.

COLONIA ESCALÓN AND THE ZONA ROSA

Comedor y Pupusería Shadaii 77A Av Sur (behind Súper Selectos); map p.208. The *comedor* and *pupusería* of choice for the area's workers, with *típicos* breakfasts (US$2) and lunches (US$3–4) that are the cheapest around. Mon–Fri 7am–3pm.

Dulce y Salado 3A C Pte 3951, at 75 Av Nte ☎ 2263 2212; map p.208. Decorated like a little girl's bedroom, this small restaurant has good pancake, juice and coffee breakfasts (US$5) and great quiche (US$6.50). Mon–Sat 8am–7pm.

La Michoacana Paseo General Escalón (in a small strip mall near Plaza Argentina) ☎ 2225 3168; map p.208. Delicious fresh-fruit ice cream (US$1.50–2), hot chocolate and ices (lollies to Brits), including tamarind and chilli, beer, tequila and *mojito cubano* flavours. You'll see *Michoacana* ice-cream shops all over Central America, but it's not a chain: the name is a homage to the Mexican state (Michoacán) that claims the world's best ice cream. Daily 11am–7pm.

★ Rustico Bistro 3A C Pte (aka Shafick Handal), at Pasaje Los Pinos 3877; map p.208. Local expats judge this the best burger joint in El Salvador (if not Central America), for good reason; the main event is a half-pound, juicy patty of beef seasoned with spices, chipotle sauce and topped with bacon and cheese under a sourdough bun (served with fries). At US$9 it's not cheap, but you'll be glad you coughed up the cash (it's big enough for two to share). Daily noon–4.30pm.

DRINKING AND NIGHTLIFE

San Salvador's clubs and bars are found mainly in the western suburbs, but there are also small pockets of expat and tourist nightlife, particularly in and around *Ximena's Guesthouse* and *La Estancia* in Colonia Centroamérica,

behind Blvd de los Héroes. If you fancy mingling with the city's upwardly mobile, head for the cluster of swanky clubs and bars in the shadow of the towering *Hilton Hotel* off Blvd del Hipódromo in Colonia San Benito.

BLVD DE LOS HÉROES AND PARQUE CUSCATLÁN

El Arpa Irlandés Av A Col San José 137, on the west side of Parque San José ☎ 2225 0429; map p.207. This laidback bar is the place to come for an ice-cold Guinness (US$4) or a US$6 bucket of Pilsner. There's a pool table, and it livens up on Sat nights with rock bands, which draw a young crowd. No sign – look for the green paint and leprechaun mural. Mon–Thurs 4pm–1am, Fri 3pm–2am, Sat noon–2am.

★ Café la 'T' C San Antonio Abad 2233 ☎ 2225 2090; map p.207. Owner Anna has turned this into an enticing little arty café and bar offering monthly live music and art exhibitions. The *tiramisù* (US$3) is the best in the country and the lemon, honey and vodka-filled "Café Ivanovic" cocktail (US$2.50) is a treat. Mon–Wed 10am–9.30pm, Thurs–Sat 10am–11pm.

La Canchita Pasco 11, at Aconcagua (off C Lamatepec) ☎ 2261 0317; map p.207. This fun and feisty sports bar, which offers buckets of six bottles of beer for US$6 and has the best full-sized pool tables in town (US$1/30min), is the pick of several places in the area. Mon–Sat 10am–1am.

COLONIA ESCALÓN AND THE ZONA ROSA

La Hola Beto's Av Las Magnolias 230, at Blvd del Hipódromo ☎ 2223 6865, ⓦ laholabetos.com; map p.208. Lively restaurant and bar, popular for its tiki-style patio and terrace on the second floor. The mini-chain is known locally for its seafood (mains US$8–15), but this branch is the best for drinks, especially its Beer Revolution brews. Mon–Sat 11am–2am, Sun 11am–midnight.

NVY 2nd floor, Multiplaza shopping mall ☎ 2243 2584; map p.208. A favourite of upwardly mobile Salvadoreños, who all get dressed up, and you have to too (trousers, shirt, shoes). Expect dance music, R&B and hip-hop. Cover US$10. Wed–Sat 11pm–6am.

Los Rinconcitos Blvd del Hipódromo 310 ☎ 2298 9661; map p.208. This no-frills disco and bar (close to *Beto's*) makes a good place to start (or end) your evening. Expect live rock music at the weekend, and blaring karaoke most other nights – thankfully, it does promotions on drinks most nights, too. Mon 6pm–2am, Tues–Sat 6pm–5am.

Zanzibar Blvd del Hipódromo ☎ 2279 0833, ⓦ zanzibar .com.sv; map p.208. Inside the Centro Comercial Basilea complex of shops and restaurants, this stylish open-air bar and restaurant features live music and second-storey views across the boulevard; martinis, margaritas and mojitos from US$4.50. *Gaudí Bar*, a smart wine bar, is also part of the complex. Tues–Fri 5pm–1.30am, Sat 4pm–1.30am.

3

3

ENTERTAINMENT

Cinema There are a several multi-screen complexes – try Cinemark at the Metrocentro and Gran Via (☎ 2261 2001, ⓦ cinemarkca.com), or the eleven-screen Cinépolis (ⓦ cinepolis.com.sv) at Galerías Escalón. All show some original-language films and some dubbed (most tickets US$4.25). Independent cinema can be found at *La Luna*, C Berlin 228 on Wed–Sun, starting at around 7pm, or *Café la 'T'* (see p.213) on Wed & Thurs around 8pm.

Theatre The Teatro Presidente (next to the Museo de Arte) and the magnificently restored Teatro Nacional (see p.205) host everything from ballet to musicals to opera, at anything from free to US$30, while the Teatro Luis Poma, just inside the main arched entrance to the Metrocentro, shows locally produced plays (from US$5). Information can be found in the Friday edition and on the website of *El Diario de Hoy* (ⓦ elsalvador.com). Buy tickets online at ⓦ todoticketsv.com.

SHOPPING

Art El Árbol de Dios art gallery, at Av Masferrer Nte 575 & C la Mascota (Mon–Fri 8am–7pm, Sat 9am–6pm; free; ⓦ arboldedios.com), is the shop of El Salvador's emblematic painter Fernando Llort. Everything from prints to cooking aprons in his naïf style can be bought; most items are produced in the workshop in the back. Originals go for about half a million dollars.

Books and newspapers Librería Latinoamérica (Mon–Sat 9am–7pm, Sun 10am–6pm), on the 3rd and 7th levels of the Metrocentro, has English-language titles and US magazines. Librería La Ceiba (Mon–Sat 10am–7pm, Sun 10am–5pm; ⓦ libroslaceiba.com) is the biggest chain of bookstores, branches of which you'll find in Metrocentro, Galerías Escalón and other malls, with a reasonable range, including some books in English (average US$14 for a paperback).

Craft markets There are two good markets for artisan handicrafts: the central Mercado Ex Cuartel (Mon–Sat 7.30am–6pm, Sun 7.30am–2pm), three blocks east of the Teatro Nacional, and the higher-quality Mercado de Artesanías (daily 9am–6pm), opposite the baseball stadium on Alameda M.E. Araujo.

Malls Reputedly the largest mall in Central America, Metrocentro (ⓦ metrocentro.com) at the southern end of Blvd de los Héroes holds three storeys of boutiques, sporting-goods outlets, pricey souvenir shops, a supermarket and a food court. Galerías Escalón (ⓦ galerias.com.sv), at Paseo Gen Escalón 3700, is the same but classier. Multiplaza (ⓦ multiplaza.com) and Las Cascadas (home to Walmart; ⓦ lascascadas.com.sv) on the Carretera Panamericana just outside Santa Tecla have been overshadowed by the pristine Gran Via mall development (ⓦ lagranvia.com.sv), a few minutes further down the highway – if you want to escape Central America completely for a few hours, this genteel slice of Western consumerism is the place.

Markets Southwest of Plaza Barrios are the ever-expanding street stalls of the Mercado Central (daily 7.30am–6pm), where anything and everything can be bought for about a dollar, even on Sundays.

DIRECTORY

Banks and exchange Most banks ask for the original receipt when cashing travellers' cheques and give over-the-counter cash advances on Visa and MasterCard. Banco Hipotecario, at Av Cuscatlán between 4A & 6A C Ote, and other branches around the city, do not require the receipt. The American Express office is at Anna's Travel Company, 3A C Pte 3737, Colonia Escalón (☎ 2209 8888). Banks and ATMs are ubiquitous around the western suburbs and Blvd de los Héroes.

Embassies Most embassies are located in or around the Paseo Escalón and Zona Rosa districts. The heavily fortified US embassy is on Blvd Santa Elena, Antiguo Cuscatlán (bus #44; ☎ 2501 2999, ⓦ sansalvador.usembassy.gov). Canada is at Centro Financiero Gigante, Alameda Roosevelt y 63A Av Sur (☎ 2279 4655). British citizens should call the new embassy at the Torre Futura, Colonia Escalón, on ☎ 2511 5757 (ⓦ ukinelsalvador.fco.gov.uk). Australians should contact the Canadian embassy.

Health The city has two good hospitals: Hospital de Diagnóstico, 21A C Pte at 2A Diagonal (☎ 2226 8878, ⓦ hospitaldiagnostico.com), and its branch, Hospital de Diagnóstico, Escalón, 3A C Pte at 99A Av Nte (☎ 2264 4422). There's also a 24hr pharmacy at Farmacia Internacional, Edificio Kent, Local 6, Alameda Juan Pablo II at Blvd de los Héroes, and a 24hr Farmacia Economica on Hipódromo and Revolución. The Medicentro at 27A Av Nte & 21A C Pte has a number of doctors specializing in different fields (☎ 2225 1312). A consultation will cost around US$40.

Immigration Dirección General de Migración y Extranjería (Sección de Visas y Prórrogas), 9A C Pte & 15 Av Nte, in the Centro de Gobierno (Mon–Fri 8am–4pm; ☎ 2221 2111), is the place to get stamps, tourist cards and visas extended.

Internet Ciber Morazán, in the Centro Histórico, on Plaza Morazán near the Teatro Nacional (daily 9am–6pm). Webcity Cyber Café, perched on the outer edge of Metrosur (C Los Andes), is also open daily. You'll find a cluster of places around the UTEC campus along C Arce (try La Universitaria Librería y Ciber Café or CompuStar), though these are open Mon–Sat only (usually 9am–7pm). Expect to pay US$0.50–1/hr (the UTEC cafés are the cheapest).

Laundry Jet Cleaners operates several handy branches in the city; Paseo Gral Escalón; Blvd del Hipódromo 105; and inside the Metrocentro (typically Mon–Sat 7am–7pm; average load US$3).

Police The main station is in the Scottish-castle-like building that occupies an entire block on 10A Av Sur at 6A C Ote (☎ 2271 4422).

Post office Behind the Centro de Gobierno at 15A C Pte and Diagonal Universitaria Nte; look for the large building with "UPAE" on the side (Mon–Fri 8am–5pm, Sat 8am–noon). There is a smaller office in the lower level of the Metrocentro mall.

Around San Salvador

Northwest of the city, **Volcán San Salvador** looms over the valley, while to the south the **Puerta del Diablo** offers vistas the length of the coast. Tucked beneath the rocks, the village of **Panchimalco**'s splendid colonial church belies its predominantly indigenous populace. Some 15km east of San Salvador sits the country's largest crater lake, serene **Lago de Ilopango**, while to the west are the natural gorge and pools of **Los Chorros**, the exceptionally rare ruins of **Joya de Cerén** and the partially reconstructed pyramids and temples at **San Andrés**.

VOLCÁN SAN SALVADOR

As you travel west along the Carretera Panamericana (CA-1) from San Salvador light industrial and residential districts blend indiscernibly into **Santa Tecla**, briefly the capital in 1854 but now only of minor interest. North of Santa Tecla lie the heavily cultivated slopes of dormant **VOLCÁN SAN SALVADOR** (1960m), the fifth-highest volcano in the country. Its 558m-deep crater **El Boquerón** has a blossom-smothered floor and a smaller cone known as **Boqueroncito**, created in the last eruption in 1917. From the well-kept **Parque El Boquerón** (daily 8am–5pm; US$1) on the rim (at 1839m) are dizzying views of San Salvador, Lake Ilopango, Puerto del Diablo and the crater's interior; adventurers can tackle the walk around it (about 2hr) or down the wooded slopes inside to Boqueroncito (be warned, the climb back up can be exhausting). Early morning is the best time to go, when the views from the summit are clearest. You can also walk up to the crater, though robberies have been reported; the Policía de Turismo at the entrance may be willing to provide an escort for groups.

ARRIVAL AND DEPARTURE

By bus Bus #103 (hourly) and pick-ups run from 4A Av Sur & C Hernández in Santa Tecla (reached via the La Libertad, Santa Ana and Sonsonate buses from Terminal de Occidente), to Pueblo del Boquerón, 1km from the rim; the last bus down leaves mid-afternoon.

By taxi At least US$25 from San Salvador.

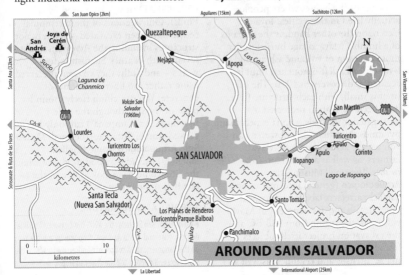

AROUND SAN SALVADOR

3

PARQUE ACUÁTICO LOS CHORROS

Six kilometres west of Santa Tecla, just off the Carretera Panamericana (CA-1), El Salvador's most popular *parque recreativo familiar*, **PARQUE ACUÁTICO LOS CHORROS** (daily 8am–4pm; US$1), is an inviting spot for a swim. Small waterfalls cascade through mossy jungle slopes into four landscaped pools; there are public changing rooms and showers – don't bring valuables – and a couple of *comedores* provide meals.

ARRIVAL AND DEPARTURE

By bus From San Salvador take bus #79 (heading to Lourdes) from 15A Av Sur & C Rubén Darío at Parque Bolívar (every 15min; 30min), or any Santa Ana bus from the Terminal de Occidente, and ask to be dropped at the gate.

JOYA DE CERÉN

Some 14km northwest of Los Chorros (on the road to San Juan Opico, which branches north off the Carretera Panamericana), the Maya site of **JOYA DE CERÉN** (Tues–Sun 9am–4pm; US$3, parking US$1) isn't quite the "Pompeii" it's hyped up to be, but it does offer a totally different perspective to all the other great Mesoamerican ruins. What remains of sites like Copán and Tikal is grand but ceremonial – there is very little evidence of the houses where people actually lived in these cities. Joya de Cerén, on the other hand, is the remains of a humble Maya village buried under more than 6m of volcanic ash around 640–650 AD, left untouched until its accidental discovery in 1976. The site itself is small, with each structure (ten have been excavated) protected in corrugated iron sheds – don't expect giant pyramids. Nowhere else, however, can you see the actual homes of Maya farmers, as well as a sweat bath (*temazal*), *in situ*. The small **Museo Sitio Arqueológico** (general information in English; artefacts labelled in Spanish only) details the development of Maya culture in the region from 900 BC and the excavation project itself; objects found here, including petrified beans, maize, utensils and ceramics, as well as

the discovery of gardens for growing a wide range of plants, have helped confirm a picture of a well-organized and stable pre-colonial society, with trade links throughout Central America. As yet, no human remains have been uncovered, which concurs with the hasty departure suggested by the number of artefacts left behind. The guided tours are highly recommended (free; some guides speak English).

ARRIVAL AND DEPARTURE

By bus Bus #108 from San Salvador's Terminal de Occidente runs right by the site – get off just after crossing the Río Sucio. If you want to go to San Andrés (see below) in the same trip, start here and take #108 back towards San Salvador as far as the Carretera Panamericana, where you can intercept a #201 (towards Santa Ana from the Terminal de Occidente) to San Andrés.

SAN ANDRÉS

A few kilometres southwest of Joya de Céren (32km from San Salvador, on the Carretera Panamericana) lies the elevated Maya ceremonial centre of **SAN ANDRÉS** (Tues–Sun 9am–4pm; US$3, parking US$1). One of the largest pre-Columbian sites in El Salvador, originally supporting a population of about twelve thousand, the site reached its peak as the regional capital around 650–900 AD (it was later used by the Pipils). Only sections of the ceremonial centre have been excavated – seven major structures including the Acropolis and a seventeenth-century Spanish indigo works – and sadly, they've been preserved using rather too liberal amounts of concrete. You can climb freely around most of the site, though the tallest pyramid ("La Campana") can only be viewed from a distance. The small **Museo Sitio Arqueológico** (some English labelling) includes a good model of what the site would have looked like in the late first millennium.

ARRIVAL AND DEPARTURE

By bus From San Salvador the #201 bus between Terminal de Occidente and Santa Ana will drop you by a black ruin on the Panamericana a couple of hundred metres from the site – you will need to tell the driver to stop.

LAGO DE ILOPANGO

Heading east from San Salvador, the Carretera Panamericana passes the city's dismal eastern slums and bends northwards. A few kilometres beyond the military airport at Ilopango, a dirt road branches south and winds down through scrubby hillsides, offering dazzling views across **LAGO DE ILOPANGO** to the peaks of Volcán San Vicente. The country's largest and deepest crater lake, resulting from one of the biggest eruptions in history in around 250 AD, Ilopango is a contrast of blue waters and tumbling, thickly vegetated cliffs. Further along the road, in the dusty hamlet of **Dolores Apulo**, the attractive (but busy at weekends) **Parque Acuático Apulo** (daily 8am–5pm; US$1) has a beach, swimming pools and fine *comedores*. Small boats tout for custom here (US$12/hr; reductions for groups) – drifting around the Isla de Amor or touring the rich lakeside communities is a pleasant way to spend a hot afternoon. The best **volcano diving** in the country also takes place under the surface of the lake, on the underwater volcanic cone La Caldera. This should be organized with El Salvador Divers (see p.211) in the capital beforehand.

ARRIVAL AND DEPARTURE

By bus Bus #15 runs from Av España and the corner of C 9 Pte & 1A Av Nte in San Salvador (every 30min or so).

LOS PLANES DE RENDEROS

Overlooking the Valle de Hamacas from the brim of the valley's southern watershed, **LOS PLANES DE RENDEROS** offers fresh air, good food and fine views. The best panoramas of San Salvador are from the *Casa de Piedra* (see below); cheaper, though, is the *mirador* lookout point off the road just before the restaurant as you come up the hill. Jaw-dropping views of the coast are the attraction at the **Puerta del Diablo**, a split rock formation (the three peaks are known as el Chulo, el Chulito and el Chulón), a forty-minute walk from the road through the somewhat grubby **Parque Natural Balboa** (Carretera Los Planes km 12; daily 8am–6pm; US$0.50, parking $1). The rock's legendary origins

– split by a bolt of lightning more than three hundred years ago – have been eclipsed by its very real role in the civil war as a place of death-squad interrogations, executions and body-dumping.

ARRIVAL AND DEPARTURE

By bus Bus #12 and #17 run up the Carretera Los Planes from Av 29 de Agosto (and the Mercado Central) in San Salvador. If you don't fancy walking to the Puerta del Diablo, you can take the bus to the last stop, at km 14.

EATING AND DRINKING

Casa de Piedra Carretera Los Planes, km 8.5 ☎ 2280 8822. An open-fronted bar/restaurant serving seafood (mains US$12) and *típicos* with weekend music or karaoke. Daily 11am–2am.

Pupusería Paty Carretera Los Planes, km 10 ☎ 2280 8856. Another tempting restaurant, this barn-like place serves some of the best and biggest *pupusas* in the country. Daily 8am–7pm.

PANCHIMALCO

Some 15km south of San Salvador, the largely indigenous town of **PANCHIMALCO** lies sleepily beneath the Puerta del Diablo. Locals are known as "*panchas*", many of them descendants of the Pipils, though traditional dress is rarely seen nowadays. The baroque **Iglesia Santa Cruz de Roma**, built in 1725, is one of the oldest surviving churches in the country and is also remarkable for its statue of a dark-skinned, indigenous Jesus. There are indigenous **crafts** for sale too, including pre-Hispanic musical instruments, at the **Casa de la Cultura** (Mon–Fri 10am–noon & 2–4pm; ☎ 2280 8767). Usually a quiet place, things become livelier during the town's annual **festivals** (see p.202). **Bus** #17 runs regularly to the town from outside the Mercado Central in San Salvador (30min).

The Pacific coast

El Salvador's **Pacific coast** is a 300km strip of palm-backed beaches, jungle-smothered cliffs, mangrove swamps and exceptional surf breaks. While the tourist potential of many of the beaches is now being developed, most stretches of

3

3

THE PACIFIC BEACHES

Potosí (Nicaragua)

HONDURAS

Río Goascorán

El Amatillo

Santa Rosa de Lima

La Unión

Conchagua

Volcán Conchagua

Golfo de Fonseca

Meanguera

Marín Pérez

Playitas

Zacatillo

Playa El Tamarindo

Conchaguita

San Miguel

Laguna de Olomega

Intipuca

Playa El Icacal

Playa Las Tunas

Playa El Esterón

CARRETERA DEL LITORAL

Playa El Cuco

Playa Las Flores

RUTA DE PAZ

Laguna el Jocotal

Jucuarán

Punta Mango

Playa El Espino

San Francisco Gotera

Usulután

Puerto El Triunfo

Bahía de Jiquilisco

Corral de Mulas

Embalse 15 de Septiembre

Río Lempa

Península San Juan del Gozo

San Vicente

Zacatecoluca

La Herradura

Playa La Puntilla

Embalse de Cerrón Grande/ Lago Suchitlán

Lago de Ilopango

Comalapa

Playa Los Blancos

Playa Costa del Sol

International Airport

Playa San Marcelino

PARQUE NACIONAL WALTER DENINGER

Costa del Sol

SAN SALVADOR

Puerto La Libertad

Playa San Diego

CARRETERA DEL LITORAL

Playa El Tunco

Playa El Zonte

Km 59

Km 61

Playa Mizata Km 87

Los Cóbanos

Los Remedios

Costa del Bálsamo

Santa Ana

Laguna de Chanmico

Sonsonate

Ahuachapán

Acajutla

RUTA DE LAS FLORES

Barra de Santiago

P A C I F I C   O C E A N

N

0 ——— 25

kilometres

coastline are still blissfully wild and unspoiled. Indeed, the allure of this part of the country lies in lounging on clean, wide swathes of volcanic sand, catching world-class waves or spending time in relatively untouched fishing villages.

Coming from San Salvador, the most accessible stretch of coast is the **Costa del Bálsamo**, extending around the small fishing town of **La Libertad**. This section boasts some of Central America's most mouth-watering surf breaks, and El Salvador's biggest gringo community. In the extreme east of the region you can watch turtles hatch at **El Cuco**, or catch early-morning *lanchas* to the tranquil islands of the **Golfo de Fonseca**.

The beaches near Acajutla (Los Cóbanos and Los Remedios) and to the west are best accessed via Sonsonate rather than along the coastal road; we've covered them elsewhere (see p.249).

PUERTO LA LIBERTAD

Just 34km south of San Salvador, **PUERTO LA LIBERTAD** (or just "El Puerto"), once a major port and still an important, if shabby, fishing town, has recently grown from surfing haven to tourist junction thanks to its position at the gateway to the Costa del Bálsamo. It's a popular place, particularly at weekends, when capital day-trippers join the local and gringo surfers to enjoy the food and sea breezes. Until the early 2000s, the town suffered from the long-term effects of drug, delinquency and gang violence, but in the last decade the place has been cleaned up, the dealers driven out, and a gleaming new *malecón* esplanade built, complete with tourist office, pleasant places to eat and drink, and live entertainment.

WHAT TO SEE AND DO

The main action in La Libertad occurs along the seafront, not the Parque Central further inland. The focus is the **Muelle** (pier) jutting out into the ocean, which hosts a lively daily fish market, and the *malecón* that stretches from the pier along the town beach, **Playa La Paz**. Playa La Paz itself is quite dirty, and becomes rocky and prone to riptides in the rainy

season. For sunbathers, the small and busy **Playa Las Flores** is 1.5km east, reachable by bus #80 or #187.

Punta Roca

La Libertad's pride and joy is the world-famous **Punta Roca** surf break, which tubes perfectly around the point a couple of hundred metres to the west of the pier. This is not a beginner's wave, and localism does exist – confrontations are best avoided by hiring a local guide (ask at your hotel or at the tourist office). Even if you don't surf, it's fun just to go and watch experts take on the wave in the morning and evening, or at any of the regular surf events held here.

If you need to work on your surf skills before hopping on a board, try some of the better beaches along the coast to the west (see p.221).

ARRIVAL AND DEPARTURE

By bus Services from San Salvador arrive at C Barrios & 4A Av Nte, two blocks inland from the pier. Buses to and from the eastern beaches go from the other side of 4A Av Nte, on Barrios. Further up that road on the corner with 1A C Pte is the stop for Sonsonate and the western beaches.

Destinations Playa San Diego, via Playa Las Flores and Parque Walter Deininger (#187; #80 direct; every 15min; 15–30min); Playa El Sunzal, via El Tunco (#80A/B, #192, #102-A, #187-A; every 15min, 4.30am–6pm; 35–40min); Playa El Zonte (#192-B to Teotepeque/#192 to La Perla; hourly 7am–7.30pm; 50min); San Miguel (#324; frequent); San Salvador, Terminal de Occidente (#102; every 10–15min, 4.30am–8pm; 1hr; microbus #102-A every 30min, 5am–6.30pm; 45min); Sonsonate, via all beaches to the west (#287; daily 6am & 1.55pm; 3hr); Zacatecoluca (#540; 7 daily; 1hr 20min) – change at Comalapa for the airport.

INFORMATION AND ACTIVITIES

Tourist information The extra-helpful Centro de Amigos del Turista (English spoken) is inside the white seafront centre opposite the pier (daily 9am–12.30pm & 1.10–5pm; ☎2346 1634), with clean public toilets opposite the entrance.

Internet You'll find several cyber cafés opposite the church on the Parque Central, two blocks inland from the pier.

Surfboards Boards can be bought, sold, rented and repaired at the Hospital de Tablas, on 3 Av Sur, between 2A C Pte and the *malecón* (7am–4pm; US$12/day).

ACCOMMODATION

AST Surf Hotel Malecón Turístico, Edificio AST #2-7, Playa La Paz, between 1A Av Sur & 3A Av Sur ☎2312 5143,

3

3

PUERTO LA LIBERTAD

Playa El Sunzal

Playa Las Flores, Playa San Dreya & Parque Walter T. Deninger

LA CALLE PONIENTE

CALLE EL CALVARIO

2A CALLE PONIENTE

2A CALLE ORIENTE

Mercado Municipal

Iglesia del Puerto

★ Bus #192 El Zonte, Tunco & Sonsonate

Bus #102 San Salvador

Banco Agricola

Despensa Familiar

Alcaldia

Bus to San Diego

Super Selectos

Parque Central

Pharmacy

CALLE BARRIOS

Hospital de Tablas

Seafood Restaurants

Market

MALECON

ATM

Playa La Paz

MALECON

PACIFIC OCEAN

Muelle

0   100
metres

▼ Punta Roca Surf Break

■ ACCOMMODATION	
AST Surf Hotel	2
Hotel Rick	3
La Posada Familiar	1

● EATING & DRINKING	
Danilo	1
El Delfin	4
Neto's Beer	2
Punta Roca	3

ⓦ astadventures.com. Adventure Sports Travel runs this plush option right on the seafront, with a range of surf packages including dorm accommodation (with a/c and wi-fi), airport transfers and three meals daily. *La Terraza*, the open-air rooftop restaurant and bar, is the best place to take in views of the bay. Dorm package, 4 nights/5 days US$675

Hotel Rick 5A Av Sur 30 ☏ 2335 3033, ⓔ eldelfin.reyes@ gmail.com. This traditional surfers' favourite is ideally located behind Punta Roca. Rooms are all en suite, with cable TV and space for surfboards. There's a/c in some, but a slightly musty smell in others. US$28

La Posada Familiar 3A Av Sur at 4A C Pte ☏ 2335 3252. Very friendly and popular place with basic rooms, some with bath, all with outdoor hammocks. They're just about the cheapest in town, but certainly not the cleanest. A small *comedor* serves meals and you can see the sea from the roof veranda. US$10

EATING AND DRINKING

The dining scene in La Libertad is relatively pricey but varied, with an inevitable emphasis on seafood. The daily market on the pier sells a good selection from the morning catch, while the cheap seafood restaurants to the east of the pier serve both raw and cooked fish (US$3–5). To the west of the pier along the *malecón* is a collection of much cleaner (and pricier) restaurants, with live music at weekends.

★ TREAT YOURSELF

Danilo Malecón, Playa La Paz (just west of the pier). If you are going to splurge on quality seafood in Libertad, seek out chef Danilo Ortega's humble-looking place, tucked in among the modern restaurants along the *malecón*. Start with a potent but refreshing *muñeco sour* (US$3), like a Peruvian *pisco sour* but made with local Muñeco liquor, before tucking into the ceviche (US$4.75), fillets of fish (from US$8) or seafood rice (US$6–7). Other mains US$13–15. Daily noon–10pm.

El Delfín 5A Av Sur, Playa La Paz (opposite *Hotel Rick*). A solid seafood joint overlooking the western end of the beach, serving heaps of paella (US$9) for dinner and shrimp omelettes (US$4) for breakfast in pleasant surroundings. Boasts the dubious benefit of Sky TV via satellite. Daily 7am–10pm.

Neto's Beer Malecón, Playa La Paz (just east of the pier). First (and best) of the cheaper places east of the pier – it's clean, serves fresh seafood and ice-cold beers. Daily 11am–11pm.

Punta Roca 5A Av Sur, Playa La Paz ☎ 2335 4342, ⓦ puntaroca.com.sv. A local institution, after which the break itself is named. There is hearty food with a Western nod ("gringo fry" US$8), and it is consistently the best place in town for a cold Pilsner (US$1.50). Daily 7am–1am.

DIRECTORY

Banks Banco Agrícola's main branch is on C Barrios, between 4 & 6 Av Nte; it also operates a 24hr ATM opposite the tourist office.

Pharmacy Centro Médico Moises, C Barrios 11-7 (Mon–Fri 7am–6pm, Sat 7am–noon; ☎ 2335 3531).

Post office 2A C Ote, between 2 & 4 Av Nte (Mon–Fri 8am–noon & 12.45–4pm, Sat 9am–noon).

Supermarkets Súper Selectos is in the Centro Comercial el Faro, on the Carretera del Litoral east of the centre; Despensa Familiar is at 4A Av Sur & 3A C Pte 9 (daily 7.30am–7pm).

COSTA DEL BÁLSAMO

Strung out on either side of Puerto La Libertad is the **COSTA DEL BÁLSAMO**, a favourite destination for surfers and day-trippers from the capital. The coast takes its name from the now-defunct trade in medicinal balsam that was once centred here, before tourism took over as the main source of income. More and more expensive beach clubs are now popping up, as international tourists gain confidence in El Salvador, but reasonable accommodation and surfing communities still dominate.

WHAT TO SEE AND DO

West of La Libertad, the Carretera del Litoral runs through thickly wooded hills and tunnels to palm-fringed black beaches. To the **east** the beaches are more disappointing, infringed upon by the expansion of the town; the sole exception is the surfer-free **Playa San Diego**, a quick escape from the intensity of La Libertad.

All kilometre distances given are for the Carretera del Litoral, along which there are markers to help you get oriented. La Libertad is the transport hub for the area (see p.219).

Playa El Tunco

The beaches just west of La Libertad are crowded with people and pricey hotels, but beyond these, at km 42, **PLAYA EL TUNCO** has a much friendlier atmosphere and the liveliest nightlife on the coast. Indeed, if you've been travelling in rural El Salvador, Tunco will come as a bit of a shock – now a fully fledged backpacker/surfer resort, sun-tanned gringos sip lattes and local agents offer shuttle buses direct to Antigua, San Salvador and Copán. The variety and wholesomeness of the food on offer (plus the amount of English spoken) certainly makes a welcome change, and Tunco remains relatively tranquil, at least on weekdays. The black-sand **beach** is pebble-strewn (the rock formation just offshore is supposed to resemble a hog, or "*tunco*"), but the waves draw plenty of surfers and it is a good spot for the inexperienced to learn. A single one-way road (Calle Principal) leads down from the Carretera making a loop through the village; there is parking where it hits the river (US$2/day), and a pedestrian-only road down to the beach (aka Calle La Bocana), where most of the action takes place. **Surf shops** will charge around US$12 for a day's board rental and US$10–15 for an hour's lesson; bodyboards are also available for US$5/hr and US$10/day.

ARRIVAL AND DEPARTURE

By plane Most hotels offer pick-ups from the airport for US$35 (there are no direct public buses; you must take a shuttle to Comalapa, then take bus #187 to La Libertad – cheap but a hassle).

By bus The easiest option from San Salvador to Playa El Tunco is to catch direct buses #102, #107 or #177 (daily 6am–7pm, every 20min; 1hr) from Parque Bolívar. You can also catch plenty of buses from La Libertad (see p.219).

ACCOMMODATION

Hotel Pupa C Principal ☎ 7529 1414, ⓔ hotelpupa @gmail.com. Justly popular hotel owned by local surfer Oscar "Pupa" Amaya, with six simple, clean, a/c

3

cabaña-style rooms with bathrooms, and a cheap dorm. It's closer to the entrance of the village than the water, but still just a short walk to the beach and bars. The leafy grounds contain a small pool, hammocks and a kitchen. Free wi-fi. Cash only. Dorm US$6, double with fan US$25, double with a/c US$30

Papaya Lodge C Principal ☎ 2389 6027, ⓦ papayalodge .com. The best-value accommodation, with good communal space, including a treehouse-like roof terrace, a kitchen, little pool, sitting areas with hammocks, DVDs and books. The large, spotless rooms have a/c or fans with private baths, or you can opt for perfectly acceptable smaller rooms with shared bath. Toss in wi-fi, parking, great staff and a shared kitchen and you can't beat it. Dorm US$10, double without bath US$18, double with bath US$25

Roots Campground Off C Principal (access via D'rocas entrance) ⓦ rootscamping.es.tl. Close to the beach, Roots has its own tents and hosts renowned Saturday-night beach parties at D'roca's. US$5

La Sombra Off C Principal (before Hotel Mopelia) ⓦ surflibre.com. Rooms – doubles with shared or private baths, and fans or a/c – are simple but clean, with a small pool, free wi-fi, cable TV and kitchen (morning coffee included). Managed by a pro-surfer, José, who offers surf lessons for US$15/hr. Minimum stay 3 nights. Dorm US$7, double with shared bath & fan US$16, double with private bath & a/c US$28

Tunco Lodge C Principal ☎ 2389 6318, ⓦ tuncolodge .com. Sparkling rooms, with or without a/c, and with shared or private bath, plus a pool, free internet and huge showers; also airport pick-ups for US$35 (US$30 from San Salvador city centre). Double with no a/c & shared bath US$30, double with a/c & shared bath US$40, double with a/c & private bath US$50

Zuzu's Hangout Guest House Carretera del Litoral km 42 ☎ 2389 6239, ⓦ zuzusplayaeltunco.com. Bare-bones hostel on the main highway, with a small dorm and a mix of doubles, free wi-fi and use of kitchen – not bad if you intend to surf all day, but this is probably a last resort. Rents boards for US$5/hr or US$10/day, lessons US$8/hr. Dorm US$10, double with shared bath US$20, double with private bath US$40

EATING AND DRINKING

Dale! Dale! Café C La Bocana. The best coffee in town (US$1–2), and the widest choice, with healthy snacks and breakfast options (granola, fresh fruits) from US$3.45. Free wi-fi. Daily 6am–5pm.

D'rocas Beach Bar & Restaurant Off C Principal ☎ 2389 6313. Party central, right on the beach, with cabañas for rent (from US$15) and a large pool (day use US$3); Thurs is ladies' night, Fri and Sat sees live music – you'll pay US$3 cover on Sat. Thurs–Sat 5pm–2am.

BREW REVOLUTION

In 2012, US expat Andy Newbom opened **Brew Revolution** (Wed–Sun 9am–5pm; ⓦ brewrevolution.com), a micro cervecería right next to the Hotel Mopelia entrance on Calle Principal. His small bar sells craft beers to drink or to go: Mercurio IPA, Venus Wit (a Belgian wheat beer with local passionfruit and pineapple) and Nyx Black Ale (a meaty black pale ale, laced with hops and coffee). Three seasonal beers rotate. Prices are US$4–4.25 for a 333ml bottle or draught. You can also drink Andy's beer in the Hotel Mopelia bar, and it is increasingly available in San Salvador – try Zanzibar (p.213).

Hotel Mopelia C Principal ☎ 2389 6265, ⓦ hotelmopelia -salvador.com. Even if you can't afford to stay here, it's worth visiting the bar, which has around forty beers on offer and a huge cocktail menu (the margaritas are especially tasty); combine with a visit to Brew Revolution at the entrance (see box above). Daily 4pm–late.

Restaurante La Bocana C La Bocana ☎ 2389 6238, ⓦ restaurantelabocana.com. The sprawling grande dame restaurant of Tunco, right at the end of the beach road, with two floors overlooking the ocean. Serves huge seafood platters (US$8–13), frozen coconuts (US$1.50) and ice-cold beers (US$7.50 per baldo), accompanied by sporadic live music. Daily 8am–10pm.

Soya Nutribar C Principal ☎ 7887 1596. Healthful, nutritious meals and drinks; natural licuados and smoothies from US$2–2.50, using fresh yoghurt and soy milk, as well as more substantial fish salads (US$5). Daily 8am–5pm.

Taco Guanaco C La Bocana ☎ 7730 5933. This two-storey palapa knocks out delicious and filling Mexican tacos for US$2 and burgers for US$1.50. You'll smell the mouthwatering aromas from the kitchen before you see it. It's usually the last place to close at weekends. Daily 7am–10pm (to sunrise Fri & Sat).

★ **Tunco Veloz** C Principal (opposite Tekuani Ka Hotel) ☎ 2319 8611. Candidate for best pizza in the country – proper thin crusts and local ingredients (the "Jala-Piña" features spicy jalapeno peppers and pineapple). Large pizzas to share US$10. Tues–Sun 5–10pm.

DIRECTORY

Banks Banco Hipotecario has an ATM (daily 8am–9pm) inside the Roca Sunzal Resort; there's also a Banco Agrícola ATM inside Surfo's & Tiki Travel in the centre of the village.
Internet Most places offer wi-fi. Your best chance of using a computer to get online is at the Mangle store or Sunzal Surf Shop in the centre.
Police Tourist Police, C Principal (☎ 2389 6102).

Playa El Sunzal

Wading across an ankle-deep estuary from El Tunco takes you to the long and wide black sands of **PLAYA EL SUNZAL** (road access at km 44.5, either side of the Sunzal River). This first section of Sunzal is close to the highway and a few high-priced hotels on the cliffs – there's a cheaper collection of *palapas* further around the headland. For **surfing**, this is the best learners' beach in the country, with long, uncrowded breaks. It's also good for sunbathing, swimming and just lounging on the sand. While this is all easily accessible from Tunco (and Tunco's surf shops are accessible from here), staying here offers the benefit of a distinctly more laidback atmosphere.

INFORMATION

Internet Across the road from *Surfer's Inn* (right on the highway), Ciber Fox (daily 8am–8pm; US$1/hr) has the fastest internet around.

ACCOMMODATION AND EATING

There's a string of *comedores* by the highway near the river – and the basic *Rancho Carolina* and *Rancho Gladys* along the *palapa* strip on the far side of the headland.

San Patricio Carretera del Litoral km 44.5 (on the highway, 250m from the beach) ☎ 2389 6107, ⓦ ranchosanpatricio.es.tl. More comfortable en-suite rooms than *Surfer's Inn*, with a splash pool and free internet. US$15

Sunzal Point Surf Lodge Carretera del Litoral km 44 (take the road to the beach before the river) ☎ 7842 8886, ⓦ surfsunzal.com. The closest hostel to the waves, right on the jungly point in the middle of Sunzal (it pioneered surfing in the area, starting in 1961). Great-value dorms, plus basic, cheap doubles, fans, hammocks and communal kitchen. Dorm US$7, double US$18

Surfer's Inn Carretera del Litoral km 44.5 (on the beach) ☎ 2389 6266. Well-shaded camping and basic, concrete en-suite rooms with access to a kitchen and fridge. Camping US$6, double US$10

★ TREAT YOURSELF

Café Sunzal *Casa de Mar Hotel*, Carretera del Litoral km 43 ☎ 2389 6020, ⓦ surfeldorado.com. This plush restaurant high above the surf at El Sunzal is definitely the place to splurge on this stretch of coast; the views are phenomenal, the breeze is cooling and the seafood is excellent. The Caribbean-style shrimp, ceviches and sashimi are especially good, but the steak with rosemary cream sauce is also a worthy house special. Mains from US$12. Sun–Thurs 11am–5.30pm, Fri & Sat 11am–9.30pm.

Playa El Zonte

Down a track just beyond the bridge at km 53, the small, surfer-dominated **PLAYA EL ZONTE** is a real gem, set apart by its stunning location between two high headlands and its friendly community vibe. Sparkling grey volcanic sands cover the beach in the dry season (divided by the river), but recede as the waves grow from March to October. The surf here is harder going for beginners than Sunzal and Tunco, better suiting those who are intermediate and above. However, this is no reason for non-surfers to avoid it, as anyone can enjoy the surroundings, swim and join evening games of football.

ACCOMMODATION AND EATING

Costa Brava Carretera del Litoral km 53.5 (high on the cliffs at the western end of the beach, just off the highway) ☎ 2302 6068 or ☎ 7025 9934. Great food and drinks from Manuel, a Spanish cable-TV chef and local celebrity. His big breakfasts (US$3.25) and excellent seafood dishes (US$6.75–12.50) are great value, though he is only usually there at weekends. Mon–Fri 8am–8pm, Sat 8am–11pm, Sun 7am–7pm.

Esencia Nativa Carretera del Litoral km 53 (turn off the highway before the bridge) ☎ 7337 8879, ⓦ esencianativa .com. Pleasant rooms around a yard containing a pool, bar

EL SALVADOR'S BEST HIDDEN BREAKS

Heading west of El Zonte along the Carretera del Litoral will bring you to three more great and often empty **surfing spots**. **Km 59**, a right-hand beach and point break, tubing when big (though poor at low tide), is often compared to Punta Roca, but without the crowds. Around the corner, **Km 61** has equally empty long breaks for longboarders. Further along, **Playa Mizata** at km 87 is a wave machine, with point and beach breaks going right and left. All three can be reached on the #197 or #287 buses from La Libertad.

3

> ### ★ TREAT YOURSELF
>
> **El Dorado Surf Resort** Playa El Zonte
> ☎ 7226 6166, ⊕ surfeldorado.com.
> Welcoming Quebecois owners and a
> great atmosphere at this top-notch surfer
> haven with clean, comfortable rooms and
> dorms. Surfers (and non-surfers) will find
> everything they need – board rental,
> lessons, longboard skateboards, even a
> training pool – and staff will even help
> guests plan their travels. One of the
> country's best treats. Dorm US$22, double
> US$72

and pizza restaurant, as well as hammocks, airy upstairs terrace, plenty of reading material and table football. The owner, Alex Novoa, really knows his surfing and will organize rental (US$10/day) and surf lessons (US$10/hr). Double with fan US$25, double with a/c US$35

Playa San Diego

Some 5km east from La Libertad along the Carretera del Litoral, languid **PLAYA SAN DIEGO**, with its light grey, seemingly endless, scrubby but generally clean stretch of sand, is deserted during the week except for a few fishermen. Views to the sea from the 7km dirt road behind the beach are blocked by ranks of private homes behind locked gates, but get off the bus outside the *Hotel Villa del Pacífico* and you can follow a path just to the left that leads down to the sand.

ACCOMMODATION AND EATING

Cheap accommodation options at San Diego are pretty poor, but there are some good budget places to eat.
Hostal Tortuga Feliz C Principal, Pasaje Ote 15 no. 158 ☎ 2542 2252. Halfway along the strip; similar prices and food to *La Finkita*, with two swimming pools and a chance to see nesting turtles crawling up the beach (tours US$6). Set breakfasts from US$3, lunch and dinner US$6. Daily 8am–10pm.
Hotel Villa del Pacífico C Principal, Pasaje 1 (right by the western end of the beach, nearest the highway) ☎ 2345 5681. The best place to stay: a/c rooms with bath, plus a restaurant and a pool set in manicured gardens. US$50
Rancho La Finkita C Principal, Pasaje 16 (half way along the strip) ☎ 2373 8730. Good-value chicken and steaks (US$3–5) as well as the obligatory fish dishes. Daily noon–10pm.

COSTA DEL SOL

Ever wondered why El Salvador's main airport is so far away from the capital? The airport was built in the late 1970s primarily to serve the nation's premier beach playground, the **COSTA DEL SOL**, a 15km peninsula with a strip of palm-fringed beaches on the southern side. Development was put on hold by the civil war, but now the coast is lined with a wall of hotels and resorts, making free beach access difficult. This and widespread price inflation makes the Costa del Sol an area that is tough on travellers with a budget, but there are some exceptions – and the beach really is magnificent.

Playa San Marcelino to Playa Los Blancos

Behind **Playa San Marcelino**, the first beach along the strip, lies a collection of enticing seafood restaurants, but for an easier route to the water, continue some 3km east to **Playa Costa del Sol**, where a *parque recreativo* (daily 7am–6pm; US$1) rents cabañas for the day. A few kilometres further on, at km 66, is **Playa Los Blancos**, where there are a couple of cheapish hotels.

ARRIVAL AND DEPARTURE

By bus Bus access to the Costa del Sol usually means a change in the humdrum town of Zacatecoluca, or just Zacate, some 45km southeast of San Salvador on the Carretera del Litoral. From here, bus #193 (twice hourly; 1hr 30min) serves La Puntilla via all beaches. You can reach Zacatecoluca from La Libertad (#540; 7 daily; 2hr), San Salvador, Terminal del Sur (#133; every 15min; 1hr) and San Vicente (#177; every 15min; 1hr).

ACCOMMODATION AND EATING

Haydee Mar Blvd Costa del Sol km 66 (about 50m before the *Mila*), Playa Los Blancos ☎ 2338 2046. This hotel has two pools, but is haunted by a deadly sense of kitsch. Good-value set meals (breakfast US$2.50, lunch US$4, dinner US$7). Rates increase by $20 at weekends. US$30
Kenny Mar Blvd Costa del Sol km 60, Playa San Marcelino ☎ 2352 5429, ⊕ restaurantekennymar.net. Award-winning restaurant serving fresh seafood and sandwiches (US$3–13) and cheaper breakfasts from US$2.50. Known for its massive and (deceptively) potent frozen strawberry daiquiris. Mon–Fri 9am–9pm, Sat & Sun 8am–9pm.

BOAT TRIPS AROUND THE ESTERO

A **boat trip** around the Estero is really the highlight of this section of coast. *Lancha* owners run trips from La Puntilla across to the **Isla de Tasajera**, around the mangrove swamps of the Estero and up the Río Lempa. You'll be approached by touts as soon as you step off the bus, but don't let yourself be led to a boat or you'll pay the "agent's" commission. It's better to go hunt a boat down yourself; it should cost no more than US$45 per boat for 2–3 hours, so try to get a group together to reduce costs.

Mini Hotel y Restaurante Mila Blvd Costa del Sol km 66, Playa Los Blancos ☎ 2338 2074. The area's best deal, with nine small but comfortable rooms with fans (five more with a/c), a swimming pool and beach access. Sells decent sandwiches for US$2. Double without bath US$12, double with bath US$20

Playa La Puntilla

At the far eastern tip of the Costa del Sol (km 78), **Playa La Puntilla** is a sleepy array of thatch-and-bamboo beach shacks with a dazzling view across the mouth of the **Estero de Jaltepeque** and the Río Lempa – most people come here for the boat trips (see box above). There is inexpensive lodging here, but it is shockingly bad. There are plenty of cheap *comedores* along the beach serving fresh seafood, though most only open at weekends.

THE EASTERN BEACHES

Wider and wilder than their western counterparts, the **eastern beaches** tend to be over-visited by Salvadoreños at the weekend but under-visited during the week – the whole stretch offers you the chance to stay in rustic surroundings where you are unlikely to see another traveller for days on end. The exception is **El Cuco**, where the active beachside community is supplemented by large annual doses of surfers during the wet season.

Puerto El Triunfo

Around 7km south of the Carretera del Litoral (and some 20km southwest of the unexceptional town of **Usulután**),

PUERTO EL TRIUNFO is a shabby port set on the north shore of the **Bahía de Jiquilisco**, separated from the ocean by the San Juan del Gozo peninsula. Formed by coastal mangrove swamps, the pristine bay features 12km of waterways and a number of jungly islands. A long, fine sandy beach forms the ocean side of the peninsula, while floating platforms can be swum to from the bay-side beach.

Corral de Mulas

From Puerto El Triunfo passenger boats (US$2) cross to El Icaco on **CORRAL DE MULAS** on the peninsula. Boats leave when full, which happens much more regularly in the early morning (last boat back around 4pm); if you miss these, renting a boat can be costly – expect to pay up to US$45. Corral de Mulas offers the opportunity to engage in old-fashioned, rural Salvadoran life – it's a great place to walk and chat to locals, and as well as camping you can ask to stay with a family when here.

ARRIVAL AND DEPARTURE

By bus Puerto El Triunfo is connected to San Miguel (#377; every 40min; 3hr) and San Salvador (#185; 6 daily; 2hr) – for Playa El Espino, change in Usulután (#363; every 10min; 1hr).

ACCOMMODATION

If you want to stay on Corral de Mulas, either with a local family or camping, ask at Puerto El Triunfo's *alcaldía* (town hall) and they will help you out.

El Jardín 1 Av Nte 4, Puerto El Triunfo ☎ 2663 6089. Between the pier and the bus station, this small, grubby place is the only formal place to stay. US$14

Playa El Espino

Once one of El Salvador's finest swathes of sand, **PLAYA EL ESPINO** is no longer a remote, undeveloped beach, with a 26km paved road from the Carretera del Litoral opening it up to visitors. Sadly, some of this redevelopment is distinctly garish, and even the beach itself has receded in recent years, the water lapping the waterside *palapas* at high tide. Weekends see crowds of day-trippers from Usulután, while during the week many businesses simply close down. What remains of the palm-fringed beach can be magical, and if

3

you are travelling by car, Espino is worth a look (ask anywhere in Usulután about the latest beach situation), but getting here by bus is not worth the hassle – make for El Cuco (see below) instead.

ARRIVAL AND DEPARTURE

By bus Access to Playa El Espino is via Usulután on the Carretera del Litoral (from Usulután take #351 or #358B, changing at Jucurán to #358; 7 daily, last one back at 4pm; 1hr 45min). Usulután is connected to Puerto El Triunfo (#363; frequent; 1hr), San Miguel (#373; frequent; 1hr 40min), San Salvador (#302; frequent; 2hr 30min), San Vicente (#417; 6 daily; 2hr) and Santiago de María, for transfers to Alegría (#392C, #35, #348 or #349; very frequent; 45min).

ACCOMMODATION AND EATING

It is best to be in a group of four or five to stay cheaply on Espino, though all accommodation is bare-bones. Book the hotels ahead at weekends. A host of *comedores* and basic restaurants on the beach sell similar dishes, though prices for seafood are high and the quality varies.

Arcos del Espino C Principal (at the entrance to the area next to the beach) ☎ 2608 0686. Basic, spotless en-suite rooms (for four people) with a/c, set around a crystal-clear pool. **US$38**

Natali 300m on right as you reach the beach ☎ 7254 9215. The a/c and en-suite rooms here – with use of a kitchen – sleep five people, including one in an indoor hammock. **US$45**

Playa El Cuco

Some 30km east of Usulután, the Carretera del Litoral turns south, descending towards the east's most famous beach community, **PLAYA EL CUCO**. The village itself is rather manic, with a beachfront crowded by tourism opportunists. The beaches to either side,

---

> ### TURTLES AND PELICANS AT TORTUGA VERDE
>
> Curious about turtles and pelicans? *La Tortuga Verde* hostel (see opposite) in El Esterón doubles as a **turtle sanctuary** and **pelican retreat**; pelicans roam the property freely (the owner helps rehabilitate injured birds), and turtles are born on the beach here year round. Guests get to help release the hatchlings into the sea – a magical experience.

however, are ravishing: the 300m breaks at **Las Flores** to the west, and the wide and empty peace of **El Esterón** to the east.

ARRIVAL AND INFORMATION

By bus The ride from San Miguel to Playa El Cuco is one of the finest bus journeys in the country, with sensational views of the valleys and Volcán San Miguel; sit on the right side of the bus on the way to El Cuco for the best view.

Destinations San Miguel (#320; twice hourly; for La Unión transfer at El Delirio; 1hr 30min); Usulután (#373; twice hourly).

Internet There are no internet cafés in El Esterón, but non-guests can use the computer or wi-fi at *La Tortuga Verde* for US$1/hr. There is a small, two-computer internet place in El Cuco next to the police station, as well as the *El Cuco Diner* (US$1/hr or free with purchase of US$3 or more).

ACCOMMODATION

Most accommodation in El Cuco itself is terrible, but there are excellent options to the east. A mini US-expat enclave has opened several good backpacker hostels in El Esterón.

La Bocanna (aka *Munda's Place*), next to *Cruz's Place*, El Esterón ☎ 7338 9646, ✉ latortugaverderest@yahoo.com. Excellent restaurant (see opposite) with basic singles and doubles, one of which has a/c (US$25), all with fabulous river views. **US$15**

> ### BOATS TO NICARAGUA
>
> *La Tortuga Verde* (see opposite) arranges taxi/ferry transport across to **Nicaragua** (Potosí) – this is a more reliable alternative to the Cruce de Golfo service (see box, p.228). The fare includes the taxi ride to La Unión, which takes 45min. Boats typically leave between 10am and 11am (Mon–Fri only), and take around 2hr 30min. Although *Tortuga* will not guarantee passage, if you pay for at least one night at the hotel, your room is free for every day you are delayed thereafter (apart from Sat & Sun, when no boats run). For 1–2 people the charge is US$75/person; it's just US$70/person for 3–4 people and US$65 for 5–6 people. Tortuga can also arrange for a private car to take you all the way to León for an additional US$125.
>
> Taking just the boat back from Potosí to La Unión is much cheaper (see box, p.228). Private boats are also available daily, for US$375 (maximum of eight people).

Cucolindo Near town along the road, El Esterón ☎ 2619 9012. This beach-fronted place is a decent budget option, with clean rooms. U$$30

Cuco Surf Dorm El Cuco ☎ 7338 9646 ⓦ cucosurfdorm .com. This bargain hostel in the centre of El Cuco (one block from the ocean) is the town's only decent option, with a six-bunk dorm, each with its own private locker (locks can be rented for US$1). Shared bathroom with shower, communal kitchen and free surfboard storage. Guests get a free coconut (claim at *Cuco Diner* next door), and cheap board rentals and surf lessons. Dorm U$$7

Rio Mar A house before the end of the beach road, El Esterón ☎ 7338 9646, ⓦ latortugaverderest@yahoo.com. For the best sea views and a pool by the ocean, snag a double room at this great restaurant (see below). Some singles available. U$$20

★ **La Tortuga Verde** C Pacífica, El Esterón ☎ 7774 4855, ⓦ latortugaverde.com. Excellent hotel, run by US-expat Tom Pollak, and right on the seafront – it features arty hidden lighting (so not to disturb turtles hatching nearby) and a restaurant overlooking the beach serving fresh fish and fruit. They have doubles, some with a/c (for $10 more), a dorm and a good-value "room & board backpacker special": a double bed in the dorm plus breakfast and lunch for US$17. They also have a turtle and pelican sanctuary (see box opposite), a tiki bar, *lanchas* that will take you to Isla Meanguera, the famous surf break of Punta Mango and Las Flores (also by car), and they coordinate with boats to Potosí in Nicaragua (see box opposite). Dorm (4 double beds) U$$10, double U$$25

EATING

★ **La Bocanna** (aka *Munda's Place*), next to *Cruz's Place*, El Esterón ☎ 7338 9646, ⓦ latortugaverderest@yahoo .com. New spot with jaw-dropping views of the ocean and the volcano across in Nicaragua; sit in the shaded patio and enjoy the fresh fish and *conchas* (local black river clams) as the sun sets (mains from US$5). Manager Munda sources her fish daily from local fishermen, and has a secret supply of green coconuts from trees imported from Thailand (much sweeter than the Central American kind). Watch the local kids play football on the beach opposite. Daily 7am–7pm.

Cruz's Place At the end of the beach road and down the right-hand cul-de-sac, El Esterón. This *comedor* has long had a reputation for quality seafood; it's unofficially named after the owner, Cruz, who goes fishing every day, and serves the catch to a faithful bunch of regulars. Enjoy superb views of the ocean while you eat (mains US$4–9). Daily 7am–7pm.

★ **El Cuco Diner** Opposite the football stadium, El Cuco ⓦ cucodiner.com. The best place to eat and drink in El Cuco itself. The menu features fabulous comfort food: bacon-and-cheeseburgers, fries, hot dogs, tofu sandwiches, milk-shakes, root beer floats, fresh fish and sloppy joe – fruit

smoothies served from the *cantina* next door (with optional shots of rum). Daily 10am–7pm.

Rio Mar A house before the end of the beach road, El Esterón ☎ 7338 9646, ⓦ latortugaverderest@yahoo.com. Another relatively new place with eye-popping views, right on the ocean. Also specializes in seafood and *conchas*, but in addition serves excellent fried chicken and hamburgers. Day visitors can use the lovely pool here for US$2. Daily 7am–7pm.

Playa Las Tunas and Playa El Tamarindo

Some 22km east of the El Cuco turn-off along the Carretera del Litoral, another side-road heads along the tooth-like **Península Punta Amapala**, pointing into the mouth of the Golfo de Fonseca. **PLAYA LAS TUNAS**, on the south side, is the first beach that you encounter, with a fine dark-sand beach and tides that wash right up into the beachside *ramadas*. It has a friendly atmosphere to it, and, budget-wise, it is your best option for accommodation on a beach between Cuco and La Unión. There's a small village here with several restaurants open for lunch only, right on the beach, selling fresh fish and oysters and offering plenty of hammocks for a post-prandial lounge.

The final beach at the northern tip of the peninsula, **PLAYA EL TAMARINDO**, is a panorama-lover's dream. The huge golden arc of sand, backed by uninterrupted palm trees, curves around the mountainous bay; sitting beneath the Volcán de Conchagua, the islands of the Golfo de Fonseca loom large, and in the distance the mountainsides of Honduras and Nicaragua are clearly visible. The beach faces a protected cove with very little wave action, making it ideal for swimming. On the downside, gangs have been taking over this area in recent years and many locals have moved away – there's not much in the way of places to stay or eat, either, so it's best as a day-trip. Check in La Unión or at La Tortuga Verde in El Cuco (see above) for the latest situation.

ARRIVAL AND DEPARTURE

By bus Buses to La Unión run along the peninsula, passing through Las Tunas (#383; three hourly); the last one back leaves at 5pm.

ACCOMMODATION AND EATING

Rancho Las Tunas Playa La Tunas ☏ 2526 5542. The highlight of the restaurants and places to stay at Tunas, perched on a rock that's surrounded by rushing water at high tide, and serving the best oysters (US$7) in the area. They also have two rather pricey rooms on the beach side, with a small pool and stupendous views. **US$45**

Tropi Tamarindo Playa El Tamarindo ☏ 2649 5082. The only accommodation on the beach is too pricey for what are little more than standard mid-range rooms, but they will let you use the pool and loungers if you spend US$10, so it's a good spot for beers and food. **US$55**

LA UNIÓN

The grimy port town of **LA UNIÓN** sits in a stunning location on a bay on the edge of the Golfo de Fonseca. There are no particular attractions here, but the town is a useful jumping-off point for trips to the beautiful islands of the **Golfo de Fonseca** (see opposite). Shops are scarce on the islands, and prices high, so it's worth stocking up before you go. Budget accommodation is limited, sketchy and not recommended in La Unión; skip the town and stay on the islands or in El Cuco instead, where you can arrange onward travel to Nicaragua (see p.226).

ARRIVAL AND INFORMATION

By bus The main bus terminal is on 3A C Pte, between 4A and 6A Av Nte, two blocks west and one north of the Parque Central. If you're travelling along the coastal highway, you will need the Terminal Los Cantones, two blocks south and one block west of the main terminal, on C San Carlos.

Departures from the main terminal San Miguel (#324; very frequent; 1hr); San Salvador (#304; twice hourly; 2hr 30min); Santa Rosa de Lima (#342; every 15min; 1hr 30min) – change here for the Honduran border at El Amatillo. There are also *especial* buses to San Miguel (#304

and others, frequent departures all day; 40min); and San Salvador (#304; 4am, 6am & 12.30pm; 2hr).

Departures from Terminal los Cantones Conchagua (#382; 4 daily; 30min); El Tamarindo, via Las Tunas (#383; every 20min; 1hr 30min).

Ferries to the Golfo de Fonseca See opposite.

Banks Banco Agrícola, 1A C Pte & Av General Cabañas, or Scotiabank, 3A C Ote & 1A Av Nte, one block downhill from the Parque (both Mon–Fri 8am–4pm, Sat 8am–noon), change money and have 24hr ATMs.

EATING

Cappuccino's 1A C Ote & 3A Av Nte, two blocks down from the Parque ☏ 2605 3091. Freshly brewed coffee and espresso, as well as tasty sandwiches and breakfasts (from US$2) – the perfect place to chill out while you wait for the boat across to Nicaragua. Mon–Sat 7.30am–7pm, Sun 7.30am–1.30pm.

De Todo supermarket 1A Av Sur between 2A & 4A C Ote. Handily located, just a block south of the Parque. Daily 7am–6pm.

CONCHAGUA

Looming to the south of La Unión is **Volcán de Conchagua** (1225m), with scintillating views across the gulf to Nicaragua and Honduras. The friendly village of **CONCHAGUA**, sitting on its northern slopes, was founded in 1543. The climate is fresher here, a pleasant relief from the heat of La Unión, and the village contains one of the oldest churches in the country, dating back to 1693 and dedicated to Santiago Apóstol.

From Conchagua pick-ups will take you to the lookout point up the **volcano** (cars pay US$5 to park; locals also charge US$2/car or US$1/person to pass through the gate on the road to the *mirador*), where there are short and long walking routes. If driving, you'll need a 4WD.

TO NICARAGUA BY BUS AND BOAT

Cruce del Golfo (ⓦ crucedelgolfo.com) boats link La Unión with **León** (US$99) and **Potosí** (US$65) in **Nicaragua** every Tuesday and Friday, but only if they have a group of ten to twelve people. You need to arrive at the harbour by 8.30am to complete immigration formalities before the boat departs; after a short break at Isla Meanguera the boat (a covered speed boat) arrives at Potosí around 11.30am. After clearing immigration (1hr), a 4WD car takes you to León in around 3hr (arriving 3.30pm), and will drop off at your hotel. *La Tortuga Verde* in El Cuco can also organize this trip (see p.227), and offers cheaper rates from Potosí back to La Unión: US$45/person for 1–2 people, US$40/person for 3–4 people, and US$35/person for 5–6 people. You'll have to take a taxi (45min; US$35) or bus (see above) to El Cuco from La Unión.

ARRIVAL AND DEPARTURE

By bus Bus #382 arrives in Conchagua from the Terminal los Cantones in La Unión (5 daily; 15min).

ACCOMMODATION AND EATING

Note that there are no stores or restaurants on the volcano, so you will need to bring your own supplies.

Pupusódromo Parque Central, Conchagua village. In the evenings you can grab a delicious *pupusa* from the collection of ten *pupuserías* along the side of the Parque. Stalls daily 9am–10pm (*pupusas* served from 6pm).

Volcán de Conchagua (CODECA) ☎ 2604 5320, ✉ ongcodeca@yahoo.com. Camping and simple accommodation with shared bathrooms at a stomach-tingling spot near the summit of the volcano. Camping US$5, double US$20

ISLAS DEL GOLFO DE FONSECA

Four delightfully secluded **islands** – Conchagüita, Martín Pérez, Meanguera and Zacatillo – sit out in the **GOLFO DE FONSECA** under the stewardship of El Salvador, all a short boat ride from La Unión. **Isla Zacatillo**, the nearest island to La Unión (9km) and once a prison, is just four square kilometres with a small fishing settlement and a few unremarkable beaches; tiny **Isla Martín Pérez** (just a half square kilometre), 1km beyond, has some sandy coves, but no facilities for visitors. Further south, visitor-friendly **Isla Conchagüita** (a circular 8.45 square kilometres) was sacked by English pirates in 1782 and remained deserted until the 1920s, when settlers finally began moving back. In its centre, on the Cerro del Pueblo Viejo, are the remains of a tiny pre-Columbian (Lenca) settlement; a path to the north of the ruins leads up to a large rock bearing engravings that some believe is a map of the gulf. Even now in the two small settlements of Conchagüita and El Líbano you can see fairer, blue-eyed, pirate descendants among the islands' inhabitants.

Rumour has it that Sir Francis Drake buried a stash of Spanish silver while at anchor on **Isla Meanguera Del Golfo**, the largest island (23.6 square kilometres) and the furthest away from La Unión (30km). There are still plenty of secluded coves to explore, as well as good swimming and boundless scope for hiking. For fantastic views of the surroundings, climb Cerro de Evaristo, the highest peak on Meanguera. The best **beach** on the islands, Playa El Majahual, is also on Meanguera (south side). Wide, tranquil and with black sand, it can be reached on foot in 45 minutes by the road south of town and the track it turns into, or by boat in ten minutes if you can persuade a *lancha* owner. For bird lovers, tiny **Isla Meanguerita** off the southeast coast of Meanguera can only be reached by *lancha*.

ARRIVAL AND DEPARTURE

By ferry *Lanchas* for the islands of the Golfo de Fonseca arrive and depart in La Unión (see opposite) on the pier jutting out from the northern end of 3A Av Nte. Public *lanchas* (US$3; 90min) depart La Unión for Meanguera around 10.30am and leave the island for La Unión around 5.30am. There is only one trip per day, so unless you plan to charter a private boat you will have to stay overnight. *Lanchas* from La Unión to Zacatillo (US$3; 20min) depart between 9 and 10am, and return in the afternoon – it's the only island you can visit as a day-trip. The only way to visit Martín Pérez is by private boat – note also that there are no public *lanchas* between the islands, so to island-hop you must return to La Unión or hire a private *lancha*. Schedules are fairly informal; if there are enough people to fill a boat to a specific island, a *lancha* will be allocated to go direct, but if not, the Meanguera *lancha* will usually make stops along the way (at Conchagüita, for example). The fare to any of the islands is usually US$3 one-way.

By private lancha Local boatmen in La Unión will rent out a *lancha* for around US$90–100/boatload to go as far as Meanguera and back, though you can commandeer one on the islands for a little less.

ACCOMMODATION AND EATING

The smaller islands – Conchagüita, Zacatillo and Martín Pérez – have no accommodation, but Meanguera is a terrific getaway spot. The two good backpacker hostels here both have great seafood restaurants with shellfish for

---

★ TREAT YOURSELF

Hotel Joya del Golfo Isla Meanguera ☎ 2648 0072, ⊕ hotellajoyadelgolfo.com. Reservations are essential for this place, a 10min walk up the hill from Meanguera's harbour. It has four wonderful rooms (a/c, cable TV) and an excellent restaurant, plus kayaks, a *lancha* to beaches and extremely friendly US/Salvadoran owners. US$79

less than US$4; they're close enough together to compare. Otherwise, *comedores* in the villages serve fresh seafood, delivered daily by a fishing fleet that floats in the bay.

El Mirador Isla Meanguera ☎ 2648 0072. This pretty hostel has spotless rooms with hard mattresses, en-suite baths, cable TV and perhaps a fractionally better view than *El Paraíso*. US$21

El Paraíso Isla Meanguera ☎ 2648 0145. Older rooms, cable TV and en-suite baths with the elusive hot-water shower. US$25

The east

3

The rough and wild terrain of **eastern El Salvador** remained relatively unexplored territory for the pre-Columbian Pipils, who did not venture far beyond the natural frontier of the Río Lempa into this land of lofty volcanoes, hot plains and mountain ranges. As a result, its Lenca inhabitants developed their society in isolation from the west, and it was only with some difficulty that the Spanish conquered this frontier in 1537.

Today, coffee production around the flower-filled mountain village of **Alegría** and the region's major cities, languid **San Vicente** and bustling **San Miguel**, create a wealth that contrasts cruelly with the rural poverty found further north. Along the **Ruta de Paz**, refugees from communities devastated by the civil war – this region saw the worst of the fighting – have in the last two decades returned to try and pick up the pieces in this wild and beautiful area. Some have turned to "war tourism" as a viable new occupation, but their ongoing struggle with poverty is often still painfully apparent. The former guerrilla stronghold of **Perquín** contains a moving war museum, while the haunting and unmissably sad village of **El Mozote** was the scene of the conflict's most horrific massacre.

COJUTEPEQUE

East of Lago de Ilopango (and some 33km from San Salvador), the Carretera Panamericana flies past the pilgrimage retreat of **COJUTEPEQUE**. There's little to see in the actual town, but a thirty-minute walk south up a zigzagging path from the centre brings you to the **Cerro de las Pavas** and the **Santuario de la Virgen de Fátima**, a shrine dedicated to the famous apparition of Mary reputed to have appeared in Portugal in 1917. The shrine, completed in 1949, attracts worshippers from across the region – devotees believe the Virgin performs miracles, and you'll see offerings piled around her main image, sent here from Spain. A Sunday **food festival** to rival Juayúa's weekend festival (see p.251) starts on the Cerro at 10am, with the imperious summit as a backdrop – be sure to try the *chorizos de cojutepeque*, local sausages famed throughout the country.

ARRIVAL AND DEPARTURE

By bus Bus #113 arrives from San Salvador (frequent; 2hr) – moving on to San Miguel or other towns further east, get off bus #113 at the Carretera Panamericana to change to #301.

ILOBASCO

Some 6km beyond Cojutepeque, a road branches north off the Carretera Panamericana through 22km of enchanting countryside to the small town of **ILOBASCO**, noted for its brightly painted earthenware decorated with animals and everyday scenes. The town's hallmark pieces are known as *sorpresas* (surprises) – detailed scenes of village life contained in small, clay shells (from US$0.50). The government arts organization **CEDART** (Mon–Fri 7.30am–4.30pm; free), on Avenida Bonilla, has a small exhibition on the evolution of ceramic art in the town, and a collection of products in its shop; they'll direct you to a potter you like, or you can just stroll around and visit shops such as ArfaBambú (daily 8.30am–5pm) or Cerámica San Pedro (daily 9am–5pm).

ARRIVAL AND DEPARTURE

By bus #111 (frequent; 1hr 30min) is the nominal service to and from San Salvador, but from the Carretera Panamericana you can change for the quicker #301 to destinations in either direction.

ACCOMMODATION

Hotel Ilobasco 4A C Pte at 7A Av Sur ☎ 2332 2563. Though tatty and overpriced, this friendly hotel will do if you have to stay. Rooms have shared bath. US$32

SAN SEBASTIÁN

Between the turnings for Ilobasco and San Vicente, another paved road leads north off the Carretera Panamericana to the small village of **SAN SEBASTIÁN**, lauded for its hammocks, patterned cloth sheets and bedspreads. The first place to start learning about the traditions and extraordinary patience involved in the town's unique craft is the **Casa de la Cultura** on Calle Molina (Mon–Fri 8am–4pm; free). Several **weaving shops** around town will let you watch the goods being produced on simple wooden looms, though you will be pressured into buying. One of the oldest and best is **Casa Durán**, just off C Molina on 12A Av Nte (Mon–Fri 9.30am–5.30pm). Soft **hammocks** are the prize item; compare prices and materials, then bargain before handing over any money. **Bus** #110 arrives from San Salvador (twice hourly) and #176 arrives from San Vicente (four daily).

SAN VICENTE

Around 60km east of San Salvador, **SAN VICENTE** is a calm, low-slung city with a rich agricultural area producing sugar cane, cotton and coffee. It's a more appealing destination than San Miguel, further along the highway – the one downside is the lack of accommodation. Vicente was sacked during the Insurrection of the Nonualcos in 1833, a doomed indigenous uprising led by Anastasio Aquino (who was later executed here), and the city still has a conspicuous military presence. The barracks are at the southwestern corner of the central Parque Cañas – rivalled only by the number of American Peace Corps trainees, who come here to prepare for forthcoming missions in El Salvador.

WHAT TO SEE AND DO

The centre is compact and laidback with a couple of intriguing sights.

Parque Cañas

The centrepiece of the central **Parque Cañas** is the eye-catching **Torre de San Vicente** (daily 8am–6pm; US$1). Inspired by – and closely resembling – the Eiffel Tower, the 40m clock tower was completed in 1930 and badly damaged by the 2001 earthquake, which killed hundreds here and flattened the entire city centre. It was reopened in 2009 – climb the spiral staircase for the best views of the city.

The **Cathedral** on the Parque was destroyed by the quake, and though it has been rebuilt in the style of the nineteenth-century original, the interior is modern and plain.

Iglesia de Nuestra Señora del Pilar

Two blocks south of the Parque, at Av Crescencio Miranda 2, the **Iglesia de Nuestra Señora del Pilar** (daily 7am–6pm) has far more character than the cathedral. The church was completed in 1769 on the site where a miraculous moving statue of the Virgin Mary persuaded one Manuela de Arce not to stab her husband, or so it's told. Salvadoran independence hero José Simeón Cañas (known as "the liberator of the slaves") was buried here in 1838. The original was restored after earthquake damage, but the modern extension next door remains the primary place of worship (you can enter the older section from a side door).

Dulcería Villalta

Make time for San Vicente's sweetest sight, the **Dulcería Villalta** (Mon–Sat 7.30am–5pm, Sun 7.30am–3pm) north of the Parque at 7A C Pte 4, just off José María Cornejo. Established in 1860, this small shop sells local handmade candies of all shapes and colours, containing local fruits, milk and molasses, and tasting a bit like fudge. Buy an assorted bag (US$2) to take away or munch in the shady garden at the back.

ARRIVAL AND DEPARTURE

By bus The bus station is on 8A C Pte & 15A Av Sur, a long walk southwest of the centre, but all local buses pass the Parque Cañas going in or out (get out when you see the tower). You can also catch a pick-up or local bus (#157; frequent; 10min) 3km up to the Carretera Panamericana to catch the more frequent #301 between San Salvador and San Miguel.

Destinations Costa del Sol (#193E; 4 daily; 2hr 30min); Ilobasco (#530; 3 daily; 1hr); San Salvador, Terminal de

Oriente (#116; frequent; 1hr 30min); Usulután (#417; 6 daily; 2hr); Zacatecoluca (#177; every 15min; 50min).

By taxi Local taxis in the Parque Cañas will take you to San Salvador or San Miguel for US$40 (bargain hard).

ACCOMMODATION

Posada Belén 12A C Pte 25, Barrio San Juan de Dios ☎ 2393 0383 or ☎ 7255 7761, ✉ belenmarisol@live.com. The only decent lodgings in town, popular with North American aid workers and presided over by the friendly Ulises and Marisol (some English spoken). Large, clean rooms with a/c and bathroom, a communal TV lounge, free wi-fi, laundry and a grill in the courtyard. US$25

EATING AND DRINKING

There are a number of bars around Parque Cañas, while the *comedores* that line the western edge are decent options for a cheap buffet lunch (*Acapulco* is the best), and *Guacamambos* is a much-loved hot-dog stand next to *Rivoly* (dogs US$1, burgers US$1.10). If you have to change buses at the Panamericana turn-off to San Vicente, try one of the *tortillas con carne* sold at the stalls here – a local favourite.

Casa Blanca 2A C Ote, just east of 2A Av Sur ☎ 2393 0549. Meat and fish dishes including *codorniz* (quail; US$7) served in a lovely shaded garden that doubles as a good place for an evening drink, though the artsy surroundings are better than the fairly average food. Daily 11am–10pm.

Comedor Rivoly 1A Av Sur, between 2A C Pte & 4A C Pte ☎ 2393 0492. A real treat, with big, fresh and tasty meat meals such as *pollo con arroz* (chicken with rice; US$3.50) on spick-and-span tables. Good breakfasts, too. Daily 7am–8.30pm.

La Nevería Parque Cañas. Welcoming ice-cream shop on the main plaza, knocking out all the usual flavours for just US$0.75 per giant scoop. Daily 11am–9pm.

Pupusería Teresita 4A C Pte, just west of 2A Av Sur. Standard but popular *pupusa* canteen serving tasty filled *pupusas* of cheese and *chicharrón* for US$0.50. Mon–Sat noon–7pm.

Taqueria Mexicana 4A C Pte, between Av Miranda & 2A Av Sur. This small, clean taco shop serves filling taco plates – tortillas, refried beans, cheese, pork and chicken – from US$2, with decent salsas on the side. Daily 11am–10pm.

DIRECTORY

Banks Banco Agrícola and Banco Hipotecario on Parque Cañas, both with ATMs and exchange facilities.

Internet Try Cyber Inser or Ciber Life, both on 4A C Pte either side of 1A Av Sur (daily 10am–7pm; US$0.75/hr).

Pharmacy Farmacia Guadalupe II has branches on 4A C Pte, off 1A Av Sur, and also on 2A Av Sur, just north of 2A C (daily 8am–7pm).

Phones Claro (Mon–Fri 8am–5pm, Sat 8am–noon) is at 2A Av Nte 3, just off the southeast corner of the Parque,

opposite the Súper Selectos supermarket.

Post office C 1 de Julio, one block south of the Parque (Mon–Fri 8am–5pm, Sat 8am–noon).

VOLCÁN CHICHONTEPEC

Looming over San Vicente is one of the most awe-inspiring volcanoes in the country, **VOLCÁN CHICHONTEPEC** (meaning "Hill of Two Breasts" in Nahuatl, and also known as Volcán San Vicente). The second-highest volcano in the country, its twin peaks rising to 2182m, it's considered dormant, with cultivated lower slopes and the steep summit left to scrub and soil. A number of paths lead up the slopes from the village of **San Antonio** on the east side and from **Guadelupe** on the northwest flank. It's a stiff, fairly dull walk of around three to four hours to the top (where there's an old army base) from any of the trails, and good walking shoes, sun protection and lots of water are essential. From the summit, however, there are mind-bending panoramic views north across the Jiboa valley, with San Vicente nestled at the bottom, and west across to Lago de Ilopango. It's possible to do the climb solo, but the paths are unmarked and confusing, so you'd be advised to hire a local guide in either village (ask at the local *alcaldía*; guides are usually free but not always available). Skip the hike altogether in the rainy season (June–Oct). **Buses** to San Antonio and Guadelupe leave every hour or so until mid-afternoon from San Vicente's market.

ALEGRÍA

The whole of the northern El Salvador seems to unfold below the lofty, floral haven of **ALEGRÍA**, 140km east of San Salvador and the highest town in the country (at around 1240m). It's also home to an extraordinary number of flower nurseries – Alegría simply erupts with blossoms during orchid season.

Laguna de Alegría

A 2km gravel road leads from the town up **Volcán Tecapa** to the green, sulphurous **Laguna de Alegría** (daily 8am–5pm; US$0.25), a spring-fed crater lake whose hot and cold waters will strip you of your dead skin if you can take the smell. It's a moderate hike along the road of about 45 minutes (going via the rough paths over the volcano rim can take much longer) – try to get there at 4pm when the water is at its highest. The surrounding area is predominantly coffee-growing country, and occasionally beans can be seen drying on the streets. There's a small shack selling basic snacks and cold beer by the lake.

ARRIVAL AND INFORMATION

Alegría is accessible from the Carretera Panamericana at El Triunfo, 36km east of the San Vicente turning, where a road leads south to Usulután, passing through the pleasant town of Santiago de María; from here a steep but paved road leads 5km up the slopes of Volcán Tecapa into Alegría. Taxis charge around US$20 to El Triunfo.

By bus Buses stop on C Masferrer, 100m or so west of the Parque Central and the main church, San Pedro Apóstol.
Destinations Santiago de María and Usulután (#348; every 30min; 15min); change at Santiago de María for the Carretera Panamericana at El Triunfo (#362; frequent minibuses; 15min).
Internet There's an internet café just off the Parque (opposite the church), on 1A C Pte & 2A Av Sur (Mon–Sat 9am–7pm; US$0.80/hr).
Tourist information Alegriá has a real, live tourist office (daily 7am–4pm; ☎2614 7171) at the northwestern corner of the Parque Central, offering all the usual information, but rarely English-speakers or maps.

ACCOMMODATION

Cabañas La Estancia de Daniel CM Araujo, 2A Av Sur (just off the Parque) ☎2628 1030, ✉fredypostecapa @yahoo.com. Inviting home surrounded by trees and flowers, with five cabañas with cable TV and free wi-fi – the amenities are almost as good as at *Entre Piedras* (see below), and prices are lower. Breakfast US$2.50. __US$10__
Casa Alegre Av C Campos ☎7201 8641, ⓦlacasaalegre .org. The coolest place to stay, with firm beds in clean rooms with a shared bathroom below the studio of the artists who own it. __US$14__
Casa del Huéspedes La Palma 1a Ave Nte (on the west side of the Parque Central) ☎2628 1012. The friendly old owners here have lovingly maintained the original old-fashioned decor. Bed sizes and firmness vary, but there are hot showers and free wi-fi. It's a better deal for solo travellers, as rates (US$10) are per person. __US$20__
Hostal Entre Piedras Parque Central ☎2605 5886, ⓦhostalentrepiedras.com. Right on the plaza, this is the best place to stay in town, with wood-panelled rooms with hot water, cable TV and free wi-fi. The restaurant is great, too (see below). __US$32__

EATING AND DRINKING

Café Entre Piedras Parque Central ☎2605 5886, ⓦhostalentrepiedras.com. The best restaurant in town, linked to the guesthouse, serving a vast range of dishes from baguettes and *churrasco* steaks (from US$7), to local "Alegría Bourbon" coffee and delicious pastries (US$1.50) to enjoy on the relaxing terrace. Daily 7.30am–10pm.
Casita de mi Abuelo C M. Araujo, just beyond 4A Av Nte. Streetside *comedor* and *tienda* serving sandwiches (US$1.25), ice cream, milkshakes and beers (US$1). Cool off or chill out in the shade. Daily noon–9pm.
Merendero Mi Pueblito C A. Masferrer (just east of the Parque, opposite the *alcaldía)* ☎2628 1038. The town's most in-vogue restaurant, with jaw-dropping views all the way to the northern border from its own *mirador*, and dishing up big portions (*pollo dorado* US$4.50) and good veg options. Daily 8am–7pm.
El Portal Parque Central. Decent *carne asada*, *pupusas*, rabbit, deer and *pelibüey* (a local breed of sheep) from US$4.50–7. It's a favourite place for locals to sip beers and enjoy the action on the Parque. Daily 9.30am–9pm.
Pupusería Cristina 4A Av Sur & Pasaje Grimaldi. The best *pupusería* in town (standard US$0.35), with a well-above-average *chicharrón*-filled option (US$0.50). Daily 4–9pm.

SAN MIGUEL

Some 135km east of San Salvador, the chaotic and blisteringly hot city of **SAN MIGUEL** is the country's third-largest city, though despite being the birthplace of several national heroes and home to some great places **to eat**, it is surprisingly short on sights and attractions. The most exciting time to visit is during the November **Carnaval**, a huge and free event, supposedly the biggest in Central America. San Miguel is a major transportation hub you can't avoid if travelling by bus, but unless you arrive late, frequent connections mean you can pass straight through – you won't miss much.

Initially the least important of the Spanish cities, San Miguel grew wealthy firstly through the profits of gold, and then on the coffee, cotton and *henequén* grown on the surrounding fertile land, leading to the nickname "The Pearl of the East". More recently it was a centre of

3

SAN MIGUEL

Terminal de
San Miguel

Farmacia
Brasil

Antiguo Teatro
Nacional

Cathedral

Claro

Alcaldía

CALLE SIRAMA ORIENTE

Casa de
Francisco
Gavidia

Parque
David J.
Guzmán

Farmacia
Brasil

Dispensa
Familiar

Scotiabank

AVENIDA JOSÉ SIMEÓN CAÑAS SUR

Casa de David
J. Guzmán

Banco
Hipotecario

Parque
Gerardo
Barrios

Market
Stalls

AVENIDA GERARDO BARRIOS NORTE

Mercado

Casa de Juan
José Cañas

Market Stalls

CALLE CHAPARRASTIQUE

Farmacia
Brasil

AVENIDA MONSEÑOR ROMERO

Capilla de la
Medalla
Milagrosa

Universitario
de Oriente

Centro Comercial
de Artesanías

Parque del
Centenario

AVENIDA ROOSEVELT NORTE

Cemetery

RUTA MILITAR

metres
0   250

⬤ 9.   ⬤ 10.   ⬤ 11. & Metrocentro

▲

▲ 4 (100m)

N

ACCOMMODATION
Caleta	4
Hotel del Centro	1
Hotel El Guanaco	3
King Palace	2

⬤ EATING
Bati Jugos Carlitos	3
Comedor y Pupusería Chilita	1
Comedor Vicky	6
Conchadromo Esmerelda	2
El Paraíso	4
Pastelería Francesa	5
La Perna	11

⬤ DRINKING & NIGHTLIFE
Mama Gallina's	8
Maya	7
El Paisa	10
Papagallo's	9

arms trading during the civil war, though today the city's grimy streets hum and rattle with more mundane forms of commerce – downtown resembles the market-smothered Centro Histórico in the capital, albeit on a smaller scale.

WHAT TO SEE AND DO

The city is laid out in the usual quasi-grid system, with the main avenida (Av Gerardo Barrios/Av José Simeón Cañas) and the main calle (C Chaparrastique/C Sirama) intersecting at **Parque Gerardo Barrios**, surrounded by market stalls. However, most of the action – shops, bars, motels and businesses – lies on the seemingly endless strip mall of the Panamericana as it bypasses the centre, best accessed by car.

Parque David J. Guzmán

Although Parque Barrios is technically the central plaza, the heart of San Miguel – and a much better place to sit – is the shady **Parque David J. Guzmán**, a block away to the northeast. It was named after the eminent nineteenth-century Migueleño biologist and member of the French Academy of Science. On the east side sits the **Catedral Nuestra Señora de la Paz** (daily 7am–7pm), started in 1862 and officially completed one hundred years later. Despite its modern elements, it is still an impressive building, with a cast-iron statue of Christ bearing his crown of thorns standing between two red-roofed bell towers. The rather bare interior offers a blissfully cool refuge from the grimy heat outside, with the famed statue of **Nuestra Señora de la Paz** (see box below) above the Italian marble altar.

Antiguo Teatro Nacional

Just south of the cathedral is the **Antiguo Teatro Nacional**, a honey-coloured Renaissance-style building completed in 1909. It's closed during the day (the ticket office is usually open just inside the lobby) but evening performances occasionally take place here, particularly during fiesta time; check the *Prensa Gráfica* at weekends.

Capilla de la Medalla Milagrosa

Of the few minor sights within San Miguel, the most appealing is the Gothic **Capilla de la Medalla Milagrosa**, at the western end of Calle 4 Pte where it joins 7A Avenida Sur. The brilliant white chapel was built in 1904 by French nuns working in the hospital that once stood next door, and is known for its pretty blue ceiling and beautiful French stained-glass windows, best seen on a clear evening. Its leafy gardens make an enticing entrance, with the walkway to the main door festooned with bright pink bougainvillea. The chapel is usually open only for services (Sun 5.30am, 8.30am & 5.30pm; usually Mon–Sat 9.30am, check on ☏2661 1831).

3

NUESTRA SEÑORA DE LA PAZ

San Miguel's stately cathedral, while rather disappointing inside, holds a revered wooden statue of **Nuestra Señora de la Paz**, the city's patroness (and since 1953, patron of El Salvador). The veneration of the Virgin Mary as "Our Lady of Peace" originated in the Spanish city of Toledo in the seventh century, though accounts differ as to how and when this particular statue arrived in San Miguel (the legend goes it washed up on a beach in 1682). It is generally held that her true moment of glory came during the eruption of Volcán Chaparrastique on September 21, 1787. On seeing a glowing river of lava advancing on San Miguel, the terrified citizens, praying to the Virgin to save them, took the statue to the door of the cathedral and presented her to the volcano. The lava changed course and the city was saved. In honour of these events, San Miguel holds two months of **fiesta**, beginning with the Virgin "descending" the volcano on September 21 and culminating in a procession through the streets, attended by thousands, on November 21. A more recent coda to the fiesta is the annual **Carnaval** held on the last Saturday in November, when free live music, fireworks and street dancing dominate the whole town. Instituted in 1958, it has quickly grown to be the largest carnival in Central America (or so locals like to claim). If you're around during the festival look out for people wandering around holding large plastic iguanas aloft – the locals are nicknamed *garroberos* (iguana eaters) due to their penchant for the lizard's meat.

3

ARRIVAL AND INFORMATION

By bus Buses arrive at the well-ordered Terminal de San Miguel on 6A C Ote between 8A & 10A Av Nte, four blocks (or a 10min walk) east of the centre.

Destinations Corinto (#327; twice hourly; 2hr); El Amatillo, via Santa Rosa de Lima (#330; frequent; 1hr 30min); El Tamarindo, via Las Tunas (#385; hourly; 1hr 30min); La Unión (#324; frequent; 1hr); Perquín (#332 & #426; hourly 9.30am–3.20pm; 3hr); Playa El Cuco (#320; every 30min, 3.10am–4pm; 1hr 30min); Puerto El Triunfo (#377; every 40min; 1hr); San Francisco Gotera (#328; frequent; 1hr); San Salvador (#301; every 15min; 3hr); Usulután (#373; frequent; 1hr 15min). *Especial* and *super especial* services also serve San Salvador (10 daily; 2hr). For San Vicente take one of these latter buses and get off at the Vicente turning on the Panamericana (just over 1hr) – you can get a taxi or local bus into the city from here.

Tourist information There is no official tourist office, but staff at the Alcaldía (town hall; Mon–Fri 9am–4pm) on the south side of Parque David J. Guzmán will help you with quick questions (Ⓦalcaldiasanmiguel.gob.sv). During Carnaval, contact the Comite de Festejos de San Miguel for programme details (Ⓦsanmiguelencarnaval.com.sv).

ACCOMMODATION

The majority of accommodation clusters around the bus terminal, inevitably a rather sleazy area. There are posher hotels away from the city centre, mostly along Av Roosevelt Sur, but you'll have to pay a lot more (*Villas San Miguel* and *Comfort Inn* are the most popular).

Caleta 3A Av Sur 601 between 9A & 11A C Pte ☎2661 3233, ✉hotelcaleta@gmail.com. Clean and quiet hotel, popular with local business travellers during the week. There's a small courtyard with hammocks, and some rooms have private bath. Staff can also help arrange surf trips to secluded beaches. **US$15**

Hotel del Centro 8A C Ote 505 at 8A Av Nte ☎2661 5473. This very friendly, helpful and spotless hotel is the best of the cheaper options around the bus terminal. The rooms are smallish but well arranged, with cushions on beds and bedside lights; all rooms have bath and TV. There's free wi-fi for guests and US$0.50 laundry washes. **US$15**

Hotel El Guanaco 8A Av Nte Pje Madrid ☎2661 8026. A giant hotel with gaudy green paintwork and kitsch cowboy decor. Its big, airy and clean en-suite rooms all have a/c and cable TV – the oversized three double-bed room for US$40 is a great deal for groups. **US$20**

King Palace 6A C Ote ☎2661 1086. Good-value and professional hotel opposite the bus terminal, with a glitzy mirrored-window facade. The clean rooms are en suite, some with balcony, cable TV, a/c and telephone. Secure parking, restaurant, fast internet (computers and wi-fi), laundry, swimming pool and rooftop gym and pool also available. **US$30**

EATING

Bati Jugos Carlitos 1A Av Nte & 4A C Pte ☎2661 0606. Carlito serves excellent snacks (US$2.50) and lunches (US$4–7) in an intimate, colourful downstairs and roomier first floor. His speciality is a wide selection of big, fresh fruit *licuados* (US$2), from melon and pineapple to tamarind and papaya. Mon–Sat 8am–5pm.

Comedor y Pupusería Chilita 8A C Ote, just east of 6A Av Nte. A barn of a neighbourhood *pupusería*, particularly popular on Fri & Sat. The *pupusas* are good (4–10pm; US$0.50), but there's also a decent selection of *comidas a la vista* (7am–3pm). Sit inside or on the breezy terrace at the back. Mon–Sat 7am–10pm.

Comedor Vicky 7A Av Nte, at C Chaparrastique. Small, friendly, bare-bones *comedor* that does an ice-cold, freshly squeezed orange juice (US$1.50) and cooked breakfast. The *sopa Gallina India* (US$2.50) is fine for lunch too. Daily 7am–9pm.

Conchadromo Esmerelda 6A Av Nte between 4A & 6A C Ote. Good, basic breakfasts and *comidas a la vista*. One of a clutch of similar food shacks in a former car park – it's cleaner and much better than it looks from the outside. Also serves cheap, cold beers. Mon–Sat 7am–10pm.

El Paraíso Parque David J. Guzmán. Well-prepared *pupusas* (US$0.50) and *comidas a la vista* (US$3) dished out in an attractive colonial building in a conveniently central location. Prices are low and quality is good. Steer clear of the juices though; they are surprisingly bad. Daily 7am–9pm.

Pastelería Francesa Parque David J. Guzmán ☎2661 8054, Ⓦpasteleriafrancesa.com.sv. This a/c local chain is the best place for a pastry, free wi-fi and decent coffee on the Parque – there is another handy branch at 1A Av Nte 302. Both Mon–Sat 7am–6pm, Sun 7am–noon.

★ TREAT YOURSELF

La Pema 5km from town on the road to El Cuco ☎2667 6055, Ⓦlapema.com. El Salvador's most renowned restaurant (named after founder "Doña Pema") will set you back around US$20 per head (without alcohol), but the huge servings of *mariscada* (US$12–15), a creamy soup of every conceivable type of seafood, and the bowls of fruit salad served as an accompaniment mean you won't feel like eating again for a while. Credit cards accepted. Daily 10am–5pm.

DRINKING AND NIGHTLIFE

By night the focus shifts to the *comedores* and fast-food chains along Av Roosevelt. Think about ordering taxis, not least because the action is quite far out of town. Return journeys can be arranged with the barmen. No journey should be over US$3.

Mama Gallina's Av Roosevelt Sur 303, btw 2A C Pte & C Chaparrastique ☎ 2661 2123. The most renowned of a clutch of bar/restaurants on Roosevelt is ostensibly a big dark hall respected for its seafood – it soon fills up. Drink rather than eat unless you really want to spend; on top of beer there's sangría (US$4.50), shots (US$7 double) and wine by the bottle (from US$20). Daily noon–midnight.

Maya C Chaparrastique 602 ☎ 2635 9347. One of several popular joints along this section of Chaparrastique, a laidback bar and café awash with the sounds of *trova*, salsa and Latin rock. Free wi-fi. Cash only. Mon–Sat 2pm–2am.

El Paisa Av Roosevelt Sur 105, opposite *Hotel Trópico Inn* ☎ 2661 0352. Popular Mexican food spot that also does steaks for US$8, though the large tacos are cheaper at US$4. It's used more as an outdoors booze hall with a big screen and a stage for live musicians at weekends. Daily 10am–2am.

Papagallo's Plaza Chaparrastique, Av Roosevelt Sur ☎ 2661 0400. The town's main nightlife venue has big Mexican dishes starting at US$3, but most come to drink and dance under the a/c. On certain nights they have live music and comedy for a US$5 entry fee, redeemable in drink. Thurs–Sun noon–2am.

SHOPPING

Centro Comercial de Artesanías Alameda Roosevelt between 4A & 6A C Pte. Less artisan than souvenir, but there are some pockets of genuine local crafts. Mon–Sat 8am–5pm.

Mercado Central Parque Barrios. A sprawling affair lined with narrow warrens filled with stalls selling food, clothes and other goods. Daily 6am–6pm.

Metrocentro Av Roosevelt Sur ⓦmetrocentro.com /inicio-SM. At the southern edge of town, this consumer vortex includes stores, banks, bookshop, supermarket, fast-food restaurants and a cinema (Cinemark); any bus heading south down Av Roosevelt will drop you outside. Shops daily 8am–7pm; Cinemark daily 5pm–2am.

DIRECTORY

Banks Banks cluster around the west side of the Parque and along 4A C: Scotiabank is at 2A Av Nte & 4A C Ote 210 (both Mon–Fri 8am–4.30pm, Sat 8am–noon).

Health Farmacia El Progresso, 4A C Ote & 6A Av Nte (Mon–Fri 8am–6pm, Sat 8am–noon; ☎ 2661 1098); Farmacia Brasil has several branches in the centre, including one on 2A C Pte just off the Parque (Mon–Fri 7am–10pm). Hospital Clínica San Francisco (Av Roosevelt Nte 408; ☎ 2661 1991) is an excellent private hospital with 24hr emergency care.

Internet Cyber Café, 11A Av Nte, between 2A C Ote & 4A C Ote (Mon–Sat 11am–7pm; US$0.80/hr).

Phones Claro, 2A C Ote & 4A Av Nte (Mon–Fri 8am–6pm, Sat 8am–4pm), at the corner of Parque Guzmán next to the Alcaldía.

Post office 4A Av Sur at 3A C Ote, south from the cathedral (Mon–Fri 8am–5pm, Sat 8am–noon).

Supermarket Súper Selectos, Galería Jardín, Av Roosevelt at C Almendros (aka 11A C Pte); Despensa Familiar in the centre on Av José Simeón Cañas just north of C Sirama Ote.

SAN FRANCISCO GOTERA

North of San Miguel, Highway CA-7 runs 30km to **SAN FRANCISCO GOTERA** (usually called "Gotera"). It's the least exciting of the towns along the **Ruta de Paz** (the section of CA-7 linking the civil war's worst affected towns), but is a pivotal transport point for the more interesting destinations beyond. There's no real reason to stay here, as onward bus connections are good, but if you have some time to kill, check out the panoramic view from the Parque Concordia.

ARRIVAL AND INFORMATION

By bus Buses, which stop just beyond the dusty and ugly main plaza, run regularly north to Perquín. Pick-ups (5am–5.30pm) cover the same route from the northern end of Av Morazán.

Destinations Cacaopera (#337; hourly; 1hr); Guatajiagua (#410; hourly; 1hr); Perquín (#332A & #328; every 30min; 1hr 30min); San Miguel (#328; every 10min; 1hr).

Bank Citibank, at 1A C Pte no. 1 bis (Mon–Fri 8am–6pm, Sat 8am–noon).

GUATAJIAGUA

Lying in the basin of an open valley 12km west of Gotera, peaceful **GUATAJIAGUA** is a wonderfully artistic Salvadoran small town. Like many other craft-based settlements, it has a unified creative output – black clay pottery and sculpture – but the products are of far higher quality than the usual souvenirs. Moreover, the town is very accessible, and as yet untainted by tourism.

Calle Principal, running west of the Parque, is the town's unofficial centre – the many **workshops** around here include that of Sarbelio Vásquez García, whose sculptures of a kneeling man you'll see imitated throughout town (ask for directions).

ARRIVAL AND DEPARTURE

By bus Buses from San Francisco Gotera (#410; hourly; 1hr) stop by the market, as does the San Miguel bus (#326; hourly; 1hr 20min), which you can pick up at Chapeltique on the highway if you're coming from the west.

CACAOPERA

The small village of **CACAOPERA**, 9.6km northeast of Gotera (hourly bus #337) on a paved side road off the Ruta de Paz (CA-7), takes its name from the Ulúa language, and refers to the heavy cultivation of cacao in the area during colonial times. Yet it is Kakawira (or Cacaopera) culture and religion (not Ulúa) that is still strongly adhered to in this region (though the language is extinct). An excellent place to learn about it is the **Museo Winakirika** (Thurs–Sun 9am–4pm; US$1), just under 1km north of the village (on the road to Joateca, on the banks of the Río Torola), which has fine exhibits on indigenous tradition and culture, as well as photos, arts and crafts; it also organizes hikes to nearby petroglyphs. Another worthy stop is the colonial **church** dating back to 1660 (though heavily restored), with walls up to 5m thick. Adjacent is a bell tower with three huge bronze bells dating from 1772. The church is the focus of festivities on January 15–17, when the villagers dance in memory of the eight *caciques* (priests) and the indigenous warrior deities Tupaica and Tumaica.

CORINTO

From Cacaopera, a scenic paved road heads northeast to the town of **CORINTO**, an important commercial hub and home to a **market** on Wednesday and Sunday that attracts vendors from neighbouring Honduras. All the usual tat is on sale, but look for hand-rolled cigars and locally grown foods. The town's main claim to fame is about fifteen minutes' walk north:

La Gruta del Espíritu Santo (Tues–Sun 9am–4.30pm; US$2), a series of caves bearing pre-Columbian reddish wall art. Though faint, the art is said to date back some ten thousand years, and the whole area makes a very pleasant stroll. If the caves are closed, call the custodian Argelio at ☎7905 2777 (Spanish only). Corinto can be reached as a day-trip from San Miguel (**bus** #327 from the main terminal), or #782 (hourly; 1hr) comes from Cacaopera.

PERQUÍN

Some 32km north of Gotera on the Ruta de Paz (CA-7), **PERQUÍN** is a small and, given its history, surprisingly friendly mountain town set in the middle of glorious walking country. During the war the town was the FMLN headquarters, and in later years Radio Venceremos was broadcast to the nation from here. Attempts by the army to dislodge the guerrillas mostly failed, leaving the town badly damaged and deserted. Today, the "town that refused to die" has repaired most of its buildings, although the scars of war are still evident and nearly everyone has a horrendous tale to tell. Recently community action has been moving away from the retrospective outlook that war tourism has created, and instituted new schools, coffee production and a young and hip annual festival, the **Festival del Invierno**, which hosts live music and events in August (since this is the rainy season, it is called the "winter festival").

WHAT TO SEE AND DO

The town itself is clumped around its pentagonal **Parque Central**, where there is a municipal basketball court. One block uphill is Calle de los Héroes, containing most of the town's attractions.

Museo de la Revolución Salvadoreña

Perquín's main draw is the poignant **Museo de la Revolución Salvadoreña** (Tues–Sun 8am–4.30pm; US$1.25), set up by former guerrillas in the wake of the 1992 Peace Accords. The curators travelled throughout the country collecting photographs and personal effects of "disappeared" guerrillas, a collection that is still growing and displayed in the first room. There is a succinct summary (in Spanish) of the escalation to the armed struggle, weaponry and examples of international propaganda aimed at bringing the events in El Salvador to the world's attention, but the most moving exhibits are the anonymous transcripts of witnesses of the El Mozote massacre (see p.240), and drawings by refugee schoolchildren, depicting the war's events as they saw them. A separate room contains the transmitting equipment and studio used by Radio Venceremos, whose clandestine broadcasts every afternoon throughout the war transmitted the guerrillas' view of events, as well as interviews and music. (After the peace accords, the station received an FM licence, and is now a commercial music station based in San Salvador, a status viewed by some as a bit of a sell-out.)

Outside the museum is the crater left by a bomb dropped on the village – standing next to it is a disarmed bomb with "Made in the USA" stencilled on the side. Behind the museum lie the remains of the helicopter that was carrying Domingo Monterrosa, architect of the El Mozote massacre, after it was blown up by the FMLN in 1984. A partial reconstruction of a guerrilla camp lies just down the road from the museum, with more bombs and bullets on display – locals charge US$1 or so to walk through some of the guerrilla tunnels uncovered here.

Cerro de Perquín

Opposite the museum, a track leads up from a parking lot to the panoramic views from the peak of the **Cerro de Perquín**. It's an easy 1km stroll to the top, where climbers can picnic and have their picture taken next to a sign marking the summit.

ARRIVAL AND INFORMATION

By bus Buses arrive on the south and west sides of the Parque Central, though it's easier to jump off before town for many of the accommodation options. Toyota pick-ups from San Francisco Gotera (US$0.25) stop one block south of the park on C San Sebastián.

Destinations San Miguel, via San Francisco Gotera (#332; 4 daily; 2hr); El Mozote (#426; 2 daily; 20min); also pick-ups to San Francisco Gotera (twice hourly; 1hr).

Tourist information There's a small but enthusiastic tourist office (Mon–Sat 8am–4pm; ☎ 2680 4086) on the outskirts of town, beyond *Posada Don Manuel*. The tourist police (see p.240) will drive you here if you ask nicely.

ACCOMMODATION

★ **Hotel Perkin Lenca** 1.5km south of town on CA-7, km 205.5 ☎ 2680 4046, ⓦ perkinlenca.com. The owner here, former aid worker Ron Brenneman, built the entire site himself, including the huge barn where excellent meals are served – *La Cocina de Ma' Anita* (US$5–10) – which is worth a visit even if you don't stay. Spotless, spacious rooms in log cabins or a newer motel-like section, hot-water en suites, firm beds, hammocks and chairs on the porches, great views, table tennis, free internet and a laundry service make this worth every cent. Breakfast is included, and advance booking is recommended; Ron offers a 20 percent discount during the week if enough rooms are available. He also sets up tours to El Mozote with ex-guerrilla guides, and runs a local educational charity. Double US$40, cabin (double) US$64

Hotel y Restaurante La Posada Signed at km 206 on CA-7, 500m south of town ☎ 2680 4037, ⓔ laposada perquin@hotmail.com. This hotel used to be a sawmill, evidenced by the lofty reception area, where simple *típicos* are served. Though the ten rooms are quite dark the beds are firm and good, there's free wi-fi and the shared bathrooms have toilet paper and seats. It stands out for its pool table, in great condition, and gym facilities. Rates include breakfast. US$20

El Ocotal Km 201 on CA-7 ☎ 2634 4083, ⓦ hotelelocotal .com. The cabins with private bath (hot showers), set in a tranquil pine forest several kilometres south of town, are a paler version of those at *Perkin Lenca*, but the restaurant is worth a trip (US$0.25 by Toyota pick-up). Sunday brunch is fun but packed out by locals (see p.240). US$35

Perquín Real At the southern end of town on CA-7 ☎ 2680 4158, ⓔ xiomvarela@yahoo.com. The best budget option in town has a row of spacious rooms with at least two double beds in each. Shiny new individual shower stalls are a plus, though there is no hot water. Two large (but very friendly) dogs live on site. Per person: US$8

EATING

Antojitos Marisol Av los Próceres. Though it looks something like a field hospital, this is the place if you fancy a drink or two, local soups (US$2) and good burgers and fries (US$3). Daily 8am–10pm.

Blanquita Av los Próceres ☎ 2680 4223. The best *comedor* in town, with a small selection but popular *a la vista* and cakes. Breakfast from US$2. Daily 7am–7pm.

La Muralla C de los Héroes, at the foot of the climb to the museum. The evening *pupusa* spot, frying on demand out

3

front while the townsfolk watch dubbed US soaps on the cable TV inside. Around US$2.50 for five *pupusas*. Daily 6–9pm.

El Ocotal CA-7 km 201. Good *sopas* (US$3) and a mean fried *yuca* on weekends, when it's very popular with locals. It's set in a pine forest, which somehow suits the 80s power ballads they favour on the stereo. Bring your swimsuit – you can use the pool once you've paid for something. Daily 11am–7pm.

DIRECTORY

Pharmacy Next to the post office on the west side of the Parque.

Police Politur – tourist police – opposite the church just off the Parque (☎ 2680 4040) are very helpful and friendly.

Post office On the west side of the Parque (Mon, Tues, Thurs & Fri 8am–5pm).

AROUND PERQUÍN

The area around Perquín offers very enjoyable **hiking**, the highlights of which are the route over **Cerro el Pericón** to El Mozote, taking around three hours with a stop to swim in the middle, and a two-hour loop around **Cerro Gigante**. Perquín's tourist office (see p.239) can organize guides a day in advance, some of whom have reasonable English. Paying for a guide (around US$20 per group) is tremendously worthwhile, as they are mostly ex-guerrillas who will bring the history of the landscape to life.

El Mozote

A few kilometres south of Perquín (off the CA-7, via Arambala) sits **EL MOZOTE**, the scene of the country's most horrifying wartime massacre (see box below). Families are slowly moving back, however, and a

mural by Argentine artist Claudia Bernard on the left-hand side of the church describes the village's old agricultural life and hopes for the future. On the other side, colourful mosaics of children playing form the backdrop to a heart-rending memorial garden to the young lives lost.

Although the massacre's one survivor, Rufina Amaya, passed away in 2007, newer inhabitants are continuing the guide work she did (no charge, but tipping is expected); these tours are vital to understanding the scars left from the war. You can see a bomb crater, the massacre's mass graves and the hole that Amaya hid in for five days. A moving **monument** to the victims features an iron sculpture of the silhouette of a family and a wall bearing the names of those killed. For a small fee (around US$4), local children will take you to the caves where the guerrillas were hiding out, a pleasant walk of 4–5km through forest and brush, where wildlife abounds. The caves themselves are not overly spectacular, but it was from here that **Radio Venceremos** ("We Will Overcome") was first broadcast, and as you look out over the densely forested countryside it is easy to see why the army never discovered the guerrillas' hiding place.

ARRIVAL AND DEPARTURE

By bus From Perquín you can take a pick-up to Arambala, 3km down the CA-7, where you change to a Joateca bus that leaves at 8am every morning (the return bus leaves El Mozote at 12.45pm).

On foot El Mozote can be reached on foot from Perquín, via the Cerro el Pericón.

LOS INOCENTES

In December 1981, the elite, US-trained Atlacatl army battalion entered the village of **El Mozote** and rounded up its inhabitants on the suspicion that they had been harbouring FMLN guerrillas. Earlier, the villagers had been warned by guerrillas of the army's intent, but the mayor had been assured by the government that they would be safe staying put. This was not to be: under orders to set an example and obtain information, for three days the soldiers tortured and raped the inhabitants, before **executing** them all, including the children, who were shot in front of their parents. In all, some thousand people were killed, and their bodies subsequently burned or buried in mass graves. Eyewitness testimonies – from soldiers, the survivor, guerrillas who arrived on the scene after the event – were ignored for years, and the bodies of the victims did not begin to be exhumed until 1992. Foreign groups are still working to uncover these mass-burial sites today; in some graves upwards of 85 percent of the bodies belong to children. On the right side of Mozote church, a small garden for "the innocent ones" commemorates the tragedy of their lost lives.

INTO HONDURAS: EL AMATILLO

Beyond Santa Rosa, the road connects with the Carretera Panamericana to run to the border over the Río Goascora at **El Amatillo**. The border crossing is easy and free but busy, and teeming with moneychangers – who generally do slightly better rates than the bank here – and beggars. On the Honduran side, buses leave regularly until late afternoon for Tegucigalpa and Jícaro Galán, and there are also direct buses to Choluteca, for onward connection to the Nicaraguan border along the Carretera Panamericana.

SANTA ROSA DE LIMA

Travelling 40km east of San Francisco Gotera through hot, low hills, you come to **SANTA ROSA DE LIMA**, a messy but thriving place with a large weekly market, a cheese industry and a well-maintained church. Besides the Wednesday **market** there's not much to do here, but it's a convenient stopover if you're crossing late from Honduras.

ARRIVAL AND INFORMATION

Buses Buses stop at the western end of 6A C Pte.
Destinations El Amatillo (#346; every 20min; 1hr 30min); La Unión (#304 or #342; frequent; 1hr 30min); San Miguel (#330; frequent; 1hr); San Salvador (#306; twice hourly; 4hr).
Bank Citibank, Av General Larios 14 (Mon–Fri 8am–6pm, Sat 8am–noon).

ACCOMMODATION AND EATING

Comedor Chayito 6A C Pte & 1A Av Sur. A very clean place which does a good, cheap *comida a la vista* (from US$2). Mon–Sat 7am–4pm.
Taquería El Tabasqueño Carretera Ruta Militar (CA-18), next to the Puente Las Cadenas. Popular taco joint on the main highway, doubling as a car wash. Munch on tacos, *carne asada* and pork ribs (*costilla de cerdo*) from US$2. Daily 7am–10pm.
El Tejano Amigo Colonia Altos de Santa Rosa, 100m north of the Estadio Municipal (just off CA-18) ☎ 2641 4242, ✉ hoteltejanoamigo@hotmail.com. Your best bet for a comfy night's sleep, with a/c, bath and cable TV. US$25

The north

North of San Salvador, hilly pastures and agricultural land give way to the remote, rugged and sparsely populated Chalatenango and Cuscatlán provinces, a region of poverty and pride that was until recently all but closed to outsiders. The Spanish found few natural riches to attract them this far north, and successive generations of *campesinos* have vainly struggled to make a living. This harsh terrain created fertile ground for dissent and support for the FMLN, who controlled large parts of the department of Chalatenango for significant periods during the 1980s. Both army and guerrillas struggled to take control, leaving devastated communities in their wake and refugees fleeing across the border to Honduras. The legacy of the region's wartime status was not exclusively detrimental, however, and the effect of the subsequent repopulation has been the reinvention and modernization of its big towns. Each now has a very singular character: colonial **Suchitoto** is the darling of culture and tourism; **La Palma** is a mountainous escape with a legion of artisans; and bustling **Chalatenango** is a centre of rural commerce.

SUCHITOTO

Cobbled and colonial **SUCHITOTO** perches like a crown on the ridge above the southern edge of Lago de Suchitlán, 47km north of San Salvador. The left-leaning but increasingly gentrified town was made a site of National Cultural Heritage in 1997, and today you will find arts and cultural venues dotted around all Suchitoto's streets. There are food and arts **festivals** every weekend, and the month-long festival of culture in February draws the country's best painters, orchestras, performers and poets.

During the 1980s, the area was the scene of bitter fighting as the army struggled to dislodge FMLN guerrillas from their nearby mountain strongholds. Upwards of ninety percent of the inhabitants left the town, which was largely resettled by ex-guerrillas after the war. Today life here is generally quiet,

3

Lago de Suchitlán, Museo de Alejandro Cotto, ❶ & ❶

SUCHITOTO

■ ACCOMMODATION
Blanca Luna	5
El Gringo Hostel	4
Hostal Vista al Lago	2
Palancapa	1
Villas Balanza	3

Museo Comunitario La Memoria Vive

Parque San Martín

Museo de la Moneda

Teatro de las Ruinas

Police Station

Galería de Pascal

Telecom

Casa de Cultura

Alcaldía

Parque Centenario

Pharmacy

Bus from San Salvador

Bus to Lago Suchitlán

Iglesia Santa Lucía

Museo De Los 1000 Platos Y Mas

Suchitoto Adventure Outfitters

● EATING
Artex Café	9
La Posada	3
Rinconcito del Gringo	7
El Tejado	2
Villa Balanza	4

● DRINKING & NIGHTLIFE
Centro Arte para la Paz	6
La Fonda del Mirador	1
Lupita del Portal	8
El Necio	5

N

0	100
	metres

San Salvador (47km)

Volcán Guazapa & Cascada Los Tercios

with its quality restaurants, bars and luxury hotels offering a welcome respite from rough travelling.

WHAT TO SEE AND DO

Suchitoto has some of the finest examples of colonial architecture in the country, so before getting stuck into the cafés and shops it's worth taking a stroll to admire the low red-tiled adobe houses lining the town's streets and around its tranquil plazas.

Around the Parque Central

Overlooking the Parque Central and inaugurated in 1857, the **Iglesia Santa Lucía** has an impressive Neoclassical facade, a particularly fine wooden altar and strange, hollow wooden columns inside. The quirky **Museo De Los 1000 Platos Y Mas**, 3A Av Nte 1, behind the church (Tues–Sat 8am–5.30pm; US$2) contains a gaudy collection of plates, decorated with everything from florid Victorian designs to images of President Lincoln. The **Casa de Cultura** (Mon–Fri 9am–5pm; free), a block north of the church (Pasaje Sta. Lucia 9),

has displays on local history and information on local walks.

Museo de la Moneda

The shaded **Parque San Martín**, a couple of blocks northwest of the church, commands stunning views across the blue waters of the lake. Nearby, the **Museo de la Moneda** (Tues–Sun 8am–5pm; US$2; ☎2335 1094), 4A C Pte 9, contains examples of **UDIS** ("Unidad de Intercambio Solidario Suchitotense"), the "official" currency of Suchitoto established in 2007 as a sort of voucher system to boost the local economy. It's legal tender (at par with the US$), though it has never really caught on. The museum also displays coins and notes from all over the world, as well as a comprehensive history of Salvadoran tender.

Museo de Alejandro Cotto

Northeast of town, Avenida 15 de Septiembre leads down to the lakeshore, passing the **Museo de Alejandro Cotto** (Sat & Sun 2–6pm; US$4), a beautifully restored colonial house with a fine collection of local paintings, sculpture, indigenous artefacts and musical instruments. The owner, Cotto himself, is a famous Salvadoran writer and filmmaker, and is often in residence. The entrance price, while relatively steep for El Salvador, goes towards funding the February arts and culture festival.

Museo Comunitario La Memoria Vive

The small **Museo Comunitario La Memoria Vive** (Tues–Sun 8am–3pm; US$2; ☏2335 1080), 2A C Pte 5, was opened in 2010, dedicated to the history, culture and art of Suchitoto. Small exhibitions highlight the effect of the civil war, Pipil civilization, the creation of Lago de Suchitlán in 1976 (it's actually a reservoir), the local Festival del Maíz and fiesta of the Virgen de Santa Lucía.

Lago de Suchitlán

It's worth travelling the couple of kilometres from the town centre to **Lago de Suchitlán**, where you can swim in clear, cool waters and enjoy a relaxing drink at a couple of small lakeside bars. A small boat sometimes runs around the lake, or local fishermen may be persuaded to take you out onto the water. Boat tours (1hr; US$30) head out to **Isla de los Pájaros** in the middle of the lake, the home of a range of fish-eating birds. To get to the lake, walk north on Avenida 15 de Septiembre from the Parque Central and keep going, or take a minibus from the corner of that road and 4A Calle Poniente (10min; US$0.35).

Los Tercios

Another worthy excursion is the **Cascada Los Tercios**, a waterfall that flows over unusual hexagonal basaltic columns – note that the water level gets low in the dry season. You can be dropped off the Lago de Suchitlán minibus on the lakeshore, near a trail that leads to the waterfall, or walk to it by following the signposts south out of town (30min).

Salto El Cubo

Salto El Cubo, with its chilly twin pools, is a better waterfall for swimming than Los Tercios. It's a pleasant twenty-minute

walk west of town – go to the western end of Calle Morazán, then follow the signs down the track.

Volcán Guazapa

The roads up and around **Volcán Guazapa**, a former guerrilla stronghold to the south of the town, still bear witness to the crumbling remains of the trenches and dugouts used by both sides, now quietly submerged beneath green vegetation. **Horseriding** is popular in this area and hacks across the volcano can be organized through the tourist office (US$18/person on horseback, US$10 on foot; 6hr; requires minimum number of participants). Check the condition of the horses before you go, as some aren't in great shape. You'll need to take a taxi or bus #107 or #163 (to Aguilares; get off at La Clínica La Mora) to the starting point, 8km out of town.

ARRIVAL AND DEPARTURE

By boat Small car ferries from San Francisco Lempa (30–40min; 10 daily or when ferry is full; US$1.50, cars US$5), across Lago de Suchitlán, arrive at the boat dock, 1.5km north of town along C Al Lago, with shops, cafés and toilets in the visitors' centre. A frequent microbus runs to the Parque Central (US$0.35). From San Francisco Lempa buses travel on to Chalatenango at around 6am, 7.25am, noon & 2.45pm.

By bus Buses stop at 1A C Pte.

Destinations Aguilares (#163; every 40min; 1hr) for transfer to Chalatenango (#125) & La Palma (#119); San Martín (#129; 10 daily; 1hr) for Cojutepeque (#119) or San Miguel (#301); San Salvador, Terminal de Oriente (#129; every 15min; 1hr 30min).

INFORMATION AND TOURS

Tourist information Centro de Amigos del Turista Suchitoto, Av 5 de Noviembre & C San Martín 2 (Mon–Fri 9am–5pm, Sat & Sun 9am–1pm; ☏503 2335 1835, ⓦsuchitoto.travel), is possibly the best tourist office in the country.

Tour operators Suchitoto Adventure Outfitters (☏2335 1429, ⓦsuchitotoadventureoutfitters.com), based in the *Lupita del Portal* café on the main square, organize waterfall jumping (US$80 per group of 1–4; 3hr 30min), as well as tours of the town (US$100 per group of 1–4; 3hr), kayaking, horseriding and excellent tours of guerrilla battlefields. Owner René Borbón speaks good English and is a mine of information. The town's other main source of advice is Roberto Broz Moran at *El Gringo* (see p.244), who also organizes tours (☏7860 9435, ⓦelgringosuchitoto

.com) covering everything from how to make *pupusas* (US$10; 45min) to city walking tours (US$5; minimum 3 people) and boat tours of the lake (US$35; 2hr 30min). He also runs a pick-up service to the airport (US$65), San Salvador (US$35) and other places in El Salvador.

ACCOMMODATION

Blanca Luna One block south of the Parque ☎ 2335 1661, ✉ blancaluna21@hotmail.es. The most central of the cheap hotels has two or three double beds in the basic rooms, as well as fan, cable TV and en suites. None too clean but not bad value, and an airy roof terrace makes up for the scruffy rooms, with hammocks and climbing bougainvillea. The artist manager's paintings decorate the walls. US$14

El Gringo Hostel C Francisco Morazán 27 ☎ 2327 2351, ⊕ elgringosuchitoto.com. Newish and cosy hostel with two private rooms and one dorm (5 single beds); free wi-fi (and two computers), cable TV in lounge, kitchen, laundry (US$5/load) and a restaurant (see below). Discounts for longer stays. Dorm US$7, double US$18

Hostal Vista al Lago 2A Av Nte 18 ☎ 2335 1357. The rooms here are small and cubicle-esque, with passable beds and a shared bathroom, but the owners are relaxed, the cosy courtyard has a bar and serves food, and the bench overlooking the lake is possibly the best spot in town for an evening drink. Double US$16

Palancapa Final Av 15 Septiembre, in front of La Gruta ☎ 7848 3438, ✉ palancapa@gmail.com. New hotel with two pricey private rooms, hand-carved wooden beds, ceiling fans, private bathrooms with hot water and free wi-fi. A superb camping area, with views over the lake, is also available, with shared showers and free wi-fi. All rates include breakfast. Camping per tent US$7, double US$65

Villas Balanza Parque San Martín ☎ 2335 1408, ⊕ villabalanzarestaurante.com. Very clean, wood-finished rooms down the hill behind the restaurant of the same name on the edge of town. The en-suite rooms have a splendid view of the lake, there's a shared kitchen for guests and good free wi-fi. US$50

EATING

Artex Café Plaza Central ⊕ artexcafe.com. Not only does this place have the best coffee in town (they'll sell you bags for US$4.50) but also fast internet (US$1/hr), excellent cultural information (the café is run by a nonprofit organization promoting the arts) and outdoor tables for a beer (Pilsner US$1.50). Tues–Fri 8am–6pm, Sat 8am–7pm.

★ **Rinconcito del Gringo** C Francisco Morazán 27 ☎ 2327 2351. From the same gringo, Roberto Broz Moran, who runs the *El Gringo Hostal*, this largely Tex-Mex restaurant offers fresh juice smoothies (US$2.50), gourmet *pupusas* (US$1) and big, spicy portions (meals US$2.50–7). Admire the expressive paintings by artist Trudy Myrrh in the on-site gallery. Free wi-fi. Daily 8am–8pm.

El Tejado 3A Av Nte 58 ☎ 2335 1769. Big meat and chicken dishes (US$6) are served in a pleasant garden with an unrivalled lake view. The best thing is the giant and clean swimming pool where you can cool off on hot days; you may be asked for a US$3 supplement for this. Mon–Fri 10am–5pm, Sat 9am–9pm, Sun 9am–5pm.

Villa Balanza *Villa Balanza* hotel, Parque San Martín ☎ 2335 1408, ⊕ villabalanzarestaurante.com. This open-sided barn restaurant has rustic antique-ranch decor, with romantic tables in a corner alcove overlooking the lake. The food is good, with breakfasts and lunches (chicken *suprema* US$7) served by waitresses in "traditional" milkmaid outfits. Daily 7am–10pm.

DRINKING AND ENTERTAINMENT

Suchitoto is a great place to go out – largely safe and with lots of choice. That said, if you're female and on your own in *El Necio* you should expect the all-too-usual attention. There are also plenty of opportunities to enjoy excellent cultural events.

Centro Arte para la Paz 2A C Pte 5 ☎ 2335 1080, ⊕ capsuchitoto.org. The venue for the Museo Comunitario La Memoria Vive (see p.243) also hosts a range of arts events, including film, theatre and concerts.

La Fonda del Mirador Av 15 de Septiembre 85 ☎ 2335 1126. The largely expensive menu has some cheap and filling treats (seafood salad US$4), but it really comes into its own as a spot for early evening drinks with stunning sunset views of the lake. Daily 11am–7pm.

Lupita del Portal Parque Central ☎ 2335 1429. Laidback café and bar with outdoor tables, specializing in gourmet *pupusas* (roasted garlic and basil or cheese and spinach; US$1.50), tasty sweet pasties and a potent *chaparro* (*aguardiente*, or cane liquor). Owner René Barbón runs Suchitoto Adventure Outfitters (see p.243) from here, one of the best tour operators in the country. Daily 7am–9pm.

El Necio 4A C Pte 9 ☎ 7504 5490. The only out-and-out bar in town is a local favourite, serving beers (US$1.50) and spirits amid guerrilla decor. The name ("the fool") is taken from the first nickname given to Ernesto "Che" Guevara, and this place, decorated with FMLN, Che and

John Lennon posters, certainly exudes revolutionary chic. Wed–Sun 4pm–2am.

SHOPPING

Galería de Pascal 4A C Pte 2B, next to *Hotel Los Almendros* (just north of the plaza). A large exhibition space that sells original paintings, which are naturally very expensive, as well as local artisanal work. Mon–Fri 10am–6pm, Sat 10am–7pm, Sun 9am–6pm.

DIRECTORY

Banks There is, surprisingly, no bank or ATM here (at the time of writing), so bring plenty of cash if you want to stay a while.

Internet *Rinconcito del Gringo* (see opposite) offers free wi-fi and two internet computers for restaurant and *hostal* clients.

Pharmacy Farmacia Santa Lucía (daily 8am–noon & 2–6pm), on the corner of C Francisco Morazán and Av 5 de Noviembre, is well stocked.

Police The tourist police have a good presence in town; the office on the corner of Av 15 de Septiembre and 4A C Pte (☎ 2335 1141) is open 24hr.

AGUILARES AND CIHUATÁN

Some 35km north of the capital, on the border-bound Troncal del Norte (CA-4), the pleasant workaday town of **AGUILARES** has nothing more to offer than a relaxing snack in the garden at *Río Bravo* on the Parque. Archeology buffs might want to pass through, however, as 4km to the north sit the ruins of **CIHUATÁN** (Tues–Sun 9am–4pm; US$3; ⊚cihuatan.org), the most important Postclassic site in the country. Originally covering an area of around four square kilometres, Cihuatán (meaning "Place of Women" in Nahaut) was founded sometime after the first waves of Pipils (or Toltecs) began arriving in El Salvador in the tenth century and destroyed for reasons unknown around 1200 AD. The excavations, which include stepped pyramids and a pelota court bearing a clear Mexican influence, were officially opened in 2007, along with a very informative bilingual museum. To really get into it, it's worth reading the information on the website before going.

Take any **bus** from Aguilares (10min) or the capital (around 1hr) to Chalatenango or La Palma and ask to be dropped at the gates – they're right on the highway.

CHALATENANGO

Around 18km north of Aguilares, on the Troncal del Norte, is a major crossroads at the scrubby junction of **Amayo**.

The road east from here (CA-3) leads through agricultural and pasture lands along the northern fringes of Lago de Suchitlán to **CHALATENANGO**, an important centre of rural trade. The town has the rough-and-ready feel of a frontier settlement, an atmosphere enhanced by the fortress-like army barracks on the main square. During the early 1980s it was under FMLN control, and though much of the town's physical damage has been repaired, the barracks still has bullet holes in its walls. Nowadays, though, Chalatenango is a bustling and very friendly place.

WHAT TO SEE AND DO

Chalatenango lies in a beautiful setting – southeast of the La Peña mountains, overlooking the distant Cerro Grande to the west and Lago de Suchitlán to the south – and much of its attraction lies in day-trips to the surrounding area (see p.246). However, the daily **market** that seals off Calle San Martín every morning from 5am to 1pm is full of fresh, locally grown produce and cowboy attire, which you'll see even more of when the Friday horse fairs come to town. Twenty minutes from the centre to the east is the **Parque Recreativo Agua Fría** (daily 8am–5pm; US$1), with artificial pools, a water slide and a café in a pleasant park.

ARRIVAL AND DEPARTURE

By bus All buses arrive and depart from along 3A Av Sur, a couple of blocks south of the Parque Central.
Destinations Concepción Quetzaltepeque (#300B; every 30min; 20min); La Palma – take the San Salvador bus and change at Amayo (#119; every 30min; 3hr); San Francisco Lempa (#542; 5 daily; 45min); San Salvador, Terminal de Oriente (#125; frequent; 2hr).

ACCOMMODATION

Hotel La Ceiba Behind the garrison building and down the hill on 1A C Pte ☎2301 1080. Standard features for the price (cable, en suite, a/c), though a bit run-down. <u>US$20</u>

La Posada del Jefe C El Instituto ☎2335 2450. The furthest option from the centre is just about adequately clean, though rooms are dark and poky, and – despite its enviable hilltop location – there are no views over the town. At the price and at ten blocks' slog uphill beyond the church to the east of the centre, it's a bit steep. **US$25**

EATING AND DRINKING

For an evening drink, the stall on the south side of the church on C San Martín does cheap beer as well as burgers, and stays open until 11pm. There are plenty of open-air pizzerias among the craft stalls on the square, with eat-in tables or takeaway (US$4–5).

Comedor Blanquita C Morazán & Av Libertad. A good *comedor* serving the usual *comida típica*, as well as burgers and chips (US$3), though a visit to the toilet might put you off your food. Daily 7am–7pm.

3

Comedor Carmary 3A Av Sur. This *comedor* is popular at lunchtime, serving the locally favoured *a la vista* (US$3–4), with vegetarian options too. Mon–Sat 7am–2pm.

Sarita 1A Av Sur. The countrywide ice-cream chain offers plenty of different flavours – or try a Giga, their cheaper but just as tasty version of a Magnum (US$1.25). Daily 11am–7pm.

AROUND CHALATENANGO

The villages **north of Chalatenango** are spread across forested mountains and rarely visited. More adventurous travellers may want to explore beyond the artisan town of **Concepción Quetzaltepeque**; find out more beforehand by asking at the tourist office or local experts in Suchitoto (see p.243). By the Lago de Suchitlán, **San Francisco Lempa** is a great little stop before crossing the lake to Suchitoto.

Concepción Quetzaltepeque

Some 12km northwest of Chalatenango, the village of **CONCEPCIÓN QUETZALTEPEQUE** is notable for its **hammock** industry. Workshops lining the village's main street and homes around the village turn out colourful items in nylon and, less commonly, cotton and *mezcal* fibres for prices at about half those in San Salvador. Most producers sell in the market at Chalatenango at roughly the same bargain rate as in the workshops here. The annual hammock festival takes place November 10–12.

San Francisco Lempa

The little lakeside town of **SAN FRANCISCO LEMPA** is home to the pier for ferries to and from Suchitoto (see p.241). The town itself is very pleasant for a dock community, but holds no real interest. In the vicinity, however, are an excellent restaurant and a great camping spot.

ACCOMMODATION AND EATING

Hacienda Grande 3km west of San Francisco Lempa along the shore ⓣ 2375 1447, ⓦ haciendagrande.webs.com. Probably the nicest camping in the country (they have five tents to lend out), next to a swimming pool and restaurant. They also have horses you can take out on your own (US$4/hr). Per person **US$5**

Tao Tao Next to San Francisco Lempa's pier ⓣ 2399 3118. This restaurant, worth a visit even if you're not getting a ferry, serves tasty, big, predominantly seafood dishes (*camerones* soup US$5) on its lakeside veranda. They can also sort out boats and tourist information – including how to walk, or get a boat, to *Hacienda Grande* (see above). Its best feature, though, is the booming jukebox; bring plenty of quarters. Daily 8am–8pm.

LA PALMA

Beyond Amayo, the Troncal del Norte (C-4) winds up the Cordillera Metapán Alotepeque to the Honduran border through an abundance of vertiginous, pine-clad mountain vistas (for the best views sit on the left-hand side of the bus on the way up). Some 8km short of the border lies the serene village of **LA PALMA**, supposedly named after the indigenous custom of building houses out of palms. The climate is cooler here and the peace is only broken during the annual fiesta of **Dulce Nombre de María**, in the third week of February. But under the surface the village's plentiful *artesanías* are hives of industry, reproducing the brightly painted, naïf-style representations of people, villages and farming life and religion made famous by Salvadoreño artist **Fernando Llort** (Llort lived here 1971–80), on wooden and ceramic handicrafts and toys, which are now sold all over the world.

WHAT TO SEE AND DO

The **crafts industry** is the economic mainstay of the village, with **workshops** lining the main road. Most sell their goods on the spot and are pretty relaxed

LA PALMA

■ ACCOMMODATION	
Hostal Quecheláh	2
Hotel La Palma	3
Piedra del Bosque	1

● EATING & DRINKING	
Del Pueblo	2
La Estancia	3
Pupusería La Palma	1

about visitors turning up to watch; prices are cheaper than in San Salvador and the items make great gifts. The **Museo Fernando Llort**, at the western end of town, displays a selection of Llort's colourful paintings (Mon–Fri 8am–4pm, Sat 8am–noon; free; ☏ 2335 9076).

Hiking trails

North of La Palma are several fine **hiking trails**, including El Salvador's highest mountain, **Cerro Pital** (2730m), 10km away on the Honduran border. A rough road branches east just before La Palma to run to Las Pilas on the lower slopes of the mountain; a dirt road also leads up from the village of **San Ignacio**. Hiking to the summit is an adventure of two or three days, for which you will need to be fully equipped – the owners of the *Hotel La Palma* (see below) are a good source of information on shorter walks and guides, and run their own excursions around the hillsides.

ARRIVAL AND INFORMATION

By bus There is no bus station as such. You can ask to get off at either end of town or in the centre; the bus goes along 2A Av Nte on the way up to the border, and calles Delgado and Barrios on the way back down.

Destinations Chalatenango (#119; every 30min; 1hr); El Poy, Honduras border (#119; every 30min; 30min); San Ignacio (#119; every 30min; 15min); San Salvador, Terminal de Oriente (#119; every 30min; 3hr 30min).

Tourist information The Centros de Amigos del Turista (Mon–Fri 9am–5pm; ☏ 2335 9076) is on the north side of the Parque Central.

ACCOMMODATION

★ **Hotel La Palma** Barrio el Tránsito, Troncal del Norte km 84 ☏ 2335 9012. Supposedly the oldest functioning hotel in El Salvador (since 1944), this friendly and good-value place at the entrance to town has clean and bright rooms, with hot-water en suites, nicely decorated with huge Llortist murals. Singles cost US$18. There's a reasonably priced restaurant (specializing in *gallina india*, a local chicken dish), free wi-fi and a pool and hammock area. __US$35__

Piedra del Bosque C a La Loma (across the river from C Independencia) ☏ 2335 9067 or ☏ 7722 2465. Charming

3

owner Óscar built this entire eco-complex, with extremely basic hillside cabins, a river-fed swimming pool, a restaurant, hammocks, camping space, collection of archeological finds, craft shop, and bonfires in the evening. Óscar will talk you through everything stone by stone. Camping **US$10**, double **US$25**

EATING

Del Pueblo 2A Av Sur. A family-run establishment with bags of character, carved wooden chairs and handmade candles, *Del Pueblo* serves a good-value menu featuring mostly meats and one of the best *típico* breakfasts around (US$4–5). Daily 8am–9pm.

La Estancia C Gerado Barrios 35 ☎ 2335 9049. Great little restaurant in the centre, decorated with rustic murals and cooking up all the usual Salvadoran classics as well as the house special – *pollo al vino* (chicken fried in red wine). Mains from US$6. Daily 7am–10pm.

Pupusería La Palma C Barrios at C Libertad ☎ 2335 9063. The town's best *pupusería* is small, always busy with locals and serves soft and flavoursome *pupusas* (US$0.50), as well as *típicos* all day. Daily 7am–10pm.

SHOPPING

Galería de Arte Alfredo Linares C Barrios ☎ 2335 9049. A small gallery where the internationally established naïf artist exhibits with other local painters. The fine watercolour and pen-and-ink originals are a little steep, but there are also poster prints for US$10 and postcards for US$1.50.

Semilla de Dios 3A C Pte at 5A Av Nte ☎ 2335 9098. An artistic production line built around Llort's iconic, colourful naïf style. It is mostly exported, so there isn't a huge amount of hand-painted stuff for sale, but you can see how the work is made.

DIRECTORY

Bank Banco Azteca, C Barrios 34 (Mon–Fri 8am–4pm, Sat 8am–noon).

Internet Palma City Online, next to the supermarket on 2A Av Sur, has a fast connection (daily 11am–7pm; US$0.50/hr).

Pharmacy Farmacia San Rafael, C Barrios & 1A C Pte (Mon–Fri 8am–12.30pm & 1.30–6pm).

Post office On 1A C Pte (Mon–Fri 8am–5pm, Sat 8am–noon).

The west

The rich landscape of **western El Salvador** is in many ways the most enticing part of the country, with rolling mountain chains and valleys dominated by vibrant green expanses of coffee plantations. Spared from the most violent hardships of the conflict of the 1980s, the friendly towns and cities of the west have a relatively well-developed tourist infrastructure that makes travelling here easier than in other regions.

The Carretera Panamericana runs between San Salvador and the main city of the west, **Santa Ana**, but the primary access route to the southern part of the region leads through the sweaty town of **Sonsonate**, 65km west of the capital. From here, buses head off in several directions: down to the coast for the untouched beaches of **Los Cóbanos**, **Los Remedios** and **Barra de Santiago**; to the tranquil forest reserve at **Parque Nacional El Imposible**; and northwest into the mountains. High above the plains, **Apaneca**, **Ataco** and **Juayúa** are picture-perfect Salvadoran towns, harbouring talented communities of local and foreign artists. Closer to Santa

INTO HONDURAS: EL POY

Crossing the border to **Honduras** at **El Poy** (daily 6am–5pm), 11km from La Palma, is straightforward and quick: the #119 bus from La Palma and San Salvador drops you within sight of the gate. Many trucks use this route, but private traffic is light; crossing early in the day is advisable. The last bus #119 from the border for La Palma and San Salvador leaves at 4.15pm. On the Honduran side, buses run the 10km to Nueva Ocotepeque (see box, p.404) every 40min or so until 5pm, departing from just the other side of the gate that marks the beginning of Honduras.

THE WEST BY BUS: SONSONATE CONNECTIONS

SONSONATE, set in tobacco and cattle-ranching country, prickles with heat in the day and menace at night. It has a history of gang problems, and since there is nothing here to see, its main feature is the **bus terminal**.

Destinations Ahuachapán, via all towns on the Ruta de las Flores (#249; every 15min, 6.15am–6pm; 2hr); Barra de Santiago (#285 direct/#259 getting off at the turning off the Carretera del Litoral; 2 daily/frequent; 1hr 20min/1hr); Parque Nacional El Imposible main entrance (#259; frequent; 1hr 20min); Los Cóbanos (#257; every 30min, 5.30am–6pm; 40min); La Libertad, via the Costa del Bálsamo (#287; daily 5.55am & 3.30pm; 3hr; US$1.50); La Hachadura, Guatemala border (#259; every 10min, 4.30am–7.30pm; 1hr 45min); San Salvador (#205; every 15–20min, 4.30am–5pm; 1hr 30min); Santa Ana (#216 via Los Naranjos/#209B via El Congo; every 20min/hourly; 1hr 15min/1hr 45min).

Ana lie the peaks of **Cerro Verde**, **Volcán Santa Ana** and **Volcán Izalco**, the sublime crater lake of **Lago de Coatepeque**, and the pre-Columbian site of **Tazumal**. In the north of the region, near the Guatemalan border, the accommodating little town of **Metapán** gives access to the **Bosque Montecristo**, where hiking trails weave through unspoilt cloudforest amid some of the most remote and perfectly preserved mountain scenery in the region.

LOS CÓBANOS AND LOS REMEDIOS

With idyllic white sands, warm water and gentle waves, **LOS CÓBANOS** is the ideal place for just lounging on the beach, though it's also the only **reef-diving** spot in the country. Just 25km south of Sonsonate, via a fast highway, it is a favourite weekend destination for Salvadoreños, when it is better to round the headland at the west end of the small bay to the quieter beach of **LOS REMEDIOS**. Although rather rocky, the pretty, gently curved beaches here make a nice contrast to the dark, palm-fringed expanses further down the coast.

ARRIVAL AND DEPARTURE

By bus #257 leaves Sonsonate every thirty minutes for Los Cóbanos until early evening, and there are also occasional direct buses from San Salvador (#207); the last bus leaves the beach at 5pm.

TOURS

Los Cóbanos Tours (☎ 2417 6825) runs boat trips (daily 8am–3pm; 3hr; US$37) off the coast into the Área Natural Protegida Complejo Los Cóbanos in search of dolphins, sea turtles and humpback whales (best Nov–Jan).

El Salvador Divers (ⓦ elsalvadordivers.com) runs dive trips out to the reef – arrange these in advance or in San Salvador.

Grupo Calle Real (☎ 2260 4314, ⓦ senderoselsalvador .com) arranges cheap packages for groups of eight or more and a variety of tours for just two people or more (snorkelling US$12; boat tours US$37).

ACCOMMODATION AND EATING

Budget accommodation is limited along the beaches. The best places to eat are the fishermen's restaurants that line the shore. The delicious fish is caught in the morning and cooked at lunch.

Los Cóbanos Village Lodge Los Remedios ☎ 2420 5248, ⓦ loscobanosvillagelodge.com. Clean *palapas* with balconies onto the beach and a dorm with seven beds. They also provide breakfast, use of the pool, and rent out snorkel gear and kayaks. Dorm US$12, double US$59

BARRA DE SANTIAGO

West of the rough and shabby port town of Acajutla, the Carretera del Litoral runs on to the Guatemalan border at La Hachadura (see box, p.250), with the slopes of the Cordillera Apaneca rising to the north and rolling pasturelands to the south. After 35km an unmarked track leads south to **PLAYA BARRA DE SANTIAGO**, a gorgeous, sandy strip of land separating the ocean from a protected estuary and mangrove reserve inland. The peninsula is occupied by a scruffy fishing village, but the expanse of beach is delightfully empty and the locals still seem a little surprised to see visitors. Barra de Santiago is also a major **turtle-nesting** area – visit from August

3

INTO GUATEMALA: LA HACHADURA

From the Barra de Santiago turning the Carretera del Litoral continues the last few kilometres to **La Hachadura**, a 24hr border crossing used by international buses heading for Mexico and reached via bus #259 from Sonsonate (1hr 45min). There's a small *hospedaje* on the Guatemalan side, and buses to Guatemala City (4hr; last bus 3pm), stopping at Esquintla along the way, leave from a point 1km down the road.

through November and you can see giant sea turtles laying eggs along the beach.

ARRIVAL AND DEPARTURE

By bus Bus #259 from Sonsonate passes the turning from the Carretera, where pick-ups go to the village; or Lena of *Capricho Beach House* can organize a lift. You can also wait for direct buses (#285) that go twice a day from Sonsonate.

TOURS

Julio César Local expert Julio (☎7783 4765) runs illuminating birdwatching boat trips (US$45) around the mangroves and to a small archeological site, Isla El Cajete, where obsidian arrowheads, ceramics and other remains have been found dating from the Postclassic period (700–1524); he is also very knowledgeable on local flora and fauna.
Canoe trips *Capricho Beach House* can organize canoe trips into the nature reserve.

ACCOMMODATION AND EATING

As with Los Remedios, the best places to eat are local fishermen's shacks that line the shore.
Capricho Beach House Final C Principal & 39 Av Sur, 3km from Barra de Santiago village ☎7860 8632, ⓦximenasguesthouse.com/en-capricho.html. The place to stay, related to *Ximena's* in San Salvador (see p.212). Choose between firm metal beds in the dorms, and en-suite doubles with fan or a/c. There's an outdoor kitchen for guests and a restaurant (6am–9pm). Free wi-fi. Dorm US$12, double US$47.20

PARQUE NACIONAL EL IMPOSIBLE

Just off the Carretera del Litoral near the Guatemalan border, a bone-shaking road snakes its way 13.5km up to one of El Salvador's greatest hidden glories, the forest reserve of **PARQUE NACIONAL EL**

IMPOSIBLE, so called because of the early hazards in transporting coffee by mule pack down from its sheer heights and steep gorges to the coast. Covering more than 31 square kilometres and rising through three climatic zones across the Cordillera de Apaneca, the reserve contains more than four hundred species of tree and 1600 species of plant, some unique to the area. You may glimpse some of the more than three hundred bird species here, including the emerald toucanet, trogons, hummingbirds and eagles, while the park provides a secure habitat for a diverse range of animals, including anteaters, the white-tailed deer and ocelot, plus more than five hundred different species of butterfly, including the dazzling blue morpho.

Clearly marked **trails**, offering a variety of walks lasting from two hours to a full day, set off from the park's visitors' centre (see opposite). It's not advisable, however, to try to explore deeper within the densely forested park without a **guide** (see below).

ARRIVAL AND DEPARTURE

Exploring El Imposible can be time-consuming and expensive without your own transport; there are no cheap accommodation options near the main entrance and most of the San Salvador operators (see p.211) run expensive tours here. If travelling by public transport you'll need to spend the night. It is actually easier to approach from Tacuba in the north (see p.257).
By bus The main park entrance is accessed from the Desvío Ahuachapío turn-off on the Carretera del Litoral, halfway between the Sonsonate–Acajutla road and Cara Sucia, and about 13.5km from the park itself on a gravel road. Bus #259 from Sonsonate stops at the turn-off to the park (5km before Cara Sucia) on its way to the Guatemalan border (at La Hachadura) – get off here and catch the 11am or 2pm pick-up, or 3.30pm bus (#811) to San Miguelito (daily), a short walk from the park gate. Pick-ups make the return journey at 5.30am and 6.30am; the bus departs at 7.30am.
By motorcycle taxi Another option is to use local motorcycle taxis or tuk-tuks in Cara Sucia (US$10–20 to the park entrance – you'll have to negotiate hard to get US$10).

INFORMATION

Entry fee and guides There's a US$6 entry fee (parking is an additional US$1/day) to enter the reserve, which is managed by SalvaNatura (33 Av Sur 640, Col Flor Blanca, San Salvador; ☏ 2279 1515, ⊛ salvanatura.org) – you're meant to visit their office in San Salvador to pay and arrange a guide beforehand, but you can usually do it by phone or just turn up and plead ignorance. Heading away from the official trails without a guide you'll get lost within minutes. Guides are free, but will ask for a US$10 tip – this is just suggested, but it's customary to leave at least US$5.

Visitor centre In the old Hacienda San Benito, 100m inside the main entrance, is the solar-powered Centro de Visitantes Mixtepe (daily 7am–5pm; free) with information boards about the park's wildlife, tour guides on hand and a small souvenir store.

ACCOMMODATION AND EATING

There are *comedores* inside the park, and a restaurant in the *hostal*.

Camping SalvaNatura allows camping on three sites, with small campfires and rinsing (but not washing) possible in the river. The campsite near the visitor centre offers grills, picnic tables and toilets. Per person US$3

Hostal El Imposible Inside the park, 800m from the main entrance ☏ 2279 1515. A comfy, eco-neutral (solar-powered) hostel, with five comfortable cabañas, a springwater pool and a very good restaurant, *Restaurante El Ixcanal*. US$30

NAHUIZALCO

The population of the village of **NAHUIZALCO**, 10km north of Sonsonate on the Ruta de las Flores (see box below), is mostly descended from the region's indigenous peoples, although few wear traditional dress any longer. The town thrives on the manufacture of **wicker** and **tule** (a type of plant) handicrafts, with workshops lining the main street. Some of the pieces are small enough to take home, and gentle bargaining is acceptable. The government arts

organization **CEDART**, 3A C Pte 3 (in front of the Parque), is a helpful place to start and has a shop (Mon–Fri 7.30am–4.30pm; ☏ 2453 0618). There's also a candlelit **night market**, with food and craft stalls open to around 10pm.

ARRIVAL AND INFORMATION

By bus Bus #249, which runs the length of the Ruta de las Flores from Sonsonate to Ahuachapán (every 15min), stops at the highway turn-off, which is a 500m walk downhill to the centre; bus #53-D goes direct to the village from Sonsonate.

Services There are no hotels here. The cheap food stalls in the market around the Parque are usually open during the day.

JUAYÚA

Beyond Nahuizalco, the air freshens as the road winds its way up to the enchanting colonial town of **JUAYÚA** (pronounced "why-YOU-ah"), once in the heart of a major coffee-producing area. When coffee prices slumped in the early 1990s, Juayúans started the **food festivals** (*ferias gastronómicas*) that now dominate the centre every weekend. The town itself is safe at night, clean and crammed with traditional adobe houses adorned with florid street murals by local painters, while the coffee-growing countryside offers plenty of activities to work off the weekend's indulgences.

WHAT TO SEE AND DO

On Saturdays and Sundays the main plaza and roads leading onto it are lined with the **feria gastronómica**'s food stalls; look out for iguana, paella, snake, Chinese and Mexican dishes, frogs, excellent seafood and chocolate-covered

---

RUTA DE LAS FLORES

Beginning at the northern edge of the Parque Nacional El Imposible and stretching east for more than 70km from the Guatemalan border, the glorious mountains of the Cordillera Apaneca are covered in a patchwork of coffee plantations and acres of pine forest. The so-called "**Ruta de las Flores**", covering the area between Concepción de Ataco and Nahuizalco, is named after the abundant white coffee flowers visible during May and the wild flowers that colour the hills and valleys from October to February. This stretch is one of the country's biggest attractions, home to a string of cool and pleasant towns with good accommodation, restaurants and sights, the highlights of which are **Juayúa**'s now-famous *ferias gastronómicas*, the high Laguna Verde and the strongly artistic community of **Ataco**.

3

frozen fruit on sticks (US$1). The festival has been so successful with day-trippers that half of Juayúa seems to own a stall or food cart – if you can't visit on a weekend you'll still find a few plying their wares during the week.

Templo del Señor de Juayúa

On the west side of the main plaza (Parque Unión) stands the magnificent **Templo del Señor de Juayúa** (daily 6am–noon & 2–6pm; free). It was rebuilt in colonial style in 1956, and houses the Black Christ of Juayúa, thought to have been carved around 1580 by Quiro Cataño, sculptor of the Black Christ of Esquipulas in Guatemala (see box, p.337). Consequently, the town is something of a pilgrimage site, particularly during the January 8–15 festival.

Reptilandia

Reptilandia (daily 9am–6pm, usually closed noon–1pm; US$0.50, parking US$1), one block south of the church on 6A C Pte, is an enthusiastic if slightly amateurish mini zoo containing reptiles and insects from El Salvador and elsewhere in the tropics. More than twenty snakes, bearded dragons and Australian lizards slither around glass cases, while scary-looking tarantulas and scorpions pose for photographs.

Los Chorros de la Calera

Just 2km out of town (take the street to the left of the mermaid statue), **Los Chorros de la Calera** (free) is the town's local swimming spot, featuring three waterfalls with two artificial pools, the top one deep enough to jump in, and connected by a couple of water-filled tunnels. You can walk there (a steep twenty-minute hike down a rocky jungle hillside), or take a tuk-tuk (motorcycle taxi; US$1). On weekdays locals recommend you organize a free tourist police escort (see below).

ARRIVAL AND DEPARTURE

By bus On weekdays, the Sonsonate-to-Ahuachapán buses stop on the east side of Parque Unión, but at weekends they are pushed out to Pasaje San Juan, three blocks west along 4A C Pte. Other buses stop at the Izalco

turning, where you can take a motorcycle taxi (tuk-tuk) into the centre ($0.35).

Destinations Ahuachapán, stopping at Apaneca and Ataco (#249; every 30min; 1hr 15min); San Salvador, Terminal de Occidente (#205, normal 1hr 45min; *especial* 1hr 15min); Santa Ana (#209 via Cerro Verde; frequent; 1hr); Sonsonate (via Nahuizalco #249; every 30min; 45min; direct #53; every 30min; 15min).

INFORMATION AND TOURS

Tourist office The well-stocked and enthusiastic tourist office, on the eastern side of the Parque (daily 8am–5pm), offers excellent maps, but has limited English.

POLITUR The tourist police office is at 1 Av Nte, just north of C Merceditas (☎ 2469 2510).

Tours There are trekking, horseriding, geysers and coffee tours to be enjoyed locally – organize trips with your accommodation.

ACCOMMODATION

The town is largely quiet during the week, but at weekends you should book ahead.

Casa de Huespedes "Doña Mercedes" 2A Av Sur & 6A C Ote 3–6 ☎ 2452 2287. Cheerful place with comfortable rooms, hot water and cable TV. The shared bathrooms are very clean – en suites cost just US$5 more. <u>US$30</u>

Hostal Casa Mazeta 2A Av Nte & C 1 Ote ☎ 2406 3403, ⓦ casamazetajuayua.blogspot.com. A friendly and popular addition to Juayúa's backpacker scene, two blocks from the Parque; the English owner (Darren Clarke) offers clean rooms (shared or private bath), dorms and cheap hammock space under cover. Accommodation is arranged around a leafy little garden, plus there's a lounge area, DVDs, free wi-fi, laundry and kitchen. Dorm <u>US$9</u>, double <u>US$22</u>

★ **Hotel Anáhuac** 1A C Pte & 5A Av Nte ☎ 2469 2401, ⓦ hotelanahuac.com. The best choice in town and probably the best hostel in the country, run by young and friendly couple César and Janne. Immaculately clean rooms, comfortable beds, powerful hot-water showers, a lovely courtyard with hammocks, vibrant modern art on the walls, free wi-fi, a good DVD collection, book exchange and tours organized. Dorm <u>US$9</u>, double <u>US$25</u>

El Mirador 4A C Pte (at the western end of town) ☎ 2452 2432, ⓦ elmiradorjuayua.com. A large hotel near the Parque, with friendly hostess and hard mattresses in clean but gloomy en-suite rooms (some singles; US$17.50) with cable TV and fan around a two-storey atrium. Good wi-fi and laundry available. <u>US$32.50</u>

EATING AND DRINKING

El Cadejo Café 4A C Pte, between 2 Av Sur & Av Daniel Cordón Sur. This cosy, lively little bar/café, spilling out onto

3

★ TREAT YOURSELF

Restaurante R & R C Mercedes 1–2, at 1
Av Nte (a block north of the Parque)
☎ 2452 2083. One of the best restaurants
in the region, decorated with vivid murals.
Chef Carlos Caceres fuses Central
American cuisine with Western staples
(red bean pasta, *carne de café*), liberally
doused in local herbs and spices. Mains
around US$10–15, slightly less for veggie
options. Mon–Sat 7am–10pm.

---

the street, hosts great live music on Saturday. Their range
of coffees (from $1) and their *capitán mojitos* (from
US$3.85) are specialities – after a couple of the latter the
day-glo paintings will dance before your eyes. They also
serve sandwiches (from US$7), burgers (US$8.50) and
excellent pastas (US$6). Thurs–Sun 11am till late.

El Mirador 4A C Pte (at the western end of town) ☎ 2452
2432. Come here for breakfast on the third floor. They
have pancakes (US$1.50) and fruit salads as well as the
típicos (try the *frijoles borrachos*, "drunken beans"), and
the panoramic views – only slightly marred by the glass
– are a good morning eye-opener. Mon–Fri 7am–10pm,
Sat & Sun 7am–2.30pm.

Panadería y Cafetería Festival 4A C Ote (south side of
the Parque). This basic canteen serves good coffee,
traditional Spanish cakes (US$1.50) and fine breakfasts
(from US$2.50). Daily 7am–10pm.

Pupusería Doña Cony 2 Av Sur, at 6A C Ote ☎ 2452
2256. Although a tad pricier than other *pupuserías*, at
$0.60 each, these *pupusas* are made fresh while you wait,
and stuffed full of beans, cheese, *chicharrón* and *ayote*
(calabaza squash). Daily 7am–5pm.

Taquería Guadalupana C Merceditas Cáceres, at Av
Daniel Cordón ☎ 2452 2195, ⊕ taqueriaguadalupana
.com. Big portions of top-notch Mexican food – daily deals
for US$2.99. *Tacos al pastor* (US$2.40) are a favourite.
Tues–Sun 10.30am–9.30pm.

DIRECTORY

Bank Scotiabank (Mon–Fri 8am–4pm, Sat 8am–noon),
by the weekend bus stop at the western end of 4A C Pte,
has an ATM.

Supermarkets Selectos supermarket, C Merceditas &
Daniel Cordón; Despensa Familiar, 2A C Ote & Daniel
Cordón (both daily 8am–7pm).

APANECA

A short ride further along CA-8 from
Juayúa lies **APANECA**, another captivating
mountain town, founded by Pedro de

Alvarado in the mid-sixteenth century.
Despite being popular with weekend
visitors, tourism is far less developed here
than in Juayúa or Ataco – there are fewer
cafés and hotels, and the town is a little
shabby around the edges.

WHAT TO SEE AND DO

There's little to do in Apaneca itself, and
during the week you're likely to have the
place – and the wonderful surrounding
mountain scenery – all to yourself.

Laguna Verde

It's an enjoyable and not too strenuous
walk through woods and fincas to the
Laguna Verde, a small crater-lake 4km
northeast of town. Fringed by reeds and
surrounded by mist-clad pine slopes, the
lake is a popular destination, and at
weekends you're likely to share the path
with numerous families and groups of
walkers. From the highway on the
southern edge of town, follow the
well-signed dirt road, and keep going
straight up. The hamlet just above the
lake, reached after about ninety minutes,
has gasp-inducing views from
Ahuachapán to Cerro Artillería on the
Guatemalan border.

Adventure sports

Apaneca has become the unlikely base for
a couple of adventure sports outfits in
recent years. **Apaneca Aventura Buggy
Tours** (☎ 2614 7034) operates off-road
buggy rides (*cuadrimoto*; 2–5hr; from
US$50/person) from its office at 4A Av
Nte and C Los Platanares (Tues–Sun
8.30am–5pm). **Apaneca Canopy Tours**,
Av 15 de Abril at C Central, offers zipline
tours (Tues–Sun: June–Oct 9.30am,
11.30am, 3pm & 7pm; Nov–May
9.30am & 11.30am; US$35/person;
☎ 2433 0554) over lush forests and coffee
plantations (with a plantation tour
included) – its longest cable runs for
280m and the highest is 125m off the
ground. Make reservations in advance for
buggy and canopy tours.

ARRIVAL AND INFORMATION

By bus Services to and from Ahuachapán, via Ataco (#249;
every 30min; 45min); San Salvador, Terminal de Occidente

(#205; 1hr 45min), and Sonsonate, via Nahuizalco (#249; every 30min; 1hr 15min).

Internet Cibernautica, on the far side of the Parque (daily 8am–6.30pm; US$0.50/hr).

Tourist office It is literally an office, on the Parque Central, at 1A Av Sur (Sat & Sun 9am–5pm, in theory; ☎ 2401 8675), with some leaflets and a very helpful man at his desk. A kiosk, opposite, is also manned at weekends.

ACCOMMODATION

Hostal Rural Las Orquídeas 4A C Pte between 1 Av Sur & Av Central ☎ 2433 0061. Well-signposted hostel with seven clean, simple rooms with hot shower, decorated with an odd assortment of antiques. US$15

Hotel Colonia 1A Av Sur by 6A C Pte ☎ 2433 0662. This pretty hotel at the north end of town does indeed have a colonial-looking courtyard. The hotel is furnished with sofas and hammocks, and the good en-suite rooms have sturdy mattresses. US$20

★ **Laguna Verde Guest House** 3.5km from town, in the hamlet by Laguna Verde, left of the school ☎ 7859 2865. In a magnificent position on the edge of the El Cuajusto crater and a short walk from Laguna Verde, the "guest house" is in fact two delightfully remote structures: the white igloo with four bunks and a kitchenette is a good, if a little damp-smelling, novelty, but the cabin is a better pick, with views down to Ahuachapán that are beautiful at night. No one lives on site, so calling ahead is essential. Dorm US$14, double US$35

EATING

Cheap eats are on offer at the Mercado Municipal on 1A Av Sur, opposite the small *parque*; other than *Comedor y Pupusería Edith* (see below), however, most of the food stalls tend to open at lunch or weekends only.

Café Café Av 15 de Abril, at C Menéndez (front of the Casa de la Cultura) ☎ 2263 2413, ✆ cafecafe.com.sv. Roberto Cuadra (who has a celebrated, very expensive restaurant in San Salvador) specializes in "creole Peruvian" cuisine – *ceviche*, shrimp soup, baked pig, rabbit with garlic and the like (mains from US$8). Sat 11.30am–9.30pm, Sun 11.30am–5pm.

Comedor y Pupusería Edith Mercado Municipal, 1A Av Sur. The market food stall with the longest hours, serving *pupusas*, snacks and locally made meringues. Daily 9am–7pm.

★ **El Jardín de Celeste** Km 94 CA-8 (the road to Ataco) ☎ 2433 0281, ✆ eljardindeceleste.com. Don't believe the hype: Ataco's renowned *La Cocina de mi Abuela* on 1A Av Nte is not what it once was and most people now rate this hotel's restaurant to be the best around. It's not as expensive, serving very well-prepared *típicos* like *pollo con arosa* as well as international dishes for under US$10, and with its own plant nursery on site, the surroundings are pretty good too. Daily 7am–6.30pm.

ATACO

Unlike its quiet neighbour Apaneca (twenty minutes away), **ATACO** (full name Concepción de Ataco) is vibrant and lively, with an artistic community unlike anywhere else in the country. Some good, cheap accommodation and restaurants have emerged over recent years, giving it the feel of an up-and-coming destination.

WHAT TO SEE AND DO

You'll see artisans at work throughout the town, and vast, exuberant murals smothered over adobe walls and homes.

Diconte & Axul

The lauded **Diconte & Axul** handicraft store, on the corner of 2A Av Sur and C Central Ote 8 (Mon–Thurs 9am–6pm, Fri–Sun 9am–7pm, ring the doorbell on weekdays; ☎ 2450 5030), is owned by Álvaro Orellana and Cristina Pineda, whose boldly coloured, manga-influenced **paintings** of cats, moons and fish cover several buildings both here and in San Salvador (under the name "Axul"). The shop, in a house built in 1910, sells stylish canvases, masks, wooden figures and boxes for surprisingly little – it's best known for fabrics produced using traditional treadle looms (you can see the looms at the back). It also has a good café (see opposite).

On the opposite street corner is **Artesanías Madre Tierra** (Mon–Sat 9am–6pm), its exterior walls painted in similar day-glo designs and selling a similar mix of local and Guatemalan handicrafts, souvenirs and weavings.

Swimming spots

Hotels can arrange guides to take you to the enticing swimming spots of the 50m **Salto de la Chacala** (on the Río Matala between Ataco and Apaneca), as well as the **Balnerario Atzumpa** (daily 7am–4pm; US$0.25), 2km from town on the road to Ahuachapán, for around US$10/person.

ARRIVAL AND DEPARTURE

By bus Buses come and go from beside the market on the corner of 2A C Pte & 4A Av Nte. From Terminal de Occidente in San Salvador, you can take the *especial* #205 (1hr 15min) or *normal* #205 (1hr 45min). You can also take bus #249 from Ahuachapán or Sonsonate (via Apaneca and Juayúa).

ACCOMMODATION

Posada de Don Oli 1A Av Sur ☎ 2450 5155. This family-run hotel has swings in its pretty courtyard, hot water, and breakfast included. It's a great deal for groups – the two rooms each sleep four. US$50

Segen Hostel 3A C Pte 1 (a block north of the main plaza) ☎ 2450 5832, ✉ segenhostel@hotmail.com. Rooms here are small but neat and tidy; the dorms come with bunk beds. The best deal in town for backpackers. Dorm US$10, double US$35

EATING AND DRINKING

The weekend capital trade means food and drinks here can be relatively pricey. The *portales* on the north side of the Parque are lined with bars and restaurants, while there's a tiny market selling fresh fruit and veg on 2A Av Sur, one block down from the Diconte & Axul store.

The Brother Parque Central (no phone). This popular local food cart can be found most afternoons and evenings on the north side of the Parque, serving mouthwatering *tortas* and hamburgers (US$1–1.20). Times vary, but usually Mon–Sat noon–7pm.

Café del Sitio At the back of the Diconte & Axul store, 2A Av Sur & C Central Ote 8. Drinks and snacks (the spaghetti is a speciality; US$2–7) served in a lovely little garden. Mon–Thurs 9am–6pm, Fri–Sun 9am–7pm.

Doña Mercedes Av Central Sur (opposite the market). A large canteen with smart wooden tables that does an excellent range of *pupusas* (US$0.50 each), as well as good *tortas* and imported beers. Daily 7am–3pm.

★ **House of Coffee** Av Central Sur 13 ☎ 2450 5353. By far the best place for an espresso or cappuccino, with coffee sourced directly from the Escalon family's local plantation – order a fluffy crêpe with your drink (from US$2). Mon–Fri 9am–7pm, Sat & Sun 9am–10pm.

Portland Grill Bar C Central Pte & 1A Av Sur 1 ☎ 2450 5823. The coolest place to drink in town, with a vast menu of beers, cocktails and wines (US$1.50 specials), a pool table and an extensive menu of international dishes from US$4.75. Sun–Thurs 11.30am–10pm, Fri & Sat 11.30am–11pm.

Sibaritas C Emilia Aguilera & Av Central Sur ☎ 2450 5756. Gorgeous restaurant in an old house, but not as expensive as you might think: US$2.50 drink specials and breakfasts from US$5. The theme is Latino-Caribbean fusion, combined with Mediterranean flavours and dishes (pastas, marinated fish and pork). Fri noon–8pm, Sat 8am–10pm, Sun 8am–8pm.

Xochikalko 2A Av Nte (just north of the plaza) ☎ 2541 6593. Top-notch Salvadoran restaurant serving traditional dishes such as *gallo en chichi* and *sopa de gallina india* as well as pizzas, burgers and soups (mains US$8–15). Mon–Sat noon–10pm.

AHUACHAPÁN

From Apaneca the CA-8 tumbles down 13km or so to the city of **AHUACHAPÁN**, the western terminus of the Ruta de las Flores. It's one of the oldest Spanish settlements in the country, and, like most towns in the area, its wealth grew from the coffee trade. Lauded Salvadoran poet **Alfredo Espino** was born here in 1900, during the coffee boom – his only book, *Jícaras Tristes*, is one of the most published collections of poetry in the country.

Today the main industry is geothermal electricity generation, at one time supplying seventy percent of the country's power, while the city centre retains an air of peaceful charm, with tight streets and elegant *parques*. Nonetheless, Ahuachapán is principally a springboard for surrounding attractions.

WHAT TO SEE AND DO

Confusingly, the **Parque Central** is not at the exact centre, but along the main road into town (6A C Pte) and Avenida Francisco Menéndez (three blocks north of the intersection of the two main streets, Calle Gerardo Barrios and Menéndez). A bronze statue of Menéndez (the ex-President was born here in 1830) graces the southern side of the plaza under the palm trees, while across the street an arcade of cobblers ply their trade. On the east side is the indoor Mercado Municipal.

Iglesia Parroquia de Nuestra Señora de la Asunción

The imposing white edifice of the **Iglesia Parroquia de Nuestra Señora de la Asunción** on the Plaza Concordia (five blocks south of Parque Central on Av Menéndez), with intricate stained glass and a wooden ceiling, dominates the centre of the city and acts as the focus for the annual fiesta in the first week of February. By the side of the church you can view the famously whimsical **murals** of local artists Fabio and Bruno Jiménez, along the **Pasaje La Concordia**.

The ausoles

Some 5km east of town, near the hamlet of El Barro, are the **ausoles** (geysers) that form the basis of the local geothermal industry. The plumes of steam hang impressively over the lush green vegetation and red soil – particularly photogenic in the early morning light. Access to the area is via the turn-off signed "Los Ausoles" on the road to Apaneca – get a pick-up or take the bus that leaves twice daily from the market. The power plant itself is off-limits, but locals will allow you access to their land for a small fee, from where you can get a better view. **Eco Mayan Tours** (Paseo General Escalón 3658, Colonia Escalón, San Salvador; ☎2298 2844, ⓦecomayantours.com) provides tours to the *ausoles*, including a chance to roast corn over them, and a tour of the plant (US$30 from Ahuachapán or U$75 to and from San Salvador).

Termales Santa Teresa

At the **Termales Santa Teresa** (daily 8am–6pm; ☎2413 2173, ⓦtermalesdesantateresa.com), hot springs just 2km outside Ahuachapán (off the road to Ataco) have been fed into three gorgeous tiled pools. It costs US$10 to soak all day long, and most weekdays you'll have the place to yourself.

ARRIVAL AND DEPARTURE

By bus The terminal, a chaotic affair, is on Av Comercial, between 10A and 12A C Pte, eight blocks from the Plaza Concordia. Little moto-taxis (tuk-tuks) are a cheap way to get around town (pay no more than US$1).

Destinations Chalchuapa, for Tazumal (#210; frequent; 30min); Las Chinamas–Guatemala border (#263; every 15min, 6am–5pm; 30min); Santa Ana (#202/#210; frequent; 1hr); San Salvador (#202; frequent; 3hr 30min); Sonsonate (#249; every 15min; 2hr 30min); Tacuba (#264/#15; every 20min; 40min).

ACCOMMODATION

La Casa Blanca 2A Av Nte, at C Barrios Pte 1–5 ☎2443 1505, ⓔcasablancahuachapan@hotmail.com. A good-value option, housed in a well-decorated colonial building with eight large, clean rooms, all with bath, cable TV and free wi-fi (a/c rooms are US$11 extra). The restaurant is set around a relaxing courtyard. <u>US$42</u>

Casa de Mamapán 2A Av Sur, at Pasaje La Concordia (in front of Parque Concordia) ☎2413 2507, ⓦlacasademamapan.com. Built in 1823, this cosy hotel has a prime location on Plaza Concordia, with seven homey en-suite rooms all with a/c, cable TV and free wi-fi. The small café opens onto the mural-smothered Pasaje LaConcordia (the hotel is similarly adorned). <u>US$53</u>

EATING AND DRINKING

Café El Imposible Pasaje La Concordia. This no-frills local café is a cool place to hang out amid the wild murals on this stretch of the *pasaje* – grab a coffee, pastry or cold beer. Daily 7am–10pm.

Casa Grande 4A Av Nte 2, at 4A C Ote ☎2443 0363. There's plenty of character in this restaurant, with loud music blaring and a standard menu featuring some game specialities including venison (*venado*) and rabbit (*conejo*) for less than US$6. Daily noon–10pm.

★ **La Estancia** 1A Av Sur 1–3, at C Barrios ☎2443 1559. Housed in an elegantly decaying former coffee mansion built in 1910, this *comedor* gets a star for the sheer wonderful bizarreness of the surroundings – and a rare glimpse of colonial Salvador. The food is so-so – well-prepared *comida* at standard prices (US$2–6.50) from an incongruous buffet-style kitchen at the back – but you eat in the grand old rooms. Daily 7am–6pm.

Mixta "S" 2A Av Sur, just north of the Parque Concordia. Serving "*mixtas*" – flatbreads stuffed with meat, cheese or vegetables (US$1.95) – this clean canteen with plastic tables also offers *pupusas* (US$0.65), *churrasco* (steak) plates (US$4.75) and a big selection of fruit juices. Daily 9am–11pm.

Pastelería Roxana 2A Av Sur 1–2 ☎2426 1269, ⓦpasteleriaroxana.com.sv. Great place for cakes and coffee, with a new, modern interior and a pink facade – local specialities include *semitas* (bran or pineapple cakes) and *salpores de almidón* (small biscuits). The local chain was founded in 1969, down the road in Chalchuapa. Daily 9am–6pm.

El Sin Rival 2A Av Sur (east side of Parque Concordia) ⓦelsinrival.com.sv. Not quite as good as the Santa Ana

INTO GUATEMALA: LAS CHINAMAS

From Ahuachapán, a reasonably good and very scenic road (CA-8) runs the 20km or so to the **Guatemalan border** on the Río Paz, just past **Las Chinamas** (local bus #11AH from Ahuachapán; every 15min; 1hr). You'll have to walk across the bridge and up the hill to reach the buses that run to Guatemala City from Valle Nuevo (see box, p.338) on the Guatemalan side (500m), though moto-taxis will whisk you there for a small fee. International buses between Santa Ana, San Salvador and Guatemala City also pass through this border crossing; passports are normally checked on the bus, but there will be a short wait on both sides of the border. The mobs of moneychangers on the Guatemalan side will take hefty commissions if they can, so make sure you know the current **exchange rate** before agreeing on an amount.

original (see p.260), this branch still offers refreshing ice cream (coconut, tamarind, orange) served in a distinctive flat (and pink) cone. Some seating inside. Single scoops US$0.75. Daily 11am–9pm.

DIRECTORY

Banks Scotiabank and Citibank face each other on the corner of C Gerardo Barrios & Av Francisco Menéndez, with money exchange, travellers' cheque-cashing and ATMs (both Mon–Fri 8am–4pm, Sat 8am–noon).

Internet Ciber Sharks, 2A Av Sur, just north of Parque Concordia (daily 10pm–6pm; US$0.75/hr).

Pharmacy Farmacia Central, 2A Av Sur & C Barrios (daily 8am–noon & 2–6pm; ☎ 2443 0158).

Post office 1A C Ote & 1A Av Sur (Mon–Fri 8am–5pm, Sat 8am–noon).

Supermarket Despensa Familiar, Av Central Sur Lote 1 (daily 7am–7pm), is by the bus terminal.

TACUBA

Some 15km west of Ahuachapán lies the tranquil mountain village of **TACUBA**, reached via a winding and scenic road with tantalizing views of coffee plantations and the Parque Nacional El Imposible (see p.250). An important settlement existed here long before the Spaniards arrived, and the village retains strong folkloric traditions, although you'll only really notice these at fiesta time.

WHAT TO SEE AND DO

The village is small and welcoming, but the only thing to see is the ruined colonial **church**, the **Iglesia Santa María Magdalena de Tacuba**, which was much less ruined before the 2001 earthquake. Built between 1605 and 1612 in an elegant Baroque style, it was flattened for the first time by an earthquake in 1773. Either the guard or Manolo of Imposible Tours (see box below) will let you in to walk through and climb up the remaining structure. The real draw of Tacuba is, however, its back route into the dramatic **Parque Nacional El Imposible** (see p.250).

ARRIVAL AND DEPARTURE

By bus From Ahuachapán Tacuba can be reached by bus #264 or minibus #15 (every 15min; 45min).

ACCOMMODATION AND EATING

Hostal Mamá y Papá 10A C Pte & 1A Av Sur 1 ☎ 2417 4268. The mama and papa in question are Mr and Mrs González, parents of Manolo (see box below) and very good hosts. Shared hot showers, clean and comfortable rooms (with very thin walls), morning coffee and shady hammocks add to the appeal, and the roof terrace is a nice place to watch the sunset with a beer. Dorm US$8, double US$20

Miraflores 2A Av Nte, at 7A C Ote ☎ 2417 4746, ✉ miraflores@hotmail.com. A good option if *Mamá y Papá* is full, this bright and breezy place has a flower-filled

IMPOSIBLE TOURS

Based in Tacuba, **Imposible Tours** (☎ 2417 4268, ⊛ imposibletours.com) is one of the best tour operators in the country, due in most part to good-humoured and charismatic leader Manolo González, whose ceaseless enthusiasm comes from a genuine desire to get to know everyone he guides. The company's hallmark tour takes you along the back route through **Parque Nacional El Imposible** along a series of occasionally staggering waterfalls and sheer-walled canyons, though the setup is flexible. Other options include **mountain biking** along ridges to the coast, several day-treks and wallowing in hot **volcanic springs** with a beer or two. Tours start from US$25–30/person.

courtyard ringing with birdsong. Try to get an en-suite room (cold water only) – they're brighter (with two windows). Rates include two meals. <u>US$25</u>

TAZUMAL AND CASA BLANCA

Northeast from Ahuachapán, the road drops down onto a broad and scenic plain to the town of **CHALCHUAPA** and the towering archeological site of **Tazumal**, the most impressive Mesoamerican ruin in the country.

Tazumal

Tazumal (Tues–Sun 9am–4pm; US$3; ☎2444 0010) lies on the southern edge of Chalchuapa – the highway passes on the north side, so if driving you must pass through the town to get to the ruins. The main showstopper is a vast fourteen-stepped ceremonial pyramid, influenced by the style of Teotihuacán in Mexico. Though the site certainly possesses its own enigmatic beauty and is easily the most impressive ancient ruin in El Salvador, as a whole it is – by comparison with sites in Honduras and Guatemala – rather small, and parts have been rather sloppily restored. The site was occupied for more than 750 years, mostly in the Late Classic period (600–900 AD). Earlier remains, dating back to 100–200 AD, have been found beneath the pyramid. The Maya abandoned the city around the end of the ninth century, during the collapse of the Classic Maya culture, and, unusually, Pipils moved in and occupied the site, building a pyramid dating back to the Early Postclassic (900–1200 AD) and another pelota court, in the northwest corner of the site. Tazumal was finally abandoned around 1200 AD. The **Museo Sitio Arqueológico** (same hours; Spanish only) displays artefacts discovered during excavations, including some stunning ceramics, but you'll need to read Spanish to make the most of it.

Casa Blanca

Aficionados should check out the smaller, grassy ruins of **Casa Blanca** (Tues–Sun 9am–4pm; US$3; US$1 parking; ☎2408 4641), an important Maya centre between 200 BC and 250 AD, just a five-minute taxi ride from Tazumal (it's right on the main highway on the north side of Chalchuapa). Visit in mid-winter and the site is smothered in pink *madrecacao* blooms. There's also a small exhibit here on traditional indigo production and tie-dye cloth making – enthusiastic women provide demonstrations (Spanish only).

ARRIVAL AND DEPARTURE

By bus #218 from Ahuachapán drops passengers off at a small plaza a few blocks from the centre of Chalchuapa; from here, walk uphill for about four blocks and follow the sign for Tazumal (you'll see the souvenir shops before the ruins). If driving, just park on the street outside (ask anyone for directions if you miss the signs).

SANTA ANA

El Salvador's second city, **SANTA ANA** lies in a superb location in the Cihautehuacán valley. Surrounded by jungle-smothered peaks, with the slope of Volcán Santa Ana rising to the southwest, the gently decaying colonial streets exude a restrained, provincial calm that is generally only ruptured during the July fiesta, when a host of events bring the streets to life. It's the most relaxed of El Salvador's cities, with the most elegant Parque Central in the country and a decent nightlife, though the natural attractions of **Lago de Coatepeque**, the forest reserve of **Cerro Verde**, and the **Santa Ana and Izalco volcanoes** all beckon.

WHAT TO SEE AND DO

Santa Ana's **historic centre** possesses arguably the finest main plaza in the country: the **Parque Libertad** is neatly laid out with a small bandstand, where people gather to sit and chat in the early evening.

Catedral de Santa Ana

On the eastern edge of the Parque is the magnificent **Catedral de Santa Ana** (Mon–Sat 6.30am–noon & 2–5.30pm, Sun 7am–noon & 2–5.30pm; free), an imposing neo-Gothic edifice completed in the early twentieth century. It's the second cathedral to occupy this site: a Spanish settlement was initially founded here in July 1569, when Bishop Bernardino de Villapando arrived en route from Guatemala. Completed seven years later, this church occupied the site of the present cathedral until it was destroyed in the early twentieth century to make way for the new building.

Inside the cathedral, the high naves, rather unsympathetically painted in pink and grey, soar upwards, and images – some dating back four hundred years – line the walls to the altar. Inset into the walls are plaques from local worshippers giving thanks to various saints for miracles performed.

Teatro Nacional

On the northern edge of the Parque, the **Teatro Nacional**, completed in Renaissance style in 1910, was funded by taxes on local dignitaries. Once the proud home of the country's leading theatre companies, the building became a cinema in the 1930s before falling into disuse. Now restored to something resembling its former glories, it once again hosts recitals and concerts, as well as exhibitions and plays (see p.261). Guided tours (US$1.50) are in Spanish; you can usually wander around unaccompanied (Mon–Sat 8am–noon & 2–6pm).

Museo Regional del Occidente

On the second block down Avenida Independencia from the Parque, the **Museo Regional del Occidente** (Tues–Sun 9am–noon & 1–5pm; US$1) provides a comprehensive introduction to the region's history and archeological sites, though the best bit is the room dedicated

3

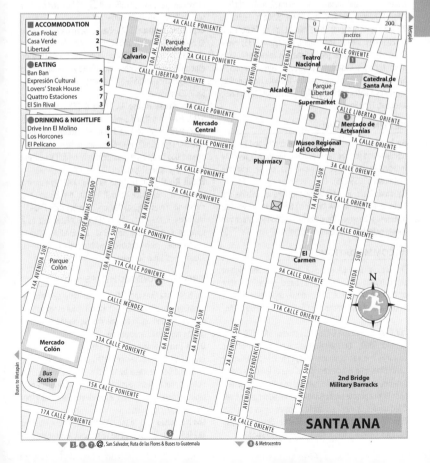

ACCOMMODATION
Casa Frolaz 3
Casa Verde 2
Libertad 1

EATING
Ban Ban 2
Expresión Cultural 4
Lovers' Steak House 5
Quattro Estaciones 7
El Sin Rival 3

DRINKING & NIGHTLIFE
Drive Inn El Molino 8
Los Horcones 1
El Pelícano 6

SANTA ANA

to the various evolving forms of legal tender in the country, from 1828 right up to the dollar – fitting, considering this was once the local office of the Banco de Central de Reserva.

ARRIVAL AND DEPARTURE

By bus The main Terminal Mercado Colón is on 10A Av Sur between 13A & 15A C Pte. Buses for Metapán (#325) arrive and depart two blocks west of the main terminal, in front of the Despensa Familiar supermarket, and international Puerto Buses to and from Guatemala arrive and depart from 25A C Pte between 6A & 8A Av Sur, just north of *Casa Frolaz*. King Quality and Ticabus (to and from Guatemala) usually stop at the Shell petrol station on the outskirts of the city (confirm before you leave; taxis will take you to the gas station for US$4–5).

Destinations Ahuachapán (#210; frequent; 1hr); Chalchuapa (#218; frequent; 30min); Guatemala City, Guatemala (standard/first class; hourly/2 daily; 4hr/3hr 30min); Juayúa (#238; daily 6.45am, 9.50am, 12.30pm, 2.30pm, 4pm, 5.35pm; 1hr 30min); Lago de Coatepeque (#220; every 30min; 1hr 30min); Metapán (#235; every 20min; 1hr 15min); Parque Nacional Los Volcanes (#248; 6 daily; 1hr); San Cristóbal (#248; every 20min; 1hr); San Salvador (#201; frequent; 1hr 30min); Santa Elena, Belize, via Flores, Guatemala (daily; 9hr); Sonsonate (#216/#209; frequent; 1hr 15min/1hr 45min).

GETTING AROUND

By bus Bus #51 runs between the centre and the bus terminal, and you can take any bus going up and down Av Independencia to get between the centre and the Metrocentro (US$0.25).

By taxi There are stands on the Parque, outside the Metrocentro and on 10A Av Sur, by the market, or you can hail one on the street. They should cost US$4–5, which you should politely agree beforehand.

ACCOMMODATION

The area around 8A and 10A Av Sur has the highest concentration of cheap and basic places to stay, co-dependent on the vice industry operating on the streets at night. Book ahead for *Casa Frolaz* or *Casa Verde*.

★ **Casa Frolaz** 29A C Pte 42B, between 8A & 10A Av Sur ☎2440 5302, ✉casafrolaz@yahoo.com. One of the country's finest accommodation options is in the house of Javier Díaz, who is a descendant of one of the city's oldest families, a painter of international repute and a perfect host. With a private kitchen, laundry, hot water and a fruit-filled garden, a stay here could be three times the price. Free wi-fi but no computers. Shuttle buses to Copán (US$30). Camping US$5, dorm US$8, double US$20

★ **Casa Verde** 7A C Pte between 8A & 10A Av Sur ☎7860 7180, ⓦhostalverde.wordpress.com. Excellent option close to the centre, and quite different from the standard of neighbouring hotels. Spotless rooms on an open courtyard and (two) very well-equipped kitchens, with free wi-fi. There are board games, free water and coffee, help-yourself beers (US$1.25), rooftop terrace and a laundry, and the young owners (both Carlos) are keen and helpful. Dorm US$12, double US$27

Libertad 4A C Ote 2, at 1A Av Nte ☎2441 2358, ✉javal@navegante.com.sv. Great location right by the cathedral with gigantic, quite clean and basic rooms with TV, some with bathroom. Free wi-fi. Bring your own padlock for the doors. Dorm US$10, double US$15

EATING

Ban Ban Av Independencia Sur 52 ☎2447 1865. The best bakery in town (opened in the 1970s), with a second outlet in the Metrocentro. Serves sandwiches for lunch, and cakes, pastries and coffee all day. Indoor and outdoor seating. Free wi-fi. Daily 8am–7pm.

Expresión Cultural 11A C Pte between 6A & 8A Av Sur ☎2440 1410. An arts and cultural centre, bookshop and internet café in a bohemian, leafy courtyard. They do especially good sandwiches (including a veggie option), as well as full meals (US$7–8) and desserts (US$3–4). Mon–Sat 7.30am–9pm.

Lovers' Steak House 4A Av Sur & 17A C Pte ☎2440 5717. A meat grill and Santa Ana institution that serves huge portions of steak and seafood, accompanied by a *bocadillo* (appetizer), as well as wine or beer. Mains cost around US$12, but you will definitely be full when you leave. Daily noon–10pm.

El Sin Rival C Libertad Ote ☎2441 0042, ⓦelsinrival.com.sv. A cool place to chill out in the centre, this *sorbetería* serves original flavours of sorbet (US$0.70–1); blueberry is the best. The mini-chain started out as a *sorbetes* cart opened in 1951 by Emiliano Rivera Landaverde, soon dubbed "without rival". Mon–Fri 10am–9pm, Sat & Sun 9am–9pm.

DRINKING AND NIGHTLIFE

Much of Santa Ana's nightlife is outside of the centre to the south, so take a taxi (US$3–4). Heading out of town, taxis are easily found on Av Independencia; on the way back, get the barman to arrange one.

Drive Inn El Molino 25A Av Sur, at Carretera Antigua ☎2447 2029, ⓦdriveinnelmolino.com. A little out of town and best reached by taxi, this big and well-known club has pool tables, live music, food and dancing. The best night is Thurs, but it's lively all weekend. Tues–Sat 11pm until the early morning.

Los Horcones Next to the cathedral on Parque Libertad ☎2484 7511. The best views in the city, with seats on a

Quattro Estaciones 29A C Pte & 10 Av Sur 42-B ☎ 2440 1564. This smart local favourite distinguishes itself from the pricier options nearby by its fine cooking rather than the size of its portions. It has an Italian influence, with good bruschetta and spaghetti dishes, as well as a fine wine menu and coffee selection. US$18–20 per head. Mon–Thurs noon–9pm, Fri & Sat noon–10.30pm.

rickety terrace facing the cathedral and plaza. There are drinks promotions on Saturdays, and there's often dancing too. Mon–Thurs & Sun 10.30am–9pm, Fri & Sat 10.30am–2am.
El Pelícano Av Moraga Sur 12, 1km south of town ☎ 2449 0386. A small bar with good food, including more than sixty appetizers (US$2–3) – you'll only need three to fill you up. They play pop music and regularly host karaoke. Daily 11am–2am.

ENTERTAINMENT

Cinema Cinemark, in the Metrocentro, shows dubbed or subtitled Hollywood blockbusters.
Theatre The beautifully restored Teatro Nacional (see p.259) has a calendar of classical music, theatre and performance arts (☎ 2447 6268). Check listings in the Friday *Prensa Gráfica* or stop by to find out times. Tickets should be under US$4 a show.

DIRECTORY

Banks There is a clump of banks around 2A Av Nte behind the Alcaldía.
Internet Time Out (10am–7 or 9pm; US$1/1hr) is on 10A Av Sur & 29A C Pte.
Market The Mercado Central (daily 7am–5pm) is on 8A Av Sur between 1A & 3A C Pte, and the Mercado de Artesanías (Mon–Sat 8.30am–6pm), with a range of national crafts, is on 1A Av Sur.

INTO GUATEMALA: SAN CRISTÓBAL

Crossing to **Guatemala** at **San Cristóbal** is quick and easy: it's open 24hr, and there are frequent buses from Santa Ana (#36; 1hr) to the crossing. There are no official exchange facilities, but the touting moneychangers can offer reasonable rates. On the Guatemalan side, buses run to Asunción Mita, with connections to Guatemala City.

Phones Claro, C Libertad Ote, at 5A Av Nte (Mon–Fri 8am–6pm, Sat 8am–4pm).
Post office Av Independencia at 7A C Pte (Mon–Fri 7.30am–5pm).
Supermarkets La Despensa de Don Juan (8am–8pm), on the southeast corner of the Parque (1A Av Nte, at C Libertad Ote), has a good selection; there is also a Despensa Familiar at 8A C Ote1–3 (daily 7am–7pm).

LAGO DE COATEPEQUE

From El Congo junction, 14km southeast of Santa Ana, a winding branch road descends to the truly stunning crater-lake of **LAGO DE COATEPEQUE**. The views are so mesmerizing that it's worth getting off the bus at the *mirador*, 4km from the water's edge, to take your time soaking them in, and then walking down the rest of the way. As much of the shore is bounded by private houses, access to the water itself is difficult. **Boat rides** are available at *Restaurante Rancho Alegre* (see below), costing from US$20/person for a thirty-minute trip around the lake, while jet skis are US$25/30min.

3

ARRIVAL AND DEPARTURE

By bus Buses #220 and #240 leave Santa Ana for the lake (every 30min; 1hr). If you're heading back to San Salvador, take the Santa Ana bus as far as El Congo then walk down the slip road to the main highway and catch any bus running from Santa Ana to the capital.

ACCOMMODATION AND EATING

Accommodation on the lake is limited and poor – you are better off visiting as a day-trip.
Rancho Alegre Cantón La Laguna, Caserío La Bendición (along the lake) ☎ 2441 6071, ⓦ restauranterancho alegresv.com. This waterside restaurant and hotel rents simple rooms for four or six people, all with a/c and hot water bathrooms. The restaurant (daily 9am–8pm) serves the usual mix of local and international dishes (breakfasts from US$4.50; mains US$7.50), with lively bands playing at the weekend (margaritas US$4.25). U̲S̲$̲4̲0̲
Torremolinos C Principal, 200m on the right down the road alongside the lake ☎ 2441 6037, ⓦ torremolinos lagocoatepeque.com. This ageing but relatively comfortable hotel, with large, clean rooms, two pools and a small private beach, can feel rather neglected, especially on a weekday, and some of the beds need replacing – check your room first. They also arrange boat trips, but rates are much higher than at *Rancho Alegre*. U̲S̲$̲4̲0̲

PARQUE NACIONAL LOS VOLCANES

Around 14km southeast of Santa Ana on the Panamericana, a narrow road rises up from the El Congo junction through coffee plantations, maize fields and pine woods to the **PARQUE NACIONAL LOS VOLCANES** (daily 8am–5pm; US$1; Ⓦsalvanatura.org). Here you can conquer the three dizzying volcanic peaks of Cerro Verde, Santa Ana and Izalco, or just enjoy the flora and fauna on a more relaxing hike through pristine mountain forests.

WHAT TO SEE AND DO

The oldest volcano in the park, **Cerro Verde**, is now a softened, densely vegetated mountain harbouring a wealth of wildlife – park activities centre around the car park near the top. **Santa Ana**, the highest volcano in the country at 2365m, has erupted out of its dormant state, while **Izalco**, one of the youngest volcanoes in the world, is an almost perfect, bare lava cone of unsurpassed natural beauty, and a very novel climb (the best views of it are from Santa Ana). The climb up Santa Ana is much easier than Izalco, and has more shade.

Volcán Cerro Verde

Dense forest fills the crater of the long-extinct **Volcán Cerro Verde**, inside of which a now-rare mix of Salvadoran flora and fauna combine, like a big bowl of nature soup. The numerous species of **plants**, including pinabetes and more than fifty species of orchid, are best viewed in season (for most species, between November and March), while armadillos and white-tailed deer are shy and hard to see year-round. Agoutis, which look like long-legged guinea pigs, can be found rummaging in the forest floor, but it's the **birds** that are most regularly spotted. Hummingbirds and toucans are commonly seen, as is the turquoise-browed motmot (*torogoz* – El Salvador's national bird), identifiable by its pendulous, racketed tail.

From the main car park, go clockwise along the main trail, the *sendero natural*, for an enjoyable walk of around 45 minutes through the green calm of the forest. *Miradores* along the way overlook Volcán Santa Ana and, far below, Lago de Coatepeque. Smaller trails branch off through the trees if you want to explore. The trails are clear and very well managed, but can get busy at weekends.

Volcán Santa Ana

A path branches left from a signed turn ten minutes into the *sendero natural* from the car park, and leads eventually to the summit of **Volcán Santa Ana**, known also as "Ilamatepec" (Nahuat for "old lady mountain"), with a sulphurous crater lake at the summit. In October 2005 the old lady turned out to be a bit more vigorous than her name suggests, erupting violently, killing two people in a boiling mudslide that broke off down its side and spitting rocks, some the size of cars, in a 2km radius. A second eruption was predicted, though has never materialized, and evacuated communities have long since moved back. The trail to the summit was closed for several years, but is now open; guided climbs follow the same format as Volcán Izalco (see below), but check with Corsatur (☎2243 7835) for an update in case of further eruptions. Tours depart at 11am sharp from the Caseta de Guías in the car park, with a mandatory guide and a couple of uniformed policemen costing around US$8.

Volcán Izalco

Sitting in contrast to the green slopes around it, the bleak, black volcanic pile of majestic **Volcán Izalco** began as a small hole in the ground in 1770. The volcano formed rapidly over the next two centuries, during which time its lava plume, known as the "lighthouse of the Pacific", was used by sailors to navigate. Then in 1966, just as a new hotel was built at its base, the plume dried up. Now guided tours leave daily at 11am from the car park for the steep climb to the top (3–4hr; tip US$5–8); be there at 10.30am for the tour briefing. The guides are compulsory, for your safety, set up in response to muggings. A marked trail leads from the lookout down for about thirty minutes to a saddle between Volcán Santa Ana and Volcán Izalco. From here it takes at least an hour to climb the barren moonscape of volcanic scree to the summit. Bring water and good shoes.

ARRIVAL AND DEPARTURE

By bus Sonsonate-bound bus #248 runs to the car park (Tues–Thurs 8.30am, Fri–Sun 7.30am; returning daily 3pm) from Santa Ana's Vencedora terminal. The last bus from the car park leaves at 5pm but runs to El Congo only, from where you can pick up services to Santa Ana or San Salvador.

ACCOMMODATION

Camping If you have your own tent, you can camp for free around the visitors' centre in the car park, though there are no dedicated facilities, so bring food and water; ask a warden to tell you where to set up.

METAPÁN

Some 40km north of Santa Ana, the small, amicable town of **METAPÁN** is scenically situated on the edge of the mountains of the Cordillera Metapán–Alotepeque, which run east along the border with Honduras. Metapán was one of only four communities that supported Delgado's first call for independence in 1811; the town is the birthplace of **Isidro Menéndez** (1795–1858), a key figure in El Salvador's independence movement and often credited with drafting the country's first constitution. With low-set, gently whitewashed buildings, it is one of the more pleasant of Salvadoran provincial towns, the market less unsightly than most and confined to the outskirts well away from the centre. The main reason for staying in Metapán, however, is as a base for the international reserve of **Parque Nacional Montecristo**, jointly administered by the governments of El Salvador, Honduras and Guatemala.

WHAT TO SEE AND DO

At the Parque Central, the **Iglesia de la Parroquia San Pedro Apóstol**, completed in 1743, is one of El Salvador's finest colonial churches, with a beautifully preserved facade. Inside, the main altar is flanked by small pieces worked in silver from a local mine while the ornately decorated cupola features paintings of San Gregorio, San Augustín, San Ambrosio and San Gerónimo. On the south side of the plaza, the colonnaded **Alcaldía** is an attractive building in its own right, watched over by two statues of teeth-baring jaguars symbolizing the strength and suffering of the indigenous people of the department. The west side, rather bizarrely, forms one of the stands of the town's football stadium, though it's cunningly disguised with a neo-colonial colonnaded facade and balcony restaurant, which also offers a good people-watching perch over the square.

Parque Acuático Apuzunga

Just outside Metapán on the nearby Guajoyo River (on the road to Santa Ana), the **Parque Acuático Apuzunga** (Sat & Sun 7am–5pm; ☎ 2483 8952, ⓦ apuzunga.com) offers five naturally fed swimming pools (US$3), ziplining (US$10), camping and rafting with professional river guides (US$50/person).

ARRIVAL AND DEPARTURE

By bus Buses arrive at the main terminal on the Carretera Internacional, five or six blocks from the centre down C 15 de Septiembre, which heads past the market and most of the hotels towards the centre.

Destinations Anguiatú and the Guatemalan border (#211A/#235; every 30min; 30min); San Salvador (#201A; 6 daily; 2hr); Santa Ana (#235; every 20min; 1hr 30min).

ACCOMMODATION

Hostal de Metapán Carretera Internacional, at 9A C Ote ☎ 2402 2382, ⓦ hostaldemetapan@hotmail.com. Rafael and Estrella have created a spotless, central guesthouse with eight rooms including en-suite doubles with a/c, free wi-fi, parking, free coffee and breakfast. US$16

Hostal Villa Limón Carretera Internacional (near the border) ☎ 2442 0149, ⓔ hostalvillalimon@hotmail.com. Three rustic but pleasant log cabins (for up to 6 people) equipped with kitchens and grill (wood fire), fridge and microwave. There's also a camping area with grills and toilets. The owners operate a zipline through the jungle (US$15), and offer meals (US$4–7). Camping per person US$5, cabin US$55

EATING

Antojitos La Nueva Esperanza Off the Parque on Av Benjamin Valiente. Excellent, lofty food hall in a colonial building, with seven dishes of *comida a la vista* a day (US$2–3). Daily 7am–10pm.

Balompié Café 3A Av Nte ☎ 2416 4140, ⓦ balompiecafe .com. Soccer fan (*balompié* means soccer) Amadeo

3

INTO GUATEMALA: ANGUIATÚ

Some 13km north of Metapán, **Anguiatú** is a generally smooth border crossing to **Guatemala**. Open 24hr, it's the most convenient crossing if you're heading for Esquipulas in Guatemala or the Copán ruins in Honduras. Regular buses run from the Guatemalan side to Chiquimula until 5.30pm. If you're coming in the other direction note that the last bus to Metapán leaves at 6.30pm.

Gonzalez, "Prince of Pupusas", runs a couple of famed *pupusa* joints in San Francisco as well as this branch in his home town; check out the balcony with views of the church. Wed–Sun 10am–1pm.

Taquería Guadalajara Carretera Internacional (in front of *Hotel San José*) ☎ 2402 4399. Quality Mexican food – beef tacos, *al pastor*, quesadillas and burritos, as well as giant *tortas* (grilled baguettes), from US$2.50. Daily noon–9pm.

DIRECTORY

Banks Scotiabank, with ATM, at Av Ignacio Gómez & C 15 de Septiembre (Mon–Fri 8am–4.30pm, Sat 8am–noon); Citibank, Av Isidro Menéndez & 3A C Pte (Mon–Fri 8.30am–6.30pm, Sat 8.30am–noon).

Supermarket Súper Selectos (7am–7pm) is near the bus terminal on Carretera Internacional.

PARQUE NACIONAL MONTECRISTO

The enchanting **PARQUE NACIONAL MONTECRISTO** reserve (daily 7am–3pm) rises through two climatic zones to the **Punto Trifinio**, the summit of Cerro Montecristo (2418m), where the borders of Honduras, Guatemala and El Salvador converge. The higher reaches of Montecristo, beginning at around 2100m, are home to an expanse of virgin **cloudforest**, with an annual rainfall of 2m and one hundred percent humidity. Orchids and pinabetes thrive in these climatic conditions, while huge oaks, pines and cypresses, some towering to higher than 20m, swathed in creepers, lichens and mosses, form a dense canopy preventing sunlight from reaching the forest floor. **Wildlife** abounds, with howler and spider monkeys the most visible (and audible) mammals, and jaguars and other large mammals hiding out. **Birds**, including hummingbirds, quetzals, toucans and the regional endemic bushy-crested jay, are

more easily seen. Walking straight to the summit is a truly rewarding climb of around four hours; the path from Los Planes leads through the cloudforest, however, and you can branch off in any direction – bring warm clothing and good footwear. Note that the upper reaches of cloudforest are **closed** to visitors from May to October. Trails also lead from just below **Los Planes** (1890m) to the peaks of Cerro el Brujo and Cerro Miramundo.

ARRIVAL AND INFORMATION

By tour Various operators in San Salvador (see p.211) run tours (US$30–50/person) to the park.

By taxi or pick-up Occasional pick-ups make the 5km journey up from Metapán for a negotiable fee; the best place to catch them is at the turning to the Parque Central, by *Hotel San José* on the Carretera Internacional. You could also try to get into a group of four and organize a taxi from around Metapán's Parque (US$45 return).

On foot You're not allowed to enter Parque Nacional Montecristo on foot.

Entrance fee and registration The park entrance is 5km from Metapán. Pay the entrance fee (US$6, plus US$1.50 for a vehicle) here. After another 2km you come to the Casco Colonial, formerly Hacienda San José, where the wardens are based and where you have to register; it has an interesting collection of natural history and archeological exhibits, as well as a small orchid garden. In theory, you need permission to enter the park from the Ministerio de Medio Ambiente in San Salvador (☎ 2223 0444), but if you're on an organized tour your guide will take care of this; otherwise you can call the Ministerio or just turn up and plead ignorance.

ACCOMMODATION AND EATING

Camping There are free camping areas at Los Planes, 14km from the Casco Colonial (with toilets and picnic tables, but no equipment, so bring food and water), and two simple cabañas sleeping up to eight each. Camping free, cabin <u>US$35</u>

Restaurant Also at Los Planes is a small restaurant serving *típicos* (US$3).

CHICHICASTENANGO MARKET

Guatemala

HIGHLIGHTS

❶ **Antigua** The former capital, boasting colonial buildings and ruined churches. **See p.288**

❷ **Lago de Atitlán** Breathtaking, steep-sided crater lake. **See p.298**

❸ **Highland villages** Traditional highland villages offering insight into Maya life. **See p.309**

❹ **Río Dulce Gorge** Stunning jungle-clad river system with numerous tributaries. **See p.343**

❺ **Lanquín and Semuc Champey** Idyllic turquoise waters and caves to explore. **See p.354 & p.355**

❻ **Tikal** Once a great Maya metropolis, now an incomparable site. **See p.366**

HIGHLIGHTS ARE MARKED ON THE MAP ON PP.268–269

ROUGH COSTS

Daily budget Basic US$25/occasional treat US$40

Drink Beer (330ml) US$2, coffee US$1

Food Tostada US$0.50

Hostel/budget hotel US$8/US$16

Travel Antigua–Panajachel (78km) by public bus: 2hr 30min, US$4

FACT FILE

Population 15 million

Languages Spanish, 23 indigenous languages

Capital Guatemala City (population: 3 million)

Currency Quetzal (Q)

International phone code ☎502

Time zone GMT –6hr

Introduction

Guatemala is simply loaded with natural, historical and cultural interest. In established destinations – Antigua, Lago de Atitlán, Flores – you'll have your choice of Western comforts and convenient transport options. Get off the beaten track and opportunities for activities like jungle trekking, exploring ancient Maya ruins and cooling off in crystalline pools and waterfalls abound. Whatever preconceived notions you have, throw them away – you'll be surprised by the variety of beguiling experiences the country has to offer.

Guatemala's landscape, defined by extremes, is dramatic and wildly beautiful. Rising steeply from the Pacific coast, and contributing to the country's status as the most mountainous Central American nation, is a chain of volcanoes (some still smoking). In many **highland villages** these behemoths are just a fact of life. Then there are the **lowlands** – on the flat, steamy Pacific side you'll find black-sand beaches, turtles and mangroves, while the tropical Caribbean coast is fringed with coconut palms. **El Petén**, the country's least populous yet largest department, fosters everything from savanna to rainforest, and is extraordinarily rich in both **Maya ruins** and wildlife. Guatemala also has some superb cities: **Antigua** is home to irresistible colonial architecture and a plethora of restaurants, cafés and Spanish schools, while **Quetzaltenango** is the de facto capital of the highlands and another important study centre. Even **Guatemala City**, avoided by many, possesses its own gritty charm.

The country's landscape has had an undeniable effect on the history and lifestyle of its people. **Indigenous groups** (mostly Maya) are in the majority here, especially in the highlands; villages such as Todos Santos Cuchumatán, Chichicastenango and Nebaj are renowned for riotously coloured textiles and some of the most sense-assaulting **markets** in the world. Throughout the country you'll find that Guatemalans (or Chapines, as they call themselves), while perhaps more reserved than some of their neighbours, are polite, helpful and welcoming at every turn.

WHEN TO VISIT

As with all mountainous countries, Guatemala's **climate** is largely governed by **altitude**. Many places of interest (including Antigua, Lago de Atitlán, Cobán and the capital) are between 1300 and 1600m, where the climate is temperate: expect warm days and mild evenings. Low-lying Petén is a different world, with steamy conditions year-round, and the Pacific and Caribbean coasts are equally hot and humid.

The rainy season is roughly between May and October. Precipitation is often confined to the late afternoon, and the rest of the day is frequently warm and pleasant. As a rule, it's only in remote areas that rain can affect travel plans. The **busiest times** for tourism are during July and August, between Christmas and mid-January, and around Easter, when Holy Week (Semana Santa) celebrations are quite a spectacle to behold.

CHRONOLOGY

c. 2500 BC Proto-Maya period. Agricultural communities are formed and an early Maya language spoken.

1800 BC Preclassic Maya culture emerges in the forests of Petén.

1000 BC Early settlement at sites including Nakbé and El Mirador.

300–150 BC Colossal temple construction at El Mirador, which enters its greatest era as 70m-high temples are built.

150 AD Preclassic cities in the Mirador Basin are abandoned.

300–900 AD Classic Period of Maya culture sees astounding advances in architecture, astronomy and art, and development of political alliances.

378 AD Tikal defeats Uaxactún; Teotihuacán influence permeates the Petén.

682 AD Hasaw Chan K'awil begins 52-year reign at Tikal, which becomes a "superpower" of Maya world. Vast temple construction programmes commence.

750 AD Population peaks at around 10 million in Maya region.

780 AD Warring increases and Maya cities gradually decline.

1200s Toltecs invading from Mexico institute a militaristic society that fosters highland tribal rivalries.

1523 Conquistador Pedro de Alvarado arrives, and takes advantage of tribal rivalries to bring the Maya under Spanish control.

1540 The last of the highland tribes are subdued.

1541 Guatemala's capital (today's Antigua) presides over the provinces of modern-day Costa Rica, Nicaragua, El Salvador, Honduras and Chiapas.

1773 Antigua is destroyed by an earthquake; the capital is relocated to its present-day site.

1821 The Captain-General of Central America signs the Act of Independence and Guatemala briefly becomes a member of the Central American Federation.

1847 Guatemala declares itself an independent republic.

1871 Rufino Barrios starts a liberal revolution, which heralds sweeping social change but crushes dissent and marginalizes the rural poor.

1901 The United Fruit Company begins to grow bananas in Guatemala. It monopolizes railway and port facilities, and establishes a pervasive political presence.

1944 Guatemala embarks on a 10-year experiment with "spiritual socialism".

1952 Law redistributing United Fruit Company land is passed, to the benefit of 100,000 peasant families.

1954 The CIA sets up an invasion of Guatemala to overthrow its "communist-leaning" government.

1955–85 Military governments send the country into a spiral of violence, economic decline and corruption.

1976 Huge earthquake leaves 23,000 dead, 77,000 injured and a million homeless. Presence of guerrilla groups increases in the wake of the destruction.

1978 Lucas García takes over, escalating the civil war and massacring some 25,000 peasants, intellectuals, politicians, priests and protesters.

1982 Efraín Ríos Montt stages a successful coup. His Civil Defence Patrols polarize the country, trapping peasants between armed forces and guerrilla groups.

1985 The first legitimate elections in thirty years are won by Vinicio Cerezo, but the army is still clearly in control.

1992 Civil war rumbles on. Rigoberta Menchú is awarded the Nobel Peace Prize for campaigning on behalf of Guatemala's indigenous population.

1996 Peace accords are signed on December 29.

1998 Bishop Juan Gerardi is assassinated two days after publishing an investigation of wartime atrocities.

1999 Alfonso Portillo takes office. His reign is plagued by corruption, and the country is left virtually bankrupt.

2004 Newcomer Oscar Berger is inaugurated president; the economy makes some teetering progress.

2007–11 Guatemala's first left-leaning president in fifty years, Alvaro Colom, is elected. Drug traffickers and street gangs challenge the rule of law.

2012 Ex-general Otto Pérez begins presidency with iron-fist mandate to tackle crime.

2013 Pérez declares that the war on drugs has failed and presses for an international debate on decriminalization.

ARRIVAL AND DEPARTURE

The vast majority of Guatemala's visitors arrive at the modern **La Aurora International Airport** (GUA) in the

LAND AND SEA ROUTES TO GUATEMALA

Mexico borders Guatemala at Ciudad Hidalgo–Tecún Umán and El Carmen–Talismán (see box, p.331), both close to the Mexican city of Tapachula. Ciudad Cuauhtémoc–La Mesilla (see box, p.330) is convenient when travelling from San Cristóbal de Las Casas. There are also two routes connecting Palenque and Flores: Frontera Corozal–La Técnica/Bethel via the Río Usumacinta and El Ceibo–El Naranjo (see p.374).

Entering Guatemala from **Belize**, there's either the land crossing in Petén at Benque Viejo del Carmen–Melchor de Menchos (see box, p.87) or two boat routes: Punta Gorda to Puerto Barrios and Punta Gorda–Lívingston (see p.98).

Coming from **El Salvador**, most Guatemala City-bound traffic uses the Las Chinamas–Valle Nuevo border (see box, p.257), while the La Hachadura–Ciudad Pedro de Alvarado (see box, p.250) route is convenient for Guatemala's Pacific coast. There are also two border crossings at Anguiatú (see box, p.264) and at San Cristóbal Frontera (see box, p.261); both access the eastern highlands.

The two main borders with **Honduras** are at El Florido (see box, p.413), which connects Copán with Chiquimula, and Corinto–Entre Ríos (see box, p.421), which links Puerto Cortés with Puerto Barrios.

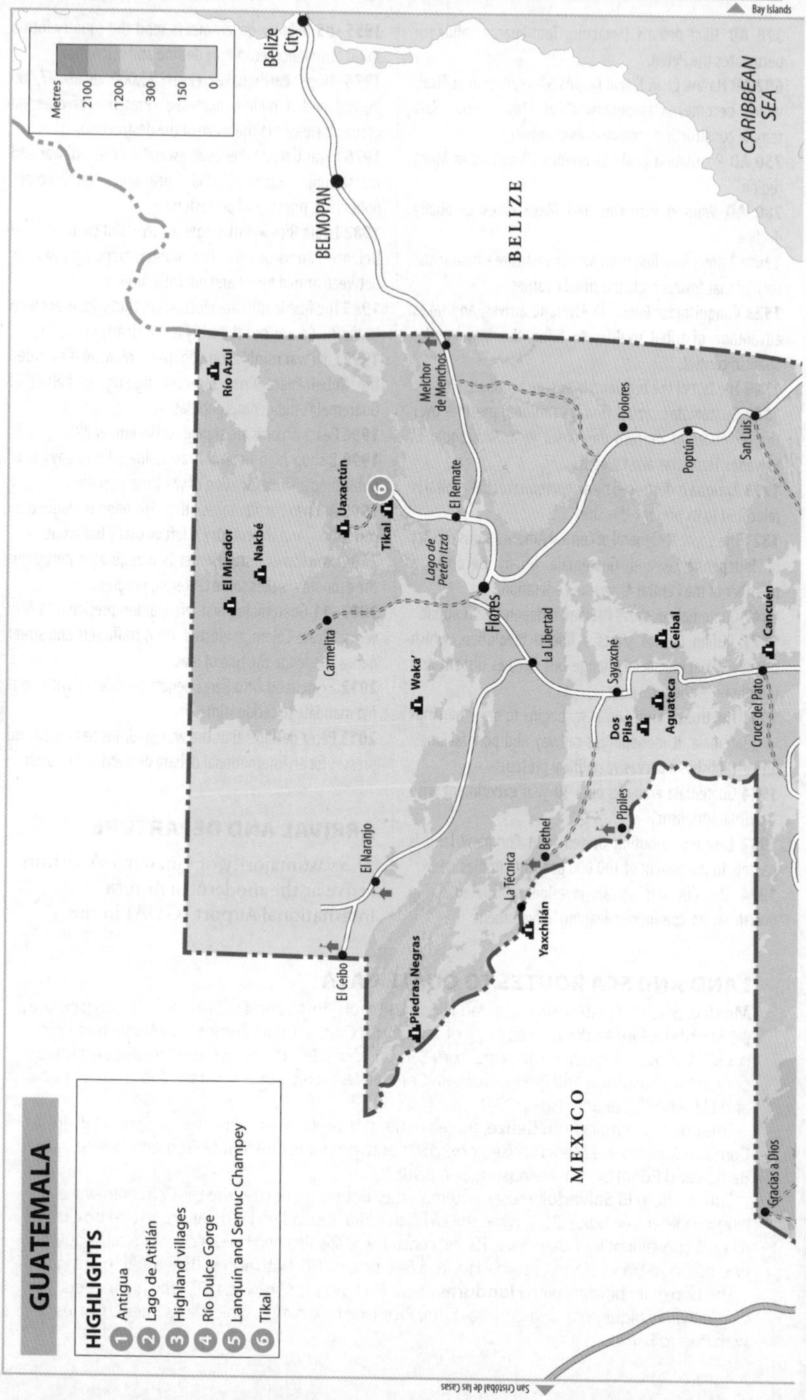

4

Bay Islands

CARIBBEAN SEA

BELIZE

Belize City

BELMOPAN

Metres
2100
1200
300
150
0

Río Azul

Melchor de Mencho

Dolores

San Luis

Poptún

Uaxactún

El Remate

6

Tikal

Nakbé

El Mirador

Lago de Petén Itzá

Flores

Carmelita

La Libertad

Sayaxché

Ceibal

Cancuén

Waka'

Dos Pilas

Aguateca

Cruce del Pato

El Naranjo

Pipiles

Bethel

La Técnica

Yaxchilán

El Ceibo

Piedras Negras

MEXICO

Gracias a Dios

San Cristóbal de las Casas

GUATEMALA

HIGHLIGHTS

1 Antigua
2 Lago de Atitlán
3 Highland villages
4 Río Dulce Gorge
5 Lanquín and Semuc Champey
6 Tikal

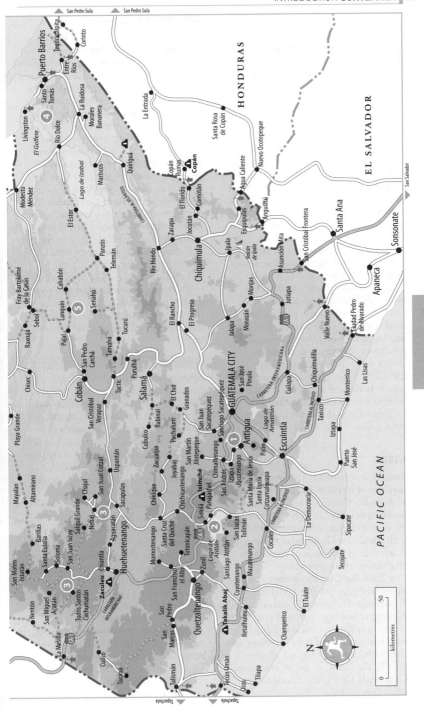

southern suburbs of Guatemala City. Most long-haul flights arrive from the US: Delta (⬛delta.com) flying from Atlanta/Los Angeles; United (⬛united .com) from Houston/Newark; and American Airlines (⬛aa.com) from Dallas–Fort Worth/Miami. TACA (⬛taca.com) also connects Chicago, Los Angeles, Mexico City, Miami, Orlando (seasonally) and San José with the Guatemalan capital, while Spirit Airlines (⬛spirit.com) fly from Fort Lauderdale and Interjet (⬛interjet.com.mx) from Mexico City. Iberia (⬛iberia.com) also offers direct flights from Madrid. **Flores airport** in Petén is currently only served by Tropic Air (⬛tropicair.com) and TAG airlines (⬛tag.com.gt) from Belize City.

You can enter Guatemala by **land** from Chiapas and Tabasco in Mexico, as well as Belize, Honduras and El Salvador. Many travellers choose to take cross-border shuttles or long-distance **bus** services, though it's also possible to use local transport – you'll always find buses waiting at the border to take you to the next town (cross early in the day to ensure more choice of departures). Unofficial fees of a dollar or two are routinely charged by border officials to enter Guatemala at all land borders.

There are two **sea routes** to Guatemala from Belize.

VISAS

Visas are not currently required by the majority of travellers (including citizens of Australia, Canada, New Zealand, South Africa, the UK, US and almost all Western European countries). Check with the closest Guatemalan embassy well in advance of your trip, or consult the visa section at ⬛minex.gob.gt.

In 2006 the **CA-4 agreement** was set up to facilitate visa-free travel in Guatemala, Honduras, El Salvador and Nicaragua (see box, p.30). If your Guatemala tourist card is coming to an end, you can extend it by travelling to either Mexico or Belize, which are outside the CA-4, or get an extension in Guatemala City at the immigration office (see p.288).

GETTING AROUND

Expect to get what you pay for when it comes to Guatemalan **transport**: options available range from the country's "chicken buses" (see box, p.32) to privately operated shuttles. If you're in a hurry, you can also expect to be frustrated – despite frequent services and an improved road network, delays are still common. An epidemic of speedbump-building (even on major highways like the CA-13 between Río Dulce Town and Flores) means that journey times can be painfully slow. Be aware, too, that safety remains a major issue when travelling in Guatemala; premium services are not necessarily more secure. Highway robberies have decreased markedly in recent years due to an increase in highway patrols, but tourist vehicles remain lucrative targets.

Traffic accidents are also common. If you're feeling uncomfortable with your driver, consider asking him to slow down (if a private shuttle), or if on public transport, get off and wait for the next bus.

BY BUS

Buses in Guatemala are incredibly crowded, but they're also cheap and the easiest way to get around. In urban and rural areas alike, **second-class buses** – known as *camionetas* to Guatemalans and "chicken buses" to foreigners (see box, p.32) – are numerous. Second-class buses generally start and stop at the local terminal (often in the same place as the local market) and will drop you off wherever you like en route. They don't generally have schedules (except on more remote routes), instead leaving every thirty minutes or when full. Pay your **fare** (expect it to be about Q8/hr) to the *ayudante* (conductor) on the bus. It pays to be open to help from locals when trying to negotiate your passage – the *ayudantes* are invariably friendly, knowledgeable and for the most part honest.

In many areas **microbuses**, or *micros*, supplement (or have replaced) chicken buses. They cost roughly the same. These minibuses can depart from a central bus station, private terminal or just a bus stop.

First-class, or **Pullman**, buses are more comfortable and make fewer stops. Each passenger has a seat, and tickets can be bought in advance. Some Pullman companies stop en route to pick up passengers if they have space, but most only pause very infrequently at designated bus terminals. Pullmans usually leave from the bus company's office rather than a town's main bus terminal (except for some services in Guatemala City). Expect to pay about Q10–15 per hour of travel.

All the main tourist routes are also served by convenient **shuttle buses** that will whisk you around for a price (Antigua–Panajachel, for example, costs between Q75 and Q100). Tickets are booked (best the day before) through a travel agent or your hotel. You'll be picked up from your accommodation and dropped off where you choose.

Shuttles are best used for relatively short journeys – for longer trips Pullmans are far more comfortable. Some shuttle bus operators (the Lanquín–Flores route is notorious) pack passengers in the aisles between seats on little stools – not much fun when the journey time is more than eight hours and there are twenty people aboard a non-air-conditioned minibus.

BY CAR

Driving in Guatemala is not for the faint-hearted, though if you prepare yourself for some alarming local practices it can be a highly enjoyable way to get around. The main routes are paved, but minor roads are often extremely rough and landslides are common in the rainy season. **Parking** and **security** are the main problems; in the larger towns you should always use a guarded car park. **Petrol** costs around Q35 a gallon, **diesel** a little less. **Renting a car** costs from as little as Q240 a day for a small vehicle, but watch out for extra charges (excesses on any damage caused can be huge). All major rental firms have an office at the airport in Guatemala City (see p.283).

If you plan to visit the more remote parts of the country, then you might **hitch a ride** with a pick-up or truck from time to time. You'll usually have to pay for your lift – around the same as the bus fare. This said, hitching is never entirely safe, and carries obvious risks.

Motorcycle taxis, or tuk-tuks, are common in most towns and villages, but not in big cities (including the capital and Quetzaltenango). A short ride usually costs Q5, a longer trip Q10 or so. Clarify that the price is for the journey, not per person. **Taxis** are also readily available, but cost more (around Q40 for a 3km trip). Except in Guatemala City, meters are nonexistent so it's essential to **fix a price** before you set off.

BY BIKE

Cycling is the most exhilarating way to see Guatemala, but the country's mountainous terrain makes it very challenging. If you set out and it all gets too much, you can change to a bus – most buses will carry bikes on the roof. You can rent mountain bikes in Antigua, Panajachel and Quetzaltenango, as well as several other cities. Repair shops are fairly widespread.

4

ADDRESSES IN GUATEMALA

Like the majority of towns and cities in Central America, Guatemala's streets generally follow a **grid system**, with the occasional diagonal thrown in for variety. In most towns, **avenidas** run north–south and are numbered from 1 Avenida (on either the west or east side of town), while **calles** run east–west (and will start at 1 Calle in the north). Even small towns will centre on a plaza (with the exception of waterside settlements such as Panajachel and Lívingston). In larger towns the ever-expanding street network is divided into **zonas**, each of which may have its own separate set of numbered calles and avenidas (ie, 1 Calle may exist in more than one *zona*). **Addresses** in Guatemala are given listing first the calle or avenida that the property is on, followed by a number signifying the calle/avenida that intersects to the north/west. The final number given is the property number. For example "6 Av 9–14, Zona 1" is in Zona 1, on 6 Avenida south of 9 Calle, house number 14.

Several tour agencies, including in Antigua, Santa Cruz La Laguna and Quetzaltenango, offer escorted mountain bike tours, which are an excellent way to see the countryside.

BY BOAT

Small, speedy, motorized boats called **lanchas** are the main form of water transport. The two definitive boat trips in Guatemala are through the Río Dulce gorge system, starting in either Lívingston or Río Dulce Town, and across Lago de Atitlán. The Monterrico, Lago de Petexbatún and Lago de Petén Itzá regions also offer the possibility of excellent boat excursions.

BY PLANE

The only internal **flight** most tourists are likely to take is from Guatemala City to Flores (from Q1800 return), with two airlines, TACA and TAG, offering daily services. Virtually any travel agent in the country can book you a ticket.

ACCOMMODATION

Accommodation in Guatemala comes in different guises: *pensiones*, *posadas*, *hospedajes* and hotels. The names don't actually mean much, however, as they're approximately the same thing, although in general hotels are towards the top end of the price scale and most *hospedajes* and *pensiones* towards the bottom. Budget options are plentiful and even in tourist centres you can sleep for as little as Q25 in a dorm. **Hostels and lodges** tailored to backpackers are springing up across the country; most have dorms and camping facilities as well as private rooms. Wherever you stay, **room prices** are fixed by Inguat, the tourist board (see p.275), and there should be a tariff posted by the door of your room. You should never pay more than this posted rate.

Rates rarely include breakfast; however, many moderately priced rooms (Q130–220) come with cable TV and hot-water showers (though actually only emit a trickle of luke-warm water). Only on the coasts and in Petén will you need a **fan** or **air conditioning**, while you'll need

heavy-duty blankets in the highlands. A **mosquito net** is sometimes provided in lowland areas, but if you plan to spend time in Petén or on either coast it's probably worth investing in one.

Camping facilities are rare and it's not worth bringing a tent unless you're a complete canvas addict. Lanquín, Laguna Lachúa, Poptún, El Remate and Tikal have campsites.

FOOD AND DRINK

You can be well fed in Guatemala for just a few dollars a day. Cheap eats are abundant, from fresh produce at markets to street stalls selling tasty snacks. **Lunch** is the main meal for locals; you'll get a two-course lunch, with a drink, for Q20–30 in *comedores* throughout the country. These *menú del día* or *almuerzo* set menus are usually served from noon to 3pm. **Breakfast** is also good value, if fattening, with traditional *desayunos* including a combination of eggs, beans, tortillas, cheese, fried plantains and cream. Most places in tourist centres also offer continental options for slightly more money. Alternatively, fresh fruit can be bought from street vendors, and muffins and breads from bakeries, cutting your breakfast bill considerably. **Evening meals** in restaurants are generally more expensive (from Q40).

Maya cuisine is at the heart of Guatemalan cooking. Maize is an essential ingredient, appearing most commonly as a **tortilla**, which is like a small, thick corn wrap. **Beans** (*frijoles*) are served either refried (*volteados*) or whole (*parados*). Chillis, usually in the form of a spicy sauce (*salsa picante*), are the final ingredient. When Guatemalans talk about "comida típica" you can be sure that these three ingredients will feature on the plate.

Popular **market snacks** include *pupusas* (thick stuffed tortillas topped with crunchy, grated salad vegetables) and tostadas (corn crisps smeared with avocado, cheese and other toppings). On the Caribbean coast there is a distinct **Creole cuisine**, heavily based on fish, seafood, coconuts, plantains and banana. *Tapado* (a coconut-based fish or shellfish soup) is the signature dish in these parts. In small towns and rural areas across the country, you can expect your choice to be confined to rice, tortillas and beans, and fried chicken or grilled beef. Vegetarians receive a mixed bag; Guatemala City offers some gems (even for vegans), and tourist hubs such as Flores, Antigua and Lago de Atitlán present interesting veggie menus too. Elsewhere, options can be quite limited.

DRINK

Bottled water (*agua pura*) is available almost everywhere and cheapest if bought in 500ml plastic bags (*bolsitas*), which cost Q1 each in shops.

Guatemalan **coffee** is great – unfortunately, most of it is exported. In tourist centres espresso machines are becoming very common – expect to pay Q10–15 for a cappuccino – but off the gringo trail very weak or instant coffee is the norm. During the day locals drink water or **refrescos**, water-based drinks with some fruit flavour. **Fizzy drinks** like Coca-Cola or Fanta (all called *aguas* or *gaseosas*) are also popular. For a healthy treat, order a **licuado**: a thick, fruit-based smoothie made with either water or milk (milk is safer).

The national **beer** (*cerveza*) is Gallo, a medium-strength, bland lager that comes in 330ml or litre bottles (around Q15 and Q30 respectively in a bar; much less in a supermarket). Brahma, another lager, is also widely available, while Moza, a dark brew with a slight caramel flavour, is worth trying, too. Better still, and served in traditional bars, is a *mixta* – a mix of draught clear (*clara*) and dark (*obscura*) beers. **Rum** (*ron*) and **aguardiente**, a clear and lethal sugar-cane spirit, are also popular and cheap. Ron Botran Añejo is an acceptable brand (around Q50 a bottle), or for a real treat order a glass of the fabulously smooth Zacapa rum. Hard drinkers will soon get to know Quetzalteca, a local *aguardiente*. Chilean and Argentine **wines** are popular in tourist centres: a glass costs from Q20 in a bar; bottles start at about Q75.

CULTURE AND ETIQUETTE

Perhaps more than in other Central American countries, **religious doctrine** – Catholic, Evangelical Protestant, indigenous spiritual beliefs – continues to influence cultural behaviour in Guatemala. Consequently, Guatemalans are fairly modest, reserved folk. This is particularly true of the Maya, who can be suspicious of outsiders; tradition rules in indigenous communities. The dominant Ladino (Latin American) culture is generally less rigid, thanks to the more immediate effects of globalization. Women show more skin, and the Latin American **machismo** is more obvious. Even this, though, is pretty inoffensive – the odd comment or whistle from men trying to impress their friends – and can be ignored by female travellers.

Homosexuality is not illegal, though it is frowned upon by many. There are small gay communities in Guatemala City, Antigua and Quetzaltenango, but few public meeting places.

It would be a mistake to take Guatemalan reserve for unfriendliness, and you're likely to receive gracious hospitality from all levels of society. **Politeness** is valued highly by Ladino and Maya society alike, and there is a pleasantry for nearly every occasion – you will endear yourself to locals by returning these. "Buen provecho", for example, is usually exchanged among strangers in restaurants; it literally translates to "I hope your meal is of good benefit to

---

GUATEMALAN WORDS AND PHRASES

Baa Right! (often used at the start of sentences, or on its own as an affirmative)
Buena onda Cool
Fijase It's like this… (often used to preface why something hasn't gone according to plan)
Chapín/Guatemalteco/Guatemayan Guatemalan/Ladino/Maya

… AND GESTURES

Rubbing one's elbow signifies that somebody is cheap.
Pulling one's collar signifies that someone has clout/power.

4

you!" Be prepared, though, for the fact that **noise pollution** and **personal space** are almost foreign concepts: it is quite usual to be woken by firecrackers at 5am, evangelical PA systems blare for hours, and you can expect a good deal of pushing and shoving on buses and around markets.

Tipping in restaurants and *comedores* is not expected, but is certainly appreciated.

SPORTS AND OUTDOOR ACTIVITIES

Football (soccer) is the country's top spectator sport, by far. The two big local teams, both from Guatemala City, are Municipal and Communications. Admission to games is inexpensive (starting at Q25 or so). Football also provides for easy cross-cultural conversation, as most Guatemalan men are well versed on the topic and have a favourite team in the Spanish Primera Liga. The website ⓦguatefutbol.com (Spanish only) details fixtures and results.

Guatemala is a paradise for outdoor activities. With a sturdy pair of shoes, you can **hike** volcanoes, jungles and national parks, and sections of Lago de Atitlán. **Caving** is also popular, especially in the area north of Cobán where there are great caverns and underground rivers to explore: Lanquín (see p.354), Kan'ba (see p.355) and Finca Ixobel (see p.358) are the places to head for. Finca Ixobel, Antigua and San Pedro La Laguna also make good bases for exploring the countryside on horseback. Wildlife- and **birdwatching** can be very rewarding in Guatemala, as the nation is home to ten percent of the world's registered species and encompasses twenty ecosystems and some three hundred microclimates. National parks and reserves good for wildlife include Tikal (see p.366), Monterrico (see p.335), Cerro Cahuí (see p.365), the Biotopo del Quetzal (see p.349) and the vast Reserva de la Biósfera Maya around El Mirador (see p.372). Other, more eclectic, activities include **cycling** in the highlands, **altitude diving** in Lago de Atitlán's volcanic lake (see

p.308) and **surfing** on the Pacific coast (see p.330). You can also **sail** from Río Dulce – one popular route takes you to Belize's more remote cayes.

COMMUNICATIONS

Guatemalan **postal services** are fairly efficient by Latin American standards, and even the smallest of towns has a *correo* (post office); hours are generally Monday to Friday 8am to 5pm. Airmail letters generally take around a week to the US, and a couple of weeks or so to Europe. Post coming into Guatemala is fairly reliable too, though note that there is no longer any **poste restante** service.

There are no **area codes** in Guatemala. To call a number from abroad simply dial the international access code, followed by the country code (ⓞ502) and the number (all of which are eight-digit). The cheapest way to make an **international phone call** from Guatemala is usually from an internet café set up with Skype or web-phone facilities. Some places include Skype calls in the cost of renting a terminal, but most charge a little extra. Local calls are cheap, and can be made from either a communications office or a phone booth (buy a Ladatel phonecard).

Many North American and European **mobile phones**, if unlocked, will work in Guatemala; all you'll need is a local SIM card (Tigo and Claro are the most popular networks and have excellent coverage). Phones can also be bought locally from as little as Q150 (including around Q75 of calling credit). Keep an eye out for the "double" and "triple" offer days, when you can get two to three times the top-up credit you pay for.

The country is very well connected to the **internet**, though don't expect lightning connection speeds. Most small towns have at least a couple of internet cafés, while the cities have dozens. Rates vary between Q4 and Q20 an hour. Many hotels and hostels also provide internet facilities. **Wi-fi** (nearly always free for customers and hotel guests) is very common in all the main tourist centres, though again speeds can be pedestrian.

EMERGENCY NUMBERS

ASISTUR (tourist assistance) ☎ 1500
Fire ☎ 122 or ☎ 123
Police ☎ 110 or ☎ 120
Red Cross Ambulance ☎ 125

CRIME AND SAFETY

Personal safety is a valid concern for visitors to Guatemala. The vast majority of the nearly two million tourists who come every year experience no problems at all, but general crime levels are high, and it's not unknown for criminals to target visitors.

Ask before taking **photographs** in indigenous areas, and be particularly careful not to take pictures of children without permission from their parents. (In remote regions wild rumours circulate that tourists steal children, or their organs.) **Muggings** and acts of **violent crime** are common in Guatemala City; there's not too much danger in daylight, but use taxis at night. There have also been a few cases of armed robbery in Antigua and around Lago de Atitlán.

All this said, relatively few tourists actually have any trouble. However, it's essential that you minimize your chances of becoming a victim. **Petty theft** and **pickpocketing** are likely to be your biggest problems – as anywhere, theft is most common in bus stations and crowded markets. As a rule, ask for local advice on safety issues. If you do plan to be in a risky spot, don't take more than you can afford to lose – many travellers carry "decoy" wallets with just a small amount of cash to satisfy muggers. You could also consider buying pepper spray,

ASISTUR

ASISTUR (☎ 1500) is a nationwide network of English-speaking staff employed to help tourists. Most ASISTUR employees are extremely helpful and will liaise with local police. Some can also organize a police escort to accompany travellers along highways known for banditry. You can find a list of local representatives and their phone numbers on the Inguat website ⓦ visitguatemala.com.

ATM SCAMS

A number of travellers have reported **ATM scams** in Guatemala, particularly in Antigua. Card holders are finding their bank accounts drained of cash, days or even months after they've used a cash machine. It's probable that scammers are "skimming" or using cloned cards. Check your balance regularly and consider changing your pin code when you return to your home country.

which is available locally in camping stores and Los Próceres mall in Guatemala City (see p.287).

If you become a victim of crime you should first contact **ASISTUR** (see box below) who will assign a representative to help you out. You'll also have to file a report with the police, though be aware that the force has a poor reputation for efficiency and crime solving. In Antigua, Panajachel and Tikal there are well-established **tourist police** forces.

Drugs (particularly marijuana and cocaine) are quite widely available. Don't partake: **drug offences** are dealt with severely – even the possession of marijuana could land you in jail.

HEALTH

Guatemala's **pharmacies** can provide many over-the-counter medications, and some pharmacists can diagnose ailments and prescribe the appropriate pills. However, pharmacists are not qualified medics – so make sure your Spanish is correct.

Even in remote communities there are basic **health centres**, although you may find only a nurse or health worker available. In case of serious illness, head for a city and a private **hospital**. Guatemala's doctors often speak English, and many were trained in the US. You must travel with medical insurance (see p.42), as without it you'll need to pay for any hospital treatment up front.

INFORMATION AND MAPS

The national **tourist board**, Inguat (ⓦ visitguatemala.com), with offices in

4

GUATEMALA ONLINE

ⓦ**guatemala-times.com** News and features about Guatemala in English.

ⓦ**guatemalaweb.com** Everything from ATM locations to Maya ceremonies, though some information is out of date.

ⓦ**http://lanic.utexas.edu/la/ca/ guatemala/** The University of Texas provides a comprehensive Guatemala portal offering access to news sources and academic resources.

ⓦ**revuemag.com** The *Revue*'s website has fully downloadable files of the monthly magazine, including back copies.

ⓦ**visitguatemala.com** Official Inguat site.

Guatemala City, Panajachel, Antigua, Flores and Quetzaltenango, gives out glossy brochures and will try to help you with your trip, but don't expect too much independent travel advice. The main office in Guatemala City (see p.284) has a library of information about tourism and can also provide you with a good country map.

Specialist travel agents and hostels are often excellent sources of information.

MONEY AND BANKS

The Guatemalan currency, the **quetzal** (Q), has been very stable against the dollar for the last decade. The **exchange rate** at the time of writing was Q7.82 to US$1. **US dollars** are also accepted in many of the main tourist centres; prices for hotels and tours are often quoted in dollars. That said, you certainly can't get by with a fistful of greenbacks and no quetzals. Euros and other foreign currencies are tricky to cash; try foreign-owned hotels or stores.

Debit and credit cards are very useful for withdrawing currency from bank ATMs but are not that widely accepted elsewhere, so don't count on paying with them except in upmarket hotels and restaurants. Beware expensive surcharges (5 to 10 percent is sometimes added) if you do want to pay by a card in many places.

ATMs are very widespread, even in small towns – though note that in Antigua,

especially, there have been reports of ATM scams (see box, p.275). Charges of Q15–20 per withdrawal are common, but those using the 5B network, including Banrural, did not charge at the time of research. You could consider having a few **travellers' cheques** (American Express preferably, and in US dollars) as a backup, but they are becoming hard to cash these days. Note that currency exchange counters at Guatemala City airport offer appalling rates (see p.283). At the main land-border crossings there are usually banks and a swarm of moneychangers who generally give fair rates for cash.

Bank hours are extremely convenient, with many opening until 7pm (and some as late as 8pm) from Monday to Friday and until 12.30pm or 1pm on Saturdays.

Student discounts are rare in Guatemala but some museums do offer reduced entry rates. You'll need an International Student Identity Card (ISIC).

OPENING HOURS AND HOLIDAYS

Most offices and shops are **open** between 8am and 5pm, though some take a break for lunch. **Archeological sites** are open every day, usually from 8am to 5pm (Tikal maintains longer hours), while most museums open Tuesday to Sunday from 9am to 4pm. **Sundays** remain distinguishable – many businesses close and transport is less frequent, though tourist centres such as Antigua keep

PUBLIC HOLIDAYS

Jan 1 New Year's Day
March/April Semana Santa – Easter Week
May 1 Labour Day
June 30 Army Day, anniversary of 1871 revolution
Aug 15 Guatemala City fiesta (capital only)
Sept 15 Independence Day
Oct 12 Discovery of America (only banks are closed)
Oct 20 Revolution Day
Nov 1 All Saints' Day
Dec 25 Christmas

buzzing. On **public holidays** (see box opposite) virtually the entire country shuts down, and though some buses do run it's not the best time to be travelling.

FESTIVALS

Traditional **fiestas** are one of the great excitements of a trip to Guatemala, and every town and village, however small, devotes at least one day a year to celebration. Many of the best include some specifically local element, such as the giant kites at **Santiago Sacatepéquez** (see p.298), the religious processions in Antigua and the wild horse race in **Todos Santos Cuchumatán** (see p.328). At times virtually the whole country erupts simultaneously. The following is a selection of some of the most interesting regional and national festivals.

January 23–24 The town fiesta in Rabinal, in Baja Verapaz, renowned for pre-colonial dances.

March/April Semana Santa (Easter week) is celebrated nationwide. Particularly impressive processions take place in Antigua, Guatemala City, Santiago Atitlán and San Cristóbal Verapaz. Every Sunday of Lent sees massive street processions in Antigua, which culminate with the main event on Easter Sunday.

July 25 Cubulco, Baja Verapaz, hosts the Palo Volador, a bungee-jump-style ritual.

July 31–Aug 6 Cobán celebrates the national folklore festival.

August 15 Guatemala City fiesta.

November 1 All Saints' Day, with celebrations all over, but most dramatic in Todos Santos Cuchumatán and Santiago Sacatepéquez, where massive kites are flown.

December 7 Bonfires (the Burning of the Devil) take place throughout the country.

December 21 Huge traditional fiesta in Chichicastenango.

Guatemala City

Spilling across a highland basin, surrounded on three sides by jagged hills and volcanic cones, **GUATEMALA CITY** is the largest city in Central America, home to more than three million people. Characterized by an intensity and a vibrancy that simultaneously fascinate and alarm, Guatemala's capital is a shapeless and swelling metropolitan mass,

---

ADDRESSES IN GUATEMALA CITY

The system of street numbering in the capital can be confusing – and is often complicated by the fact that the same calles and avenidas can exist in several different zones. Always check the zone first and then the street. For example, "7 Av 9–14, Zona 10" is in Zona 10, on 7 Avenida between 9 and 10 calles, house number 14.

---

and the undisputed centre of the country's politics, power and wealth. Not even a wild imagination will be able to make it out as a pleasant environment – indeed, for many travellers time spent in the capital is an exercise in damage limitation, struggling through bus fumes and crowds. However, once you get used to the pace, Guatemala City can offer some surprises, including a satisfying variety of restaurants, authentic bars, a sprinkling of interesting sights as well as multiplex cinemas and shopping plazas. It is important to note, though, that the city's **crime rate** is one of the highest in Central America. While daytime is relatively safe, conditions deteriorate after dark, when you should be vigilant and take taxis to get around.

WHAT TO SEE AND DO

Despite the daunting scale of Guatemala City – it consists of 25 sprawling zones – the key areas of interest are quite manageable. Broadly speaking, the city divides into two distinct halves. The northern section, centred on **Zona 1**, is the old part of town, and undeniably the most exciting part of the capital. A squalid world of low-slung, crumbling nineteenth-century townhouses, faceless concrete blocks, low-rent stores, broken pavements and car parks, it has a certain brutal allure. South of 18 Calle, Zona 1 merges into **Zona 4**, home to the Municipalidad, tourist and immigration offices and the Teatro Nacional.

The southern half of the city, beyond the Torre del Reformador, begins with **zonas 9 and 10** and is the modern, wealthy part of town, split in two by

4

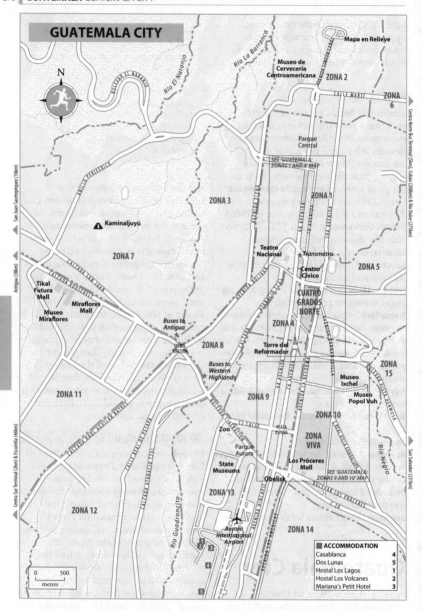

GUATEMALA CITY

N

Mapa en Relieve

Río La Barranca

Río El Naranjo

Museo de
Cervecería
Centroamericana

ZONA 2

CALLE MARTI

ZONA 6

Centro Norte Bus Terminal (5km), Cobán (206km) & Río Dulce (275km)

Parque
Central

SEE 'GUATEMALA:
ZONAS 1 AND 4' MAP

ZONA 3

ZONA 1

Kaminaljuyú

ZONA 7

Teatro
Nacional

Transmetro

ZONA 5

Centro
Cívico

CUATRO
GRADOS
NORTE

Tikal
Futura
Mall

Miraflores
Mall

ZONA 4

Museo
Miraflores

Buses to
Antigua

ZONA 8

Torre del
Reformador

ZONA 15

TREBÓL
JUNCTION

Museo
Ixchel

Buses to
Western
Highlands

Museo
Popol Vuh

ZONA 11

ZONA 9

ZONA 10

Zoo

12 CALLE

PLAZA
ESPAÑA

ZONA
VIVA

Parque
Aurora

Río Negro

State
Museums

Los Próceres
Mall

SEE 'GUATEMALA:
ZONAS 9 AND 10' MAP

Obelisk

San Salvador (231km)

ZONA 13

ZONA 12

Río Guardoncito

Aurora
International
Airport

ZONA 14

0   500

metres

■ ACCOMMODATION	
Casablanca	4
Dos Lunas	5
Hostal Los Lagos	1
Hostal Los Volcanes	2
Mariana's Petit Hotel	3

San Juan Sacetepéquez (16m)

Antigua (38km)

Centra Sur Terminal (2km) & Escuintla (46km)

Avenida La Reforma. Here you'll find exclusive offices, international hotels, private museums and, in the **Zona Viva**, Guatemala's most expensive clubs, boutiques, restaurants and cafés. Continuing south, **zonas 13 and 14** are rich leafy suburbs and home to the airport, zoo and the state museums.

Parque Central

The windswept expanse of the vast **Parque Central**, at the northern end of

Zona 1, is full of life, especially on Sundays and public holidays as people and pigeons, shoe-shiners and raving Evangelicals jostle for space.

On the west side of the square is a concrete bandstand, the Concha Acústica, where you can enjoy a variety of marimba and classical music performances (Wed 4–6pm & Sat 3.30–5pm; free). Most of the city's major sights – including the cathedral, Palacio Nacional and two semi-restored colonial arcades, the Pasaje Aycinena and Pasaje Rubio (leading off the park's south side) – lie nearby.

Palacio Nacional
Just north of the Parque Central is the striking **Palacio Nacional** (entrance by guided tour only, conducted in Spanish or English; daily 9.30am–4pm; hourly; 40min; Q40), a lavish, pale-green palace built in the 1940s by president Jorge Ubico and nicknamed "El Guacamole" by locals. It housed the government's executive branch for about fifty years but today hosts cultural exhibitions.

The tour gives you a brief look at the interior, with its two Moorish-style interior courtyards (one containing an eternal flame dedicated to the heroes of Peace Accords). You'll also see striking murals depicting warring Spaniards and Maya and the principal state reception room, complete with a suitably grandiose chandelier embellished with four cut-glass quetzals.

Cathedral
On the east side of the Parque Central sits the blue-domed **cathedral** (daily 7am–noon & 3–7pm), completed in 1868. Its solid, squat design was intended to resist the force of earthquakes and has, for the most part, succeeded. Inside there are three main aisles, austere colonial paintings and intricate altars housing an array of saints. The cathedral's most poignant aspect is outside, however: etched into the twelve pillars that support the entrance railings are the names of thousands of the dead and "disappeared" victims of the country's civil war.

Mercado Central
Guatemala City's best market, the **Mercado Central** (Mon–Sat 6am–6pm, Sun 9am–1pm), spreads out underground beneath a car park east of the cathedral between 8 and 9 avenidas and 6 and 8 calles. The place is a riot of colour, with the obligatory handicrafts, souvenirs, fruit and vegetable displays and some impressive fresh-flower arrangements.

Sexta Avenida
Sexta Avenida (6 Av) was the city's main commercial artery for decades, lined with glamorous department stores, cinemas and cafés. People from all over the city would promenade the Sexta to see and be seen. But the character of the street took a downturn in the 1980s, as stalls choked the pavements and many businesses closed.

In 2009, the city authorities implemented a regeneration programme, clearing the street traders, planting trees and pedestrianizing the avenida (except for cycles and a tourist tram) between the Parque Central and 18 Calle, making Sexta a delight to stroll once again. Be sure to stop by the well-kept **Parque Concordia**, the fabulously elaborate facade of the **Iglesia de San Francisco** and renovated Art Deco splendour of the **Teatro Lux** as you explore the heart of Zona 1.

Palacio de Correos
The Baroque **Palacio de Correos**, south of the Parque Central on 7 Avenida between 11 and 12 calles, is one of the city's most arresting buildings, with an elaborately restored terracotta-and-cream facade. Don't miss the adjoining decorative bridge, built in the same Baroque style, which spans 12 Calle.

Casa Mima
South of the post office, at the corner of 8 Avenida and 14 Calle, **Casa Mima** (Mon–Sat 10am–5pm; Q20) is an immaculately restored, late nineteenth-century Guatemalan townhouse with original furnishings from various design movements. The decor offers a fascinating glimpse into a wealthy household, with lavish rooms kitted out with gilded

4

1 (700m) ▲   ▲ ① Parque Minerva & Mapa en Relieve (1.75km)

■ ACCOMMODATION

Chalet Suizo	3
La Coperacha	1
Hotel Ajau	4
Hotel Santoña	5
Hotel Spring	2

★ BUS STOPS

ADN	B
Transmetro Terminal Plaza Barrios	C
Transmetro	E
Transportes Galgos	D
Transurbano buses to Centra Norte	A

Parque del Centenario

Palacio Nacional

ATM

Parque Central

Mercado Central

Biblioteca Nacional

Cathedral

Teatro Lux

San Miguel de Capuchinas

Laundry

Palacio de Correos

Museo de los Músicos Invisibles

Iglesia de San Francisco

Police Headquarters

Parque Concordia

Casa Mima

ZONA 1

Mercado Sur

CENTRO CÍVICO

Museo del Ferrocarril

Teatro Nacional

Estadio Nacional Mario Flores

Municipalidad

Banco de Guatemala

Centro Comercial

ⓘ

Immigration

CUATRO GRADOS NORTE

Centro Cultural de España

ZONA 4

● EATING

Café de Imeri	3
Café León	13
Café Música	15
Café Saúl	12
Cafetalito	11
El Cuscún	9
Kafé Katok	14
Rey Sol	10
Rocque Rosito	7

● DRINKING & NIGHTLIFE

Bad Attitude	1
Blanco y Negro	6
Las Cien Puertas	6
Genetic Majestic Club	16
El Gran Hotel	8
La Luna	5
El Portal	4
Tacos Tequila	2

Iglesia Yurrita

Jardín Botánico

Torre del Reformador

N

0   250
metres

GUATEMALA CITY: ZONAS 1 AND 4

Trébol Junction (1.25km) & Kaminaljuyo (3km)

4

mirrors, chandeliers, oriental rugs, hand-painted wallpaper and curios including a gloriously detailed dolls' house and a ninety-year-old "talking machine" (a gramophone). The house even has a private chapel complete with a fabulous wooden altar.

Museo de los Músicos Invisibles

The quirky **Museo de los Músicos Invisibles**, 13 Calle (Mon–Sat 8am–6pm; Q25 including tour), dedicated to the "invisible musician", showcases an incredible collection of automated and wind-up antique musical instruments: organs, music boxes, juke boxes, gramophones, Art Deco radios, mechanical saxophones and harmonicas and even a vinyl-cutting machine. All are in perfect working order, as demonstrated on the guided tour (Spanish only). There's a great little café here too (see p.285).

Mapa en Relieve

North of the Parque Central, in Zona 2's Parque Minerva, the **Mapa en Relieve** (daily 9am–5pm; Q25; ⓦmapaenrelieve .org) is a huge, open-air relief model of Guatemala. The map's vertical scale has been somewhat exaggerated, but still highlights the dramatic landscape of the highlands, shedding new light on those perilous mountain bus journeys.

Museo de Cervecería Centroamericana

Just to the south of the Mapa on 3 Avenida Norte, **Cervecería Centroamericana** (Mon–Thurs 8.30am–5pm; free tours 9am, 11am & 2.30pm; book on ☎2289 1555) is Guatemala's largest brewery. Beer has been produced here for 125 years; today, around a dozen varieties are brewed, including Dorada, Victoria and Gallo (Guatemala's most popular brew). The museum, containing some interesting antique curios and photographs related to the history of beer-making in Guatemala, is interesting enough, but the highly informative tour allows you access to the plant, gazing into the vast stainless-steel vats and viewing the bottling process. The tour finishes, appropriately, with a glass or two of complimentary Gallo.

Centro Cívico

At the southern end of the old city, beyond sleazy 18 Calle and around 6 and 7 avenidas, the distinctively 1960s architecture of the **Centro Cívico** area marks the boundary between zonas 1 and 4. Looming over 7 Avenida is the **Banco de Guatemala** building, bedecked with bold modern murals and stylized glyphs recounting the history of the nation and the conflict between Spanish and Maya. Just south of here is the main Inguat office (see p.284). On a small rise to the west of 6 Avenida is the futuristic **Teatro Nacional**, designed to resemble a ship (see p.287).

Jardín Botánico

The city's **Jardín Botánico** (Mon–Fri 8am–3pm, Sat 9am–noon; Q10), at the northern end of Avenida La Reforma, is part of San Carlos University. It's a beautiful evergreen space with quite a selection of species, all neatly labelled in Spanish or Latin. An anachronistic natural history museum, the **Museo de Historia Natural** (same hours), also sits within the grounds; the collection, mainly mangy stuffed animals, is pretty dull.

Torre del Reformador

South of the Centro Cívico, at the junction of 7 Avenida and 2 Calle, in Zona 9, is the landmark **Torre del Reformador**, Guatemala's stunted version of the Eiffel Tower. The steel structure was built in honour of President Barrios, whose liberal reforms transformed the country between 1871 and 1885. Just to the north, at the junction with Ruta 6, is the **Iglesia Yurrita** (Tues–Sun 8am–noon & 3–6pm), built in a weird neo-Gothic style reminiscent of a horror-movie set.

Museo Ixchel and Museo Popol Vuh

The campus of the University Francisco Marroquín, reached by following 6 Calle Final off Avenida La Reforma, is home to two excellent private **museums** (both Mon–Fri 9am–5pm, Sat 9am–1pm; combined ticket Q50). The **Museo Ixchel** (ⓦmuseoixchel.org) shouldn't be missed if you're a fan of textiles, or just can't get enough of Guatemalan traditional dress: its collection is dedicated to Maya

4

GUATEMALA CITY: ZONAS 9 AND 10

Iglesia Yurrita
ZONA 4
ZONA 5
Jardín Botánico
Torre del Reformador
US Embassy
ZONA 9
Hedman Alas
Laundry
Centro Gerencial Las Margaritas
PLAZA ESPAÑA
ZONA VIVA
Pullmantur
Los Próceres Mall
Obelisk
ZONA 10
Museo Ixchel
Museo Popol Vuh
Hospital Centro Médico
Oakland Mall
BLAZA ISRAEL

0 — 250 metres

N

EATING
Café de Jabes — 5
Paco's Café — 1
Pitaya — 3
Sopho's — 2
Tacontento — 4

DRINKING & NIGHTLIFE
Kahlua — 6
Rattle & Hum — 7

ACCOMMODATION
Hostal Plaza — 2
Quetzalroo — 1

4

African lions, Bengal tigers, hippos, giraffes, elephants, monkeys and all the Central and South American big cats, including some well-fed jaguars. As zoos go, it's not bad and the grounds are a delight. It's also open on full-moon nights, the ideal time to see nocturnal animals.

Museo Nacional de Arqueología y Etnología

Opposite the Parque Aurora is a complex of three state-run museums, of which the **Museo Nacional de Arqueología y Etnología** (Tues–Fri 9am–4pm, Sat & Sun 9am–noon & 1.30–4pm; Q60; Ⓦmunae.gob.gt) is the best. The collection includes a world-class selection of Maya treasures, though the layout and displays are very much in need of an update. Noteworthy pieces include spectacular jade masks from Abaj Takalik, a stunning wooden temple-top lintel from Tikal and priceless artefacts from Piedras Negras, one of the remotest sites in Petén. Stele 12, dating from 672 AD, depicts a cowering captive king begging for mercy, and there's an enormous carved stone throne from the same site, richly engraved with glyphs and decorated with a two-faced head.

Museo Nacional de Arte Moderno

Opposite the archeological museum, the **Museo Nacional de Arte Moderno** (Tues–Fri 9am–4pm, Sat & Sun 9am–noon & 1.30–4pm; Q50) also suffers from poor presentation, but does boast some imaginative geometric paintings by Dagoberto Vásquez, and a collection of startling exhibits by Efraín Recinos, including a colossal marimba-cum-tank sculpture. There's also a permanent collection of Cubist art and massive murals by Carlos Mérida, Guatemala's most celebrated artist.

Kaminaljuyú

Way out on the western edge of the city lies Zona 7, which wraps around the ruins of pre-colonial **Kaminaljuyú** (daily 8am–4pm; Q50). Archeological digs have uncovered more than three hundred mounds and thirteen ball courts here,

culture, with emphasis on traditional weaving. Stunning hand-woven fabrics include some impressive examples of ceremonial costumes, with explanations in English, plus information about techniques, dyes, fibres and weaving tools.

The excellent **Museo Popol Vuh** (Ⓦpopolvuh.ufm.edu.gt) next door is home to an outstanding collection of archeological artefacts collected from sites all over the country. The small museum is divided into Preclassic, Classic, Postclassic and colonial rooms, and all the exhibits are top quality. Particularly interesting is a copy of the Dresden Codex, one of very few surviving written and illustrated records of Maya history.

Parque Aurora

In Zona 13, **Parque Aurora** houses the city's **zoo** (Tues–Sun 9am–5pm; Q25; Ⓦaurorazoo.org.gt). Here you can see

though unlike the massive temples of the lowlands, these structures were built of adobe, and most of them have been lost to erosion and urban sprawl. Today the site is little more than a series of earth-covered mounds; to learn more about the city, visit the Museo Miraflores (see below).

Museo Miraflores

The **Museo Miraflores** (Tues–Sun 9am–7pm; Q40; ⓦmuseomiraflores.org), a ten-minute walk south of the Kaminaljuyú ruins on Calzada Roosevelt, is dedicated to the ancient city; displays explain its history and its importance as a trading centre. To get there from the city centre, take any bus headed to "Tikal Futura" or Antigua.

ARRIVAL AND DEPARTURE

Arriving in Guatemala City is always a bit disconcerting. Wherever you arrive, you should *always* take a taxi to your destination in the city (unless it's a block or two away), or use the Transmetro. Viajes Tivoli, 6 Av 8–41, Zona 9 (☎2386 4200, ⓦviajestivoli.com), is a good all-round travel agent with competitive rates for international and domestic flights.

BY PLANE

Aurora airport The modern and efficiently run airport (☎2334 7680) is in Zona 13 some way south of the centre, but close to Zona 10.

Transport into the city The easiest way to get from and to the airport is by taxi. You can pre-pay your fare from a taxi desk; Zona 10 costs about Q70, Zona 1 around Q90. Note, however, that most guesthouses in Zona 13 offer free pick-ups. Don't, under any circumstances, risk taking the city buses that leave from outside the airport, because of security concerns.

Getting to Antigua Regular shuttle buses run to Antigua (Q80/person, three minimum) until about 10pm. A taxi to Antigua is about Q275.

Currency exchange All the official-looking Global Exchange currency exchange booths offer derisory rates (25 percent lower than the banks') and represent a total scam. Seek out a Banrural bank (daily 8am–9pm) instead – there are branches in the Arrivals and Departures areas – where you can change US dollars and euros at fair rates. There are no ATMs in Arrivals, but two in the Departures hall.

BY BUS

To/from the north and east Most buses to the north and east of the country (including Flores, Cobán, Chiquimula and Puerto Barrios) use the impressive new Centra Norte terminal (ⓦcentranorte.com.gt), 8.5km northeast of Zona 1. It's secure and very well organized, with buses leaving from designated bays below an upmarket shopping mall. But it's a long, long way from the centre of town (Q100–120 in a taxi, or Q2 in a Transurbano bus #311 to the Parque Colón or 18 C in Zona 1) along heavily congested roads – allow 1hr for the journey.

To/from Antigua and western highlands Chicken buses for the western highlands use bus stops (there's no terminal) at 41 Calle between 7 Av and 11 Av, Zona 8, which

---

BUS COMPANIES IN GUATEMALA CITY

ADN Mayan World (ADN) 8 Av 16–41, Zona 1 (☎2251 0610, ⓦadnautobusesdelnorte.com).

Buses del Sol (BS) *Hotel Crowne Plaza*, Av Las Américas 9–08, Zona 13 (☎2422 5000 ⓦbusesdelsol .com).

Fuente del Norte (FN) Two terminals: Centra Norte, for Flores; Calzada Aguilar Batres 7–55, Zona 12, for Tecún Uman border (☎7447 7070, ⓦgrupofuentedel norte.com).

Hedman Alas (HA) 2 Av 8–73, Zona 10 (☎2362 5072, ⓦhedmanalas.com).

King Quality (KQ) 18 Av 1–96, Zona 15 (☎2369 7070, ⓦking-qualityca.com).

Línea Dorada (LD) Centra Norte (☎2415 8900, ⓦlineadorada.info).

Litegua (L) Centra Norte (☎2220 8840, ⓦlitegua .com).

Los Halcones (LH) Calzada Roosevelt 37–47, Zona 11 (☎2439 4911, ⓦtransportesloshalcones.com).

Monja Blanca (MB) Centra Norte (☎2238 1409, ⓦtmb.com.gt).

Pullmantur (P) *Holiday Inn*, 1 Av 13–22, Zona 10 (☎2363 6240, ⓦpullmantur.com).

Rápidos Zaculeu (RZ) Calzada Roosevelt 9–34, Zona 7 (☎2473 5081).

Rutas Orientales (RO) Centra Norte (☎2253 7282).

Tica Bus (TB) Calzada Aguilar Batres 22–55, Zona 12 (☎2473 1639, ⓦticabus.com).

Transportes Alamo (TA) 12 Av A 0–65, Zona 7 (☎2471 8626).

Transportes Galgos (TG) 7 Av 19–44, Zona 1 (☎2232 3661, ⓦtransgalgosinter.com.gt).

Transportes Velásquez (TV) 0 C 31–70, Zona 7 (☎2439 55 53).

Transportes La Vencedora (V) 3 Av 1–38, Zona 9 (no phone/website).

4

is very close to Trébol Transmetro stop. Pullman buses for Quetzaltenango, Huehuetenango and the La Mesilla border use private terminals; most are located in Zonas 1 and 7. Note that to/from Antigua it's far easier, quicker and safer to take a shuttle bus (Q70–90); but it is possible to connect with second-class services at Trébol Transmetro stop.

To/from southern Guatemala Chicken buses for southern Guatemala (including the border with El Salvador, Monterrico and the Mexican border) plus Santiago Atitlán use a purpose-built terminal called Centra Sur in Zona 12 (also known as Cenma), 14km south of the Parque Central. This has a Transmetro stop directly above it, a new shopping plaza under construction and good security. A few Pullman buses to the Mexican border run from Centra Sur, but most still operate from private terminals closer to the centre.

Domestic destinations Antigua (second class from 21 C & 2 Av, Zona 3, via Trébol junction, every 15min until 6.30pm; 1hr–1hr 30min); Chichicastenango (second class from 41 C Zona 8, every 30min; 3hr); Chiquimula (RO: every 30min; L: daily, 2.45pm; 3hr 30min); Cobán (MB: hourly; 5hr); Florido border (L: daily, 2.45pm; 4hr 45min); Esquipulas (RO: every 30min; 4hr 30min); Flores (FN: 15 daily; LD: 3 daily; ADN: 2 daily; 8–9hr); Huehuetenango (LD: 4 daily; LH: 6 daily; TV: 5 daily; RZ: 2 daily; 6hr); La Mesilla (LD: 3 daily; 7hr 30min); Monterrico (second class from Centra Sur, 2 daily; 3hr 30min; or travel via Iztapa which has hourly onward connections); Nebaj (second class from 41 C Zona 8; 5 daily; 5hr 15min); Panajachel (second class from 41 C Zona 8; hourly until 3pm; 3hr); Puerto Barrios (L: 19 daily; 5hr 30min–6hr 30min); Poptún (take a Flores bus; 7hr); Quetzaltenango (ADN: 2 daily; TA: 6 daily; LD: 2 daily; TG: 3 daily; FD: 1 daily; 4hr); Río Dulce Town (L: 5 daily; 5hr; or catch a Flores bus); San Pedro la Laguna (second class from 41 C Zona 8; 7 daily; 3hr 45min); Santiago Atitlán (second class from Centra Sur; 7 daily; 3hr); Tecún Umán (FN: 6 daily; 6hr).

International destinations Copán, Honduras (HA: 2 daily, 5am & 8.30am; FN: 1 daily 6.15am; 5hr); La Ceiba, Honduras (HA: daily 5am & 8.30am; 12hr); Managua, Nicaragua (BS: daily 1.30am; TB: 2 daily; 18–28hr); San Pedro Sula, Honduras (FD: daily 6.15am; HA: daily 5am & 8.30am; RO: daily 5.30am & 1.30pm; 8–9hr); San Salvador, El Salvador (V: hourly; BS: 2 daily; TB: 2 daily; P: 3–4 daily; KQ: 2 daily; 5hr); Tapachula, Mexico (KQ: 1 daily; LD: 1 daily; TB: 1 daily; TG: 6 daily; 6hr); Tegucigalpa, Honduras (HA: daily 5am & 8.30am; 12–13hr; or the following, all of which involve a stopover in San Salvador, around 36hr in total: KQ: daily 7am & 3.30pm; P: daily 7am; TB: daily 6am).

BY CAR

Car rental Two good local companies are Tabarini, 2 C A 7–30, Zona 10 (☎ 2444 4200, ⓦ tabarini.com), and Adaesa, Calzada Aguilar Batres 8–12, Zona 11 (☎ 2472 1122, ⓦ adaesa.com).

GETTING AROUND

BY BUS

Transmetro Guatemala's excellent new Transmetro bus network operates on dedicated lanes that are closed to all other traffic. The articulated buses are modern, air-conditioned, wheelchair-friendly and only stop every kilometre or so along specific routes. Transport police provide security. The green line (#CC) runs north–south from Plaza Barrios, 18 C in Zona 1, along 6 Av through zonas 4 and 9 to Zona 13, returning along 7 Av. The orange line (#70) connects Plaza Barrios and the Centro Cívico with points to the southwest, along Av Bolívar via the Trébol junction and down to the Centra Sur bus terminal. It's useful for connecting with buses to/from the western highlands and zonas 1 and 4.

Transurbano Slower Transurbano buses do not use designated lanes; take bus #311 to/from Centra Norte and Parque Colón, Zona 1 (which is five blocks east of the Parque Central).

BY TAXI

There are both metered and non-metered taxis. Metered taxis are comfortable and fairly cheap; Amarillo (☎ 2470 1515) is highly recommended and will pick you up from anywhere in the city. The fare from Zona 1 to Zona 10 is about Q40. Always take taxis after dark.

INFORMATION AND TOURS

Tourist information The main Inguat tourist office (Mon–Fri 8am–4pm; ☎ 2331 1333, ⓦ visitguatemala .com) is at 7 Av 1–17, Zona 4, and has English-speaking staff and plenty of brochures.

Tours Quetzalroo (see opposite) offer an excellent half-day walking tour of the centro histórico for just Q40 per person. Non-guests are welcome to join.

ACCOMMODATION

The capital is much more expensive than the rest of Guatemala. Firstly choose the zone where you want to base yourself. Zona 1 is not a great area to be hunting for a room late at night, but it's safe enough in the day and early evening. Zona 13, very near the airport, has some good options (and most places offer free airport pick-ups and drop-offs) but it's a quiet, suburban location with no restaurants close by. Zona 10 is a relatively safe upmarket part of town with a glut of restaurants and bars; there's one good budget option here too.

ZONA 1 AND 2

Chalet Suizo 7 Av 14–34 ☎ 2251 8191; map p.280. In the heart of the city a block from Sexta Av, this secure established place has spacious, spotless rooms (with or without private bathroom) with quality beds and fresh linen. Filling meals are available and there's wi-fi. **Q160**

La Coperacha 4 Av 2–03 ☎ 2232 1414 or ☎ 5855 2950, ⊜ coperacha.guate@gmail.com; map p.280. Seven blocks north of the Parque Central, this hostel, occupying a fine old adobe house, has five rooms and a dorm. The young Guatemalan managers look after their guests well, with bikes for rent, a kitchen and good travel information. Popular with artists and musicians. Dorm Q75, double Q150

Hotel Ajau 8 Av 15–62 ☎ 2232 0488, ⊜ hotelajau @hotmail.com; map p.280. Replete with old-school ambience, this simple hotel has a grand lobby and 41 rooms (all with TV, and many en suite). There's a *comedor* for breakfast and evening meals, plus wi-fi. Q130

Hotel Santoña 8 Av 15–13 ☎ 2232 6455; map p.280. An efficient, modern hotel with spacious, clean, featureless, rooms (all twins or doubles) with cable TV. Q220

Hotel Spring 8 Av 12–65 ☎ 2230 2858, ⓦ hotelspring .com; map p.280. A solid choice, this large rambling, secure place has been hosting travellers and Peace Corp workers for decades. Most of the 43 rooms are spacious and many have private bathroom and cable TV. The pretty central courtyard is a nice focal point for meeting other guests. Breakfast is available, plus laundry and wi-fi. Q150

ZONAS 9 AND 10

Hostal Plaza Plaza Aeropuerto 13–92, off 6 Av A, Zona 9 ☎ 5417 2143, ⓦ hostalplaza.page.tl; map p.282. A few blocks from the Zona Viva, this well-run new place has helpful family owners. The attractive singles and doubles boast bright bedspreads and there's an attractive patio for drinks. Q235

Quetzalroo 6 Av 7–84, Zona 10 ☎ 5746 0830, ⓦ quetzalroo.com; map p.282. Owner Manuel is a font of knowledge about his city and is switched on to travellers' needs. Located in an apartment block, *Quetzalroo* offers good accommodation, three shower rooms, a guests' kitchen, TV lounge, laundry room and a fun, communal vibe. Airport pick-ups, internet and a light breakfast are gratis, with excellent city tours offered for just Q40. Dorm Q140, double Q275

ZONA 13

Casablanca 15 C C 7–35 ☎ 2261 3129, ⓦ hotel casablancainn.com; map p.278. Tasteful, stylish guesthouse with light, airy and spacious rooms, most en suite. There's a well-stocked bar and an attractive sitting room. Breakfast, airport transfers and wi-fi are included. Q385

★ **Dos Lunas** 21 C 10–92 ☎ 2261 4248, ⓦ hotel doslunas.com; map p.278. A very welcoming and efficient guesthouse run on a quiet suburban street, managed by fluent English-speaker Lorena Artola and her Dutch husband Henk, who take great care of guests. The attractive rooms are spotless, and rates include airport transfers, internet terminals and wi-fi, and breakfast. Excellent evening meals (from Q50) are also offered, and transport and

tourist advice is second to none. Book well ahead. Dorm Q120, double Q240

Hostal Los Lagos 8 Av 15–85 ☎ 2261 2809, ⓦ loslagoshostal.com; map p.278. New B&B just 400m from the airport with good-quality rooms and dorms. Staff are friendly and informative; free airport transfers and drinking water are offered. Dorm Q120, double Q315

Hostal Los Volcanes 16 C 8–00 ☎ 2261 3040, ⓦ hostallosvolcanes.com; map p.278. Just 600m from the airport, this B&B has clean rooms and a seven-bed dorm, a pleasant lounge and garden. All rooms have cable TV and rates include breakfast, airport transfers and internet/ wi-fi. Dorm Q120, double Q120

Mariana's Petit Hotel 20 C 10–17 ☎ 2261 4105, ⓦ marianaspetithotel.com; map p.278 A well-managed, welcoming guesthouse very close to the airport with inexpensive rates, a quiet location, free airport transfers and free wi-fi. Q325

EATING

You'll find cheap eats scattered around Zona 1, while in Zona 10 the emphasis is more on refined dining. Wherever you are, street vendors and fast-food chains are never far away.

ZONA 1

Café de Imeri 6 C 3–34 ☎ 2232 3722; map p.280. Popular European-style café with alpine decor and filling breakfasts, pasta, sandwiches, baguettes and an excellent *menú del día* (Q28). Mon–Sat 8am–6pm.

★ **Café León** 8 Av 9–15 ☎ 2251 0068, ⓦ cafeleon.net; map p.280. Atmospheric old-school café with gleaming espresso machines and vintage photographs that's a downtown hotspot for Guatemala's chattering classes. It's all about the coffee and conversation here, with treacle-thick espresso and milky *café con leche*, though they do serve breakfasts, cakes (*cubiletes*, *empanadas*) and *rollados* (pastries stuffed with fillings including spinach and cheese). The second Zona 1 branch at 12 C 6–23 is more spacious but a little less atmospheric. Mon–Fri 8am–6pm, Sat 9am–1pm.

Café Música 8 Av 10–6 ☎ 2232 2423; map p.280. Inside the Museo de Músicos Invisibles, this is a very civilized café-restaurant for a filling Guatemala breakfast (Q35) or tasty set lunch (Q28) of *comida casera*. Tables are grouped around a lovely little grassy patio, and there's a live pianist from noon till 3pm daily. Also good for a coffee or a beer. Daily 7am–6pm.

Café Saúl Teatro Lux, 6 Av & 11 C ☎ 2379 8718; map p.280. Astonishing new café in an old cinema foyer complete with movie theatre-style seats, classic film posters and vintage projection equipment. The menu is a bit pricey but includes nutritious juices, good crepes (around Q50), salads and a tasty antipasti selection (Q59) that's enough for two. Daily 8am–8pm.

4

Cafetalito 8 Av 10–68 ⓦ elcafetalito.com; map p.280. Modern café, with all the familiar coffee combinations, plus granitas and frapuccinos and some Guatemalan arabica bean choices (including Huehuetenango and Cobán). Panini and snacks are also served. Mon–Sat 8am–6pm.

El Cuscún 7 Av & 10 C ☎ 2232 1003; map p.280. Huge new warehouse-style space complete with giant photographic murals and a canteen feel. Offers very reasonably priced breakfasts and *menús del día* (Q20–25). Mon–Fri 6am–3pm.

Kafé Katok 12 C 6–61 ☎ 7840 3387, ⓦ ahumadoskatok .com; map p.280. Rustic-style place with huge wooden beams and chunky tables that specializes (appropriately enough) in hearty country cooking, especially grilled meats. Come hungry for the set lunch (Q55), or tuck into a sandwich (Q27) or a few tapas. Mon–Wed 6am–8pm, Thurs–Sun 6am–9pm.

Rey Sol 11 C 5–51 ☎ 2232 3516; map p.280. Vegetarian café-restaurant serving a good choice of lunch dishes that might include lasagne (Q21), a stir-fry or Mexican-style options. Doubles as a health-food store, selling good bread, *empanadas*, granola, soya milk, herbal teas and veggie snacks. Mon–Sat 7.30am–7pm, Sun noon–4pm.

Rocque Rosito 8 Av & 9 C ☎ 2232 7343; map p.280. A spacious café with banquette seating and stylish sofas that's ideal for a coffee or juice and a quick bite – try a crêpe or a sandwich. Mon–Sat 7.30am–6pm.

ZONA 10

Café de Jabes 14 C 4–12 ☎ 2363 4150; map p.282. Ever-popular *comedor* serving Guatemalan breakfasts and the best-value lunch in Zona Viva, such as *bistek* or *pollo dorada* with vegetables. Set meals (Q24) include soup, tortillas and a drink. Daily 7am–3pm.

Paco's Café 1 Av 10–43; map p.282. Tiny, very welcoming *comedor* that's a winner for a traditional breakfast, snack (tacos are just Q7) or a filling set lunch: Q20 buys you a bowl of soup, grilled meat with rice, vegetables and tortillas, a drink and a dessert. Mon–Fri 7am–3pm.

Pitaya 13 C Av 2–75 ☎ 2334 3884, ⓦ pitayajuice.com; map p.282. Hip new juice bar, with amazing selection of healthy blends (including wheatgrass shots, lots of smoothies and supplements including Omega 3 and ginseng) as well as salads (try the *griega* for Q30), wraps and breakfasts. Mon–Fri 7.30am–6.30pm, Sat 9am–5pm.

Sopho's Fontabella Plaza, 12 C & 4 Av ☎ 2419 7070; map p.282. Inside an upmarket courtyard-style shopping mall, this bookstore/café (see opposite) is a delightfully civilized place to browse a book or magazine, sip a *café con leche* and snack on a sandwich or cake. Daily 8am–7pm.

Tacontento 2 Av & 14 C ☎ 2360 2815, ⓦ tamarindos .com.gt; map p.282. Inexpensive in Zona 10, this place knocks out decent tacos and Mexican classics; eat in the lively dining room or on the streetside terrace. The lunch

special (Q30) includes soup, three tacos and a drink. Daily noon–3pm & 7pm–midnight.

DRINKING AND NIGHTLIFE

Guatemala City isn't going to win any prizes for its nightlife. Essentially it comes down to two choices: gritty Zona 1, which has some highly atmospheric old bars and raucous student places, and Zona 10's *Zona Viva*, largely the domain of wealthy Guatemaltecos and bursting with upmarket bars and clubs. It's best not to stroll around Zona 1 late at night, but Zona 10 is considered safe enough. For information on Guatemala's club and DJ scene consult ⓦ electronik.net.

ZONAS 1 AND 2

Bad Attitude 4 C 5–10 ☎ 5206 9510; map p.280. Heavy rock music venue showcasing heavy/death/metal/thrash/alternative rock bands on Thurs and Sat, while on Fri it's everything from reggae to trance. Free entrance some nights; maximum cover will be Q40 (includes a drink). Thurs–Sat 5.30pm–1am.

Blanco y Negro Pasaje Aycinena, 9 C between 6 & 7 Av; map p.280. This place really jumps on weekends when lovers of Afro-Caribbean music descend en masse for the Jamaican dancehall, ska and punta sounds. Also electronic and dubstep DJ nights. Tues–Sat 6pm–1am.

Las Cien Puertas Pasaje Aycinena, 9 C between 6 & 7 Av; map p.280. Bohemian bar in a beautiful, shabby colonial arcade with graffiti-plastered walls. Popular with artists, students and political activists. Good Latin music and reasonable prices. Mon–Sat 5pm–1am.

El Gran Hotel 9 C 7–64; map p.280. Hugely popular bar-cum-cultural centre that draws a young, studenty crowd with indie, protest rock bands, electronica artists and club nights. On weekend nights the atmosphere is raucous and a lot of fun. Cover charge is Q25–50, with two or three live bands per week. Also film evenings and a café during the day. Mon–Sat 9am–midnight.

La Luna Pasaje Aycinena, 9 C 8–59 ☎ 2253 8728, ⓦ cafepianolaluna.com; map p.280. Small, sociable little bar in a faded historic building that has live music (Tues–Sat) – mainly *trova*, acoustic and rock. Doubles as a café in the day when snacks are served. Mon–Wed 10am–midnight, Thurs–Sun 10am–1am.

★ **El Portal** Pasaje Rubio, 9 C between 6 & 7 Av; map p.280. One of Che Guevara's old drinking haunts, and the decor (and clientele) is little changed since the revolutionary era. Order a *chibola* of *cerveza mixta*, munch on a few (complimentary) *boquitas* and soak up the scene: hard drinkers glued to bar stools and wandering *trios* of musicians prowling the tables, mariachi style. Mon–Sat 11am–10pm.

Tacos Tequila 7 Av 5–47 ⓦ tacostequila.com; map p.280. A bohemian drinking den *par excellence*, serving draught beer and bar snacks like *tacos al pastor*. You should find the place buzzing shortly after opening time, making it a good spot for pre-dinner drinks. Mon–Thurs 5–11pm, Fri & Sat until midnight.

ZONA 4

Genetic Majestic Club Vía 3 & Ruta 3; map p.280. The capital's premier (mainly) gay club is packed on weekends, when a young, fashionable crowd gathers to groove to trance, house and Latin anthems. There are three floors and a VIP section, themed nights and go-go dancers. The 1am closing time is sometimes extended. Thurs–Sat 8pm–1am.

ZONA 10

Kahlua 1 Av 15–07 ☎4736 2278; map p.280. Well-established, four-storey club that draws a young, raving crowd. Sounds range from electronica and reggaetón to mainstream Latin dance. Thurs–Sat 7pm–1am.

Rattle & Hum 4 Av 16–11 ☎2366 6524, ⓦrattlen humbar.com; map p.280. Upmarket Australian-owned bar, popular with both expats and locals, with a sociable atmosphere and live music (Tues & Wed) and bar grub including chicken wings and nachos. There's a huge selection of shots and cocktails. Daily noon–1am.

ZONA 15

Stage Club Ruta El Salvador km 14.5 ⓦstageclub.com .gt. Guatemala City's leading club hosts eclectic nights, with DJs playing house, hip-hop and urban Latin music. Cover charges vary from Q40 to Q120 (including a drink) depending on the night. It's on the edge of the city, 14km from the centre. Thurs–Sat 8pm–1am.

ENTERTAINMENT

For full listings of cultural events in the city, see ⓦcultura .muniguate.com or consult supplements in the national press (best are *Prensa Libre* and *El Periódico*).

CINEMA

You'll find Hollywood blockbusters and art-house films in the capital. For English audio with Spanish subtitles, head for the shopping-mall multiplexes.

Centro Cultural de España Vía 5 1–23, Zona 4 ⓦcceguatemala.org; map p.280. The Spanish Cultural Centre has an innovative selection of European and independent Latin American movies, plus occasional classics. Also hosts plays and cultural events.

Cinépolis Oakland Mall, Diagonal 6 13–01, Zona 10 ⓦcinepolis.com.gt. This multi-screener has the best-quality audio-visuals in the city, and even offers "butler service", which gets you a leather chair and drinks brought to your seat.

LIVE MUSIC AND THEATRE

La Bodeguita del Centro 12 C 3–55, Zona 1 ☎2230 2976. Guatemala City's bohemian heart, this barn-like

place emblazoned with revolutionary art hosts live music (particularly *trova* and protest rock), poetry and all manner of left-field events. Free during the week, with cover around Q40 at weekends. Tues–Sat 7pm–1am.

Teatro Nacional ⓦteatronacional.com.gt; map p.280. The national complex has several theatres, including an amphitheatre, and stages some diverse and prestigious events.

Trovajazz Vía 6 3–55, Zona 4 ⓦtrovajazz.com. Intimate venue that showcases quality jazz, blues, acoustic and *trova*. Entrance is around Q40 for most acts. Closed Mon.

SHOPPING

Los Próceres 16 C 2–00, Zona 10 ⓦproceres.com; map p.282. Conveniently located mid-range mall, with four floors and more than two hundred stores, including many budget clothes, electrical and phone shops, some food stalls and a multi-screen cinema. Daily 8am–10pm.

Oakland Mall Diagonal 6 13–01, Zona 10 ⓦoaklandmall .com.gt; map p.282. Upmarket mall with stores including Diesel, Apple and Zara, a good food court and free wi-fi. Daily 8am–10pm.

Markets Best is the Mercado Central, in an underground warren between 8 & 9 Av and 6 & 8 C. The city's biggest market is at Centra Sur (the terminus of the Transmetro route). There is also the touristy Mercado de Artesanías opposite the zoo in Zona 13.

Sopho's Fontabella Plaza, 2 C & 4 Av, Zona 10 ⓦsophosenlinea.com; map p.282. Good bookshop selling English-language fiction and travel guides, with a pleasant café.

DIRECTORY

Banks In addition to those at the airport (see p.283) ATMs are widespread across the city. Very few banks change travellers' cheques. Cash advances on Visa/MasterCard can be obtained at banks including Banco Industrial, 7 Av & 11 C, Zona 1. You can exchange euros at Banco Internacional, Av Las Américas 12–54, Zona 13, and Banrural, at the airport.

Embassies Most embassies are in the southeastern quarter of the city, along Av La Reforma and Las Américas: Australia, contact the Canadian embassy; Belgium (honorary), 6 Av 16–24, Zona 10 (☎2385 5234); Belize, 5 Av 5–55, Zona 14 (☎2367 3883); Canada, 13 C 8–44, Edificio Edyma Plaza, Zona 10 (☎2363 4348, ⓦcanadainternational.gc.ca); Honduras, 19 Av A 20–19, Zona 10 (☎2366 5640); Mexico, 2 Av 7–57, Zona 10 (☎2420 3400, ⓦsre.gob.mx/guatemala); New Zealand (honorary), 13 C 7–85, Zona 10 (☎2431 1705); South Africa (honorary), 11 Av 30–24, Zona 5 (☎2332 6953); Sweden, Edificio Reforma 10, Av La Reforma 9–55, Zona 10 (☎2384 7300, ⓦswedenabroad.com); United Kingdom, Torre Internacional, 16 C 0–55, Zona 10 (☎2380

7300, @ukinguatemala.fco.gov.uk); United States, Av La Reforma 7–01, Zona 10 (☎2326 4000, @guatemala .usembassy.gov).

Health The Centro Médico, 6 Av 3–47, Zona 10 (☎2332 3555), is a private hospital with 24hr cover and English-speaking staff. Central Dentist de Especialistas, 20 C 11–17, Zona 10 (☎2337 1773), is the best dental clinic in the country.

Immigration The main immigration office (*migración*) is at 6 Av & Ruta 3, Zona 4 (☎2411 2411). Visas can be extended here for another ninety days; you'll need copies of your passport, proof of funds (such as a credit card) and a passport-style colour photograph.

Internet There are plenty of internet cafés throughout the city, particularly in Zona 1. Expect to pay around Q5/hr.

Laundry Lavandería el Siglo, 2 C 3–42, Zona 1 (Q40 for wash and dry; Mon–Sat 8am–6pm).

Police The police headquarters are in the fortress building on 6 Av, Zona 1. However, if you actually need anything, go to the yellow-and-blue office on the corner of 11 Av and 4 C, Zona 1.

Post office The main post office is at 7 Av and 12 C, Zona 1 (Mon–Fri 8.30am–5.30pm, Sat 9am–noon).

Antigua

A visit to the colonial city of **ANTIGUA** is a must for any traveller in Guatemala. Nestled in a valley between the Agua, Acatenango and Fuego volcanoes, the city was founded in 1541 and built on a grand grid pattern as befitting a capital. Antigua grew in importance over the next two hundred years, peaking in the mid-eighteenth century, before being largely destroyed by an earthquake in 1773. Since then, it's become something of an open-air architectural museum, with many of its major remaining structures and monuments preserved as ruins – the impressive churches and magnificent buildings on view today date back to the Spanish empire. Local conservation laws are strict, ensuring that the city will remain in its current atmospheric state, and continue to draw in thousands of visitors every year. Long favoured by travellers as an antidote to hectic, nearby Guatemala City, in recent years Antigua has seen its population joined by both large numbers of Guatemaltecos from "la capital" and many expats attracted by the city's sophisticated and relaxed ambience. Tourists of every nationality fill the town, along with numerous foreign students attending the city's language schools. With smart restaurants and wine bars catering to this international, cosmopolitan crowd, Antigua's civilized world can at first seem quite bourgeois, but like most travellers, you will probably end up staying a lot longer than planned.

WHAT TO SEE AND DO

Antigua is laid out as a grid, with avenidas running north–south, and calles east–west. Each street is numbered and has two halves, either a north (*norte/nte*) and south (*sur*) or an east (*oriente/ote*) and west (*poniente/pte*) with the city's main plaza, the **Parque Central**, at their centre. Despite this apparent simplicity, most people get lost here at some stage. If you're confused, remember that Volcán Agua, the one closest to town, is almost directly south.

SEMANA SANTA IN ANTIGUA

Antigua's **Semana Santa (Holy Week)** celebrations are some of the most impressive and remarkable in all Latin America. The celebrations start on Palm Sunday with a procession representing Christ's entry into Jerusalem, and continue through to Good Friday, when processions re-enact the progress of Christ to the Cross. Setting out at about 8am from La Merced, Escuela de Cristo and the village of San Felipe, and accompanied by solemn dirges and clouds of incense, penitents carry images of Christ and the Cross on massive platforms. Initially garbed in either purple or white, after 3pm, the hour of the Crucifixion, the penitents change into black. Some of the images they carry date from the seventeenth century, and the procession itself is thought to have been introduced in the early years of the Conquest. Check the exact details of events with the tourist office (see p.293), and reserve a hotel well in advance if you want to stay in the city.

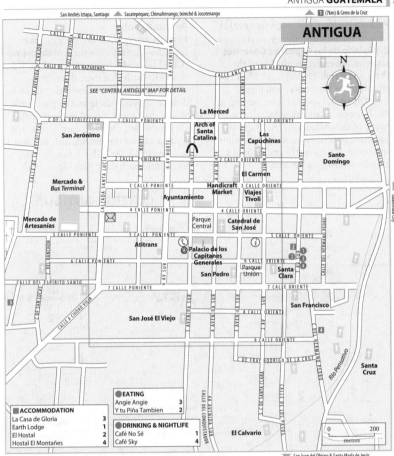

ANTIGUA

N

SEE "CENTRAL ANTIGUA" MAP FOR DETAIL

Guatemala City

4

■ ACCOMMODATION	
La Casa de Gloria	3
Earth Lodge	1
El Hostal	2
Hostal El Montañes	4

● EATING	
Angie Angie	3
Y tu Piña Tambien	2

● DRINKING & NIGHTLIFE	
Café No Sé	1
Café Sky	4

San Juan del Obispo & Santa María de Jesús ▼

Parque Central

Antigua's focal point is its main plaza, the **Parque Central**. It's a popular hangout, with both visitors and locals congregating, chatting and relaxing on its many benches around the central **Fuente de Las Sirenas** fountain, built in 1739.

Catedral de San José

Of the structures surrounding the plaza, the **Catedral de San José**, on the east side, is the most arresting. Built in 1670, the cathedral was quite elaborate for its time and location – it boasted an immense dome, five aisles, eighteen chapels and an altar inlaid with mother-of-pearl, ivory and silver – but the 1773 earthquake almost destroyed the building. Today only two of the original interior chapels remain; take a peek inside and you will find a gold cloister and several colonial images. To get some idea of the vast scale of the original building, check out the ruins to the rear (enter from 5 C Ote; daily 9am–5pm; Q5) where you'll find a mass of fallen masonry and rotting beams, broken arches and hefty pillars. Buried beneath the floor are some of the great names of the Conquest, including Bishop Marroquín, Pedro de Alvarado and his wife, and the historian Bernal Díaz del Castillo. At the very rear of what was once the nave, steps lead down to a burial vault that's regularly used for Maya religious ceremonies – an example of the coexistence of pagan and Catholic beliefs that's so characteristic of Guatemala.

4

Palacio de los Capitanes Generales

One of the oldest buildings in Antigua, the **Palacio de los Capitanes Generales** takes up the entire south side of the Parque Central. Dating to 1558, it's been rebuilt more than once, and been through several incarnations, serving as the Mint for all of Latin America, the home of the colonial rulers, dragoon barracks, stables, law courts, ballrooms and more. It's currently undergoing a lengthy renovation project.

Ayuntamiento

Directly across from the Palace of the Captains-Generals sits the **Ayuntamiento** (City Hall), which dates from 1740. It's so solidly built that even three centuries of earthquakes have taken little toll on its double-arcaded facade and mighty walls. When the capital moved to Guatemala City following the 1773 earthquake, the Ayuntamiento was abandoned, but was restored in 1853. Today it houses two museums (both daily 9am–4pm; both

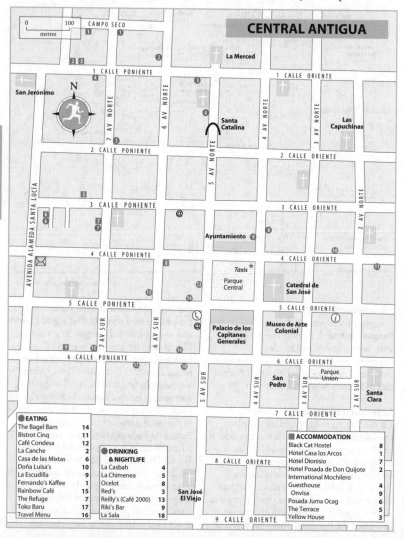

CENTRAL ANTIGUA

La Merced

San Jerónimo

Santa Catalina

Las Capuchinas

Ayuntamiento

Parque Central

Taxis

Catedral de San José

Palacio de los Capitanes Generales

Museo de Arte Colonial

San Pedro

Parque Unión

Santa Clara

San José El Viejo

● EATING	
The Bagel Barn	14
Bistrot Cinq	11
Café Condesa	12
La Canche	2
Casa de las Mixtas	6
Doña Luisa's	10
La Escudilla	9
Fernando's Kaffee	1
Rainbow Café	15
The Refuge	7
Toko Baru	17
Travel Menu	16

● DRINKING & NIGHTLIFE	
La Casbah	4
La Chimenea	5
Ocelot	8
Red's	3
Reilly's (Café 2000)	13
Riki's Bar	9
La Sala	18

■ ACCOMMODATION	
Black Cat Hostel	8
Hotel Casa los Arcos	1
Hotel Dionisio	7
Hotel Posada de Don Quijote	2
International Mochilero Guesthouse	4
Onvisa	9
Posada Juma Ocag	6
The Terrace	5
Yellow House	3

VOLCÁN PACAYA

Volcán Pacaya, one of Guatemala's many cones, is a spectacular Strombolian volcano (characterized by low-level, intermittent explosions). Though technically closer to Guatemala City than to Antigua, it's nonetheless more commonly reached from the latter – indeed, it is *the* trip to make in the area. Depending on Pacaya's activity level, you may be able to scale its slopes.

You can only visit the volcano on a **guided tour** (prices start at Q70 for budget tours), which are offered daily (leaving 2pm) by virtually all travel agents and tour operators in town. Tours entail an hour's climb up the volcano where you can, quite literally, poke at the lava flows with a stick (make sure you wear good shoes, as thin soles can melt). Bring marshmallows for toasting. The views at sunset are breathtaking – remember to bring a torch, as it will be nearly dark when you walk down. The volcano sits inside Pacaya National Park, for which entry is an additional Q40. Note that sulphurous fumes and high winds can occasionally make the ascent impossible.

The budget tours described here can feel impersonal and rushed, as you're herded in a large group from a packed minibus up the crater and back again. If you want to experience the volcano differently, contact the recommended tour operators (see p.293), who can organize bespoke trips.

Q30): the **Museo de Santiago**, in the section of the building that was once the city jail, contains a collection of colonial artefacts, while the **Museo del Libro Antiguo**, in the rooms that held the first printing press in Central America, displays a replica of the press and some copies of the works produced on it. From the upper floor of the Ayuntamiento there's a wonderful **view** of the three volcanoes that surround the city – it's especially fine at sunset.

Iglesia de San Francisco

Southeast of the Parque Central on 1 Avenida Sur is the colossal **Iglesia de San Francisco** (daily 6am–6pm). One of the oldest churches in Antigua, dating from 1579, during the colonial period it served as a vast religious and cultural centre that included a school, a hospital, music rooms, a printing press and a monastery. All of this was lost, though, in the 1773 earthquake. Restoration of the chapel started in 1960, and today very little remains of what was once the original monument.

Inside the church is the tomb of **Hermano Pedro de Betancourt**, a Franciscan from the Canary Islands who founded the Hospital of Belén in Antigua, and is credited with powers of miraculous intervention. Pope John Paul II made him Central America's first saint in 2002.

The **ruins** (daily 9am–4.30pm; Q5) of the monastery to the rear are among the most impressive in Antigua, with colossal fallen arches and pillars strewn over extensive gardens and grassy verges. Don't miss the curious museum here and its "hall of miracles" which contains dozens of crutches and walking sticks left behind by grateful pilgrims, who credit Hermano Pedro with divine healing.

Parque Unión

One block west and one block north of San Francisco is **Parque Unión**, flanked on each end by a church (both daily 8am–4.30pm). The one on the western side is **San Pedro**, dating from 1680, and the one to the east is **Santa Clara**, a former convent with a fine ornate facade. In colonial times the latter was a popular place for aristocratic ladies to take the veil – the hardships were not too extreme, and the nuns gained a reputation for their fine cooking. In front of Santa Clara is a large open-air *pila* (washhouse).

Las Capuchinas

At the junction of 2 Calle Oriente and 2 Avenida Norte are the remains of **Las Capuchinas** (daily 9am–5pm; Q40), dating from 1726, once the largest and most beautiful of the city's convents. These ruins are among Antigua's best preserved, and yet least documented: the Capuchin nuns who lived here were not allowed any contact with the outside world. Food was passed to them by means of a turntable, and they could only speak to visitors through a grille. You should wander through the ruins – they are beautiful, with fountains, courtyards, massive pillars and a unique tower, or "retreat", which has eighteen tiny cells set into the walls on the top floor and a cellar that probably functioned as a meat storage room. The convent was damaged following the 1751 earthquake, and in 1773 the sisters left the premises.

The impressive new **museum** here beautifully showcases some terrific religious art and ecclesiastical artefacts including colonial-era sculptures and portraits.

Santa Catalina and La Merced

A couple of blocks west of Las Capuchinas, spanning 5 Avenida Norte, the **arch of Santa Catalina** is all that remains of yet another convent, this one founded in 1609. The arch was built so that the nuns could walk between the two halves of the establishment without being exposed to the outside world. At the end of the street, just to the north, the church of **La Merced** boasts one of the most intricate facades in the entire city. Look closely and you'll see the outline of a corncob, a motif probably added by the original Maya labourers. The church is still in use, and the cloisters and gardens, including a monumental fountain, are open to the public (daily 8am–5pm; Q5).

Cerro de la Cruz

Northeast of Antigua, the **Cerro de la Cruz**, a hilltop with a giant cross, has commanding views of the city and Volcán Agua. It was something of a mugging hotspot for years, but an increased police presence has meant it's now considered safe. A tuk-tuk here costs Q20.

Santo Domingo

Once forming the largest monastery in Antigua, the immense complex of **Santo Domingo** is today largely occupied by a luxury hotel. Substantial parts of the gorgeous grounds have been sensitively converted into a **cultural zone** (Mon–Sat 9am–6pm, Sun 11.45am–6pm; Q50), which includes several small museums, the monastery ruins, various subterranean crypts, artisans' workshops, exhibitions of local textiles and crafts, a re-creation of an early pharmacy and an art exhibition space.

The **Museo Colonial** harbours an exquisite array of religious artefacts and treasures from the Spanish era including a breathtaking collection of golden crowns, silver lecterns and chalices. You can then tour the monastery's four **crypts**, including the Calvary crypt which has an impressive mural of Christ and the crucifixion. The crypts are dotted around the ruined remains of Santo Domingo's 68m-long **church**. Inside the complex's **Archeological Museum** are some impressive Maya ceramics, including intricately painted drinking vessels, funerary urns and incense burners in an exhibition room that has walls painted with scenes from the

---

LANGUAGE SCHOOLS IN ANTIGUA

Antigua is an extremely popular place to attend **language school**. Listed here are only a few of the many schools offering Spanish courses.

Antigüena Spanish Academy1 C Pte 10 (☎7832 7241, ⓦspanishacademyantiguena.com).

APPE 1 C Ote 15 (☎7882 4284, ⓦappeschool.com).

Centro Lingüístico Internacional Spanish School Av del Espíritu Santo 6 (☎7832 1039, ⓦspanishcontact.com).

Centro Lingüístico Maya 5 C Pte 20 (☎7832 0656, ⓦclmaya.com).

Christian Spanish Academy 6 Av Nte 15 (☎7832 3922, ⓦlearncsa.com).

Guate Linda Language Center 7 Av Norte 76 (☎4360 5238, ⓦguatelindacenter.com).

Ixchel Spanish School 4 Av Norte 32 (☎7832 3440, ⓦixchelschool.com).

Ixquic 7 Av Nte 74 (☎7832 2402, ⓦixquic.edu.gt).

Probigua 6 Av Nte 41B (☎7832 2998, ⓦprobigua.org).

San José El Viejo 5 Av Sur 34 (☎7832 3028, ⓦsanjoseelviejo.com).

Spanish Academy Sevilla 1 Av Sur 17 C (☎7832 5101, ⓦsevillantigua.com).

Tecún Umán Spanish School 6 C Pte 34A (☎7832 2792, ⓦtecunuman.centramerica.com).

famous murals of Bonampak. The neighbouring **Museum of Maya Art and Modern Glass** has exhibitions of Maya artefacts and ceramics together with contemporary glassworks that are supposed to have been influenced by them – a slightly bizarre concept.

ARRIVAL AND DEPARTURE

By bus Antigua's second-class bus terminal is beside the market. Very few travellers now take local buses to Guatemala City, partly due to security concerns and partly because they use an inconvenient terminal in the capital in Zona 3, 1.5km west of the centre. If you're heading to the western highlands catch the first bus to Chimaltenango and transfer there. The following buses all leave from the main terminal, except the Panajachel bus (which leaves from 4 C Poniente 34) and Hedman Alas (ⓦ hedmanalas .com) buses to Copán, Honduras (2 daily; US$35–65), which leave from *Hotel de Don Rodrigo*, 5 Av Norte 17.

Destinations Chimaltenango (every 20min; 40min); Escuintla (every 30min; 1hr 15min); Guatemala City (every 15min; 1hr–1hr 30min); Panajachel (7am daily; 2hr 30min); Santa María de Jesús (every 30min; 20min).

By shuttle bus Shuttle buses drop off/pick up passengers at their hotels. Minibuses can be booked through most travel agents, including Atitrans. Shuttles typically cost triple the price of public buses, but they are more comfortable.

Destinations Chichicastenango (2 daily; 2hr 30min); Cobán (daily; 6hr); Copán, Honduras (daily; 6hr); El Tunco, El Salvador (daily; 5hr); Lanquín (daily; 9hr); Guatemala City (8 daily; 1hr–1hr 30min); Monterrico (8am daily; 2hr 30min); Panajachel (2–3 daily; 2hr 30min); Quetzaltenango (daily; 3hr 45min); San Cristóbal de las Casas, Mexico (daily; 11hr).

GETTING AROUND

By taxi Taxis wait on the east side of the cathedral, or you can call ⓣ 7832 0479; a local journey is about Q30.
By tuk-tuk Tuk-tuks charge Q10 per trip.
Bike rental Maya Mountain Bike Tours and Old Town Outfitters (see below) rent mountain bikes (from around Q125/day). La Ceiba, 6 C Pte 6 (ⓣ 7832 4168, ⓦ ceibarent .com), rents scooters for Q350/day and 250cc trail bikes for Q425/day.
Car rental La Ceiba (see above) offers small cars (like a Daihatsu Charade) for Q230/day; 4WDs start at Q360/day.

INFORMATION AND TOURS

Tourist information The Inguat office (Mon–Fri 8am–5pm, Sat & Sun 9am–5pm; ⓣ 7832 5682, ⓔ antigua@inguat.gob.gt) is presently at 5 C Ote 11, but may move back to its usual location on the south side of the Parque Central. The English-speaking staff are

extremely helpful. Otherwise, check out the noticeboards in hostels and restaurants including *Doña Luisa's* restaurant (see p.295) and the *Rainbow Reading Room* (see p.296) for everything from private language lessons to apartment rental.

Tour operators Maya Mountain Bike Tours, 1 Av Sur 15 (ⓣ 7832 3383, ⓦ guatemalaventures.com), offers a wide range of biking and hiking trips as well as bike rental; Old Town Outfitters, 6 C Pte 7 (ⓣ 7832 4171, ⓦ adventure guatemala.com), runs mountain-biking, rock-climbing, kayaking and hiking trips, and offers tent, sleeping bag and bike rental. Elizabeth Bell, 3 C Ote 28 (ⓣ 7832 2046, ⓦ antiguatours.net), offers excellent twice-daily historical walking tours of Antigua (Q160).

Travel agents There are dozens of travel agents in Antigua, many of a low quality. Atitrans, 6 Av Sur 8 (ⓣ 7832 3371, ⓦ atitrans.net), runs shuttle bus connections all over Guatemala and has a good reputation for reliability. Viajes Tivoli, 4 C Ote 10 (ⓣ 7832 4274 or ⓣ 7832 4287, ⓦ viajestivoli.com), is a good all-rounder.

ACCOMMODATION

Antigua has lots of excellent budget accommodation, including many good hostels. You'll also see rooms and apartments advertised on café noticeboards. During Semana Santa the whole town is fully booked, but even if you haven't reserved you can usually find a room in a family home (locals with spare rooms approach travellers at the bus station). All the following places have free wi-fi for guests.

HOSTELS

Black Cat Hostel 6 Av Nte 1A ⓣ 7832 1229, ⓦ blackcathostels.net; map p.290. One of the most sociable hostels in town, very much geared to a young backpacking crowd with decent dorms (some en suite). There's also a movie room and a free, gut-busting breakfast. Dorm Q̲6̲5̲, double Q̲1̲6̲0̲

★ **Earth Lodge** ⓣ 5664 0713, ⓦ earthlodgeguatemala .com; map p.289. High above Antigua, this spectacular rural retreat has sweeping views of the Panchoy valley and its volcanoes. Accommodation options include A-frame cabañas, a wood-cabin dorm and tree houses. Wholesome meals are served (dinner is eaten family-style) and there's a Maya-style sauna and good walking trails. Consult their website for transport information (you can arrange a pick-up from Antigua). Dorm Q̲4̲5̲, cabin Q̲1̲7̲0̲

★ **El Hostal** 1 Av Sur 8 ⓣ 7832 0442, ⓦ elhostal.hostel .com; map p.289. The best hostel in town has spacious rooms and dorms that offer comfort and style in an elegant converted colonial house. The communal bathrooms (with superb hot-water showers) are spotless, and there's a great central courtyard for chilling, a juice bar and water refills (just Q1). Rates include an excellent breakfast. Dorm Q̲7̲8̲, double Q̲2̲3̲5̲

4

Hotel Dionisio 3 C Pte ☎5644 9486, ⓦhotel dionisioantigua.com; map p.290. Offering a quiet location and great value, *Dionisio* has spacious dorms and rooms (those without bathroom are small and simple) with good mattresses, lockers and hot water. You'll find free coffee, a kitchen, friendly staff, a sunny terrace and a recommended travel agency here too. Dorm Q50, double Q150

International Mochilero Guesthouse 1 C Pte 33 ☎7832 0520, ⓦinternacionalmochilero.com; map p.290. This long-running place has cheap rates, especially for private rooms (very basic but OK), as well as a large garden. Check out the old musical instruments in the hall, including a marimba. Dorm Q50, double Q120

Onvisa 6 C Pte 40 ☎5909 0160, ⓔonvisatravel@hotmail .com; map p.290. Locally owned hostel with very cheap, clean and fairly spacious dorms (most with three or four beds) set around a pretty patio. The private rooms, with antique floor tiles and cable TV, are great value too. Dorm Q45, double Q130

The Terrace 3 C Pte 24B ☎7832 3463, ⓦterracehostel .com; map p.290. Sociable hostel run by helpful staff that has an amazing roof terrace, the perfect spot for barbecues (Wed & Sun) and a glass of ale (they sell microbrew beers). Breakfast is included, there's a guests' lounge with TV/DVD player, and good tours of the Antigua region. Dorm Q65, double Q205

Yellow House 1 C Pte 24 ☎7832 6646, ⓔyellow houseantigua@hotmail.com; map p.290. This welcoming solar-powered hostel is a good choice, boasting a lovely rustic-style roof terrace with hammocks, greenery and views. The four bathrooms mean that you shouldn't have to wait long for a *ducha*. Accommodation varies: the three-bed dorms are the best value, while the cabin-like upstairs rooms are lovely. Rates include use of kitchen and a good buffet breakfast. Dorm Q60, double Q175

HOTELS AND GUESTHOUSES

La Casa de Gloria C San Luquitas 3B ☎4374 1391, ⓔlacasadegloria@yahoo.com; map p.289. Sociable guesthouse about 10min walk southwest of the Parque Central, with five private rooms and a kitchen. Run by a welcoming young Guatemalan (a salsa and Spanish teacher), it's a great option if you're after a local experience. Q60

Hostal El Montañes C del Hermano Pedro 19 B ☎7832 3046 or ☎5308 6223, ⓦhostalelmontanesantigua.com; map p.289. With beautifully presented rooms, most en suite, this welcoming B&B has character and comfort. There's an elegant guests' lounge, with a piano and TV/DVD player and a pretty front garden. Breakfast is filling. It's away from the centre but close to the bars and restaurants on 1 Av Sur. Q360

Hotel Casa los Arcos Callejón Camposeco (off 7 Av Nte) ☎7832 7813, ⓔcasa_losarcos@hotmail.com; map p.290. A family-owned guesthouse with a good choice of modern, spotless rooms (nine en suite), all with hand-woven bedspreads and cable TV. It's a great deal for singles (rooms are Q120 per person). There's a guests' kitchen. Q240

Hotel Posada de Don Quijote 1 C Pte 22 ☎7832 0775, ⓦposadaquijote.com; map p.290. Run by a friendly, house-proud Guatemalan woman, this small hotel has simple, well-kept rooms priced per person (Q100 or Q120 with private bathroom). Breakfast included. Q200

★ **Posada Juma Ocag** Alameda Santa Lucía Nte 13 ☎7832 3109, ⓦposadajumaocag.com; map p.290. A lovely little guesthouse a stone's throw from the market, with immaculately presented rooms decorated with local fabrics. The owners are very accommodating, security is good, and there's a little upper terrace and laundry service. Q190

EATING

CAFÉS

The Bagel Barn 5 C Pte ⓦthebagelbarn.com; map p.290. An intimate café serving nine kinds of bagel (including oregano, all-grain and sesame), with lots of tempting combo options. Prices start at Q18. There's free wi-fi, and films shown at 4.15pm and 7pm. Daily 6am–10pm.

Café Condesa West side of the Parque Central ☎7832 0038; map p.290. An Antiguan institution, this classy café has a gorgeous cobbled patio, smart dining rooms and gurgling fountains. Great for breakfasts (from Q28) and superb salads (small Q28, large Q46) – order the green leaves with toasted macadamia nuts and outstanding home-made corn bread. Sun–Thurs 7.30am–8pm, Fri & Sat 7.30am–9pm.

Fernando's Kaffee 7 Av Nte 43D ☎7832 6953, ⓦfernandoskaffee.com; map p.290. The hospitable English-speaking Guatemalan owner is a complete bean-head who selects and roasts (on the premises) his own arabica coffee from small estates and also makes gourmet chocolate. Breakfasts (from Q20), sandwiches (Q22), light lunches and wonderful juices, smoothies and cakes are also available. Daily 8am–8pm.

Rainbow Café 7 Av Sur 8 ☎7832 1919, ⓦrainbow cafeantigua.com; map p.290. Attractive courtyard café/ restaurant offering a tempting choice of imaginative salads, Mexican and vegetarian dishes. The "early bird" breakfast is Q25 and the set lunch costs Q35. There's a good secondhand bookshop and live events (music, political and cultural lectures) most nights. Daily 7am–11pm.

The Refuge 7 Av Norte 18A ☎4118 4904; map p.290. Excellent new café that advertises "coffee is all we do." Not quite true – you can grab a cup of *mate* (Argentine tea) or a *galleta* (biscuit) here as well – but the emphasis is definitely on perfectly prepared espressos and the like. Mon–Fri 7.30am–7pm, Sat 8am–6.30pm.

Y Tu Piña También 1 Av Sur 11 ⓦytupinatambien.com; map p.289. Popular with Antigua's creative crowd, this zany-looking café has winsome blended fruit juices and good breakfast options (from Q15) that all include juice and a coffee. Also good wraps, waffles, baguettes, omelettes, salads and soups. Free wi-fi. Mon–Fri 7am–8pm, Sat & Sun 8am–8pm.

RESTAURANTS

★ **Angie Angie** 1 Av Sur 11A ☎ 7832 3352; map p.289. Terrific garden restaurant with superb grilled meats (including flavoursome cuts like *entraña* – thick skirt steak), imaginative salads, fresh pasta and tapas-style options (Q30–40) including *camarones* (squid) and delicious Argentine sausage. Tables are set around a log fire at night. Daily 8am–10pm.

La Canche 6 Av Nte 42; map p.290. For a very local experience, chow down at one of the lino-topped tables inside this humble store-cum-*comedor*. Filling Guatemalan *comida típica* (Q12–20 a meal) is the order of the day – take your pick from the steaming pots. Tables are shared; if there's space someone will shout "¡hay lugar!". Mon–Sat 11am–8.30pm.

Casa de las Mixtas 1 Callejón, off 3 C Pte; map p.290. Authentic, filling Guatemalan *comedor* grub: extensive breakfast options and hearty portions of grilled meats and *caldos* (soups) at reasonable prices. Daily 8am–4pm.

Doña Luisa's 4 C Ote 12 ☎ 7832 2578; map p.290. Still going strong, this is one of Antigua's most renowned café-restaurants, set in a historic colonial mansion. The menu is pretty basic – sandwiches (from Q27), burgers (Q30) and salads – but the in-house bakery is superb. Pastries, cakes and fresh bread can be bought from the adjoining shop. Daily 7.30am–9.30pm.

La Escudilla 4 Av Nte 4 ☎ 7832 1327; map p.290. Given the gorgeous colonial surrounds, the prices at this courtyard restaurant are very moderate. Offers a choice of breakfasts (try the "Kill Hangover" for Q30), Mexican and European dishes. The lunch deal (Q27) is a serious bargain. Also home to *Riki's Bar* (see beow), which is ideal for an aperitif. Daily 8am–10pm.

Toko Baru 6 C Pte 21 ☎ 4079 2092; map p.290. Tiny, friendly place with just three tables that offers a pretty

---

★ **TREAT YOURSELF**

Bistrot Cinq 4 C Ote 7 ☎ 7832 5510, Ⓦ bistrotcinq.com; map p.290. Very classy, Parisian-style bistro that delivers on every level, with highly accomplished, technically adept French cooking, atmospheric decor that combines contemporary and colonial influences, and professional, informed service. The menu is short and to the point, with classics (most Q90–130) like *filet mignon au poivre*, and always some excellent daily specials and fish dishes. Daily noon–10.30pm.

---

authentic stab at Middle Eastern favourites like *falafel* and *sharma* kebabs, plus Asian dishes including chicken tikka, satay and spring rolls. Tues–Sat noon–9pm, Sun 1–8pm.

Travel Menu 6 C Pte 14 ☎ 5682 9648; map p.290. Intimate candlelit place with very moderate prices that caters to all tastes with Western and Guatemalan dishes (try a *plato típico*). House wine is Q20 a glass. They also show NFL games and movies some nights. Daily noon–10pm.

DRINKING AND NIGHTLIFE

There are bars throughout Antigua. Two of the main areas are around the arch on 7 Av Nte and over on 1 Av Sur. The city's dance scene is fairly small but lively; however, all places (including clubs) officially close at 1am.

BARS

★ **Café No Sé** 1 Av Sur 11C ☎ 5501 2680, Ⓦ cafenose .com; map p.289. The mantra at this famous bar is "because every dive needs a town". Draws an intoxicating mix of characters – Guatemalan artists and writers, gringo wasters, travellers and boozy expats – plus the odd stray dog. There's live acoustic music virtually nightly and a (semi-) secret mescal bar: order the house brand, *Ilegal*. Daily 1pm–1am.

Café Sky 1 Av Nte ☎ 7832 7300; map p.289. On the top deck of a sky-blue structure on the east side of town, this bar is the best bet for sunset, with volcano views *par excellence*. Order a cold *cerveza* or treat yourself to a Margarita (Q35) and you're set. Daily 8am–10pm.

La Chimenea 7 Av Nte & 2 C Pte ☎ 7832 4805; map p.290. This long-running bar is popular with young Guatemalans, and serves pretty authentic food too. It's a good bet for happy hour when there are cocktail specials. Mon–Sat 11am–1am.

Ocelot 4 Av Nte 3 ☎ 5658 9028; map p.290. Probably Antigua's classiest bar, *Ocelot* is a great place for a relaxed drink, with elegant furnishings, gingham floor tiles, seductive cocktails (around Q30) and live music most nights. There's an excellent quiz (trivia) on Sunday evenings while on Monday Mojitos are just Q15. Daily 12.15pm–1am.

Red's 1 C Pte 3; map p.290. Large British-owned sports bar with pool tables and a dart board, good beer selection and a pub grub menu that takes in local, Mexican, Indian curries and English comfort food like shepherd's pie. Daily 10am–midnight.

Reilly's (Café 2000) 6 Av Norte 2; map p.290. Antigua's Irish bar's winning formula is very straightforward: a gregarious atmosphere, free-flowing beer and lots of drinks promotions. Everyone calls it *Reilly's* but due to silly local laws the sign says *Café 2000*. Daily noon–1am.

Riki's Bar 4 Av Nte 4 (inside *La Escudilla*) ☎ 7832 1327; map p.290. Intimate bar with an inexpensive happy hour and an eclectic music policy; expect a mix of jazz, lounge and electronica. Daily noon–1am.

CLUBS

La Casbah 5 Av Nte 30 ☎ 7832 2640, ⓦ lacasbahantigua
.com; map p.290. The only real club in town, the *Casbah*
attracts a mix of well-heeled locals and up-for-it gringos
with DJs spinning Latin house, reggaetón and salsa via a
powerful sound system. Cover around Q30. Tues–Sat
9pm–1am.

La Sala 6 C Poniente 9 ☎ 7832 9524; map p.290. Recently
refurbished, this is an atmospheric bar and live music
venue. Bands (Latin/funk/rock/reggae) play several times
a week and there's a big salsa club night on Sundays. Food
served during the day. Daily noon–1am.

ENTERTAINMENT

Cinemas The following places show Western and Latin
American films daily: *The Bagel Barn* (see p.294);
Cooperación Española, 6 Av Nte (☎ 7832 1276, ⓦ aecid-cf
.org.gt), and El Sitio (see below), which is good for art-
house movies. Weekly listings are posted on noticeboards
all over town.

Cultural institutes ⓦ antiguacultural.com is useful.
Cooperación Española (see above) promotes all manner of
cultural events: films, exhibitions, lectures and workshops,
and its library is a terrific resource. El Sitio, 5 C Pte 15
(☎ 7832 3037, ⓦ elsitiocultural.org), has an active
theatre, art gallery and café and regularly hosts exhibitions
and concerts.

SHOPPING

Good supermarkets include La Bodegona, 4 C Pte &
Calzada Santa Lucía, and La Despensa, Calzada Santa Lucía
between 4 and 5 C.

Casa del Conde West side of the plaza. Bookshop with a
decent collection of English-language novels and non-
fiction, travel guides and photographic books.

Dyslexia Books 1 Av Sur 11. A good option for
secondhand books, run by knowledgeable people who are
happy to recommend reading matter.

Markets The main mercado (daily 7am–5.30pm) by
the bus terminal is fascinating. Browse the Latino CDs
and Hollywood DVDs and shop for unusual tropical fruit
or fake footie gear. Just south of here, the Mercado de
Artesanías is a tad touristy, so bargain hard. There's
another handicraft market next to the El Carmen church
on 3 Av Nte.

Nim Pot 5 Av Nte 29 ☎ 7832 2681, ⓦ nimpot.com. An
astounding, warehouse-sized place, more of a museum
than a store, stuffed with all manner of Guatemalan crafts:
rare and everyday *huipils* and weavings from every corner
of the nation, masks, ceremonial outfits, as well as books,
souvenirs and even Maximón mannequins.

Rainbow Reading Room 7 Av Sur 8. Small store,
stocking (mainly) used books at fair prices. You can grab a
coffee while you're here.

DIRECTORY

Banks There are several ATMs in town, including on the
west side of the plaza. Banco Industrial is at 4 C Pte 14.

Health 24hr emergency service at the Hospital Privado
Hermano Pedro (☎ 7832 1190). Dr Marco Antonio Bocaleti
has a surgery on 3 Av Nte 1 (☎ 7832 4835) and speaks
English and German. Ivory Pharmacy is at 6 Av Sur 11
(daily 7am–10pm; ☎ 7832 5394).

Internet Dozens of internet cafés (Q4–8/hr). Funky
Monkey, 5 Av Sur 6, is open daily till 12.30am and has
quick connections.

Laundry Rainbow Laundry, 6 Av Sur 15 (daily
7.30am–8pm).

Police The headquarters are outside town. If you're a
victim of a crime in Antigua, contact English-speaking
ASISTUR rep Abraham Martínez (☎ 5578 9835), who will
help you deal with the police and file a report.

Post office Alameda de Santa Lucía, opposite the bus
terminal (Mon–Fri 8am–6pm).

Telephones You can netcall on good lines at Funky
Monkey (see above) for Q1/min to North America and Q3 to
Europe, Australia, New Zealand and the rest of the world.

AROUND ANTIGUA

The countryside **around Antigua** is
extremely beautiful. The valley is dotted
with small villages, ranging from the
ladino coffee centre of Jocotenango to the
indígena village of Santa María de Jesús.
For the more adventurous, Agua and
Acatenango volcanoes offer strenuous but
superb hiking, best done with a specialist
agency (see p.293). Northwest of Antigua
is **Santiago Sacatepéquez**, renowned for
its annual Festival of the Day of the Dead,
when beautiful, intricately decorated kites
– some with a diameter of up to 7m
– soar through the skies. Further west are
the ruins of **Iximché**, the "Place of the
Maize Tree", where you can visit what
remains of a pre-Columbian archeological

> ## CRIME AROUND ANTIGUA
>
> Visitors to the areas around Antigua should
> be aware that **crime against tourists**
> – including violent robbery and rape – is
> not common but does occur. Keep
> informed by taking local advice, and try to
> avoid walking alone at night, or to isolated
> spots during the day. ASISTUR (see box,
> p.275) will accompany you free of charge,
> or even give you a ride to many sites.

site. All of these sites (except the last) are less than an hour from Antigua.

Santa María de Jesús and Volcán Agua

Heading south from Antigua, a good paved road snakes through the coffee bushes and past the village of San Juan del Obispo before arriving in **SANTA MARÍA DE JESÚS**. Perched on the shoulder of **Volcán Agua**, the village is some 500m above the city, with brilliant views over the Panchoy valley and east towards smoking Volcán Pacaya. Though the women wear beautiful purple *huipiles*, the village itself is of minimal interest – most people come through here on their way up Agua, the easiest and most popular of Guatemala's major cones to climb. It's an exciting ascent with a fantastic view to reward you at the top. The trail starts in Santa María de Jesús: it's a fairly simple climb on a clear (often garbage-strewn) path, taking five to six hours, and the peak, at 3766m, is always cold at night. There is shelter (though not always room) in a small chapel at the summit, and the views certainly make it worth the struggle.

As there have been (occasional) robberies reported on the outskirts of Santa María, it's best to team up with an Antigua adventure sports outfit (see p.293) and not attempt the hike on your own.

Buses run from Antigua to Santa María (every 30min or so 6am–6pm).

Jocotenango

Despite being rather unattractive, the suburb of **JOCOTENANGO**, just 3km north of Antigua, does boast a couple of interesting sights, both of which are grouped in the **Centro La Azotea** cultural centre (Mon–Fri 8.30am–4.30pm, Sat 8.30am–2.30pm; Q50, including tour in English; ⓦcentroazotea.org). **Casa K'ojom**, which forms one half of the centre, is a purpose-built museum dedicated to Maya culture, especially music. Displays clearly present the history of indigenous musical traditions, beginning with its pre-Columbian origins and moving through sixteenth-century Spanish and African influences – which brought the marimba, bugles and drums – to today. Other rooms are dedicated to the village weavings of the Sacatepéquez department and the cult of Maximón (see box below). Next door, the 84-acre **Museo de Café** plantation dates from 1883, and offers the chance to look around a working organic coffee farm. All the technicalities of husking, sieving and roasting are explained, and you can sample a cup of the home-grown brew after the tour. A free hourly **shuttle bus** runs between the cathedral in Antigua and the Azotea.

San Andrés Itzapa

Beyond Jocotenango, the Antigua–Chimaltenango road ascends the Panchoy valley, past small farming villages, before a side road branches off to **SAN ANDRÉS ITZAPA**. San Andrés is known as the home of the cult of **San Simón** (or Maximón), the "evil saint" – a kind of combination of Judas Iscariot and Pedro

---

THE CULT OF MAXIMÓN

Despite being just 18km from Antigua, few tourists visit the shrine of the "evil saint" **San Simón** (or Maximón), in San Andrés Itzapa, and you may feel more welcome here than at his other places of abode, which include Zunil (see p.324) and Santiago Atitlán (see p.303). To reach the saint's "house" ("Casa de San Simón") – which is only open from sunrise to sunset – head for San Andrés' central plaza, turn right when you reach the church, walk two blocks, then up a little hill, where you should spot street vendors selling charms, incense and candles.

Once you've tracked down the shrine, you'll find that Maximón lives in a peculiar world, his image surrounded by drunken men, cigar-smoking women and hundreds of burning candles, each symbolizing a request. You may be offered a *limpia*, or soul cleansing, which, for a small fee, involves being beaten by one of the resident women with a bushel of herbs. A bottle of *aguardiente* is also demolished: some is offered to San Simón, some of it you drink yourself and the rest is consumed by the attendant, who may spray you with alcohol (from her mouth) for your sins.

de Alvarado – who is housed in his own pagan chapel (see box, p.297).

There are direct **buses** from the Antigua terminal to San Andrés (every 2hr). Alternatively, catch a bus to Chimaltenango (every 20min) and ask to be dropped off at the entrance to the town.

Santiago Sacatepéquez

SANTIAGO SACATEPÉQUEZ, 20km northeast of Antigua on the Carretera Interamericana, is renowned for its fiesta honouring the **Day of the Dead** (Nov 1). On this day, colourful, massive paper kites with bamboo frames – some take months to create – are flown in the town's cemetery, symbolizing the release of the souls of the dead from agony. Teams of young men struggle to get the kites aloft while the crowd looks on with bated breath, rushing for cover if a kite comes crashing to the ground. At other times of the year, there's little to see or do here – if you find yourself passing through on a Tuesday or a Sunday you might visit the town market, but that's about it.

To reach Santiago Sacatepéquez, catch a **bus** to San Lucas Sacatepéquez (buses running between Antigua and Guatemala City pass through), and then change there – many buses shuttle back and forth between the two.

Chimaltenango

The grim, traffic-plagued town of Chimaltenango is an ugly transport hub on the Interamericana. Frequent **buses** arrive from both Guatemala City and Antigua; you can change here for buses to destinations in the highlands. Services to Antigua leave every twenty minutes between 6am and 7pm from the turn-off on the highway.

Iximché

The Maya site of **Iximché** (daily 8am–5pm; Q50) sits on a beautiful exposed hillside about 5km south of the small town of **TECPÁN**, northwest of Antigua. These are the ruins of the pre-Conquest capital of the Kaqchikel Maya, who allied themselves with the conquistadors in the early days of the

Conquest. Time and weather have taken their toll, though, and the majority of the buildings – which once housed more than ten thousand people – have disappeared, and just a few low pyramids, plazas and ball courts are left. Nevertheless, the site – protected on three sides by steep slopes and surrounded by pine forests – is quite peaceful; the grassy plazas make excellent picnic spots and you may have the place to yourself during the week. George W. Bush stopped here in 2007 on a visit to Guatemala to take in a Maya ceremony, though not all the locals were impressed; after he'd left, Maya shamans performed a cleansing ritual to rid the site of what they called "bad energy". The ruins are still used for Maya worship: ceremonies, sacrifices and offerings take place down a small trail behind the final plaza.

Take any **bus** travelling along the Carretera Interamericana between Chimaltenango and Los Encuentros and ask to be dropped at Tecpán. Regular buses shuttle back and forth from Tecpán's plaza to the ruins. Plan to be back on the Carretera Interamericana before 5.30pm to be sure of a bus. Tecpán itself is of no interest, but there are a number of restaurants and guesthouses, if you get stuck.

Lago de Atitlán

Lago de Atitlán, one of the most visited destinations in Guatemala's western highlands, was described by Aldous Huxley in 1934 as one of the most beautiful lakes in the world – and it

---

CRIME AROUND LAGO DE ATITLÁN

Though **crime** against tourists is rare, hikers have been sporadically robbed on paths around Lago de Atitlán and on the trails that climb the volcanoes. Take precautions: hire a local guide or walk in a large group. In the more remote areas, where foreigners are a much rarer sight, incidents are extremely uncommon.

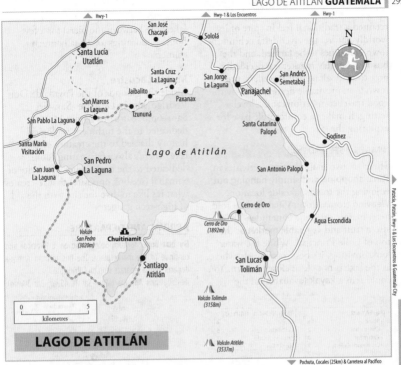

Map labels: Hwy-1 · Hwy-1 & Los Encuentros · Hwy-1

San José Chacayá
Sololá
Santa Lucía Utatlán
Santa Cruz La Laguna
San Jorge La Laguna
San Andrés Semetabaj
Jaibalito
Paxanax
Panajachel
San Marcos La Laguna
Tzununá
San Pablo La Laguna
Santa Catarina Palopó
Santa María Visitación
Godínez
San Pedro La Laguna
San Juan La Laguna
Lago de Atitlán
San Antonio Palopó
Cerro de Oro
Volcán San Pedro (3020m)
Chuitinamit
Cerro de Oro (1892m)
Agua Escondida
Santiago Atitlán
San Lucas Tolimán
Volcán Tolimán (3158m)

0 — 5 kilometres

LAGO DE ATITLÁN

N

Volcán Atitlán (3537m)

Pochuta, Cocales (25km) & Carretera al Pacífico

Patzicía, Patzún, Hwy-1 & Los Encuentros & Guatemala City

4

really is exceptionally scenic. Atitlán is of interest both for its majestic setting (it's hemmed in by three volcanoes and steep hills) and for its cultural appeal – the lake's shores are dotted with thirteen diverse yet traditional Maya villages. With the exception of cosmopolitan **Panajachel** and **San Pedro La Laguna**, most of the pueblos are subsistence farming communities, and you can hike or take a boat between them; highlights include visits to **Santiago Atitlán**, where Maya men still wear traditional dress, and **Santa Cruz** and **San Marcos**, both of which are on excellent walking trails.

PANAJACHEL

Not too long ago **PANAJACHEL**, known locally as "Pana", was a quiet little village of Kaqchikel Maya, whose ancestors settled here centuries ago. These days, it's an established resort town, highly popular with foreigners and holidaying Guatemalans. Yet somehow it has

RISING HIGH

Atitlán's beauty remains overwhelming, but recent pressures are decidedly threatening. Sediment analysis has shown that the lakewater has risen and fallen in cycles for hundreds of years, but after the **tropical storm Agatha** in 2010 Atitlán rose 5m in eighteen months, an unprecedented event that caused businesses to flood and beaches and paths to disappear, and destroyed livelihoods. Some reckon landslides caused by Agatha blocked underwater drainage channels – but for Maya with centuries of local knowledge it was less of a surprise; their villages sit high above the shore, and many sold lakefront land to foreigners. For visitors, the impact so far has been pretty minimal, with just a handful of lakeside hotels losing land. By 2013 lake levels seemed to be stabilizing again, with a rise in the wet season followed by a drop in the dry, but of course the situation could change.

retained a traditional feel in spite of its worldly nature: the river delta behind the town continues to be farmed, and the bustling Sunday market is a decidedly non-touristy affair. For travellers, the town is an inevitable destination – with good travel connections and a lovely setting, it makes a comfortable base for exploring the lake.

WHAT TO SEE AND DO

There are two main daytime activities in Pana: **shopping** and simply **hanging out**, enjoying the town's lakeside location. **Weaving** from all over Guatemala is sold here, mainly on Calle Santander. There is also a fruit and vegetable **market** at the top of Calle Principal. While the water looks inviting, it's best to swim elsewhere, as the lake is not clean close to town. You could rent a **kayak** (available on the lakeshore between the piers) for a few hours – mornings are usually much calmer.

Museo Lacustre

Inside the grounds of the Posada de Don Rodrigo, **Museo Lacustre** (Sun–Fri 8am–6pm, Sat 8am–7pm; Q35) is dedicated to the turbulent geological history that led to the creation of the lake. There's also a fascinating room dedicated to the underwater Maya site of Samabaj (see box opposite) that re-creates what it's like to dive the site with the aid of high-tech gadgetry.

ARRIVAL AND DEPARTURE

By bus Buses to/from Sololá stop on C Principal and continue to the marketplace. The bus to/from Antigua departs from a separate stop on C Principal.
Destinations Antigua (Mon–Sat 10.45am; 2hr 30min);

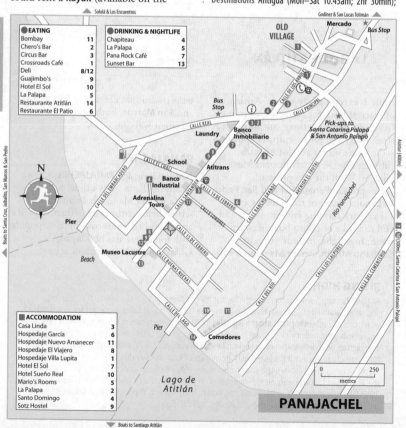

EATING
Bombay	11
Chero's Bar	2
Circus Bar	3
Crossroads Café	1
Deli	8/12
Guajimbo's	9
Hotel El Sol	10
La Palapa	5
Restaurante Atitlán	14
Restaurante El Patio	6

DRINKING & NIGHTLIFE
Chapiteau	4
La Palapa	5
Pana Rock Café	7
Sunset Bar	13

ACCOMMODATION
Casa Linda	3
Hospedaje García	6
Hospedaje Nuevo Amanecer	11
Hospedaje El Viajero	8
Hospedaje Villa Lupita	1
Hotel El Sol	7
Hotel Sueño Real	10
Mario's Rooms	5
La Palapa	2
Santo Domingo	4
Sotz Hostel	9

PANAJACHEL

Lago de Atitlán

SAMABAJ

In December 2011 news emerged that the remains of an important ceremonial Maya settlement, dubbed **Samabaj**, had been discovered opposite the tiny village of Cerro de Oro on the south side of Lake Atitlán.

Samabaj is highly unusual on many fronts. Most of the Maya remains found in the Atitlán region date back 500 years or so, but Samabaj was a Preclassic Maya site that thrived more than 2000 years ago and was a place of pilgrimage, located on an offshore island. Around 250 AD, an abrupt rise in Atitlán's lakewater flooded Samabaj, preserving the monuments (including several stelae and altars) around 16m below the surface. Links have been established with the Preclassic Maya superpower of El Mirador, way to the north in Petén.

In the future it could be possible to dive the remains of Samabaj – contact Iguana Perdida (see p.308). Or you can view many of the discoveries for yourself in Panajachel's Museo Lacustre (see opposite).

Chichicastenango (6 daily; 1hr 30min); Cocales (6 daily; 2hr); Guatemala City (8 daily; 3hr); Quetzaltenango (7 daily; 2hr 30min).

GETTING AROUND

By tuk-tuk Tuk-tuks (Q5/person) are everywhere in Pana.

By boat Most lakeside villages are served by *lanchas* – small, fast boats, which depart about every 30min. Panajachel has two piers. The main pier, at the end of C del Embarcadero, serves the villages on the northern side of the lake: Santa Cruz (about 15min), Jaibalito (20min), Tzununá (30min) and San Marcos (40min). This pier is also home to direct (15min) and non-direct (50min) boats to San Pedro, from where you can easily get to San Juan. The second pier, at the end of C Rancho Grande, is for Santiago Atitlán (25min by *lancha*) and lake tours. The last boats on all routes leave around 7.30pm. Tourists pay Q10 for a short trip, or Q15–20 for a longer journey. Locals pay less. Some *lancheros* try to charge more for the last boat of the day.

By bike Emanuel, C 14 de Febrero, rents mountain bikes (Q70/day).

INFORMATION AND TOURS

Tourist information Inguat, C Principal (Mon–Fri 9am–5pm, Sat 9am–1pm; ☎2421 2953, ✉info-panajachel@inguat.gob.gt), has English-speaking staff and hotel information.

Travel agents Atitrans, Anexo Hotel Regis, C Santander (☎7762 0146, ⊕atitrans.net) is a professional nationwide agency offering tours of the region and shuttle buses; Adrenalina Tours, C Santander (☎7762 6236, ⊕adrenalina tours.com) has shuttle bus connections and highland tours.

ACCOMMODATION

There's no shortage of cheap accommodation in Pana, although most places are *hospedajes* as opposed to hostels with dorms.

Casa Linda Down an alley off the top of C Santander ☎7762 0386. A few steps from the main drag, this family-managed place has a quiet location and a gorgeous central garden to enjoy. There are 21 neat, simple, well-priced rooms, with balcony or veranda – they're priced per person, so solo travellers get a great deal. **Q120**

Hospedaje García C 14 de Febrero 2–24 ☎7762 2187. Sacrificing aesthetics for functionality, this large concrete place has tons of basic, clean, spartan rooms in various blocks. **Q100**

Hospedaje Nuevo Amanecer C Ramos, opposite the Santiago dock ☎7762 0636. This *hospedaje* has pleasant rooms and sparkling bathrooms with hot water and cable TV. Safe parking in the courtyard too. **Q200**

Hospedaje El Viajero C off Santander ☎7762 0128. Peaceful place with an excellent location close to the lakeshore. All rooms are en suite, with cable TV. There's a (basic) guests' kitchen, laundry and free internet access. It's priced per person, and a good deal for single travellers. **Q160**

★ **Hospedaje Villa Lupita** Callejón El Tino ☎7762 1201. Superb *hospedaje* that may be a hike from the lake but its old town location is quiet and everything is beautifully set up. The pretty, very clean and good-value rooms (some with private bathroom) have a splash of local colour thanks to the highland rugs and blankets, and come with reading lights and good mattresses. Guests get free drinking water and coffee and can expect a warm welcome from the family owners. **Q110**

Hotel El Sol Ctra Santa Catarina Palopó ☎7762 6090, ⊕hotelelsolpanajachel.com. A Japanese-owned hotel with super-clean accommodation: an eight-person dorm with lockers plus four immaculate rooms. While you're here, make sure to enjoy the delicious food (see p.302). The only slight drawback is the location, 1km east of the centre. Dorm **Q60**, double **Q200**

Hotel Sueño Real C Ramos, opposite the Santiago dock ☎7762 0608. An excellent choice if you want to be close to the shore, this hospitable Maya-owned place has beautifully decorated, immaculate rooms, most with

4

private bathroom and some with lake views and private terrace. Free wi-fi. **Q180**

Mario's Rooms C Santander ☎ 7762 1313. This place maintains high standards and the accommodation has character, with attractive if smallish rooms (some with private bathroom) overlooking a slim, sunny garden courtyard bursting with pot plants. Free wi-fi, breakfast and drinking water. Staff are very accommodating. **Q220**

La Palapa C Santander ☎ 4568 8033. Reasonable bunk-bed accommodation in large rooms at the rear of this popular bar; you won't have to stagger far to your bed. Dorm **Q50**, double **Q170**

Santo Domingo Down a path off C Monterrey ☎ 7762 0236. Basic yet agreeable age-old travellers' stronghold with a garden ideal for chilling. It's run by friendly people who look after the compact, modernish rooms, some with en-suite bathrooms, well. Free wi-fi and 24hr hot water. **Q105**

Sotz Hostel Off C Santander ☎ 5258 1555, ⓦ sotzhostel .com. Comfortable new hostel with a great location close to the shore and a garden to enjoy. There's a pleasant four-bed dorm and private rooms (with or without bathroom). It's run by a friendly gringo couple who also offer tours. Dorm **Q80**, double **Q200**

EATING

Panajachel has an abundance of restaurants, most of them on C Santander. For really cheap, authentic Guatemalan food, head to the *comedores* close to the market; there are good fish restaurants by the Santiago dock.

Bombay Halfway along C Santander ☎ 7762 0611. An inviting vegetarian place where the menu features a hit-list of global classics: falafel, Indonesian *gado-gado*, pasta and Mexican dishes, most priced at Q40–60. Wed–Mon 11am–9pm.

Chero's Bar C de los Árboles ☎ 7762 0254. No-frills *pupusería* run by a guy from El Salvador where dishes are prepared right in front of you. A good feed is around Q20. Always lively as it doubles as a sociable bar with lots of drink specials. Daily 11am–11pm.

★ **Crossroads Café** C del Campanario 0–27 ☎ 5292 8439, ⓦ crossroadscafepana.com. A temple to the arabica

---

★ **TREAT YOURSELF**

Circus Bar C de los Árboles ☎ 7762 2056, ⓦ circusbar.com.gt. Serving the best pizza (from Q50) in Pana, this atmospheric restaurant is divided into little sections with walls covered in circus memorabilia. Also offers good salads, bruschettas, pasta and grilled meats. Full bar including cocktails (and mocktails) and live music (jazz, salsa, flamenco, bolero, *trova*) every night at 7.30pm. Daily noon–midnight.

---

coffee bean, this welcoming, modest little Old Town place is run by an American perfectionist who selects, blends and roasts his own beans from the Guatemalan highlands and far beyond. Also offers herbal teas, rich hot chocolate and delicious fresh pastries and cakes (try the almond and blueberry). Tues–Sat 9am–1pm & 2.30–6pm.

★ **Deli** Bottom of C Santander ☎ 7762 2585. The most delightful garden setting for a bite to eat in Pana, and also serves some of the best food. Healthy breakfasts, sandwiches, salads, Mexican dishes and *tempe* (Indonesian wholebean tofu); most dishes are Q25–40. There's a second branch halfway up C Santander with the same menu. Wed–Mon 7am–6pm.

Guajimbo's C Santander ☎ 7762 0063. South American-style *churrasco* restaurant, serving up huge portions of prime cuts of beef and chicken (mains from Q48) as well as cheaper options like *choripan* (a chorizo sandwich, Q24). Live music some evenings. Mon–Wed & Fri–Sun 8am–10pm.

Hotel El Sol Ctra Santa Catarina Palopó ☎ 7762 6090, ⓦ hotelelsolpanajachel.com. The restaurant at this Japanese-run hotel serves authentic, delicious miso soup, soba and ramen, sushi and tempura for between Q40 and Q80 a meal. Note that fresh sushi is not always available (though warm sake is). Daily 7am–9.30pm.

La Palapa C Santander ☎ 4568 8033, ⓦ lapalapa.com.gt. If you're in town on a Saturday the lunchtime barbecue here (noon–4pm) is a must, with terrific marinated grilled meats and a large salad bar; around Q40 a feed. Daily 7am–1am.

Restaurante Atitlán Lakeside, by the Santiago pier. For fish or seafood with a lake view head to this thatched-roofed place. Offers big portions of Guatemalan favourites: try *camarones especial Atitlán*. Daily 8am–9pm.

Restaurante El Patio Towards the top of C Santander ☎ 7762 2041. A lovely front patio, set just off the street, is the main appeal here. The menu offers pretty standard Guatemalan grub, but it's famous for its Monday *caldo*. Portions are massive and the *licuados* (shakes) are cheap (Q10). Daily 8am–9pm.

DRINKING AND NIGHTLIFE

Pana's mini *Zona Viva* (around the southern end of C de los Árboles) buzzes on weekend nights. Many places have happy hours, and either live music or a DJ. The *Circus* bar (see above) has live music nightly.

Chapiteau Southern end of C de los Árboles ☎ 7762 2056, ⓦ panajachel.com/chapiteau. Disco with a lively dance floor on weekend nights. Salsa instructors are often at hand early in the evening to sort out your steps. Cover around Q25. Wed–Sat 7pm–1am.

La Palapa C Santander ☎ 4568 8033, ⓦ lapalapa.com.gt. Huge bar with live music (blues, rock, *trova* and acoustic) four times a week. Filling food (including breakfasts and good grilled meats) is also served and trivia (quiz) nights are popular. Daily 7am–1am.

Pana Rock Café Towards the top of C Santander ☎7762 2144, ⓦpanarockcafe.com. A kind of *Hard Rock Café* tribute bar with "Pana Rock Café" T-shirts for sale and an old American school bus converted into a sitting area with tables. It's a popular place to watch sports games, and there are numerous drinks specials. Live rock music on weekend nights. Daily 8am–1am.

Sunset Bar By the lake ☎7762 0003. This appropriately named bar is worth considering as a spot to enjoy a cocktail or cold *cerveza* towards the end of the day. Daily 11am–midnight.

ENTERTAINMENT

Solomon's Porch C Principal ☎7762 6032. Check this barn of a place out for films, live music and cultural and environmental lectures, including talks by Maya activists. Also a pool table, café-restaurant and free wi-fi. Tues–Sat noon–10pm.

DIRECTORY

Banks Banco Industrial, C Santander (Mon–Fri 9am–6pm, Sat 9am–1pm), has an ATM, and there's a 5B ATM at the north end of this road too.

Books Librería Libros del Lago, C Santander 9 (daily 9am–7pm; ☎7762 2788), has a good selection of English-language books on Maya culture, Guatemala, maps and guidebooks. Get Guated Out (see below) has a good stock of used books.

Health Dr Edgar Barreno speaks good English; his surgery is down the first street that branches to the right heading north off C de los Árboles (☎7762 1008).

Internet You'll find lots of internet cafés in Pana, including Get Guated Out (see below). Rates are around Q4–6/hr.

Language schools Pana has two language schools where you can study Spanish, though rates are cheaper in San Pedro la Laguna (see p.304). Escuela Jabel Tinamit, Callejón las Armonias (☎7762 6056, ⓦjabeltinamit.com), and Jardín de América, off C El Chali (☎7762 2637, ⓦjardindeamerica.com), are both professional.

Laundry Lavandería Santander, C Santander opposite *Pana Rock Café* (Mon–Sat 7am–8pm), charges Q5/pound.

Police For emergencies, first contact ASISTUR (☎5874 9450), who will help you deal with the police.

Post office C Santander & 15 de Febrero.

Telephones Get Guated Out, C de los Árboles (☎7762 0595), charges Q1/min for webcalls to all landlines worldwide and Q3 to all mobiles.

AROUND PANAJACHEL

It's well worth taking the time to explore the area **around Pana**, the best connected of all the lake towns. The landscape surrounding the different villages is so diverse that it's easy to forget they all look over the same lake.

Sololá

Perched on a natural balcony overlooking Lago de Atitlán, **SOLOLÁ** is a fascinating settlement, largely overlooked by the majority of travellers. It is probably the largest Maya town in the country, with a majority of residents still wearing traditional costume – the women covered in striped red cloth and the men in their outlandish "space cowboy" shirts, woollen kilt-like aprons and wildly embroidered trousers. Although the town itself is nothing much to look at, its Friday **market** is one of Central America's finest, drawing traders from all over the highlands, as well as thousands of local Maya. There's also another, smaller, market on Tuesdays.

To **get to** Sololá, take a bus from Panajachel (every 30min 5am–7pm).

SANTIAGO ATITLÁN

SANTIAGO ATITLÁN, a microcosm of Guatemala's past, sits sheltered on the side of an inlet on the opposite side of the lake from Panajachel. The largest of the lakeside villages, it's one of the last bastions of traditional life, serving as the main centre for the Tz'utujil-speaking Maya. During the day it's a fairly commercial place and you should expect some sales pressure from vendors, but by mid-afternoon, when the boats have left, things become much quieter.

It's worth taking a few hours to wander around – and if you want to get away from the foreign crowds that pervade other parts of the lake, consider staying for a night or two.

WHAT TO SEE AND DO

There's not much to do in Santiago other than stroll around and soak up the atmosphere. During the day the town's main street, which runs from the dock to the plaza, is lined with weaving shops and souvenir stands.

Market day is Friday, with a smaller event on Sunday.

Museo Cojolya

The one museum in town, the **Museo Cojolya** (Mon–Fri 9am–4pm, Sat 9am–1pm; free; ⓦ cojolya.org), about 100m up the main drag from the dock on the left, takes textiles as its subject. Inside you'll find excellent displays about the tradition of backstrap weaving in Santiago. At 11am and 1pm guided tours (English and Spanish; donation requested) set off from the museum to visit the homes of local weavers.

Santiago church

Santiago's whitewashed Baroque Catholic **church**, which dates from 1571, is an essential visit. The huge central altarpiece culminates in the shape of a mountain peak and a cross, which symbolizes the Maya world tree. On the right as you enter, there's a stone memorial commemorating **Father Stanley Rother**, who died here in 1981, defending his parishioners against the military and death squads.

Casa de Maximón

Folk Catholicism plays an important role in the life of Santiago – one of the few places where Maya still pay homage to **Maximón**, the "evil" saint (see box, p.297), known locally as Rilej Mam. Every May he changes residence – any child will take you to see him: just ask for the "Casa de Maximón". It costs Q2 to enter his current home and Q10 to take his picture.

ARRIVAL AND INFORMATION

By boat *Lanchas* link Santiago with both San Pedro (15min) and Panajachel (20min); they leave when full.
By bus The town is well connected by bus to Cocales and Guatemala City's Centra Sur terminal (7 daily, 3am–4pm; 3hr). Microbuses also leave very regularly for San Lucas Tolimán.
Tourist information Santiago does not have a tourist office. Consult the excellent website ⓦ santiagoatitlan .com for history and information in English.

ACCOMMODATION

Casa de las Buganvillas Opposite Clínica Rxiín Tnamet in Cantón Chechiboy, about 5min east of the church ☎7820 7055. Spacious, spotless en-suite rooms with attractive wooden furniture. There's a good rooftop restaurant here too. **Q170**

Hospedaje Colonial Rosita Just south of the church ☎5397 7187. This simple, secure *hospedaje* has no-frills rooms, a vigilant owner and fairly clean communal bathrooms. **Q100**
Hotel Chi-Nim Ya On the left uphill from the dock ☎7721 7131. A long-running place with simple rooms (some with private bath) set around a courtyard. **Q110**

EATING

Comedor Brendy In the centre of town by the main square. For authentic, inexpensive Guatemalan cooking this *comedor* can't be beaten. Specializes in filling set lunches (from Q18), including great *pollo dorada* and rich *caldos*. Daily 7am–7pm.
El Horno 400m up from the dock, on the left ☎7762 2394. Grab a snack from this excellent bakery, which has a fine selection of crusty baguettes and sandwiches, salads and cakes (including carrot and German chocolate cake). Daily 7am–5pm.

CHUITINAMIT

Opposite Santiago Atitlán, on the lower flanks of the San Pedro volcano, the Postclassic Maya ruins of **Chuitinamit** are worth a quick visit. This modest site, originally called Chiya, was the fortified capital of the Tz'utujil before the conquistador Alvarado and his Kaqchikel allies laid waste to the place in 1524 – arriving in a flotilla of three hundred canoes. Sadly, the site is in pretty poor shape today as locals have re-carved the stone monuments, creating cartoon-like figures, and have even added a Virgin Mary! That said, Chuitinamit is still actively used by shamans for ceremonies, and its position high above the lake affords panoramic views. The paths around the site are littered with Maya ceramic fragments and obsidian arrowheads and blades.

ARRIVAL AND DEPARTURE

By boat To get to Chuitinamit you'll need to hire a boat (around Q100 for a return trip of 1hr) from the dock in Santiago; it's a steep 10min hike up to the ruins.

SAN PEDRO LA LAGUNA

Around to the west of Volcán San Pedro lies the village of **SAN PEDRO LA LAGUNA**, considered by many travellers as the place to be. It's *the* party destination on the lake, with happening bars playing everything from reggae to trance till the early hours of the morning. All this raving has spawned a pretty serious drug culture, and although the town has clamped down in recent years, tensions remain.

If you've no interest in the high life, you'll still find plenty to do in San Pedro, with yoga classes, some good language schools and plenty of hiking trails. It's the kind of place people love or hate – come and make your own mind up.

WHAT TO SEE AND DO

As the lake water is quite polluted around San Pedro, the town's two **swimming pools**, both close to the Santiago dock, are popular places to cool off. You'll also find **thermal pools** between the two boat docks for relaxing. **Volcán San Pedro**, which towers above the village at some 3020m, can be climbed in around four hours. Drop by the visitor centre on the lower slopes of the peak, and hire a **guide** (Q100), which is essential as the foliage is dense and the route very difficult to find. There's another great hike to **Indian Nose**, with arguably an even better perspective of Atitlán – contact the Excursion Big Foot and Casa Verde tour operators (see below) for a guide. For something less strenuous, considering taking out a **kayak**.

ARRIVAL AND DEPARTURE

By boat There are two docks in San Pedro. All boats from Panajachel and villages on the north side of the lake, including Santa Cruz and San Marcos, arrive and depart from the Panajachel dock on the north side of town. Boats from Santiago Atitlán use a separate dock to the southeast, a 10min walk away.

By bus The public bus stop for all arrivals and departures is in front of the church. Buses connect San Pedro with Quetzaltenango (7 daily; 2hr 15min) and Guatemala City (9 daily, last at 2pm; 3hr 45min). Minibuses (about every 20min) link the town with San Juan, San Pablo and San Marcos, or you can hire a tuk-tuk. Casa Verde Tours (see below) run shuttles to Antigua (2hr 45min), Chichicastenango (1hr 30min), Cobán (9hr), Guatemala City (3hr 45min), Huehuetenango (4hr), Lanquín (11hr), Quetzaltenango (2hr 15min) and San Cristóbal de las Casas in Mexico (11hr).

INFORMATION AND TOURS

Tourist information There's no tourist office. Contact the tour operators for information.

Tour operators Excursion Big Foot (☎ 7721 8203), just left of the Panajachel dock, organizes hikes, horses (Q50/

hr; guide included) and bicycles (Q50/day). Casa Verde Tours, above the Panajachel dock (☎ 5837 9092, ⓦ casaverdetours.com), offers kayak hire (Q10/hr) and trips to a zipline canopy in Santa Clara above the lake (Q175) as well as horseriding, and hikes to Indian Nose and Volcán San Pedro; precise prices depend on numbers, but rates are reasonable.

ACCOMMODATION

San Pedro has some of the cheapest accommodation in Latin America, with lots of choice, and you rarely need to book ahead.

Casa Blanca 300m right of Pana dock ☎ 5012 8032. New place with a spectacular lakefront location. The clean, spacious rooms all have sweeping views and there's free wi-fi and a good café; it's popular with Israelis. Dorm __Q50__, double __Q140__

Hotel Gran Sueño 200m left of the Pana dock ☎ 7721 8110. Run by a welcoming local family, this mini-hotel, set back from the road, has eleven spotless, inviting rooms, some on the small side. Plus free wi-fi and drinking water and a pretty garden. __Q175__

Hotel Nahual Maya 250m left of the Pana dock ☎ 7721 8158. Whitewashed colonial-style place with two floors of very well-kept, attractive, en-suite rooms; all have plenty of natural light. Popular, so book ahead. __Q180__

Hotel Pinocchio Between the docks ☎ 5845 7018. Excellent-value, well-swept rooms in a large concrete block. There's a huge garden, welcoming staff, free wi-fi and a guests' kitchen. __Q75__

Hotel San Antonio Left of the Pana dock and towards the end of the road ☎ 5823 9190. A good mustard-coloured place where all the inviting rooms have TV and bathroom, and there's free wi-fi and a café too. __Q120__

Mr Mullet's 150m left of the Pana dock ☎ 4419 0566. New hostel owned by a friendly young Dutch couple who are busy renovating an old hotel. They offer simple, clean rooms with good mattresses and four-bed dorms; bathrooms (with hot water) are shared. There's a lovely garden at the rear for chilling, a cheap café downstairs, free wi-fi and a planned bar. Dorm __Q30__, double __Q80__

★ **TREAT YOURSELF**

Casa Lobo Lakeshore 1.5km south of Santiago dock ☎ 5950 9294, ⓦ casalobo .org. Very tasteful place with stone bungalows, each equipped with huge beds, artwork, kitchenette and verandas set in a lovely garden. The hospitable German owners whip up a mean, healthy breakfast. It's about a 20min walk from town, right on the lakeshore – ideal for anyone who wants to get away from it all. __Q290__

Yo Mama's Casa Between the docks ☏ 4687 1378. Boasting a distinctly boho vibe, a wonderful garden and a well-equipped guests' kitchen, this rustic hostel draws plenty of visiting artists and musicians. As a hangout it's enticing, but sleeping facilities are very basic – ancient mattresses below a tin roof. Dorm Q30, double Q80

Zoola Left of the Pana dock ☏ 5543 4111 or ☏ 5847 4857, ⓦ zoolapeople.com. Israeli-owned lakeside hostel popular with young travellers, with pleasant, well-designed dorms and rooms. Some aspects, including the great chill-out space shaded by canvas, (tiny) lakeside pool and Middle Eastern food, are great, but the stoner vibe, bangin' techno and slow service won't appeal to all. Minimum two-night stay. Dorm Q35, double Q110

EATING

San Pedro's restaurants have an international flavour, with good options for vegetarians. You'll find *comedores* and a food market in the centre of town.

D'Noz By Pana dock ☏ 5578 0201. English-owned bar-restaurant that offers a global menu – bagels, Indian, Guatemalan and Chinese – friendly service, free films (8.30pm nightly), free wi-fi and a long happy hour (5–8pm). Daily 8am–1am.

Home Between the docks. This new vegetarian restaurant enjoys a leafy garden setting with tables under trees and a menu that takes in tofu stir-fries, wraps, lentil dishes and a set lunch for Q28. *Licuados* cost just Q10, or Q15 with yoghurt. Tues–Sun 8am–4pm.

Hummus-Ya Left at the Pana dock ⓦ hummusya.com. Huge place serving authentic Israeli and Middle Eastern food including *shakshuka* (Q30), falafel (Q25) and *malawach* as well as steaks. Doubles as a bar (see below). Thurs–Tues 9am–midnight.

Idea Connection Between the docks ☏ 7721 8356. Superb, very welcoming Italian-owned garden café with delicious breakfasts (Q25–30), muffins and croissants, great coffee and fast free wi-fi. Doubles as a cybercafé, and has a Wii and an X-Box. Daily 7.30am–5.30pm.

Mr Mullet's 150m left of the Pana dock ☏ 4419 0566. Streetside café with some of the cheapest meals in town: try a Dutch pancake with cheese (Q10). Free wi-fi and friendly staff. Daily 8am–6pm.

★ **La Puerta** Between the docks ☏ 5098 1272. The best food in San Pedro, courtesy of an accomplished cook, who trained at *Isla Verde* in Santa Cruz (see p.308). There's a stunning, very relaxing garden setting, and the healthy, creative menu takes in delicious breakfasts, home-made pasta (from Q35), excellent salads (from Q32) and snacks like *quesadillas*. Daily 7.30am–9pm.

Zoola *Zoola* hotel ☏ 5847 4857. The food – Israeli, Western and Guatemalan – is very good, but service can be extremely slow. Relax on the cushions and play backgammon as you wait. Daily 8am–10pm.

DRINKING AND NIGHTLIFE

San Pedro's vibrant bars are concentrated on the trail between the docks, and around the Pana dock. Most places have happy hours. After the 1am curfew "after parties" start up, often with DJs.

Alegre Pub Above Pana dock ☏ 7721 8100, ⓦ thealegrepub.com. Pub showing European football, NFL and NBA games, and serving comfort grub such as Sunday roasts, shepherd's pie and burgers. Mon 5pm–1am, Tues–Sat 9am–1am, Sun 9am–11pm.

El Barrio Between the docks ☏ 4424 6941, ⓦ elbarriosp .com. With an intimate little bar and garden area, this place is busy during its extended (5–8pm) happy hour. Hosts a quiz (trivia) on Wednesdays and an all-you-can-eat Saturday brunch for Q40. Mon–Fri & Sun 5pm–1am, Sat 9am–1am.

Buddha Bar Between the docks ☏ 4178 7979. This four-storey American-owned bar is popular for its live music (everything from *cumbia* to country), DJ and comedy events, pool tables, dart board, films and general *craic*. Daily 9am–1am.

Hummus-Ya Left at the Pana dock ⓦ hummusya.com. Huge bar-restaurant (see above) that regularly host live bands. Mon, Tues & Thurs–Sun 9am–midnight.

DIRECTORY

Banks Banrural just south of the market has an ATM. There's a 5B ATM by the Pana dock.

Internet *D'Noz* by the Pana dock is one of a dozen or so places with web and Skype access. You can burn photos to disk and they offer laptop repairs.

Language schools Co-operativa Spanish School, uphill from the Santiago dock (☏ 5398 6448, ⓦ co-operative schoolsanpedro.com), is very well regarded. Casa Rosario, south of Santiago Atitlán dock (☏ 5613 6401, ⓦ casarosario .com), Corazón Maya, 1.5km south of Santiago dock (☏ 7721 8160, ⓦ corazonmaya.com), and San Pedro Spanish School, between the piers (☏ 5715 4604, ⓦ sanpedrospanishschool .com), are also good.

Post office Behind the church in the town centre (erratic hours).

SAN JUAN LA LAGUNA

Just 2km west of San Pedro, the tranquil village of **SAN JUAN LA LAGUNA** specializes in the weaving of *petates*, lake-reed mats and textiles: two large co-ops, Las Artesanías de San Juan, signposted on the left from the dock, and the Asociación de Mujeres de Color, on the right, have weaving for sale. Almost next door, *Restaurant Chi'nimaya* (see opposite) is a shrine to **Maximón** (see box, p.297), the "evil saint", dressed in local garb.

ARRIVAL AND DEPARTURE

Regular pick-ups run between San Pedro and San Juan, or you can walk.

ACCOMMODATION AND EATING

Hospedaje Estrella del Lago Next to Asociación de Mujeres de Color. Attractive, simple rooms and a kitchen open to guests. Rates are charged per person. **Q140**

Restaurant Chi'nimaya Centre of the village. A quiet *comedor* a short walk uphill from the dock.

SAN MARCOS LA LAGUNA

SAN MARCOS LA LAGUNA, on the northwest shore of the lake, is the most bohemian place around Atitlán, home to legions of foreigners of an artistic and spiritually minded persuasion. If you're enticed by holistic centres, rebirthing classes and all things esoteric, this is the place for you. The village has a decidedly relaxed feel – there's no real bar scene – so it's a perfect place to read a book in your hammock and enjoy the natural beauty of the lake. The bulk of hotels and restaurants are close to the water, while the Maya village sits on higher ground further away from the shore.

WHAT TO SEE AND DO

Apart from a huge stone **church**, built to replace the colonial original destroyed in the 1976 earthquake, there are no sights as such (though the sartorial tastes of some of the gringo residents are amusing). The long-established *Las Pirámides* yoga and meditation centre (see below) and **San Marcos Holistic Centre** (ⓦsanmholisticcentre.com), which offers massage, reflexology, kinesiology and natural remedies, are two key attractions. You'll also find a surplus of masseurs, and many places offer **yoga**, including *La Paz* (see below) for Hatha and Vinyasa.

The recent rise in Atitlán's lakewater (see box, p.299) means that you might struggle to find a good spot to **swim** from, but there are wooden jetties by the shore. On a clear day, views of the lake's three **volcanoes** (including double-coned Tolimán) are sublime, while in the distance you can glimpse the grey peak of Acatenango near Antigua.

ARRIVAL AND DEPARTURE

By boat *Lanchas* from other lakeside villages, including San Pedro (10min; last boat 5pm), Santa Cruz and Pana (25min; last boat 7.30pm), pull up at the dock, which is about a 5min walk from the centre of town.

By bus and shuttle bus If you're travelling by public bus to Quetzaltenango it's best to travel via San Pedro; to Guatemala City and Antigua it's quickest via Panajachel. Casa Verde (☎5837 9092, ⓦcasaverdetours.com), inland from the dock, organizes shuttle bus connections to all these destinations.

ACCOMMODATION

San Marcos has some good accommodation, though few with rock-bottom rates. To access most places, get off at the westernmost dock, by *Posada Schumann*: all accommodation is signposted from there.

Aaculaax Shorefront, west of the dock ☎5729 6101, ⓦaaculaax.com. Eco-fantasy hotel, built from thousands of recycled bottles, plastic and wood, which incorporates lots of stained glass and artistic touches including murals and sculptured concrete. Most accommodation is pricey, but there are a few excellent budget rooms and the restaurant is superb. **Q120**

Hospedaje Panabaj Up in the Maya village, behind the town hall ☎5483 1225. No frills, just two floors of simple rooms and shared bathrooms in a functional block. **Q75**

Hotel Quetzal In the Maya village ☎4146 6036, ⓦhotelquetzal-gt.com. Swiss/Guatemalan-owned place with quality rooms, some of them en suite, decorated with local textiles. The owner is a baker, so be sure to try his delicious breads. A good deal for solo travellers, as you pay per person. **Q125**

Kaivalya Yoga Hostel ☎3199 1344, ⓦyoga retreatguatemala.com. More of a yoga retreat than a hostel, this new place has a couple of two-bed dorms and three little rooms – all bathrooms are shared. It's ideal for those wanting to get stuck into some serious yoga, meditation or *kirta* (Indian chanting), and there's a kitchen and free wi-fi. It's an alcohol- and meat-free zone. Dorm **Q50**, double **Q120**

La Paz ☎5702 9168, ⓦlakeatitlanlapaz.com. Very spacious, rustic cottages, a superior six-bed, two-storey dorm, good home cooking, yoga classes and inexpensive Spanish lessons. There's a lovely leafy garden with hammocks and swings. Dorm **Q50**, double **Q150**

Las Pirámides ☎5202 4168, ⓦlaspiramidesdelka.com. Meditation retreat set in leafy grounds. Courses (lasting a day, week or month) include Hatha yoga, healing and meditation techniques. Accommodation is in comfortable, though not huge, pyramid-shaped cabañas; rates include courses but not food (which is delicious and vegetarian). **Q320**

★ **Posada del Bosque Encantado** ☎5208 5334, ⓦhotelposadaencantado.com. This wonderful place has four huge, gorgeous adobe cottages each with two beds,

4

facing a lovely garden. There's also a good café, *temascal* (sauna) and hammocks. **Q175**

Tul y Sol ☎5293 7997. Two very spacious and superb-value rooms at the rear of a lakeside restaurant. You get a huge bed, nice wooden furniture, bathroom, lake views from a shared balcony and even a free breakfast and wi-fi. It's a total bargain for single travellers, as rates are charged per person. **Q100**

EATING

Comedor Mi Marquensita Susi In the Maya village. Simple, local place serving filling *comida típica* at very reasonable prices.

La Fé Inland from dock ☎5994 4320. Large garden restaurant with a keenly priced, eclectic menu that takes in tapas, curries, sandwiches (from Q22), home-made soups and burritos, burgers and kebabs. Portions are very generous and service is friendly. Daily 7.30am–midnight.

Moon Fish On main road, west side of the village. Garden restaurant famous for its burritos and falafel, salads and sandwiches. The organic house coffee (Q8) is fabulously smooth. Daily 8am–6pm.

Seiko's By the football field. Quirky, authentic Japanese-owned garden restaurant ideal for delicious noodle dishes, veggie tempura, sushi, onigiri, miso soup and warm sake. Daily 5.30–10pm.

JAIBALITO

JAIBALITO, an isolated lakeside settlement nestling between soaring *milpa*-clad slopes, remains resolutely Kaqchikel – very little Spanish is spoken, and few of the local women have ever journeyed much beyond Lago de Atitlán – though the opening of a few hotels means that outside influence is growing.

From Jaibalito it's a thirty-minute walk to Santa Cruz along a glorious, easy-to-follow path that parallels the steep hillside.

ACCOMMODATION AND EATING

La Casa del Mundo ☎5218 5332, ⓦlacasadelmundo.com. Excellent lodge that sits pretty on a little peninsula with panoramic lake views from its cute cottages, and great food. **Q275**

★ **Posada Jaibalito** ☎5598 1957, ⓦposada-jaibalito.com. Very inexpensive, good-value option with a superb six-bed dorm (with lockers and en-suite bathroom), great private rooms, tasty Guatemalan food (Q16–28) and very cheap drinks – treat yourself to a shot of 23-year-old Ron Zacapa. Free wi-fi. Dorm **Q35**, double **Q95**

SANTA CRUZ LA LAGUNA

Set well back from the lake on a shelf 100m or so above the water, **SANTA CRUZ LA LAGUNA** is the largest of the lake's northwest villages, with a population of around four thousand. There isn't much to see in the village itself, apart from a fine sixteenth-century church, and most people spend their time by the bucolic lakeshore, which is fringed with mature trees, dotted with holiday homes and a handful of lovely hotels.

It's a fine base for swimming, chilling out with a book, or exploring the tough but spectacular inland **hiking** trails. Local Maya guide Pedro Juan Solis (☎5355 8849, ⓦtours-atitlan.com), who speaks fluent English, knows the area like the back of his hand and arranges walks and mountain-bike trips. You can rent **kayaks** for Q15/hour from Los Elementos (☎5359 8328, ⓦkayakguatemala.com), west of the dock.

ARRIVAL AND DEPARTURE

By boat *Lanchas* connect Santa Cruz with Panajachel (6am–7pm; about every 30min). The last one to/from San Pedro leaves at 5pm.

ACCOMMODATION AND EATING

★ **Iguana Perdida** On the shore ☎5706 4117, ⓦlaiguanaperdida.com. Offering yoga classes, massage, a TV lounge and the only PADI scuba-diving school on the lake, this is one of the most convivial places in Lago de Atitlán. Many guests stay much longer than planned, and volunteer workers are always needed. There are basic dorms and budget rooms, as well as more luxurious options, but it's the gorgeous, peaceful site overlooking the lake that really makes this place. Dinner (Q50) is a wholesome, three-course communal affair. Dorm **Q35**, double **Q80**

> ★ **TREAT YOURSELF**
>
> **Isla Verde** Western corner of Santa Cruz bay ☎5760 2648, ⓦislaverdeatitlan.com. This gorgeous place, nestled in a tranquil spot, has lovely little A-frame bungalows with fine lake views. There's a sublimely situated decked restaurant that juts over the lake, and the slow-food cuisine here is as good as it gets in Guatemala, with healthy, nutritious meals in the Q40–70 range, good-quality wine and wonderful juices and smoothies. Bungalows **Q270**

The western highlands

Guatemala's **western highlands** are home to some of the most dramatic and breathtaking scenery in the country. The area also has the highest concentration of one of the Americas' largest indigenous groups, the **Maya**. Languages and traditional costume still remain largely intact – probably the most striking dress of all is that worn in **Todos Santos Cuchumatán**. From the wild mountains surrounding **Nebaj** to the bustling colourful market of **Chichicastenango**, you are bound to be captivated by the region's sublime scenery, culture and colour. The western highlands are also home to the country's second-most populous city, **Quetzaltenango**, which draws numerous language students and voluntary workers. Travelling in remote parts of the highlands can be arduous, but the main highways are all paved.

CHICHICASTENANGO

CHICHICASTENANGO, Guatemala's "mecca del turismo", is known best for its twice-weekly **markets**, which are some of the most colourful in the country. It also offers an insight into indigenous Maya society in the highlands. Over the years, Maya culture and folk Catholicism have merged here, with indigenous rituals continuing often under the wings of the church. You'll also see traditional weaving, mostly by the women, who wear beautiful, heavily embroidered *huipiles*. For the town's **fiesta** (Dec 14–21), and on Sundays, a handful of *cofrades* (elders of the religious hierarchy) still wear traditional clothing and carry spectacular silver processional crosses and incense burners.

WHAT TO SEE AND DO

Although Chichi's main attraction is undoubtedly its vibrant markets, the town also offers other sights of cultural interest.

Markets

Most visitors come to Chichicastenango for its **markets**, which fill the town's central plaza and all surrounding streets on Sundays and Thursdays. Fruit and vegetable vendors congregate inside the covered Centro Comercial (which adjoins the plaza); most of the other stalls sell

4

HIGHLAND HISTORY

The **Maya** have lived in the Guatemalan highlands for some two thousand years. The Spanish arrived in the area in 1523, making their first permanent settlement at **Iximché** (see p.298), the capital of their Kaqchikel Maya allies. Not long after, conquistador **Pedro de Alvarado** moved his base to a site near modern-day Antigua, and gradually brought the highlands under a degree of Spanish control. Eventually, **Antigua** also served as the administrative centre for the whole of Central America and Chiapas (now in Mexico). In 1773, however, the city was destroyed by a massive earthquake and the capital was moved to its present site.

The arrival of the Spanish caused great hardship for the native Maya. Not only were their numbers decimated by Spanish weaponry, but waves of infectious diseases also swept through the population. Over time, indigenous labour became the backbone of the Spanish Empire, with its **indigo** and **cacao** plantations. The departure of the Spanish in 1821 and subsequent **independence** brought little change at village level. *Ladino* authority replaced that of the Spanish, but Maya were still required to work the coastal plantations and at times were press-ganged to work, often in horrific conditions.

In the mid-1960s, **guerrilla movements** began to develop in opposition to Guatemala's military rule, seeking support from the highland population and establishing themselves in the area. The Maya became the victims in this process, caught between the guerrillas and the army. Some 440 villages were destroyed; around 200,000 people died and thousands more fled, seeking refuge in Mexico. Despite the harsh conditions and terrific adversity, the Maya survived: traditional costume is still worn in many areas (particularly by women), a plethora of indigenous languages is still spoken and some remote areas even still observe the 260-day Tzolkin calendar.

WESTERN HIGHLANDS

0 ————— 25
kilometres

N

MEXICO

4

San Cristóbal de las Casas

San Cristóbal de las Casas
Gracias a Dios • Yalambojoch
Nentón
La Mesilla
San Antonio
Huista
La Democracia
San Sebastián Coatán
San Miguel Acatán
Santa Ana Huista
Jacaltenango
Concepcion
San Mateo
Ixtatán
Barillas
Santa
Eulalia
San Rafael la
Independencia
Soloma
San Juan Ixcoy
San
Martín
Todos Santos
Cuchumatán
San Pedro
Necta
Santiago
Chimaltenango
San Juan Atitán
Paquix
SIERRA
Cuilco
Ixtahuacán
Colotenango
Chiantla
Motozintla
San Gaspar
Ixchil
Zaculeu
Huehuetenango
SIERRA MADRE
San José
Ojetenan
Concepción
Tutuapa
Malacatancito
Tacaná
Ixchiguán
Sibinal
*Volcán
Tacaná*
Tejutla
Tajumulco
*Volcán
Tajumulco*
San Pedro
Sacatepéquez
San Bartolo
Pologuá
San Carlos
Sija
Momóstenango
San Marcos
Sibilia
San Francisco
El Alto
Palestina
de los Altos
San Cristóbal Totonicapán
Totonicapán
El Rodeo
San Andrés Xecul
Cuatro Caminos
Malacatán
Olintepeque
Salcajá
Talismán Bridge
El Tumbador
Quetzaltenango
Cantel
Tapachula
San Martín
Sacatepéquez
Almolonga
Zunil
**Fuentes
Georginas**
Río Suchiate
*Volcán
Lacandón*
*Volcán
Chicabal*
*Volcán
Santa
María*
Santa María de Jesús
Hidalgo
Tecún Umán
Coatepeque
Colomba
*Volcán
Santiaguito*
CARRETERA AL PACÍFICO
Ocós • Tilapa
Takalik Abaj
El Asintal
Cuyotenango
Chicacao
Retalhuleu
Mazatenango
*PACIFIC
OCEAN*
Río Cuilco
Río Nacapoxloc

Champerico   *Escuintla*

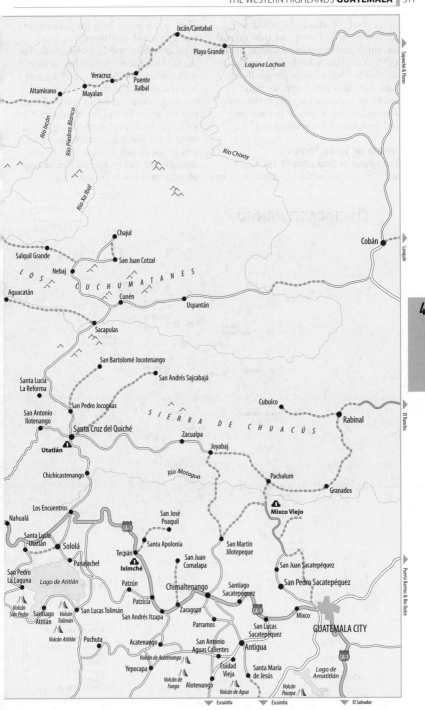

Sayaxché & Flores

Lanquín

4

El Rancho

Puerto Barrios & Río Dulce

textiles and souvenirs. The crowds are eclectic – you'll be surrounded by myriad foreigners and commercial traders, as well as Maya weavers from throughout the highlands – but many of the goods are geared to the tourist trade, so initial prices are high and haggling is essential. The trading starts early in the morning, and goes on until mid-afternoon.

Iglesia de Santo Tomás

The **Iglesia de Santo Tomás**, on the southeast corner of the plaza, was built in 1540 and is now a local religious centre, home to a faith that blends pre-Columbian and Catholic rituals. For the faithful, the entire building is alive with the souls of the dead, each located in a specific part of the church. Before entering, it's customary to make offerings in a fire at the base of the steps or to burn incense. Don't enter the building by the front door, which is reserved for *cofrades* and senior church officials; use the side door instead and be warned that **taking photographs** inside the building is

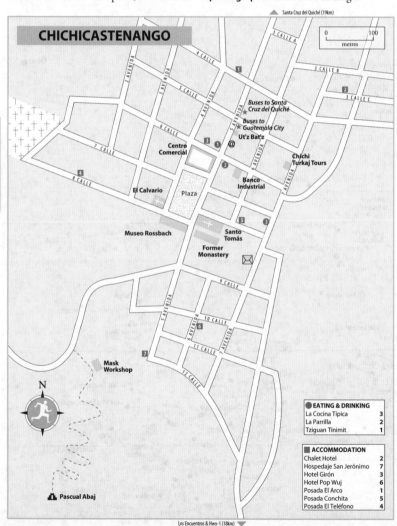

CHICHICASTENANGO

Santa Cruz del Quiché (19km)

Buses to Santa Cruz del Quiché
Buses to Guatemala City
Ut'z Bat'z
Centro Comercial
Chichi Turkaj Tours
Banco Industrial
El Calvario
Plaza
Museo Rossbach
Santo Tomás
Former Monastery
Mask Workshop
N
Pascual Abaj

EATING & DRINKING
La Cocina Típica	3
La Parrilla	2
Tziguan Tinimit	1

ACCOMMODATION
Chalet Hotel	2
Hospedaje San Jerónimo	7
Hotel Girón	3
Hotel Pop Wuj	6
Posada El Arco	1
Posada Conchita	5
Posada El Teléfono	4

considered deeply offensive – don't even contemplate it. The candles scattered around the floor at the entrance are put here by Maya in honour of their ancestors, some of whom are buried beneath the church.

Beside the church is a former **monastery**, now used by the parish administration. It was here that a Spanish priest, Francisco Ximénez, became the first outsider to be shown the Popol Vuh, the Maya holy book; it is said that the Maya became interested in worshipping here after Ximénez began to read the book in the early eighteenth century.

Museo Rossbach

On the south side of the plaza, often hidden by stalls on market day, the **Museo Rossbach** (Tues, Wed, Fri & Sat 8am–12.30pm & 2–4pm, Thurs 8am–4pm, Sun 8am–2pm; Q5) houses a broad collection of pre-Columbian artefacts, mostly small pieces of ceramics (including some demonic-looking incense burners), jade necklaces and earrings, and stone carvings (some of which are two thousand years old). Also on show are some interesting old photographs of Chichi and local weavings, masks and carvings.

Pascual Abaj

Many of the hills that surround Chichicastenango are topped with shrines. The closest of these, **Pascual Abaj**, is less than 1km south of the plaza and regularly visited by outsiders. The shrine comprises small altars facing a stern pre-Columbian sculpture. Offerings are usually overseen by a shaman, and range from flowers to sacrificed chickens, always incorporating plenty of incense, alcohol and incantations. Remember that any ceremonies you may witness are deeply serious – keep your distance and be sensitive about taking photographs. To get to Pascual Abaj, walk down the hill beside Santo Tomás, take the first right, 9 Calle, and follow this as it winds its way out of town. You'll soon cross a stream and then a well-signposted route takes you past a mask workshop, continuing uphill for ten minutes through a pine forest.

ARRIVAL AND INFORMATION

By bus Chichi doesn't have a bus terminal, but all buses stop by the corner of 5 C and 5 Av north of the centre.
Destinations Guatemala City (every 30min; 3hr); Quetzaltenango (7 daily; 2hr 30min); Santa Cruz del Quiché (every 30min; 30min).
By shuttle bus Chichi Turkaj Tours (☏ 5070 6580, ✉ chichiturkajtours@yahoo.com) at 7 Av 05–31 offers shuttle buses to Lago de Atitlán, Antigua and Guatemala City.
Internet Internet Digital, 5 Av 5–60, just north of the plaza.
Tourist information There's no tourist information office.

ACCOMMODATION

There are a few good budget hotels in town. These can be in short supply on Saturday nights before the Sunday market, but you shouldn't have a problem at any other time (except on fiesta days). Prices can also rise on market days, though at other times you can usually negotiate a good deal.
Chalet Hotel 3 C 7–44 ☏ 7756 1360, ⓦ chalethotelguatemala.com. A good highland inn, this little hotel has attractive, smallish, en-suite rooms decorated with Mayan crafts. It's solar-powered, there's free wi-fi and you can eat your breakfast (Q20) on a roof terrace overlooking the town. **Q190**
Hospedaje San Jerónimo 5 Av & 12 C ☏ 7756 1838. A well-run, quiet *hospedaje* where the clean rooms all have private hot-water bathrooms, and some a balcony. **Q110**
Hotel Girón 6 C 4–52 ☏ 7756 1156. Spacious, pine-trimmed rooms in the heart of town with clean bathrooms, free wi-fi and safe parking. **Q140**
Hotel Pop Wuj 6 Av between 10 & 11 C ☏ 7756 2014. Pleasantly decorated, spotless, en-suite rooms. The most expensive doubles have huge beds. There's a restaurant downstairs. **Q160**
Posada Conchita 8 C 6–14 ☏ 7756 1258. This colonial-style place has real charm, with huge rooms, all en suite, with fireplaces and decorative Mayan artefacts. Very good rates for single travellers. **Q220**
Posada El Teléfono 8 C 1–64 ☏ 7756 1197. Friendly, functional guesthouse where the basic but tidy rooms are

---

★ TREAT YOURSELF

Posada El Arco 4 C 4–36 ☏ 7756 1255. This solar-powered guesthouse, run by a hospitable English-speaking Guatemalan, has charm and character, and a beautiful garden with stunning views of the Quiché mountain ranges to the north. The seven large, attractive rooms have good wooden beds and reading lights; rooms 6 & 7 have access to a pleasant terrace. **Q240**

4

accessed via rickety stairways. Many have fine highland views, and the communal bathrooms are kept clean. **Q80**

EATING AND DRINKING

There are plenty of good-value Guatemalan *comedores* available in Chichicastenango, especially in the plaza on market day. Many restaurants are quite pricey, however, as they're geared to day-tripping Westerners.

La Cocina Típica 7 Av. No-frills *comedor* from the plastic fantastic school of decor, offering filling set lunches for Q20. Daily 7am–4pm.

La Parrilla 6 C & 5 Av ☎4472 3982. Set in a little courtyard, this is a good place to get away from the market crowds. There's an excellent selection of grilled meats, including succulent, flavoursome *pinchos* (kebabs) for Q55, which will feed two. Daily 7am–8.30pm.

Tziguan Tinimit 5 Av & 6 C ☎7756 1144. Most of the grilled meat, pasta and pizza dishes are in the Q40–70 range, but portions are huge and there's always a good daily special (like *pollo dorada*; Q30). They serve espresso coffee. Daily 7am–9.30pm.

SHOPPING

Ut'z Bat'z 5 Av 5–24 ☎5008 5193, ⊛enmisalsa.com. An excellent handicraft co-operative that applies fair-trade principles to benefit female weavers (most are widows). Also sells quirky bags, purses and scarfs. Wed 1–5pm, Thurs, Sat & Sun 9am–5pm.

DIRECTORY

Bank Banco Industrial, 6 C (Mon, Wed & Fri 10am–4pm, Thurs & Sun 9am–5pm, Sat 10am–3pm), has an ATM.
Post office 7 Av & 8 C (Mon–Fri 8.30am–5pm, Sat 9am–1pm).

SANTA CRUZ DEL QUICHÉ

SANTA CRUZ DEL QUICHÉ, known locally as "Quiché", is capital of its eponymous department, and half an hour north of Chichicastenango. A good paved road connects the two towns, running through pine forests and ravines. The town has a busy street market but few attractions other than the minor Maya ruins of K'umarkaaj nearby, and foreigners are a rare sight. In the central **plaza** there's a large colonial **church**, built by the Dominicans with stone from K'umarkaaj. In the middle of the plaza, a defiant **statue** of the K'iche' hero, Tecún Umán, stands prepared for battle. His position is undermined somewhat by the ugly urban tangle of hardware stores, bakeries and trash that surrounds the square.

K'umarkaaj (Utatlán)

Early in the fifteenth century, the K'iche' king Gucumatz (Feathered Serpent) founded a new capital, **K'umarkaaj**. A hundred years later, the Spanish arrived, renamed the city **Utatlán** and then destroyed it. Today you can visit the ruins, 3km to the west of Santa Cruz del Quiché.

Once a substantial city, there has been little restoration at **the site** (daily 8am–5pm; Q40), and just a few of the main structures are still recognizable, most of them buried beneath grassy mounds, but it is impressive nonetheless. The one-room **museum** has a scale model of what the original city is thought to have looked like. You should be able to make out the main plaza, three temple buildings, foundations of a circular tower and the remains of a large ball court. Beneath the plaza are several tunnels containing shrines – *costumbristas* (traditional Maya priests) still come to these altars to perform **religious rituals**. If a ceremony is taking place you'll hear the murmurings of prayers; don't disturb the proceedings by approaching too closely.

Microbuses from the terminal pass the ruins every fifteen minutes. To **walk**, head south from the plaza along 2 Avenida, and then turn right down 10 Calle, which will take you all the way out to the site – it's a pleasant forty-minute stroll.

ARRIVAL AND DEPARTURE

By bus Buses pull into the bus terminal, which is about four blocks south and a couple east of the central plaza. The street directly north of the terminal is 1 Av, which takes you into the heart of the town.
Destinations Guatemala City (every 30min, 3.30am–5pm; 3hr 30min) via Chichicastenango (30min) and Los Encuentros (1hr); Nebaj (10 daily; 2hr 30min); Quetzaltenango (9 daily; 3hr); Totonicapán (4 daily, 6am–3pm; 1hr 30min); Uspantán (7 daily, 8am–4pm; 3hr 30min).

ACCOMMODATION

Hotel Rey Kiche 8 C 0–39 ☎7755 0827, ⊕hotel reykiche@gmail.com. A brick-faced hotel with large, plain singles, doubles and triples with firm beds, TV, desk and wardrobe. There's a *comedor* here too (breakfast and dinner only). **Q190**

Hotel San Andrés 0 Av 9–04 ☎ 7755 3057, ✉ hotelsan _andres@hotmail.com. Three-storey hotel with spacious, clean rooms, all with cable TV and private bathroom with tub. __Q140__

EATING

Café San Miguel Opposite the church ☎ 7755 1488. Old-fashioned café-restaurant with filling local food, including *empanadas* and sandwiches (from Q12). The pastries can be very dry, though. Daily 7am–9pm.

Loven Pastería South side of the Parque. Inside a little shopping plaza, this café has espresso coffee, burgers, sandwiches and snacks (Q15). Daily 7.30am–8pm.

SACAPULAS

Just over an hour from Quiché, spectacularly situated on the Río Negro and beneath the foothills of the Cuchumatanes, lies the little town of **SACAPULAS**, with a small colonial church and a good market every Thursday and Sunday. A two-minute walk outside of town, upriver, takes you to some small **salt flats**; several roadside stallholders will sell you bags of black salt (Q2), which is said to have medicinal properties.

ARRIVAL AND DEPARTURE

By bus Buses to Quiché (every 30min; 1hr) run until around 5.30pm. There are also buses to Nebaj (7 daily; 1hr 45min), Huehuetenango (5 daily; 2hr) and Uspantán (7 daily; 2hr).

ACCOMMODATION AND EATING

Comedor y Hospedaje Tujaal Riverside ☎ 5983 5698. The basic rooms are manageable for a night but not in great shape. At least you can dine with a view here, as the popular restaurant has sweeping vistas over the Río Negro. __Q130__

Hospedaje y Restaurante Río Negro Just south of the bridge ☎ 5385 7363. A bit grim, with small dark rooms and shared bathrooms. __Q100__

NEBAJ

NEBAJ, a bustling market town with a dwindling number of attractive old adobe houses and plenty of new concrete structures, is the centre of Ixil country (see box below). Though the pretty central plaza is well kept, the surrounding streets are riddled with potholes and none too clean. Nebaj is remote, but it's well worth a visit for the glimpse it affords of the traditional Ixil way of life. The weaving, especially, is spectacular, with the women's *huipiles* an artistic tangle of complex geometric designs in superb greens, yellows, reds and oranges. There are some wonderful **hikes** in the surrounding region, too.

WHAT TO SEE AND DO

The **plaza** is the community's focal point, lined by its major shops and municipal buildings. The **market area**, which sprawls southeast of the plaza, is worth investigating. On Thursdays and Sundays the town explodes, as out-of-town traders visit with secondhand clothing from the US, stereos from Taiwan and Korea and chickens, eggs and produce from across the highlands. The town **church** on the plaza is also worth a look – inside its door on the left are dozens of crosses, forming a memorial to those killed in the civil war. If you're here for the second week in August, you'll witness the **Nebaj fiesta**,

THE IXIL REGION

The three small towns of **Nebaj**, **Chajul** and **Cotzal**, high in the Cuchumatanes, form the hub of the **Ixil-speaking region**, a massive area of around 140,000 inhabitants whose language is not spoken anywhere else. For all its charm and relaxed atmosphere today, the region's history is a bitter one. After many setbacks, the Spanish finally managed to take Nebaj in 1530, but by then they were so enraged that not only did they burn the town to the ground, but they condemned the survivors to slavery. Independence didn't improve conditions – the Ixil people continued to be regarded as a source of cheap labour, and were forced to work on the coastal plantations. In the late 1970s and early 1980s, the area was hit by horrific violence when it became the main theatre of operation for the **EGP** (the Guerrilla Army of the Poor). Caught up in the conflict between the guerrillas and the military, the civilians suffered terribly. Despite this bloody legacy, the region's fresh green hills are some of the most beautiful in the country, and the three towns are friendly and accommodating.

which includes processions, dances, drinking, fireworks and a marimba-playing marathon.

There are several beautiful **hikes** in the hills around Nebaj, for which guides can be arranged at *El Descanso* (see below).

ARRIVAL AND INFORMATION

By bus All buses pull into the terminal, two blocks southeast of the plaza.

Destinations Acul (regularly 5.30am–5pm; 25min); Chajul (regularly 5.30am–5pm; 40min); Cobán (daily microbus 5am; 6hr – or take any bus to the Cunén junction and catch an onward connection there); Cotzal (regularly 5.30am–5pm; 50min); Guatemala City (4 daily; 6hr); Huehuetenango (take any bus and change in Sacapulas); Santa Cruz del Quiché (10 daily; 2hr 30min).

Tourist information *El Descanso* restaurant (see below), an excellent community tourism initiative, can arrange numerous treks (from Q125/day).

ACCOMMODATION

Grand Hotel Ixil 2 Av 9–15 ☎7756 0036. This family-run place in a tranquil location southeast of the plaza has spacious, comfortable and well-presented en-suite rooms, all with TV and facing a courtyard garden. __Q130__

Hospedaje Ilebal Tenam Calzada 15 de Septiembre ☎7755 8039. Efficiently run *hospedaje* with more than thirty cheap rooms, ranging from tiny but tidy to smarter options with TV and private bathroom. It's about 400m northeast of the plaza along the road to Cotzal/Chajul. __Q65__

Hotel Villa Nebaj Calzada 15 de Septiembre 2–37 ☎7755 8115, ⓦvillanebaj.com. Yes, it's an architectural oddity (monstrosity?), but this garish four-storey place is extremely comfortable – all the clean, attractive rooms have quality beds, bedside lights, cable TV and decorative highland textiles. Those without private bathroom are a real bargain. __Q85__

Hotel del Centro Naab'a 3 C 3–18 ☎7755 8101, ⓔnaabacentro@yahoo.com. Spotless, welcoming place with 24 very clean rooms; all are slightly spartan but comfortable and have bathroom, TV and good beds. __Q115__

Popi's 5 Av 3–35 ☎7756 0092. Two blocks north of the square, this is a sociable home-from-home for travellers that has two decent dorms (with six/eight beds) and a couple of private rooms. The management has recently changed but the home-cooked food at the restaurant and travel and cultural information remain excellent. All profits fund the NGO Mayan Hope. Dorm __Q40__, double __Q110__

EATING

Local specialities include *boxboles* (maize dough steamed in *güisquil* – squash – leaves with herbs) and *pollo pulique* (chicken cooked with tomatillos and spices).

Comedor Elsin East side of the Parque. Classic *comedor*, humble and filled with cooking smoke, offering hearty food at low prices. Daily 7am–8pm.

El Descanso Two blocks northwest of the plaza on 3 C ☎5847 4747. Huge café-restaurant-hub that's a popular hangout for backpackers and development workers, with sofas, free wi-fi, and a long menu, including good breakfasts (from Q22) and decent-enough mains including pasta, Mexican dishes, sandwiches and grilled meats. There's also beer and wine by the glass. Daily 8am–10pm.

Popi's 5 Av 3–35 ☎7756 0092. This hostel (see above) offers excellent-value food including sandwiches with home-baked bread, plenty of veggie dishes and near-legendary apple pie. Live music some nights. Daily 7am–9pm.

Taco Express 3 C 3–18. Tiny, clean little place ideal for inexpensive Mexican snacks (three tacos cost Q10). Also *gringas* (tortillas and chopped salad), burritos and burgers. Daily 9am–9pm.

DIRECTORY

Bank Banrural, on the plaza, has an ATM.

Internet *El Descanso* restaurant (see above) has lots of terminals.

Language school Nebaj Language School (☎5847 4747, ⓦnebaj.info), based in the *El Descanso* restaurant.

ACUL

One of the most interesting hikes from Nebaj takes you to the village of **ACUL**, about a ninety-minute walk away. Starting from the church in Nebaj, cross the plaza and head along 5 C past *Hotel Turansa*. At the bottom of the dip, beyond *Tienda y Comedor El Oasis*, the road divides: take the right-hand fork and head out of town along a dirt track. This switchbacks up a very steep hillside, and heads over a narrow pass into the next valley, where it drops down into Acul. The village was one of the country's original so-called "model villages" into which people were herded after their homes had been destroyed by the army during the civil war.

ACCOMMODATION AND EATING

Hacienda San Antonio On the outskirts of the village ☎5305 6240, ⓦquesochancol.com. Wonderful, alpine-lodge-like run by an Italian–Guatemalan family who make some of the country's best cheese, Chancol, which they sell at pretty reasonable prices. They also rent out delightful rustic rooms. __Q320__

Posada Doña Magdelena ☎5782 0891. Charming little place where the owner also serves tasty, inexpensive meals. **Q50**

SAN JUAN COTZAL

SAN JUAN COTZAL, the second of the three Ixil towns, is about forty minutes from Nebaj. The town sits in a gentle dip in the valley, which is sheltered somewhat beneath the Cuchumatanes and often wrapped in a damp blanket of mist. Cotzal attracts very few Western travellers, though there is some great hill-walking nearby. Intricate turquoise *huipiles* are worn by the Maya women here, who also weave bags and rope from the fibres of the maguey plant.

The **community tourism** project Tejidos Cotzal (☎5428 8218, ⓦtejidoscotzal.org), just behind the marketplace, can hook you up with a guide to show you around this lovely region, its waterfalls and hilltop Maya shrines, cottage industries (including candle making) and introduce you to local weavers. Tours cost just Q100 for a two-day adventure well off the gringo trail. **Market days** (Wed & Sat) are a particularly good time to visit, when there's more transport and life in the town.

ARRIVAL AND DEPARTURE

By bus Regular buses connect Cotzal for Nebaj until 5.30pm. It's possible to also visit Chajul the same day if you get an early start from Nebaj.

ACCOMMODATION AND EATING

El Maguey ☎7765 6199. A basic but decent place to stay, where they also serve good meals. **Q100**

CHAJUL

CHAJUL, made up mainly of old adobe houses, with wooden beams and red-tiled roofs blackened by the smoke of cooking fires, is the most determinedly traditional and least bilingual of the Ixil towns. The women wear earrings made of old coins strung up on lengths of wool, and dress in bright reds and blues, while boys still use blowpipes to hunt small birds, a skill that dates from the earliest of times. The colonial church is home to the **Christ of Golgotha** and the focus of a large

pilgrimage on the second Friday of Lent, a particularly good time to be here. Staff at the office of charity Limitless Horizons (☎5332 6264, ⓦlimitlesshorizonsixil .org), next to the Salon Municipal, can direct you to local guides for **hiking** (and skilled volunteers are always in need).

ARRIVAL AND DEPARTURE

There are regular bus, microbus and pick-up connections between Nebaj and Chajul until 5pm (40min). There are fewer transport options from Cotzal, but you shouldn't have to wait too long for a ride.

ACCOMMODATION AND EATING

You can stay with a local family – many rent out beds – or at the *posada*.
Posada Vetz K'aol ☎7765 6114. Well set up for travellers, with bunk beds in dorms and tasty, cheap grub. **Q60**

QUETZALTENANGO

QUETZALTENANGO, Guatemala's second city, sits in a beautiful mountain valley ringed by volcanoes. In pre-Columbian times the town belonged to the Mam Maya people, who named the town Xelajú, meaning "under the rule of the ten mountains" – hence the name, **Xela** (pronounced "Shay-La"), by which the city still goes. It was the Spaniards who dubbed the city Quetzaltenango, roughly translated as "the land of the quetzal". Xela went on to flourish during colonial times, thanks in large part to the area's abundant coffee crops, but a massive earthquake in 1902 destroyed nearly the entire city. Subsequently almost completely rebuilt (all the Neoclassical buildings that you can see today date to this time), Xela is once again one of the country's major centres. Nonetheless, it manages to preserve an air of subdued, dignified calm, and remains popular among travellers, especially language students looking for more of an authentic Guatemalan experience than their counterparts in Antigua.

4

WHAT TO SEE AND DO

There aren't many sights in the city itself, but if you have an hour or two to spare then it's worth wandering through the

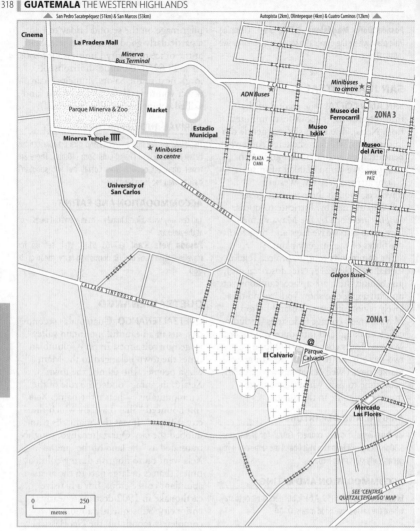

streets, soaking up the atmosphere and taking in a museum or a market. The city is divided into zones; you'll primarily be interested in zonas 1 and 3, home to the central plaza and the (second-class) bus terminal, respectively. Most places are within walking distance, except the bus terminal and railway terminal museums.

Parque Centro América

The **Parque Centro América**, with a mass of mock-Greek columns and imposing bank facades, is at the centre of Xela.

There's none of the buzz of business that you'd expect, though, except on the first Sunday of the month when the plaza hosts a good artisan market with blankets, baskets and piles of weavings for sale. On the west side of the plaza is the impressive **Pasaje Enríquez**, planned as a sparkling arcade of upmarket shops but now home to a number of good bars and restaurants.

Casa de la Cultura

At the southern end of the plaza is the **Casa de la Cultura** (Mon–Fri 8am–noon

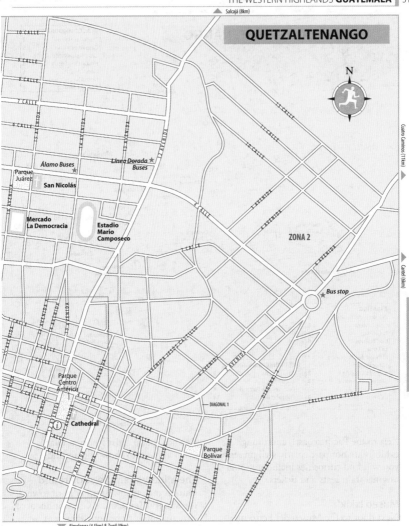

& 2–6pm, Sat & Sun 9am–5pm; Q6), the city's blatant architectural homage to ancient Greece. On the ground floor you'll find a room dedicated to the marimba, along with assorted documents, photographs and pistols from the liberal revolution and the state of Los Altos. Upstairs are modest Maya artefacts, historic photographs and a bizarre natural-history room that has curious displays of stuffed bats, pickled snakes and assorted freaks of nature including a four-horned goat.

Mercado La Democracia

Around 750m northwest of the plaza, the **Mercado La Democracia** is a vast covered complex with stalls daily selling local produce and lots of inexpensive clothing.

Museo del Ferrocarril

A trio of modest museums reside, in Xela's former railway terminal, 2km northwest of the centre. The **Museo del Ferrocarril** (Mon–Fri 8am–noon & 2–6pm, Sat 8am–1pm; Q6) is dedicated to the long-gone railway (which once connected

CENTRAL QUETZALTENANGO

■ ACCOMMODATION
Black Cat Hostel	2
Casa Argentina	5
Casa Renaissance	7
Hostal Don Diego	3
Hostal Miguel	6
Hostal Siete Orejas	1
Pensión Andina	4

● EATING
El Balcón del Enríquez	8
Café Baviera	5
El Cuartito	12
Dos Tejanos	6
La Luna	9
El Pasaje Mediterraneo	7
Sabor de la India	1
Sagrado Corazón 1	3
Sagrado Corazón 2	13
Tilde	10
Ut'z Hua	2
Xela Café Gourmet	11

● DRINKING & NIGHTLIFE
Bajo La Luna	9
El Cuartito	12
Discoteca La Parranda	4
Pool and Beer	14
Salón Tecún	8

Xela to the Pacific coast), and though exhibits are not particularly well presented you will find curiosities including some original train seats and tickets.

Museo Ixkik'

Next door to the Museo del Ferrocarril the more impressive **Museo Ixkik'** (daily 9am–1pm & 3–6pm; Q25) concentrates on Maya costume, with examples of fine *traje* from across the highlands and one room devoted to Xela itself. Guides are often here to explain each weaving's meaning.

Museo del Arte

The third museum in Xela's old railway terminal, the **Museo del Arte** (Mon–Fri 9am–1pm & 3–7pm; Q15) has an important collection of more than 200 paintings from artists including Efraín

Recinos. Local artist Rodrigo Díaz is often at hand to show you around.

The Minerva Temple and around

Out on the northwestern edge of town, the **Minerva Temple** is a Greek-influenced structure built to honour President Barrios's enthusiasm for education. Below the temple are the sprawling daily produce **market** and the **Minerva Bus Terminal**. It's here that you can really sense the city's role as the centre of the western highlands, with *indígena* traders from all over the area doing business. Just behind the market, **La Pradera** shopping plaza boasts more than one hundred stores and a multiplex cinema.

ARRIVAL AND INFORMATION

By bus Unfortunately, most buses arrive and depart from nowhere near the centre of town. Second-class

TOURS FROM QUETZALTENANGO

Xela has several excellent tour operators offering some fascinating trips around the region.

Adrenalina Tours Inside Pasaje Enríquez, Parque Centro America ☏ 7761 4509, ⊚ adrenalinatours .com. Long-established, professionally run company with some excellent tours around Xela and in remote parts of the Huehuetenango department; prices depend on numbers taking the tour. They also run shuttle buses and offer volcano climbs (Chicabal and Volcán Santa María).

Altiplano's 12 Av 3–35 ☏ 5247 2073, ⊚ altiplanos .com.gt. Reliable locally owned operator with trekking and tour programmes to villages around Xela and

beyond. They also buy and rent camping gear and are skilled at organizing custom-made trips.

Quetzaltrekkers *Casa Argentina*, 12 Diagonal 8–37 ☏ 7765 5895, ⊚ quetzaltrekkers.com. Terrific trekking organization that offers several outstanding hikes, including a three-day trek from Xela to Atitlán (minimum donation Q600) and a two-day ascent of Tajumulco (Q400), plus rock climbing (Q300). All profits go to Asociación Escuela de La Calle (⊚ escueladelacalle.org), a charity for street children.

---

buses pull into the chaotic Minerva Bus Terminal on the city's northwestern edge; to get to the main plaza, walk 300m through the market stalls to 4 C and catch a microbus marked "Parque". There are four companies operating first-class buses to and from the capital (4hr), each with their own private terminal: ADN, 7C & 24 Av, Zona 3 (☏ 6649 2089, ⊚ adnautobusesdelnorte.com); Línea Dorada, 12 Av 5–13, Zona 3 (☏ 7767 5198, ⊚ lineadorada.info); Álamo, 14 Av 5–15, Zona 3 (☏ 7767 7117); and Galgos, C Rodolfo Robles 17–43, Zona 1 (☏ 7761 2248). For the latest schedules check out ⊚ xelawho.com or ⊚ xelapages.com.

Destinations Chicken buses leave when full (every 30min–1hr) for Chichicastenango (3hr); Cuatro Caminos (30min); Guatemala City (4hr 15min); Huehuetenango (2hr); La Mesilla (4 daily; 4hr); Momostenango (1hr 30min); Panajachel (2hr 30min); San Pedro La Laguna (2hr 15min) and Retalhuleu (1hr). There are also buses to Zunil and the Rotonda (both every 15min) from 10 C in the city centre, as well as from the main terminal. For Antigua, take any Guatemala City-bound bus and change in Chimaltenango. Twelve daily Pullman buses link Xela with Guatemala City (4hr), operated by four companies from private terminals (see above).

Tourist information The Inguat tourist office, Parque Centro América (Mon–Fri 9am–5pm, Sat 9am–1pm; ☏ 7761 4931, ⊚ info-xela@inguat.gob.gt), is not particularly helpful. You'll find the tour operators (see box above) a better source of local information. To find what's on, pick up a copy of *Xela Who* (⊚ xelawho.com), available in many of the popular bars and cafés.

ACCOMMODATION

Black Cat Hostel 13 Av 3–33 ☏ 7761 2091, ⊚ black cathostels.net; map p.320. Set in a historic building just north of the main Parque, this hostel has a sociable vibe, and a hip bar (happy hour 5–10pm) with retro sofas. The dorms are fine, shared bathrooms are clean, but the private

rooms are very average and overpriced. Rates include a massive breakfast. Dorm **Q60**, double **Q160**

Casa Argentina 12 Diagonal 8–37 ☏ 7761 2470 or ☏ 7761 0010, ⊚ casargentina.xela@gmail.com; map p.320. This huge place, Xela's original budget hotspot, could definitely use a makeover but still remains a friendly, sociable base for backpackers. Rooms (all with cable TV) are basic but adequate, but the (vast) dorm is a last resort (unless you're totally into crowds). There's a kitchen, sun terrace and café and it's also the home of Quetzaltrekkers (see box above). Dorm **Q25**, double **Q70**

★ **Casa Renaissance** 9 C 11–26 ☏ 7761 8005, ⊚ casarenaissance.com; map p.320. Welcoming Dutch-owned place in a fine old town house with five huge rooms, original floor tiles, free tea, coffee and water, sunny patios, fast wi-fi, good bathrooms and a TV lounge stocked with more than a thousand DVDs. The showers are gas-heated. **Q110**

Hostal Don Diego 6 C 15–12 ☏ 5308 3616, ⊚ hostaldondiegoxela.com; map p.320. This secure place has twenty simple, cheap rooms (none en suite). There's free wi-fi and purified water. Dorm **Q45**, double **Q120**

Hostal Miguel 12 Av 8–31 ☏ 7765 5554, ⊚ learn2 speakspanish.com; map p.320. Nine very simple, cheap rooms in a slightly ramshackle old house; one has a private bathroom. There's a living room with TV, kitchen and free wi-fi. It's inside a recommended Spanish language school. **Q55**

Hostal Siete Orejas 2 C 16–92 ☏ 7768 3218, ⊚ 7orejas .com; map p.320. Flashpacker-style place with very high-quality, spacious rooms, each with hand-carved beds, good mattresses and a wooden chest of drawers. Continental breakfast is gratis. Dorm **Q75**, double **Q230**

Pensión Andina 8 Av 6–07 ☏ 7761 4012; map p.320. Offers good value, with neat, smallish well-scrubbed rooms, all with private bathrooms and reliable hot water, set around a covered courtyard. **Q100**

4

EATING

CAFÉS

Café Baviera 5 C 13–14 ☎7761 5018; map p.320. Anachronistic, pine-panelled coffeehouse with old photos of Xela on the walls. Fine for a coffee (from Q7), and they also offer cakes, snacks and sandwiches. Daily 8am–8pm.

★ **El Cuartito** 13 Av 7–09 ⓦ elcuartitocafe.tumblr.com; map p.320. A very hip little joint with quirky decor – all crooked bookshelves, bottle lights and interesting art and photography. Good coffee and cakes, with snacks including bagels (from Q22) and salads. It's more of a bar in the evening. Free wi-fi. Daily 7am–11pm.

La Luna 8 Av 4–11 ☎5174 6769; map p.320. Crammed with curios including a collection of 1930s radios and antiques, *La Luna* has seven different varieties of drinking chocolate (Q6) – though note that they're (outrageously) pre-sweetened to local tastes. Snacks are also served (around Q25). Mon–Fri 10am–9pm, Sat 4–9pm.

Tilde 10 Av 5–33 ☎4444 7796; map p.320. Hip boutique-cum-café-cum-bar with a short menu of snacks and meals, plus great coffee. Tues–Sat 11am–8pm, Sun 11am–4pm.

Xela Café Gourmet 6 C Av 9–26; map p.320. Just off the Parque, this smart café has a broad choice of espresso-based coffees and a menu that takes in panini and burgers. Daily 8am–8pm.

RESTAURANTS

El Balcón del Enríquez Inside the Pasaje Enríquez ☎7765 2296; map p.320. For a perfect view of the Parque Centro América, this restaurant is unbeatable. Great for breakfast (from Q20), when you can perch yourself on a stool and watch the city coming to life. Most meals are a bit pricey, but the set lunch (Q25) is good value. There's also a full bar. Daily 8am–10pm.

Dos Tejanos Inside the Pasaje Enríquez ☎7765 4360; map p.320. Great Mexican-American food (meals from around Q40); expect huge portions and big flavours. Daily 8am–11pm.

Sabor de la India 15 Av 3–64 ☎7765 0101; map p.320. This Indian-owned place serves up filling and pretty authentic dishes and lots of vegetarian options including a good thali (Q60). The premises lack atmosphere, though. Tues–Sat noon–10pm, Sun 5–9pm.

Sagrado Corazón 1 14 Av 3–08; map p.320. Small, informal place that's a great spot to try Guatemalan specialities like *pepián* or *jocón* (meat cooked with peppers and tomatillos) or *estofado de pollo* (chicken stew). Daily 8am–7.30pm.

★ **TREAT YOURSELF**

★ **TREAT YOURSELF**

El Pasaje Mediterraneo Inside the Pasaje Enríquez ☎5515 6724 or ☎5825 1782; map p.320. Classy tapas restaurant with two atmospheric dining rooms and an excellent menu of Mediterranean dishes, including favourites from Spain, Greece, Turkey and Italy. Portions are very generous – reckon on three or four tapas (most are Q30–40) for two people. There's a decent wine and excellent service. Mon–Sat noon–10pm.

LANGUAGE SCHOOLS IN QUETZALTENANGO

Quetzaltenango has many excellent **language schools**, and if you're looking for a full-immersion experience it's ideal, as few people speak English in town. Good schools include the following:

Casa de Español Xelajú Callejón 15, Diagonal 13–02, Zona 1 (☎7761 5954, ⓦ casaxelaju.com).

Celas Maya 6 C 14–55, Zona 1 (☎7761 4342, ⓦ celasmaya.com).

Centro Bilingüe Amerindia (CBA) 12 Av 10–27, Zona 1 (☎7761 8535, ⓦ cbaspanishschool.com).

La Democracia 9 C 15-05, Zona 3 (☎7767 0013, ⓦ lademocracia.net).

Educación para Todos Av El Cenizal 0–58, Zona 5 (☎5935 3815, ⓦ spanishschools.biz).

Inepas 15A Av 4–59, Zona 1 (☎7765 1308, ⓦ inepas .org).

Juan Sisay 15 Av 8–38, Zona 1 (☎7765 1318, ⓦ juansisay.com).

Kie Balam Diagonal 12 4–46, Zona 1 (☎7761 1636, ⓦ kiebalam.com).

Madre Tierra 13 Av 8–34, Zona 1 (☎7761 6105, ⓦ madre-tierra.org).

Miguel de Cevanates 12 Av 8–31, Zona 1 (☎7765 5554, ⓦ learn2speakspanish.com).

El Nahual 28 Av 9–54, Zona 1 (☎5606 1704, ⓦ languageselnahual.com).

La Paz 2 C Callejón 16 2–47, Zona 1 (☎4018 2180, ⓦ xelapages.com/lapaz).

Pop Wuj 1 C 17–72, Zona 1 (☎7761 8286, ⓦ pop-wuj.org).

El Portal 9 Callejón A 11–49, Zona 1 (☎7761 5275, ⓦ spanishschoolelportal.com).

Proyecto Lingüístico Quetzalteco de Español 5 C 2–40, Zona 1 (☎7765 2140, ⓦ hermandad.com).

Sakribal 6 C 7–42, Zona 1 (☎7763 0717, ⓦ sakribal .com).

Sagrado Corazón 2 9 C & 11–16; map p.320. Large, popular *comedor* that scores highly for its honest Guatemalan grub, particularly dirt-cheap breakfasts. The set lunch (around Q20) is a winner too, and there's always a veggie version available. Daily 8am–8pm.

Ut'z Hua 12 Av & 3 C ☎7768 3469; map p.320. A good choice for authentic, tasty Guatemalan cuisine, including *jocón* (chicken with sesame and pumpkin seeds, tomato and coriander), local sausages, fried fish and seven kinds of highland soup. Reckon on Q30–40 for a feed. Daily 8am–9pm.

DRINKING AND NIGHTLIFE

The main areas for nightlife and dancing in central Xela are 14 Av A (which is lined with bars) and Pasaje Enríquez.

Bajo La Luna 8 Av 3–72 ☎7761 2242; map p.320. Basement wine bar with relaxed background music that's perfect for a quiet drink. You can nibble on a cheese platter (from Q25) while you sip. Thurs–Sat 8pm–1am.

El Cuartito 13 Av 7–09 ⊛elcuartitocafe.tumblr.com; map p.320. In the evening this café becomes a key hangout with live music (blues/folk/reggae/funk) most nights. Daily 7am–11pm.

Discoteca La Parranda 14 Av 4–41; map p.320. You can strut your stuff here to salsa on Wednesdays (when there are free classes), while from Thursday to Saturday it's a mix of hip-hop, reggaetón and Latin electronica. Wed–Sat 7pm–1am.

Pool and Beer 12 Av 10–21; map p.320. Pool tables and table football are available in this spacious bar with subdued lighting. Electronic DJs spin their stuff here occasionally.

★ **Salón Tecún** Inside the Pasaje Enríquez ☎7761 2832; map p.320. Number one in Xela, this ever-popular pub-like institution is a favourite of both locals and travellers. There's a sociable interior, bench seating inside the arcade and they also serve good grub. Daily 8am–1am.

ENTERTAINMENT

Casa N'oj Parque Central America ☎7768 3139. Art exhibitions, films and lectures in a wonderful restored building.

Cinemas Blue Angel, 7 C 15–79, Zona 1, has a daily video programme (Q10) at 8pm with a large selection of movies (mainly Hollywood blockbusters and cult films). There's a multi-screen cinema by La Pradera mall, near the Minerva terminal.

Teatro Municipal 14 Av A & 1 C ☎7761 2218. Recitals, dance and theatre performances, concerts and exhibitions.

DIRECTORY

Bank Banrural (Mon–Fri 9am–6pm, Sat 9am–1pm) on the Parque Centro América has an ATM.

Bike rental The Bike House, 15 Av 5–22, Zona 1, has

mountain bikes (Q40/24hr or Q100/week); the Vrisa bookstore (see below) offers similar rates.

Books Vrisa, 15 Av 3–64, stocks thousands of used titles. North & South, 15 Av & 8 C, Zona 1, has a good choice of political, social and anthropological books on Guatemala, as well as a café.

Health Hospital San Rafael, 9 C 10–41, Zona 1 (☎7761 4414 or ☎7761 2956).

Internet There are dozens of places in Xela for internet connections and wi-fi, including Xela Pages, 4 C 19–48, Zona 1 (Mon–Fri 8am–8pm, Sat 10am–6pm; Q3–6/hr).

Laundry Lavandería Tikal, Diagonal 13 8–07 (Mon–Sat 8am–5pm; Q25 for a typical load, washed and dried in 2hr).

Police Contact Ángel Quiñonez (☎4149 1104), the very efficient ASISTUR rep for the Xela area.

Post office 15 Av & 4 C (Mon–Fri 8.30am–5.30pm, Sat 9am–1pm).

Supermarket Despensa Familiar, 3 Av & 7 C, in the centre of town (daily 7.30am–8pm).

Telephones Xela Pages (see above) offers Skype calls.

AROUND QUETZALTENANGO

Based in Quetzaltenango, you could easily spend a week or two exploring the highlands, perhaps on a guided tour (see box, p.321). There are numerous smaller towns and villages nearby, mostly indigenous agricultural communities and weaving centres with colourful weekly markets, as well as some lovely hot springs. The area also offers excellent hiking. The most obvious climbs are **Volcán Santa María**, towering above Quetzaltenango itself, and up **Volcán Chicabal** to its sublime crater lake. Straddling the coast road to the south is **Zunil** and the hot springs of **Fuentes Georginas**, overshadowed by more breathtaking volcanic peaks, while to the north are **Totonicapán**, capital of the department of the same name, and **San Francisco El Alto**, a small town perched on an outcrop overlooking the valley. Beyond that lies **Momostenango**, the country's principal wool-producing centre and a centre of Maya culture.

Volcán Santa María

Due south of Quetzaltenango the perfect cone of **Volcán Santa María** (3772m) looms over most of the Xela valley. The view from the top is, as you might expect, truly spectacular, with nine other volcanoes visible on clear days, including the smoking summit of Santiaguito directly below. You can climb the volcano as a day-trip, but for the best views you need to be on top at dawn, either sleeping on the freezing peak, or camping at the site below and climbing the final section in the dark by torchlight. Either way, you need to make sure you're acclimatized to the altitude for a few days before attempting the climb. It is highly recommended you go with a guide; they can be organized at most of the tour operators in Quetzaltenango (see box, p.321).

Laguna Chicabal

One spectacular excursion (and less strenuous than the trip to Volcán Santa María) is to **Laguna Chicabal**, a crater lake set in the cone of the Chicabal volcano, about 25km southeast of Xela.

The hike, a two-hour trek from San Martín Sacatepéquez, starts just before the village; get your bus driver to drop you off at the right spot on the highway, where you'll see a sign to the lake. On the way you'll pass the entrance to the reserve (Q20). Once you enter the reserve, a signposted route to the left leads to a *mirador (*from where there are stunning views of the emerald lake and the volcanoes of Santa María and Santiaguito, Tajumulco and Tacaná), or, alternatively, you could take the precipitous path straight down to the shore. Small sandy bays bear charred crosses and bunches of fresh-cut flowers, marking sites of ritual sacrifice. Every May 3 *costumbristas* gather here for ceremonies to mark the fiesta of the Holy Cross; never disturb any rituals that are taking place. Swimming is not permitted.

ARRIVAL AND DEPARTURE

By bus Get a Coatepeque-bound bus (every 30min; 40min) from Quetzaltenango's Minerva terminal to the town of San Martín Sacatepéquez. Be back at the highway for your return bus to Xela by 5pm.

ACCOMMODATION

Cabins There are rustic cabins at the entrance to the reserve. Per person Q40—70
Camping You can camp for free on the Laguna Chicabal shore, though you'll have to bring your own supplies.

Zunil

Some 10km south of Quetzaltenango is the village of **ZUNIL**, a vegetable-growing market town hemmed in by steep hills and a sleeping volcano. The main plaza is dominated by a beautiful white colonial church with a richly decorated facade; inside, an intricate silver altar is protected behind bars. The women of Zunil wear vivid purple *huipiles* and carry bright shawls – the plaza is awash with colour during the Monday market. Just below the plaza is a **textile co-operative**, where hundreds of women market these weavings. **Maximón**, the "evil saint" (see box, p.297), has a strong following locally; his mannequin is usually paraded through the streets during Holy Week, dressed in Western clothes and smoking a cigar. Virtually any child in town will take you to his current abode for a quetzal.

ARRIVAL AND DEPARTURE

By bus Buses to Zunil run from Quetzaltenango's Minerva Bus Terminal (every 30min or so), though some also leave from closer to the centre of town, stopping beside the Shell petrol station at 10 C & 9 Av in Zona 1.
Tours Tour operators in Xela (see box, p.321) run trips to Zunil.

Fuentes Georginas

High in the hills, 8km from Zunil, are the **Fuentes Georginas** (daily 8am–6pm; Q40), a set of luxuriant hot springs. Surrounded by fresh green ferns, thick moss and lush forest, the baths are sublime, and to top it all there's a restaurant and bar. It's a blissful place to spend a few hours soaking away the chicken bus blues or recovering from a volcano climb in the heavenly steaming pools.

ARRIVAL AND DEPARTURE

By bus There's a dedicated shuttle bus service from Xela: buses (Q140 return; daily 9am & 2pm; 30min) leave from the Fuentes office, 14 Av & 5 C, Zona 1. Otherwise, minibuses (Q80 one-way) head up from Zunil on demand.

ACCOMMODATION AND EATING

Bungalows ☎ 5704 2959. Stone bungalows are available for the night, complete with bathtub, two double beds, fireplace and barbecue. Q330
Restaurant The springs have their own restaurant – meals around Q60, snacks Q30 – and a well-stocked bar.

Totonicapán

A one-hour bus journey from Xela, **TOTONICAPÁN** is capital of one of the smaller departments, a pleasant if unremarkable provincial town. As you enter Toto you pass one of the country's finest *pilas* (communal washing places), ringed with Gothic columns. Surrounded by rolling hills and pine forests, the town stands at the heart of a heavily populated and intensely farmed region. Toto's Tuesday and Saturday morning **markets** fill its two plazas to bursting. The town is an important centre of commercial weaving, producing much of the jasped cloth worn as skirts by indigenous women throughout the country. Totonicapán is best done as a day-trip from Xela; **buses** shuttle from the Minerva terminal and back every fifteen minutes or so, via the Cuatro Caminos junction.

San Francisco El Alto

The small town of **SAN FRANCISCO EL ALTO** overlooks the Quetzaltenango valley from a lovely hillside setting just north of Totonicapán. The view alone is worth a visit, with the great plateau stretching out below and Volcán Santa María on the horizon, but the main reason for a trip here is the **Friday market**, possibly the biggest in Central America and attended by traders from every corner of Guatemala – many arrive the night before, and some start selling by candlelight from as early as 4am. Throughout the morning a steady stream of buses and trucks fills the town to bursting; by noon the market is at its height, buzzing with activity; things start to thin out in the early afternoon.

The market is separated into a few distinct areas. At the very top of the hill is an open field used as an **animal market**, full of everything from pigs to parrots. Buyers inspect the animals' teeth and tongues, and at times the scene degenerates into a chaotic wrestling match, with livestock and men rolling in the dirt. Below, around the town's plaza, the stalls are dominated by textiles and clothing, mainly *ropa americana* as well as vegetables, fruit and pottery. For really good views of the market and the surrounding countryside, pay the church caretaker a quetzal and climb up to the church roof.

Buses connect Quetzaltenango and San Francisco every twenty minutes from the Minerva terminal; the first is at 6am, and the last bus back leaves at about 5pm (45min).

Momostenango

Some 22km from San Francisco is **MOMOSTENANGO**, a small, isolated town and the centre of wool production in the highlands. The main reason for visiting is to take in the town's **Sunday market**, which fills the town's two plazas. Momostecos travel throughout the country peddling their blankets, scarves and rugs – years of experience have made them experts in the hard sell and given them a sharp eye for tourists. The town is also famous for its unconventional folk-Catholicism, and there are many Maya **shamans** working here. While you're here you could also walk to the *riscos*, a set of bizarre pumice pillars, or beyond to the **hot springs** of Pala Chiquito, about 3km away to the north.

Visits are best done as day-trips from Quetzaltenango, or you could head on to Huehuetenango. **Buses** run from the Minerva terminal in Quetzaltenango, passing through Cuatro Caminos (every 30min, 6am–5pm; 1hr 45min). There are additional services on Sundays, for the market.

HUEHUETENANGO

Bustling **HUEHUETENANGO**, capital of the department of the same name, lies at the foot of the Cuchumatanes mountain range. A small city, it's pretty relaxed, but heavy traffic, much of which thunders through the town centre, reduces this appeal somewhat. There are no real sights, but the area around the central square is attractive, surrounded by shaded walkways and administrative offices. A few blocks east, around 1 Avenida, the **market area** is always alive with activity, its streets packed with Maya from remote corners of the highlands. Few travellers stay long in Huehue, but if you're heading to or from Mexico or Todos Santos Cuchumatán you'll probably find yourself

4

here to change buses. While you're in town, it's easy to take in the minor ruins of **Zaculeu** close by (see opposite).

ARRIVAL AND INFORMATION

By bus The bus terminal is halfway between the Carretera Interamericana and the centre. Minibuses make constant trips between the town centre and the bus terminal until late, though the frequency decreases after dark. Buses to Zaculeu leave from the corner of 2 C and 7 Av. For Todos Santos, there are also microbuses (roughly every 40min) from El Calvario, 1 Av and 1 C. Some first-class buses use their own private terminals.

Destinations from main terminal Aguacatán (every 30min; 40min); Barillas (9 daily; 6hr 30min); Guatemala City (every 30min; 6hr); La Mesilla, Mexican border (second-class, every 30min; 2hr); Nebaj – take an Aguacatán or Sacapulas bus and change; Quetzaltenango (every 30min; 2hr); Sacapulas (2 daily, 11.30am & 12.30pm; 2hr); Todos Santos (12 daily; 2hr 15min).

Destinations: private buses Línea Dorada, Av Kaibil Balam 8–70 (2 daily pullmans to Guatemala City, 1 daily to La Mesilla; ☎7768 1566, ⓦlineadorada.info); Los Halcones, 10 Av 9–12 (6 daily to Guatemala City; ☎7765 7986, ⓦtransportesloshalcones.com); Transportes Velásquez, main terminal (5 daily to Guatemala City; ☎7764 7594); Zaculeu Futura, 6 C & 9 Av (2 daily to Guatemala City; ☎7764 1535).

Information and tours There is no tourist office in Huehue. Adrenalina Tours, 4 C 6–54 (☎7768 1538, ⓦadrenalinatours.com), is an excellent source of information, with trips that include a guided walk to a cheese farm and Zaculeu (Q100), Chiabal, San Juan Atitán and two-day trips to Laguna Yalambojoch.

ACCOMMODATION

Hotel Gobernador 4 Av 1–45 ☎7764 1197. A warren of basic, bare rooms (some en suite), none of them fancy, but all of them cheap. The shared bathrooms are clean enough. **Q70**

Hotel Mary 2 C 3–52 ☎7764 1618. Friendly, secure place: the 25 rooms, all with private bath and TV, are ageing but decent enough for a night. There's a *comedor* too. **Q135**

Hotel Maya 3 Av 3–55 ☎7764 0369. Concrete hotel with sizeable en-suite rooms with good beds. **Q175**

Hotel Zacaleu 5 Av 1–14 ☎7764 1086, ⓦhotelzacaleu .com. A classy colonial-style hotel with spacious if old-fashioned rooms set around a lovely leafy courtyard (and a less appealing newer section). Don't miss the fantastic old bar, with piano. Good rates for solo travellers. **Q225**

Todos Santos Inn 2 C 6–74 ☎5432 3421. This place maintains good standards with well-scrubbed if spartan rooms, all with cable TV. Those upstairs are fairly bright and cheery, those downstairs less so. The shared bathrooms are clean. **Q115**

HUEHUETENANGO

ACCOMMODATION	
Hotel Gobernador	1
Hotel Mary	3
Hotel Maya	5
Hotel Zacaleu	2
Todos Santos Inn	4

EATING	
La Cabaña del Café	1
Café Bougambilias	2
Cafetería Las Palmeras	3
Mi Tierra	4
Museo del Café	5

THE CUCHUMATANES

The largest non-volcanic peaks in Central America, the **Sierra de los Cuchumatanes** rise from a limestone plateau close to the Mexican border, reaching their full height of more than 3800m above Huehuetenango. This is magnificent mountain scenery, ranging from wild, exposed craggy outcrops to lush, tranquil river valleys. While the upper slopes are almost barren, scattered with boulders and shrivelled cypress trees, the lower levels are fertile, planted with corn, coffee and sugar. In the valleys are hundreds of tiny villages, simply isolated by the landscape. These communities are still some of the most traditional in Guatemala, and a visit, either for a market or fiesta, offers one of the best opportunities to see Maya life.

The most accessible of the villages in the vicinity, and the only one yet to receive a steady trickle of tourists, is **Todos Santos Cuchumatán**. Mountain trails from Todos Santos lead to other villages, including the equally traditional pueblo of **San Juan Atitán**.

Be wary of taking pictures of people in this region, particularly children. Rumours persist locally that some foreigners steal babies, and a tragic misunderstanding led to the death of a Japanese tourist here in 2000.

EATING

La Cabana del Café 2 C 6–50 ☎ 7764 8903. Welcoming log cabin-like café with wonderful coffees (from Q6); all beans are from the Huehue region. Snacks and cakes are also served. Daily 8am–9pm.

Café Bougambilias Opposite the church ☎ 7764 0105. This four-storey pink and lurid green *comedor* is a good place for breakfast – try the highland-style *mosh*: porridge with cinnamon, wheat and sugar. Daily 7am–9.30pm.

Cafetería Las Palmeras Opposite the church ☎ 5783 2967. Very popular, clean and efficiently run restaurant that offers fine-value lunch deals (Q25), which all include soup and a *refresco*. Dishes include *tortilla de carne* and (on Sat only) delicious *tamales* for Q5 a hit. Daily 7am–9.30pm.

Mi Tierra 4 C 6–46 ☎ 7764 1473. Intimate café-restaurant set in a covered patio. There's plenty of choice on the menu (Q20–40), with popular Guatemalan dishes, Mexican classics (like fajitas and nachos) and breakfasts. Mon–Sat 7am–9pm, Sun 2–9pm.

★ **Museo del Café** 4 Av 7–40 ☎ 7764 1128, ⓦ cafemuseohuehue.com. Dedicated to the coffee bean, this fine museum-cum-restaurant is loaded with coffee paraphernalia: storage sacks on the walls, machinery, photographs of coffee fincas and lots of café curios. More than twenty types of coffee are offered, and it's also a good choice for breakfast (from Q20), or lunch and dinner dishes (such as enchiladas or pasta); the *menu del día* is Q25. Free wi-fi. Mon–Sat 7am–9.30pm.

DIRECTORY

Bank G&T Continental on the main square (Mon–Fri 8am–7pm, Sat 8am–1pm) has an ATM.

Internet Internet Milenio, 4 Av 1–54 (Q5/hr).

Language school Xinabajul, 4 Av 14–14, Zona 5 (☎ 7764 6631, ⓦ spanishschoolinguatemala.com).

ZACULEU

A few kilometres west of Huehuetenango are the ruins of **Zaculeu** (daily 8am–5pm; Q50), once the capital of the **Mam**, who were one of the principal pre-Conquest highland Maya tribes. Zaculeu includes several large temples, plazas and a ball court, all restored pretty unfaithfully by the United Fruit Company in 1946–47: the walls were recoated with white plaster, a technique seldom used for restoring pre-Columbian buildings, as it leaves them lacking the roof-combs, carvings

ZACULEU'S HISTORY

The site of **Zaculeu**, first occupied in the fifth century, is thought to have been a religious and administrative centre for the Mam, and the home of the elite; the bulk of the population most likely lived in small surrounding settlements or else scattered in the hills.

In 1525 conquistador Pedro de Alvarado dispatched an army to conquer the area; the approaching Spanish were met by about five thousand Mam warriors, but the Mam leader, **Kaibal Balam**, quickly saw that his troops were no match for the Spanish and withdrew them to the safety of Zaculeu, where they were protected on three sides by deep ravines and on the other by a series of walls and ditches. The Spanish army settled outside the city and besieged the citadel for six weeks until starvation forced a surrender.

and stucco mouldings that would have adorned the structures. Nonetheless, Zaculeu has a unique atmosphere – surrounded by pines, and with fantastic views of the mountains, its grassy plazas make excellent picnic spots. There's a small **museum** at the site (same hours), with examples of some of the unusual burial techniques used and some ceramics found during excavation. To get to Zaculeu from Huehuetenango, take one of the **buses** that leave every thirty minutes from close to the school, at 7 Avenida between 2 and 3 calles – make sure it's heading for "Las Ruinas".

AGUACATÁN

It's 22km east from Huehue to **AGUACATÁN**, a small agricultural town strung out along a very long main street, and the only place in the country where the Akateko and Chalchitek languages are spoken. It is best done as a day-trip, preferably in time to see Aguacatán's huge Sunday **market**, which actually gets under way on Saturday afternoon, when traders arrive early to claim the best sites.

WHAT TO SEE AND DO

On Sunday mornings, a steady stream of people pours into town, cramming into the **market** and plaza, and soon spilling out into the surrounding area. Around noon the tide turns as the crowds start to drift back to their villages, with donkeys leading their drunken drivers home.

Aguacatán's other attraction is the source of the **Río San Juan**, which emerges fresh and cool from beneath a nearby hill, making a good place for a chilly dip. To get there, walk east along the main street out of the village for about 1km, until you see the sign. From the centre it takes about twenty minutes.

ARRIVAL AND DEPARTURE

By bus Buses and microbuses connect Huehuetenango to Aguacatán (6am–6pm, roughly every 30min; 40min). Beyond Aguacatán the road runs out along a ridge, with fantastic views stretching out below, eventually dropping down to the riverside town of Sacapulas, 90min away (see p.315); very regular microbuses ply this route until 5pm.

TODOS SANTOS CUCHUMATÁN

The village of **TODOS SANTOS CUCHUMATÁN** is many travellers' favourite place in Guatemala. The beauty of the alpine surroundings is a key attraction: the entire region is crisscrossed with excellent trails, offering fantastic **hiking**. Highland Maya culture is all-pervading here: the vast majority of Todosanteros are indigenous and speak Mam as their first language, and the ancient 260-day Tzolkin calendar is still observed. Most houses have a low mud-brick structure outside, called a *chuj*, which is similar to a sauna, with a wood fire lit under the rocks; family members use the steam generated to cleanse themselves. The local costume is incredible: the men wear straw hats, red-and-white-striped trousers and pinstripe shirts decorated with pink and blue collars, while the women wear dark blue *cortes* and intricately woven purple *huipiles*.

WHAT TO SEE AND DO

The village itself is pretty – a modest main street with a few shops, a plaza and a church – but is totally overshadowed by the looming presence of the Cuchumatanes mountains. Todos Santos sits at an altitude of 2460m, and it can be very chilly up here when the mists set in. Though most of the fun of this place is in simply hanging out, it would be a shame not to indulge in a traditional *chuj* **sauna**; most of the guesthouses will prepare one

ALL SAINTS' DAY IN TODOS SANTOS

The **All Saints' Day** fiesta (Nov 1) in Todos Santos Cuchumatán is one of the most famous in the country. The all-day horse race on All Saints' Day attracts large crowds, and is characterized by a massive stampede as the inebriated riders tear up the course, some still slugging on liquor bottles. On the "**Day of the Dead**" (Nov 2), the action moves to the cemetery, with marimba bands and drink stalls set up among the graves – a day of intense ritual that combines grief and celebration. By the end of the fiesta, the streets are littered with drunken revellers and the jail packed with brawlers.

HIGHLAND MARKET DAYS

Make an effort to catch as many highland market days as possible – they're second only to local fiestas in offering a glimpse of the traditional Guatemalan way of life.

Mon Chimaltenango; Zunil.

Tues Chajul; Nebaj, Totonicapán.

Wed Chimaltenango; Santiago Sacatepéquez, Todos Santos Cuchumatán.

Thurs Chichicastenango; Nebaj; Sacapulas; San Juan Atitán; San Lucas Tolimán.

Fri Chajul; Chimaltenango; Nebaj; San Francisco El Alto; Santa María de Jesús.

Sat Todos Santos Cuchumatán; Totonicapán.

Sun Chichicastenango; Momostenango; Nebaj; San Juan Atitán; San Lucas Tolimán; San Martín Sacatepéquez; Santa María de Jesús.

---

for you. If you want to take a shirt, pair of trousers or *huipil* home, you'll find an excellent co-op selling quality **weavings** next to the *Casa Familiar*.

Museo Balam

The **Museo Balam** (Mon–Sat 7am–8pm; Q5), east of the plaza, is definitely worth a visit, with such eclectic local objects as old pottery and statues, old traditional hats made of beeswax and a hundred-year-old marimba.

Qman Txun

Above the village – follow the track that goes up behind the *Comedor Katy* – is the small Maya site of **Qman Txun** where you'll find a couple of mounds sprouting pine trees. The site is occasionally used by *costumbristas* for the ritual sacrifice of animals.

ARRIVAL AND INFORMATION

By bus Buses and microbuses from Huehuetenango (2hr 15min) pass right through the centre of town.

Tourist information The Hispanomaya Spanish School, 150m south of the plaza, is a good source of tourist information; they have a book exchange, show videos and can also organize guided walks. There are two excellent community websites – ⓦ stetson.edu/~rsitler /TodosSantos and ⓦ todossantoscuchumatanes.weebly .com – dedicated to the Todos Santos region.

ACCOMMODATION AND EATING

Plenty of families rent out rooms very cheaply – ask at the Hispanomaya Spanish School (see below). *Comedores* are scattered around the market. Note that Todos Santos is a dry town; no alcohol is served except to guests of the *Casa Familiar*.

Comedor Katy One block from the square. There's always something bubbling on the hearth at this simple *comedor*

with excellent food (meals from Q15). Daily 7.30am–7.30pm.

Hospedaje Casa Familiar Above the plaza ☎ 7783 0656 or ☎ 5580 9579, ⓔ wovent@gmail.com. This renovated hotel is the best in town, with attractive rooms with valley views, TV, woven bedspreads and private hot-water bathrooms. Warm up in the guests' lounge around the fireplace or enjoy a *chuj* on the roof terrace. The café is recommended for both Western or Guatemalan food, though quite pricey (meals Q20–40) compared to the local places. Wine and beer are available to guests. Q110

Hotelito Todos Santos Just above the plaza beyond *Comedor Katy* ☎ 7783 0603 or ☎ 5327 9313. Popular with Guatemalans in town on business, this little hotel has fifteen small, plain and tidy tiled-floor rooms (some with bathroom) and a good *comedor*. They'll prepare a *chuj* here on request. Q95

DIRECTORY

Exchange On the square, Banrural (Mon–Fri 8am–5pm, Sat 7–11am) changes US dollars. There are no ATMs in town.

Internet Café Internet on the main drag (daily 8am–8pm; Q8/hr).

Language school Hispanomaya Spanish School (☎ 5163 9293, ⓦ hispanomaya.weebly.com), 150m south of the plaza.

AROUND TODOS SANTOS

It would be a real shame to miss out on one of the many **hikes** that can be done around Todos Santos – make sure you spend some time exploring the surrounding areas, home to some of the country's most breathtaking and dramatic scenery.

San Juan Atitán

The village of **SAN JUAN ATITÁN** is five to six hours on foot from Todos Santos via a wildly beautiful, isolated highland trail. It's

4

best to go with a guide: Hispanomaya Spanish School in Todos Santos (see p.329) organizes hikes. Follow the path that bears up behind the *Comedor Katy*, past the ruins and high above the village through endless muddy switchbacks until you get to the ridge overlooking the valley where, if the skies are clear, you'll be rewarded by an awesome view of the Tajumulco and Tacaná volcanoes. Take the easy-to-follow central track downhill from here past some ancient cloudforest to San Juan Atitán. Market days are Mondays and Thursdays. There is irregular **transport** back from San Juan Atitán to Huehue (around 6 daily pick-ups; 1hr).

You can **stay** in San Juan Atitán, in a couple of cheap *hospedajes*, or continue west along the valley from Todos Santos to **San Martín** and on to **Jacaltenango**, a route which also offers superb views. There's basic accommodation and a Banrural bank (with ATM) in Jacaltenango, so you could stay the night and then catch a bus back to Huehuetenango in the morning. Some buses from Huehue also continue down this route.

The Pacific coast

The **Pacific coast**, a strip of 250km of black volcanic beaches, is known in Guatemala as La Costa Sur. Once as rich in wildlife as the jungles of Petén, it's now the country's most intensely farmed region, with coffee grown on the volcanic slopes and entire villages effectively owned by vast cotton, sugar cane, and African palm plantations. A few protected areas try to preserve some of the area's natural heritage; the **Monterrico Reserve** is one of the most accessible of these, a swampy refuge for sea turtles, iguanas, crocodiles and an abundance of birdlife. It also encompasses a beachside village with a near-endless stretch of clean, dark sand. Close to the Mexican border, the empty sands at the tiny beach resort of **Tilapita** are another good alternative for some hammock time, and perhaps the odd boat excursion through the coastal mangrove forest.

You can glimpse the impressive art of the Pipil around the town of **Santa Lucía Cotzumalguapa**, and the Maya site of **Takalik Abaj** is worth a detour on your way to or from Mexico, or as a day-trip from Quetzaltenango. Otherwise, the region's pre-Columbian history isn't as visible as in other parts of the country.

The main route along the coast is the **Carretera al Pacífico**, which runs from the Mexican border at Tecún Umán into El Salvador at Ciudad Pedro de Alvarado. It's the country's swiftest highway and you'll never have to wait long for a bus. Venture off this road, however, and things slow down considerably.

TILAPA AND TILAPITA

Most travellers arriving in Guatemala's extreme west forgo the beaches in these parts and head straight from the border to Quetzaltenango or Guatemala City. But for total relaxation, a day or two in tranquil **Tilapita** will be time well spent.

Tilapa

South of Tecún Umán (see box opposite), a paved road paralleling the border passes endless palm-oil and banana plantations to the humble little village of **TILAPA**. The dark-sand beach here has a relatively gently shelving profile; lifeguards are only posted on weekends, though.

The coastline forms part of the **Reserva Natural El Manchón**, which covers some 30km of prime turtle-nesting beach and extends around 10km inland to embrace

---

INTO MEXICO: EL CARMEN AND TECÚN UMÁN

There are two border crossings with **Mexico** in the coastal region, both open 24hr. The northernmost is the **Talismán Bridge**, also referred to as **El Carmen**. On the Mexican side, a constant stream of minibuses and buses leaves for Tapachula (30min). Coming from Mexico, there are regular buses to Guatemala City until about 7pm; if heading towards Quetzaltenango or the western highlands, take the first minibus to Malacatán or Coatepeque and change there.

Further south and leading directly onto the Carretera al Pacífico, the **Tecún Umán–Ciudad Hidalgo** crossing is favoured by most Guatemalan and virtually all commercial traffic. If you're Mexico-bound, there are very frequent bus services to Tapachula (40min) over the border. There's a steady flow of buses to Guatemala City along the Carretera al Pacífico via Retalhuleu, and also regular direct buses to Quetzaltenango until 3pm (3hr 30min).

Three companies – King Quality, Ticabus and Línea Dorada – run direct buses between Tapachula in Mexico and Guatemala City (see p.283).

---

a belt of swamp and mangrove, which is home to crocodiles, iguanas, kingfishers, storks, white herons, egrets and an abundance of fish. Speak to one of the local boatmen in Tilapa or Tilapita about taking a tour (around Q120/hr) of the canals and lagoons.

Tilapita

On the other side of an estuary from Tilapa is the even tinier, and more agreeable, beach settlement of **TILAPITA**. Here there's a real opportunity to get away from it all and enjoy a superb stretch of clean, dark sand and the ocean (with not too much undertow). Just next to the *El Pacífico* hotel is a small **turtle hatchery**, with protected enclosures where eggs are buried until they hatch, and some information boards (the Olive Ridley turtle is the main visitor here, between June and October).

ARRIVAL AND INFORMATION

By bus Regular buses connect Coatepeque on the Carretera al Pacífico and Tilapa (every 30min, last bus returns at 6pm; 2hr). If you're travelling along the Pacific highway, just wait at the Tilapa junction on the highway for a connection.

By boat Boatmen buzz you up the canal that connects Tilapa and Tilapita (10min; Q10); it's possible to wade over at low tide.

Information ⓦ playatilapa.com.

ACCOMMODATION AND EATING

There's a row of beach *comedores* dispensing surf-fresh prawns and deep-fried fish (around Q50 a meal), plus Gallo beer in Tilapa.

El Pacífico Just off Tilapita beach ☏ 5940 1524. Owned by charming local couple Siria and Alex Mata, this hotel has functional, large rooms, all with decent mattresses, fans and showers – though you might want to bring your own mosquito net. The 18m swimming pool is filled with water at weekends. Good food, including fresh fish (try the *caldo de mariscos*), is served, and the hotel is always well stocked with cold beers. **Q100**

RETALHULEU

4

RETALHULEU, usually referred to as **Reu** (pronounced "Ray-oo"), may be one of the largest towns in the area, but that doesn't mean it's exciting. However, it is something of a transport hub, with virtually all **buses** running along the coastal highway stopping at the Retalhuleu terminal, a ten-minute walk from the plaza. If you find yourself with time on your hands, take a look at the **Museo de Arqueología y Etnología**, on the plaza (Tues–Sat 8.30am–1pm & 2–5pm, Sun 9am–12.30pm; Q15), home to an amazing collection of anthropomorphic figurines, mostly heads, and some photographs of the town dating back to the 1880s.

ARRIVAL AND DEPARTURE

By bus From Reu there are buses to Guatemala City (every 30min; 3hr), the Mexican border (every 30min; 1hr 30min) and Quetzaltenango (every 30min; 1hr 15min), plus regular buses to Champerico (1hr) and the beach at El Tulate (1hr 45min) until about 6.30pm.

ACCOMMODATION AND EATING

Cafetería La Luna On the plaza. Good breakfasts (from Q18) and lunches (Q25).

Hotel América 8 Av 9–32 ☏ 7771 1154. The best bet for budget accommodation, with smallish rooms with cable TV and private bathroom. **Q145**

TAKALIK ABAJ

TAKALIK ABAJ (daily 7am–5pm; Q50) is among the most important Mesoamerican sites in the country and one of the few that has both Olmec and Maya features. Though the remains of two large **temple platforms** have been cleared, it's the sculptures and stelae found carved around their base, including rare and unusual representations of frogs and toads (monument 68) and an alligator (monument 66), that make a trip here worthwhile. Among the finest carvings is stele 5, which features two standing figures separated by a hieroglyphic panel that has been dated to 126 AD. Look out for giant Olmec-style heads too, including one with great chipmunk cheeks. Royal tombs unearthed in 2002 and 2012 confirmed that following the Olmec, the site was later occupied by the Maya.

To get to Takalik Abaj, take a local **bus** from Reu 15km west to the village of El Asintal, from where you can take a pick-up (Q5) to the site, 4km away.

CHAMPERICO

A fast highway runs the 40km or so south from Reu to the beach at **CHAMPERICO**, which, though it doesn't feel like it, is the country's third port, and best visited as a day-trip. The town enjoyed a brief period of prosperity many decades ago when it was connected to Quetzaltenango by rail, though there's little sign of this now apart from a rusting pier. The dark-sand **beach** is impressive for its scale (though watch out for the dangerous undertow), but perhaps the best reason for visiting is **seafood**; there are rows of beachside *comedores*, all offering deep-fried prawns and fresh fish for around Q60 a head. Don't wander too far from the busiest part of the beach – muggings have occurred in isolated spots here. **Buses** run between Champerico and Quetzaltenango every hour or so until 6pm (2hr 15min), and there are also very regular connections to Retalhuleu.

SANTA LUCÍA COTZUMALGUAPA AND AROUND

The nondescript coastal town of **SANTA LUCÍA COTZUMALGUAPA** functions as a good base to explore three mysterious Pipil **archeological sites** that are scattered around the surrounding cane fields. Bear in mind, though, that getting to them all isn't easy unless you have your own transport or hire a taxi.

WHAT TO SEE AND DO

Three **archeological sites** around Santa Lucía are all that remains of the Pipil civilization, an indigenous non-Maya culture with close links to the Nahuatl tribes of Central Mexico. To this day, it is unclear as to how these people, now known for their intricate stone carvings, came to live in this area (possibly as early as 400 AD), as it was largely inhabited by the Maya. It is possible, although not advisable, to visit the sites on foot passing through cane fields – but beware that this can be dangerous, as muggers hide in the fields. It is much safer to hire a **taxi** in the plaza in Santa Lucía – to visit all three sites in a couple of hours reckon on at least Q100. You can also get to the Museo El Baúl by **bus** (every 30min); take one heading to Colonia Maya from either the bus terminal or the park in Santa Lucía.

Bilbao

Unearthed in 1860, the site of **Bilbao** has four sets of stones visible *in situ*, two of which perfectly illustrate the magnificent precision of the Pipil carving techniques, beautifully preserved in slabs of black volcanic rock. A path leading left into the cane brings you to two large stones carved with bird-like patterns, with strange circular glyphs arranged in groups of three: the majority of the glyphs are recognizable as the names for days once used by the people of southern Mexico.

Finca El Baúl

Finca El Baúl lies about 5km beyond Bilbao. The hilltop site has two stones, one a massive half-buried stone head with wrinkled brow and patterned headdress. In front of the stones is a set of small altars on which local people make animal sacrifices, burn incense and leave offerings of flowers. The next stones of interest are at the **finca** itself, in the **Museo El Baúl** (admission free), a few kilometres further away from town, where the carvings include some superb heads, stone skulls, a massive jaguar, the emblem of Santa Lucía, and an extremely well-preserved stele of two boxers (monument 27) dating from the Late Classic period. Alongside all this antiquity is the finca's old steam engine, a miniature machine that used to haul the cane along a system of private tracks.

Finca Las Ilusiones

The site at **Finca Las Ilusiones** is on the other side of town from Finca El Baúl and Bilbao. Here another collection of artefacts and some stone carvings has been assembled in the **Museo Cultura Cotzumalguapa** (Mon–Fri 8am–4pm, Sat 8am–noon; Q15). Two of the most striking figures within are the pot-bellied statue (monument 58), probably from the middle Preclassic era, and a copy of monument 21, which bears three figures, the central one depicting a ball player. To **get here**, head out of town east along the highway for about 1km, and follow the signs on the left.

ARRIVAL AND INFORMATION

By bus Pullman buses passing along the highway will drop you at the entrance road to Santa Lucía Cotzumalguapa, a 10min walk from the centre, while second-class buses go straight into the terminal, a few blocks from the plaza. Buses to the capital leave the terminal every 30min until 4pm, or you can catch a bus from the highway.
Banks You'll find plenty of banks around the main plaza.

ACCOMMODATION AND EATING

There are lots of places to eat near the main plaza.
Hotel Internacional Just south of the main highway ☎ 7882 5504. There are no decent budget options in the centre, but this place has spacious, fan-cooled rooms which will more than suffice for a night. Q155

SIPACATE AND PAREDÓN

The low-key village of **SIPACATE** is located inside the **Parque Natural Sipacate-Naranjo**, a mangrove coastal reserve. The black-sand beach here is separated from the village by the black waters of the Canal de Chiquimulilla; boats ferry a steady stream of passengers to the waves. Some of the best **surf** in the country here is about 5km to the east on the empty sands of neighbouring **Paredón** beach, where there's a new travellers' lodge. The beach break here averages 2m and is consistent between December and April, though note that conditions can be tough for beginners.

ARRIVAL AND DEPARTURE

By bus Regular buses to Sipacate (8 daily; 2hr) leave Siquinalá, just west of Santa María Cotzumalguapa, on the Carretera al Pacífico. There are also two daily buses from the Centra Sur terminal in Guatemala City to Sipacate (4hr). Once you're in Sipacate village you need to catch a public boat to reach the beach. (It's a little complicated to reach Paredón from Sipacate, but the *Paredón Surf House* website has clear instructions.)
By shuttle bus From Antigua direct shuttles operated by *Paredón Surf House* head to Paredón (2hr; Q120); these tend to run on weekends only. Contact them to book your place.

ACCOMMODATION AND EATING

El Paredón Surf Camp Beachside in Paredón ☎ 4593 2490, ⓦ surf-guatemala.com. This simple setup has dorms (with mosquito nets and lockers) and basic accommodation. Food is prepared by a local family and boards and kayaks can be rented; surf lessons are Q120/hr. You must contact them first so they can prepare for your arrival. Transport can be organized from Antigua. Dorm Q50, double Q160, apartment Q300
Paredón Surf House Beachside in Paredón ☎ 4994 1842, ⓦ paredonsurf.com. Really putting the Guatemalan surf scene on the map, this fine new place has beautifully designed thatched bungalows with Bali-style outdoor bathrooms and a great loft dorm with quality mattresses. There's a small oceanside pool, tasty grub (lunch around Q40, dinner Q80) and a full bar. Surf lessons are Q120/hr and there are boards for rent. Horseriding and canoe tours can be arranged. Get in touch and transport can be organized from Antigua. Cash only. Dorm Q80, bungalow Q340

ESCUINTLA

Sitting at the junction of the two main coastal roads from the capital, **ESCUINTLA** is the largest of the Pacific towns, typified by relentless heat and traffic. Unfortunately, it's also the most dangerous, and the only reason you should find yourself in town is to change buses.

ARRIVAL AND DEPARTURE

By bus Buses to Guatemala City leave from 8 C & 2 Av. For other destinations, there are two terminals: for places en route to the Mexican border, buses run through the north of town and stop by the large Esso station (take a local bus up 3 Av); buses for the coast road are best caught at the main terminal on the south side of town, at the bottom of 4 Av. Buses leave every 30min for the eastern border and hourly for Antigua.

ACCOMMODATION

Hotel Costa Sur 12 C 4–13 ☏ 5295 9528. If for some reason you're stuck here, check into this good-value, clean and orderly place. **Q145**

MONTERRICO

The tiny beachside settlement of **MONTERRICO** enjoys one of the finest settings on the Pacific coast. Scenically, things are reduced to a strip of dead-straight sand, a line of powerful surf and an enormous curving horizon. The village is scruffy but friendly and relaxed, separated from the mainland by the waters of the Chiquimulilla canal, which weaves through a fantastic network of **mangrove swamps**. Be sure to take care in the waves as there's a vicious **undertow**.

If you're looking for a really tranquil experience, try to avoid visiting on a weekend when Monterrico is much busier with visitors from Guatemala City.

WHAT TO SEE AND DO

Monterrico's long stretch of **beach** is perfect for kicking back with a book and watching one of the many beautiful sunsets that tinge the sky pink. Squadrons of pelicans – flying in formation and nicknamed the "Monterrico air force" by locals – skim

MONTERRICO

Boats to La Avellana

Lagoon

Minibuses/buses to Iztapa & Guatemala City

Izapa (25km)

Airstrip

Farmacia

High School

Proyecto Lingüístico Monterrico

Banrural

Shuttle buses to Antigua

Pick-ups & Buses to Hawaii

Super Monterrico

Tourist Police

Parque

CECON Turtle Hatchery

Hawaii (8km)

0   500
metres

PACIFIC OCEAN

ACCOMMODATION
Brisas del Mar	1
Café del Sol	2/6
Hotel el Delfín	3
Hotel el Mangle	5
Johnny's Place	4

EATING & DRINKING
Bar Bambas	1
Johnny's Place	3
Taberna El Pelícano	2

over the ocean, angling their wings to clip the crest of the wave as they glide along the coastline.

Biotopo Monterrico-Hawaii nature reserve

Natural beauty aside, Monterrico's other attraction is the **Biotopo Monterrico-Hawaii nature reserve**, which embraces the village, the beach – an important **turtle** nesting ground – and a large slice of the mangrove swamps behind. The reserve is actually home to four distinct types of mangrove, which act as a kind of marine nursery, offering small fish protection from their natural predators, while above the surface live hundreds of species of bird and a handful of mammals, including raccoons and armadillos, plus iguanas, caimans and alligators. The best way to explore the reserve is in a small *cayuco* (kayak); these are best organized via your guesthouse or down at the dock itself. The reserve's **visitors' centre** (daily 8am–noon & 2–5pm; Q40), just off the beach between *Hotel El Mangle* and the *Pez d'Oro* hotel, has plenty of information about the environment (Spanish only), and sections where endemic species including sea turtles, caimans, iguanas and other lizards are bred for release into the wild. There's a short interpretive **trail** through the grounds of the centre to explore too.

ARRIVAL AND INFORMATION

By bus The bus stop is just south of the dock, a 5min walk from the beach. From Guatemala City's Centra Sur terminal buses leave for Monterrico (2 daily; 3hr 30min), Iztapa (6 daily) and Puerto San José (every 20min). There are very regular microbus links between Puerto San José and Iztapa (every 30min; 30min) and Iztapa and Monterrico (every 30min; 1hr) until 6pm.

By shuttle bus Most visitors arrive on the daily shuttle buses that link Antigua with Monterrico (2hr 45min; Q80) and drop off/pick up from hotels.

By boat Boats leave for La Avellana (8 daily; 30min; passengers Q6, cars Q90), from where there are connections to Taxisco (see box, p.336) on the coastal highway.

Tourist information There is no tourist office. Proyecto Lingüístico Monterrico (see p.336) and *Johnny's Place* (see below) are the best sources of information on the ground, or consult ⓦ monterrico-guatemala.com.

ACCOMMODATION

Expect to pay a little more here than in many places in Guatemala. At weekends it's best to book ahead (and price rises of 20 percent are common). All places listed below are right on or just off the beach.

Brisas del Mar Turn left just before the beach ☏ 5517 1142. This hotel, about 100m inland from the beach, looks a bit uninspiring, but the 26 functional bungalows (with fan or a/c) are excellent value, in decent condition and have private bathroom. All face a garden with two pools. Q80

Café del Sol Turn right at the beach and walk for 250m ☏ 5050 9173, ⓦ cafe-del-sol.com. Enjoys a lovely beach-facing aspect, with sunbeds facing the ocean. It's a well-run place with inland and beachside blocks (avoid rooms in the bar-restaurant, which lack privacy). There's a small pool at the rear. Q300

★ **Hotel el Delfín** 50m right at beachfront ☏ 5702 6701, ⓦ hotel-el-delfin.com. Rambling place owned by an enthusiastic, welcoming American-Guatemalan couple who are switched on to travellers' needs. Many rooms are cell-like but all have fans and mosquito nets and there's a pool, bar and cheap food. Q80

Hotel el Mangle Turn left at the beach ☏ 5514 6517. Relaxed lodge with charming, attractive fan-cooled rooms, all with mosquito nets, bathrooms and little terraces with hammocks. Prices have risen steeply recently, so bargain hard. The central garden area has a small pool. Q190

Johnny's Place Turn left at the beach ☏ 5812 0409, ⓦ johnnysplacehotel.com. For years this place has been a backpacker favourite, and the prime beachside location and chill-out zone (a *palapa* with hammocks) are enticing. Offers a well-designed new beachside block (with modish rooms and beach-facing suites), rough'n'ready ageing bungalows and dorms, plus some a/c rooms and a family-sized apartment. The party vibe has been turned down a notch but the bar here still rocks on weekends. Dorm Q45, double Q160

EATING AND DRINKING

You'll find a row of traditional Guatemalan places on C Principal just before you hit the beach, all offering huge portions of fried prawns and fresh fish for about Q50–60 a plate.

> ★ **TREAT YOURSELF**
>
> **Taberna El Pelícano** Behind *Johnny's Place* ☏ 4001 5885. The creative Swiss chef here serves up fine European food, including fresh pasta (Q45), seafood and grilled fish (around Q80). The attractive thatched premises have atmosphere (including wonderful wooden dining tables) that makes up for the lack of sea views. Wed–Sat noon–2pm & 5–9pm, Sun noon–3pm & 6–9pm.

INTO EL SALVADOR: CIUDAD PEDRO DE ALVARADO

Very regular buses run along the coastal highway to the border with **El Salvador** at **Ciudad Pedro de Alvarado**. From Taxisco the border is just over an hour away. The crossing is fairly quiet but there are onward buses (every 30min) and a few basic *hospedajes* on both sides of the frontier.

Bar Bambas Behind *Johnny's Place*. Likeable thatched-roofed bar that's good for a cold beer and a game of pool. There's a bass-heavy sound system. Mon–Thurs 5–11pm, Fri–Sun 11am–1am.

Johnny's Place Turn left at the beach ☎ 5812 0409, ⓦ johnnysplacehotel.com. This waveside café is renowned for its *ceviche* (Q80/lb), which is available prepared three different ways, and also offers sandwiches and burgers. Doubles as a bar and there's some DJ and dance action most weekends. Daily 7am–10pm.

DIRECTORY

Banks There are two banks; Banrural has an ATM, as does the Super Monterrico store on C Principal.

Language school Proyecto Lingüístico Monterrico (☎ 5475 1265, ⓦ monterrico-guatemala.com/spanish-school), on the main drag, offers inexpensive one-on-one Spanish instruction (20hr for Q750).

The eastern highlands

The **eastern highlands**, southeast of the capital, are probably the least-visited part of Guatemala. The landscape lacks the appeal of its western counterpart – the peaks are lower and the towns, whose residents are almost entirely Latinized, are nearly universally featureless. You're unlikely to want to hang around for long. **Esquipulas** is worth a visit, though, for its colossal church, home to the Cristo Negro Milagroso (Miraculous Black Christ), and the most important pilgrimage site in Central America. It's conveniently positioned very close to the border with Honduras and El Salvador. There's also the idyllic crater lake on top of the **Volcán de Ipala**, whose isolation adds to its appeal.

CHIQUIMULA

Perennially hot and dry, the town of **CHIQUIMULA** is an unattractive, bustling *ladino* stronghold. Few travellers spend the night – if you've just arrived in Guatemala, things only get better from here. Although the centre itself is nothing to boast about, the little **Parque Calvario** square, a couple of blocks south of the main plaza, is a pleasant enough spot with a few cafés and restaurants.

ARRIVAL AND INFORMATION

By bus The sprawling bus terminal is in the market area around 1 C between 10 & 11 Av, Zona 1.

Destinations Anguiatú (every 30min; 1hr); El Florido border (every 30min; 1hr 30min); Esquipulas (every 20min; 1hr); Guatemala City (every 30min until 6pm; 3hr 30min); Ipala (hourly; 1hr); Puerto Barrios (hourly; 4hr 30min); Santa Elena, for Flores (5 daily; 7hr 30min).

Facilities Banks and internet cafés are dotted around the main plaza.

ACCOMMODATION

Hotel Hernández 3 C 7–41 ☎ 7942 0708, ✉ chapin54 @yahoo.com. Long-standing favourite that's been hosting travellers for years, this maze-like place is run efficiently by a friendly family. Dozens of orderly, clean rooms, in several different price categories, spread along long corridors – you pay a lot more for a/c and TV. There's a small pool at the rear for cooling off. **Q120**

Posada Don Adán 8 Av 4–30 ☎ 7942 0549. A genteel, old-fashioned family-run hotel. The a/c comes in handy when the temperature is soaring. Free parking. **Q155**

EATING AND DRINKING

The nicest places to eat are on Parque Calvario, a trendy, youthful hangout two blocks south of the main plaza. Inexpensive *comedores* are around the central market, just east of the main plaza.

Jalisco Parque Calvario. Pleasant little café with a couple of tables set outside; try the Mexican dishes (from Q20). Daily 7.30am–7pm.

Parrillada de Calero 7 Av 4–83 ☎ 7942 5639. A bustling open-sided place specializing in barbecued meats: *lomito*, *pollo* and *carne de res*. Also serves good breakfasts. From Q40 a meal. Daily 11am–10pm.

VOLCÁN DE IPALA

Reached down a side road off the main highway between Chiquimula and Esquipulas, the **VOLCÁN DE IPALA** (1650m) may at first seem a little disappointing – it looks more like a hill than a grand volcano. However, the cone is filled by a beautiful little **crater lake** ringed by dense tropical forest – you can walk round the entire lake in a couple of hours. It's well worth heading here if you're looking for some peace; if you visit on a weekday it should be pretty quiet.

ARRIVAL AND INFORMATION

By bus Buses between Chiquimula and Agua Blanca pass the trailhead at El Sauce (km 26.5), from where it's 90min to the summit.

Entrance fee Staff at the visitor centre on the volcano's slope collect a Q15 entrance fee.

ESQUIPULAS

ESQUIPULAS is home to the most important Catholic shrine in Central America. For the past four hundred years pilgrims from all over the region have flocked here to pay their respects to the **Cristo Negro Milagroso** (Miraculous Black Christ), whose image is found in the town's magnificent basilica. The principal day of **pilgrimage** is January 15; if you're in town at this time make sure you book accommodation in advance (or commute from Chiquimula). The rest of the town is a messy sprawl of cheap hotels, souvenir stalls and restaurants that have sprung up to serve the pilgrims.

THE BLACK CHRIST OF ESQUIPULAS

In 1595, following the indigenous population's conversion to Christianity, the town of Esquipulas commissioned famed colonial sculptor Quirio Cataño to carve an image of Christ. Sculpted in a dark wood, the image acquired the name **Cristo Negro** (Black Christ). Rumours of its miraculous capacities soon spread – according to the religious authorities, the first miracle took place in 1603, but it wasn't until 1737, when the archbishop Pardo de Figueroa was cured of an illness, that its healing properties were recognized. It has ever since been the object of the most important religious pilgrimage in Central America.

WHAT TO SEE AND DO

The **Black Christ** is the focus of the town, and is approached through the church's side entrance, beyond a little area full of candles that are lit upon exiting the building. Pilgrims stand reverently in line, slowly making their way towards the image. The walls are plastered with anything and everything – golden plaques with engraved messages to Christ, passport-sized photos that the pious slip into large picture frames, interwoven gold and silver necklaces that viewed from a distance form the image of Jesus. Pilgrims mutter prayers as they approach the image: some kneel, while others briefly pause in front of it, before getting moved on by the crowds behind. They leave walking backwards so as to show their respects to Christ by not turning their back on Him.

ARRIVAL AND DEPARTURE

By bus All buses leave from 11 C, the main drag. Rutas Orientales (for Guatemala City and Flores) and María Elena (for Flores) bus terminals are just west of the central plaza, on 11 C.

Destinations Copán – catch a bus for Chiquimula (every 20min; 45min) and another from there to the El Florido border post (see box, p.413); El Salvador border at Anguiatú (every 30min, 6am–5pm; 1hr); Flores (5 daily; 8hr 30min); Guatemala City (every 30min; 4hr 30min); Honduras border at Agua Caliente (every 30min, 6am–5.30pm; 30min).

ACCOMMODATION

Hotels in Esquipulas fill up quickly on weekends, when prices (which are always negotiable) increase. Cheap places are clustered just north of the main road, 11 C.

La Favorita 2 Av 10–15 ☎ 7943 1175. Basic, cell-like and very inexpensive rooms. Pay a little more and the quality jumps markedly, and you'll score a private bathroom too. It's a 2min walk from the church. **Q85**

Hospedaje Esquipulas 1 Av & 11 C A ☎ 7943 2298. No frills, just plain, smallish rooms with private bathroom that are perfectly adequate for a night. **Q135**

Hotel Villa Edelmira 3 Av 8–58 ☎ 7943 1431. Pleasant, family-run hotel with excellent rates for singles. **Q120**

EATING AND DRINKING

Many of the cheaper restaurants and *comedores* are on 11 C and the surrounding streets.

Restaurante Calle Real 3Av & 10 C ☎ 7943 2405. A block north of the main drag, this large *comedor* serves up generous portions of grilled meats, soups and Chapin-style breakfasts with all the trimmings. Daily 7am–9pm.

4

INTO EL SALVADOR: ANGUIATÚ, SAN CRISTÓBAL FRONTERA AND VALLE NUEVO

There are three border crossings with El Salvador in the region of Esquipulas.

ANGUIATÚ

Buses run to the **Anguiatú** crossing from Chiquimula (every 30min, 6am–6pm; 2hr) and Esquipulas (from 6 Av & 11 C, Zona 1; every 30min, 6am–6pm; 1hr). From the Anguiatú border, buses go to **Metapán** (every 30min, 6am–6pm; 20min), where you can get a connection to San Salvador and Santa Ana.

SAN CRISTÓBAL FRONTERA

Buses connect El Progreso and Jutiapa with the San Cristóbal border crossing (2hr), from where you can get a bus to Santa Ana (1hr). Regular buses travel between Guatemala City and El Progreso.

VALLE NUEVO

Several companies operate very regular bus connections from Guatemala City (see p.283), travelling via **Valle Nuevo** for El Salvador.

Restaurante La Frontera Opposite the park. There's usually a bustle about this large place, which has a good selection of local dishes, including fish and tasty *carne a la plancha*. Daily 6.30am–9.30pm.

Izabal

The eastern section of Guatemala, the department of **Izabal**, has a decidedly sultry, tropical feel, with rainforest reserves, a Caribbean coastline, a vast lake and a dramatic gorge system to explore. As you approach the coast, skirting the Maya ruins of **Quiriguá**, the landscape dramatically changes from dry, infertile terrain to lush, green vegetation. Although **Puerto Barrios** is nothing more than a port town, the relaxed settlement of

Lívingston, home to the black Garífuna people, has a unique blend of black Caribbean and Guatemalan cultures.

QUIRIGUÁ

Sitting in an isolated pocket of rainforest, surrounded by a forest of banana trees, the small Maya site of **QUIRIGUÁ** is home to some of the finest Maya carvings anywhere. Only Copán, across the border in Honduras (see p.409), offers any competition to the site's magnificent stelae, altars and so-called "zoomorphs", covered in well-preserved and superbly intricate glyphs and portraits.

WHAT TO SEE AND DO

Entering the site (daily 8am–4.30pm; Q80), you emerge at the northern end

---

THE HISTORY OF QUIRIGUÁ

Quiriguá's **early history** is still relatively unknown, but during the Late Preclassic period (250 BC–300 AD) migrants from the north established themselves as rulers here. In the Early Classic period (250–600 AD), the area was dominated by Copán, just 50km away, and doubtless valued for its position on the banks of the Río Motagua, an important trade route, and as a source of jade. It was during the rule of the great leader **Cauac Sky** that Quiriguá challenged Copán, capturing its leader 18 Rabbit in 738 AD and beheading him, probably with the backing of the "superpower" city of Calakmul. Quiriguá was then able to assert its independence and embark on a building boom: most of the great stelae date from this period. For a century Quiriguá dominated the lower Motagua valley. Under **Jade Sky**, who took the throne in 790, Quiriguá reached its peak, with fifty years of extensive building work, including a radical reconstruction of the acropolis. Towards the end of Jade Sky's rule, in the middle of the ninth century, the historical record fades out, as does the period of prosperity and power.

of the **Great Plaza**. By the ticket office is a small **museum** (daily 7am–4pm; free), which explains the site's history (see box opposite) and discovery. Quiriguá is famous for the **stelae** scattered across its Central Plaza, seven (A, C, D, E, F, H and J) of which were built during the reign of Cauac Sky and depict his image. The nine stelae are the tallest in the Maya world – the largest of all is Stele E, elevated 8m above ground and weighing 65 tonnes. Note the vast headdresses, which dwarf the faces, as well as the beards, an uncommon feature in Maya life. As you make your way towards the **acropolis**, you will be able to make out the remains of a **ball court** on your right, before reaching six blocks of stone carved with images representing animal and human figures: the **zoomorphs**. Have a look at the turtle, frog and jaguar.

ARRIVAL AND DEPARTURE

By bus The ruins are some 70km beyond the junction at Río Hondo, and 4km down a turn-off from the main road. All buses travelling between Guatemala City and Flores or Puerto Barrios pass by. There's a fairly regular bus service connecting the highway and the site itself, plus assorted motorbikes and pick-ups.

On foot It's probably best not to walk to the site, as this is a pretty isolated region.

ACCOMMODATION AND EATING

The village of Quiriguá, just south of the turn-off, has a few places to stay.

Hotel y Restaurant Royal ☎ 7947 3639. Decent, inexpensive place with clean, spacious rooms and a good *comedor*. **Q60**

> ★ **TREAT YOURSELF**
>
> **Posada de Quiriguá** ☎ 5349 5817, ⓦ geocities.jp/masaki_quirigua. Japanese-owned guesthouse, beautifully run by Masuki, with lovely, immaculately clean rooms in a fertile garden setting. The four "single" rooms have a double bed and can accommodate a couple comfortably, while the two doubles are much more spacious. The food is a real highlight, with wonderful Guatemalan and Japanese meals (dinner Q80), and good vegetarian choices too. **Q200**

PUERTO BARRIOS

PUERTO BARRIOS is not somewhere you'll want to hang around for too long – probably just long enough to hop on a boat to your next destination. Named after President Rufino Barrios in the 1880s, the port fell into the hands of the United Fruit Company and was used to ship UFC bananas to the US. Puerto Barrios fell into a long decline in the late twentieth century, but a new container facility has revived its fortunes to a degree. However, the town retains a seedy feel, with potholed streets, a clutch of strip bars and iffy characters. The one sight worth a peek is the remarkable **Hotel del Norte** (see p.340), Barrios' last surviving Caribbean architectural landmark, with timber corridors warped by a century of storms and salty air – be sure to take a look at the colonial-style bar and dining room.

ARRIVAL AND INFORMATION

By boat All boats use the dock at the end of 12 C. If you're heading to Belize, remember to clear *migración* (7am–7pm) first and pay your Q80 exit tax; the office is on 12 C, a block inland from the dock.

Destinations Lívingston (daily 6.30am, 7.30am, 9am, 11am, 2pm & 5pm; additional services leave when full; 30min); Punta Gorda, Belize (daily 10am, 1pm & 2pm; 1hr 15min).

By bus There's no purpose-built bus station in Puerto Barrios but all buses leave from near the central market. Bus schedules are posted at the Litegua terminal (6 Av & 9 C; ⓦ litegua.com). Litegua runs comfortable a/c services to Guatemala City (19 daily; 5hr 30min–6hr 30min), though only three of these are speedy *directos*. Chicken buses, roughly hourly, for both Chiquimula (4hr 30min) via Quiriguá (2hr), and those to Río Dulce (2hr), leave from 6 Av & 9 C. Microbuses for the Entre Ríos Honduran border (every 30min; 1hr) leave from the market area.

Tourist information There's no tourist office.

ACCOMMODATION

Barrios is not very backpacker-friendly: there are few decent cheap places.

Hotel La Caribeña 4 Av between 10 & 11 C ☎ 7948 0384. Rambling place with a variety of reasonable rooms (some with a/c) and a good seafood restaurant here. **Q120**

Hotel Europa 2 3 Av & 12 C ☎ 7948 1292. Motel-style place very conveniently located for the dock with decent (if

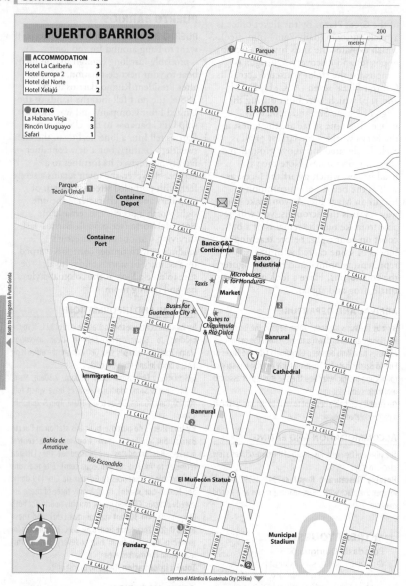

PUERTO BARRIOS

ACCOMMODATION

Hotel La Caribeña	3
Hotel Europa 2	4
Hotel del Norte	1
Hotel Xelajú	2

EATING

La Habana Vieja	2
Rincón Uruguayo	3
Safari	1

EL RASTRO

Parque Tecún Umán

Container Depot

Container Port

Banco G&T Continental

Banco Industrial

Taxis

Microbuses for Honduras

Market

Buses for Guatemala City

Buses to Chiquimula & Río Dulce

Banrural

Cathedral

Immigration

Bahía de Amatique

Banrural

Río Escondido

El Muñecón Statue

N

Fundary

Municipal Stadium

Boats to Livingston & Punta Gorda

Carretera al Atlántico & Guatemala City (293km)

4

---

ageing) clean rooms with two beds and TV with either fan or a/c. Priced per person, so single travellers get a good deal. **Q160**

★ **Hotel del Norte** 7 C & 1 Av ☎ 7948 0087. Highly atmospheric Caribbean hotel, built entirely from wood. Unfortunately the facilities are pretty historic too, and many of the rooms lack bathrooms, but with this much faded style and heritage on offer the comfort levels are

adequate enough. There's a swimming pool, and the location, overlooking the Bahía de Amatique, is magnificent. Meals, served in a mahogany-panelled restaurant, are disappointing, however. **Q175**

Hotel Xelajú 8 Av between 8 & 9 C ☎ 7948 1117. Yes, it looks like a prison, but the manager is friendly, rooms (some with bathroom) are clean and it's very secure and cheap. **Q80**

INTO HONDURAS: ENTRE RÍOS

Microbuses (every 30min, 6.30am–4.30pm; 1hr) for the border crossing to Honduras at **Entre Ríos** depart from the Puerto Barrios marketplace. Once there, you may be asked for an unofficial "exit tax" (Q20 or so) on the Guatemalan side and an entry fee of a similar sum on the Honduran side. Buses leave the border post of **Corinto** for Puerto Cortés (hourly; 2hr) via Omoa. The border crossing is open 24hr.

EATING

For *comedores* and juice stands head to the market where you'll find *pan de coco* (coconut bread) and *tortillas de harina* (wheat tortillas stuffed with meat and beans).
La Habana Vieja 13 C between 6 & 7 Av ☏ 7948 0695. Run by very welcoming Cuban exiles, this atmospheric restaurant has meat dishes including *chuletas "baby" del cerdo* (pork chops; Q55) and a bargain-priced set lunch for Q25. There's an a/c interior and small street terrace. Mon–Sat 11am–11pm.
Rincón Uruguayo 7 Av & 16 C ☏ 7948 6803. Excellent place excelling in *parrilladas* (South American-style barbecues) and with outside seating. About Q60 a head for a serious feast. Mon–Sat 10am–10pm.
Safari North of the centre on the seafront, at the end of 5 Av ☏ 7948 0563. A huge place with a *palapa* roof and bayside seating. It's pricey, but portions are enough for two: seafood platters (Q110), *ceviche* (Q80), *tapado* (Q95). Daily 11am–9.30pm.

DIRECTORY

Banks Banco Industrial, 7 Av & 7 C, and Banco G&T Continental, 7 C between 6 & 7 avs, both have ATMs.
Immigration For Belize, clear *migración* before buying a ticket; the office is a block east of the dock on 12 C.
Internet Red Virtual, 17 C & 9 Av, offers access for Q5/hr (daily 8am–9.30pm).

LÍVINGSTON

Lying at the mouth of the Río Dulce and only accessible by boat, **LÍVINGSTON** is unlike anywhere else in Guatemala – it's largely inhabited by the **Garífuna** (see box, p.90), or black Carib people, whose communities are strung out along the Caribbean coast between southern Belize and northern Nicaragua. The town is a little scruffy, and has a slightly edgy vibe at times, with a few resident hustlers eager to scrounge a beer or sell

you ganja. But the vast majority of the population is relaxed and welcoming, and the local culture is certainly fascinating: a unique fusion of Guatemalan and Caribbean life, with a lowland Maya influence for good measure. Be sure to try the delicious *tapado* (seafood soup) and other local treats while you're in town.

WHAT TO SEE AND DO

Lívingston is a small place with not much to do other than kick back and relax. The local **beaches**, though safe for swimming, are not the stuff of Caribbean dreams, with dark sand and greyish water. The sole exception is wonderful, white-sand **Playa Blanca**, though this is privately owned and can only be visited on a tour (see p.342).

The most popular trip around town is to **Las Siete Altares**, a group of waterfalls about 5km to the northwest, a good spot to take a dip and have a picnic. Robberies have occurred here occasionally, however, and though no incidents have been reported for some time, it's best to hire a local guide or visit as part of a tour. Boardwalks have recently been constructed so you can access the most impressive upper section easily.

ARRIVAL AND DEPARTURE

BY BOAT

The only way to get to Lívingston is by boat, either from Puerto Barrios, the Río Dulce or Belize; they arrive at the main dock on the south side of town. Combined boat/shuttle bus tickets are sold by Exotic Travel to Antigua, Copán (both Q320), San Pedro Sula (Q375) and La Ceiba (Q470).
For Río Dulce Town Boats leave daily at 9am and 2pm. Tickets (Q135) for the trip up the river can be booked by any travel agent or hotel in Lívingston. The journey takes around 2hr 30min – all boats stop at some hot springs, Isla de los Pájaros (a bird sanctuary) and cruise past the Castillo de San Felipe – but are otherwise eager to get to Río Dulce Town quickly. To really get the most out of the stunning gorge scenery you need to do a more leisurely cruise – ask at *Casa de la Iguana* (see p.342) for a boatman.
For Puerto Barrios *Lanchas* leave for Puerto Barrios (5 daily; additional services leave when full; 30min; Q35).
For Belize Two weekly boats run to Punta Gorda (Tues & Fri 7am; 1hr; Q200).

4

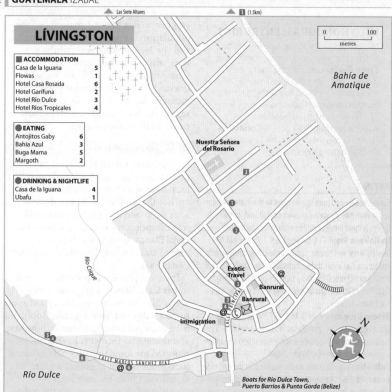

INFORMATION AND TOURS

Tours If you want an educative, highly informed walking tour of the Garífuna *barrio*, contact Philip Flores (also known as Polo) on ☎ 4806 0643.

Travel agents Exotic Travel (☎ 7947 0049, ⓦ blue caribbeanbay.com), in the same building as the *Bahía Azul* restaurant (see opposite), is the best travel agent in town. They can arrange trips (minimum six people) around the area, including visits to the Siete Altares (daily; Q80), Playa Blanca (Q120) and the Sapodilla Cayes off Belize for snorkelling (Q430 plus exit fees).

ACCOMMODATION

Make sure you book ahead during holidays; at other times you should easily be able to find a bed.

★ **Casa de la Iguana** Turn left at the dock and walk for 5min ☎ 7947 0064, ⓦ casadelaiguana.com. Party hostel with a winning formula of drinking games, hedonism and all-round merriment dreamed up by the inimitable Rusty, the British owner. All accommodation – a couple of dorms and attractive private cabañas with bathrooms – is in well-constructed wooden buildings set around a large grassy plot. There's local and Western grub and excellent travel information. Dorm Q35, cabaña Q140

Flowas On the beach, about 2km west of the centre ☎ 7947 0376, ✉ infoflawas@gmail.com. Run by a bohemian Spaniard, this beachside place has good two-storey bungalows and a restaurant with local and Spanish food. It's a very relaxing setting, but about a 30min walk from the centre; taxis will drop you close to the front gate for around Q15. Dorm Q75, single/double Q170

★ **Hotel Casa Rosada** About 400m left of the dock ☎ 7947 0303, ⓦ hotelcasarosada.com. A very inviting waterfront hotel run by a hospitable couple from Guatemala and Belgium with a huge, lush garden to enjoy. The small, cheery wooden cabins have twin beds, nets and nice hand-painted detailing. Bathrooms are all shared but kept very clean. Excellent, wholesome meals are served. Q160

Hotel Garífuna Turn left off the main street towards the *Ubafu* bar and walk 250m ☎ 7947 0183, ✉ quiqueboss@hotmail.com. A clean, secure guesthouse with tidy, slightly old-fashioned rooms, managed by a hospitable Garífuna family. Q80

Hotel Río Dulce C Principal ☎ 4022 8680. Gorgeous old wooden Caribbean-style property with functional, simple rooms and dorms in the main building and more expensive options at the rear. Dorm Q̲3̲5̲, single/double Q̲1̲0̲0̲

Hotel Ríos Tropicales C Principal ☎7947 0158 or ☎5755 7571, ⓦmctropic.webs.com. Very well-presented rooms, some very spacious and with tasteful furniture and art (around Q180), others much simpler but still a great deal. There's a sunny patio at the rear with sofas and a little espresso bar at the front. Free wi-fi. Q̲6̲5̲

EATING

Prices tend to be higher than in most parts of Guatemala. Make sure you try *tapado* (seafood soup with coconut, the local speciality) – reckon on about Q90 for a huge bowl.

Antojitos Gaby Turn left at the dock and walk for 250m. A cheap, clean little *comedor* with a couple of streetside tables, serving good seafood (including *sopa caracol*), fish and pasta. Free wi-fi. Daily 7am–9.30pm.

Bahía Azul C Principal ☎7947 0151. Popular café-restaurant in a fine old Caribbean building, with an inexpensive menu (try the *coco burguesa* – a burger in coconut bread) and an excellent terrace for watching the world go by. Daily 7.30am–10pm.

Buga Mama Left at the dock ☎7947 0981. A lovely wooden Caribbean building with a huge rear waterside deck. Good shrimp, *tapado*, pasta and salads (in the Q40–100 range). Staff are trained as part of the Ak' Tenamit development project, a good cause, but service can be spotty. Free wi-fi. Daily 7am–10pm.

Margoth C de la Iglesia ☎7947 0019. Perhaps the best place to try *tapado*, this large Garífuna-owned place also serves very tasty seafood and a wide array of local dishes. Daily 7am–10pm.

DRINKING AND NIGHTLIFE

Casa de la Iguana C Marcos Sánchez Díaz ☎7947 0064, ⓦcasadelaiguana.com. The gringo bar scene here (happy hour 6–8pm) has a lively vibe and can be a riot, with anything from drinking games to mud-wrestling. Daily until 1am.

Ubafu C de la Iglesia. This intimate bar is a key place for live music, especially Garífuna *punta*. Bands play at weekends and the odd weekday too. Daily 6pm–1am.

DIRECTORY

Bank Banrural on C Principal has an ATM and changes dollars.

Immigration About 200m up the main drag (daily 7am–7pm). Get your exit and entry stamps and pay your departure tax (Q80) here.

Internet Many places have wi-fi. Rapid Internet is 400m north of the dock (daily 8am–9pm).

Taxis Available from the dock; fares are Q10–15 to anywhere in town.

Lago de Izabal and the Río Dulce

Fringed by lush forests, wetlands and some outstanding natural attractions, **Lago de Izabal** is a beautiful tropical area with plenty to keep you occupied for a few days. The lake empties into the spectacular **Río Dulce** gorge system, which you can explore by boat from a jungle guesthouse. **El Estor** serves as a good base to access the beautiful nature reserve to the west of the lake, which is home to numerous species of wildlife and secluded spots. The area also encompasses one of the country's most curious natural phenomena, the Finca El Paraíso **hot-spring waterfall**.

THE RÍO DULCE GORGE

From Lívingston, the river leads into an astonishingly beautiful system of **gorges**. Tropical vegetation and vines cling to the walls, and the birdlife is outstanding, with white herons, sea eagles, pelicans and parrots darting over the water.

WHAT TO SEE AND DO

To really get the most out of the stunning region around these gorges you need to **stay locally**, and explore the myriad tributaries slowly – not glimpse it from the speeding *lanchas* that zip between Lívingston and Río Dulce Town. Fortunately there are now three excellent ecolodges (all with kayaks for rent) to allow you to do just that.

Beyond the gorge the river opens up into the **Golfete** lake, the north shore of which has been designated the **Biotopo de Chocón Machacas** (daily 8am–5pm; Q50). This reserve has some specially cut trails where you might catch sight of a bird or two, or, if you've time and patience to spare, a tapir or jaguar. If you're very lucky you may even see a **manatee** here; dawn is the best time.

ACCOMMODATION

Around 7km inland from Lívingston, just west of the main gorge section, there's a trio of fine ecolodges. Boats

4

LAGO DE IZABAL AND RÍO DULCE AREA

Puerto Cortés

CARIBBEAN SEA

Omoa

Cuyamel

Tegucigalpita

HONDURAS

SIERRA DEL MERENDÓN

Finca La Inca

Corinto

Canal Inglés

Laguna Santa Isabel

BIOTOPO PUNTA DE MANABIQUE

Entre Ríos

Punta Manabique

Puerto Barrios

Santo Tomás

Cayos del Diablo

Livingston

Siete Altares

Río Dulce

CERRO SAN GIL

Cerro San Gil (1267m)

MONTAÑAS DEL MICO

CARRETERA AL ATLÁNTICO

Morales/Bananera

BIOTOPO CHOCÓN MACHACAS

El Golfete

Cuatro Cayos

Río Chocón Machaca

Río Dulce

La Ruidosa Junction

Río Motagua

BELIZE

Río Sarstún

Modesto Méndez

Castillo San Felipe

Río Dulce San Felipe

Mariscos

Denny's Beach

Quiriguá

Quiriguá

Los Amates

Lago de Izabal

SIERRA DE SANTA CRUZ

Finca El Paraíso

Boquerón Canyon

El Estor

RESERVA BOCAS DEL POLOCHIC

Selempim

Río Zarigua

Río Polochic

RESERVA SIERRA DE LAS MINAS

N

0 | 10
kilometres

Belize (Punta Gorda) ◄

Poptún & Tikal ◄

Sebol ◄

▼ Panzós, Tactic & Cobán

▼ Guatemala City

ACCOMMODATION	
Finca Tatin	1
Hotelito Perdido	3
Round House	2

travelling between Río Dulce and Lívingston (see below) will drop you off at any of these places.

Finca Tatín 400m up the Río Tatín ☏ 4148 3332, ⓦ fincatatin.centroamerica.com. Fine jungle lodge with an eight-bed dorm (above the bar), private rooms and two-storey cabins set in dense rainforest. It's well set up for travellers, offering healthy food (the communal dinner is Q60), table tennis, tubes, hammocks, walking trails, wi-fi and even a gym and yoga space. Dorm Q40, single/double Q110, cabaña Q200

Hotelito Perdido 300m up the Río Lámpara ☏ 5725 1576, ⓦ hotelitoperdido.com. Set in a verdant tropical garden, this intimate place has split-level wooden cabañas, dorm beds and a relaxed vibe. Dorm Q45, single/double Q160, cabaña Q200

★ **Round House** 1km west of Río Dulce gorge ☏ 4294 9730, ⓦ roundhouseguatemala.com. Excellent new place, run by a very welcoming, well-travelled English-Dutch couple with high-quality accommodation, a sociable vibe and great cooking (a filling, flavoursome dinner is Q50). There's a small pool (ideal for volleyball) and great swimming in the *río* itself. Manatees are often seen directly offshore in the early morning. Dorm Q45, single/double Q110

RÍO DULCE TOWN

Still commonly referred to as Fronteras, the town of **RÍO DULCE** is not a place you'll want to hang around long. Once the stopover for ferries on their way to El Petén – a gargantuan concrete bridge now spans the river – this tiny transit town is unlovely and plagued by traffic. Nonetheless, there are pretty creeks and marinas popular with yachties nearby, and many travellers find a hotel away from the town itself and explore the sights around Lago de Izabal before heading down to Lívingston.

ARRIVAL AND INFORMATION

By boat The dock is under the north side of the bridge. For Lívingston via the Río Dulce gorge, *colectivo* boats leave at 9.30am and 1.30pm; there are additional services until 4pm (2hr; Q135). Pick-ups from local hotels can be arranged for no extra cost. The boatmen usually cruise up to the Castillo de San Felipe for photographs (but do not stop there), slow down at an islet to see nesting cormorants and pelicans; then stop for 15min at a place where hot springs bubble into the river and at another where water lilies are profuse.

By bus All buses stop on the north side of the bridge, which is where you will also find the Litegua, Línea Dorada, ADN and Fuente del Norte bus offices. Minibuses to El Estor leave from a side road just north of the Río Dulce bridge.

Destinations El Estor (every 45min; 1hr 30min); Flores (every 30min; 3hr 30min); Guatemala City (every 30min; 5hr); Lanquín (4WD daily 1.30pm from *Sun Dog Café*; 5hr; Q140); Poptún (every 30min; 1hr 45min); Puerto Barrios (hourly; 2hr).

Tourist information ⓦ mayaparadise.com has good links and listings covering the Río Dulce region.

ACCOMMODATION

All the following places will come and pick you up by boat from the north side of the bridge in Río Dulce Town.

Casa Perico 3km northeast of the bridge ☏ 5930 5666. Up a small lakeside inlet, this rustic Swiss-owned jungle hideaway has a relaxed atmosphere and is popular with budget travellers. It's not a party spot. All the buildings are wooden, built on stilts and connected by walkways. Meals cost around Q30, the set dinner is Q55. You'll find kayaks for rent and trips are offered around the *río*. Dorm Q45, single/double Q115

Hacienda Tijax Just across from the dock ☏ 7930 5505, ⓦ tijax.com. Nicely located on the lakefront, with a pool. There's a range of accommodation, from small A-frame cabins to large bungalows, and the restaurant food is tasty, if a little overpriced. Also offers a canopy jungle walk, hiking trails and horseriding. Cabin Q240

Hostal del Río North of the bridge, by *Sun Dog Café* ☏ 5527 0767. If you just want a bed for the night, this place is fine, with eight clean, functional rooms all with bathrooms and some with a/c. Q120

Hotel Backpackers Underneath the south side of the bridge ☏ 7930 5480, ⓦ hotelbackpackers.com. This huge, rickety wooden structure has large dorms and some mediocre doubles. Unfortunately, it lacks atmosphere and is noisy (due to both bridge and river traffic), which is a shame as it's owned by the nearby Casa Guatemala children's home, and many of the young staff are former residents. Dorm Q40, double Q120

★ **TREAT YOURSELF**

Tortugal 4 min by water-taxi from bridge ☏ 5306 6432, ⓦ tortugal.com. A great selection of very good accommodation, all attractively presented and well finished. The two dorms have quality mattresses, mosquito nets and lockers. Above the river-facing restaurant (meals Q45–75) there's a chill-out area with pool table and library. Free kayaks for guests. Dorm Q110, room/bungalow Q320

4

EATING AND DRINKING

There's a strip of undistinguished *comedores* on the main road close to the bus stop.

Bruno's Under the north side of the bridge ☎ 7930 5721. The area's most popular yachtie hangout, with a wide menu of local and international grub including sandwiches, seafood (from Q50) and pasta. The happy hour (4–7pm) features Victoria beer for just Q7. Free wi-fi and a pool. Daily 8am–11pm.

★ **Sun Dog Café** Down a lane on north side of bridge ☎ 5760 1844. Excellent little place run by a friendly Swiss guy and serving great thin-crust pizza (from a wood-fired oven) starting at Q50, baguettes and sandwiches (on delicious home-made bread) and espresso coffee. Also offers wine, and all spirits are double shots. Free wi-fi. Mon & Wed–Sun noon–10pm.

DIRECTORY

Banks Banrural and Banco Industrial have ATMs.
Internet You can access the internet at the *Río Bravo* restaurant north of the bridge.

CASTILLO DE SAN FELIPE

Looking like a miniature medieval castle, the **CASTILLO DE SAN FELIPE** (daily 8am–5pm; Q25), 1km upstream from the Río Dulce bridge, marks the entrance to Lago de Izabal, and is a tribute to the audacity of British pirates, who used to sail up the Río Dulce to raid supplies and harass mule trains. The Spanish were so infuriated by this that they built the fortress to seal off the entrance to the lake, and a chain was strung across the river. Inside there's a maze of tiny rooms and staircases, plenty of cannons and panoramic views of the lake.

LAGO DE IZABAL

Guatemala's largest lake, the **LAGO DE IZABAL**, is most definitely worth a visit – not only does it boast great views of the highlands beyond its shores, but the west of the lake on the Bocas del Polochic is also home to untouched forests and bountiful wildlife. Most hotels in Río Dulce Town (see p.345) will organize a lake cruise taking in the main sights, or you can explore the north shore by bus along the road to El Estor.

The **hot-spring waterfall** (daily 8am–5pm; Q12) near the *Finca El Paraíso*, 25km from Río Dulce and 300m north of the road, is a truly remarkable phenomenon, with near-boiling water cascading into cooled pools, creating a steam-room environment in the midst of the jungle. There is also a series of caves above the waterfall, their interior of different shapes and colours (remember to bring a torch). Buses and pick-ups travel in both directions until about 6pm.

Some 7km further west is the hidden **Boquerón canyon**, with near-vertical cliffs rising more than 250m; villagers (including Hugo, a *campesino*-cum-boatman) will paddle you upstream in a canoe for a small fee. Hiking trips into the canyon can be organized too; speak to *Casa Perico* or *Sun Dog Café* in Río Dulce Town (see p.345) or tour operators in El Estor (see below).

EL ESTOR

Supposedly given its name because of the English pirates who came up the Río Dulce to buy supplies at "the store", the tranquil lakeside town of **EL ESTOR** lies 6km west of El Boquerón. Few tourists make it to this corner of the lake, so it's a great place to escape the gringo trail. The town is ideally positioned to capitalize on the vast **ecotourism** possibilities of the lake and its surrounding areas, but the recent resumption of nickel mining on the western fringes of El Estor has raised the threat of pollution.

ARRIVAL AND INFORMATION

By bus Buses arrive and depart from 3 C west of the Parque Central. Microbuses (every 45min; 1hr 30min) connect El Estor with Río Dulce Town until 6pm. There are 6 daily buses to Cobán (7hr) via Tactic. Some public transport (1–2 daily) struggles up towards Lanquín via Cahabón, though this route is very mountainous and can be near-impossible to drive during heavy rains. The one guaranteed departure for Lanquín is a private 4WD truck (Q140; 4hr), which passes through town around 2.30pm. You can check all schedules at *Café El Portal* on the main square.

Tour operators *Café El Portal* organizes tours, as does Hugo at *Hotel Ecológico* and Óscar Paz at *Hotel Vista del Lago*. All can arrange boats and guides to explore the surrounding countryside, plus fishing trips on the lake.

ACCOMMODATION AND EATING

Café El Portal On the east side of the square ☎ 7818 0843. For genuine Guatemalan food, including filling *típico* breakfasts (Q20), this busy little place is ideal. Daily 7am–9pm.

Hotel Ecológico Cabañas del Lago 1.5km east of the centre ☎ 4037 6235 or ☎ 7949 7245. Set in a tranquil shady lakeside plot, these wooden bungalows are functional yet comfortable; some have three beds. There's a private sandy beach, good swimming, a guests' kitchen and bountiful wildlife around (lots of birds, spider monkeys and some iguanas). The restaurant has sweeping views and serves delicious meals (Q40–80). Drop by *Hugo's* restaurant in the plaza for a ride here. **Q180**

Hotel Vista del Lago Facing the lake ☎ 7949 7205. This fine old wooden building is claimed to be the original "store" that gave the town its name. The rooms, with bathroom, are clean but perfunctory – ask for one on the upper storey. Owner Óscar Paz is a good source of information and can set up tours. **Q170**

Posada Don Juan On the main square ☎ 7949 7296. A solid budget choice, this concrete hotel has clean, plain rooms with fan, some en suite. Great value. **Q80**

★ **Ranchón y Cabañas Chaab'il** 3 C, east of the main square ☎ 7949 7272. A good choice, with cabaña-style rooms with fans and mossie nets, chunky wooden beds and private bathrooms; most enjoy lake views. The restaurant (daily 7.30am–9.30pm) offers a lakeside setting for a meal (from Q40) of grilled meats and lots of seafood. **Q160**

DIRECTORY

Bike rental You can rent bikes at 6 Av 4–26 (Q80/day).
Bank Banrural on C Principal has an ATM.

RESERVA BOCAS DEL POLOCHIC

The **RESERVA BOCAS DEL POLOCHIC** is one of the richest wetland habitats in Guatemala, and shelters around 300 species of bird and a large number of mammals, reptiles, amphibians and fish. The ecosystem is one of the few places in the country where you can find manatees and tapirs, and you're bound to spot (or certainly hear) howler monkeys.

ARRIVAL AND INFORMATION

By boat To get to Selempím, on the edge of the reserve, catch a public *lancha* from El Estor (Mon, Wed & Sat; Q45) or hire a private *lancha* (around Q700).

Tour operators Locals organize treks into the foothills of the Sierra de las Minas or can take you kayaking around the river delta. Defensores de la Naturaleza, 5 Av & 2 C, El Estor

(☎ 7949 7130, ⓦ defensores.org.gt), who manage the reserve, organize excellent tours deep into the heart of the refuge.

ACCOMMODATION AND EATING

Selempím Lodge Contact Defensores de la Naturaleza (see above) to book ☎ 7949 7130, ⓦ defensores.org.gt. This large mosquito-screened wooden house has bunk beds and mossie nets. Guides are available to lead you on guided walks up into the foothills of the Sierra de las Minas and conduct kayak tours of the river delta. Rates include three substantial meals. **Q150**

The Verapaces

The twin departments of the **Verapaces** harbour some of the most spectacular mountain scenery in the country, yet attract only a trickle of tourists. **Alta Verapaz**, in particular, is astonishingly beautiful, with fertile limestone landscapes and mist-soaked hills. The mountains here are the wettest and greenest in Guatemala – ideal for the production of the cash crops of coffee, cardamom, flowers and ferns. To the south, **Baja Verapaz** could hardly be more different: a low-lying, sparsely populated area that gets very little rainfall.

Many travellers completely bypass Baja Verapaz, whizzing through on Carretera 14 from Guatemala City to Cobán and

4

VERAPACES HISTORY

The history of the Verapaces is quite distinct from the rest of Guatemala. The Maya here resisted the Spanish so fiercely that eventually the conquistadors gave up, and the Church, under the leadership of **Fray Bartolomé de las Casas**, was given the role of winning the people's hearts and minds. By 1542 the invincible **Achi** Maya had been transformed into Spanish subjects, and the King of Spain renamed the province Verapaz (True Peace). Nonetheless, the Verapaces remain very much *indígena* country: Baja Verapaz has a small Achi outpost around the town of Rabinal, and in Alta Verapaz the Maya population is largely **Poqomchi'** and **Q'eqchi'**.

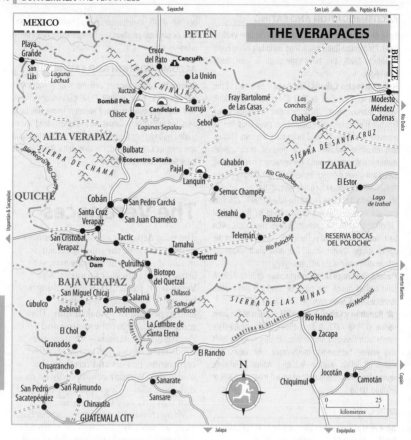

the rest of Alta Verapaz. There are, however, a few sights worth stopping off for en route. Clustered around the village of Purulhá are **sacred caves**, **waterfalls** and the **Biotopo del Quetzal**. To the west of the highway the **Salamá valley** drops dramatically away, leading to the sleepy department capital and beyond.

North of the La Cumbre junction for Salamá and the quetzal reserve is the departmental border with Alta Verapaz, and shortly thereafter the city of **Cobán**, where you'll find great cafés and restaurants and a good range of budget accommodation. Heading further towards Petén, take time to check out some of the interesting community tourism projects that showcase Alta Verapaz's limestone landscape, as well as its living Maya heritage. The star attraction in the area, however, has to be the natural wonder of **Semuc Champey**, just outside the village of **Lanquín**.

MARKET DAYS IN THE VERAPACES

Mon Salamá, Senahú, Tucurú
Tues Chisec, Cubulco, Lanquín, Purulhá, Rabinal, San Cristóbal Verapaz
Fri Salamá
Sun Chisec, Cubulco, Lanquín, Purulhá, Rabinal, San Jerónimo, Santa Cruz, Tactic

---

SALAMÁ

From the La Cumbre junction on Carretera 14, a paved road drops steeply towards the secluded Salamá valley.

SALAMÁ itself, capital of the department, is a quiet town, where you are unlikely to bump into other tourists. There isn't a great deal to see, but it does have a lively twice-weekly **market** (Mon & Fri) and makes a handy base for visiting the Chilascó waterfall and Achi Maya town of Rabinal to the west.

ARRIVAL AND DEPARTURE

By bus Buses from/to Guatemala City's Centra Norte terminal arrive/depart from the plaza. Minibuses use a dusty car park off 6 Av, one block west.

Destinations Chilascó (4 daily; 6.30am, 10.30am, noon & 5.30pm; 1hr 45min); Cobán (hourly; 2hr 15min); Guatemala City (every 30min; 3hr); Rabinal (every 30min; 45min).

ACCOMMODATION AND EATING

Deli-Donus 5 C 6–61 ☎7940 1121. Attractive café-restaurant ideal for coffee and a slice of home-made cake. Also good for breakfasts (around Q20) or a sandwich. Daily 7.30am–8pm.

Hotel Real Legendario 8 Av 3–57 ☎7940 0501, ⓦhotelreallegendario.com. A fairly modern, efficiently run hotel where the twenty well-presented rooms have comfortable beds, private hot-water bathrooms and cable TV. There's a little *comedor* here for breakfast, as well as internet and free wi-fi. **Q162**

Posada Don Maco 3 C 8–26 ☎7940 0083. Hospitable family-run place where the well-scrubbed, neat rooms have private bathrooms, cable TV and nice decorative touches. However, they keep squirrels in cages in the yard. **Q155**

SALTO DE CHILASCÓ

Just north of the La Cumbre junction, at km 144.5, a track leads east from the highway, towards the dramatic scenery of the **Sierra de las Minas**. After 12km you reach the village of **Chilascó**, where the community administers the impressive **SALTO DE CHILASCÓ** (last entry 1pm; Q40), one of the highest **waterfalls** in Guatemala, plunging 200m in two drops close to the entrance of Sierra de Las Minas. From Chilascó you walk via a steep, muddy mule path heading down to a ridge flanked by broccoli plantations. After 1km the path plunges down into the forested valley. The well-maintained trail offers picnic sites with views towards the Chilascó falls and information panels on the local flora (rare orchids, giant bromeliads and ferns), liquidambar forest and fauna.

Don't miss the **Saltito**, a delightful smaller waterfall halfway down, where you can bathe in the plunge pool and admire the stunning views. At the base of the main falls, water cascades onto huge boulders and seemingly disappears into the cavernous valley beyond the trail's end.

ARRIVAL AND DEPARTURE

By bus or pick-up There are buses from Salamá (see above) to Chilascó, and occasional pick-ups and trucks also cover the route from the CA-14 highway. The last bus back to the highway leaves the village at 3pm.

ACCOMMODATION AND EATING

Dorm accommodation (Q40) and food are available in Chilascó village.

BIOTOPO DEL QUETZAL

Back on CA-14 towards Alta Verapaz and Cobán, the road sweeps around endless tight curves below forested hillsides. Just before the village of **Purulhá** (km 161) is the **BIOTOPO DEL QUETZAL** (daily 7am–4pm; Q30), an 11.5-square-kilometre nature reserve designed to protect the habitat of the endangered bird. The reserve comprises steep and dense rain- and cloudforest, pierced by waterfalls, natural pools and the Río Colorado. There are two **hiking** trails, one an easy one-hour circuit, and the other a half-day Stairmaster. Trail maps are sold at the information centre at the park entrance.

The best time to catch a glimpse of the quetzal is March–April at either dawn or dusk. Since the reserve is not open during these hours it's definitely worth spending the night to increase your viewing opportunities.

To the north of the Biotopo, just past Purulhá at km 167 on the highway, are the sacred **Chicoy Caves** (daily 9am–5pm; Q25), where there are towering stalagmites of up to 20m. Maya religious rituals are still regularly performed here.

ARRIVAL AND DEPARTURE

By bus Buses to and from Cobán pass the reserve entrance every 30min.

THE RESPLENDENT QUETZAL

The **quetzal**, Guatemala's national symbol, has a distinguished past but an uncertain future. From the earliest of times, the bird's feathers have been sacred: to the Maya the quetzal was so revered that killing one was a capital offence, and the bird is also thought to have been the *nahual*, or spiritual protector, of the Maya chiefs. When Tecún Umán was slain by conquistador Alvarado, the quetzal is said to have landed on his chest, and consequently obtained its red breast from the Maya's blood.

Today the quetzal's image permeates the entire country: as well as lending its name to the nation's currency, citizens honoured by the president are awarded the Order of the Quetzal, and the bird is also considered a symbol of freedom, since caged quetzals die in confinement. Despite all this, the sweeping tide of deforestation threatens the existence of the bird.

The heads of males are crowned with a plume of brilliant green, while the chest and lower belly are a rich crimson and trailing behind are the unmistakeable oversized, golden-green tail feathers, though these are only really evident in the mating season. The females, on the other hand, are an unremarkable brownish colour. Quetzals can also be quite easily identified by their strangely jerky, undulating flight.

ACCOMMODATION AND EATING

Ranchitos del Quetzal Just 100m north of the entrance to the reserve ☎ 5191 0042 or ☎ 2331 3579. A convenient if basic place to stay. The very hospitable family owners were cunning enough to nurture the habitat of the quetzal's favoured foods and nesting places, so it's now one of the prime places to view the plumed legend. They have a good *comedor* (meals Q20–30) and the breakfasts are legendary. <u>Q130</u>

INTO ALTA VERAPAZ

Beyond the Biotopo del Quetzal, Carretera 14 crosses into the department of Alta Verapaz. The first place of any size is **Tactic** – a small, mainly Poqomchi'-speaking town adjacent to the main road, which most buses pause at. The colonial **church** in the centre of the village, boasting a Baroque facade decorated with mermaids and jaguars, is worth a look, as is the Chi-Ixim chapel high above the town.

About 10km beyond Tactic is the turn-off for **San Cristóbal Verapaz**, a pretty town almost engulfed by fields of coffee and sugar cane, set on the banks of the Lago de Cristóbal. From here a (mostly) paved road continues to **Uspantán** in the western highlands.

COBÁN

Though not as visually impressive as other Guatemalan colonial cities, the welcoming mountain town of **COBÁN** is the perfect base for some fantastic day-trips to surrounding forests, rivers, caves and natural swimming pools. The town's microclimate is such that locals say that it rains for thirteen months a year here – heavy downpours are actually quite rare, but Cobán is famous for its drizzle (known as *chipi chipi*). Cobán is also an important coffee-growing centre; you can tour fincas that provide beans for the town's cafés.

WHAT TO SEE AND DO

There are several interesting attractions in and around town. Cobán is centred on an elevated **plaza**, with the **Cathedral** gracing its eastern side. The central area is divided into four zones, which are separated north–south by 1 Calle and east–west by 1 Avenida.

Finca Santa Margarita

For a closer look at Cobán's principal crop, take the guided tour offered by the **Finca Santa Margarita**, 3 C 4–12, Zona 2 (Mon–Fri 8am–12.30pm & 1.30–5pm, Sat 8am–noon; Q35), a coffee plantation just south of the centre of town. The interesting tour (in English or Spanish) covers the history of the finca, examining all the stages of cultivation and production. You also get a chance to sample the crop and, of course, buy some beans.

El Calvario

A short stroll northwest from the town centre on 3 Calle is the church of **El**

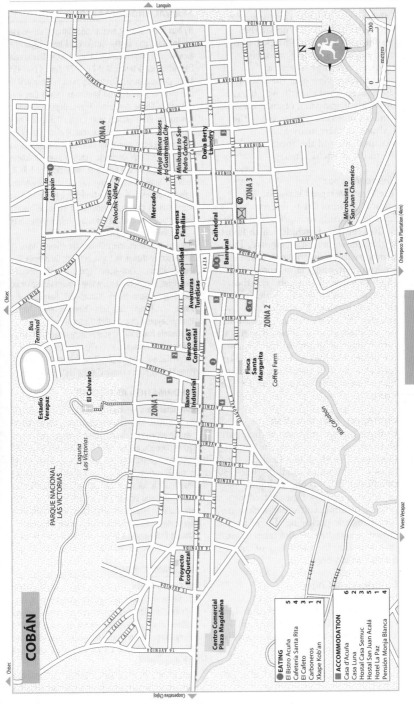

COBÁN

PARQUE NACIONAL
LAS VICTORIAS

Laguna
Las Victorias

Estadio
Verapaz

El Calvario

ZONA 1

Banco
Industrial

Banco G&T
Continental

Bus
Terminal

Buses to
Polochic Valley

Buses to
Lanquín

Mercado

Municipalidad

Aventuras
Turísticas

ZONA 4

Despensa
Familiar

Cathedral

Banrural

PLAZA

Doña Berty
Laundry

Monja Blanca buses
to Guatemala City

Minibuses to San
Pedro Carchá

ZONA 3

ZONA 2

Finca
Santa
Margarita
Coffee Farm

Río Cahabón

Microbuses to
San Juan Chamelco

Proyecto
EcoQuetzal

Centro Comercial
Plaza Magdalena

N

0   200
metres

Lanquín

Chixoc

Chixoc

Cooperativa Chijol

Chimpeco Tea Plantation (4km)

Vivero Verapaz

4

● EATING
El Bistro Acuña   5
Cafetería Santa Rita   4
El Cafeto   1
Carboneros   3
Xkape Kob'an   2

■ ACCOMMODATION
Casa d'Acuña   6
Casa Luna   2
Hostal Casa Semuc   3
Hostal San Juan Acalá   5
Hotel La Paz   1
Pensión Monja Blanca   4

4

Calvario, one of Cobán's most intriguing sights. Steep steps lead up via the Stations of the Cross – blackened by candle smoke and decorated with scattered offerings. There's a commanding view over the town from the whitewashed church, which has a distinctly pagan aura, often filled with candles, incense and corn cobs. The Calvario attracts many Maya worshippers, and the Sunday services are in the Q'eqchi language.

Vivero Verapaz

The **Vivero Verapaz** (Mon–Sat 9am–noon & 2–4pm; Q10), a former coffee finca just outside town, is now dedicated to the growing of **orchids**, which flourish in the sodden mountain climate. The plants are carefully grown in a shaded environment, and a farm worker will show you around and point out the most spectacular blooms, which are at their best between November and January. It's a forty-minute walk to the nursery: leave the plaza on Diagonal 4, turn left at the bottom of the hill, cross the bridge and follow the road for 3km; taxis charge Q20, or you can jump on a *micro* heading for **Tontem** from 3 Calle, Zona 2.

Chirrepeco Tea Plantation

Coffee is not the only crop in these parts, and 4km southeast of town the **Chirrepeco Tea Plantation** (daily 8am–4.30pm; tour including guide Q30; ⓦtechirrepeco.com) offers a highly enjoyable roundup of the tea farming process: planting, cultivation techniques, harvesting and packaging. There's a small museum, and the tour also takes in some caves sacred to the Maya and, of course, finishes with a brew.

Co-operativa Chijoj

Some 7km west of Cobán is the **Co-operativa Chijoj** (Mon–Fri 8am–4pm; Q50), a community-run coffee farm. Tours here include ziplining across a river and a full explanation of coffee production. To get here, take a *micro* heading west to **Chijoj** from 3 Calle, Zona 2 (Q2).

ARRIVAL AND DEPARTURE

By bus Unfortunately, most public transport arriving in Cobán drops you on the outskirts of town (with the exception of Monja Blanca buses to/from Guatemala City, which use a terminal at 2 C 3–77, Zona 4 (⊕7951 1793, ⓦtmb.com.gt). The muddy main bus terminal to the north of the city, also known as Campo Dos, has services to Chisec, Sayaxché, Flores, Uspantán, Nebaj, Salamá and Playa Grande. From Campo Dos it's a 20min walk (or Q20 taxi ride) to the central plaza. Buses for Lanquín use a bus stop at the junction of 3 Av and 6 C on the northeast side of town. For San Juan Chalmeco *micros* leave from the bridge at the bottom of 1 Av A, Zona 3. Note that the highway west to Uspantán suffered serious damage in a landslide a few years ago; *micros* still ply the road regularly, but it involves a scary descent down an unstable mountainside; services may not run during heavy rains.

Destinations Chisec (every 30min; 1hr 45min); Flores (1 daily, 1pm or change in Sayaxché; 6hr); Guatemala City (every 30min, 2am–6pm; 5hr); Lanquín (hourly, 6am–6pm; 2hr); Nebaj (1 daily, 5am or travel via Uspantán; 6hr); Playa Grande (every 30min; 4hr); Raxrujá (every 30min; 2hr 15min); San Juan Chalmeco (every 10min; 15min); Sayaxché (hourly; 4hr); Uspantán (hourly; 3hr).

By shuttle bus Book via your hotel or contact Aventuras Turísticas (see below).

Destinations Antigua (3 daily, 8am, 8.30am & 10am; 6hr); Flores (3 daily; 6hr); Lanquín (3 daily; 2hr).

INFORMATION AND TOURS

Tour operators Aventuras Turísticas, 1 C 3–25, Zona 1 (⊕7951 2008, ⓦaventurasturisticas.com), offers trips all over the Verapaces including Semuc Champey and Laguna Lachúa. Proyecto EcoQuetzal, 2 C 14–36, Zona 1 (⊕7952 1047, ⓦecoquetzal.org), arranges off-the-beaten-path treks to the Chicacnab cloudforest and boat trips along the beautiful Río Ik'Bolay; you stay with Q'eqchi communities and the income helps provide a sustainable living for villagers, who also serve as guides. Many of Cobán's hotels also provide tour services, with shuttles and trips to nearby attractions.

Tourist information There is no tourist office in town. Staff at *Casa Luna* are very helpful, however.

ACCOMMODATION

★ **Casa d'Acuña** 4 C 3–11, Zona 2 ⊕7951 0449, ⓦcasadeacuna.com. A wonderfully refined place to stay, with excellent four-bed dorms and a couple of private doubles (all with shared bathrooms) set to one side of a simply gorgeous courtyard restaurant (see opposite). Make sure you indulge in a meal while you're here. Dorm __Q55__, double __Q110__

Casa Luna 5 Av 2–28, Zona 1 ⊕7951 3528, ⓦcoban travels.com. This backpacker haunt is well run by Lionel, a fluent English-speaker, and his family. There are spacious rooms and a dorm (none with private bathroom) around a pleasant courtyard garden with hammocks, and there's a TV lounge. Tours and shuttle buses can be booked, and breakfast is included. Dorm <u>Q60</u>, double <u>Q160</u>

Hostal Casa Semuc 3 Av 2–12, Zona 2 ☎ 7951 4505. Just below the plaza, this hotel offers secure, high-quality budget accommodation in a lovely old house. There's a good dorm, plus eleven smallish, very clean private rooms with good mattresses. An airy guests' living room with sofas and PC access (Q5/hr) completes the picture. Dorm <u>Q55</u>, double <u>Q110</u>

Hostal San Juan Acalá 6 Av 2–50, Zona 3 ☎ 7952 1528. Dependable little hotel where cleanliness is taken very seriously. All the eleven rooms have good beds, highland blankets and wooden furniture, private bathroom and TV. <u>Q170</u>

Hotel La Paz 6 Av 2–19, Zona 1 ☎ 7952 1358. A safe, pleasant budget hotel, run by a very vigilant señora with clean rooms that face an open corridor or courtyard sitting areas. There's a small *comedor* downstairs. <u>Q115</u>

Pensión Monja Blanca 2 C 6–30, Zona 2 ☎ 7951 1900 or ☎ 7952 0531. Agreeably old-fashioned with plenty of inviting rooms, many with private bathrooms; the hot water is reliable. The courtyard gardens are lovingly tended, and don't miss the Victorian-style tearoom for breakfast. <u>Q165</u>

EATING

Cobán has a choice of excellent European-style restaurants and cafés and basic *comedores*. You'll find the cheapest food around the market, but as it's closed by dusk, in the evening you should head to the street stalls set up around the plaza.

Cafetería Santa Rita 2 C 1–36, Zona 2 ☎ 7952 1842. Classic, friendly *comedor* ideal for cheap, filling *comida típica*, including huge breakfasts. Daily 8am–8pm.

★ TREAT YOURSELF

El Bistro Acuña Casa d'Acuña 3 C 3–17, Zona 2 ☎ 7951 0449, ⓦ casadeacuna.com. One of Guatemala's most enjoyable and classy restaurants, with tables dotted around a lovely garden courtyard and more than one atmospheric dining room. It's fantastic for breakfast (from Q28), lunch or dinner, with mains costing Q60 for pasta up to around Q130 for exquisite fish and meat dishes. Informed, friendly waiters in starched white uniforms add to the refined appeal and the wine list includes many tempting half-bottles. Daily 8am–10pm.

El Cafeto 2 C 1–36, Zona 2 ☎ 7951 2850. Right on the plaza, this cosy little place serves coffee (from the local Chijoj finca) and is a good bet for breakfast: a traditional plate with two eggs, plantain and cream is Q18. Sandwiches, burgers, hot dogs and pastas are also served. Daily 7.30am–8pm.

Carboneros 6 C 3–40, Zona 4 ☎ 5000 9005. This suburban "Casa de Carne y Más" serves up delicious grilled meats cooked over charcoal at very moderate prices: plates of chicken, beef or pork are just Q20 or so. Daily 10am–9pm.

Xkape Koba'n Diagonal 4 5–13, Zona 2 ☎ 7951 4152. A wonderful, quirky café-restaurant in a gorgeous old house where the walls are decorated with *huipiles* and local art. There's a very inventive menu with snacks like *tamales* (Q15) and many local recipes including the famous local *kak-ik* turkey soup (Q60), and *kakaw-ik* (a chocolate milk drink flavoured with vanilla, chilli and honey). Mon–Sat 8am–6pm.

DIRECTORY

Cinema Inside Plaza Magdalena (at the western end of C 1).

Banks G&T Continental and Banco Industrial on 1 C west of the plaza both have ATMs.

Internet There's a good internet café inside the *Hostal Doña Victoria*, 3 C 2–38, Zona 3.

Language schools Cobán is a popular place to learn Spanish. Oxford Language Center, 4 Av 2–16, Zona 3 (ⓦ olcenglish.com), is well regarded and has attractive premises.

Laundry Doña Berty Laundry, 2 C 6–10, Zona 3 (daily until late); wash and dry service in 2hr for Q30.

Shopping The lively daily market is centred on the junction of 3 C & 1 Av at the meeting of zonas 1 & 3, and extends uphill to the streets behind the cathedral, where you can find cheap street food. For supermarket shopping head to Despensa Familiar just north of the cathedral, or Plaza Magdalena on the town's western outskirts. For souvenirs, *Casa d'Acuña* and *Xkape Kob'an* (see above) sell an excellent range of local crafts and produce, including several single-estate coffees.

AROUND COBÁN

The area surrounding Cobán is both craggy and lush, with limestone bedrock and a surface of patchwork fields. There are still some areas of forest, mainly to the southeast, but the Maya population of Alta Verapaz has turned most of the land over to the production of maize, coffee, cardamom and ferns. It's worth venturing into this rural heartland of Guatemala to explore traditional market towns and their surrounding villages, as well as fresh-water swimming pools and stalactite caves.

San Juan Chamelco

A few kilometres southeast of Cobán, easily reached by regular *micros*, **SAN JUAN CHAMELCO** is the most important Q'eqchi' settlement in the area. However, Chamelco's focal point is its hilltop **church**, a huge, open-plan space with timber-frame roof and several Jesus effigies with bloody stigmata. The best time to visit the village is the week preceding its annual **fiesta** (June 23), when celebrations include folk dancing in traditional dress and the arrival of numerous saints from neighbouring San Pedro Carchá, brought to greet the holy effigies from Chamelco's own church.

Just outside Chamelco are the **Grutas del Rey Marcos**, an extensive cave network (daily 7am–5pm; Q40, including the services of a guide, hard hat and boot rental). You can take a tour that explores up to 100m into the caverns, which are full of stalagmites that uncannily resemble various familiar objects. To reach the caves, catch a *micro* from the church in Chamelco headed for Santa Cecilia.

Microbuses congregate behind the church on the hilltop and head to Cobán and the surrounding Maya villages.

Ecocentro Sataña

On the road to Chisec, half an hour outside Cobán, is the **Ecocentro Sataña** (daily 9am–5pm; Q20), a bathing complex that includes both natural and man-made swimming pools in a jungle setting, with gardens and picnic areas as well as a restaurant at weekends. Take any *micro* headed to Chisec.

Balneario las Islas

At the town of San Pedro Carchá, 5km east of Cobán, is the **Balneario las Islas**, another natural pool with a river tumbling into it. To get to Carchá there are regular departures from the car park opposite the Monja Blanca terminal in Cobán. The Balneario is about fifteen minutes east of town – locals should be able to direct you.

LANQUÍN

From Cobán a paved road heads east, almost as far as the Q'eqchi' village of **LANQUÍN** (the last 11km are along a painfully slow and bumpy dirt track). The journey is stunningly beautiful, in spite of the evident deforestation – sit on the right side of the bus for the best views. The nearby natural wonder of **Semuc Champey** is now well and truly on the backpacker trail, and consequently some excellent accommodation and activity options have sprung up. Most visitors stay at least two nights (either in Lanquín or around Semuc), with weekends and holidays being especially busy.

WHAT TO SEE AND DO

Lanquín itself is a sleepy place, superbly sheltered beneath towering green hills.

Grutas de Lanquín

As you enter Lanquín from Cobán you pass the impressive cave system, the **Grutas de Lanquín** (daily 8am–6pm; Q30), from where the Río Lanquín emerges. You should refrain from using flash photography inside (or outside) the cave as it unsettles the bats that live here. At dusk every day thousands fly out of the cave to feed – you can watch them for free from the entrance car park or anywhere along the riverbank. Tubing down the river from the cave is very popular and a blissful way to experience a tropical river; all the hostels organize tours – after heavy rains the river can be fairly feisty.

ARRIVAL AND DEPARTURE

By bus Buses arriving from Cobán (roughly hourly) pass the central junction in the village and continue to Cahabón (1hr 15min). Buses also struggle north between the Pajal junction and Fray Bartolomé de Las Casas (every 90min; 3hr) via a rough road, though ongoing road improvements will speed up this route again in the next few years; check with your hotel for the latest information. Buses for Cobán (roughly hourly; 2hr) depart from the central junction.

By shuttle bus Note that service standards on the shuttle bus routes is poor, and minibuses are usually packed and uncomfortable. Coming from Antigua involves travelling at night (which is not recommended). On arrival in Lanquín, don't listen to what local hustlers tell you about places (like *Zephyr* that don't pay commission) being full. There's also one daily 4WD shuttle minibus to Río Dulce Town (Q160).

Destinations Antigua (3 daily; 8hr 30min); Cobán (3–4 daily; 2hr); Flores (2 daily; 9hr).

INFORMATION AND TOURS

Bank and exchange Banrural, just south of the Parque, changes dollars. Many lodges will give you a cash advance (for a hefty commission of around 7 percent).

Tour operators Most of the lodges offer tours, including tubing down the Río Lanquín (Q50) and Semuc (Q170 including entrance).

Tourist information *El Retiro* and *Zephyr Lodge* offer good practical information.

ACCOMMODATION AND EATING

Comedor Shalom In the village. An excellent local place with three or four daily-changing set-meal deals (Q20–30), friendly local staff and clean surrounds. Daily 7am–8pm.

Posada Ilobal Beyond the market in the village centre ☎ 7983 0014. Locally owned, with five simple, clean and airy rooms with shared bathroom, some with valley views, this is a good option if you'd rather not be surrounded by gangs of gap-year students. There's a nice garden, too. Q90

La Poza Riverside Guesthouse A 15min walk east of Lanquín ☎ 4685 5766, ✉ lapoza@rocketmail.com. Stunning four-bedroom riverside house that's a great deal for groups, with a deck overlooking the Río Lanquín, tubes, table tennis, a sauna and extensive grounds. There are discounts for longer stays. House Q700

El Retiro On the banks of the Río Lanquín ☎ 4513 6396, ⓦ elretirolanquin.com. This near-legendary riverside lodge has undergone a change of ownership and standards have slipped somewhat. The setting remains lovely, however, and accommodation is well designed, consisting of four-bed dorms, cabins and rooms, some with private bathrooms. Tubing and hiking trips are offered and buffet-style dinners are served. Dorm Q45, double Q100

★ **Zephyr Lodge** Down a little dirt lane, just north of village centre ☎ 5168 2441, ⓦ zephyrlodgelanquin.com. Top dog in Lanquín, this expertly designed hostel-lodge sits pretty on a hill with stunning views over the Lanquín river valley and evergreen Verapaz hills. All the accommodation has character and comfort, staff are switched on and the food is great, with plenty of veggie choices. Cocktails are the best in town. It's a sociable place with a good balance between bar action and tranquillity. Reserve ahead – it's usually full. Dorm Q45, double Q150

PARQUE NACIONAL SEMUC CHAMPEY

One of the most beautiful natural destinations in Guatemala, **SEMUC CHAMPEY** (daily 8am–6pm; Q50), 12km southeast of Lanquín, is a shallow staircase of sublime turquoise pools suspended on a natural limestone bridge. This idyllic spot sits at the base of a towering jungle-clad valley and makes a wonderful destination for a blissful day's wallowing and swimming. Just a few years ago very few visitors made it to this remote part of Guatemala, but the secret is now definitely out, and the pools are very much a key stop on the backpacking trail between Tikal and the western highlands. That said, you can usually find a peaceful corner without too much difficulty. Most travellers choose to visit Semuc as part of a **tour**, which avoids having to wait for infrequent public transport.

There are security guards at the site, but it's best not to leave your belongings unattended. You'll find a small café (reasonable meals are around Q40) and there are vendors selling drinks and snacks at the entrance.

ARRIVAL AND DEPARTURE

By pick-up To get to Semuc Champey without a tour you'll need to catch a pick-up or truck from Lanquín (roughly hourly until 4pm; 45min).

ACCOMMODATION

El Portal 100m from Semuc ☎ 5319 6848, ⓦ hostalelportaldechampey.com. Community-owned

---

THE KAN'BA CAVES

It's well worth a visit to the privately owned **KAN'BA CAVES** (guided tour only, 8am, 10am, 1pm & 3pm; Q50), on the riverbank close to the entrance to the Semuc Champey National Park. Best for adrenaline junkies, tours here are run without hard hats and torches – you swim one-handed while holding stubby candles aloft. Sharp rocks and slippery surfaces add to this treacherous assault course, which will leave you shivering and happy to emerge into the daylight. Some tubing is usually included at the end of the tour.

lodge that enjoys an elevated plot with fine views down to the Río Cahabón. The accommodation is inviting, with well-built screened wood cabañas with hammocks and balcony, cosy private rooms and an eight-bed dorm. Bathrooms are well presented. There's great birding and good food but electricity is only 6–10pm. Tubing and other trips are offered. Dorm Q40, double Q90

Utopia Eco Hotel 3km before Semuc ☎ 3135 8329, ⊛ utopiaecohotel.com. Terrific new ecolodge in a remote, beautiful location that enjoys a lovely riverside plot on the banks of the Cahabón. There's rustic accommodation and camping, inexpensive (vegetarian only) food, a communal vibe and lots to do including hikes, tubing and Spanish lessons. Dorm Q40, double Q100, cabin sleeping two Q300

CHISEC

CHISEC is a small town, bisected from north to south by CA-14. There's not much here – in fact, the huge plaza seems to account for half the town. However, it makes a convenient base for visiting nearby attractions and has several hotels.

WHAT TO SEE AND DO

Just outside Chisec are a couple of wonderful natural attractions.

B'omb'il Pek

Some 2km north of town, with an office on the highway, is the entrance to the **B'omb'il Pek** caves, accessible on community-run tours (daily 8am–3pm; 2hr; Q80). The first "cave" is actually a sinkhole, with vertical sides clad in jungle. You can rappel down (for an extra Q25), or use a slippery wooden staircase. Maya ceremonies are performed here. The second cave is only accessed via a tiny entrance, which you'll have to squeeze through horizontally; those with a larger physique will not be able to make it. Inside there's an ancient painting of two monkeys, thought to represent the hero twins of the Popol (see p.313). A pleasant addition to the tour involves inner tubing for thirty minutes (Q30) on the nearby **Río San Simón**, which cuts a tiny gorge through the rock. Very regular *micros* pass the tour office on the highway, shuttling between Chisec and Raxrujá.

Lagunas Sepalau

Some 10km east of Chisec are the beautiful **Lagunas Sepalau** (daily 7am–5pm; Q60 including guide). Set among a protected forest reserve, these three lovely lagoons are ringed by towering rainforest. Guides escort you along a trail, pointing out wildlife (iguanas and monkeys are sometimes seen) and medicinal plants, and can provide you with canoes for paddling across the lakes. The pristine lake waters are perfect for swimming. To get here from Chisec either catch the 10am microbus or hitch a ride with a pick-up (Q5). There's more traffic returning in the afternoon, when you shouldn't have to wait too long for a ride.

ARRIVAL AND DEPARTURE

By micro From Cobán, *micros* run right past the plaza, then continue north past *La Estancia*.

Destinations Cobán (every 30min; 1hr 45min); Playa Grande (hourly; 2hr); Raxrujá (every 30min; 30min). Some northbound *micros* also continue on to Sayaxché.

ACCOMMODATION AND EATING

Café La Huella On the main road, just off the north side of the plaza. A decent *comedor* providing filling meals and carb attacks. Reckon on Q25 for lunch or dinner; breakfast is less. Daily 7am–8pm.

Hotel La Estancia 700m north of the centre ☎ 5514 7444, ⊛ hotelestanciadelavirgen.com. Huge concrete hotel with four floors of plain, functional rooms with cable TV and either a/c or fan. There's a good restaurant and small swimming pool. Q150

Restaurante Bombil Pek On the highway, at the southern end of the village ☎ 4853 3565. Large, clean, welcoming place, excellent for something a little more fancy than *comida típica* – try the fish. Around Q35–50 a meal. Daily 7.30am–8.30pm.

RAXRUJÁ

The small town of **RAXRUJÁ** provides a handy base for visiting the nearby **Candelaria cave network** and the Maya ruins of **Cancuén**. The town itself, however, is no beauty: little more than a sprawl of buildings along the roadside, centred at the junction where the paved road ends and rough tracks lead to La Unión and **Fray Bartolomé de las Casas**.

ARRIVAL AND DEPARTURE

The direct road south to the Pajal junction (for Lanquín) is steadily being upgraded and paved. When finished, it'll be a short cut to Semuc Champey.

By micro *Micros* to and from Cobán (every 30min; 2hr 15min) via Chisec (30min); Playa Grande (hourly; 2hr 15min); and Sayaxché (every 90min; 2hr 30min).

ACCOMMODATION AND EATING

Doña Reyna Just north of the main junction in the centre. It looks a bit grim and dark from the street, but the food (meals from Q20) is fresh, tasty and filling. Daily 6.30am–9pm.

★ **Hotel Cancuén** Towards the western end of town ☎ 5764 0478, ⓦ cuevaslosnacimientos.com. Excellent place with broad selection of fine-value, clean, neat rooms; bathrooms have cold water in the cheaper options, but as this is a tropical-hot town, that won't matter. Dr César, the friendly owner, also offers great tours to the Cuevas de los Nacimientos (see below) and to Cancuén ruins. There's a small *comedor* on site, plus internet access (Q10/hr). **Q55**

AROUND RAXRUJÁ

The limestone hills around Raxrujá are riddled with **cave** networks and subterranean rivers. Also nearby is the rarely visited Maya ruin of **Cancuén**.

The Candelaria caves

Forming a core section of 22km, the spectacular **Candelaria cave system** is the longest underground complex in Latin America. (If subsidiary streams, galleries and systems are included then it measures more than 80km.) It's quite straightforward to visit part of this cave network, but rather confusingly, there are four possible entrances. Two are community run (**Candelaria Camposanto** and **Mucbilha'**) and two – the most impressive sections – are privately owned (**Cuevas de Candelaria** and **Cuevas de los Nacimientos**).

The Cuevas de Candelaria contain some truly monumental caverns, including the 200m-long Tzul Tacca cave. To reach this cave complex, hop on a *micro* heading west from Raxrujá. At the large "Cuevas de Candelaria" sign, about 5km from town, a path leads south towards a resort complex containing some overpriced rustic bungalows. You don't have to be a guest to visit the caves. A one-hour group tour on foot is Q30 per person, or by inner tube Q100. Usually you can tag

onto a group if they have one visiting and simply pay per head. Otherwise, you need a minimum of three to obtain the above rates.

Hotel Cancuén in Raxrujá (see above) offers a full-day tour (Q150; minimum four people) to Los Nacimientos (ⓦ cuevaslosnacimientos.com), where you can visit the crystalline Cueva Blanca, as well as float for several hours through creepy bat-filled caverns on a tube.

Cancuén

North of Raxrujá is the large Maya site of **CANCUÉN** (daily 8am–4pm; Q50), where a huge Classic-era palace, which had 170 rooms, has been unearthed. You can also see the remains of an impressive bathing pool (which was used for ritual purification). Uniquely, Cancuén seems to have lacked the usual religious and defensive structures characteristic of Maya cities, instead existing as an essentially secular trading city. The vast amounts of jade, pyrite, obsidian and fine ceramics found recently indicate that this was actually one of the greatest trading centres of the Maya world, with a paved plaza (which may have been a marketplace) covering two square kilometres. Cancuén is thought to have flourished because of its strategic position between the great cities of the lowlands, like Tikal and Calakmul, and the mineral-rich highlands of southern Guatemala. There's a trail with good information panels (in English), and a visitors' centre.

ARRIVAL AND DEPARTURE

By pick-up and lancha To get to Cancuén, pick-ups (approximately hourly) leave Raxrujá for the *aldea* of La Unión, 12km to the north, where boatmen will take you by *lancha* for the 30min ride along the Río Pasión to the site. Unfortunately it's an expensive trip – around Q300 for the whole boat – but it can accommodate up to sixteen people. It's also possible to travel via the village of La Isla, but connections here are not as good.

PARQUE NACIONAL LAGUNA LACHUÁ

In the far northwest corner of Alta Verapaz is the frontier town of Playa Grande and the nearby natural attraction

4

of **PARQUE NACIONAL LAGUNA LACHUÁ** (daily 7am–4pm; Q40; ☎7861 0086), a sublime spot to get off the beaten track for a day or two of tranquillity and swimming in pristine water. The lake is a near-perfect circle of crystal water, ringed by a tropical forest reserve that's home to a host of wildlife, including jaguars, ocelots, otters and tapirs.

ARRIVAL AND INFORMATION

By bus The road is completely paved between Cobán and the entrance to Lachúa. From Cobán *micros* bound for Playa Grande pass the entrance (every 30min; 2hr 45min), and there are fast links from both Chisec and Raxrujá.

Visitors' centre You pay your entrance fee and accommodation costs at the visitors' centre on the road. It is also possible to leave your backpack here and take just a smaller bag on the sweaty 4km walk through the jungle to the lakeside lodge.

ACCOMMODATION

Park accommodation The scrupulously maintained national park provides camping facilities and a lodge with mosquito-netted bunks. There are good cooking facilities and drinking water, but you need to bring your own food. Camping <u>Q25</u>, lodge <u>Q50</u>

Petén

The low-lying northern department of **Petén**, once the Maya heartland, occupies about a third of Guatemala's territory but is home to just three percent of its population. In the last thirty years there has been a wave of immigration to the area, initially encouraged by the government in an attempt to cultivate this wild land. Vast swathes of rainforest have been cleared for ranching and commercial logging, despite the fact that forty percent of the department is officially protected by the **Maya Biosphere Reserve**. However, most sights of note are at least still shrouded in jungle, and you will doubtless witness some of Petén's remarkable wildlife.

Petén also boasts an incredible number of **Maya sites** – several hundred ruined cities have been mapped in the region, though most are still buried beneath the forest. The superstar attraction is **Tikal**, but other, less-visited highlights include

atmospheric **Yaxhá** and the immense **El Mirador**.

The lakeside towns of **Flores** and **Santa Elena** form the hub of the department, while to the east is the peaceful alternative base of **El Remate**. The caves and scenery around **Poptún**, on the main highway south, also justify exploration, while down the other road south, **Sayaxché** is surrounded by yet more Maya sites.

POPTÚN AND AROUND

Heading north from the Río Dulce the paved highway to Flores cuts through a degraded landscape of small *milpa* farms and cattle ranches that was jungle a few decades ago. Many travellers choose to stop along the way at the sublime *Finca Ixobel* (see below) outside the small town of **POPTÚN**. There's no particular reason to stay in the town itself, but you may well pause to top up the finances (there are several banks with ATMs). The area **around Poptún** also offers excellent opportunities to visit little-known attractions, including the Naj Tunich caves, Las Cataratas waterfalls near the village of Mopán and the minor archeological sites of El Chal, Ixcún and Ixtontón.

ARRIVAL AND DEPARTURE

By bus and minibus Minibuses shuttle between Poptún and Santa Elena (for Flores) until 6.30pm, while a constant stream of buses and minibuses heads south to Río Dulce and on to Guatemala City all day and night.

Destinations Guatemala City (every 30min; 7hr) via Río Dulce Town; Santa Elena (every 30min; 1hr 45min).

ACCOMMODATION

★ **Finca Ixobel** About 5km south of Poptún ☎5410 4307, ⓦfincaixobel.com. Surrounded by pine forests in the foothills of the Maya Mountains, this working farm doubles as an idyllic lodge for travellers, a supremely beautiful and relaxing place where you can swim in the pond, walk in the forest and stuff yourself with delicious (mostly organic and home-grown) food. The finca is run ecologically, using solar power. You run a tab (dinner costs Q35–60), paying when you leave – which can be a rude awakening. There's hiking, horseriding (Q100), tubing, cave excursions (Q40) and trips to Naj Tunich and Ixcun ruins. Microbuses and chicken buses will drop you off at the entrance gate from where it's a 15min walk; after dark, take a tuk-tuk from Poptún (Q15). Dorm <u>Q40</u>, double <u>Q120</u>, tree house <u>Q120</u>

FLORES AND SANTA ELENA

Despite the legions of tourists that pass through, the charming town of **FLORES** – gateway to the Mundo Maya and the capital of Petén – has retained an easy pace and a sedate, old-world atmosphere. This tiny island (joined by a 500m causeway to the shore) on Lago de Petén Itzá has historically been a natural point of settlement. It remained the capital of the Itzá Maya until 1697, when the Spanish finally forced the town (then known as Tayasal) under their control. Across the causeway, **SANTA ELENA** and adjoining San Benito are home to the gritty business of Guatemalan life, with sprawling markets and multiple hardware stores.

Flores boasts the lion's share of quality restaurants and decent budget accommodation, while Santa Elena is the region's transport hub and home to several banks and characterless expensive hotels. You will inevitably pass through Santa Elena on your way in and out of Flores, but there is no particular reason to visit here other than to check out the market, which chaotically surrounds the old (still partly used) bus terminal.

ARRIVAL AND DEPARTURE

By plane The airport is 3km east of the causeway. Tuk-tuks/taxis charge Q20 for a ride between the airport and town.

Destinations Belize City (3 daily; 45min) – two with Tropic Air (☎ 7926 0348, ␍ tropicair.com), one with TAG (☎ 2360 3038; ␍ tag.com.gt; Cancún (1 daily, TAG; 1hr 30min); Guatemala City (3 daily; 50min; around Q1800 return); two with TACA (☎ 2470 8222, ␍ taca.com), one with TAG (demand is heavy for these flights in peak periods, and over-booking is common. Reserve well in advance and arrive promptly for check-in). A direct daily flight to Palenque, Mexico, is also planned by TAG.

By bus You'll be dropped off at Santa Elena's large modern Terminal Nuevo on 6 Av, about 2km south of the causeway. Some local buses also use bus stops at the market in Santa

FLORES' COYOTES

Many travellers experience the hard sell on arrival in Flores from local ticket touts, known as **coyotes**. These guys know every trick in the book to persuade you to spend your money with them. Be especially aware on tourist shuttles arriving from Belize and Mexico, when you are likely to be travel-weary and green (ie, new to the country). Most *coyotes* speak excellent English and will bamboozle you with their seemingly exhaustive knowledge of your future travel options. Many susceptible backpackers are persuaded to book hotel rooms, tours and onward travel arrangements before even setting foot on Flores Island. In some cases *coyotes* have been found selling completely fake tickets; even if you do receive the service you've paid for, you will almost certainly have paid over the odds, as *coyotes* take a cut. Always buy tickets from a legitimate tour operator or hotel staff, and don't hurry – if you shop around you're likely to get the best price and service.

Elena, and San Juan Travel have their own private terminal on 6 Av in Santa Elena.

Destinations from Terminal Nuevo Belize City (1 daily, 7am, Línea Dorada; 5hr); Chiquimula (5 daily; 7hr 30min); El Ceibo border (12 daily; 4hr); El Remate (every 30min; 45min); Guatemala City (3 daily, 11am, 9pm & 10pm, with ADN; 3 daily, 10am, 9pm & 9.30pm, with Línea Dorada; 16 daily with Fuente del Norte; 2 daily with Rápidos del Sur; 9hr); La Técnica via Bethel (5 daily; 4hr 30min); Melchor de Menchos (*micros* every 30min; 2hr 15min); Poptún (hourly; 2hr); San Pedro Sula, Honduras (1 daily, 5.45am, with Fuente del Norte; 2 daily, 6am & 10am, with María Elena; 12–14hr); San Salvador (1 daily, 5.45am, with Fuente del Norte; 12hr); Sayaxché (every 30min; 2hr); Tikal (6 daily; 1hr 30min); Uaxactún (2 daily; 2hr 30min). Most buses to Guatemala City stop in both Poptún and Río Dulce en route. For Copán in Honduras catch a bus heading for San Pedro Sula. There are also some services around Lago de Petén Itzá, to San Andrés and San José from here.

Destinations from Market terminal Carmelita (2 daily, 5am & 1pm; around 3hr); San Andrés (every 45min; 30min); San José (every 45min; 35min). There are also buses to destinations across Petén, including Poptún and Sayaxché, from here.

By shuttle bus You can book shuttle buses through hotels and travel agents.

Destinations Belize City (2 daily, 5am & 7.30am; 5hr; Q160); Chetumal (1 daily, 5am; 8hr; Q275); Lanquín via Cobán (2 daily; 9hr; Q125); Palenque (1 daily, 5am; 8hr; Q240); Tikal (1hr; Q70 return).

GETTING AROUND

Canoes *La Villa del Chef* (see p.362) rents canoes for Q20/hr.

Lanchas You can hop across to the Tayasal Peninsula by *lancha* for a quetzal or two; they run on a regular basis until 11pm from the dock on Flores' northeast shore. Boatmen also offer easy and half-day trips to explore the lake by *lancha*. They tend to hang out around the southwest corner of the island, close to *Hotel Petenchel* and near the dock for San Miguel. Look for Miguel, who was born in Flores in 1925 and has some great stories.

Taxis and tuk-tuks For short hops, tuk-tuk drivers charge Q5–10 for anywhere in the Flores/Santa Elena/San Benito area.

INFORMATION AND TOURS

Tourist information There's no shortage of information sources in Flores, but be careful who you listen to as there

TOUR OPERATORS IN FLORES

Flores has dozens of tour operators, many of them pretty average. For **Tikal**, it's easiest to book your bus via your hotel, as no matter who you book with you're likely to end up on a shuttle operated by San Juan Travel, 6 Av, Santa Elena (☎5847 4729). This agency does not have the best reputation, but has recently improved; however, it's best to just use them for shuttle buses only. Three of the best agencies are:

Martsam Travel C 30 Junio ☎7867 5093, ⓦmartsam.com. Trips to sites including Waka' (El Perú), Yaxhá and Aguateca.

Mayan Adventure Inside *Café Arqueológico Yaxhá*, C 15 de Septiembre ☎5830 2060, ⓦthe-mayan -adventure.com. Superb trips to Yaxhá and La Blanca

(Q370/person for four people) and ruins including Nakúm, San Clemente and Nixtun Ch'ich'.

Turismo Aventura 6 Av & 4 C, Santa Elena ☎7926 0398, ⓦtoursguatemala.com. A good all-rounder with tours to many Maya ruins in Petén, and also cheap airline tickets.

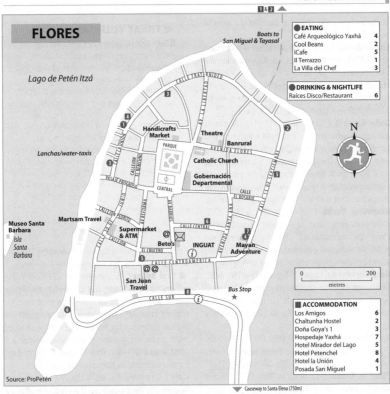

FLORES

Lago de Petén Itzá

Boats to
San Miguel & Tayasal

Lanchas/water-taxis

Handicrafts
Market

Theatre

Banrural

PARQUE

AVENIDA FLORES

Catholic Church

Gobernación
Departmental

CALLE
EL ROSARIO

CENTRAL

Museo Santa
Barbara

*Isla
Santa
Barbara*

Martsam Travel

Supermarket
& ATM

Beto's

INGUAT

Mayan
Adventure

San Juan
Travel

Bus Stop

CALLE SUR

Causeway to Santa Elena (750m)

Source: ProPetén

● EATING

Café Arqueológico Yaxhá	4
Cool Beans	2
iCafe	5
Il Terrazzo	1
La Villa del Chef	3

● DRINKING & NIGHTLIFE

Raíces Disco/Restaurant	6

N

0	200
	metres

■ ACCOMMODATION

Los Amigos	6
Chaltunha Hostel	2
Doña Goya's 1	3
Hospedaje Yaxhá	7
Hotel Mirador del Lago	5
Hotel Petenchel	8
Hotel la Unión	4
Posada San Miguel	1

4

SANTA ELENA

Maya
Mall

1 CALLE

San Juan
Travel

SANTA
ELENA

Turismo
Aventura

SAN
BENITO

CALLE PRINCIPAL

Banco
Agromercantil (ATM)

Banco Industrial
(ATM)

Market

Terminal
Viejo

Airport, Tikal & Belize

Terminal Nuevo (500m)

are *coyotes* about (see box opposite). *Los Amigos* hostel is probably the best source of advice for budget travellers. Otherwise Inguat has an office on C Centro América (Mon–Fri 8am–4pm; ☎2421 2957) and a desk at the airport (Mon–Sat 7.30–11am & 3.30–7.30pm).

ACCOMMODATION

There are several good budget places in Flores itself, making it unnecessary to stay in noisier and dirtier Santa Elena. For even more tranquillity, try sleepy San Miguel just across the lake.

Los Amigos C Central ☎7867 5975, ☜amigoshostel .com. Flores' main backpacker base has plus points including the courtyard garden, sociable vibe, inexpensive rates, veggie food, free wi-fi, DVD collection, secure charge points for mobile phones and travel advice. Not so great are the cramped dorms and rooms, cleanliness (ashtrays are rarely emptied), slowish service and the 4am Tikal tour exodus every morning (forget all thoughts of a peaceful lie-in). Dorm Q45, double Q110

Chaltunha Hostel Across the lake in San Miguel village ☎4219 0851, 🌐chaltunhahostel.com. You get a welcoming vibe and stunning lake views at this hotel in sleepy San Miguel, with comfortable screened rooms, basic dorms, good cooking and excellent travel advice. Call the owner for a free boat pick-up from Flores. Dorm Q75, double Q230

Doña Goya's 1 C La Unión ☎7867 5513, 📧hospeda jedonagoya@yahoo.com. Budget hotel offering no-frills but spacious dorms and reasonably large doubles (you pay more for a view). The rooftop terrace is a huge bonus and you'll find a small breakfast room and computers with internet downstairs. A second branch of *Doña Goya's* is 20m around the corner. Both have wi-fi. Dorm Q35, double Q80

Hospedaje Yaxhá C 15 Septiembre ☎5830 2060, 🌐cafeyaxha.com. Good new budget accommodation above the recommended *Café Arqueológico Yaxhá* restaurant with well-presented clean rooms, all with private bathroom, powerful fans and free wi-fi. Q100

Hotel Mirador del Lago C 15 Septiembre ☎7867 5409. Basic rooms have fan, screened windows and bathroom but no view; those facing the lake also have cable TV. Plus inexpensive water refills, friendly staff, internet, laundry service and a small restaurant. Q80

Hotel Petenchel C Sur ☎7867 5450. This little place has a row of good, clean, double rooms with hot-water bathroom, fan and TV. There's a little café here, too. Q125

Hotel la Unión C La Unión ☎7867 5531. Offering excellent value, this well-maintained hotel has clean, bright rooms with private bathroom and fan. Those with direct lake views cost a bit extra. Q100

Posada San Miguel Across the lake in San Miguel village ☎7867 5312, 📧posadasanmiguel1@gmail.com. Delightful family-run posada that represents great value. Large lakeside rooms have attractive furnishings, private bathroom, TV and stunning views. There is a small beach directly out front and a simple *comedor* downstairs. *Lanchas* connect San Miguel with Flores every few minutes. Q125

EATING AND DRINKING

You'll find a good selection of restaurants in Flores, though prices are high compared to the rest of Guatemala. Be aware that some local restaurants still serve wild game (such as *venado*, *pavo silvestre*, *coche de monte* or *tepescuintle*) – this is best avoided, as it is most likely to be poached from reserves. For economical eats, head for the stalls on the plaza (7am–10pm).

★ **Café Arqueológico Yaxhá** C 15 Septiembre ☎5830 2060, 🌐cafeyaxha.com. An interesting café, with a menu that boasts many pre-Hispanic dishes of Maya origin using ingredients like yucca and squash (most mains Q40–60). The walls are covered with posters and photos relating to local Maya sites, to which Dieter, the German owner, runs

excellent tours. Evening slide shows about the Maya are well worth attending too. Free wi-fi. Daily 7am–9pm.

★ **Cool Beans** C 15 Septiembre ☎5571 9240. A fine café-restaurant with tables that spill down to the lakeside garden. They're trying a lot harder than most here: the excellent breakfasts feature home-made bread and jam and real butter, sandwiches are huge (try the shredded carrot, bacon and guacamole) and mains are delicious (most around Q40–60). They also serve draught beer, espresso coffee and cocktails. Mon–Sat 7am–10pm.

iCafé C Centro América. Yes, it looks like a Guatemalan *Starbucks* but this is a good spot if you're after a coffee – a full selection includes frappaccinos, and they also offer chai tea, smoothies and cakes (try the cheesecake pie). Daily 7am–8.30pm.

Raíces Disco/Restaurant Western end of C Sur ☎5521 1843. The restaurant is a pricey affair that packs in the tour groups but the bar-disco is the only game in town for dance floor action. Sun–Thurs 8am–10pm, Fri & Sat till 1am.

La Villa del Chef C La Unión, Flores ☎7926 0296. Elegant place with a lovely vista over the lake from its huge windows and terrace seating. Food presentation, portions and quality are very good: both the beef and veggie burgers are wonderfully flavoursome, or try the lake fish. Watch out for extra charges for bread and water (at least profits benefit development projects in Petén). Popular for happy hour drinks (like vodka mango, Q10). Daily 7am–10pm.

DIRECTORY

Banks In Flores, there's an ATM inside the supermarket on C 30 de Junio. You'll find many more banks in Santa Elena, including Banco Agromercantil junction on 6 Av and 4 C, which has an ATM. There's also an ATM inside the Terminal Nuevo bus station.

INTO BELIZE: MELCHOR DE MENCOS

There is regular transport from Santa Elena to the **Belize** border at **Melchor de Mencos** (every 30min; 2hr 15min) from the Terminal Nuevo; most buses make a stop in the market area on their way west. It is also possible to take direct services to Belize City and beyond (see p.359). The border is fairly straightforward, although you'll probably be charged a Q20 unofficial exit tax. Moneychangers should give you a fair rate. Once in Belize you'll need to take a taxi (US$3) for the short journey to Benque Viejo del Carmen, from where it's a thirty-minute bus journey to the pleasant town of San Ignacio, or three hours to Belize City (last bus leaves at 6pm).

Health Centro Médico Maya, 4 Av near 3 C, Santa Elena (☏ 7926 0180), is a professional place, and some staff speak a little English.

Internet and telephone There are several internet cafés along C Centroamérica. The best are Petén Net and Tikal Net, which have fast connections and discounted international phone calls.

Language schools Academia de Español Dos Mundos (c/o *Café Yaxhá*; ☏ 5830 2060, ⓦ flores-spanish.com) has one-on-one, group and crash courses in Spanish. On the other side of the lake, the villages of San José and San Andrés (see box, p.364) also have schools.

Laundry Cheapest is Beto's on Av Barrios (wash and dry Q25). Since he runs sunrise tours to Tikal, the shop is often closed until noon.

Shopping As well as the plethora of tourist shops, there is a handicrafts market on the Parque Central (9am–9pm).

LAGO DE PETÉN ITZÁ

While the majority of visitors to Flores rightly prioritize a visit to Tikal, there is a string of other worthwhile day-trip excursions in the region surrounding **LAGO DE PETÉN ITZÁ**.

From Flores it's possible to visit a number of nearby attractions by *lancha*. The tiny **museum** (daily 9am–5pm; Q10), on an island just off Flores' western shores, houses a collection of Maya pottery, while at **ARCAS**, an animal rescue NGO 5km east of San Miguel village (daily 8am–4pm; Q50; ⓦ arcasguatemala.com), you can volunteer and learn about wildlife protection in Petén, walk an interpretive trail and view animals that cannot be released into the wild. Beyond ARCAS, the **Petencito Zoo** (daily 8am–5pm; Q25) is home to (among others) crocodiles, tigers and some zippy – though dodgy – waterslides. For the best *lancha* prices you'll need to get a group together and haggle fairly fiercely. Estimate about Q100/hr.

Peninsula Tayasal

Incredibly, this attractive peninsula, just a five-minute *lancha* ride across the lake from Flores, is largely overlooked by the tourist dollars flooding into that town. The village of **San Miguel** and nearby **El Mirador** and **Playita El Chechenal** make for an easy excursion. Regular *lanchas* leave from the northeast shores of Flores to San Miguel. To reach the *mirador* it's a twenty-minute, fairly isolated walk. Follow the lakeshore west past the village, turn uphill after the last buildings, then follow the track up until it evens out to a shaded trail and take the left branch (keeping the lake to your left). Eventually you'll reach a clearing from where concrete steps lead up to the wooden lookout tower. There are fantastic views of the lake and its settlements. Back down at the clearing you can follow another trail for ten minutes around the northern side of the peninsula (keeping the lake to your left), until you reach a signposted left turn for La Playita. You can see the turquoise water beckoning you and there is a quiet beach area with picnic benches and toilets. To return to San Miguel village, simply turn left at the end of the beach road and follow the track for fifteen minutes to complete your circuit.

Grutas Ak'tun caves

Just north south of Santa Elena, past the bus terminal, is the entrance to the **Grutas Ak'tun-Kan**, or serpent caves (daily 8am–5pm; Q20). Bring your own torch and decent shoes, as the interior is dark and pretty slippery. The cave comprises a series of small passageways and some stalactites apparently resembling well-known people and objects. There are, however, no snakes. A tuk-tuk to the caves is Q10.

4

4

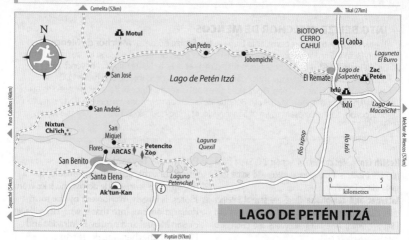

LAGO DE PETÉN ITZÁ

Nixtun Ch'ich'

Spread over a peninsula about 4km west of Flores, the extensive Maya ruins of **Nixtun Ch'ich'** have barely been touched by archeologists. It's an enormous site, with dozens of small temple mounds and a triadic temple complex (ZZ1) more than 30m in height that was a magnificent ceremonial centre. The 60m-long **ball court** ranks as one of the largest ever found in the entire Maya world. A 2007 dig revealed millennia of occupation, beginning before 1000 BC and extending into the early eighteenth century. Nixtun Ch'ich' is situated on private land (some of which is owned by Manuel Baldizón, Guatemalan presidential candidate in 2012) used for cattle ranching. Virtually all the mounds you see were once temples, but there's been no excavation or restoration so the site looks like a series of grassy hillocks.

Wear good boots and expect to encounter cow dung and plenty of mud after heavy rains. The only access to this intriguing site is via one of the late afternoon boat tours (Q155 per person) offered by Mayan Adventure (see box, p.360) in Flores.

San Andrés and San José

Across the lake from Santa Elena and Flores are the quiet villages of **SAN ANDRÉS** and **SAN JOSÉ**, both of which have good language schools. The villages' roads slope steeply up from the shore, lined with colourful buildings. San José, in particular, has an impressive array of facilities (including a water park and music stadium), and a lovely public beach. The village is also undergoing something of a cultural revival: Itzá, the pre-Conquest Maya tongue, is being taught in the large school.

LANGUAGE SCHOOLS IN SAN ANDRÉS AND SAN JOSÉ

Most visitors come to San Andrés and San José to study or volunteer at one of the local **language schools**. You'll pay around Q1500 per week for twenty hours of one-to-one lessons, food and lodging and a homestay with a local family. Very few locals here speak English so you can progress quite quickly. Good schools include:

Eco Escuela de Español ☎5940 1235. A community-run, long-established school in San Andrés.

Escuela Bio Itzá ☎7928 8056, ⓦbioitz.com. Based in San José, part of a project for the conservation of the Itzá biosphere and culture. Activities include volunteer work in the botanical garden and preparing natural medicines and cosmetics.

Escuela Nueva Juventud ☎5711 0040, ⓦvolunteerpeten.com. Just outside San Andrés.

ARRIVAL AND INFORMATION

By microbus Regular microbuses connect Santa Elena with both villages (every 30min to both; 30min to San Andrés, 40min to San José).

Facilities San José has a bank with ATM and several *comedores* serving *comida rápida*.

EL REMATE

The tranquil village of **EL REMATE** lies midway between Flores and Tikal on the northeastern corner of Lago de Petén Itzá. The lake is a beautiful turquoise blue here and many of the budget hotels offer swimming access – extremely welcome after a sweaty morning climbing Tikal's jungle temples. The village itself is a lovely place to take a break from the rigours of the road, with little traffic and a lot of nature to enjoy.

WHAT TO SEE AND DO

On the north shore of the lake, fifteen minutes' walk from the centre of El Remate, the **Biotopo Cerro Cahuí** (daily 7am–4pm; Q35) is a 6.5-square-kilometre wildlife conservation area comprising lakeshore, ponds and some of the best examples of undisturbed tropical forest in Petén. There are hiking trails (4km and 6km), a couple of small ruins and two thatched *miradores* on the hill above the lake; pick up maps and information at the gate where you sign in. It's best to visit the park in the early morning, when it's cooler and wildlife is most active.

ARRIVAL AND DEPARTURE

By bus and microbus Getting to El Remate is easy: every minibus to Tikal (around 15 per day from Flores/Santa Elena) passes through the village. Coming from the Belize border, get off at the Ixlú junction – from here you can walk (it's 2km away) or wait for a ride to El Remate. For accommodation on the northern lakeshore road you will need to walk.

Destinations Flores (around 15 daily; 45 min); Tikal (around 15 daily; 40min). San Juan Travel (see box, p.360) operates two daily shuttles buses for Belize City (Q160) and onward connections to Chetumal, Mexico.

INFORMATION AND TOURS

Exchange There are no banks, but you can change dollars (US and Belize) at *La Casa de Don David* in the village centre.
Internet There's a little internet place right by the junction in the heart of the village.

Tourist information Several hotels, including *La Casa de Don David* and *Mon Ami*, provide good information.
Tours Santiago Billy, owner of *Mon Ami* (see below) has lived in the Petén area for years and offers good tours in his Land Rover to Maya sites including Yaxhá, Nakúm and Aguateca as well as horseriding. Prices depend on numbers, but if you can get a group together rates per person drop considerably.

ACCOMMODATION

El Remate has plenty of budget deals and a few mid-range options, too. You'll pay slightly more for lake views or access, but the setting is so idyllic it's probably worth it.
La Casa de Don David Village centre ☎7928 8469, ⓦlacasadedondavid.com. Efficiently run mid-range guesthouse, owned by a welcoming Guatemalan-American family, offering spotless rooms (most with a/c) that face a huge garden that extends down towards the lakeshore. Meals are served on an elevated deck that makes the most of the views, and the birdlife is outstanding. There's excellent independent travel advice and books and magazines to browse. Rates include a meal (breakfast or dinner). **Q360**
Casa de Doña Tonita 800m down the road to Cerro Cahuí on the right ☎5701 7114. One of the cheapest deals in town, this basic place has four clapboard rooms, built above the lake, with great views, plus a reasonable six-bed dorm. There's tasty budget-friendly food in the *comedor* and the owners look after their guests well. The lakeside location is superb. Dorm **Q30**, double **Q70**
Hostal Hermano Pedro Down off the main road opposite the football pitch ☎5719 7394, ⓦhhpedro.com. Large wooden house with a profusion of good rooms (most with private bath) that open onto a communal decked balcony. There's wi-fi, a *comedor* and a complimentary breakfast (though no view of the lake). **Q170**
Hotel Sun Breeze Lakeside, in the centre of the village ☎7928 8044, ⓔsunbreezehotel@gmail.com. Recent construction means that this hotel no longer has lake views, but it remains an excellent budget choice with very well-presented, screened rooms (some with private bath). The friendly owners offer tours, transport and laundry service. **Q110**
★ **Mon Ami** 300m beyond *Dona Tonita's* ☎7928 8413, ⓦhotelmonami.com. A superb French-owned guesthouse with gorgeous, well-constructed rooms and bungalows scattered around a tranquil, forested plot of land. All the accommodation has style and character, enhanced by the use of local textiles and artistic flourishes, while the dorm is probably the most attractive in Guatemala. There's excellent swimming from the dock. Be sure to treat yourself to a meal here too (see p.366). Dorm **Q50**, double **Q200**

4

★ **TREAT YOURSELF**

Restaurant Las Orquideas 800m along the road to Cerro Cahuí ☎5701 9022. Superb Italian-owned restaurant, a casual place where your welcoming hosts prepare food around an open kitchen. They serve fine pizza, pasta, bruschettas and full meals such as carpaccio and baked lake fish, plus wine by the glass and espresso coffee. Around Q60–120 a head. Tues–Sun 11am–9.30pm.

Posada del Cerro 300m beyond *Mon Ami* ☎5376 8722, ⓦposadadelcerro.com. Above the lakeshore, this stylish family-owned guesthouse makes a tempting flashpacker base with fine-quality rooms blending modern fittings with natural materials in a jungle setting. Some bathrooms are not en-suite. Very tasty meals are offered, though breakfast is not included. Dorm Q100, double Q375

EATING

Most places to eat are on the main road, though many hotels also have their own restaurants. *La Casa de Don David*, in the village centre, features a specials board tailored towards the palates of international guests.

Mon Ami 300m beyond *Dona Tonita's* ☎7928 8413, ⓦhotelmonami.com. The best food in town is served in this charming hotel's lake-facing *palapa*. It's not cheap, but the quality is outstanding and if you choose carefully (pasta is Q30–40) you won't break the bank. There's always a good set lunch for Q35 and wine available by the bottle and glass. Free wi-fi. Daily 7am–9pm.

Restaurant Cahuí Opposite *Hostal Hermano Pedro*, near the football pitch. Worth trying for breakfasts (from Q20), *comida típica*, burgers and pasta (meals from Q30). There's a well-stocked bar too, and the fine lake-facing terrace makes a great place for a sundowner. Daily 8am–9pm.

Restaurant El Muelle South of *Restaurant Cahuí* ☎5514 9785. This smart restaurant's menu is not cheap, though there are snacks (sandwiches, burgers and nachos) for less than Q30, and you get free use of the fantastic lakeside swimming pool if you eat here. Daily 7.30am–9.30pm.

TIKAL

Towering above the rainforest, **TIKAL** is possibly the most spectacular and visually impressive of all Maya ruins. The site is dominated by six giant temples, steep-sided pyramids that rise up to 64m from the forest floor. In addition, literally thousands of other structures, many half-strangled by giant roots and still hidden beneath mounds of earth, demand exploration. The site itself is deep in the jungle of the **Parque Nacional Tikal**, and the forest is home to all sorts of wildlife, including howler and spider monkeys, toucans and parakeets, coatis and big cats. Perhaps early explorer Sylvanus Morley coined the most fitting description of Tikal: "Place Where the Gods Speak". The sheer scale of the place is astounding and its jungle location spellbinding. Whether you can spare as little as an hour or as long as a week, it's always worth the trip.

WHAT TO SEE AND DO

Tikal is vast. The **central area**, with its five main temples, forms by far the most impressive section; if you start to explore beyond this you can wander seemingly endlessly in the maze of smaller, unrestored structures and complexes. Whatever you do, Tikal is certain to exhaust you before you exhaust it. Rather too many visitors congregate to witness the sunrise from Temple IV when the forest canopy bursts into a frenzy of sound and activity. However, as the park officially opens at 6am, if you arrive independently at this hour you can witness much the same atmosphere, yet without the hundred-strong crowd of snap-happy tourists, from other spots; Mundo Perdido is a good choice. There are two official park **museums**, the Museo Lítico (daily 9am–4pm; Q10) and the Museo Tikal (Mon–Fri 9am–5pm, Sat & Sun 9am–4pm; Q10), which house some of the artefacts found in the ruins, including jade jewellery, ceramics and obsidian flints, as well as numerous stelae.

From the entrance to the Great Plaza

From the site map at the entrance, a path branches right to **complexes Q and R**. The first pyramid, with a line of eight stelae in front of it, is also known as the Temple of Nine Mayan Gods. Bearing left after Complex R, you approach the **East Plaza**; in its southeast corner stands an imposing temple, beneath which were found the remains of several severed heads, the victims of human sacrifice. From here a few short steps bring you to the **Great Plaza**, the heart of the ancient city. Surrounded by four massive structures, this was the focus of ceremonial and religious activity at Tikal for around a thousand years. Beneath the grass lie four layers of paving, the oldest of which dates from about 150 BC. **Temple I** (or Jaguar Temple), towering 44m above the plaza, is the hallmark of Tikal. The skeleton of ruler Hasaw Chan K'awil (682–721 AD) was found in the tomb at the temple's core, surrounded by an assortment of jade, pearls, seashells and stingray spines. There's a reconstruction of the tomb (*tumba* 116) in the Museo Tikal. Standing opposite, like a squat version of Temple I, is **Temple II**, known as the Temple of the Masks for the two grotesque masks, now heavily eroded, which flank the central stairway. The **North Acropolis**, which fills the whole north side of the Great Plaza, is one of the most complex structures in the entire Maya world. In true Maya style it was built and rebuilt on top of itself, and beneath the twelve temples that can be seen today are the remains of about a hundred other structures.

Central Acropolis

On the southeastern side of the Great Plaza is the **Central Acropolis**, a maze of tiny interconnecting rooms and stairways. The buildings here are usually referred to as palaces rather than temples, although their precise use remains a mystery. Behind the acropolis is the palace reservoir, which was fed with rainwater by a series of channels from all over the city.

From the West Plaza to Temple IV

Behind Temple II is the **West Plaza**, dominated by a large Late Classic temple on the north side, and scattered with various altars and stelae. From here the Tozzer Causeway leads west to **Temple III** (60m), still covered in jungle vegetation. Around the back of the temple is a huge palace complex, of which only the **Bat Palace** has been restored.

At the end of the Tozzer Causeway is **Temple IV**, at 64m the tallest of all the Tikal structures, built in 741 AD. Twin ladders, one for the ascent, the other for the descent, are attached to the sides of the temple. Its summit, with stupendous views over an ocean of rainforest, is unmatched, with the roof combs of the great temples piercing the canopy and intermittent roars of howler monkeys resonating across the

4

THE RISE AND FALL OF TIKAL

900 BC First known settlement at Tikal.

500 BC Evidence of early stone buildings at the site.

250 BC Early pyramid built in the Mundo Perdido.

c.10 AD Great Plaza begins to take shape and Tikal is an established major site with a large permanent population.

c.250 AD Continuous eruption of the Ilopango volcano causes devastation and disrupts trade routes.

292 AD First recorded date on stelae at Tikal.

378 AD Tikal, aligned with Teotihuacán, defeats rival Uaxactún.

550 AD Tikal conquers neighbouring city-states and establishes an influence reaching as far as Copán in Honduras.

562 AD Caracol defeats Tikal in a "star war", probably in alliance with the city of Calakmul, a formidable new power to the north.

682–810 AD Tikal's legendary leader Hasaw Chan K'awil revives the city with a series of incredible victories deposing sequential kings of Calakmul. The Great Plaza is remodelled and five great temples built.

869 AD Ceremonial construction ceases at Tikal; the population dwindles.

1000 AD Tikal abandoned.

1848 AD Ruins of Tikal officially rediscovered by a government expedition.

1956 AD Project to excavate and restore the buildings started.

1984 AD Most major restoration work completed.

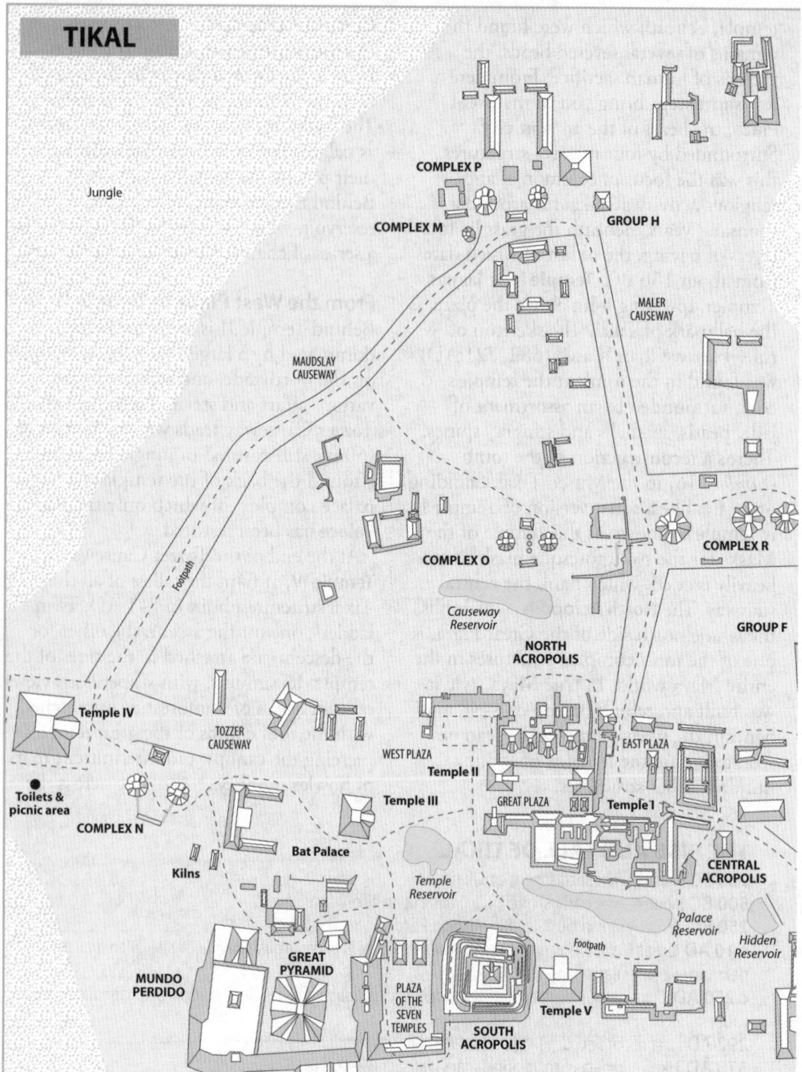

TIKAL

Jungle

COMPLEX P

COMPLEX M

GROUP H

MALER
CAUSEWAY

MAUDSLAY
CAUSEWAY

COMPLEX O

COMPLEX R

Causeway
Reservoir

GROUP F

NORTH
ACROPOLIS

Temple IV

TOZZER
CAUSEWAY

WEST PLAZA

EAST PLAZA

Temple II

Toilets &
picnic area

COMPLEX N

Temple III

GREAT PLAZA

Temple 1

CENTRAL
ACROPOLIS

Kilns

Bat Palace

Temple
Reservoir

Palace
Reservoir

Hidden
Reservoir

footpath

MUNDO
PERDIDO

GREAT
PYRAMID

PLAZA
OF THE
SEVEN
TEMPLES

Temple V

SOUTH
ACROPOLIS

Jungle

0   200
      metres

Footpath

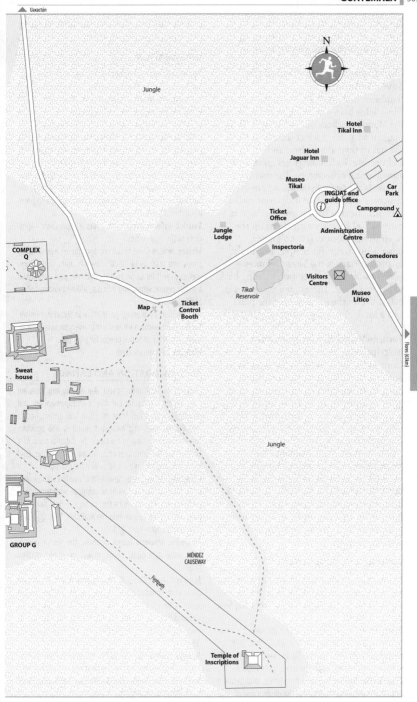

Uaxactún

N

Jungle

Hotel
Tikal Inn

Hotel
Jaguar Inn

Museo
Tikal

INGUAT and
guide office

Car
Park

Campground

Ticket
Office

Administration
Centre

Jungle
Lodge

Comedores

Inspectoría

COMPLEX
Q

Visitors
Centre

Tikal
Reservoir

Museo
Lítico

Map

Ticket
Control
Booth

4

Flores (63km)

Sweat
house

Jungle

GROUP G

MÉNDEZ
CAUSEWAY

Footpath

Temple of
Inscriptions

jungle. However, it's become such a popular place for sunrise that you may want to opt for a less obvious location.

Mundo Perdido and Plaza of the Seven Temples

Southeast of Temple IV, a trail passes some Maya kilns before winding round down to the **Mundo Perdido**, or Lost World. This magical and very distinct section of the site has its own atmosphere and architecture, its buildings designed as an astronomical observatory. The main feature is the **Great Pyramid**, a 32m-high structure whose surface hides four earlier versions, the first dating from perhaps as early as 500 BC. After accidents on the steep stone staircase, it is no longer possible to climb this temple. Just to the east is the **Plaza of the Seven Temples**, which forms part of a complex dating back to before Christ. There's an unusual triple ball court on the north side of the plaza and a lot of archeology work ongoing here.

Temple V and the Temple of the Inscriptions

Continuing east, you pass the unexcavated South Acropolis before you reach the 58m-high Temple V. Construction of this great monument started around 600 AD. It's possible that it was dedicated to the rain god Chaac, due to the six large masks found on the roof comb.

Finally, there's the **Temple of the Inscriptions**, also known as Temple VI, reached via a ten-minute hike through the forest along the Méndez Causeway. The temple (only discovered in 1951) is famous for its 12m roof comb, at the back of which is a huge but rather faint hieroglyphic text.

ARRIVAL AND DEPARTURE

It's wise to arrive early at Tikal when the air is fresh and heat less intense, but note that it's rare to witness an impressive sunrise over the ruins due to mist rising from the humid forest.

From Flores The easiest way to reach the ruins is via one of the tourist minibuses (Q70 return) that pick up passengers from every hotel in Flores, Santa Elena and El Remate, as well Flores airport, starting from 3.30am.

From Belize If you're travelling from Belize, change buses at Ixlú, the three-way junction at the eastern end of Lago

de Petén Itzá, from where there are plenty of passing minibuses (Q35 one-way) all day long.

INFORMATION

Opening hours and tickets Tikal is open daily 4am–8pm, and has three kinds of entrance tickets. The vast majority of visitors choose to buy a standard ticket (6am–6pm; Q160) which will give most people sufficient time at the site. There are also sunrise (4am–8am; Q100) and sunset (6–8pm; Q100) tickets, for which you have to be accompanied by an official guide, at additional cost. So if you want to arrive at dawn, catch the sunrise (though see the warning above) and leave at 4pm, you'll need two tickets (Q100 and Q160). Note that if you're staying at a hotel (or the campsite) inside the national park you still have to pay for entrance tickets (even if you do not enter the ruins area).

Tourist information Inguat has a desk (6am–4pm) close to the ticket office.

Visitor centre Close to the entrance there's a post office, shops and stalls (which sell souvenirs, hats, sun cream, memory cards for cameras, film, batteries and water) and a visitor centre, where you'll find a café-restaurant, toilets and luggage storage.

Guides There's a licensed guide office in the visitor centre. Guides, most of whom are excellent and very knowledgeable, charge Q350 for up to five people for a 4hr tour.

Website Ⓦ tikalpark.com.

ACCOMMODATION AND EATING

Most backpackers choose to visit Tikal as a day-trip. There are three hotels at the ruins but they're all expensive and not especially good value. However you'll find decent, secure camping facilities, and hammock rental is also possible. There's nowhere cheap to eat inside the national park. Your best bet are the *comedores* opposite the visitor centre. Cold soft drinks and snacks are sold around the ruins.

Camping Behind the new administration centre and main car park. Well-maintained campsite with toilets and cold showers. You can rent a tent under a shelter, and good hammocks with mossie nets are available. Tent Q50 plus Q50/person, hammock Q35

Comedor Impero Maya Opposite the visitor centre. Tasty local-style eggs, beans, grilled meat and chicken (from Q35).

Jaguar Inn ☎ 7783 3647, Ⓦ jaguartikal.com. Tents here come with an inflatable mattress, sheets and pillow, but space is very limited so book ahead. Their bungalows, sleeping two, are decent, though pricey, and have a hot-water bathroom, fan and porch. Camping Q120, bungalow Q575

Jungle Lodge ☎ 2476 8775, Ⓦ junglelodgetikal.com. This attractive lodge with a good restaurant and pool has a few basic rooms with shared bath and a five-bed dorm. Dorm Q100, double Q275

AROUND TIKAL

Dotted throughout the Petén jungle are literally hundreds of **Maya ruins**. With tourism booming in the region many of these are becoming more accessible via a selection of trips offered by Flores- and El Remate-based operators. To see these more remote sites independently you will need plenty of time to account for sporadic transport schedules. In addition, some larger, still unexcavated sites require a local guide simply to navigate the ruins themselves.

Uaxactún

Some 23km north of Tikal, strung out by the side of a disused airstrip, are the village and ruins of **Uaxactún** (pronounced "Wash-ak-toon"). The overall impact of the place may be a little disappointing after the grandeur of Tikal, but you'll probably have the site to yourself. The most interesting buildings are in **Group E**, east of the airstrip, where three low reconstructed temples, built side by side, are arranged to function as an observatory. Viewed from the top of a fourth temple, the sun rises behind the north temple on the longest day of the year and behind the southern one on the shortest day. On the other side of the airstrip is **Group A**, a series of larger temples and residential compounds, some of them reconstructed, a ball court and some impressive stelae.

ARRIVAL AND DEPARTURE

By bus Buses leave Santa Elena (1pm & 3pm; 2hr 15min), passing through Tikal en route to Uaxactún. Return buses leave Uaxactún at 6am and 4pm.

ACCOMMODATION AND EATING

Aldana's Friendly, family-run place with bare-bones wooden rooms and camping. Tours of the region and food are offered. Camping Q15, double Q40

Campamento Ecológico El Chiclero 7926 1095, campamentoelchiclero@gmail.com. Welcoming place offering simple rooms with decent mattresses and nets, camping and hammock space; bathrooms are shared but clean. Owner Antonio Baldizón also organizes 4WD trips (in the dry season Feb–June) to ruins of Río Azul and Naachtún. His wife Neria prepares excellent food – large meals cost Q50. Hammock Q30, camping Q30, double Q140

Yaxhá

Midway between El Remate and Melchor de Menchos, some 12km off the highway, is the partly restored site of **Yaxhá** (daily 6am–5pm; Q80). The site is rarely visited, but is very well managed with an impressive collection of reconstructed temples and palaces and numerous stelae. Yaxhá's greatest attraction is its stunning location on the northern shores of the tranquil **Yaxhá lagoon** (no doubt the site was originally chosen with this in mind). Many of the remains are from the Preclassic period, and there's a terrific example of triadic temple arrangement at the North Acropolis where you'll probably have a 2000-year-old ceremonial centre to yourself. Views over the lake from the top of **Temple 216**, the site's largest structure, are unforgettable, with 360-degree vistas over an intact rainforest. You ought to be lucky enough to see (and hear) plenty of monkeys too.

ARRIVAL AND DEPARTURE

By shuttle bus ADN (see box, p.283) claim to offer buses (2 daily, 6am & 8am; Q100) from Santa Elena that will drop you off at Yaxhá, but they don't offer a return service.

By pick-up There is no public transport to the park entrance. However, on the main road, in the village of La Máquina, it should be possible to negotiate a price for a pick-up (approx Q40) or hitch a ride. Ask at the *tienda* opposite the school.

Tours Many Flores-based tour operators offer trips to the Yaxhá area; the highly recommended two-day tours run by Mayan Adventure (see box, p.360) cost Q1500 (minimum four people); these also include the ruins of Nakúm or La Blanca.

ACCOMMODATION

Camping The campsite by the lakeshore has recently been upgraded and now has a (cold) shower block.

El Zotz

Some 30km southwest of Uaxactún, along a rough track passable by 4WD, is **El Zotz**, a large Maya site set in its own nature reserve. A royal tomb, dating from around 400 AD, was discovered here in 2010 beneath the El Diablo pyramid, containing the king buried with the tiny corpses of six infants (possibly sacrificial victims). Totally unrestored, and smothered by vegetation, El Zotz had been systematically looted, although there are guards on duty today. Zotz means "bat" in Maya and each evening at dusk you'll see tens, perhaps hundreds, of thousands of **bats** of several species emerge from a cave near the campsite – one of the most remarkable natural sights in Petén. From the tops of El Zotz's jungle-shrouded temples it's also possible to see the roof combs of Tikal.

To **get here** you can rent vehicles, supplies and equipment in Uaxactún, or take a three-day tour from Flores (ask at *Los Amigos* to form a group). The tour involves approximately six hours of walking per day and two nights camping in the jungle, and finishes at the ruins of Tikal.

Waka' (El Perú)

It's possible to reach the Maya ruins of **Waka'** (previously known as El Perú) independently but you'll need a tent, a good grasp of Spanish and plenty of initiative. The ruins are largely unreconstructed but mainly date from the Classic period when the city was allied to Calakmul. A royal tomb unearthed here in 2004 contained the remains of a queen, who was buried along with stingray spines (used for ritual bloodletting).

A chicken bus leaves Santa Elena's market terminal at 10am for **Paso Caballos** (4hr), from where you can hike or take a boat to the site, and where local guides may also be hired. It may be easier to take a **tour**; companies based in Flores (see box, p.360) offer tours of Waka', often dubbed the "Scarlet Macaw Trail" on account of the large concentrations of the critically endangered birds that live in the forests around the site.

El Mirador

Only accessible by foot, mule or helicopter, the colossal Preclassic site of **El Mirador** is perhaps the most exotic and mysterious of all Petén's Maya sites. Still buried in the forest, way north of the remote village of Carmelita, this massive city matches Tikal's scale, and may even surpass it. By 1000 BC a settlement was thriving here, and by 450 BC impressive temple construction had begun, the city peaking in influence between 350 BC

> ### TOURS TO EL MIRADOR
>
> For the time being, **getting to El Mirador** is a substantial undertaking, with most backpackers opting to take a five- or six-day **tour** from Flores (although during the rainy season this may not be possible). Tours involve up to eight hours of arduous jungle trekking per day; you'll need plenty of repellent to kill off the mosquitoes, ticks and other nasties. Tours offered by *Los Amigos* in Flores (see p.361) provide horses or mules to carry your food and equipment, and cost US$275 per person for a group of five.

and 100 AD when it was unquestionably the superpower of Mesoamerica, eclipsing the Olmecs in Mexico and lording it over the entire Maya region. Fittingly, Mirador's name in Preclassic Maya times is thought to have been Te Tun ("The Birthplace of the Gods").

The core of the site covers some sixteen square kilometres, stretching between two massive pyramids that face each other across the forest. One of these, **La Danta**, sits on a vast stone base platform measuring 600m by 300m, the pyramid itself reaching 79m above the forest floor – the tallest pre-Columbian structure in the Americas.

The area around El Mirador is riddled with smaller Maya sites, and as you look out across the forest from the top of either of the main temples you can see others rising above the canopy on all sides – including giant Calakmul in Mexico. Although much of the site is still buried, archeologists are currently excavating and have already uncovered fantastic Maya artwork inside some temples. It is likely that in the coming decades El Mirador will be opened up to more tourism – there's even talk of a monorail through the jungle.

SAYAXCHÉ

The small town of **SAYAXCHÉ**, on the banks of the Río de la Pasión, is a handy base for visiting the nearby archeological sites of Ceibal, Aguateca and Dos Pilas. The complex network of rivers and swamps that cuts through the surrounding area has been an important trade route since Maya times and there are several ruins in the area. There's no bridge, so all road transport has to use a ferry to shuttle across the river.

WHAT TO SEE AND DO

The Maya sites of **Ceibal**, **Aguateca** and **Dos Pilas** are in an isolated pocket of the country and are seldom visited. If you only have the time (or finances) for one ruin, Aguateca is the most impressive. Whether you choose to arrive by boat or by trekking, the journey through the jungle gives all these ruins a special *Heart of Darkness* aura. Trips can be organized via Flores tour operators (see box, p.360); the friendly *Restaurant Yaxkín* (see p.374) also offers useful advice.

Ceibal

Surrounded by forest and shaded by huge ceiba trees, the ruins of **Ceibal** (daily 6am–5pm; Q50) are a mixture of cleared open plazas and untamed jungle. Though many of the largest temples lie buried under mounds, Ceibal does have some outstanding and well-preserved carving: the two main plazas are dotted with lovely **stelae**, centred around two low platforms. During the Classic period Ceibal was unimportant, but it grew rapidly between 830 and 930 AD, apparently after falling under the control of colonists from what is now Mexico. This is evident in the fantastic Mexican-influenced carving displayed here.

Lago de Petexbatún: Aguateca and Dos Pilas

To the south of Sayaxché is **Lago de Petexbatún**, a spectacular expanse of water ringed by dense forest and containing plentiful supplies of snook, bass, alligator and freshwater turtle. The shores of the lake abound with birdlife and animals (including howler monkeys) and there are a number of Maya ruins.

Aguateca (daily 7am–5pm; Q50), perched on a high outcrop at the southern tip of the lake, is the furthest away from Sayaxché but the most accessible. Extensive restoration work is still ongoing

at this intriguing site, which is split in two by a natural chasm. The atmosphere is magical, surrounded by dense tropical forest and with superb views of the lake from two *miradores*. Throughout the Late Classic period, Aguateca was closely aligned with (or controlled by) nearby Dos Pilas, and military victories were celebrated at both sites with remarkably similar stelae – look out for Stele 3 here, which shows Dos Pilas ruler Master Sun Jaguar in full battle regalia. In the late eighth century, these Petexbatún cities began to lose regional control, and despite the construction of 5km of walls around the citadel (the remains are still visible today), Aguateca was overrun in 790 AD.

The resident guards will provide you with stout walking sticks – essential as the slippery paths here can be treacherous – before escorting you around the steep trails, past palisade defences, stelae, temples and palaces (including the residence of Aguateca's last ruler, Tante K'inich) and a barracks.

Dos Pilas, where restoration is ongoing, is buried in jungle west of the Lago de Petexbatún. Once the centre of a formidable empire in the early part of the eighth century, with a population of around ten thousand, it has some tremendous stelae, altars and four short **hieroglyphic stairways** decorated with glyphs and figures around its central plaza.

ARRIVAL AND DEPARTURE

By bus Minibuses and buses from Santa Elena and Raxrujá arrive at the Río de la Pasión. A ferry (Q3 per head) takes you over the river.

Destinations Cobán (2 daily; 4hr 30min); Flores (every 15min; 1hr 45min); Raxrujá (every 30min; 2hr 30min).

Boats and tours Plenty of boatmen offer trips to the ruins – you'll have to be patient and bargain hard. Try Viajes Don Pedro (☎7928 6109) on the riverfront or the owners of *Restaurant Yaxkín* (see p.374) and *Yaxkín Chel Paraíso*.

Getting to Ceibal Ceibal is reachable by land or river. It's easy enough to make it here and back to Sayaxché in an afternoon by boat; haggle with the boatmen at the waterfront and you can expect to pay around Q450 (for up to five people). The boat trip is followed by a short walk through towering rainforest. By road, Ceibal is just 17km from Sayaxché. Any transport heading south out of town passes the turn-off, from where an 8km track leads to the

INTO MEXICO

There are two popular routes into **Mexico** from Petén.

VIA BETHEL/LA TÉCNICA

Buses (roughly hourly, 5am–3pm; 4hr) leave Santa Elena's Terminal Nuevo for Bethel and La Técnica. At Bethel it's relatively easy to find a shared *lancha* heading downstream (around Q50/person; 30min) to Frontera Corozal. Alternatively, it's cheaper to get off the bus, obtain your exit stamp in Bethel and continue on the same bus for a further 12km to the tiny settlement of La Técnica, where you can cross the Usumacinta (boats leave when full; 5min; Q10) to Corozal on the opposite bank. La Técnica lacks accommodation or other facilities. Agencies in Flores (see box, p.360) offer cross-border tickets on **shuttle buses** direct to Palenque using this route (8hr, around Q240).

Lanchas leave regularly from Frontera Corozal on the Mexican side to the world-class ruins of **Yaxchilán**, a stunning 45-minute journey along the Usumacinta River; it's normally possible to join a group to save costs (around US$20/person return). Back in Frontera Corozal, there are simple *hospedajes* and places to eat. If you're travelling independently from here you'll find a flow of minibuses (roughly hourly) to Palenque from the highway, 18km west of Corozal. *Colectivo* taxis (US$3/person) run between the town and the highway bus stop. (If you're on a shuttle bus package to Palenque all this is taken care of for you, and the taxi price is included in the ticket.)

VIA EL CEIBO

A second, northern route to Mexico has recently become popular as road connections have improved. It's now the fastest and cheapest way to get to Palenque from Flores. From the main bus terminal in Santa Elena catch a bus for the border at **El Ceibo** (12 daily; 4hr; Q40). Minibuses leave the Mexican side of the border for Tenosique (1hr 15min; US$3.50), where you change and catch another minibus for Palenque (1hr 45min; US$6). If you choose this route, note that it is used by Central American migrants heading to *El Norte* and there's plenty of military in evidence. Get an early start and avoid getting stuck for the night in El Naranjo (the nearest town in Guatemala to El Ceibo), which is a rough place with little to recommend it.

site through the jungle. Alternatively, hire a pick-up for the full journey for around Q275 return – ask at *Restaurant Yaxkín* (see below).

Getting to Aguateca A beautiful 2–3hr boat ride (Q475, up to six people) can get you to within a 20min walk of the ruins. Alternatively, it's usually possible to access the site via the village of Nacimientos (no facilities other than *tiendas*), from where it's an hour or so's walk; the trail may not be passable in the rainy season, however. A *micro* leaves Sayaxché at 2pm directly to Nacimientos, and from the highway junction of Las Pozas, south of Sayaxché, there's more transport.

Getting to Dos Pilas To get to Dos Pilas from the lakeshore you have to trek 12km on foot (or on horseback).

INFORMATION

Banks There are several ATMs in town.

Internet You can get online at the internet café on Sayaxché's plaza.

Tourist information *Restaurant Yaxkín* (see below) offers free travel advice and has a big map of the area painted on the wall. Better still, if you're staying for a few days, head to the hotel *Yaxkín Chel*, where Don Rosendo Girón is an authority on the region.

ACCOMMODATION AND EATING

You can camp at the Ceibal site, but there are no toilets or drinking water.

Hotel La Pasión 50m up from the dock, Sayaxché ☎ 4056 5044. Spacious, well-presented rooms with cable TV, bathroom and fan. There's free coffee in the pleasant lounge area. **Q110**

Hotel Del Río 300m north of the dock, Sayaxché ☎ 7928 6138. Efficient, secure hotel with very spacious, clean rooms (some with a/c) and a very friendly host family. **Q175**

Oasis 1km west of Sayaxché in Barrio San Miguel. Part-hardware store, part-civilized, a/c café that serves snacks like hot dogs and nachos. It has the only espresso machine in town. Mon–Sat 8am–8pm.

Restaurant Yaxkín One block up from the dock, on the left, Sayaxché. Friendly, family-run restaurant that serves up *comida típica* and good burgers (Q25) and sandwiches. Offers impartial tourist information too. Daily 7am–8pm.

Yaxkín Chel Paraíso Barrio Esperanza, six blocks up and five across (southeast) from Sayaxché dock ☎ 4053 3484. Rustic bungalows and a restaurant (serving good Mexican food and fish) in a verdant garden, where the family grows cocoa, pepper and tropical flowers. Owner Chendo can arrange tours and transport. **Q120**

MAYA RUINS, COPÁN

Honduras

HIGHLIGHTS

❶ **Lago de Yojoa** Hide in caves, fly over waterfalls, enjoy the beauty. **See p.398**

❷ **Gracias** Among Honduras's oldest towns, and gateway to Parque Nacional Celaque. **See p.401**

❸ **Copán** Step back in time at these spectacular Maya ruins. **See p.409**

❹ **Olancho** Tackle Honduras's most stunning and challenging terrain. **See p.413**

❺ **La Mosquitia** Isolated and undisturbed land, where nature still rules. **See p.433**

❻ **Bay Islands** A unique personality and world-famous diving: Honduras's top destination. **See p.436**

HIGHLIGHTS ARE MARKED ON THE MAP ON P.377

ROUGH COSTS

Daily budget Basic US$35/occasional treat US$55

Drink *Nacional* beer US$1.50, coffee US$1

Food *Almuerzo típico* US$4

Hostel/budget hotel US$10/US$20

Travel Copán–San Pedro Sula (140km) by bus: 3hr, US$7

FACT FILE

Population 7.7 million

Languages Spanish, English in the Bay Islands

Currency Honduras lempira (L)

Capital Tegucigalpa (population: 1.8 million)

International phone code ☎ 504

Time zone GMT –6hr

5

Introduction

All too often, Honduras receives short shrift on travellers' Central American itineraries: most visitors either race to see the Maya ruins at Copán or the palm-fringed beaches of the Bay Islands, and skip the rest of the country. And while these are two beautiful, worthy sights, there's much more to Honduras – from the wetlands of La Mosquitia to the subtropical shore of the Golfo de Fonseca, this is a land of inspiring, often untouched natural beauty – and a longer visit will pay ample rewards.

The capital, **Tegucigalpa**, is somewhat underwhelming, but home to the best facilities and services in the country, while 100km south of the city lies the volcanic **Isla El Tigre**, a little-visited but worthwhile getaway. An essential detour on the way north to the city of **San Pedro Sula** is the **Lago de Yojoa** region, which offers birdwatching, caves and a 43m waterfall. To the west, colonial towns like **Santa Rosa de Copán** and **Gracias** offer fantastic restaurants, hot springs and access to indigenous villages, while the sparsely populated region of **Olancho** – Honduras's "Wild East" – and the **Sierra de Agalta** national park has the most extensive stretch of virgin

cloudforest in Central America. On the Caribbean coast, **Tela** and **Trujillo** are good-sized towns with great beaches, while **La Ceiba**, larger and with thriving nightlife, is the departure point for the **Bay Islands**, home to world-class diving and a rich cultural mix.

Gradually, Honduras is waking up to its potential as an **ecotourism** destination – its network of national parks and preserves is extensive – as well as the likely benefits of an increased tourist infrastructure for the country's struggling economy (it's the second-poorest country in Central America, with more than half the population living below the poverty line). The pick of Honduras's natural attractions is the biosphere reserve of the **Río Plátano** in **La Mosquitia**. Encompassing one of the finest remaining stretches of virgin tropical rainforest in Central America, the region is largely uninhabited and a trip here really does get you off the beaten track.

The country's development, however, has been held up by political instability and the (largely unchecked) violent activities of international **drug cartels**, which use the country as a staging post. Security in Honduras is a serious issue (see p.383).

WHEN TO VISIT

The **climate** in Honduras is generally dictated by **altitude**. In the central highlands, the weather is pleasantly warm in the daytime and cool at night. The hot Pacific and Caribbean coasts offer the relief of breezes and cooling rain showers, while San Pedro Sula and other lowland towns can be positively scorching in summer.

Honduras's **rainy season**, "winter" (*invierno*), runs from May to November (most markedly June and July). In much of the country it rains for only a few hours in the afternoon, though along the northern coast and in Mosquitia rain is possible year-round. October and November are the only months you might want to avoid in these parts: in the middle of the **hurricane season** (generally said to begin in August), this is when you're most likely to be affected by storms.

CHRONOLOGY

1000 BC Maya settlers move into the Río Copán valley.

100 AD Construction of the city of Copán begins.

426 AD Maya royal dynasty is founded. Copán, the civilization's centre for artistic and scientific development, controls area north to the Valle de Sula, east to Lago de Yojoa and west into present-day Guatemala.

900 AD Maya civilization collapses, and Copán is

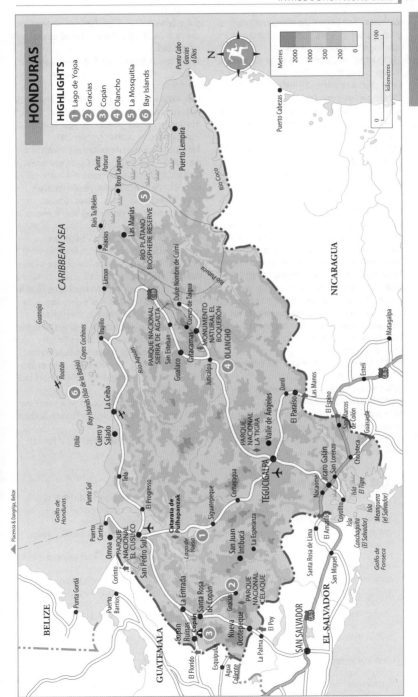

HONDURAS

HIGHLIGHTS

1. Lago de Yojoa
2. Gracias
3. Copán
4. Olancho
5. La Mosquitia
6. Bay Islands

5

abandoned. Lenca becomes the predominant indigenous group, settling in small, scattered communities and absorbing other indigenous cultures.

1502 Christopher Columbus arrives on the island of Guanaja, naming it "Isla de Pinos" (Island of Pines). First Catholic Mass in Latin America is held on August 14.

1524 Hernán Cortés sends Cristóbal de Olid from Mexico to claim the isthmus in Cortés's name; the man arrives himself one year later, founds Puerto Cortés and Trujillo, then returns to Mexico.

1524–71 Indigenous population declines from 400,000 to around 15,000.

1536 Pedro de Alvarado arrives from Guatemala to govern the territory. Lempira, a Lenca chieftain, amasses a 30,000-man force, which rebels against the Spanish. Comayagua is destroyed.

1539 Lempira is assassinated and the Spanish hold on Honduras is assured. Gold and silver are discovered in the country's interior and mining begins. The *encomienda* labour system is put in place, assuring social stratification.

1573 Comayagua, rebuilt, is designated the capital.

1800 With mines failing and droughts destroying agricultural harvests, the economy enters a crisis period. Society is deeply divided, and the country still has no national printing press, newspapers or university.

1821 Honduras gains independence from Spain, but is annexed by Mexico.

1823 Provinces of Central America declare themselves an independent republic. Civil war begins.

1830 Honduran Francisco Morazán elected president of the Republic after defeating Conservative forces in Guatemala.

1839 Honduras and Nicaragua go to war against El Salvador. Morazán resigns, and the Central American Republic is essentially finished. Independence is not kind to Honduras's economy or infrastructure, and intense rivalry between Liberals and Conservatives keeps the country in an almost permanent state of political and military conflict.

1876 Liberal Dr Marco Aurelio Soto is elected president. Improves infrastructure and encourages foreign investment.

Late 1800s Banana industry develops with arrival of US fruit companies, which gain control of national infrastructure; private interests dominate government. Tegucigalpa becomes national capital in 1880.

1956 A coup introduces the military as a new element in the country's hierarchy of power. Civilian government is reinstated in 1957, but a new constitution that year gives the military the right to disregard presidential orders.

1963 Another coup brings Colonel Oswaldo López Arellano to power as provisional president; he remains in power for twelve years.

1969 So-called "Football War" breaks out on the Honduras–El Salvador border (see box below).

1975 The "Bananagate" scandal (the payment of more than US$1 million to government officials by United Brand in return for reductions on export taxes) forces López to resign. Under his successors – all high-ranking military officials – the country becomes even more stratified.

1981 Honduras becomes focus for US-backed Contra war in Nicaragua; relationship between military and government grows closer; human-rights violations rise.

1989–98 Following US withdrawal, the economy collapses completely, but power is slowly wrested back from the military.

1998 Hurricane Mitch hits Honduras, killing more than 7000. President Carlos Flores declares Honduras has been set back fifty years.

2005 Manuel Zelaya of the Liberal Party of Honduras is elected.

THE FOOTBALL WAR

In one of the more bizarre conflicts in modern Latin American history, on **July 14, 1969**, war broke out on the Honduras–El Salvador border. Ostensibly caused by a disputed result in a **soccer match** between the two countries, the conflict also stemmed from tensions generated by a steady rise in **illegal migration** of *campesinos* from El Salvador into Honduras in search of land.

In April 1969 the Honduran government had given settlers 30 days to return to El Salvador, and then begun forced expulsions – the result was the break-out of sporadic violence. In June, the two countries began a series of qualifying matches for the 1970 World Cup. The first game, held in Tegucigalpa, was won by Honduras, with a score of 1–0. At the second game (won 3–0 by El Salvador), held in San Salvador, spectators booed the Honduran national anthem and attacked visiting Honduran fans. The third, deciding, match was then pre-empted by the El Salvadoran army bombing targets in Honduras, and advancing up to 40km into Honduran territory.

After three days, around 2000 deaths and a complete breakdown of diplomatic relations, the Organization of American States (OAS) negotiated a ceasefire, establishing a 3km-wide demilitarized zone along the border. Tensions and minor skirmishes continued, however, until 1980, when a US-brokered peace treaty was signed. Only in **1992** did both sides finally accept an International Court of Justice ruling demarcating the border in its current location.

5

LAND AND SEA ROUTES TO HONDURAS

Honduras has land borders with Guatemala, El Salvador and Nicaragua, and sea crossings with Belize. There is a US$3 exit tax at each one.

From **Guatemala**, there are three crossings. The most frequently used is at El Florido for Copán (see box, p.413); there is also a crossing at Agua Caliente (see box, p.404), used by buses from Esquipulas, and one at Corinto–Entre Ríos (see box, p.341), which connects Puerto Barrios and Puerto Cortés.

El Salvador has two crossings: El Amatillo (see box, p.241) in eastern El Salvador, and El Poy in western El Salvador (see box, p.248).

There are three crossings from **Nicaragua**. The easiest is Las Manos (see box, p.476), for Tegucigalpa; the others are at El Espino and Guasaule (see box, p.473).

From **Belize**, there are weekly boats from both Placencia and Dangriga to Puerto Cortés (see p.96).

2006 Honduras signs the Central America Border Control Agreement (see box, p.30).

2009 Manuel Zelaya is ousted from government in a move seen by many as a coup and by others as a legitimate action. Porfirio Lobo of the conservative National Party is elected president in November. Honduras is suspended from the Organization of American States (OAS).

2011 Zelaya and Lobo sign an agreement that allows the former to come out of exile and return to the country. The move leads to Honduras's re-entry into the OAS.

2012 Xiomara Castro, Zelaya's wife, is announced as the presidential candidate of the Libre party for the 2013 elections.

ARRIVAL AND DEPARTURE

Visitors **flying** to Honduras have their choice of airports. The three most commonly used are: **Toncontín International (TGU)**, outside Tegucigalpa (reputedly one of the most dangerous airports in the world, for its difficult runway); **Ramón Villeda Morales International (SAP)**, southeast of San Pedro Sula; and **Juan Manuel Gálvez International (RTB)**, on Roatán. All three are served by direct flights from other Central American capitals, as well as North American (namely Miami, Houston and Atlanta) and South American destinations. Airlines such as United (wunited.com) and TACA (wtaca.com) ply these routes. In addition, CanJet (wcanjet.com) operates flights between Toronto and Montreal to Roatán, and SOSA (waerolineassosahn.com) operates flights between La Ceiba and Grand Cayman, from where you can connect to the UK and elsewhere in

Europe. There's a departure tax of around US$39 for international flights.

You can enter Honduras by **land** from Guatemala, El Salvador and Nicaragua. International services such as Tica Bus (wticabus.com) offer long-haul trips from other Central American cities, but you can also travel via slower, cheaper local transport. If you do come by local bus, you'll have to disembark, cross the border on foot and change buses on the other side. The only **sea routes** to Honduras are from Belize.

VISAS

Citizens of Australia, Canada, Japan, New Zealand, the UK, the US and most European countries do not need visas for stays in Honduras of up to ninety days. **Tourist cards**, given on entry, are good for stays of between thirty and ninety days. The card is a yellow slip of paper that needs to be returned when you leave, or stamped if you extend your stay.

Honduras is part of the **CA-4 border control agreement**, which means you can move freely within Honduras, Guatemala, El Salvador and Nicaragua for up to ninety days (see box, p.30).

GETTING AROUND

Most budget travellers in Honduras depend on the bus, though there are security issues to be aware of (see box, p.380). To reach the popular Bay Islands you will need to fly or take a boat.

5

ADDRESSES IN HONDURAS

Honduras's major cities are mainly laid out in a **grid**, with a park or plaza at the centre. Here calles run east–west, and avenidas north–south. In some towns, such as Santa Rosa de Copán Ruinas, street names are followed by the designation "**NO**", "**NE**", "**SO**" or "**SE**" (northwest, northeast, southwest and southeast respectively), depending on their location around the central park. Note that smaller towns (including Copán) don't have **street names**, so addresses tend to be given in terms of landmarks. Exact **street numbers** tend not to exist anywhere; a city address written in the Guide as "C 16, Av 1–3", for example, means the place you're looking for is on Calle 16, between avenidas 1 and 3, while "Av 1, C 11–13" means it's on Avenida 1, between calles 11 and 13.

BY BUS

Bus services in Honduras are fairly well organized, with frequent departures from the main transport hubs of Tegucigalpa, San Pedro Sula and La Ceiba, as well as a network of local services. These local, or "**chicken**" buses (see box, p.32) are the cheapest, but also get packed and stop frequently, so can be quite slow. **Rapiditos** also serve local routes. Usually minibuses, they are much quicker but a little more expensive than chicken buses. On the longer intercity routes there's usually a choice of services, with an increasing number of luxurious air-conditioned **express buses** (*ejecutivos* or *lujos*), plus comfortable services with a few scheduled stops (*directos*). **Fares** are extremely low on most routes, at around US$1–2 an hour or less, though they can triple on some of the really smart services – travelling between Tegucigalpa and La Ceiba can cost as much as US$37. For the express buses (notably Hedman Alas, the smartest operator: ⓦ hedmanalas .com), you should buy tickets in advance when possible; if you are getting on at smaller destinations the conductor will

come through and collect the fare. The frequency of buses slows down considerably after lunch, so you should try to be at your final destination by 4pm to avoid getting stranded.

BY CAR

If your budget will stretch, **renting a car** can open up the country's more isolated areas. Including insurance and emergency assistance, **rates** start at around US$45 a day for a small car, and US$90 for larger models and 4WDs. The highways connecting the main cities are well looked after, but the numerous dirt roads in the highlands can be impassable at certain times of the year, so always seek local advice on conditions before starting out. Rental agencies can be found at the airports in San Pedro Sula, Tegucigalpa and Roatán as well as in San Pedro Sula and Tegucigalpa towns. As with bus travel, however, it's important to be aware of the safety issues: **car-jackings** and armed robberies are not uncommon; inter-city routes are not safe after dark, and it's important to seek local advice before setting off.

Taxis are generally the safest way to travel around the bigger towns and cities, and should always be used after dark; they can also be hired for longer journeys – negotiate a price up-front. They operate in all the main towns, tooting when they are available. Meters are nonexistent, so always agree on a price before getting in. Expect to pay US$2–3 for a city ride in Tegucigalpa or San Pedro, or around US$1 in smaller towns. Three-wheeled moto-taxis (similar to tuk-tuks or auto-rickshaws) are available in some parts of the country.

BUS SAFETY

It is important to be aware of the **security** situation when travelling by bus in Honduras. In some of the bigger cities, notably San Pedro Sula and to a slightly lesser extent Tegucigalpa, local buses are not safe to use. Inter-city buses have been subject to armed robberies to such an extent that many services have a soldier on board. Always take a taxi to/from bus terminals, and don't travel on any buses after dark.

Hitching is very common in rural areas, but – as everywhere else in the world – carries inherent risks and is not advisable.

Internal flights in Honduras are fairly affordable. A small number of domestic airlines (not all with the best safety records) offer competitive fares, with frequent departures between Tegucigalpa and San Pedro Sula, La Ceiba and the Bay Islands; the most established airlines are SOSA (Ⓦaerolineassosahn.com) and Isleña/TACA (Ⓦflyislena.com). A one-way ticket between Tegucigalpa and San Pedro costs around US$110, while La Ceiba to Utila or Roatán is US$75. There's a **departure tax** of US$2.50 for internal flights.

Boats are the most budget-friendly option when it comes to reaching the Bay Islands: La Ceiba is linked to Roatán and Utila by daily ferries; Trujillo has less regular services to/from Guanaja.

ACCOMMODATION

That Honduras is slowly waking up to tourism is reflected in the country's **accommodation** options. The larger cities – Tegucigalpa, San Pedro Sula – offer the widest range of places to stay, with something to suit all budgets. **Hostels** are beginning to spring up across the country, generally representing excellent value for money; Copán has some of the best budget hostels on the mainland. Of the Bay Islands, Utila is the cheapest and Roatán has a few places catering to backpackers, while Guanaja is aimed more at luxury tourists. On the mainland, US$10–20 gets you a basic room; more than US$20 will secure a well-furnished room, with extras such as TV, a/c and hot water. A 16 percent tax is occasionally added to the bill. Usually the only time you need to **reserve** in advance is at Semana Santa or during a big local festival, such as the May Carnaval in La Ceiba.

The only formal provisions for **camping** are at Omoa, Copán Ruinas and in some of the national parks. Elsewhere, pitching a tent is very much an ad hoc affair. If you intend to camp, make sure you ask permission from the landowner. Tempting though they may seem, the north-coast beaches are not safe after dark and camping here is highly inadvisable.

FOOD AND DRINK

Budget travellers can eat very well in Honduras. The best way to start the day is with a **licuado**, a sort of fruit smoothie. Many places mix them with bananas and cornflakes, so they're very filling. Most towns have **markets** where you can pick up a huge amount of fresh produce. With an eye on your budget, you'll find that eating a big **lunch** is a better option than waiting for dinner. Market areas tend to be where you will find the cheapest *comedores*, where typical *almuerzos* of rice, beans, tortillas and meat can be had for around US$3–4.50. The larger cities have a decent range of **restaurants**, including an increasing number of fast-food chains. On the whole, you'll pay US$5 for a good-sized lunch at a restaurant. The ever-popular Chinese restaurants routinely have portions big enough for two, making them a reliable budget option. Note that most shops and facilities close from noon to 2pm so that families can eat lunch together.

Some of the highlights of *comida típica* (local cuisine) in Honduras include **anafre**, a fondue-like dish of cheese, beans or meat, or a mixture of all three, sometimes served as a bar snack, and **tapado**, a rich vegetable stew, often with meat or fish added. The north coast has a strong Caribbean influence, with lots of seafood. **Guisado** (spicy chicken stew) and **sopa de caracol** (conch stew with coconut milk, spices, potatoes and vegetables) should both be tried at least once. Probably the most common street snack, sold all over the country, is the **baleada**, a white-flour tortilla filled with beans, cheese and cream; two or three of these constitute a reasonable meal.

Licuados or **batidos** are a mix of fruit juice and milk. **Tap water** is unsafe to

5

drink; bottled, purified water is sold everywhere and many hotels have water machines. The usual brands of **fizzy drink** are ubiquitous.

Honduras produces five brands of **beer**: Salvavida and Imperial are heavier lagers, Port Royal slightly lighter and Nacional and Polar very light and quite tasteless. **Rum** (*ron*) is also distilled in the country, as is the Latin American rotgut, **aguardiente**. Adventurous connoisseurs of alcohol might wish to try **guifiti**, an elixir of various plants soaked in rum, found in the Garífuna villages of the north coast.

CULTURE AND ETIQUETTE

Catholicism is the main **religion** in Honduras – though American Evangelical missionary groups are having an impact – and with it come traditional values and roles. Family is very important, and children tend to grow up and settle close to their parents, though increasingly Honduran youngsters are going to the US in order to send back some money. Anti-gay attitudes are prevalent, and while not illegal, public displays of affection between same-sex couples are frowned upon.

Hondurans are very friendly, and, on the whole, glad to have visitors in their country and keen to tell you about where they come from. Greeting shop assistants is polite, and in smaller towns a simple "buenos días" can win you new friends in no time. Of Honduras's population, 85–90 percent are ladino (a mix of Spanish and indigenous people). The rest of the country is made up of a mixture of **ethnic minorities**. Prominent groups include the Maya Chorti in the department of Copán; the Lenca, with their traditional clothing,

found along the Ruta Lenca in the area around Santa Rosa de Copán; and the Miskitos in La Mosquitia.

A ten percent **tip** is the norm for waiters and tour guides, but is not expected in taxis. **Haggling** is not widespread, but a bit of gentle negotiation can earn you a discount at a hotel or a lower price with a taxi driver.

SPORTS AND OUTDOOR ACTIVITIES

The largest spectator sport in Honduras is **football** (soccer), and the Honduran national league and the major European leagues are all keenly followed. Olimpia and Motagua from Tegucigalpa, Marathón and Real España from San Pedro Sula, and Victoria from La Ceiba are the biggest teams and usually pull in a fairly decent crowd. **Tickets** don't need to be bought in advance, as most games don't sell out.

With a number of **national parks** – most of which have accommodation and/or camping and well-marked trails – Honduras is a fantastic place to **hike**. Parque Nacional Celaque, with the highest peak in the country, is a great place to start. Meanwhile, the Bay Islands offer some of the cheapest places in the world to take PADI **diving** certification courses – both the diving and the **snorkelling** are excellent – while Lago de Yojoa has **fishing** and **birdwatching** trips.

COMMUNICATIONS

There are **post offices** in every town; letters generally take a week to the US and up to two weeks to Europe. Opening hours are usually Monday to Friday 8am to noon and 2pm to 5pm, Saturday 8am to 1pm.

International **phone** calls can be made from Hondutel offices (there's a branch in every town), but are very expensive to Europe (around L50/min) – you are much better off visiting an internet café with web-phone capabilities. Many public telephones are out of use or damaged, so for local calls (eight-digit numbers) it's better to buy a cheap **mobile phone** (US$20–30) and periodically top up the

---

HONDURAN WORDS AND PHRASES

Ando hule I'm broke
Bola A dollar
Jalón A pick-up
Birria A beer
Macizo Cool
La riata Something/someone useless

credit (*recarga*), which can be done in most small shops. Alternatively, you could visit an office of mobile-phone provider Claro (the largest provider in Latin America – ⓦclaro.com.hn) to see if your phone will accept a foreign SIM card. All landline numbers start with a 2, while mobile numbers start with different digits (3, 8 or 9) according to the provider.

Internet cafés can be found in most towns; the average rate is L20–30/hr, or more on the Bay Islands. Many hotels provide internet/wi-fi access for guests, usually for free.

CRIME AND SAFETY

The security situation in Honduras has deteriorated dramatically in recent years, largely thanks to the activities of violent **drug gangs** ("maras"). San Pedro Sula has been dubbed the most violent city in the world, thanks to a horrifically high murder rate, and Tegucigalpa is not far behind. **Street crime** is a real concern throughout the country; as well as numerous cases of pickpocketing and robberies, some tourists have been killed (sometimes as a result of resisting a mugging). That said, the vast majority of travellers who visit Honduras do so safely, and you can reduce the likelihood of being a victim of crime by using **common sense** and caution. Leave your valuables at home (or in the safe of your hotel). Don't walk around cities or bigger towns unless you're very sure of your surroundings; see also our warning about **bus travel** (see box, p.380). After dark take a taxi, even for short distances. Steer well clear of rough neighbourhoods (local advice on where not to go is invaluable): for example, the Comayagüela district in Tegucigalpa, particularly around the market, and the streets south of the old railway line in San Pedro Sula are both considered very dangerous. Going around in groups is safer than exploring on your own.

The Bay Islands are considered safer than the mainland, and rural areas are generally safer than urban areas, though far from crime-free; taking the usual precautions and seeking advice from locals are vital. Hiking alone or walking on isolated stretches of beach (or indeed any stretch of beach at night) is inadvisable.

If you are the victim of a crime the **police** are unlikely to be of much help, but any incidents of theft should be reported for insurance purposes (ask for a *denuncia*).

The websites of the British Foreign Office (ⓦfco.gov.uk) and the US Department of State (ⓦstate.gov) have up-to-date security information and advice on Honduras; check both before travelling.

HEALTH

The Honduras Medical Centre, Av Juan Lindo in Tegucigalpa, is considered one of the best **hospitals** in the country; in San Pedro Sula head for the Hospital Centro Médico Betesda, Av 11A NO between C 11A and 12A NO. Facilities in rural areas tend to be much more limited, though most towns have at least one **pharmacy** (some of which are open 24hr), and staff, who can issue prescriptions, tend to be very helpful. In general, it's worth trying to learn a little emergency Spanish, as English is not widely spoken. Basic medical care is relatively inexpensive (certainly when compared with the US); for serious problems or emergencies it's best to head for a **private hospital** (or even, if possible, one in your home country).

Honduras has one of the highest rates of AIDS in Central America, so it is especially important to take all the usual precautions when it comes to sex. Make sure, too, if you seek medical help that all instruments are sterilized.

INFORMATION AND MAPS

The national tourist office, the **Instituto Hondureño de Turismo** (ⓦletsgohonduras .com), is fairly helpful. The main office,

---

EMERGENCY NUMBERS

Cruz Roja (ambulance) ☎195
Fire ☎198
International operator ☎197
Police ☎199 (☎*199 from a mobile)

5

HONDURAS ONLINE

ⓦ **honduras.com** The country's official website and one of the best.

ⓦ **hondurastips.hn** The definitive guide to the country, also published as an indispensable magazine (available free in hotels) detailing all the sights and latest developments of interest to tourists.

ⓦ **travel-to-honduras.com** General site covering a range of subjects – everything from business and tourism to Spanish schools and volunteer work.

in the Edificio Europa in Tegucigalpa (see p.390), can provide general **information** about where to go and what to see in the country. They also have booths at the Tegucigalpa and San Pedro Sula airports, and a free information service in the US (☏ 1 800 410 9608). Most towns you'll visit will have a municipality-run tourist office. These vary in helpfulness; the better ones sell maps, can arrange homestays and can tell you the cheapest places to stay. **National parks** and reserves are overseen by the government forestry agency, **ICF** (ⓦicf.gob.hn). If you intend to spend much time in any of the parks, it's worth visiting one of their offices for detailed information on flora and fauna. *Honduras Tips* (ⓦhondurastips.hn), a free bilingual magazine found in the better hotels and tourist offices, has fairly up-to-date information on hotel **listings** and bus routes – it is updated every few months. The magazine also has maps of most towns in the country.

The best **map** of Honduras is published by Reise Know-How (ⓦreise-know-how .de), and can be bought in bookshops or online; unfortunately, the chance of finding it in Honduras is unlikely.

MONEY AND BANKS

Honduras's currency is the **lempira** (L), which consists of 100 centavos; at the time of writing, the exchange rate was L19.5 to US$1. Coins come as 1, 2, 5, 10, 20 and 50 centavos and notes as 1, 2, 5, 10, 20, 50, 100 and 500 lempiras. In heavily touristed areas – Copán, the Bay Islands – **US dollars** are widely accepted, but on the whole lempiras are the standard currency.

You will need **cash** for day-to-day expenses, though credit/debit cards are accepted at smarter hotels and restaurants (there is often a hefty charge levied for credit/debit card payments, especially on the Bay Islands). ATMs are widespread, though acceptance of foreign **debit cards** can be hit-and-miss. Make sure before you leave home that your PIN is four digits or fewer; your card will be rejected if it is longer. As a rule Visa is more widely accepted than other cards. Beyond the usual charges for using your card abroad, there are no additional ATM charges. Visa cardholders can also get **cash advances** in several banks, including Banco Atlántida; MasterCard is sometimes accepted but not to be relied upon.

Honduras has a number of national **banks**, of which the biggest are Banco Atlántida, Banco de Occidente and BAC/ Credomatic. Many banks change **travellers' cheques** – American Express is the most widely accepted brand (in US dollars). When cashing travellers' cheques you will often be asked to show proof of purchase receipts and your passport.

OPENING HOURS AND PUBLIC HOLIDAYS

Business hours for **shops** are generally Monday to Friday 9am to noon and 2pm to 4.30 or 5pm, and Saturday from 9am to noon. **Banks** in larger towns are generally open 8.30am to 4.30pm and until noon on Saturdays, while those in smaller towns shut for an hour at lunch; moneychangers generally operate longer hours. **Museums** often stay open at lunch,

PUBLIC HOLIDAYS

Jan 1 New Year's Day
Easter week Semana Santa
April 14 Day of the Americas
May 1 Labour Day
Sept 15 Independence Day
Oct 3 Birth of Francisco Morazán
Oct 12 Discovery of America
Oct 21 Armed Forces Day
Dec 25 Christmas

but close at least one day each week. On **public holidays** (see box opposite), almost everything closes, and public transport generally operates on a reduced schedule.

FESTIVALS

Honduras's calendar is full of **festivals**, featuring everything from small local events to major national parties. The following are just a few highlights.

January 25–February 4 Pilgrims flock to Tegucigalpa to worship and celebrate the Virgen de Suyapa.
March–April Semana Santa (Easter) is a major celebration throughout Honduras, with many of the cities hosting sizeable parades.
April 6–12 Punta Gorda celebrates the arrival of the Garífuna.
May La Feria de San Isidro or Carnaval in La Ceiba, during the week leading up to the third Saturday. Festivities culminate in a street parade through the city centre, followed by live music until the early morning.
June 29 San Pedro Sula holiday.

Tegucigalpa and around

Situated 1000m above sea level, deep in a mountain valley, the Honduran capital of **TEGUCIGALPA** is not, at least on first impression, the most welcoming city. The winding, narrow streets are thick with motorized traffic, and the sidewalks full to the gills with shoppers and loafers. That said, unlike other capital cities in the region, Tegucigalpa isn't totally without charm, and its colonial feel and cool climate actually make it an ideal starting point, allowing you to get to grips with the Honduran pace of life.

Tegucigalpa's first mention in records is in the 1560s, when silver deposits ("tegucigalpa" means "silver mountain" in the Nahuatl language) were found in the hills to the east. It was given town status in 1768, and named a city in 1807. With wealth from the country's mines pouring in, the city's location at the centre of key trade routes became highly advantageous, and Tegucigalpa soon rivalled the then

capital, Comayagua. In 1880, the Liberal President Soto officially shifted power to Tegucigalpa, and in 1932 Comayagüela became a part of the capital. Since then, the nation's economic focus has shifted to San Pedro Sula, but Tegucigalpa continues to function as the nation's political and governmental centre.

Surrounded by reminders of its past – crumbling colonial buildings and decaying nineteenth-century mansions – the city today is a vibrant, noisy place. A handful of churches and a fantastic history museum will easily keep you entertained for a day or two. That said, **street crime** is a serious problem (see p.383), so take common-sense precautions.

WHAT TO SEE AND DO

The heart of Tegucigalpa's **old city** is the pleasant Parque Central, **Plaza Morazán**; a number of interesting churches and museums, plus many hotels, lie within easy walking distance of the square. East from the centre, two major roads, Avenida Jeréz (which becomes Avenida Juan Gutemberg and then Avenida La Paz) and Avenida Miguel Cervantes (which becomes Avenida República de Chile), skirt the edges of upmarket **Colonia Palmira**.

Running west from Plaza Morazán, the pedestrian-only **Calle Peatonal** is lined with shops, cafés and the fabulous Museo para la Identidad Nacional (see p.386). Further west of the old centre, the character of the city rapidly becomes more menacing as you approach the banks of the Río Choluteca.

Plaza Morazán

Plaza Morazán is the centre of life for most people who live and work in the capital. Shaded by a canopy of trees, and populated with shoe-shiners and other vendors, it's an atmospheric, if not particularly peaceful, place. A **statue** at the centre of the square commemorates national hero Francisco Morazán, a soldier, Liberal and reformer who was elected president of the Central American Republic in 1830. On the eastern edge of the plaza, the recently refurbished facade of the **Catedral San Miguel** (daily 8am–6pm; free), completed in 1782, is

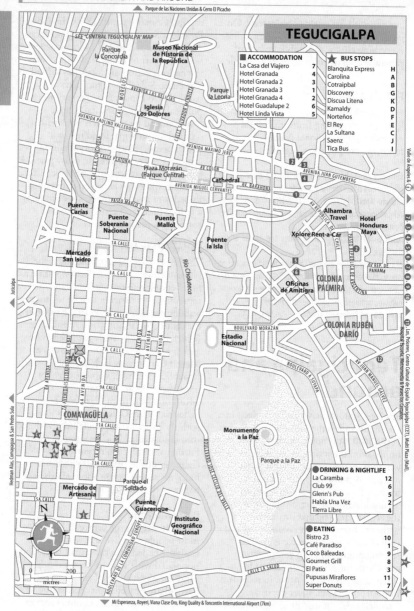

Parque de las Naciones Unidas & Cerro El Picacho

TEGUCIGALPA

ACCOMMODATION
La Casa del Viajero	7
Hotel Granada	4
Hotel Granada 2	3
Hotel Granada 3	1
Hotel Granada 4	2
Hotel Guadalupe 2	6
Hotel Linda Vista	5

BUS STOPS
Blanquita Express	H
Carolina	A
Cotraipbal	B
Discovery	G
Discusa Litena	K
Kamaldy	D
Norteños	F
El Rey	E
La Sultana	C
Saenz	J
Tica Bus	I

DRINKING & NIGHTLIFE
La Caramba	12
Club 99	6
Glenn's Pub	5
Había Una Vez	2
Tierra Libre	4

EATING
Bistro 23	10
Café Paradiso	1
Coco Baleadas	9
Gourmet Grill	8
El Patio	3
Pupusas Miraflores	11
Super Donuts	7

Mi Esperanza, Royeri, Viana Clase Oro, King Quality & Toncontín International Airport (7km)

one of the best preserved in Central America. Inside, look out for the magnificent Baroque-style gilded altar and the baptismal font, carved in 1643 from a single block of stone by indigenous artisans.

Museo para la Identidad Nacional

The permanent exhibition at the excellent **Museo para la Identidad Nacional**, Calle Peatonal (Mon–Sat 9am–5pm, Sun 10am–4pm; L60; ☎ 2238 7412, ⓦ min .hn), focuses on the history of Honduras.

Starting with the geographical formation of Central America, the displays move chronologically through the Maya civilization and colonial era to the various post-colonial presidents and their influence on the country. The museum's highlight is a 3D tour of Copán (Tues–Fri 10am, 11.30am, 2pm & 3.30pm; Sat 10am, 11.30am, 1pm, 2pm & 3.30pm; Sun 11.30am, 1pm, 2pm & 3.30pm; L30) that re-creates how the Maya kingdom would have looked at the height of its power.

Iglesia San Francisco

Three blocks east of Plaza Morazán, on Avenida Paz Barahona, the **Iglesia San Francisco** is the oldest church in the city, first built by the Franciscans in 1592, although much of the present building dates from 1740. No longer a functioning church, these days it houses a **museum** dedicated to the Honduran armed forces (Mon–Fri 8am–4pm; free). The signage is all in Spanish.

Galería Nacional de Arte

Just south of the Parque Morazán and next to the Iglesia La Merced on Calle Bolívar, the **Galería Nacional de Arte** (Mon–Sat 9am–4pm, Sun 9am–2pm; L30; ☎2237 9884) is home to an extensive and interesting collection of Central American art. Displays on the ground floor range from prehistoric petroglyphs and Maya stone carvings to religious art, while rooms upstairs house an ambitious selection of modern and contemporary Honduran art, including some works by Pablo Zelaya Sierra, one of the country's leading twentieth-century artists. Originally serving as a convent during the seventeenth century, and later as the national university, the building has a Neoclassical facade that sits rather uncomfortably alongside the stained concrete bulk of the **Congreso Nacional**, the country's seat of government next door.

Iglesia Los Dolores

A few blocks northwest from the central plaza, the pleasant, white, domed **Iglesia Los Dolores** (daily 8am–6pm; free), completed in 1732, sits next to the small **Plaza Los Dolores**. Its Baroque facade is

decorated with a representation of the Passion of Christ, featuring a crowing cock and the rising sun; inside, the elaborate gold altar dates from 1742. A choir usually sings at 6pm on Saturdays and Sundays. The plaza itself is crowded with cheap, shabby stalls.

Colonia Palmira and around

The upscale **Colonia Palmira** neighbourhood is home to most of the capital's foreign embassies, luxury hotels, top restaurants and swanky residences. A particular landmark, the modern **Hotel Honduras Maya**, is on the Avenida República de Chile, in Colonia Palmira, fifteen minutes' walk east from the centre. A kilometre beyond the hotel, an overpass gives access to eastward-bound **Boulevard Morazán**, Tegucigalpa's major commercial and entertainment artery. No city buses run along here, so you'll have to walk or take a taxi. On Calle 1, the **Centro Cultural de España Tegucigalpa** (CCET; Tues–Sun 10am–8pm; ☎2238 2013, ⊛ccet-aecid.com), housed in an attractive modern building, puts on a stimulating programme of music, art exhibitions and talks.

Cerro El Picacho

To the north of Plaza Morazán, older suburbs – previously home to the wealthy middle classes and rich immigrants, now long gone – edge up the lower slopes of **Cerro El Picacho**. Grab a picnic and escape to the **Parque Naciones Unidas El Picacho** for fantastic views over the city. At the top stands the open-armed **Cristo del Picacho**, illuminated at night in a dazzle of coloured lights. Take a bus from in front of *Hotel Granada 2* or a taxi (around L150); it's a twenty-minute journey.

Comayagüela

The brown waters of the polluted Río Choluteca form the border of Tegucigalpa's twin, **Comayagüela**, which sprawls away through down-at-heel business districts into industrial areas and poor *barrios*. Such is its dangerous reputation that tourists are not advised to spend any more time here than it takes to change buses.

5

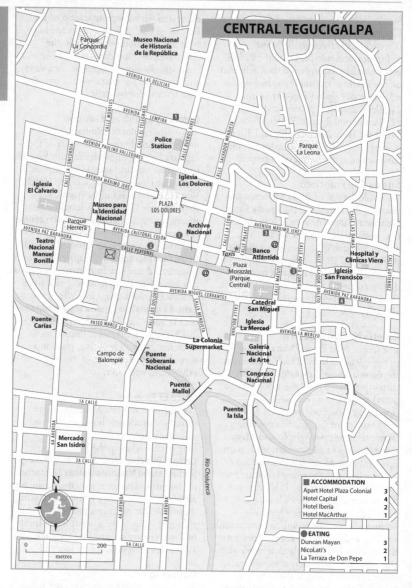

CENTRAL TEGUCIGALPA

ACCOMMODATION	
Apart Hotel Plaza Colonial	3
Hotel Capital	4
Hotel Iberia	2
Hotel MacArthur	1

EATING	
Duncan Mayan	3
NicoLati's	2
La Terraza de Don Pepe	1

ARRIVAL AND DEPARTURE

By plane Toncontín International Airport, 7km south of the city, sees international (see p.379) and domestic flights. Taxis (around L200 into the city centre; US dollars are generally accepted) wait outside the terminal. Bus #24 also passes the airport, running through Comayagüela and Tegucigalpa.

Domestic destinations La Ceiba (Isleña/TACA & SOSA, 3 daily; 50min); Roatán (Isleña/TACA & SOSA, 1–2 daily; 1hr 10min); San Pedro Sula (Isleña/TACA, 2 daily; 50min).
By bus There is no main bus station; each international or intercity bus company has its own terminal (see box opposite), most of them scattered around Comayagüela. Whichever station you use, take a taxi to your drop-off point.

Domestic destinations Choluteca (B hourly 3.30am–4pm; luxury ME 6am, 10am, 2pm & 6pm; normal ME hourly 4am–6pm; R, S 1–2 hourly 4am–5.45pm; 2hr 30min–3hr 30min); Comayagua (LS; hourly 6am–1.30pm; 1hr 30min–2hr); Copán Ruinas (HA; 5.45am & 10am via San Pedro Sula; 8hr); Juticalpa (direct D hourly 6.15am–4.15pm; 2hr; normal D hourly 6.45am–5pm; 3hr); La Ceiba (HA 5.45am, 10am & 1.30pm; K 7.30am, 12.30am & 3.30pm; V 6.30am, 9.30am & 1.30pm; 5hr 30min–7hr); La Esperanza (CA; hourly 5am–4.50pm; 4hr); La Guama (for Lago de Yojoa) (N 1–2 hourly 6am–2.30pm; ER 7.30am, 9.30am, noon & 2pm; 2hr 30min); San Pedro Sula (CN hourly 8.45am–4.15pm; ER 7.30am, 9.30am, noon & 2pm; HA 5.45am, 10am, 1.30pm & 5pm; N 1–2 hourly 6am–2.30pm; RE every 30min 5.30am–6.15pm; V Mon–Fri & Sun 6.30am, 1.30pm, 3.30pm & 6.15pm, Sat 6.30am, 9.30am, 1.30pm & 3.30pm; 3hr 30min–4hr); Santa Rosa de Copán (HA 5.45am & 1.30pm; LS 6am, 7.30am, 8.30am & 10am; 7hr); Siguatepeque (N 1–2 hourly 6am–2.30pm; ER 7.30am, 9.30am, noon & 2pm; 2hr); Tela (take a La Ceiba-bound bus; HA 5.45am, 10am & 1.30pm; K 7.30am, 12.30pm & 3.30pm; V 6.30am, 9.30am & 1.30pm; 5hr); Trujillo (C 2 daily, 6.10am & 8.20am; 5hr 30min).

International destinations Guatemala City (HA 2 daily, 5.45am & 10am; KQ 1 daily, 5.30am; TB 1 daily, 6am, with overnight in El Salvador; 12–14hr); Managua (KQ 1 daily, 5.30am; TB 1 daily, 9.30am; around 8hr); Panama City (TB; 1 daily, 9.30am with overnights in Nicaragua and Costa Rica; 2 days); San José (TB; 1 daily, 9.30am with overnight in Managua; 1 day); San Salvador (KQ 1 daily, 5.30am; TB 1 daily, 5.30pm; 7hr).

GETTING AROUND

By bus Chicken buses run the urban routes. Route names and numbers are painted on the front, and you pay your fare on the bus. No buses pass close to Plaza Morazán or Blvd Morazán. However, buses are not especially safe (see box, p.380), and tourists are often targeted by pickpockets. Don't use the buses after dark; take a taxi instead.

By taxi Taxis are usually white with numbers painted on the side. A short ride within the city costs around L50–80 during the day, a little more at night. *Colectivo* taxis gather at predetermined stops (*puntos*); the most central one is on C Palace just north of Plaza Morazán. They generally leave when full with passengers going to a similar area of the city. Though you may have to wait a bit, they are cheaper than standard taxis. Always use a taxi to get around after dark.

BUS COMPANIES AND STOPS

Tegucigalpa does not have a central bus terminal. Instead, each bus company has its own office and bus stop – most are in Comayagüela (see p.387). Take a taxi when travelling to and from this area. The following are the main operators.

Blanquito Express (**B**; ☎ 2225 1502) Direct to Choluteca from its stop in Barrio Villa Adela.

Carolina (**CA**) To La Esperanza from Av 7 (Solidaridad de Cuba), C 7–8.

Costeños (**CN**) Normal services to San Pedro Sula from Av 7, C 11–12.

Cotraipbal (**C**; ☎ 2237 1666) Direct to Trujillo from Av 7, C 11–12.

Discovery (**D**; ☎ 2222 4256) Normal services to Juticalpa from Av 7, C 12–13.

Discua Litena (**DL**; ☎ 2230 2939) Direct services to El Paraíso (for Nicaragua) from Col Kennedy, near Mercado Jacaleapa.

El Rey (**ER**; ☎ 2237 1462) Normal services to La Guama and San Pedro Sula from C 12, Av 7–8.

El Rey Express (**RE**; ☎ 2237 8561) Direct services to San Pedro Sula from the same spot as El Rey.

Hedman Alas (**HA**; ☎ 2237 7143) Direct and luxury services to La Ceiba and San Pedro Sula from Av 11, C 13–14.

Kamaldy (**K**; ☎ 2220 0117) Services to La Ceiba from the corner of Av 8 & C 12.

King Quality (**KQ**; ☎ 2225 5415) Luxury services to Guatemala City (Guatemala), Managua (Nicaragua) and San Salvador (El Salvador) from Blvd Comunidad Económica Europea, Barrio La Granja.

La Sultana (**LS**; ☎ 2237 8101) Normal services to Santa Rosa de Copán and Comayagua from Av 8, C 11–12.

Mi Esperanza (**ME**; ☎ 2225 1502) Luxury and normal services to Choluteca from C 23–24, Barrio Villa Adela.

Norteños (**N**; ☎ 2237 0706) Normal services to La Guama and San Pedro Sula from C 12, Av 6–7.

Royeri (**R**; ☎ 2225 2863) Normal services to Choluteca from C 23–24, Barrio Villa Adela.

Saenz (**S**; ☎ 2213 9200 or ☎ 2231 3112) First-class services to Choluteca from the small Centro Comercial Centroamerica on Blvd Centroamerica.

Tica Bus (**TB**; ☎ 2220 0579, ✺ ticabus.com) Luxury services to Guatemala City (Guatemala), Managua (Nicaragua), Panama City (Panama), San José (Costa Rica) and San Salvador (El Salvador) from C 16, Av 5–6.

Viana Clase Oro (**V**; ☎ 2239 8288) Luxury services to La Ceiba and San Pedro Sula from Las Cascadas mall on Blvd Fuerzas Armadas.

5

INFORMATION

Tourist information The tourist office is in Edificio Europa, Av Ramón Ernesto Cruz, Colonia San Carlos (Mon–Sat 9am–5pm ☏ 2222 2124).

Travel agent Alhambra Travel (☏ 2220 1704, ⓦ alhambratravel.net) on Av República de Chile in the "*area comercial*" close to *Hotel Honduras Maya*, is quick, friendly and efficient.

ACCOMMODATION

As the capital, Tegucigalpa's accommodation is generally pricier than elsewhere in Honduras.

Apart Hotel Plaza Colonial Av Máximo Jeréz, behind Plaza Morazán ☏ 2222 7727 or ☏ 2237 9159; map p.388. A haven of calm away from the capital's busy streets, with nice details like a fountain on the ground floor and carved wooden bed frames. All rooms are en suite, and rates include breakfast. Ten percent discount for cash payments. **L812**

Hotel Capital Av Miguel Cervantes ☏ 2220 0156; map p.388. Clean, family-run hotel with simple rooms with big windows that let in plenty of natural light. **L450**

Hotel Granada Av Juan Gutemberg at Av Cristóbal Colón ☏ 2237 2381, ⓔ hotelgranadategucigalpa@yahoo.com; map p.386. A consistently popular budget option, *Hotel Granada* has basic but clean rooms; the better ones are en suite and come with TVs. **L500**

Hotel Granada 2 & Hotel Granada 3 Opposite each other on Subida Casa Martín, just off Av Juan Gutemberg *Grenada 2* ☏ 2238 4438, *Grenada 3* ☏ 2237 8066; map p.386. Just around the corner from the original *Hotel Granada*, and under the same management, these hotels are both solid choices. All rooms, which include several triples and quads, are en suite. **L550**

Hotel Granada 4 Facing *Granada 3* ☏ 2237 4004; map p.386. The newest and nicest of the *Granada* hotels: all rooms have TV and private bath, and free internet/wi-fi is available in the lobby area. **L600**

Hotel Guadalupe 2 Av Juan Manuel Galvez 324 ☏ 2238 5009, ⓔ hotelguadalupe@cablecolor.hn; map p.386. In a safe, residential area, this hotel has 14 rooms, all with private hot-water baths. Communal areas have comfy sofas, and wi-fi is available, as well as a/c, at a price. **L450**

Hotel Iberia Plaza Los Dolores ☏ 2237 9267; map p.388. Rooms are basic but very clean. There's little natural light, no a/c, and hot water is only available 6–8am, but sharing a bathroom makes things very cheap. **L350**

Hotel Linda Vista C Las Acacias 1438, Colonial Palmira ☏ 2238 0188, ⓦ lindavistahotel.net; map p.386. Although a little worn around the edges, this hotel has cosy en-suite rooms and wonderful city views. It's just beyond the Edificio Italia on the opposite side of the road, in an unmarked yellow building with a red garden wall. Rates include breakfast. **US$65**

Hotel MacArthur Av Lempira 454 ☏ 2237 9839, ⓦ hotelmacarthur.com; map p.388. Neat en-suite rooms with TVs and fans (a/c costs around US$10 extra) at this lower mid-range hotel, which also boasts a nice pool area. Rates include breakfast. **US$49**

EATING

The centre has all the usual fast-food chains and cheap and cheerful cafés, as well as a few good-value restaurants with meals for less than L100; smarter restaurants are to be found in Colonia Palmira and along Blvd Morazán.

CAFÉS

Bistro 23 Second floor of the Nova Centro mall on the Los Próceres site; map p.386. Three or four options (from around L120) daily, such as fish chowder and Greek moussaka. Mon–Wed & Sun 11am–8pm, Thurs–Sat 11am–2am.

Café Paradiso Av Paz Barahona 1351 ☏ 2237 0337; map p.386. Attractive café-bar, popular with local artists, in a colonial-era building with art on the walls and a nice outdoor seating area. The menu runs from coffee and croissants to beer and pastas (from around L100). It's gay-friendly, and film and literary events are often staged in the evenings. Mon–Sat 10am–10pm.

Coco Baleadas Los Próceres mall; map p.386. A Honduran take on the classic sandwich bar, offering coconut *baleadas* (see p.381) with a choice of twenty or so fillings. You can get a *baleada* and a soft drink for under L60. Daily 7am–10pm.

Gourmet Grill At the back of The Bakery Center on Paseo República de Argentina, Colonia Palmira; map p.386. Cheerfully decorated with primary colours, padded banquettes and zebra print throughout. Huge breakfasts (L100–200) – from waffles to eggs Benedict – are the order of the day. You probably won't need lunch.

NicoLati's C Peatonal; map p.388. A chain-like atmosphere but pleasant nonetheless, with good coffee,

---

★ TREAT YOURSELF

La Casa del Viajero Lomas del Guijarro, Av Enrique Tierno Galvan 2884, 80m beyond the Instituto Sagrado Corazon ☏ 2231 0431, ⓦ casadelviajero.com; map p.386. This colonial-style house once belonged to a Honduran president and you can well imagine it: standing on the terrace, looking out over the city, you'll feel like the king of all you survey. Inside, it's huge, tiled throughout and teeming with plants; the rooms all have a/c, TVs and mini-fridges. There's a communal kitchen, and free wi-fi, buffet breakfast and shuttle-bus tour service. It's a 10min walk downhill to Bvd Morazán. **US$70**

sandwiches and crepes (from L60), plus free wi-fi. There's another branch in Plaza Miraflores.

Super Donuts Blvd Morazán; map p.386. In spite of the name, this place is locally revered for its varied breakfast menu, from the basic eggs and ham to beer-stewed *frijoles borrachos* and banana-leaf-wrapped corn, meat and rice, known as *nacatamales*. Dishes from L20.

RESTAURANTS

Duncan Mayan Av Cristóbal Colón; map p.388. In a new location but as popular as ever. The central of the three large rooms would be a pleasant courtyard but for the covering of corrugated plastic. Mains L100–160. Open till 10pm.

El Patio Far eastern end of Blvd Morazán ☎ 2221 4141; map p.386. Meat may not be Honduras's strong point, but they make a good stab at it in this cavernous banqueting hall. Try the *pincho olanchano*, a mix of beef, chorizo and pork – the cowboys from Honduras's own Wild East would be proud. Mains L160–320. Daily 11am–midnight.

Pupusas Miraflores 2 Blvd Suyapa; map p.386. Good, inexpensive restaurant crammed with locals, specializing in tacos, *pupusas* (from L20) and *flautas* ("flute" tacos). Try the *loroco* flower-filled *pupusa* when it's in season. Take a taxi here – drivers should know it. Daily 11am–10pm.

La Terraza de Don Pepe Av Cristóbal Colón ☎ 2237 1084; map p.388. On two floors above a fried-chicken shop, this *comida típica* restaurant has plenty of character with once-grand, now faded dining rooms and a slip of a balcony. The dishes of the day (around L80–100) are good options. Daily 8am–10pm.

DRINKING AND NIGHTLIFE

Use taxis when going out at night. Most bars in the centre are fiercely local, so you're best off heading to Colonia Palmira and Blvd Morazán. Head also to Paseo Los Próceres (closed Sun), a peculiar strip of bars at the large Los Próceres site, housed in units that were intended for clothing boutiques. *Café Paradiso* (see opposite) is also worth stopping by for an early evening drink.

BARS

Glenn's Pub C Av 1A, Colonia Palmira; map p.386. Better than its bland name might suggest, this is a tiny, satisfyingly grungy place. It's not easy to spot – look out for it just beyond the triangular traffic island with trees. Open 6pm–late.

Había Una Vez Near *Hotel Honduras Maya*, Paseo República de Argentina; map p.386. An artsy café-bar with original work displayed on the brightly painted walls (and colanders for lampshades). A beer will set you back around L35, and there's some decent food on offer too. Daily 6pm–2am.

Tierra Libre C 3A, Colonia Palmira; map p.386. Formerly known as *Cinefilia*, *Tierra Libre* shows (non-Hollywood) movies every Tues and hosts live bands at the weekend.

Local beers L30, as well as a few international brands such as Leffe. Mon–Sat 5pm–midnight.

CLUBS

La Caramba Col Rubén Darío, opposite Cybex gym; map p.386. Live music specialists, with "salsa Saturdays", jazz, reggae and rock nights. Drinks from L30. Thurs–Sat 7pm–2am.

Club 99 Blvd Morazán, behind a *Subway* and just beyond an enormous *KFC*; map p.386. Formerly *Bambu*, this place attracts tourists, students and foreign volunteers. Entrance around L150. Wed, Fri & Sat from 9pm.

ENTERTAINMENT

The website ⊛ agendartehonduras.com is a helpful up-to-the-minute resource for cultural events listings.

Cinema The modern Multi Plaza complex (see below) has an eight-screen cinema, Cinemark, showing subtitled Hollywood blockbusters.

Football The Estadio Nacional, at the western end of Blvd Morazán, hosts international and domestic football games. Buy tickets at the stadium. Depending on the teams playing and whether you are in a sunny or shady spot, tickets start at around L100.

Theatre The Teatro Nacional Manuel Bonilla (☎ 2222 4366, ⊛ teatromanuelbonilla.hn) is a 15min walk west of Parque Morazán along Calle Peatonal; ask at the box office inside for details of current shows.

SHOPPING

La Colonia South of the Plaza on C Bolívar ⊛ lacolonia .hn. Supermarket selling everything you need to make lunch, as well as toiletries and alcohol. Daily 7am–8pm.

Metromedia Av San Carlos beyond C República de Mexico; smaller branch in Multi Plaza. Bookstore with a wide range of English-language fiction, nonfiction and travel titles, as well as secondhand books and US newspapers and magazines. There's a café on site. Mon–Sat 10am–8pm, Sun noon–6pm.

Multi Plaza Av Juan Pablo II, 1.5km southeast of Colonia Rubén Darío ⊛ multiplaza.com. Mall with international shops, a huge food court with the usual fast-food chains, a Paiz supermarket and a cinema. Tigo and Claro stores here sell SIM cards and mobile phones. Daily 8am–10pm.

DIRECTORY

Banks Most banks will change dollars and travellers' cheques. Banco Atlántida, on Plaza Morazán (with 24hr ATM) and elsewhere, gives advances on Visa cards. ATMs are commonplace.

Car rental Advance Rent A Car (☎ 2235 9531/9528) at the airport; X Plore Rent A Car (☎ 2239 0134), near *Hotel Maya*, Colonia Palmira.

Embassies Belize, ground floor of *Hotel Honduras Maya*,

5

Av República de Perú & C 3 (Mon–Fri 9am–1pm; ⓣ 2238 4616); Canada, Edificio Financiero Banexpo 3, Col Payaqui, Blvd San Juan Bosco (Mon–Fri 9am–3pm; ⓣ 2232 4551); Costa Rica, Residencial El Triángulo, 1A C, Casa 3451 (Mon–Fri 8am–3pm; ⓣ 2232 1768); El Salvador, Colonia Altos de Miramontes, Casa 2952, Diagonal Aguan (Mon–Fri 8.30am–noon & 1–3pm; ⓣ 2232 4947); Guatemala, Colonia Lomas de Guijarro (Mon–Fri 8.30am–3pm; ⓣ 2231 1543); Mexico, Colonia Lomas del Guijarro, Av Eucalipto (Mon–Fri 8–11am; ⓣ 2232 0141); Nicaragua, C 11, Block M1, Colonia Lomas del Tepeyac (Mon–Fri 8.30am–1pm; ⓣ 2232 1966); Panama, Edificio Palmira 200, Colonia Palmira (Mon–Fri 8am–1pm; ⓣ 2239 5508); UK, Centro Financiero Banexpo 3 piso, Colonia Payaqui (Mon–Thurs 8am–noon & 1–4pm, Fri 8am–3pm; ⓣ 2232 0612); US, Av La Paz (Mon–Fri 8am–5pm; ⓣ 2236 9320).

Hospitals Hospital y Clínicas Viera (ⓣ 2237 3160, ⓦ hospitalyclinicasviera.hn), Av Colón, by C Las Damas, is a reliable private health-care provider. There are emergency departments (24hr) at the public Hospital Escuela, Blvd Suyapa (ⓣ 2232 6234), and Hospital General San Felipe, C La Paz by the Bolívar monument, though neither has the best reputation.

Immigration Dirección General de Migracíon, Av La Paz, near the US Embassy (Mon–Fri 8.30am–4.30pm).

Internet Cybercafé Colonial, C Matute. Prices are around L20/hr.

Laundry Superc Jet, Av Juan Gutemberg beyond Parque Finlay (Mon–Sat 8am–5pm).

Police Go to the FSP office on C Buenos Aires, behind Los Dolores church, with any problems.

Post office The post office is at C Peatonal at C El Telégrafo, three blocks west of Plaza Morazán (Mon–Fri 8am–7pm, Sat 8am–1pm).

AROUND TEGUCIGALPA

There are several places a short bus ride away from Tegucigalpa where you can while away an afternoon, or even a day or two. The famous **Basílica de Suyapa** takes only twenty minutes to reach, or for a really adventurous couple of days you could take yourself off to **Valle de Ángeles** for a morning before going on to the **Parque Nacional La Tigra** to hike.

Basílica de Suyapa

Some 6km east of Tegucigalpa's centre, the monolithic white bulk of the **Basílica de Suyapa** (daily 9am–5pm; free) rises from the flat plains. Built in the 1950s, it is home to the **Virgen de Suyapa**, patron saint of Honduras. The statue of the Virgin was discovered by two *campesinos* in 1743. The story goes that after bedding down for the night, one of them noticed he was lying on something, but without looking to see what the offending object was, threw it to one side. Within a few minutes, however, the object had returned. The next day, the two carried the little statue down to Suyapa where, placed on a simple table adorned with flowers, the Virgin began to attract worshippers.

Today you can see the tiny statue (just 6cm tall) behind the wooden altar in **La Pequeña Iglesia**, the original eighteenth-century chapel behind the Basílica. According to legend, each time she is placed in the larger Basílica, the Virgin mysteriously returns to the simple chapel, built by Captain José de Zelaya y Midence in thanks for the recovery of his health.

City **buses** to Suyapa run regularly from the Mercado San Isidro in Comayagüela (20min).

Valle de Ángeles

Continuing east from the Basílica de Suyapa, the road rises gently amid magnificent scenery, winding through forests of slender pine trees. Some 22km from the capital is **VALLE DE ÁNGELES**, a former mining town now reincarnated as a handicraft centre and scenic getaway for *capitalanos*. Surrounded by forested mountains, the small town slumbers during the week, then explodes with activity at weekends. The town is chiefly noted for its quality carved wooden goods, and it's a nice place to while away a couple of hours.

ARRIVAL AND DEPARTURE

By bus Buses leave Tegucigalpa for Valle de Ángeles from a car park near the San Felipe Hospital (every 45min until 6pm; 45min–1hr) and terminate a couple of blocks from the town's Parque Central. The last return bus leaves around 5.30pm.

EATING

Restaurante Manolo On the Parque Central. Your best bet in Valle de Ángeles, with freshly cooked, tender meat prepared on the outside grill. Go for a steak or the *anafre*, Honduran fondue with beans and cheese (mains from around L80).

Parque Nacional La Tigra

The oldest reserve in Honduras, **Parque Nacional La Tigra** (daily 8am–5pm; US$5) was designated a national park in 1980. Just 22km from Tegucigalpa, its accessibility and good system of trails make it a popular destination; however, much of the original cloudforest has been destroyed through heavy logging, so what you see is generally secondary growth. Parts of the park still shelter oak trees, bromeliads, ferns, orchids and other typical cloudforest flora, along with **wildlife** such as deer, white-faced monkeys and ocelots – though they tend to stick to parts of the park that are out of bounds to visitors. The **trails** are well laid out, and provide some easy hiking, either on a circular route from the visitors' centre or across the park between the two entrances. **Guides** (US$5–15/day) are also available, though they only speak Spanish. You can visit the park as a day-trip but it's worth staying a couple of nights.

The park has two entrances. The western side is reached via the village of **Jutiapa**, 17km east of Tegucigalpa. Though slightly easier to reach from the capital, this entrance has few facilities. The second entrance is best reached via the village of **San Juancito** from where you can walk or get a pick-up the 5km to the park.

ARRIVAL AND INFORMATION

Via Jutiapa Take the El Hatillo bus from the corner of C Finlay & C Cristóbal (50min) in Tegucigalpa.

Via San Juancito Direct buses run to San Juancito from Mercado San Pablo, Barrio El Manchen (3 daily; 2hr) in

Tegucigalpa or from Valle de Ángeles (3 daily; 2hr; pick-ups are also available). From San Juancito it is a steep 5km hike up the mountain to the visitors' centre; pick-ups are sometimes available for around L300.

Visitors' centre The visitors' centre has simple accommodation (US$10/person) and the friendly warden is usually around to provide information and trail maps.

Southern Honduras

Stark, sun-baked coastal plains stretch south from Tegucigalpa all the way to the Pacific Ocean. Though a world away from the clean air and gentle climate of the highlands, this region is nonetheless beautiful in its own right, defined by a dazzling light and ferociously high temperatures. Traditionally a poor region, it's also a little-visited one, with the foreigners who do pass through usually in transit to Nicaragua or El Salvador. If you're really looking to get off the gringo trail, this is the place to do it.

The chief attraction in the area – and well worth a visit – is **Isla El Tigre**, a volcanic island set in the calm waters of the **Golfo de Fonseca**, while the colonial city of **Choluteca** offers a change of pace from the frenzy of the capital and makes a convenient stopover en route to Nicaragua.

The main transport junction in this part of the country is the village of **Jícaro Galán**, at the intersection of Highway CA-5 and the Carretera Panamericana,

---

INTO NICARAGUA: LAS MANOS

The **Las Manos** border crossing, some 120km from Tegucigalpa, is the most convenient place to enter **Nicaragua** from the capital. Buses run to the town of El Paraíso (Discua Litena; hourly 6am–6pm; 2hr 15min), 12km from the border, from where minibuses and pick-ups shuttle to the border every thirty minutes or so. With an early enough start, it's possible to reach Managua (see p.457) the same day. Taxi drivers hawking for business may well tell you that no buses run to the border from El Paraíso, but this is not true. However, if you don't want to wait around for one of the buses, you could take a taxi for about US$5–6.

The border post itself is a collection of huts housing the immigration and customs officials. Both sides are open daily until 5pm and crossing is generally straightforward. There are no banks, but eager moneychangers accept dollars, lempiras and Nicaraguan córdobas. There's a US$3 exit tax to leave Honduras. On the Nicaraguan side, trucks leave every hour for Ocotal, from where you can pick up buses to Estelí and Managua.

5

some 70km south of Tegucigalpa. Buses stop here to exchange passengers before continuing west to the border with El Salvador at El Amatillo, 42km away (see box opposite), or east to Nicaragua.

ISLA EL TIGRE

Boats depart the fishing village of **Coyolito**, on the coast of the Golfo de Fonseca, southwest of Jícaro Galán, for the volcanic **ISLA EL TIGRE**, whose conical peak rises sharply against the sky across the sparkling water. With good beaches, calm waters and constant sunshine, it's an ideal spot to hide away for a couple of days.

WHAT TO SEE AND DO

The island's only town is **AMAPALA**, once the country's major Pacific port and now a decaying relic of the nineteenth century. Looking up from the dock, you'll see ageing wooden houses clustered along the hillside, while the restored church in the **Parque Central** shows signs of the island's desire to get on the tourist map. Nonetheless, during the week there's every chance you'll be the only visitor on the island.

From the southern side of the island there are stunning **views** across the gulf to Volcán Cosiguina in Nicaragua, and in some places to Isla Meanguera and mainland El Salvador. The island's peak can be climbed in a steep and very hot two- to three-hour **walk**; ask for directions to the start of the trail, opposite the naval base, about 15 minutes' walk southwest of Amapala.

Beaches

An 18km road runs all the way around the island, giving access to some glorious deserted **beaches**; it takes four or more hours to walk the whole thing, or you can take one of the moto-taxis that hang around the end of the dock in Amapala (around L300 for a trip around the island).

A 45-minute walk or L10–20 moto-taxi ride (avoid the car taxis that may be waiting at the end of the pier – find a red moto-taxi near the square) east from the Parque Central takes you to **Playa El Burro**, where you can while away the afternoon people-watching – children and taxi drivers play football on the beach before cooling off in the sea. Popular **Playa Grande**, a L10–20 ride west of the plaza, is backed by rows of *comedores* serving freshly barbecued fish at the weekend. A further ten minutes west is **Playa Negra**, a pretty volcanic sand beach.

ARRIVAL AND INFORMATION

By bus and boat Mi Esperanza runs buses from Tegucigalpa to Choluteca (1–2 hourly; 3hr 30min), which can drop you off at Jícaro Galán on the Carretera Interamericana (look out for the Dippsa fuel station). Local buses (every 15min; 1hr) shuttle between here and Coyolito. From Coyolito, regular taxi boats (the last one departs around 6pm; 15min) run to/from Amapala's dock. You can also sometimes be dropped off at Playa El Burro.

Bank The nearest ATM is in San Lorenzo, between Coyolito and Choluteca.

Tourist information The tourist office on the pier (Mon–Sat 9am–5pm; ☎ 9823 8579) has a basic hand-drawn map of the island on the wall that you can copy or photograph.

ACCOMMODATION AND EATING

Accommodation standards are fairly low, though a good option is to contact the tourist office to arrange a homestay (from L200/person/night).

Aquatours Marbella Playa El Burro ☎ 2795 8075. A rather run-down, overpriced hotel with acceptable attached, a/c rooms and a murky-looking pool. **L1000**

El Faro Victoria At the end of the Amapala dock. Atmospheric place with a terrace that sits over the water. There's good food, including fried fish and *curiles* cocktail (local clams marinated in their own blood, lime juice and *chismol*, which is similar to salsa). Most mains L70–200. Mon–Thurs 7–10pm, Fri–Sun noon–3pm & 7–10pm.

Veleros Casa de Huéspedes Playa El Burro ☎ 2795 8040 or ☎ 9898 2285. Friendly guesthouse with a handful of spick-and-span rooms. The attached *palapa*-roofed beach café is a great place to watch the world go by; try the shrimp *ceviche*. Mains around L100–150. **L400**

CHOLUTECA

Honduras's fourth-largest city, with a population of around 160,000, **CHOLUTECA** has a fine old colonial centre, which is its main attraction. Most places of interest are grouped around the **Parque Central**, itself a pleasant place to enjoy the evening air. Dominating the square, the imposing seventeenth-century **cathedral** is worth a look for its elaborately constructed wooden ceiling. On the southwest corner of the square is the birthplace of **José Cecilio del Valle**, one of the authors of the Central American Act of Independence in 1821; the town's authorities have started to turn the building into a municipal museum. It is Valle's statue that stands in the middle of the square. Once you've seen the centre, there's not much reason to hang out in the heat, and most people move on fairly quickly.

ARRIVAL AND INFORMATION

By bus The main terminal is ten blocks northeast of the Parque Central (a 20min walk or L20–30 taxi ride). Mi Esperanza also has a stop down the street from the main terminal. Both Mi Esperanza and Blanquito Express run regular buses to/from Tegucigalpa (2–3 hourly; 2hr 30min–3hr 30min). There are also buses to Nicaragua and El Salvador (see box below).

Banks Banco Occidente, one block south of the Parque Cental, has a 24hr ATM, as does Banco Atlántida, on Av J.C. del Valle at the corner with C F.D. Roosevelt.

Internet Try Global Cyber in Pasaje Sarita, near *Espresso Americano*.

ACCOMMODATION AND EATING

Bonsai Av Valle ☏ 2782 2648. The rooms vary quite widely at this low-cost hotel, so make sure you look at a few before checking in; the better ones have private bathrooms and a/c. The grassy courtyard that most rooms open onto saves the place from drabness. **L425**

Paseo Metropolitano On the Panamericana. This restaurant is a reliable spot for a hearty, good-value Honduran-style lunch or dinner.

Santa Rosa Av La Rosa between C Williams & C Paz Barahona ☏ 2782 0355. The simple rooms – all with private bathrooms and fans; the more expensive ones (around L425) have a/c and TVs – are clean but characterless. There are some hammocks on the patio to lounge in. **L200**

The central highlands

With gritty San Pedro Sula to the north and the sprawl of Tegucigalpa to the south, the appeal of Honduras's central highlands lies in their relative serenity. Whether it's an early-morning birding trip on **Lago de Yojoa** or a twilight stroll around former capital **Comayagua**, this is

---

INTO NICARAGUA AND EL SALVADOR: EL ESPINO, GUASAULE AND EL AMATILLO

Choluteca is a transport hub for most of the country's border crossings with Nicaragua and El Salvador. There's a US$3 exit tax at each of the crossings.

INTO NICARAGUA

For **Nicaragua**'s **El Espino** border, El Rey Express buses (3 daily; 1hr) run the 110km from Choluteca to San Marcos de Colón. From there frequent *colectivo* taxis (around L20) go to El Espino and the border, 10km away. The border post itself (daily 8am–5pm) is quiet and straightforward, with moneychangers on both sides. On the Nicaraguan side, regular buses run to Somoto, 20km from the border. White *rapiditos* leave Choluteca for **Guasaule** (every 30min, 6am–5pm; 40min). There's regular transport from Guasaule on to Chinandega, León and Managua.

INTO EL SALVADOR

For **El Salvador**, local buses run from Choluteca to **El Amatillo** (hourly 3.15am–5.45pm; 2hr 15min). This point of entry (open 6am–10pm) teems with border traffic, moneychangers and opportunistic beggars. Crossing, however, is straightforward. A bank on the El Salvadoran side changes dollars and lempiras, but you'll get slightly better rates from the moneychangers as long as you're careful. If coming **from Tegucigalpa** you don't need to go all the way to Choluteca – just change at Jícaro Galán onto the Choluteca–El Amatillo service. Over the border in El Salvador, buses (every 10min until around 6.30pm) leave for Santa Rosa de Lima – 18km away, and the closest place offering accommodation (see p.241) – and San Miguel, 58km away (see p.363).

5

a region for relaxation. The one exception is the **Catarata de Pulhapanzak**, a 43m waterfall that you can clamber behind and explore, or simply admire the crashing white water from the comfort of a picnic spot.

COMAYAGUA

Once the capital of Honduras, faded **COMAYAGUA** lies just 85km north of Tegucigalpa. Santa María de Comayagua, as it was first known, was built in 1539, and quickly gained prominence thanks to the discovery of **silver** nearby, becoming the administrative centre for the whole of Honduras. Following independence, however, the city's fortunes began to decline, particularly after Tegucigalpa was designated alternative capital of the new republic in 1824, and especially when President Soto permanently transferred the capital to Tegucigalpa in 1880. Although Comayagua is today a relatively

rich and important provincial centre, its rivalry with Tegucigalpa has hardly waned over the centuries. The main reason to visit is the architectural legacy of the colonial period, in particular the dramatic cathedral overlooking the Parque Central.

WHAT TO SEE AND DO

Most sights of interest are within a few blocks of the large, tree-lined **Parque Central**, which is graced by a fountain and a pretty bandstand. It's a great place to watch city life, especially in the evenings, when music plays out of speakers. The centre is relatively compact and orientation straightforward.

Iglesia de la Inmaculada Concepción

On the southeast corner of the Parque Central is the recently renovated **cathedral** (Mon–Sat 9.30am–noon & 2–5pm, Sun 9.30am–5pm; free), whose intricate facade consists of tiers of niches containing statues of the saints. More

ACCOMMODATION

America Inc	3
Hotel Casa Grande B&B	1
Hotel Norymax Colonial	4
Hotel Siesta Real	2

COMAYAGUA

0 — 100 metres

Museo Arqueológico

PLAZA SAN FRANCISCO

Iglesia San Francisco

Parque Central

Iglesia de la Inmaculada Concepción

Casa de Cultura

Museo Colonial de Arte Religioso

Supermarket

HSBC

General Market

PLAZA LA MERCED

Iglesia de la Merced

N

EATING & DRINKING

Comidas Rápidas Venecia	5
Gota di Limon	1
La Princesita	4
Restaurante Plaza Colonial	2
Villa Real	3

properly known as **Iglesia de la Inmaculada Concepción**, it was the largest church of its kind in the country during the colonial period, housing sixteen altars, though only four of these survive today. The cathedral's bell tower, built between 1580 and 1708, is considered one of the outstanding examples of colonial Baroque architecture in Central America, and is home to the twelfth-century **Reloj Arabe**, one of the oldest clocks in the world. Originally made for the Alhambra in Granada, Spain, the timepiece was presented to the city in 1582 by King Philip II.

Museo Colonial de Arte Religioso

The small **Museo Colonial de Arte Religioso**, a block southeast of the Parque Central, was closed at the time of research, though hopefully should reopen in the not to distant future.

Casa de Cultura

The **Casa de Cultura**, on the south side of the Parque Central (Mon–Fri 9am–5pm, Sat & Sun 9am–noon; free; ⓦmunicomayagua.com), hosts changing exhibitions, usually related to the city's history. Its location makes it a nice place to hide from the sun for a while.

Museo Arqueológico

One block north of the Parque Central, on Plaza San Francisco, the **Museo Arqueológico** (daily 8.30am–4pm; US$4) occupies a single-storey building that used to be the government palace. The small but interesting range of permanent exhibits includes a pre-Columbian Lenca stele, some terrific jade jewellery and a colourful Semana Santa display.

Iglesia de la Merced

Three blocks south of the Parque Central is another colonial church, the **Iglesia de la Merced** (daily 7am–8pm; free). Built between 1550 and 1558 (though its facade dates only to the early eighteenth century), this was the city's original cathedral, holding the Reloj Arabe until 1715, when the new cathedral was consecrated. In front of the church is the very pretty **Plaza La Merced**.

ARRIVAL AND INFORMATION

By bus Most buses drop passengers off on the highway at the top of "the Boulevard", which connects CA-5 to the centre; the stop is about 1km from the Parque Central – either a L15 taxi ride or 20min walk. Some buses come directly to the town centre with various stops in the streets south of the Parque. There are regular buses to/from Tegucigalpa (with La Sultana hourly; 1hr 30min–2hr) and San Pedro Sula (with La Sultana & Mirna 1–2 hourly; 2hr 30min–3hr 15min). For Lago de Yojoa, catch any San Pedro Sula-bound bus and ask for La Guama.

Bank HSBC on Av 1 NO has an ATM and changes travellers' cheques.

Internet La Red, on the Parque Central, is a conveniently located cyber café; its computers have Skype.

Tourist information Tourist information and a map are available at the Casa de Cultura (Mon–Sat 9am–5pm; ☏ 9749 3086). There is an interesting map on the side of the small souvenir cabin in front of La Red internet café (see above), with photographs depicting noteworthy buildings in town.

ACCOMMODATION

America Inc Av 1 NO, just south of C 1 NO ☏ 2772 0360, ⓦhotelamericainc.com. A big, faded mid-range hotel with welcoming staff. If you haggle you might get a room for a similar price to those at the town's budget hotels, but if you can't get a discount, it's not really worth stretching the budget for. L804

Hotel Norymax Colonial C Manuel Bonilla near Av 1 NE ☏ 2772 1703. One of the better budget hotels in town: rooms vary in quality (some have more natural light and better furnishings) so ask to look at a few. L450

Hotel Siesta Real Blvd 4 Centenario ☏ 2772 3690. A friendly, clean, family-run place in a dark pink building with white railings; note that latest check-in is 10pm. L500

EATING AND DRINKING

An extensive general market three blocks south of the Parque Central sells meat and fish, with stalls around the main building for fresh fruit and vegetables. You can easily

> ### ★ TREAT YOURSELF
>
> **Hotel Casa Grande B&B** Two blocks north of the Parque Central, C 7 NO ☏ 2772 0772, ⓦhotelcasagrande comayagua.com. The most atmospheric hotel in town, *Casa Grande* is a beautiful colonial mansion with a colonnaded, flower-filled courtyard and individually decorated en suites filled with tasteful period furniture. Rates include breakfast. L1140

5

pick up an *almuerzo* for around L50 in the surrounding *comedores*.

Comidas Rápidas Venecia Av 1 NO, one block south of the Parque Central. A simple café, but clean and friendly with low-cost mix-and-match breakfasts and lunches (around L40–60). Closed evenings & Sun.

Gota de Limón C 5 NO, one block east of the Parque Central ☎ 2772 8446. There's a vibrant, clubby feel to this restaurant-bar, which serves economical *comida típica* and has live DJs (mainly playing reggaetón) at night. However, be aware that sex workers are said to frequent the place, perhaps because of the presence of American military from the local base. Beers around L30–40. Tues–Sat 9am–midnight, Sun 6pm–midnight.

La Princesita Blvd 4 Centenario, C 4–5 NO. It may be decorated with a princess-themed wallpaper border, but their *baleadas* are definitely for grown-ups. Try the "super" with beans, cheese, egg, chorizo, shredded chicken and *encurtido* (pickles). You can have a good feed here for less than L50.

Restaurante Plaza Colonial Next to the cathedral, on the eastern side of the Parque Central. You couldn't ask for a better spot, right on the square – grab an outside table. Inside is also nice, with film posters and flamenco imagery. The menu features a good mix of Honduran and international dishes (mains L180–220). Daily 7.30am–9pm.

Villa Real A block southeast of the Parque Central on Av 1 NE ☎ 2772 0101. The food is unreliable, but this atmospheric place is definitely worth a visit for a drink (local beers around L30). It's set in a beautifully restored colonial home with a large garden courtyard; note the shrine to Barcelona FC in a display cabinet. Closed Sun & Mon.

LAGO DE YOJOA

Beyond Comayagua, the highway descends from the mountains and the air becomes appreciably warmer. Some 67km north of Comayagua sits the spectacular, sparkling blue **LAGO DE YOJOA**, a natural lake approximately 17km long and 9km wide. Its reed-fringed waters, sloping away to a gentle patchwork of woods, pastures and coffee plantations, are overlooked by the mountains of **Cerro Azul Meámbar** to the east and **Santa Bárbara** to the north and west. Both of these contain small but pristine stretches of **cloudforest** and are protected as national parks. The bowl of the lake is a microclimate and attracts more than four hundred species of **bird**, one of the highest concentrations in the country.

> ### NATURE TOURS OF LAGO DE YOJOA
>
> If it's nature you're after, contact the very knowledgeable Malcolm (✉ malcolmbirdwatch@hotmail.com), the resident bird expert at *D&D Brewery* (see opposite), who runs fantastic early-morning **tours** on the lake (L250). With so many species of bird – including herons, kingfishers and hawks – as well as bats, iguanas and otters, this is a great introduction to the lake. He also offers two-day guided walks up Santa Bárbara mountain (L1500), exploring the dense cloudforest at 1400–2000m, with the possibility of spotting quetzals.

During the week, the waters – and surrounding hotels – are virtually empty, making this a supremely relaxing place for a couple of days of rowing, birdwatching and general outdoor exploring. However, at weekends the lake is a favourite with middle-class *hondureños*, and the peace can be shattered by the crowds and the buzz of jet skis.

WHAT TO SEE AND DO

The area around Lago de Yojoa offers some of the most **adventurous activities** of the region: you can hike through the cloudforests of the national parks, get wet crawling behind a 43m waterfall, explore some dark and mysterious caves or get up close to the local wildlife (see box above).

Las Cuevas de Taulabé

The **Taulabé caves** (8am–4pm; L40) make an easy and interesting stop off the CA-5 at km 140. More than 12km of tunnels and caverns have so far been explored, but only 400m have paths and lighting. You can walk through the caves on your own, but local guides also hang around (negotiate a price beforehand – generally L50–70). The caves can be slippery, so make sure you wear suitable shoes. All local **buses** running along the CA-5 will drop you off here; it's also easy to catch a bus on to La Guama for the lake or back to the junction at Siguatepeque for connections to the west.

Parque Nacional Cerro Azul Meámbar

Continuing north beyond the Taulabé caves, the highway divides at the small town of **La Guama**, from where a dirt road runs east for another 7km to the entrance to **Parque Nacional Cerro Azul Meámbar** (daily 7am–5pm; US$5; ☏9865 9082 or ☏2608 5506, ⊛paghonduras.org). Named after its highest peak, the blue-hued Cerro Azul Meámbar (2047m), this is one of the smaller and most accessible national parks, with a core of untouched cloudforest. The **visitors' centre** at the park's entrance has information on a number of short walking trails. Anyone planning to hike should be prepared for precipitously steep gradients in the upper reaches of the reserve, with dense vegetation and tumbling waterfalls. The excellent marked **trails** – you don't really need a guide – are suitable for day-trips, though it is worth staying overnight so that you can see the forest in the early morning.

Taxi fares to the park from La Guama vary wildly, with around L250 the cheapest you can hope for. **Buses** that ply the route to Santa Elena may also take you on to the entrance to the lodge for around L200. It is money well spent, given the steep one-hour walk from Santa Elena, and the occasional assaults that have been reported along this route.

Peña Blanca

The village of **PEÑA BLANCA**, north of the lake, is the commercial focus for the area. Approaching from the south on CA-5, ask for the *desvío* (turn-off) to Peña Blanca, just after La Guama; from here you can catch one of the frequent *rapiditos* or local buses to Peña Blanca itself. The El Mochito bus from San Pedro Sula also passes through Peña Blanca.

There are various useful services here: Internet Exploradores is on a small dirt road that runs down the side of Minisuper Surticasa; Banco Occidente changes dollars and travellers' cheques, though there is currently no ATM; and if you're hungry, you could do worse than try the pizza served above Mercado El Mexicano.

Catarata de Pulhapanzak

The absolute highlight of this region is the privately owned **Catarata de Pulhapanzak** (daily 7am–6pm; L50), a stunning, 43m-high cascade of churning white waters on the Río Lindo. Probably the prettiest waterfall in the country, the cascade is at its most dazzling in the early mornings, when rainbows form in the rising sun. It's easy enough to explore on your own, but to really get the most out of your visit take advantage of the fantastic **guided tours** run by the staff (L200; wear sturdy shoes), which are not for the faint-hearted. They'll take you jumping or diving in and out of pools, ducking behind the falls and climbing in and out of the caves behind the curtain of water. The canopy tour (L500) is also recommended: a network of five ziplines works its way down the river until you are flying through rainbows above the waterfall. Do not be tempted to swim in the area of water immediately above the falls as there have been fatalities.

The falls are an easy, partly uphill, fifteen-minute walk from the village of **San Buenaventura**, 8km north of Peña Blanca; **buses** between El Mochito and San Pedro Sula run hourly, passing through both Peña Blanca and San Buenaventura en route. A football field inside the waterfall site entrance fills with locals at the weekend and a restaurant offers cheap fish or fried chicken.

ACCOMMODATION AND EATING

Catarata de Pulhapanzak cabins ☏3319 7282, ⊛letsgopulha.com. A collection of (rather pricey) cabins in a great location close to the falls. You can also camp (bring your own gear), and there's a café-restaurant for refreshments. Camping <u>US$10</u>, Cabin <u>US$110</u>

El Cortijo del Lago On the road to Peña Blanca, 2km from La Guama ☏9906 5333, ⊛elcortijodellago.com. This lodge can accommodate up to thirty people in dorms, private rooms and cabins – one popular room on the lake feels like a birdwatching hut. A good restaurant serves dishes such as tilapia fillet with *chismol*, rice and vegetables picked fresh from the garden. Dorm <u>L150</u>, double/cabin <u>L600</u>

★ **D&D Brewery** A little way outside Peña Blanca on the road to San Pedro Sula; take the El Mochito bus from San Pedro Sula until you see the *D&D Brewery* sign ☏9994 9719, ⊛ddbrewery.com. This marvellous brewery/

5

restaurant/lodge, set in a thickly wooded area near the lake, is a real treat. There's a pool, the tropical garden teems with birds and plants, and the home-brewed beer packs a tangy punch. Accommodation ranges from dorms and basic but well-maintained rooms to atmospheric cabins sleeping up to six; if you have a tent, you can also camp in the grounds. Advance booking recommended. Camping L60, dorm L120, double L300, cabin L600

Panacam Lodge 7km from the highway between San Pedro Sula and Tegucigalpa, La Guama turn-off ☎ 9865 9082, ⓦ paghonduras.org. The park has some fantastic accommodation, from simple dorms to wooden cabins with hot-water bathrooms, and is well signposted from La Guama. Bring your own equipment if you want to camp. Rates include breakfast. Camping L100, dorm L200, double L1000

The western highlands

The **western highlands** of Honduras present a picturesque landscape of pine forests, sparsely inhabited mountains and remote villages. The departments of **Lempira** and **Intibucá** contain the highest concentration of indigenous peoples in the country, and many of the towns in the region make up the so-called **Ruta Lenca**. Around the village of **La Esperanza** particularly, look out for Lenca women wearing traditional coloured headdresses while working in the fields.

Cobbled, colonial **Gracias** makes a relaxing base for hikes in the pristine cloudforest reserve of the **Parque Nacional Celaque**. An easy bus ride away is **Santa Rosa de Copán**, which is also a relaxing place to stay and still unspoilt, despite its growing popularity with tourists and its proximity to the famous **Copán ruins**.

LA ESPERANZA

Just north of the town of Siguatepeque, a good paved road heads west from CA-5 to the village of **LA ESPERANZA**, the centre of commerce for western Honduras and the capital of the department of Intibucá. During the week there's nothing much of interest here, but the town livens up considerably during the colourful **weekend market** (Sat & Sun), when Lenca farmers from surrounding villages pour into town. It's likely that if you're heading to Gracias you'll need to **stay overnight** in La Esperanza due to the lack of buses.

ARRIVAL AND INFORMATION

By bus Buses running between Tegucigalpa and San Pedro Sula can drop you off at the *desvío* (turn-off) to La Esperanza, just north of Siguatepeque. Buses (every 2hr; 2hr) run between the *desvío* and the town until mid-afternoon.

Bank La Esperanza, in the centre of town, has one ATM that takes Visa cards.

Internet Communicaciones Vasquez, opposite *Opalaca* restaurant.

ACCOMMODATION AND EATING

El Fogón Close to the Parque Central. Popular restaurant-bar with a hearty mix of Honduran and international dishes, as well as live music (and sometimes karaoke) in the evenings. Closed Sun.

Gran Hotel La Esperanza Four blocks southeast of the Parque Central ☎ 2783 0068. For a touch of comfort, this establishment has attractive en-suite rooms with TV and plush bedding. L700

Hotel Mina Four blocks east of the Parque Central ☎ 2783 1071. Prices are a bit lower here than at *La Esperanza*, though the smart exterior is not quite matched by the rather pokey rooms inside. L600

SAN JUAN INTIBUCÁ

A bumpy 52km north of La Esperanza, the village of **SAN JUAN INTIBUCÁ** is slowly finding its way onto the tourist map thanks to a local **cooperativa** promoting the area's Lenca traditions. Information about tours and demonstrations is available from *Hotel Guancascos* in Gracias (see opposite) or Gladys Nolasco (☎ 2754 7150 or ☎ 9786 1012, ⓔ glaisra7@yahoo.com), who can be found at a building marked *Docucentro Israel copias y mas*, a five-minute walk from the main square, opposite a small fruit and vegetable market. Options include participating in the roasting of coffee beans, hikes to nearby waterfalls and cloudforests, and observing the production of traditional handicrafts.

San Juan Intibucá is linked by fairly regular **buses** to both Gracias (every 1–2hr; 45min–1hr) and La Esperanza (hourly; 1hr–1hr 30min).

GRACIAS

Founded in 1536 by Spanish conquistador Juan de Chávez, **GRACIAS** lies in the shadow of the nearby **Parque Nacional Celaque**. It's a hot and dusty cobbled town, but well located for day-trips to surrounding natural attractions, including the park and some natural **hot springs** (daily 5am–11pm; L60), about an hour's walk south or around L60 each way in a moto-taxi – you can arrange for one to come and collect you for the return leg. These are small pools purpose-built for bathing in the 36–39° waters; an on-site *comedor* serves basic meals.

ARRIVAL AND INFORMATION

By bus The bus terminal is three blocks west of the Parque Central. There are buses to/from Santa Rosa de Copán (with various companies every 20–30min; 1hr 15min) and San Pedro Sula (with Gracianos, Toritos & Cooperative Transportes Lempira 4 daily; 4–5hr).
Bank Banco Occidente, one block west of the Parque Central (Mon–Fri 8am–4pm, Sat 8–11.30am), changes dollars and travellers' cheques, and has an ATM.
Internet Try Ecolem, in front of *Guancascos* hotel.
Shopping Lorendiana, two blocks southwest of the Parque Central, sells beautifully bottled pickles, preserves and other food delicacies.
Tourist information An office in the centre of the Parque Central (daily 8am–noon & 1–4.30pm) sells maps and provides basic information, though staff at *Hotel Guancascos* (see below) are more helpful. ⓦ colosuca.com is also worth a look.

ACCOMMODATION

Erick One block north of the Parque Central ⓣ 2656 1066. Rooms are clean but basic, with pipes for showers. Some bathrooms are only separated by a half-wall, so don't provide a great deal of privacy. Guests can store bags here when hiking in the national park. **L̲280**
Hotel Guancascos East side of Castillo San Cristóbal ⓣ 2656 1219, ⓦ guancascos.com. An eco-friendly hotel with a collection of well-kept rooms (all have TVs, fans and private bathrooms). There's a good restaurant (see below) and a tourist information office on site, and guided tours are offered of the national park. **L̲550**

EATING AND DRINKING

Guancascos *Hotel Guancascos*, east side of Castillo San Cristóbal ⓣ 2656 1219, ⓦ guancascos.com. Diners enjoy a superb view from the terrace, especially if you make it for an early breakfast. Highlights include the home-baked bread and the chocolate brownies. Expect to pay around L60–120 for a meal. Daily 7am–10pm.
Kandil Kafe y Bar Three blocks from the Parque Central. An unexpectedly fashionable place, given the town's sleepy and traditional feel. It's crisply painted, with minimal furnishings, and the pizzas (around L100) with prosciuto or *loroco* (a local flower that is used as a herb) are particularly recommended. Tues–Thurs 7–10pm, Fri & Sat 7pm–midnight.
Riconcito Graciano Two blocks west and south of the Parque Central. The menu features dishes made solely from local ingredients (mains around L100), served in an atmosphere about as rustic as can be. You might find yourself drinking fresh *noni* (a so-called "miracle" fruit) juice, eating meat with a *loroco* flower sauce, or sampling *pinol*, which has been described as Lenca chocolate. Daily 7am–9pm.
El Señor de la Sierra Parque Central. The name of this café refers to Lempira, whose image graces their drinks menu. There's free wi-fi, the coffee's good, and there are usually one or two snack options (about L20).

PARQUE NACIONAL CELAQUE

PARQUE NACIONAL CELAQUE protects one of the largest and most impressive expanses of virgin cloudforest in Honduras. Thousands of years of geographical isolation have resulted in several endemic species of flora. Locals also claim that the park is home to more quetzals than all of Guatemala, though you'll still have to keep a sharp eye out to see one. The focus of the park is the nation's highest peak, **Cerro Las Minas** (2849m).

WHAT TO SEE AND DO

Inside the park, there are rambles and hikes of all experience levels to choose from. The most exciting and scenic option is the 6km marked **trail** up to the summit of Cerro Las Minas. In the upper reaches of the park much of the main trail consists of 40-degree slopes, so this is not a hike for the unfit. If the peak is your aim, you'll need to **camp** at one of the two designated spots along the way (see p.402). The cloudforest proper doesn't begin until after

5

Campamento El Naranjo, so try to make it this far. **Guides** aren't necessary for the main trail, but you'll need one if planning to undertake the more difficult treks on the southern slopes.

ARRIVAL AND INFORMATION

The park is best approached from Gracias; the entrance is an 8km walk west from town.

On foot Take the dirt road from Gracias through the village of Mejicapa (around 1.5–2km from Gracias), from where a marked track leads uphill to the entrance.

By pick-up Pick-ups from Gracias are sometimes available.

Entrance fee and opening times The park is open daily 8am–4pm. Pay your entrance fee (L50) at the visitors' centre, which is near the Río Arcagual.

Information and guides *Hotel Guancascos* in Gracias (see p.401) functions as an unofficial information centre for the park. As well as selling maps, they can arrange lifts up to the lodge, gear and guides.

ACCOMMODATION AND EATING

When it comes to equipment, sleeping bags, decent boots and a change of warm clothing are essential.

Camping There are two designated camping spots on the way to the peak, *Campamento Don Tomás* and *Campamento El Naranjo*. **L60**

Doña Alejandra Just outside the lodge entrance, at the visitors' centre. If you haven't brought your own supplies, head here for dinner (until 7pm; dishes around L50–60).

Lodge At the visitors' centre. If you prefer to stay somewhere a bit more solid than a tent, you could try the basic lodge at the visitors' centre, offering bunkrooms and showers. **L150**

SANTA ROSA DE COPÁN

It's an easy ninety-minute bus ride 45km northwest from Gracias to **SANTA ROSA DE COPÁN**, a colourful colonial relic built on the proceeds of the tobacco industry. Unusually for a town of this size, the majority of its streets are still cobbled, which gives it a traditional feel. While fresh in the mornings and evenings, the town heats up steadily during the day.

WHAT TO SEE AND DO

In the centre of town is the delightful, shady **Parque Contreras**, the Parque Central, with a beautiful cathedral on its eastern side. **Calle Real Centenario**, lined with shops and restaurants, runs along the southern edge of the Parque, past the town's central **market** a couple of blocks east.

Flor de Copán Cigar Company factory

Santa Rosa de Copán was chosen in 1765 as the headquarters of the Royal Tobacco Factory and the golden weed continues to play a role in the local economy. The **Flor de Copán Cigar Company** maintains offices in the town centre – in the original Royal Tobacco building on Calle Real Centenario – but their **factory** is 2km northwest of the town centre, about 300m after turning right out of the bus station. Around thirty thousand hand-rolled cigars are produced daily, and **tours** in Spanish and English are available, but you'll need to book with the tourist office (see below) a day ahead (Mon–Fri 10am & 2pm; US$2).

Beneficio Maya

Colonia San Martín, a short taxi ride away, is home to the **Beneficio Maya** (w cafecopan.com) coffee finca. A family-run business, they offer tours during the coffee season (Nov–Feb; US$2), which should be booked via the tourist office (see below), and welcome visitors year-round.

ARRIVAL AND DEPARTURE

By bus The bus terminal is just off the highway, 2km northwest of the centre. Taxis (around L25) and the yellow buses marked *urbanos* (city buses) run regularly to the Parque Contreras.

Destinations Copán (travel via La Entrada); La Entrada (local services; every 30min; 45min); Gracias (various companies every 20–30min; 1hr 15min); Nueva Ocotepeque (La Sultana; hourly; 2hr); San Pedro Sula (Hedman Alas, La Sultana, Congolón and local services; 2–3 hourly; 3hr 30min); Tegucigalpa (Hedman Alas and La Sultana; 6 daily; 7hr).

INFORMATION

Internet You can get online at the tourist office (see below), Zona Digital on Av 3 NE and Bonsay Cyber Café on C Real Centenario.

Tourist information The tourist office in the centre of the Parque Contreras (Mon–Sat 8am–noon & 1.30–6pm) has city maps and helpful staff.

Tour operators Max Elvir of Lenca Land Trails (☎ 9997

5340, @lencatours@gmail.com), a local guide, offers a number of excellent tours, including trips to Parque Nacional Celaque, indigenous villages and hot springs, all for around US$40–60.

ACCOMMODATION

A great option in Santa Rosa de Copán is to organize a homestay through the tourist office (around L160–200 per night).

Alondra's Tu Hotel Av 2 SO ☎ 2662 3583. The ground-floor rooms are a little dark at this lower-mid-range hotel, but those upstairs are much brighter. There's a spacious communal area, free internet/wi-fi, and coffee, juice and pastries are available at breakfast. L600

Blanca Nieves Av 3 NE ☎ 2662 1312. A decent option – the simple en-suite rooms are larger and better value than those with shared facilities. L350

Hotel Escalon Av 2 & C 3 SO ☎ 2662 0652, ⓦhotel escalon.com. Pot plants line the hallways of this small hotel that has clean but rather stark singles, doubles and triples; all have private bathrooms and TVs, though some get more natural light than others. L350

El Rosario Av 3 NE ☎ 2662 0211. The rooms here are clean, though some are a little dark and cell-like, with cold-water bathrooms separated from bedrooms by just a shower curtain. L320

EATING

Santa Rosa has a glut of eating establishments. Cheap *comedores* line the bus station and upstairs in the Mercado Central, where filling *almuerzos* can be had for around L50. In the evenings street vendors sell *tamales* and tortillas around the market and Parque Contreras. There are several places to sample the excellent local coffee.

Cafe La Taza C Real Centenario Av 3–4 NO. Small, homely café proudly displaying their certification of good coffee practice ("high grown"). Wi-fi is available, too. Coffee L30–40. Mon–Sat 9am–7pm.

Doña Toya Av 4 C1–2 NO. The walls are flaking, the floor is chipped and yet this place has a charming, friendly feel. The nourishing, tangy *atol chuco* – a savoury corn-based drink (L10–15) – is served in carved bowls, and fried or boiled *yuca* with *chicharrón* (crispy fried pork rinds) will set you back around L50. Daily 8am–10.30pm.

Kaldi's Koffee Av 1 NE, just south of the cathedral. The perfect place for a stimulating coffee (from L20) with varieties from as far away as Ethiopia and Thailand, as well as – of course – Honduras. Mon–Sat 10.30am–7pm.

El Rodeo Av 1 SE. Huge steakhouse serving the best barbecued meat in town: a mixed grill comprising steak (including *puyaso*, or top *sirloin*), chorizo, pork chop, chicken and sides, plus drinks, feeds four and costs around L500.

Bus Terminal (2km), Flor de Copán Cigar Company (2km), Colonia San Martin & Beneficio Maya

Boulevard Jorge Bueso Arias, Copán, Gracias & San Pedro Sula

● **EATING**
Café La Taza	3
Doña Toya	1
Kaldi's Koffee	4
El Rodeo	7
Ten Napel Café	2
Weekends Pizza	5

● **DRINKING**
Los Cuates	8
Flamingos	6

Parque Contreras

Royal Tobacco Company

Manzanitas Supermarket

Buses to Bus Terminal

Cathedral

Pharmacy

Market

Banco Occidente

N

Mercado Santa Teresa

■ **ACCOMMODATION**
Alondra's Tu Hotel	3
Blanca Nieves	1
Hotel Escalon	4
El Rosario	2

SANTA ROSA DE COPÁN

0   100
metres

5

INTO EL SALVADOR AND GUATEMALA: EL POY AND AGUA CALIENTE

Buses to both El Salvador and Guatemala pass through **Nueva Ocotepeque** (hourly from Santa Rosa de Copán; 2hr). It's a dirty, busy town, and most people change buses and move on quickly, but if you get stuck, the *Hotel Turístico*, up from the bus stop (☎2653 3639; L400) is a solid choice. The Banco de Occidente, near the bus stop, changes currencies and travellers' cheques, but you'll get better rates for Guatemalan quetzales at the border.

TO EL SALVADOR

For **El Poy** (**El Salvador**), *rapiditos* run the 7km from Nueva Ocotepeque (every 15min 6am–6pm; 10min). El Poy itself is drab and dusty, but the crossing is straightforward, as the immigration windows are next to each other in the same building just a short walk from where the bus drops you. Banpaís (Mon–Fri 8am–noon & 1–5pm) will change currencies. There are buses to La Palma, the nearest town over the border, and San Salvador (every 30min until 4.30pm).

TO GUATEMALA

For **Agua Caliente** (**Guatemala**), yellow local buses make the trip from Nueva Ocotepeque (every 30min until 6.30pm; 30min). There are no banking or accommodation facilities on the Honduran side. Over in Guatemala, minibuses (every 20min until 6pm) leave for Esquipulas (see p.337).

Ten Napel Café C 1 Av 2–3 NO. A lovely café with a fantastic garden, wi-fi, and bags of coffee, cigars and maps of the town for sale, plus good sandwiches, bagels and cakes. If you fancy a treat, try the tiramisu or the passion fruit cheesecake (around L50). Mon–Sat 8am–7pm.

Weekends Pizza Av 4 NO & C 2 SO. This deservedly popular place serves the best pizza (from L150) in town, as well as pastas and sandwiches. Wed–Sun 9am–9pm.

DRINKING

Los Cuates C 1 SE, Av 4 SE. A Mexican bar and restaurant with happy-hour offers on food and drink (7–9pm) and karaoke on Thurs. Beer costs around L30. The kitchen is open until 11pm, and the bar until 2am.

Flamingos Av 1 SE, half a block south of the Parque Contreras. This smart restaurant-bar offers a two-for-one deal on *boquitas* (snacks) Wed–Fri and has a daily happy hour (8–10pm) for drinks (from L25).

DIRECTORY

Banks Banco Occidente, south of the Parque, has a 24hr Visa/Plus ATM and also changes cash dollars and travellers' cheques. There's a second ATM opposite Manzanitas supermarket.

Pharmacy Farmacia Cruz Roja, C 1 & Av 3 NE (daily 8am–6pm).

Post office On the west side of the Parque (Mon–Fri 8am–noon & 2–5pm, Sat 8am–noon).

Shopping Manzanitas supermarket (in an unmarked, large yellow building), C Real Centenario & Av 2 NO (Mon–Sat 8am–7.30pm, Sun 8am–2pm). The Mercado Santa Teresa, in Barrio Santa Teresa, a 10min walk east of Parque Contreras, sells fresh fruit and vegetables.

COPÁN RUINAS

A charming town of steep cobbled streets and red-tiled roofs set among green hills, **COPÁN RUINAS** has more to offer than just its proximity to the infamous archeological site of Copán. Despite the weekly influx of visitors, Copán Ruinas has managed to remain largely unspoilt. Many travellers are seduced by the relaxed atmosphere, clean air and rural setting, and end up spending longer than planned, studying Spanish, eating and drinking well or exploring the region's other minor sites, hot springs and beautiful countryside.

WHAT TO SEE AND DO

Half a day is enough to take in virtually all the in-town attractions. The **Parque Central** is lined with banks, municipal structures and a simple, whitewashed Baroque-style church.

Museo Regional de Arqueología

On the west side of the plaza is the **Museo Regional de Arqueología** (daily 9am–5pm; US$3), housing some impressive Maya carvings from the Copán region, including glyph-covered altars T and U and **Stele 7**, discovered just 100m from the Parque Central. There are also two remarkable **tombs**, one of which contains the remains of a female shaman, complete with jade jewellery, an entire puma skeleton, the skull of a deer, and two human sacrificial victims.

The Municipalidad

In the **municipalidad** on the Parque Central is a fantastic photography exhibition (Mon–Fri 8am–4pm; free) donated by Harvard University's Peabody Museum, detailing, in beautifully reproduced prints, the first archeological expeditions to Copán at the turn of the twentieth century.

ARRIVAL AND DEPARTURE

By bus Buses from the east generally terminate by a small football field at the entrance to town. Buses from Guatemala enter town from the west and stop just before the Parque.

Destinations Agua Caliente (regular buses 5am–4pm; last return to Copán at 4pm; 1hr); Antigua (with Hedman Alas,

via Guatemala City, 2.20pm; 6hr); La Entrada (local buses every 45min until 5pm; 1hr); Guatemala City (Hedman Alas 2 daily; 7hr); San Pedro Sula (Hedman Alas & Casasola 8 daily; 3hr). For Tegucigalpa, Tela and La Ceiba, you have to travel via San Pedro Sula. For Santa Rosa de Copán and Gracias, you have to go via La Entrada.

By shuttle bus Basecamp (see below) runs daily shuttle buses to Guatemala (Guatemala City & Antigua; US$20) and El Salvador (several destinations including San Salvador; US$36).

INFORMATION AND TOURS

Internet There are several internet cafés in town, including Maya Connections, just south of the plaza, and La Casa de Todo, on the corner south of *Los Gemelos*.

Tourist information Copán Connections and Basecamp (see below) are both excellent sources on the local area and the country as a whole.

Tour operators Basecamp (☎ 2651 4695, ⓦ basecamphonduras.com), in the *ViaVia* café (see p.406),

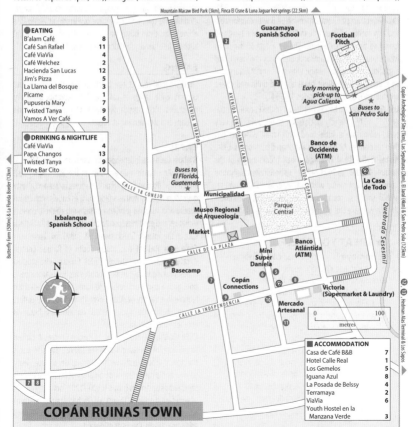

Mountain Macaw Bird Park (3km), Finca El Cisne & Luna Jaguar hot springs (22.5km)

EATING
B'alam Café	8
Café San Rafael	11
Café ViaVia	4
Café Welchez	2
Hacienda San Lucas	12
Jim's Pizza	5
La Llama del Bosque	3
Picame	1
Pupusería Mary	7
Twisted Tanya	9
Vamos A Ver Café	6

DRINKING & NIGHTLIFE
Café ViaVia	4
Papa Changos	13
Twisted Tanya	9
Wine Bar Cito	10

Guacamaya Spanish School

Football Pitch

Early morning pick-up to Agua Caliente

Buses to San Pedro Sula

Banco de Occidente (ATM)

La Casa de Todo

Buses to El Florido, Guatemala

Municipalidad

Museo Regional de Arqueología

Parque Central

Ixbalanque Spanish School

Market

Mini Super Daniela

Banco Atlántida (ATM)

Basecamp

Copán Connections

Victoria (Supermarket & Laundry)

Mercado Artesanal

N

0   100
metres

COPÁN ARCHEOLOGICAL SITE (1km), Las Sepulturas (2km), El Jaral (4km) & San Pedro Sula (125km)

Quebrada Sesesmil

Hedman Alas Terminal & Los Sapos

Butterfly Farm (500m) & La Florida Border (12km)

ACCOMMODATION
Casa de Café B&B	7
Hotel Calle Real	1
Los Gemelos	5
Iguana Azul	8
La Posada de Belssy	4
Terramaya	2
ViaVia	6
Youth Hostel en la Manzana Verde	3

COPÁN RUINAS TOWN

5

offers a range of hikes (US$10–45) lasting up to 8hr, horseriding trips (from US$15), including to Finca el Cisne (see box, p.408), canopy tours (US$45), and excursions to Macaw Mountain Bird Park (US$10) and Luna Jaguar hot springs (US$55 for up to eight people). The town tour (US$10) is particularly good: owner Gerardo explains what really makes Copán Ruinas tick, politically and economically. Copán Connections (☏2651 4182, ⓦcopanconnections.com) is a one-stop source of information on Copán and popular destinations like Lago de Yojoa and the Bay Islands. They also offer wider tours of Honduras, transfers, house rentals, flight bookings, and numerous tours including one that combines Macaw Mountain with the Miramundo coffee finca (US$70).

ACCOMMODATION

Some of the best hostels in this region are to be found in Copán. Steer clear of the touts who attempt to shepherd you into hotels upon arrival.

★ **Casa de Café B&B** At the southwest edge of town, overlooking the Río Copán valley ☏2651 4620, ⓦcasadecafecopan.com. Charming B&B with comfortable and airy rooms, all with nice individual touches, fans, and sparkling private bathrooms. There's a fabulous garden where you can lie in a hammock and enjoy the views, and a spacious communal lounge with a TV, small library and wi-fi access. An excellent breakfast and unlimited coffee and tea are included in the rates. US$64

Los Gemelos Two blocks northeast of the Parque Central ☏2651 4077. Friendly backpacker stronghold. The very basic rooms are a little tired with small windows but they're spotless. All have fans and shared bathrooms. L300

Hotel Calle Real Two and a half blocks north of the Parque Central ☏2651 4230, ✉hotelcallereal@yahoo .com. Well-kept rooms with hot water and fan or a/c, set within shady surroundings; the garden and hammock-slung area make this place even better value. L450

★ TREAT YOURSELF

Terramaya Two and a half blocks north of the Parque ☏2651 4623, ⓦterramayacopan.com. From the outside, the whitewashed walls, terracotta roof and wrought-iron metalwork of Terramaya have a reassuring solidity, while from the moment you step through the heavy wooden doors, it's all about comfort and relaxation (there's even a pillow menu). There's a massage pavilion outside in the beautiful garden, and some of the rooms have balconies overlooking the Copán River valley and archeological park. Rates include breakfast. US$99

Iguana Azul At the southwest edge of town, overlooking the Río Copán valley, next to the *Casa de Café* ☏2651 4620, ⓦiguanaazulcopan.com. An excellent, spotless budget choice, with three private rooms and two very pleasant dorms (eleven beds in total). Amenities include a pretty garden, hot-water bathrooms, laundry facilities and free wi-fi. Dorm L150, double L320

La Posada de Belssy One block north of the Parque Central ☏2651 4680, ⓦlaposadadebelssy.com. With a small pool and nice hangout area at the top of the building, hot-water bathrooms, communal kitchen and free coffee, this is a solid choice. A laundry service is available. Breakfast costs L50. L300

ViaVia Two blocks west of the Parque Central ☏2651 4652, ⓦviaviacafe.com. This hotel-cum-café-cum-tourist office, part of an international chain and under hospitable Belgian management, has simple but spotless rooms with private bathrooms and fans. Wi-fi and salsa classes are free, and they offer yoga and movie shows for a fee. US$16

Youth Hostel en la Manzana Verde One and a half blocks north of the Parque Central ☏2651 4652, ⓦviaviacafe.com. Under the same ownership as *ViaVia* (see above), this clean hostel has six-bed dorms, a communal kitchen, free laundry facilities and free wi-fi. US$6

EATING

There's a food market one block west of the Parque, and Copán's wide range of cafés and restaurants generally maintains high standards. Most places open around 7–8am and stop serving at 10pm.

CAFÉS

B'alam Café C La Independencia, one block south of Parque Central. An intimate café attached to the *Yat B'alam* hotel, with a tiled floor and tiny terrace. It serves coffee and a tasty quesadilla cake, as well as snacks such as bagels with cream cheese and jalapeño jelly and pittas with chicken, cheese, tomatoes and *papalinas* (potato chips), plus a Middle Eastern take on the *baleada*. Snacks from L50. Daily 7am–7pm.

Café San Rafael Two blocks south of Parque Central ⓦcafesanrafael.com. Owner Carlos Guerra, who studied cheesemaking in California, produces his own camembert, brie, gouda and mozzarella – to name just a few – which feature in a variety of dishes here (from L50). The coffee, grown, harvested and roasted on Guerra's finca, is excellent too. Daily 8am–8pm.

Café ViaVia Two blocks west of Parque Central. Attached to the hotel of the same name (see above), this café-bar is the town's social hub, with a streetside terrace, leafy garden and a menu featuring an array of breakfast dishes, sandwiches and main meals (L100–120), including plenty of vegetarian options. There's a daily happy hour (5–7pm) and a range of evening activities such as film screenings and salsa classes. Closes at midnight.

5

★ TREAT YOURSELF

Hacienda San Lucas 1.8 km south of Parque Central ☎ 2651 4495, ⓦ haciendasanlucas.com. Wonderful converted farmhouse set in the hills south of town, with breathtaking views over the valley. In the evening, hundreds of candles are lit all over the grounds and you can watch the night unfold over the ruins. The food, meanwhile, is some of the best you'll find in Honduras: five-course traditional meals (from US$30) featuring dishes such as *tamales* and *adobo* sauce are on offer, as well as dishes such as a *tamale* plate which includes home-made cheese, *encurtido*, beans and fresh tortilla. Reservations essential for lunch and dinner. Daily 7am–10pm.

Café Welchez Northwest corner of Parque Central ⓦ cafehonduras.com. Boasts some of the world's smallest balconies, which offer great views of the square. Inside, wood panelling adds a distinguished feel. Gourmet coffee (L20–40) and desserts (try the German chocolate cake) are the focus. Coffee tours can be arranged.

Picame One block northeast of Parque Central ⓦ picamecopan.com. A friendly Honduran/Dutch-run café that's perfect for breakfast (from around L80), from *típico* to pancakes with fruit salad and honey. Take on their legendarily huge burritos if you dare. Daily 7am–9pm.

Vamos a Ver Café One block south of Parque Central. Busy garden café, popular with travellers thanks to affordable and delicious home-made soups, sandwiches (under L100), snacks and fruit juices.

RESTAURANTS

Jim's Pizza (Pizza Copán) Half a block south of Parque Central. Locals and tourists flock to this Texan-run joint to indulge in delicious, generous pizzas and pasta (from L160). Takeaway is available, and live US sport is shown on the big screens.

La Llama del Bosque Two blocks west of Parque Central. Slightly old-fashioned restaurant (the first to open in Copán) with a reasonably priced menu including local breakfasts, meat and chicken dishes, *baleadas* and snacks (most dishes L60–120).

Pupusería Mary One block southwest of Parque Central, though planning to move to a site near the football field. This great local restaurant specializes in *pupusas* served with pickles made from everything from cauliflower to chilli. A drink and a couple of *pupusas* costs less than L50.

★ **Twisted Tanya** One block south of Parque Central ⓦ twistedtanya.com. Some of the best food in the town, with mains such as slow-roasted pork, spicy chicken curry

and seafood pasta. Three courses cost US$22; individual dishes are US$4 upwards. The "backpackers' special" menu (3–6pm; US$6–10) has offerings such as home-made beef ravioli, as well as two-for-one cocktails. Mon–Sat 2–10pm.

DRINKING

In addition to those listed below, *Cafe ViaVia* (see opposite) and *Twisted Tanya* (see above) are also excellent nightspots.

Papa Changos 10min walk south of Parque Central. Things don't really get going much before 10pm, when they start playing a mix of merengue and other Latin beats. Its safety record is not impeccable, however, so take advice in town. Fri & Sat 8pm–5am.

Wine Bar Cito One block south of Parque Central. Cushioned bottle-crates for seats and low lighting make this a cosy spot for a drink. Head chef Hans describes their tapas as "Maya flavours, European technique". Daily 5pm–midnight; happy hour 5–7pm.

SHOPPING

La Casa de Todo One block east of the Parque Central. Shop and internet café with a selection of English-language books for sale or exchange, and every souvenir imaginable including jewellery and ceramics. Daily 7/8am–9pm.

Mercado Artesanal C La Independencia, one block south of the Parque, opposite *Yat B'alam*. Tourist-friendly market selling T-shirts, handicrafts and the like. Open daily in the afternoon.

Supermarkets Try Mini Super Daniela on the Parque, or Victoria one block south.

Twisted Tanya One block south of Parque Central ⓦ twistedtanya.com. This excellent restaurant (see above) also sells a good selection of gifts.

DIRECTORY

Banks Banco de Occidente (Mon–Fri 8.30am–4.30pm, Sat 8.30–11.30am & 1–4pm) and Banco Atlántida (Mon–Fri 9am–5pm, Sat 9am–noon) both have 24hr ATMs.

Language schools Guacamaya (☎ 2651 4360, ⓦ guacamaya.com), two blocks north of the plaza, offers a week-long course for US$225 which includes 20hr of one-on-one tuition, homestay accommodation, a day-trip and university credits. Without the homestay it's US$140. Ixbalanque (☎ 2651 4432, ⓦ Ixbalanque.com), three blocks west of the Parque, is another option; a week-long course, including a homestay, costs US$250. Both schools can also organize volunteering opportunities.

Laundry La Casa de Todo (see above) has a one-day service, or try the service at the back of Victoria supermarket.

Massage Basecamp (see p.405) can arrange foot, hand, neck and shoulder and full-body massages (US$13–50).

5

Post office Behind the Museo Regional de Arqueología (Mon–Fri 8am–4pm, Sat 8am–noon).

AROUND COPÁN RUINAS

While the main draw for travellers to Copán is the nearby ruins, there's a lot more on offer to help you while away a few days. **Nature parks** give visitors the chance to walk among beautiful butterflies and exotic birds, a local family-run farm can show you how your morning cup of coffee came into existence, and lesser-known archeological sites like **Las Sepulturas** can be gratifyingly quiet.

Enchanted Wings Butterfly House

A twenty-minute walk west of the Parque Central, along the road to Guatemala, stands the **Enchanted Wings Butterfly House and Nature Centre** (daily 8am–4.30pm; L115), owned by an American enthusiast and his Honduran wife. You will be shown any butterflies they are currently breeding before entering a large enclosure where you're surrounded by fluttering wings. Types to look out for include the speckled brown "giant owl" and the scarlet-and-yellow "helicopter". Butterflies hatch in the morning hours, so time your visit accordingly. For your best chance to see orchids flowering in the adjacent enclosure, visit between February and April or July and August.

Macaw Mountain Bird Park

Around 3km north of the Parque Central (around L30 each way in a moto-taxi), the **Macaw Mountain Bird Park** (daily 9am–5pm; US$10; ☎2651 4245, ⓦmacawmountain.com) is home to parrots, macaws and toucans rescued from captivity. Your ticket gives you entrance for three days – with walk-through aviaries, a stunning forest location and a natural pool for swimming, it's worth the entrance fee.

Las Sepulturas

Some 2km east of Copán along the highway is the smaller archeological site of **Las Sepulturas** (daily 8am–4pm;

US$15, includes entrance to Copán), the focus of much interest in recent years because of the information it provides on daily domestic life in Maya times. Eighteen of the forty-odd residential compounds at the site have been excavated, yielding a hundred buildings that would have been inhabited. Smaller compounds on the edge of the site are thought to have housed young princes, as well as concubines and servants. It was customary to bury the nobility close to their residences, and more than 250 tombs have been excavated around the compounds. One of the most interesting finds – the tomb of a priest or shaman, dating from around 450 AD – is on display in the museum in Copán Ruinas town.

Luna Jaguar hot springs

Some 22km north of Copán, set in lush highland scenery dotted with coffee fincas and tracts of pine, the **Luna Jaguar spa resort** (daily 9/10am–9/10pm) is a great place to relax. Here thermal waters pour into the cold-water river, creating natural pools and showers. L40 will get you into the man-made pools, but across the river, with another L200 entrance fee, you enter a world fit for a Maya king, with pools and footbaths all around.

★ TREAT YOURSELF

If you want to get a real insight into the local way of life, take a day-trip or stay overnight at **Finca El Cisne** (☎2651 4695 or ☎9920 4836, ⓦfincaelcisne.com), 23km north of Copán. Owner Carlos Castejón's family has worked the land here since 1885, and they now invite guests to explore their working farm, which is involved in the production of cardamom, coffee and cattle. Day-long tours (from US$75) include transport to and from the finca, fantastic scenic horseriding, swimming in the Río Blanco and a trip to the Luna Jaguar hot springs. Overnight tours (from US$95) include accommodation, breakfasts and dinners. Visits can be arranged through the Basecamp office in Copán Ruinas (see p.405).

COPÁN

Set in serene, rolling hills 45km (as the crow flies) from Santa Rosa de Copán, **COPÁN** is one of the most impressive of all Maya sites. Its pre-eminence is not due to size – in scale it's far less impressive than sites such as Tikal or Chichén Itza – but to the overwhelming legacy of artistic craftsmanship that has survived over so many centuries. Copán now ranks as the second-most visited spot in the country after the Bay Islands.

Museum of Maya Sculpture

Opposite the visitors' centre at the ruins (see p.412) is the terrific **Museum of Maya Sculpture** (daily 8am–4pm), arguably the finest in the entire Maya region, with a tremendous collection of stelae, altars, panels and well-labelled explanations in English. Entrance is through an impressive doorway made to look like the jaws of a serpent; you then pass through a tunnel signifying the passage into *xibalba*, or the underworld.

THE HISTORY OF COPÁN RUINS

Once the most important **city-state** on the southern fringes of the Maya world, Copán was largely cut off from all other Maya cities except **Quiriguá**, 64km to the north in Guatemala (see p.338). Archeologists now believe that settlers began moving into the Río Copán valley from around 1400 BC, taking advantage of the area's rich agricultural potential, although construction of the city is not thought to have begun until around 100 AD. For those interested in finding out more, *Vision del Pasado Maya* by Fash and Fasquelle, available from the museums, is an excellent historical account of the site's history in Spanish.

426 AD Yax K'uk Mo' (Great Sun First Quetzal Macaw), a warrior-shaman, establishes the basic layout of the city. Yax K'uk Mo's son Popol Hol creates a cult of veneration for Yax K'uk Mo' which continues for more than fifteen generations.

553 AD Golden era of Copán begins with the accession of Moon Jaguar, and the construction of his magnificent Rosalila Temple.

578–628 AD Reign of Smoke Serpent.

628–695 AD Reign of Smoke Jaguar.

695–738 AD 18 Rabbit reigns and oversees the construction of the Gran Plaza, the final version of the ball court and Temple 22 in the East Court, creating much of the stonework for which Copán is now famous. Following 18 Rabbit's capture and decapitation by Quiriguá's Cauac Sky, construction at Copán comes to a halt for seventeen years.

749–763 AD Smoke Shell reigns and completes the construction of the Hieroglyphic Stairway.

760 AD Copán's population booms at around 28,000, the highest urban density in the entire Maya region.

763–820 AD Yax Pasaj, Smoke Shell's son, commissions Altar Q, which illustrates the entire dynasty from its beginning.

776 AD Yax Pasaj completes the final version of Temple 16.

822 AD Ukit Took' assumes the throne; the only monument to his reign, Altar L, was never completed. Skeletal remains indicate that the decline of the city was provoked by inadequate food resources created by population pressures.

1576 Don Diego de Palacios, a Spanish court official, mentions the ruins of a magnificent city "constructed with such skill that it seems that they could never have been made by people as coarse as the inhabitants of this province" in a letter.

1834 Explorer Juan Galindo writes an account of the ruins.

1839 John Stephens, the US ambassador to Honduras, buys the ruins. Accompanied by Frederick Catherwood, a British architect and artist, he clears the site and maps the buildings. *Incidents of Travel in Central America, Chiapas and Yucatán* is published by Stephens and Catherwood, and Copán becomes a magnet for archeologists.

1891 British archeologist Alfred Maudsley begins a full-scale mapping, excavation and reconstruction of the site, sponsored by Harvard University's Peabody Museum.

1935 Washington's Carnegie Institution diverts the Río Copán to prevent it carving into the site.

1959–60 Archeologists Heinrich Berlin and Tatiana Proskouriakoff begin to decipher the site's hieroglyphs, leading to the realization that they record the history of the cities and the dynasties.

1977 Instituto Hondureño de Antropología e Historia starts running a series of projects, including tunnelling, with the help of archeologists from around the world.

1989 Rosalila Temple, buried beneath Temple 16, is discovered.

1993 Papagayo Temple, built by Popol Hol and dedicated to his father Yax K'uk Mo', is discovered.

1998 Yax K'uk Mo's tomb is discovered.

5

Once out of the tunnel you are greeted by a full-scale, flamboyantly painted replica of the magnificent **Rosalila Temple**, built by Moon Jaguar in 571 AD and discovered intact under Temple 16. A vast crimson-and-jade-coloured mask of the Sun God, depicted with wings outstretched, forms the main facade. Other exhibits concentrate on aspects of Maya beliefs and cosmology, while the upper storey houses many of the finest original sculptures from the Copán valley, comprehensively displaying the skill of the Maya craftsmen.

Plaza Central and Gran Plaza

Straight through the avenue of trees from the warden's gate lie the **Plaza Central** and **Gran Plaza**, large, rectangular arenas strewn with the magnificently carved and exceptionally well-preserved stelae that are Copán's outstanding features. The northern end of the Gran Plaza was once a public place, the stepped sides bordered by a densely populated residential area. **Structure 4** in the centre of the two plazas is a modestly sized pyramid-temple.

Dotted all around are Copán's famed **stelae** and altars, made from local andesite. Most of the stelae represent **18 Rabbit**, Copán's "King of the Arts" (stelae A, B, C, D, F, H and 4). Stele A (731 AD) has 52 glyphs along its sides including the emblem glyphs of the four great cities of Copán, Palenque, Tikal and Calakmul – a text designed to show that Eighteen Rabbit saw his city as a pivotal power in the Maya world. The original is now in the museum. **Stele B** (731 AD) depicts Eighteen Rabbit bearing a turban-like headdress intertwined with twin macaws, while his hands support a bar motif, a symbol designed to show the ruler holding up the sky. **Stele C** (730 AD) is one of the earliest stones to have faces on both sides. Two rulers are represented here: facing the turtle-shaped altar (a symbol of longevity) is Eighteen Rabbit's father Smoke Jaguar, while on the other side is Eighteen Rabbit himself. **Stele H** (730 AD), perhaps the most impressively executed of all the sculptures, shows Eighteen Rabbit wearing the latticed skirt of the Maize God, his wrists weighed down with jewellery, while his face is crowned with a stunning headdress.

Ball court

South of Structure 4, towards the Acropolis, is the I-shaped **ball court** (738 AD), one of the largest and most elaborate of the Classic period, and one of the few Maya courts still to have a paved floor. Dedicated to the great macaw deity, both sloping sides of the court are lined with three sculptured macaw heads. The rooms overlooking the playing area are thought to be where priests and the elite watched the game.

Hieroglyphic Stairway

Protected by a vast canvas cover just south of the ball court is the famed **Hieroglyphic Stairway**, perhaps Copán's most astonishing monument. The stairway comprises the entire western face of the Temple 26 pyramid, and is made up of some 72 stone steps; every block forms part of the glyphic sequence – around 2200 glyph blocks in all, forming the longest-known Maya hieroglyphic text. Since their discovery at the end of the nineteenth century and a well-meaning reconstruction in the 1930s, the blocks have become so jumbled their true meaning is unlikely ever to be revealed. It is known that the stairway was initiated to record the dynastic history of the city; some of the lower steps were placed by Eighteen Rabbit in 710 AD, while Smoke Shell rearranged and completed most of the sequences in an effort to reassert the city's dignity and strength in 755 AD. At the base of the stairway the badly weathered **Stele M** depicts Smoke Shell and records a solar eclipse in 756 AD.

Temple 11

Adjacent to the Hieroglyphic Stairway, and towering over the extreme southern end of the plaza, are the vertiginous steps of **Temple 11** (Temple of the Inscriptions). At its base, **Stele N** (761 AD) represents Smoke Shell. The depth of the relief has protected the nooks and crannies, and in some of these you can

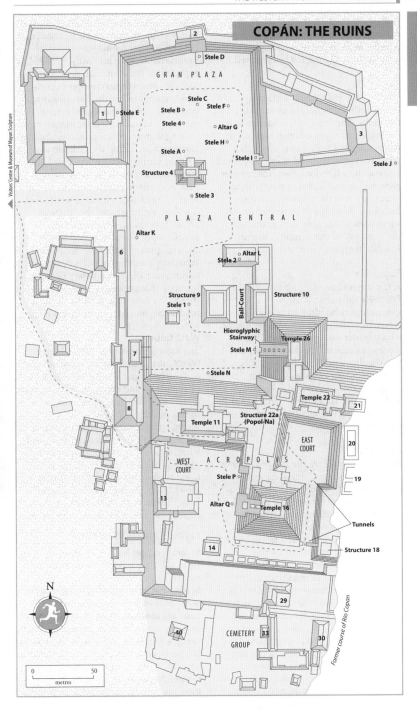

COPÁN: THE RUINS

5

still see flakes of paint – originally the carvings and buildings would have been painted in a whole range of bright colours, but only the red has survived.

Acropolis

South of the Hieroglyphic Stairway monumental temples rise to form the **Acropolis**. This lofty inner sanctum was the reserve of royalty, nobles and priests where religious rituals were enacted, sacrifices performed and rulers entombed. For over four hundred years, the temples grew higher and higher as new structures were built over the remains of earlier buildings. A warren of excavated tunnels, some open to the public, bore through the vast bulk of the Acropolis to the Rosalila Temple and several tombs.

Popol-Na

A few metres east of Temple 11 are the **Popol-Na** (Structure 22A), a governmental building with interlocking weave-like brick patterns, and **Temple 22**, which boasts some superbly intricate stonework around the door frames and was the site of religious blood-letting ceremonies. The decoration here is unique in the southern Maya region, with only the Yucatán sites such as Kabáh and Chicanna having carvings of comparable quality.

East Court

Below Temple 22 are the stepped sides of the **East Court**, a graceful plaza with life-sized jaguar heads – the hollow eyes would have once held jade or polished obsidian. Dominating the Acropolis, **Temple 16**, built on top of the **Rosalila Temple**, is the tallest structure in Copán, a 30m pyramid completed by the city's sixteenth ruler, Yax Pasaj, in 776 AD. It was Maya custom to ritually deface or destroy obsolete temples and stelae. Yax Pasaj's extraordinary care to preserve the Rosalila Temple beneath illustrates the importance of the previous centre of worship during a period that marked the apogee of the city's political, social and artistic growth. The discovery of the Rosalila Temple has been one of the most exciting finds of recent years.

You can now view the brilliant original facade of the buried temple by entering through a short **tunnel** – an unforgettable, if rather costly (US$15), experience. The admission price also includes access to two further tunnels, which extend below the East Court and past some early cosmological stucco carvings – including a huge macaw mask – along with more buried temple facades and crypts including the Galindo tomb.

At the southern end of the East Court is **Structure 18**, a small, square building with four carved panels, and the burial place of Yax Pasaj, who died in 821 AD. The diminutive scale of the structure reveals how quickly decline set in. The tomb, empty when excavated by archeologists, is thought to have been looted on a number of occasions. South of Structure 18, the **Cemetery Group** was formerly thought of as a burial site, though it's now known to have been a residential complex for the ruling elite.

West Court

The second plaza of the Acropolis, the **West Court**, is confined by the south side of Temple 11 and Temple 16. At the base of Temple 16 and carved in 776 AD, **Altar Q** celebrates Yax Pasaj's accession to the throne on July 2, 763 AD. Six hieroglyphic blocks decorate the top of the altar, while the sides are embellished with 16 cross-legged figures representing previous rulers of Copán. All point towards a portrait of Yax Pasaj, which shows him receiving a ceremonial staff from the city's first ruler, Yax K'uk Mo', thereby endorsing Yax Pasaj's right to rule.

ARRIVAL AND INFORMATION

On foot From Copán Ruinas centre the ruins are an easy 15min walk along a shaded pavement following the highway.

By moto-taxi You can grab a moto-taxi from the Parque Central to take you to the ruins (5min; L20).

Hours and admission The site is open daily 8am–5pm (last entry 4pm). The US$15 admission fee includes entrance to the complex of ruins and the Museum of Maya Sculpture, as well as to the smaller site of Las Sepulturas (see p.408). The ticket is valid for three days.

Tourist information On entering the site, the visitors' centre, where you pay your entrance fee, is to your left.

INTO GUATEMALA: EL FLORIDO

The **Guatemalan border** is just 12km west of Copán, and crossing at the **El Florido** border post – usually busy with travellers coming to and from the ruins – is pretty easy, though it can be slow. Minibuses and pick-ups leave for El Florido (about every 30min until around 4pm) from just west of the Parque Central, at the corner of Av Mirador and C 18 Conejo. Hedman Alas, Copán Connections (see p.406) and Basecamp (see p.405) in Copán Ruinas have direct daily shuttles to Antigua and Guatemala City, with connections to Río Dulce. The ever-present moneychangers at the border handle dollars, lempiras and quetzales at fairly good rates. From the border, buses leave (every 30min; last bus 4pm; 1hr 15min) for Chiquimula (see p.336), 57km away down a smooth paved road.

From here it's a 200m walk east to the warden's gate, where your ticket will be checked and you'll be greeted by squabbling macaws.

Tour guides Guides are available and are generally well worth the fee – they do an excellent job of bringing the ruins to life; get together with other visitors to spread the cost (around US\$25/2hr).

LA ENTRADA

Northeast from Copán the CA-11 winds its scenic way through lightly wooded mountains and fertile pasture to **LA ENTRADA**, an unpleasant junction town 55km from Copán, useful only for its bus connections to San Pedro Sula, Santa Rosa and Copán Ruinas.

ACCOMMODATION

Hotel San Carlos Junction of CA-11 & CA-4 ☎ 2898 5228, ⓦ hotelsancarlos.com. If you get stuck in La Entrada, opt for this, the best of the available accommodation. Rooms are at least comfortable and secure with en-suite bathroom. **L650**

Olancho

Stretching east of Tegucigalpa to the Nicaraguan border and north into the emptiness of La Mosquitia, the sparsely populated uplands of **Olancho** are widely regarded as the "Wild East" of Honduras: an untamed frontier region with a not entirely undeserved reputation for lawlessness. Over time, everyone from the first Spanish settlers to the Honduran government has had trouble imposing law and order here, and in many respects today is no different: the region's profitable cattle-ranching industry (which has encroached into national parks and other protected areas) and the logging of its massive forests (much of which is done illegally) have led to the creation of a powerful local oligarchy supported by military and police connivance. As a result, environmental issues have been sidelined, and activists have been threatened and even killed.

Despite Olancho's size – it makes up a fifth of Honduras's total territory – tourist attractions are few, and its high, forested mountain ranges interspersed with broad valleys make getting from place to place difficult and slow. However, these same ranges harbour some of the country's last untouched expanses of tropical forest and cloudforest: the national parks of **El Boquerón** and **Sierra de Agalta** are awe-inspiring. Along the valleys, now given over to pastureland for cattle, are scattered villages and towns. Both **Juticalpa**, the department capital, and **Catacamas**, at the eastern end of the paved road, are good bases for exploring the region.

Olancho's **climate** is generally pleasant, with the towns at lower altitudes hot during the day and comfortably cool at night; up in the mountains it can get extremely cold after dark. Once off the main highway, **travelling** becomes arduous, with the dirt roads connecting villages served by infrequent and invariably slow public transport.

JUTICALPA

Situated towards the southern end of the Valle de Catacamas, about 170km from Tegucigalpa, **JUTICALPA** is a pleasant little provincial city where the streets are busy

5

night and day with bustle and commerce – it can be a refreshing place to spend a few days. The focal point is the leafy **Parque Banderas**, which includes a small pool of rather disgruntled-looking turtles. The majority of facilities are on the streets around here. The general **market** stretches for a few blocks to the west, along Calle Perulapan. When the town's attractions have worn thin, try the **cinema** at Calle 1, Avenida 2–3.

ARRIVAL AND INFORMATION

By bus Juticalpa's two bus terminals are just off the highway on 1 Av SE, which leads straight to the centre, a 15min walk north. Local buses run from the terminal on the right side of the road (facing town), while direct buses to Tegucigalpa and the north coast use the other side.
Destinations Catacamas (20 plus daily; 40min); La Ceiba (2 daily; 9hr); Tegucigalpa (hourly; 3hr).
Banks Several banks dot the perimeter of Parque Banderas.
Internet You can get online at Brothers Internet on Av 5.
Tourist information The ICF agency (formerly COHDEFOR) is set back from the road on Av 7 near C 14 (erratic hours, but in theory Mon–Fri 9am–5pm ☎ 2785 2253). Boss Daniel Cerma is very helpful (though he speaks only Spanish).

ACCOMMODATION

Hotel El Paso Blvd Los Poetas ☎ 2785 2311. A decent budget choice with a mix of rooms: all have private bathrooms, but only the more expensive options have a/c and hot water. Noise can be a problem, so bring earplugs. **L470**
Hotel Honduras Walk up C 2 from the square, turn left down Av 7 and it's on the left between C 2 & C 3 ☎ 2785 1580. Very clean and well-looked-after hotel; rooms come with either fan or a/c. **L420**

EATING

Juticalpa's range of restaurants is pretty modest, though there's a healthy profusion of inexpensive *comedores* and street-food stalls around Parque Banderas.
La Fonda On the highway, near the petrol station, a 30min walk from the town centre. Reliable place for good-value, no-nonsense Honduran food (dishes L70–150). Daily 8am–9pm.

MONUMENTO NACIONAL EL BOQUERÓN

Some 20km east of Juticalpa, **MONUMENTO NACIONAL EL BOQUERÓN**, one of the last remaining tracks of **dry**

tropical forest in Honduras, is home to a wide variety of wildlife, including more than 250 species of bird.

WHAT TO SEE AND DO

To see the forest properly, you'll want to hike the moderately strenuous main **trail** through the reserve. The trail runs from where the bus drops you off near the Puente Boquerón bridge to a point a few kilometres west of the main entrance; the walk is manageable in one day if you get an early start.

Follow the track starting on the left-hand side of the Río Olancho – though it crosses over several times, so be prepared to wade – and after about a kilometre the path enters the gorge, eventually emerging onto the floodplain at the other side. From here it is around two more easy hours through level pastureland to the village of **La Avispa**. Beyond the village, the path loops steeply uphill and through the cloudforest section of the park; you have a pretty good chance of seeing some of the country's elusive bird and animal life here, including mixed flocks of brightly coloured trogons and quetzals that feed together at fruit trees. The reserve is also the only known Honduran location of the white-eared ground sparrow, fairly easily seen in the undergrowth. Beyond the cloudforest the walk is downhill all the way, with the path finally emerging a few kilometres later on the highway at Tempisque, west of the main entrance.

ARRIVAL AND INFORMATION

By bus Monumento Nacional El Boquerón is about halfway between Juticalpa and Catacamas. Any bus going between the two towns can drop you near the start of the main trail, by the Boquerón bridge. After you're done trekking, you can easily flag down buses to either place on the main highway.
Reserve information The reserve is easily accessible as a day-trip from Juticalpa, though there are facilities should you want to camp (free). It is advisable to visit the ICF (formerly COHDEFOR) office in Juticalpa before setting out (see above), as the trail can be hard to follow, especially after heavy rainfall, and there are no rangers or information facilities once you reach the park. Bring your own food and water.

CATACAMAS

CATACAMAS, midway along the Valle de Catacamas beneath the southern flanks of the Sierra de Agalta, is a smaller version of Juticalpa. The fact that it's at the end of one of the paved roads through the region contributes to the affable, small-town charm of the place. It certainly has a more spectacular setting than its larger neighbour: a short walk up to the **Mirador de la Cruz**, fifteen minutes from the centre on the northern side of town, gives superb views over the town and valley.

WHAT TO SEE AND DO

The main reason for coming out this far is to visit the local **Cuevas de Talgua**, one of the country's foremost historical sites.

Cuevas de Talgua

Located 8km northeast of town on the banks of the Río Talgua, the **Cuevas de Talgua** (daily 9am–5pm; US$6) are notable for the discovery here of a **prehistoric burial ground** featuring hundreds of skeletons arranged in chambers deep underground. Though the burial ground itself is out of bounds to visitors, the rest of the site has been developed for tourists, with a **museum** telling the tale of the finds and trails leading through the caves. To get here, take the local **bus** from Catacamas to Talgua (3 daily, 7am, 11am & 3pm; 20min). The last return bus leaves Talgua at 4pm. Taxis generally quote around L200–250, but try to pay no more than L150.

ARRIVAL AND INFORMATION

By bus Buses terminate four blocks south of Catacamas's Parque Central; the Parque itself, dominated by a giant ceiba tree, is a short walk away up a slight hill. There are frequent buses to Juticalpa (20 plus daily; 40min) and Tegucigalpa (20 plus daily; 3–4hr).

Banks There are banks around the Parque Central and in the streets just to the north.

Tourist information Jorge Yanes at the IHAH (Instituto Hondureño de Antropología e Historia; ☎ 2799 3090, ⊕ ihah.hn), opposite the *municipalidad* on Av Piedra Blanca, is very knowledgeable about all things Olancho and La Mosquitia and can arrange tours. Town maps can be bought at *Hotel Plaza María*.

Tour operators Olancho Tours (☎ 9811 7451, ⊕ olanchotours@yahoo.com) offers excursions throughout the region; contact them by phone or email.

ACCOMMODATION

La Colina Av SW, just off the corner of the Parque ☎ 2799 4488. The best budget hotel in town, with reasonably comfortable rooms set round a courtyard; all come with private bathrooms, TVs and fans. L350

Hotel Plaza Maria Av 3 between C 3 & C 4 ☎ 2799 4832, ⊕ plazamaria.com. *Plaza Maria* offers comfortable en-suite rooms with TVs, a pool and free wi-fi. The helpful manager speaks English. Breakfast included. L1102

Oriental Close to *La Colina*, just off the southwest corner of the Parque ☎ 2799 4038. Basic but orderly rooms, some with private bathrooms. L300

EATING

As de Oro Three blocks south of *Hotel Plaza María* on Av 3. Described as a *restaurante típico olanchano*, As de Oro is popular with locals. Among the dishes (L50–200) are a few options not for the faint-hearted including the euphemistically named *huevos de toro a la plancha* and the somewhat more direct *sopa de testículo*.

Francel *Hotel Plaza María*, Av 3 between C 3 & C 4. The buffet restaurant at this hotel (see above) offers an array of items such as breaded fish fillet, rice, chorizo and various other meats. A plateful costs around L100. Clean, friendly and particularly good for breakfast. Daily 7am–9.30pm.

PARQUE NACIONAL SIERRA DE AGALTA

Draped across the sweeping ranges of the Sierra de Agalta, the vast **PARQUE NACIONAL SIERRA DE AGALTA** shelters the most extensive stretch of **virgin cloudforest** remaining in Central America. Though the area has been designated a protected area since 1987, large stands of pine and oak in the lower parts of the park have nonetheless still been logged, and much of the land cleared for cattle pasture. The higher reaches of the mountains, however (including Honduras's fourth-highest peak, La Picucha), are so remote that both vegetation and wildlife have remained virtually untouched. Here a typical cloudforest of oaks, liquidambar and cedar, draped in vines and ferns, covers the slopes up to about 2000m, where it gives way to a dwarf forest.

5

In addition to the flora, the park's isolation ensures a protected, secure environment for a biologically diverse range of **mammals** and **birds**, many of them extremely rare. Tapirs, jaguars, ocelots, opossums and three types of monkey are among the species of mammal recorded. More evident are the birds, of which more than four hundred species have been sighted.

ARRIVAL AND INFORMATION

By bus The easiest points of entry for the park are along the northern edge of the Sierra, via the small towns of Gualaco and San Esteban, which you can reach off Highway C-39 between Juticalpa and Trujillo. The daily bus from Juticalpa (1 daily, 4am; 1hr 30min to Gualaco; 3hr 30min to San Esteban; 8hr to Trujillo) passes by both towns – just ask the driver to stop so you can hop off. Accessing the park trails from either town requires a significant hike.

By pick-up Pick-ups from the market in Juticalpa also make the trip to the park.

Tour operators Hiring a guide is highly recommended, and pretty much essential for hiking the difficult trails: ask at the IHAH office in Catacamas (see p.415), Gualaco or San Esteban. In Gualaco ask for Francisco Urbina (☎9901 3400, ✉chicourbina@yahoo.com) at the *municipalidad*; he charges around US$30/person. From the Catacamas side, Calixto Ordoñez (☎9783 8259, ✉calixtoo77@yahoo.com) offers tours, including a hike up La Picucha, for a negotiable L500/person.

ACCOMMODATION

Camping Note that there's no accommodation in the park other than official camping spots, for which you'll need to bring all equipment and supplies.

The north coast

Honduras's **north coast** stretches for some 300km along the azure fringes of the Caribbean. A magnet for Hondurans and foreign tourists alike, the region provides sun, sea and entertainment in abundance, especially in the coastal towns of **Tela**, **La Ceiba** and **Trujillo**, with their broad expanses of beach, clean warm waters, plentiful restaurants and buzzing nightlife. San Pedro Sula, the region's major inland city and transport hub, provides amenities of a strictly urban kind. Dotted along the north coast

between these main towns are a number of laidback **villages** blessed with unspoilt **beaches**. Populated by the **Garífuna** people, descendants of African slaves and Carib people (see box, p.90), these villages are often very much removed from the rest of Honduran culture and society, and can feel like visiting an entirely different country.

When beach life loses its appeal, there are several **natural reserves** to visit in the region. The national parks of **Cusuco**, **Pico Bonito** and **Capiro y Calentura**, whose virgin cloudforest shelters rare wildlife, offer hiking for all levels; the wetland and mangrove swamps at **Punta Sal** and **Cuero y Salado** require less exertion to explore.

The region's **rainy season** generally runs from November to January, while the hurricane season is August to October. Obviously, it's best to visit outside of these times but you won't necessarily be battered incessantly by rain or winds if you do visit during this period. Temperatures rarely drop below 25–28°, but the heat is usually tempered by ocean breezes. **Transport** is reasonably good, with frequent buses along the fast, paved highway that links the main coastal towns; as usual, reaching the remoter villages and national parks requires some forward planning.

SAN PEDRO SULA

The country's second city and driving economic force, **SAN PEDRO SULA** sprawls across the fertile Valle de Sula ("Valley of the Birds" in Usula dialect) at the foot of the Merendón mountain chain, just an hour from the coast. Flat and uninspiring to look at, and for most of the year uncomfortably hot and humid, this is a city for getting business done, rather than sightseeing. It has also been dubbed the most violent city in the world, thanks to the burgeoning activities of **drug gangs** and traffickers. Take special precautions here (see p.383).

San Pedro Sula is the **transport hub** for northern and western Honduras, however, which means a visit here is usually unavoidable, even if only to pass through.

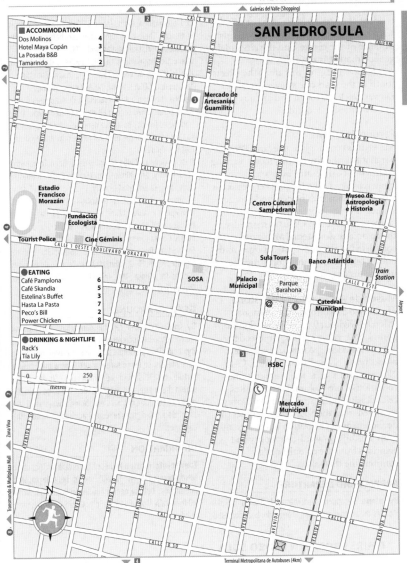

SAN PEDRO SULA

Galerías del Valle (Shopping)

ACCOMMODATION
Dos Molinos	4
Hotel Maya Copán	3
La Posada B&B	1
Tamarindo	2

EATING
Café Pamplona	6
Café Skandia	5
Estelina's Buffet	3
Hasta La Pasta	7
Peco's Bill	2
Power Chicken	8

DRINKING & NIGHTLIFE
Rack's	1
Tía Lily	4

Estadio Francisco Morazán
Fundación Ecologista
Tourist Police
Cine Géminis
CALLE 1 OESTE (BOULEVARD MORAZÁN)
Mercado de Artesanías Guamilito
Centro Cultural Sampédrano
Museo de Antropología e Historia
Sula Tours
Banco Atlántida
Train Station
SOSA
Palacio Municipal
Parque Barahona
Catedral Municipal
HSBC
Mercado Municipal

0   250
metres

N

Transmundo & Multiplaza Mall
Zona Viva
Airport
Terminal Metropolitana de Autobuses (4km)

Luckily **facilities** – an international airport, foreign consulates and a wide range of hotels, restaurants and shops – rate alongside those in Tegucigalpa.

WHAT TO SEE AND DO

San Pedro's dangerous reputation generally precedes it, causing most tourists to get in and out as quickly as possible. There are a few sights, however, though it is important to exercise caution and common sense when taking them in.

San Pedro's centre is in the southwest sector of the city. Running west from the **Parque Barahona**, Calle 1 is also known as Boulevard Morazán for the twelve blocks before it meets the **Avenida Circunvalación** ring road, which separates the city centre from San Pedro's wealthier

5

residential districts. Most of what you'll want to see in the city is within walking distance of the centre, and the city's main general **market** is towards the southeastern edge of this area. The streets south of the market and over the old railway track are rough and are not places to be wandering around.

Parque Barahona

San Pedro's central plaza, the large **Parque Barahona**, is the city centre's focus, teeming with vendors, shoeshine boys and moneychangers. The Parque's centrepiece is a large fountain with bridges and bronze statues of washerwomen beating their clothes on the rocks. On its eastern edge, the colonial-style **Catedral Municipal**, completed in the mid-1950s, is open to the public, but there's nothing of particular interest inside.

Museo de Antropología e Historia

The **Museo de Antropología e Historia** (Mon & Wed–Sat 9am–4.30pm, Sun 9am–3pm; US$2; ☎ 2557 1496, ⓦ museode antropologiadesanpedrosula.com), a few blocks north of the Parque at Av 3, C 4 NO, is worth a visit. The museum's fine collection of pre-Columbian sculptures, ceramics and other artefacts, the majority recovered from the Sula valley, outlines the development of civilization in the region from 1500 BC onwards; weaponry and paintings from the colonial period continue the theme.

ARRIVAL AND DEPARTURE

By plane Aeropuerto Internacional Ramón Villeda Morales, the north coast's point of arrival for both domestic

and international flights (see p.379), lies 12km southeast of the city. There is no public transport between the city and the airport; taxis cost around L200.

Domestic destinations La Ceiba (SOSA, 1 daily; 30min); Roatán (SOSA & Isleña/TACA, 1–2 daily; 2hr 35min); Tegucigalpa (SOSA & Isleña/TACA, 2 daily; 50min).

By bus The Terminal Metropolitana de Autobuses is 5km south of the town centre; all services listed below leave from here. The city buses are dangerous (see box, p.380), so take a taxi from the terminal to the centre; they should cost less than L100.

Destinations La Ceiba (20 plus daily; 3hr); Comayagua (1–2 hourly; 2hr 30min–3hr 15min); Copán Ruinas (8 daily; 3hr); La Entrada (25 daily; 1–2hr); Gracias (4 daily; 4–5hr); Guatemala City & Antigua (5 daily; 7–8hr); Managua (1 daily; 12hr); Ocotopeque (5 daily; 5hr); Pulhapanzak & Lago de Yojoa (14 daily; 1hr 30min); Puerto Cortés (every 30min; 1hr); San Salvador (1 daily; 6hr); Santa Rosa de Copán (2–3 hourly; 3hr 30min); Siguatepeque (1–2 hourly; 3hr); Tegucigalpa (every 30min; 3hr 30min–4hr); Tela (1–2 hourly; 1hr 30min); Trujillo (hourly; 5–6hr).

GETTING AROUND

By bus City buses can be dangerous and are not recommended. It's quicker and safer to get a taxi.

By taxi The plentiful taxis are licensed but none have meters, so make sure you settle on a price before setting off. It should be about L50–70 for travel within the centre, and around L100–150 to go from the centre to the edge of town. You should always use a taxi after dark (and they're often advisable during the daytime).

INFORMATION

Tourist information In theory, the *policía turística* office (Blvd Morazán & Av 12 NO) should be able to offer information, but the nearby Fundación Ecologista, Av 12 NO (generally Mon–Fri 9am–5pm; ☎ 2552 1014), is more helpful.

TOURS FROM SAN PEDRO SULA

There are numerous **tour agencies** in San Pedro Sula. Some of the best include:

Eli Gonzalez ⓔ naturalhonduras@yahoo.com. An independent tour guide with more than twenty years' experience.

Jungle Expedition *Banana Inn* hotel, near the airport ☎ 9762 6620, ⓦ junglexpedition.org. Reliable outfit offering excellent hikes into Parque Nacional El Cusuco (US$40–80), plus shuttle buses thoughout the country, trips to Copán and mountain biking.

Mesoamérica Travel Col Juan Lindo, Casa 709,

C 8 Av 32 NO ☎ 2558 6447 or ☎ 2558 6258, ⓦ mesoamerica-travel.com. A 15min taxi ride from the centre (around L80–100), this company offers tours throughout the country, including La Mosquitia, and responds promptly to enquiries.

Sula Tours *Gran Hotel Sula*, northern side of the Parque Central ☎ 2545 2660 or ☎ 9618 1305, ⓦ hotelsula.hn. A number of different tours, to destinations far and wide, starting at US$35.

Travel agent Transmundo (☏ 2553 5072 or ☏ 2553 5513, ⊛ transmundohn.com), Edificio Plaza del Carmen, Bo Suyapa, C 6, Av 16–17 SO, can book flights and arrange car rental.

ACCOMMODATION

San Pedro, the second-largest city in Honduras, is one of the fastest-growing in Latin America. Don't be tempted by any of the super-cheap hotels – most aren't secure and can be dangerous.

Dos Molinos Bo Paz Barahona C 13, Av 8–9 SO 34 ☏ 2510 0335 or ☏ 9960 0857, ⊛ dosmolinos.hostel.com. The principal appeal in this unmarked green house is the friendly, homely atmosphere. The en-suite rooms have high ceilings and big TVs, and there's a communal kitchen. Rates include wi-fi and breakfast. US$39

Hotel Maya Copán C 4, Av 5–6 ☏ 2553 2049, ⊛ hotelmayacopanhn.com. Warm, characterful place, hung with traditional blankets on the walls and old photos of Honduras (as well as London's Big Ben). Internet/wi-fi access, a/c, and a *típico* breakfast are included. US$65

La Posada B&B Col Universidad C 21, Av 9 Casa 172 ☏ 2566 3312, ⊛ laposadahn.com. This spacious place feels like a modern suburban home. The comfortable en-suite rooms all have a/c and TVs, and there are pleasant communal areas where you can mingle with other guests. Rates include bus terminal pick-up/drop-off, wi-fi, purified water and breakfast. US$58

Tamarindo Bo Los Andes C9, Av 10–11 NO ☏ 2557 0123, ⊛ tamarindohostel.com. This popular hostel, a 5min drive from the centre, has slightly stuffy dorms, clean bathrooms, a communal kitchen, barbecue area, and a swimming pool. The private rooms are nice, but rather overpriced. Service can be a little sloppy. Dorm US$13, double US$36

EATING

★ **Café Pamplona** Parque Barahona. A San Pedro institution, with wood, brick and tiled decor and a Spanish flavour. Tasty and inexpensive breakfasts, snacks such as *baleadas*, and more substantial meals are available (dishes from L50). Mon–Fri 7am–7/8pm, Sun 8am–2pm.

Café Skandia Gran Hotel Sula, on the northern side of the Parque Central. Open all day, every day, the *Skandia* feels like a Scandinavian take on a diner, with everything in cool blues and white. There's a terrace with palm trees and a pool. The menu features North and Central American staples (L50–150). Daily 24hr.

Estelina's Buffet Mercado Guamilito. It's said that if you don't eat at this stall when you're in San Pedro, you haven't been to San Pedro: these expert *baleadas* (from L20) are the real deal. Mon–Sat 9am–4.30pm.

Hasta La Pasta Barrio Río de Piedras, C 7 SO, between Av 18 & 19 ☏ 2550 3048, ⊛ hastalapasta.com. One of the city's top Italian restaurants, in a new location, with an extensive menu of soups (the *sopa de mariscos* is particularly good), salads, pastas, pizzas, seafood and steaks (mains L85–325). Mon–Thurs 11am–10.30pm, Fri & Sat 11am–11pm, Sun 11am–9pm.

Peco's Bill Av 15, C 6 NO. This rambling, open-sided place feels like an overgrown tree house, and is as popular with drinkers as it is with diners. Grilled meat (from L100), from steaks to pork chops, is the order of the day here; adventurous diners can sample the *mondongo* (tripe) stew. Tues–Sun 11am–11pm.

Power Chicken Near the junction of Av 15 and Av Circunvalación on the southern edge of the *Zona Viva* (see below). Residents of the city will not hear a bad word said about this place, and they're right: this is fast food at its finest. Spicy chicken, ribs, steak, fried plantain, *yuca* – it's all here, with mains around L60–90. Mon–Thurs 9am–9.30pm, Fri–Sun 9am–9pm.

DRINKING AND NIGHTLIFE

All of San Pedro Sula's action is, in theory, out in the so-called *Zona Viva*, which is how the area around the southern half of avenidas 15 and 16 is known. It can often feel about as *viva* as a ghost town, however. In general, the clubs in this area are safer than the bars, which can get very dangerous. Always take a taxi to and from the *Zona Viva*.

Rack's Bo Los Andes, C11, Av 11 NO, near Parque Benito Juárez. A foreigner-friendly sports bar with pool tables and a deck out front. Live bands sometimes play at weekends. A beer costs around L30, and there's a range of bar snacks (such as buffalo wings) for lining your stomach.

Tía Lily C 2A, Col Moderna. An open-sided bar hidden behind dense greenery, this is on the edge of the *Zona Viva* but feels rather cosy, and the food's good too. Try the chorizo with beans, *chismol* (salsa) and *tajadas* (fried bananas/plantains) – perfect beer (L30–40) food.

ENTERTAINMENT

Centro Cultural Sampedrano C 3, Av 3 NO ☏ 2553 3911, ⊛ centrocultural-sps.com. This cultural centre regularly hosts concerts and plays; the building also houses the public library.

Cinema Near the *Zona Viva* is the four-screen Cine Géminis, at C 1 & Av 12 NO; there's another cinema with lots of screens at Multiplaza mall. Both show subtitled movies.

SHOPPING

Numerous malls are dotted around the city centre, and a couple of shops on C Peatonal, just off the Parque Central, sell similar stuff to the Guamilito craft market, though prices are higher.

5

Mercado de Artesanías Guamilito Av 8, C 6–7 NO. Indoor market with numerous stalls selling hammocks, ceramics, leatherwork and wooden goods.

Mercado Municipal Between Av 4–5 SO & C 5–6 SO. Stalls spilling onto the streets for several blocks; you can find a bit of everything here.

Metro Nova First floor of Galerías del Valle, C 25, north of the town centre. A good selection of English-language books, though they're not cheap.

DIRECTORY

Banks Banco Atlántida has a number of branches downtown, including one on the Parque Central with an ATM; there are several other banks along C 2 between Av 5 and 6. HSBC is at C 4 and Av 5 SO.

Car rental Molinari, in the *Gran Hotel Sula* on the northern side of the Parque Central (☏2533 2639); Omega, Av 3, C 3–4 NO (☏2552 7626).

Consulates Belize, on the road to Puerto Cortés (☏2551 6247); El Salvador, Av 11, 5–6 NO (☏2557 5591); Germany, C 1, 8–9 SO (☏2553 1244); Mexico, C 2, Av 20–21 SO (☏2552 3672); Netherlands, Av 15, C 7–8 (☏2557 1815); Nicaragua, Av 5, Av 4–5 SO (☏2550 0813); Spain, Av 2, C 3–4 NE (☏2553 2480); UK, C 2, Av 18–19 NO (☏2550 2337); US, in the Banco Atlántida building on the northern side of the Parque (☏2236 9320 or ☏2238 5114).

Hospital The Hospital Centro Médico Betesda is at Av 11, C 11–12 NO.

Internet Diosita.net, in a little arcade just off C Peatonal, next to *Espresso Americano*. Cyber Café Pro on the first floor of Galerías del Valle, C 25, north of the town centre, has good computers and quick connection.

Post office C 9, Av 3 SO (Mon–Fri 7.30am–5pm, Sat 8am–noon).

PUERTO CORTÉS

North of San Pedro Sula, Highway CA-5 runs through the flat agricultural lands and lush tropical scenery of the Sula valley. After 60km the four-lane highway reaches the coast at **PUERTO CORTÉS**, Honduras's main port. There's nothing here to entice, and you'll likely pass through only to change buses en route to Omoa or to hop aboard a boat for Belize.

ARRIVAL AND DEPARTURE

By bus Several companies run buses between San Pedro Sula and Puerto Cortés, including the reliable Citul, whose terminal is a block north of the main plaza at Av 4 & C 4. Other buses arrive at the nearby Transportes Citral terminal.

INTO BELIZE BY BOAT

In theory, several companies run **boats** between **Belize** and Honduras (see p.90), although in reality the timetables are inconsistent and boats rarely leave on time. One-way tickets cost around US$60.

The Nesymein Neydy service (☏2223 1200, ✉mundomayatravels @yahoo.com) to Dangriga is scheduled to leave from Puerto Cortés's Laguna de Pescadería (3km southeast of town under the bridge near the fish market) every Monday at 11am, but you should be at the dock at 9am. The "D" express (☏2665 0726, ⊕belizeferry.com) leaves from the same spot, and at the same time, for Independence and Placencia – again, it's best to get there in plenty of time. The return journeys for both are on Friday.

Destinations Corinto (for Guatemala; every 45min; 4hr); Omoa (every 30min; 1hr); San Pedro Sula (every 30min; 1hr).

By boat There are ferries to Independence and Placencia in Belize (see box above).

ACCOMMODATION AND EATING

Budget accommodation is hard to come by, and there is also little choice in terms of places to eat.

Hotel El Centro Av 3, C 2–3 ☏2665 1160. This economical hotel is the best bet for budget travellers, offering small but clean en-suite rooms with a/c. **L575**

Repostería Plata Av 3 & C 2. Popular with locals for their buffet meals, this place has the added advantage of being open on Sun, when all other restaurants are closed. Mains from L60.

OMOA

Spreading inland from a deep bay at the point where the mountains of the Sierra de Omoa meet the Caribbean, **OMOA** was once a strategically important location in the defence of the Spanish colonies against marauding British pirates. Its popularity with travellers has waned in recent years, thanks to a gas company's decision to construct jetties here to protect their tanks. This has altered the current of Omoa bay, causing the beach to shrink – it is estimated that 60 percent has disappeared over the course of four years. The best beach now is to be found behind the fort.

WHAT TO SEE AND DO

Omoa's one outstanding sight, the restored **Fortaleza de San Fernando de Omoa** (Mon–Fri 8am–4pm, Sat & Sun 9am–5pm; US$4), stands amid tropical greenery in mute witness to the village's colourful history. Now isolated 1km from the coast, having been beached as the sea has receded over the centuries, the triangular fort was originally intended to protect the port of Puerto Barrios in Guatemala. Work began in 1759 but was never fully completed due to a combination of inefficiency and a labour shortage. The steadily weakening Spanish authorities then suffered the ignominy of witnessing the fortress be temporarily occupied by British and Miskito military forces in October 1779. A small museum on site tells the story of the fort and displays a selection of military paraphernalia including cannons and period weaponry.

ARRIVAL AND INFORMATION

By bus/moto-taxi Buses between Puerto Cortés and Corinto pass the southern end of the village at a crossroads, though some go all the way to the beach, where you'll find most of the action. Moto-taxis ply the 2km stretch from the crossroads to the beach.

Destinations Corinto (for Guatemala; every 20min; 8am–4pm; 1hr); Puerto Cortés (every 30min; 1hr).

Bank Banco de Occidente, just off the highway, can advance cash on your cards but doesn't have an ATM.

ACCOMMODATION

Fisherman Along the beach road ☎ 2658 9224. A good budget option with some of its eleven rooms right on the

---

INTO GUATEMALA: CORINTO

Moving on from Omoa to **Guatemala** is an excruciatingly slow journey along the notoriously bumpy road leading southwest to **Corinto**, 2km from the border. Corinto has its own *migración* (daily 8am–5.30pm). Pick-ups shuttle to and from the border, from where you can catch a minibus (every 30min) to Guatemala; there's usually an exit fee of US$1–2 charged. Minibuses pass through the village of Entre Ríos, for Guatemalan *migración*, to Puerto Barrios, an hour from the Honduran border.

---

beach, but make sure you view a few before deciding. All have cold-water private bathrooms. **L500**

Roli's Place Along the main road about 200m from the sea ☎ 2658 9082, ⦿ omoa.net. Excellent budget place with comfortable rooms as well as camping, hammocks and dorms; they also have kayaks, bikes and laundry facilities. There's a useful map of Omoa on the website. Hammocks and camping **L60**, dorm **L100**, double **L330**

EATING AND DRINKING

La Champa de Monchin Beside the pier. The dishes here are as cheap as can be, with prices from L10: chicken tacos, *baleadas*, and conch or shrimp soup are some of the highlights.

Eddy's Grill Asados On the main road between the beach and the highway. A friendly, family place, where you can sit on the tiled terrace outside the house or on plastic garden chairs in the garden. The meat may be a bit chewy, but it's certainly flavoursome. Dishes from L70.

Sueños de Mar At the western end of the beach road (turn right at the beach) ⦿ suenosdemar.com. You'll find hearty, home-cooked food, Canadian style, at this guesthouse-restaurant. Breakfasts (L80–120) include imported Virginia ham, while "smokies" in a bun are well worth a try. Breakfast and lunch 8am–5pm, bar open until 8pm.

TELA

Sitting midway around the Bahía de Tela, surrounded by sweeping beaches, **TELA** has a near-perfect setting. In the past, the town has suffered from a reputation for violence, but a pilot force of tourist police is substantially cleaning up the town's image. Whether you choose to partake in the nightlife or not, the wealth of fantastic **natural reserves** – including Punta Sal – within minutes of the town makes Tela well worth a visit. The town is also one of the main destinations for Hondurans during **Semana Santa** (Easter Holy Week): it's best to book several weeks or months ahead for that period.

WHAT TO SEE AND DO

Today's Tela is a product of the banana industry. In the late nineteenth century United Fruit built a company town – **Tela Nueva** – here, on the west bank of the Río Tela; the old town became known as **Tela Vieja**. These distinctions still stand. The old town, which lies about 2km

5

north of the highway and two blocks from the beach on the east bank of the river, encompasses the **Parque Central** and main shopping area. Five blocks west from the Parque Central is the Río Tela, beyond which lies Tela Nueva. A fifteen-minute stroll covers practically everything there is to see.

Beaches

It's the **beaches** that most people come for; those in Tela Vieja, though wide, are more crowded than the stretch of pale sand in front of the hotel *Villas Telamar* in Tela Nueva. Even better beaches can be found along the bay outside town – if you walk far enough in either direction you should be able to have one entirely to yourself.

ARRIVAL AND INFORMATION

By bus Most local bus services use the terminal on the corner of Av 9 and C 9 NE. Buses to the surrounding villages use the terminal two blocks north at C 11 and Av 8 NE. There are buses to La Ceiba (every 30min; 2hr 30min) and San Pedro Sula (8 daily; 2hr). You can also get to San Pedro Sula by taking a taxi out to the highway south of town and flagging down one of the buses coming from La Ceiba.

Tourist information The tourist office is in the municipal building off the southeast corner of the Parque Central (Mon–Fri 8am–6pm, Sat 8am–noon; ⓦ telahonduras.com).

Tour operators Garifuna Tours, just off the Parque Central (ⓣ 2448 2904, ⓦ garifunatours.com), run trips to Punta Sal (US$34), Punta Izopo (US$29), Laguna de los Micos (US$39), as well as the "EcoPass" tour, which includes visits to both places plus Pico Bonito for US$99. Run by the English-speaking Ferdinand Florentino, Eco di Mare (ⓣ 2439 0110, ⓣ 9932 3552 or ⓣ 9855 8311, ⓦ ecodimaretours.com) offers a similar range of tours. Its office is next to *Mamma Mia!*, opposite the parking lot for Banco Atlántida, Av 4, C 9 NE.

ACCOMMODATION

Many of Tela's older hotels are quite run-down. There are, however, a number of newer, better-value places opening up as the town becomes more of a fixture on the backpacker trail. Many of these tend to get busy at weekends, when it pays to book ahead.

Bertha's Av 2, C 6–7 ⓣ 2448 3020. Seventeen rooms, all passably clean, with those upstairs a little brighter. Unfortunately it only has cold-water bathrooms. **L350**

Hotel Gran Central Southern end of Av 6 ⓣ 2448 1099, ⓦ hotelgrancentral.com. You'll receive a very friendly Gallic welcome here from Luc and Véronique. The rooms (all a/c and with private bathrooms and safes) have been decorated with some flair; some have a terrace, shuttered windows and high ceilings. There's also a larger suite sleeping up to five. Double **US$50**, suite **US$120**

Hotel Marsol Av 2 near C 9 ⓣ 2448 1781 or ⓣ 2448 1782, ⓦ hotelmarsolteia.com. A reliable choice, though not the

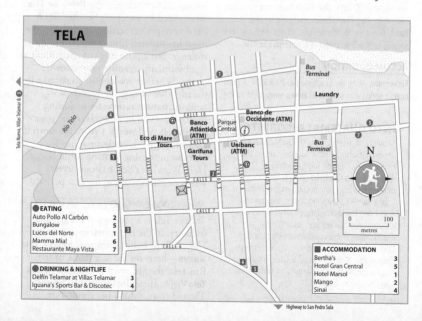

TELA

Bus Terminal

Laundry

Banco de Occidente (ATM)

Banco Atlántida (ATM)

Parque Central (i)

Eco di Mare Tours

Garifuna Tours

Unibanc (ATM)

Bus Terminal

N

Río Tela

Tela Nueva, Villas Telamar & ⑤

CALLE 11
CALLE 10
CALLE 9
CALLE 8
CALLE 7
CALLE 6

AVENIDA

0   100
metres

Highway to San Pedro Sula

most stylish of places (the curtains are particularly gaudy). The rooms come with a/c, TV and private bathrooms. US$52
Mango Corner C 8 & Av 5 ☎ 2448 0338, ⓦ mangocafe.net. A travellers' favourite. The cheaper rooms here come with fan, while the more expensive ones have a/c and TVs. Rooms are clean and there's a small communal terrace, but prices are a bit high. Bike rental and Spanish classes available. US$24
Sinai Southern end of Av 6 ☎ 2448 1486. A good, friendly option, though some way from the beach. The "showers" in the private bathrooms though are basically just tubes. L400

EATING

Tela has an interesting mix of places to eat, with foreign-run restaurants that cater to European and North American visitors competing with locally owned seafood places. One staple that shouldn't be missed is the delicious *pan de coco* (coconut bread) sold by Garífuna women and children on the beach and around town.
Auto Pollo Al Carbón Western end of C 11, by the bridge. Informal place on the doorstep of the Caribbean Sea with a grimy sort of beachside view, serving rotisserie chicken and not much else (from L50).
Bungalow C 9, three and a half blocks east of the Parque Central. An eight-sided wooden affair decorated with American memorabilia, perhaps because owner and chef Norman Taylor grew up in New Orleans. Barbecue ribs, spaghetti with shrimp and pork chops with Cajun rice are among the dishes (from L80) on offer. Thurs–Tues 11am–midnight.
Luces del Norte Corner C 11 & Av 5. Popular with tourists and locals alike, *Luces del Norte* offers a good range of seafood dishes (L100–250), including an array of conch-based meals. Daily 7am–10pm.
Mamma Mia! Av 4, C 9–10. Very friendly Italian-owned pizza and pasta spot with some seafood and meat dishes as well as a wide range of breakfast options. Mains L80–200. Mon–Sat 8am–9pm, Sun 11am–9pm.
Restaurante Maya Vista C 9, Av 9–10. Attached to a hotel on a hillside, so you can enjoy great ocean views as you dine. The menu features a mix of fish, seafood, steaks and pasta (mains from L100). Daily 7am–9pm.

DRINKING AND NIGHTLIFE

Tela has a thriving nightlife, at weekends at least, when the bars along C 11 behind the beach host crowds listening to salsa, reggae and mainstream dance music.
Delfín Telamar at Villas Telamar 1km west of town, in Tela Nueva. This is the place to go for a tranquil drink while enjoying the sea breezes. It's also home to the *Guarumas Lounge Bar*, a lively spot open most nights till 11pm.
Iguana's Sports Bar & Discotec Av 2, C 10–11, up by the bridge in the northwest of town. This lively disco really

gets going at weekends and is a popular hangout for both locals and travellers. Opens 8pm.

DIRECTORY

Banks There is a Unibanc ATM on the southern side of the Parque. Banco de Occidente, on the eastern side of the Parque, has an ATM and does cash advances, while Banco Atlántida, on the corner of Av 4 & C 9, has an ATM and can change travellers' cheques.
Internet The unnamed bright-red building on Av 6 just south of *Espresso Americano* offers internet access.
Language school *Mango* (see above) has a Spanish school (20hr/US$139) and offers good combined classes-accommodation deals.
Laundry Lavandería San Jose is at the eastern end of C 10.
Post office Av 4, C 7–8, two blocks south of the Parque Central.

AROUND TELA

Tela is a good base for a number of attractions. These include the **Garífuna villages** along the bay on pristine beaches on either side of town, the **Punta Sal** wildlife reserve, and **Lancetilla**, probably the finest botanical reserve in Latin America, just 5km south of town. To get to any of these places, you can take taxis or rely on local buses, but renting a bike is probably the most enjoyable way to get around; ask at Garífuna Tours (see opposite) for rental information.

Garífuna villages

The **Garífuna communities** of the north coast have an entirely different history and culture from the mestizo people who represent the majority of Hondurans. The villages, located on quiet and expansive stretches of beach, are an interesting getaway for a few hours. Weekends are the best time to visit them, when people congregate to perform the traditional, haunting and melodic drum-driven rhythms of Garífuna music.

Heading west from Tela, a dirt road edges the bay between the seafront and the **Laguna de los Micos**, which forms the eastern edge of Punta Sal (see p.424). Some 7km along this road is the sleepy village of **Tornabé**, and, beyond that, **Miami**, which is set on a fabulous stretch of beach at the mouth of the lagoon. Though Tornabé has a few brick-built

5

houses, Miami consists of nothing but traditional palm-thatched huts.

ARRIVAL AND DEPARTURE

By bus Buses (hourly 6am–5pm; 30min) run to Tornabé to/from the eastern end of C 10 in Tela. From Tornabé pick-ups (Mon–Sat 6.30am & 12.30pm, returning 8am & 2pm; 30min) run to Miami.

ACCOMMODATION

Rooms Local families in Tornabé and Miami may rent out basic rooms if you ask around, but otherwise accommodation is limited.

Parque Nacional Jeanette Kawas (Punta Sal)

The **Parque Nacional Jeanette Kawas** (daily 6am–4pm; US$5; ⓦprolansate .org), commonly known as **Punta Sal**, is a wonderfully diverse **reserve** encompassing mangrove swamps, coastal lagoons, wetlands, coral reef and tropical forest, which together provide habitats for an extraordinary range of flora and fauna. Jeanette Kawas, for whom the reserve is named, was instrumental in obtaining protected status for the land, in the face of intense local opposition; her murder, in 1995, has never been solved.

Lying to the west of Tela, curving along the bay to the headland of Punta Sal (176m), the reserve covers three lagoons: **Laguna de los Micos**, on the park's eastern side; **Laguna Tisnachí**, in the centre; and the oceanfront **Laguna El Diamante**, on the western side of the headland. More than one hundred species of bird are present, including herons and storks, with seasonal migratory visitors bumping up the numbers; animals found in the reserve include howler and white-faced monkeys, wild pigs, jaguars and, in the marine sections, manatees and marine turtles. Boat trips along the Río Ulúa and the canals running through the reserve offer a superb opportunity to view the wildlife at close quarters. Where the headland curves up to the north, the land rises slightly to Punta Sal; a **trail** over the point leads to small, pristine **beaches** at either side.

It's possible to visit parts of Punta Sal independently – you can rent a **boat** in Miami (see p.423) to explore the Laguna de los Micos and surrounding area – though most people opt to join an organized **tour** (see p.422). You could also **hike** the scenic 8km from Miami to the headland along the beach, though you should check the security situation first and certainly not attempt it alone.

Jardín Botánico de Lancetilla

The extensive grounds of the **Jardín Botánico de Lancetilla** (Mon–Fri 7.30am–3pm, Sat & Sun 8am–3pm; US$6), 5km south of Tela, started life in 1925 as a United Fruit species research and testing station, and over time has grown into one of the largest collections of fruit and flowering trees, palms, hardwoods and tropical plants in the world. There are also 365 recorded species of bird. Guided **tours** of the arboretum and birdwatching tours are available, and visitors are also free to wander along the marked **trails**; maps are available at the **visitors' centre** at the entrance to the park. A small, refreshing swimming hole in the Lancetilla River is at the end of one of the trails.

ARRIVAL AND INFORMATION

By bus To get to Lancetilla, take a San Pedro Sula-bound bus from Tela for a couple of kilometres to the signposted turn-off; ask the driver to drop you. From here, the park is a further 3km.

By taxi or bike A taxi from Tela costs around L80–100 each way, or you could rent a bike from *Mango* (see p.423).

Visitors' centre Park entrance (ⓣ 2448 1740).

ACCOMMODATION AND EATING

Visitors' centre Park entrance ⓣ 2448 1740. There's a *comedor* and a small hostel at the visitors' centre. **L400**

LA CEIBA

Some 190km east along the coast from San Pedro Sula, steamy **LA CEIBA**, the lively capital of the department of Atlántida, is the gateway to the Bay Islands. Although the town is completely bereft of architectural interest and its sandy beaches are strewn with rubbish, it does enjoy a remarkable setting at the steep slopes of the Cordillera Nombre de Dios. La Ceiba is home to a cosmopolitan mix of inhabitants, including a large Garífuna community,

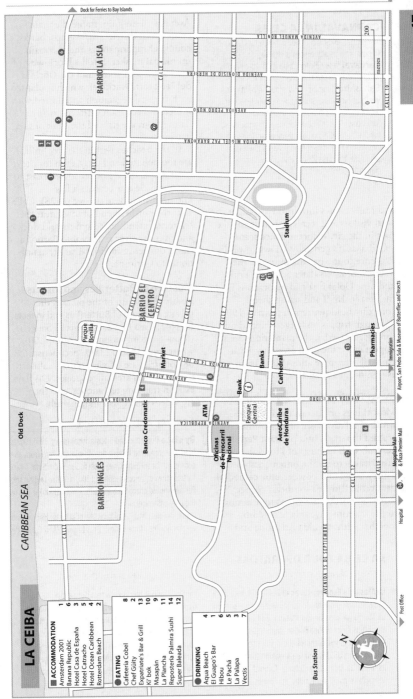

LA CEIBA

CARIBBEAN SEA

Dock for Ferries to Bay Islands

Old Dock

BARRIO LA ISLA

BARRIO INGLÉS

BARRIO EL CENTRO

Parque Bonilla

Market

Banco Credomatic

Oficinas de Ferrocarril Nacional

ATM

Parque Central

Bank

Banks

Cathedral

AeroCaribe de Honduras

Pharmacies

Stadium

AVENIDA MANUEL BONILLA

AVENIDA DIONISIO DE HERRERA

AVENIDA PEDRO NUFIO

AVENIDA MIGUEL PAZ BARAHONA

AVENIDA 14 DE JULIO

AVENIDA ATLANTIDA

AVENIDA SAN ISIDRO

AVENIDA REPUBLICA

AVENIDA SAN ISIDRO

AVENIDA 15 DE SEPTIEMBRE

CALLE 1, CALLE 2, CALLE 3, CALLE 4, CALLE 5, CALLE 6, CALLE 7, CALLE 8, CALLE 9, CALLE 10, CALLE 11, CALLE 12, CALLE 13

Airport, San Pedro Sula & Museum of Butterflies and Insects

Immigration

Megaplaza Mall & Plaza Premier Mall

Hospital

Post Office

Bus Station

Magaplaza Mall

0 — 200 metres

N

◼ ACCOMMODATION	
Amsterdam 2001	1
Banana Republic	6
Hotel Casa de España	3
Hotel Catracho	5
Hotel Ocean Caribbean	4
Rotterdam Beach	2

◼ EATING	
Cafetería Cobel	8
Chef Güity	2
Expatriate's Bar & Grill	13
Ki'bok	10
Masapán	9
La Plancha	11
Repostería Palmira Sushi	14
Super Baleada	12

● DRINKING	
Aqua Beach	4
El Guapo's Bar	1
Hibou	6
Le Pachá	3
La Palapa	5
Vectis	7

5

CARNAVAL IN LA CEIBA

The most exciting time to be in La Ceiba (book well in advance) is during **Carnaval**, a week-long bash held every May to celebrate the city's patron saint; **San Isidro**. Dances and street events in various *barrios* around town culminate in an afternoon parade on the third Saturday. The 200,000 or so partygoers who attend Carnaval every year flock between the street events and the clubs on Calle 1 in the Zona Viva, where the dancing continues until dawn.

and really comes into its own at night, with visitors and locals gathering to take part in the city's vibrant **dance scene**.

Ceiba, as it's generally known, owes its existence to the banana industry: the Vaccaro Brothers (later Standard Fruit and now Dole) first laid plantations in the area in 1899 and set up their company headquarters in town in 1905. Although fruit is no longer shipped out through La Ceiba, the plantations are still important to the local economy, with crops of pineapple and African palm now as significant as bananas.

WHAT TO SEE AND DO

Most things of interest to visitors lie within a relatively small area of the city, around the shady and pleasant **Parque Central**, with its busts of Honduran historical heroes. The unremarkable whitewashed and powder-blue **cathedral** sits on the Parque's southeast corner. Running north from the Parque almost to the seafront, Avenida San Isidro, together with Avenida Atlántida and

Avenida 14 de Julio, frame the main commercial district, with shops, banks, a couple of supermarkets and the main municipal market. Stroll a block west of the Parque and you'll find the **Oficinas del Ferrocarril Nacional**, which is planted with tropical vegetation and dotted with museum-piece train carriages, many dating from the days of the peak of the banana trade.

All the **beaches** within the city limits are too polluted and dirty, even for the most desperate. It's better to head east to the much cleaner beaches a few kilometres out of town (see p.428). Calle 1, at the northern end of town near the seafront, extends east from the old dock and over the river estuary into **Barrio La Isla**, a quieter residential district, mainly home to Garífuna.

Museum of Butterflies and Insects

About 1km south of the plaza is the private **Museum of Butterflies and Insects**, Etapa 2, Casa G-12, Colonia El Sauce (Mon–Sat 8am–noon & 1–4pm; L60), where more than 12,000 specimens from 68 countries are on view, though almost three-quarters are native species. Displays explain trapping techniques, and there are videos in English and Spanish.

ARRIVAL AND DEPARTURE

By plane Domestic and international (see p.379) flights land at Aeropuerto Internacional Golosón, 9km from the centre, off the main highway west to San Pedro Sula. A taxi to/from the centre costs around L200; *colectivo* taxis at the Parque should charge around L20, or about L80 if you're the only passenger.

Domestic destinations Ahuas (AeroCaribe de Honduras 6 weekly; journey time varies); Brus Laguna (AeroCaribe de

LA CEIBA TOUR OPERATORS

A couple of well-run companies offer tours to the surrounding area and further afield.

La Moskitia Ecoaventuras ☎ 2441 3279 or ☎ 9929 7532, ⊛ lamoskitia.hn. Jorge Salaverri is an expert on La Mosquitia and the Río Plátano, and his company also offers tours to Pico Bonito (from US$35), Cuero y Salado and Cayos Cochinos (both from US$53), plus rafting (from US$35) and sea-kayaking (from US$35). Its office is located in Colonia Toronjal 2 close to Megaplaza mall: turn right at *Pollitos La Cumbre*,

continue for two blocks then turn right again.
Omega Tours Río Cangrejal valley, 19km from La Ceiba ☎ 2440 0334 or ☎ 9631 0295, ⊛ omegatours .info. Extensive range of tours including rafting, kayaking, horseriding (from US$76) and trips to Cayos Cochinos and La Mosquitia. All start at their lodge (see p.429), which borders both Pico Bonito and Nombre de Dios parks, and prices include a night's stay.

Honduras 6 weekly; journey time varies); Guanaja (AeroCaribe de Honduras 6 weekly; journey time varies); Puerto Lempira (AeroCaribe de Honduras 6 weekly; journey time varies); Palacios (AeroCaribe de Honduras 6 weekly; journey time varies); Roatán (SOSA 4 daily; 30min); San Pedro Sula (SOSA 1 daily; 30min); Tegucigalpa (Isleña/TACA & SOSA 3 daily; 50min); Utila (SOSA 3 weekly; 20min).

By boat Ferries to and from Roatán and Utila in the Bay Islands use the Muelle de Cabotaje municipal dock, about 5km east of the city. A shared taxi to the dock should cost L100–200 total; buses to the dock (every 30min; 20–40min) leave from outside *Banana Republic*.

Destinations Roatán (☎ 2445 1775, ⌨ roatanferry.com; daily 9.30am & 4.30pm to Roatán, 7am & 2pm to La Ceiba; 1hr 20min; tickets from L550); Utila (☎ 2425 3390, ⌨ utilaprincess.com; daily 9.30am & 4pm to Utila, 6.20am & 2pm to La Ceiba; around 1hr; tickets from L448).

By bus or taxi Long-distance and local buses arrive at and depart from the main terminal, 2km west of the centre; local buses run into town, while taxis, usually shared, charge around L30/person.

Destinations Guatemala City (2 daily; 11hr); Olanchito (for Juticalpa; 12 daily; 3hr); San Pedro Sula (20 plus daily; 3hr); Tegucigalpa (hourly; 5hr 30min–7hr); Tela (every 30min; 2hr 30min); Trujillo (20 plus daily; 3hr–4hr 30min).

INFORMATION

Internet Café Internet in the Megaplaza mall food court, or Servi Office Internet, Barrio La Isla, C 4.
Taxis Expect to pay L30–50 for a taxi ride in La Ceiba during the day, a bit more after 8pm.
Tourist information There's a tourist office on C 8, one block east of the Parque Central; some staff speak English. ⌨ holaceibita.com has information on the city.

ACCOMMODATION

La Ceiba has a range of budget places to stay. The only problem is deciding whether you want to be near the centre or closer to the nightlife along C 1. Prices rise around Carnaval time in May, when reserving ahead is essential.
Amsterdam 2001 1 C, Av Barahona, Barrio La Isla ☎ 2443 2311, ✉ zaal_xx_12@hotmail.com. The dorms are dilapidated but the private rooms with fans are adequate (some have attached bathrooms). The 12-bed dorm is up a perilous metal staircase (go easy on the beer). Dorm L̲1̲5̲0̲, double L̲3̲0̲0̲
Banana Republic Av República, C 12–13 ☎ 2441 9404, ⌨ jungleriverlodge.com. Once the heart of the backpacker scene in La Ceiba, *Banana Republic* is starting to show its age – and some of the dorm bunks are out in a corridor – but is still a decent option. There's free wi-fi/internet access and a communal kitchen, and staff are very helpful. Dorm U̲S̲$̲8̲, double U̲S̲$̲1̲5̲

★ **Hotel Casa de España** Av 14 de Julio, C 4–5 ☎ 2454 0210 or ☎ 9725 8973, ⌨ hotelcasadespana.com. Impeccably clean hotel, dotted with plants and other homely elements. The comfortable en-suite rooms can be a bargain if you're able to haggle the price down a bit. Opt out of breakfast, though, which adds more than L100 to the cost. L̲7̲5̲0̲
Hotel Catracho Barrio Solares Nuevos, C 12 ☎ 2440 2312 or ☎ 2440 2313, ⌨ hotelcatracho.com. A clean, modern hotel with rooms at a fair price, this place is saved from blandness by the pool and deck area. Only a minute's walk from *Expatriates* bar (see below), too. L̲3̲5̲0̲
Hotel Ocean Caribbean C 5, between Av San Isidro & Av Atlántida ☎ 2443 1857 or ☎ 2454 0330. Although the exterior of this hotel is a little shabby, inside you will find a friendly, family-run place. The rooms all come with TV, fan and cold-water bathrooms. L̲5̲0̲0̲
Rotterdam Beach C 1, Av Barahona, Barrio La Isla ☎ 2440 0321. Next door to *Amsterdam 2001*, with eight clean and neat rooms with fan and private cold-water bathrooms. Noise can be an issue. L̲3̲2̲0̲

EATING

Cafetería Cobel C 7. This Ceiba institution features a simple, meat-heavy menu offering the usual steaks and chops plus a range of soups, and a selection of cakes and pastries. Lunch/dinner from L60. Mon–Sat 7am–6pm.
Chef Güity C 1. With looks like this – mismatched tablecloths, rickety chairs, faded soccer photos – the food at this Garífuna *palapa* restaurant has got to be good, and it generally is, particularly the king fish and the *tapado garífuna* (a typical stew). Mains from L100.
Expatriate's Bar & Grill C 12, two blocks east of Av San Isidro. A huge, thatched bar-restaurant slickly run by Frenchman Jérome Marchand. Food ranges from healthy organic to the tastily stodgy (such as German sausage in a bun with fries). Mains from L100. Good beers and cocktails too. Mon–Sat 11am–midnight, Sun 11am–10/11pm.
★ **Ki' bok** Two blocks east of the Parque between C 9 & C 8. A friendly, good-value little café with art on the walls and a homely feel. The menu ranges from burgers to spaghetti with shrimps, with several vegetarian options. Dishes from L75.
Masapán C 7, on the corner of Av La República. Popular self-service cafeteria with a cheap buffet of Honduran and North American-style food (dishes from L15). Mon–Sat 7am–7pm, Sun 7am–3pm.
La Plancha Two blocks east of the Parque between C 9 & C 8 ☎ 2443 2304. Classy joint with green tablecloths and framed cowhides on the walls. They're proud of their meat here, and rightly so: it has a tenderness that's rare in Honduras and they'll cook it just the way you want it. A steak and sides will set you back around L250. Daily 11am–2pm & 5–11pm.
Repostería Palmira Sushi C del Hospital D'Antoni 4, opposite Uniplaza mall ☎ 2442 0312. In this unlikely

5

merging of traditional Honduran bakery and sushi restaurant, owner-chef Jaime incorporates ingredients from Manchego to plantain in his Japanese cuisine. Start with edamame or gyoza, then try the San Pedro Sula roll with a fried tempura and sesame coating, filled with crispy breaded shrimp and spicy avocado salsa. Dishes from L50. Mon–Sat noon–9pm, Sun takeaway only, 4–8pm.

Super Baleada Corner Av Colón & C 12. The cheapest meal you're likely to have in La Ceiba and surely one of the best. *Baleadas* from L10.

DRINKING AND NIGHTLIFE

La Ceiba has long had a reputation as the place to party, though the economic downturn in the city in recent years means it's not as lively as it was. Still, there are several good options for a night on the town. The action takes place along C 1, which runs parallel to the seafront. Nicknamed the *Zona Viva* due to its preponderance of bars and clubs, the area hums several nights a week, though weekends are really explosive. Just stroll down the street to see what's going on and where the crowds are. Beyond the *Zona Viva*, *Expatriate's Bar and Grill* (see p.427) is a good place for an evening drink.

Aqua Beach 1 C, Av Barahona, Barrio La Isla. Sit upstairs and watch city life go by while listening to the waves lap onto the beach and munching on Honduran and Mexican dishes (from L100). Mon–Thurs 11.30am–4am, Fri & Sat 11.30am–5am, Sun 4pm–4am.

El Guapo's Bar C 1. This is right next door to the sprawling *Snake* bar and shares the same *palapa* feel. Hugely popular on Fri and Sat nights, it has a fantastic atmosphere, especially when the karaoke takes over. Daily happy hour 5–7pm; the food's a bit pricey though.

Hibou C 1. This dance club is currently the place that has teenagers and twenty-somethings patiently queueing for entry (from L100).

Le Pachá Opposite *Vectis* on C 1. A huge space covered in massive stretched awnings, right on the beach. The music is a mix of reggaetón, merengue and bachata. Beer from L35. Wed–Fri & Sun 10am–10pm; closes later on Sat.

La Palapa Just off C 1. Very popular spot in the *Zona Viva*, known for its large dance floor. Sat nights are especially exciting: live bands perform a mix of merengue, reggae and rock. Tues–Sun from 6pm.

Vectis C 1. A smallish, popular place, open to the street, which plays loud reggae and rock and also hosts cover bands.

DIRECTORY

Banks Most of the banks are on C 9 and Av 14 de Julio one block east of the Parque. The Megaplaza mall also has several banks and ATMs.

Cinema Cines Premiere, in Plaza Premier on the opposite side of the road from Megaplaza, shows subtitled movies, as does Cines Millenium inside the mall itself.

Health Hospital D'Antoni (☎ 2443 2264) is at the southern end of Av Morazán. Two good pharmacies are Auto Farmacia Zaz (24hr) and Farmacia Mary Ann (daily 8am–11pm), both on C 13, near Av 14 de Julio.

Immigration Immigration is between C 17 & 18 on Av 14 de Julio.

Language schools Centro Internacional de Idiomas (Col Toronjal II, Etapa 5, Block 15, Casa L–13; ☎ 2441 1715 or ☎ 9984 2008, ⓦ hondurasspanish.com) is a good Spanish school. Rates are US$250 weekly for 20hr of one-to-one tuition and homestay, including all meals (US$150 without the homestay). The school can also help organize volunteer placements.

Post office Av Morazán, C 13–14.

Shopping The main general market is on Av Atlántida, C 5–7. The huge Megaplaza mall is in the southern outskirts of town beyond the hospital.

AROUND LA CEIBA

The broad sandy beaches and clean water at **Playa de Perú** and the village of **Sambo Creek** are easy day-trip destinations east of La Ceiba. A trip to explore the cloudforest within the **Parque Nacional Pico Bonito** requires more planning, although the eastern edge of the reserve, formed by the **Río Cangrejal**, is still easily accessible, and also offers opportunities for swimming and whitewater rafting. Finally, a trip to the serene islands of the **Cayos Cochinos** is thoroughly worthwhile.

Playa de Perú

Some 10km east of the city, **Playa de Perú** is a wide sweep of clean sand that's popular at weekends. Any local **bus** running east up the coast (towards Trujillo) will drop you at the highway-side turn-off, from where it's a fifteen-minute walk to the beach. About 2km beyond the turning for Playa de Perú, on the Río María, there's a series of **waterfalls** and **natural pools** set in lush, shady forest. A path leads from Río María village on the highway, winding through the hills along the left bank of the river; it takes around thirty minutes to walk to the first cascade and pool, with some muddy sections and a bit of scrambling during the wet season.

Sambo Creek

There are deserted expanses of white sand at the friendly Garífuna village of **Sambo**

Creek, 8km beyond the Río María. As well as the beach and a clutch of low-key seafood restaurants, there is **Sambo Creek Canopy Tours and Spa**, 500m beyond the village, which offers ziplining and hot springs (daily 8am–4pm; ☎3355 5481). Boats to Cayos Cochinos also depart from Sambo Creek.

ARRIVAL AND DEPARTURE

By bus Olanchito or Juticalpa buses from La Ceiba will drop you at the turn-off to Sambo Creek on the highway, a couple of kilometres from the village; slower buses run all the way to the village centre from La Ceiba's terminal (every 30min; 45min).

ACCOMMODATION AND EATING

Paradise Found Playa Helen ☎9861 1335, ⓦparadise foundlaceiba.com. An excellent accommodation option – the food is great too: try the ribs smoked with fruitwood. **US$59**

Parque Nacional Pico Bonito and Río Cangrejal

Directly south of La Ceiba, the Cordillera Nombre de Dios shelters the **Parque Nacional Pico Bonito** (daily 6am–4pm; US$7), a remote expanse of tropical broadleaf forest, cloudforest and – in its southern reaches, above the Río Aguan valley – pine forest. Taking its name from the awe-inspiring bulk of Pico Bonito (2435m), the park is the source of twenty **rivers**, including the Zacate, Bonito and Cangrejal, which cascade majestically down the mountains' steep, thickly tree-covered slopes. The park also provides sanctuary for an abundance of wildlife, including armadillos, howler and spider monkeys, pumas and ocelots. The lower fringes are the most easily accessible, with a few **trails** laid out through the dense greenery.

The easiest way to get into the park is to enter via the luxury *Lodge at Pico Bonito* (☎2440 0389, ⓦpicobonito .com), a world-class **jungle lodge** with bungalow accommodation (US$334), gourmet cuisine, a pool and a sublime setting in the foothills of the forest reserve. Trails from the lodge snake up through the tree cover to a lookout from where Utila is visible, and down to beautiful river bathing pools. You don't

have to be a guest at the lodge to access the park and trails, but you will have to pay a US$33 fee, which includes lunch and a guide.

The **Río Cangrejal**, which forms the eastern boundary of the park, boasts some of the best rapids in Central America; **whitewater rafting** and **kayaking** trips are organized by tour companies (see box, p.426). There are also some magnificent swimming spots, backed by gorgeous mountain scenery, along the river valley.

ARRIVAL AND DEPARTURE

By bus Buses and *rapiditos* (every 30min or so; 30–45min) run between La Ceiba and the village of El Pino, 12km away, from where the *Lodge at Pico Bonito* is signposted, 3km away up a dirt side-road. Alternatively, tour companies in La Ceiba (see box, p.426) operate day- and overnight trips.

ACCOMMODATION

Eco Jungle Lodge Near the Río Cangrejal, bordering both Pico Bonito and Nombre de Dios parks ☎2440 0334 or ☎9631 0295, ⓦomegatours.info. Omega Tours (see box, p.426) runs this excellent lodge which has camping, cabins (sleeping up to six) and rooms, and a restaurant-bar. Camping **US$11.60**, double **US$46.40**, cabin **US$116**

Refugio de Vida Silvestre Cuero y Salado

Some 30km west from La Ceiba, the **Refugio de Vida Silvestre Cuero y Salado** (daily 8.30am–3.30pm; US$10; ☎2440 1990) is one of the last substantial remnants of wetlands and mangrove swamps along the north coast. The reserve is home to a large number of endangered animals and bird species,

5

including manatees, jaguars, howler and white-faced monkeys, sea turtles and hawks, along with seasonal influxes of migratory birds.

ARRIVAL AND INFORMATION

By bus, moto-taxi and motocarro By far the easiest way to visit the reserve is on an organized tour from La Ceiba. To get here independently (a journey of around 1hr 15min), catch a bus (hourly 6.20am–3.30pm; 30min) from La Ceiba to the village of La Unión, 20km or so west. From here, take a moto-taxi (10min; around L30) to the El Bambú Estación del Motocarro then take a *motocarro* (a very rudimentary train – a little like a tuk-tuk on rails; 30min; L100) to the visitors' centre.

Tours It's best to arrange canoe tours through a travel agency or FUCSA (see below).

Fundación Cuero y Salado FUCSA is a good source of information on the park, and can organize boat trips and guides for independent travellers; its La Ceiba office (generally Mon–Fri 9am–5pm) is in Barrio La Merced on C 15, Av Ramón Rosa, Edificio Daytona (☎ 2443 0329 or ☎ 2440 1990, ✉ fucsa@televicab.net, cuero_salado@yahoo.com or canp82@yahoo.es).

Cayos Cochinos

Lying 30km offshore, the **Cayos Cochinos** (**Hog Islands**; US$10 if visiting independently, US$5 with a tour group) comprise thirteen privately owned cayes and two thickly wooded islands – **Cochino Mayor** and **Cochino Menor**. Fringed by a reef, the whole area has been designated a **marine reserve**, with anchoring on the reef and commercial fishing both strictly prohibited. The small amount of effort it takes to get to the islands is well worth it for a few days' utter tranquillity.

ARRIVAL AND DEPARTURE

By bus and boat You will have to shell out a bit to travel to the islands, especially if you're on your own. The only

> ### DIVING IN THE CAYOS COCHINOS
>
> Based in Sambo Creek (see p.428), **Pirate Islands Divers** (☎ 3228 0009 or ☎ 9563 9172, ⊕ pirateislandsdivers.com) is run by PADI Master Instructor Tony Marquez and offers two-tank diving trips (from US$80), open-water courses (from US$326), four-dive overnight trips (from US$178) and snorkelling trips (US$39).

feasible way to get there is with the fishermen who sail from the Garífuna villages of Sambo Creek (see p.428) or Nueva Armenia (40min; around US$30/person return). Buses from La Ceiba run to Sambo Creek (every 30min; 45min) and Nueva Armenia (6 daily; 2hr).

Tours Several tour companies in La Ceiba offer day-trips and overnight stays, starting from around US$39 per person (see box, p.426). If arranging a tour, ask whether the price quoted includes the entrance fee.

ACCOMMODATION AND EATING

Chachauate hut Organized accommodation on the two islands is limited to overpriced resort-style places. However, villagers in the traditional Garífuna fishing village of Chachauate on Lower Monitor Caye have allocated a hut for visitors to sling their hammocks in and they will also cook meals for you. Basic groceries are available in the village, but there is no running water and electricity and toilets are latrines. Per person __US$5–10__

TRUJILLO

Perched above the sparkling waters of the palm-fringed Bahía de Trujillo, backed by the beautiful green Cordillera Nombre de Dios, **TRUJILLO** immediately seduces the small number of tourists who make the 90km trip from La Ceiba. Beautifully relaxed, the city has a very different feel from its big north-coast neighbours, La Ceiba and Tela.

The area around present-day Trujillo was populated by a mixture of Pech and Tolupan groups when Columbus first disembarked here on August 14, 1502; the city itself was founded by Cortés's lieutenant, Juan de Medina, in 1525, though it was frequently abandoned due to attacks by European pirates. Not until the late eighteenth century did repopulation begin in earnest, aided by the arrival, via Roatán, of several hundred Garífuna. In 1860, a new threat appeared in the shape of US filibusterer and adventurer William Walker, who briefly took control of the town. Executed by firing squad three months later by the Honduran authorities, he is buried in Trujillo's cemetery.

WHAT TO SEE AND DO

Apart from its wonderful **beaches**, much of Trujillo's charm lies in meandering through its rather crumbly streets. The town proper stretches back five or so blocks south of the **Parque Central**, which is just 50m from cliffs overlooking the sea. On the north side of the square is a bust of Juan de Medina, the town founder. Southwest from the centre, a couple of blocks past the market, is the **Cementerio Viejo**, where Walker's grave lies overgrown with weeds – collect the key to the gate from the office in the fort.

Beaches

The town's most outstanding attractions by far are its **beaches**, which have long stretches of almost pristine sand. The glorious sweep of the **Bahía de Trujillo** is as yet unaffected by excessive tourist development, and its calm, blue waters are perfect for effortless swimming. The beaches below town, lined with *champas* (thatch-roofed, open-sided huts), are clean enough, but the stretches to the east, beyond the disued airstrip, are emptier. It's also possible to walk east along the beach to the reserve of **Laguna de Guaimoreto** or west to the Garífuna village of **Santa Fe**.

Fortaleza de Santa Bárbara

In town, near the Parque Central, is the sixteenth-century **Fortaleza de Santa Bárbara** (daily 8am–noon & 1–4pm; US$3), site of William Walker's execution. The low-lying fort hangs gloomily on the edge of the bluffs, overlooking the coastline that it singularly failed to protect against pirates. The museum charts the town's often-colourful history, and has an exhibition room on Garífuna culture.

Museo y Piscinas Riveras del Pedregal

Turn right beyond the Cementerio Viejo and a ten-minute stroll brings you to the privately run **Museo y Piscinas Riveras del Pedregal** (daily 7am–5pm; L50), an eccentric collection of rusty junk. Almost all of the original pre-Columbian ceramics once held by the museum have been sold off, though the replacement replicas are pretty convincing. Outside, the wheels of an American jumbo jet that crashed in the area in 1985 can be seen. Behind the building are a couple of small, naturally fed swimming pools.

Parque Nacional Capiro y Calentura

Directly above the town lies the dark-green swathe of the **Parque Nacional Capiro y Calentura** (daily 6am–5pm; free). The reserve's huge cedars and pines

TRUJILLO

0 — 200 metres

Bahía de Trujillo

Fortaleza de Santa Bárbara

Banco Atlántida

Parque Central

Laundry

Pharmacy

Market

Cementerio Viejo

Museo y Piscinas Riveras del Pedregal

& Barrio Cristales

Bus Terminal & Laguna de Guaimoreto

N

ACCOMMODATION
Casa Alemania	1
Casa Kiwi	2
Emperador	3
Plaza Centro	4

EATING
Café y Sabores	6
Café Vino Tinto	4
Campamento	3
El Delfin	1
Rogue's Galeria	2

DRINKING & NIGHTLIFE
Karao's	5
La Truxillo	7

Parque Nacional Capiro y Calentura

tower amid a thick canopy of ferns, flowering plants and vines. As a result of the devastation wrought by Hurricane Fifi in 1974, much of the cover is secondary growth, but it still provides a secure habitat for howler monkeys, reptiles and colourful birdlife and butterflies. You can walk into the reserve by following the dirt road past the *Villas Brinkley* – it winds, increasingly steeply, up the slope of Cerro Calentura to the radio towers just below its summit; a 10km walk, this is best done in the relative cool of early morning. Alternatively, you could negotiate with a taxi driver to take you to the top and then walk down. Unfortunately there aren't any trail maps, so you'll have to do a bit of exploring.

ARRIVAL AND INFORMATION

By boat An intermittent ferry service (1hr 30min) operates between the old pier in central Trujillo and Guanaja; ask locally for the latest schedule.

By bus The bus terminal is to the east of town, at the bottom of the hill leading into the centre. From here infrequent urban buses head up the hill to the Parque Central, or you can take a taxi (around L30).

Destinations La Ceiba (20 plus daily; 3hr–4hr 30min); Puerto Castilla (7 daily, last one 6pm; 45min); San Pedro Sula (hourly; 5–6hr; 10hr); Tocoa (24 daily; 2hr 30min).

Tourist office There's a small office (sporadic opening hours) on the eastern side of the Parque, next door to the Fortaleza de Santa Bárbara office.

ACCOMMODATION

There's not much in the way of budget accommodation in town, but there are a couple of excellent places in glorious settings just outside the centre.

Casa Alemania 1km east of town ☎ 2434 4466. An extraordinary range of options is on offer here, from tiny backpacker rooms and camping all the way up to a penthouse. There's also a book exchange, housed in an attractive library-like room. **US$38**

★ **Casa Kiwi** 7km east of town ☎ 2434 3050, ⓦ kiwihosteltrujillo.com. One of the best hostels on the north coast, right on the beach. The clean dorms include a hot-water shower; there are also private rooms and a/c cabins sleeping up to four, plus an on-site restaurant (serving great burgers) and a bar that stays open as long as you like. Staff are knowledgeable about travel to La Mosquitia. Dorm **L140**, double **L280**, cabin **L680**

Emperador By the market ☎ 2434 4446. The town's best budget hotel, run by an extremely friendly family. Rooms

are clean – albeit rather small – and have en-suite bathroom, TV and fan. **L450**

Plaza Centro By the market, opposite *Emperador* ☎ 2434 3006. The fresh white linen is the most eye-catching aspect of these drab rooms, but they're kept in decent order and are fairly spacious. **L520**

EATING

Café y Sabores One block south of the Parque. Doors and windows are propped wide open in this diner-like place, allowing for nice, breezy breakfasts (around L50), lunches and (early) dinners. Good *licuados* too. Mon–Sat 6am–8pm.

Café Vino Tinto Just off the Parque Central. This sweet place has an open-sided seating area overlooking the bay, hung partly with white drapes. Try the delicious *tostones rellenos* – slices of fried plantain with various toppings – or the beef kebabs. Mains from L80. Tues–Sun 9am–11pm.

Campamento 4km west of Trujillo on the road to Santa Fe. In a lovely beach location, shaded by palm trees, this restaurant-bar serves up fresh fish and seafood, as well as a few more unusual dishes such as agouti steaks. Daily 7am–10pm.

El Delfín On the strip fronting the beach. More impressive than the other *champas* along this stretch. Choose between the tiled, indoor dining area, or sand between your toes outside. The service is efficient and the king crab *a la ojo* (L200) superb. Weekends only.

Rogue's Galería On the beach below town. Commonly referred to as *"Jerry's"*, this engaging American-owned bar/restaurant features superb seafood and has plenty of hammocks for daytime chilling. Mains from around L80. Daily 7am–10pm.

DRINKING AND NIGHTLIFE

Karao's Southeast of the Parque. This well-worn disco charges around L50 for entry.

La Truxillo Up the hill towards the western side of town. Certainly the most popular place at weekends, when it heaves to Latin American rhythms and the bar fills up with a young crowd. Entrance at least L50.

DIRECTORY

Bank Banco Atlántida, on the Parque, gives Visa cash advances and has a 24hr ATM.

Internet Ciber Café, on the eastern end of the main road running through town.

Language school Local teacher Vicente Lopez (☎ 2434 4944) is recommended. He can also be contacted through *Casa Kiwi*.

Laundry A block northwest of the market.

Pharmacy Two blocks south of the Parque.

Post office Three blocks south of the southeast corner of the Parque.

AROUND TRUJILLO

Expanses of white-sand **beach** stretch for kilometres around the bay from Trujillo. All beaches are clean, wide and perfect for swimming; don't take anything valuable with you, though, and don't venture onto them after dark.

Aguas Calientes

Taking a hot bath in the heat of the Caribbean may not strike everyone as an appealing thought, but a soak in the clean and very hot mineral waters of the **Aguas Calientes** springs (L50), 7km inland from Trujillo, feels delightfully decadent. It's closed most of the time, but ask the caretaker of the hotel *Aguas Calientes* (where the pools are located) if you can use them. Any **bus** heading to Tocoa will drop you off at the entrance; the last return bus leaves at around 5.30pm.

La Mosquitia

Occupying the northeast corner of Honduras is the remote and undeveloped expanse of **La Mosquitia** (often spelt "Moskitia"). Bounded to the west by the mountain ranges of the Río Plátano and Colón, with the Río Coco forming the

border with Nicaragua to the south, this vast region comprises almost a fifth of Honduras's territory. With just two peripheral roads and a tiny population divided among a few far-flung towns and villages, entering La Mosquitia really does mean leaving the beaten track. There are few phones in the region, and all accommodation is extremely basic, often without electricity and with latrine-style toilets. Food is usually limited to rice, beans and the catch of the day, so if you're making an independent trek, bring enough food with you for your party and guides. Getting around requires a spirit of adventure, but the effort is well rewarded.

To the surprise of many who come here expecting to have to hack their way through jungle, much of La Mosquitia is composed of marshy coastal wetlands and flat savanna. The small communities of **Palacios** and **Brus Laguna** are access points for the **Río Plátano Biosphere Reserve**, the most famous of five separate reserves in the area, set up to protect one of the finest remaining stretches of virgin tropical rainforest in Central America. **Puerto Lempira**, to the east, is the regional capital. The largest ethnic group inhabiting La Mosquitia is the **Miskitos**, numbering around 30,000, who spoke a unique form of English until as recently as a few generations ago. There are much smaller

---

LA MOSQUITIA HISTORY AND POLITICS

Before the Spanish arrived, La Mosquitia belonged to the **Pech** and **Sumu**. Initial contact with Europeans was comparatively benign, as the Spanish preferred to concentrate instead on the mineral-rich lands of the interior. Relations with Europeans intensified when the **British** began seeking a foothold on the mainland in the seventeenth century, establishing settlements on the coast at **Black River** (now Palacios) and **Brewer's Lagoon** (Brus Laguna), whose inhabitants – the so-called "shoremen" – engaged in logging, trading, smuggling and fighting the Spanish.

Britain's claim to La Mosquitia, made nominally to protect the shoremen, though really intended to ensure a transit route from the Atlantic to the Pacific, supposedly ended in 1786, when all Central American territories except Belize were ceded to the Spanish. In the 1820s, however, taking advantage of post-independence chaos, Britain again encouraged settlement on the Mosquito Coast and by 1844 had all but formally announced a protectorate in the area. Not until 1859 and the British–American Treaty of Cruz Wyke did Britain formally end all claims to the region.

The initial impact of mestizo Honduran culture on La Mosquitia was slight. Since the creation of the administrative department of Gracias a Dios in 1959, however, indigenous cultures have gradually become diluted: Spanish is now the main language, and the government encourages mestizo settlers to migrate here in search of land. Pech, Miskito and Garífuna communities have become more vocal in recent years in demanding respect for their cultural differences and in calling for an expansion of health, education and transport infrastructures.

5

communities of **Pech**, who number around 2500, and **Tawahka** (Sumu), of whom there are under a thousand, living around the Río Patuca.

ARRIVAL AND GETTING AROUND

A number of companies in La Ceiba, San Pedro and Tegucigalpa offer tours to La Mosquitia, and travelling independently is by no means impossible, as long as you're prepared to go with the flow. Transport to and within La Mosquitia is mainly by air or water: Puerto Lempira, Belén and Brus Laguna are currently connected to La Ceiba by regular flights, while *lanchas* ply the waterways connecting the scattered villages. Bear in mind that all schedules, especially those of the boats, are subject to change, delay and cancellation; transport on the rivers and channels is determined by how much rain has fallen.

Tour operators The excellent La Moskitia Ecoaventuras in La Ceiba (see box, p.426) offer tours starting from US$250 (five days; excluding transport to the region). Mesoamérica Travel (see box, p.418), based in San Pedro Sula, offer a relatively "budget" five-day tour (excluding flights) from US$210. Another option is Omega Tours, near La Ceiba (see box, p.426), whose all-inclusive tours last from three (from US$520) to 13 (US$1470) days. La Ruta Moskitia (☎2406 6782, ⌨larutamoskitia.com) offers excellent advice on visiting the region, as well as a range of tours and lodges throughout the region that bring real benefits to the local communities.

Boat travel Travelling around the region by boat is pricey, with *expreso* boats much more expensive than multiple-stop *colectivo* boats. Direct services from Palacios to Rais Ta/Belén are currently around L800–1000 per boat and can hold up to ten people (1hr 30min); Rais Ta/Belén to Las Marías L3000–3500 (4–5 person boat; 5hr) or to Brus Laguna L1500–2000 per boat (2hr); Brus Laguna to Las Marías costs about L3500–4000 (4–5 person boat; 6hr). Prices to Las Marías include the charge for the driver spending two nights with you there. For *colectivo* services, the per-person rates are: Palacios to Rais Ta/Belén L150 (2–3hr); Rais Ta/Belén to Río Plátano L50 (overland; 45min); Río Plátano to Brus Laguna L200 (1hr 30min). There are no *colectivo* services to Las Marías.

By plane Flights to La Mosquitia depart from La Ceiba only (see p.426). AeroCaribe (☎2442 1097, ☎2442 1085, ☎2442 1088 or ☎2442 2569, ⌨aerocaribehn .com), based at La Ceiba's airport, currently run the only service into the region, flying to Brus Laguna, Ahuas and Puerto Lempira (1 daily Mon–Sat). Timetables are not strictly observed; take local advice as to their reliability at the time of your visit. SOSA (⌨aerolineasosahn.com) have offered travel into the region in the past and it's worth checking their website for developments. Central

American Airlines has already suffered one serious crash and cannot be recommended.

Ground transport Getting to the region by land – the cheapest option – is possible, but progress is extremely slow. Take the bus from Trujillo to Tocoa, then a pick-up to Batalla (hourly 7am–noon; 4–5hr). From Batalla, *colectivo* boats leave for destinations within La Mosquitia, such as the sister communities of Rais Ta/Belén (1–2hr). If heading for Las Marías (see opposite), you will need to spend the night in one of these communities. Returning, you should spend the night in Batalla, from where early-morning trucks depart for Tocoa, or in Rais Ta/Belén before taking the 4am *colectivo* boat to Batalla (around L150). The *Casa Kiwi* hostel in Trujillo (see p.432) is a good place for information on entering by road and meeting others who are preparing to make the trip. Note that during the rainy season this trip becomes much more difficult. Some Spanish makes negotiating the various connections and inevitable delays much easier.

PALACIOS

Sited on what was once the British settlement of Black River, **PALACIOS** lies just west of one of the Río Plátano Biosphere Reserve's three coastal lagoons, Laguna Ibans. This is frequently the starting point for organized trips to the Río Plátano Biosphere Reserve, and, for independent travellers, a logical place from which to begin exploration of the region.

WHAT TO SEE AND DO

Dotted along the Caribbean shoreline around Palacios is a cluster of interesting **Garífuna villages**, including **Batalla**, just to the west of town across the Palacios lagoon, and **Plaplaya**, about 8km to the east, where a **turtle project** has been established. Highly endangered giant leatherbacks, the largest species in the world (reaching up to 3m in length and 900kg in weight), nest in the beaches around the village between April and June. **Rais Ta** and **Belén** are also worth visiting.

ACCOMMODATION

Hotel Moskitia ☎9996 5648 or ☎9996 9659, ⌨hotelmoskitia.com. This is the most modern and comfortable hotel in town, complete with a bar and restaurant on site. **L450**

Río Tinto In the centre of Palacios. You'll find adequate rooms at this ramshackle place run by local Don Felix Marmol. **L200**

5

RÍO PLÁTANO BIOSPHERE RESERVE

The **RÍO PLÁTANO BIOSPHERE RESERVE** is the most significant nature reserve in Honduras, sheltering an estimated eighty percent of all the country's animal species. Visitors usually come to experience the rare tropical rainforest, but the reserve's boundaries – which stretch from the Caribbean in the north to the Montañas de Punta Piedra in the west and the Río Patuca in the south – also encompass huge expanses of coastal wetlands and flat savanna grasslands. Sadly, even its World Heritage status hasn't prevented extensive destruction at the hands of settlers: up to 60 percent of forest cover on the outer edges of the reserve has disappeared in the last three decades.

To get the most out of the park you should head for the small Pech and Miskito village of **Las Marías**, where plenty of prospective **guides** are available to help you explore the river and surrounding jungle for US$10–15 a day. One pleasant, if rather wet, trip you can make is by *pipante* (pole-propelled canoe), five hours upstream to rock **petroglyphs** at Walpaulban Sirpi, carved by an unknown people – these are more or less at the heart of the reserve. The journey itself is the main attraction, along channels too shallow for motorized boats to pass; in sections you'll be required to leave the boat and make your way through the undergrowth. *Pipantes* require three guides each, but carry only two passengers and cost around US$30 (excluding guides).

ARRIVAL AND INFORMATION

Arrival and departure Getting to the heart of the Río Plátano reserve requires travelling up the Río Plátano to the village of Las Marías (see opposite).

Tourist information For general information about the reserve, contact the tour operators who work within the region (see box, p.426).

ACCOMMODATION

Hospedaje Doña Justa Las Marías. Simple *hospedaje*. Meals are served. **L200**

Hospedaje Ovidio Las Marías. Basic *hospedaje* with meals included. **L200**

BRUS LAGUNA

Some 30km east along the coast from Palacios, on the southeastern edge of the Laguna de Brus, is the friendly Miskito town of **BRUS LAGUNA**. The town is mostly seen by visitors as they are coming or going – regular **flights** (see p.426) connect the town with La Ceiba, and guides and boats can be hired for multi-day trips, travelling up the Río Sigre into the southern reaches of the Río Plátano reserve.

ACCOMMODATION

La Estancia Main street, near the water ☎ 2433 8043 or ☎ 2898 7959. Basic rooms with en-suite bathroom. **L300**

Laguna Paradise Centre of Brus Laguna ☎ 2433 8039 or ☎ 2898 7952. A handful of acceptable rooms. **L300**

PUERTO LEMPIRA

Capital of the department of Gracias a Dios, **PUERTO LEMPIRA** is the largest town in La Mosquitia, with a population of eleven thousand. Set on the southeastern edge of the biggest of the coastal lagoons, Laguna de Caratasca, some 110km east of Brus Laguna, the town survives on government administration and small-scale fishing and shrimping. Like Brus Laguna, Puerto Lempira is mostly used by travellers as a transit hub – flights connect it with the rest of Honduras, and it's close to the border with Nicaragua.

INFORMATION

Bank Banco Atlántida, next to *Hotel Flores*, changes travellers' cheques and gives Visa cash advances.

Information Mopawi (☎ 2433 6022, ⊚ mopawi.org), the Mosquitia development organization, has its headquarters in the town, three blocks south of the main dock.

ACCOMMODATION

Gran Hotel Flores In the centre of town ☎ 2433 6421. The best of the accommodation options, with small rooms all with a/c and bathroom. **L350**

Hospedaje Santa Teresita Centre of town, opposite *Gran Hotel Flores* ☎ 2433 6008. Clean but basic accommodation. **L250**

5

The Bay Islands

Strung in a gentle curve 60km off the north coast, the **Islas de la Bahía**, with their clear waters and abundant marine life, are the country's main tourist attraction. Fringed by a coral reef, the islands are the perfect destination for inexpensive, water-based activities – diving, sailing and fishing top the list – or just relaxing. Composed of three main islands and some 65 smaller cayes, the chain lies on the **Bonacca Ridge**, an underwater extension of the Sierra de Omoa mountain range. **Roatán** is the largest and most developed of the islands, while **Guanaja**, to the east, is a bit smarter. **Utila**, the closest to the mainland, is a backpacker hotspot.

The Bay Islands' history of conquest, pirate raids and constant immigration has resulted in an unusual society. The original inhabitants were recorded by Columbus in 1502, but the indigenous population declined rapidly as a result of enslavement and forced labour. Following a series of pirate attacks, the Spanish evacuated the islands in 1650. Roatán was left deserted until the arrival of the Garífuna in 1797. These 300 people, forcibly expelled from

DIVING SAFETY IN THE BAY ISLANDS

Diving safety is taken seriously by all professional dive schools in the Bay Islands. Make sure that you understand – and get along with – your instructors. Before signing up, check that classes have no more than six people, that the equipment is well maintained and that all boats have working oxygen and a first-aid kit. Also ask to see a card proving the instructor is qualified to teach the course (PADI, BSAC or whatever), and not merely a dive master. Anyone with asthma or ear problems should not be allowed to dive. Be aware that schools advertising discount rates may be cutting corners.

the British-controlled island of St Vincent following a rebellion, were persuaded by the Spanish to settle in Trujillo on the mainland, leaving a small settlement at Punta Gorda on Roatán's north coast. Further waves of settlers arrived after the abolition of slavery in 1830, when white Cayman Islanders and freed slaves arrived first on Utila, later spreading to Roatán and Guanaja.

Today, the islands retain their **cultural separation** from the mainland, although

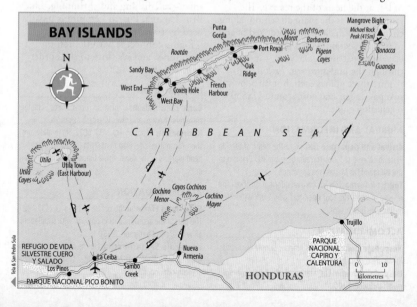

BAY ISLANDS

the presence of Spanish-speaking Hondurans and North American and European expats, who are settling in growing numbers, means the reshaping of the culture continues. A distinctive form of Creole English is still spoken on the streets of Utila and Guanaja, but Spanish has taken over as the dominant language in Roatán. The huge growth in visitors since the early 1990s – a trend that shows no signs of abating – has been controversial, as the islanders' income, which traditionally came from fishing or working on cargo ships or oil rigs, now relies heavily on tourism. Concern is also growing about the environmental impact of tourism.

UTILA

The smallest of the three main Bay Islands, **UTILA** is also the cheapest and one of the best places in the world to learn to dive (and even if you don't want to don tanks, the superb waters around the island offer great swimming and snorkelling possibilities), factors which combine to make it one of Central America's best destinations for budget travellers.

WHAT TO SEE AND DO

The island's principal **main road**, a twenty-minute walk end to end, runs along the seafront from **The Point** in the east to **Sandy Bay** in the west. **Utila Town** (also known as East Harbour) is the island's only settlement and home to the majority of its two-thousand-strong population.

Diving

Most visitors come to Utila specifically for the **diving**, attracted by the low prices, beautifully clear water and rich marine life. Even in winter, the water is generally calm, and common sightings include nurse and hammerhead sharks, turtles, parrotfish, stingrays, porcupine fish and an increasing number of dolphins. **Whale sharks** also continue to be a major attraction – the island is one of the few places in the world where they frequently pass close to shore.

On the north coast of the island, **Blackish Point** and **Duppy Waters** are both good sites; on the south coast the best spot is **Airport Caves**. The schools (see box, p.439)

will be happy to spend time talking to you about the merits of the various sites.

It's worth spending a morning walking around checking out all the schools. You want to feel comfortable with your decision, as diving can be dangerous – it is imperative that you get along with your instructor (see box opposite).

Swimming and snorkelling

The best **swimming** near town is at the **Blue Bayou**, a twenty-minute walk west of the centre. You can also snorkel further out; there's a US$1.50 charge to use the area, which also boasts a small sandy beach. Closer to town, where the road ends beyond *Driftwood*, **Chepes Beach** offers a narrow strip of sand, shallow water and a bar. East of town, **Bando Beach** (or **Airport Beach**) offers good snorkelling just offshore, as does the little reef beyond the **lighthouse**. The path from the end of the airstrip up the east coast of the island leads to a couple of small coves – the second is good for swimming and sunbathing.

Utila Iguana Station

The **Utila Iguana Station** (Mon, Wed & Fri noon–5pm; L60; ☎2425 3946, ⓦutila-iguana.de), signposted from the road five minutes west of the dock, is a breeding centre for the endangered Utila spiny-tailed iguana, found only on the island and facing extinction. Guided tours explain the life cycle of the species. It's worth a visit, especially if you need a break from all the diving.

Utila Cayes

The **Utila Cayes** – eleven tiny outcrops strung along the southwestern edge of the island – were designated a wildlife refuge in 1992. **Suc Suc** (or Jewel) **Caye** and **Pigeon Caye**, connected by a narrow causeway, are both inhabited, and the pace of life is even slower than on Utila. Small *lanchas* regularly shuttle between Suc Suc and Utila (US$8), or can be rented to take you across for a day's snorkelling (US$20). Ask at *The Buccaneer* (see p.440) or call Steve Christiensen (☎2425 3988).

Water Caye, a blissful stretch of white sand, coconut palms and a small coral

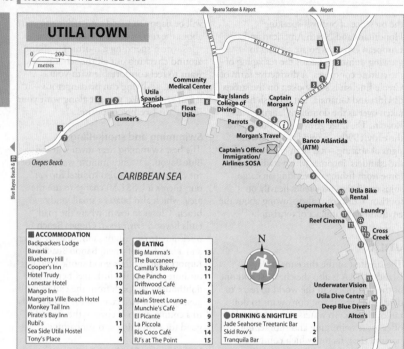

UTILA TOWN

Iguana Station & Airport · Airport

ROCKY HILL ROAD · MARY LYN · COLA DE MICO ROAD

Community Medical Center · Utila Spanish School · Float Utila · Bay Islands College of Diving · Captain Morgan's · Parrots · Morgan's Travel · Bodden Rentals · Banco Atlántida (ATM) · Gunter's · Captain's Office/ Immigration/ Airlines SOSA

Chepes Beach

CARIBBEAN SEA

Utila Bike Rental · Supermarket · Laundry · Reef Cinema · Cross Creek · Underwater Vision · Utila Dive Centre · Deep Blue Divers · Alton's

Blue Bayou Beach & 10

0 — 200 metres

N

■ ACCOMMODATION
Backpackers Lodge	6
Bavaria	1
Blueberry Hill	5
Cooper's Inn	12
Hotel Trudy	13
Lonestar Hotel	10
Mango Inn	2
Margarita Ville Beach Hotel	9
Monkey Tail Inn	3
Pirate's Bay Inn	8
Rubi's	11
Sea Side Utila Hostel	7
Tony's Place	4

● EATING
Big Mamma's	13
The Buccaneer	10
Camilla's Bakery	12
Che Pancho	11
Driftwood Café	7
Indian Wok	5
Main Street Lounge	8
Munchie's Café	4
El Picante	9
La Piccola	3
Rio Coco Café	14
RJ's at The Point	15

● DRINKING & NIGHTLIFE
Jade Seahorse Treetanic Bar	1
Skid Row's	2
Tranquila Bar	6

reef, is even more idyllic. Captain Hal charges around US$45 for return trips to Water Caye (ask for him at Parrots; see box opposite).

ARRIVAL AND INFORMATION

By plane The airstrip is 3km north of Utila Town at the end of the island's second main road, Cola de Mico Rd, which heads inland from the dock. Taxis wait for arriving flights. SOSA (book through Morgan's Travel, which has an office in the dock; ☎ 2425 3161, ⓦ utilamorganstravel .com) flies between Utila and La Ceiba (3 weekly; 20min). Island Air (☎ 9558 8683, ⓦ guanajaair.com) operates flights on small planes between Utila, Roatán and Guanaja, as well as San Pedro Sula and La Ceiba.

By boat All boats dock in the centre of Utila Town. Daily ferries (☎ 2425 3390, ⓦ utilaprincess.com) run to La Ceiba (6.20am & 2pm; 1hr; depart La Ceiba 9.30am & 4pm). Tickets (one-way L448–472) are usually available on the day. There were no scheduled boat services between Roatán and Utila at the time of writing, but one may well start up again in the future.

Tourist information Captain Morgan's dive shop (see box opposite) is often used as an unofficial information point. ⓦ aboututila.com is another useful source of information about the island.

GETTING AROUND

Scooters and quad bikes Scooters cost around US$35–40/day; golf carts and quad bikes go for around US$60/day; try Bodden (☎ 2425 3245, ⓔ boddenlance@yahoo .com), near the dock on Cola de Mico Rd.

Bikes Bodden, *Rio Coco Café* and Utila Bike Rental, southeast of the dock, all rent out bikes (L75–100/day).

ACCOMMODATION

Utila has more than enough affordable accommodation. With the exception of Semana Santa and parts of the high season, there's always somewhere available. Most of the dive schools (see box opposite) have affiliated lodgings, and enrolling in a course invariably gets you a few free or discounted nights. There are no designated places to camp except on the cayes. Electricity is expensive on the island so opting out of a/c will make things cheaper.

EAST OF THE DOCK

Cooper's Inn 5min from the dock ☎ 2425 3184. One of the best budget places on the island, with orderly rooms (all with fans), some with private bathrooms. **US$12**

Hotel Trudy South end of the main road ☎ 2425 3103, ⓦ underwatervision.net. Owned by Underwater Vision dive shop (see box opposite), this place has smart four-bed dorms and some private rooms. The bar area is one of

Utila's social hubs. Dorm US$8, double US$35
Rubi's Next door to the Reef cinema ☎ 2425 3240, ⓦ rubisinn.com. This is one of the most popular mid-range places on the island. There's a communal kitchen, a pleasant beach and lots of trees dotted around the grounds. Rooms 6 and 12 have ocean views. US$25

COLA DE MICO ROAD

Bavaria Up on the hill, just past the *Mango Inn* ☎ 2425 3809. A nice wooden porch runs around the outside of the building and all but one of the rooms have cold-water bathrooms (L50 extra for hot water). US$15
Blueberry Hill On the left side of the road, right before *Jade Seahorse* ☎ 2425 2199. Locally owned, no-frills hotel renting out rooms and apartments. The family who own it are usually at church on Saturdays, so it can be difficult to get a room then if you turn up without a reservation. L300
Monkey Tail Inn Just beyond *Jade Seahorse* ☎ 2425 2781. Owned and run by the affable Tonia, this guesthouse has a collection of simple, fairly scruffy rooms with shared cold-water bathrooms and communal kitchens. US$8
Tony's Place Opposite *Mango Inn* ☎ 2425 3376. The eight rooms here feel a little barren but are incredibly cheap, and the two shared bathrooms and kitchen are clean. L200

WEST OF THE DOCK

Backpackers Lodge Down an alley opposite Gunter's Dive Shop ☎ 2425 3350. Ten passable rooms (eight private rooms and two dorms) with shared bathrooms. Enquire at Gunter's Dive Shop. Dorm L100, double L200

★ **TREAT YOURSELF**

Mango Inn 5min from the dock ☎ 2425 3335, ⓦ mango-inn.com. A beautiful, well-run place, timber-built and set in shady gardens. They offer thatched, a/c cabins sleeping up to four, plus pleasant dorms (only available to divers from Utila Dive Centre). There's a good pizza restaurant on site. Double US$60, cabin US$90

Margarita Ville Beach Hotel Opposite *Driftwood* ☎ 2425 3366, ⓔ margaritavillehotel@yahoo.com. Very pleasant, big rooms, a wide terrace all around the house and hot water throughout. Recommended. US$25
Pirate's Bay Inn 4min from the dock ☎ 2425 3818, ⓦ piratesbayinn.com. This new hostel has clean, sparsely furnished dorms as well as spick-and-span private rooms with fans (a/c costs US$10 extra) – the latter are normally reserved for divers on Captain Morgan package deals, but are available to non-divers during quiet periods. Dorm US$9, double US$39
Sea Side Utila Hostel Opposite Gunter's Dive Shop, 8min from the dock ☎ 2425 3150. Just about the best budget accommodation on the island. Three-person dorms come with spotless bathrooms, and there are also a few private rooms (with fans or a/c). There's a communal kitchen and a nice balcony upstairs, where you can take in the Caribbean sunsets. Dorm L100, double L300

DIVE SCHOOLS IN UTILA

Open-water courses cost around US$280–300; prices are supposed to be fixed but in reality some schools charge more and some less. The price normally includes accommodation for at least part of the course, and discounted accommodation afterwards. Fun dives cost around US$35. There's a US$4 reef conservation fee to pay too.

Alton's 2min west of the airstrip ☎ 2425 3704, ⓦ diveinutila.com. Accommodation on site (discounted following courses), and use of kitchen. It has a conch nursery and a stringent ecological policy.
Bay Islands College of Diving 5min west of the dock, next to *Utila Lodge* ☎ 2425 3291, ⓦ dive-utila.com. Professional school, with an indoor training pool and the island's only hyperbaric chamber on site.
Captain Morgan's On the corner opposite the dock ☎ 2425 3349, ⓦ divingutila.com. Accommodation provided at *Pirate's Bay Inn* and the *Lonestar Hotel*.
Cross Creek 5min east of the dock ☎ 2425 3397, ⓦ crosscreekutila.com. Based in the hotel of the same name.
Deep Blue Divers 10min west of the dock ☎ 2425 3511, ⓦ deepbluediversutila.com. Based at the hotel

of the same name, where accommodation is provided.
Gunter's 8min west of the dock ☎ 2425 3350, ⓦ ecomarineutila.com. A small, relaxed operation that offers a "lazy boat" for late risers. Its dock is a favourite haunt of sea horses.
Parrots 2min west of the dock ☎ 2425 3772, ⓦ diveparrotsutila.com. Free accommodation and a dynamic environment.
Underwater Vision ☎ 2425 3103, ⓦ underwatervision.net. Good accommodation provided at *Hotel Trudy*.
Utila Dive Centre Near the end of the road west of the dock, close to the bridge ☎ 2425 3326, ⓦ utiladivecentre.com. Perhaps the best reputation for quality and safety, and courses are a bit pricier as a result. Free dorm accommodation at *Mango Inn*.

5

UTILA CAYES

Camping Water Caye. Camping is allowed here – a caretaker turns up every day to collect the fee. You'll need to bring a tent, food, equipment for a fire and water. **US$2**

Lonestar Hotel Jewel Caye ☎ 9925 1093. If the area around the dock is too hectic for you, try the *Lonestar Hotel*, which has four nicely kept rooms with fans and attached hot-water bathrooms. **L350**

EATING

Lobster and fish are excellent on the islands (though it's a good idea to ask about the reef-friendliness and sustainability of what's being served), and then there's the usual rice, beans, chicken, and US and European food. Prices are higher than on the mainland: for low-cost eating, head for the evening stalls on the road by the dock, which do a thriving trade in *baleadas*. Many restaurants stop serving at around 9.30pm.

EAST OF THE DOCK

Big Mamma's 5min from the dock. Clean, inexpensive and popular with the nearby dive shops, with some dishes (such as pizza slices) on display at the counter. Snacks from L30. Thurs–Tues 11am–3pm & 6–9.30pm.

The Buccaneer 3min from the dock. Formerly known as the *Bundu Café*, this barn-like place has a good range of breakfast options (L60–140), plus burgers, sandwiches and nachos, plus ice-cream sundaes and alcoholic coffees. The sofa by the book exchange is a good place to park yourself on a rainy afternoon. Open till 10pm.

Camilla's Bakery 5min from the dock. A good spot for a snack or picnic supplies, this bakery has everything from croissants and bagels to banana bread and pecan pie (all around L40–50). It shares the premises with *Pizza Nut* restaurant. Tues–Sat.

★ **Che Pancho** 4min from the dock. Underneath Reef Cinema in a shady courtyard, this friendly little café serves huge, top-notch smoothies (L35–50), hot dogs (L25–40; try the Argentine *choripan* with *chimichurri* sauce), sandwiches and snacks. There's normally also a home-baked cake or two. Mon–Sat 8.30am–6pm.

Main Street Lounge 1min from the dock, above the *El Casino* bar and pool hall. Located in what feels like an old wooden American house, with a porch that's a great spot to keep an eye on comings and goings. Pasta, steak, seafood and Mexican dishes also feature on the menu (mains from around L85), and there are often good beer/cocktail promotions. Opening hours are erratic.

El Picante 2min from the dock. One of the smarter restaurants in town, *El Picante* produces tasty Mexican food (L100–200) – from fajitas to enchiladas. Sun–Thurs 11am–10pm, Fri 11am–5pm, Sat 6–10pm.

Rio Coco Café Beside the bridge, 8min from the dock. The best coffee (L20–40) in Utila is served at this café, alongside delicious home-made chocolate chip cookies

and savoury muffins. Mon–Fri 7am–2pm.

RJ's at The Point Beside the bridge, 8min from the dock. You can have anything you want – snapper, marlin, wahoo, king fish, steak, burgers – as long as it's grilled. Get there early as it fills up quickly. Mains from around L100. Wed, Fri & Sun 5.30–10pm.

WEST OF THE DOCK

Driftwood Café 10min from the dock, right at the end of the path. The food here is excellent, and they have one of the most peaceful jetties on the island. Menu highlights include burgers, baja fish tacos, pulled pork sandwiches, and fish soup (all around L100–200). The kitchen is open until 9pm, the bar until 10pm. Tues–Sun.

Indian Wok 3min from the dock. This restaurant vows not to use fish from the reef, which means its sushi (served on Tues) is guilt-free. Indian and Thai-style curries, satay, spring rolls and other Asian dishes are on offer too. Mains around L100–180. Sun–Thurs 6–9.30pm.

Munchie's Café 1min from the dock. A real mix of dishes – from local breakfasts to seafood kebabs – served in an 1864 house with an iguana garden out back and a nice porch. Mains L65–200.

La Piccola 1min from the dock. The island's only Italian restaurant serves excellent bruschetta and mains (around L120–250) such as gorgonzola and walnut ravioli or the excellent filet mignon with mushroom sauce. Sadly the quality of the service doesn't always match that of the food. Tues–Sun 5–10pm.

DRINKING AND NIGHTLIFE

Despite its tiny population, Utila is a hedonistic party island. A Honduran beer will set you back around L30. Most of the restaurants (including *Driftwood Café*) double as bars, and some of the hotels (notably *Mango Inn*) are also good drinking spots.

★ **Jade Seahorse Treetanic Bar** A short walk up the Cola de Mico Rd. The most eccentric place on the island. Run by an American artist, this hotel/restaurant/bar is a maze of colour and reflective surfaces that really comes alive at night. Open until around 1am.

Skid Row's Next door but one to *Sea Side Rooms*. Though it feels a little like somewhere they repair boat parts, this is a small, friendly place full of expat seadogs boozing throughout the day. Some of the cheapest beers on the island, plus good food. Daily 10am–10pm.

Tranquila Bar Behind Parrots, 2min west of the dock. Lively, low-lit bar over the water, packed with locals and backpackers most nights.

DIRECTORY

Bank Banco Atlántida, opposite the dock, has an ATM.
Books *The Buccaneer* and *Che Pancho* both have book exchanges, though choices are limited.

Cinema Reef Cinema, above *Che Pancho*, has one screening daily at 7.30pm.

Health The Community Medical Center is 2min west of the dock (Mon–Fri 10.30am–3.30pm).

Immigration At the captain's office (Mon–Fri 9am–noon & 2–4.30pm).

Internet Caye Caulker Cyber Café, 4min east of the dock.

Language School Central America Spanish School has an outpost on Utila (☎ 2443 6453, ⓦ ca-spanish.com).

Laundry Alice's Laundry is next to the Caye Caulker Cyber Café. Utila Bike Rental (see p.438) also offers a laundry service.

Post office At the main dock.

Snorkelling Bodden and *Rio Coco Café* (among other places) rent out snorkelling equipment (around L100/day).

Yoga and meditation Yoga Utila (☎ 9779 0521, ⓦ yogautila.com) runs daily classes in a studio above Bush Supermarket, 4min east of the dock, as well as sunset sessions at Deep Blue Divers. If you're after an immersive meditation experience, Float Utila (☎ 2425 3827, ⓦ floatutila.com), 4min west of the dock, offers reportedly the world's largest sensory deprivation floatation tank. A 60min session costs US$50.

ROATÁN

Some 50km from La Ceiba, **ROATÁN** is the largest of the Bay Islands, a curving ridged hump almost 50km long and 5km across at its widest point. A popular stopoff for cruise ships, Roatán can be a hard place to enjoy if you're on a tight budget – expect your spending to go way above average. The island's accommodation mostly comes in the form of all-inclusive luxury resort packages, although there are a few good deals to be found in **West End**. Like Utila, Roatán is a superb **diving** destination, and also offers some great hiking, as well as the chance to do nothing except laze on a beach. **Coxen Hole** is the island's commercial centre.

Note that credit-card transactions are subject to a 16 percent fee in all establishments on the island.

WHAT TO SEE AND DO

Roatán's abundance of great diving and superb beaches often takes away from the charm of the island's smaller towns and **villages**, which are worth exploring to get a sense of what it would have been like before the tourists arrived.

Coxen Hole

COXEN HOLE (also known as Roatán Town) is uninteresting and run-down; most visitors come here only to change money or shop. All of the town's practical facilities and most of its shops are on **Main Street**, near where the buses stop.

Sandy Bay

Midway between Coxen Hole and West End, **SANDY BAY** is an unassuming community with a number of attractions. The **Institute for Marine Sciences** (daily 7am–5pm; L20; ☎ 2445 3049, ⓦ anthony skey.com), based at *Antony's Key Resort*, has exhibitions on the marine life and geology of the islands and a museum with useful information on local history and archeology. There are also **bottlenose dolphin shows** (Fri–Sun 10.30am; L100/US$5), or you can enjoy "encounters" in waist-deep water (daily 8am, 10am, 1pm & 2.30pm; US$62 for 30min). Across the road, several short nature trails weave through the jungle at the **Carambola Botanical Gardens** (daily 8am–5pm; US$10; guided tours cost an extra US$5; ☎ 2445 3117, ⓦ carambolagardens.com), a riot of beautiful flowers, lush ferns and tropical trees. A thirty-minute hike to the summit of Carambola Mountain gives a view of the coral in the ocean beyond.

West End

With its calm waters and incredible sandy beaches, **WEST END**, 14km from Coxen Hole, makes the most of its ideal setting at the southwest corner of the island. From the beautifully sheltered **Half Moon Bay** at the northern end of town, a sandy track runs 1km or so along the water's edge, past guesthouses, bars and restaurants geared towards independent travellers of all budgets. The year-round community of sun-worshippers and dive shops gives the village a laidback charm during the day and a vibrant, party feel after dark.

West Bay

Some 2km southwest of West End, towards the extreme western tip of Roatán, is the stunning white-sand beach of **West Bay**, fringed by coconut palms

5

ROATÁN: WEST END

N

Roatán Institute
for Deep Sea
Exploration

Book Nook

Native Sons
Laundry

Half Moon Bay

Coconut Tree Divers

ATM

ATM

Roatán
Divers

Captain Van's
Rentals

Roatán Rentals
Ocean Connections

West End
Divers

CARIBBEAN
SEA

Water Taxi to
West Bay

Green Hole & ATM

West Bay

Barefoot Charlie's

0   200
metres

◼ ACCOMMODATION	
Burke's Place	1
Chillie's	5
Cocolobo	3
Georphi's Tropical Hideaway	10
Mariposa Lodge	7
Milkas	8
Posada Arco Iris	4
Posada Las Orquídeas	2
Sea Breeze Inn	6
Splash Inn Dive Resort	9

● EATING		
Argentinian Grill	1	
Cannibal Café	6	
Creole's Rotisserie Chicken	12	
Earth Mama's	5	
Escondido Café	8	
Fresh	4	
Linga Longa	3	
Pollo Caribeño	7	
Rudy's	13	
Tong's Thai Island Cuisine	10	
● DRINKING & NIGHTLIFE		
Blue Marlin	9	
Foster's	14	
Nova	11	
Sundowners	2	

French Harbour

Leaving Coxen Hole, the paved road runs northeast past the small secluded cove of Brick Bay to **FRENCH HARBOUR**, a busy fishing port and the island's second-largest town. Less run-down than Coxen Hole, it's a lively and interesting place to spend a few hours.

Oak Ridge

From French Harbour the road cuts inland along a central ridge to give superb views of both the north and south coasts of the island. After about 14km the road reaches **OAK RIDGE**, a fishing port with wooden houses strung along its harbour – it's attractive in a bleak sort of way. There are some nice, unspoiled beaches to the east of town, accessible by *lanchas* from the main dock, and other nearby communities can be reached by boat cruises through the mangroves. Boatmen offer trips to Port Royal, the mangroves and Morat for US$50 or to Pigeon Cayes for US$200 (up to ten people).

Punta Gorda

About 5km from Oak Ridge on the northern coast of the island is **PUNTA GORDA**, the oldest Garífuna community in Honduras. The best time to visit is for the anniversary of the founding of the settlement on April 12, when Garífuna from all over the country attend the celebrations. At other times it's a quiet and slightly dilapidated little port with no buildings of note, though the black, white and yellow of the Garífuna flags brighten things up.

Port Royal

The road ends at **PORT ROYAL**, on the southern edge of the island, where the faint remains of a fort built by the English can be seen on a caye offshore. The village lies in the **Port Royal Park and Wildlife Reserve**, the largest refuge on the island, set up in 1978 in an attempt to protect endangered species such as the yellow-naped parrot.

The eastern tip of Roatán is made up of mangrove swamps, with a small island, **Morat**, just offshore. Beyond is **Barbareta Caye**, which has retained much of its virgin forest cover.

and washed by crystal-clear waters. There's decent snorkelling at the southern end of the beach, though the once-pristine reef has suffered in recent years from increasing river run-off and the close attentions of unsupervised day-trippers.

From West End, it's a pleasant 45-minute stroll south along the beach and over a few rock outcrops; alternatively, you can take one of the small *lanchas* that leave regularly from the jetty near West End Divers (US$3/50L each way; three-person minimum).

WATERSPORTS AROUND WEST END

The waters around West End offer fantastic watersports – primarily **diving**, and superb **snorkelling** in the reef just offshore, but with plenty of other activities available.

DIVING

Diving courses in West End are available for all levels, and prices are officially standardized. A four-day PADI Open Water course will cost about US$280, with some schools offering discounted accommodation. You will also have to buy a manual (US$35). Fun dives costs US$35–40 a dive, with ten-dive packages around US$300. All divers must also buy a US$10 pass, which is valid for a year. Recommended West End-based **schools** include: West End Divers (☎ 2445 4289, ⊛ westenddivers.info); Ocean Connections (⊛ ocean-connections.com); Coconut Tree Divers (☎ 2445 4081, ⊛ coconuttreedivers.com); Native Sons (☎ 2445 4003, ⊛ nativesonsroatan.com) and Roatán Divers (☎ 8836 8414, ⊛ roatandiver.com).

SNORKELLING

The best **snorkelling** spots around West End are at the mouth of Half Moon Bay and at the Blue Channel, which can be accessed from the beach 100m south of *Foster's* bar; you can rent equipment (around US$10/day) from many of the dive schools and some shops along the main road.

WATERSPORTS

You can rent **sea kayaks** from the *Sea Breeze Inn*, close to the entrance road; expect to pay US$18 for a single kayak and US$21 for a double per day. They also offer **waterskiing** (US$85/hr). Alfredo (contactable through *Sea Breeze Inn* or on ☎ 9866 4582) offers **fishing trips** for around US$70/hr for a minimum of two hours. Captain Danillo offers **glass-bottomed-boat tours** (US$25 per person), leaving from the jetty opposite Coconut Tree Divers.

ARRIVAL AND DEPARTURE

By plane Regular domestic and international flights (see p.379) land at Roatán's international airport, on the road to French Harbour, 3km east of Coxen Hole. There are information and hotel reservation desks, car rental agencies (Avis ☎ 2445 0122) and a bank at the airport. A taxi to/from West End costs L400.

Domestic destinations La Ceiba (SOSA; 4 daily; 30min); San Pedro Sula (SOSA & Isleña/TACA 1–2 daily; 2hr 35min); Tegucigalpa (SOSA & Isleña/TACA 1–2 daily; 1hr 10min). Island Air (☎ 9558 8683, ⊛ guanajaair.com; contact for timetables) also operates flights on small planes between Utila, Roatán and Guanaja, as well as San Pedro Sula and La Ceiba.

By boat Roatán's harbour, known as Brick Bay, sits directly between the towns of Coxen Hole and French Harbour. A taxi to/from West End costs L400. Daily ferries run to La Ceiba (7am & 2pm; in the opposite direction 9.30am & 4.30pm; 1hr 20min; L550–574 standard class, L650–674 first class; ☎ 2445 1775, ⊛ roatanferry.com). You can usually buy tickets on the day, if you turn up about an hour in advance. There were no scheduled boat services between Roatán and Utila at the time of writing, but there's a good chance one will start up in the future.

GETTING AROUND

By bike, moped, motorbike or car Captain Van's (☎ 2445 4076, ⊛ captainvans.com), at the southern end

of Half Moon Bay, rents out bicycles (US$10/day), mopeds (US$39/day), motorbikes (US$55–65/day) and cars (US$55–65/day); taxes are extra for all of the motorized vehicles. Another option is Roatán Rentals, a short walk south.

By minibus There are two minibus routes covering all of the island's main settlements. Bus #1 (every 30min) goes from Coxen Hole to French Harbour, stopping in Oak Ridge; the last bus from Oak Ridge leaves between 4.30pm and 6pm. Buses from Oak Ridge pass through Punta Gorda. Bus #2 (every 15min) goes from Coxen Hole to Sandy Bay, stopping in West End. The price depends on how far you're going, and journey times depend largely on the driver.

By taxi It's never hard to find taxis and *colectivos* in Roatán, though as with everything else, it is often a lot more expensive than on the mainland.

By water-taxi Water-taxis run from West End to West Bay, leaving from the jetty near *Splash Inn* (L50 each way).

ACCOMMODATION

In the low season (April–July & Sept to mid-Dec) discounts may be available, particularly for longer stays.

WEST END

Burke's Place At the northern end of the main beach road ☎ 2445 4146. One of West End's best deals, *Burke's* has three apartments with private bathrooms and kitchenettes. <u>US$25</u>

5

Chillies Half Moon Bay ☎ 445 4062, ⓦ nativesonsroatan .com/chillies. *Chillies* is a well-set-up budget choice with a range of accommodation options (all but the most expensive cabins, which sleep up to six, have cold-water bathrooms) and a communal kitchen. Dorm US$11.60, double US$25.50, cold-water cabin US$30, hot-water cabin US$37

Georphi's Tropical Hideaway Towards the southern end of the main beach road ☎ 2445 4205, ⓦ georphi.com. One of the better-value deals on the island, this is a sort of rustic resort, with dorms and cabañas. Dorm US$11.60, cabaña US$23.20

Mariposa Lodge On a side street halfway down the main beach road ☎ 2445 4460, ⓦ mariposa-lodge.com. A quiet and very comfortable mid-range place with a mix of a/c rooms and apartments (which sleep up to four). Room/ apartment US$80

Milkas Set back off the main beach road ☎ 2445 4241 or ☎ 9781 3733. Very basic but impeccably clean, this is a reliable budget option. Choose between three-bed dorms or newer, more spacious private rooms. Dorm US$10, double US$25

Posada Arco Iris Half Moon Bay ☎ 2445 4264, ⓦ roatanposada.com. Set in attractive gardens just off the beach, with excellent, imaginatively furnished and spacious rooms, studios and tastefully decorated apartments, all with fridge and hammocks; a/c costs US$15 extra per night. There's also an attached Argentine restaurant (see below). Double US$55.60, studio US$62.60, apartment US$76.50

Posada Las Orquídeas At the northern end of the main beach road ☎ 2445 4387, ⓦ posadalasorquideas.com. There's a serene feel to this rather smart secluded hotel. Rooms all have fridges and fans; those with a/c and sea views cost extra; #14 is the pick of the bunch. US$55.70

Sea Breeze Inn Just south of Half Moon Bay, behind the *Cannibal Café* ☎ 2445 4026, ⓦ seabreezeroatan.com. Popular place, if slightly overpriced, offering a mix of (rather cramped) rooms, and better-value studios and

apartments with kitchenettes. Avoid the noisy ground-floor rooms. A/c costs US$5–10 extra. Double US$25, studio US$45, apartment US$55

Splash Inn Dive Resort Half Moon Bay ☎ 2445 4110, ⓦ roatansplashinn.com. A reliable mid-range hotel providing spotless rooms with TVs and a/c, plus a decent Italian-inspired restaurant and a dive school. US$72

EATING

There's a good range of places to eat in West End, with fish and seafood featuring heavily – take advice from the dive shops as to the most reef-friendly choices. Prices are on the high side. Prices quoted below are in the currency used by each establishment; you can pay with either dollars or lempiras at all. Most places open daily from the morning until 9–11pm; exceptions are noted in the reviews below.

WEST END

Argentinian Grill Half Moon Bay. An Argentine-style steakhouse serving good barbecued meat: the *bife de chorizo* is particularly succulent. On Sundays, a *parrillada* – an Argentine mixed grill for two – is often on offer. Steaks L235–500. Tues–Sun.

Cannibal Café Just south of Half Moon Bay, in front of the *Sea Breeze Inn*. This split-level Mexican joint is famous for its filling "Big Kahuna" burritos (L192–290) – if you can eat three in an hour they're on the house. Tacos, quesadillas, fajitas and chimichangas (L65–290) are also available.

Creole's Rotisserie Chicken Towards the southern end of the main beach road. If you're looking for value for money, this is the place. As the name suggests, chicken (L70 for a quarter, L220 for the whole bird) is the focus here, though the quesadillas are good too.

Earth Mama's Half Moon Bay, just off the main beach road. Tranquil garden café serving healthy breakfast and lunch options, as well as huge smoothies (L100–120). Tues–Sun 8am–4pm.

Escondido Cafe Just south of Half Moon Bay. Breezy first-floor café with good breakfast (including filled muffins, French toast and massive banana pancakes for L80–100) and lunch options (sandwiches and "rice bowls"), plus good coffee (you can even get a flat white). Wed–Mon 7.45am to mid-afternoon.

Fresh Alba Plaza, a 20–30min walk from West End in Gibson Bight, just before Sandy Bay. Well worth the stroll from West End, this café serves excellent coffee (L30–60), sandwiches and bagels (L90–120), and fresh bread, cakes, pastries and cookies to eat in or take away. Mon–Fri 7am–5pm, Sat 7am–7pm.

Linga Longa Half Moon Bay, just north of the mini roundabout. *Linga Longa* has a pleasant deck area overlooking the sea, and a varied menu that runs from crepes and sandwiches to curries and stir-fries (L120–300). You can also buy bags of Roatán-grown coffee beans.

★ TREAT YOURSELF

Cocolobo Northwest of Half Moon Bay ☎ 9898 4510, ⓦ cocolobo.com. The best hotel in West End, Cocolobo has a peaceful location a 15min walk north of the centre. The spacious, tastefully decorated rooms have private terraces (and hammocks) overlooking the sea, and there are also self-contained cottages sleeping up to four people; a/c costs US$12.50 extra. The infinity pool and large deck area are added bonuses. Room rates include breakfast; cottage rates do not. Double US$157, cottage (for two people) US$122

Tong's Thai Island Cuisine Just south of Half Moon Bay. For something a little different, try this Thai restaurant, which knocks up tasty (if sometimes slightly oversweet) red, green and penang curries, pad thai, fried rice, spicy soups and a range of other dishes. The candlelit tables out on the jetty are particularly romantic in the evening. Mains L260–420. Daily noon–3pm & 5.30–9.30pm.

Pollo Caribeño Just south of Half Moon Bay. A roadside shack with a few stools, serving economical Honduran food, including breakfast options, *baleadas*, "lunch plates", fried chicken and a range of snacks (L25–100).

Rudy's Towards the southern end of the main beach road, next to *Georphi's Tropical Hideaway*. Locally renowned spot for breakfast (US$3–5) – the banana pancakes are particularly good. *Rudy's* also serves shots and smoothies of the local so-called "miracle fruit", *noni*. Sun–Fri 6am–5pm.

DRINKING AND NIGHTLIFE

Drinking in West End can drain your pocket fast, so seek out half-price happy-hour deals, some of which last until 10pm. Expect to pay around L45 for a beer.

WEST END

Blue Marlin Just south of Half Moon Bay. A popular bar-restaurant that often serves as the first stop after *Sundowners* (see below) closes and the crowds start heading down the beach. The food (mains L170–370) is good too: try the shrimp fried rice. Mon–Thurs noon–midnight, Fri & Sat noon–2am.

Foster's At the second of the big piers to the south of town. Set on its own pier, *Foster's* is a West End institution. There's a daily happy hour (4–7pm), and Fri nights are particularly rowdy. Opening times vary.

Nova A 5min walk south of Half Moon Bay. With fluorescent strings dangling from the ceiling and swinging chairs at the bar, this atmospheric place sees DJs play electro breakbeat and drum'n'bass, but also Latin and 80s music. Fri night is especially lively. Mon–Thurs 11am/noon–midnight, Fri & Sat 11am/noon–2am.

Sundowners Half Moon Bay. The happy hour (5–7pm) at this tiny beach bar, popular with both locals and tourists, is a good way to kick off the night. Daily 10am–10pm.

DIRECTORY

Banks In Coxen Hole, Banco Atlántida and the HSBC near the small square have ATMs. In West End there is an ATM at the Coconut Tree Minisuper, right by the mini roundabout triangle, and a third in the supermarket at the petrol station a 10min walk east of the mini roundabout triangle. Neither is particularly reliable.

Books Book Nook (Thurs–Tues 11am–5pm) has a good selection of novels and travel books (including a few *Rough Guides*) to buy or rent. Barefoot Charlie's, a cyber café located towards the southern end of West End, also has a selection of books.

Immigration The *migración* is near the small square on Main Street in Coxen Hole, in a green building.

Internet Most hotels and many restaurants and bars offer free wi-fi. For cyber cafés, try Barefoot Charlie's (see above).

Laundry There's a small laundry (Sun–Fri) close to *Linga Longa* restaurant.

Post office In a blue building near the *migración* and the small square on Main Street in Coxen Hole (Mon–Fri 8am–4pm).

Supermarket HB Warren, near the small square in Coxen Hole, is the largest supermarket on the island, plus there's a small and not too impressive general market just behind Main Street. There are several small supermarkets in West End.

Yoga *Earth Mama's* (see opposite) runs daily yoga sessions (US$6.50–10).

GUANAJA

GUANAJA, some 25km long and just 4km wide at its largest point, is divided into two unequal parts by a narrow canal – the only way to get between the two sections of the island is by water-taxi, which adds both to the atmosphere and to the cost of living. The island is very thinly populated and receives relatively few travellers. Note that sandflies and mosquitoes are endemic throughout the island, so arrive prepared to deal with them.

WHAT TO SEE AND DO

Most of Guanaja's 12,000 inhabitants live in **Bonacca** (also known as **Guanaja Town**), a crowded settlement on a small caye a few hundred metres offshore. It's here that you'll find the island's shops, as well as the bulk of the less unreasonably priced accommodation. The only other settlements of any substance are **Savannah Bight** (on the east coast) and **Mangrove Bight** (on the north coast).

Bonacca

Wandering around the warren of tight streets, walkways and canal bridges in

5

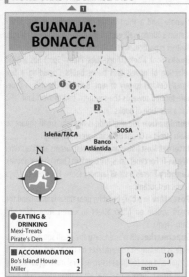

GUANAJA: BONACCA

Isleña/TACA
SOSA
Banco Atlántida

N

● EATING & DRINKING
Mexi-Treats — 1
Pirate's Den — 2

■ ACCOMMODATION
Bo's Island House — 1
Miller — 2

0 — 100
metres

BONACCA makes for an interesting half-hour or so – though government plans to eliminate the town's tiny waterways for new roads means the town may not be the Honduran Venice for much longer. Virtually all the houses in town are built on stilts – vestiges of early settlement by Cayman Islanders – with the main causeway running for about 500m east–west along the caye.

Hiking

Though Guanaja's Caribbean pine forests were flattened by Hurricane Mitch in 1998, there's still some decent hiking to be found. A wonderful trail leads from Mangrove Bight up to **Michael Rock Peak**, the highest point in the Bay Islands (412m), and down to Sandy Bay on the south coast, affording stunning views of Guanaja, Bonacca and the surrounding reef. Fit walkers can do the trail in a day, or you can camp on the summit, provided you bring your own provisions.

Beaches

Some of the island's finest white-sand beaches lie around the rocky headland of **Michael's Rock**, near the *Island House Resort* on the north coast, with good snorkelling close to the shore.

Diving

Diving is excellent all around the main island, but particularly off the small cayes to the east, and at **Black Rocks**, off the northern tip of the main island, where there's an underwater coral canyon. The **Mestizo Dive**, off Soldado Beach, south of Michael's Rock, was opened in 2002 to mark the 500th anniversary of Christopher Columbus's visit, with sunken statues of the explorer and national hero Lempira on a reef surrounded by genuine Spanish colonial artefacts, including a cannon.

ARRIVAL AND DEPARTURE

By plane The Guanaja airstrip is on the larger, northern section of the island, next to the canal. If you have pre-booked a resort on the island you will be met at the airport. AeroCaribe de Honduras has regular flights to/from La Ceiba (6 weekly; journey time varies). Island Air (☎ 9558 8683, ⊛ guanajaair.com) also operates flights on small planes between Utila, Roatán and Guanaja, as well as San Pedro Sula and La Ceiba.

By boat An intermittent ferry service (1hr 30min) operates between Trujillo and Bonacca and Mangrove Bight; call Captain Roy (☎ 9962 6163 or ☎ 9600 2235) or ask locally for the latest schedule.

INFORMATION AND TOURS

Bank You can change dollars and get cash advances at Banco Atlántida, southeast of the dock in Bonacca.

Tour operators To get to some of the underwater sites you'll have to contact one of the hotel-based dive schools: *Bo's Island House Resort* (see below) usually has the best rates.

ACCOMMODATION

Bo's Island House Near Michael's Rock ☎ 2453 4240, ⊛ bosislandhouse.com. A good option if *Miller* is full, *Bo's Island House* has clean, well-ventilated rooms, all with hot-water bathrooms. Rates include full board; good week-long diving packages available too. **US$100**

Miller Halfway along the main causeway, Bonacca ☎ 9847 0746. The building itself is slightly run-down, but the rooms are in reasonable condition; most have hot water and, for a little extra, a/c and TVs. **L1200**

EATING AND DRINKING

Mexi-Treats Towards the western end of the main causeway, Bonacca. This restaurant is one of the best in town, serving up tasty Tex-Mex dishes. Mains from L120. Mon–Fri.

Pirate's Den Near *Mexi-Treats*, Bonacca. Good for fresh seafood, daily lunch specials and Fri barbecues. Mains from L120. Wed–Mon.

BEACH AT SAN JUAN DEL SUR

Nicaragua

HIGHLIGHTS

❶ **León** Hot sun, black volcanoes and a revolutionary past. **See p.467**

❷ **Granada** A tourist-friendly colonial jewel. **See p.484**

❸ **San Juan del Sur** Surf by day, party by night. **See p.491**

❹ **Isla de Ometepe** Hike mysterious twin volcanoes in Lago de Nicaragua. **See p.496**

❺ **Río San Juan** Pristine tropical forest and the El Castillo ruins. **See p.502**

❻ **Little Corn** Perfect, pint-sized Caribbean getaway. **See p.509**

HIGHLIGHTS ARE MARKED ON THE MAP ON P.449

ROUGH COSTS

Daily budget Basic US$20/occasional treat US$50

Drink Beer US$1, coffee US$0.50

Food *Comida corriente* US$3

Hostel/budget hotel US$7/US$16

Travel Managua–Chinandega by bus (130km): 2hr, US$3

FACT FILE

Population 6 million

Languages Spanish, Creole and indigenous

Currency Nicaraguan córdoba (C$)

Capital Managua (population: 1.8 million)

International phone code ☏ 505

Time zone GMT –6hr

6

Introduction

Wedge-shaped Nicaragua may be the largest nation in Central America but, despite recent growth, it remains one of the least visited. Still, many travellers who spend any time here find that Nicaragua's extraordinary landscape of volcanoes, lakes, mountains and vast plains of rainforest helps make it their favourite country on the isthmus. Compared to the Maya ruins of Guatemala or the national parks of Costa Rica, Nicaragua offers few traditional tourist attractions – almost no ancient structures remain, and years of revolution, civil war and natural disasters have laid waste to museums, galleries and theatres – and a chronic lack of funding, high inflation and unemployment have impoverished the country's infrastructure. It's these same qualities, though, that make Nicaragua an incorrigibly vibrant and individualistic country, with plenty to offer travellers prepared to brave its grubby highways, cracked pavements and crammed public transport.

Virtually every visitor passes through the capital, **Managua**, if only to catch a bus straight out – while the city has an intriguing atmosphere and a few sights, it's hard work, and many quickly head for **Granada**, with its lakeside setting and wonderful colonial architecture. A smattering of **beaches** along the Pacific coast, notably cheery **San Juan del Sur**, continues to attract the **surfing** and backpacking crowds, while the beautiful **Corn Islands**, just off the coast of **Bluefields**, offer idyllic white-sand beaches framed by windswept palm trees and the azure Caribbean Sea. Culture and the arts are very much alive in Nicaragua, too; visit **Masaya**'s Mercado Nacional de Artesanía to find some fantastic-value high-quality crafts, or stay on the **Solentiname archipelago** and learn about the primitive painting traditions that have flourished there.

Buzzing **León** is often considered the country's cultural capital – look for the famous **murals** depicting Nicaragua's turbulent political history. Ecotourism, volcano-viewing and hiking are the attractions of the **Isla de Ometepe**, with its thrilling twin peaks rising out of the freshwater lake, while further east, up the lush Río San Juan, sits **El Castillo**, a small town with a great fortress. In the central region, where much of the country's export-grade coffee is grown, the climate is refreshingly cool; hiking and birdwatching are the main activities near the mountain town of **Matagalpa**.

Stepping off Nicaragua's beaten track is appealingly easy – the peaceful waters of the **Pearl Lagoon** and lush highlands of **Miraflor** reserve are fine spots for exploration, but really are just the tip of the iceberg. More than anything, the pleasures and rewards of travelling in Nicaragua come from interacting with its inhabitants – who tend to be engagingly

> ### WHEN TO VISIT
>
> Nicaragua has two distinct **seasons**: the dry summer (*verano*) and the wet winter (*invierno*). **Summer** (Dec–April) can be extremely hot and often uncomfortably dry. Fewer travellers come in the **rainy season** (May–Nov) – which alone could be a reason for choosing to put up with the daily downpour. On the **Pacific coast**, rain often falls in the afternoons from May to November, although the mornings are generally dry. The **central mountain region** has a cooler climate with sporadic rainfall all year, while the **Atlantic coast** is wet, hot and humid year-round, with September and October the height of the tropical storm season.

witty and very hospitable. This is a country where a bus journey can turn into a conversational epic and a light meal into a rum-soaked carnival, a stroll round the street can be interrupted by a costumed giant and a marching band, and a short boat ride can seem like a trip into another world.

CHRONOLOGY

1000 AD Aztec migrate south after the fall of Teotihuacán (Mexico), following a prophecy that they would settle where they found a lake with two volcanoes rising from it – Isla de Ometepe.

1522 The Spanish arrive and name the region "Nicaragua", after the indigenous groups living there.

1524 Spanish establish the settlements of Granada and León.

1821 Nicaragua gains independence from Spain as part of the Central American Federation.

1838 Nicaragua becomes an independent nation (save the Atlantic coast, which is claimed as British territory).

1855 American adventurer William Walker takes control of the government.

1857 Walker is overthrown by joint efforts of Nicaragua, Costa Rica, Guatemala and the US. He is later executed in Honduras.

1857–93 "The Thirty Years": a period of relative prosperity. US companies come to dominate the Nicaraguan government.

1893 General José Zelaya seizes control, establishing a dictatorship.

1909 Civil war breaks out. Four hundred US marines land on the Caribbean coast. Zelaya resigns.

1912–25 US military bases are established.

1927 Augusto Sandino leads a guerrilla campaign in protest at the US military presence. US takes over Nicaraguan military and develops Nicaraguan National Guard.

1934 Under orders of National Guard commander General Anastasio Somoza, Sandino is assassinated.

1937 Somoza "elected" president, commencing forty-year dictatorship.

1956 Somoza is assassinated by Rigoberto López Pérez. One of Somoza's sons, Luís, becomes interim president, and another, Anastasio, head of the National Guard.

1961 Frente Sandinista Liberación Nacional (FSLN), or Sandinista National Liberation Front, is founded.

1967 Luis Somoza dies; his brother Anastasio becomes president.

6

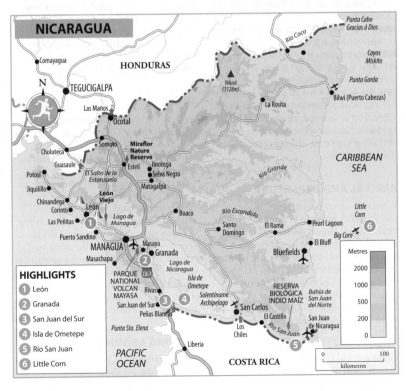

6

1972 Massive earthquake flattens Managua, killing some 10,000.

1978 Opposition leader Pedro Chamorro is assassinated by National Guard; demonstrations and fighting spread across the country.

1979 Sandinistas gain control of the country, and Somoza is forced to flee. Revolution is officially won on July 19. Liberal Sandinistas are in control of government.

1981 Unhappy with Nicaragua's left-wing policies and communist ties, the US funds Contra troops in an anti-Sandinista campaign.

1984 FSLN's Daniel Ortega wins presidential election.

1988 FSLN and Contras sign a ceasefire.

1990 Violeta Chamorro defeats Daniel Ortega to become Latin America's first female president. US cuts off aid to Contras.

1996 Right-wing ex-lawyer Arnoldo Alemán, former mayor of Managua, becomes president.

1998 Hurricane Mitch devastates the region.

2001 Alemán's vice president, Enrique Bolaños, is elected.

2002–03 Alemán is jailed on charges of embezzlement and money laundering.

2004–05 The World Bank and Russia clear much of the country's debts, as part of the Heavily Indebted Poor Countries Initiative.

2006 Former president Ortega wins the November elections and returns to power.

2009 Ortega announces he will run for president in late 2011, after the Supreme Court lifts the constitutional ban on back-to-back electoral terms.

2010 Periodic tensions over the disputed Río San Juan flare after Nicaraguan dredging of the river. Troops are mobilized but no shots fired; the UN ruling orders both Nicaragua and Costa Rica to keep their distance.

2011 Ortega is re-elected, amid widespread accusations of voting irregularities.

ARRIVAL AND DEPARTURE

If arriving on an international flight, you'll land at **Augusto C. Sandino International Airport (MGA)** in Managua. As well as flights from neighbouring capitals such as San José and San Salvador (served mainly by COPA and TACA), Managua receives direct flights from major US hubs Atlanta, Miami and Houston through Spirit Airlines, Continental, American Airlines and Delta.

You can enter Nicaragua by land from Honduras and Costa Rica (see box below). International **buses** pull into Managua,

---

> ### LAND AND SEA ROUTES TO NICARAGUA
>
> Nicaragua shares borders with Costa Rica and Honduras. The busiest Nicaraguan land entry/exit point is at Peñas Blancas (see box, p.172), on the southern border with **Costa Rica**. Los Chiles in Costa Rica provides a water crossing further east, to San Carlos on the Río San Juan. The two main border crossings with **Honduras** in the north, meanwhile, are at Guasaule and El Espino (see box, p.395) and Las Manos (see box, p.393), with the latter providing the quickest access to Tegucigalpa.

often via Granada and Rivas (if coming from the south); it's also possible to take local services to and from the border. There is a **water crossing** from the border at Los Chiles, Costa Rica (see box, p.177), to San Carlos; from here it is a five- to seven-hour bus ride or an hour-long plane ride on to Managua. It is also possible to cross from La Unión in El Salvador (see p.228) to Potosí in Nicaragua, either by arranging to cross with local fishermen, or with the passenger service Cruce del Golfo (ⓦcrucedelgolfo.com US$65).

VISAS

As part of the **CA-4 agreement** (see box, p.30), visitors are granted ninety days of travel within Nicaragua, Honduras, Guatemala and El Salvador. Australian, British, Canadian, US and most EU nationals do not currently require **visas** to visit Nicaragua. You do, however, need a **tourist card**, which allows for stays of thirty to ninety days depending on your nationality and costs US$10 (payable upon arrival). The permitted length of your visit will be hand-written on the entry stamp in your passport; while all tourist cards allow for thirty days' entry, it is only this hand-written number that counts.

GETTING AROUND

Public transport, especially buses, is geared toward the domestic population. It's very cheap but quite uncomfortable.

BY BUS

The standard local **buses** in Nicaragua are the usual old North American school buses, though an increasing number of express minibuses and coaches also serve the more popular routes – only a few córdobas more, they are less crowded, stop less frequently and occasionally even have air conditioning. Most **intercity buses** begin running between 4am and 7am, departing about every thirty minutes, or when the bus is full, with last buses leaving by 5 or 6pm. **Bus stops** are usually at the local market – only Estelí and Managua have anything approximating a modern terminal – and fares are very cheap. You'll pay US$1–4 for anything up to three or four hours, with longer journeys to the Atlantic coast costing up to US$20. There is often a list of fares displayed at the front of the bus. You can usually keep your **luggage** with you, although especially on busy services it may end up on the roof or in a pile at the back of the bus. It should be safe, but it's worth keeping valuables on your person. Most buses have a conductor and a helper (*ayudante*) as well as a driver – in most instances, you'll pay the conductor once the bus is moving. If you have a lot of luggage, you may be charged extra, but it should never be more than the price of a single fare to your destination.

Timetables for key routes can be viewed on ⓦthebusschedule.com/EN/ni/index.php. Alternatively, your accommodation should be able to fill you in.

SHUTTLE BUSES

Nicaragua's buses are cheap and safe, but if you're in a group, in a rush, or want to travel later in the day you may want to consider a **shuttle** – cars or minibuses that head between the tourist hotspots. The trip from Managua airport to San Juan del Sur, for example, will set you back around US$65 between two or US$130 among six – compared to US$2.50 on the slow bus (though you'd also need to make your way across town from the airport to the bus station – around US$5 per person in a taxi). Most tour companies can arrange this, or try the shuttle companies direct on ⓦadelanteexpress.com or ⓦpaxeos.com.

BY CAR

Taxis – many on their last legs – are most often seen in cities, but they also make long-distance journeys; a good deal, especially if in a group. In Managua, most taxi fares are US$1–3 during the day and US$2–5 at night. Outside the capital, in-town fares vary, but are usually around US$0.50–1. Always agree on the fare before getting into the cab, and don't be afraid to haggle if the rate seems high – at Managua's bus terminals, overcharging foreigners is the norm.

Renting a car is probably the best way to explore the country's many beaches. Rates average US$40 a day for the cheapest models. Outside Managua and the main west-coast highway, you'll want something robust and preferably 4WD. Rental is most reliable in Managua – Alamo, Avis, Hertz and Thrifty all have offices at the airport. You need a valid licence, passport and a credit card. Make

---

ADDRESSES IN NICARAGUA

Nicaraguan towns are usually set up on a vague **grid system**, with a commercial build-up around the *parque central* and main streets, and residential neighbourhoods sprawling outwards from the centre. Only main streets are labelled with signs, and smaller towns do not have any street names at all, depending instead on their direction from the main square: calles go east–west and avenidas north–south, with a central calle and avenida acting as the grid's axis. Calles and avenidas **northeast** of the main park are generally designated *noreste* (NE), those **northwest** are *noroeste* (NO), **southeast** are *sureste* (SE) and southwest *suroeste* (SO). There is also no set numbering system for streets in Nicaraguan towns. Addresses refer to locations' proximity to **local landmarks**, such as churches, roundabouts, shopping centres, banks, restaurants and petrol stations.

6

sure you take out full-cover **insurance**. Bear in mind when driving that road signage is quite poor, and you'll need to ask directions frequently. And as with other Central American countries, don't drive at night – it's less a question of crime than the lack of lighting, which disguises potholes, sudden deviations in the road or even the road disappearing altogether, as well as cattle straying onto the highway.

Although it's generally safe to **hitch** a ride with a pick-up truck (but not advisable otherwise), it's only common among locals in the countryside where there is little or no other transport. Most pick-up trucks will happily stop and let you jump in the back – just bang on the roof when you want to get off. If you're driving in the countryside yourself, it's almost rude not to stop and pick up people walking in the same direction.

BY BOAT

Boats provide vital links around Nicaragua's numerous waterways and two large lakes. On the Atlantic coast, they are the main means of transport. For travellers the most useful routes are those between Bluefields and either Pearl Lagoon or El Rama (both of which are served by small boats called *pangas*), and the cargo boat which goes between Granada and San Carlos, stopping at Ometepe. San Carlos can also be accessed by boat from the border crossing at Los Chiles.

BY PLANE

Nicaragua's domestic airline, La Costeña (☎2263 2142, ⍟lacostena.com.ni), operates fairly reliable **flights** around the country, with Managua the inevitable hub. Routes run from the capital to locations including San Carlos, Bluefields, the Corn Islands and Puerto Cabezas (the latter two are hard to reach *without* flying), and also run from Bluefields to the Corn Islands and Puerto Cabezas. A return will set you back US$80–180, and can be bought by phone or online, as well as at the airport.

If the flight is full, there's a chance you'll be **bumped** – rare but not inconceivable, especially if you're travelling to or from the Corn Islands around Christmas or Easter. To be safe, call the airport you're departing from (numbers are given throughout the Guide) the day before you fly to confirm your booking. If you are bumped, your reservation will be valid for the next flight. Luggage occasionally gets left behind, especially on the smallest planes, but is almost always on the next scheduled arrival.

ACCOMMODATION

Most budget travellers to Nicaragua at some point find themselves in a Nicaraguan **hospedaje** – a small and usually pretty basic pension-type hotel, most often family-owned and run. Simple *hospedajes* charge around US$5–15 for a double. For this you get a bed and fan; in many places you'll have to share a bathroom, and breakfast is not normally included. **Hostels** (US$5–10 for a dorm bed) are common in backpacker hotspots like León and Granada but rare elsewhere. **Hotels** (from US$20) tend to be more luxurious, with air conditioning, cable TV and services like tours and car rental; you are less likely to see these in very small towns. **Camping** is pretty rare thanks to the low cost of accommodation. If you're determined to camp, the most promising areas are beach spots around San Juan del Sur, Isla de Ometepe and the Corn Islands.

FOOD AND DRINK

As in the rest of Central America, **lunch** (around 11.30am–1.30pm) is the main meal. Central markets in Nicaraguan towns are guaranteed to have snack spots, with several small **comedores** or **cafetines** offering cheap **comida corriente** (everyday food) – a set lunch of meat, rice and salad, for around US$3. Throughout the country **streetside kiosks** sell hot meals; you'll soon become familiar with their plastic tablecloths, paper plates and huge bowls of cabbage salad. The food is cheap – around US$2 – but generally well prepared. **Restaurants** are more expensive (around US$6), and generally open daily for lunch and dinner from noon–9pm in smaller towns and until 11pm in the cities of Managua, Granada and León.

Nicaraguan **cuisine** is based around the ubiquitous **beans**, **rice** and **meat**, and everything is cooked with oil. Lunch usually includes **chicken**, **beef** or **pork**, most deliciously cooked *a la plancha*, on a grill or griddle, and served with beans, rice, plantain and shredded cabbage salad. For breakfast and dinner the rice and beans are generally fried together to make **gallo pinto**, served with an egg for breakfast or **cuajada** (curd cheese) for dinner. Roast chicken, pizza and Chinese food also crop up in the bigger towns.

On the Atlantic coast the cuisine becomes markedly more **Caribbean**. Here rice is often cooked in mild coconut milk, and the staple fresh **coconut bread** is delicious. **Rondon** is a stew of *yuca*, *chayote* and other vegetables, usually with fish added, which is traditionally eaten at weekends.

In the rest of the country weekends are the time to eat **nacatamales**, parcels of corn dough filled with vegetables, pork, beef or chicken, which are wrapped in a banana leaf and steamed for several hours, or **baho** – beef, green plantain and yuca slow-cooked in a huge pot.

Tropical **fruit** is abundant, cheap and delicious, and throughout the country you'll see **ice cream**-sellers pushing their Eskimo carts. The quality isn't great, but you will find an extraordinary range of flavours, including many made with local fruits and nuts.

DRINK

Given Nicaragua's heat, it's just as well that there's a huge range of cold drinks, or **refrescos** (usually shortened to *frescos*), available. These are made from grains, seeds and fruits, which are liquidized with milk or water. Some unusual ones to look for include *cebada*, a combination of ground barley and barley grains mixed with milk, coloured pink and flavoured with cinnamon and lots of sugar; *pinolillo*, a spiced corn and cacao drink; and *semilla de jícaro* (or "hickory seed"), which looks and tastes a bit like chocolate. Just about every fruit imaginable is made into a *fresco*,

including watermelon, passion fruit, papaya, *pitaya* (dragon fruit) and melon.

You might want to ask whether your *fresco* is made with purified water, as **tap water** is generally worth avoiding, especially outside major cities. Alongside a fairly standard mix of soft drinks, **bottled water** is found everywhere; if you buy a drink to take away it will usually come in a plastic bag – bite off the corner, and you're off. Nicaragua has two local brands of **beer**, Victoria and Toña, both light and refreshing lagers. For spirits, it is common in bars to buy local Flor de Caña **rum** by the bottle. It comes in dark and white, gold, old, dry and light, and is an excellent buy at just US$5–10 per bottle. It's usually brought to the table with a large bucket of ice and lemons, but you can mix it with soft drinks for something a little less potent.

CULTURE AND ETIQUETTE

Nicaraguans are generally courteous and appreciate this trait in visitors, and it is considered polite to address strangers with "Usted" rather than "Tú" (or its local form "Vos"). You will often hear the term *Adiós* (literally, "to God") used as a greeting – hardly surprising in a country where ninety percent of the population is Christian. The older generations in particular are often religiously conservative in appearance and manner. *Machista* attitudes are still prevalent, and female travellers, especially those travelling solo, may be harassed by catcalls from local (usually young) men; this is best ignored.

With regard to **tipping**, posher restaurants, especially the tourist dens of

> ### NICARAGUAN WORDS AND PHRASES
>
> **Adiós** Used as a greeting in passing, as well as the standard "goodbye"
> **Chele/a** ("che-le"/"che-la") White or pale-skinned person (from *leche*: milk)
> **Dale pues** ("dah-leh pweh") Literally, "give it, then", it's used to say "OK", "go on", "fine", "it's on", etc
> **Naksa/Aisabi** "Hello"/"Goodbye" in the Miskito language

6

Granada and León, will add a ten- to fifteen-percent service charge to the bill – you don't have to pay it. If someone carries your bag, they'll probably expect C$5–10 for their trouble. Outside of the tourist areas, most Nicaraguans don't tip and taxi drivers don't expect a tip.

Haggling is the norm in markets and with street vendors, but not in shops.

SPORTS AND OUTDOOR ACTIVITIES

Nicaragua's national sport is **baseball**, and every town has a field and numerous, active leagues. Ask your local taxi driver about league games, for which most of the town will turn out in support. **Football** (soccer) is played by children in the street, but lacks the popularity here that it has in other Latin countries.

Visiting **surfers** are drawn to the country's Pacific coast, where there seems to be an endless run of deserted beaches with great breaks; the most popular area (with good tourist amenities) is around **San Juan del Sur**, near the Costa Rican border – you'll find the most surf camps, teachers, and board sales or rentals in this area. Nicaragua also offers excellent **hiking**, with stunning volcanoes, like those on **Isla de Ometepe** and mountains around Estelí and Matagalpa. On the Atlantic coast, **diving** and **snorkelling** are a must, particularly on the **Corn Islands**, where you can reach wrecks and reefs from right off the beach. Nicaragua is also the only country in the world currently offering **volcano-boarding** – using a customized plank to ride the ashes on the Cerro Negro volcano near León.

COMMUNICATIONS

Most towns have **post offices** (generally Mon–Fri 8am–1pm), although there are few on the Atlantic coast. A postcard to the US is C$15, C$20 to Europe.

There are virtually no coin-operated **phones** in Nicaragua, and you're best off using phones in internet cafés or *pulperías* (small neighbourhood shops), where the shop owner will "hire" you use of his phone. Phone numbers within Nicaragua changed from seven to eight digits a few years back, but you'll still see some in the old format – just add a "2" (landline) or "8" (mobile) to the number. Calling Nicaragua from abroad, the **country code** is ☎505.

If you decide not to bring your own phone, you could buy a **mobile phone** for as little as US$15; Movistar (Ⓦmovistar .com) and Claro (Ⓦclaro.com.ni) have pay-as-you-go packages. Both have an outlet in the airport.

You'll find **internet cafés** in even the smallest towns. Rates – generally C$10–15/hr – often rise in smaller or more remote towns, where connections can also be painfully slow. **Wi-fi** is increasingly common, even in cheaper accommodation, and is usually free for customers. If you bring a laptop, you might want to buy **surge protector**, as power surges can happen. As a precaution, unplug anything electrical if the electricity goes off; most surges happen when it comes back on.

CRIME AND SAFETY

Nicaragua is the second-poorest country in the Americas, and unemployment is rife. You'll almost certainly encounter street kids, but you're far more likely to be greeted with courtesy than aggression, and Nicaragua remains **safer** than many of its neighbours. You should take care in Managua, however (see box, p.457).

Petty theft can be a problem – keep an eye on your bags and pockets, especially on buses. **Muggings** have occurred in tourist stretches like the beaches of San Juan del Sur and at day-trip destinations around Granada – your accommodation should be able to advise you, and cabs are plentiful. Larger hotels will have safes where you can leave valuables. Wherever you are, **women** should be wary of going out alone at night, though the chief threat is being harassed by groups of drunken men.

The **police** in Nicaragua are generally reliable, but watch out for the traffic police (*policía de tránsito*), who are infamous for targeting foreigners and

EMERGENCY NUMBERS

Fire ☎ 115 (or ☎ 911 from mobile phones)
Police ☎ 118
Red Cross ☎ 128
Traffic police ☎ 119

who will take any chance to threaten you with a fine (*multa*) in the hope that you'll pay them off. Often even ordinary police officers will try stopping you, but if they are not traffic police, they can't fine you, so stand your ground. To **report a crime** you must go to the nearest police station. If you need a police report for an insurance claim, the police will ask you to fill out a *denuncia* – a full report of the incident. If the police station does not have the *denuncia* forms, ask for a *constancia*, a simpler form, signed and stamped by the police. This should be sufficient for an insurance claim.

Visitors to Nicaragua should in theory carry their **passports** on them at all times, though checks are rare and a photocopy is usually acceptable.

HEALTH

Serious medical situations should be attended to at a **hospital** – most towns and cities have one. In an emergency, if possible, head to Managua. Failing this, find a Red Cross (*Cruz Roja*) post, health centre (*centro de salud*) or pharmacy (*farmacia*) for advice. **Pharmacies** are generally open daily between 8am and 5pm, and in each town they take turns to stay open all night; in an emergency out of hours ask which pharmacy *esta de turno* (is on duty).

INFORMATION AND MAPS

The national tourist board, **INTUR** (ⓦintur.gob.ni), has **information** offices throughout the country, with the largest in Managua. Although staff are usually friendly, they generally only speak Spanish and can't offer much besides colourful leaflets. They may stock *Anda Ya!*, a free quarterly booklet that's packed with advertorial, but also has some useful maps and details of travel frequencies. Tourist information centres and most hotels have free **maps** which come with lots of advertisements but are generally accurate.

MONEY AND BANKS

Nicaragua's **currency** is the **córdoba** (C$), which is divided into 100 centavos; at the time of writing, the exchange rate was C$24 to US$1, but it devaluates at a set rate each day, so check the current rate at ⓦbcn.gob.ni. Notes come in denominations of 10, 20, 50, 100, 200 and 500 córdobas; coins come in denominations of 1, 5 and 10 córdobas, and 25 and 50 centavos. Get rid of C$500 notes when you can, as they can be difficult to change. Small US dollar bills are accepted for most transactions, as long as they are not marked or torn, and accommodation and tour prices are usually quoted in dollars – although US$100 bills can usually only be changed at a bank.

Banks are usually open Monday to Friday from 8am to 4pm; many are also open on Saturday mornings until noon. Most will change US dollars, and some change euros, and colones (from Costa

NICARAGUA ONLINE

ⓦ**hechomagazine.com** Snazzy site that's useful for news on nightlife and culture, with a Managua focus.
ⓦ**nicaliving.com** Expat forum with some useful travel tips and news.
ⓦ**nicaraguadispatch.com** Respected English-language journalism and editorial on all things Nica.
ⓦ**rightsideguide.com** Good for information on sights on the Caribbean coast.
ⓦ**vianica.com** General information on sights and travel.
ⓦ**visit-nicaragua.com** INTUR's tourism promotions site, with general information on tourist attractions, cultural activities and amenities.

6

Rica) but no other currency. **Moneychangers** (*coyotes*) operate in the street, usually at the town market, and are generally reliable – though it helps to have an idea of what you expect to get back before approaching them.

Travellers' cheques are only changed by the Banco de América Central (**BAC**) – even here you'll struggle with anything but US-dollar cheques – and they're probably not worth bothering with. **Credit cards** such as Visa, MasterCard and Amex are generally accepted in more expensive hotels and restaurants and can also be used to pay for car rental, flights and tours. BAC, Bancentro, Banco ProCredit and Banpro's **ATMs** all accept foreign-issue cards, and in most reasonable-sized towns you will find at least one of these, distributing cash in dollars or córdobas. That said, you can't rely on ATMs alone and, especially out of the major centres, you'll have little alternative but to carry a decent amount of cash. There are currently no ATMs on Little Corn Island or Solentiname, or in Pearl Lagoon or San Juan de Nicaragua.

OPENING HOURS AND PUBLIC HOLIDAYS

Shops and **services** in Nicaragua observe Sunday closing: on other days you'll find most places open from 8am to 4pm, though many government-run services, such as tourist information, post offices and immigration, are open from 8am to 1pm. **Businesses**, **museums** and **sites** close for lunch, normally between noon

and 2pm, before reopening again until 4 or 5pm. Supermarkets, smaller grocery shops and the small neighbourhood shops called *pulperías* or *ventas* generally stay open until 8pm. **Bars** and **restaurants** tend to close around 11pm or midnight, except for nightclubs – most of which are in Managua – which stay open until 2am or later. Public holidays (see box below) see almost everything shut down, so don't plan on visiting tourist attractions over those dates.

FESTIVALS

Nicaragua's calendar includes plenty of **festivals**, from local events to national fiestas and raucous *hípicas* (horse parades). In addition, each town in Nicaragua has its own patron saint whose saint's day is observed with processions and celebrations – these may well combine old customs inherited from the Aztecs with mestizo traditions, including the masked *viejitos* ("old ones" – young and old alike wearing masks of old men and women). Nicaraguans also love to dance, and you will probably see folkloric dances in the streets, usually performed by children. The calendar here lists just a few highlights.

March–April At Easter the whole country packs up and goes to the beach: buses are crammed, hotel rooms are at a premium, and flights to the Corn Islands are fully booked. Semana Santa (Holy Week) processions, in which crowds follow *pasos* (depictions of Christ and the Virgin), are the biggest in Granada.

May The Atlantic coastal town of Bluefields celebrates Palo de Mayo, an adapted May Day fiesta flavoured with Caribbean reggae and soca – a fusion of dance and folklore.

July 19 The holiday marking the Revolution is still celebrated ardently by Sandinistas and is usually accompanied by parades and marches. In Managua, the Plaza de la Revolución fills with Sandinista supporters, who gather in memory of the historical events.

December 31 Throughout much of the country, New Year's Eve is mainly celebrated in the home, although San Juan del Sur is known for drawing a crowd of young revellers. Bear in mind you'll find most things closed on January 1.

PUBLIC HOLIDAYS

Jan 1 New Year's Day
Easter week Semana Santa
May 1 Labour Day
May 30 Mother's Day
July 19 Anniversary of the Revolution
Sept 14 Battle of San Jacinto
Sept 15 Independence Day
Nov 2 All Souls' Day (Día de los Muertos)
Dec 7 & 8 Inmaculada Concepción
Dec 25 Christmas

Managua and around

Hotter than sin and crisscrossed by anonymous highways, there can't be a more visitor-unfriendly capital than **MANAGUA**. Less a city in the conventional sense than a conglomeration of neighbourhoods and commercial districts, Managua offers few sights and cultural experiences – in fact, most visitors are so disturbed by the lack of street names and any real centre that they get out as fast as they can.

Not even the city's setting on the southern shore of **Lago de Managua** is particularly pleasant: the area is low lying, swampy and flat, relieved only by a few eroded volcanoes. It also, unfortunately, sits on top of an astounding eleven **seismic faults**, which have shaken the city severely over time. The result has been a cycle of ruin and rebuilding, which has created a bizarre and postmodern mixture of crumbling ruins inhabited by squatters, hastily constructed concrete structures and gleaming new shopping malls and hotels. The old city centre, damaged further in the **Revolution** of 1978–79 and never thoroughly repaired, remains eerily abandoned.

All this said, there *are* things to enjoy here, although being a tourist in Managua does require a good degree of tenacity. As Nicaragua's largest city and home to a quarter of its population, the city occupies a key position in the nation's economy and psyche, and offers more practical services than anywhere else in the country.

6

WHAT TO SEE AND DO

For the visitor, sprawling Managua can thankfully be divided into a few distinct areas. The **old ruined centre** on the lakeshore is the site of the city's tourist attractions, including the few impressive colonial-style buildings that have survived all the earthquakes. **Lago de Managua**, which forms such a pretty backdrop to this part of the city, is unfortunately severely **polluted** from sewage and regular dumpings of waste.

Just to the south is the city's main landmark, the **Crowne Plaza Hotel**, whose white form, reminiscent of a Maya pyramid, sails above the city. Walking just west of the *Crowne Plaza* and twelve or so blocks south of the old ruined city centre brings you to the backpacker-frequented **Barrio Martha Quezada**, home to rock-bottom prices and international bus connections. A further 1km south, around **Plaza España**, you'll find many of the city's

SAFETY IN MANAGUA

Managua has its problems with poverty, theft and violence. The areas around the **Carretera a Masaya** are relatively clean and safe, while many locals will warn you away from hostel-packed **Barrio Martha Quezada**. Like most of the city, however, that district is safe enough to **walk around** in the daytime, if sketchy in the evening. **Cabs** are a good idea anyway, given Managua's perplexing layout and their low prices, and are worth investing in at night, especially if you're on your own.

That said, you need to be careful with taxis, as cab-based **express muggings** have occurred. This scam sees tourists befriended (often by a woman) on the buses coming into Managua and helped into a cab at the terminal with several other passengers, before being threatened with a knife, usually by another male passenger, driven around ATMs and forced to withdraw cash until their money runs out and they are finally dropped on the city fringes. In the unlikely event this happens to you, don't resist, but report the crime at INTUR in Managua as soon as possible (see p.463). If in doubt, don't get into a packed cab or one without a red-and-white number plate, try to sit in the front and, if you don't like the look of something, don't be afraid to find another vehicle – the vast majority of drivers want nothing more than to overcharge you slightly, and seeking one out yourself is a better bet than letting yourself be directed into one. Away from the main terminals you're on safer ground catching a cab, and if they open the door to let another passenger in, don't panic – shared rides are the norm.

6

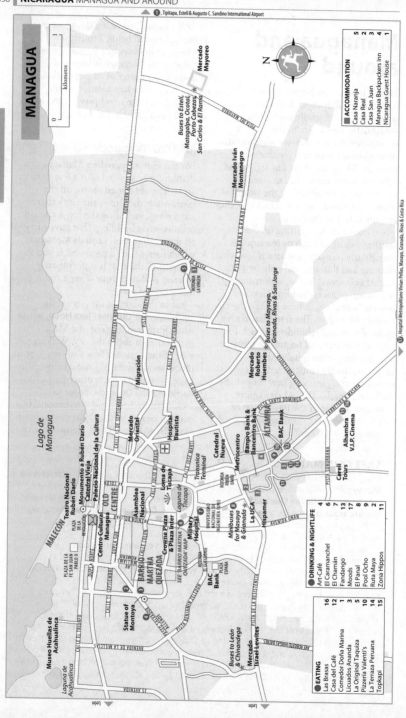

MANAGUA

0 — 1 kilometre

Tipitapa, Estelí & Augusto C. Sandino International Airport

Lago de Managua

Museo Huellas de Acahualinca

Laguna de Acahualinca

MALECÓN

Teatro Nacional
Rubén Darío

Monumento a Rubén Darío

Catedral Vieja

Palacio Nacional de la Cultura

PLAZA DE LA
FE SAN JUAN
PABLO II

PLAZA
DE LA
REVOLUCIÓN

OLD CENTRE

Centro Cultural
Managua

BARRIO
MARTHA
QUEZADA

Statue of
Montoya

BAC
Bank

PLAZA
ESPAÑA

Buses to León
& Chinandega

Mercado
Israel-Lewites

Asamblea Nacional

Loma de Tiscapa

Laguna de
Tiscapa

Military
Hospital

Transnica
Terminal

UNIVERSIDAD
NACIONAL DE
INGENIERÍA (UNI)

Minibuses
for Masaya
& Granada

La UCA

Hispamer

Mercado
Oriental

Migración

Hospital
Bautista

Catedral
Nueva

Metrocentro

Banpro Bank &
Bancentro Bank

BAC Bank

Cereli
Tours

ALTAMIRA

Alhambra
V.I.P. Cinema

Mercado
Roberto
Huembes

Buses to Masaya,
Granada, Rivas & San Jorge

RONDA
LA VIRGEN

Mercado Iván
Montenegro

Mercado
Mayoreo

Buses to Estelí,
Matagalpa, Ocotal,
Puerto Cabezas,
San Carlos & El Rama

Hospital Metropolitano Vivian Pellas, Masaya, Granada, Rivas & Costa Rica

● EATING

Las Brasas	16
Casa del Café	12
Comedor Doña Marina	1
Licuados Ananda	3
La Original Taquiza	5
Pizzería Valenti's	10
La Terraza Peruana	14
Topkapi	15

● DRINKING & NIGHTLIFE

Art-Café	4
El Caramanchel	6
El Chamán	7
Fandango	13
Moods	17
El Panal	8
Pool Ocho	9
Ruta Maya	2
Zona Hippos	11

N

banks, airline offices and a well-stocked La Colonia supermarket. In the southeast of the city, a new commercial district has grown up along the **Carretera a Masaya**, the main thoroughfare through the southern part of the city. East of here lie the **Metrocentro** shopping centre and upmarket residential suburb of **Altamira**.

Plaza de la Revolución

At the heart of the old centre is **Plaza de la Revolución**, a battered, intriguing and often eerily empty square flanked by city landmarks, including the cathedral ruins, the Palacio Nacional and the park containing **Carlos Fonseca's tomb** (marked by an eternal flame). The tomb, which serves as a memorial to the FSLN founder, is fringed by a row of huge black-and-red flags. Each year on July 19 thousands of Sandinista supporters make a pilgrimage to the area, paying homage to the revolution and the ensuing movement.

Catedral Vieja

On the eastern side of the Plaza de la Revolución stands the wreckage of the ash-grey Catedral Santiago de los Caballeros. Known as the **Catedral Vieja**, the ruins are a compelling and oddly romantic monument to a destroyed city. Birds fly through the interior, where semi-exposed murals and leaning stone angels with cracked wings still line the walls. Plans to restore the cathedral are continually being shelved; for now, the building remains officially closed to visitors.

Palacio Nacional de La Cultura

The lovely blue-marble and cream-stucco exterior of the **Palacio Nacional**, on the south side of the plaza, holds a darker history. During the long years of Somoza rule the columned building was the seat of government power: Colombian writer Gabriel García Márquez called it "*el partenón bananero*" – the banana parthenon. Then, on August 22, 1978, Sandinista commandos disguised as National Guard soldiers ran through its corridors to capture the deputies of the National Assembly, a cinematic coup d'état that effectively brought down the Somoza dictatorship.

Today, the Palacio, still a functioning government building, also houses the national library and archives, while the ground floor intersperses small, relaxing gardens with a **museum and art gallery** (daily 9am–4pm; C$80). There's a good display of Nicaraguan handicrafts, colourful murals and large sculptures, plus a few pre-Columbian artefacts. The museum frequently holds dance, poetry and *artesanía* events; ask at reception.

Teatro Nacional Rubén Darío

Perched like a huge white futurist bird north of the Plaza de la Revolución, the **Teatro Nacional Rubén Darío** (Mon–Fri 9am–5pm; ☎2222 7426, ⓦtnrubendario.gob.ni) is

---

NAVIGATING MANAGUA

In a city where nobody uses **street names** (if they actually exist) or addresses, it's helpful to have your destination given to you in terms of neighbourhood and distance from a **landmark** – taxi drivers will most easily find places in relation to a well-known city fixture. For destinations around Barrio Martha Quezada, use the Crowne Plaza, Tica Bus terminal or Montoya statue as a reference point; the Metrocentro shopping centre and La Union supermarket are useful landmarks around Zona Hippos and Los Robles.

Distances are measured in metres as much as in blocks – in local parlance, 100m is a city block, or **cuadra**. Sometimes an archaic measure, the **vara**, is also used: one vara (a yard) is interpreted as roughly equivalent to a metre. To confuse the issue still further, many Managuans do not use the cardinal points in their usual form: north becomes al lago – towards the lake; al sur is south; arriba – literally, "up", is to the east; and abajo, "down", is to the west. So, "del Hotel InterContinental (now the Crowne Plaza, although many people still use its old name) una cuadra arriba y dos cuadras al lago" means one block east and two blocks north of the Crowne Plaza.

6

Managua's main cultural venue, hosting foreign and Nicaraguan theatre, dance and opera groups. It's worth going inside just to see the massive chandeliers, marble floors and stirring view out to the lake from the enormous windows upstairs. There is a small permanent art exhibition in the foyer (free), and theatre buffs might be interested in a tour (US$1; call ahead), which takes you around otherwise closed parts of the building. South of the theatre is the **Monumento a Rubén Darío**, a striking sculpted memorial to the famous poet (see box, p.469).

Malecón

North of the theatre, an attempt has been made to spruce up the previously seedy lakeshore boardwalk, or **malecón**, with bars and food kiosks, plus a couple of fairground rides. A statue of Latin American liberator **Simón Bolívar** sits in the middle of the nearby roundabout, guarding the shorefront's entrance. The area gets quite lively at weekends, though it's fairly deserted during the week except for ambling teenage couples. There are pleasant views to the north, where **Volcán Mombotombo** and **Mombotombito** sit side by side against the horizon on the far shore of the lake, 50km away.

Plaza de la Fe San Juan Pablo II

Just south of the *malecón* is the **Plaza de la Fe San Juan Pablo II**, a large square whose central obelisk commemorates Pope John Paul II's two visits to Nicaragua. At its lake end sits the Concha Acústica or "acoustic shell" statue (resembling a large white wave), which serves as a stage for concerts and shows. The plaza is rarely busy and is one of the fiercest suntraps in the city, though it looks better at night when floodlighting adds some definition to its vast expanse.

Museo Huellas de Acahualinca

Volcán Mombotombo's capacity for destruction is evoked in the **Museo Huellas de Acahualinca** (daily 9am–4pm; US$4, $1 to take photos), just west of the *malecón* in Barrio Acahualinca (take a taxi or bus #112). A rudimentary affair, it nonetheless offers a fascinating glimpse into the area's history. Alongside fragments of pottery and boards on fauna and geology, a series of great pits reveals animal and human footprints from prehistoric nomads – preserved in volcanic ash, the footprints have been dated to around 6000 years ago.

Loma de Tiscapa

Directly behind the landmark *Crowne Plaza*, you can get some perspective on

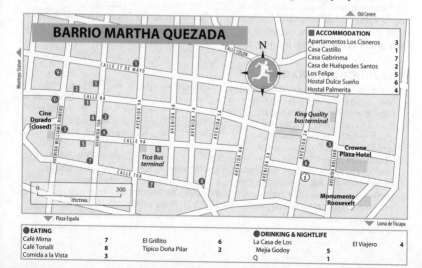

BARRIO MARTHA QUEZADA

▲ Old Centre

N

◄ Montoya Statue

CALLE COLON

CALLE 27 DE MAYO

@

CALLE 8A

@

Cine Dorado (closed)

AVENIDA WILLIAMS ROMERO

AVENIDA 10A

AVENIDA 9A

AVENIDA 8A

AVENIDA 7A

AVENIDA 5A

CALLE 9A

Tica Bus terminal

King Quality bus terminal

AVENIDA 4A

AVENIDA 3A

AVENIDA BOLIVAR

Crowne Plaza Hotel

CALLE 10A

0   300
metres

▼ Plaza España

Monumento Roosevelt

▼ Loma de Tiscapa

ACCOMMODATION
Apartamentos Los Cisneros	3
Casa Castillo	1
Casa Gabrinma	7
Casa de Huéspedes Santos	2
Los Felipe	5
Hostal Dulce Sueño	6
Hostal Palmerita	4

●EATING
Café Mirna	7	El Grillito	6		
Café Tonalí	8	Típico Doña Pilar	2		
Comida a la Vista	3				

●DRINKING & NIGHTLIFE
La Casa de Los Mejía Godoy	5	El Viajero	4
Q	1		

both Managua's dramatic history and its weird, battered cityscape in the **Loma de Tiscapa**, or Tiscapa Historical National Park (Mon–Sat 8am–5.30pm, Sun 9am–5.30pm; US$1). The fifteen-minute walk up the hill takes you via a series of posters detailing the rise and fall of Somoza's National Guard, then past the elegant white pillars of the Monumento Roosevelt and a decapitated statue of Justice before winding round and up to a silhouetted statue of **Sandino**. Nearby lie a tank and statue donated to Somoza by Mussolini. Photos detail the disastrous earthquakes of 1931 and 1972, while a display in the tunnels of the former prison goes into gory details of Somoza's infamous *noches de tortura* (torture nights).

The **views** of the city from here are excellent, stretching north to Lago de Nicaragua and the distant volcanoes and south beyond the new cathedral towards Masaya. Adventurous types can enjoy them on a so-called **canopy tour** (Tues–Sun 9am–5.30pm; US$15; ☎8872 2555) from the top of the hill. Three cables cover more than 1km, allowing you to glide high above the city and the picturesque – but polluted – **Laguna Tiscapa**, which sits below the Loma de Tiscapa's summit.

Carretera a Masaya and the Metrocentro

About 1km south of the laguna lies Managua's biggest concentration of residential and commercial neighbourhoods and most of its westernized nightlife. The main thoroughfare through this part of the city is the **Carretera a Masaya**, hemmed in to the east by the embassy neighbourhood of Altamira and to the west by La UCA, or the Universidad Centroamericana. It's on this road, just south of Pista Juan Pablo II, where you'll find the bland but blissfully cool **Metrocentro** shopping centre, which offers shops, ATMs, a food court, banks, a cinema and the *InterContinental Metrocentro* hotel.

Catedral Nueva

A short walk from the Metrocentro shopping centre, in the middle of a field,

is the Catedral Metropolitana de la Purísima Concepción, known simply as the **Catedral Nueva** (usually daily 6.30am–6pm), a striking and brutal piece of architecture whose roof resembles a collection of large concrete hand grenades. Inside there's a bleeding figure of Christ encased in glass, but the milling worshippers are more compelling than the cavernous interior.

6

ARRIVAL AND DEPARTURE

As the transport hub of the country, Managua is virtually impossible to avoid. From here you can get almost anywhere by bus, while flights put the otherwise inaccessible parts of the country on the map.

BY PLANE

Airport The Augusto C. Sandino International Airport is 11km east of Managua; on arrival, you'll have to pay US$10 for a tourist card (see p.30). Designated airport taxis wait just outside the terminal doors; reportedly safer than normal taxis, and always a/c, these charge US$15–20 for journeys to most parts of the city. If you cross the street from the airport you can catch a normal taxi, which shouldn't cost more than US$7 – though take care to avoid scams (see box, p.457). There are several ATMs, and the BanPro has a window where you can change dollars, but not travellers' cheques. You'll find car rental agencies in the arrivals hall. The domestic terminal sits at the main terminal's western end.

International flights Copa (ⓦcopaair.com) and Taca (ⓦtaca.com) between them have international flights to San José, Panama City, Guatemala, San Salvador and Tegucigalpa.

Domestic flights Domestic airline La Costeña (☎2263 2142, ⓦlacostena.com.ni) runs one or more flights a day to San Carlos, Bluefields, Puerto Cabezas and the Corn Islands; advance reservations are recommended, either at the airport office or via agencies across the city. Costeña tickets can only be reserved by phone or email – it's often worth confirming your flight over the phone before you fly too.

BY BUS

Domestic buses Domestic buses arrive at one of the several crowded, noisy and generally chaotic urban marketplaces that also serve as bus terminals: from Masaya, Granada, Rivas or other southern destinations, chicken buses come into the Mercado Huembes near the Carretera a Masaya on the southeastern edge of the city and express minibuses arrive and depart from La UCA, near Metrocentro; buses from the north and east – including Estelí, Matagalpa, Ocotal, San Carlos and El Rama – arrive at the terminal in the Mercado Mayoreo in Barrio Concepción,

6

TOUR OPERATORS IN MANAGUA

Organized tours are generally best arranged locally – we've listed operators throughout the Guide. If you've only got a short spell in the country and don't fancy the rigours of Nicaragua's clamorous bus terminals and ramshackle taxis, though, various places can arrange trips from Managua. These are usually pricey, but can get you to remote areas fast and will pick you up from your hotel or the airport. **Careli Tours**, opposite Colegio La Salle, Planes de Altamira (☎ 2278 6919, ⓦ carelitours.com), are good for expensive best-of-Nicaragua-type packages (US$200–1200), lasting up to a fortnight, as well as trips combining Nicaragua and Costa Rica. Otherwise, operators in León and Granada can help – try the likes of Green Pathways and Va Pues (see box, p.470) or Tierra Tour and Nicaragua Adventures (see box, p.487).

near the airport; buses from the northwest towns of León and Chinandega use the busy Mercado Israel Lewites in the southwest of the capital. Taxis crowd the arriving buses, but be careful (see box, p.457). Leaving Managua, the busiest domestic bus routes run to the provincial cities, particularly León in the northwest and Granada in the south. Other main routes run to Matagalpa, Estelí, Masaya and Rivas, the last for connections to the Costa Rican border and the beach town of San Juan del Sur. Buses to the Atlantic coast can be grievously affected by the weather – in the rainy season in particular, times are elastic and journeys can be decidedly wearing. Below, where we list buses as having regular departures (hourly or more frequent), these run from 5am–6pm unless otherwise stated.

Domestic destinations Bluefields (from Mercado Iván Montenegro; express departure daily 9pm, arriving in Rama around 3am for the early-morning *panga* to Bluefields; 10hr); Chinandega (from Mercado Israel Lewites; standard departures every 30min; 2hr 30min; express departures every 30min; 1hr 40min); El Rama (from Mercado Mayoreo; 5 daily [second-class]; 8hr); Estelí (from Mercado Mayoreo; standard departures every 30min; 3hr; express departures hourly; 2hr); Granada (from Mercado Huembes second-class departures every 15min; 1hr 20min; from Mercado Huembes express departures every 15–20min; 1hr); León (from Mercado Israel Lewites; second-class departures every 15–30min; 2hr; express departures every 15–20min; 1hr 30min); Masaya (from Mercado Huembes second-class departures every 20min; 1hr; from La UCA express services every 15–20min; 40min); Matagalpa (from Mercado Mayoreo; second-class departures every 30min; 3hr; express services hourly; 2hr); Ocotal (from Mercado Mayoreo; second-class departures hourly; 3hr 30min); Puerto Cabezas (from Mercado Mayoreo; second-class departures noon & 5pm; 18–25hr); Rivas (from Mercado Huembes; second-class departures every 25min; 2hr 25min; express services every 30min; 2hr); San Carlos (from Mercado Mayoreo; 7 daily second-class departures; 5–7hr); San Jorge (from Mercado Huembes; express departures every 30min; 2hr).

International buses Three major companies serve Central America's capitals; most international services come

into Barrio Martha Quezada in central Managua. The Tica Bus station (☎ 2222 6094, ⓦ ticabus.com) sits two blocks east and one block south of the old Cine Dorado, while the King Quality station (☎ 2228 1454, ⓦ kingqualityca.com) is nearby on C 27 de Mayo, opposite Plaza Inter. Transnica buses (☎ 2277 2104, ⓦ transnica.com) depart from 300m north and 50m east of the Rotonda Metrocentro.

International destinations Guatemala City (King Quality 2 daily, 2.30am & 3.30am; 17hr; Tica Bus 1 daily, 5am, with overnight in San Salvador; 31hr); Panama City (Tica Bus 1 daily, noon, with overnight in San José; 32hr); San José (King Quality 1 daily, 2.30am; 9hr; Tica Bus 3 daily, 6am, 7am & noon; 10hr; Transnica 4 daily, 5am, 7am, 10am & 1pm; 9hr); San Salvador (King Quality 2 daily, 3.30am & 11.30am; 11hr; Tica Bus 1 daily, 4.45am; 11hr; with Transnica 2 daily, 3.30am & 11.30pm; 10hr); Tegucigalpa (King Quality 2 daily, 3.30am & 11.30am; 9hr; Tica Bus 1 daily, 5am; 8hr; Transnica 3 daily, 3.30am, 5am & 11.30am; 8hr).

GETTING AROUND

By bus Buses, generally labelled with a route number, cover the main city routes. The fares are dirt cheap (around C$5), but pickpocketing is common, so be alert. Fares are paid in cash, on board – use coins and smaller bills whenever possible. If unsure of your destination, ask the driver to point out stops, which are unmarked. Services start at 5am and continue until 10pm, becoming less frequent from about 6pm onwards. Useful buses include #109 (running from the *malecón* to Mercado Huembes), #110 (Mercado Israel Lewites, La UCA and Mercado Iván Montenegro) and #112 (Mercado Israel Lewites to the *malecón*).

By taxi Legitimate taxis have red-and-white striped licence plates and are officially registered. Cheap and plentiful, they will probably be your main mode of transport, with most trips costing around C$20–60 and the journey from Barrio Martha Quezada to the airport around C$150 (agree on a price before setting off and do your best to haggle, especially with taxis waiting at bus terminals). Drivers always like to have more than one passenger at a time, and will stop to pick up and drop off people en route – if travelling alone, it's safest to sit next to the driver (see box, p.457). Taxis will honk at you as a matter of course, whether you want one or not.

INFORMATION

Tourist information There is an under-stocked INTUR desk at the airport. The INTUR headquarters (Mon–Fri 8am–1pm & 2–5pm; ☎ 2254 5191, ⍟ intur.gob.ni) are in central Managua, one block west of the *Crowne Plaza*. The staff are well intentioned and some speak English, but don't have much in the way of hand-outs or information on accommodation or tours. You should be able to pick up a free map of the city, if available – for everything else, your hotel will probably be of far more use. You can also try the CIT office opposite, but it's much of the same.

ACCOMMODATION

Barrio Martha Quezada, where most international buses arrive, is the place for backpacker-friendly *hospedaje*-type accommodation; most places are scattered in the quiet streets on either side of the Tica Bus terminal. Elsewhere in the city, you'll find more secure and modern districts than Martha Quezada, notably in the relatively swish area around the Metrocentro.

BARRIO MARTHA QUEZADA AND AROUND

Apartamentos Los Cisneros One block north and one and a half blocks west of the Tica Bus terminal ☎ 2222 3535, ⍟ hotelloscisneros.com; map p.460. The sole upmarket option in the heart of Martha Quezada, offering bright standard rooms and chalet-style apartments with hot water, fridge, cooker and optional fan or a/c. It's an extra US$5 to use the kitchen appliances, but the fee is waived for stays of a week or more. Double US$26, two-person apartment US$40

Casa Castillo One block west and one and a half blocks north of Tica Bus ☎ 2222 2265; map p.460. Hospitable, family-run *hospedaje* with seven basic, clean rooms with private bath; those right at the back and upstairs are larger and quieter. US$14

Casa Gabrinma One block south and half a block east of Tica Bus ☎ 2222 6650; map p.460. Welcoming guesthouse with a chatty owner whose cute, vaguely monastic rooms – all with ceiling fans – are set around a series of leafy inner courtyards. US$10

Casa de Huespedes Santos One block north and one and a half blocks west of Tica Bus ☎ 2222 3713, ⍟ casadehuespedessantos.com.ni; map p.460. Big, ramshackle *hospedaje* that feels like a youth club when it's full and a shed when it's empty, with hammocks, easy chairs, funky art on the walls and an indoor patio with cable TV. Some of the 28 scruffy rooms are on the gloomy side – try to get one upstairs, where ventilation is better. All have ceiling fans, and some come with private bath. US$7

★ **Los Felipe** One and a half blocks west of Tica Bus ☎ 2222 6501, ⍟ hotellosfelipe.com.ni; map p.460. This clean, peaceful hotel has 27 clean and compact rooms nestled amid an urban jungle of foliage. All come with private bath and TV, and there's wi-fi and laundry available alongside optional a/c and a swimming pool (9am–5pm). US$15

Hostal Dulce Sueño One and a half blocks east of Tica Bus ☎ 2228 4125, ✉ hospedajedulcesueno@yahoo.es; map p.460. Helpful budget place in a secure courtyard. Try to get one of the two brighter upstairs rooms, which sit alongside a rooftop area with hammocks where you can squint over Martha Quezada's tin roofs and ponder your next excursion. There's a kitchen and fridge too. US$16

Hostal Palmerita One block west and half a block north of Tica Bus ☎ 2222 5956; map p.458. Simple, faded hostel that draws a mostly Nica clientele. Nothing special, but the seven rooms are a reasonable deal. Private bathrooms cost an extra US$2. US$16

ELSEWHERE IN THE CITY

Casa San Juan C Esperanza 560, behind La UCA ☎ 2278 3220, ✉ sanjuan@cablenet.com.ni; map p.458. Welcoming mid-range guesthouse in a quiet neighbourhood. The spotless rooms come with a/c, cable TV and well-equipped modern, private bathrooms. Breakfast is included and other meals are available with advance notice. The hotel is popular, so reserve in advance. US$55

Managua Backpackers Inn 100m south of the old *Chamán* nightclub, Los Robles ☎ 2267 0006, ⍟ managuahostel.com; map p.458. A well-located, friendly hostel with tidy dorms and private rooms, some with en-suite bathroom. The courtyard garden with a pool, shaded by a mango tree and surrounded by deck chairs

---

★ **TREAT YOURSELF**

Casa Naranja Planes de Altamira ☎ 2277 3403, ⍟ hotelcasanaranja.com; map p.458. Smart, quiet and charming upmarket option, its cool corridors dotted with furniture and musical instruments. Rooms have hot water and TVs, and some come with nice little outdoor areas too. Breakfast included. US$100

Casa Real Two blocks west and two blocks south of the Rotunda Rubén Darío ☎ 2278 3838, ⍟ casareal.com; map p.458. Spotless, family-run hotel with spacious, clean rooms (with TV, a/c and private bath) grouped around a leafy inner lounge with huge hammocks; the upstairs rooms are brighter, with balconies. Breakfast included. US$75

6

and hammocks, is tranquil, although the nearby nightlife can be noisy. There's a large communal kitchen and TV room, free wi-fi and laundry services. Dorm US$12, double US$29

Nicaragua Guest House Two blocks south and two and a half blocks west of Rotonda La Virgen ☎ 2249 8963, ⊚ 3dp.ch/nicaragua; map p.458. A small guesthouse in a good location for the airport and most buses, with basic rooms, all en suite with TV and a fan or a/c, and a cool courtyard garden. The upside is that it's a safe three-block walk away from the new Multicentro Las Americas shopping centre, the downside is the 11pm curfew. US$20

EATING

Wherever you walk in Managua – on the street, at the bus stop or even under a shady tree – you will find someone selling a drink or *comida corriente*. Good, cheap food on the hoof is also easy to get in any of the major markets – look out for *pupusas*, a Salvadoran concoction of cheese, tortillas, sauce and meat. Managua also has a surprisingly cosmopolitan selection of restaurants: Chinese, Spanish, Mexican, Japanese, Italian, Peruvian, North American – even vegetarian. Americanized fast food is virtually everywhere, but cafés are thin on the ground and tend to be frequented by expats and wealthier locals. As for picnic food and self-catering, well-stocked supermarket chains La Colonia and La Unión sell a large selection of local and imported food including organic produce. You can also buy a lot of the basics at local *pulperías*, small shops set up in people's houses. Fruit and vegetables are cheapest at the weekend markets, when the growers come into town to sell their produce.

BARRIO MARTHA QUEZADA AND AROUND

Café Mirna One block west and south of the Tica Bus terminal; map p.460. This compact, likeable, family-run place has become something of an institution over its thirty-year history, though the service can be uneven. Come for decent *típica* or gringo breakfasts, or the *comida casera* buffet (C$70) at lunchtime. Mon–Sat 6.30am–2pm, Sun 7am–2pm.

Café Tonallí Two blocks east and half a block south of Tica Bus; map p.460. Principally a bakery selling specialist breads (from C$30), with a few tables in a leafy garden where you can enjoy good breakfasts – muesli, fruit and yoghurt (C$45), fresh coffee (C$10) and croissants baked on the premises – plus healthy lunches like veggie lasagne and pesto. Daily 7am–noon.

Comida a la Vista Two blocks west of the Tica Bus station; map p.460. Definitive lunch-only buffet joint – the only thing bigger than the huge plates of satisfying *comida típica* (around C$80 with a drink) is the queue, which can sprawl from the busy counter through the restaurant hall

and out into the street. If the buzz of the main room isn't to your taste, try the pleasant area upstairs.

El Grillito Just north of the INTUR office; map p.460. There aren't too many spots in Martha Quezada that might tempt you in for both a meal and a drink: *El Grillito* won't win any prizes, but with bright murals, reasonably priced beers (C$25) and seafood and grilled meat (from C$100) served on its open terrace, it's a reasonable place to while away one of Managua's hot nights.

Licuados Ananda Next to the Montoya statue; map p.458. This restaurant and juice bar, set around a covered patio and garden, is a veritable oasis in Managua's concrete chaos. The varied veggie menu includes a good-value *plato del día*, nice bread and superb smoothies (C$40) – try the papaya. A meal plus drink will cost C$70–80.

Típico Doña Pilar One block east of *Casa de Huespedes Santos*; map p.458. Simple plastic chairs and a large grill set up on the sidewalk every evening, offering *quesadillas*, enchiladas and lip-smacking grilled chicken for a mere C$70 (drink included).

METROCENTRO AND AROUND

Casa del Café One block north of Carretera a Masaya, by the Mexican Embassy ⊚ casadelcafe.com.ni; map p.458. This branch of a local chain serves reasonable coffee (from C$30) and snacks (cheese croissant C$70); the draw is the foliage-shaded balcony, a rare bit of tranquillity in this achingly modern stretch of town. Mon–Fri 7am–9pm, Sat 8am–9pm, Sun 8am–4pm.

Pizzeria Valenti's One block east of *Domino's Pizza*, house no. 6 ☎ 2278 7474, ⊚ pizzavalenti.com; map p.458. The outside patio is a decent place to enjoy a thin-crust pizza – they're filling and good value considering the area. A meal and a beer will cost about C$150.

La Terraza Peruana Planes de Altamira No. 14, 150m south of *Ola Verde* ☎ 2278 0013, ⊚ laterrazaperuana.com; map p.458. Upmarket Peruvian restaurant with a relaxing shaded terrace. The tasty and substantial dishes include a dozen varieties of *ceviche*, Chinese chicken (C$115) and rice with seafood (C$269).

ELSEWHERE IN THE CITY

Las Brasas Around the corner from *Topkapi* ☎ 2277 5568, ⊚ restaurantelasbrasas.com; map p.458. The popular buffet lunch, serving good Nica food, is a bargain at C$92. Dinner is more expensive (around C$200), but it's worth coming for a drink (beer C$20–30). Wed is karaoke night; live music every Thurs.

Comedor Doña Marina Opposite the airport, one block east of *Las Mercedes Hotel*; map p.458. There's no sign, so look out for the blue-green *comedor* full of airport workers filling up on chicken, beef (both C$50) or whole fish (C$60), with piles of rice and plantain chips. Twice as filling and half the price of a sandwich at the airport.

La Original Taquiza Half a block west of La Virgen roundabout; map p.458. You can't miss this place right on the highway. It keeps expanding, but you can still expect to queue on a weekend for their tasty Mexican tacos (around C$125 for a filling portion). Daily 11am–midnight.

Topkapi Opposite the Alhambra cinema; map p.458. Simple fast food at a good price (beef with jalapeño sauce C$155, thin-crust pizza C$70, beer C$30). It's been open since 1974, so it must be doing something right.

DRINKING AND NIGHTLIFE

Managua's nightlife is given a shot in the arm with the continuing return of the "Miami Boys" – wealthy families who fled revolutionary Nicaragua – who have helped drive the demand for upmarket bars and discos. As well as the plusher options, the city offers a reasonable choice of cheaper places to drink and dance – most places only charge a few dollars cover and drinks are either included or cost around C$20–60. You can expect to hear merengue, salsa, reggaetón, pop, house and even Nica *rancho* music (not unlike American country). Most bars shut between midnight and 2pm, and clubs start filling up from 10pm – Saturday is the busiest evening of the week.

BARS

Art-Café Opposite the Las Palmas park ☎ 2607 5104; map p.458. A café/bar/cultural space, with a yummy Mexican menu on Sun (around C$68), as well as live music shows where you'll hear everything from reggae to heavy metal. Cover US$40–80.

El Caramanchel Three blocks south and half a block west of Plaza Inter ☎ 8931 4199; map p.458. Frequented by a lively international crowd, this "cultural bar" is decorated with Mexican tapestries, old beer ads and odd artworks. It hosts several live gigs a month as well as occasional poetry readings, theatre and photography exhibitions, but it's worth a visit just for a drink or for the tasty local food (from C$40). Free entry, beer from C$25. Wed–Sun 6pm–3am.

La Casa de Los Mejía Godoy Colonia Los Robles, opposite the *Crowne Plaza* ☎ 2222 6610, ⓦ losmejiagodoy.zonaxp .com; map p.460. The brainchild of Nicaraguan guitarist and song-writing brothers Luís Enrique and Carlos Mejía Godoy, this is a cultural centre and bar rolled into one. There's an art gallery, a CD/bookstore and a café/bar selling *comida típica* (around C$140). Thurs sees young local musicians jam, and if the brothers aren't performing on Fri & Sat, there's likely to be a quality replacement. Cover from C$200.

★ **Fandango** Half a block north of *La Terraza Peruana*, Planes de Altamira; map p.458. This is where the pros from Managua's dance schools come to let off steam. Grab a beer (C$33) and maybe some tapas (very limited menu; C$170) and watch in awe. Wed–Sat 3pm–2.30am.

El Panal Opposite the Universidad Nacional de Ingeniería, tucked away behind the copy shops in a disused container; map p.458. There's live music on Sat afternoons and Wed evenings, but it's worth popping in for a beer (C$24) any day to mingle with the young poets and writers of Managua. *Comida corriente* is less than C$100. Take a taxi. Mon–Sat until 11pm/midnight.

Pool Ocho Los Robles, behind the Casa Pellas building; map p.458. While visiting pool halls is not generally a good idea in Nicaragua, this one is safe and well lit. Bar food costs around C$130, beer C$35 and the pool tables cost C$40/30min – less than $2, but expensive enough to attract only serious players. Daily 2pm–1am.

Ruta Maya 150m east of the Montoya statue ☎ 2268 0698, ⓦ rutamaya.com.ni; map p.458. Long-standing cultural centre/bar that hosts a diverse cross section of the city's musical and artistic talent and tends to attract an older, more sophisticated crowd. Seating is outdoors under a big marquee; traditional Nica food is also available (C$100–200). Gig tickets are usually C$120. Open Thurs, Fri & Sat.

El Viajero C 9A, a block west of the Tica Bus terminal; map p.460. Your best bet for an unfussy beer or four (C$44/litre) in Barrio Martha Quezada. Expect cheesy Nica pop and some uproariously drunk locals.

Zona Hippos Av Gabriel Cardenal, a block west of the *Hilton Princess* hotel; map p.458. Not one bar but a whole street-full. The Americanized joints, including *Woody's* and *Hippos*, are good for the daily 5–7pm happy hour, but walk further down the street for some artier establishments. *El Tercer Ojo* has a good clothes shop out the back, *El Garabato*, opposite, offers a lunchtime buffet for less than C$100.

CLUBS

El Chamán 200m south of the *Tiscapa* restaurant, off Av Simón Bolívar ⓦ chamanbar.net; map p.458. One of the biggest clubs in town, and arguably the most iconic: it's built in the shape of a Maya pyramid. Caters to a younger crowd, with Latin, hip-hop and pop playing on the three nicely decorated floors. There's regular live music and the occasional rock-centric talent contests are worth a look. Ladies' night Thurs C$30 women, C$200 men (open bar on beer and rum for all). Wed & Fri C$50 (no open bar), Sat C$200 for men and women (open bar). Wed–Sat 8pm–4am.

Moods Second storey of the Galerías Santo Domingo; map p.458. Exclusive and swanky *Moods* has quality DJs spinning dance music, a vast range of drinks and a hip crowd (dress up, or getting in may be a hassle). Entry C$250. Wed–Sat 9pm–6am.

Q C 27 de Mayo; map p.460. Friendly, relaxed gay club, playing mainstream US and Latin pop, which can be heaving at the weekend. It's one of only three gay clubs in town: nearby *Lollipop* and *Tabú* have a similar vibe. Entry around C$100. Thurs–Sun from 9pm.

6

6

CINEMA AND THEATRE

Cinema Alhambra V.I.P. (see box above), Cinemark Metrocentro (☎ 2271 9037, ⓦ cinemarkca.com), Cinemas Inter in Plaza Inter (☎ 2222 5122), Cinemas Galerías in Galerías Santo Domingo (☎ 2276 5065). American blockbusters (usually with subtitles).

Teatro Nacional Rubén Darío ☎ 2222 7426, ⓦ tnrubendario.gob.ni; map p.459. One of the best theatres in Central America (see p.459), with a main auditorium seating 1200 people, exhibition space and occasional experimental theatre in the basement. Events are scheduled most weekends. Bus #109 stops right in front.

SHOPPING

Hispamer One block east, one block south and then one block east again from UCA ☎ 2270 4409, ⓦ hispamer.com .ni. The largest selection of academic, fiction and nonfiction titles (in Spanish) in Nicaragua. There's a small shelf of classic and modern English-language fiction too. Mon–Fri 9am–6pm, Sat 9am–noon.

Mercado Oriental A few blocks southeast of the old centre. A small, lawless city-within-a-city where you can buy just about anything, but need to keep a close eye on your pockets and an even closer eye on your back – Nicaraguans will tell you that this is one of the most dangerous places in the country. If you must go, take someone with you and leave your valuables in your hotel. In the streets around the entrance to the market are many shops selling furniture – including beautiful rocking chairs – and electrical goods.

Mercado Roberto Huembes Near the Carretera a Masaya in the south of the city. Safer than the Mercado Oriental to wander around, with an excellent crafts section. There's a huge range of hammocks – everything from a simple net one (C$140) to a luxury, two-person, woven cotton option (from C$800). Products made of leather and skins are in abundance, but choose carefully as

many of the species used are endangered. Paintings in the style of the artists' colony on the Solentiname islands are available here, along with many fine pen-and-ink drawings and abstract works. You can buy Nicaraguan cigars as well as pottery and wicker products (*mimbre*) such as baskets, mats, chairs and wall-hangings.

DIRECTORY

Banks Central banks that exchange foreign currency include Banpro and Bancentro, both on the Carretera a Masaya near the *Hotel Princess*, and BAC (Banco de América Central), Plaza España. ATMs accepting foreign cards (Visa, MasterCard and Cirrus) can be found at these banks and in most malls, as well as in many petrol stations and at the airport.

Embassies and consulates Canada, C El Nogal 25, Bolonia (☎ 2268 0433, ✉ managua@international.gc.ca); UK, one block north of the Military Hospital (☎ 2254 5454); US, km 5.5, Carretera Sur (☎ 2252 7100, ⓦ nicaragua.usembassy.gov).

Health Hospital Bautista, in Barrio Largaespada (☎ 2249 7070, ⓦ hospitalbautistanicaragua.com), is your main option; Hospital Metropolitano Vivian Pellas, km 9.75, Carretera a Masaya, 250m west (☎ 2255 6900, ⓦ metropolitano.com.ni), is more sophisticated and more expensive. Both are private, with 24hr emergency departments. Medco is one of the larger pharmacy chains, with branches at Bello Horizonte and Plaza España. Alternatively, try the 24hr pharmacy at the Hospital Bautista.

Immigration The main office is two blocks north of Los Semáforos de la Colonia Tenderí (Mon–Fri 8am–1pm; ☎ 2244 3989), and there's another in the Metrocentro and Multicentro Las Americas (Mon–Fri 10am–4pm, then 4–6pm for picking up passports only; Sat & Sun 10am–1pm; ☎ 2244 3989). All can renew visas (US$10 for thirty days).

Internet There are plenty of internet cafés around town – in Barrio Martha Quezada, try Sistema Internet, Av Williams Romero, one block north of Cine Dorado (C$12/ hr), or Internet Santos half a block away (C$12/hr).

Post office Palacio de Correos, Plaza de la Revolución (Mon–Fri 8am–1pm, Sat 8am–noon).

The northwest

Nicaragua's Pacific **northwest** is hot and dry, with grassy plains punctuated by dramatic volcanoes. The largest city in the northwest, and once the capital of Nicaragua, is **León**, the birthplace of the Sandinistas and a lively town with a dynamic tourist scene. The northwest's sweeping **coastline** is just as appealing, with surf beaches and breezes that relieve the sometimes vicious heat. **Chinandega** offers no such relief, but is a convenient base near the Honduran border.

LEÓN

The capital of Nicaragua until 1857, **LEÓN**, 90km northwest of Managua, is now a provincial city, albeit an energetic, architecturally arresting one. A significant element in the city's healthy buzz is the presence of the **National University** (the country's premier academic institution) and its large student population, swelled by the ranks of young people studying at León's various other colleges. León's colonial architecture is arguably as impressive as Granada's; there's also an impressive range of tours, an entertaining

backpacker scene and the best **art gallery** in the country.

Yet for all its buzz, León has a violent history. The original León was founded by Hernández de Córdoba in 1524 at the foot of Volcán Momotombo, where its ruins – now known as **León Viejo** (see p.472) – still lie. The city was moved northwest to its present-day location after León Viejo's destruction by an earthquake and volcanic eruption in 1609. In 1956, the first President Somoza was gunned down in León by the martyr-poet Rigoberto López Pérez. During the Revolution in the 1970s, the town's streets were the scene of several decisive battles between the Sandinistas and Somoza's forces, and many key figures in the Revolution either came from León or had their political start here. Although many

6

LEÓN

EATING
Asados Pelibuey	5
Café La Rosita	3
Cafetín San Benito	9
El Desayunazo	1
Hong Kong	11
Pan y Paz	8
Taquezal	12
Terraza Mediterraneo	2

DRINKING & NIGHTLIFE
El Alamo etc	7
Camaleón	4
La Olla Quemada	10
Vía Vía	6

ACCOMMODATION
Bigfoot	5
Chilli Inn	1
Hostal Guardabarranco	4
Hostal d'Oviedo	8
Hostel Sonati	2
Lazybones	3
La Tortuga Booluda	7
Vía Vía	6

Bus Terminal

Subtiava & Las Peñitas

Parque San Juan — Iglesia de San Juan

Laundry Express

Sanoti

La Recolección

Quetzaltrekkers

Bigfoot Tours

La Merced — UNAN

La Unión

Banpro supermarket (ATM)

Green Pathways

Casa Rigoberto López Pérez

INTUR

BAC (ATM)

Galería Héroes y Mártires

BDF (ATM)

Mausoleo Héroes y Mártires

Centro de Arte Fundación Ortiz-Guardián

Parque Rubén Darío

Parque Central

Mercado

CALLE CENTRAL RUBÉN DARÍO

Museo Archivo Rubén Darío

Museo de la Revolución de León

Cathedral

Va Pues

N

La Veinte Uno

La Antigua Iglesia San Sebastián

Río Chiquito

0	200
	metres

Managua & Discoteca Dilectus

years have passed since then, and most of the Sandinista graffiti has been painted over, the city continues to wear its FSLN heart on its sleeve: the street signs read "León: ciudad heroica – primera capital de la revolución", and a few fine examples of the city's famous murals remain.

León's heart is the **Parque Central**, which is shadowed by the largest cathedral in Central America. **Calle Central Rubén Darío** runs along the Parque's northern edge, cutting the city in two from east to west, while **Avenida Central** runs between the Parque and Cathedral north to south. Splendidly and unusually, León has street signs, though people will usually still give you directions in relation to a landmark.

Parque Central

The **Parque Central** lies at the intersection of Calle Central Rubén Darío and Avenida Central. Centring on a statue of General Máximo Jeréz guarded by four lions, it's visited by a constant stream of locals, street vendors and tourists. If you value your hearing, avoid the square at 7am and noon, when a ludicrously loud siren wails across the city – a throwback to the days when workers flocked in to León's booming cotton factories.

Cathedral

The city's most obvious attraction is its colossal **Cathedral** (open from sunrise to late evening), a gorgeous, battered, cream-coloured structure whose volcano-blackened turrets tower over the heart of León. Now a UNESCO World Heritage Site, the building was begun in 1747 and took more than a century to complete. You can climb up to the roof (Mon–Sat 8.30am–noon & 2–4pm, Sun 6.30–8am & 10.30am–5pm; US$2) for stunning views across to the surrounding volcanoes. Inside, don't miss the tomb of local hero **Rubén Darío**, Nicaragua's most famous writer and poet, which is guarded by a statue of a mournful lion.

Museo de la Revolución de León

On the western side of the park is one of the city's Sandinista strongholds, the **Museo de la Revolución de León** (daily 8am–5pm; C$30). You'll be shown around the airy, decaying building by an FSLN combat veteran, who'll talk you through the extensive collection of photos, articles and news clippings documenting the Revolution, its historical antecedents and its aftermath. It's an affecting tour, though you'll need some Spanish to make sense of things. You may be allowed onto the roof, which has cracking views of León.

Mausoleo Héroes y Mártires

The northeast corner of the Parque is home to the **Mausoleo Héroes y Mártires**, a star-shaped monument dedicated to those who died fighting for freedom during the civil war, surrounded by a large mural colourfully detailing Nicaragua's history from pre-Columbian times to the ending of the civil war.

La Recolección

Two blocks north and one block east of the Parque is one of Nicaragua's finest colonial churches, **La Recolección**, with a beautiful Mexican Baroque facade dating from 1786, and some fine mahogany woodwork inside.

Parque Rubén Darío

Followers of Nicaragua's second religion, poetry, might want to head for the **Parque Rubén Darío**, a block west of the Parque Central, which is home to a statue of the rather sombre-looking poet dressed in suit and bow tie.

Centro de Arte Fundación Ortiz-Guardián

Sitting on Calle Central Rubén Darío, a little to the west of Parque Rubén Darío, is the **Centro de Arte Fundación Ortiz-Guardián** (Tues–Sat 10am–6pm, Sun 8am–4pm; C$20, C$30 with guided tour), an expansive art gallery in two renovated colonial houses. The collection features an engrossing cross section of Latin American art, including pre-Hispanic and modern ceramics and some impressive modern art.

Museo Archivo Rubén Darío

A few blocks west of the Centro de Arte Fundación Ortiz-Guardián is the

RUBÉN DARÍO

Born in 1867 in a village outside Matagalpa, the writer **Rubén Darío** is one of Nicaragua's most famous sons. *Azul …*, published in 1888, became particularly influential and is often cited as a cornerstone for the birth of Spanish-language modernism. Nearly a century after his death in 1916, he remains one of the region's most influential poets.

Museo Archivo Rubén Darío (Mon–Sat 8am–noon & 2–5pm, Sun 8am–noon; donations requested), housed in a substantial León residence that was the home of the poet's aunt, Bernarda. Inside, the lovingly kept rooms and courtyard garden are home to wonderfully frank plaques detailing Darío's tempestuous personal life and diplomatic and poetic careers, along with personal possessions and commemorative items, such as Rubén Darío lottery tickets.

Galería Héroes y Mártires

The **Galería Héroes y Mártires** (Mon–Fri 9am–5pm, Sat 9am–noon; contributions welcome), a block north and half a block west of the Parque Central, houses wall after wall of simple, moving black-and-white photos of Nicaraguans (men and women, young and old) killed fighting for the Sandinista cause during the civil war.

La Veinte Uno

Three blocks south of the cathedral lie the ruins of **La Veinte Uno**, the National Guard's 21st garrison and scene of heavy fighting in April 1979. The garrison now houses two very different museums, which together go by the long-winded title of **Museo de Leyendas y Tradiciones Coronel Joaquín de Arrechada Antigua Cárcel de La Veinte Uno** (daily 8am–noon & 1–5pm; C$50). One half of the building houses a collection of ghoulish figures from Nicaraguan folklore, including a chariot-riding grim reaper and a giant crab, while the other focuses on the garrison's ugly past, with a small collection of revealing black-and-white photos taken during and after the Somoza era. Captions in Spanish document the torture that went on inside.

Subtiava

Four kilometres west of the city centre is the *barrio* of **Subtiava**, which long predates León and is still home to much of the city's indigenous population. It is also the site of one of the oldest **churches** in the country. Recently renovated, the small adobe building is not always open, but worth a visit if you're catching a bus to or from the beach at Las Peñitas (see p.471).

ARRIVAL AND INFORMATION

By bus Buses arrive at the anarchic, traffic-clogged terminal, eight blocks northeast of the centre, from where you can hop in a taxi (standard fare anywhere in town is C$20) or walk into town.

Destinations Chinandega (frequent; leaves when full; 50min); Estelí (3 daily; 2hr 30min); Guasaule (1 daily, 4am; 3hr 30min); Las Peñitas (14 daily; 50min); Managua (every 15min; 1hr 15min–2hr); Matagalpa (3 daily; 3hr); San Isidro (for more frequent Matagalpa and Estelí connections; 24 daily; 2hr).

Tourist information INTUR, 2A Av NO (Mon–Fri 8am–1pm), has a few leaflets and maps and general tour information – the hostels and tour companies are usually more helpful.

ACCOMMODATION

Budget accommodation in León has really taken off in the last few years, and there is now an abundance of good-value hostels.

Bigfoot Av 2 NE ☎ 8917 8832, ⓦ bigfootnicaragua.com. Opposite *Vía Vía*, this sociable place is popular with a

THE GIGANTONA OF SUBTIAVA

In November and December, be sure not to miss the posses of young boys hammering away at snare drums while a huge **Gigantona** (a papier-mâché, Rio Carnaval-style figure of an elegant colonial-era woman, directed from underneath by a teenager) weaves among them. Traditionally, the boys are given a few córdobas for a recital of poetry, typically that of national bard Rubén Darío. The gigantonas are judged during the festivities of La Purísima (a festival celebrating the Virgin Mary's conception) on December 7, with the best winning a prize.

TOURS IN LEÓN

As you might expect from a backpacker-friendly city with volcanoes, beaches and mangroves within striking distance, León is packed with tour operators. The headline activity is **volcano-boarding**, in which you'll truck off to the ash-covered slopes of Cerro Negro early in the morning, spend a good hour slogging up its alien, gas-belching curves and then skid down on a board that generally moves at a fairly gentle pace despite the fierce gradient, although some boards are faster – and damp days can be especially quick. Almost every operator offers it – Quetzaltrekkers give you two runs (most operators only offer one), Bigfoot are allegedly the fastest and Va Pues offer some proper (if battered) snowboards.

Trips from León can also take in the wet ride through the canyon at **Somoto**, near the Honduran border, treks up the **San Cristóbal and El Hoyo volcanoes**, the ruins of **León Viejo** (see p.472) and more; and Spanish lessons can be arranged. Rates for excursions are a fairly standard US$30 per day, and are given on companies' websites, though you may be able to haggle, especially with a larger group. The companies below are all established and reliable.

Bigfoot Tours *Bigfoot* hostel, Av 2 NE ☎ 8917 8832, ⌨ bigfootnicaragua.com. Fun firm mostly focusing on volcano-boarding and surf trips to Isla Los Brasile, though other trips can be arranged.

Green Pathways Av 2 NE ☎ 2315 0964, ⌨ greenpathways.com. Country-wide adventures, including turtle-watching and volcano-scaling.

Quetzaltrekkers 2A C NE ☎ 2311 6695, ⌨ quetzaltrekkers.com. Friendly, reliable bunch offering volcano treks around the country, including a full-moon lava hike up Volcán Telica. All profits go towards supporting street children in León. Food and drink is included in tour prices. Sun & Mon 2–6pm; Tues–Sat 10am–6pm.

Sonati 3A C NE ☎ 2311 4251, ⌨ sonati.info. Relatively inexpensive non-profit-making company, operating from the hostel of the same name, whose volcano trips are supplemented by visits to the swamps of Isla Juan Verano and various birdwatching trips.

Va Pues 2A C SO ☎ 2315 4099, ⌨ vapues.com. This moderately upmarket operator has country-wide tours, trips to local fincas and – of course – volcano-boarding.

younger backpacker crowd. The huge dorms are fairly clean, and there's a large kitchen and a small foot-shaped pool. The pleasant veggie café has breakfasts at C$60. Dorm US$6, double US$13

Chilli Inn 1 Av NO ⌨ chilliinn.com. The self-styled "Party Hostel in León", doing their damnedest to live up to the title. Every guest gets two free cocktails, and there are nightly activities from free salsa classes to pub crawls in an old VW van. Free wi-fi. US$6

Hostal Guardabarranco Av 2 NE ☎ 2311 7124, ⌨ hostalguardabarranco.net Just a few doors up from *Bigfoot* and *Vía Vía*, but much quieter, this clean, family-run place offers the best of both worlds – you can party down the street, and still get a good night's sleep. Free wi-fi and use of kitchen. Dorm US$6, double US$17

Hostal d'Oviedo Av 1 SO ☎ 2311 3766. Small, quiet hostel downhill from the town centre with friendly Nica owners and a homely front room with easy chairs. There's wi-fi, a kitchen and a fridge too. Dorm US$7, double US$18

Hostel Sonati 3A C NE ☎ 2311 4251, ⌨ sonati.info. Non-profit hostel linked to the tour operator of the same name, with animal-themed rooms and dorms, a flower-filled courtyard, a kitchen and a quieter atmosphere than some places in town. Dorm US$5, double US$15

Lazybones Av 2 NO ☎ 2311 3472, ⌨ lazybonesleon.com. The clean and comfortable dorms at this large hostel are arranged around an airy courtyard with hammocks and a pool table, while the mellow back-courtyard boasts a swimming pool. The doubles and triples are pretty good too – try to get one of the upstairs rooms with a balcony. There's free organic coffee and tea, plus wi-fi. Dorm US$8, double US$20

★ **La Tortuga Booluda** 1A C SO ☎ 2311 4653, ⌨ tortugabooluda.com. Great little hostel that's a lovely place to relax during the day as well as lay your head down at night. Just a few blocks from the centre, it still feels set apart, and the free pancake breakfasts, kitchen facilities, wi-fi and pool table complete the package. Dorm US$7, double US$18

Vía Vía Av 2 NE ☎ 2311 6142, ⌨ viaviacafe.com. Opposite *Bigfoot*, and just as popular. The on-site bar and restaurant are probably the biggest draws of this Belgian-owned branch of the hostel chain, but the tiled colonial corridors also hold two reasonable dorms and some pleasant private rooms. Dorm US$7, double US$19

EATING

León boasts a cosmopolitan and ever-increasing range of places to eat and drink, from pizza joints and seafood restaurants to chic café-bars and bohemian hangouts. Most of the restaurants close around 10pm, while the trendier places stay open until the small hours, especially at weekends.

★ TREAT YOURSELF

Terraza Mediterraneo 2A Av NO. Recently refurbished, never-ending restaurant with comfy sofas and a huge open-air seating area out back. You don't have to spend a fortune (pizzas C$100–390), but If you're in the mood for a treat try the lobster flambé in brandy (C$400) followed by the Belgian chocolate dessert (C$95). They also have a good wine list and a range of cocktails (C$50–210) – for a very special occasion, a bottle of Moët & Chandon Imperial will set you back C$3200. Mon & Wed–Sun 5.30pm–midnight.

Asados Pelibuey 2A Av NO. A handful of tables and platefuls of delicious chicken, beef and other *comida corriente* (from C$50) at this excellent little place, run by a women's co-operative.

Café La Rosita Av Central. It's worth getting a coffee here just for the views from the roof terrace. Free wi-fi, lunch and a *fresco* C$80. Mon–Sat 7.30am–9pm.

Cafetín San Benito 2A Av NE. Tasty juices and a solid buffet will set you back a paltry C$30 in the café out front or courtyard out back. There's Chinese food (from C$40) too. Closed Sun.

El Desayunazo 2A Av NO. This green-tabled front room, half colonial elegance, half greasy spoon, serves decent grub to gringos. Nica breakfast C$45, English breakfast C$95. Daily 6am–noon.

Hong Kong 1A C SO. Choose between reasonably priced Nica grub (chicken and pork plates will set you back C$50–80) and salty-but-filling Chinese dishes (chop suey C$65). Closed Mon.

Pan y Paz 1A C NO ⓦpanypaz.com. The French owner grew up in a bakery, and you won't find better bread in Nicaragua. Prices are reasonable (quiche and salad C$60, sandwiches from C$45, coffee from C$8), and there's free wi-fi and a relaxing courtyard where you can while away the afternoon. Mon–Sat 7am–7pm.

Taquezal 1A C SO. Rustic but stylish café-bar with candlelit tables and a good menu featuring decent vegetarian pasta dishes, Chinese food, wonderful iced tea with lemon and a fine selection of espresso drinks. Mains from C$70. It gets dancier later in the evening, when you may have to pay a C$50 cover charge. Closed Sun.

DRINKING AND NIGHTLIFE

León is second only to Managua in the party stakes, thanks in large part to its many students, and Fridays and Saturdays are usually fairly happening. Most of the restaurants are good for a beer too.

El Alamo/Don Señor/La Cabaña/El Mirador 1A Av NO. Not one, not two, but (confusingly) four bars in one! Choose a different entrance to the same building and you could find yourself in a sports bar, chill-out room, karaoke bar, or disco. The best bet for food is the sports bar, *El Alamo*, where you can get a reasonable steak (C$135) and beer (C$26).

Camaleón 2A C NE. León's after-party spot. It's not the classiest place, but when everywhere else closes you can head here and carry on dancing and drinking (beer C$30) till daybreak.

★ La Olla Quemada C Central Rubén Darío ⓦlaollaquemada.com. You'll find big speakers and a lively, mostly local crowd at this scruffily funky bar, which is busiest on Wed (live music), Thurs (Salsa night) and Sun (films).

Vía Vía 2A Av NE. The bar-restaurant at this popular hostel is regularly full, especially when there's live music (every Fri) or a quiz night (fortnightly Mon). Its selling point is its lively atmosphere (complete with pool table) but they also do decent Mexican and European food (mains from C$70, breakfast from C$45).

DIRECTORY

Banks There's a cluster of banks on the corner of 1 C NE and 1A Av, all with ATMs.

Internet There are scores of internet cafés: CyberFlash .com, opposite *Vía Vía*, has a quick connection (C$10/hr) and can also burn pictures from your camera to disk.

Language schools Most of the hostels and tour companies, including Va Pues (see box opposite), offer lessons and homestays; Nicaragua Spanish Language Schools (ⓦnicaraguaspanishschools.org) are an established institution.

Laundry Most hostels will wash clothes, or try the friendly Laundry Express, Av Central & 4A C NO (C$145/ large load).

Post office 3 Av NO, C 3–4.

AROUND LEÓN

Worthwhile day-trip destinations from León include the Pacific beach of **Las Peñitas**, west of the city and easily accessible by bus, and more out-of-the-way UNESCO World Heritage Site of **León Viejo**.

Las Peñitas and Poneloya

Surfers come to **Las Peñitas**, 20km west of León, for reliable Pacific waves, although the village's relaxed vibe is enjoyable whether you're bound for board or hammock. The water here is fairly

6

rough, due to a combination of powerful waves and riptides, but you can swim reasonably safely. **Poneloya**, 2km north, is a different story: ask locals about riptides (*corrientes peligrosos*) before venturing into the water, and never swim alone. Nearby **Isla Juan Venado** is a nature reserve and turtle-nesting site.

ARRIVAL AND DEPARTURE

Most travellers come to Las Peñitas as a day-trip from León. Buses leave León's Terminal Poneloya (see p.469) every hour (until 6pm; 55min). The last bus back to León leaves at 6.45pm. A taxi will cost around US$12.

ACCOMMODATION AND EATING

Accommodation in town is limited, but there are several simple places right on the black-sand beach. Both *Barco de Oro* and *Quetzal Playa* offer surfboard rental and can help arrange fishing trips and excursions to Isla Juan Venado.

Barco de Oro On the beach ☎ 2317 0275, ⍟ barcadeoro .com. Formerly a nightclub frequented by Somoza, this place is now a tranquil travellers' haven. The basic rooms have rustic wooden beds, en-suite bathrooms and a lovely upstairs balcony for sunset-watching. There's quality seafood on offer in the restaurant. Dorm US$7, double US$24

Quetzal Playa Hostel On the beach ☎ 2317 0260, ⍟ playa.quetzaltrekkers.org. Linked to a non-profit tour operator and run by volunteers, offering new, airy dorms with a/c (for an extra charge). Dorm US$7, double US$27

Surfing Turtle Lodge Isla Los Brasiles, just across from Poneloya beach ☎ 8905 3237, ⍟ surfingturtlelodge.com. The main draw here is to see sea turtles lay their eggs, so check if it is the right time of year. It's well signposted in Poneloya – you need to get the boat (US$1) from next to *Chepe's* bar (clean, reasonably priced and friendly). Camping (tent provided) per person US$5, dorm US$10, double US$30

León Viejo

Founded in 1524, **León Viejo** (Mon–Fri 9am–5pm, Sat & Sun 9am–4pm; C$45), 32km east of the modern city and now designated a UNESCO World Heritage Site, was the original site of León, before it was destroyed by an earthquake and volcanic eruption on December 31, 1609. Among the ruins excavated since the site's discovery in 1967 are a cathedral, monastery and church; the graves of Nicaragua's first three bishops and of the country's founder, **Francisco Fernández de Córdoba**, were also

uncovered. It's a modest site, although a wander around the half-restored buildings and accompanying plaques gives you a good idea of just how bloody Nicaragua's colonial history was. The surroundings are almost as fun: for much of the year the woods are rich with birds and butterflies, and the old fort, located just east of the main ruins, offers tremendous views of Lago de Managua and brooding Volcán Momotombo.

ARRIVAL AND DEPARTURE

Unless you visit with a tour, getting to the site is half the fun. You'll first need to head to La Paz Centro, a village about 60km north of Managua – buses leave León every 30min or so. Some will drop you off on the motorway just outside town: from there get a motorized rickshaw to La Paz Centro's bus terminal for a few córdobas. Buses run (roughly hourly) from the terminal via various small villages to the site itself, which sits a few hundred metres from the route's terminus, Puerto Momotombo. The total journey there can take anything from 90min to double that – set off early.

CHINANDEGA

CHINANDEGA, 35km northwest of León, is primarily a working city. Set on a plain behind looming Volcán San Cristóbal, the area's dry, kiln-like climate is ideal for growing cotton, the area's main economic activity, along with Flor de Caña **rum**, Nicaragua's export-grade tipple, produced in a distillery on the outskirts of town. Chinandega is generally visited on the way to the Honduran border and, with wildlife-rich volcanoes nearby and a decidedly untouristed vibe, it's not a bad place to stop off. Most action centres on the **Parque Central**, which has an odd miniature fort at its centre, and Parroquia Santa Ana, a faded but peaceful church opposite its northern end.

The **coast west** of here is truly beautiful and unspoilt, with great surfing and kayaking. There is some laidback accommodation in the village of **Jiquilillo** – check out ⍟ rancho-esperanza.com.

ARRIVAL AND DEPARTURE

By bus Buses arrive at the market southeast of the centre. Destinations Guasaule (regular service, leaving when full; 1hr); Jiquilillo (5 daily from the El Mercadito terminal – get

---

INTO HONDURAS: GUASAULE

Crossing into **Honduras** via **Guasaule** can be chaotic. You'll get a fair bit of attention from touts – you will usually get better rates closer to the border, so if you are changing cash, it's worth waiting. You can get buses here from Chinandega and there may be a direct service from Managua – ask at your accommodation. The exit tax is currently US$2 (it's US$10 to enter Nicaragua), and the border post is open 24 hours.

It's just under 1km between the Nicaraguan border post and the Honduran side, across an impressive bridge, and it's easily walkable, though you'll be repeatedly offered bicycle taxis (C$20) from Guasaule bus station. From the border there's a direct bus to Tegucigalpa every 2hr.

There's another crossing at **El Espino**, which is connected to the small town of Somoto by frequent buses. Somoto, home to a smattering of accommodation and a canyon (which you can visit on tours from León and Estelí), is served by regular buses from Estelí and hourly departures from Managua's Mercado Mayoreo. Border fees are standard and the crossing relatively quiet.

---

a taxi from the main terminal; 1hr 30min); León (every 15min; 1hr 30min); Managua (every 20min; 1hr 40min–2hr 30min).

INFORMATION

Banks There are several ATMs, including a BAC a block east and half a block south of the Parque Central.

Tourist information There's an INTUR office (Mon–Fri 8am–1pm) opposite the BAC, where you can get info on climbing volcanoes and visiting the area's quiet beaches. Don Alvaro at *Hotel Casa Grande* can organize walking trips to San Cristóbal (US$25/person) and a stay in his family farm on its slopes. Ibis Kayaking (☎8961 8548, ⊕ibiskayaking.com) offer trips for a day or more to the spectacular mangrove estuaries of the Padre Ramos reserve, on the coast to the west of Chinandega.

ACCOMMODATION

Don Mario Two blocks north and one block east of the Parque Central ☎2341 4054. This lovely, relaxing little place is the best option in town, with welcoming rooms, neat en suites, wi-fi and a shared kitchen. **US$19**

Hotel Casa Grande A block and a half east of the Parque Central ☎8266 0184. Basic, cheap rooms above a friendly family home (laundry service available). Owner Don Alvaro is a good bet for tours (see above). **US$15**

EATING AND DRINKING

The competing sound systems of a series of bars at the northeast end of the Parque Central play everything from folk laments to Euro pop, and are your best bet for an evening drink.

Fritanga La Parrillada One block south of the Parque Central. Classic *comida corriente* café, its deliciously smoky meats cooked on a barbecue on the pavement. Meal and drink C$65 at lunchtime.

★ **"The Shawarma place"** Northeast corner of the Parque Central. This place doesn't actually have a name, but it's a word-of-mouth favourite, so ask around. Delicious kebab chicken with salad and chips, all wrapped up in a giant flour tortilla for only C$50. Sit in or outside where you can watch all the comings and goings in the park.

The central highlands

North of Managua, the **central highlands** sweep up from sea level in a lush procession of mountainous hillsides, bright-green coffee plantations and cattle-flecked alpine pastures, stretching north to the Honduran border and east to the jungles and mines of the interior. The climate here is fairly temperate and the soil productive, with plenty of tobacco plantations and an economy based on coffee, grains, vegetables, fruit and dairy farming. The 150km journey north from Managua to **Estelí**, the northeast's largest city, is one of the most inspiring in the country, as the Carretera Interamericana winds through the grassy Pacific plains, skirting the southern edge of Lago de Managua before climbing slowly into a ribbon of blue mountains. East of here is **Matagalpa**, a town of steep slopes and coffee shops, while around the two sit fincas and reserves that merit deeper exploration.

ESTELÍ

The largest town in the north, at first sight **ESTELÍ** can seem downtrodden. But this low-key city is an engaging place and

6

ESTELÍ

Texaco Star Mart & Miraflor Nature Reserve ▲

EATING

Café Luz	3
La Casita	9
Coffe Café	6
Licuados Ananda	5
Mocha Nana Café	7
Pa'Pikar	1
El Quesito	4
El Rincón Pinareño	8
Vuela Vuela	2

ACCOMMODATION

Los Arcos	1
Hospedaje Chepito	7
Hospedaje Luna	2
Hostal Sonati	4
Hostal Tomabú	6
Miraflor	3
Sacuanjoche	5

El Salto de la Estnzuela & Bus Terminals ▼

a hotbed of political activity. Notorious for its staunchly leftist character, Estelí saw heavy fighting and serious bloodshed during the Revolution. Somoza bore a particular grudge against the town's inhabitants, and waged brutal offensives on the city. The scars have not really healed, either on the bombed-out buildings that still dot the streets or in people's minds, and the region remains a centre of Sandinista support.

Estelí's relatively rural setting makes it a good base for trips. **El Salto de la Estanzuela** – a secluded waterfall within walking distance of the centre – makes for a great day out, while the wonderful **Miraflor nature reserve** is just under 30km away.

WHAT TO SEE AND DO

Although Estelí lacks the stunning mountain views of Matagalpa, the centre of town is a nice place to wander, and the climate is refreshingly cool. Much of the pleasure lies in soaking up the atmosphere, particularly along **Avenida Central**, whose southern end sees shops' wares spill out onto the street, including cowboy boots and the local farmers' favourite, Western-style hats.

Parque Central

The town's **Parque Central** isn't as nice as some others in the country, but is nonetheless busy from dawn until dusk. The **cathedral** on the eastern side of the Parque has a rather austere facade but an interesting interior, with bright windows and lots of artwork. The south side of the Parque is dominated by the **Centro Recreativo Las Segovias**, which puts on regular music and sporting events, particularly basketball games.

Galería de Héroes y Mártires

Just south of the Parque Central is the tiny **Galería de Héroes y Mártires** (officially daily 9am–5pm but can be sporadic; C$20), a simple yet moving museum devoted to the Revolution and to the many residents of Estelí who died fighting in it. The women who work at the Galería are, for the most part, mothers and widows of soldiers who were killed.

Casa de Cultura

The **Casa de Cultura** (☎ 2713 3021), a cultural venue a block south of Parque Central, hosts local art exhibitions, dancing and music events. Across the street, the **Artesanía Nicaragüense** has a reasonable selection of crafts, pottery and cigars.

ARRIVAL AND DEPARTURE

By bus Estelí has two bus terminals: Cotran Sur, at the southern entrance to town, serves destinations south of Estelí, while Cotran Norte, 100m north, serves destinations north of Estelí, plus most express buses to León and one daily Managua bus. Some buses may also drop you at the Shell Estelí or the Shell Esquipulas (in true Nica style, they are no longer Shell garages, but the name is still used to give directions). You can also catch buses to the Miraflor reserve (see p.477).

Destinations León (3 daily from Cotran Norte; 1 daily, 6.45am from Cotran Sur; 2hr 30min; alternatively, get on any bus to Matagalpa and get off at San Isidro); Managua (15 daily from Cotran Sur; 2–3hr); Masaya (2 daily, 2pm & 3pm from Cotran Norte; 2hr 30min); Matagalpa (every 30min from Cotran Norte; 1hr 45min); Ocotal (12 daily from Cotran Norte; 2hr).

By taxi A taxi into town from any of the main bus stops should cost around C$10–15 per person.

INFORMATION AND TOURS

Tour operators UCA Miraflor, Av 4 NE, C 4 NE (☎ 2713 2971, ⓦ miraflor.org), can, in theory, arrange accommodation in the Miraflor reserve (see p.477) and give you information on getting there independently. The friendly TreeHuggers (☎ 8496 7449), based in *Hospedaje Luna* (see below), is a better option, with more English spoken. They can arrange homestays with local families in Miraflor, offer general advice, bike rental, information on Spanish classes and cigar tours and can also help organize trips to other destinations including the canyon at Somoto, near the Honduran border.

Tourist information INTUR, C1 NE (Mon–Fri 8am–1pm; ☎ 2713 2468, ⓔ esteli@intur.gob.ni), has some information on transport links and tours.

Banks There's a bank on every corner of C Transversal and Av 1 SO.

Internet There are plenty of places in town; try Cyber on Av 1 SE (C$10/hr; Mon–Sat 8am–6pm).

ACCOMMODATION

Budget accommodation is mostly on the simple side, with a few decent options around the Parque Central and the real cheapies clustered around the scruffy shopping streets to the south.

Hospedaje Chepito Av Central ☎ 2713 3784. Small, family-run *hospedaje* with decent camp beds and clean concrete floors. The rooms are a bit cell-like, but this is the best cheapie in town. US$5

★ **Hospedaje Luna** Av 2 NE ☎ 8441 8466, ⓦ cafeluzyluna.com. Estelí's main backpacker hostel is a likeable place with a social conscience and what is probably the town's most useful information office ("TreeHuggers") within its walls. The dorms and private rooms are clean, if basic, there's a good book exchange and wi-fi and the associated *Café Luz*, opposite, is a decent hangout too. Dorm US$7, double US$25

Hostal Sonati 3 blocks east of the Cathedral ☎ 2713 6043, ⓦ sonati.org. Non-profit organization with another hostel in León. New, clean dorms, plus doubles with private bathroom and hot water. Dorm US$6, double US$25

Hostal Tomabú Av Central ☎ 2713 3783, ⓔ hostal tomabu.esteli@gmail.com. With its bright courtyard, towel-toting rooms and pot plants, this feels a cut above its nearby rivals. US$18

Miraflor Av Central ☎ 2713 2003. Small hotel with homely, terracotta-coloured rooms, overhead fan and decent bathroom. There's also a restaurant and bar on site. It's a good deal, especially if you're travelling in a group (a five-bed room costs US$30). US$18

Sacuanjoche Av 1 SE ☎ 2713 2482. Bright rooms with comfy beds, tiled floors, clean bathrooms and varnished wooden ceilings, all set around a pretty patio just south of the centre. US$12

★ TREAT YOURSELF

Los Arcos Av 1 SE ☎ 2713 3830, ⓦ familiasunidas.org/arcos/introduction .htm. Nice, businesslike hotel with a great central location that's a good bet if you fancy a spot of mild luxury. Breakfast is included, a/c is available, and there's a series of courtyards and terraces in which to relax. Profits go to helping disadvantaged young people, too. US$45

EATING

Café Luz Av 2 NE ⓦ cafeluzyluna.com. Civilized tourist den, and a good place to socialize. Most produce is organic and grown by local co-operatives, and everything is on offer, from good black coffee (C$10), yoghurt (C$18) and *nacatamales* (C$45) to juices and beer.

La Casita 5min walk past the hospital on the right. Right on the southern edge of town, and a convenient stop if you're visiting El Salto, this charming café has beautifully carved tables, a botanic garden out back and some fairly slow service. Sit by the tinkling stream (surprisingly tranquil despite the nearby motorway), snack on small loaves of bread with honey (C$21) and drink lassis (C$16), pots of chai (C$20) and the like.

Coffe Café C Transversal. Simple coffee shop serving sandwiches and other light snacks. One of the best places in town for breakfast (plate of fresh fruit C$60).

Licuados Ananda C Transversal. Arranged, rather surreally, around a disused swimming pool, this relaxing outdoor café has mostly veggie mains (dish of the day C$50, smoothies C$22), a reasonable range of smoothies and filling breakfasts.

Mocha Nana Café C Transversal ☎ 2713 3164. This laid-back café, with outdoor seating, is one of the few places in the country you can get a decent cup of real English tea (C$25). Frequent live music at the weekend – look out for posters around town. Panini C$60, bagel with hummus C$40.

Pa'Pikar 2 blocks north of the Cathedral. Eccentric, colourful place serving sandwiches, gyros, curly fries and all sorts of treats you won't find elsewhere (C$30–70). Mid-afternoon till late.

El Quesito 2 blocks east of the Cathedral ☎ 2713 0547. Try local dairy-based specialities, such as *quesillo* (string cheese) and *cuajada* (curd cheese), as well as the ubiquitous tacos and *nacatamales*. Breakfasts C$15–50; lunch C$70–90; supper C$45–50. Yoghurt (C$25) and other treats also available to take away.

★ **El Rincón Pinareño** Av 1 SE. Popular Cuban restaurant, serving filling sandwiches with chips and well-cooked steaks (C$70–200). Head upstairs for a balcony seat. Closed Mon.

Vuela Vuela Corner of C 3 NE & Av 1. This bright café-bar and separate restaurant is an NGO initiative, with profits going to help disadvantaged youths back into the job market. The menu veers from Spanish (seafood paella C$320) to American (cheeseburger C$70), and the coffee (C$20) is pretty decent.

AROUND ESTELÍ

Estelí is blessed with beautiful natural surroundings, some – like the appealing waterfall of **El Salto de la Estanzuela** – an

INTO HONDURAS: LAS MANOS

The **Las Manos** border crossing for **Honduras** is less busy and less hassle-prone than the trip via Guasaule (see box, p.473). The exit fee is US$2; there is a US$10 fee to enter Nicaragua. The post is open 24hr, but vehicles can only cross between 8am and 5pm. To get here, take one of the regular buses from Managua or Estelí to the small town of Ocotal, and change for the bus to Las Manos (every 45min; 30min). Continuing on, there are regular buses from Las Manos to the nearest town, El Paraíso (every 30min; 30min), where buses leave to Tegucigalpa (every 15min). There are two direct buses a day from the border to Tegucigalpa (9.20am & 2.20pm).

easy day-trip. The gorgeous **Miraflor** reserve to the north is worth staying in for a night or more.

El Salto de la Estanzuela

El Salto de la Estanzuela is one of the few waterfalls in Nicaragua easily accessible on foot from a major centre of population. Located in the **Reserva Natural Tisey-Estanzuela**, it's reached on a lovely two-hour walk through green, rolling hills – although it's also possible to drive right to the foot of the falls. The path begins just beyond the hospital at the southern edge of town – it's a fairly dull forty-minute walk to get here, and you may want to get a bus (C$4) from the eastern end of the Parque Central. Turn right at the *Kiosko Europeo* and follow the path around to the left for 4km or so until you see a sign for "Comunidad Estanzuela"; go through the gate on the right-hand side and follow the path for another 1km (you can cut off early if you want to explore the lovely but litter-strewn stretch above). The falls themselves – 35m or so in height – are located at the bottom of a steep flight of steps and cascade spectacularly into a deep pool perfect for swimming in. Don't go directly underneath the falling water as rocks do occasionally fall down, especially after heavy rainfall. Nearby is **El Mirador**, one of the most spectacular viewpoints in all Nicaragua; on a clear day it's possible to see volcanoes as far away as El Salvador.

Miraflor nature reserve

The wonderful **Miraflor nature reserve**, 28km northeast of Estelí, covers 206 square kilometres of forest, part of which is farmed by a group of agricultural co-ops – more than five thousand locals currently produce coffee, potatoes, milk, cheese and exotic flowers in and around the protected area. One of the project's main aims is to find sustainable ways in which farming and environmental protection can coexist; the emphasis is firmly upon community-centred tourism.

The reserve itself comprises several different **ecosystems**, ranging from savanna to tropical dry forest and humid cloudforest. To best appreciate this diversity it's advisable to stay for at least two or three days, either walking or horseriding between the zones and staying with different families each night – a very satisfying back-to-basics experience. Guides can take you to waterfalls, swimming spots, viewpoints, flower gardens and caves once inhabited by the ancient Yeluca and Cebollal mountain peoples. In terms of flora and fauna, Miraflor is one of the richest reserves in the country, with over three hundred species of bird including quetzal, *guardabarranco* (the national bird of Nicaragua) and *urraca*, a local type of magpie, as well as howler monkeys and reclusive mountain lions. There are also over two hundred species of orchid.

ARRIVAL AND INFORMATION

By bus To get to the reserve, take a bus from Estelí. For El Coyolito, La Pita and El Cebollal, all villages within the reserve, head to the Texaco Star Mart (on the Interamericana just north of the centre – any taxi can take you) for 6am or 1pm; for Yalí, La Rampla or Puertas Azules, head to Cotran Norte for 6am, noon or 3pm.

Guides and accommodation UCA Miraflor and *Hospedaje Luna* in Estelí (see p.475) can arrange your trip and advise you on different areas' strengths. Both can book good, Spanish-speaking local guides (C$15 per group) and accommodation (C$15 for three starchy but delicious meals a day, plus a bed in a farmhouse). Due to the altitude, it gets chilly on an evening – come prepared.

MATAGALPA

Known as "La Perla del Septentrión" – "Pearl of the North" – **MATAGALPA** is spoken well of by most Nicaraguans, principally, perhaps, because of its relatively cool climate: at about 21–25°C, it's considered *tierra fría* in this land of 30°C-plus temperatures. Located 130km northeast of the capital, this small, quiet town is a gateway to the blue-green mountains and coffee plantations that surround it, whether you fancy a short hike into the hills or a longer trip to fincas like the famous **Selva Negra** to the north.

WHAT TO SEE AND DO

Matagalpa's services, hotels and restaurants are spread out between the seven blocks that divide the town's two principal squares: **Parque Morazán** to the north and the smaller **Parque Darío** seven blocks to the south. The town's

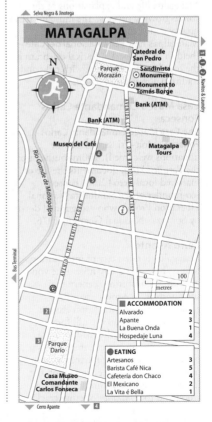

ACCOMMODATION	
Alvarado	2
Apante	3
La Buena Onda	1
Hospedaje Luna	4

EATING	
Artesanos	3
Barista Café Nica	5
Cafetería don Chaco	4
El Mexicano	2
La Vita é Bella	1

6

main thoroughfares, **Avenida José Benito Escobar** and **Avenida Central**, link the two.

Parque Morazán

At the northern end of town, sunny **Parque Morazán** fronts the **Catedral de San Pedro**, dating from 1874. Unusually, the cathedral was constructed side-on, with its bell towers and entrance facing away from the Parque. A large **Sandinista monument**, consisting of three men firing guns, stands on one corner of the eastern side, with a monument to *Matagalpino* Tomás Borge, one of the founders of the Sandinista party, on the opposite corner.

Museo del Café

One and a half blocks south of the Parque Morazán, the **Museo del Café** (Mon–Fri 8am–12.30pm & 2–5.30pm; free) houses some old photos of Matagalpa life and explanations of the coffee-growing process. The museum sells quality coffee and is also behind Matagalpa's new **Feria Nacional del Café** (held in November), a festival celebrating the town's coffee expertise with talks and traditional music and dance.

Casa Museo Comandante Carlos Fonseca

The **Casa Museo Comandante Carlos Fonseca** (Mon–Fri 8am–5.30pm; donations welcomed), 100m southeast of the Parque Darío, documents the life of martyred local hero Carlos Fonseca (co-founder of the Sandinista National Liberation Front), who was gunned down by Somoza's National Guard in 1976.

Cerro Apante

Matagalpa is not a city of intoxicating beauty, but several day-hikes take you out into the inspiring scenery that surrounds it. The most accessible explores **Cerro Apante**. From Parque Darío head south up the hill for thirty minutes, following the road into the reserve itself. Turn left at the rangers' cottage, where you'll probably have to pay the C$30 entry fee, and climb the (at times steep) path through pleasant woodland to a *mirador* offering cracking

views of the town and the crown of mountains that surrounds it. You can continue along the ridge, but the summit proper is private property – signs warn you off the final climb up some wooden stairs. The walk should take less than three hours in total. Guides are available for C$250 for the three hours, but need to be arranged in advance (Arcenio Brenes, ☏8651 3727).

ARRIVAL AND DEPARTURE

By bus Matagalpa's south bus terminal is southwest of the city centre; it's about a 10min walk to Parque Darío.
Destinations Estelí (every 30min; 1hr 30min); León (3 daily; 3hr; for a more frequent service, take any bus towards Estelí and change at San Isidro); Managua (every 20min; 2–3hr); Masaya (2 daily; 3hr).

INFORMATION AND TOURS

Tourist information INTUR (Mon–Fri 8am–1pm) on Av Central can offer a few fliers and maps.
Tour operators Helpful Matagalpa Tours, one block southeast of Parque Morazán (☏ 2772 0108, ⊛ matagalpa tours.com), offers excursions to the surrounding area, including tours of local coffee and chocolate farms and treks in the hills. Newer Nativos, based in *La Buena Onda* hostel (⊜ nativotour@hotmail.com), can organize city tours (US$13), walks up Cerro Apante (US$15) and trips to waterfalls and fincas.

ACCOMMODATION

Alvarado Just north of Parque Darío on Av José Benito Escobar ☏ 2772 2830, ⊜ hotelalvarado@gmail.com. This charming, family-run hotel above a pharmacy has en-suite wood-panelled rooms with TV and fan; some are on the small side (and two lack windows). US$13
Apante East side of Parque Darío ☏ 7272 6890. Tasteful rooms with TV, modern beds, and colourfully tiled, hot-water bathrooms. Some are a lot larger than others, for the same price, so ask to see a few before choosing. US$13
★ **La Buena Onda** One block north and two blocks east of the Cathedral ☏ 2772 2135, ⊛ hostelmatagalpa.com. Smart, welcoming hostel with solid facilities – wi-fi, book exchange, hot water, free coffee and kitchen for guests' use. Nativos tours are based here too (see above). Dorm US$8, double US$25
Hospedaje Luna One block south and half a block east of the Museo Carlos Fonseca ☏ 8496 3408 or ☏ 2772 6806, ⊛ cafeluzyluna.com. Part of the Estelí-based organization (see p.475), committed to sustainable development, and a good source of tourist information. Wi-fi and free pancake breakfast. Dorm US$7, double US$20

EATING

Artesanos Next to Matagalpa Tours. Appealing café-bar with a relaxed daytime vibe and a nice buzz at night, when it's pretty much *the* place to come. The food menu has just five options (C$50–180). Tues–Sun 4pm–2am.

Barista Café Nica Av José Benito Escobar ☎ 2772 6338, ⓦ baristacafenica. Modern coffee shop with free wi-fi and good service. Decent cappuccino C$30, panini C$75–100. During Happy Hour (8–9pm) you can get a plate of chicken wings and five beers for C$250.

Cafetería don Chaco 1.5 blocks south of Parque Morazán on Av José Benito Escobar. Intimate little restaurant serving up a range of Nicaraguan dishes. The breakfasts (C$50) will set you up nicely for a day's walking and there are healthy smoothies (C$25–40) and mains (around C$110) too.

★ **El Mexicano** One block north and two blocks east of the Cathedral, opposite *La Buena Onda*. Authentic, reasonably priced (starters under $2; mains $2–3) Mexican food on regularly changing seasonal menus. The Mexican chef/owner and his Nicaraguan wife are very accommodating – just ask if you fancy something that's not on the menu, or want to eat vegetarian food. Free wi-fi.

★ **La Vita é Bella** Tucked down an alleyway behind *La Buena Onda* ☎ 2772 5476. The chef is from Tuscany, the lasagne (C$130), pasta (C$70–100) and bread are all home-made and the pizza is perhaps the best in the country (C$120–150). There's a relaxing courtyard at the back. Tues–Sun noon–10pm.

DIRECTORY

Banks You'll find a couple of banks with ATMs on Av Central just south of Parque Morazán.

Internet G-Net Cyber Café (C$12/hr), Av José Benito Escobar, has reasonably fast connection (Mon–Fri 8am–5pm, Sat 8am–3pm).

Laundry Cuenta Conmigo, 2.5 blocks north of *La Buena Onda* (C$60 for up to 10kg; Mon–Fri 8am–noon & 2–5pm; ☎ 2772 6713, ⓦ cuentaconmigo.info). Charitable organization providing help for people with mental illnesses. Volunteer opportunities also available.

AROUND MATAGALPA

Matagalpa has an exceptional natural setting, and most of the area is only accessible on tours (see opposite). You can get a good feel for it in the grounds of the **Selva Negra**, where footpaths weave through the thick tropical forest.

Selva Negra

North of Matagalpa, the **SELVA NEGRA** (US$2.50, US$5 if staying overnight) is a stretch of dark blue, pine-clad mountains named by the area's German immigrants in the nineteenth century after their homeland's Black Forest, thanks to the physical resemblance and its spring-like climate. An amazing variety of **wildlife** flourishes in these pristine tropical forests, including more than eighty varieties of orchid, many birds, sloths, ocelots, margay, deer, snakes, mountain lions and howler monkeys.

The **trails** range from short strolls around the central lake to the thigh-burning La Mosquitia, which ascends to 1570m. It's perfectly feasible to come up from Matagalpa early in the morning and pack most of them into a day's hiking.

The owners of the *Selva Negra* hotel (see below) have grown **coffee** here since 1891, and the finca still produces some of the best export-grade coffee in the country; the estate employs 250 workers, most of whom live nearby. Various **tours** of the operation run daily, including horseback treks (US$10/hr), and there's a small museum too.

ARRIVAL AND DEPARTURE

By bus To get here from Matagalpa, hop on one of the buses to Jinotega (every 30min) and ask to be let off at Selva Negra. The hotel and office is a 20min walk away – head 100m uphill, turn right at the tank and continue up the track.

ACCOMMODATION AND EATING

Selva Negra 10km north of Matagalpa ☎ 2772 3883, ⓦ selvanegra.com. Many visitors to the area stay in this faded but prestigious hotel, which offers an accessible route to the forest and mountains. Options include good-sized doubles, individually designed cabañas and perfectly adequate dorms. There's a pricey restaurant on site (though your entry fee doubles as a voucher for food and drink), serving good coffee and traditional German food as well as local options – avoid the disappointing Sunday buffet. Dorm <u>US$15</u>, double <u>US$45</u>, cabaña <u>US$85</u>

The southwest

The majority of Nicaragua's population lives in the fertile **southwest** of the country. Bordered by Lago de Nicaragua to the east and the Pacific to the west,

6

and studded with **volcanoes** – Volcán Masaya, Volcán Mombacho and the twin cones of Ometepe's Concepción and Maderas – the southwest is otherwise a flat, low, grassy plain, home to what is left of Nicaragua's beef industry, while coffee plantations can be found at higher altitudes.

Masaya, 29km south of Managua, and **Granada**, 26km further south, are the region's key cities; Masaya's excellent crafts market attracts virtually everyone who comes to Nicaragua, while the nearby **Parque Nacional Volcán Masaya** offers the most accessible volcano-viewing in the country. The picturesque "**Pueblos Blancos**", or White Towns, lie on the road connecting Managua, Masaya and Granada; the latter, with its fading classical-colonial architecture and lakeside setting, is Nicaragua's most beautiful and touristy city, and makes a good base for exploring nearby attractions such as the **Isletas de Granada** and **Volcán Mombacho**. Some 75km south of Granada, **Rivas**, the gateway to Costa Rica, is of little interest in itself, though many travellers pass through on their way to Isla de Ometepe (see p.496) and the popular beach town of **San Juan del Sur**.

MASAYA

Set midway between Managua and Granada and shadowed by the hulking form of Volcán Masaya, **MASAYA**'s stirring geography and regular festivals would make it an enjoyable stop even if it weren't also the centre of Nicaragua's **artesanía production**. During the Sandinista years, Masaya developed its crafts tradition into a marketable commodity, and the city is now the best place in the country to buy hammocks, rocking chairs, traditional clothing, shoes and other souvenirs. Most visitors come here on day-trips from Managua or Granada, easily manageable on the bus, but Masaya is a pleasant place to overnight too.

WHAT TO SEE AND DO

Masaya is an attractive place to explore on foot: there's not too much traffic in

the streets and all the sights are within walking distance of each other.

Parque Central

What little action there is in downtown Masaya takes place in the local hangout, the **Parque Central**, where – with the help of Spanish finance – **La Parroquia de La Asunción** church (daily 6am–7pm) has been renovated. Its cool interior boasts a lovely wooden ceiling and images of various Central American saints, swathed in coloured satin and wilting gold lamé.

Iglesia de San Jerónimo

The ramshackle **Iglesia de San Jerónimo**, 600m north of the Parque Central (opening hours vary but there should be someone to let you in), is the best example of colonial architecture in Masaya. The statue of San Jerónimo on the altar depicts an old man wearing a loincloth and a straw hat, with a rock in his hand and blood on his chest, evidence of self-mortification. The tower is officially closed to the public awaiting renovation, but it's worth asking if they'll let you up to see the panoramic views of the city and surrounding area, with volcanoes rearing grandly from the plains.

Mercado Nacional de Artesanía

Two blocks east of the Parque Central sits the **Mercado Viejo** (daily 8am–6.30pm), which has been converted into the grandly named **Centro Cultural (Antiguo Mercado de Masaya) – Mercado Nacional de Artesanía**. Behind the large, fortress-style walls lies a complex network of stalls selling paintings, many in the naïf-art tradition of the Solentiname archipelago, as well as large, excellent-quality hammocks, carved wooden bowls, utensils and animals, simple wood-and-bead jewellery, cotton shirts, straw hats and leather bags and purses. It's a fun place for a potter even if you're not going to buy anything – safe, not too hustly and dotted with drinks stalls and restaurants. The weekly **Jueves de Verbena** party night (see box, p.482) takes place here too. Check out the giant wall map of the country, which shows the places in Nicaragua where crafts are

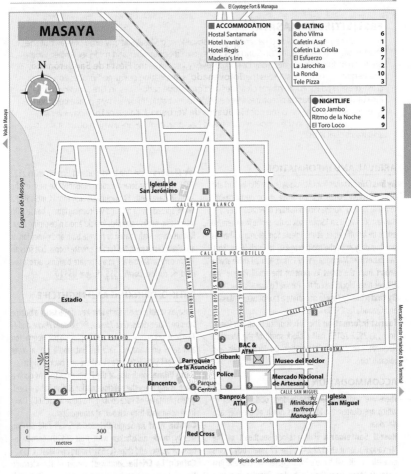

MASAYA

ACCOMMODATION	
Hostal Santamaría	4
Hotel Ivania's	3
Hotel Regis	2
Madera's Inn	1

● EATING	
Baho Vilma	6
Cafetín Asaf	1
Cafetín La Criolla	8
El Esfuerzo	7
La Jarochita	2
La Ronda	10
Tele Pizza	3

● NIGHTLIFE	
Coco Jambo	5
Ritmo de la Noche	4
El Toro Loco	9

6

produced. If your Spanish is up to it, ask about visiting artisans at work in their homes and workshops. Many of the crafts on sale come from designs that originated in the indigenous *barrio* of **Monimbó**, fifteen minutes' walk south of the market, where you'll find more produce on sale around Iglesia de San Sebastián.

Museo del Folclor

Inside the Mercado Nacional de Artesanía, the **Museo del Folclor** (daily 9am–5pm; US$2) is a modern building displaying a variety of national costumes and masks from around the country. Interesting information (in Spanish only, but there are plans to offer tours in

English) explains the origin and meaning of many of the traditional dances and costumes you'll doubtless come across on your travels.

Laguna de Masaya

On the western side of town, seven blocks from the Parque Central, **Laguna de Masaya** beckons. Despite its crystalline appearance and appealing, forested slopes, the lake is heavily polluted with sewage effluent from the town. It's still worth the walk, though, as the waterfront **malecón** has stunning views of the smoking cone of Volcán Masaya (see p.483) and most of the town's late-night bars and clubs.

6

FESTIVITIES IN MASAYA

You may see processions and hear music in festival-loving Masaya at any time of year, but the most exciting time to visit is on Sundays between mid-September and mid-December, when the town indulges in a ninety-day period of revelry known as the **Fiesta de San Jerónimo**. The beginning of the fiesta sees the **Torovenado**, a fascinating costumed procession of cross-dressing dancers, mythical creatures and grotesque caricatures. In late January, the **Fiesta de San Sebastián** features a large-scale mock battle followed by a peace ceremony. A more recent invention is the popular **Jueves de Verbena**, held every Thursday evening throughout the year in the renovated Mercado Nacional de Artesanía, which offers stalls, food and traditional music.

ARRIVAL AND INFORMATION

By bus Chicken buses from Managua (every 20min; 1hr) and Granada (every 20min; 45min) arrive at the dusty, chaotic terminal next to Masaya's main market (Mercado Nuevo) to the east of town; it's a 15min walk to the centre from here, so ask to be let off earlier, at the Iglesia San Jerónimo. There is one bus daily from the main terminal to Estelí (6am; 3hr). Minibuses from Managua (every 15min; 40min) arrive at and depart from the street in front of the small Parque San Miguel, three blocks east of the Parque Central.

By taxi It's fairly easy to negotiate a taxi between Masaya and Granada for C$150–200.

Tourist information The INTUR office (Mon–Fri 9am–noon; ☎2522 7615), half a block south of the Mercado Nacional, can provide information on local hotels and volcano tours.

ACCOMMODATION

There are several reasonable budget options, most of which are clustered a few blocks north of the Mercado Nacional.

Hostal Santamaría Half a block southeast of the Mercado Nacional ☎2522 2411. The 22 small, tidy rooms here, all en suite with cable TV, are quiet and cool and just a stone's throw from the old market. Popular with Nica travellers. US$20

Hotel Regis Av Sergio Delgadillo ☎2522 2300, ✉hotelregismasaya@hotmail.com. A spotless bargain with cell-like, wood-panelled rooms with thin partition walls, and a neat little courtyard. 10pm curfew. US$8

★ TREAT YOURSELF

Hotel Ivania's Two blocks north and one and a half blocks east of the Mercado Nacional ☎2522 7632, ⊛hotelivanias.com. Smart, modern option a short walk from the centre, with a clientele of foreign travellers and local business folk. It offers bright furnishings, hot water, parking, a/c, cable TV and a bar, set around a mellow courtyard. Breakfast included. US$45

★ Madera's Inn One block north of *Hotel Regis* ☎2522 5825, ⊛hotelmaderasinn.com. Probably the best of the lot in Masaya, with 13 bright and cosy rooms, including a dorm, spread over a tidy and welcoming family house with interesting nooks and knick-knacks and a nice dining area. Rooms come with shared or private bath and either fan or a/c. Breakfast is included for the private rooms, but so is an 11pm curfew. Dorms are in a separate building across the road, no curfew. Dorm US$5, double US$20

EATING, DRINKING AND NIGHTLIFE

Masaya's social scene is fairly low-key. If you fancy a boogie later on, three clubs, *Coco Jambo*, *Ritmo de la Noche* and *El Toro Loco*, get going on the *malecón*, playing pop, reggaetón and salsa until around 3am Fri–Sat. You'll pay a cover change of C$50–100; get a taxi there and back at night.

Baho Vilma South side of the Parque Central. As good a place as any to try the delicious national dish Baho – beef, green plantain and yuca cooked in a huge pot (C$60). Daily from noon until they sell out, at around 2pm.

Cafetín Asaf Av Sergio Delgadillo. Small café serving freshly made milkshakes with fruit (C$20) or not-so-healthy burger and chips (C$65). Filling breakfasts C$55.

Cafetin La Criolla Southwest corner of the Mercado Nacional. Hearty, popular market cheapie – stuff yourself on chicken, plantain, rice and a drink for C$85 and watch tourists and locals browse and haggle.

El Esfuerzo Half a block east of the Parque Central. Small coffee shop that's a good spot to fill up at breakfast or lunch: the gigantic cheese pasties (C$25), or sandwiches (C$55) should see you right.

La Jarochita Av Sergio Delgadillo, north of La Asunción ☎2522 0450. A charming Mexican restaurant where you can dine on fajitas, burritos and quesadillas (C$85–130), all washed down with tequila or a cold beer (C$25). Head upstairs for the pleasant balcony.

La Ronda Overlooking La Asunción and the Parque Central. An airy bar and restaurant drawing a local crowd with cheap beer (C$24, C$42 for a litre) and televised sport. The food (steak with jalapeños C$165, substantial chicken salad C$95) is pretty decent too.

Tele Pizza Av San Jerónimo. Tasty, decent-sized pizzas for

C$105–215, as well as pastas (C$105–155) and salads (C$130) served from a pink front room and restful courtyard.

DIRECTORY

Banks Banks and ATMs are plentiful in Masaya; there's a handy Banpro machine by the Mercado Nacional de Artesanía, and a branch of BAC opposite the police station where you can change dollars and travellers' cheques.

Internet There are various spots around town: try Cyber Jet, opposite *Hotel Regis* (C$12/hr).

Post office There's a tiny office one block north of the Mercado Nacional next to the BAC (Mon–Fri 8am–4pm, Sat 8–11am).

AROUND MASAYA

Attractions around Masaya include the town's namesake **volcano** and a crater lake, **Laguna de Apoyo**, which can be explored on foot and with a guide. The nearby **Pueblos Blancos**, meanwhile, are famous for artisanal crafts, including pottery, which is made in small workshops throughout the villages, while the historical site of **Coyotepe** is a must for anyone interested in the nation's political history.

Coyotepe

Three kilometres out of town on the road to Managua is the old fort of **COYOTEPE** (daily 8am–5pm; US$2 plus tip for guide). Built on a hilltop by the Somoza regime to house political prisoners, the abandoned structure commands stunning views of Masaya and the volcanoes of Masaya and Mombacho, and also offers an eerie reminder of the atrocities carried out here by Somoza's National Guard: when Sandinistas stormed the fort during the Revolution, the National Guard responded by slaughtering all those inside. It's now administered by Nicaragua's Boy Scouts, who will illuminate the tunnels on a torchlit tour and tell you grim tales about Nicaragua's recent past.

ARRIVAL AND DEPARTURE

By bus From Masaya, take any Managua-bound bus and ask to be let off at the entrance, from where a winding path leads up to the fort. On your return, simply flag any Masaya-bound bus down from the roadside (some stop on the highway just outside Masaya).

By taxi A cab from Masaya will cost C$20 or so.

Parque Nacional Volcán Masaya

Just outside Masaya, the **PARQUE NACIONAL VOLCÁN MASAYA** (daily 9am–4.45pm; C$100; ☎2528 1444) offers you the chance to peer into the smoking cone of a volcano, as well as some stunning long-distance views. Gazing warily over the smoke-blackened rim into the crater's sulphurous depths, you can well imagine why the Spaniards considered this to be the mouth of hell itself – the large white cross above the crater marks the spot where a Spanish friar placed a cross in the sixteenth century to exorcize the volcano's demonic presence. This is still one of the most active volcanoes in the world; the last eruption occurred in 2001, but plumes have been spotted since then, and signs advise drivers to park their cars facing downhill in case a quick getaway is required.

From the entrance (see p.484), it's a 1.5km walk up the road to the **Centro de Interpretación Ambiental** (daily 9am–4pm), home to an exhibition outlining the area's geology, agriculture and pre-Columbian history, along with an interesting 3D display of the country's chain of volcanoes. From the centre you're best off hitching or getting a spot in one of the regular minibuses going up to the **crater** (C$25 each way – they are less frequent in the afternoon so arrive early if you can), as it's a fairly steep 5km hike up a paved road. Walking down is more pleasant, although in theory (and despite the lack of any kind of danger) you must be accompanied by a guide along this stretch – if you're not, a ranger will probably follow you down, at a discreet distance, on a bike. The rangers at the crater can point out a few short walks around the area that you can take unaccompanied, and also offer guided **tours** of two trails, Sendero Los Coyotes and Sendero de Las Pencas, as well as highly recommended **night hikes** (5–7/8pm; US$10; book in advance), including a visit to the subterranean **Cueva Tzinancanostoc**, where you'll see bizarre lava formations and a bat colony and, if you're lucky, a chance to see the lava glowing deep in the main crater.

6

Look out for the stunted bromeliads common to high-altitude volcanic areas, and the famous *chocoyos del cráter*, small green parrots that have thrived in an atmosphere that should be poisonous.

ARRIVAL AND DEPARTURE

By bus The park entrance lies between km 22 and km 23 on the Managua–Granada highway, about 4km north of Masaya. You can get off any bus (except the express) between Managua and Masaya or Granada at the entrance – you'll pass Coyotepe (see p.483) on the way.

By taxi Alternatively, you could hire a taxi from Masaya (about C$200 return). Arrive early if you want to catch a minibus to the crater (see p.483).

Pueblos Blancos

Scattered within 15km of Masaya are the "**Pueblos Blancos**" or White Towns: **Nindiri, Niquinohomo, Masatepe, Catarina, Diria** and **Diriomo**. The name comes from the traditional whitewash used on the villages' houses – called *carburo*, it is made from water, lime and salt – as well as a past tradition of practising white magic in the area. The white buildings are pretty, but there's not much more to see: although each town has its own specific artisan traditions and fiestas, and local identity is fiercely asserted, they seem remarkably similar, sleepy towns with a few people hanging out around nearly identical central squares. **CATARINA** is the prettiest, the main draw being **El Mirador** (US$1), a lookout at the top of the village that stares right down into the blue waters of the collapsed crater lake of Laguna de Apoyo, with Volcán Masaya looming behind it. Restaurants, cafés and *artesanía* stalls have sprung up around the viewpoint.

ARRIVAL AND DEPARTURE

By bus A regular local bus runs from Masaya's main bus terminal to Catarina (roughly every 30min; around 30min). From Granada (around 25min), buses to Niquinohomo pass through the town, or alternatively you can take any Masaya or Managua bus and ask to be let off at the Catarina turning, from where you'll need to take another short bus ride to the edge of the village.

Laguna de Apoyo

The volcanic **Laguna de Apoyo** draws tourists with its mineral-rich waters,

tropical rainforest and stunning views. Nature-lovers will be entranced by the rare **flora and fauna**, including howler monkeys, armadillos and toucans, and divers can check out the lake's unique fish, but it's a pleasant place just to relax and sip a few beers, too. Its popularity means stretches get a bit party-centric on busy days, and others are under threat from developers despite its natural reserve status, but it remains a stunning place.

ARRIVAL AND DEPARTURE

By bus Masaya has direct buses part-way to the lake, departing at around 10am and 3pm.

From Granada Most tourists visit from Granada, whether on a tour (see box, p.487), or using the *Bearded Monkey* or *Hostel Oasis* shuttles (C$40–60 return).

ACCOMMODATION

Estación Biológica ☎ 8882 3992, ⓦ gaianicaragua.org. You can stay at this research centre, which also offers PADI courses and voluntary work. Dorm US$10, double US$21
Monkey Hut ☎ 8887 3546 or ☎ 8366 9986, ⓦ themonkeyhut.net. Many backpackers head to this place for day-trips, paying US$7 to use the hammocks, kayaks, kitchen and buzzing bar, which means the accommodation can feel like an afterthought. Dorm US$12, double US$29

GRANADA

Set on the western shore of Lago de Nicaragua, some 50km southeast of Managua, **GRANADA** was once the jewel of Central America. The oldest Spanish-built city in the isthmus, it was founded in 1524 by Francisco Fernández de Córdoba, who named it after his hometown in Spain. During the colonial period Granada became fabulously rich, its wealth built upon exploitation: sited just 20km from the Pacific, the city was a transit point for shipments of gold and other minerals mined throughout the Spanish empire. In the mid-nineteenth century Granada fell to American adventurer William Walker, who briefly gained control of the city – and, by default, the entire country. Granada paid dearly for the eventual overthrow of Walker; as he retreated in the face of international resistance, he burned the city practically to the ground.

6

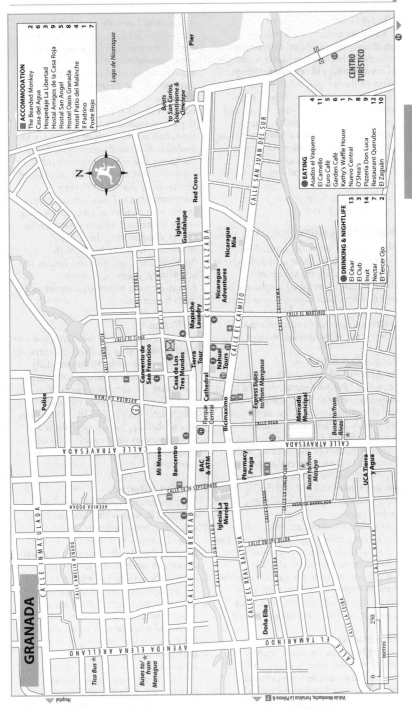

GRANADA

ACCOMMODATION
The Bearded Monkey	2
Casa del Agua	6
Hospedaje La Libertad	3
Hostal Amigos de la Casa Roja	9
Hostal San Angel	5
Hostel Oasis Granada	8
Hotel Patio del Malinche	4
Il Padrino	1
Poste Rojo	7

EATING
Asados el Vaquero	4
El Camello	11
Euro Café	5
Garden Café	6
Kathy's Waffle House	1
Nuevo Central	7
O'Shea's	8
Pizzeria Don Luca	9
Restaurant Querubes	12
El Zaguán	10

DRINKING & NIGHTLIFE
El César	13
El Club	3
Inuit	14
Nectar	7
El Tercer Ojo	2

Lago de Nicaragua

Pier

Boats to San Carlos, Solentiname & Ometepe

CENTRO TURISTICO

Red Cross

Iglesia Guadalupe

CALLE LA CALZADA

Nicaragua Mia

Nicaragua Adventures

CALLE SAN JUAN DEL SUR

CALLE EL CISNE

CALLE SANTA LUCIA

CALLE CORRAL

CALLE EL ARSENAL

CALLE LA LIBERTAD

Mapache Laundry

Convento de San Francisco

Casa de Los Tres Mundos

Tierra Tour

Cathedral

CALLE EL CAIMITO

CALLE EL MARTIRIO

CALLE CHICHIGUA

Nahual Tours

AVENIDA GUZMAN

Police

Parque Central

Bicimaximo

Express buses to/from Managua

CALLE VEGA

Mercado Municipal

Buses to/from Rivas

CALLE ATRAVESADA

Mi Museo

Bancentro

BAC & ATM

Pharmacy Praga

Buses to/from Masaya

CALLE 14 DE SEPTIEMBRE

AVENIDA BODAN

CALLE INMACULADA

CALLE AMELIA BENARD

CALLE ELENA ARELLANO

AVENIDA ELENA ARELLANO

Tica Bus

Buses to/from Managua

CALLE LA LIBERTAD

Iglesia La Merced

CALLE EL CONSULADO

CALLE EL REAL XALTEVA

CALLE OBISPO ULLOA

CALLE LA HOYADA

CALLE CONCEPCION

AVENIDA BARRICADA

UCA Tierra y Agua

CALLE LA CEIBA

CALLE NUEVA

Doña Elba

EL TAMARINDO

AVENIDA

0 metres 250

Hospital

Volcán Mombacho, Fortaleza La Pólvora & 7

Volcán Mombacho, fortaleza La Pólvora & 7

N

6

Today Granada is central to the Nicaraguan government's tourism ambitions. Its popularity with foreign visitors has led to a large-scale restoration of the stunning old **colonial buildings**, many of them repainted in pastel shades, and a burgeoning network of foreign-owned bars, restaurants and hostels has sprung up. This manageable, gringo-packed city also makes a **good base** from which to explore the lake, volcanoes, Zapatera archipelago and Isla de Ometepe, while more adventurous travellers might head from here to San Carlos, the Solentiname islands (see p.501) and beyond.

(see p.501)

WHAT TO SEE AND DO

There are few "must see" attractions in Granada itself, but most of the pleasure is simply in strolling the streets and absorbing the colonial atmosphere – be sure to take a peek through open front doors along Calle La Calzada to see the magnificent interior courtyards that adorn some of the private houses.

Parque Central

At the centre of town sits the attractive, palm-lined **Parque Central**, peopled by an engaging mix of tourists, stalls, itinerants and clumping horses. A few small kiosks sell snacks, and an ice-cream seller wanders around ringing his handbell in search of trade. On the east side of the Parque is the large, graceful **cathedral** (open daily to the public as a house of worship), built in 1712 and damaged in the 1850s during William Walker's violent reign.

As well as the cathedral, many of the city's most captivating historic houses line the square. The palatial red house with white trim on the corner of Calle La Calzada, across from the cathedral, is the **Bishop's Residence**, with a columned upstairs veranda typical of the former homes of wealthy Granadino burghers.

Convento de San Francisco

Dating from the sixteenth century but rebuilt in 1867 after Walker's attack, the historic **Convento de San Francisco** is two blocks northeast of the cathedral.

The attached **cultural centre** (Mon–Fri 8am–4pm, Sat 9am–4pm; US$2) has been converted into Nicaragua's best pre-Columbian museum, housing various displays and many of the **petroglyphs** recovered from Isla Zapatera. Hewn from black volcanic basalt in about 1000 AD, these statues depict anthropomorphic creatures – half man, half lizard, turtle or jaguar – which probably had ritual significance for the indigenous peoples who inhabited the islands. It was also from the confines of this convent that in 1535 **Frey Bartolomé de Las Casas**, apostle of the indigenous peoples of Central America, wrote his historic letter to the Spanish Court, condemning the Indians' mistreatment at the hands of the Spanish. The Convento also houses the city **library**; many of Walker's filibusterers are buried in the catacombs in its basement.

Mi Museo

Set in a fine converted colonial house one block northwest of the Parque Central on the Calle Atravesada, **Mi Museo** (daily 8am–5pm; free) is a private collection of more than five thousand pieces of pre-Columbian ceramics, the oldest of which dates back to 500 BC. There's not much labelling, but the jars, plates and urns of various sizes, mostly depicting birds, crocodiles and toads, are intriguing.

Iglesia La Merced

For panoramic views of Granada's rooftops, as well as the lake and volcano, climb the **tower** (daily 8am–12.30pm & 2–6pm; US$1 – pay the attendant in the stairwell) at **Iglesia La Merced** (technically La Iglesia de Nuestra Señora de Las Mercedes – The Church of Our Lady of Mercy), which sits two blocks west of the Parque Central on Calle 14 de Septiembre. Yet to receive a lick of new paint, the sooty front and serene interior give it a shabby-chic charm. The tower is accessed at the front of the church on the left. If you suffer from vertigo, you may be put off by the tiny winding staircase with low railings that leads you upstairs. Once up top, there's a wraparound balcony where you can take photos or simply soak up the view.

Fortaleza La Pólvora

A pleasant fifteen-minute stroll west of La Merced takes you past a few smart churches to the old fort of **La Pólvora** (officially daily 8am–5pm, though it's not always open), which has a grand gate and good views. On the way you'll pass the small **Doña Elba** cigar factory (Mon–Thurs 8am–5pm), where you can have a go at rolling the product and take the result home – tip the worker who shows you around.

Lago de Nicaragua

The shoreline of **Lago de Nicaragua** is about 1km east of the Parque Central. As you head down the wide boulevard of Calle La Calzada, past churches and baseball diamonds, the stretch gets more and more dilapidated until you arrive at the shore, which has a huge vista of the lake, but feels eerily empty unless you happen to arrive as the boat from San Carlos or Ometepe is docking. To the south a small park lines the lake, a few hundred metres beyond which is the entrance to the **Centro Turístico** (C$10 entry occasionally imposed), a group of lakeside bars and cheap restaurants that's ironically far more popular with locals than visitors. It's deserted on weekdays but popular at weekends, especially in the evenings, when the nightlife gets going. If heading here after dark, get a taxi back into town.

ARRIVAL AND INFORMATION

By boat The boat from San Carlos (14hr) and Ometepe (4hr) docks at the pier at the bottom of C La Calzada (Mon & Thurs 2pm). A/c first-class tickets – the only ones that can officially be sold to foreigners – are C$104 to Ometepe, C$219 to San Carlos. They're available on the day of travel from the dock office at the bottom of C La Calzada – arrive by noon to be safe or call ahead (☎ 2552 2966). The journey is notoriously cold and uncomfortable – come prepared.

By bus Buses from Managua (every 20min; 40min) come into the terminal west of town, 700m from the Parque, from where you can walk or grab a taxi into the centre (C$10). Services from Rivas (every 45min; 1hr 30min) and points south pull up at the market, a short walk southwest of the centre. Buses from Masaya (frequent; 45min) pull up a block west of the market. If you're travelling from Costa Rica, the Tica Bus for Managua will stop and let you off at its Granada office on Av Elena Arellano, 1km northwest of the centre, but you may not be able to board there. Check when you buy your ticket.

Tourist information Granada's better-than-average (in the sense that it might actually prove useful) INTUR office (Mon–Fri 8am–1pm; ☎ 2552 6858, ✉ granada@intur .gob.ni) is on C Corral, and stocks information on climbing local volcanoes and other attractions.

GETTING AROUND

By bike Bicimaximo, next door to the cathedral (ⓦ bicimaximo.com; US$6/US$3 day/half-day), are your best bet, and several hostels and tour agencies also rent out bikes.

By taxi Taxis line up in the northwest corner of the Parque. Any trip in Granada should cost C$10–20.

TOUR OPERATORS IN GRANADA

Guides hang around the larger hostels, and can be a reasonable bet as long as you ensure you know what you're getting for the price. The established operators below offer greater experience and professionalism, though.

Nicaragua Adventures C El Consulado ☎ 2552 8461, ⓦ nica-adventures.com. Long-standing, reliable company owned by European expats that offers trip-planning and shuttles and tours across Nicaragua, as well as Granada-specific activities like half-day kayak tours of Las Isletas, day-trips to Masaya and city tours.

Tierra Tour C La Calzada two blocks east of the cathedral ☎ 2552 8723, ⓦ tierratour.com. Professional, Nica-owned company (with offices in León too)

offering shuttles, kayak tours of the Isletas (US$25/ person), as well as city and volcano tours, diving in Laguna de Apoyo (US$65), and night tours of Masaya volcano (US$35 inc. entrance fee).

UCA Tierra y Agua ☎ 2552 0238, ✉ turismo @ucatierrayagua.org. This government-run co-operative can help organize homestays around Granada, notably around the Charco Muerto region, taking in crafts, horseriding and walking trails (bed and breakfast from US$5, guided tours from US$5).

ACCOMMODATION

The Bearded Monkey C 14 de Septiembre ☎ 2552 4028, ⓦ thebeardedmonkey.com. Granada's best-known backpacker hostel is worth visiting for its cool, verdant courtyard bar even if you don't stay here. The large dorms are perfectly decent, and there are private rooms and hammocks too. It's a big, busy place – watch your valuables and expect some noise. Dorm US$5, double US$15

★ **Casa del Agua** Av Guzmán ⓦ casadelaguagranada .com. Dinky, smart place with a handful of rooms and a kitchen encircling a cool little pool. It's small enough that you'll end up talking to everyone and offers a surprisingly mellow experience given its just-off-the-square location. US$24

Hospedaje La Libertad C 14 de Septiembre ☎ 8408 0003, ⓦ la-libertad.net. A pleasant set of dorms, this one distinguished by some nice old *baños* and free use of the kitchen, but the big draw is that guests get free use of the nearby gym. It's Nica-owned, with tours including trips to a few remote beaches. Dorm US$5, double US$12

Hostal Amigos de la Casa Roja C Estrada ☎ 2552 2085, ⓦ nicaraguamiahostal.com. Well-run, central hostel. Guests have use of the communal kitchen and wi-fi, and laundry services are also available (US$4–6). Dorm US$8, double US$20

Hostal San Angel Av Guzmán ☎ 2552 4591, ✉ maria campos118@hotmail.com. This welcoming, family-run hostel, which stretches either side of *Casa del Agua*, offers quiet and tidy, if slightly dark rooms, all en suite with good mattresses and fans. Breakfast included. US$24

Hostel Oasis Granada C Estrada, 100m north of Masaya bus terminal ☎ 2552 8006, ⓦ nicaraguahostel.com. A self-proclaimed "backpackers' paradise", this imaginatively conceived hostel offers comfortable dorm beds and private rooms in a restored colonial house. There's also free wi-fi, plus DVDs, tours, a bar and even a tiny swimming pool. Dorm US$9, double US$20

Il Padrino 2 blocks north of El Convento de San Francisco ☎ 8895 6789, ⓦ lamesadelpadrino.com. Elegant hotel with a laidback arty vibe, spacious doubles and a beautiful garden. Even if you don't stay, it's worth popping by to see

> ### ★ TREAT YOURSELF
>
> **Hotel Patio del Malinche** C Caimito near C El Cisne ☎ 2552 2235, ⓦ patiodelmalinche.com. An immaculate colonial conversion set around a tropical courtyard (with a good pool). The staff are helpful and rooms feature cool tiled floors, high ceilings and original wood beams, a/c and wi-fi, and those upstairs have fantastic views of the Mombacho volcano. Full breakfast included. US$75

if the Italian owner has opened his planned restaurant. US$42

Poste Rojo Pozo del Oro ☎ 8903 4563, ⓦ posterojo.com. Located 10km out of Granada near Volcán Mombacho, this funky collection of treehouses offers hammocks, dorms and doubles on the edge of the rainforest, with some great views. They also run yoga classes (Tues) and full-moon parties, and can organize tours to nearby Mombacho and beyond. Take a bus from Granada's market to Rivas, Nandaime or Diriomo, or get the free daily noon shuttle from *The Bearded Monkey*. Hammock US$4, dorm US$8, double US$20

EATING

Granada offers an increasingly cosmopolitan variety of places to eat, with lots of Italian and Spanish food. Most places have wi-fi. Budget travellers can grab a quick but basic bite at the town market, and in the early evening a couple of small food stands open up on the Parque, selling cheap and filling meat and rice dishes. Most of the gringo-orientated places sit at the western end of C La Calzada, where prices are higher, but there's a nice buzz most evenings.

★ **Asados el Vaquero** 50m east of *El Club*. This Nicaraguan husband-and-wife team make creative use of local ingredients. If you're feeling adventurous try grilled kidneys (C$60) or heart (C$70), or play it safe with pork tenderloin (C$140). Beers are cheap (C$25) and you can choose to sit on a bale of hay as you dine. Tues–Sun noon–11pm.

El Camello C El Camito. Food from the Mediterranean and further east. Most ingredients (including the lamb) are grown on the owner's farm. Kafta sandwich (C$110) and Thai green curry (C$150) are not to be missed. Beer C$25. Closed Tues.

Euro Café Northwest corner of the Parque. Pleasant, central café with decent coffees (from C$20), smoothies (C$54) and meals (soy burger C$69, salad C$100). The back courtyard is fun, with free ping-pong for customers, a bookstore/exchange and Seeing Hands, a non-profit organization that trains blind people as masseurs (a good massage costs from C$5).

★ **Garden Café** C La Libertad and C El Cisne. This cool haven from the bustling streets is tucked inside yet another colonial conversion. There's an extensive breakfast menu (*huevos al pesto* C$95) as well as tasty and imaginative smoothies (C$50), salads and sandwiches (around C$100), and free wi-fi, and the leafy courtyard comes complete with tinkling fountain.

Kathy's Waffle House Opposite the San Francisco convent on C El Arsenal ⓦ kathyswafflehouse.com. A breakfast institution in Granada offering good coffee and tasty grub, although service can be slow. The waffles (C$100), eggs, *gallo pinto* and toast (C$100) and filling

> ★ **TREAT YOURSELF**
>
> **El Zaguán** C Cervantes, directly behind the cathedral. Tucked down a little side street just off C La Calzada, this grill-house has one of the best reputations in town. The restaurant is set in a converted house with a large, open-air courtyard, and the mouthwatering menu includes top-quality steak and fish – try the melt-in-your-mouth sirloin or fresh guapote. Most mains are C$250–350.

lunches (burger C$120) are served on a beautifully shaded terrace looking across to the convent. Daily 7am–2pm.

Nuevo Central C La Calzada. The interior, dominated by a long bar, is nice enough, but like most people on La Calzada you'll probably be on the paved street breathing in the night air and ignoring the hawkers. The food and drink – omelettes (C$65), burgers (C$65) and lovely, juicy burritos (C$90) – is decent and relatively cheap for the location.

O'Shea's C La Calzada ⓦ osheaspubgranada.com. So you didn't come to Nicaragua to eat fish and chips, but when it's on the menu with shepherd's pie and Irish stew for the same price as your average rice and beans (all C$120), why not? Wash it down with Guinness (C$90) and/or Jameson (C$60). For a treat, try the new *O'Shea's Bistro* next door (Sat & Sun only) for good home-cooked recipes from America's Deep South.

Pizzeria Don Luca C La Calzada, opposite *Zoom*. Popular and unpretentious, with pleasingly authentic Italian food. Be warned, though: the *pequeña* size is just that. Pizza from C$60, pastas from C$125. Closed Mon.

Restaurant Querubes Half a block north of the market on C Atravesada. A *buffet típica*, where hefty portions of rice, beans, plantain, salad and *churrasco* or grilled chicken come to C$90. The lunch menu has fewer options than the evening one; both offer food comparable in quality to La Calzada's offerings, for half the price.

DRINKING AND NIGHTLIFE

Most travellers in search of alcohol and company tend to head either to the buzzing bar at *The Bearded Monkey* or to C La Calzada (for a super-cheap night, buy your drinks from the supermarket on La Calzada – they will open bottles for you, lend you glasses, and even have a couple of tables). There are also some great venues for a night out, with music ranging from acoustic Nicaraguan folk to the ever-present strains of reggaetón. The Centro Turístico (see p.487) is the place to head late on – take a taxi.

El César On the lakefront in the Centro Turístico. Granada's largest club has a party setting under an open-air *rancho*. Latin and disco dominate. Cover charge C$20–30. Fri–Sun till 3am.

El Club *El Club* hotel, C de La Libertad & Av Barricada. Open for food and drink daily (*huevos rancheros* C$60, pasta C$125), this place turns into a bar and club from Thurs–Sat, when the slightly over-the-top DJ booth oversees some serious boogying. There are strippers on Thurs, and a jacuzzi out back. Nightly.

Inuit On the lakefront in the Centro Turístico. When *El César* shuts, around 3am, the party usually heads to this place at the other end of the lakefront. Daily, Sat & Sun 24hr.

Nectar C La Calzada. Small cocktail bar with groovy art, a nice courtyard, decent juices, sandwiches, soups and salads for under C$100 and cold beer (C$35). Happy hour 4–7pm. Closed Mon.

El Tercer Ojo C El Arsenal, opposite the Convento de San Francisco. Tapas bar and deli with a funky, cushion-strewn interior set in a lovely colonial building. The global food isn't cheap, and you might prefer to stick to the booze – beer is C$36 but happy hour (6–8pm) offers good deals on rum, sangría and wine.

DIRECTORY

Banks All banks in town change dollars. The Banco de América Central (BAC), on the corner of C Atravesada and La Libertad, will change travellers' cheques, and also has one of many ATMs in the city.

Health The Praga pharmacy on C Real Xalteva is well stocked (daily 7am–10pm), while the Hospital Privado Cocibolca (ⓣ 2552 2907) is just outside town on the highway to Managua.

Internet Cafés have sprung up all over town; the Alhambra on C La Libertad (daily 8am–10pm; C$20/hr) is central and pleasant enough.

Language schools There are plenty of places to learn Spanish in Granada – UCA Tierra y Agua (see box, p.487) can set you up with a rural homestay for the full cultural experience. Ask at tour offices or your accommodation for options in the city, or try the highly recommended Nicaragua Mia, C el Caimito (ⓣ 2252 0347, ⓦ nicaragua miaspanish.com), who offer one-on-one and group lessons.

Laundry Try Mapache on the corner of C La Calzada and C El Cisne (ⓣ 2522 6711), or La Lavandería (ⓣ 2252 0018) just north on C El Cisne. Both also offer pick-up and delivery.

Post office C El Arsenal (Mon–Sat 8am–noon & 1–5pm).

AROUND GRANADA

Although Granada is a jumping-off point for trips to Ometepe (see p.496) and Solentiname (see p.501), there are a couple of worthwhile **day-trips** closer to town.

6

Isla Zapatera and Las Isletas

About 20km south of Granada, scattered about Lago de Nicaragua, are more than three hundred and fifty islands all believed to have been formed from the exploded top of Volcán Mombacho. Many of the pre-Columbian artefacts and treasures you find in museums throughout the country came from this group, which must have been of religious significance for the Chorotega-descended people who flourished here before the Conquest. The smaller islands, **Las Isletas**, make for a varied boat tour. Some are home to monkeys, one has a small fortress built by the Spanish conquistadors; one or two have private mansions, and on others you will see women washing their clothes in the lake in front of their ramshackle houses.

At 52 square kilometres, **Isla Zapatera** is the largest of the islands, skirted by attractive bays and topped by a much-eroded extinct volcano. Guides should be able to show you **El Muerto** (The Dead), a site full of the remains of tombs, several **petroglyphs** and the scant remains – a few grassy mounds and stones – of **Sozafe**, a site sacred to the Chorotegas. These apart, there's really very little to see, bar lovely views of the lake.

ARRIVAL AND DEPARTURE

Tours Every tour operator in Granada (see box, p.487) runs half-day boat tours to Las Isletas from US$25 per person – some can also arrange more tranquil kayak trips. The easiest way to visit Zapatera is with a travel agency, such as Tierra Tour in Granada (see box, p.487), who offer informed but costly archeological excursions.

Lanchas Cabaña Amarilla Cheaper than the tour operators is Lanchas Cabaña Amarilla (☎8878 0763) at the far southern end of the Centro Turístico, a 20min walk beyond the entrance – unless you're on the waterfront anyway it's easiest to get a taxi down here. From here tours of Las Isletas cost US$20/hr (not/person) for groups of 1–8 people. They even have a bar where you can stock up before heading out.

Volcán Mombacho

The slopes of the rather lovely **RESERVA NACIONAL VOLCÁN MOMBACHO** (daily 8am–5pm; US$15 including transport, add US$3 to walk to the summit) are home to one of only two **cloudforests** in

Nicaragua's Pacific region (the other is at Volcán Maderas on Isla de Ometepe). The reserve is run by the **Fundación Cocibolca** (ⓦmombacho.org), whose interesting **research station and visitors' centre** at the volcano's summit acts as the centre for the study and protection of the reserve's flora and fauna – which includes three species of monkey, 22 species of reptile, 87 species of orchid, 175 species of bird and some fifty thousand species of insect. The air is noticeably cooler up here, the views of the lakes and volcanoes around are tremendous, and several **trails** skirt the four craters at the top of the volcano.

ARRIVAL AND DEPARTURE

By bus To get to the volcano take any bus from Granada bound for Rivas or Nandaime and ask to be let off at the turn-off for the park (at Intersection El Guanacaste). From the turn-off it's a 2.5km walk to the entrance, from where it is a further 5.5km to the top. Alternatively, you can take the "Eco-truck" to the summit from the reserve entrance (Mon–Wed 8.30am & 10am, Thurs–Sun 8.30am, 10am, 1pm & 3pm; included in the ticket price).

Tours Most visitors choose the easier option of a tour from Granada (see box, p.487), which start from around US$35/ person and typically include a visit to a coffee finca. For canopy tours Miravalle, at the volcano entrance (ⓔcanopymiravalle@yahoo.com), is your best bet (US$28/person).

ACCOMMODATION

Fundación Cocibolca Ecoalbergue ☎2248 8234, ⓦmombacho.org/eco.htm. Simple rooms where you can bunk down. Dinner, breakfast and transport from Granada are included in the rates. Per person <u>US$40</u>

RIVAS

Most travellers, experiencing **RIVAS** as a dusty bus stop on the way to or from Costa Rica, San Juan del Sur or Ometepe, are unaware of the pivotal role it played in Nicaraguan history. Founded in 1736, it became an important stop on the route of Cornelius Vanderbilt's Accessory Transit Company, which ferried goods and passengers between the Caribbean and the Pacific via Lago de Nicaragua – the town's heyday came during the California Gold Rush, when its streets were full of prospectors travelling with the Transit Company on their way to the goldfields of the western US. Modern-day Rivas isn't anything special, and can seem scarily deserted at night, but it's not a bad place to get stuck, especially if you fancy a taste of the real Nicaragua between gringo-tastic Granada and San Juan del Sur.

WHAT TO SEE AND DO

The colonial church near the Parque Central, **La Parroquia San Pedro**, is worth a visit, primarily for a fresco featuring a maritime-themed depiction of Catholicism triumphing over the godless communists. The desperately underfunded **Museo de Antropología e Historia de Rivas** (Mon–Fri 8am–noon & 2–5pm, Sat 8am–noon; C$40) sits four blocks west and two north of the Parque, with fine views of the rest of the town. Inside you'll find artefacts of the local Nahua Nicarao people dating from the fourteenth to sixteenth centuries, prehistoric bones (thought to be from a mammoth), some frightening stuffed animals and a few dusty 78rpm records from the early twentieth century.

ARRIVAL AND DEPARTURE

By bus Chicken buses pull into the ragged station in the market, a few blocks northwest of the town centre. Express buses to/from Managua (every 20min; 1hr 45min) stop on the highway, just outside town (get a bike taxi for C$10). Both Transnica and Tica Bus pass through Rivas (by the Texaco station) en route to San José, Managua and beyond. Destinations Granada (every 45min; 1hr 30min); Managua (*ruteado* every 20min; 3hr); Peñas Blancas (every 40min; 45min); San Juan del Sur (every 30min; 45min–1hr).

By taxi A taxi anywhere in town will set you back around C$10. A shared taxi from the market to San Jorge (see below) should be about C$15 and to San Juan del Sur C$50 (both/person).

To Isla de Ometepe The quickest route out to Isla de Ometepe (see p.496), in Lago de Nicaragua, is via San Jorge, which is just east of Rivas on the lakeshore. From Rivas, San Jorge is best reached by shared taxi (see above) and is accessible on direct buses (every 30min) from Managua's Mercado Huembes. There's not much to the town, although it does have a small beach and a reasonable hotel (see below).

ACCOMMODATION

Hospedaje Lidia One block north and two and a half blocks east of Parque Central ☎ 2563 3477. Rooms (some with private bath), sleeping up to five, spin off two pleasant courtyards at this decent family-owned option. It's convenient for the Tica Bus, if further from the market than most. Traditional breakfast US$3. **US$18**

Hostal El Chinica Half a block south of Parque Central ☎ 2563 1109, ✉ hostalelchinica@gmail.com. A haven in this grubby town: central, clean and well run. All rooms are en suite, with a/c and cable TV. You can also order room service from the family's Chinese restaurant round the corner. **US$35**

Hotel Hamacas San Jorge, east of Rivas on the lakeshore ☎ 2363 0048, ⊛ hotelhamacas.com. A short walk from the ferry terminal, this is a pleasant place to lay your head. Rates include breakfast. **US$30**

EATING AND DRINKING

A quick, cheap meal can be picked up at any of the comedores in the market, where you'll find good chicken, pork or beef and rice dishes for around C$50.

El Mesón Four blocks south of the market, behind Iglesia San Francisco. Classic lunch-only buffet joint, serving good daily specials for around C$50.

Repostería Don Marcos 100m east of the Parque Central's northern edge. Excellent for breakfast or stocking up for a long bus ride; a coffee and a piping-hot pastry will set you back C$20.

Vila's Rosti-Pizza On the southwest corner of the Parque. Probably your best bet for an evening, with a giant kids' playground inside and great people-watching from the tables outside. Chow down on *pollo a la plancha* (C$155) or passable pizza (C$130).

DIRECTORY

Banks There is a handful of banks in town: BAC (Mon–Fri 8.30am–4.30pm, Sat 8.30am–noon), two blocks west of the Parque, will change travellers' cheques and dollars. There are several ATMs around the Parque.

Health Clínica María Inmaculada, on the north side of the Parque, is open daily.

Internet Cafés are all over Rivas; try Cyber Plus (C$10/hr) just off the northwest corner of the Parque.

SAN JUAN DEL SUR

In the mid-1800s the sleepy fishing village of **SAN JUAN DEL SUR** was a crucial transit point on Cornelius Vanderbilt's trans-isthmian steamboat line, on which people and goods were transported to Gold Rush-era California. The town is enjoying a second wave of prosperity, thanks to its popularity with wave-hunting Westerners, and you'll

6

SAN JUAN DEL SUR

● EATING
"Chicken Lady"	7
El Gato Negro	3
Margarita's	5
Pelican Eyes	8
V.I.P	6

● DRINKING & NIGHTLIFE
Arribas	2
Crazy Crab Beach Club	1
Iguana Bar	4

■ ACCOMMODATION
Casa 28	1
Casa Oro	5
Hospedaje Eleonora	2
Hostel Esperanza	7
Hotel Estrella	3
Rebecca's Inn	6
Sueños del Mar	4

BAC Bank
Arena Caliente
San Juan del Sur Surf and Sport
Mercado
Tica Bus Ticket
Bus stop
Farmacia Santa Ana
Banco Pro Credit & ATM
Neptune Watersports
Bancentro
Andrea's Laundry
BDF Bank
Parque Central
Bampo Bank

▼ Refugio de Vida Silvestre La Flor

find few places in Nicaragua more geared up to backpackers.

Located in a lush valley with a river running down to the town's beach, the setting is beautiful; the beach itself is a long wide stretch of fine dark sand running between two cliffs. With excellent seafood restaurants, gringo-packed bars and an increasing number of good places to stay, San Juan is the kind of place where a two-day stay can turn into a two-week reverie. The locals are mostly happy with the attention, but there are occasional reports of muggings on the quieter beaches – get local advice before heading off on your own.

WHAT TO SEE AND DO

The lack of conventional sights in San Juan del Sur means that most people are engaged either in sunning themselves on the beach or undertaking something more energetic in the surrounding azure seas. While the waters around town aren't the cleanest, the stunning cliffs, reserves and beaches just along the coast are easily accessible.

Watersports

Surfing is the most popular sport in town, and you can easily rent boards and arrange transport – the town beach is surfable but not spectacular, and the good beaches are too far to walk to. Head for **Remanso** (to the south, and good for beginners), **Maderas** (to the north, popular with experienced surfers) or a number of further-flung options. Almost anywhere in town can arrange this – transport should set you back around US$5 and board hire about US$10. Water-taxis to playas Maderas and Majagual (12km to the north) leave from the area in front of *Hotel Estrella* at 10am or 11am daily, returning at 4pm or 5pm (40min; US$10 return) – a taxi will cost about the same.

The beaches, inlets and bays of the coast are ripe for exploration, and **sailing** and **fishing** trips are almost as popular as surfing – *Casa Oro* arrange backpacker-oriented fishing tours, and local tour companies (see box opposite) all have trips of their own. San Juan isn't quite the Corn Islands, but there's still plenty of diving here: try Neptune Watersports.

Other activities

For **frisbee golf**, Marsella Valley Nature Center (near Marsella Beach; ☎8805 6951, ⊚marsellavalley.com) has a twelve-"hole" course surrounded by nature trails, and offers accommodation. **ATV** rental can be arranged through a few hostels, including *Casa 28* (see below).

Refugio de Vida Silvestre La Flor

The **Refugio de Vida Silvestre La Flor**, 19km south of San Juan del Sur (C$200 entrance fee; if travelling direct, contact the national environment agency, MARENA ☎2563 4264), is a guarded reserve dedicated to protecting the **sea turtles**, primarily the Olive Ridley species, that nest here in large numbers between July and February. The night-time nestings themselves are an amazing spectacle, and the reserve also has good surf, a beautiful white sandy beach and a stand of shady trees, plus more great empty beaches within walking distance. Most hostels and operators can organize a trip here from San Juan – getting here independently (either via one of the water-taxis opposite *Hostel Estrella*, or by bus from the main stop) can be tricky and you're best asking in town for frequencies. Mosquitoes and sandflies are abundant – take repellent. Camping overnight (there are a few tents here to rent) is an expensive C$500 per tent.

ARRIVAL AND INFORMATION

By bus Buses from/to Rivas (every 30min; 45min–1hr) and Managua (3 express [3hr] and 3 *ruteados* [4hr] daily) pull up outside the market.

By taxi A shared taxi from/to Rivas should only cost you C$50 per person.

Tourist information The INTUR office (Mon–Fri 9am–1pm) sits on the western corner of the Parque. Various websites offer news and information – ⊚sanjuansurf.com is the pick of the bunch.

Bike rental Bikes can be rented at many hotels, including *Hospedaje Elizabeth* (opposite the bus stop) for US$6–8/day.

ACCOMMODATION

Like Granada, San Juan del Sur is witnessing a major expansion of tourist accommodation, with big, sociable places bunched on the waterfront and mellower, smaller establishments tending to sit a few streets back. Bear in mind that many places raise their prices in high season (around Christmas and Easter), when it might be worth reserving in advance.

Casa 28 Half a block south of *El Gato Negro* ☎2568 2441, ⊚marvincalde@hotmail.es. A reasonable, chilled-out budget option offering fifteen basic rooms with a fan, shared bath and optional a/c. US$14

★ **Casa Oro** One block west of the Parque ☎2568 2415, ⊚casaeloro.com. Sprawling backpacker den offering everything the homesick surfer might require, from pizza delivery and DVD nights to wave reports, board rental, a beach shuttle (US$4 return) and a funky rooftop terrace. Dorms are decent, there's a kitchen, and beach, sailing and surf trips can be arranged. Dorm US$7.50, double US$25

Hospedaje Eleanora Just east of the market ☎2568 2191. Likeable family-owned cheapie offering six rooms, all with private bathrooms, and a small hammocked balcony. More mellow than the big beachside hostels too. US$16

Hostel Esperanza Three blocks west and half a block

TOUR OPERATORS IN SAN JUAN DEL SUR

There's plenty of competition in San Juan del Sur, and most operators offer similar deals at similar prices. It's easy to organize trips via accommodation – if in doubt, try *Casa Oro*, *Hostel PachaMama*, *Casa 28* or *La Casa Feliz* – but several other tour and rental companies are worth considering.

Arena Caliente Next to the market ☎8815 3247, ⊚arenacaliente.com. Friendly place offering surf lessons, rental and transport, plus fishing trips (US$30). Lodging and packages can also be arranged.

Neptune Watersports Half a block south of the market ☎2568 2752, ⊚neptunenicadiving.com. San Juan's diving specialists can take you below the waves (US$85 for a two-tank dive) and also run fishing trips (US$45/hr for a group of up to eight).

San Juan del Sur Surf and Sport Half a block west of the market ☎2568 2022, ⊚sanjuandelsursurf.com. This long-standing local operator offers fishing trips (a boat of your own from US$275/half day), tours to Refugio La Flor (US$30), ATV rentals and a nearby canopy tour (US$30) plus – of course – surf rental and lessons.

6

south of the Parque ☎8760 4343, ⓦhostelesperanza
.com. Relaxed, somewhat chaotic hostel with
unexceptional rooms but a tremendous beachfront
location. There's a barbecue, hammocks and wi-fi too.
Breakfast included. Dorm US$8, double US$18

Hotel Estrella On the beachfront, two blocks west of
the market ☎2568 2210, ⓔhotelestrella1929@hotmail
.com. With a downstairs area devoted to selling on
secondhand ovens and fridges, this hotel may be quirky,
but it also has a plum location right on the beachfront and
reasonable prices. The rooms at the back are nothing
special and bathrooms are shared, but snag yourself a
front balcony and you're sorted. Breakfast is included.
Numerous tours are run from here too, including fishing
trips for US$40/hr. US$16

Rebecca's Inn Just off the northwestern edge of the
Parque ☎8675 1048. A pink-fronted family-run inn with
colourful, clean, wood-panelled rooms (fan and shared
bath) and friendly service. US$20

Sueños del Mar Just southeast of the market ☎2568
2079. Cosy TV room, kitchen and outdoor bamboo shower.
The rooms are small but the vibe is friendly. Continental
breakfast included. Dorm US$6, double US$16

EATING

San Juan del Sur is a great place to eat seafood – a whole
baked fish costs about C$170, while fresh lobster starts at
around C$250. There are plenty of bars and restaurants
along the beachfront, though the same dishes are
considerably cheaper and often equally tasty at the
comedores inside the market (C$70 for a big plate).

★ **"Chicken Lady"** *Asados Juanita*, at the central
market. A word-of-mouth travellers' favourite, this streetside BBQ serves lip-smacking chicken plates to eat in or
take away from C$70. Evenings only.

El Gato Negro 50m east of *Iguana Bar*. A colourful, mellow
café and bookshop with a reasonable menu (muffins C$25,
sandwiches C$100) and organic coffee (C$30 with refills).

★ **TREAT YOURSELF**

Pelican Eyes A block and a half east of the
Parque Central ⓦpelicaneyesresort.com.
Pelican Eyes is one of the plushest hotels in
the area, but you don't have to shell out for
the rooms (US$180–430) to get an eyeful
of its greatest asset: the magical sunset
views into the bay. Tramp up the stone
steps, sip the pricey but mighty fine
cocktails (from US$6), or slip into one of the
three infinity pools (US$5). Happy hour
(Wed 5–8pm) offers two-for-one drinks.

Margarita's Opposite the market. Another San Juan
institution. Almost as cheap as the market (mains C$70,
breakfast C$40), but friendlier, cleaner and just plain
nicer.

V.I.P Half a block south of *Casa 28*. The best pizza in town
(C$110–170), nothing more, nothing less. Beers C$25.
Wed–Sun 4–10pm.

DRINKING AND NIGHTLIFE

The seafront bars are perfectly located for soaking up the
sunset with a cold beer. As well as *Crazy Crab*, several clubs
and bars are open as late as 3 or 4am – all cater to a lively
mix of locals, tourists and resident surfers.

Arribas 100m north of *Iguana Bar*. Buzzy beachside place
where you can sip your beer (C$30) on the sands.

Crazy Crab Beach Club 500m north of *Iguana Bar*. Salsa
classes from 9pm, but it only really gets busy after 1am,
when everyone who hasn't gone to bed yet shakes their
stuff to a merry mix of salsa and pop. Beer C$20. Entry
C$30 on Sat, free otherwise. Thurs–Sun until sunrise.

Iguana Bar On the beachfront square, a block north of
Hotel Estrella. This place is booming at night, when the
huge bamboo balcony overlooking the beach and bay fills
with flirting locals and foreign beach bums. There's

INTO COSTA RICA: PEÑAS BLANCAS

Crossing the border at **Peñas Blancas**, 35km from San Juan del Sur, can be a time-consuming
process when countless migrant workers head back to see their families; don't be surprised if it
takes up two hours – you'll be there most of the day if you try to do it around Christmas or
Semana Santa.

Local buses from Rivas go all the way to the border; if you're leaving from San Juan del Sur, take
the Rivas bus only as far as the highway at La Virgen and then catch a connecting bus – there's
no need to go all the way back to Rivas. If you're travelling on to a Central American capital, you
can also head back to Rivas and catch a Transnica or Tica Bus as it passes through (see p.491).

The crossing is open daily 6am to 8pm, and packed with touts offering money-changing and
to fill out your forms for you. You'll be charged an exit tax of US$2. There is a US$10 fee to enter
Nicaragua. It's a fairly easy 1km walk (a moto-taxi will charge around C$20, a taxi a bit more) to
the Costa Rican *migración* where you'll have to pay a US$3 municipal tax before hopping on
the regular onward transport to San José.

reasonable food during the day (clams C$100, fish C$150), while a beer is C$30.

DIRECTORY

Banks Banks have popped up all over town, and there are several ATMs. Bancentro, south of the market, and Banco Pro Credit, one block east of *Hotel Estrella* (both Mon–Fri 8am–noon & 1–4.30pm, Sat 8am–noon), will change US dollars but not travellers' cheques.

Health Farmacia Santa Ana, half a block south of the market, is open daily.

Internet Connexion Cyber, opposite *El Mercado* (Mon–Sat 7am–10pm, Sun 7am–9pm), and Cyber Manfred, opposite *El Gato Negro* (daily 8am–9pm), both charge C$20/hr and have phones.

Laundry Several hostels have DIY facilities (washboards, not machines) and there are several independent laundries charging about US$3–5 per load; try Andrea's, just south of *Casa Oro*.

Lago de Nicaragua

Standing on the shore and looking out onto vast **Lago de Nicaragua**, it's not hard to imagine the surprise of the Spanish navigators who, in 1522, nearly certain they were heading towards the Pacific, found the lake's expanse instead. They weren't too far off – merely a few thousand years – as both it and Lago de Managua were probably once part of the Pacific, until seismic activity created the plain that now separates the lake from the ocean. Several millennia later, by the time the Spanish had arrived, the Lago de Nicaragua was the largest **freshwater sea** in the Americas after the Great Lakes: fed by freshwater rivers, the lake water gradually lost its salinity, while the fish trapped in it evolved into some of the most unusual types of fish found anywhere on earth, including freshwater shark and swordfish. Locally, the lake is still known by its indigenous name, Cocibolca ("sweet sea").

It's easy to be captivated by the natural beauty and unique cultures of the **islands** that dot the southwest sector of the lake, including twin-volcanoed **Isla de Ometepe** and the scattering of small islands that make up the **Solentiname archipelago**. On its eastern edge the lake is fed by the 170km **Río San Juan**, which you can boat down to the remote **El Castillo**, an old Spanish fort surrounded on all sides by pristine jungle. The Río San Juan and El Castillo are reached via the largest town on the east side of the lake, **San Carlos**, a bug-ridden settlement mainly used by travellers as a transit point.

6

6

Making your way around the lake can be quite an undertaking: Lago de Nicaragua is affected by what locals call a "short-wave phenomenon" – short, high, choppy waves – caused by the meeting of the Papagayo wind from the west and the Caribbean-generated trade winds from the east. Crossing can be hell for those prone to seasickness. You'll need to be prepared for the conditions and patient with erratic boat schedules.

ISLA DE OMETEPE

Almost everyone who travels through Nicaragua comes to **ISLA DE OMETEPE**, Lago de Nicaragua's largest island, to experience its lush scenery and tranquil atmosphere. Ometepe's name comes from the Nahuatl language of the Chorotegans, the original inhabitants of Nicaragua, who called it Ome Tepetl – "the place of two hills" – for its two volcanoes. The island has probably been inhabited since the first migration of indigenous groups from Mexico arrived in this area, and a few stone sculptures and **petroglyphs** attest to their presence on the island. Even from the mainland, taking in the

sight of its two cones, you can tell it's a special place.

The higher and more symmetrical of the two is **Volcán Concepción** (1610m), Nicaragua's second-highest volcano. Much of the island's 40,000-strong population live around the foot of Volcán Concepción, where you'll find the main towns of **Moyogalpa** and **Altagracia**. Smaller, extinct **Volcán Maderas** (1394m) is less perfectly conical in shape, but clothed with precious **cloudforest**, where you're likely to spot such **wildlife** as white-faced (*carablanca*) and howler (*mono congo*) monkeys, green parrots (*loro verde*) and blue-tailed birds called *urracas*. Almost all activities on the island are based in the outdoors: **walking**, **hiking**, **volcano-viewing**, **volunteering** and **horseriding** are among the most popular.

WHAT TO SEE AND DO

Most people are here to visit Ometepe's iconic twin volcanoes, but there's plenty to do elsewhere, from chilling at lodges and stretching out on beaches – notably **Playa Santo Domingo** – to exploring waterfalls and pre-Columbian remains.

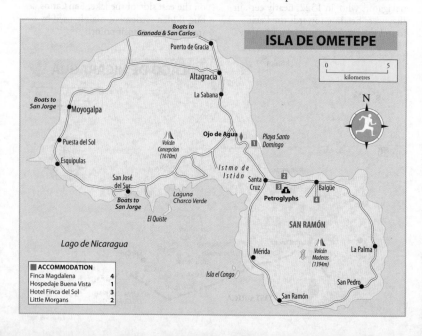

ISLA DE OMETEPE

Boats to Granada & San Carlos
Puerto de Gracia
Altagracia
La Sabana
Boats to San Jorge
Moyogalpa
Puesta del Sol
Esquipulas
Volcán Concepción (1610m)
Ojo de Agua
Playa Santo Domingo
San José del Sur
Istmo de Istián
Santa Cruz
Balgüe
Petroglyphs
Laguna Charco Verde
Boats to San Jorge
El Quiste
SAN RAMÓN
Lago de Nicaragua
Mérida
Volcán Maderas (1394m)
La Palma
Isla el Congo
San Pedro
San Ramón

0   5
kilometres

N

ACCOMMODATION
Finca Magdalena	4
Hospedaje Buena Vista	1
Hotel Finca del Sol	3
Little Morgans	2

Moyogalpa

Moyogalpa, the largest town on the island, sits on the northwest side of Volcán Concepción. It's convenient for the ferry and has a few decent bars and restaurants, while its popularity with backpackers means it's not a bad place to arrange a tour or shoot the breeze for an evening. After you've walked up the hill and looked at the dock, there's not much sightseeing to do – the **museum** (daylight hours; C$40), on the right just before the church at the top end of town, houses a few artefacts and petroglyphs.

Altagracia

While there's also little to detain travellers in **Altagracia**, a sleepy town set slightly inland on Ometepe's northeastern side, it is quieter and less touristed than Moyogalpa. The **Parque Central** is ringed by several pre-Columbian statues found on the island, while the **Museo de Ometepe** (Mon–Fri 8am–noon & 1–4pm, Sat 9am–3pm, Sun 9am–1pm; C$30), off the west side of the park, houses a few more local archeological finds.

Volcán Concepción

The main **hike** (8–10hr return) up **Volcán Concepción** starts from just outside Altagracia. Much of the climb is extremely steep and it's compulsory to hire a **guide** (see p.498) for the upper sections. Several **trails** wind up, and all

SAN DIEGO DE ALCALÁ

Every year during the third week of November, Altagracia celebrates the week-long **fiesta of San Diego de Alcalá**, in honour of the village's patron saint. If you're passing through on November 17 you may be lucky enough to see one of the highlights of the festival, the **Baile del Zompopo** ("dance of the leaf-cutter ant"). The locals set out from the church in a traditional procession through the streets, parading aloft an image of San Diego. Participants act out the distinctive dance with tree branches held aloft – representing the indigenous leaf-cutter ant – while moving to traditional drum rhythms.

are quite an exercise – start early and bring plenty of water – with an exposed and rocky stretch towards the summit that gets very windy. The cloudforests of the lower slopes are gorgeous (keep an ear out for howler monkeys), and the dramatic views from the top, encompassing neighbouring Volcán Maderas and the expanse of surrounding Lake Nicaragua, are genuinely breathtaking.

Playa Santo Domingo

Stretching for more than 1km on the east side of the narrow isthmus separating the two volcanoes is the grey-sand **Playa Santo Domingo**. This is the best place to swim on the island, and many volcano-climbers and hikers spend a day soaking up some sun here. The beach is accessed from the recently resurfaced main road circling Concepción.

Volcán Maderas

The **hike** (7–8hr return) up the verdant slopes of dormant **Volcán Maderas** is less arduous than the steep climb up and down Concepción, though it can nonetheless be a muddy and slippery walk – guides are mandatory (see p.498). The final stretch down into the crater is not for the faint of heart; the rocks are almost sheer and you'll have to use a rope. Birds and monkeys can be heard (if not seen) all the way up, and the summit gives stunning views of Concepción and the lake. The crater itself is eerily silent and still, its lip covered by a mixture of dense, rainforest-like vegetation and a few bromeliad-encrusted conifers. Make sure you take plenty of water, sunscreen and perhaps a swimming costume; the crater lagoon is swimmable, if pretty mucky.

The rest of the island

If you have time, it's worth exploring the quiet villages dotted around the lower slopes of Maderas. **Petroglyphs** are scattered over this part of the island, with one group clustered between the hamlets of Santa Cruz and La Palma – ask at *Finca Magdalena* (see p.499) for a guide (US$6). A two- or three-hour hike from the *Finca Magdalena* will take you to the pleasant, but extremely cold, **San Ramón waterfalls**. The naturally fed pools at **Ojo de Agua** (the waterhole), a twenty-minute hike from Villa Paraíso near Playa Santo Domingo, also merit a visit. If you've just hiked a volcano, there's nothing more refreshing than climbing on the rope swing and diving in to one of the rainforest-shaded pools.

ARRIVAL AND DEPARTURE

BY BOAT

The only way to travel between Isla de Ometepe and the mainland is by a fairly bumpy boat trip. Moyogalpa's dock is at the bottom of the town's steep and narrow main street and Altagracia's is 2km out of town ($10/person in a minivan). The third port, at the village of San José del Sur, is less convenient – you'll probably have to get a taxi.

From San Jorge The majority of travellers arrive by ferry (C$40–69) or less comfortable *lancha* (C$30–40) via San Jorge, northeast of Rivas (see p.491). There are roughly hourly departures between San Jorge and Moyogalpa and a twice-daily ferry from San Jorge to San José del Sur, though itineraries change regularly – check at the INTUR office in Granada (see p.487) or on ⓦepn.com.ni.

From Granada There are currently two boats a week from Granada to Altagracia (Mon & Thurs 2pm; 4hr; C$104; return Wed & Sat 12.30am). The journey is not great, however – the lake is often very choppy and tourists have to buy a "first class" ticket, sitting in an icily cold a/c section of the boat.

From San Carlos Two boats a week run from San Carlos to Altagracia (Tues & Fri 2pm, arriving midnight; C$210; return Mon & Thurs 7.30pm). The same caveats apply to this trip as to the boats from Granada.

GETTING AROUND

The roads around the island have recently been resurfaced, so getting around is not the nightmare it once was. At the time of writing, there is an airport under construction, with talk of direct flights from Costa Rica, as well as Managua.

By bike and motorcycle Ometepe is one of the best places in Nicaragua to cycle, even if the state of the roads takes a little bit of getting used to. Ask at your accommodation or UGO (see below) for the best place to rent bicycles or motorbikes and check the condition of your bike carefully before you get on it – some operators have been known to claim you've wrecked their machines and refuse to give you back your deposit.

By bus Buses connect Moyogalpa and Altagracia (roughly hourly until 6pm; 1hr–1hr 30min), taking in Playa Santo Domingo. A handful of services connect the two towns with Mérida and Balgüe (2 daily) and Mérida (3 daily) – check with your accommodation, as schedules fluctuate.

By taxi Minibus taxis are mostly found in Moyogalpa, but charge a whacking C$600 for a trip to Mérida – a good option if travelling in a group. You can also hire these drivers/minibuses for the day; beware, however, of drivers telling you that the last bus has already left in order to get your custom.

INFORMATION

Tour operators There's no INTUR office on the island but you won't be short of advice – all accommodation will be able to point you towards a tour and in some you'll be approached by informal guides. These can be a reasonable bet for a simple trip – but in all cases, check exactly what you're getting. For something more substantial it's worth speaking to UGO (on the left, just as you exit the dock at Moyogalpa, ☎ 2827 7714), a confederation of guides who can take you all over the island – trips cost US$10–40/person, depending on how large your group is and what you're after.

ACCOMMODATION

In Moyogalpa and Altagracia, most rooms are simple, concrete and dry-wall cubicles, while those at the various fincas and haciendas can be charmingly rustic, with lots of polished wood and hammocked balconies. Many of the latter are splendidly located – but you may have to rely on their catering, as many are pretty isolated.

MOYOGALPA

Hospedaje Central Three blocks east (uphill) and one south of the dock ☎2569 4262, ⓦhostelometepe.com. Likeable, creaky hostel with a lively on-site bar and restaurant, *El Indio Viejo* (see opposite). There are reasonable doubles (a/c and bath US$3 extra), wi-fi throughout, and a relaxing, hammock-bedecked courtyard.

PUESTA DEL SOL HOMESTAYS

For an authentic Ometepe experience, consider arranging a homestay with a local family. For US$20 per night (including all meals or US$7 bed only), one of ten families in the **Puesta del Sol** collective will take you in and share their home with you. The group (☎8619 0219, infrequently updated website ⓦpuestadelsol.org) has small plots of land growing organic herbs, fruits and other plants from its base 2km from Moyogalpa, and makes wine and tea from hibiscus. Visitors can learn about cultivation, experience life with a typical Nica family and arrange visits to Ometepe's sights – bike and canoe rental can also be arranged.

Most work is done by volunteers and there are links to ecological and spiritual projects that the grizzled owner will fill you in on if you ask. Hammock US$3, dorm US$5.50, double US$15

Hospedaje Cool Vibe Three blocks east and one and a half blocks south of the main dock in Moyogalpa. New *hospedaje* with a young (cool) vibe, kitchen facilities, and a garden with hummingbirds. Dorm US$7, double US$15

★ **The Landing Hotel** 50m east (uphill) from the dock ☎ 2569 4113, ✉ hbsaussy@gmail.com. Smart hotel with a decent downstairs bar and restaurant (pasta C$100, fillet of fish C$120), helpful staff and splendid views from the upstairs terrace. The comfortable rooms – both en suite and with shared bath – are a stone's throw from the dock, and good value too. Dorm US$7, double US$15

ALTAGRACIA

Hotel Castillo 100m south and 50m west of the Parque Central ☎ 2552 8744. Basic but spotless rooms, some with private bath, as well as a good restaurant, large hammocks, an internet café (C$25/hr) and a bar showing sports. The latter gets busy when there's sport on, but the courtyards remain mellow enough with their hammocks and rocking chairs. You pay US$5 extra for private bath, another US$15 for a/c. US$10

Hotel Central Two blocks south of the Parque Central ☎ 2552 8770. Probably the best choice in town, with excellent-value rooms, some with a balcony and private bath (extra US$16), and sweet little cabañitas. There's also a restaurant and bicycle rental (C$120/day). Double US$14, cabaña US$20

THE REST OF THE ISLAND

Finca Magdalena Take the bus from Altagracia to Balgüe, from where it's a 20min walk up a signposted path ☎ 8498 1683, ✆ fincamagdalena.com. This welcoming old hacienda, converted by the Sandinistas into an organic coffee co-operative (and still going strong), has stunning views across the lake. The no-frills accommodation consists of hammocks or camping, large dorm rooms, partitioned private rooms, and a private en-suite hut. A restaurant serves hearty meals and organic coffee, while tours take you round the plantations and to nearby waterfalls and petroglyphs. Camping US$3.50, dorm US$4, double US$11.50, hut US$23

Hospedaje Buena Vista Playa Domingo ☎ 2569 4868. Probably the best budget bet near lovely Playa Domingo, with simple rooms, a cheap and cheerful *comedor* next door and a more tranquil vibe than the boozier options elsewhere on the island. US$20

Little Morgans Between Santa Cruz and Balgüe ☎ 8611 7973, ✆ littlemorgans.com. Groovy lodge by the lakeside that combines cool views from the tree house with a party vibe come evening – the simple cabañas are quieter than

★ **TREAT YOURSELF**

Hotel Finca del Sol Opposite *Little Morgans* ☎ 8364 6394, ✆ hotelfincadelsol .com. Places claiming to be eco-friendly abound, but this one's genuine – your power really does come from solar panels, your toilet waste is turned into compost and there is a maximum of ten guests at a time (so book ahead). Accommodation is in one of three private en-suite cabins, with their own private seating/hammock area – perfect for watching the sun set behind the volcano. Bike rental is available and recommended for exploring nearby Santa Cruz and Balgüe. A hearty, healthy breakfast costs around $5.50. US$40

the dorm beds. Buses run to Balgüe from Altagracia and Moyogalpa; otherwise you'll need to get a cab (US$30 per group). Dorm US$8, cabaña US$25

EATING AND DRINKING

The best choice of places to eat and drink is in Moyogalpa; Altagracia has a handful of others, with a shack on the north side of its Parque Central offering classic, hearty fodder for around C$50. Out of town, most of the fincas and haciendas have excellent on-site restaurants. There's not a huge party scene on Ometepe; Moyogalpa is the liveliest after dark.

MOYOGALPA

The American A block east (uphill) from the main dock. Bright café serving gringo-style food like hot dogs (C$45), chilli con carne (C$100) and clam chowder (C$80), plus breakfasts, smoothies and coffee (C$20). Also has rooms for rent with a/c. Open from 6am for breakfast.

★ **The Cornerhouse** A block up the hill from the dock, opposite the petrol station ☎ 2569 4212, ✆ thecorner houseometepe.com. A cool vibe, due mainly to the friendly owners. Breakfast menu (C$50–105), delicious sandwiches (around C$100) and smoothies (C$30). There are also four rooms for rent on a first-come-first-served basis.

El Indio Viejo *Hospedaje Central*, three blocks east (uphill) and one south of the dock ☎ 2569 4262, ✆ hostelometepe.com. This bar and restaurant is the most sociable joint on the island, and the main backpacker hangout, offering breakfast for C$40–100, mains for C$75–150 and beer for C$25.

Restaurante Ranchitos Opposite *Casa Familiar*. This long, narrow bamboo-clad *rancho* offers a cracking Nica-style menu of meat and seafood plates (C$160–230), with decent sides, plus pizza (from C$110). The tilapia's so good you'll be slurping its bones till they bring the bill.

Timbo al Tambo 100m uphill (east) from docks. A funky little café-bar with a cool half-raised dance floor playing Latin music to a lively local crowd. Beer C$20, mojito C$30.

ALTAGRACIA

Hotel Kencho Just south of the Parque Central. Reasonable, airy restaurant below the adequate hotel of the same name, where you can chomp down on chicken (C$70), grilled fish (C$120) or *desayuno típico* (C$50).

ELSEWHERE ON THE ISLAND

★ **Café Campestre** On your left as you arrive in Balgüe ☎ 8725 8447, ⓦ ometepe.info. The British owner bought a farm here twelve years ago and now serves his organic produce in the restaurant. If you need a curry fix, it's worth making the trip to Balgüe just to eat here (Thai and Indian curries C$100–135), and if you're lucky, there'll even be some home-brewed beer (C$25). There are also two rooms for rent (doubles $15) and local tours available.

DIRECTORY

MOYOGALPA

Banks Banpro, Bancentro and Banco ProCredit have branches in Moyogalpa; all change US dollars and have an ATM.

Health Emergencies can be attended to at the Héroes y Mártires Hospital, just outside Moyogalpa on the road to Altagracia.

Internet Ciber Café, one block uphill (east) from the dock on the left (C$16/hr), or Cyber Ometepe, opposite the bank (C$15/hr).

ELSEWHERE ON THE ISLAND

Internet Altagracia's only option is Cyber Vajoma, in the *Hotel Castillo* (C$15/hr). Most of the fincas and haciendas also offer (often slow) internet access.

Laundry Services are provided by many hotels.

SAN CARLOS

Sleepy, bedraggled **SAN CARLOS**, at the southern end of Lago de Nicaragua and the head of the Río San Juan, has to be one of the most unprepossessing towns in the whole country. Despite its position as one of the main transit towns for the lake area, and the odd bit of renovation work around the dockfront, an air of apathy pervades its ramshackle buildings and battered streets. That said, the people are friendly and most visitors end up spending at least one night here – generally en route to the **Solentiname archipelago**, to **El Castillo** and points further south along the **Río San Juan** or to Costa Rica via Los Chiles, although San Carlos itself is an access point to the wild and relatively untouched Los Guatuzos reserve.

ARRIVAL AND DEPARTURE

By plane La Costeña (☎ 2583 0048) flies from Managua to San Carlos (40min), landing at the tiny airstrip just north of town. It's a 20min walk into town; a taxi (5min) should cost about C$20.

By boat Solentiname boats (see p.502) use the main dock in San Carlos, while those for Granada, El Castillo, Sabalos, San Juan del Norte, Ometepe and Los Chiles use the dock on the east side, by the Petronic station – pay your US$2 exit fee at *migración*, just west of the municipal dock. Boats from Granada arrive in San Carlos around 4am at the eastern dock by the Petronic station; from here it's a 10min walk or 2min taxi ride to any of the town's accommodation. You can either strike out to find a hotel, or wait around (for about 1hr) for boats on to El Castillo – they use the same dock. Boats back to Altagracia/Granada currently leave on Tues and Fri at 2pm (10hr/14hr) – arrive early to pick up tickets.

By bus The bus station is by the eastern dock, opposite a cluster of *comedores*. Services to Chinandega, however (Sun & Thurs 3pm), don't leave from the bus station – take a taxi.

Destinations El Rama (1 daily, 8am; 6hr); Granada (leaves San Carlos Tues & Fri 3pm & 4pm; leaves Granada Mon & Thurs 11am & 3pm); Managua (7 daily; 5–7hr).

INTO COSTA RICA: LOS CHILES

There are currently three boats (usually 10.30am, 1.30pm [not Sun] & 4pm; US$10) leaving from the east *muelle* (dock) in San Carlos for the scenic hour-plus chug to **Los Chiles** in Costa Rica. It's best to aim for one of the earlier services, as the later ones can be unreliable, and it's easiest to get your exit stamp from the customs office at the dock before departure (US$2). Coming the other way the charge is US$10. The actual border post is just outside Los Chiles; you'll need to walk a few hundred metres down to the immigration office to get an entry stamp to Costa Rica at the Los Chiles *muelle*, then either hop in a taxi or walk a further kilometre to the bus stop. It's a world away from the chaos of Nicaragua's other borders.

INFORMATION

Tourist information There's a small INTUR office in the main dock building (Mon–Fri 8am–1pm ☏ 2853 0301), where you can get up-to-date information on Solentiname and points south on the Río San Juan. They post a boat timetable with current prices outside. The CANTUR office (Mon–Fri 8am–5pm ☏ 2583 0266), one block east of INTUR above a shop, also provides tourist information, along with a free map of town.

Tour operators *Hotel Cabinas Leyko* can organize wildlife trips, or try Ryo Big Tours (☏ 8828 8558, ✉ ryobigtours@hotmail.com), in the same office as CANTUR, for excursions to the Los Guatuzos reserve or further up the river.

ACCOMMODATION

San Carlos has a lot of transient traffic, which is reflected in its spartan hotels. There's little to choose between the few vaguely acceptable and not overly bug-ridden, sinister or noisy places in town.

Hotel Cabinas Leyko Two blocks west of the Parque ☏ 2583 0354, ✉ leykou7@yahoo.es. The best budget rooms in town, which isn't saying much. The decent, if slightly damp, wooden rooms come with wall fan or a/c (a/c costs extra), screened windows and shared or private bath. There's also a balcony with rocking chairs and lake views. <u>US$13</u>

Hotel Seledith 1 block north of *Cabinas Leyko* ☏ 2583 0376. Simple, clean rooms with TV and shared balcony. Access is via a gate beside the shop below. Double with bath <u>C$800</u>, double without bath <u>C$300</u>

Hotelito Carmina Opposite *Restaurante Kaoma*. Quiet, safe and clean family-run hostel. All rooms are en suite with cable TV. The 9pm curfew might be negotiable. <u>C$500</u>

EATING

Criollo del Lago Right opposite the plaza by the waterfront. A popular spot for simple, well-priced food. Breakfast (C$40–60), lunch (C$70–80) and supper (C$50 for *gallo pinto*, eggs and cheese). They don't sell beer, but nor do they mind if you shout over to the waitress and buy one from the *comedor* next door.

Restaurante Don Leo Next to and part of the same business as *Cabinas Leyko*. Attentive staff for such a simple café, with English spoken. Breakfast C$70, sandwiches C$80, mains from C$100. They can also arrange tours.

Restaurante el Granadino One block uphill from the *muelle municipal*. Probably the best restaurant in town, set on a huge wooden balcony overlooking the main square and dock. Steaks, fish and chicken from C$100.

Restaurante Kaoma On the waterfront, a block up from the *muelle municipal*. Good, filling seafood and vegetarian (on request) plates for C$100–250, with a bit of a buzz come the evening.

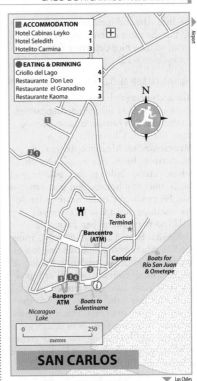

ACCOMMODATION
Hotel Cabinas Leyko	2
Hotel Seledith	1
Hotelito Carmina	3

EATING & DRINKING
Criollo del Lago	4
Restaurante Don Leo	1
Restaurante el Granadino	2
Restaurante Kaoma	3

SAN CARLOS

DIRECTORY

Banks There's a Bancentro with an ATM two blocks up from the waterfront and a Banpro ATM in one of the hexagonal huts on the waterfront.

Internet A couple of internet cafés sit near the Parque Central, two blocks up from the waterfront.

SOLENTINAME ARCHIPELAGO

Lying in the southeast corner of Lago de Nicaragua, the **SOLENTINAME ARCHIPELAGO** is made up of 36 islands of varying size. For a long time it was the islands' colony of naïf-art **painters** that brought it fame – priest and poet Ernesto Cardenal lived here for many years before becoming the Sandinistas' Minister of the Interior in the 1980s, and it was his promotion of the archipelago's primitive art and artisan skills that led to the government declaring Solentiname a national monument in 1990 – but today the islands are better known for their unspoilt natural beauty and remarkable

6

wildlife. The archipelago's **isolation** keeps all but the most determined travellers away, so it's a nice departure from the backpacker trail.

WHAT TO SEE AND DO

The archipelago's largest islands are also the most densely inhabited: **Mancarrón**, **La Venada**, **San Fernando** (also referred to as Isla Elvis Chavarría) and **Mancarroncito**. Most people stay on Mancarrón, home to a simple church whose interior holds vibrant paintings of birds, trees and houses, and make trips to San Fernando and other nearby islands. It's worth paying a visit to the small MUSAS **museum** on San Fernando (Mon–Sat 8am–12.30pm & 2.30–5pm; US$2), where you'll find information on the local wildlife, petroglyphs, medicinal plants and, of course, the local artisanal process. Make sure you bring plenty of cash with you – there's no ATM on the islands. Other than that, you're best off interspersing long periods of relaxation with the odd hike along the many trails – where you'll see plenty of birdlife – and a few spots of fishing.

ARRIVAL AND DEPARTURE

By boat A "ferry" goes to Mancarrón (also calling at La Venada and San Fernando) from San Carlos twice a week (Tues & Fri 1pm; 2hr; C$80), although it's best to check departure times at the dock. Returning to San Carlos, boats depart from Mancarrón at 4.30am on Tues and Fri. At the time of writing, there is also a daily "tourist" service between San Carlos and Solentiname, but this is subject to change (check ⓦ transol.com.ni or ☎ 8828 3243 before travelling).

ACCOMMODATION AND EATING

Almost all accommodation offers inclusive meals; failing that, owners will point you to the nearest hotel that has a dining room – there are no dedicated restaurants on the islands.

MANCARRÓN

El Buen Amigo ☎ 8869 6619. A clean, basic and friendly *hospedaje* located up the hill just out of town. Traditional food from C$80. US$10

Hostal Los Pececitos Castillo Opposite *El Buen Amigo* ☎ 8684 5701, ⓔ victodani@yahoo.es. Family-run *hostal* – all rooms with shared bathroom. Meals available US$4. US$16

SAN FERNANDO

Hotel Familiar Vanessa Just left of the main dock ☎ 8680 8423, ⓔ jose.sequeirapineda@gmail.com. Simple, friendly, family-run *hostal* with shared bathroom. Meals can be cooked to order. US$15

Mire Estrellas Beside the lake ☎ 8894 7331. Cheap, simple rooms with a hammocked balcony on the lake. You can eat at the restaurant of the pricey *Hotel Cabañas Paraíso*, opposite. US$20

RÍO SAN JUAN

The mighty 170km-long **RÍO SAN JUAN** is one of the most important rivers in Central America. In colonial times it was the route by which the cities of Granada and León were supplied by Spain and emptied of their treasure by pirates, and optimists still claim it could one day form the basis of a canal to rival Panama's. It's the site of regular squabbles between Nicaragua and Costa Rica (see p.450), although you wouldn't know it while drifting down its sinuous and gloriously verdant length: the only settlements nearby are remote and sleepy villages whose inhabitants make their living by fishing and farming. **Ecotourism** offers one of the few sources of income: pack a waterproof, insect repellent and a stout pair of boots, and get ready for grand castles, intriguing tours and giant grilled river shrimp.

WHAT TO SEE AND DO

Most travellers see the Río San Juan from a boat between **San Carlos** (see p.500) on the eastern shore of Lago de Nicaragua and the old Spanish fort and town of **El Castillo**, the only real tourist attraction in the area. **Wildlife** is abundant along the river, and travellers who venture up- or downstream will certainly spot sloths, howler monkeys, parrots and macaws, bats, storks, caimans and perhaps even a tapir.

El Castillo

The full name of the Río San Juan's historic fort is La Fortaleza de la Inmaculada Concepción de María, though everyone refers to it simply as **El Castillo**. Lying on a hillock beside a narrow stretch of the Río San Juan, the fort was built by the Spanish as a defensive measure against the pirates who continually sacked Granada in the seventeenth century. It was more or less effective for a hundred years, until a British force led by a young Horatio Nelson finally took it in 1780, after which it was abandoned for nearly two centuries. The neatly restored structure boasts an interesting small **museum** (daily 8am–1.40pm; C$45, plus C$25 to take photos or C$50 for video) with dusty armaments of the period, information on the area's history and a few random artefacts found during the restoration of the castle, and a **library** (closed at weekends) with more than a thousand books on the history of the castle and the Río San Juan area.

Reserva Biológica Indio Maíz

Downstream from El Castillo, heading out towards the Caribbean, the northern bank of the Río San Juan forms part of the 3000-square-kilometre **Reserva Biológica Indio Maíz**, the largest nature reserve in Nicaragua. The climate here is very wet and hot, with the vast expanses of dense rainforest sheltering many species, including the elusive manatee, jaguars, tapirs, scarlet macaws, parrots and toucans. The pristine Indio Maíz vegetation stands in sharp contrast with the Costa Rican side, where agriculture and logging have eroded the forest.

San Juan de Nicaragua

Located at the mouth of the mighty Río San Juan, just as the Río Indio branches off northwards, Greytown was one of the first places European explorers/pirates (depending on your point of view) arrived. Nearby **San Juan de Nicaragua** (aka San Juan del Norte, aka Greytown), however, is perhaps the youngest town in Central America, established in the early 1990s when a mishmash of families displaced by the war decided to return to Nicaragua. All that is left of old Greytown is an overgrown graveyard and a dredger brought by Cornelius Vanderbilt in the 1800s with hopes of creating an inter-oceanic canal.

ARRIVAL AND DEPARTURE

BY PLANE

La Costeña (☎ 2263 2142) runs flights from Managua and San Carlos on Thurs & Sun, which arrive at the tiny airport where the old town of Greytown once stood. The only way to/from the airport is by private *panga*. Arrange in advance through your accommodation, or call *Hotelito Evo* (US$10/person; ☎ 2583 9019). Planes are small and flights regularly sell out, so if you're planning to travel along the river and then hop on a plane back to Managua, you'd be better off booking the flight before you set off – or be prepared to spend a few more days in San Juan. There is a US$2 airport tax payable at all national airports.

BY BOAT

El Castillo Boats travel between El Castillo and San Carlos (see p.500) six times daily (leaving San Carlos 6.30am, 8am, 10.30am, noon, 2pm & 3pm; leaving El Castillo 5am, 6am, 7am, 11.30am, 2pm & 3.30pm; 2–3hr; C$77–140), stopping off at Sábalos en route. Lodges can also organize transport. During the week there may be more daytime departures, while on Sunday afternoon departures are unreliable – check at the docks.

Reserva Biológica Indio Maíz You can hire a private boat from El Castillo (around US$25 one-way) to get to the research station, or board any boat travelling between San Carlos and San Juan de Nicaragua (they have to stop here as there is a checkpoint, but for the return journey you may find that boats are already full by this point). A couple of operators in El Castillo also offer tours (see below).

San Juan de Nicaragua *Pangas* to/from San Carlos arrive/leave from the dock at the north end of town (fast boats Mon & Fri 8am, Thurs & Sun 5am; 7hr; C$610; slow boats Thurs, Sat & Sun 5am; 10–12hr; C$329). All boats make the return trip from San Carlos the following day. There are no regular services to/from Bluefields; *Hotelito Evo* is currently the only tour operator licensed to make private trips there (US$600 for groups of 8–10).

INFORMATION AND TOURS

EL CASTILLO

Tourist information The Asociación Municipal de Ecoturismo El Castillo runs a small tourist office just up

6

from the dock (Mon–Sat 8am–noon & 2–6pm; ☎8652 6020). They offer canoe trips (US$70 for up to five people; 3–4hr) and walking tours in the Indio Maíz biological reserve, and atmospheric sunset cayman-spotting trips (US$45 for four people). Nena Tours (☎8821 2135, ⓦnenalodge.com), operating from the lodge of the same name (see below), offers an English-speaking alternative, with tours of the reserve (US$70 for four people), trips in a traditional dug-out canoe (US$15/person) and cayman-spotting (US$45 for four).

ACCOMMODATION

The trip to and from El Castillo can be completed in a day, but the small and friendly village around the fort offers several accommodation options and is a charming place to rest up, especially if you've been travelling hard and fast via San Carlos. Just over halfway between San Carlos and El Castillo, the small riverside town of Sábalos offers several rather wonderful lodges – the only drawback is that you'll be dependent on their food and tours, which are more expensive than those in El Castillo.

SÁBALOS

★ **Grand River Lodge** Along the river, a couple of km before Sábalos ☎8936 3919, ⓦhotelgrandriverlodge .com. Tiny wooden cabins with charming open-roofed shower rooms. There's a real family atmosphere, with the owner happy to show guests around his cocoa plantation, and horseriding and kayaking can be arranged. Rates include breakfast; other meals C$70. **US$20**

★ **Hotel Kateana** One block north of the dock, on the right-hand side. The sweet young owner will go out of her way to accommodate you. If you've had your fill of rice and beans, she can tell you where to find cheap vegetables and lend you her kitchen. Laundry service available. Rates include a light breakfast. Double: with shared bath **C$400**, with private bath **C$450**

Hotel Sábalos ☎2271 7424, ⓦhotelsabalos.com.ni. A great hotel just up the river from *Sábalos Lodge*. The en-suite rooms are rather plain, but immaculately tidy, set over the river and accessed from a large, wooden porch. A wide variety of tours can be arranged, too. **US$36**

Sábalos Lodge 45km from San Carlos ☎8850 7623, ⓦsabaloslodge.com. A rustic-chic ecolodge with en-suite *cabinas* in wild jungle grounds inhabited by howler monkeys and hummingbirds; stay in one of the larger, riverfront thatched huts for a real Tarzan experience. The (costly) tours include kayak trips down the river, birdwatching and treks. Breakfast is included; lunch and dinner are available on request from the restaurant (US$12). **US$35**

EL CASTILLO

Albergue El Castillo On the hill by the entrance to the ruins ☎8924 5608. Simple, comfortable rooms with mosquito

nets and fans in a huge, wooden cabin-style hotel with balcony and great river views – get a room upstairs. Breakfast is included, as is wi-fi – C$20/hr for non-guests. **US$30**

Hospedaje Universal Just left of the dock ☎8666 3264. This family-run hostel has small, clean wood-partitioned rooms and shared showers, along with a wooden balcony with hammocks right on the river. **US$10**

Nena Lodge 5min from the dock, on the left ☎8821 2135, ⓦnenalodge.com. Neat, tidy rooms in a friendly, family-run hostel that also offers tours. **US$14**

RESERVA BIOLÓGICA INDIO MAÍZ

★ **Refugio Bartola** ☎8376 6979 or ☎8873 8586. A scientific research station offering eleven comfortable en-suite wooden rooms. Rates include three good meals a day. **US$110**

SAN JUAN DE NICARAGUA

★ **Cabinas Monkey** Just northwest of the dock ☎8601 3451. Beautiful wooden cabins set in a colourful garden, each with private bathroom and TV. **US$20**

Hotelito Evo Fourth street back from the waterfront, three blocks west of the mobile phone tower ☎2583 9019. The town's first hostel, with the parents gradually handing the business down to their sons. It's the best place in town for tours – the boys grew up on the river and know all the waterways. Rates include breakfast; other meals are available. **US$18**

EATING

Options are limited in Sábalos but El Castillo has a few decent spots. In San Juan de Nicaragua, there are some pleasant places to eat along the waterfront and a couple of gems inland.

EL CASTILLO

Borders Coffee Right on the dock. The tables are upstairs on a lovely wooden open-air deck alongside easy chairs and an incongruous cross-trainer. Sip beer (C$25), great milkshakes and proper coffee (C$20), and dine on reasonable food ("American" breakfast C$80, mixed grill C$150).

Restaurante Vanessa A few hundred metres along from the dock on the left. Mellow and faintly classy (for El Castillo) riverside spot offering fried fish (C$160) and river shrimp (C$280), plus a reasonable drinks range.

Soda La Orquidea 30m on the right from the dock. Has a sweet little upstairs balcony for typical breakfasts (C$50), tasty chicken (C$120) and the chef's speciality river shrimp (C$300).

SAN JUAN DE NICARAGUA

Fritanga It has no name, but can be found by the sports hall on the main street – follow your nose. Big portions of flame-grilled chicken with plantain chips (C$70); for something smaller try the enchiladas (C$30). Wed–Sun evenings.

Soda Lolito Opposite *Hotelito Evo*. Don Lolito is one of the few people living in San Juan who was born and raised in old Greytown, and is a mine of information (in English and Spanish) about its history. He needs a bit of notice, but this is the place to come for authentic Caribbean food and drinks, including *rondon* (C$180) and *sopa pecaminosa* (a "sinful" seafood soup; C$200).

The Atlantic coast

Nicaragua's low-lying **Atlantic coast** makes up more than half the country's total landmass. It's mostly composed of impenetrable mangrove swamps and jungle, and as such only a few places in the region attract visitors in any number: **Bluefields**, a raffish port town, the idyllic **Pearl Lagoon** just to the north, and the **Corn Islands**, which boast sandy beaches, swaying palm trees and a distinctly Caribbean atmosphere. Outside these areas, the coast remains an untouristed tangle of waterways and rainforests, and should be approached with caution and negotiated only with the aid of experienced locals and good supplies of food, water and insect repellent. Indeed, there is only one actual town in the northern half of the coast – **Puerto Cabezas**. Few travellers make the trip (flying is the only real transport option), but the impoverished town has a unique feel and is the best access point for the Miskito-speaking wildernesses of the northeast.

The possibilities for ecotourism in this vast, isolated coastal region are obvious, though a scarcity of resources and a lack of cooperation between central and local government have so far stymied all progress, while the long-discussed highway linking Managua and Bluefields has failed to leave the drawing board.

EL RAMA

Downtrodden **EL RAMA** is a major transit point to the Atlantic coast – beyond here roads are limited, and you'll mostly travel

6

HISTORY AND POLITICS ON THE ATLANTIC COAST

The Atlantic coast never appealed to the Spanish conquistadors, and repelled by disease, endless jungle, dangerous snakes and persistent biting insects, they quickly made tracks for the more hospitable Pacific zone. As a result, Spanish influence was never as great along this seaboard as elsewhere. English, French and Dutch buccaneers had been plying the coast since the late 1500s, and it was they who first made contact with the **Miskito**, **Sumu** and **Rama** peoples who populated the area. Today the **ethnicity** of the region is complex, and the east can feel like another country. The indigenous peoples mixed with slaves brought from Africa and Jamaica to work in the region's fruit plantations, and while many inhabitants are Afro-American in appearance, others have Amerindian features, and some combine both with European traits. Creole **English** is still widely spoken.

During the years of the **Revolution** and the Sandinista government, the FSLN met with suspicion on the Atlantic coast, which had never really trusted the government in Managua. The region was hit hard by conflict, and half the Miskito population went into exile in Honduras, while a much smaller number made their way to Costa Rica. In 1985 the Sandinistas tried to repair relations by granting the region political and administrative autonomy, creating the territories **RAAN (Región Autonomista Atlántico Norte)** and **RAAS (Región Autonomista Atlántico Sur)**, though this only served to stir up further discontent, being widely seen as an attempt to split the Atlantic coast as a political force. Improvements to infrastructure (notably the resurfacing of the road to El Rama and the extension of the route right the way to Pearl Lagoon) show that the government has not forgotten the east coast, and tourism offers a route out, of sorts, but its profits remain focused on a handful of accessible destinations. As the jungles of the northeast are sacrificed for farmland and more Spanish-speakers from the west move to the Atlantic, this damp, diverse region is losing some of the qualities that make it so distinctive and appealing – but for now, this great, troubled region remains a land apart.

6

by boat or plane. Most travellers only stop long enough to change from the Managua bus to a boat for Bluefields, or vice versa. The bus station sits in the town's low-key centre, and *pangas* leave from the small jetty two blocks south and one block west of here. The river curves northeast towards the Atlantic from the dock, enclosing the rest of El Rama – if you fancy a wander, **Año Santo** church is a pleasant enough destination, just two blocks east of the bus station.

ARRIVAL AND INFORMATION

By boat A sporadic and very slow ferry service (5–7hr; C$140) runs along the Río Escondido between El Rama and Bluefields. Opt instead for the high-speed *pangas* (2hr; C$250) that run daily from 5.30am, with several departures in the early morning and a couple more heading downstream until around 1pm – with sufficient demand another may leave later in the afternoon. There are also boats to Big Corn Island (see p.509).

By bus There are services to and from Managua (5 express daily; 8hr), Pearl Lagoon (1 daily, 4pm; 5hr) and San Carlos (1 daily, 4.10am; 6hr).

Facilities Continue north from Año Santo church to the crossroads and you'll spot a Bancentro bank to your left and an internet café down the road to your right.

ACCOMMODATION AND EATING

The market, right by the bus station, has a decent *comedor*, and there are a couple of other options.

Eco-Hotel El Vivero A couple of kilometres outside town on the road from Managua ☎ 2517 0318. The best option if you're intending to spend any time in El Rama, with nice a/c rooms in a large wooden building set in the jungle. Ask the bus to drop you off or get a cab (C$20). **US$30**

El Expresso One block west and three blocks north of the bus station. A cool and somewhat clinical refuge from grubby El Rama, this big-windowed restaurant offers tender chicken and decent shrimp (both C$180).

Kingstown Ranch Opposite *El Expresso*. There's a cool balcony upstairs where you can eat for around C$130 or sip beer (C$20) come the evening, when music and karaoke liven things up, and a highly rated *comedor* downstairs during the day.

BLUEFIELDS

There are no fields, blue or otherwise, near steamy **BLUEFIELDS**, the only town of any size on the country's southern Atlantic Coast. It acquired its name from a Dutch pirate, Abraham Blauvelt, who holed up here regularly in the seventeenth century, and it still has something of the fugitive charm of a pirate town, perched on the side of a lagoon at the mouth of the Río Escondido, though this is about the only allure it holds. Indeed, listen to some travellers' tales of constant rainfall, murderous mozzies and menacing streets, and you might never come here at all.

But despite being undoubtedly poor, frequently wet and utterly beachless, Bluefields can be an intriguing place to stop over on your travels around the area. Fine river views and a hospitable, partly Creole-speaking population reward those who do visit. Avoid the portside "hotels" and hustlers and get a taxi if you head out of the small central area, and you should be just fine – indeed, Bluefields' karaoke-country- and reggae-based nightlife can be pretty engaging if you keep half an eye out.

The few streets in Bluefields are named, though locals resort to the usual method of directing from landmarks: the Moravian church, the *mercado* at the end of Avenida Aberdeen and the *parque* to the west of town are the most popular ones.

WHAT TO SEE AND DO

Take a *panga* from behind the market to **El Bluff** (leave and return when full; 30min; C$41). There are few amenities here, but there is a beach on the far side and a *comedor*. **Bluefields Museum** on Calle Central (Mon–Fri 8am–noon & 2–5pm; $2) has an interesting collection around the history of the indigenous communities on the Atlantic coast, as well as a library and bookshop.

ARRIVAL AND INFORMATION

By plane The small airport (☎ 2572 2500) is about 3km south of town – take a taxi (around C$20). There are daily flights to and from Managua and Big Corn Island and flights (Mon, Wed & Fri) to Puerto Cabezas.

By boat Boats arrive and leave from the dock about 150m north of the town's Moravian church, although you may be dropped at the market too. There's a C$5 port fee on top of ticket prices. *Pangas* head to Rama (daily from 5.30am, with several departures in the early morning and a few more heading upstream until around noon, with occasional afternoon departures; C$250) and Pearl Lagoon (Mon–Sat 9am, with sporadic departures until around 4pm, Sun 9am only; 1hr; C$170). Several ferries head to

Big Corn – the *Bluefields Express* (Wed 9am; 5–7hr; C$210) is your best bet, as the rest leave from El Bluff, outside Bluefields, making connections tricky. From the docks you can walk to all accommodation in Bluefields' small centre.

Tourist information The small INTUR office, in a pink building south of the centre (Mon–Fri 8am–1pm; ☎ 2572 0221), has a few brochures but isn't much help.

ACCOMMODATION

Lodging in Bluefields is underwhelming, with gloomy, noisy, overpriced rooms the norm. The cheaper, more basic establishments attract a rough local clientele – one reason why some places have a curfew.

Hotel Aeropuerto By the airport ☎ 2572 2862. Perfectly located if you're flying out the next day. The rooms are large, but some are dark and musty while others have wood panelling and windows leading onto a balcony with great views of the lagoon – ask to see a selection. A/c $1 extra. There's a fair range of food on offer at the downstairs restaurant too. __US$14__

Hotel Caribbean Dream C Central ☎ 2572 0107, ✉ reyzapata1@yahoo.com. The snazziest option in the centre, not that that's saying a huge amount: all rooms are en suite, with TVs and optional a/c. Bag one of the brighter rooms upstairs, which lead onto a pleasant balcony. __US$18__

La Isleña A block east of the Parque Central ☎ 2257 2070, ✉ hotelbluefields@gmail.com. Simple rooms set off a cool courtyard in a relatively quiet part of town. A/c US$9 extra. __US$11__

EATING

Except for seafood, which is as plentiful and fresh as anywhere along the coast, Bluefields doesn't offer a great deal of choice on the eating front. The cheapest eats are, naturally, found in the market.

Bella Vista Five blocks south and one block east of the Moravian church. Set in an atmospheric wooden building with great views, right on the lagoon, *Bella Vista* serves tasty and relatively inexpensive pork ribs (C$130), shrimp (C$160) and more, and is a decent bar too (beer C$25, rum C$15).

Cafetin Los Pipitos A block west of the market. A good place for breakfast – pancakes (C$70), *nacatamales* (C$60) and *gallo pinto* with eggs (C$80). Also coffee and a good selection of cakes.

Chez Marcel One block south of the Parque. The tablecloths, plastic flowers and a/c indicate that this is one of the fanciest restaurants in town, but the prices aren't too bad – try the chicken in wine (C$140) or fried snook (C$150), or push the boat out towards lobster thermidor (C$300).

La Ola A block west of the market. Munch on tasty *ceviche* (C$90), chicken and chips (C$85) and *pescado a la plancha* (C$150) on the breezy balcony or in the functional downstairs space, which comes complete with "no hay credito" signs and groggy-looking men sipping beer (C$25).

BLUEFIELDS N

■ ACCOMMODATION
Hotel Aeropuerto 3
Hotel Caribbean Dream 2
La Isleña 1

● EATING
Bella Vista 7
Cafetín los Pepitos 6
Chez Marcel 3
La Ola 5
Pelican Bay 1
Tia Irene 2

● DRINKING & NIGHTLIFE
Cima Karaoke Bar
& Cima Club 4
Flotante 8
Four Brothers 9

Airport & 3

★ **Pelican Bay** Beyond *Tia Irene's*, overlooking the bay right at the end of the street. Packed with locals eating whole fish (C$180) or seafood stew (C$250). There's no dance floor, but it's a decent place to listen to music and sink a few beers (C$25).

Tia Irene *Bluefields Bay Hotel*, Barrio Pointeen ☎ 2572 2143. This tropical, bamboo-clad *rancho* sits on the water and is packed to the rafters with locals on the weekends, when the small dance floor comes alive. You can eat anything from sandwiches (C$35) to lobster (C$280), and gaze upon the rusty hulks and palm trees that surround Bluefields while sipping a margarita (C$60).

DRINKING AND NIGHTLIFE

Bluefields' nightlife features an interesting mix of promenading couples, likely lads, drunken policemen, pool halls and karaoke. Country and western, soca and reggae dominate the dance floors. Travel in groups at night.

Cima Karaoke Bar 50m west of Bancentro. You'll probably hear this popular bar, a reggae and soca stronghold with speakers blasting into the street, before you see it. Cover charges (C$30) only apply on weekends. (*Cima Club*, next door, has no cover charge, but a slightly rougher crowd.) Upstairs bar & club daily; downstairs karaoke Thurs–Sun.

Flotante Five blocks south of the Moravian church. This waterfront building on stilts has an indoor dance floor and cracking views over the (almost) unspoilt bay. With beer from C$15 and piña coladas at C$50, this is a popular spot on the weekends. There's music in the evenings and food from 2pm.

6

¡MAYO YA! FESTIVAL

During the month of May, particularly in the last week, the streets of Bluefields are taken over by **¡Mayo Ya!** or **Palo de Mayo**, one of the most exciting fiestas in the country. Derived from the traditional May Day celebrations of northern Europe and celebrating the arrival of spring, ¡Mayo Ya! features a mixture of reggae, folklore and indigenous dance that young Blufileños pair ingeniously with the latest moves from Jamaica. The celebrations wrap up with the election of the Mayaya Goddess, the queen of the festivities.

★ **Four Brothers** On the southern side of town (a short taxi ride). This big, groovy shed is the granddaddy of the Caribbean music scene in Bluefields, and commands a loyal, largely Creole crowd. Thurs–Sun.

DIRECTORY

Banks There are several ATMs in town, with a Banpro opposite the Moravian church and a Bancentro just around the corner.

Internet Atlantic Cyber, 50m south of the Moravian church, and Cyberzone, a block and a half east of the park (Mon–Fri 8am–7.30pm), offer internet access for C$10/hr.

Laundry Atlantic Dry Clean. Round the corner from *Hotel Caribbean Dream* (C$130 for 12 items machine washed and dried).

PEARL LAGOON

Mellow, manageable and just a short hop from Bluefields, **PEARL LAGOON** (Laguna de Perlas) is a slowly growing spot on Nicaragua's tourist map. It's connected to El Rama and thence Managua by road, but most visitors arrive on a bouncy but magical boat ride that takes you through tangled mangroves into a vast, shallow lagoon. In its southern corner, the village of Pearl Lagoon has sandy streets, quality seafood and a friendly Creole populace who make their living from fishing and tourism. Once you've seen the **big gun** that looks out over Pearl Lagoon's small wharf, you've seen the sights, but it makes a fine base for fishing trips, longer excursions and sitting happily on your backside, sinking beer and lobster and watching the sun set.

Those who fancy exploring can head out to the remote **Pearl Cayes** where the

water really is crystal clear (for all its charms, Pearl Lagoon is a little more silty), or walk/cycle inland to **Awas**, a Miskito village about 3km west with a small beach and a decent restaurant. (It's best to head back before dark.)

ARRIVAL AND DEPARTURE

By boat *Pangas* to/from Bluefields take about 1hr. One leaves the small wharf at 6.30am and there are sporadic departures later in the day. Arrive early to put your name on the passenger list.

By bus The bus from El Rama arrives at the basketball court around 9pm daily and leaves at 5.30am (5hr). Try to get there around 5am if you want a seat.

INFORMATION AND TOURS

Tourist information INTUR office in the green building by the wharf (Mon–Fri 8am–1pm).

Tours For tours, you are best off dealing direct with operators. Fishermen at the dock offer trips, and most accommodation can point you in the right direction, but there are a couple of established players too. The friendly *Queen Lobster* restaurant (contact Pedro on ☎ 8499 4403) offers fun combined fishing and cooking classes (US$25), trips to the Pearl Cayes (US$200 for 2–4 people) and sports fishing in Top Lock Lagoon with a stay on the family farm. George Fox (head right from the dock towards *Casa Ulrich* and his house is on the left) has trips to Orinoco and the Wawashang Reserve, and out to the Pearl Cayes – a group of four will pay around US$200 for the day.

Bike rental *Queen Lobster* rents bicycles (C$20/hr).

Internet Taylor Cyber, 100m north of the wharf, offers a good connection (sporadic opening hours; C$20/hr).

ACCOMMODATION

Cool Spot Turn left out of the wharf and left again back down to the waterfront to a yellow house with no sign; ask for Doña Cherry ☎ 8662 4270. No-frills accommodation with shared bath. The friendly owner may show you how to bake coconut bread and make *rondon*. **C$150**

Green Lodge 100m south of the wharf ☎ 2572 0507, ✉ williamsdes60@yahoo.com. This popular choice offers creaking rooms in the main house and newer lodgings in a modern annexe in an overgrown garden. All rooms have TV, and there are fine hammocks for chilling. **US$15**

★ **Hospedaje Ingrid** One block west and three blocks south of *Green Lodge*, set back from the path ☎ 2572 5007 or ☎ 8725 6606. Several small but pleasant cabins alongside a family home. All have private bathrooms and TV. **C$200**

Queen Lobster 200m north of the wharf ☋ queenlobster .com. This excellent restaurant (see opposite) offers two beautiful cabins over the water with TV and hot water – a good option if you fancy a treat. **US$30**

EATING AND DRINKING

Spices and seafood make Pearl Lagoon a fine place to eat. Just south of the dock are two bakeries (open early until they sell out), offering delicious soda cake, coconut and cheese pasties from C$5. Most restaurants are also decent options for a sundowner, and there are a couple of proper bars with the Atlantic coast's traditional soundtrack of country and reggae .

Bar Relax A block west (inland) from *Green Lodge*. This groovy bar is a decent place to see the locals shake their stuff on the dance floor and guzzle beer (C$20) in the covered outdoor area.

Casa Ulrich 300m north of the dock. The filet mignon (C$300), grilled fish (C$150) and other main meals get plaudits at this hostel/restaurant, and the elevated deck is a fine place to sink a few beers (C$25) too.

★ **Queen Lobster** 200m north of the wharf ⓦ queenlobster.com. This charming round hut over the water offers excellent Creole cuisine – it's one of the few places you can get *rondon* (C$150) without pre-ordering – lobster (C$230) and a tasty chicken salad (C$100). Tours and cooking classes are on offer, along with accommodation (see opposite).

THE CORN ISLANDS

Lying 70km off the country's Atlantic coast, the **CORN ISLANDS** (Las Islas de Maíz) offer white beaches, warm, clear water and a Caribbean vibe – the kind of place you come to intending to stay for a couple of days and end up hanging around for a week or more.

Like many parts of the Caribbean coast, during the nineteenth century both larger **Corn Island** and tiny **Little Corn** were a haven for **buccaneers**, who used them as a base for raiding other ships in the area or attacking the inland towns on Lago de Nicaragua. These days it's drug-runners who use the islands, unfortunately, as part of the transportation route for US- and Europe-bound cocaine.

WHAT TO SEE AND DO

Big Corn is home to virtually all the islands' services, has a reasonable selection of hotels and restaurants, and is large enough to ensure that – if you're prepared to head far enough – you can get your own patch of beach. More backpackers head straight to idyllic **Little Corn**, though if you have time you might want to try them both out. Reached by a quick but bouncy *panga* from the bigger island, "La Islita" is extremely quiet, with **rustic** tourist amenities – bring sunscreen, mosquito repellent, a torch and money. Set on just three largely undeveloped square kilometres, with a population of just over a thousand, the island boasts lush palm trees and beautiful **white-sand beaches**, great snorkelling and diving, good swimming and, above all, plenty of peace and quiet – with no cars on the island, traffic consists of bikes, dogs and wheelbarrows.

Big Corn

It's possible to walk round the entire island of **BIG CORN** in about three hours. **Brig Bay** stretches south from the dock and main town past shacks and perfectly serviceable sands. **Long Bay**, across the airstrip heading east, is quieter and less populated and there are plenty of places to swim in either direction. North of Long Bay is **South End**, where there's some coral reef good for snorkelling – there's more on the northeast corner near the village of Sally Peachy. The southwest bay, **Picnic Center**, is a fine stretch of sand near a loading dock – there's a huge party here during Semana Santa, when crowds of people come over from Bluefields and the locals set up stalls to sell food and drink.

About 1.5km offshore to the southeast, in about 20m of clear water, is the wreck of a Spanish galleon, while the beach in front of *Paraíso Beach Hotel* boasts three newer wrecks, lacking the historical excitement of the galleon but with excellent marine life within wading distance of the shore.

Little Corn

If you're going to work up the energy to do anything at all on **LITTLE CORN**, it's likely to be **diving** or **snorkelling**; the island has around nine square kilometres of glorious, healthy reef to explore. Little Corn is even easier to navigate than its larger neighbour; all *pangas* arrive at and depart from **Pelican Beach**, while most backpackers stay on **Cocal Beach** on the east side of the island. The north end is even more remote and quieter than the rest of the island, and best suited to couples or families. There's great snorkelling both here and off Iguana Beach, just south of Cocal Beach – ask your accommodation for advice, as some reefs are a fair swim away.

6

6

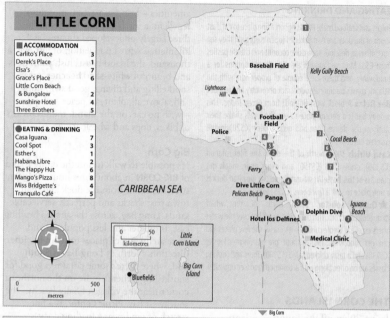

LITTLE CORN

■ ACCOMMODATION

Carlito's Place	3
Derek's Place	1
Elsa's	7
Grace's Place	6
Little Corn Beach & Bungalow	2
Sunshine Hotel	4
Three Brothers	5

● EATING & DRINKING

Casa Iguana	7
Cool Spot	3
Esther's	1
Habana Libre	2
The Happy Hut	6
Mango's Pizza	8
Miss Bridgette's	4
Tranquilo Café	5

Baseball Field
Kelly Gully Beach
Lighthouse Hill
Football Field
Police
Cocal Beach
Ferry
Dive Little Corn
Pelican Beach
Panga
Dolphin Dive
Iguana Beach
Hotel los Delfines
Medical Clinic

CARIBBEAN SEA

N

0	50
kilometres	

Little Corn Island

Bluefields
Big Corn Island

0	500
metres	

▼ Big Corn

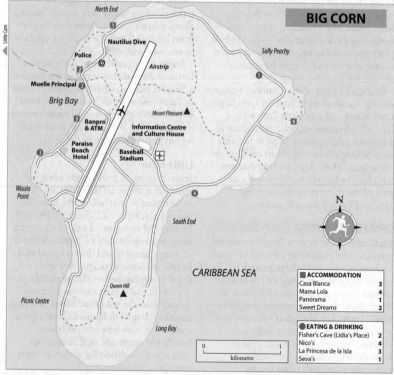

Little Corn ◄

BIG CORN

North End
Nautilus Dive
Police
@
Airstrip
Sally Peachy
Muelle Principal
Brig Bay
Banpro & ATM
Mount Pleasant
Information Centre and Culture House
Paraiso Beach Hotel
Baseball Stadium
Waula Point
South End

N

CARIBBEAN SEA

Picnic Centre
Queen Hill
Long Bay

0	1
kilometre	

■ ACCOMMODATION

Casa Blanca	3
Mama Lola	4
Panorama	1
Sweet Dreams	2

● EATING & DRINKING

Fisher's Cave (Lidia's Place)	2
Nico's	4
La Princesa de la Isla	3
Seva's	1

ARRIVAL AND DEPARTURE

BIG CORN

By plane The easiest and quickest route takes you in an often-tiny plane to/from Managua (1hr) or Bluefields (30min), both offering great views. La Costeña (☎2263 2142, ☻lacostena.com.ni) operates two flights daily from Managua to Corn Island. Depending on the number of passengers, the same flights will stop at Bluefields, or there will be separate departures around the same time. There is a US$2 airport tax payable at all national airports. Taxis await incoming flights and can take you to your hotel or the jetty for Little Corn (10min); a taxi to anywhere on the island costs US$1.

By boat Cargo boats and freight ferries head to the island. The *Bluefields Express* (Wed 9am; 5–7hr; C$210) leaves from docks in Bluefields, while the *Río Escondido* (☎8437 7209; 5–7hr; C$210) departs El Bluff on Wed at 9am (returning Thurs at 9am). If you want to miss out Bluefields, try *Captain D* (☎8202 0306; 12hr; C$400 with bed), which leaves El Rama at 8pm on Tues and Corn Island at 11pm on Sat, with a brief stop at El Bluff. Boats arrive at the *muelle principal* on the west side of the island. A harbour tax of C$3 must be paid at the harbour entrance on Big Corn.

LITTLE CORN

By boat A regular *panga* leaves the *muelle principal* at the northern end of Brig Bay on Big Corn (10am & 4.30pm daily, returning from Little Corn 6.30am & 1.30pm; 30min; C$140) – flights generally wait for the *panga*, and vice versa, so you're unlikely to miss your connection. The ride is rough and can be very wet – waterproof your bag if you can. The boat drops you off on Little Corn's western side, amid the island's only real cluster of population and facilities.

INFORMATION AND TOURS

BIG CORN

Tourist information There's a small INTUR office in the Culture House just east of the airport and plans to have tourist information at the *muelle principal*.

Tour operators Trips can be arranged through *Paraíso Beach Hotel*, the small resort on the west of the island (☎2575 5111, ☻paraisoclub.com), who also rent scuba gear and golf carts. Nautilus Dive (☎2575 5077, ☻nautilus-dive-nicaragua.com) offer dives with boat, guide and complete equipment for US$85/person, as well as fishing trips and snorkel tours for US$25 (min 2 people). Dorsey Campbell (☎8909 8050) lives in the relaxed hamlet of Sally Peachy; US$20 will get you equipment for as long as you want, plus Dorsey's formidable expertise.

LITTLE CORN

Tour operators Two friendly, PADI-certified dive outfits offer a similar range of activities and prices – from single-tank dives (US$35) to trips to Blowing Rock (US$95) and five-day packages (US$150). Dolphin Dive (☻dolphindivelittlecorn.com) is run from the fancy *Hotel Los Delfines* and also offers kitesurfing (☻kitelittlecorn .com), while Dive Little Corn is just south of *Miss Bridgette's* (see p.513). Snorkel and kayak rental costs around US$10/day – you can also rent snorkels at most accommodation on the island.

ACCOMMODATION

Things get busy, and prices rise, during the Christmas/New Year period and around Semana Santa. If you're here at quieter times, it may be worth haggling.

BIG CORN

Much of Big Corn's accommodation is rather anonymous, with options spread between built-up Brig Bay and the quieter beaches that sprawl around the island – you'll need taxis to get to these.

Casa Blanca 100m south along the rough beach track skirting Brig Bay ☎8629 4529. A windswept *hospedaje* that feels fairly isolated (despite being just a 10min walk from town), with inexpensive but tiny wooden rooms. Fans and mosquito nets supplied. There are also pleasant verandas with hammocks. <u>US$10</u>

Mama Lola Near *Casa Canada* and the baseball diamond on the east side of the island ☎8356 4615, ✉mamalolacon1@yahoo.com. This colourful beach-set hotel looks like a squat postmodern lighthouse, and has cracking views across the island and out to sea. The doubles are clean enough, and the upstairs bar (beer C$25) is a great place to contemplate the Caribbean. <u>US$35</u>

Panorama 20m north of the Nautilus Dive shop ☎2575 5065. Fairly anonymous block housing several spotless rooms, as well as a sweet veranda. The pricier rooms with a/c also come with hammocked porches and wicker rocking chairs. <u>US$15</u>

Sweet Dreams Right by the harbour ☎2575 5195. The location makes this orange-hued hotel a good bet for those heading off to Little Corn. The first-floor rooms are smallish but tidy, mostly en suite and all with TV, and there's a restaurant attached. Double: with shared bath <u>US$15</u>, with private bath <u>US$20</u>

LITTLE CORN

Head to the east and north sides of Little Corn if you want tranquillity and great snorkelling on your doorstep. A 20min walk away, in the main village, a couple of inexpensive options vie for your custom. Many places only have electricity in the evenings and at night.

Carlito's Place Cocal Beach ☻carlitosplacelittlecorn .com. A friendly beachfront backpacker hangout with individual en-suite *cabinas*. Meals are served in a cheery

6

Derek's Place North Little Corn ⓦ dereksplacelittlecorn.com. A handful of rustic-chic, wood-and-bamboo *cabinas* on stilts, complete with solar panels, ingenious fold-out tables and walls built from bright glass bottles, set among palms overlooking the beach. A treat for anyone after relaxed privacy. Hearty communal meals cost US$8.50 for lunch or from US$12 for dinner. Derek also runs snorkelling and diving trips. Double: with shared bath **US$40**, with private bath **US$50**

Little Corn Beach & Bungalow Cocal Beach, Little Corn ⓦ littlecornbb.com. This neat place, set at the mellow north end of Cocal Beach, offers neat shipwreck-themed bungalows with nice touches (from the recycled rainwater to the little foot-baths by the door), and a friendly and professional restaurant (breakfast US$3.50, dinner US$9–15) that's a fine place to chill, with coffee and free wi-fi for guests. Bunkhouse **US$40**, bungalow **US$84**

pink space from around C$50, and there's a pool table (C$10). **US$20**

Elsa's Cocal Beach ☎ 8859 4048. An island institution, with simple, clean double cabañas and smaller rooms in thatched huts on the beach. Some cheaper rooms were being rebuilt at the time of writing, following a fire. Cabaña **US$25**

Grace's Place Cocal Beach ✉ coolspotlittlecorn@hotmail .com. These Rasta-flag-coloured bamboo huts are the most popular of the three budget-cabaña spots along this pleasantly breezy stretch of beach. They aren't particularly distinctive, but the attached *Cool Spot* bar-restaurant is fun. **US$25**

Sunshine Hotel 200m north of the ferry ☎ 8495 6223. Hostel-style accommodation in a rather grand building (in Little Corn terms), offering ten rooms (with two double beds in each), pool and ping-pong tables, wi-fi, a kitchen for guests, a cool shared balcony and among the cheapest snorkel hire on the island (US$3/day). **US$20**

Three Brothers 150m north of the ferry on the right ☎ 8927 0721. This simple guesthouse is just a short walk from the beachfront bars and restaurants. Rooms are clean and secure, there's an on-site grocery, and you can use the kitchen. **US$10**

EATING AND DRINKING

It's easy to fill up on fish, prawns or lobster for reasonable prices (C$100–200), although service can be slow. For inexpensive meals, there are several nameless *comedores*

in Big Corn by the dock, which serve large plates of *comida típica* for C$100. On Little Corn, *Elsa's*, *Cool Spot* (at *Grace's Place*) and *Carlito's Place*, on the east side, all serve up cold beers and dishes for C$120–180.

BIG CORN

Fisher's Cave, aka Lidia's Place Beside the harbour entrance. Seafood specialists in the thick of Big Corn's action. Perch in the courtyard dining area and go for classic Caribbean *rondon* (C$520 for four), lobster in tomato sauce (C$224) or a land-lubbing dish of chicken breast (C$200).

Nico's On the east side of the island – get a taxi. Popular beachside nightspot, with a small waterfront balcony and heaving dance floor where you join locals in "sexy dancing" to reggaetón and Caribbean rhythms, or swaying to country music. Beer C$25. Thurs, Sat & Sun.

★ **Seva's** Sally Peachy. Locally renowned restaurant with a veranda facing the azure sea, serving tasty grilled fish (C$160), and a big and tender plate of fish, chicken and lobster (C$330), as well as standard breakfasts (C$60).

LITTLE CORN

Casa Iguana On the lower east side of the island ⓦ casaiguana.net. A busy little bar-restaurant offering US$6 breakfasts, lunch US$8, snacks and hot food during the day, as well as sophisticated US$15 three-course dinners (which need to be reserved in advance). Most food comes from their farm and garden – which also provides the mint for their mojitos (US$3.50). A range of cabinas (US$35) is also available.

Cool Spot Cocal Beach, right next to *Grace's Place*. On the beach at the heart of the east side's backpacker accommodation, *Cool Spot* serves up chicken with pasta (C$130), chilli prawns (C$280) and more, and has more buzz and more tables than anywhere else on the east side of the island.

★ **Esther's** The small pink house on the path from the school to the baseball field. Esther's *pan de coco*, or coco bread, is famous on the island, and comes out of the oven here at about 2.15pm.

La Princesa de la Isla Just south of *Paraíso Beach Hotel*, Big Corn ☎ 8854 2403. Serving delicious, authentic Italian meals, including superb home-made pastas and desserts like *pannacotta* (four courses from US$18–22), plus tasty breakfasts (US$6), all concocted by an Italian chef. Lunches and dinners are cooked upon request – give them notice or you may have to wait a while. The *Princesa* also offers nicely rustic rooms (US$55) and *cabinas* (US$70).

Habana Libre At the dock. The most touristy spot on the island – mainly due to the prices (from C$200 for mains – you'll have to order seafood specials in advance). It's a decent bet for cocktails too. Closed Mon.

The Happy Hut In the "village" behind *Tranquilo Café*. The name pretty much nails it – this simple club is the place to dance to reggae at weekends.

Mango's Pizza Just south of Dolphin Dive. A (possibly welcome) change from rice, beans and all things coconut: the cheesy pizzas (C$150 medium, C$180 large) are also available for takeaway.

★ **Miss Bridgette's** Opposite the dock. Renowned for good seafood at the best prices on the island, *Miss Bridgette's* is always busy; lobster and *rondon* go for C$240 (the latter requires advance notice), while big breakfasts are C$100.

Tranquilo Café Just north of Dolphin Dive. This likeable (if not cheap) place is one of the island's main hangouts. There's wi-fi (US$2/20min), reasonable diner food, tasty organic coffee and a range of beers (C$48) and cocktails. There's a gift shop and book exchange too. Things can get busy in the evenings (especially on bonfire nights – usually Wed and Sat), when the music gets turned up and wide-eyed divers knock back mojitos.

DIRECTORY

Bank On Big Corn, the Banpro, south of the centre on the road from the airport, has an ATM. There's no bank at all on Little Corn.

Health Assistance can be found at the hospital on Big Corn, or the medical clinic just south of Dolphin Dive on Little Corn.

Internet Access on Big Corn is provided by Miss Normis opposite the port. On Little Corn, *Hotel Los Delphines* charges a whacking C$60/hr. Higher-end places to stay and many bars, including *Tranquilo Café*, also offer free wi-fi for customers.

BILWI (PUERTO CABEZAS)

Small and scruffy **PUERTO CABEZAS**, or **BILWI**, as it's been officially named in defiance of central governmental control (the name means "snake leaf" in the Mayangna-Sumo indigenous tongue), is the most important town north of Bluefields and south of La Ceiba in Honduras. Everyone seems to have come to this town of thirty thousand people in order to do some kind of business, whether it be a Miskito fisherman walking the streets with a day's catch of fish dangling from his hand, a lumber merchant selling planks to foreign mills, or the government surveyors working on the all-season paved road through the jungle that may one day link the town with Managua. The people are mostly welcoming, and more used to foreigners than you might expect, thanks to a relatively heavy NGO presence.

6

WHAT TO SEE AND DO

The town's amenities are all scattered within a few blocks of the Parque Central, a few hundred metres west of the seafront. The water at the small local **beach** below the hotels can be clear and blue if the wind is blowing from the northeast, although the townspeople usually head to Bocana beach a few kilometres north of town; taxis can take you here for about C$15. The river water is not safe to bathe in and you need to watch your belongings as there are often a few dodgy characters around.

THE RAAN: NORTHERN NICARAGUA

The northern reaches of Nicaraguan Mosquitia – the famous **Mosquito Coast** – is one of the most impenetrable and underdeveloped areas of the Americas. No roads connect the area with the rest of the country, and the many snaking, difficult-to-navigate rivers and lagoons, separated by thick slabs of jungle, prevent the casual traveller – or any non-local, for that matter – from visiting the area. Bordered at its northern extent by the **Río Coco**, Nicaragua's frontier with Honduras, La Mosquitia is dotted by small settlements of the indigenous – mainly Miskito – peoples. The area was highly sensitive during the war years of the 1980s, when Contra bases in Honduras sent guerrilla parties over the long river border to attack Sandinista army posts and civilian communities in La Mosquitia and beyond. The Sandinistas forcibly evacuated many Miskitos from their homes, ostensibly to protect them from Contra attacks, but also to prevent them from going over to the other side.

Few travellers come to **Bilwi/ Puerto Cabezas**, the only town of any size and importance in the area. Heading out beyond Cabezas is difficult, but with determination, a good guide, a water purification kit and a good mozzie net, you can use it as a springboard to get even further from the tourist routes and into isolated Miskito communities – Waspám, near the Honduran border, is the biggest.

6

The southern horizon is broken by the atmospheric outline of the **muelle viejo** (old pier), a twenty-minute walk through the *barrios* (take a taxi), where you'll find fishermen and rusting ships. It was built in 1924 and saw guns delivered for the civil war and trussed-up turtles pulled in for their meat; now access is limited by a wire fence.

Puerto Cabezas is also the headquarters for **YATAMA** (Yapti Tasba Masraka Nanih Aslatakanka, which translates roughly as "Children of the Mother Earth"), a political party which fights for the rights of the indigenous Atlantic Coast peoples, and which is fiercely opposed to central government, whether Conservative, Liberal or Sandinista.

ARRIVAL AND DEPARTURE

By plane Flights from Managua (1hr 30min) and Bluefields (50min) touch down at the airstrip (☎2792 2282) 2km north of the town centre. Taxis will cost no more than C$20 per person. Drivers wait at the airport when flights are due to arrive.

By bus The bus terminal is a taxi ride (C$15) west of town. The bus journey to/from Managua (2 daily; 18–30hr depending on how much it's been raining) is notoriously hellish, and impossible after very heavy rain.

INFORMATION AND TOURS

Banks The Banpro, a block south of the Parque Central, has an ATM, and there are Bancentros at the airport and just east of the market.

Health Clinica y Farmacia Sukia, 100m south of Banpro (Mon–Fri 8am–6.30pm, Sat 8am–noon).

Internet Access is available at several cafés; try Servinet y Comunicaciones Saballes, just south of Banpro (C$15/hr).

Tourist information The INTUR office (Mon–Fri 8am–1pm) behind the market can provide information about local hotels and restaurants.

Tour operators AMICA (Mon–Fri 8am–noon & 2–5.30pm; ☎2792 2219, ✉asociacionamica@yahoo.es), four blocks south of the Parque Central, focus their energies on improving the lives of the region's indigenous women. They're your best bet for local trips, heading to the lagoon-side fishing village of Haulover, the long black-sand beach at Wawa Bar and the small community of Karata, most of whose members were displaced in Honduras and Costa Rica during the war but many of whom have now returned.

ACCOMMODATION

Puerto Cabezas is one place it's worth spending a bit – there's a real jump in quality and it's nice to have comfortable digs in this shabby town.

★ **Hotel Casa Museo Juith Kain** 400m north of the INTUR office ☎2792 2225, ✉casamuseojudithkain @hotmail.com. One of the prettier options in town, offering bright rooms with high ceilings, folksy bedspreads, hot water, wi-fi and a choice of fan or a/c. A free museum (donations welcome) details the history of the Mosquito Kingdom from when the British educated and crowned kings to rule this part of Nicaragua, to its integration into the rest of Nicaragua and subsequent autonomy following the civil war. It also houses examples of the art, clothes and traditional tools and implements used by the various indigenous groups. **US$12**

Hotel Cortijo 1 100m north of the Parque and **Hotel Cortijo 2** on the street behind ☎2792 2659, ✉cortijoaa @yahoo.com.mx. Both have cool and comfortable wooden rooms (all with fan or a/c and private bath). #1 has wi-fi (which guests at #2 can come and use for free), while #2 has a wooden jetty running down to the sea and balconies in the back rooms ($2 extra) overlooking the ocean. They also have a laundry service and do decent breakfasts with real coffee. **US$25**

Hotel Liwa Mair On the small cliffs that overhang the beach ☎2792 2225. Under the same management as *Casa Museo*, with well-equipped and generally spacious rooms. Those upstairs have wonderful private balconies with hammocks. **US$20**

Hotel Perez 100m north of *Cortijo 1* ☎8615 4000. This ageing place boasts carpeted floors, European-style glass windows and a quirky reception. The best rooms, which you'll pay more for, are out back around the old wooden balcony. Meals (C$60 and up) are also available. **US$16**

Hotel Tangney A block and a half east of the Banpro ☎8943 9891. Ramshackle guesthouse with slightly shabby rooms, a cool balcony and fans but no mozzie nets – if you want cheap prices, it's adequate. **US$11**

EATING AND DRINKING

Comedor Abril Opposite Banpro. Cheap, home-style restaurant serving a decent, filling lunch for C$70.

Comedor Aqui Me Quedo Opposite the Parque Central. Classic beef, chicken and *gallo pinto* done well for C$80 including *fresco*, in this simple pit stop that's well set for gazing over the market.

★ **Kabu Payaska** On a bluff 2km north of town. This great sweep of a terrace over the beach is a cracking place to feast on delicious lobster *a la plancha*, fresh fish or chicken (C$180), or to just enjoy a beer (C$25) or two. Get a taxi here and back – they will call one for you.

Restaurante Malecón 300m south of *Hotel Liwa Mair*. Appealing beachfront restaurant and bar specializing in seafood; lobster and shrimp dishes cost C$200–210, while the cold beers are C$22. A good place to view the Old Pier. Things get funkier at night, when there are sometimes DJs and karaoke.

VOLCÁN BARÚ, CHIRIQUÍ HIGHLANDS

Panama

HIGHLIGHTS

❶ **Casco Viejo** Panama City's captivating old quarter seeps faded grandeur. **See p.527**

❷ **Panama Canal** Explore this incredible engineering feat by boat or train. **See p.542**

❸ **Guna Yala** Experience the traditional culture of the Guna. **See p.558**

❹ **Isla Cañas** Witness a rare sea turtle *arribada* **See p.570**

❺ **Chiriquí Highlands** Cool mountain air, fine coffee and untouched cloudforest. **See p.574**

❻ **Bocas del Toro** Dive, surf and snorkel in the warm Caribbean. **See p.583**

HIGHLIGHTS ARE MARKED ON THE MAP ON PP.518–519

ROUGH COSTS

Daily budget Basic US$35/occasional treat US$50

Drink Beer US$1.50, *café con leche* US$2.50

Food *Arroz con pollo* US$3.50

Hostel/budget hotel US$12/US$30

Travel Panama City–Bocas del Toro by bus (600km): 10hr, US$29

FACT FILE

Population 3.5 million

Language Spanish

Currency US dollar (US$)

Capital Panama City (population: 1.2 million)

International phone code ☎507

Time zone GMT –5hr

Introduction

A narrow, snake-shaped stretch of land that divides oceans and continents, Panama has long been one of the world's greatest crossroads – far before the construction of its famous canal. Though its historical ties to the US have led to an exaggerated perception of the country as a de facto American colony, Spanish, African, West Indian, Chinese, Indian, European, and several of the least assimilated indigenous communities in the region have all played a role in the creation of the most sophisticated, open-minded and outward-looking society in Central America. The comparatively high level of economic development and use of the US dollar also make it one of the more expensive countries in the region, but the wildlife-viewing and adventure-travel options are excellent.

7

Cosmopolitan and contradictory, **Panama City** is the most striking capital city in Central America, its multiple personalities reflected in the frenzied energy of its international banking centre, the laidback street-life of its old colonial quarter, its polished nightlife and the antiseptic order of the US-built Canal Zone. Located in the centre of the country, it is also a natural base from which to explore many of Panama's most popular destinations, including its best-known attraction, the monumental **Panama Canal**. The colonial ruins and Caribbean coastline of **Colón Province** are also within reach of the capital. Southeast of Panama City stretches **Darién**, the infamously wild expanse of

rainforest between Central and South America, while to the north, along the Caribbean coastline, **Guna Yala** is the autonomous homeland of the Guna, who live in beautiful isolation on the coral atolls of the **Guna Yala Archipelago**. West of Panama City, the Carretera Interamericana runs through the Pacific coastal plain, Panama's agricultural heartland. This region lures travellers intrigued by the folkloric traditions and nature reserves of the **Azuero Peninsula**, also a major surf destination, and the protected cloudforests of the **Chiriquí Highlands** on the Costa Rican border. The mostly uninhabited Caribbean coast west of the canal meets Costa Rica near the remote archipelago of **Bocas del Toro**, a popular holiday destination thanks to its largely unspoiled rainforests, beaches, coral reefs, surfing hot spots and easy-going vibe.

WHEN TO VISIT

Panama is well within the tropics, with temperatures hovering at 25–32°C throughout the year, and varying only with **altitude** (the Chiriquí Highlands are generally 15–26°C). Visiting Panama during the **dry season** (late-Dec to April; known as *verano*, or summer) maximizes your chance of finding sunny days. However, seasonal climatic variation is really only evident on the Pacific side of the country's mountainous spine. The average annual rainfall here is about 1500mm; on the Caribbean, about 2500mm falls, spread more evenly throughout the year. From May to December, the storms of the Pacific's winter (*invierno*) **rainy season** are intense but rarely extended.

CHRONOLOGY

1501–02 European explorers Rodrigo de Bastidas and Christopher Columbus visit modern-day Panama.

1510 Conquistador Diego de Nicuesa establishes Nombre de Dios, one of the earliest Spanish settlements in the New World.

1513 Vasco Núñez de Balboa crosses Panama, becoming the first European to see the Pacific Ocean.

1519 Panama City is founded on August 15 by conquistador Pedro Arias de Ávila (known as Pedrarias).

1596–1739 Spanish colonies and ships, loaded with treasure from indigenous Central and South American empires, are attacked several times by British privateers. Henry Morgan sacks Panamá Viejo in 1671.

1746 Spain re-routes treasure fleet around Cape Horn, but trade remains Panama's dominant economic activity.

1821 Panama declares independence from Spain, and joins the confederacy of Gran Colombia (Bolivia, Peru, Ecuador, Venezuela, Colombia and Panama).

1830 Panama becomes a province of Colombia after the dissolution of Gran Colombia.

1851 US company begins building railroad across Panamanian isthmus; project is completed in 1855.

1881 French architect Ferdinand de Lesseps begins excavations for the Panama Canal, which turns out to be an unmitigated disaster. Some 20,000 workers die before the venture is abandoned in 1889.

1903 Backed by the US, Panama declares separation from Colombia. French engineer Philippe Bunau-Varilla signs a treaty with the US, essentially selling rights to the canal, and giving the US control of the Canal Zone "in perpetuity".

1914 The canal is completed. More than 75,000 people have a hand in its construction.

1939 Panama ceases to be a US protectorate, but tensions continue to build between Panama and the US territory of the Canal Zone.

1964 "Martyrs' Day" flag riots, precipitated by a student protest, leave 21 Panamanians dead and over 500 injured in the Canal Zone.

1968 General Omar Torrijos Herrera, Chief of the National Guard, overthrows president Arnulfo Arias and imposes a dictatorship.

1977 Torrijos signs new canal treaty with US President Jimmy Carter, who agrees to transfer the canal to Panamanian control by December 31, 1999.

1983 Colonel Manuel Noriega becomes de facto military ruler. He is initially supported by the US, but also cultivates drug-cartel connections.

1988 US charges Noriega with rigging elections, drug smuggling and murder; Noriega declares state of emergency, dodging a coup and repressing opposition.

1989 Guillermo Endara wins the presidential election, but Noriega seizes presidency. US troops invade Panama and oust Noriega, but also kill and leave homeless thousands of civilians.

1992 US court finds Noriega guilty of drug charges, sentencing him to forty years in prison.

1999 Mireya Moscoso, the widow of former president Arnulfo Arias, is elected as Panama's first female president. US closes military bases and hands full control of the canal to Panama in December.

2003 A country-wide strike over mismanagement of the nation's social-security fund shuts down public services and turns violent.

2004 Martín Torrijos, son of former dictator Omar Torrijos, is elected president.

2004 The canal, under Panamanian management, earns record revenues of one billion US dollars.

2006 Referendum on a US$5.2 billion plan to expand the Panama Canal is passed by an overwhelming majority. Panama and the US sign a free-trade agreement.

2007 Work begins on the Panama Canal expansion project.

2008 Noriega is released from prison in the US but following extradition to France is sentenced to seven more years in prison for money laundering.

2009 Right-wing supermarket multimillionaire Ricardo Martinelli is elected president in landslide victory; initially popular for increasing the minimum wage and introducing pensions, by 2012 his popularity plummets due to corruption scandals, violent clashes with indigenous populations, and the soaring cost of living.

2011 Noriega is extradited back to Panama to serve another twenty years for murder and money laundering.

7

LAND AND SEA ROUTES TO PANAMA

Panama has three land routes from **Costa Rica**: the main border crossing along the Interamericana is at Paso Canoas (see box, p.190), while a less-frequented border outpost is at Guabito, on the Caribbean coast (see box, p.143), which allows for access to the Bocas archipelago. There's a rarely used border post in the Chiriquí Highlands at Río Sereno (8am–5pm; reached by bus from Volcán).

Though you can take local transport and switch buses at the border, the slightly costlier fares on international services run by Tica Bus (W ticabus.com) give you a better shot at an efficient and hassle-free passage (though border waits can be long). In addition to official documents, travellers at the border crossing will often be asked to show an onward or return ticket. If travelling on a one-way ticket, *migración* is likely to require advance purchase of your bus fare back to San José.

TO AND FROM COLOMBIA

Crossing by land to or from **Colombia** is both forbidden and dangerous. While there are no official **sea crossings**, it is possible to book passage on private yachts and passenger boats heading for Colombia, stopping in Guna Yala on the way (see box, p.550), or to fly to Puerto Obaldía, a town at the far eastern end of Guna Yala on the Caribbean coast, and make a short trip by speedboat to Capurganá, just over the border in Colombia (see box, p.562).

7

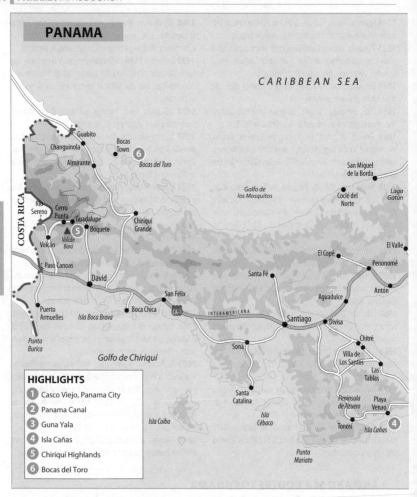

PANAMA

CARIBBEAN SEA

COSTA RICA

Guabito
Changuinola
Almirante
Bocas
Town
6 *Bocas del Toro*

Río
Sereno
Cerro
Punta
Guadalupe
5 Boquete
Volcán
*Volcán
Barú*
*Chiriquí
Grande*

*Golfo de
los Mosquitos*

San Miguel
de la Borda
Coclé del
Norte
*Lago
Gatún*

Paso Canoas
David
San Félix
Boca Chica
Isla Boca Brava

El Copé
Penonomé
El Valle
Antón
Santa Fé
Aguadulce
INTERAMERICANA
Santiago
Divisa
Chitré
Villa de
Los Santos
Las
Tablas
Playa
Venao
*Península
de Azuero*
Tonosí
4 *Isla Cañas*

Puerto
Armuelles
*Punta
Burica*
Golfo de Chiriquí
Soná
Santa
Catalina
Isla Coiba
*Isla
Cébaco*
*Punta
Mariato*

HIGHLIGHTS
1 Casco Viejo, Panama City
2 Panama Canal
3 Guna Yala
4 Isla Cañas
5 Chiriquí Highlands
6 Bocas del Toro

ARRIVAL AND DEPARTURE

International **flights** arrive at **Tocumen
International Airport (PTY)** in Panama
City. Services arrive daily from the US
(most are routed through Atlanta, Dallas/
Fort Worth, Houston or Miami) and
other Central and South American cities;
KLM and Iberia fly from Amsterdam and
Madrid, respectively. Flights from San
José, in neighbouring Costa Rica, often
stop in David before continuing on to
Panama City. The recently upgraded
airport in David is expected to see direct
international flights from and to the US
at some point.

You can cross into Panama by **land** from
Costa Rica (see box, p.517), but due to
security concerns it's not possible to do so
from Colombia. Instead, backpackers are
increasingly booking passages by **boat**
(see box, p.550).

VISAS

Travellers from Australia, Canada,
Ireland, New Zealand, the UK or the
US **do not require a visa** to enter
Panama. Passports are generally stamped
for three or six months and extensions
cannot be granted unless applying for a

different kind of visa, such as a residency permit.

GETTING AROUND

Although the canal corridor and the western Pacific region are covered by a comprehensive road network served by regular **public transport**, eastern Panama, Guna Yala and Bocas del Toro are each linked to the rest of the country by just a single road. Access to the islands of Bocas del Toro and Guna Yala is by plane or boat, and boats also provide the main means of transport between the islands,

as well as along the rivers of the Darién region. Crossing the isthmus by train is also possible between Panama City and Colón.

BY BUS

Where there are roads, **buses** are the cheapest and most popular way to travel. Panama City is the hub of the network, with regular buses to Colón, Metetí in Darién, Almirante (for Bocas del Toro) and all the western cities and towns. Buses vary in comfort and size, from modern, a/c Pullmans to smaller "coaster" buses and old US school buses – Central

7

ADDRESSES IN PANAMA

Panama's towns are mainly laid out in a **grid pattern**. Calles run north–south, and avenidas east–west. Both calles and avenidas are generally numbered in order, calles north to south and avenidas west to east. In larger cities – Panama City and David in particular – roads, especially major thoroughfares, usually have two or more names. In smaller towns and villages exact **street numbers** or even names tend not to exist, so addresses are frequently given in terms of landmarks.

America's ubiquitous "chicken buses" (see p.32). Smaller towns and villages in rural areas tend to be served by less frequent minibuses, pick-up trucks and flat-bed trucks known as **chivas** or *chivitas*, converted to carry passengers, while Colón and David are also served by express buses, which are more expensive, more comfortable and faster. ⓦthebusschedule.com/pa is a fairly reliable source to check **bus timetables**.

Most buses are owned either by individuals or private firms, and even when services are frequent, **schedules** are variable. Cities and larger towns have bus terminals; otherwise, buses leave from the main street or square. You can usually flag down through-buses from the roadside, though they may not stop if they are full or going a long way. In general, you can just turn up shortly before departure and you should be able to get a seat, though the express buses to and from David, buses from Bocas del Toro, as well as international buses to and from Costa Rica, are definitely worth **booking in advance**. **Fares**, as elsewhere in Central America, are good value: bank on paying around US$2 per hour of travel, more for the more luxurious long-distance buses; the most you'll have to pay is US$29 for the overnight, ten-hour ride from Panama City to Almirante.

BY CAR

Starting at around US$50 a day or US$300 a week (almost double for 4WD), **car rental** is reasonably priced but not cheap. However, having your own vehicle is a good way of seeing parts of the country not well served by public transport, especially the canal corridor and the Azuero Peninsula. All of the main rental companies are based at Tocumen International Airport, and also in the city centre; some also have offices at Albrook airport and the airport in David; National Panamá (ⓦnationalpanama.com) is popular with locals as it offers some of the cheapest rentals in the country.

Driving in Panama is pretty straightforward, though even the paved roads in the canal corridor and the west can be badly maintained. The main roads on the Azuero Peninsula are in good condition, however, as is the road across the cordillera to Bocas del Toro, and the secondary roads to Cerro Punta, Santa Fé, Boquete and El Valle. **4WD** is rarely necessary except during the rainy season and in more remote rural areas. Police **checkpoints** appear throughout the country, mainly on provincial borders, and normally you are only required to slow down. If the police ask you to stop, in most cases they will just want to know your destination and see your licence and/or passport.

Hitching is possible, but carries all the obvious risks. Private cars are unlikely to stop for you on main roads, though in more remote areas, hitching is often the only motor transport available, and there is little distinction between private vehicles and public transport – drivers will pick you up, but you should expect to pay the same kind of fares you would for the bus.

In larger cities, like Panama City and David, **taxis** are plentiful and inexpensive. Most intra-city rides will cost US$1–2 (US$2–5 in the capital). There are many unlicensed cab drivers patrolling the streets who are willing to negotiate on prices, but who may engage in unscrupulous practices. Even licensed cab drivers won't hesitate to exploit an obviously unsavvy, lost or needy tourist. Specifically, be wary of price hikes on the Amador Causeway in Panama City.

BY BOAT

Scheduled **ferries** run from Panama City to Isla Taboga as well as between Bocas del Toro and Almirante. Motorized

water-taxis and **dugout canoes** are important means of transport in Bocas del Toro, Darién and Guna Yala, though the only scheduled small-boat services are the water-taxis in Darién (between Puerto Quimba and La Palma, or La Palma and Garachiné) and between Almirante and Bocas. Otherwise, you'll either have to wait for somebody going your way, or hire a boat. The latter can be expensive – US$150 for a motorized dugout with a small engine from La Palma to Sambú, for example – but obviously works out more cheaply the more there are of you. Make sure you find out the approximate price per gallon for diesel and the number of gallons needed per journey from a disinterested party before starting to negotiate a price. Hiring a dugout canoe also opens up possibilities for wilderness adventure – up jungle rivers to isolated villages or out to uninhabited islands.

BY PLANE

Cities and larger towns are served by regular **flights** with Air Panama (ⓦairpanama.com), currently the only domestic carrier, which flies to David, Bocas, parts of Darién, as well as to Guna Yala and to the Pearl Islands. With the exception of the more isolated areas, though, most destinations are so close to Panama City that it's scarcely worth flying; not least because it's very expensive (at the time of writing, high-season return flights between Panama City and Bocas cost US$236). Flights can be bought online, or over the phone using a credit card.

BY BIKE

Cycling is a popular way to get around in western Panama, where roads are generally paved and traffic scarce (away from the Interamericana and other major routes), and towns usually have a shop offering parts and simple repairs. Other good roads for cycling include all those on the Azuero Peninsula and the roads to Cerro Punta and El Valle, off the Interamericana.

BY TRAIN

The **Panama Canal Railway** (ⓦpanarail .com), which runs alongside the canal between Panama City and Colón, offers an excellent way of seeing the canal and the surrounding rainforest (see p.544).

ACCOMMODATION

Most areas in Panama offer a wide choice of places to stay. In general, the cheapest **hotel** rooms, normally a simple en-suite double (with one double bed – *cama matrimonial*) with cable TV and a/c costs US$30 a night, although **hostels** – most common in well-travelled spots like Bocas Town, Boquete, David and Panama City – will put you up for around US$9–13/person. In **Panama City**, where many hotels target business travellers, prices tend to be slightly higher, while at the very low end of the market some hotels – euphemistically termed **drive-in motels** and auto-hotels – cater largely to Panamanian couples, with hourly rates. Locally referred to as a "Push", each unit is accessed by a push-button garage door to provide couples with privacy. These are often the least expensive lodgings but not recommended for a solid night's sleep.

For popular hostels, particularly in the city, you will need to **book in advance**, especially during public holidays, fiestas, Carnaval and even right through the high season (Dec–April). During these times hotel prices can double, and many places are booked out months in advance. The ten percent **tourist tax** charged on hotel accommodation is not always included in the quoted price but has been factored into the prices that we have quoted throughout the chapter.

There are no official **campsites** in Panama, but you will find several hostels that allow you to pitch your tent for around US$6/person, and you can camp in the national parks, though facilities will be limited. That said, camping is never really necessary – even in the smallest villages there's almost always somewhere you can bed down for the night. If you do camp, either a **mosquito net** or mosquito coil (*mechita*) is essential in the lowlands. Almost all the national parks have ANAM (see p.525) **refugios** where you can spend the night for US$5–10, though this fee is not always charged. These refuges are usually pretty

7

basic, but they do have bunk beds, cooking facilities and running water.

FOOD AND DRINK

Street vendors are less common in Panama than elsewhere in Central America. The cheapest places to eat are the ubiquitous canteen-like **self-service restaurants** (sometimes called *cafeterías*), which serve a limited but filling range of Panamanian meals for around US$3–4; these usually open for breakfast and stay open late. Larger towns generally have several upmarket **restaurants** with waiter service, where a main dish may cost upwards of US$6 (from US$8 in Panama City), as well as US-style fast-food places. There is often a seven percent **tax** to pay on meals; some also add on a ten percent service charge. These costs have been factored in when we have quoted prices throughout this chapter. Large **supermarkets** in the major cities offer a good range of cold and hot snacks to eat in or take out.

Known as **comida típica**, traditional Panamanian cooking is similar to what you find elsewhere in Central America. Rice and beans or lentils served with a little chicken, meat or fish form the mainstay, and *yuca* (cassava) and plantains are often served as sides. The national dish is **sancocho**, a chicken soup with *yuca*, plantains and other root vegetables flavoured with cilantro – similar to coriander though more pungent. **Seafood** is plentiful, excellent and generally cheap, particularly *corvina* (sea bass), *pargo rojo* (red snapper), lobster and prawns. Fresh tropical **fruit** is also abundant, but rarely on the menu at restaurants – you're better off buying it in local markets. Popular **snacks** include *carimañolas* or *enyucados* (fried balls of manioc dough filled with meat), *empanadas*, *tamales*, *patacones* (fried, mashed and refried plantains) and *hojaldres* (discs of deep-fried leavened bread). Toasted sandwiches called *emparedados* or *derretidos* are also very popular, appearing on most menus, from humble cafeterias to high-end cafés.

The diverse **cultural influences** that have passed through Panama have left their mark on its cuisine, especially in Panama City, where there are scores of international restaurants – Italian, Greek and Chinese being the most numerous. Almost every town has at least one Chinese restaurant, often the best option for **vegetarians**. Perhaps the strongest outside influence on Panamanian food, though, is the distinctive **Caribbean** culture of the West Indian populations of Panama City, Colón Province and Bocas del Toro. Speciality dishes involve seafood and rice cooked with lime juice, coconut milk and spices.

DRINK

Coffee is excellent where grown locally (in the Chiriquí Highlands) and generally good throughout Panama, made espresso-style and served black or with milk as *café americano*. The **drinking water** of Panama City is so good that it is known as the "Champagne of the Chagres". Iced water, served free in restaurants, along with tap water in all towns and cities except Bocas del Toro, Guna Yala, Darién and remote areas, is perfectly safe. **Chichas**, delicious blends of ice, water and tropical-fruit juices, are sometimes served in restaurants and by street vendors, and are not to be confused with *chicha fuerte*, a potent fermented maize brew favoured by *campesinos* and indigenous populations, who prepare it for ceremonial occasions. **Batidos**, delicious when prepared with fresh fruit, are thick milkshakes. Also popular are **pipas**, sweet water from green coconuts served either ice-cold or freshly hacked from the palm tree. Fresh **fruit juices** are highly recommended, but it's best to make sure not too much sugar is added.

Beer is extremely popular in Panama. Locally brewed brands include Panamá, Atlas, Soberana and Balboa; imported beers such as Budweiser, Heineken and Guinness are available in Panama City. For a quicker buzz, many Panamanians turn to locally produced **rum** – Carta Vieja and Abuelo are the most common brands – though the national drink is Seco Herrerano (known as *seco*), an even more potent sugar-cane spirit. Imported whiskies and other spirits are widely available and you can get **wine** in most major towns.

CULTURE AND ETIQUETTE

Panama, like much of the rest of Latin America, is **socially conservative**, with a vast majority of the population reported to be Roman Catholic. Thanks to the country's history, more religions are present than in other parts of the region, but the combination of a largely Catholic cultural identity, marked economic stratification and other ingrained colonial legacies has produced a country and people who appreciate rules and accept established social castes. This is not to say, however, that Panamanian society is stagnant. The history of a US presence, widespread access to global media and entertainment, and relatively diverse demographics as well as recent economic expansion, have all contributed to making Panama a country familiar with change.

Macho attitudes, however, do prevail. For women travelling in Panama, unsolicited attention in the form of whistles and catcalls is almost inevitable, though easily ignored. Overall, the Caribbean and indigenous areas of Panama hold less macho and more relaxed attitudes, though revealing clothing is not tolerated (except on the beach). Though attitudes toward homosexuality are gradually softening – it was decriminalized in 2008 – by and large same-sex relationships are kept under wraps.

Tipping is only expected in more expensive places, where a tip is sometimes included in the final bill, or where service has been particularly good. It's not usual to **haggle** in shops, but prices are more negotiable in markets, especially if you're buying a lot, and you'll often need to bargain when organizing transport by boat or pick-up truck.

SPORTS AND OUTDOOR ACTIVITIES

With every important match being televised and broadcast on radio, both European and Latin American **football** (soccer) leagues have a broad fan base and are closely followed in Panama, but **baseball** (*beisbol*) is Panama's official national sport. There are twelve teams in the national league, and home teams are sacred to their impassioned fans, making the experience of attending a game lively and culturally rich (see ⓦfedebeis.com .pa). The season runs from January to April. Panama City's stadium, 8km northeast of the city centre – and named after Major League Baseball Hall-of-Fame player and Panamanian native Rod Carew – is never full, other than during the play-offs; tickets cost around US$5.

Hiking, rafting, surfing and diving are probably the most common and easily accessible of the outdoor activities. Boquete, in the Chiriquí Highlands, provides an ideal departure point for **hikes** up Volcán Barú (see p.581), Panama's highest point, as well as for **rafting** trips down ríos Chiriquí and Chiriquí Viejo

7

PANAMANIAN WORDS AND PHRASES

Panamanian slang shows the nation's culturally diverse roots, with a strong flow of foreign words making their way into mainstream vocabulary.

Buay Boy in Caribbean English
Bukoo Many, taken from the French "beaucoup"
Chucha Vulgar term for a woman's private parts, commonly used as an exclamation like "damn"
Chuleta Used when someone is very surprised, in order not to say "chucha"
En serio? No way!/Seriously?
(Esa) Vaina (This) "thing" or "stuff"; can be substituted for a word you don't know, for example "me gusta esa vaina" or "I like this stuff"
Offi Affirmative/yes, derived from "official"
Palos Local slang for dollars
Priti Pretty
¿Que Xopá? What's up? Panamanians love to play with vocabulary; this term comes from "Que pasó", mixing the letters of "pasó" and replacing "s" with "x", making "xopá"

7

(see p.579). Isla Coiba is a world-renowned **dive** site for experienced divers (see p.572), while Bocas del Toro also has a good reputation, with trips ranging from all-day snorkel tours to underwater exploration of shipwrecks and spectacular reef walls. Bocas can also have excellent **surf**, though it is seasonal and less consistent than on the Pacific coast, where Santa Catalina has the most popular break, and is considered world class. ⓦwannasurf.com lists the best breaks.

Panama is also one of the world's top destinations for **birdwatching;** areas in the former Canal Zone (see p.542) and the Chiriquí Highlands (see p.574), for example, are home to numerous colourful exotic species. It's well worth engaging the services of an expert on birding trips; local Spanish-speaking guides charge around US$30/half-day, not including transport. You'll pay up to three times that for a bilingual naturalist guide, though the price will usually include use of a telescope and private transport.

COMMUNICATIONS

Other than in remote areas, Panama's **communications** network is good. **Letters** posted with the Correo Nacional (COTEL) cost US$0.45 (US$0.35 for postcards) to both the US and Europe, and should reach their destination within a couple of weeks. Even though **post offices** can be found in most small towns, it's best to post mail in Panama City.

Panama's privatized telephone company is owned by Cable & Wireless. **Local calls** are cheap, and there's a wide network of payphones that take phonecards sold in shops and street stalls; a *Telechip* card allows you to make both local and international calls. Local numbers should have seven digits; local mobile numbers have eight digits and begin with a "6" or a "5". Many internet cafés also provide international phone calls for between US$0.05–10/minute to North America or Europe. You can make **international reverse charge calls** from payphones via the international operator (ⓣ106).

Mobile phone coverage is growing, and even covers remote stretches of the Darién

and Guna Yala, with the Móvil and Digicel networks having the best coverage outside of the capital. It's easy to buy a local SIM card in Panama City (around US$3) and replace the card in your own phone with it, although you may need a "hacker" to unlock your phone for use of the Panamanian networks.

You should be able to find an **internet** café almost anywhere you go; rates are normally US$1/hour. Wi-fi is commonly available and free in hostels and most hotels, especially in Panama City.

CRIME AND SAFETY

Panama has something of an unjust reputation as a dangerous place to travel. Although **violent crime** does occasionally occur, it is usually in particular city areas, as in most countries, and Panama is far safer than most other countries in Central America. Nonetheless, you should take special care in **Colón** and some districts in **Panama City**, and more generally late at night in cities, or when carrying luggage; take a taxi. Outside these two cities, the only other area where there is any particular danger is near the **Colombian border** in Darién and Guna Yala. This frontier has long been frequented by guerrillas, bandits and cocaine traffickers, and several travellers attempting to cross overland to Colombia have been kidnapped or killed – or have simply disappeared. It is possible to visit some areas of Darién safely, including parts of the national park, but always seek advice before travel (see p.553). Note, too, that some of the boats that ply the coast may be involved in smuggling.

If you become the victim of a crime, report it immediately to the local **police** station, particularly if you will later be making an insurance claim. In Panama City and Colón the **tourist police** (*policía de turismo*) are better prepared to deal with foreign travellers and more likely to speak some English – in Panama City they wear white armbands.

Although by law you are required to carry your **passport** at all times, you will rarely be asked to present it except when in transit; the tourist police recommend

EMERGENCY NUMBERS

Ambulance ☎ 225 1436 or ☎ 228 2187
(*Cruz Roja*) or ☎ 269 9778
Fire ☎ 103
Police ☎ 104
Tourist Police (Casco Viejo, Panama City)
☎ 270 3365

that when walking around the towns and cities it's better to carry a copy of your passport (including the page with the entry stamp).

HEALTH

Medical care in Panama is best sought in the two largest cities: Panama City and David. Panama City has a handful of top-notch **hospitals** with many US- and European-trained doctors and English-speaking staff (see p.540). As most doctors and hospitals expect payment up front, frequently in cash, check your health insurance plan or buy supplementary travel insurance before you leave home. Note, too, that tourists entering the country via Tocumen International Airport are entitled to a new **free health insurance policy**, which is valid for thirty days. Ask for the brochure at the ATP information booth on arrival.

Pharmacies are numerous and often stay open late; in addition, 24hour supermarkets Rey, Romero and Super 99 usually have 24hour pharmacies. Hospitals and occasionally health clinics have pharmacies on site, and many types of medicines are available over the counter, without a prescription.

INFORMATION AND MAPS

Good, impartial information about Panama is hard to come by once you're in the country. The biggest network of information is the **Panamanian Tourist Institute** (ⓦ visitpanamav2.com) or the **Autoridad de Turismo Panamá** (ATP ⓦ atp.gob.pa), which has its main office in Panama City and many provincial branches; their ATP offices offer flyers and pamphlets but the quality of information varies enormously and staff rarely speak English. *The Visitor/El Visitante* (ⓦ thevisitorpanama.com), a free, weekly **tourist promotion magazine** in English and Spanish, is available online and at ATP offices and tourist venues throughout Panama, and lists attractions and upcoming events. Several **tour operators** based in Panama City (see box, p.536) can give you advice on the rest of the country, in the hope of selling you a tour.

Panama's **national parks** and other protected areas are administered by the National Environment Agency, **ANAM** (ⓦ anam.gob.pa). Their regional offices are often very helpful – though again you'll need some Spanish – and are an essential stop before visiting areas where permission is needed, or if you want to spend the night in a *refugio* and/or hire a guide.

The best **maps** of Panama are the *International Travel Map of Panama* and the *National Geographic* one (both available online). In the country,

PANAMA ONLINE

ⓦ **almanaqueazul.org** A green portal (in Spanish), promoting ecological and sustainable tourism within Panama.

ⓦ **anam.gob.pa** Official ANAM website page (click on the icon for *Áreas Protegidas*) with links to info in Spanish on all the national parks and many of the other reserves.

ⓦ **extremepanama.com** A great portal, with links to independent tour operators, organized by region and activity.

ⓦ **panamainfo.com** Comprehensive portal providing listings of hotels, restaurants and tourist activities across the country.

ⓦ **thevisitorpanama.com** Website of *El Visitante/The Visitor*, a dual-language, weekly publication.

ⓦ **visitpanama.com** Panamanian Tourist Authority (ATP) site, with information on attractions and links to hotels, airlines and tour agencies.

7

large-scale maps are available at the Instituto Geográfico Nacional Tommy Guardia (Mon–Fri 8.30am–4pm) on Avenida Simón Bolívar, opposite the entrance to the university in Panama City. The *Rutas de Aventuras* series of maps (Ⓦrutasdeaventuras.com), covering most cities and tourist areas in Panama, are widely available in bookshops and souvenir stores throughout the country for around US$4.

MONEY AND BANKS

Panama adopted **US dollars** (referred to interchangeably as *dólares* or *balboas*) as its currency in 1904, and has not printed any paper currency since. The country does, however, mint its own coinage: 1, 5, 10, 25 and 50 **centavo** pieces which are used alongside US coins, plus a new US$1 coin. Both US$100 and US$50 bills are often difficult to spend, so try to carry nothing larger than a US$20 bill. It is difficult to **change foreign currency** in Panama – change any cash into US dollars as soon as you can. Foreign banks will generally change their own currencies.

Travellers' cheques are impossible to change, so you're better off with a credit card, and a debit card for ATM withdrawals. The three major **banks** are Banco Nacional, Banco General and HSBC. Almost all branches have **ATMs**, as do many large supermarkets; all ATMs demand a US$3 levy on every transaction. Major **credit cards** are accepted in most hotels and restaurants in Panama City and the larger provincial towns, though hardly anywhere in Bocas del Toro. Visa is the most widely accepted, followed by MasterCard. Some shops will charge an extra five percent if you pay by credit card.

OPENING HOURS AND PUBLIC HOLIDAYS

Opening hours vary, but generally businesses and government **offices** are open Monday to Friday from 8am to 4pm. **Post offices** are open Monday to Friday 8am to 5pm, and Sat 8am to noon, while the major **banks** are generally open from 8am to 3pm Monday to Friday, and from 9am to noon on Saturday. **Shops** are usually open Monday to Saturday from 9am to 6pm.

Panama has several national **public holidays** (see box below), when most government offices, businesses and shops close. Panama City and Colón also each have their own public holiday, and there is one public holiday for government employees only. When the public holidays fall near a weekend many Panamanians take a long weekend (known as a *puente*) and head to the beach or the countryside – it can be difficult to find hotel rooms during these times. Public holidays that fall midweek are sometimes moved to a Monday or Friday to avoid disrupting the working week. Several of these public holidays also coincide with **national fiestas** that continue for several days.

FESTIVALS

The following lists a few highlights on Panama's festivals calendar. There are even more festivals on the Azuero Peninsula (see box, p.567).

January Feria de las Flores y del Café in Boquete (date varies).

February Comarca de Guna Yala (Feb 25) celebrates the Guna Revolution of 1925, their independence day; Carnaval (Feb/March) celebrated all over the country, but especially in Las Tablas and Panama City, with an aquatic version in Penonomé; Festival de los Diablos y Congos, biennially in Portobelo (2013, 2015, date varies).

PUBLIC HOLIDAYS

Jan 1 New Year's Day
Jan 9 Martyrs' Day
Feb/March (date varies) Carnaval
March/April Good Friday
May 1 Labour Day
Aug 15 Foundation of Panama City (Panama City only)
Nov 2 All Souls' Day
Nov 3 Independence Day
Nov 4 Flag Day (government holiday only)
Nov 5 National Day (Colón only)
Nov 10 First Cry of Independence
Nov 28 Emancipation Day
Dec 8 Mother's Day
Dec 25 Christmas

March/April Semana Santa. Celebrated everywhere, but most colourfully in La Villa de Los Santos, Pesé and Guararé, on the Azuero Peninsula.

April Feria de las Orquideas in Boquete (date varies); Feria International del Azuero in La Villa de Los Santos (date varies).

June Corpus Christi (date varies) in La Villa de Los Santos.

July Nuestra Señora del Carmen (July 16) on Isla Taboga; Patronales de La Santa Librada and Festival de la Pollera in Las Tablas (July 20–22).

August Festival del Manito Ocueño (date varies) in Ocú.

October Festival of Nogagope (Oct 10–12) on Isla Tigre, Comarca de Guna Yala; Feria Guna (mid-Oct) on Isla Tigre; Festival de la Mejorana (five days mid-Oct) in Guararé; Fiesta de Cristo Negro (Oct 21) in Portobelo.

November 10 The "First Cry of Independence", Independence Day, celebrated as part of "El Mes de la Patria". Cities and towns across the nation put on parades featuring school drumming troupes and majorettes, which the whole population comes out to watch.

Panama City

Few cities in Latin America can match the diversity and cosmopolitanism of **PANAMA CITY**: polyglot and postmodern before its time, its atmosphere is, surprisingly, more similar to the mighty trading cities of Asia than to anywhere else in the region. The city has always thrived on commerce; its unique position on the world's trade routes and the economic opportunity this presents has attracted immigrants and businesses from all over the globe. With nearly a third of the country's population living in the urbanized corridor between Panama City and Colón, the capital's metropolitan melting pot is a study in contrasts.

The city's layout, too, encompasses some startling incongruities. On a small peninsula at the southwest end of the Bay of Panama stands the old city centre of **Casco Viejo**, a breezy jumble of ruins and restored colonial buildings; 4km or so to the northeast rise the shimmering skyscrapers of **El Cangrejo**, the modern banking and commercial district. West of the old centre, the former US Canal Zone town of **Balboa** retains a distinctly North American character, while eastward from El Cangrejo, amid sprawling suburban

slums, stand the ruins of **Panamá Viejo**, the first European city on the Pacific coast of the Americas. Isles of tranquillity far from the frenetic squalor of the city include **Isla Taboga**, the "Island of Flowers", some 20km off the coast; the islets of the Amador Causeway alongside the Pacific entrance to the canal; and the **Parque Nacional Metropolitano**, an island of tropical rainforest within the capital. Panama City is also a good base for day-trips to the canal and the Caribbean coast as far as Portobelo.

WHAT TO SEE AND DO

The old city centre of **Casco Viejo** (also known as Casco Antiguo or San Felipe) is the most picturesque and historically interesting part of Panama City and houses many of its most important buildings and several museums. Declared a UNESCO World Heritage Site in 1997, it is gradually being restored to its former glory after decades of neglect. For views of the modern city and ships waiting to cross the canal, head for the bougainvillea-shaded **Paseo Las Bóvedas**, running some 400m along the top of the old city's defensive wall between the Plaza de Francia and the corner of Calle 1 and Avenida A.

To the west, the **Amador Causeway** (*Calzada de Amador*) marks the entrance to the canal and the former Canal Zone, comprised of the causeway and the town of Balboa. East along the bay from the old city centre, the pulsing and chaotic commercial heart of the capital lies in the neighbouring districts of **Bella Vista**, **El Cangrejo** and **Punta Paitilla**, where the

7

STREET NAMES IN PANAMA CITY

Getting around Panama City can be disconcerting, so it's often best to take a taxi to your accommodation. Confusingly, many streets have at least two names: Avenida Cuba, for instance, is also Avenida 2 Sur, and the road commonly known as Calle 50 is also Avenida 4 Sur or Avenida Nicanor de Obarrio. We have used the most common names throughout this account.

PANAMA CITY AND AROUND

7

■ ACCOMMODATION
Hostal Amador Familiar	3
Panama by Luis	2
Panama Hat B&B	1

Eastern Panama ▲

Tocumen International Airport

Western Panama ▲

Colón ◀

Gamboa ◀

VÍA TOCUMEN (AV DOMINGO DÍAZ)

CORREDOR SUR

VÍA ESPAÑA

TRANSÍSTMICA

CORREDOR NORTE

PARQUE NATURAL METROPOLITANO

Museo Antropológico Reina Torres de Araúz

Albrook Airport (domestic)

Train Station

Albrook Bus Terminal

COROZAL

BALBOA

CERRO ANCON
199m

BRIDGE OF THE AMERICAS

CALZADA DE AMADOR (AMADOR CAUSEWAY)

Museo de la Biodiversidad

Isla Perico

Isla Naos

Punta Culebra Nature Center

Isla Flamenco

Isla Taboga ▶

EL CANGREJO

BELLA VISTA

CASCO VIEJO

PUNTA PAITILLA

AV JUAN

PARQUE II

AV BALBOA

AV CENTRAL

Bahía de Panamá

SEE 'CENTRAL PANAMA CITY MAP'

Panamá Viejo

P A C I F I C   O C E A N

Panama Canal

N

0 — 2 kilometres

majority of banks, hotels, restaurants, shops and luxurious private residences can be found.

Casco Viejo and El Cangrejo are joined by **Avenida Central**, the city's main thoroughfare. Running north of the old centre, its name changes to **Vía España** as it continues through the downtown districts of Calidonia and La Exposición and the residential neighbourhood of Bella Vista. Several other main avenues run parallel to Avenida Central: Avenida Perú, Avenida Cuba, Avenida Justo Arosemena and, along the seafront, **Avenida Balboa**, which has recently been subsumed into the four-lane **Cinta Costera**.

Plaza Catedral

Elderly men chat amiably among the shaded benches and gazebos of cobblestoned **Plaza Catedral**, which sits at the heart of Casco Viejo and the old city. It's also known as Plaza de la Independencia, in honour of the proclamations of independence from both Spain and Colombia that were issued here. The western side of the plaza is dominated by the classical facade of the **cathedral** (daily 8am–2pm). Built between 1688 and 1796, it was constructed using stones and three of the bells from the ruined cathedral of Panamá Viejo (see p.541).

Across the square from the cathedral towers the half-restored facade of the **Hotel Central**, built to replace the *Grand Hotel*, which was, in its time, the plushest hotel in Central America. Southeast of the cathedral is the Neoclassical Palacio Municipal, whose small **Museo de Historia Panameña** (Mon–Fri 9.30am–3.30pm; US$2) offers a cursory introduction to Panamanian history.

Museo del Canal Interoceánico

The excellent **Museo del Canal Interoceánico** (Tues–Sun 9am–6pm; US$2; ☎211 1649, ⓦmuseodelcanal .com), on the south side of the Plaza Catedral, explains in great detail the history of the country's trans-sthmian waterway. Photographs, video footage and historic exhibits – including the

original canal treaties – document everything from the first Spanish attempt to find a passage to Asia to the contemporary management of the canal. All displays are in Spanish, but there are audioguides in English and French (US$5), or you can hire an English-speaking guide (US$5/person for 3–10 people); book **tours** in advance.

Palacio Presidencial

On the seafront two blocks north of the Plaza Catedral along Calle 6, the **Palacio Presidencial**, built in 1673, was home to several successive colonial and Colombian governors. In 1922 it was rebuilt in grandiose neo-Moorish style under the orders of President Belisario Porras, who also introduced white Darién herons to the grounds, giving the palace the nickname of "Palacio de las Garzas". The birds and their descendants have lived freely around the patio fountain ever since and have now been joined by a couple of cranes, donated by the South African government. The streets around the palace are closed to traffic and pedestrians, but the presidential guards allow visitors to view the exterior of the palace between 8am and 5pm daily (except Tues) via a checkpoint on Calle 4.

Plaza Bolívar

Two blocks east of the Palacio Presidencial is **Plaza Bolívar**, an elegant square dedicated in 1883 to Simón Bolívar, whose statue, crowned by a condor, stands in its centre. Bolívar came here in 1826 for the first Panamerican Congress, held in the chapter-room of the old **monastery** on the northeast corner of the square, now the **Salón Bolívar**, a small museum whose centrepiece is a replica of the Liberator's bejewelled ceremonial sword. The whole building has been beautifully restored and currently houses government offices but you can visit for free (Mon–Fri 9am–4pm); go through the door marked "Ministerio de Relaciones Exteriores", to the right of the building's main courtyard entrance.

Next door stands the church and monastery of **San Francisco**, built in the seventeenth century but extensively

7

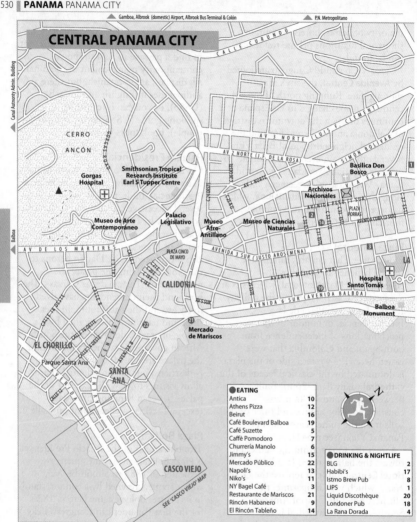

CENTRAL PANAMA CITY

CALLE CURUNDÚ

Canal Authority Admin. Building

CERRO
ANCÓN

AV 3 NORTE LUIS F. CLEMENT

AV 2 NORTE (J.F. DE LA ROSA)

VIA SIMÓN BOLÍVAR

Basílica Don
Bosco

VIA ESPAÑA

Smithsonian Tropical
Research Institute
Earl S Tupper Centre

AV 1 NORTE

Gorgas
Hospital

Archivos
Nacionales

PLAZA
PORRAS

AVENIDA PERÚ 2 SUR

AVENIDA CUBA (3 SUR)

Museo de Arte
Contemporáneo

Palacio
Legislativo

Museo
Afro-
Antillano

Museo de Ciencias
Naturales

AV DE LOS MÁRTIRES

PLAZA CINCO
DE MAYO

AVENIDA 3 SUR (JUSTO AROSEMENA)

LA

Balboa

CALLE OESTE

CIBE
CIBE
CIBE
CIBE

CALIDONIA

AVENIDA MÉXICO (4 SUR)

Hospital
Santo Tomás

AV 5 SUR

AVENIDA 6 SUR (AVENIDA BALBOA)

Balboa
Monument

CALLE 19 OESTE
CALLE 18 OESTE

CALLE CENTRAL

CALLE 16 OESTE

EL CHORRILLO

Parque Santa Ana

SANTA
ANA

Mercado
de Mariscos

CALLE 12 OESTE

CASCO VIEJO

SEE 'CASCO VIEJO' MAP

● EATING	
Antica	10
Athens Pizza	12
Beirut	16
Café Boulevard Balboa	19
Café Suzette	5
Caffè Pomodoro	7
Churrería Manolo	6
Jimmy's	15
Mercado Público	22
Napoli's	13
Niko's	11
NY Bagel Café	3
Restaurante de Mariscos	21
Rincón Habanero	9
El Rincón Tableño	14

● DRINKING & NIGHTLIFE	
BLG	2
Habibi's	17
Istmo Brew Pub	8
LIPS	1
Liquid Discothèque	20
Londoner Pub	18
La Rana Dorada	4

modified subsequently. Since the impressive tower is collapsing, the place has been closed for years awaiting unforthcoming restoration.

Teatro Nacional

Just south of Plaza Bolívar on Avenida B is the **Teatro Nacional** (Mon–Fri 9.30am–5.30pm; US$1; ☎262 3525), designed by Genaro Ruggieri, the Italian architect responsible for La Scala in Milan. Extensively restored in the early 1970s, the splendid Neoclassical interior is richly furnished and decorated in red and gold, with French crystal chandeliers, busts of famous dramatists and a vaulted ceiling painted with scenes depicting the birth of the nation by Panamanian artist Roberto Lewis. Official opening hours are rarely adhered to, but if the door is open, you can usually take a look around; alternatively, try to catch a performance here (see p.540).

Plaza de Francia

The **Plaza de Francia** lies at the southeastern tip of the peninsula, a couple of hundred

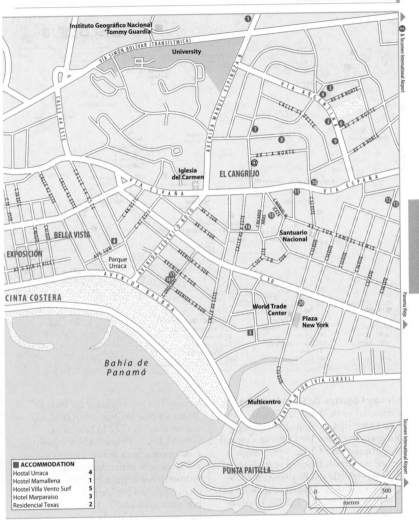

ACCOMMODATION	
Hostal Urraca	4
Hostel Mamallena	1
Hostel Villa Vento Surf	5
Hotel Marparaiso	3
Residencial Texas	2

metres from the theatre, and beyond the ruined shell of the **Club de Clases y Tropas** – the former recreation centre for Noriega's national guard, which was bombed during the US invasion. Enclosed on three sides by seaward defensive walls, it's the site of a **monument** dedicated to the thousands of workers who died during the disastrous French attempt to build the canal (see p.542). The Neoclassical **French Embassy** building, fronted by a statue of former president Pablo Arosemena, stands on the north side of the square. The elegant

building to the east is home to the **National Cultural Institute**. During the colonial period the square was a military centre, with the now restored vaults under the seaward walls – known as **Las Bóvedas** – serving as the city's jail; built below sea level, it is claimed that they would sometimes flood at high tide, drowning the unfortunate prisoners within.

Iglesia y Convento de Santo Domingo

Two blocks west along Avenida A from the corner with Calle 1 stands the ruined

7

CASCO VIEJO

EATING	
Buzios	12
Café Coca-Cola	4
Caffè Per Due	9
Diablo Rosso Café	11
Granclement	5
Super Gourmet	8

DRINKING & NIGHTLIFE	
Habana Panamá	1
Mojito's (sin mojitos)	7
Platea	6
La Rana Dorada	2
Relic	3
Villa Agustina	10

ACCOMMODATION	
Hospedaje Casco Viejo	5
Luna's Castle	2
Magnolia Inn	3
Panamericana	4
White Lion	1

Iglesia y Convento de Santo Domingo, completed in 1678 and famous for the **Arco Chato** (flat arch). Just 10.6m high but spanning some 15m with no external support, the Arco Chato (open irregular hours) was reputedly cited as evidence of Panama's seismic stability when the US Senate was choosing whether to build an interoceanic canal through Nicaragua or Panama.

Iglesia de San José and Plaza Herrera

On Avenida A at the corner with Calle 8 is the **Iglesia de San José**. Built in 1673 and since remodelled, the church is exceptional only as the home of the legendary Baroque Golden Altar, one of the few treasures to survive Henry Morgan's ransacking of Panamá Viejo in 1671 – it was apparently painted or covered in mud to disguise its real value.

One block west of San José, Avenida A emerges onto **Plaza Herrera**, a pleasant square lined with nineteenth-century

houses. This was originally the Plaza de Triunfo, where bullfights were held, but was renamed in 1922 in honour of General Tomás Herrera, whose equestrian monument is at its centre. Herrera was the military leader of the short-lived independence attempt in 1840; he went on to be elected president of Colombia, but was assassinated in 1854. Note that beyond the plaza lies the no-go slum area of **El Chorillo**, which was devastated during the US invasion of Panama, leaving hundreds dead and thousands homeless.

Avenida Central

Avenida Central runs north all the way from the waterfront in the old city centre, through the scary, off-limits *barrios* of Santa Ana and El Chorillo – so don't venture down the side streets – towards the more modern portion of the city. The pedestrianized, ten-block stretch between **Parque Santa Ana**, a small park, and Plaza Cinco de Mayo is the liveliest and most popular **shopping** district for the city's less wealthy residents. Blasts of air conditioning and loud music pour from the huge superstores that line the avenue, while hawkers with megaphones attempt to entice shoppers inside with deals on clothing, electronics and household goods. Nowhere is the diversity and vitality of the city more evident.

Plaza Cinco de Mayo

As Avenida Central emerges onto **Plaza Cinco de Mayo**, the pedestrianized section ends and the maelstrom of traffic takes over again. The plaza is actually two squares rolled into one. The first has a small monument to the volunteer firemen killed while fighting an exploded gunpowder magazine in 1914; *bomberos* occupy a revered position in a city that has so often been devastated by fire. To the south of the plaza stands a forlorn Neoclassical building that was once the Panama Railroad Pacific terminal. The second square, Plaza Cinco de Mayo proper, borders the legislative palace compound, identifiable by a black, monolithic monument. Heading north from here, Avenida Central splits, with the north fork called Avenida Central and the south called Avenida Justo Arosemena (Av 3 Sur).

Museo Afro-Antillano

At the corner of Avenida Justo Arosemena and Calle 24 is a wooden former church, now the **Museo Afro-Antillano** (Tues–Sun 9am–4pm; US$1; ☎ 262 5348), dedicated to preserving the history and culture of Panama's large West Indian population. It's very small, but the exhibits – photographs, tools and furniture – give a good idea of the working and living conditions of black canal-workers.

Mercado del Mariscos

Even if you don't smell the **fish market** from a distance, the vultures circling outside are a sure indication that you've reached the city's seafood hub, on Avenida Balboa close to the entrance to Casco Viejo. Inside you'll find a fantastic selection of Panama's marine life on ice, with lime, and ready to consume. The market is open daily (6am–5pm) but closed the third Monday of the month for fumigation.

Balboa

To the southwest of Calidonia and El Chorrillo, Panama City encompasses the former Canal Zone town of **Balboa**, administered by the US as de facto sovereign territory from 1903 to 1979. Balboa retains many of the characteristics of a US provincial town: clean and well ordered, it stands in stark contrast to the chaotic vitality of the rest of the city, though it conceals a troubled past.

Along the border of the former Canal Zone runs **Avenida de Los Mártires**. An extension of Avenida 4 de Julio and often

---

THE AFRO-ANTILLANOS

Some five percent of Panama's population are **Afro-Antillanos** – descendants of the black workers from the English- and French-speaking West Indies who began migrating to Panama in the mid-nineteenth century to help build the railroad and canal. Widely considered second-class citizens or undesirable aliens, Afro-Antillanos worked and lived in appalling conditions under French and American control. Most of the twenty thousand workers who died during the French canal attempt were West Indians, and the mortality rate was four times higher among black workers than white during US construction.

Throughout the twentieth and into the twenty-first century, successive Panamanian governments have ignored the needs of Afro-Antillanos, and they remain among the most marginalized segments of the population. In spite of this, they maintain a vibrant and distinct **culture** whose influence is widely felt in contemporary Panamanian society. Many second- and third-generation Afro-Antillanos still speak the melodic patois of the West Indies, and the street Spanish of Panama City and Colón is peppered with Jamaican slang. Unique Protestant beliefs imported from the West Indies continue to thrive, heavily spiced Caribbean dishes permeate Panamanian cuisine, and the music, from jazz in the 1950s to "reggaespañol" in the 1990s, has made an indelible mark on the region.

called by the same name, the road is named in honour of the young Panamanians, mostly students, killed by the US military during the flag riots of 1964. A sculpture by González Palomino, depicting three people climbing a flagpole, was erected here in 2004 as a tribute to the fallen; above it rises **Cerro Ancón**, crowned by a huge Panamanian flag that is visible throughout the city. An early morning or late afternoon walk to the top (30min from the gate; US$6 taxi ride) will reward you with great **views** of both the canal and the city and likely sightings of **toucans** in the treetops.

Museo de Arte Contemporáneo

Some 200m east of the entrance to Cerro Ancón, on Avenida de Los Mártires, is a turn-off that leads to Gorgas Road. This winds around the side of Cerro Ancón to the Canal Authority Building in Balboa Heights (see below), about twenty minutes away on foot. Just off Gorgas Road to the right, the **Museo de Arte Contemporáneo** (Tues–Sun 9am–5pm; US$5, free Sun 9am–1pm; ☎262 2012, ⓦmacpanama .org), housed in a former Masonic temple, has a small collection of modern paintings and engravings by Panamanian and Latin American artists, as well as temporary international exhibitions.

Canal Authority Administration Building

On Gorgas Rd in Balboa Heights, the **Panama Canal Authority Administration Building** (daily 8am–11pm; free) was built during the canal construction and is still home to the principal administration offices. Inside, four dramatic murals by US artist William Van Ingen depict the story of the canal's construction under a domed ceiling supported by marble pillars.

At the rear of the building, where a Panamanian flag now flutters, a broad stairway runs down to the **Goethals monument**, a white megalith with stepped fountains that represent the canal's different locks, erected in honour of George Goethals, chief engineer from 1907 to 1914 and first governor of the Canal Zone. Beside the monument is **Balboa High School**, whose ordinary appearance belies the dramatic events it has witnessed. It was here in 1964 that Zonians attacked students attempting to raise the Panamanian flag, triggering the **flag riots** that left a group of young Panamanians dead. During the 1989 invasion, the school was used as a detention camp for Panamanian prisoners, some of whom were allegedly executed by US soldiers.

Calzada de Amador (Amador Causeway)

West of Balboa, the **Calzada de Amador**, originally designed as the canal's Pacific breakwater, runs 6km out into the bay, linking the mainland with the tiny islands of **Naos**, **Perico** and **Flamenco**. It's a popular weekend escape for the city's wealthier residents, who come here to jog, swim, stroll, rollerblade or cycle – you can rent bikes (see p.536) – and to enjoy the sea air and the views of the city and the canal. The northern sector of the causeway is being redeveloped into a complex – still under construction – which will comprise luxury bars, restaurants and hotels, and a marina, as well as the much vaunted **Museo de la Biodiversidad** (ⓦbiomuseopanama.com), a "biodiversity exhibition centre" designed by architect Frank Gehry. Building began in 2004 but has been plagued with controversy, and there is still no opening date in sight.

At the southern side of Punta Culebra, a small promontory at the end of Naos, 4km along the Causeway, and next to the unexciting **Punta Culebra Nature Center** (Tues–Thurs & Sun 10am–6pm, Fri & Sat 10am–8pm; US$5; ⓦstri.org), is the departure point for passenger ferries to Isla Taboga (see p.541) and for some of the canal transit tours (see p.542). Beyond, Perico and Flamenco are home to more shops, bars, restaurants and a marina.

Parque Natural Metropolitano

A couple of kilometres north of central Panama City, the 2.65-square-kilometre **Parque Natural Metropolitano** (daily 6am–6pm; ⓦparquemetropolitano.org) is an unspoilt tract of tropical rainforest that is home to more than two hundred species of birds and mammals, including Geoffroy's tamarin monkeys, white-tailed deer, sloths and agoutis. It's possible to complete the four main **trails** in just a few hours; the best of these is the combined La Cienaguita and Mono Titi trail (3km), which leads to a *mirador* with views across the forest to the city. As elsewhere, the best time to see wildlife, particularly birds, is early in the morning – there's nothing to stop you from coming in earlier than the official opening time. The **park office** (daily 7am–4.30pm; US$4; ☏ 232 5552) and main entrance are on Avenida Juan Pablo II; no buses pass the entrance, though buses from Albrook bound for Corundú can drop you nearby, and a taxi from El Cangrejo should cost about US$4. Three-hour **guided tours** can be arranged to help you spot the early bird (US$50 for up to four people; book in advance at the office).

ARRIVAL AND DEPARTURE

BY PLANE

International flights Tocumen International Airport (☏ 238 4322) lies about 24km northeast of Panama City. Taxis to the city cost US$28 for one or two people, or US$11/person with three or more people sharing. When leaving Panama, save the taxi fare to Tocumen by taking the Metrobus labelled "Tocumen via Corredor Sur" from outside the Albrook bus terminal (every 20min 5.20am–10pm, then hourly; 30–40min; US$1.25), picking up passengers at a stop just under the flyover to the south of Plaza Cinco de Mayo and along the Cinta Costera, and dropping them off just outside the international airport.
Domestic flights All domestic flights (Air Panama; ☏ 316 9000, ☏ airpanama.com) leave from Marcos A. Gelabert Airport (☏ 315 0241) – better known as Albrook airport – which lies roughly 3km, or a 15min taxi ride, northwest of the centre. Taxis from Albrook to the city should cost around US$6 from just outside the terminal building, but are much cheaper if flagged down on the road across from the terminal.
Destinations Bocas del Toro (3 daily; 1hr); Contadora, Pearl Islands (1 daily; 20min); David (4 daily; 1hr); Jaqué (Mon & Fri; 1hr); Guna Yala (daily flights to Achutupo, Corazón de Jesús, Mulatupo, Playón Chico (30min–1hr 15min); also to Puerto Obaldía (Tues, Sat & Sun; 1hr); Sambú via Garachiné (Wed & Sat; 50min).

BY BUS

International buses International services from Costa Rica, with Ticabus (☏ 314 6385, ☏ ticabus.com) and Panafront (☏ 314 6885 or ☏ 6564 6889), arrive at and

depart from the Albrook bus terminal (simply referred to as "*el terminal*"), 3km northwest of the city centre and very near the domestic airport. Taxis, which can take you into town from around US$4, and local city-bound buses (US$0.25) leave from the ground floor, in front of the terminal. Ticket offices for onward domestic travel (you can buy a ticket, in person, up to three days in advance of travel) are inside the building, along with toilets, ATMs and a 24hr cafeteria. Buses depart from the back of the terminal.
Destinations Paso Canoas, on the border (Panafront: hourly 7.30am–10.30pm; 9hr); San José (Ticabus: 2 daily; 11am [executive class]; 16hr; 11pm [economy class]; 18hr).
Domestic buses The Albrook bus terminal (see above) is also the transport hub for all domestic buses.
Destinations Almirante and Changuinola, for Bocas (2 daily, 8pm & 8.30pm; 10/11hr); Chitré (hourly; 4hr); Colón (local departures every 20min; 2hr; express departures every 30min; 1hr 30min); David (hourly; 7hr, plus 2 express departures daily; 5hr 30min); El Valle (every 30min; 2hr 30min); Gamboa (8 daily; 45min); Las Tablas (every 2hr; 4hr 30min); Metetí (7 daily until 4.30pm; 5hr); Miraflores Locks (take Paraíso or Gamboa bus); Paraíso (every 30–45min; 20min); Paso Canoas (hourly; 9hr) plus 2 express departures daily (7hr); Penonomé (every 15min; 2hr 15min); Santiago (every 30min; 3hr 30min); Soná, for Santa Catalina (6 daily; 5hr); Yaviza (7 daily until 11.30am; 6hr).

GETTING AROUND

By bus Buses head almost everywhere in the city from Albrook bus terminal, many passing through Plaza Cinco de Mayo, the nearest point to Casco Viejo, before heading towards El Cangrejo and Bellavista. There are two types of public buses. Best known, but being phased out, are the chicken buses (see box, p.32) – known in Panama as *diablos rojos*, or red devils, because of the devil-may-care attitude of many of the drivers. These cost just US$0.25 per ride, payable on exit, and operate from 6am to midnight. Though they operate fixed routes, there are no fixed timetables; destinations are painted on the windscreen. Newer, a/c Metrobuses (☏ mibus.com.pa) operate the same hours and also cost US$0.25, though this will rise to US$0.75 once they have completely replaced the *diablos rojos*. You need a pre-paid card (*tarjeta*), which you swipe on entry and exit, to ride the Metrobus. Cards are available at supermarkets (such as El Rey on Via España and El Machetazo on Av Central) as well as at the Albrook bus terminal and from a kiosk on Plaza Cinco de Mayo. The initial card costs US$2 and then you need to buy credit.
By taxi Taxis are plentiful and cheap, if prone to hiking prices for tourists. Fares are theoretically based on a zone system, though few taxi drivers adhere to it. Most city rides

7

7

will cost about US$2–3 for one or two people, maybe closer to US$4 to the bus terminal. Taxis from Albrook bus terminal into town tend to be pricier, especially at night. No trip should cost more than US$5, except to the Amador Causeway (often around $10), where drivers do not expect to get a client for the return journey, and to Tocumen International Airport (US$25–30). If a driver doesn't want to go your way, you'll be quoted a vastly inflated price, which is meant to either put you off or make it a worthwhile trip for them.

By bike The safest place to ride a bicycle in Panama City is on the Amador Causeway. For rentals head to *Las Pencas* restaurant, close to the Museo de la Biodiversidad (see p.534), where Bicicletas Moses (noon–6pm in high season; otherwise weekends only; ☏ 211 3671) will kit you out for US$3–4/hr. Rali-Carretero, Via España at Av Argentina (☏ 263 4136) and on Av Balboa (☏ 263 4136), has spare parts and a maintenance centre.

INFORMATION

Tourist information For simple queries, ask at the international or domestic airport booths. The central tourist office, Av Samuel Lewis & Ortega, Edif. Central, 2nd Floor (☏ 526 7000, ☒ atp.gob.pa), is not geared up to actually dealing with tourists; you'll get more information from the city's hostels, where you'll also be able to book travel and accommodation for trips including to Guna Yala, the canal and beyond, and boat trips to Colombia.

ACCOMMODATION

A growing number of budget travellers bed down in Casco Viejo. The restoration of many of the area's colonial buildings makes it a pleasant retreat from the congestion and the pollution of the rest of the city – though there's constantly some construction noise to contend with – and the nightlife is pretty good. The Calidonia/La Exposición area offers unexceptional but affordable modern hotels and *residenciales*, while further east along Via España, the districts of Bella Vista and El Cangrejo, the hub of the city's nightlife and commercial activity, have a couple of hostels, some mid-range options and the expensive chain hotels. In high season (Dec–April) it's highly advisable to book in advance no matter where you're staying; hostels, in particular, are almost always booked up. It's also best to exercise caution in all neighbourhoods after dark.

CASCO VIEJO

Hospedaje Casco Viejo C 8A 8–31 by Iglesia San José ☏ 211 2127, ☒ hospedajecascoviejo.com; map p.532. Well kept and surprisingly spacious, this *hospedaje* may be lacking in colonial charm but is a calm option in the old town, though staff often speak only limited English. There's a small, shared kitchen, free basic breakfast (toast and coffee) and wi-fi, though the place suffers from periodic water problems. Dorm __US$11__, double __US$25__

Luna's Castle C 9A Este between Av B & Av Alfaro ☏ 262 1540, ☒ lunascastlehostel.com; map p.532. Perfect for

---

TOUR OPERATORS IN PANAMA CITY

Panama City boasts a number of decent tour operators, though many are only really worth considering for excursions in the former Canal Zone and along the central Caribbean Coast. For trips further afield, it's often more convenient, and cheaper, to engage a local operator in the nearest tourist centre – highlighted in the relevant sections of this chapter. Several hostels also organize inexpensive tours.

Advantage Panama ☒ advantagepanama.com/ darienadventure. Specializing in birdwatching and involved in important conservation work, this company offers a good-value four-day "Darién Adventure" tour.

Ecocircuitos Albrook Plaza, 2nd Floor, No 31, Ancón ☏ 315 1305, ☒ ecocircuitos.com. Actively promotes sustainable tourism and offers a range of day- and multiday tours with multilingual, naturalist guides, including trekking across the isthmus, kayaking and birdwatching.

Emberá Tours ☏ 250 1165 or ☏ 6519 7121 ☒ emberatourspanama.com. Run by Garceth Cunampio, an English-speaking Emberá guide who organizes excursions to villages up the Chagres (from US$150 for an overnight trip for 1 to 4 people), as well as birdwatching trips to the Darién.

My Friend Mario C Arnoldo Cano, La Chorrera ☏ 253

6500 or ☏ 6615 2271, ☒ myfriendmario.com. Popular outfit offering relatively inexpensive tours (US$45– 85), including to the Canal Zone, taking in the forts at Portobelo and San Lorenzo, and to an Emberá village up the Río Chagres.

Panama Organica ☏ 6079 6825, ☒ panama organica.com. Small outfit offering customized budget tours to hard-to-access areas such as Darién and Guna Yala, working with local communities and independent operators. Can also help arrange transport to Colombia and day-trips from Panama City.

Scuba Panamá Av 6 Norte at C 62A ☏ 261 3841, ☒ scubapanama.com. The country's oldest outfit offers countrywide diving excursions – including the popular and gimmicky two oceans in one day (US$288) – equipment sale and rental, and diving instruction. They also have accommodation in Portobelo (see p.550).

partying 'packers, but not the best option for a weary traveller in need of sleep, this colonial maze of high-ceilinged rooms has a busy kitchen, loads of chill-out spaces with wi-fi, and a cinema, framed by a kaleidoscope of vibrant artwork. Experienced gringo owners and friendly young staff will arrange your onward travel (including boats to Colombia). The *Relic* bar is downstairs (see p.539). Pancake breakfast included. Dorm US$13, double US$30

Magnolia Inn C 8 & Boquete, behind the cathedral ☎ 202 0872, ⊛ magnoliapanama.com; map p.532. Lovingly restored, two floors of this colonial mansion are part boutique hotel, part luxury hostel. Though the hotel rooms are expensive (from US$160) the deluxe six-bed dorm offers excellent value, boasting a/c, excellent mattresses and reading lights, plus a beautifully furnished dining and lounge area to relax in. Dorm US$15

★ **Panamericana** Plaza Herrera ☎ 202 0851, ⊛ panamericanahostel.com; map p.532. Beautifully restored colonial mansion enlivened by artistic touches in fluorescent paint, with shared balconies and a great rooftop terrace-bar offering panoramic views of Casco Viejo. Large airy rooms with high ceilings and excellent beds, plus spacious hot showers and a comfy TV lounge and decent-sized kitchen downstairs make this a top choice. The only downside, currently, is that the old ventilation slats above the doors let in the noise – to be resolved soon, we're told. Dorm US$13, double US$35

White Lion C12 between Av B & Eloy Alfaro ☎ 212 0094, ⊛ hotelyhostelwhitelion-pty.com; map p.532. Down a dingy side street, a bright hotel lobby-cum-café fronts this surprisingly spacious hotel-hostel. Spartan, new rooms with a/c, cable TV, fridge and bathroom are good value for the location; the hot dorms have thin mattresses. There's a rooftop disco Fri & Sat. Dorm US$13, double US$29

CALIDONIA AND LA EXPOSICIÓN

Hotel Marparaiso C 34 at Av Justo Arosemena, La Exposición ☎ 227 6767, ⊛ marparaisopma.com; map pp.530–531. A stay of two nights, booked in advance, includes transport from the airport. There's a downstairs restaurant and free wi-fi. Rooms sleeping up to six people are homey rather than modern, and the street noise can be bothersome, but it's one of the best budget options in this sketchy area. US$40

Residencial Texas C 31 between Av Peru & Cuba, beside the national lottery ☎ 225 1467, ✉ hoteltexas@mixmail .com; map pp.530–531. Friendly, secure place offering good-value rooms with spotless tiled bathrooms, decent hot showers and good mattresses, though the furniture is tired. US$38

BELLA VISTA AND EL CANGREJO

Hostal Urraca C 44 2–112, Parque Urraca ☎ 391 3972, ⊛ posadaurraca.com; map pp.530–531. A newish hostel

in a very central location, incongrously hemmed in by high-rises, where tidy little dorms (with a/c), good-value singles, and much pricier doubles (with shared or private bathroom) share bright communal spaces. Plus wi-fi, a communal kitchen, laundry services, free basic breakfast and tourist info. Dorm US$18, double US$70

Hostel Villa Vento Surf C 47 ☎ 397 6001, ⊛ hostel villaventosurf.com; map pp.530–531. Modern hostel in the heart of the banking district, but within reach of restaurants and nightlife. There's one private room with shared bathroom, and five rather small dorms (with fan; a/c costs an extra US$5) with comfortable bunks. The pool and BBQ patio area are the big draws and the place has a kitchen, lockers and wi-fi. Dorm US$13, double US$50

Panama Hat B&B (formerly Casa del Carmen) C Primera El Carmen 32 ☎ 263 4366, ⊛ lacasadecarmen.net; map p.528. Attracts a wide age range with their restful patio and garden, and free services including breakfast, internet, shared kitchen, laundry, hot water and barbecue area. Strongly recommended and usually full, so book ahead. Dorm US$17, double US$50

ELSEWHERE IN THE CITY

Hostal Amador Familiar C Akee, off Av Amador, behind *Tamburelli's*, Balboa ☎ 314 1251, ⊛ hostalamadorfamiliar .com; map p.528. Converted three-storey Canal Zone building attracting foreign and Panamanian visitors. Simple, compact dorms (with a/c) and en-suite rooms (with fan or a/c) with hot showers, plus a back patio area for the DIY breakfast – included. Special airport transfer rates and wi-fi. Dorm US$15, double US$30

Hostel Mamallena C Primera, Casa de la Junta Comunal por el Colegio Javier, Perejil ☎ 6676 6163, ⊛ mamallena .com; mappp.530–531. Popular, well-run hostel with clean dorms and small private rooms (all with a/c), as well as a communal kitchen – where you can make your free breakfast pancakes all day! – and a funky courtyard garden with hammocks. Good info and travel assistance. Dorm US$13, double US$33

Panama by Luis C Benito Reyes Testa, opposite Condominio Davinci, San Francisco ☎ 393 6275, ⊛ panamabyluis.com; map p.528. A small house tucked away on a quiet residential street; the not-so-inviting facade belies a more pleasant interior with funky modern touches. Clean dorms (fan or a/c) and private rooms, with a/c, cable TV and shared bathroom, have good mattresses; plus, there's a comfortable TV lounge and a kitchen in the back yard. Can arrange tours and onward travel, including trips to Guna Yala. Dorm US$13, double US$36

EATING

Panama City's cosmopolitan nature is reflected in its restaurants: anything from US fast food to Greek, Italian, Chinese, Japanese and French can easily be found, and

7

excellent seafood is widely available. Cheap takeaway meals are also available from the Rey supermarket (open 24hr) on Vía España.

CASCO VIEJO AND SANTA ANA

Café Coca-Cola Plaza Santa Ana, C 12 at Av Central; map p.532. The self-proclaimed "oldest restaurant in Panama" and something of an institution among the city's older residents, who gather to drink coffee, read the paper and discuss the news. Filling Panamanian staples (*ceviche*, chicken with rice, soups) from US$4.50, and generous breakfasts. The people-watching is fabulous; the food is variable. Daily 7am–11pm.

Caffè Per Due Av A at C 3 ☎ 6512 9311; map p.532. Cosy café that keeps its prices affordable: thin, crispy pizzas, salads and cakes. Tues–Sat 8.30am–10pm, Sun from 9.30am.

★ **Diablo Rosso Café** C 6 at Av A ☎ 262 1957; map p.532. Also home to the Diablo Rosso Art Gallery, this trendy boutique café has an eclectic, Mediterranean-influenced menu of large and delicious panini and Quinoa-rich salads (US$5–10). Displaying a collection of quirky furniture, art, designer clothing and accessories – all of which are for sale – the place also hosts film screenings (Tues & Wed 11am–7pm). Thurs–Sat until 9pm.

Granclement Av Central at C 4; map p.532. Head here when you're feeling indulgent; US$2.75 may seem pricey for a scoop of ice cream, but this French-style artisanal ice cream, served in a waffle cone, is to die for, from creamy rich chocolate concoctions to mouthwatering sorbets. Daily noon–8.30pm.

Super Gourmet Av A at C 6 ☎ 212 3487, ⊛ supergourmet cascoviejo.com; map p.532. A café and deli serving tasty baguette sandwiches (US$4–5.50), excellent daily specials (US$6), and the best coffees in the old town. Mon–Sat 8am–5pm, Sun 10am–4pm.

CALIDONIA AND LA EXPOSICIÓN

Café Boulevard Balboa Av Balboa at C 30 Este; map pp.530–531. The spartan 1970s interior is enlivened by a

---

> ★ **TREAT YOURSELF**
>
> **Buzios** C 1 Las Bóvedas ☎ 228 9045; map p.532. A top spot for unpretentious, alfresco dining on a patio with lush tropical plants draped with fairy lights. The food is Mediterranean, with a seafood bias, accompanied by mellow Brazilian music. Try the chicken and mango in coconut cream, or the snapper with plantain on a bed of oriental vegetables (mains from around US$12), and leave room for the mouthwatering fruit mousse. Tues–Sun noon–10.30pm.

---

smart lunchtime crowd of local politicians and office workers. Although specializing in toasted sandwiches (US$4.50–8), the lengthy menu also includes filling Panamanian dishes (from US$6), such as *ceviche de corvina*. Mon–Sat 6.30am–1am.

Mercado Público Av B & Av Balboa; map pp.530–531. Seek out the food court, where you can choose from a dozen *fondas* serving hot, heaped platefuls of noodles or rice with bits of meat, seafood and veg for under US$3. Mon–Sat 6am–3pm.

Restaurante de Mariscos Av Balboa above the Mercado de Mariscos ☎ 212 3898; map pp.530–531. Pick a fresh seafood dish from their own menu, or buy something from the stalls downstairs and get them to cook it for you, served with rice or *patacones*. Daily 11am–6pm.

El Rincón Tableño Av Cuba at C 31; map pp.530–531. One of the city's ubiquitous cafeteria-style restaurants, serving *comida típica* with relish and at economical prices (under US$5). Try the *sancocho*, Panama's favourite meat-and-veg soup. Daily 6am–4pm.

BELLA VISTA AND EL CANGREJO

Antica Vía España & C Eusebio A Morales; map pp.530–531. Popular ice-cream parlour serving authentic *gelati*, inexpensive slabs of cake or sandwiches (under $2), hot chocolate and decent espresso coffee. Mon–Sat 10am–9pm, Sun from noon.

Athens Pizza C 57 Este, off Vía España, opposite *Napoli's* ☎ 223 1464; map pp.530–531. Tasty, filling meals from around US$7. The Greek dishes, including salads (US$7), are abundant and the pizza is great comfort food. Wed–Mon 11am–late.

Beirut C 49A Este at Av 3 Sur, opposite the *Marriott*; map pp.530–531. A largely Lebanese menu (from US$4) with bowls of tasty hummus and *baba ganoush* for US$5, and halal *shawarma* and *kofta* plates for US$12. Popular with wealthy locals for its good service, hookah pipes and occasional belly-dancing at weekends. Daily noon–late.

Café Suzette Vía Argentina ☎ 393 2257; map pp.530–531. Fluffy sweet and savoury crêpes (most US$5–8) are the mainstay of this friendly little café, which also serves a small selection of soups, salads and sandwiches. Wi-fi. Daily 8am–9pm.

Caffè Pomodoro C 49B Oeste in *ApartHotel Las Vegas*; map pp.530–531. Extremely popular Italian restaurant, with outdoor seating in an enclosed tropical garden. One of several venues owned by local celebrated chef Willy Digelmann, with a menu of antipasti, salads, pastas and pizzas from US$6. Daily 7am–midnight.

Churrería Manolo Vía Argentina 12; map pp.530–531. Café specializing in sweet, cigar-shaped *churro* pastries for around a dollar, as well as serving coffees, *emparedados* and more substantial mains (US$8–11).

Jimmy's C Manuel Icaza, off Vía España; map pp.530–531.

Enjoy the comfy seating while you peruse the wide-ranging, affordable menu of Panamanian and Greek dishes – meat and fish mains from US$6, or *sancocho* for under US$5. Daily specials and light bites also available. Mon–Sat 7am–11pm.

Napoli's C 57 Este Obarrio, off Vía España ☎ 263 8800; map pp.530–531. The place for pizza, as far as middle-class Panamanians are concerned, and frequently bulging at the seams. You can get a 10" pizza from US$6 or a monster family one for around US$15, plus there are mid-priced salads and pasta dishes. Order a takeaway and save yourself the tax. Tues–Sun 11am–11pm.

Niko's Just off Vía España, opposite Plaza Regency; map pp.530–531. Busy 24hr cafeteria with branches all over the city (notably in the bus terminal) serving a wide choice of Panamanian and international fast food. Much of the large menu, from grilled meat and fish to sandwiches, pizza and strong coffee, can be tasted for under US$5. Takeaway available.

★ **NY Bagel Café** Cabeza de Einstein, C Felipe Motta at Vía Argentina; map pp.530–531. The exposed brick walls and large open kitchen lend a touch of the Big Apple to this popular hangout for travellers, expats and Panamanians. *NY* serves a wide variety of home-made bagels with home-made cream cheese (US$3), breakfasts and burgers, fruit smoothies, good coffee and more. Mon–Fri 7am–8pm, Sat 8am–8pm, Sun 8am–3pm.

Rincón Habanero Vía Argentina, opposite *El Trapiche* ☎ 202 0872; map pp.530–531. Great little tucked-away Cuban-owned restaurant with images and sounds of old-time Havana on the walls and plasma TV. Plantain, beans and rice all feature heavily on the modestly priced menu, and the mojitos are a must. Mon–Sat noon–10.30pm.

DRINKING AND NIGHTLIFE

Panama City is a 24hr metropolis, and its residents like nothing better than to drink and dance into the early hours. At one end of the great range of places to go are the *cantinas* and bars around Av Central: hard-drinking dives where women are scarce. Most of the upmarket places are found around El Cangrejo – around C Uruguay in particular – Amador and Casco Viejo, though the colonial centre also has some less expensive, more bohemian spots. Nightlife in the Amador Causeway centres on the Zona de la Rumba – a secure, walled enclave of glitzy bars, restaurants and clubs, with pricey drinks and a non-too-cheap taxi fare to factor in. Once in a particular neighbourhood, it's easy and relatively safe to walk between venues at night. Most clubs are closed on Mondays and Tuesdays and don't get going until around midnight. Cover charges, mostly levied on weekends and for live acts, tend to be high, but often include several free drinks.

CASCO VIEJO AND AMADOR

Habana Panamá Eloy Alfaro at C 12; map p.532. Evoking classic Havana, this is the spot to swing your

hips to live salsa (playing from around 11pm). US$2 entry. Fri & Sat.

★ **Mojitos (sin Mojitos)** Plaza Herrera; map p.532. This small, intimate cellar-like bar, buzzing with expats, locals and travellers, is a must for a night out in Casco Viejo, offering cheap drinks (though no Mojitos!) and tasty home-made meat and veggie burgers. Tues–Sat 6pm–late.

Platea C 1, in front of the old *Club Unión* ☎ 228 4011; map p.532. Upscale intimate live-music bar underneath the expensive *Scena* restaurant. Pricey but good food and drinks. From 8pm, music (Thurs jazz, Fri salsa, Sat rock) from 9.30pm.

Relic *Luna's Castle*, C 9A Este between Av B & Av Alfaro ☎ 262 1540, ⌨ lunascastlehostel.com; map p.532. With its crypt-style interior and breezy courtyard, which heaves until the wee hours, *Relic* pulls in a healthy mix of locals and travellers. Mon–Sat from 8.30pm.

Villa Agustina Av A, between Plaza Herrera & C 8; map p.532. Trendy outdoor party venue set in a painted and plant-filled courtyard illuminated by pretty lights. It's a hot spot in the dry summer months – less so in the rainy season – popular with backpackers and locals, with cheap booze and occasional big-name DJ events blasting out *música variada*, heavily laced with *electrónica*. Cover charge for events. Thurs–Sun 6pm until late.

BELLA VISTA AND EL CANGREJO

BLG Transístmica; map pp.530–531. *BLG* serves the gay community, and everyone else, unlimited drinks with the US$5+ cover charge. A well-known party spot, with excellent DJs. Wed–Sat.

Habibi's Off C Uruguay; map pp.530–531. Right in the thick of things, *Habibi's* has seemingly limitless indoor and outdoor seating perfect for enjoying hookahs, cocktails (from US$5) and pricey Lebanese snacks.

Istmo Brew Pub Av Eusebio A. Morales; map pp.530–531. If you're craving something other than the standard local *cerveza*, try the half open-air, half covered *Istmo* – all the beer is brewed on site (US$3–5) in beautiful copper kegs. The pool table and televised football matches are further pluses. Daily 4.30pm until late.

LIPS Av Manuel Batista, upstairs in the Centro Comercial Splash; map pp.530–531. Gay dance hot spot with a busy calendar of events, featuring themed evenings, foam parties and drag acts. Cover charge from US$5. Wed–Sun.

Liquid Discothèque C 50 Plaza New York; map pp.530–531. *Liquid* plays a range of music, from europop to house, for a well-dressed crowd on its huge dance floor. Cover charge usually US$5–8. Thurs–Sat.

Londoner Pub C Uruguay; map pp.530–531. A slightly over-modernized take on the British pub, with beers on tap (from US$4), darts and flat-screen TVs showing football. It's missing the cosy corners of a true pub, but its location draws a crowd on busy nights. Mon–Sat from 5pm.

7

La Rana Dorada Vía Argentina at Einstein's Head; map pp.530–531. Brasserie-bar popular with young expats and wealthy Panamanians, serving beer, cocktails (from US$4) and food (from US$5). The home-brewed beer and the trendy location has the crowds spilling out onto the street. Its equally popular sibling bar in Casco Viejo is tucked beside *Habana Panama*. Daily noon–late.

ENTERTAINMENT

Most theatre productions are in Spanish, and can be found advertised outside theatre buildings and in *La Prensa*. Rock concerts and the like happen at the convention centres of ATLAPA (W atlapa.gob.pa) and Figali Convention Center (W figaliconventioncenter.com). Check the papers, as well as W quehacerhoypanama.com, W thepanamanews.com and W prensa.com, for entertainment listings, including live music and theatre.

Cinema There are many cinemas showing current, mainly subtitled, Hollywood blockbusters (generally from around US$4); check W cinespanama.com for schedules. Try Cinemark, in the Albrook Mall, across from the bus terminal, and in Multicentro on Av Balboa, near Punta Paitilla.

Dance For a taste of traditional Panamanian dance served up for tourists, pass by *Los Diabólicos* in C 1 Casco Viejo or head for *Las Tinajas* in Bellavista (W tinajaspanama.com). Tickets for many events are available online at W tuboleto .com or at the Blockbuster video store on Vía España at Vía Argentina.

Teatro Balboa Stevens' Circle, Balboa ☎ 228 0327. Jazz, folk dancing and theatre productions sponsored by the National Cultural Institute.

Teatro Nacional Av B, Plaza Bolívar, Casco Viejo (☎ 262 3525). Opera and ballet productions.

SHOPPING

There are several souvenir shops lining Vía Veneto in El Cangrejo, and a handful of shops catering to tourists clustered along C 1 in Casco Viejo – the best is the Galería de Arte Indigena. Av Central, the pedestrian zone running between Plaza Cinco de Mayo and Casco Viejo, is the place to go for low prices on any type of goods.

Crafts Mercado de Buhonerías y Artesanías (Mon–Sat 9am–6pm) is on Plaza Cinco de Mayo behind the old railway building, while the Centro de Artesanías International on the Amador Causeway, next to the Figali Convention Centre (Mon–Sat 9am–6pm, Sun 10am–5pm), has a good selection from Panama and other Latin American countries.

Exedra Books Vía Brazil at Vía España. Large, modern bookshop with café and free wi-fi. Mon–Sat 9.30am–8.30pm, Sat 9.30am–7pm, Sun 11am–5pm.

Gran Morrison Vía España, El Cangrejo. English-language books on Panama, with a souvenir section.

Librería Argosy Vía Argentina at Vía España. Mostly used books, with titles in Spanish and English.

Malls Albrook Mall across from the Albrook bus terminal; MultiPlaza Mall at Vía Israel & C 50; Multicentro on Av Balboa at Plaza Paitilla.

DIRECTORY

Banks and exchange The Banco Nacional de Panamá and HSBC – each with several outlets across the city, including on Vía España in El Cangrejo – allow cash withdrawals on credit cards; most banks also have 24hr ATMs. Foreign currency is more difficult to change – foreign banks will generally change their own currency, and there is a licensed exchange house, Panacambios (Mon–Fri 8am–4pm; ☎ 223 1800), in the Plaza Regency Building on Vía España, opposite the Rey supermarket.

Car rental Most major rental companies have desks at the airport and some have offices along Vía Espana; National Panama (W nationalpanama.com) is a local company with branches at both airports.

Embassies Australia – seek advice from Canadian embassy; Canada, Torres de las Americas, Tower A, 11th floor, Punta Pacífica (☎ 294 2500); Costa Rica, Av Samuel Lewis, Edif. Omega, 3rd floor (☎ 264 2980); UK, MMG Tower, C 53, Marbella (☎ 297 6550); US, Av Demetrio Basilio Lakas, Clayton (☎ 317 5000).

Health Hospitals include Hospital Nacional, Av Cuba, C 38/39 (☎ 207 8100); Centro Médico Paitilla, C 53 & Av Balboa (☎ 265 8800); and Hospital Punta Pacífica, Bld Pacífica & Vía Punta Darién (☎ 204 8000). Pharmacies are found all over the city and often have a big green sign with a cross; Farmacia Arrocha is popular – the largest branch is on Vía España in front of *El Panamá* hotel, and there is others on Vía Argentina and one in Punta Paitilla. City-wide branches of El Rey supermarket (24hr) and Super 99 often have 24hr pharmacies.

Immigration The *migración* is in Tumba Muerto outside the city centre (Mon–Fri 9am–4pm; ☎ 507 1800, W migracion.gob.pa); you won't need to go there unless you have overstayed your visa or want to change status.

Internet There are many internet cafés throughout the city, especially in El Cangrejo around Vía Veneto, C 49B Oeste, a block up from Vía España (around US$1/hr).

Language schools Berlitz, C 47, Edificio Marbella (☎ 265 4800, W berlitz.com); ILERI, Vía La Amistad, El Dorado (☎ 260 4424); Spanish Panama, off Vía Argentina, El Cangrejo (☎ 213 3121, W spanishpanama.com).

Police Emergencies ☎ 104; tourist police ☎ 211 3365.

Post office The most central post office is on Av Central at C 34, opposite the Don Bosco basilica; there's another in El Cangrejo in the Plaza de la Concordia shopping centre on Via España (both Mon–Fri 7am–6pm, Sat 7am–3pm).

Telephones Public phone booths throughout the city take phonecards; some take coins. The main Cable & Wireless office (Mon–Fri 7.15am–6.30pm, Sat 7.30am–2pm) is in the Banco Nacional building on Via

España. Most internet cafés offer cheap international calls for about US$0.05–10/min.

AROUND PANAMA CITY

Two contrasting attractions provide welcome escapes from the frenetic pace of the capital: to the east, a short bus ride away, lie the ruins of **Panamá Viejo**, once the premier colonial city on the isthmus; to the southwest, and an hour by boat, tropical **Isla Taboga** provides a peaceful setting for some gentle hiking and beach-lounging.

Panamá Viejo

On the coast about 8km east of the city centre stand the ruins of **PANAMÁ VIEJO**, the original colonial city founded by Pedro Arias de Ávila in 1519. Abandoned in 1671 after being sacked by Henry Morgan and his band of pirates, many of its buildings were later dismantled to provide stones for the construction of Casco Viejo, and in recent decades much of the site has been built over as the modern city has spread eastward – another new major road was being built through the site at the time of writing. Despite this encroachment, a surprising number of the original buildings still stand.

The best place to start a visit is the **museum** (Tues–Sun 9am–5pm; US$3, US$6 with entrance to ruins; ☎224 2155, ⓦpanamaviejo.org) on Vía Cincuentenario near the ruins, where exhibits explain the changes that have taken place since this was a tiny Indian village around 500 BC. Only one section of the ruins, the former **Plaza Mayor**, requires an entry fee. The major draw here is the three-storey square stone tower of the cathedral, built between 1619 and 1629. It has a modern stairway with a lookout at the top and is flanked by the square **cabildo** (town hall) to the right and the bishop's house to the left. Nearby, and free to the public, is the site of La Merced, the church and monastery where Francisco Pizarro took communion before embarking on the conquest of Peru in 1531. La Merced was once considered Panama City's most beautiful church, and survived Morgan's burning of the city by his use of it as a headquarters.

To **get to** Panamá Viejo, either take a taxi (US$3–4) or catch any bus marked "Panamá Viejo" or "Vía Cincuentenario" from along the Cinta Costera.

Isla Taboga

Some 20km off the coast and about an hour away by boat, tiny **ISLA TABOGA** is one of the most popular retreats for Panama City residents, who come here to enjoy the island's clear waters, peaceful atmosphere and verdant beauty. Known as the "Island of Flowers" for the innumerable fragrant blooms that decorate its village and forested slopes, Taboga gets very busy at weekends, particularly during the summer, but is usually quiet during the week.

Taboga's one **fishing village** is very picturesque, with narrow streets, whitewashed houses and dozens of gardens filled with bougainvillea and hibiscus. Most visitors head straight for a section of **beach**, either right in front of the village or in front of the defunct *Hotel Taboga*, to the right of the pier as you disembark. The water is calmer here and the view of Panama City is magnificent, though the rubbish that frequently washes up on the beach is unsightly.

Behind the village, forested slopes rise to the 300m peak of **Cerro Vigía**, where a viewing platform on top of an old US military bunker offers spectacular 360-degree views. It's about an hour's climb through the forest to the *mirador* – follow the path some 100m up behind the church until you find a sign marked "Sendero de los Tres Cruces", beyond which the trail is easy to follow. It's a great area for spotting poison dart frogs and tarantulas, especially after some rain. The other side of the island is home to one of the largest brown pelican breeding colonies in the world and, together with the neighbouring island of Urabá, forms a protected wildlife refuge.

ARRIVAL AND DEPARTURE

By boat Daily departures on the *Calypso Queen* passenger ferry (US$13 return; ☎314 1730) leave for Isla Taboga from next to the Punta Culebra Nature Centre on Isla Naos on the Amador Causeway (8.30am, returning 4.30pm), with extra ferries at 10.30am and 3pm at weekends and on public holidays.

ACCOMMODATION AND EATING

Though you can stay on Taboga (see ⓦtaboga .panamanow.com), the island is easily explored in a day. **Acuario** C Abajo, a few hundred metres along from the jetty. The best of several restaurants on Taboga, this small upstairs place serves some of the most delicious seafood on the island (from US$7).

7 The Panama Canal and Colón Province

Stretching 80km from Panama City in the south to Colón in the north, the **Panama Canal** is a work of mesmerizing engineering brilliance. One of the largest and most ambitious human endeavours, the waterway allows massive vessels – which otherwise would have to travel all the way south around Cape Horn – to traverse the isthmus in less than one day. East of the canal spreads the rainforest of **Parque Nacional Soberanía**, the greatest possible contrast to its mechanical might. Delve into the park's humming, humid atmosphere on one of its many accessible pathways, and you'll discover unparalleled biodiversity. **Colón**, at the Atlantic entrance to the canal, and only a boat or train or bus ride away from Panama City, seems like a different world from the capital – a brief tour of the poverty-stricken city from the safety of a taxi leaves you in no doubt about the canal's socioeconomic importance, and the depth of Panama's social inequalities. Some 45km northeast of Colón lies another port – **Portobelo** – whose glory days are even more distant. Its riches once proved irresistible to such pirates as Sir Francis Drake and Henry Morgan, and its once-mighty fortifications are now atmospheric ruins.

THE PANAMA CANAL AND THE CANAL ZONE

The **PANAMA CANAL** really is amazing, both physically and in concept. The basis of the country's modern economy, it's also the key to much of its history: were it not for the US government's determination to build the waterway, Panama might never have come into existence as an independent republic. Construction on the project began in the late nineteenth century, initiated by the French, but their efforts were abandoned in 1893, having taken the lives of nearly 22,000 workers through disease. The US took up the construction just over ten years later, aided by more powerful machinery than the French had been using, and improved understanding of malaria, yellow fever and the engineering that was necessary. The job was finally finished in 1914, the isthmus having been breached by the 77km-long canal, with vessels raised from and lowered to sea level by three sets of locks totalling 5km in length.

From 1903 to 1977, the strip of land that extends 8km on either side of the canal was de facto US territory, an area known as the **Canal Zone**. After more than ninety years the waterway was finally handed over to Panamanian jurisdiction at midnight on December 31, 1999, to be managed thereafter by the Autoridad del Canal de Panamá (ACP). In 2006 a proposal for a US$5 billion expansion of the canal, due to be completed in 2015, was approved first by President Torrijos and then by public referendum. The ACP claims that the expansion will directly benefit Panama's people, though critics contend that the country will be crippled by debt – the project will be paid for by increased tolls, supplemented by US$2.3 billion in loans – and that only the elite of society will benefit.

GETTING TO AND AROUND THE PANAMA CANAL AND CANAL ZONE

By boat The most interesting way to explore the canal and its surroundings is by boat; though large commercial vessels are charged around US$126,000 to make the transit, you can pay a great deal less. Panama Canal Tours (☎226 8917, ⓦpmatours.net) and Canal & Bay Tours (☎209 2009,

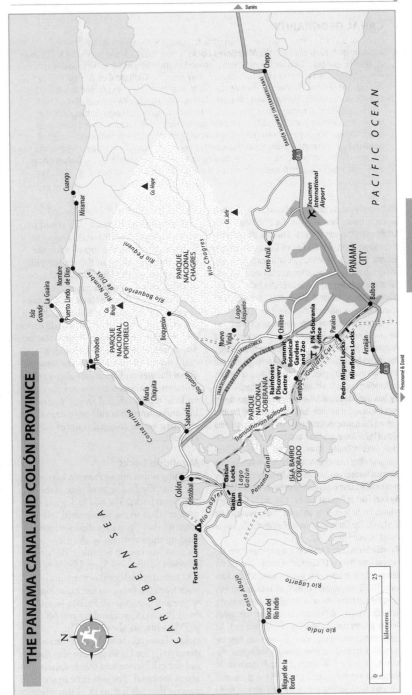

THE PANAMA CANAL AND COLÓN PROVINCE

7

CANAL GEOGRAPHY

From the Bahía de Panamá on the country's Pacific coast, the canal runs at sea level approximately 6km inland to the **Miraflores Locks**, where ships are raised some 16.5m to Lago de Miraflores. About 2km further on, ships are raised another 10m to the canal's maximum elevation of 26.5m above sea level, after which they enter the **Gaillard Cut**. This 14km slice through the shifting shale of the continental divide was the deepest and most difficult section of the canal's construction and was plagued by devastating landslides and loss of life.

The canal channel continues for 38km across the broad expanse of **Lago Gatún**, once the largest artificial lake in the world. Covering 420 square kilometres, it is tranquil and stunningly beautiful; until you see an ocean-going ship appear from behind one of the densely forested headlands, it's difficult to believe that this is part of one of the busiest waterways in the world. At the lake's far end ships are brought back down to sea level in three stages by the **Gatún Locks**, after which they run 3km through a narrow cut into the calm Caribbean waters of Bahía Limón.

7

W canalandbaytours.com), both in Panama City, offer half-day partial transits (generally Thurs–Sat in high season, Fri & Sat the rest of the year) of the canal through Miraflores and Pedro Miguel locks, into the Gaillard Cut, and finishing in Gamboa (US$135). These tours are well worth the outlay, and include excellent bilingual commentary and a full lunch. Full transit, including Lago Gatún and Gatún Locks, is usually offered once a month (US$175–185). A much more affordable option, although unreliable, is to get taken on as a linehandler aboard one of the private yachts that transit the canal. Law requires four linehandlers on each boat. It's a straightforward role, but it carries genuine responsibility. You will not be paid, unless experienced, although food and drink are usually supplied. Your best chance of getting linehandling work is to register with W panlinehandler.com.

By bus Gamboa-bound SACA buses from Panama depart from the far end of the main bus terminal and take the road running 26km along the canal, past the Miraflores and Pedro Miguel locks (20min to either), to the town of Gamboa near Lago Gatún (50min). Buses pass the Parque Nacional Soberanía office (see opposite) and the entrances to Summit Botanical Gardens and Zoo (see opposite). Colón is served by even more frequent buses from Panama City (see p.535).

By taxi Taxis in Panama City can take you to Miraflores, waiting for an hour or so and then taking you back for US$15–20. The Gatún Locks, on the Caribbean side, can be visited via Colón (see p.546).

By train One of Central America's only passenger trains, the Panama Canal Railway (7.15am from Corozal – arrive at the terminal 30min in advance to secure a ticket; 5.15pm from Colón; US$25 one-way; T 317 6070, W panarail.com) runs along the east side of the canal. Though the line is primarily for moving freight, a daily commuter passenger train makes the 1hr journey from Panama City to Colón and back. An observation carriage gives widescreen views and there are open-sided sections between carriages throughout the train. A taxi to the train station at Corozal, 2km north of Albrook bus terminal (see p.535), costs US$4–6, or you could take a bus to the terminal and a shorter taxi ride from there.

WHAT TO SEE AND DO

A day-trip from Panama City could see you scanning the rainforest canopy for harpy eagles from the top of a former radar station, taking in the engineering masterpiece of the **Miraflores Locks**, or visiting an indigenous Emberá community in **Parque Nacional Chagres**. If you're in the mood for hiking, try out the celebrated routes of **Camino de Cruces** and the Pipeline Road in **Parque Nacional Soberanía**. A cool and comfortable early-morning train ride on the **Panama Canal Railway** to Colón (see above) gives wonderful panoramic views of the canal and the rainforest, and from the city it's a hot and bumpy bus ride northeast along the coast to the colonial ruins of **Portobelo**.

Miraflores Locks

Heading north out of Panama City along the canal, the first sight of note is the **Miraflores Locks**. The first lock gates here are the tallest in the whole canal system. Even so, they open in just two minutes, guiding ships through by electric locomotives known as mules. The **visitor complex** (daily 9am–5pm; US$5–8; T 276 8325, W pancanal.com) is a ten-minute walk from the point on the main road where any Gamboa- or Paraíso-bound **bus** from Panama City can drop you off (see p.535) – just ask the driver. The US$5 ticket allows access to the observation decks only; for US$8 you can also check out the exhibitions and watch a short film about the canal. The best time to see ships passing through is 8am to 11am, when they come up from the Pacific side, and after 3pm, when they complete their transit from the Atlantic side. There is an overpriced café here, as well as an expensive restaurant and a souvenir shop.

Summit Botanical Gardens and Zoo

At a fork in the road 9km beyond the Miraflores Locks is the office for Parque Nacional Soberanía (see below). The left fork, heading towards Gamboa, brings you to **Summit Botanical Gardens and Zoo** (daily 9am–3pm; US$5; ☎232 4850). Any Gamboa-bound **bus** from Panama City (see opposite) can drop you off at the entrance.

Established by the US in 1923, the gardens house more than fifteen thousand plant species spread throughout the landscaped grounds, as well as a popular zoo, which more recently has been populated by rescue animals. Star attractions include a tapir and a jaguar, and a harpy eagle was due to arrive at the time of press.

Gamboa

Some 8km north of the botanical gardens lies the curious town of **GAMBOA**, which became the centre for the canal's dredging in the 1930s. With its wooden buildings and derelict baseball diamond, it feels like an abandoned, small American town. The Smithsonian Tropical Research Institute has a small dock, 1km beyond Gamboa's central park, which is the jumping-off point for trips to Isla Barro Colorado (BCI), the principal site for their research (see below). Just before the Smithsonian dock, a road signposted off to the right leads to the entrance to **Pipeline Road** in Parque Nacional Soberanía (see below).

ARRIVAL AND INFORMATION

By bus Buses run from Panama City to Gamboa (8 daily; 45min).
Bank There's an ATM by the entrance to the dredging division, in Gamboa's central park, by the bus stop.
Food There's a small grocery shop (daily 8am–7pm) just off the central park, and informal food stalls to feed the dredging division workers.

Parque Nacional Soberanía

Stretching along the eastern flank of the canal, the 220-square-kilometre **PARQUE NACIONAL SOBERANÍA** (daily 6am–6pm) provides essential protection for the rainforest-covered watershed that is vital for the canal's continued operation. Just thirty minutes from Panama City by road, Soberanía is the most easily accessible national park in Panama and is popular with both locals and visitors. Most spend just a few hours exploring one of the trails, which are mostly well marked and pass over rugged terrain cloaked in pristine rainforest, offering reasonable odds of seeing monkeys and innumerable birds as well as smaller mammals such as sloths and agoutis.

You can collect **trail** information and pay the entrance fee at the **park office** (Mon–Fri 7am–4pm; ☎232 4192; US$5), where the road to Gamboa branches off the main road from Panama City. Indicate to the bus driver that you want to go to the park office. If you ring in advance you may be able to engage the services of a park warden as a guide (around US$40–50/day for two people).

All the trails have something to recommend them, but a few stand out. The 24km **Pipeline Road** (Camino del Oleoducto), accessed from Gamboa, is world famous for its **birding** opportunities; you can also visit the excellent, but costly, nearby Rainforest Discovery Centre (US$20 10am–4pm, US$30 6–10am; ⦿pipelineroad.org), whose highlight is a canopy observation tower. **Plantation Road**, which begins at a right-hand turn-off 1.5km past the Summit Botanical Gardens and Zoo (see above) – tell the bus driver where you want to get off – follows a stream and offers great birdwatching. It runs some 4km to an intersection with the 10km **Camino de las Cruces**, the only trail for which you would need a guide. The Camino is a remnant of the cobbled track that the Spanish colonists used to transport their goods and treasures to Portobelo on the Caribbean coast.

Isla Barro Colorado

As the waters of Lago Gatún began to rise after the damming of the Chagres in 1913, much of the wildlife in the surrounding forest was forced to take

7

refuge on points of high ground, which eventually became islands. One of these, **ISLA BARRO COLORADO** (BCI), administered by the Smithsonian Tropical Research Institute, is among the most intensively studied areas of tropical rainforest in the world. Though the primary aims of the reserve are conservation and research, you can arrange visits through the STRI (one tour daily Tues, Wed & Fri–Sun; US$70, students US$40; ☎212 8951, ⊛stri.org) – contact them well in advance. The tour lasts between four and six hours and most guides speak English (double-check when booking). The cost covers the boat from Gamboa pier, the tour and lunch on the island.

Parque Nacional Chagres

East of the older highway that connects Panama City with Colón – the Transístmica – lies **Parque Nacional Chagres**, 1290 square kilometres of mountainous rainforest comprising four different life zones that are home to more than three hundred bird species and several Emberá communities displaced by the flooding of Lago Bayano, further east. Day-trips to the park (see below) include transport – bus from Panama City – followed by a glorious trip by motorized dugout up the **Río Chagres**, a rainforest walk, a traditional meal, and the opportunity to buy handicrafts directly from producers. Note that sometimes these Emberá villages can be overrun with cruise ship groups (Dec–April); you'll find fewer visitors in the Emberá communities of the **Darién** (see box, p.554).

ARRIVAL AND DEPARTURE

Tours Parque Nacional Chagres is tricky to get to independently but the Emberá–Drúa community is one of several villages that organizes tours (⊛trail2.com/embera; US$70 for a day-trip, or US$120 for an overnight stay, with a minimum of four people; often cheaper with larger groups). Alternatively, go with a Panama City tour operator (see box, p.536).

COLÓN

Officially founded by the Americans in 1852, as the Atlantic terminus of the Panama Railroad, **COLÓN**, at the Atlantic entrance to the Panama Canal, is all rubble and attitude. The city is dangerously poor, with a bad record of violent crime, set in a crumbling colonial shell that begs for a renovation it is unlikely ever to see. Colón's fortunes have fluctuated with those of the railway, and later the canal. Despite its status as Panama's main port, not to mention the financial success of both the canal and the Free Zone (established in 1949), very little of the money generated stays here, and many people who work in these areas live in Panama City. In the face of extreme poverty and unemployment levels, the crime rate – particularly **drug-related crime** – has rocketed.

For many, Colón's edginess will not appeal in the slightest, and a visit will only be a necessary evil in order to visit the nearby **Gatún Locks** or **Fort San Lorenzo** or the **Costa Arriba** (though even then it could be avoided entirely by changing buses at Sabanitas). Many people come solely to shop at the **Colón Free Zone** – a walled enclave where goods from all over the world can be bought at very low prices – and assiduously avoid the rest of the city. However, the combination of a luxurious rail trip from Panama City followed by a taxi tour of this unique and decaying place can be fascinating, giving powerful insights into what the canal and the railroad have meant physically and economically to the country.

WHAT TO SEE AND DO

The best and safest way to explore Colón is by taxi (see box below), taking in the main streets, the historic *New Washington Hotel* (see opposite) and the adjacent dark-stone Episcopalian **Christ Church by the Sea**, the first Protestant church in Central America, built in the mid-1860s for the railroad workers. You get great views of ships waiting to enter the canal from the seafront.

The southeast corner of Colón is occupied by the **Zona Libre**, or Free Zone (⊛colonfreezone.com). Covering more than a square kilometre, this is the second-largest duty-free zone in the world after Hong Kong, with an annual turnover of more than US$10 billion. Colón's residents are not allowed in unless they work here, but you and your wallet are free to enter if you present your passport at the gate, though the place holds minimal interest for the casual shopper.

Near the Free Zone an enclave known as **Colón 2000**, which comprises a handful of souvenir shops and restaurants, has been established in the hopes of luring passengers from the many cruise ships that pass through the canal.

ARRIVAL AND INFORMATION

By boat Yachts transiting the canal dock at the Shelter Bay Marina (w shelterbaymarina.com) in the former Fort Sherman, west of Colón, on the road to Fort San Lorenzo.
By bus The bus terminal is on the corner of Av del Frente & C 13.
Destinations Gatún Locks (every 20min until 5pm; 20min); La Guaira for Isla Grande (6 daily; 2hr–2hr 30min); Miramar (6 daily; 3hr); Nombre de Dios (6 daily; 2hr–2hr 30min); Panama City (daily every 20–30min, 4am–10pm; 1hr 30min–2hr); Portobelo (daily every 30min until 9pm; 1hr 30min).
Tourist information The ATP office on C 1 (Mon–Fri 8.30am–4.30pm; 475 2300) has little useful information.
Taxis Most trips in the city will cost US$1. You can also hire drivers for around US$12/hr, plus a bit more for stopping and starting, to take you around the city.

ACCOMMODATION

If you are going to stay overnight, it's worth splashing out on a more expensive hotel with armed security and a restaurant so you won't have to go out after dark.

> ### SAFETY IN COLÓN
>
> Colón's reputation throughout the rest of the country for **violent crime** is not undeserved, and if you come here you should exercise extreme caution – mugging, even on the main streets in broad daylight, does happen. Don't carry anything that may attract attention or that you can't afford to lose, try to stay in sight of the police on the main streets and take **taxis** rather than walk. Many drivers will give tours of the city (about US$12/hr); consider hiring one if you want to explore. Asking for Pablo (who speaks English and Spanish) at the *Hotel Internacional* (see below) is a good option.

Hotel Internacional Av Bolívar & C 12 447 0111 or 447 0112. A good deal in one of the safest streets in the city, within a stone's throw of the bus station. Rooms are basic but clean and comfortable with a/c, cable TV and wi-fi. There are also a couple of PCs, a sporadically open rooftop bar and a reasonable restaurant (mains US$6–8; closed Sun). Breakfast included. US$39

Hotel Meryland C 7, opposite Parque Sucre 441 7055, w hotelmeryland.com. Little atmosphere, but it's tucked away in a leafy and relatively safe patch of the city and is a cut above all other options. Smartly tiled, spacious and professionally staffed, with en-suite, a/c rooms and large, firm beds. The restaurant serves filling soups and a good selection of mains (from US$8). US$55

EATING AND DRINKING

Though Colón's kitchens are known for their Caribbean influence and heavy reliance on seafood, spices and coconut milk, most authentic places are too riskily situated to visit safely.
Café Maritano's Colón 2000. This place lies in wait for cruise-ship passengers craving a fancy coffee; grab a latte with a slab of cake or pasty for US$3. Daily 7am–7.30pm.
Grand Café Colón 2000 433 2092. Sporting a vaguely Middle Eastern decor, Lebanese menu and hookah pipes, this venue offers a breezy terrace overlooking the cruise-ship terminal and an a/c interior. Buzzy and professional but pricey; the menu includes falafel (US$8), curried vegetables plus meat and fish dishes (from US$9). Daily 7.30am–11pm.
New Washington Hotel At the northernmost end of Av del Frente 441 7133. Built in 1913, this old hotel is doing its best to live in the past, and has clung onto its chandeliers and marble stairs. The rooms are overpriced (from US$60) but you could always come for a drink on the seafront veranda and watch the ships in the bay.
Nuevo Dos Mares C 5, between Av Central & Arosemena 445 4558. Specializing in Caribbean cuisine, with a wide range of tasty fish and seafood dishes (from US$8), served with coconut rice, fried *yuca* or *patacones*. Make sure you take a taxi there and organize a pick-up time. Mon–Sat noon–7.30pm.

DIRECTORY

Banks Banco Nacional, Av Bolívar near C 10. The safest ATM is inside the 24hr Super 99 in Colón Zone 2000.
Car rental Hiring a car for the day is a good idea if you want to visit the locks and San Lorenzo. You'll find Budget, Avis and Hertz in Colón Zone 2000.
Hospital Hospital Manuel Amador Guerrero (441 5060), between C 10 & 11 at Paseo Gorgas, by Colón 2000.
Pharmacy In the Super 99 supermarkets, on Av Bolívar or in Colón 2000.

7

AROUND COLÓN

If you don't fancy a taxi tour of Colón, get straight onto a bus to the mighty **Gatún Locks** or splash out on a taxi to the beautiful and atmospheric **Fort San Lorenzo**.

Gatún Locks

From Colón, a road runs 10km southwest to the **Gatún Locks** (daily 8am–3.45pm; US$5), where ships transit between Lago Gatún and Bahía Limón. The nearly 2km-long locks, which raise and lower ships the 26.5m between the lake and sea level in three stages, are among the canal's most monumental engineering features. The **observation platform** at the visitors' centre is so close to the canal that you could speak quite easily to anyone on the deck of the ships – your best chance of having a chat is between 8am and 11am, and after 3pm. The locks can also be visited as part of a tour (see p.542).

ARRIVAL AND INFORMATION

By bus Buses bound for the Costa Abajo from the Colón terminal will drop you just before the traffic lights at the swing bridge across the canal, by a road branching off to the left.

By taxi A taxi from Colón costs about US$5 each way, plus more for wait time.

Tourist information The visitors' centre, which also has an ATM and gift shop, is a 1km walk down the side road from the point at which the bus stops.

Fort San Lorenzo

With a spectacular setting on a promontory above the Caribbean and overlooking the mouth of the Río Chagres, **Fort San Lorenzo** (8.30am–4.30pm; US$5) is the most impressive Spanish fortification still standing in Panama. Until the construction of the railway, the Chagres was the main cargo route across the

> If you plan to visit Portobelo or points further east, be aware that there are **no ATMs** beyond Colón and nearby Sabanitas, where there's an ATM in the supermarket – make sure to take money out before making your way along the coast.

isthmus to Panama City, and thus of enormous strategic importance to Spain. The first fortifications to protect the entrance to the river were built here in 1595, but the fort was taken by Francis Drake in 1596 and, though heavily reinforced, fell again to Henry Morgan's pirates in December 1670. Morgan then proceeded up the Chagres and across the isthmus to ransack Panama City. The fortifications that remain today were built in the mid-eighteenth century. The site as a whole is imposing, with a moat surrounding stout stone walls and great cannons looking out from the embrasures, all of it kept in isolation by the dense rainforest all around.

ARRIVAL AND INFORMATION

By car or taxi The fort can only be reached by car or taxi. With wait time it is a US$35–40 return trip from Colón, 1hr each way, passing through rainforest and the former US training base of Fort Sherman, which until 1999 was home to the 17,000-acre US Army Jungle Warfare Training Center and is now the location of the Shelter Bay Marina (ⓦshelterbaymarina.com). You might also consider renting a car for the day from Colón. Note that if a vessel is passing through Gatún Locks, you may be stuck on either side for around 45min.

Food The Shelter Bay Marina is a good place to stop off for a bite to eat.

PORTOBELO

The **Costa Arriba**, stretching northeast of Colón, features lovely beaches, excellent diving and snorkelling, and the historic towns of Nombre de Dios and **PORTOBELO** ("beautiful harbour"). Though Portobelo today has a somewhat stagnant atmosphere, the remnants and ruins of its former glories retain an evocative power. More powerful still – at least to the thousands of pilgrims who come to gaze on it – is the agonized face of the small **Black Christ** statue in the Iglesia de San Felipe (see box opposite).

Every two years in early March, Portobelo hosts the hugely enjoyable Afro-colonial **Festival de Congos y Diablos** (ⓦdiablosycongos.org), with smaller celebrations over the weekends leading up to it. Originating from *cimarrones*

PORTOBELO HISTORY

After the town of Nombre de Dios was destroyed by Francis Drake in 1597, Portobelo was founded to replace it as the Atlantic terminus of the **Camino Real** – the route across the isthmus along which the Spanish hauled their plundered treasures. Portobelo's setting on a deep-water bay was supposed to make it easier to defend from the ravages of pirates, and for 150 years it played host to the famous **ferias**, grand trading events held when the Spanish treasure fleet came to collect the riches that arrived on mule trains from Panama City. Unsurprisingly, the pirates who scoured the Spanish Main – most famously Henry Morgan – could not resist the wealth concentrated in the royal warehouses here. Eventually the Spanish decided enough was enough: the treasure fleet was rerouted around Cape Horn and Portobelo's star began to fade.

– outlawed bands of escaped slaves (see box, p.554) – in the sixteenth century, these colourful explosions of drumming, dancing, devil costumes and satirical play-acting were originally aimed at mocking their former colonial rulers.

WHAT TO SEE AND DO

Most of Portobelo is pretty down-at-heel. Other than the highly revered **Cristo Negro**, which fills the town every October (see box below), the **ruins** are the main attraction. Walking into Portobelo along the road from Colón brings you to the well-preserved **Santiago Battery**, which still features fourteen rusting but menacing cannons. The road then leads to the main tree-shaded **plaza**.

Casa Real de la Aduana

Just off the main plaza stands the impressive **Casa Real de la Aduana** (daily 8am–4pm; US$5), the royal customs house, which has been restored with Spanish help and now houses a small, rather overpriced museum outlining the history of the town. It was the largest civil building in colonial Panama and stored the Camino Real treasure awaiting transport to Spain.

Iglesia de San Felipe

On the square, 100m along the main road, beyond the Casa Real de la Aduana, the large, white **Iglesia de San Felipe** (daily 8am–4pm) houses Panama's most revered religious icon, the *Cristo Negro*, or Black Christ (see box below). Tucked away behind the church, a small museum (under restoration at the time of writing) exhibits an intriguing display of some of the opulent claret and purple robes donated each year to the Black Christ. Outside the church is the tiny **Mercado San Felipe**, a small cluster of stalls selling religious (often quite kitsch) paraphernalia, most of which depicts the image of *El Cristo*, and a variety of Panamanian *artesanía*.

San Geronimo Battery

Looking out onto the bay behind the Church of San Felipe are the town's most impressive ruins, those of the **San Geronimo Battery** – creep to its outermost edge and peep out through the arrow slats.

THE BLACK CHRIST OF PORTOBELO

Without question the most revered religious figure in Panama is the **Black Christ** or *Cristo Negro* in Portobelo, which draws tens of thousands of pilgrims to the town every October. A small effigy carved from black cocobolo wood with an anguished face and eyes raised to heaven, the Black Christ is reputed to possess miraculous powers. The origins of the icon still remain something of a mystery. Some say that it was found floating in the sea during a cholera epidemic, which ended after the Christ was brought into the town; others maintain it was on a ship bound for Colombia that stopped at Portobelo for supplies and was repeatedly prevented from leaving the bay by bad weather, sailing successfully only when the statue was left ashore. Every year on October 21 up to fifty thousand devotees, known as Nazareños and dressed in purple robes, come to Portobelo – a number walking or crawling the last few kilometres – for a huge procession that is followed by festivities throughout the night.

ARRIVAL AND INFORMATION

By bus Buses for Portobelo leave from Colón; if you're coming from Panama City and want to avoid Colón, change at the El Rey supermarket in Sabanitas, 14km before Colón. Buses from Colón arrive near the Church of San Felipe in the centre of town, within a few minutes' walk of the main sights and accommodation. Through buses pick up and drop off on the main road opposite the park.

Destinations Colón (every 30min until 6pm; 1hr 30min); La Guaira (6 daily; 30min–1hr); Nombre de Dios (6 daily; 30min–1hr).

Internet On the square near the church (Mon–Fri 9am–5pm; US$1.25/hr).

Tour operators The hotel *Coco Plum* (see below) can organize diving. Otherwise, Scuba Panama, in Panama City (☎ 261 3841, ⊕ scubapanama.com), has its dive centre on the road into Portobelo from Colón, which also has reasonable accommodation open to non-divers. *Captain Jack's* (see below) can arrange passage by yacht to Colombia.

Tourist information There's a large ATP office (Mon–Fri 9.30am–5.30pm; ☎ 448 2200) on the main street, opposite the Mayor's office.

ACCOMMODATION AND EATING

Las Anclas *Coco Plum*, on the road into Portobelo ☎ 448 2102. The most charming restaurant in the area specializes in fish (US$9–13) – try the mxed seafood in coconut milk (US$11) with alternatives including burgers. Also offers breakfast (from US$4). Daily 8am–8pm, until 9pm at weekends.

Captain Jack's 200m up the hill from the main road in the town centre ☎ 448 2009, ⊕ hostelportobelo.com. Rather cramped place with four dank fan-ventilated dorms with good mattresses, usually packed with travellers arriving from, or waiting for, a boat to Colombia. It also hosts a surprisingly pricey, though good, restaurant. Tuck into Thai chicken curry, pasta or seafood mains (from US$12) on the breezy veranda, which offers nice views of the church and bay. Breakfasts (from US$4.50) are more affordable. Restaurant Wed–Mon 11am–11pm. Dorm **US$13**

Ofiuras Hostal On the road into Portobelo ☎ 448 2400. A small family-run business set on the water's edge, with a handful of clean, simple rooms with fans and cable TV (US$10 extra for a/c); the friendly owners also run local boat tours. **US$30**

★ **Panadería Nazareño** On the main street. This bargain bakery is open all day and sells juices for a dollar, tasty sandwiches from US$3 and a delicious variety of fresh bread. Closed Mon.

Restaurante Ida On the square near the church. Offers meat stews and fried fish dishes (from US$4), and can rustle up a veggie-friendly plate of rice, beans and plantain for just over US$3. Daily 7am–7pm.

AROUND PORTOBELO

Isla Grande is a well-established getaway for Panamanians and tourists alike, while a more adventurous trip may explore the little-visited, windswept **beaches** further east.

Parque Nacional Portobelo

The **PARQUE NACIONAL PORTOBELO** encompasses the town and surrounding coast, although the area receives little protection or responsible management and you don't need permission from

---

INTO COLOMBIA BY BOAT

One of the most popular and adventurous ways to get to and from **Colombia** is by private yacht or catamaran, either to Cartagena, from Portobelo or Puerto Lindo, or to Sapzurro, just over the Colombian border from Puerto Obaldía (see box, p.562). Prices range from US$450–600 (generally including all meals and water), with boats varying in comfort, size and number of passengers. Taking the Cartagena route, the boat spends three days in the Guna Yala archipelago, before taking on the rougher open water to Cartagena. The newer Sapzurro route is usually cheaper, avoids the rougher open seas and spends more of the journey island-hopping in Guna Yala. Note that there are fewer departures between December and February/March as the seas are particularly rough and dangerous and some captains avoid sailing during this period. **Hostels** in Panama City (see p.536) usually have up-to-date information on boat departures. You are strongly advised to get a sense of a captain's reputation before signing on – there are nightmare tales of drunken captains, vastly overcrowded boats, poor seamanship and, worst of all, drug-running. Hostels should be able to advise you, but view their advice critically – they often get commission on sailings – and make sure you, also consult other travellers who have made the journey. There is also now an occasional **express boat** service from Carti in Guna Yala to Puerto Obaldía or Capurganá (see box, p.562).

ANAM to enter. It does have good **beaches** and some of the best diving and snorkelling on the Caribbean coast, including coral reefs, shipwrecks and, somewhere in front of Isla de Drake, the as-yet-undiscovered grave of Francis Drake, buried at sea in a lead coffin after he died of dysentery in 1596. Most of this area can only be reached by sea; you can either hire a boatman in Portobelo, Isla Grande, or **Puerto Lindo**, a fishing village 14km northeast of Portobelo (also the best option for accommodation), or join an excursion; PADI-certified dive trips take place within the park (see opposite).

ACCOMMODATION AND EATING

There are a couple of decent budget lodgings in the fishing hamlet of Puerto Lindo, 14km northeast of Portobelo; you can get there on the La Guaira-bound bus from Colón (6 daily) via Portobelo, so it's within striking distance of both.

Casa X Water's edge by the yacht club, Puerto Lindo. A handful of plastic tables by the bay, where you can enjoy fresh, inexpensive seafood dishes with salad, *patacones* or rice (US$8), and wash them down with a glass of wine. Daily noon–8pm.

Hostel Puerto Lindo Centre of Puerto Lindo ✉ hostelpuertolindo@gmail.com. Locally owned, simple, friendly hostel offering dorm beds and private rooms (a couple with a/c), all with shared cold-water bathrooms. Use of kitchen and a small garden with a hammock area, plus kayaks for rental. Dorm US$7, double US$16

Hostel Wunderbar At the western entrance to Puerto Lindo ☎ 448 2426 or ☎ 6626 8455, ✉ hostelwunderbar .com. A range of dorm beds and doubles (some with a/c) in a large, Guna-style house and a less appealing modern concrete building. There's a kitchen, and a basic grocery, restaurant and bar nearby. The pool table and traditional *cayucos* (dugout canoes) for rent are nice touches, but the ongoing construction work does detract from the ambience somewhat. Hammock US$9, dorm US$11, double US$45

Isla Grande

Some 12km northeast along the coast from Portobelo, a side road branches off left and runs a few kilometres to the tiny village of **La Guaira**. Here *lanchas* provide transport to **ISLA GRANDE**, a short 300m hop from the mainland. A hugely popular weekend resort for residents of Colón and Panama City, topped by a rickety 200-year-old **lighthouse**, the island has become rather spoilt by unchecked development and the gradually receding beach, but it's a pleasant enough day-trip if you're killing time in Portobelo or Puerto Lindo waiting for a boat to Colombia.

Isla Grande fills up at weekends, and peaks during national holidays; during the week it is so quiet you can struggle to find a place open to serve you food. The only real sand **beach**, known as "La Punta", is around the island to the southwest, and you'll need to pay US$3 to use most of it (entry gives you access to *Hotel Isla Grande*'s showers and lounge chairs). Around to the east by *Sister Moon* you'll find a reef break that's good for **surfing**. There's also some **snorkelling** round the northern part of the island by the *Bananas Village Resort*.

ARRIVAL AND DEPARTURE

By bus and boat *Lanchas* (US$2.50) shuttle over to Isla Grande from La Guaira, which is served by infrequent and unreliable buses from Colón, via Portobelo (6 daily; from Portobelo, last returning around 1pm).

EATING

Restaurante Teleton On the main stretch of Isla Grande's seafront. This restaurant offers one of the island's more reasonably priced dining experiences: seafood mains with *patacones* cost around US$8.

Darién

The sparsely populated 17,000 square kilometres that make up **Darién** are one of the last great, untamed **wildernesses** in America. The beginning of an immense forest that continues almost unbroken across the border into the Chocó region of Colombia and down the Pacific coast to Ecuador, this was the first region on the American mainland to be settled by the Spanish. Although they extracted great wealth from **gold mines** deep in the forest at Cana, they were never able to establish effective control over the region, hampered by the almost impassable terrain, the fierce resistance put up by its inhabitants and European pirates and bands of *cimarrones* (see box, p.554).

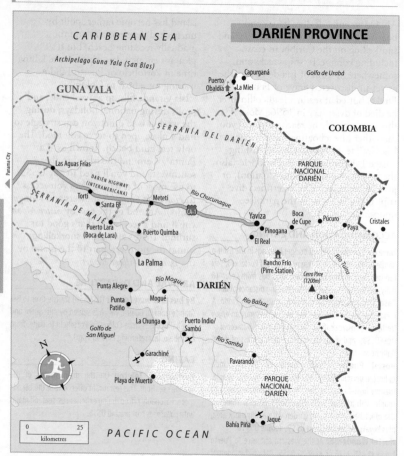

DARIÉN PROVINCE

CARIBBEAN SEA

Archipelago Guna Yala (San Blas)

GUNA YALA

Golfo de Urabá

Capurganá
Puerto
Obaldía
La Miel

SERRANÍA DEL DARIÉN

COLOMBIA

PARQUE
NACIONAL
DARIÉN

Panama City

Las Aguas Frías

DARIÉN HIGHWAY
(INTERAMERICANA)

SERRANÍA DE MAJÉ

Torti
Santa Fe

Metetí

Río Chucunaque

CA-1

Puerto Lara
(Boca de Lara)

Puerto Quimba

Yaviza

Boca
de Cupe   Púcuro

Cristales

Pinogana
El Real

Paya

La Palma

Río Mogué

DARIÉN

Rancho Frío
(Pirre Station)

Cerro Pirre
(1200m)

Río Tuira

Punta Alegre

Mogué

Río Balsas

Cana

Punta
Patiño

La Chunga

Puerto Indio/
Sambú

Golfo de
San Miguel

Río Sambú

N

Garachiné

Pavarandó

PARQUE
NACIONAL
DARIÉN

Playa de Muerto

0   25
kilometres

PACIFIC OCEAN

Bahía Piña   Jaqué

The **Interamericana** is the only road that takes the plunge and enters the region, but it goes no further than the small town of **Yaviza**, 276km east of Panama City. Along the border with Colombia, the **Parque Nacional Darién**, the largest and most important protected area in Panama, safeguards vast swathes of forest that support one of the most pristine and biologically diverse ecosystems in the world, as well as a large indigenous population.

Until quite recently, the combination of drug trafficking and the decades-long Colombian **civil war** spilling over into Panama has made the border area utterly treacherous. The Marxist guerrillas of the Colombian Revolutionary Armed Forces (FARC) have long maintained bases close to the border in Darién, but right-wing paramilitary groups backed by powerful landowners and drug traffickers have taken to pursuing them, terrorizing isolated Panamanian communities they accuse of harbouring the guerrillas. Given the **security concerns** affecting the border area, including parts of the national park and the Comarca Emberá–Cemaco, a visit to southwestern Darién is the safest way to experience the ecology and culture of the region independently. The two most **popular routes** into the area are via Yaviza and **El Real** to the ranger station at Rancho Frío (also called Pirre Station), or to the twin Emberá/Afro-Darienite settlement of **Puerto Indio/Sambú** up the

Río Sambú, usually accessed via La Palma. Once in Darién, you can ask for news of recent incidents or developments.

ARRIVAL AND DEPARTURE

TOURS

Most people who travel to Darién go with a tour. A couple of operators in Panama City (see box, p.536) run affordable trips and can help arrange travel in the region.

INDEPENDENT TRAVEL

Travelling independently is feasible, though at the time of writing the government was increasing travel restrictions. Going it alone does require some knowledge of Spanish and a certain leap of faith – you can't plan every last detail before you leave – but the very fact that it is not a simple undertaking is what makes it so special. More of your money will go to the host indigenous populations if you travel independently and organize your stay and excursions with villages once there.

Darién National Park office Before making the journey to Darién it's a good idea to check the current safety situation at the park office in Yaviza (Mon–Fri 8am–4pm; ☎ 299 4495). ANAM also has a park office in El Real (same hours; no phone).

Red tape At the time of writing, the government had introduced new restrictions on travel for foreigners in Darién. In theory you need to get permission from SENAFRONT (Freephone within Panama ☎ 800 2762, ✆ senafront.com) – the frontier police – in Panama City a couple of weeks in advance. This long and tedious process involves detailing exactly when, where and why you want to visit (and even then you may get nowhere). Alternatively, you can try your luck and hop on the bus; if you get past the security checkpoints as far as Yaviza or La Palma you're likely to find a more sympathetic reception at the national park office, for example. However, you may equally be stopped and sent back to Panama City. To increase your chance of getting through the checkpoints, make sure you have a precise itinerary (whatever the reality) to give to the police.

By plane Air Panama (☎ 316 9000, ✆ airpanama.com) offers flights to Darién, to Bahía Piña and Jaqué in the far south of the region as well as to Sambú and Garachiné, both of which lie near the Gulf of San Miguel and are good starting points for boat-based exploration of the more accessible – and safer – parts of Darién.

By bus Buses run from Panama City to Metetí and Yaviza (see p.554).

GETTING AROUND

By boat Once you've arrived in Darién, boats are the best, and sometimes the only, way to get around. Locals use *piraguas* – motorized dugout canoes – as well as slightly more modern *lanchas*. Fuel prices have risen steadily over the last few years, so in order to keep costs down you will need to be prepared to hang around, sometimes for a couple of days, to take one of the scheduled departures that is already heading in the direction you want to go (trading, fishing or community boats) – you are effectively hitching a ride, rather than chartering a boat and crew. A ride from La Palma to Sambú could be as little as US$20/person if you travel this way, compared to upwards of US$150/boat if you have to hire someone's services. Before hopping aboard a boat, especially when chartering a vessel for an excursion, check its seaworthiness, including the engine size and the availability of life-jackets, as the Gulf of San Miguel can be rough.

THE DARIÉN HIGHWAY

East of Panama City the **DARIÉN HIGHWAY** (the Interamericana) is now paved all the way to Yaviza, though lack of maintenance and heavy rainfall at certain times of year mean that you're

---

KITTING YOURSELF OUT IN DARIÉN

Whether you visit Darién with a tour operator or on your own, you should pack wisely.

Clothing You will need trousers and long-sleeved shirts, partly to keep the huge variety of insect life at bay, but also because it can get quite cool during the night. Do not take or wear anything that resembles army fatigues or has a camouflage pattern.

Equipment You'll be able to pick up basic provisions (including bottled water), but it is advisable to pack a small supply of food even so, plus a ration of bottled water, and water-purifying tablets. If you're sleeping on a floor in a village you will need something to sleep on, in or under, and a mosquito net. Bring a cover for your pack for boat travel and damp conditions. Binoculars will greatly enhance your chance of appreciating the area's abundant birdlife.

Medication You should start taking anti-malaria medication well before you arrive. Note that chloroquine is not sufficient in Darién – check the exact requirements with your doctor before your trip. Also ensure you have insect repellent and anti-histamine cream, to sooth your bites.

Money There are only two banks in the region, both with ATMs: at Metetí and La Palma. It's a good idea to bring a large stash of US$1 bills.

7

THE PEOPLE OF DARIÉN

Darién's **population** is made up of three main groups: black, indigenous and colonist.

Other than a few Guna communities, the **indigenous** population of Darién is composed of two closely related but distinct peoples, the **Wounaan** and the more numerous **Emberá**, both semi-nomadic South American rainforest societies. Recognizable by the black geometric designs with which they traditionally decorate their bodies, the Emberá-Wounaan, as they are collectively known, have been migrating across the border from Colombia for the past two centuries. Only since the 1960s have they begun to settle in permanent villages and establish official recognition of their territorial rights in the form of a *comarca*, divided into two districts: the **Comarca Emberá Cemaco**, in the north, and the **Comarca Emberá Sambú**, in the southwest.

The **black people** of Darién, descended from *cimarrones* and released slaves, are known as **Darienitas** or **libres** (the free) and are culturally distinct from the Afro-Antillano populations of Colón and Panama City (see box, p.533).

The **colonists** (*colonos*), meanwhile, are the most recent arrivals, poor mestizo peasants forced to look for new land to cultivate after having degraded their own lands in the central Panamanian provinces of the Azuero Peninsula through overgrazing cattle. Many colonists still wear their distinctive straw sombreros as a badge of identity and maintain the folk traditions of the regions they abandoned. The construction and subsequent improvement of the Darién Highway has facilitated the colonists' access to new land, which has inevitably brought them into conflict with the indigenous populations, as some make illegal encroachments into indigenous territory.

---

bound to experience some bumpy patches along the way. Just before the large reservoir that is Laguna Bayano, the highway passes through the quiet village of El Llano, where a side road leads up towards **Guna Yala** (see p.558). From the lake the highway rolls on for 196km through a desolate, deforested landscape, passing Emberá-Wounaan hamlets, with their characteristic open-walled houses raised on stilts, and half-hearted roadside settlements. The highway ends on the banks of the Río Chucunaque at **Yaviza**, the start of the Darién Gap, though most buses only go as far as **Metetí** (see below).

Metetí and Puerto Quimba

Some 50km before the highway ends in jungle it passes through **METETÍ**, a small roadside settlement that leads on to Yaviza or southwest to the jumping-off point for most Darién exploration, at **PUERTO QUIMBA**.

ARRIVAL AND INFORMATION

By bus For most buses, including those from Panama City (every 40min 4am–4.40pm; 4–6hr), Metetí's miniature Terminal de Transporte de Darién (1.5km down the road to Puerto Quimba) is the end of the road. The *chiva* (daily 6am–4.30pm, every 40min; 30min) that shuttles back and forth between Metetí and Puerto Quimba also leaves from this terminal. Minibuses also run regularly to and from Yaviza until around 5pm (1hr).

By water-taxi Water-taxis (daily 7.30am–5pm; 30min; US$4) to La Palma depart from Puerto Quimba's dock area – a dirt road with space for vehicles to park, a pier, a police hut (where you may have to present your passport) and a tiny bar.

Banks Metetí is one of the last stops for cash before entering the jungle, with a branch of the Banco Nacional and a 24hr ATM on the Interamericana 2km before the junction.

ACCOMMODATION AND EATING

If you miss your onward connection you can stay at one of the basic hotels in Metetí – note that, like the rest of the town, they suffer from frequent water outages. The best restaurant, serving cheap *comida típica*, is at the bus station (daily 7am–4pm). Ventas Metetí is a well-stocked supermarket at the junction.

Hospedaje 2 Hermanos Morenos Puerto Quimba road, near the bus terminal ☎ 299 6512. A handful of basic cement rooms with fan. **US$10**

Hotel Felicidad On the Interamericana, 1km before the Puerto Quimba junction ☎ 299 6544. Despite its inconvenient location, this hotel, with clean en-suite rooms with a/c, gets top billing and has an on-site restaurant. **US$27**

Yaviza

Edgy, run-down **YAVIZA** marks the end of the Interamericana and the beginning of the Darién Gap. If the police on the highway allow you to visit, then the town can be used as a gateway into the **Parque Nacional Darién** (see opposite). It is advisable to check in with the police in Yaviza before moving on.

ARRIVAL AND INFORMATION

By bus Buses run from Panama City to Yaviza (6 daily until 11.30am; 5–7hr). If you miss the last bus to Yaviza, catch a Metetí bus (see opposite) and change there.

Getting to Parque Nacional Darién To get to the park from Yaviza, head down to the riverbank in the morning, when there are likely to be lots of motorized dugout canoes (*piraguas*) trading goods. Provided transport is headed downriver, you can usually get an inexpensive ride to El Real (around US$8/person; US$80–140 to charter a boat), a settlement some 15km down the Río Chucunaque (then a couple of kilometres up the Río Tuira), the most convenient access point to the park.

Darién National Park office C 5 (Mon–Fri 8am–4pm; ☏ 299 4495). Check here for the current safety situation in the region, and to arrange transport into the park.

ACCOMMODATION

Hotel Yadarien On the main cement path into town ☏ 299 4334. If you have to stay the night, this basic place, with twenty en-suite rooms with a/c and beds in varying states of repair, is your best bet. U̲S̲$̲2̲5̲

PARQUE NACIONAL DARIÉN

Covering almost 5800 square kilometres of pristine rainforest along the border with Colombia, **PARQUE NACIONAL DARIÉN** is possibly the most biologically diverse region on earth – more than five hundred bird species have been reported here. Inhabited by scattered indigenous communities, the park contains the largest expanse of forest in Central America that has not been affected by logging and provides a home for countless rare and endangered species, including jaguars, harpy eagles and several types of macaw. Parts of the park are safe to visit, but the **security** situation can change rapidly so phone ahead to the park office in Yaviza (see above) to confirm safe entry points into the park.

ARRIVAL AND INFORMATION

Permission To enter the park you are supposed to seek permission from SENAFRONT in Panama City (see p.553) as well as from the Darién National Park office in Yaviza (see above; US$5). Note that most of the rangers speak only Spanish.

Transport Ask at the park office about transport into the park – the most popular destination is the ranger station at Rancho Frío, accessed via the ANAM office in El Real (transport will cost US$30 from El Real).

Guides You can arrange guides – essential, given the extreme wilderness and lack of infrastructure of the area – at the park office (around US$20/day). Ensure you have the necessary supplies (see box, p.553), which are best acquired in Yaviza, including food for the guide.

LA PALMA

LA PALMA's spectacular setting, overlooking the broad mouth of the Río Tuira, surrounded by densely forested mountains and with ruined colonial forts for neighbours, makes it a worthy capital of Darién Province, however small. Brightly painted houses are cake-layered down a steep slope to the waterfront and the town's only **street**, a narrow strip of concrete. The rubbish that clings to the pilings by the water's edge makes the place less scenic than it might be, and there's not a whole lot to do other than soak in the views before moving on.

INTO COLOMBIA: THE DARIÉN GAP

The **Darién Gap** is a band of dense and entirely untamed rainforest, 100km or so in length, that keeps the northern strand of the Interamericana (Panamerican Highway) from joining up with the southern strand. Crossing the Gap was, for many years, one of the most celebrated adventures in Latin America. However, for some years its undertaking has been **banned** by the Panamanian authorities while travellers who have ignored this ruling have disappeared or been killed attempting the trip. It's also worth remembering that there is a **war** raging across the border in Colombia.

Currently the Panamanian authorities do not allow civilians to travel east of Boca de Cupé. The two ways to travel to Colombia are via Guna Yala (see box, p.562) and along the Caribbean coast (see box, p.550), or along the Pacific coast, by catching a ride in one of the commercial boats that leaves Panama City or La Palma for Jaqué, and then from there to Colombia. This latter route is not recommended as boats are very infrequent, and will be extremely basic, may lack sufficient life-jackets, or may not be robust enough for the sea when rough.

7

Although you can easily work out how much transport to La Palma will cost, it's far less easy to estimate what any onward travel is likely to set you back – it will be by boat, and the price of fuel is steadily rising and even scheduled departures are erratic. The opportunities to come into contact with **indigenous communities** are greater in the Sambú area, but getting there from here can be expensive if there's no scheduled transport or you can't find enough travel companions to keep the cost down. While you're here, check in with the **police** who can update you on any developments or incidents in the region.

ARRIVAL AND INFORMATION

By boat Boats and water-taxis from Puerto Quimba (6am–4.30pm; 30min; US$4) arrive at the passenger dock below the main street, opposite mini-mercado La Virgen del Carmen. Return boats to Puerto Quimba are met by the *chiva* back up to Metetí (see p.554). Get to the dock at least 30min before the first or last boat leaves. Boats to Sambú/Puerto Indio (US$20) usually travel Mon, Wed & Fri. You will also need to arrange boat travel to visit the sights around La Palma (see below).

Bank Banco Nacional (Mon–Fri 8am–3pm), at the far end of town (take a right from the water-taxi dock), has a 24hr ATM.

Hospital There is a small hospital (☎ 299 6219) behind the main street, to the left of the passenger dock.

Internet There are a couple of internet cafés (US$2/hr) on the main street.

Tourist information The helpful ATP office is in the MICI office (Ministerio de Comercio e Industrias; Mon–Fri 8.30am–4.30pm; ☎ 292 5337) opposite the bank.

ACCOMMODATION AND EATING

Accommodation is extremely basic in La Palma, and there is little culinary joy to be had. Most places keep irregular hours and often close very early.

Hospedaje Tuira 100m to the right from the passenger dock ☎ 299 6490. This waterfront building has very basic rooms, with a fan and worn mattresses. A/c costs US$10 more. US$10

★ **Hotel Biaquiru Bagara** 100m on the left from the dock ☎ 299 6224. This family-run place above a general store is simple but handsome. En-suite rooms with a/c are wood-panelled with bamboo ceilings, and the huge upstairs terrace offers hammocks and breezy sea views. US$25

Restaurante Nayelis On the main drag, 100m to the right of the dock. Probably the best eating option in town, with cheery plastic tablecloths and table decorations, serving inexpensive Panamanian and Dominican dishes.

AROUND LA PALMA

Exploring La Palma's **surroundings** in the **Golfo de San Miguel** and beyond requires a bit of preparation and can be accomplished in several ways.

ARRIVAL AND GETTING AROUND

Information Ask at the MICI office in La Palma (see above) for boat travel information.

By cargo boat Sometimes a cargo boat delivering and collecting goods in Darién's villages will be heading in a convenient direction, in which case you may be able to jump aboard for a fee of US$10–20.

By private boat You might also pay someone to take you to your destination directly, though this would probably mean adding a zero to the price above. If you're travelling solo, chartering a private boat from La Palma to Sambú would be costlier than flying from Panama City.

By fishing boat Hitching rides with fishermen is the cheapest way to visit nearby communities, beaches and islands – just be sure to check out the condition of the boat beforehand and arrange your pick-up before disembarking.

ARTESANÍA AND SEAFOOD: RICHES OF DARIÉN

Darién's **Golfo de San Miguel**, where the flow of jungle rivers meets the abundant Pacific Ocean, is a nutrient-rich, predator-safe environment in which **seafood** flourishes. Calamari, giant shrimp, sea bass, snapper, black conch, oysters and lobsters are only a few of the marine treats you'll find in many a fisherman's catch – though sadly they don't often make it into the region's restaurants.

The other speciality of the region is the *artesanía* made by the Wounaan and Emberá communities: weavings of delicately intricate baskets, plates and masks are made with dyed and natural grasses to create stunning works of art; incredibly intricate carvings are also fashioned out of tagua (vegetable ivory) or cocobolo wood. You can visit indigenous communities, meet the artists and directly support the communities by buying local pieces. Many of the finer items, often sold to exclusive shops in Panama City, where the prices are hiked, take several months to create.

THE SETTLING OF NEW EDINBURGH

In the late 1600s, the Scots gambled half the country's wealth on a colony in Darién in the hopes of transforming **Scotland** into a trading power to rival England. A fleet of five ships and 1200 men set sail in July 1698 and, arriving in the Caribbean, attempted to trade goods and restock the ships, though their wigs, shoes, stockings, thick cloth and Bibles found few takers in the tropics. The fleet finally anchored in Caledonia Bay, and for five months the Scots worked hard to build **New Edinburgh**, hindered by low rations and disease. The only help they received came from the local Guna. When, after ten months, the promised supply ships failed to materialize, the Scots set sail for home. Only one ship, the *Caledonia*, made it back to Scotland. Refusing to believe the rumours that the colony had been abandoned, the company directors had already sent a second fleet of four ships, as poorly equipped as the first, but shortly after their arrival in Panama in 1700, they drew the attention of the Spanish based in Portobelo. Small **battles** soon broke out – with the Guna lending their military muscle to the Scots – but within six months the Scots finally surrendered to the Spanish. They were allowed to evacuate with full military honours, but none of the ships made it back home. The venture crippled Scotland financially, leaving the kingdom at the mercy of rival England. Several years later, in 1707, England agreed to compensate all those who had subscribed to the venture in return for the creation of a joint kingdom of England and Scotland.

Punta Alegre

You may be able to find a boat from La Palma headed towards the Afro-Darienite fishing village of **PUNTA ALEGRE**, otherwise you'll need to charter a private boat. The trip takes you 17km southeast of La Palma, a fantastic hour or two across the Gulf of San Miguel, passing forested islands and a wild coastline fringed with mangroves and deserted beaches. Once in the village, there's not much to do other than visiting the shell-strewn, jungle-fringed beaches.

SAMBÚ

The small riverine town of **SAMBÚ**, the most developed settlement for many kilometres around in this part of the jungle, is the best place to base yourself for affordable exploration in Darién. Although there's little to do in the town itself, a day spent among the locals lends valuable insight into the simple and tough livelihoods of those inhabiting this culturally diverse and isolated community. Moreover, the boat trip up the sinuous Río Sambú is a thrill in itself.

WHAT TO SEE AND DO

Exploring the area around Sambú is most rewarding if you are flexible about where you want to go. Activities range from day-trips **hiking** in the surrounding rainforest, or **fishing** and **birdwatching** on the river, to overnight stays in Emberá communities such as **Villa Queresia** – or, when water levels are high enough, remote **Pavarandó**, a village marking the last navigable point of the Río Sambú. Your accommodation may be able to fix you up with a guide, and you can organize a guide via the tourism committee in Puerto Indio (see below) if you want to explore the *comarca* itself.

Puerto Indio

A rickety suspension bridge on the edge of the town leads to **PUERTO INDIO**, the administrative centre of the **Comarca Emberá–Wounaan Sambú**. This indigenous territory resides under its own legal jurisdiction, separate from Panamanian law. Locals are deeply protective of their culture and serious about the formalities of receiving visitors. Upon crossing the bridge, the architecture visibly shifts from Sambú's concrete constructions to traditional stilted huts with single-log ladders, though the centre of social life in the late afternoon centres on the basketball court. Visitors should report to the *Cacique Regional* Tinto Quintana (regional chief), or a senior member of the tourism committee, in order to pay the US$10 entry fee. The tourism committee can organize tours of Puerto Indio, rainforest hikes, including a visit to a harpy eagle nest, plus overnight trips to Villa Queresia, and to more remote communities.

ARRIVAL AND INFORMATION

By boat Community boats from La Palma to Sambú (Mon, Wed & Fri; 2hr 30min; US$20) leave the passenger dock at around 8am.

By plane Air Panama (@airpanama.com) flights arrive from, and depart for, Panama City twice a week (Wed & Sat) at the airstrip right by the town.

Registration All tourists arriving in Sambú must register with the police, at the airstrip.

Health There is a health centre across the airstrip, opposite the police station.

Phone The community payphone (@333 2512) is at the end of the airstrip.

ACCOMMODATION AND EATING

Benedicta's Behind a shop close to the airstrip. Sturdy cane building where good breakfasts and filling lunches of *comida típica* are prepared, for around US$3–4. Evening meals are a case of what's left over. Daily 7am–8pm.

Hotel & Restaurante Mi Sueño At the end of the airstrip. Eleven simple, fan-ventilated wooden rooms with thin mattresses and shared showers, plus a communal balcony overlooking the airstrip. The occasionally functioning restaurant offers cheap meals. US$12

Restaurante Marantha On the main path before the bridge. Basic portions of lentils or beans with beef or fish from US$3–4.

Villa Fiesta At the end of the airstrip @6687 2271. Fairly comfortable good-value option, offering three en-suite rooms with a/c, which can accommodate 2–4 guests, with firm mattresses and a mini-fridge. US$25

Guna Yala

Stretching nearly 400km, **Guna Yala** – the autonomous *comarca* (territory) of the Guna people – takes in the narrow band of mainland Panama north of the Serranía de San Blas and the sweep of nearly four hundred tropical islands that is the **Guna Yala Archipelago** (often referred to as San Blas or Kuna Yala). Only about forty of the minute islands are inhabited; some strain to contain towns, while others are little more than sandbanks that a lone family has made their home. The administrative capital, **El Porvenir**, lies on a small, narrow island off the tip of the peninsula at the far western end of the *comarca*.

Changes in recent years, including a direct road from Panama City and mobile phone reception for many of the islands, have opened up **travel** in the region, while increasing pressure on the fragile environment and on traditional cultural values.

The Guna gradually made their way here over the centuries, migrating first from Colombia to the Darién region sometime in the sixteenth century. Abandoning that area after years of struggles with the Spanish and the Emberá tribe, they settled afresh along the coast and on the islands in the nineteenth century, but it took what they call "the Tule Revolution" in 1925 to have the territory recognized as theirs alone. To this day, no non-Guna may live in the *comarca*; it's a privilege just to enter it and an even greater one to hop among the islands, soaking up their beauty, and to spend the night in the community, perhaps sleeping in the same room as a Guna family. Learning a little about their cultural heritage and observing the fascinating ins and outs of island life are excellent reasons to come here – even if you can't stand idyllic beaches.

WHAT TO SEE AND DO

You're most likely to base yourself on one of the tiny uninhabited islands in western Guna Yala – all of which are palm-topped and encircled by thin white-sand beaches. Accommodation options on each one offer day-trips, usually for a fee, to other picturesque, uninhabited islands. Good bets include the tiny **Isla Perro** (Achutupo – Dog Island; US$2); a cargo ship was wrecked in the shallows here in the 1940s, making for great snorkelling. Snorkels can be rented on the beach (US$3). **Isla de las Estrellas**, its shallows dotted with its namesake starfish – is also popular.

The **Cayos Holandéses**, however, are generally considered to offer the most spectacular underwater scenery. Protected by an outer reef, they offer natural swimming pools showcasing an array of sponges and corals that attract rays, reef sharks and a plethora of

GUNA CULTURE

Guna society is regulated by a system of highly participative **democracy**: every community has a *casa de congreso* where the *onmakket*, or congress, meets regularly. Each community also elects a *sahila*, usually a respected elder, who attends the Guna General Congress twice a year. The General Congress is the supreme political authority in Guna Yala, and in turn appoints three *caciques* to represent the Guna in the national government.

Colonial missionaries struggled in vain to Christianize the Guna, who cling to their own **religious beliefs**, based above all on the sanctity of Nan Dummad, the Great Mother, and on respect for the environment they inhabit. Though Guna men wear standard Western clothes, **Guna women** wear gold rings in their ears and noses and blue vertical lines painted on their foreheads; they don headscarves and bright bolts of trade cloth round their waists, their forearms and calves are bound in coloured beads and their blouses are sewn with beautiful reverse-appliqué designs known as **molas**.

Given that no non-Guna is permitted to own property on the islands and that **tourism** is a prickly issue, your status as an outsider is symbolic and your behaviour will probably be scrutinized. Cover up on the inhabited islands and cut out public displays of affection. You must ask permission from the **saila** (chief) to visit inhabited islands in the less touristy central and eastern islands of the *comarca* – ask the advice of people you meet to find a contact – and to take photographs, which are banned on some islands, as is alcohol.

In 2011 the general congress passed a law to standardize the Guna alphabet, removing the letters "p", "t" and "k". From that point on the area previously known as Kuna Yala was now called Guna Yala.

7

rainbow-coloured fish. At the outer limit of the *comarca*, 30km from shore, they are inaccessible when the seas are rough (especially Dec–Feb) and the extra fuel needed to reach here means a day-trip here usually carries a hefty supplement.

Other excursions are sometimes made to an inhabited island, or to the mainland to visit a **Guna cemetery** or to go for a walk through the rainforest to a **waterfall**.

All of the islands are privately "owned" by the Guna, and when your hotel drops you off for an afternoon of sun-drenched laziness you will be approached for your payment of a visitor tax, usually US$2–5 – check with your guide beforehand, as it may be included in the price of the trip. When going on an excursion, be sure to bring **water** and something to do, whether it's a book, a pack of cards or snorkelling gear (though some islands do have snorkelling gear for rent).

Carti

Carti refers to a group of islands and an area on the mainland at the western end of Guna Yala. **Carti Sugdub** (Sugdub is also frequently used) is the most populated island in western Guna Yala,

with a health centre, school, library and a couple of small restaurants.

The island is crowded, with little to do aside from visit the small, interesting **museum** (US$5; US$3 if you go with a Guna guide). Fascinatingly cluttered, it's covered floor-to-ceiling with drawings and paintings in various styles – some by children – representing different aspects of Guna culture, myth and history. If you're lucky enough to be visiting in the days leading up to the anniversary of the 1925 Guna revolution on February 25, you can catch dramatizations of the clashes that took place between the Guna and the Panamanian authorities, for which a number of the islanders dress, disconcertingly, as police officers.

Swimming is not an option on Carti Sugdub, as much of the waste ends up in the surrounding waters.

Icodub

Also known as Isla Aguja (or Needle Island), **Icodub** is topped with dreamy coconut palms and fronted by a lovely beach with a beach volleyball court. Prices are slightly higher here than on many of the other western islands, as facilities are slightly more developed. You should avoid weekends in the dry season

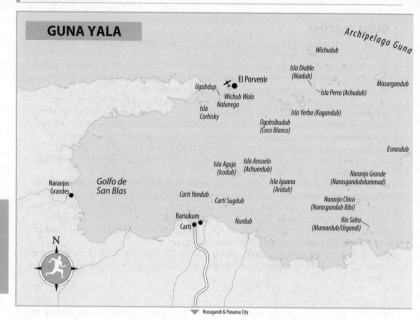

GUNA YALA

Archipelago Guna

Wichudub

Isla Diablo (Niadub)

El Porvenir

Ugubdup

Wichub Wala

Nalunega

Isla Corbisky

Isla Perro (Achudub)

Masargandub

Isla Yerba (Kagandub)

Ogobsibudub (Coco Blanco)

Esnasdub

Isla Aguja (Icodub)

Isla Ansuelo (Achuerdub)

Isla Iguana (Aridub)

Naranjo Grande (Narasgandubdummad)

Naranjos Grandes

Golfo de San Blas

Carti Yandub

Carti Sugdub

Naranjo Chico (Narasgandub Bibi)

Barsukum

Carti

Nurdub

Río Sidra (Mamardub/Urgandi)

N

Nusugandi & Panama City

and holiday periods, however, when the island is inundated with visitors from Panama City. Day-trippers to the island are charged US$5.

Isla Iguana

Providing a simple castaway experience, slender **Isla Iguana** (or Aridub) is fairly undeveloped and quiet, with a palm-shaded beach and volleyball court.

Nurdub

With no beach or palm trees to speak of, the tiny islet of **Nurdub**, shared by six families, offers a different type of experience from the other islands. There are good opportunities to learn about Guna life here – provided you speak some Spanish.

Senidup

Offering some of the cheapest and most popular lodging in Guna Yala, postage-stamp-sized **Senidup** can be circumnavigated in a matter of minutes – at a leisurely amble along a pristine beach. It is divided into two lots of accommodation, either side of a chainlink fence.

Naranjo Chico

Narasgandub Bibi, or **Naranjo Chico**, which both translate as "Little Orange Island", is a backpacker favourite, with several options for bedding down, a spread of lush vegetation sprinkled with hibiscus flowers, and a lovely swathe of a coconut-palm-fringed beach.

ARRIVAL AND INFORMATION

The easiest way to experience the Guna Yala Archipelago is to book a package deal to an island in western Guna Yala through one of the Panama City hostels (see p.536) – you could also contact reliable Guna guide Eric Brown (☎6722 8685, ⓦpecaritours.com). It is possible to visit independently, for around the same price.

Entry fee All visitors, including non-Guna Panamanians, have to pay an entry fee to the *comarca* (US$10 for foreigners, including US$2 tax), collected at the entry point to the *comarca*; this is not usually included in any package.

Supplies The prices given here for accommodation, and those quoted for tours, are per person per night, and include three basic meals. Meal portions are often quite small in the really budget places, so it's a good idea to bring extra snacks, and large containers of water with you, as water is not potable in Guna Yala – be sure to take the empty containers back out with you. When travelling by road, whether travelling independently or on a package

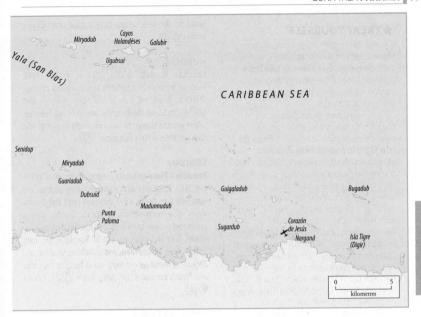

7

deal, you will usually stop off at a supermarket en route, where you can stock up on supplies.

Electricity Bring a torch, as electricity, if there is any, is usually switched off at around 10pm.

INDEPENDENT TRAVEL

By plane Air Panama (☎ 316 9000, ⊛ airpanama.com) provides daily flights from Albrook airport in Panama City from around US$75 one-way. In the archipelago, the principal airstrip for visitors is on El Porvenir (under renovation at the time of writing). Other destinations include Achutupo, Corazón de Jesús, Mulatupo, Playón Chico (30min–1hr 15min) and Puerto Obaldía (see box, p.562). Flights theoretically leave around 6am and island hop but are frequently delayed or cancelled, and there are sometimes flights not listed on the website, so phone in advance. To book a return flight when in the archipelago, you can ring Air Panama and reserve on a credit card, which is swiped on arrival in Panama City. Luggage exceeding 12kg incurs a surcharge of one percent of the published fare.

By 4WD You can book transport for US$25 each way (the standard price) by calling Guna Yala transport in Panama City (☎ 225 4900 or ☎ 225 2387) to arrange a pick-up at your hostel or hotel.

Accommodation Most lodgings accept independent bookings and will pick you up from the jetty at the old Carti airstrip, or at Barsukum river dock (where you'll pay a US$2 "river tax"). With more expensive lodging there's no charge for this ride – just confirm in advance; otherwise you'll pay

US$20–30 return from the dock to your island lodging depending on where you're staying. All the accommodation that we have listed below can also be booked through the Panama City hostels (see p.536).

TOURS

Budget tours Budget tours to the region usually comprise transport from Panama City by 4WD to the Carti or neighbouring Barsukum dock (3hr), pick-up from here by the owners of the accommodation you have been booked into, and transport by boat to the designated island. A night's stay as part of a package costs from US$20–35 at the budget end of the scale, which includes three basic set meals. Most lodgings also offer excursions to other islands (from US$5–30, depending on demand, distance to the island and the quality of the boat).

ACCOMMODATION AND EATING

CARTI SUGDUB

Hospedajes There are several *hospedajes* in Carti Sugdub, but given the wealth of uncrowded *islitas* nearby – where you can loll on empty beaches and snorkel in crystalline waters – you are unlikely to find a reason to spend the night.

Restaurants Carti Sugdub has a handful of restaurants that serve up fried chicken, rice, salad and lentils for around US$4.

ICODUB

Cabañas Icodub ☎ 6660 7908. Accommodation is in tents – mattress, pillow and sheets provided – or in a

---

★ TREAT YOURSELF

If you're interested in Guna culture, and want to escape the backpacker scene, you can't do better than a stay on **Isla Tigre** (or Digir), one of the most traditional communities, which still practises many communal activities.

The Guna dance originated here, and the island attracts dance troupes from all over the *comarca* in the annual **Feria de Isla Tigre** in mid-October. A slender, elongated island, it is partitioned into two: the village proper with a wide sandy main street, and the grassy tourism-designated area, which contains seven simple cane cabañas, a sliver of beach, a rancho hung with hammocks, and an excellent bar-restaurant offering some of the best food in the *comarca*; the bar is also a good place to meet some of the (male) villagers. To get here you'll need to fly to Corazón de Jesús (US$75), from where it's a 40min boat ride to the island (US$40). To reserve, ring one of the community's public telephones (☎317 1209) or just turn up.

---

handful of cane cabañas, some of them en suite, with use of hammocks and deckchairs for an additional few dollars. You get a proper tiled toilet/shower block here, and a tiled restaurant – seafood, pork and chicken are usually on the dinner buffet menu, but you have to pay extra for lobster or *langostinos*. Tent US$35, cabaña: shared bathroom US$45, cabaña: en suite US$60.

ISLA IGUANA
Cabañas Iguana ☎6807 2764 or ☎6151 7379. A clutch of cane-and-thatch huts, and a small bar-restaurant on a raised wooden deck, serving tasty seafood. Dorm US$35, cabaña US$50

NURDUB
Cabañas Nurdub ☎6803 7033 or ☎6054 4348. Lodgings are in six immaculately kept traditional cabañas. There's no beach, but there are daily trips to islands with beaches, including the beautiful and deserted Piderdup, where you can arrange to camp overnight as part of your package. Rates include excursions. US$60

SENIDUP
Franklin's Place (officially *Cabañas Dubesenika*) ☎299 690 2863. Party spot with eighteen tightly packed cane huts with sand floors, a dirt-volleyball court and dreamy views of a palm-framed Caribbean. Guests share a communal shower/toilet area, and luxuries such as juice, snacks, beer and cigarettes can be bought at the main "office". Rates include (basic and sometimes small) meals. Because of the larger numbers, island-hopping boat trips and fishing excursions are cheap. Dorm US$26, cabaña US$35

NARANJO CHICO
Cabañas Eneida (☎6723 0436, ✉narasganduparon507 @hotmail.com). Probably the nicest of the budget lodgings, with decent cane cabañas, more serviceable toilets and showers than most, good food and a pleasant beachside dining area. Campers can bring their own tent and food, or do a meal deal for an extra US$15. Camping US$25, dorm US$20, cabaña US$55

Cabañas Robinson (☎6721 9885). The engaging Arnulfo Robinson runs what are probably the cheapest cane huts in the whole of western Guna Yala – so don't expect much. Shared makeshift shower and bathroom and rock-bottom-priced excursions too. Dorm US$20, cabaña US$25

INTO COLOMBIA: PUERTO OBALDÍA

You can enter **Colombia** by boat via **Puerto Obaldía**, a remote border outpost at the far southeastern edge of Guna Yala, served by light aircraft from Panama City. Air Panama flies three times a week (Tues, Sat & Sun; 1hr; US$94); seats go quickly so book in advance. After going through customs and providing the Colombian consulate with proof of onward travel, you can take a **boat** (about US$10) to Capurganá, a small fishing village and holiday resort on the Colombian coast, where DAS (ⓦdas.gov.co) will stamp your passport. You can also reach **Puerto Obaldía** or Capurganá by using the occasional speedboat service from Carti offered by Andutu in Panama City (Av Justo Arosemena & C 34; ☎6060 9104, ⓦandutu.com). The 7hr journey costs US$125, or US$165, including taxes and land transfer from Panama City. From Capurganá, ADA (ⓦada-aero.com) flies to Medellín and other destinations in Colombia. There are also boats from Capurganá across the Gulf of Urabá to Turbo (US$30). From Turbo you can catch one of the regular light aircraft flights to Medellín and Cartagena, or continue your journey by bus. There are places to change money around the border, but they charge hefty commission, so it is best to change only a small amount; Turbo is the first place with an ATM.

Central Panama and the Península de Azuero

Central Panama is a strikingly diverse region. Heading west from Panama City the **Interamericana** runs along a narrow plain squeezed between the Pacific and the slopes of the Cordillera Central. Your bus will barely have hit top speed before you can hop off and spend some time sprawled on one of the abundant **beaches** just south of the Interamericana. Though they're fine for a weekend escape from Panama City, they don't compare with the offerings on the islands of the Golfo de Chiriquí, Bocas del Toro or Guna Yala. It is, however, worth heading north off the Interamericana to spend a night in the relative cool of **El Valle**, a popular weekend getaway for wealthy Panama City residents, before venturing further into spectacular mountain scenery round the village of **El Copé** and the **Parque Nacional Omar Torrijos**.

At the border of Coclé Province, 193km from Panama City, the road forks at **Divisa**: the Interamericana continues west to Santiago, the capital of Veraguas Province, but consider turning south down the Carretera Nacional into the **Península de Azuero**, which hosts some of the country's most vibrant festivals in the colonial towns of Guararé and Las Tablas, contains some splendid surfing beaches, and has two fascinating islands – Isla Iguana and Isla Cañas – to explore.

EL VALLE

About 100km west of Panama City, a twisty road climbs up into the cordillera to **EL VALLE**, a small village in a fertile valley that was once the crater of a volcano. At 600m above sea level, El Valle is comparatively cool, and the surrounding countryside is good for walking or horseriding. Renowned for its flowers – particularly orchids – the area is a popular retreat for wealthy Panama City residents at weekends, when the place is awash with 4WDs, 4WDs and golf carts and golf carts.

WHAT TO SEE AND DO

Most of the village's amenities can be found on **Avenida Central** (also called Avenida Principal), along with signposts pointing the way to local attractions, mostly located on the outskirts of the village. In the centre, the modest daily **market** draws the biggest crowds, especially on Sundays, when locals sell fruit, flowers and crafts. A small **museum** (Sun 10am–2pm but ask in the shop across the road at other times; US$0.50), run by nuns, houses exhibits on local history and folklore and stands next to the church of San José. Beyond the church by the Río Anton, a side road leads to the enjoyably quirky **thermal baths** (daily 8am–5pm; US$2.25), or *pozos termales*, reputed to have medicinal powers – they are best avoided on summer weekends and during holidays. Meanwhile, to see wonderful specimens of the orchids that grow around here, explore the **APROVACA Orchid Nursery**, signposted off to the left from the main road as you enter the town (daily 9am–4pm; US$2).

El Chorro Macho

One of the most worthwhile sights in the vicinity of El Valle, **El Chorro Macho** is a 35m waterfall in a private reserve (daily 8am–5pm; US$4), with **ziplines** (8am–3.30pm; US$54) fitted around it. However, with just five ziplines, one of which crosses the waterfall, it's only worth a trip if you aren't heading for Boquete, which boasts the country's best canopy adventure. To get here, take a local bus headed for La Mesa from Avenida Central, or walk (thirty minutes along the main road round to the right at the western end of town).

El Nispero zoo and plant nursery

Head 1km up a signposted side road off Avenida Central to visit the **El Nispero zoo and plant nursery** (daily 7am–5pm;

7

7

US$5). The animals aren't the happiest-looking creatures, but it's a great spot to view the many orchids that grow here, as well as Panama's endangered golden frog.

Hiking trails

Innumerable trails climb up into the **cloudforests** of the surrounding mountains. Best known is the trail that peaks at **La India Dormida**, a mountain ridge looming west of the valley, whose silhouette quite strikingly resembles a woman lying on her back. The passage to the **Piedra Pintada** (US$1.50 community fee), an ancient rock with petroglyphs, is somewhat less visited, with a series of waterfalls to cool you down on the way. **Cerro Gaital**, which dominates the town and is often swathed in mist, is an even greater challenge.

ARRIVAL AND INFORMATION

By bus Buses pull in at the covered market on Av Central. There are direct buses from Panama City (every 30min 7.30am–6.30pm; 2hr 30min); the last bus back to the capital leaves from the market at 6pm. Coming into El Valle from the west, get off at "*la entrada*" at Las Uvas and catch a bus up to El Valle; heading back west, catch a Panama City or San Carlos bus (every 20min) to the junction with the Interamericana (40min). Your best bet is to take a bus to Penonomé and change there.

Tourist information The small, helpful ATP office is in a kiosk next to the market; they can provide you with a map and will ring for accommodation, but your hostel owner will probably have as much knowledge about tourist activities in the area. Also check ⓦ el-valle-panama.com.

Bike rental *Don Pepe's*, by the market, and a few other places rent bicycles (US$2/hr, US$10/day).

Banks Banco Nacional has an ATM on Av Principal, near the turn-off for El Nispero; there's also an ATM in the supermarket.

Internet There are computers in the public library (Mon–Sat 8.30am–3.30pm; US$1/hr) and an internet café at the eastern end of Av Central.

ACCOMMODATION

Accommodation prices in El Valle reflect its popularity among wealthy Panamanians, who flock here for Carnaval, public holidays and weekends. That said, there are still several options catering to travellers on a tighter budget; most accept cash only.

★ **APROVACA Orchid Nursery** Signposted left off Av Central, on the way into town ☎ 983 6472. Excellent value and a quiet place to stay – either in the comfortable

six-bed dorm, with interior bathroom and a small kitchen, patio area and laundry facilities, or in their spotless en-suite room. Rates include wi-fi and entry to the orchid nursery. Dorm <u>US$12</u>, double <u>US$30</u>

Cabañas Potosí 150m past the church, take the road to the right, then the fork to the left and continue for 1.5km ☎ 983 6181. Comfortable, good-looking rooms in smart concrete cabañas with plenty of birdlife in the garden. Also camping across the road (bring your own tent) with bathroom and kitchen facilities. Camping per tent <u>US$10</u>, double <u>US$54</u>

La Casita de Don Daniel At the foot of La India Dormida ☎ 6615 5511. Friendly, family environment with three inexpensive double rooms and a riverside campsite, where you can rent a tent (US$15) or pitch your own, with use of bathrooms and communal kitchen. Local crafts are sold on site, while the weekends offer live music and snacks. Camping per tent <u>US$10</u>, double <u>US$30</u>

Santa Librada Av Central ☎ 983 5052. Reasonable budget option at the back of the restaurant, opening onto a small garden. A handful of basic rooms of variable quality share cold showers. <u>US$35</u>

EATING

Panadería y Dulceria Cano Av Central. Just the place to stock up on sticky buns, cakes and bread to keep you going on a hike. Daily 7.30am–8pm.

Restaurante Mar de Plata Av Central below *Hotel Don Pepe* ☎ 983 6425. Neat and airy, serving tasty dishes, including fried *ceviche*, from a varied menu (mains from US$7), to be washed down with delicious fresh fruit juices and *batidos*. Daily 7am–late.

Restaurante Massiel Av Central. Friendly efficient place serving *comida típica* and fast food – chicken with rice is US$4 and hamburger combos go for much the same. Also good for breakfast. Daily 7am–8pm.

Restaurante Santa Librada *Santa Librada*, Av Central. Probably the best inexpensive option in town, serving Panamanian favourites such as *pollo guisado* (chicken stew) for under US$4. Daily 7am–8.30pm.

PENONOMÉ AND AROUND

Founded in 1581 as a *reducción de Indios* – a place where conquered indigenous groups were forcibly resettled so as to be available for labour service – and briefly the capital of the isthmus after the destruction of Panamá Viejo, **PENONOMÉ** was named after Nomé, a local chieftain cruelly betrayed and executed here by the Spaniards after years of successful resistance. Now the capital of Coclé Province, Penonomé doesn't have much to see apart from a small museum, though it makes a good enough base for exploring the surrounding area, and if you're in the area during Carnaval, make sure you catch Penonomé's unique **aquatic parade**.

WHAT TO SEE AND DO

From the junction with the Interamericana, Penonomé's busy commercial **main street**, referred to as either Vía Central or Avenida Arosemena, runs a few hundred metres to the **Plaza 8 de Diciembre**. Featuring a statue of Simón Bolívar and the inevitable bandstand, the square is flanked by government buildings and the Iglesia de San Juan Bautista. A few blocks southwest, a small **museum** (Tues–Sat 9am–5pm; US$1) exhibits pre-Columbian ceramics and colonial religious art.

Chiguirí Arriba

Of the potential destinations in the mountains, **Chiguirí Arriba**, 29km to the northeast, makes an easy day-trip from Penonomé. There are plenty of good hiking trails, spectacular views, plump red chickens running about and Cascada Tavida, a 30m waterfall nearby – local children may guide you there for a small tip.

ARRIVAL AND DEPARTURE

PENONOMÉ

By bus Buses that travel the Interamericana pick up and drop off in Penonomé opposite the *Hotel Dos Continentes* at the junction with Av Arosemena (Vía Central). Buses from Panama City leave every 15min (2hr 15min) south of the Interamericana at that junction. Large buses from Panama City bound for Chitré (hourly; 1hr 30min), Las Tablas (hourly; 2hr) and Santiago (every 30min; 1hr 30min) make a pit stop at the *Restaurante Universal* on the Interamericana and will take passengers if they have space.

By minibus From the market area, *chivas* and *busitos* (minibuses) head off into the mountains, aiming for Chiguirí Arriba (every 15min 6am–6.30pm; 1hr) and El Copé (every 25min until 9pm; 1hr).

ACCOMMODATION AND EATING

PENONOMÉ

Hotel Dos Continentes Junction Av Arosemena (Vía Central) & Interamericana, opposite the bus terminal ☎ 997 9325, ⓦ hoteldoscontinentes.net. Large, sprawling place offering un-ironically retro en-suite rooms, with a/c,

sleeping up to four. The very popular restaurant serves good food: try the shrimp omelette and *patacones* (US$5) and steak and fish dishes (from US$6). They also serve *bollo* – plantain mashed and then compacted into chunks (tastier than it sounds). Rooms are more expensive at weekends. **US$30**

Panadería El Paisa Vía Central, just before the church. Busy bakery with a large selection of bread, pastries and sandwiches (US$1–4), plus outdoor seating where you can soak up the town's atmosphere. Daily 6am–9pm.

Restaurante Gallo Pinto #1 A block south of the church. Cheery checked tablecloths and a bustling central location make this branch more alluring than its other locations in town. The kitchen whips up *comida típica* like beef *guisado* (stew) and full breakfasts with popular bean-and-rice combo *gallo pinto* (US$3–4). Daily 6am–8pm.

PARQUE NACIONAL OMAR TORRIJOS

Straddling the continental divide just over 30km northwest of Penonomé is the little-visited but spectacular **Parque Nacional Omar Torrijos** (often called "El Copé" after the nearby village of the same name; US$5), named after Panama's flamboyant populist leader whose plane mysteriously crashed into one of the park's highest peaks. Scenery ranges from mist-shrouded cloudforest to abundant subtropical vegetation, offering excellent opportunities for birdwatching and hiking, and the park is chock-full of wildlife.

ARRIVAL AND DEPARTURE

By bus and minibus To get here, take a bus from Penonomé to El Copé, where you can connect with a sporadic local minibus to the village of Barrigón. From here you'll need to hike the remaining 4km up to the park entrance, or hire a 4WD pick-up (around US$15).

Guides and tours To make the most of the area, and to enjoy the services of a guide, it's a good idea to stay in the park or nearby, either in Barrigón or in the small community of La Rica, which, a day's trek over the continental divide, enjoys a verdant setting laced with waterfalls; contact the Navas family (see p.566). AGLAC Ecotours (ⓦ aglacecotours.com) also offers a range of inexpensive guided excursions (US$15–25/person).

ACCOMMODATION

ANAM refugio Park entrance. A refuge offering bunks, kitchen and camping space – bring your own food and

7

sleeping bag and wrap up warm. Camping <u>US$5</u>, bunk <u>US$10</u>

BOCA bunkhouses Barrigón, 4km from the park entrance, contact Sr Arcia ☎ 6809 6372. A couple of simple bunkhouses by the waterfall in Barrigón, managed by a local environmental group. <u>US$10</u>

★ **Navas family** Barrigón ☎ 983 9130. The welcoming and experienced Navas family offer simple rooms in their home, excellent guiding services (for an extra charge) and meals. Per person, including meals <u>US$35</u>

CHITRÉ

The capital of Herrera Province and the largest town on the Azuero Peninsula, **CHITRÉ** is a slow-paced market centre studded with colourful discount stores. Other than the market and a museum, there's not much to see here, but the town is the peninsula's main transport hub and a good base for exploration.

WHAT TO SEE AND DO

Chitré centres on the bandstand, trees and benches of **Parque Unión**. The square is flanked on one side by the gleaming white **Catedral San Juan Bautista**, with its impressive, vaulted wooden roof and extensive gilded wooden panelling.

Museo de Herrera

Chitré cathedral faces down Avenida Herrera – walk down a block and turn left onto Calle Manuel Correa and you'll reach the **Museo de Herrera** (Tues–Sat 8am–noon & 1–4pm, Sun 8am–noon; US$1), three blocks away. This is probably the best museum outside Panama City, set in an elegant colonial mansion, exhibiting a collection of pre-Columbian pottery from the surrounding area with a good display on local folklore and customs, featuring traditional masks, costumes and musical instruments.

ARRIVAL AND INFORMATION

By bus Buses to and from Panama City and other destinations pull in at the terminal on the southern outskirts of town, 1km (or a 15min walk) from the centre. Local buses run to the centre from the bus terminal; buses returning to the bus terminal can be boarded at the main square, or outside the museum.

Destinations Las Tablas (every 15min; 45min); Panama City (hourly; 4hr); Santiago (every 30min; 1hr 20min).

Tourist information There's a CEFATI office in the Parque Industrial La Arena, on the road into town (☎ 974 4532).

ACCOMMODATION

Don't expect to find anywhere to stay during Santa Librada or Carnaval (see box opposite).

Hotel Rex Opposite Parque Unión ☎ 996 2391. The fanciest spot in central Chitré, overlooking the park but with faded furnishings. A/c rooms come with breakfast in the on-site restaurant. <u>US$45</u>

Hotel Santa Rita C Correa & Av Herrera, north of the cathedral ☎ 996 4610. Run by the same family for over a hundred years, this friendly, central hotel has lost its period charm but its spotless, though rather dark, fan-ventilated rooms are excellent value (a/c is US$5 more). <u>US$23</u>

Miami Mike's Corner of Av Herrera & C Correa, north of the cathedral ☎ 910 0628, ⓦ miamimikeshostel.com. The only real hostel in town, with a massive roof terrace, cheerfully painted themed rooms and an affable American owner, who's happy to provide you with travel info. Also a communal kitchen, living room, wi-fi and lockers – but cleanliness is not high on the agenda. Dorm <u>US$10</u>, double <u>US$26</u>

EATING

El Anzuelo Paseo Enrique Geenzier ☎ 910 1030. With a rambling outdoor eating area, this place is full of contented diners and plates that are empty but for fish heads. Fish dishes (including croaker, dorado and mahi, not just the ubiquitous *corvina*) from US$9. Tues–Sun noon–11pm.

Panadería Chiquita Av Herrera. Large open-fronted café; a popular spot to grab a sticky bun or *empanada* with a Styrofoam cup of coffee or *chicha* for under US$1.50. Daily 5am–10pm.

Pizzería Ebeneezer A couple of blocks southwest of the church. Appealing place with indoor and patio seating serving inexpensive pizzas from US$4, alongside tacos, burritos and the odd Greek dish. Mon–Sat 11.30am–10pm, Sun 4–10pm.

Restaurante El Aire Libre Av Obaldía, Parque Unión on the corner opposite the church. Small restaurant, often overflowing at lunchtime, serving an inexpensive *menu del día* for just over US$3 and other dishes for US$3–4. Daily 6am–9pm.

DIRECTORY

Banks There's a Banco de Ahorros on Parque Unión (Mon–Fri 9am–3.30pm, Sat 9am–noon) with 24hr ATM, and a branch of Banco Nacional (Mon–Fri 9am–3pm, Sat 9am–noon) on Paseo Enrique Geenzier, northwest of the town centre.

FESTIVALS IN THE PENÍNSULA DE AZUERO

Jutting out into the Pacific Ocean, the **Península de Azuero** was one of the first regions of Panama to be settled by Spanish colonists. The towns and villages you come across – the main recommended bases include Chitré, Las Tablas and Pedasí – in this dry, scrubby landscape hum with their colonial heritage, visually manifested in the traditional handicrafts and folk costumes of the region, but the real giveaway is the gusto with which the people throw themselves into their **religious fiestas**. Usually honouring a particular patron saint, many of these date back almost unchanged to the days of the early settlers. Religious processions are accompanied by traditional music, fireworks and costumed folk dances, which are as pagan as they are Catholic. As the night wears on the *seco* tends to flow and DJs take over. Listed below are just a few of the major events; every village and hamlet has its own fiesta, and there's almost always one going on somewhere.

Jan 6 Fiesta de los Reyes and Encuentro del Canajagua, Macaracas.
Jan 19–22 Fiesta de San Sebastián, Ocú.
Feb (date varies) Carnaval in Las Tablas (and everywhere else in the country).
March/April (date varies) Semana Santa, celebrated most colourfully in La Villa de Los Santos, Pesé and Guararé.
Late April Feria International del Azuero, La Villa de Los Santos.
May/June (date varies) Corpus Christi, La Villa de Los Santos.
June 24 Patronales de San Juan, Chitré.
July 20–22 Patronales de La Santa Librada and Festival de la Pollera, Las Tablas.
Aug (second week) Festival del Manito in Ocú.
Late Sept Festival de la Mejorana, Guararé.
Nov 10 The "First Cry of Independence", La Villa de Los Santos.

Internet Intercopimp, C Melitón Martín (Mon–Fri 8am–6pm, Sat 8am–2pm; US$0.50/hr).
Pharmacy Farmacia Universal, C Melitón Martín & Av Herrera, opposite the cathedral (Mon–Sat 8am–8pm, Sun 8am–noon).

LAS TABLAS

LAS TABLAS, south along the peninsula's coast from Chitré, was founded in the seventeenth century by refugees fleeing by sea from Panamá Viejo after Henry Morgan and his band of pirates sacked it. The settlers dismantled their ships to build the first houses, hence the town's name, which means "the planks".

Though you wouldn't believe it if you turned up at any other time of year, this quiet, colonial market town hosts the wildest **Carnaval** celebrations in Panama. For five days in February the place is overwhelmed by visitors from all over the country, who come here to join in the festivities. The town divides into two halves – **Calle Arriba** and **Calle Abajo** – to fight a pitched battle with water, paint and soot on streets awash with *seco*, Panama's vicious firewater. Less raucous but just as colourful is the fiesta of **Santa Librada** in July, which includes the **Festival de la Pollera**, celebrating the peninsula's embroidered, colonial-style dresses. Produced in the surrounding villages, they are something of a national symbol.

WHAT TO SEE AND DO

In addition to its few sights, Las Tablas is also a choice spot to experience the extremely festive atmosphere of a **baseball** match (Jan–May) at the Estadio Olmedo Solé.

Iglesia de Santa Librada

On the main square, known as **Parque Porras**, the **Iglesia de Santa Librada** is the most popular sight in Las Tablas. The church has a magnificent golden altar illuminating an otherwise dull interior, with a figurine of the patron saint, set in the facade's apex, overlooking the square.

Museo Belisario Porras

In a lovely colonial building diagonally across the square from the church, the tiny **Museo Belisario Porras** (Tues–Sat

7

9.30am–4pm, Sun 8am–noon; US$1)
houses an array of belongings and articles
pertaining to Panama's most revered
president, who was born here in 1856.
An enthusiastic guide will proudly
explain (in Spanish only) the considerable
achievements of the great man and the
significance of items on display, including
presidential correspondence and several
splendid outfits worn by Porras – a
lovingly assembled collection, best suited
to history buffs.

ARRIVAL AND DEPARTURE

By bus Buses from Panama City arrive at and leave from
the bus terminal on Av Laureano López, near the Shell
station, a few blocks from the main square (hourly; 4hr
30min). Buses from Chitré (every 15min until 7pm; 45min)
drop off at Parque Porras, then pull up on Av Porras a few
blocks beyond the square, outside a supermarket, behind
the minibuses that run to Pedasí (every 45min
6am–6.45pm; 45min). Return buses to Chitré can be
flagged down on C Espino, which runs parallel to Av Porros.
The daily bus to Playa Venao (1.30–2pm; 1hr 30min)
leaves half a block north of the plaza round the corner from
Pharmacy Miriam. To head west from Las Tablas, take a
Panama City bus and get off at Divisa. Cross over the
highway to catch westbound buses for either Santiago
(30min from Divisa), roughly the halfway point between
Panama City and David, or David itself. Alternatively, take a
bus to Chitré, where you can get a direct connection to
Santiago.

ACCOMMODATION

If you want to come for Carnaval, you'll have to book
several months in advance, though people do rent out
rooms in their houses to make up for the shortfall in
accommodation, and you could always join the hordes
that sleep in the park.

Hotel Piamonte Av Porras ☎ 923 1903. Rooms vary in
quality, so ask to see a few; the smaller, cheaper rooms in
the annexe over the road – without hot water or wi-fi –
offer better value. There's also a restaurant. U̲S̲$̲3̲8̲

Hotel Sol del Pacífico C Cano ☎ 994 1280. An
uninspiring concrete bunker, with simple en-suite rooms
with double bed and a/c, or pricier ones with three beds
(US$55) and mini-fridge. U̲S̲$̲3̲0̲

EATING AND DRINKING

Bamboo Parque Porras ☎ 923 1910. New venue offering
upmarket, yet cheap, drinks and snacks on an upstairs
balcony, with atmospheric views of the park and town
below. DJs and live music, especially on Fri. Wed–Sun
from 4pm.

Los Portales Av Porras. This place has a small terrace for
dining right on the pavement, offering fine people-
watching, though too close for comfort during Carnaval. A
little overpriced, but the cooking is good quality. Dishes
US$5–8.

Portofino Parque Porras. Offering *emparedados* plus
chicken and beef stew and rice dishes, *Portofino* also does a
fine line in *batidos,* all for a few dollars. Daily 7.30am–9pm.

★ **Restaurante El Caserón** C Augustín Bautista. The
fancy joint in town, with lots of wood and cheery red
tablecloths, charging surprisingly modest prices. Their
mixed meat grills (US$5–8), the house speciality, are
highly recommended. Daily 7am–11pm.

DIRECTORY

Banks Banco Nacional, near the bus station on Av López
(Mon–Fri 8am–3pm, Sat 9am–noon). Av Porras is awash
with banks and ATMs.

Pharmacy There are two on Parque Porras.

Post office C Francisco González, three blocks north of
the square on a road parallel to Av López (Mon–Fri
7am–5pm, Sat 7am–1pm).

PEDASÍ

It's 42km south through cattle country
from Las Tablas to **PEDASÍ**, a friendly,
quiet little village that is fast becoming a
surf destination, best known as a
jumping-off point for Isla Iguana, Isla
Cañas and a wealth of beaches in the
surrounding area.

WHAT TO SEE AND DO

Other than having a quick peek at the
unlikely chandeliers in the **church** on the
town square, activities in Pedasí involve
day-trips to the **islands and the nearby
surf breaks** (see opposite).

Playa El Arenal

Playa El Arenal, a very long, very empty
and very flat beach, is just a thirty-minute
walk from town (US$2 by taxi).

ARRIVAL AND DEPARTURE

By bus Buses pull up on the main street that runs through
the town in front of *The Bakery*. Buses for Las Tablas (every
45min; 45min) leave from beside the supermarket. The
three daily services for Cañas village (7am, noon &
2.50pm; 45min) pass Playa Venao; two depart from the
main street and the last bus passes through en route from
Las Tablas. Bus timetables are subject to change, so check
with locals for current schedules.

By taxi Taxis hang out beside the supermarket, charging the following rates: Playa Arenal US$2.40; Playa de los Destiladores US$7; Playa Venao US$24; Isla Cañas US$30.

INFORMATION AND TOURS

Tourist information The ATP office (Mon–Fri 9.30am–5.30pm; ☎ 995 2339) is on the second left as you enter the village from the north.

Tours Shokogi, an Israeli-run outfit, offers trips in the area as well as kitesurfing and SUP. (Stand Up Paddle, a cross between surfing and kayaking) lessons and rentals (☎ 6921 1532, ⓦ surfpedasi.com). Most lodgings can rustle up a boat for you.

Banks Banco Nacional and Caja de Ahorros, both on the main street, have ATMs.

Laundry By the petrol station on the main road (Mon–Sat 7am–noon & 1–7pm).

ACCOMMODATION

★ Dim's Hostal Main street ☎ 995 2303. This long-established option has pretty, cosy en-suite rooms with dainty curtains and comfortable beds. There's a hammock-slung patio in the lush garden out back with a large, palm-thatched roof anchored to the trunk of a mango tree – a nice place for a beer and a snooze. Prices include breakfast, a/c, wi-fi and TV. US$53

Peak Hostel Main street ☎ 995 2776, ⓔ kadoshi19944@ gmail.com. Run by the owners of the tour operator Shokogi, this hostel currently offers a very hot dorm (no fan and metal roof, though this may change) with foam mattresses, plus a couple of arty, painted en-suite rooms with monsoon showers and a/c. There's also a nice courtyard, small kitchen and TV room. Dorm US$10, double US$55

Residencial Moscoso Main street ☎ 995 2203. Well acquainted with backpackers, the *Moscoso* is clean and inexpensive – the reception is in the owner's living room. Simple fan-ventilated rooms (a/c US$10 more) have shared or private bathroom. US$15

EATING

PEDASÍ

Dulcería Yely Main street, opposite *Residencial Moscoso*. Legendary cake shop with a cabinet full of delicious cakes (US$0.75) and crispy pastry *empanadas* (US$0.30), to be enjoyed with a cup of *chicha* or a shot of coffee. Daily 6am–9pm.

Maudy's Café Main street. *The* breakfast spot in town, with locally made yoghurt, granola and fruit plates for US$4, and smoothies and toasties from US$2.50. Good coffee and wi-fi, too. Daily 8am–5pm.

Restaurante El Ejecutivo C Las Tablas, across from the square. The cheap choice, with *típica* breakfasts for

US$3 and greasy Chinese dishes for US$4–5. Daily 8am–10pm.

Tiesto On the main square ☎ 995 2812. Airy place with a high roof and a stone arch that offers sandwiches and good-quality brick-oven pizzas. Wed–Mon 2–10pm.

PLAYA EL ARENAL

Coco's The beach. Owned by a local co-operative and serving delicious fried fish (US$4 with patacones), fresh from the fishermen's nets, at rock-bottom prices – an experience enhanced by the view, the beer and the sense of calm.

AROUND PEDASÍ

Pedasí is a great base from which to explore the area's fascinating marine attractions. You can set off in search of whales, iguanas and sea turtles, safe in the knowledge that you can come back and lay your head somewhere cosy.

Isla Iguana

Some 7km off the coast of Pedasí lies **Isla Iguana** (US$10), an uninhabited wildlife reserve managed by the state and surrounded by the most extensive **coral reefs** in the Bahía de Panamá, making it one of the best sites for **snorkelling** and **diving** in the country. The island has white-sand beaches, crystalline waters and a vast colony of magnificent frigate birds, and between June and December you may see **whales**. Despite the island's name, iguanas have become scarce due to the locals' fondness for their meat – though since the island was declared a national park, their numbers have been increasing.

ARRIVAL AND DEPARTURE

By boat You can hire a boat to bring you to the island from Playa El Arenal (see opposite). Fishermen charge about US$60 for a return trip (20–30min each way); at weekends you may find other visitors to share the cost. Avoid summer weekends and holiday periods, though, when the place is overrun with visitors, and remember to arrange a pick-up time with your boatman.

ACCOMMODATION AND EATING

Camping You can camp on the island but you'll need to be self-sufficient and note that, other than toilets, there are no facilities. Per person US$5

Food Take all the food and drink you need.

Playa Venao

Surfers' beach **Playa Venao** lies thirty minutes by car (45min by bus) from Pedasí. The beautiful bay is still relatively undeveloped, although it has recently become home to a new hotel and two designer *rancho*-restaurants, which serve overpriced food and drink; both businesses also rent surfboards and sell wax.

ACCOMMODATION

La Choza 200m from the beach break; contact *Hotel El Sitio* ☎ 832 1010, ⓦ playavenaohostel.com. Compact, comfortable fan-ventilated rooms, a breezy balcony and intimate garden-*rancho* kitchen facilities. Dorm U̲S̲$̲1̲5̲, double U̲S̲$̲4̲0̲

Isla Cañas

Archeological evidence suggests that people have been coming to the area now designated as the **ISLA CAÑAS WILDLIFE RESERVE** to hunt turtles and harvest their eggs for many centuries, although the island was only settled in the 1960s. Since 1988, the hunting of turtles here has been prohibited and a co-operative has been established to control the harvest. Members watch over the beaches at night and collect the eggs as soon as they are laid, keeping eighty percent for sale and consumption and moving the rest to a nursery where the turtles can

---

★ **TREAT YOURSELF**

Hostel Eco-Venao On a bluff across from Playa Venao on the main road between Pedasí and Cañas ☎ 832 5030, ⓦ ecovenao.com. Harmonize with your surroundings and support sustainable ecological development of the area with a stay here. The property encompasses a large patch of wild jungle mountainside that has been reforested, and offers great views. Accommodation ranges from an eco-campsite and a dorm to private rooms and *cabinas*. The attractive on-site bar-restaurant serves superb food (mains from US$9); otherwise stock up in Pedasí or Las Tablas and use the communal kitchen. Two–night minimum stay and prices hiked 25 percent for holiday periods. Camping U̲S̲$̲7̲, dorm U̲S̲$̲1̲2̲, double U̲S̲$̲3̲3̲, *cabina* U̲S̲$̲5̲5̲

THE ISLA CAÑAS ARRIBADA

Isla Cañas has one of the few beaches in the world that sees the phenomenon known as the **arribada**, when thousands of female sea turtles simultaneously come ashore to lay their eggs. It's still not entirely understood what triggers this mass exodus from the sea at one particular moment, though smaller numbers emerge at other times, too, within a roughly ten-day period on either side of a full moon (when tides are highest, allowing the turtles to lay their eggs further up the beach).

Whether or not your visit coincides with an *arribada* (usually Aug–Nov), if you come between May and January you'll almost certainly see olive ridley or green turtles – with a small chance of spotting loggerhead and hawksbill – laying their eggs at night. From December to March there's also a chance of seeing leviathan-like leatherbacks, which can weigh over 800kg.

---

hatch and return to the sea in safety.

A night-time **turtle walk**, at least half an hour in each direction along the beach, will set you back about US$15/group. Torch use is stringently rationed as the turtles are frightened by the piercing beams. The long, near-silent walk along soft sand, the lapping water and the incredible number of stars may just lull you to sleep on your feet. Contact Sr Fernando Domingues (☎ 6716 4095), who can advise and who offers crocodile-spotting boat trips round the mangroves at low tide, among other excursions.

The functional but unmemorable **main village** on Isla Cañas is prepared for visitors – as are the mosquitoes and sandflies.

ARRIVAL AND DEPARTURE

If you're not setting out with a tour – several lodgings in Pedasí organize them, or visit the ATP office (see p.569) – getting to and from Isla Cañas is not as straightforward as you might hope.

Buses to Cañas village Two daily buses from Pedasí (7am, noon; 1hr 30min) go to Cañas village; you could also flag down the 1.30–2pm bus from Las Tablas, which passes along the main street of Pedasí (2.15–2.50pm). Returning from Cañas village, two daily buses run to

Pedasí (9am, 3pm), and one leaves at 8am for Tonosí (35min), from where you can connect for Las Tablas (every 90min Mon–Thurs & Sat 6am–4.30pm, Fri 6am–5pm, Sun 7.30am–4pm; 1hr 30min).

By taxi You could take a taxi from Pedasí for around US$30, but make sure the driver takes you the extra couple of kilometres beyond the village to the dock for the island. There are no taxis in Cañas village.

Boats to the island For a couple of extra dollars, buses to Cañas village may take you to the "dock" – essentially the point where the road ends and the mangrove swamp begins, and which is the jumping-off point for the island – or you may be able to persuade someone in the village to drive you there (also for a few dollars). When you arrive at the dock there may be a boat waiting if the tide is in. If there is none, smack loudly on the metal wheel rim that is hung up in a tree near the edge of the swamp. This will alert people on the island (it is very close) and someone will come to get you.

ACCOMMODATION AND EATING

Cabañas Contact Sr Domingues (see opposite) or ring the public phone ☎ 995 8002 and ask for Pablo Pérez. Windowless cement cabañas – some with fans, or, for US$10 more, others with a/c – are available. U̲S̲$̲2̲0̲

Rooms Several families on the island rent out basic rooms.

Restaurant There's a small restaurant near the island dock, where you can eat for around US$4.

Veraguas Province

Although many travellers only see Veraguas while en route between David and Panama City, there are a growing number of reasons to stop here, from the stunning marine life in **Parque Nacional Coiba** and the glorious mountains of **Santa Fé** to the pounding surf of **Santa Catalina**. Travel in the area is relatively simple as most destinations are accessed from the Interamericana, with the majority of attractions within easy reach of the provincial capital **Santiago**.

SANTIAGO

The halfway point between Panama City and David, **SANTIAGO** has few sights apart from its main square, which hosts the pretty **Catedral Santiago Apóstol** and a modest one-room archeological **museum** (Tues–Sat 9am–4pm; free), but if you're headed for Santa Fé or Santa Catalina you may have to stop over if you miss the last bus.

ARRIVAL AND DEPARTURE

By bus Buses between Panama City and David stop at *Restaurante Los Tucanes*, a roadside pit stop on the Interamericana in Santiago, a 10min walk from the bus terminal, with bathrooms, a café and pharmacy. You can sometimes get a seat on these buses but rarely at weekends or during holiday periods. A new, direct, (though less comfortable) Coaster service to David now departs from a stop diagonally across the street from the bus terminal (every 1hr 30min; 3hr). Inside the terminal you can catch a bus for Santa Fé (every 30min until 6.30pm; 1hr–1hr 30min) and Soná (every 20min; 1hr) – where you can connect with the Santa Catalina-bound bus (5am, noon & 4pm; 2hr).

ACCOMMODATION

Residencial Camino del Sol Across from the bus station ☎ 998 2114. These lodgings may not be very inspiring, but they're clean, functional and cheap. U̲S̲$̲2̲8̲

SANTA FÉ

The laidback mountain village of **SANTA FÉ** has become popular as a retreat from the "backpacker trail" – which ironically has put it firmly on the must-do list. Like El Valle, the village enjoys lush hillsides and a cool microclimate, but the scenery is far more impressive and, unlike El Valle, Santa Fé is a genuine thriving village – rather than a weekend playground for Panama City's elite. It is famous for its **co-operatives**, which were founded in the late 1960s by a young Colombian priest named Héctor Gallego, who wanted to help local farmers get a fair price for their goods. For reasons that are unclear he was persecuted and eventually murdered by General Noriega's henchmen but his presence lives on here: a statue of him marks the village entrance and a foundation in his name continues to help local farmers.

There's a wealth of **outdoor activities** here, including hiking, tubing, horseriding and waterfall trips; to

7

organize these, contact staff at *La Qhia* (see below), who will put you in touch with a local guide.

ARRIVAL AND INFORMATION

By bus Buses arrive from Santiago and leave from the bus station in Santa Fé, 100m down from *Hostal La Qhia* at the top end of the village (every 30min until 6.30pm; 1hr–1hr 30min).

Information and tours 100m up the road from *Hostal La Qhia*, the Fundación Héctor Gallego offers internet access (US$1/hr) and can fix up a tour of the coffee co-operative (in Spanish) or organize a birding or hiking guide.

ACCOMMODATION AND EATING

★ **Hostal La Qhia** 100m up from the bus station ☎ 954 0903, ☒ panamamountainhouse.com. Dorms and private rooms come with use of the large hammock-strewn *rancho*, where you can take in the views of surrounding hills even if you don't want to hike them. Dorm US$11, double US$39

Restaurante El Terminal By the bus station. Probably the best of several local restaurants, serving hot tasty chicken or pork stew with plenty of lentils and rice – all for under US$4. Daily 6am–4pm.

Restaurante El Cooperativo de Turismo Village centre. Staying open later than most, this is a popular spot for a beer as well as inexpensive chicken and rice. Daily 7am–8pm.

SANTA CATALINA AND AROUND

Boasting world-class surf and beautiful beaches, **SANTA CATALINA** is considered by many to have the most impressive waves in Panama. Catalina's popularity has skyrocketed in the last decade, through **surf tourism** and as the jumping-off point for **Isla Coiba**, which offers

similarly world-class diving, but the distance from major cities and airports has left this small fishing village fairly well preserved.

WHAT TO SEE AND DO

The village and most of its businesses – many owned by expats – are based around the **main street**, the road from Soná, which ends where the concrete meets Santa Catalina **beach**. It is an unimpressive pebble-strewn strip, where the fishermen pull up their boats and unload their catch, and where boats leave for **Coiba**. Most of the accommodation and restaurants are located off what is often called the **beach road**, which deviates left at the public phone box, ending 2km later in the swath of sand that is **Playa del Estero**. This is a far nicer beach, where most of the **surf** classes take place. If you can't afford to go to Coiba, you'll find plenty of decent snorkelling and nice white sands at the nearby islands of **Santa Catalina** and **Cébaco**.

Parque Nacional Coiba

Blessed with a striking abundance of marine biodiversity, the group of 38 islands that make up **Parque Nacional Coiba** (including the namesake) has become one of Panama's most popular national parks, although strict conservation laws and limited access mean that tourism here is still relatively underdeveloped. For independent travellers, Santa Catalina is the closest destination from which you can access the park, on **tours** run by locals (see

---

SANTA CATALINA ACTIVITIES

In addition to those listed below, other activities in Santa Catalina include horseriding, yoga and massage – ask at *Buena Vida* (see opposite) – or sailing around on a catamaran (☒ coibasailing.com).

Diving Trips to Coiba and nearby dive sites can be arranged through Scuba Coiba (☒ scubacoiba.com) or Coiba Dive Center (☒ coibadivecenter.com), from around US$65/person.

Kayaking Kayaks can be rented from Rolo's (US$15). Highly recommended kayaking tours are available from Fluid Adventures, (☒ fluidadventurespanama.com), who offer a day-trip to Isla Santa Catalina (US$40/

person) and more expensive multiday adventures paddling and camping on Coiba.

Surfing Boards can be rented (from US$10–15/day) at most camps (see opposite) or with Surf and Shake (☒ surfandshake.com) on the beach road. Lessons (usually 1hr 30min–2hr) range from US$20–30 and may include use of the board for the rest of the day.

below). To really have a chance of spotting wildlife, you should arrange to stay overnight (see below), so that you can get into the forest at first light. So far, the only accommodation is on **Isla Coiba** – a former penal colony, and the park's largest island. For more, see ⓦ coibanationalpark.com.

ARRIVAL AND DEPARTURE

By bus Santa Catalina is accessed by Soná-bound buses, direct from Panama City's Albrook bus terminal (8 daily; 5hr), or from Santiago's main terminal (every 20min; 1hr), before changing in Soná for onward buses to Santa Catalina (daily 5am, noon & 4pm; 2hr). Return buses to Soná leave Santa Catalina at 7am, 8am & 2pm. There are also eight daily buses to Panama City from Soná (5hr), but you can catch a more comfortable ride from Santiago.

By taxi Taxis from Soná cost US$35–40, and hang around the bus station to catch travellers who can't be bothered to wait for the bus, or who have missed the last one.

INFORMATION AND TOURS

Tourist information There's no tourist office but there are two good village websites: ⓦ visitsantacatalina.com, ⓦ santacatalinabeach.com.

Coiba tours Various fishermen advertise outside their houses about tours to Coiba. Rates are agreed, so there's little point in shopping around; a day-trip will cost US$55/person (minimum of six), not including park fee (US$20) or food – various places, such as Buena Vida and La Vieja Panadería, can do you a packed lunch. It is also possible to stay on Coiba (see below).

Banks Note that there is no ATM in Santa Catalina, and that the one in Soná often runs out of cash during busy periods.

Internet Several hostels and restaurants in Santa Catalina offer wi-fi.

ACCOMMODATION

SANTA CATALINA

A large number of surf camps and budget hostels have kept prices low and availability likely, although the best lodgings have views of, and easy access to, the break and need to be booked in advance. Most only offer cold- or tepid-water showers.

Blue Zone Beachfront off the Beach Rd ⓦ bluezonepanama.com. A snug surfers' hangout with a handful of rooms, tiny, shared kitchen and hammock-strung *rancho* overlooking the sea. Rooms are small and dark with squidgy mattresses and mosquito nets. Surf and scuba lessons and rentals can be organized here, and there are reductions for long-term stays. Camping per person US$5, dorm US$10, double US$20

Brisa Mar Near the beach on the main road ☎ 6500 1450,

ⓦ brisamarpanama.com. Six basic en-suite rooms above the *Dive Stop* bar, surprisingly well insulated against the music. Rooms are very clean, spacious and light, with good mattresses, fans or a/c (US$11 extra) and well-screened windows. US$22

Cabañas La Sirena Off the beach road next to *Jammin'*; contact *Rolo's*. Six neat, clean rooms with decent mattresses, pine furniture and a/c, accommodating from one to four people. US$40

Mama Inés Beach road just before Playa del Estero ☎ 6923 6695, ⓦ santacatalinasurfpoint.com. Friendly, family-run hostel set around a small garden on a bluff overlooking the beach. There are a handful of private rooms and two dorms – one with a/c for a couple of extra dollars. Also a couple of tents with mattresses for rent, with just about space to squeeze in your own. Good café on site, too. Camping per person US$5, dorm US$8, double US$8

Oasis Playa del Estero, at the back of the beach ☎ 6588 7077, ⓦ oasissurfcamp.com. A more luxurious option. Clean, cheerfully painted bungalows with fan or a/c (for US$10 more), and private porches right on the beach beneath shady trees. The place also has a decent restaurant, though it charges tourist prices. Camping is possible in their tents, with mattresses supplied (US$4/person), or in your own. Camping per person US$6, bungalows US$40

★ **Rolo's** Just before Santa Catalina beach ☎ 6494 3916, ⓦ rolocabins.net. Spotless cabins with decent pine furniture and a/c, complete with balconies and hammocks, as well as dorms (for 2 to 3 people) with shared kitchen. Boat trips, surf lessons and board and kayak rentals can be arranged. Dorm US$10, double US$40

PARQUE NACIONAL COIBA

ANAM ranger station Isla Coiba ☎ 998 0615. The only accommodation in the national park, offering basic shared cabins with a/c (6–11pm), provided the generator is working. ANAM charges US$15 for the use of the kitchen, and you need to take supplies from Santa Catalina and budget to feed your boatman/guide. Per person US$20

EATING AND DRINKING

Buena Vida *Buena Vida* hotel, on the road into the village. Pleasant terrace café enlivened by orginal mosaics and wrought-ironwork created by the artistic owners. Open for healthy breakfasts – vast fruit platters or a "Greek scramble" (US$4–6) – and lunches, which include interesting salads (US$6–7.50). Wi-fi US$3/hr. Daily 6.30am–2pm.

Dive Stop Near the beach on the main road, under *Brisa Mar*. Dark, unpromising-looking local watering hole with TV that does surprisingly decent burritos, tacos and quesadillas for US$3–6, or *ceviche* for just US$2. Daily 10am–10pm.

Jammin' Off the beach road. The surfers' social hub in a pleasant garden setting, dishing out excellent thin-crust pizzas baked in a wood-fired oven, washed down with an ice-cold beer accompanied by a steady dose of reggae. Wed–Mon from 6.30pm.

Mama Inés Beach road just before Playa del Estero ☏ 6923 6695, ⓦ santacatalinasurfpoint.com. Perched on a bluff with a great sea view, this is an ideal location for lunch or a relaxing drink. Daily 8am–8pm.

El Pacífico Down by Santa Catalina beach, below *Rolo's*. With a partial view of the beach, this is a pleasant spot for breakfast: you can get fluffy eggs or juicy beefsteak with *hojaldres* for around US$3, and inexpensive mains from US$4 later in the day, served with beans and rice or chips and salad. Daily 7am–10pm.

Surfer's Paradise Off the beach road 1.5km from the junction. Boasting Santa Catalina's best viewpoint, from a cliff overlooking the sea, this is the spot to enjoy a sundowner. The amiable owner, Italo, also does a weekly all-you-can-eat Brazilian BBQ, usually on Saturdays (US$15), a must for hard-core carnivores. Daily 8am until late.

La Vieja Panadería Main road, opposite *Buena Vida*. Fantastic bakery-café selling delicious croissants, pains au chocolat, muffins and the like (sold out by 10am in high season) and a range home-made breads and buns. The café does the usual range of breakfasts, and deli-sandwiches and salads for lunch, enhanced by the best espresso coffee in town. Can make packed lunches (US$6.50) for trips to Coiba. Wed–Mon 6.30am–5pm.

Chiriquí Province

West of the Península de Azuero lies the rich agricultural province of **Chiriquí**. Here you'll find **David**, Panama's second city and a crossroads for travellers heading through Central America. North of David, you can escape the flat heat of the city and take refuge up in the cool of the **Chiriquí Highlands**, a beautiful region of cloudforests, fertile valleys and impressive mountain scenery. The varied landscapes all share the same basic characteristics of head-clearing air, cold nights and a deep, relentless green. National parks here – including **Volcán Barú** and **La Amistad** – are well protected, offering wonderful natural encounters and endless hiking opportunities. The substantial town of **Boquete** has many attractions of its own – particularly coffee- and flower-related – but it's also a great base for activities, from rafting to hot-spring soaks. In contrast, the lowlands of the **Golfo de Chiriquí** hold other pleasures: from the laidback beach scene at **Las Lajas**, a broad belt of sand midway between Santiago and David, to **Isla Boca Brava**, further west, which affords access to islands with white-sand beaches and bird-rich mangroves. Western Panama is also home to the country's most numerous indigenous group, the **Ngöbe**, whose women are instantly recognizable by their traditional, brightly coloured, long cotton dresses.

DAVID

Three Spanish settlements were founded in this area in 1602; **DAVID** was the only one to survive repeated attacks from indigenous groups. It developed slowly as a marginal outpost of the Spanish Empire, but in 1732 it was overrun and destroyed by British-backed Miskito groups raiding from Nicaragua. As settlement of Chiriquí increased in the nineteenth century, David began to thrive once again. Today, despite being a busy commercial city – the second largest in the country after Panama City – it retains a sedate provincial atmosphere. Hot and dusty, its unexceptional modern architecture spreads out on a grid, with recent attempts to restore original colonial structures in the east side. While it is not so much a destination in itself, plenty of travellers stop here en route to or from Panama City, Costa Rica, Boquete or Bocas del Toro, and find they enjoy the visit. At Carnaval, of course, things spice up considerably, and David also has a festival all of its own: the **Feria de San José** thunders its way through ten raucous days every March.

WHAT TO SEE AND DO

David centres on **Parque Cervantes**, a fine, tree-shaded place to people-watch with a cup of freshly squeezed sugar-cane juice (*caña*) perked up with tropical lemon, or a dose of coconut water (*agua de pipa*). Three blocks southeast of the park lies the oldest part of the city, where the **crumbling** colonial mansion that was home to successive generations of the distinguished

DAVID

ACCOMMODATION
Bambú Hostel	4
Hostal Chambres en Ville	2
Hostel Kibbutz de Rita	5
Hotel Toledo	1
The Purple House Hostel	3

EATING
Boca Chica	5
Casa Vegetariana	3
El Fogón	2
MultiCafé No. 2	6
Restaurante La Típica	8
El Rincón Libanés	7

DRINKING & NIGHTLIFE
Hypnosis	10
Top Place	1/4/9

7

Obaldía family, and former city museum, has sadly been left to decay. A couple more blocks southeast lies the city's ancient bell tower, and the **cathedral** – worth a peek inside to take in the garish modern murals.

ARRIVAL AND DEPARTURE

By plane The airport is about 5km out of the city; taxis cost around US$4. Air Panama (☎ 316 9000, ⓦ airpanama .com) has daily flights between David and Panama City (4 daily; 1hr) and three flights a week to San José, Costa Rica (Mon, Wed & Fri; 1hr). After a recent multimillion-dollar upgrade, it's expected that the airport will also see direct flights to and from the US.

By bus Buses from Panama City, Almirante, Boquete, Cerro Punta and Paso Canoas, as well as Tracopa international buses from San José, pull in at, and leave from, the terminal on Paseo Estudiante.

Destinations Almirante (take Changuinola-bound buses and ask to be let off at the entrance to Almirante); Boquete (every 20min until 9.45pm; 45min); Cerro Punta (every 15min until 8pm; 2hr); Changuinola (Thurs–Tues every 25min, Wed every 55min, 5am–7pm; 4hr 30min); Las Lajas (every 45min; 1hr 15min); Panama City (roughly hourly 6.30am–8.15pm; 7hr; express 10.45pm & midnight; 6hr); Paso Canoas (every 10min 4.30am–9.30pm; 1hr 20min).

INFORMATION AND TOURS

Tourist information The ATP office (Mon–Fri 9am–4pm; ☎ 775 4120), between C 5 & C 6, is friendly, but you'll get more useful information at the hostels.

Tours Moty at Panatourguide (ⓦ panatourguide.com), based in *Kibbutz de Rita* (see p.576), is trilingual and offers extensive tours of Chiriquí from US$50/person.

ACCOMMODATION

★ **Bambú Hostel** C de la Virgencita, Urbanisación San Mateo Abajo ☎ 730 2961, ⓦ bambuhostel.com. Southwest of the centre, a 5min taxi ride from the bus station, the funky *Bambú* is owned by a fun-loving former rock star. There is a variety of dorm and private accommodation options, including a wooden jungle house in the large garden, which contains fruit trees, a swimming pool and a bar. There's also a shared kitchen, laundry room, free wi-fi and lots of extras. Camping/hammock US$8,

7

dorm <u>US$10</u>, double <u>US$32</u>

Hostal Chambres en Ville Diagonally across from La Universidad Latina ☎775 7428 or ☎6404 0203, ⓦchambresenville.info. A good choice for couples and mature travellers, with cosy en-suite private rooms that are a little dark, but brightened up with colourful murals. The large open-air kitchen leads to a fruit-filled garden, complete with hammocks and a decent-size swimming pool – though the caged toucan might upset some visitors. French spoken. <u>US$28</u>

Hostel Kibbutz de Rita 5min from the centre, Urbanisación Santa Lucia ☎6677 6622, ⓦhostel-kibbutz -de-rita. Run by a friendly Panamanian/Israeli couple with a passion for wildlife, *Rita's* has a few comfortable rooms with shared (US$45) or private bathroom, and a makeshift zoo, with a large variety of rescued birds and monkeys living in the garden. Breakfast included. <u>US$60</u>

Hotel Toledo Av 1 Este between calles D & E Norte ☎774 6732. Friendly, good-value hotel offering spotless en-suite rooms – all with hot water, a/c and cable TV – a stone's throw from the bus terminal. <u>US$33</u>

The Purple House Hostel C Sur at Av 6 Oeste ☎774 4059, ⓦpurplehousehostel.com. David's original hostel, obsessively decorated in shades of lavender. The small dorms and private rooms are clean (with or without a/c) and well kept, with internet, wi-fi and coffee on the house, plus there's a small garden and plenty of information available to browse. Dorm <u>US$10</u>, double <u>US$25</u>

EATING

Calle F Sur has a collection of street-food stalls known as the Mercados de Fritura. They open around 6pm and keep on frying tasty bits and pieces (such as *hojaldres*, or pan-fried bread, stuffed *yuca*, beef and pork) until the early hours.

Boca Chica C A Sur between avenidas 4 & 5 Este. The pleasant fan-ventilated patio is a prime spot to tuck into some tasty, good-value food, including filet mignon for under US$10. Daily 11.30am–10pm.

Casa Vegetariana C Central. A buzzing Chinese veggie pick 'n' mix cafeteria with portions of broccoli, plantain, tortilla or chow mein for US$0.20–0.50. Mon–Sat 6.30am–4pm.

El Fogón Av 2 Oeste ☎775 7091. Considered a treat by locals, with an extensive (and expensive) menu and lively atmosphere. Try the *filete de pescado a la parmesana* (US$11) or the spaghetti Bolognese (US$6.50). Free wi-fi. Daily 11.30am–11pm.

MultiCafé No 2. Next to *Hotel Castilla*. Huge and deservedly popular canteen serving tasty international standards such as lasagne, a range of Mexican-influenced dishes and Panamanian staples for a few dollars. The queues for Sunday breakfast are legendary. Mon–Sat 7am–8pm, Sun until 3pm.

Restaurante La Típica C F Sur. Bright, clean cafeteria-style restaurant, tucked behind a hedge, serving vast portions of *comida típica* and Chinese dishes from US$4. Daily 24hr.

El Rincón Libanés C F Sur. Looking as benevolently on veggies as it does on meat-eaters, this place serves hummus, moussaka and *kibbe*, among other treats. Falafel and pita will set you back US$5, as will a refreshing Lebanese salad. A selection of *meze* for one is US$13.50 – not cheap, but a welcome change from the usual Panamanian food. Daily noon–late.

DRINKING AND NIGHTLIFE

The nightlife scene is constantly changing so ask around on arrival, or just listen for music playing. Wednesdays are generally Ladies' Nights, with free or cheap entry and drinks promotions for women. There are no established gay clubs in the city.

Hypnosis Next to the Crown Casino, opposite Super 99 on C F Sur. This place, largely playing electronica, is currently in favour with David's in-crowd. It doesn't usually get going until around 11pm. Men need to dress smartly. Entry around US$5.

Top Place C F Sur, opposite Super 99 supermarket; C Central & Av Cincuentenario; Av Obaldía, near the bus terminal. Good spots for a beer and a game of pool, although solo women might be overwhelmed by all the testosterone.

DIRECTORY

Car rental Budget (☎721 0845) and Thrifty (☎721 2477), among various other companies, at the airport.

Cinema The screens at the *Gran Hotel Nacional* (C Central) and in the Chiriquí Mall show Hollywood's latest, usually in English with Spanish subtitles.

Consulate Costa Rica, Torre del Banco Universal, C B Norte & Av 1 (Mon–Fri 9am–1pm; ☎774 1923).

Banks Banco Nacional (Mon–Fri 8am–3pm, Sat 9am–noon), Parque Cervantes; Banistmo (Mon–Fri 8am–3.30pm, Sat 9am–noon) is a block away from Parque Cervantes on C Norte. Both have 24hr ATMs.

Health There are two well-regarded private hospitals: Hospital Chiriquí, C Central at Av 3 Oeste, and Mae Lewis Hospital, which is on the Interamericana. Both Super 99 and Romero supermarkets, on C F Sur, have a 24hr pharmacy; Farmacia Revilla (Mon 7am–11pm, Sun 8am–10pm) is on Parque Cervantes.

Immigration C C Sur (Mon–Fri 9am–4pm; ☎775 4515).

Internet There are plenty of internet cafés, including a 24hr one opposite Super 99 on C F Sur and Planet Internet just off Parque Cervantes (daily 8am–11pm).

Laundry C Central at Av 6 Este (daily 8am–6pm); Lavandería Lux, C F Sur at Av 3 Oeste (Mon–Sat 7am–8pm, Sun 9am–1pm).

Post office A block from Parque Cervantes on C Norte (Mon–Fri 7am–5pm, Sat 8am–3pm).

INTO COSTA RICA: PASO CANOAS

You can cross the border into **Costa Rica** at the Paso Canoas crossing, 56km west of David along the Interamericana. After passing through *migración* (7am–11pm) and customs (a formality unless you have anything to declare), you simply walk across the border, though queues for both can be long if international buses are passing through. The banks in David can be reluctant to change dollars to colones so it's best to change them at the border. There are banks (Banco Nacional de Panamá and Banco Nacional de Costa Rica) on both sides of the border that will usually change currency, as well as individual moneychangers.

ISLA BOCA BRAVA

The attractive Pacific island of **ISLA BOCA BRAVA** has two **beaches** – both quite plain – and its patch of rainforest is crisscrossed by paths that are nice to ramble around while you seek out howler monkeys, armadillos and the like. The island's small size ensures that you're not in any danger of getting lost. You can also arrange a **snorkelling** trip to nearby islands with white-sand beaches (US$120/boat).

ARRIVAL AND INFORMATION

By bus and boat Take a David-bound bus from Panama City (hourly; 7hr) or from Santiago (every 1hr 30min; 3hr), alighting at the turn-off ("*el cruce*") for Horconcitos, 36km east of David. From David take a bus to Las Lajas, Tolé or San Félix from the bus terminal. During the day taxis will take you the 14km down to the village of Boca Chica (20min; US$15), where water-taxis will transport you to the island (US$3/person). There is also an unreliable minibus service (no fixed timetable), which passes the junction on its way to and from the village of Remedios. There are three morning departures from Boca Chica, which return to Boca Chica from 12.30pm onwards. Whether arriving by bus or taxi, you'll be dropped at the dock near *Wahoo Willy's*, a bar-restaurant and hotel.
Banks With no ATM in the village you'll need to bring cash with you.

ACCOMMODATION AND EATING

Hotel y Restaurante Boca Brava ☎851 0017, ⓦhotelbocabrava.com. Hammocks, dorm beds and private rooms offering varying degrees of comfort and privacy. The rooms are fine, if a little shabby, with decent mattresses. Best of all there's a great restaurant, offering fabulous views and decent, moderately priced food (mains from US$7). Hammock US$8, dorm US$13, double US$45
Rancho Tres Cuartos 5km from Boca Chica ☎6422 4580. A simple campsite with a few basic cement cabins and breezy bar-restaurant, offering glorious views across to the Chiriquí Highlands. Boat trips and horseriding can also be organized. Camping per person US$5, cabin US$40

PLAYA LAS LAJAS

The impressive 12km band of soft tan sand that is **PLAYA LAS LAJAS** lies 124km west of Santiago and 81km east of David. At weekends and during holiday periods it attracts hordes of city-dwellers desperate to escape the heat, who fill up the handful of hotels and cabañas or camp under thatched shelters lining the back of the beach. At other times, the place is deliciously deserted. There's nothing to do but play in the waves, watch the formations of pelicans and chill out. It's perfect for wild beach camping, and there are a couple of local restaurants. A new **dive centre** offers dive trips to Coiba and Islas Secas (ⓦlaslajasbeachdivers.com) but will take people out **snorkelling** too.

ARRIVAL AND INFORMATION

By bus and taxi Westbound buses to David can drop you at the Las Lajas crossroads ("*el cruce*"), a major pit stop for drivers on a long haul, with a large supermarket. Here taxis hang around during daylight hours to take you to Playa Las Lajas, 7km away, beyond Las Lajas village (US$8). From David there are regular buses to Las Lajas (every 45min; 1hr 15min), though you'll have to pay for a taxi from the village (US$6).
Banks There is no ATM in Las Lajas.

ACCOMMODATION AND EATING

La Spiaza At the T-junction before the beach ☎6620 6431, ⓦlaspiazapanama.com. Rustic cane-and-bamboo lodgings set in a luxuriant garden following eco-friendly principles. The pizza oven is fired up on Saturdays. Dorm US$8, double US$30

BOQUETE

BOQUETE is set in the tranquil Caldera Valley, 1000m above sea level. Some 37km north of David, it is the biggest town in the **Chiriquí Highlands**, and sits smack in the middle of Panama's two coasts. The road to Boquete ends in the highlands, so those wishing to travel on to Bocas del Toro from here must go back to David before catching a bus onwards. The slopes surrounding the town are dotted with coffee plantations, flower gardens and orange groves, and rise to rugged peaks that are usually obscured by thick clouds. When these clouds clear, however – most often in the morning – you can see the imperious peak of **Volcán Barú**, which dominates the town to the northwest. Foreign investment targeting retirees from the US has flooded the area in recent years, seeing the construction of all-inclusive luxury condos and the clearing of cloudforest to make way for golf courses and retirement homes, causing various tensions within the community. For all that, Boquete remains an attractive destination offering a host of activities.

WHAT TO SEE AND DO

The main attraction of Boquete is the opportunities it affords for exploring the surrounding **countryside**. As well as the climb to the summit of the volcano – a strenuous day's walk or a couple of hours on a bone-shaking drive – there are plenty of less demanding walks you can make along the narrow country lanes.

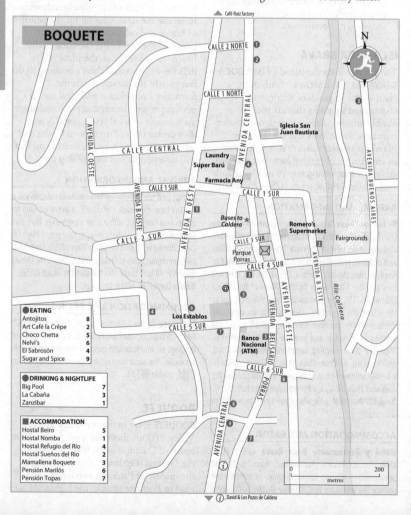

▲ Café Ruiz factory

BOQUETE

N

CALLE 2 NORTE
CALLE 1 NORTE
CALLE CENTRAL
CALLE 1 SUR
CALLE 2 SUR
CALLE 3 SUR
CALLE 4 SUR
CALLE 5 SUR
CALLE 6 SUR

AVENIDA C OESTE
AVENIDA B OESTE
AVENIDA A OESTE
AVENIDA CENTRAL
AVENIDA BUENOS AIRES
AVENIDA A ESTE
AVENIDA B ESTE
AVENIDA BELISARIO PORRAS

Iglesia San Juan Bautista
Laundry
Super Barú
Farmacia Any
Buses to Caldera
Romero's Supermarket
Fairgrounds
Parque Porras
Los Establos
Banco Nacional (ATM)
Río Caldera

EATING
Antojitos 8
Art Café la Crêpe 2
Choco Chetta 5
Nelvi's
El Sabrosón 4
Sugar and Spice 9

DRINKING & NIGHTLIFE
Big Pool 7
La Cabaña 3
Zanzibar 1

ACCOMMODATION
Hostal Beiro 5
Hostal Nomba
Hostal Refugio del Río 4
Hostal Sueños del Río 2
Mamallena Boquete 3
Pensión Marilós 6
Pensión Topas 7

0   200
metres

▼ David & Los Pozos de Caldera

BOQUETE TOURS AND ACTIVITIES

There's a wealth of nature-themed trips and tours to keep you occupied in Boquete; the operators listed below offer some of the most economical and interesting packages in town.

Boquete Mountain Safari Tours Av Central, south of the main square ☎6627 8829 or ☎6742 6614, ⓦ boquetesafari.com. Trips to the Pozos de Caldera, as well as horseback trips, coffee-tasting tours and cloudforest visits, all costing around US$35/person.

Boquete Outdoor Adventures In the Los Establos complex, corner Av Central & C 5 Sur ☎720 2284, ⓦ boqueteoutdooradventures.com. The founder of this outfit has been running whitewater kayak and rafting trips since 1997.

Boquete Tree Trek At the Los Establos complex on the corner of Av Central & C 5 Sur ☎720 1635, ⓦ boquetetreetrek.com. A twelve-line 4hr zipline tour (pick-ups Mon–Sat 8am & 1pm) across the canopy above Boquete (US$65, including transport).

Panama Rock Climbing ☎6764 7918, ⓔboqueteclimbing@yahoo.com. Run by the personable, US-certified bilingual local guide César Meléndez (US$45/person; 3hr).

One of these walks, heading out of Boquete to the north towards the hamlet of Alto Lino, takes you past the **Café Ruiz factory**, a ten-minute stroll from town. Full tours (Mon–Sat 9am & 1pm; 3hr; US$30; ☎720 1000, ⓦcaferuiz.com) explore every step of the coffee-making process; there's also a 45-minute option (8am; US$9) that limits the visit to the roasting plant.

Los Pozos de Caldera

At **Los Pozos de Caldera** (no official hours; US$5 paid to caretaker), the hot springs just outside the nearby town of Caldera, you can alternate between dips in scalding hot water and pulse-quickening splashes in the very cold river.

Guides and tour operators bring groups here (on trips that can be combined with horseriding) from around US$25 per person, but if there's a group of you, it's probably cheaper to hire a taxi from Boquete (US$30 including wait time). Alternatively, take one of the infrequent buses from Boquete to Caldera (7am, 10.45am, 1.15pm, 5pm; last bus back 4pm; 1hr); the springs are about a 45-minute walk south of town. Ask for directions once there.

Watersports

More than 35 rivers in Chiriquí Province are used for **kayaking** and **rafting**, including the Río Caldera, Río Gariché, Río Chiriquí and Río Chiriquí Viejo, with whitewater of every classification. Tour operators in town (see box above) can arrange day-trips and courses for all experience levels, for around US$80–90.

ARRIVAL AND INFORMATION

By bus Buses from David arrive at, and depart from, the main square, Parque Porras (every 25min until 9.45pm; last bus to David 7pm; 45min). Minibuses head up to the surrounding hamlets from the streets around this same square – taking one of these and then walking back to town is a good way to see the nearby countryside.

Tourist office The poorly located tourist office, on the road to David, is in the process of being relocated to the town centre. In the meantime, the privately run Boquete Visitors' Centre (daily 8am–5pm; ☎720 2545), on the same road just before the main drag, has English-speaking staff and can provide you with maps, listings and basic tourist information.

ACCOMMODATION

Accommodation prices often increase at weekends and during holidays, so check in advance.

Hostal Beiro Av Porras ☎6478 4015. Friendly local landlady offering four compact, clean en-suite rooms in an annexe, which share a small patio with a hammock and rocking chair. It's a good budget choice if you want to avoid the hostel scene. <u>US$24</u>

Hostal Nomba Av A Oeste ☎6401 6278, ⓦnomba panama.com. Very popular with backpackers, this no-frills place has two kitchens, shared bathrooms, and English-speaking staff. They can help you arrange a camping trip on the mountain or near the hot springs, and have equipment for rent. Dorm <u>US$9</u>, double <u>US$24</u>

Hostal Refugio del Río Av B Oeste ☎720 2088, ⓦrefugiodelrio.com. Handsome place by a stream, where even the dorm bedding, seemingly of crushed velvet, exceeds expectations. They also have a couple of en-suite rooms and wooden cabañas overlooking the stream. Plus internet, a flash kitchen, a lovely gazebo with barbecue pit, and a jacuzzi. Dorm <u>US$11</u>, double <u>US$28</u>

7

7

Hostal Sueños del Rio Av B Este, on the riverfront, just left of the bridge ☎6601 7771, ⓦboquetesuenosdelrio .com. This cosy if slightly dishevelled little house with rather worn furniture has en-suite dorms and private rooms with good beds. The rough-and-ready patio garden, directly over the river, has hammocks – great for catching mountain breezes. Dorm US$12, double US$28

Mamallena Boquete Parque Porras ☎720 1260, ⓦmamallenaboquete.com. The Boquete branch of *Mamallena* caters to a backpacker crowd, with tidy, small dorms and private rooms in a lovely converted wooden house in the most central location possible. Rates include pancake breakfast. Tours, bike rental (US$10/day) and transfer to Bocas (US$30). Dorm US$11, double US$28

Pensión Marilós Av A Este at C 6 Sur ☎720 1380, ✉marilos66@hotmail.com. This place feels like a home, with a pleasant dining area, intriguing paintings on the walls and tiled corridors plus a free-flying parrot. Rooms with private or shared bathroom are airy, and sheets are crisp. The helpful owner speaks English. US$20

Pensión Topas Av B. Porras ☎720 1005. The private rooms are very reasonable at this Tintin-themed hotel, and there are two smaller, budget rooms with solar-powered shared bathroom (US$24). Camping in the garden is permitted, and you can rent bikes too. The owner speaks English. Camping per tent US$6, double US$37

EATING

Antojitos Av Central. Pleasant and cheerfully decorated open-sided covered patio serving inexpensive (from US$7)

BOQUETE FESTIVALS

January's **Festival de las Flores y del Café** (ⓦferiadeboquete.com) sees Boquete's otherwise tasteful and discreet appreciation of coffee and flowers give way to lusty, noisy rejoicing. Throughout the ten-day celebrations, which coincide with the coffee harvest, the local fairgrounds explode with flower fireworks – you'll never see so many orchids – and the locals plant their own gardens accordingly. Stalls spring up selling food, handicrafts and coffee to the thousands of visitors wandering around, followed everywhere by loud, live music. In the evenings the rum is cracked open and people dance around the fairgrounds until dawn. Book accommodation well in advance and avoid the fairground area if you want to get any sleep.

The fairgrounds bloom again in April for the **orchid festival**, while the annual **jazz festival** in March is also a big crowd-puller (ⓦboquetejazzfestival.com).

★ TREAT YOURSELF

Art Café La Crêpe Av Central at C 2 Norte ☎720 1821 or ☎6769 6090. A wee gem, with brightly painted walls covered in Art Deco posters, offering superb French cuisine. Goat's cheese salad (just under US$10) and trout with almonds (US$15) are just some of the savouries on offer, while desserts include the namesake in a variety of flavours. Reservations are recommended for dinner, especially at weekends. Tues–Sun 12.30–9pm.

TexMex favourites: enchiladas, quesadillas, chilli con carne and plenty of veggie options. Mon–Sat noon–8.30pm, Sun 1–8.30pm.

Choco Chetta Av Central between C 4 & 5 Sur. Great ice cream and tasty snacks, but the signature dish is the indulgent "kebab" (*chetta* being short for *brocheta* – meaning kebab) of Cerro Punta strawberries lathered in melted chocolate. Daily 1–9pm.

Nelvi's Back of Plaza de Los Establos. Ignore the unprepossessing exterior, as *Nelvi's* arguably offers the best inexpensive Panamanian food in town, serving up breakfasts or a full lunch for around US$4. Daily 7.30am–3.30pm.

El Sabrosón Av Central between C Central & C 1 Sur. Plain and airy canteen with good Panamanian food and fish cooked to order. Rice, beans, salad and something meaty from US$3.

Sugar and Spice Av Central & C 7 Sur. This international bakery and café is a major expat meeting place, serving decent, inexpensive breakfasts (US$3–4) and salads and sandwiches using their posh breads, such as sourdough, nine-grain and rye. The host of sweet snacks includes blueberry muffins. Thurs, Fri & Sun–Tues 8am–6pm, Sat 8am–4pm.

DRINKING AND NIGHTLIFE

Big Pool The nicest of several pool halls in Boquete selling cheap beer (US$1.50 for a large Balboa) and emitting a friendly vibe. Daily 4pm until late.

La Cabaña Over the bridge and 200m north of the fairground. Try out the dark recesses of the town's main dance venue, complete with flashing lights, plasma screens and *música varieda*. Fri & Sat from 9pm.

Zanzibar Av Central at C 2 Norte. African-flavoured bar covered in animal prints and tribal artwork, where partying travellers come for cocktails (from US$4) and hookahs (US$10). Open late at weekends, when the place gets packed. Happy hour 6–7pm. Occasional live music on Sat. Mon–Sat 6pm until late.

DIRECTORY

Banks There are several banks with ATMs, including Banco Nacional (Mon–Fri 8am–3pm, Sat 9am–noon) on Av Central, and an ATM in the Los Establos complex.

Bookshop The Book Mark (Tues–Sun 9am–5pm; ☎776 1688), in Dolega on the road from David, carries a huge selection, mainly in English, both to buy (US$3–10) and exchange. Tues–Sun 9am–5pm.

Health 24hr pharmacy in Romero's supermarket behind the main square.

Internet Hastor Computers Internet Café (daily 8am–11pm; US$1/hr) is on the second floor of the building opposite *Pizza La Volcánica* on Av Central. Also has cabins for international calls.

Language schools Boquete is a popular spot to learn Spanish (approx. US$180–190/week for small-group lessons), with two good schools: Habla Ya (ⓦhablayapanama.com) comes highly recommended and is most central while Boquete Spanish by the River (ⓦlanguagecourse.net) is slightly out of town.

Post office On the main square (Mon–Fri 8am–3pm, Sat 8am–12.30pm).

PARQUE NACIONAL VOLCÁN BARÚ

Covering an area of 140 square kilometres, **PARQUE NACIONAL VOLCÁN BARÚ** runs between Boquete across the northern flank of Volcán Barú, Panama's highest peak, and Cerro Punta, Panama's highest major settlement (see p.582).

Sendero Los Quetzales

Hiking the well-known **Sendero Los Quetzales** between Boquete and Cerro Punta (10km; 4–6hr at a moderate pace with stops) can be done in both directions. The trail, which allows you to travel between the Highlands' two principal settlements through stunning scenery, is immensely satisfying, especially as it avoids a lengthy bus journey up the mountain from David and down again. There are **trailheads** at El Respingo, near Cerro Punta, and Alto Chiquero, near Boquete.

Starting from Cerro Punta you get more downhill walking, though this is much more difficult and slippery after rain. From Boquete there is more uphill, though only the last section is very steep – and it is easier to climb than descend after rain. In this direction, you also get into the forest earlier and are therefore more likely to see quetzals.

Note that, due to the large numbers of visitors combined with floods and landslides during the rainy season, the trail has been closed several times over the years. A **guide** is highly recommended, and you shouldn't attempt the hike after very heavy rain since the river you have to ford will likely be impassable.

ARRIVAL AND DEPARTURE

Tours Guides or tour operators can arrange transport, which may be included in the price, to and from the trailheads.

Hiking independently You will need to take a taxi to your start point: US$12–15 to the trailhead at the El Respingo ranger station from Cerro Punta or Guadelupe; US$6–7 from Boquete to the Alto Chiquero ranger station. Whichever direction you walk, you can arrange for pick-ups at the other end in advance. Park entry fees (US$5) are payable at either ranger station.

ACCOMMODATION

Camping You can camp at both the trailhead refuges (see below). There's also a spot midway along the trail, though it has no facilities. US$6

Refugios El Respingo and Alto Chiquero. Each ranger station has a *refugio* with bunk beds, kitchen facilities and water. To avoid having to carry your pack, get *Transportes Ferguson* in either Volcán (on the main street) or Boquete (just off the main street) to transport it by road to your next lodging for US$10. US$15

Volcán Barú

Volcán Barú is Panama's tallest mountain (3475m) and an extinct volcano that dares all visitors to take it on. From the park entrance (US$5), south of Boquete, a 13.5km-long boulder-strewn road, passable only with a customized 4WD, winds up to the cloud-shrouded peak. It's a steep and strenuous four- to eight-hour hike, and another six hours or so back to Boquete.

From the top, the cloud cover breaks every so often to reveal the sight of at least one of the oceans. Your best chance of catching the breathtaking view of both the Pacific and Atlantic is to climb in the dry season (late Dec–April), in the dark (head torch needed), setting off around midnight or 1am, to arrive at the summit at dawn. Although the trail is for the most part clear and not technical, a guide is recommended in case the weather turns foul and foggy, or someone twists their ankle.

7

Take waterproof clothing, dress in layers and wear good hiking shoes.

ARRIVAL AND INFORMATION

Tours Tours can be arranged through several operators or you can hire an independent guide; the most reliable and experienced is Feliciano González (approx US$50/person for four people, including park entry; ☎6624 9940, ✉felicianogonzalez255@hotmail.com). Some hostels provide their own guides for less, but make sure the person is experienced, has a first-aid kit, and is only taking a small group.

Climbing independently If you'd prefer to go it alone, you will need to take a minibus or a taxi (US$6 during the day, up to US$15 at night) from Boquete. This will bring you 6km to the end of the paved road and the park office (US$5 entry, payable on exit if you climb at night). You will also need plenty of food and water.

Camping There is an area close to the summit where you can set up your tent, but it has no facilities. US$6

CERRO PUNTA AND AROUND

Almost 2000m above sea level in a bowl-shaped valley surrounded by densely forested mountains, **CERRO PUNTA** is the highest village in Panama. In the eighty or so years since it was settled, the town's fertile soil has produced some eighty percent of all the vegetables consumed in Panama – there are little patches of cultivated land everywhere you look – although this agricultural boom has not done the surrounding forests any good. The town's altitude gives it a crisp atmosphere, and the taste of the food and the smell of the orchids seem all the better for it.

WHAT TO SEE AND DO

Everything in tiny Cerro Punta is spread out along the main road from David and a side road leading towards **Parque Internacional La Amistad** (see opposite). The scenery, together with the fresh mountain air, makes Cerro Punta a perfect base for **hiking** – the pristine cloudforests of the national parks of Amistad and Volcán Barú are both within easy reach and two of the best places in Central America to catch a glimpse of the elusive **quetzal**, early in the morning in the dry season (Jan–April).

Guadalupe

Local buses run from the centre of Cerro Punta to the nearby village of **GUADALUPE**, famous for its orchids, neat little gardens and its jam – made from local strawberries. Buy some at one of the roadside stalls, or tuck into a bowl of strawberries with *natilla* – a local cream concoction.

Finca Dracula Orchid Farm

You can admire the orchids at **Finca Dracula Orchid Farm** (daily 8am–5pm; US$10, including tour; ☎771 2070), signposted off the road a ten- to fifteen-minute walk beyond *Los Quetzales Lodge and Spa* (see below). The hefty entrance fee is really only worth it in March and April, when most flowers are in bloom.

ARRIVAL AND DEPARTURE

By bus Services to and from David (every 15min; until 8pm; 2hr) stop on the main road in Cerro Punta, which runs through the village, before going on a short loop of even smaller communities, including Guadalupe.

ACCOMMODATION AND EATING

Hotel Cerro Punta Main street, Cerro Punta ☎771 2020. Chalet-style lodging whose appealing rooms have pretty curtains. The windows, however, don't face the mountains, unlike at the hotel's excellent restaurant where the floor-to-ceiling windows allow you to gaze at the view as you eat carefully prepared meals – a plateful of grilled fish with chips and broccoli salad (US$8) is worth every cent. Restaurant daily 8am–8pm. US$31

★ **Hotel Los Quetzales Lodge and Spa** Guadalupe ☎771 2182, ✦losquetzales.com. This hotel accommodates backpackers, honeymooners, Panamanian families and expats, and makes it look easy. Budget travellers will find only the dorms affordable – chunky wood, quality bedding, bedside lights and really hot showers – though there are also plush rooms, suites and cloudforest cabins on offer. All guests have access to the comfy lounge and games room, full of books and sofas, warmed by a log fire, and with table tennis. Activities include spa treatments, cycling, horseriding, and walks through the surrounding cloudforest. The excellent restaurant serves delicious soups with home-made bread (US$4), and pizza and pasta for around US$8, but it's worth splurging on one of their pricier mains, accompanied by more vegetables than you are likely to see in a month elsewhere in Panama. Restaurant daily 6.30am–8pm. Camping per tent US$15, dorm US$18, double US$85

PILA restaurant At the entrance to Parque Internacional La Amistad. Run by a local women's co-operative, the restaurant serves *comida corriente* (US$2.50 for breakfast, US$5 for lunch) such as *arroz de guandú* (rice and beans) with chicken, pork or beef, which you can enjoy on a wooden balcony. Daily 8am–5pm.

PARQUE INTERNACIONAL LA AMISTAD

PARQUE INTERNACIONAL LA AMISTAD covers four thousand square kilometres of rugged, forested mountains teeming with wildlife (including five cat species), on either side of the border with Costa Rica. Although most of Panama's share technically falls in Bocas del Toro, the sliver that is in Chiriquí is best prepared for visitors, with three well-marked **trails**, including a 4km return trip to a 55m waterfall.

ARRIVAL AND INFORMATION

By taxi The park entrance is at Las Nubes. Bus services to Las Nubes are sporadic and unreliable, so you'll probably have to get a taxi (US$7) from Cerro Punta or Guadalupe, or hitch.
Entry fee The US$5 entry fee is payable at the park office, a few hundred metres beyond the entrance.

ACCOMMODATION

Camping A few hundred metres beyond the entrance. You can camp in the clearing by the park office. Per person <u>US$6</u>
Refugio Park office, a few hundred metres beyond the entrance. Bring your own food, warm clothes and, ideally, a sleeping bag, as it gets cold at night – they have some extra bedding, though. <u>US$15</u>

Bocas del Toro

Isolated on the Costa Rican border between the Caribbean and the forested slopes of the Cordillera Talamanca, **Bocas del Toro** ("mouths of the bull") is one of the most beautiful areas in Panama. It's also one of the most remote – the mainland portion of the province is connected to the rest of Panama by a single road, and the island chain offshore requires a ferry ride to reach.

Despite recent rapid development (see box below), the archipelago remains home to an **ecosystem** so complex and well preserved that it has been described by biologists as "the Galápagos of the twenty-first century". This, and the equally unusual diversity of the human population – Ngöbe-Buglé, Naso and Bribrí populate the mainland, while the islands are dominated by the descendants of **West Indian** migrants who still speak Guari-Guari, an English patois embellished with Spanish and Ngobere – make Bocas a fascinating area to visit.

ALMIRANTE

From the village of Chiriquí, 14km east of David on the Interamericana, a spectacular road crosses the continental divide, passes over the Fortuna hydroelectric dam, through the pristine forests that protect its watershed and the small town of **Chiriquí Grande**, then, 50km on, into **ALMIRANTE**.

7

BOCAS DEL TORO HISTORY

Christopher Columbus first explored the coast of Bocas del Toro in 1502 in the search for a route to Asia; later, during the colonial era, European pirates often sheltered in the calm waters of the archipelago. By the nineteenth century, English ships from Jamaica were visiting the coast frequently, but it wasn't until 1826 that West Indian immigrants founded the town of Bocas del Toro, still the province's largest settlement.

The arrival of the United Fruit **banana plantations** in the late 1800s gave the islands a measure of prosperity; by 1895 bananas from Bocas accounted for more than half of Panama's export earnings, and Bocas Town boasted five foreign consulates and three English-language newspapers. Early in the twentieth century, however, banana crops were repeatedly devastated by disease, causing the archipelago's economy to suffer.

In recent years, **tourism** and real estate speculation have come to the economic forefront in Bocas. Foreign investors have bought huge portions of the archipelago in order to develop luxury resorts and holiday homes. While this boom has enhanced the region's wealth, generating employment and income for locals, much concern still exists over how economically and environmentally sustainable it really is.

BOCAS DEL TORO

7

kilometres
0   25

N

CARIBBEAN SEA

Golfo de
los Mosquitos

Isla Escudo
de Veraguas

Isla
de Veraguas

VERAGUAS

Península
Valiente

Río Manatí

CORDILLERA CENTRAL

BOCAS DEL TORO

Archipiélago de Bocas del Toro

Parque Nacional
Marino Isla
Bastimentos

Isla Bastimentos

Cayos
Zapatillas

I. Cayo
Agua

Isla
Popa

Laguna de
Chiriquí

Chiriquí
Grande

Lago
Fortuna

**Lost &
Found**

David & Panama City

Swan Cay

Isla Colón

Bastimentos

Isla
Solarte

Bocas
del Toro

Isla
Cristóbal

Isla Carenero

Almirante

Río Changuinola

PALO SECO
FOREST
RESERVE

Boquete

David

David

Guadalupe
Cerro Punta

Volcán Barú
(3475m)

Parque Nacional
Volcán Barú

Volcán

CHIRIQUÍ

Humedales de
San San Pond Sak

Guabito

Sixaola

Changuinola

Río San San

Río Teribe

Río San San

Puerto Limón

PARQUE
INTERNACIONAL
LA AMISTAD

Co. Fábrega
(3336m)

Co. Itamut
(3279m)

Co. Echandi
(3163m)

CORDILLERA DE TALAMANCA

COSTA
RICA

Río Sereno

Paso
Canoas

San José

This ramshackle port town of rusting tin-roofed houses, propped up on stilts over the calm waters of the Caribbean, is the place to catch a water-taxi to the Bocas del Toro archipelago.

ARRIVAL AND DEPARTURE

By bus Long-distance buses to and from Panama City and Changuinola (see box, p.586), and David and Changuinola (5am–7pm Thurs–Tues every 25min, Wed every 55min; 4hr 30min), drop off and pick up passengers at "La Y" on the main coastal road, from where it's a 5min taxi ride or about a 15min walk to the dock. Local buses shuttle to and from Changuinola (every 20min 6am–10pm; 30min), and head for the bus terminal in town, but ask to get off before then at the "*parada de las lanchas*".

By water-taxi to Bocas Touts from the water-taxi companies in Almirante will lead you to one of three docks – the services at each are exactly the same (every 30min 6am–6 or 6.30pm; 30min; US$4), though you should check which company is leaving first before you buy a ticket.

By car ferry to Bocas There's a slow and unreliable car ferry to Bocas from the car ferry dock (Tues–Sun 8am; 1hr; motorbikes US$10; bicycles US$3).

CHANGUINOLA

Some 16km from the border and 29km west of Almirante through seemingly endless banana plantations, **CHANGUINOLA** is a typically hot and uninteresting banana town where almost everyone works for the Bocas Fruit Company ("the Company", successor to United Fruit and Chiquita). Only travellers heading to or from the Costa Rica border come here, though the charming **San San Pond Sak Wetlands** are reason enough to linger for a night.

Humedales de San San Pond Sak

Just 7km north of Changuinola lie the wildlife-rich **Humedales de San San Pond Sak** (San San Pond Sak Wetlands). An early morning boat trip downriver to the lagoon offers excellent birdwatching – parrots, hawks and herons abound – as well as the chance to see sloths and snakes. Even more enticing is the opportunity to catch sight of the elusive **West Indian manatee**, or sea cow. This involves a potentially lengthy stakeout on a viewing platform while being eaten alive by sandflies, but the sight of this shy and extraordinary-looking beast chomping away at banana leaves is well worth the wait. To arrange an early morning boat trip (around US$70/ boat), contact Erick Gabarrete of AAMVECONA (in Spanish; ☏6524 3399, ✉peladillo0282@hotmail.com), or ask at the ANAM office in Changuinola (two blocks from the main street).

ARRIVAL AND DEPARTURE

By bus Buses arrive at and depart from the main bus terminal on the main street in the town centre.
Destinatons Almirante (every 20min 6am–10pm; 30min); David (Thurs–Tues every 25min, Wed every 55min, 5am–7pm; 4hr 30min); Guabito (every 20min 5.30am–7pm; 30min); Panama City (see box, p.586); San José, Costa Rica (daily, 10am; 8hr).

ACCOMMODATION AND EATING

Golden Sahara Main street, 100m north of Terminal Urraca ☏758 7478. Your best bet should you need to spend the night here – not an enviable prospect – with decent, inexpensive rooms. **US$32**

Restaurante La Fortuna Main street, 100m north of Terminal Urraca, next door to *Golden Sahara*. Good Chinese

---

LOST AND FOUND: A HOSTEL WITH A DIFFERENCE

The Lost and Found On the road between David and Changuinola ☏6432 8182, ⊕lostandfoundlodge.com. A wonderful eco-friendly lodge set-up high in the cloudforest on the boundary of the La Fortuna reserve. Guests hang out on the deck, where meals are taken – the coffee you drink at breakfast is processed from berries growing a few metres away – and the observation platform sees nightly visits from local animals. Chilly weather is countered with fleece blankets, luxurious hot-water showers with serene forest views, and beer-and-foosball sessions in the bar. Wild, mostly unmarked trails offer potential wildlife encounters and can be explored at your leisure, or on one of the lodge's many tours (most US$12–25). Pick-ups from David, Boquete and Almirante can be arranged; the website details how to get here by public transport. Reductions for stays of several nights. Dorm **US$13**, double **US$33**

7

TRAVEL BETWEEN BOCAS DEL TORO AND PANAMA CITY

The overnight **bus route** from Changuinola to Almirante and Panama City is served by one company, TRANCEIBOSA (☎303 6326 in Panama City; ☎758 8455 in Changuinola; ☎758 3278 in Almirante; ☎757 9493 in Bocas), whose main office is in the Terminal Urraca in Changuinola, 200m north of the main bus terminal. Buses from Changuinola (daily 7.30am & 6pm) stop at "La Y" in Almirante at roughly 8.15am and 6.45pm. These are sometimes overbooked, and to take on the additional passenger load, TRANCEIBOSA contracts with local less comfortable **minibuses**, charging passengers the same fee they would pay for a larger bus. Buy tickets as early as possible and check that you have been assigned a seat on the full-size bus. Bocas Marine Tours (see p.588) also sells tickets for this journey. Note that the a/c on these long-distance buses is usually glacial, so wrap up warmly.

---

food in a handy location (with a/c) next to the town's best accommodation option. Daily 11.30am–10pm.

BOCAS TOWN

On the southeastern tip of Isla Colón, the provincial capital of Bocas del Toro, otherwise known as **BOCAS TOWN**, is the easiest base from which to explore the islands, beaches and reefs of the archipelago. The town, connected to the rest of the island by a narrow causeway, is busy and bustling, especially during the high season (Dec–April), when it explodes with tourists and backpackers. Rickety wooden buildings painted in cheerful colours and a friendly and laidback, mostly English-speaking population welcome you to the island's casual mêlée. The palm-fringed Caribbean beaches, decent waves, and a buzzing young nightlife have made these islands a must-see for partying backpackers.

WHAT TO SEE AND DO

Bocas Town offers a variety of aquatic activities, and an increasing number of operators (see box, p.588) offering land-based activities such as cycling, horseriding, yoga and learning Spanish.

Surfing

Surfing is the most popular activity in the area, with an abundance of spots for both beginners and experts, with various surf schools (see box, p.591) offering **lessons**, as well as board rental.

Boat tours

Endless possibilities exist for **boat excursions**. The three most common trips, sold by most tour operators for the same price (around US$20–25/person), take in a combination of **wildlife viewing** – such as seeking out the shy bottlenose dolphins in Dolphin Bay, or viewing hundreds of seabirds wheeling round

---

INTO COSTA RICA: GUABITO

From Changuinola the road runs 16km to the border with Costa Rica at **Guabito–Sixaola**, where there's little more than a few shops selling consumer goods to Costa Rican day-trippers. Local buses from Changuinola bus station can take you to Guabito (see box, p.143), or there are *colectivos* and taxis (US$7).

It's a short walk from the *migración* (daily 8am–6pm) in Guabito across a bridge to Costa Rica, where you can change currency in the town of Sixaola (see box, p.143). Note that **time changes** (shifting 1hr back) when you cross the border to Costa Rica. You can catch a bus to San José from the border (3 daily at 8am, 10am & 3pm; 6hr) or, if you just don't want to leave that Caribbean vibe behind, stop for a while in Puerto Viejo de Talamanca (see p.139) in northeastern Costa Rica (buses hourly 6am–5pm; 4hr). Note that when entering either Panama or Costa Rica, you may be asked to show proof of onward travel (such as a return air ticket). If you can't, you may be made to buy a US$13 return bus ticket.

Arriving in Guabito from Costa Rica, you can catch the bus to Changuinola until 7pm, or take a taxi (US$10 private; US$1.50 shared). Taxis also run directly to Almirante (US$25), where you can catch a water-taxi to Bocas.

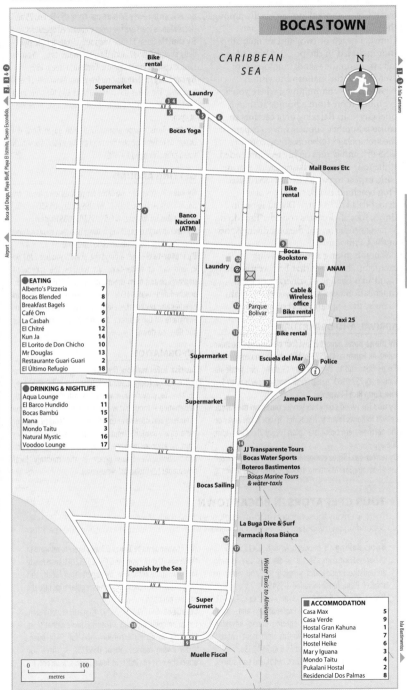

BOCAS TOWN

CARIBBEAN SEA

N

Bike rental

Supermarket

AV H

Laundry

AV G

Bocas Yoga

AV F

Mail Boxes Etc

Bike rental

Banco Nacional (ATM)

AV E

Bocas Bookstore

ANAM

Laundry

Cable & Wireless office
Bike rental

AV CENTRAL

Parque Bolívar

Bike rental

Taxi 25

EATING

Alberto's Pizzeria	7
Bocas Blended	8
Breakfast Bagels	4
Café Om	9
La Casbah	6
El Chitré	12
Kun Ja	14
El Lorito de Don Chicho	10
Mr Douglas	13
Restaurante Guari Guari	2
El Último Refugio	18

DRINKING & NIGHTLIFE

Aqua Lounge	1
El Barco Hundido	11
Bocas Bambú	15
Mana	5
Mondo Taitu	3
Natural Mystic	16
Voodoo Lounge	17

Supermarket

Escuela del Mar

Police

AV D

Supermarket

Jampan Tours

AV C

JJ Transparente Tours
Bocas Water Sports
Boteros Bastimentos
Bocas Marine Tours & water-taxis

Bocas Sailing

La Buga Dive & Surf

Farmacia Rosa Bianca

AV B

Water Taxis to Almirante

Spanish by the Sea

AV A

Super Gourmet

ACCOMMODATION

Casa Max	5
Casa Verde	9
Hostal Gran Kahuna	1
Hostal Hansi	7
Hostel Heike	6
Mar y Iguana	3
Mondo Taitu	4
Pukalani Hostal	2
Residencial Dos Palmas	8

AV SUR

Muelle Fiscal

0   100
metres

Almirante

Boca del Drago, Playa Bluff, Playa El Istmito, Tesoro Escondido,

Airport

& Isla Carenero

Isla Bastimentos

7

7

Swan Cay – **snorkelling**, especially among the rainbow-coloured coral of Cayo Crawl, a beach or two, and a lunch stop (not included in the price). Other trips take you into the islands' rainforests, or even over to the mainland to visit Ngöbe-Buglé communities, where you'll get much more from a homestay than a brief day visit. Relaxing on a **catamaran cruise** is another popular way to experience the archipelago (w bocassailing.com; US$45), and comes highly recommended. If the tour enters the Bastimentos marine park, expect to pay an extra US$10. Red Frog beach on Isla Bastimentos also demands a US$3 entry. **Diving** is big in Bocas, too; aficionados consider Escudo de Veraguas to be one of the best diving spots in the Caribbean.

When booking a tour or diving excursion, be aware that bad weather may result in a change of itinerary or even cancellation, and that beyond the main islands, the sea can get very rough.

ARRIVAL AND DEPARTURE

By plane Bocas airport is just four blocks from the main street. Air Panama (☎ 757 9841, w airpanama.com) offers flights from and to Panama City (3 daily; 1hr) while Air Nature (☎ 757 9963, w natureair.com) connects with San José, Costa Rica (4 weekly).

By bus The island's only bus service runs from the Parque Bolívar in Bocas Town to Bocas del Drago, 17km away on the northwestern tip of Isla Colón (every 2hr 7am–4pm; 30min).

By water-taxi Three companies run water-taxis between the Almirante Taxi Marítimo dock and their own jetties in Bocas Town (all every 30min 6am–6pm; US$4): Taxi 25 and Bocas Marine Tours are the more established operators.

By shuttle Bocas Marine Tours sells tickets for the twice-daily shuttle (US$32, including the water-taxi; w caribe shuttle.com) to Puerto Viejo in Costa Rica (see p.139).

By car ferry The lethargic car ferry from Almirante (Tues–Sun 8am; 1hr; bikes US$3, motorbikes US$10) pulls in at the southern end of the main street, returning to Almirante at 4pm.

By taxi Taxis charge around US$12 to go to Boca del Drago, or to head up the dirt road to Playa Bluff, for which you'll probably need a 4WD.

GETTING AROUND

By bike Bicycles are available for rent all over town; try Bocas Bikes, Av G at C 3 (US$1/hr, US$10/day, US$50/week), or IXA bikes on Av Norte & C 5 (US$2/hr, US$10/day).

By taxi Though everything in town is within easy walking distance, taxis are available (US$1/person).

By water-taxi To get around the islands, you need to hop in and out of water-taxis. As well as the scheduled transfers to and from the mainland and Red Frog Beach, unscheduled water-taxis to the various islands and beaches also dock at these jetties. Boats can be hailed from anywhere on the seafront. Just stand at the end of a pier and flag one down.

INFORMATION

Tourist information The ATP office, C 1 next to the police station (daily 9.30am–5.30pm; ☎ 757 9642), may be able to provide a map but is otherwise short on information – though it was being renovated at the time of writing and does have toilet facilities. Detailed maps of the area are available from most shops for US$4; w bocas .com is a good resource for hotel and tour operator information. *The Bocas Breeze* is the monthly local newspaper (w thebocasbreeze.com).

TOUR OPERATORS IN BOCAS TOWN

There are many tour operators in town – below is just a small selection. Tours cost US$20–30, depending on the distance to destinations and gear rental. Check whether costs include park fees.

Bocas Sailing C 3 between Av B & C ☎ 757 9710, w bocassailing.com. Spend a glorious day gliding around the islands and slipping into the water to snorkel. Picnic lunch included. US$45.

Bocas Water Sports C 3 at Av A ☎ 757 9541, w bocaswatersports.com. Professional and well-established US-run outfit offering diving, kayaking and snorkelling outings as well as equipment rental.

La Buga Dive & Surf C3 at Av B ☎ 757 9534. Friendly and fun PADI-certified outfit and surf school. Also rents out SUPs and kayaks.

J&J Transparente Tours C 3, but likely to relocate to the renovated El Pirata ☎ 6731 2525, e transparente tours@hotmail.com. Run by experienced locals, this long-established company offers regular trips into the marine park and more.

Starfleet C 1 ☎ 757 9630, w starfleetscuba.com. Canadian company with a friendly, professional team focusing on diving excursions and full PADI open-water diving courses (about US$225). Starfleet also offers the only spa in Bocas Town (high season only).

ACCOMMODATION

There's a good range of accommodation in Bocas, though it can be nearly impossible to find a room during high season without reservations. Things also fill up quickly on weekends and holidays, so it's a good idea to book accommodation in advance where you can, though many budget places don't accept reservations, in which case try to arrive by mid-morning to ensure you get a bed. Hot water is not usually provided at the budget hotels and the area suffers periodically from water shortages.

Casa Max Av G between C 4 & C 5 ☎ 757 9120, ✉ casa1max@hotmail.com. The clean, cheerfully painted en-suite rooms (with fan or a/c) have shared balconies and comfortable beds with fresh cotton sheets, giving this place a homey feel. There's a pleasant patio, a good restaurant and sound advice from the Dutch owners. The noise from *Mondo Taitu* parties across the road is the main downside. US$38

Casa Verde Av Sur & C 4 ☎ 6633 8050, ✇ casaverdebocas .com. The only seafront hostel in Bocas Town in a charming converted traditional wooden building with great bar and hammock deck overlooking the water. Superior dorms with single and double bunks, a/c and mini-fridges plus a handful of private rooms with shared showers. Dorm US$13, double US$35

★ **Hostal Gran Kahuna** C 3 at Av B, Isla Carenero ☎ 757 9038, ✇ grankahunabocas.com. Right on the beach, this is a solid budget option, attempting green practices, with four three-bed dorms with lockers and surf-board storage space, and two private en-suite rooms with a/c and great mattresses. Nice garden and social area to chill in, with comfy sofas and hammocks facing the sea. Also a moderately priced bar-restaurant. Dorm US$12, double US$45

★ **Hostal Hansi** C 2 at Av D ☎ 757 9085, ✇ hostalhansi .bocas.com. A tight German-run ship, *Hansi* is named after the owners' former friendly feline. The simple, immaculate double and single rooms (from US$11) – its speciality – with private and shared bathrooms, are spotlessly clean and good value. There's a shared kitchen. US$25

Hostel Heike C 3 between Av Central & Av E ☎ 757 9708, ✇ hostelheike.com. Dorms with shared clean, hot-water bathrooms, and small private rooms. There's also a communal kitchen, a great rooftop terrace, and free internet, wi-fi and even free beginners' Spanish lessons. Pancake breakfast included. Dorm US$10, double US$22

Mar y Iguana Feria del Mar ☎ 6047 2413, ✇ mareiguana hostel.com. A stone's throw from the beach, this cosy hostel north of Bocas Town comprises seven small private rooms (with shared or en-suite bathroom) and one dorm, all with a/c, set around a small garden – where there's room for a few tents – with a two-tier *rancho* for reading and relaxing and a good, moderately priced bar-restaurant. Camping per person US$7, dorm US$11, double US$35

Mondo Taitu Av G between C 4 & C 5 ☎ 757 9425, ✇ mondotaitu.com. The cheap booze still flows and the parties still throb through the night, but this pioneering surfer hostel/party bar – now with new owners – is showing its age. All rooms and dorms (with fan or, for a couple of dollars extra, a/c) share hot-water bathrooms, plus there's a communal kitchen and a legendary, tiny cocktail bar and lots of extras. Dorm US$11, double US$28

Pukalani Hostal 5km north of Bocas Town, close to Playa Paunch ☎ 6949 6465, ✇ pukalanihostalpanama.com. With unexceptional private rooms and four dorms, this hotel/ hostel offers the only cheap lodging on the beach – though you'll find little in the way of sand. There's a nice open bar-lounge area, a pool and *rancho* over the water which houses a bar and pool table. The bar-restaurant serves breakfast and US-style comfort food, plus there's free kayak rental, cheap bike rental and a free shuttle service into town three times a day. Dorm US$15, double US$66

Residencial Dos Palmas Av Sur & C 5 ☎ 757 9906. Bocatoreño-owned establishment offering a handful of well-kept, compact rooms each with fan, small private bathroom and electric hot-water shower, at the quieter southern tip of town. There's also a reading deck over the water. Very good value. US$28

EATING

Bocas has an excellent range of restaurants, with several international options, though consistency is an issue and prices have soared in the last few years. Lobster, conch, octopus and other locally caught specialities taste particularly delicious in local coconut milk and Caribbean spice preparations, though you should not be offered them during the off season (March–June). Tap water is not drinkable, so don't expect free iced water. Opening hours can be erratic. A large range of groceries is available at supermarkets (see p.591), though prices are higher than on the mainland.

Alberto's Pizzeria *Hotel Kala Luna*, C 5 at Av E–F ☎ 757 9066. This spacious, open-fronted restaurant serves "the best pizza in Bocas" (US$8–12) and pasta dishes. Since the place lacks ambience, order a takeaway and save yourself the 10 percent service charge. Thurs–Tues 5–11pm.

★ **Bocas Blended** C 1 at Av E, by Tropical Markets. Unmistakeable sky-blue converted bus dishing up tasty breakfasts and delectable salads and wraps filled with fresh ingredients at modest prices (US$5–7), as well as smoothies and irresistible home-made flapjacks. You can take away or "eat in", and take advantage of "wrappy hour" and excellent-value lunch combos. The best table in the house is on the bus roof, where your food is served via a dumb waiter. Unforgettable. Sun–Fri 8am–10pm.

Breakfast Bagels *Mana*, Av G between C 4 & 5, next to *Casa Max*. Breakfast bagel joint, with a large variety, from US$3.50. Mon–Sat 8am–1pm.

7

7

Café Om Av E at C 2. The Canadian/Indian owner draws from traditional family recipes, dishing up excellent curries with rice, naan and home-made chutney (from US$9). Mon–Fri 5.30–10pm.

La Casbah Av H at C 4 ☎ 6477 4727. Cosy restaurant with indoor and outdoor seating serving nicely presented Mediterranean cuisine; try the "La Casbah" salad of feta cheese, organic greens and grilled Mediterranean veg for around US$10, or the Moroccan fish salad (US$12). Tues–Sat 6–10pm.

El Chitré C 3 & Av Central. Locals trust this small cafeteria-style restaurant and so should you. *Comida típica* (from around US$2.50 for breakfast, US$4.50 for lunch or dinner) is eaten on a small patio. Daily 6am–9pm.

Kun Ja C 3 at Av C. This Chinese restaurant, with indoor and waterfront seating, is one of the friendliest budget spots in town. It serves large portions of tasty meat and seafood dishes with fried rice, chow mein or chop suey (US$6). Takeaway available. Wed–Mon noon–11pm.

El Lorito de Don Chicho C 3 at Av E, across from Parque Bolívar. *Lorito* serves tasty, inexpensive, self-service breakfast and à la carte Panamanian lunch and dinner – locals seldom eat anywhere else. An *almuerzo* is a mere US$3.60, or you can tuck into a plate of breaded shrimps or fish fillet with rice and a smidgen of salad for US$6. Mon–Sat 6.30am–10pm.

Mr Douglas C 3 at Av Central, across from Parque Bolívar. Apparently inspired by well-known US fast-food chains, *Mr Douglas* has just about every kind of greasy food you can imagine at rock-bottom prices. Burger and fries US$3. Daily 6am–midnight.

El Último Refugio Just off C 3 at Av Sur ☎ 6726 9851, ⓦ ultimorefugio.com. The building is rather flimsy, but it houses the only restaurant in town where you can watch the sun set over the mainland from the water's edge. Run by experienced gringos, this spot offers succulent mains

---

★ **TREAT YOURSELF**

Restaurante Guari Guari 2km north of town on the isthmus ☎ 6575 5513. One of the top spots to eat in all of Panama, and one place where you really have to make a reservation as there are only six patio tables within earshot of waves pounding on the beach, proving an intimate yet supremely relaxed dining experience. The daily-changing US$23 prix-fixe menu (drinks extra) gets you four mouthwatering appetizers, a fabulous main and a scrumptious dessert, beautifully prepared and served by the Spanish/German owners. With advance notice, they are happy to tweak the menu for any dietary requirements. Thurs–Mon dinner only.

(US$10–13) and delicious desserts with daily specials. Mon–Fri 6–10pm.

DRINKING AND NIGHTLIFE

Several restaurants double as music and drinking venues in the evening, plus there are a few good bars where you can relax with a cold Balboa Ice or cocktail.

★ **Aqua Lounge** Isla Carenero ⓦ bocasaqualounge .info. Just across the water from Bocas Town, a US$1 boat ride away, *Aqua Lounge* really gets going on ladies' nights (Wed & Sat), with free drinks until midnight for women, a big, starlit dance floor and a water trampoline and diving board on which to cool your heels. This Peter Pan playground hosts legendary parties, where the sandflies and mosquitoes are the only unwanted guests – come prepared with plenty of repellent. Occasional live bands. Daily 2–10pm, later on Wed & Sat.

El Barco Hundido C 1, beside the Cable & Wireless office. Locally known as the "Wreck Deck", this spot used to be the most popular hangout for locals, tourists and surfers, who came here to drink cold beer (US$2) until the early hours. Though no longer the hottest joint in town, it's still a top spot, with regular DJs playing a mix of modern r'n'b, '80s pop and the ubiquitous Bob Marley. Plus it stays open later than anywhere else. Daily 7pm–3/4am.

Bocas Bambú C 3 & Av C. A humming spot with a striking canvas of vast tent-awnings supported by thick bamboo poles, a large video screen showing surfing and pop videos, and probably the longest bar in Panama. Plus affordable daily meal specials (US$7–9), live reggae 8pm every Sat and other occasional live acts. Daily 6.30–11pm.

Mana Av G at C 4. A buzzing plant-filled patio serving reasonably priced pizzas (most US$8–9), burgers and the like, plus cheap booze and plenty of specials, and free wi-fi. Daily 1–11pm.

Mondo Taitu Av G. With all kinds of cheap, creative cocktails and drink specials, there's a frat-house-style theme party here most nights of the week. The actual bar is so small the action soon spills out into the street. Daily 7pm–late.

Natural Mystic C 3, opposite *Iguana's*. Forget the food (overpriced and nothing to write home about), this is also a good spot to warm up for the night, with happy-hour beers at US$1, and a well-positioned balcony from which you can observe the flow of partygoers on the main street below. Daily 5–10pm.

Voodoo Lounge C 3. At the southern tip of the street, come here for a local experience, with cheap drinks, a dark deck, monster speakers and dancing at weekends. Also occasional live music. Daily noon–late.

DIRECTORY

Bank Banco Nacional, C 4 (Mon–Fri 8am–3pm, Sat 9am–noon), has a 24hr ATM.

Books Bocas Bookstore, below *Café Om* on Av E & C 2, has a good selection of books in English (US$3–10), and will also buy used books. It is also a popular expat bar. Daily noon–late.

Health The island's one hospital, Av G & C 10 (☎757 9201), has 24hr emergency services. Rosa Blanca Pharmacy is on C 3 near Av A.

Internet Don Chicho Internet, C 3 (daily 7am–11pm; US$2/hr).

Language schools Spanish by the Sea, Av A at C 4 (☎757 9518, ⓦspanishbythesea.com). One of three lively and relaxed schools for travellers run by a hip Dutch/Tico family. Affordable lesson plans for extended stays (US$195/week).

Laundry At the back of a slim alley behind *El Lorito de Don Chicho* (Mon–Sat 8am–6pm; US$4/bag).

Post office The main post office is on Av E (Mon–Fri 8am–4pm, Sat 8am–noon). There's also Mail Boxes Etc., Av F (Mon–Fri 8am–5pm, Sat 8.30am–noon).

Supermarkets There are several supermarkets open from dawn until very late. Isla Colón Supermercado, C 3 & Av D, is one of the biggest. Super Gourmet (Mon–Sat 9am–7pm), Av A & C 3, carries hard-to-find items, has a decent deli counter, and is a good option for vegetarians.

AROUND BOCAS TOWN

The islands, cayes and mainland waterways surrounding Bocas Town offer wide-ranging opportunities for relaxing on pristine beaches, visiting Ngöbe-Buglé villages and diving near unspoilt coral reefs. A quick bus or taxi ride away are the beaches of the rest of **Isla Colón**, while nearby islas Carenero and Bastimentos are favoured by visiting surfers. Most visitors make a point of exploring the **Parque Nacional Marino Isla Bastimentos**, a renowned marine park that stretches across a series of islands in the archipelago.

Playa Bluff

Some twenty minutes from Bocas Town by taxi, **PLAYA BLUFF** sees some of the heaviest action at the height of the Bocas surf season. It's also a good place to observe nesting **sea turtles** (May–Sept); contact the ANABOCA office, next to ANAM (ⓦanaboca.org), to organize a visit. There are several places to stay and eat here, and the distance from town results in a more tranquil pace that is often preferred by couples and more mature travellers.

As taxis aren't plentiful and car rental is not possible, the easiest way to get around Playa Bluff is to rent a bicycle in Bocas Town (see p.588).

Boca del Drago

A popular excursion – by boat, bike or bus – leads 15km across the island to **Boca del Drago**, on the northwest tip. The main draw is nearby **Playa Estrella** (Starfish Beach), which has precious little sand but its translucent shallows are filled with its namesake, which you should be careful not to touch. Avoid the weekend crowds if possible.

ARRIVAL AND DEPARTURE

By bus A local bus shuttles back and forth from the park in Bocas Town to Boca del Drago (every 2hr; 45min).

EATING

Yarisnori Playa Estrella ☎ 6613 1934. Round off the visit with a tasty and leisurely seafood lunch (around US$9) here or at one of the other informal restaurants on the beach. Closed Tues.

Isla Carenero

Just 200m across the water from Bocas Town, tiny **Isla Carenero** is beginning to receive more visitors thanks to hostel and adult playground *Aqua Lounge* (see p.590), and the most accessible and consistent surf break in the archipelago at Punta Carenero. On the westward side of the island, a narrow concrete path goes as far as the small marina; the island is rather dingy here, and wooden houses on stilts stand over the partially waterlogged and heavily littered ground. Quieter than Bocas Town, the island has its charms, but these may be outweighed by the hefty populations of sandflies and mosquitoes that plague beachgoers.

Bibi's restaurant (see below) houses the *Escuela del Mar* (☎757 9137 or ☎6785 7984), offering **snorkel and kayak rental**, surfboard and SUP (Stand Up Paddle board) rentals and lessons, as well as surfboard repairs. The surf school also has an office in Bocas Town on C 1 across from the tourist office.

ARRIVAL AND DEPARTURE

By water-taxi To get to the island, catch a water-taxi (US$1) from the northern end of Bocas Town.

EATING

Bibi's on the Beach Great seafood (US$7–12) at this place looking out over the water at a popular beginners' surf spot; the large balcony provides the perfect refuge from the pestering insects on shore.

Isla Bastimentos

Outside the national marine park on the western tip of **Isla Bastimentos**, the small Afro-Antillano fishing community of Old

Bank, or **BASTIMENTOS**, is not really set up for mass tourism, though there are several budget lodgings and places to eat. Be sure to bring cash, though, as there's no bank or ATM on the island.

An undulating concrete path acts as the community's main thoroughfare, snaking its way between the coastline and a steep, green hillside dotted with wooden stilt houses. A jungle path, occasionally impassable after heavy rains, leads to several pristine **beaches** twenty minutes away on the other side of the island. Periodically there have been muggings on this trail so enquire about the current situation before setting out.

The future of this spectacular island remains shaky, as locals and environmental enthusiasts continue to fight with potential developers – building projects, unless very carefully planned and executed, will almost certainly cause irreparable damage to the fragile ecosystem.

ARRIVAL AND DEPARTURE

By boat Frequent boats run to and from the Bastimentos water-taxi terminal at the southern end of Bocas Town (US$2.50), and arrive at the main dock; Jampan tours also runs regular water-taxis to the dock at Red Frog Beach (US$4 single, US$7 return) on a fixed timetable. It's then a 10min walk or brief truck ride on a dirt road across private land (US$3) to the beach.

ACCOMMODATION AND EATING

Beverly's Hill Left from the main dock ☎757 9923, ⊚ beverleyshill@gmail.com, ⊛ beverlyshill.blogspot.com. A gem on the hillside, with rustic cabaña rooms (shared or private bathroom) set in a lush tropical garden that's home to the elusive red frog, and brimming with birdlife. If you can afford it, splash out on the room at the top for stunning Caribbean views (US$50). **US$22**

Hospedaje El Jaguar Off the main path, on the seafront ☎757 9383, ⊚ hosp_jaguar@hotmail.es. This hammock-strewn spot over the water is clean, comfortable and run by the Archibalds, one of the best-known families on the island. Breezy rooms are cheap and cheerful, and tours or kayak rental are available. **US$22**

★ **Hostal Bastimentos** Set back from the main path, on the hillside ☎757 9053, ⊛ hostalbastimentos.com. A sprawling maze of a backpackers' hostel affording a choice of accommodation, from dorms to posh bedrooms with a/c and hot water. There's a communal kitchen, a garden *rancho* hung with hammocks, a new bar-restaurant and a mellow vibe. Dorm US$7.50, double US$20

Palmar Tent Lodge Red Frog Beach ☎6880 8640, ⓦpalmartentlodge.com. Simple private safari tents and tent-cabin dorms (two-night min stay for all) set in rainforest at the back of the beach with solar-powered fans, lamps and showers plus an array of amenities and services. Camping (own tent, per person) US$10, dorm US$15, double in a safari tent US$50

Roots 200m right of the main dock under a mop of thatch. The most popular watering hole in town – beer goes for US$1. *Roots* also serves dynamite Caribbean dishes of fresh seafood and coconut rice for US$9–10. Daily 12.30–9pm.

Tío Tom's Just left of the main dock ☎757 9831, ⓦtiotomsguesthouse.com. A thatched wooden inn, built over water, with five cosy fan-ventilated en-suite rooms. Food, including great breakfasts, is cooked by the German owners, who also rent out kayaks and snorkel equipment and offer tours. US$22

★ **Up in the Hill** Along a well-signed path (20min) that starts going uphill near the police station. Holistic café and shop set in a private finca, producing organic cocoa and coconut-based products. Treats include icy lemonade, delectable fresh truffles and strong, fresh coffee. A charming wooden cabin is also available. US$55

Parque Nacional Marino Isla Bastimentos

Most visitors to Bocas come to explore the pristine beauty of **PARQUE NACIONAL MARINO ISLA BASTIMENTOS**, a 130-square-kilometre reserve encompassing several virtually undisturbed ecosystems that include rainforest, mangrove and coral reef supporting an immense diversity of marine life, including dolphins, sea turtles and a kaleidoscopic variety of fish.

Some of the best **beaches** in the archipelago are also in the park, on the eastern side of the island facing the open sea. Due to their powerful surf and currents, swimming here is dangerous, but they are huge, uncrowded and undeveloped. The most popular is **Red Frog Beach**, an idyllic stretch of sand that takes its name from the tiny bright-red strawberry poison-dart frogs (don't touch!) that inhabit the forest behind the beach.

Much further east, the 6km stretch of **Playa Larga** is an important nesting site for **sea turtles** (May–Sept). There's a ranger station here (US$10 park entrance); you'll need to stay overnight (see below) if you want to see the turtles lay their eggs.

Southeast of Isla Bastimentos, but still within the park, are the **Cayos Zapatillas**. Two dreamy, coral-fringed islands, the Zapatillas are excellent for snorkelling, but you must pay the park admission fee (US$10) at the ANAM station on the southern island. Camping is possible on the northern island (see below).

ARRIVAL AND DEPARTURE

By tour The easiest way to visit the marine park is with a tour operator (see box, p.588). A large number of agencies offer day-trips to beaches and snorkelling spots in and around the park, typically costing US$20–30/person (not including the park fee, which is not always collected) and including a lunch stop at an over-the-water restaurant (US$6–10). The more expensive tours often provide free cold drinks and snorkelling equipment.

By boat Alternatively, you can hire a boat in Bocas Town or Bastimentos: with a group of four or more people this could be cheaper than an agency tour and lets you decide exactly where you want to go. A typical day's excursion might include a visit to the Cayos Zapatillas in the morning, lunch and snorkelling amid the rainbow-coloured coral at Crawl Cay, and an afternoon on Red Frog Beach.

ACCOMMODATION

Cayos Zapatillas camping Contact ANAM in Bocas Town (ⓦanam.gob.pa). Camping is possible, with permission, on the pretty northern island, which has toilet and limited water (from collected rainwater) facilities. Per person US$6

ANAM refugio Playa Larga; contact ANAM or ANABOCA in Bocas Town (see p.591). A basic refuge, where you can also camp. Per person US$6

Community-based tourism

Bocas is not all about surfing, sand and partying. An increasing number of visitors are being drawn to the **community-based tourism** being offered by some of the archipelago's and mainland's **Ngöbe** communities as well as to the small **Naso** kingdom up the Río Teribe, on the boundary of the Amistad International Park (see p.583). To get the most out of the experience, consider a village homestay. The Bocas community tourism website (ⓦredtucombo.bocasdeltoro.org) and the Bocas Sustainable Tourism Alliance (ⓦdiscoverbocasdeltoro.com) give contact details and information on the activities each village offers.

Spanish

There are more than thirty languages spoken across the Central American isthmus. Fortunately for the traveller, just two dominate – Spanish, of course, but also English, spoken primarily in Belize and the Bay Islands of Honduras.

Luckily, too, **Spanish**, as spoken across Latin America, is one of the easier languages there is to learn and even the most faltering of attempts to speak it is greatly appreciated. Taking the trouble to get to know at least the basics will both make your travels considerably easier and reap countless rewards in terms of reception, appreciation and understanding of people and places.

Overall, Latin American Spanish is clearer and slower than that of Spain – gone are the lisps and bewilderingly rapid, slurred, soft consonants of the old country. There are, however, quite strong variations in accent across Central America: Guatemalan Spanish has the reputation of being clear, precise and eminently understandable even to the worst of linguists, while the language as spoken in Honduras – thick and fast – can initially bewilder even those who believed themselves to be reasonably fluent. Nicaraguans in particular take great pleasure in fooling around with language, creating new words, pronouncing certain letters differently and employing different grammar. There are enough *Nicaraguanismos* – words and sayings particular to Nicaragua – to fill a 275-page dictionary. As far as pronunciation goes, the "s" is often dropped from word endings and the "v" and "b" sounds are fairly interchangeable.

Pronunciation

For the most part, the rules of **pronunciation** are straightforward and strictly observed. Unless there's an accent, words ending in d, l, r and z are **stressed** on the last syllable, all others on the second last. All **vowels** are pure and short.

A somewhere between the "A" sound of back and that of father.
E as in get.
I as in police.
O as in hot.
U as in rule.
C is soft before E and I, otherwise hard; cerca is pronounced "serka".

ENGLISH AND CREOLE

The language you'll hear widely spoken in **Belize** may sound familiar from a distance and, if you listen to a few words, you may think that its meaning is clear. Listen a little harder, however, and you'll realize that complete comprehension is just out of reach. What you're hearing is, in fact, **Kriol**, a beautifully warm and relaxed language, spoken in various forms (as Creole) along the Caribbean coast from Belize down to Panama. This pidgin language is loosely based on English – mixed with elements of West African languages, indigenous Miskito, and some Spanish – and is similar to Jamaican Creole, or Patois. Written Kriol, which you'll come across in Belizean newspapers, is a little easier to get to grips with. There's an active movement in Belize to formalize the language, which led to the publication of the *Kriol-Inglish Dikshineri* in 2007. Luckily, almost anyone who can speak Creole can also speak English.

In the Bay Islands of **Honduras** things are much simpler. Language is English rather than Creole, and immediately understandable, albeit spoken with a unique, broad accent. Influenced by Caribbean, English and Scots migrants over the years, local inflexions turn even the most commonplace of remarks into an attractive statement. English, however, is slowly being supplanted by Spanish as the language heard on the street, as growing numbers of mainlanders make the islands their home.

G works the same way – a guttural "H" sound (like the ch in loch) before E or I, a hard G elsewhere; gigante is pronounced "higante".

H is always silent.

J is the same sound as a guttural G; jamón is pronounced "hamon".

LL sounds like an English Y; tortilla is pronounced torteeya.

N is as in English, unless there is a tilde (accent) over it, when it becomes like the N in "onion"; mañana is pronounced "manyana".

QU is pronounced like an English K.

R is rolled, **RR** doubly so.

V sounds like a cross with B, vino becoming beano.

X is slightly softer than in English, sometimes almost like SH, so that Xela becomes "sheyla"; between vowels in place names it has an H sound – México is pronounced "May-hee-ko".

Z is the same as a soft C; cerveza is pronounced "servesa".

Formal and informal address

For English-speakers one of the most difficult things to get to grips with is the distinction between formal and informal address – when to use it and to whom, and how to avoid causing offence. Generally speaking, the third-person "**usted**" indicates respect and/or a non-familiar relationship and is used in business, for people you don't know and for those older than you. Second-person "**tú**" is for children, friends and contemporaries in less formal settings. (Remember also that in Latin America the second-person **plural** – "vosotros" – is never used, so "you" plural will always be "ustedes".) In day-to-day exchanges, genuine mistakes on the part of an obviously non-native speaker will be well received and corrected with good humour.

One idiosyncrasy is the widespread use of "**vos**" in Central America. Now archaic in Spain, it is frequently used in place of *tú*, as an intimate form of address between friends of the same age. In most tenses, conjugation is exactly the same as for *tú*. In the present indicative, however, the last syllable is stressed with an accent (*tú comes/vos comés*); in "-ir" verbs in this tense, the final "i" is kept instead of changing to an "e" (*tú escribes/vos escribís*). In commands, the "vos" form drops the final "r" of the infinitive, replacing it with an accented vowel (*tú come/vos comé*). Take your lead from those around you – if you are addressed in the "vos" form it is a sign of friendship and should be reciprocated; on the other hand it is sometimes seen as patronizing to use it with someone you don't know well.

Nicknames and turns of speech

Nicknames are very common in Central America, used in both speech and writing and for any situation from addressing a casual acquaintance to referring to political candidates. Often they centre on obvious physical characteristics – *flaco/a* (thin), *gordo/a* (fat), *rubio/a* (blond).

Often, these nicknames will be further softened by **diminution** – the addition of the suffix *-ito* or *-ita* at the end of nouns and adjectives, a trend used sometimes with a passion in everyday speech. You are quite likely to hear someone talk about their *hermanito* for example, which translates as "little brother" regardless of respective ages, while *mi hijita* ("my little daughter") can as easily mean a grown woman as a child.

Also very common are **endearments**, used lightly in brief encounters and to soothe transactions. Heard in virtually every country are *(mi) amor* – used in much the same way as "love" in England and also between friends – as is *jóven* or *jovencito/a*, young one. More specific to each country (often but not always between men) are terms used to make casual questions or remarks less intrusive. *Papa* (literally "father") is used daily in Honduras, for example as in "*¿Qué hora tiene, papa?*" (What time is it?), while the Nicaraguans use *primo* (cousin). Panamanians address one another as *joven* (youth), regardless of age, and refer to friends as "*mis panas*" (my "panas", or Panamanians). In Nicaragua light-skinned or fair-haired visitors will be referred to or addressed as *chele/a*; the syllables of *leche* (milk) in reverse.

Politesse

Verbal courtesy is an integral part of speech in Spanish and one that – once you're accustomed to the pace and flow of life in Central America – should become instinctive. Saying *buenos días/buenas tardes* and waiting for the appropriate response is usual when asking for something at a shop or ticket office for example, as is adding *señor* or *señora* (in this instance similar to the US "sir" or "ma'am"). The "you're welcome" response is more likely to be *para servirle* (literally "here to serve you") rather than the casual *de nada* ("you're welcome"). The *tss tss* sound is commonly employed to attract attention, particularly in restaurants. In this very polite culture shouting is frowned upon.

On meeting, or being introduced to someone, Central Americans will say *con mucho gusto*, "it's a pleasure", and you should do the same. On departure you will more often than not be told *¡que le vaya bien!* ("may all go well"), a simple phrase that nonetheless invariably sounds sincere and rounds off transactions nicely. In rural areas, especially, it is usual to leave even complete strangers met on the path with *!Adiós, que le vaya bien!* Note that the Castilian term **coger** (to take/grab) has a very different meaning in Central and South America; here this refers to the act of sex, while the verb **tomar** is used for take/grab. Make sure you therefore say "*tomar un autobus*" (get the bus), instead of the Castilian "*coger un autobus*"!

WORDS AND PHRASES

BASIC WORDS

a lot	mucho	please	por favor
afternoon	tarde	she	ella
and	y	small	pequeño/a
bad	mal(o)/a	sir/mister	señor
big	gran(de)	thank you	gracias
boy	chico	that	eso/a
closed	cerrado/a	their	suyo/de ellos
cold	frío/a	there	allí
day	día	they	ellos
entrance	entrada	this	este/a
exit	salida	today	hoy
girl	chica	tomorrow	mañana
good	bien/buen(o)/a	what	qué
he	él	when	cuándo
her	ella	where	dónde
here	aquí	with	con
his	suyo	without	sin
hot	calor/caliente	woman	mujer/hembra
how much	cuánto	yes	sí
if	si	yesterday	ayer
information	información		
later	más tarde/después	**BASIC PHRASES**	
less	menos	Hello	¡Hola!
ma'am/missus	señora	Goodbye	Adiós
man	señor/hombre	See you later	Hasta luego
miss	señorita	Good morning	Buenos días
more	más	Good afternoon	Buenas tardes
morning	mañana	Goodnight	Buenas noches
night	noche	Sorry	Lo siento/Discúlpame
no	no	Excuse me	Con permiso/perdón
now	ahora	How are you?	¿Cómo está (usted)?/
open	abierto/a		¿Qué tal?
or	o	Nice to meet you	Mucho gusto
		Not at all/You're welcome	De nada

I (don't) understand	(No) Entiendo
Do you speak English?	¿Habla (usted) inglés?
I (don't) speak Spanish	(No) Hablo español
What?/How?	¿Cómo?
Could you ..., please?	¿Podría ... por favor?
... repeat that	... repetirlo
... speak slowly	... hablar más despacio
... write that down	... escribirlo
My name is ...	Me llamo ...
What's your name?	¿Cómo se llama usted?
I'm from	Soy de ...
... America	... Estados Unidos
... Australia	... Australia
... Canada	... Canadá
... England	... Inglaterra
... Ireland	... Irlanda
... New Zealand	... Nueva Zelanda
... Scotland	... Escocia
... South Africa	... Sudáfrica
... Wales	... Gales
Where are you from?	De dónde es usted?
How old are you?	¿Cuántos años tiene? (usted)
I am ... years old	Tengo ... años
I don't know	No sé
Do you know ...?	¿Sabe ...?
I want	Quiero
I'd like ...	Quisiera ... por favor
What's that?	¿Qué es eso?
What is this called in Spanish?	¿Cómo se llama este en español?
There is (is there)?	Hay (?)
Do you have ...?	¿Tiene ...?
What time is it?	¿Qué hora es?
May I take a photograph?	¿Puedo sacar una foto?

BASIC NEEDS, SERVICES AND PLACES

ATM	cajero automático
bank	banco
bathroom/toilet	baño/sanitario
beach	playa
bookstore	librería
border crossing	frontera
cheap hotel	un hotel barato
church	iglesia
embassy	embajada
highway	carretera
immigration office	Migración
internet café	cibercafé
lake	lago
laundry	lavandería
library	biblioteca
main street	calle principál
map	mapa

market	mercado
museum	museo
national park	parque nacional
pharmacy	farmacia
(main) post office	correo (central)
restaurant	restaurante
supermarket	supermercado
telephone office	cabina de teléfono
telephones	teléfonos
tourist office	oficina de turismo

NUMBERS

1	un/uno/una
2	dos
3	tres
4	cuatro
5	cinco
6	seis
7	siete
8	ocho
9	nueve
10	diez
11	once
12	doce
13	trece
14	catorce
15	quince
16	dieciséis
17	diecisiete
18	dieciocho
19	diecinueve
20	veinte
21	veintiuno
22	veintidos
30	treinta
40	cuarenta
50	cincuenta
60	sesenta
70	setenta
80	ochenta
90	noventa
100	cien
101	ciento uno
200	doscientos
201	doscientosuno
500	quinientos
1000	mil
1999	mil novecientos noventa y nueve
2000	dos mil
100,000	cien mil
1,000,000	un millón
first	primero/a
second	segundo/a

third	tercero/a
fourth	cuarto/a
fifth	quinto/a
tenth	décimo/a

MONTHS

January	enero
February	febrero
March	marzo
April	abril
May	mayo
June	junio
July	julio
August	agosto
September	septiembre
October	octubre
November	noviembre
December	diciembre

DAYS (DÍAS)

Monday	lunes
Tuesday	martes
Wednesday	miércoles
Thursday	jueves
Friday	viernes
Saturday	sábado
Sunday	domingo

COLOURS

black	negro/a
blue	azul
brown	marrón or café
green	verde
grey	gris
indigo	índigo/a
orange	naranja
red	rojo/a
violet/purple	violeta
white	blanco/a
yellow	amarillo/a

TRANSPORT

bus	autobús/camión
bus station	estación de autobuses
bus stop	parada de autobús
boat	barco/lancha
ferry	transbordador
dock/pier	muelle
airplane	avión
airport	aeropuerto
car	carro
4WD	tracción integral
taxi	taxi
truck	camión

pick-up	camioneta
hitchhike	hacer autostop (to hitchhike) or pedir un ride (to ask for a ride)
train	tren
train station	estación de trenes
bicycle	bicicleta (abb. bici)
motorcycle	moto
ticket	boleto
ticket office	taquilla/ boletería
I'd like a ticket to …	(Necesito) un boleto para …
How much is a … ticket from…to…?	¿Cuanto cuesta un … boleto de …a…?
… first-class	… primera clase
… second-class	… segunda clase
… one-way	… sólo ida
… return/round-trip	… ida y vuelta
I would like to rent a …	Me gustaría alquilar un/ una …
Where does … to … leave from?	¿De dónde sale …para …?
What time does the… leave for …?	¿A qué hora sale … para …?
What time does the … arrive in …?	¿A qué hora llega … en …?

DIRECTIONS

Where is …?	¿Dónde está …?
How do I get to …?	¿Como llego a …?
I'm looking for …	Estoy buscando …
Is this the way to …?	¿Es esta la carretera hacia …?
I'm lost	Estoy perdido/a
Is it far?	¿Está lejos?
left	izquierda
right	derecha
straight ahead	derecho/recto
north	norte
south	sur
east	este
west	oeste
street	calle
avenue	avenida
block	cuadra

MONEY (DINERO)

How much is it?	¿Cuánto es/cuesta?
It's too expensive	Es demasiado caro
Do you have anything cheaper?	¿No tiene algo más barato?
Do you accept …?	Aceptan …?
… credit cards	… tarjetas de crédito

… travellers' cheques	… cheques de viajero
… US dollars	… dólares americanos
I would like to change some dollars	Me gustaría cambiar unos dólares
Can you change dollars?	¿Se puede cambiar dólares?
What is the exchange rate?	¿Cuál es el tipo de cambio?

SHOPPING

I would like to buy …	Me gustaría comprar …
… a bag	… una bolsa
… a book	… un libro
… clothes	… ropas
… film	… una película
… a hammock	… una hamaca
… a hat	… un sombrero
… a jacket	… una chaqueta
… a mobile phone	… un celular
… a painting	… una cuadra
… a shirt	… una camisa
… shoes	… unos zapatos
… a skirt	… una falda
… a sleeping bag	… un saco de dormir
… socks	… unos calcetines
… a tent	… una carpa
… trousers	… pantalónes
… underwear	… ropa interior
I'm just looking	Estoy mirando
Could I look at it/that?	¿Puedo ver eso/aquello?
Please give me …	Por favor deme
… one like that	… uno asi

ACCOMMODATION

Is there a … nearby?	¿Hay … aquí cerca?
… guesthouse	… una casa de huéspedes
… hotel	… un hotel
… hostel	… un hostal
… campsite	… un camping
Do you have …?	¿Tiene …?
… a room	… un cuarto
… with two beds	… con dos camas
… a double bed	… con cama matrimonial
… a dorm room	… dormitorio compartido
… a tent	… una carpa
… a cabin	… una cabina
It's for	Es para
… one person	… una persona
… two people	… dos personas
… for one night	… una noche
… one week	… una semana
Does it have …	¿Tiene …?

… a shared bath	… baño compartido
… a private bath	… baño privado
… hot water	… agua caliente
… air conditioning	Aire acondicionado
Can one …?	¿Se puede …?
… camp (near) here	…acampar aquí (cerca)
… sling a hammock here?	… poner una hamaca aquí
… swim here?	… nadar aquí
How much is it …?	¿Cuánto es/cuesta …?
… per night	… por noche
… per person	… por persona
… per room	… por cuarto
Does the price include breakfast?	¿El precio incluye el desayuno?
May I see a room?	¿Puedo ver un cuarto?
May I see another room?	¿Puedo ver otro cuarto?
Yes, it's fine	Sí, está bien
I'd like to reserve a …	Me gustaría reservar un/ una …

HEALTH AND SAFETY

I'm ill	Estoy enfermo/a
He/she is ill	Él/Ella está enfermo/a
I'm allergic to …	Soy alérgica a …
He/she is allergic to …	Él/Ella es alérgica a …
I need to see a doctor	Tengo que ver un doctor
He/she needs to see a doctor	Él/ella tiene que ver un doctor
I need to go to …	Tengo que ir …
… the hospital	… al hospital
… a health clinic	… a una clínica
… a pharmacy	… a una farmacia
He/she needs to go to…	Él/ella tiene que ir a …
I have a …	Me duele …
… headache	… la cabeza
… stomachache	… el estómago
I have a fever	Tengo fiebre
I have hurt my…	Me hice daño …
… arm	… al brazo
… back	… a la espalda
… foot	… al pie
… head	… a la cabeza
… hand	… a la mano
… knee	… a la rodilla
… leg	… a la pierna
… neck	… al cuello
He/she has hurt	Él/ella se hizo daño …
I was bitten/ scratched by …	Me mordió/arañó …
… a dog	… un perro
… a cat	… un gato
… a snake	… una serpiente

… a mosquito	… un mosquito	tourist police	policía turística
… a spider	… una araña	ambulance	ambulancia
… a jellyfish	… una medusa	fire brigade	bomberos
He/she was bitten/ scratched by …	Le mordió/arañó un/ una …	Red Cross	Cruz Roja
I am dehydrated	Estoy deshidratado/a	Help!	¡Ayuda!
medicine	medicina	Fire!	¡Fuego!
dose/dosage	dosis	Go away!	¡Váyase!
sunscreen/sunblock	crema solar/filtro solar	Leave me alone!	¡Déjeme en paz!
bug repellent	repelente para insectos	I've been robbed	Me han robado
antibiotics	antibióticos	He/she has been robbed	Le han robado
It's an emergency	Es una emergencia	I need to fill out an insurance report	Tengo que rellenar una reclamación de seguro
police	policía	I need help	Necesito ayuda
policeman	un policía	Please can you help me?	¿Me podría ayudar por favor?
police station	comisaría		

A SPANISH MENU READER

While dishes vary by country and region, these words and terms will help negotiate most menus.

BASIC DINING VOCABULARY

almuerzo	lunch
carta (la)	menu
cena	dinner
cocina	kitchen
comida corriente	cheap set menu, usually served at lunch time
comida típica	typical cuisine
cuchara	spoon
cuchillo	knife
desayuno	breakfast
merienda	afternoon tea
mesa	table
plato	plate
plato del día	dish of the day
plato fuerte	main course
plato vegetariano	vegetarian dish
servilleta	napkin
silla	chair
taza	mug/cup
tenedor	fork
vaso	glass
La cuenta, por favor	The bill, please
¿Contiene …?	Does this contain …? (for food allergies, vegetarians, etc)
Soy vegetariano/a	I'm a vegetarian
No como carne	I don't eat meat

STAPLES

aceite	oil
ajillo	garlic butter
ajo	garlic
arroz	rice
azúcar	sugar
chile	chilli
galletas	biscuits
hielo	ice
huevos	eggs
mantequilla	butter
mermelada	jam
miel	honey
mixto	mixed seafood/ meats/salad
mostaza	mustard
pan (integral)	bread (wholemeal)
pan de coco	coconut bread
pimienta	pepper
queso	cheese
sal	salt
salsa de tomate	tomato sauce

FRUTAS (FRUIT)

banano	banana
cereza	cherry
ciruela	plum
coco	coconut
durazno	peach
fresa	strawberry
guayaba	guava
higo	fig
lima	lime
limón	lemon
manzana	apple
maracuyá	passion fruit
melón	melon
mora	blackberry
naranja	orange
papaya	papaya

pera	pear
piña	pineapple
pithaya	dragon fruit
plátano	plantain
sandía	watermelon
tamarindo	tamarind
tomate	tomato
toronja	grapefruit
uva	grapes

LEGUMBRES/VERDURAS (VEGETABLES)

aguacate	avocado
alcachofa	artichoke
apio	celery
arvejas	peas
berenjena	aubergine/eggplant
brécol	broccoli
calabaza	pumpkin
calabazín	courgette/zucchini
cebolla	onion
champiñón/hongo	mushroom
coliflor	cauliflower
curtida	pickled cabbage, beetroot and carrots
ensalada	salad
espinaca	spinach
frijoles	beans
frijoles volteados	refried beans
gallo pinto	mixed rice and beans
lechuga	lettuce
lentejas	lentils
maíz	sweetcorn/maize
menestra	bean/lentil stew
palmito	palm heart
papa	potato
papas fritas	French fries
pepinillo	gherkin
pepino	cucumber
tomate	tomato
zanahoria	carrot

CARNE (MEAT) AND AVES (POULTRY)

bistec	steak
búfalo	buffalo
carne	beef
carne de chancho	pork
cerdo	pork
chicharrones	pork scratchings, crackling
chuleta	pork chop
conejo	rabbit
cordero	lamb
filete	steak
gallina	hen

jamón	ham
lechón	roasted pig
lomo	steak
pato	duck
pavo	turkey
pollo	chicken
res	beef
ternera	veal
tocino	bacon
venado	venison

MENUDOS (OFFAL)

chunchules	intestines
corazón	heart
guatita	tripe
hígado	liver
lengua	tongue
patas	trotters

MARISCOS (SEAFOOD) AND PESCADO (FISH)

almejas	clams
anchoa	anchovy
atún	tuna
bacalao	cod
calamares	squid
camarón	shrimp
cangrejo	crab
ceviche	raw seafood marinated in lime juice with onions
corvina	sea bass
erizo	sea urchin
gambas	prawns
langosta	lobster/crayfish
langostina	king prawn
lenguado	sole
mejillónes	mussels
ostión	oyster
pargo rojo/blanco	red/white snapper
pulpo	octopus
trucha	trout

SOPAS (SOUPS)

caldo	broth
caldo de gallina	chicken broth
crema de espárragos	cream of asparagus
sopa de caracol	spicy conch stew
sopa de frijoles	bean soup
sopa del día	soup of the day
tapado	a seafood soup, served on the Caribbean coast of several countries in the isthmus

BOCADOS (SNACKS)

bocadillo	little snack
casado	meal of rice, beans, salad and meat or fish (phrase mainly seen in Costa Rica, translating to "married")
chuchito	corn-dough parcels made with beans and eggs (sometimes also pork), popular in Guatemala and El Salvador
empanada	cheese/meat pastry
hamburguesa	hamburger
nacatamales	Nicaraguan corn-dough parcels filled with vegetables, pork, beef or chicken
patacones	fried green plantains
pupusa	small, thick Salvadoran tortilla filled with cheese, beans or pork and topped with salad
salchichas	sausages
tamale	ground maize with meat/cheese wrapped in leaf
tortilla	toasted maize pancake
tortilla de huevos	omelette
tostada	toast

POSTRES (DESSERTS)

ensalada de frutas	fruit salad
flan	crème caramel
helado	ice cream
pastel	cake
piñonate	candied papaya
torta	tart
tres leches	cake made with three varieties of milk

BEBIDAS (DRINKS)

agua (mineral)	mineral water
… con gas	… sparkling
… sin gas	… still
… con/sin hielo	… with/without ice
… con limón	… with lemon

aguardiente	raw alcohol made from sugar cane
café	coffee
café con leche	milk with a little coffee
cerveza	beer
gaseosa	fizzy drink
horchata	milky, cereal-based drink sweetened with cinnamon
jugo	juice
leche	milk
licuado	fresh fruit milkshake
limonada	fresh lemonade
raspados	ice shavings with sweet topping
refresco	generic term for cold drink
ron	rum
licor	spirits
té	tea
té aromática	herbal tea
hierba luisa	lemon verbena
manzanilla	camomile
menta	mint
vino blanco	white wine
vino tinto	red wine

COOKING TERMS

a la parrilla	barbecued
a la plancha	grilled
ahumado	smoked
al ajillo	in garlic sauce
al horno	oven-baked
al vapor	steamed
apanado	breaded
asado	roast
asado al palo	spit roast
crudo	raw
duro	hard boiled
encebollado	cooked with onions
frito	fried
picante	hot, spicy
puré	mashed
revuelto	scrambled
saltado	sautéed
secado	dried

GLOSSARY

aguacero downpour

ahorita right now (any time within the coming hour)

alcalde mayor

aldea village

algodón cotton

almohada pillow

artesanía arts and crafts

bahía bay

balneario resort or spa

barranca steep-sided ravine

barrio neighbourhood, or area within a town or city; suburb

biotopo protected area of national ecological importance, usually with limited tourist access

bomba pump at a petrol station

caballo horse

cabaña literally a cabin, but can mean anything from a palm-thatched beach hut to a room; usually applies to tourist accommodation

cabina cubicle/booth/cabin

cacique chief (originally a colonial term, now used for elected leaders/figureheads of indigenous *comarcas* in Panama)

cafetería café

calzada road/carriageway

cama bed

camioneta small truck or van (in Guatemala, a chicken bus)

campesino peasant/farmer

campo countryside

cantina local, hard-drinking bar, usually men-only

carro car, equivalent of the Castilian *coche*

casa de cambio currency exchange bureau

cascada waterfall

caseta telefónica phone booth

catedral cathedral

cepillo de dientes toothbrush

chabola shack

chapín slang term for someone from Guatemala

chicle chewing gum

chorreador sack-and-metal coffee-filter contraption, still widely used

Churrigueresque highly elaborate, decorative form of Baroque architecture (usually found in churches)

cigarrillo cigarette

ciudad city

Clásico period during which ancient Maya civilization was at its height, usually given as 300–900 AD

colchón mattress

colectivo shared taxi/minibus, usually following fixed route (can also be applied to a boat – *lancho colectivo*)

colina hill (also *el cerro*)

colonia city suburb or neighbourhood, often seen in addresses as "Col"

comedor basic restaurant, usually with just one or two things on the menu, always the cheapest place to eat; literally "dining room"

conquistador "one who conquers": member of early Spanish expeditions to the Americas in the sixteenth century

convento convent or monastery

cordillera mountain range

correo aéreo air mail

corriente second-class bus

cuadra street block

cuevas caves

descompuesto out of order

Dios God

discoteca club/disco

Don/Doña courtesy titles (sir/madam), mostly used in letters, for professional people or for a boss

dolor pain/ache

edificio building

efectivo cash

ejido communal farmland

encendedor lighter (for cigarettes)

encomienda package/parcel

entrada entry/entry fee

estatua statue

extranjero foreigner

fecha date

feria fair (market); also a town fête

fiesta party

finca ranch, farm or plantation

fósforos matches

gambas buttresses; the giant above-ground roots that some rainforest trees put out

gasolina petrol

gasolinera petrol station

golfo gulf

gringo/gringa specifically American, but used widely for any white-skinned foreigner; not necessarily a term of abuse, it does nonetheless have a slightly pessimistic connotation

gruta cave

guaca pre-Columbian burial ground or tomb

hacienda big farm, ranch or estate, or big house on it

henequén fibre from the *agave* (sisal) plant, used to make rope

hospedaje very basic *pensión* or small hotel

huipil Maya woman's traditional dress or blouse, usually woven or embroidered

huracán hurricane

I.V.A. sales tax

indígena an indigenous person; preferred term among indigenous groups, rather than the more racially offensive *índio*

invierno winter (May–Oct)

isla island

jardín garden

juego de pelota ball game/ball court

ladino a vague term – applied to people it means Spanish-influenced as opposed to indigenous, and at its most specific defines someone of mixed Spanish and indigenous blood; it's more commonly used simply to describe a person of "Western" culture, or one who dresses in "Western" style, be they of indigenous or mixed blood

lanterna torch

lavabo sink

litera bunk bed

llave key

malecón seafront promenade

mar sea

mestizo person of mixed indigenous and Spanish blood, though like the term *ladino* it has more cultural than racial significance

metate Pre-Columbian stone table used for grinding corn

milpa maize field, usually cleared by slash-and-burn farming

mirador look-out point

mochila backpack

mochilero backpacker

moneda coins

montar a caballo to go horseriding

neotrópicos "neotropics": tropics of the New World

noreste northeast; often seen in addresses as "NE"

noroeste northwest

nublado cloudy

occidente west

oriente east; often seen in addresses as "Ote"

otoño autumn

paisaje landscape

palacio mansion, but not necessarily royal

palacio de gobierno headquarters of state/federal authorities

palacio municipal headquarters of local government

palapa palm thatch (used to describe any thatched/palm-roofed hut)

panadería bakery

parque park

paseo a broad avenue; also a walk, especially the traditional evening walk around the plaza

pasta de dientes toothpaste

pelota ball, or ball court

peón farm labourer, usually landless

personaje someone of importance, a VIP, although usually used pejoratively to indicate someone who is putting on airs

piscina swimming pool

planta baja ground floor – abbreviated PB in elevators

plaza square

Plateresque elaborately decorative Renaissance architectural style

poniente west; often seen in addresses as "Pte"

Postclásico period between the decline of Maya civilization and the arrival of the Spanish, 900–1530 AD

Preclásico archeological era preceding the blooming of Maya civilization, usually given as 1500 BC–300 AD

primavera spring

propina tip

pueblo town/village

puente bridge

puerta door

pulpería general store or corner store; also sometimes serves cooked food and drinks

quetzal quetzal (bird), and also the currency of Guatemala

rancho palm-thatched roof; can also mean a small-holding

recibo receipt

redondel de toros bullring, used for local rodeos

río river

ruinas ruins

sábana sheet

sacbé Maya road, or ceremonial causeway

saco de dormir sleeping bag

santo saint

seda silk

sendero path

sierra mountain range

sincretismo syncretism, the attempted amalgamation of different religions, cultures or schools of thought; mainly applied to religion and in Central America usually refers to the merging of Maya and Catholic beliefs

soda Costa Rican cafeteria or diner; in the rest of Central America it's usually called a *comedor*

sol sun

sótano basement

stele freestanding carved monument; most are of Maya origin

sudeste southeast (also *sureste*)

sudoeste southwest (also *suroeste*)

temblor tremor

temporada season: *la temporada de lluvia* is the rainy season

terremoto earthquake

terreno land; small farm

tiempo weather (can also mean time)

tienda shop

tierra land/earth

típico/típica literally "typical"; used to describe anything pertaining to a specific culture, from food to dress to art

traje traditional costume (also means suit)

vaquero cowboy

vela candle/sail (of a boat); also means "wake" or funeral gathering in Nicaragua

ventana window

verano summer (Nov–April)

vista view

volcán volcano

Small print and index

A ROUGH GUIDE TO ROUGH GUIDES

Published in 1982, the first Rough Guide – to Greece – was a student scheme that became a publishing phenomenon. Mark Ellingham, a recent graduate in English from Bristol University, had been travelling in Greece the previous summer and couldn't find the right guidebook. With a small group of friends he wrote his own guide, combining a highly contemporary, journalistic style with a thoroughly practical approach to travellers' needs.

The immediate success of the book spawned a series that rapidly covered dozens of destinations. And, in addition to impecunious backpackers, Rough Guides soon acquired a much broader readership that relished the guides' wit and inquisitiveness as much as their enthusiastic, critical approach and value-for-money ethos.

These days, Rough Guides include recommendations from budget to luxury and cover more than 200 destinations around the globe, as well as producing an ever-growing range of eBooks and apps.

Visit **roughguides.com** to see our latest publications.

Rough Guide credits

Editor: Samantha Cook
Layout: Pradeep Thapliyal
Cartography: Animesh Pathak
Picture editor: Marta Bescos
Proofreader: Jan McCann
Managing editor: Mani Ramaswamy
Assistant editor: Dipika Dasgupta
Production: Charlotte Cade
Cover design: Tim Draper, Pradeep Thapliyal

Editorial assistant: Olivia Rawes
Senior pre-press designer: Dan May
Creative operations manager: Jason Mitchell
Publisher: Joanna Kirby
Operations coordinator: Helen Blount
Publishing director (Travel): Clare Currie
Commercial manager: Gino Magnotta
Managing director: John Duhigg

Publishing information

This third edition published November 2013 by
Rough Guides Ltd,
80 Strand, London WC2R 0RL
11, Community Centre, Panchsheel Park,
New Delhi 110017, India
Distributed by the Penguin Group
Penguin Books Ltd,
80 Strand, London WC2R 0RL
Penguin Group (USA)
345 Hudson Street, NY 10014, USA
Penguin Group (Australia)
250 Camberwell Road, Camberwell,
Victoria 3124, Australia
Penguin Group (NZ)
67 Apollo Drive, Mairangi Bay, Auckland 1310,
New Zealand
Penguin Group (South Africa)
Block D, Rosebank Office Park, 181 Jan Smuts Avenue,
Parktown North, Gauteng, South Africa 2193
Rough Guides is represented in Canada by Tourmaline
Editions Inc. 662 King Street West, Suite 304, Toronto,
Ontario M5V 1M7
Printed in Singapore by Toppan Security Printing Pte. Ltd.

616pp includes index
A catalogue record for this book is available from the
British Library
ISBN: 978-1-40932-439-3
The publishers and authors have done their best to ensure
the accuracy and currency of all the information in **The
Rough Guide to Central America on a Budget**, however,
they can accept no responsibility for any loss, injury, or
inconvenience sustained by any traveller as a result of
information or advice contained in the guide.
1 3 5 7 9 8 6 4 2

MIX
Paper from
responsible sources
FSC
www.fsc.org   FSC™ C018179

Help us update

We've gone to a lot of effort to ensure that the third edition
of **The Rough Guide to Central America on a Budget** is
accurate and up-to-date. However, things change – places
get "discovered", opening hours are notoriously fickle,
restaurants and rooms raise prices or lower standards. If
you feel we've got it wrong or left something out, we'd like
to know, and if you can remember the address, the price,
the hours, the phone number, so much the better.

Please send your comments with the subject line
"Rough Guide Central America on a Budget Update" to
mail@uk.roughguides.com. We'll credit all contributions
and send a copy of the next edition (or any other Rough
Guide if you prefer) for the very best emails.

Find more travel information, connect with fellow
travellers and plan your trip on roughguides.com

Acknowledgements

Dawn Curtis Thanks to my mam, dad and brothers for a lifetime of support, to Georgina for your inspiration, and to Astrid for being there since the beginning of the adventure. Thanks to the many, many kind and hospitable people that looked after me along the way, especially Sheri and Cristiano at *Finca del Sol* for your humanity. And my oh-so-willing drinking partners who, for their own sake, shall remain nameless (Lic. Nelys Raquel Martínez Obregón). Y gracias a mi gran familia espiritual en San Isidro, San Juan del Sur, y todo el país, por su apoyo y amistad. Finally, thanks to the Rough Guides team for their patience and trust.

Sara Humphreys Thanks to Mani Ramaswamy for letting me loose once more in Panama, and to Sam Cook for sensible editing. In Panama, thanks are due to Rolo, Mike and Michelle for info on Santa Catalina, to Neil Hesketh for a reminisce in a hot tub in Boca Chica, and, above all, to Raffa Calvo, for enduring countless fact-finding missions and for his company on a rapid recce of the Darién.

Anna Kaminski I would like to thank all the people who've assisted me with my research, including my sister who put up with me on the road for two whole weeks; the wonderful Osa Wild in Puerto Jimenez/Corcovado;

Rolf of *Rainbow Valley Lodge* in Santa Elena; Daryl from Tortuguero's *Casa Marbella*; *Hotel Meli Melo* in Santa Teresa; *Tico Adventure Lodge* in Samara; *Indra Inn* in Playa Grande, and *Casa Mariposa* in San Gerardo.

Stephen Keeling Thanks to Ben Judge and Simone in San Salvador, Tom Pollak for all his excellent advice, Sam Cook for a superb editing job, Mani Ramaswamy, Alice Park and the all the crew at Rough Guides, and as always, Tiffany Wu, whose love and support made this possible.

Shafik Meghji Thanks to the many locals and travellers who helped out along the way. A special muchas gracias must go to Sam Cook for her sterling editing work, Mani Ramaswamy at RG HQ for the commission, Cristina Cunchillos of the Central American Tourism Agency for her invaluable help with planning the research trip, the Honduras Tourist Board, Jorge Salaverri for his excellent guiding and rafting skills, John Dupuis of *La Villa de Soledad* for his insight into Honduras, Jean, Nizar and Nina Meghji, and Sioned Jones for all her love and support.

Iain Stewart Many thanks to Lorena and Henk, José and Carmen, Deedle and Dave, Tom in Xela, Don David, Matt for the house in Lanquín, and to Fee, Louis and Monty for coming along for some of the ride.

Readers' updates

Thanks to all the readers who have taken the time to write in with comments and suggestions (and apologies if we've inadvertently omitted or misspelt anyone's name):

Kate Dalton, Mélissa Fradette, Glyn Garratt, Leah Heaton Jones and Alyxandria Rae

Photo credits

Index

Maps are marked in grey

Map symbols

The symbols below are used on maps throughout the book

✈	Airport	⬐	Viewpoint	T	Toilets
★	Bus/taxi	Waterfall	P	Parking
⛴	Boat	Volcano	E	Embassy/consulate
@	Internet café/access	Oasis/palm tree	▲	Mountain peak
✉	Post office	Campsite	Mountain range
ⓘ	Tourist office	⊙	Statue	Reef
☎	Telephone office	Museum	Bridge
⊞	Hospital	Fountain	Church
◆	Place of interest	Petrol station	Building
Cave	⌒	Arch	Market
Ruins	⊠	Gate	Stadium
Precolumbian ruin	Lighthouse	Park/national park
Castle	Immigration/border crossing	Beach
Fortress	Mountain refuge/lodge	Christian Cemetery
Monument	Ranger station	Marsh/swamp
Archeological site		

Listings key

▪ Accommodation

● Eating/drinking/nightlife